THE OFFICIAL PRICE GUIDE TO Antiques and Other Collectibles

**BY
THE HOUSE OF COLLECTIBLES, INC.**

We have compiled the information contained herein through a *patented computerized process* which relies primarily on a nationwide sampling of information provided by noteworthy collectible experts, auction houses and specialized dealers. This unique retrieval system enables us to provide the reader with the most current and accurate information available.

**EDITOR
THOMAS E. HUDGEONS III**

**FOURTH EDITION
THE HOUSE OF COLLECTIBLES, INC., ORLANDO, FLORIDA 32809**

IMPORTANT NOTICE. The format of **THE OFFICIAL PRICE GUIDE SERIES,** published by **THE HOUSE OF COLLECTIBLES, INC.,** is based on the following proprietary features: **ALL FACTS AND PRICES ARE COMPILED THRU A COMPUTERIZED PROCESS** which relies on a nationwide sampling of information obtained from noteworthy collectibles experts, auction houses and specialized dealers. **DETAILED "INDEXED" FORMAT** enables quick retrival of information for positive identification. **ENCAPSULATED HISTORIES** preceed each category to acquaint the collector with the specific traits that are peculiar to that area of collecting. **VALUABLE COLLECTING INFORMATION** is provided for both the novice as well as the seasoned collector: How to begin a collection; How to buy, sell, and trade; Care and storage techniques; Tips on restoration; Grading guidelines; Lists of periodicals, clubs, museums, auction houses, dealers, etc. **AN AVERAGE PRICE RANGE** takes geographic location and condition into consideration when reporting collector value. **A SPECIAL 3rd PRICE COLUMN** enables the collector to compare the current market values with the last's years average selling price . . . indicating which items have increased in value. **INVENTORY CHECKLISTS SYSTEM** is provided for cataloging a collection. **EACH TITLE IS ANNUALLY UP-DATED** to provide the most accurate information available in the rapidly changing collectors marketplace.

All of the information, including valuations, in this book has been compiled from the most reliable sources, and every effort has been made to eliminate errors and questionable data. Nevertheless the possibility of error, in a work of such immense scope, always exists. The publisher will not be held responsible for losses which may occur, in the purchase, sale, or other transaction of items, because of information contained herein. Readers who feel they have discovered errors are invited to WRITE and inform us, so they may be corrected in subsequent editions. Those seeking further information on the topics covered in this book, are advised to refer to the complete line of Official Price Guides published by The House of Collectibles.

© MCMLXXXIII The House of Collectibles, Inc.

All rights reserved. No part of this book may be reproduced or utilized in any form or by any means, electronic or mechanical, including photocopying, recording, or by any information storage and retrieval system, without permission in writing from the publisher.

Published by: The House of Collectibles, Inc.
Orlando Central Park
1900 Premier Row
Orlando, FL 32809
Phone: (305) 857-9095

Printed in the United States of America

Library of Congress Catalog Card Number: 80-84705

ISBN: 0-87637-374-0 / Paperback

TABLE OF CONTENTS

- Preface 1
- World of Antiques 2
- Building A Collection 4
- Buying From Dealers 8
- Buying At Auction Sales 12
- Buing From Other Sources 15
- Condition: A Major Influence On Value 19
- Fake! 21
- What Makes Market Trends 29
- Investing In Antiques 31
- Selling Your Antiques 35
- Selling By Auction 41
- Care And Storage 43
- What's New In Antiques? 54
- Collector Publications 55
- Building A Reference Library 59
- About The Prices In This Book 60
- How To Use This Book 61
- Alphabetical Listings A-Z .. 62
- Advertising Giveaways 62
- Almanacs 67
- American Eagles 70
- American Indian Artifacts 71
- Animation Art 75
- Art Deco 83
- Art Nouveau 85
- Autographs 87
- Autos And Automobilia 99
- Banks 120
- Barbed Wire 127
- Baseball Cards 129
- Baskets 154
- Beer Cans 157
- Bells 166
- Bicycles 169
- Bookplates 170
- Books 172
- Bottles 186
- Boxes 207
- Buttons 211
- Canes And Walking Sticks 213
- Caricatures And Cartoons 213
- Carousel Animals 214
- Cartoon Strips 215
- Cash Registers 217
- Cats 218
- Chalkware 219
- Chess Sets 220
- Christmas Tree Ornaments And Lights 221
- Circus Memorabilia 223
- Civil War Memorabilia 225
- Clocks 227
- Clothing 240
- Coca-Cola Collectibles 242
- Coins 249
- Combs 258
- Comic Art 259
- Comic Books 264
- Comic Character Spinoffs 276
- Corkscrews 287
- Coverlets 288
- Cowboy Gear 289
- Creches (Miniature Nativity Scenes) 290
- Dance Memorabilia 291
- Decoys 292
- Dogs 295
- Dolls 296
- Dollhouses 312
- Doorstops 313
- Eggs 315
- Eyeglasses 317
- Fans 317
- Farm Machinery 319
- Firearms 320
- Firefighting Equipment 336
- Fireplace Equipment 338
- Fishing Tackle 340
- Folk Art 341
- Football Cards 343
- Frogs 357
- Furniture 357
- Games 376
- Glassware 380
- Greeting Cards 480
- Horse-Drawn Carriages 483
- Hummels 485
- Inkwells And Ink Stands 497
- Insulators 499
- Irons 502
- Jars 504
- Jewelry 506
- Jukeboxes 513
- Kitchen Collectibles 517
- Knives 529
- Labels 535
- Lamps and Lighting Devices 537
- Lightning Rod Ornaments 541
- Lindenburg Memorabilia 542
- Locks And Keys 543
- Magazines 545
- Magicians' Memorabilia 550
- Maps 551
- Medals 552
- Menus 554
- Metals 555
- Militaria 575
- Model Soldiers 585
- Movie Memorabilia 586
- Music 587
- Music Boxes 594
- Musical Instruments 596
- Napkin Rings And Holders 598
- Nautical Gear 600
- Navajo Blankets And Serapes 601
- Needlework 602
- Needleworking Tools 603
- Nursery Collectibles 604
- Opera Memorabilia 606
- Orientalia 607
- Owls 614
- Paperback Books 615
- Paper Money 621
- Paperweights 630
- Penny Arcade Collectibles 631
- Pens And Pencils 632
- Pharmacy Items 639
- Phonographs And Roller Organs 639
- Photographica 642
- Plates 646
- Playing Cards 656
- Police Memorabilia 658
- Political Souvenirs 659
- Porcelain And Pottery 662
- Postcards 685
- Posters 687
- Prints 689
- Printing Collectibles ... 704
- Puppets 704
- Quilts 708
- Radio Premiums 710
- Radios 710
- Railroadiana 712
- Razors 713
- Redware 714
- Rogers Groups 715
- Royal Doulton 717
- Royalty Collectibles 721
- Rugs 722
- Science Fiction And Space 725
- Scouting Collectibles 729
- Scrimshaw 736
- Shaker Crafts And Furniture 737
- Ship Models 738
- Signs 740
- Silhouettes 741
- Sports Collectibles 743
- Stamps 748
- Stevengraphs And Silk Pictures 762
- Stock Certificates 763
- Stoneware 765
- Telegraph Collectibles 766
- Telephones 767
- Theatrical Memorabilia 769
- Tobacco Collectibles 771
- Tools 774
- Toys 777
- Trade Cards And Catalogs 795
- Tramp Art 796
- Trivets 798
- Trunks 799
- Typewriters 800
- Umbrellas 801
- Vacuum Cleaners 802
- Weather Vanes 803
- Woodenware 805
- Zodiac 808
- Index 809

ACKNOWLEDGEMENTS

The House of Collectibles would like to express its appreciation to the following individuals and or organizations for their assistance in the preparation of this publication: Phillips-Fine Art Auctioneers and Appraisers, 867 Madison Avenue, NY 10021; The Topps Chewing Gum Co., Brooklyn, NY 11232; The Fleer Corp., Philadelphia, PA 19141; Juke Box Saturday Nite, Steve Schussler, Chicago, IL 60610; Carrousel Midwest, Dale Sorenson, North Lake, WI; Clocks and Things, Cindy and Joseph Fanelli, New York, NY; Abe Kessler Appraisal Service, Queens Village, NY; Central Florida Depression Glass Club, Ruby L. Davis, Pres., Orlando, FL; Alfred J. Young, Police Academy Museum, New York, NY; Kruse Auction International Auburn, IN; Donald Z. Sokal, Airplanes, Pottstown, PA; Rita Nolth, Tacoma, WA; Michael Auclair, Lace, NYC; Selma Sternheim, Majolica, Monsey, NY; Eugene H. Brown, Lightbulbs, Dodge City, KS; George S. James Pen Fancier's Club, Washington, DC; Fridolf Johnson, Bookplates, Woodstock, NY; H.D. Lazuras, Toy Trains, Panorama City, CA; C.B. Goodman, Telegraphica, Chicago, IL.

PHOTOGRAPHIC RECOGNITION

Cover Photograph: Photographer — Bernie Markell, Orlando 32806; Location — Courtesy of Shirley's Antiques, Shirley Smith, Winter Garden, FL 32787

Color Separations; World Color, Ormond Beach, FL 32074

Pattern glass illustrations courtesy of: Bob Batty, Author of *A Complete Guide to Pressed Glass,* Pelican Publishing Co., Gretna, LA

BECOME AN "OFFICIAL" CONTRIBUTOR TO THE WORLD'S LEADING PRICE GUIDES

Are you an experienced collector with access to information not covered in this guide? Do you possess knowledge, data, or ideas that should be included?

If so, The House of Collectibles invites you to **GET INVOLVED.**

The House of Collectibles continuously seeks to improve, expand, and update the material in the **OFFICIAL PRICE GUIDE SERIES.** The assistance and cooperation of numerous collectors, auction houses and dealers has added immeasurably to the success of the books in this series. If you think you qualify as a contributor, our editors would like to offer your expertise to the readers of the **OFFICIAL PRICE GUIDE SERIES.**

As the publishers of the most popular and authoritative Price Guides, The House of Collectibles can provide a far-reaching audience for your collecting accomplishments. *Help the hobby grow* by letting others benefit from the knowledge that you have discovered while building your collection.

If your contribution appears in the next edition, you'll become an **"OFFICIAL"** member of the world's largest hobby-publishing team. Your name will appear on the acknowledgement page, *plus you will receive a free complimentary copy.* Send a full outline of the type of material you wish to contribute. Please include your phone number. Write to: **THE HOUSE OF COLLECTIBLES, INC.,** Editorial Department, 1900 Premier Row, Orlando, Florida, 32809.

PREFACE

The collecting of antiques and collectibles includes an array of objects as varied as man's interests and activities — any object produced, crafted, appreciated, or used in the past is a potential collectible. Whether an object remains as a secondhand item or becomes a valued article depends on whether anyone saves it, and if so, how many people want it. The value of such collectibles derives from the demand. Many people want stamps; very few people are eager to own old typewriters: accordingly, values for some stamps can be in the thousands or even the millions while typewriters usually sell for under $100.

Within each area of collecting, supply and demand controls the values of items for the most part. If the demand for an item exceeds the supply, prices for that object escalate: the more difficult an object becomes to attain, the more collectors will vie for it. For instance, when numerous investors bought collectibles in the late 1970's, prices rose steadily. But as the economy slowed and investors sold their collectibles, the lessened demand stagnated the prices for the majority of articles.

Still, prices for rarities and favorite items continue to climb quite dramatically for some articles. With the sluggish economy, buyers demonstrate a selectivity and carefulness not prevalent in more affluent periods. Collectors continue to buy, but with caution and great thought. Knowledgeable buyers snatch up the important rarities and items of great popularity, realizing that values will probably increase rapidly when the economy begins to heat up. As everyone becomes more prosperous, more money will be spent on collectibles. This, of course, will increase the demand for such items.

Obviously, now is the time to start a collection or add to your present one. Prices will probably not be any better for the buyer than they are presently.

The Official Price Guide to Antiques and Other Collectibles can help you decide what areas intrigue you and how to approach your hobby with intelligence. This book provides information and listings for almost two hundred different collecting areas. All of the popular fields are represented, as well as some rather unusual fields and some very recent ones. This overview shows the beginner and the specialist hobbyist possible areas that might interest him. Perhaps, you're unaware that beer can collecting is very popular or that science fiction items are avidly sought by many people. You may find items which interest you because they relate to your vocation or to a favorite activity. Gourmet cooks often delight in displaying coffee mills or spice grinders; sailing buffs enjoy accummulating nautical items; and pharmacists and doctors are often attracted to the instruments which show the development of their profession.

In this edition, new sections were added with many of the other sections expanded and revised for greater clarity. Also new are prior year prices which offer an aid to the collector in evaluating price trends. Conveniently placed next to the current price range, any price fluctuations are obvious not only for particular items, but for particular areas.

This guide will allow you to discover and enjoy with confidence the myraid world of collecting. The most attractive feature about collecting is that it becomes what each person makes it. You can choose to let collecting open doors on our past, foster esthetic appreciation, and encourage a greater understanding of man. For each hobbyist, collecting evolves into an activity shaped by their own desires, curiosity, and sensibilities. You can collect merely to decorate a room, to delve into our industrial history, or to restore old articles to their former beauty. Armed with current, up-to-date knowledge, your own individuality can mold the practice of collecting into an art — personalized by your own indelible mark.

THE WORLD OF ANTIQUES

Collectors' items exist by the multimillions. This book will introduce you to some of the more popular types, and to the world of collecting in general. In a sense, the world of antiques is a fantasyland, where objects made to be discarded are (in some cases) selling for hundreds or even thousands of dollars. But at the same time it also encompasses great art items of stirring historical interest. Collectors' items include a gallery of heroes and rogues, a panorama of mankind's changing tastes and habits, a time-machine that takes us back to the past. With collectors' items, you can recall your own youth, or America's infancy. There is scarcely a phase of life, thought, or endeavor into which the world of antiques does not reach.

The dictionary definition of "antique" and the collector's definition are two very different things. Originally, "antique" meant anything pertaining to the ancient world of Greece and Rome. It was used in the sense of "antique poetry," "antique customs," and, of course, "antique art." Even today, European collectors use the word *antiquity* to refer specifically to artifacts of the ancient world. Gradually, Americans began to apply the word "antique" to anything old. According to customs regulations, an object must be over 100 years old to rank as an antique and thereby escape the payment of customs duty if the item is in the dutiable class. Many things collected as antiques are not dutiable, such as books and coins. But when today's collectors speak of *antiques,* they're thinking more in terms of the collector interest than the age. Age of an object, when considered in relation to collectibles, is a very relative thing. A television set made in 1940 is an antique. A transistor radio of more recent date is an antique. Anything which represents an early example of its species is collectible as an antique. And you will find many such specimens listed in this book — things which are definitely collectible and have an established market value, but are much less than 100 years old.

There are other bases on which items become "collectible" in addition to age.

An object may be related to a historical event or celebrity. In collectors' parlance, "celebrity" is a far-reaching word. It includes not just statesmen and national heroes, but show business personalities, sports figures, and even cartoon characters. An object can be collectible because of exceptional design or workmanship or exceptional originality. *Prints* are an example of a collectible that includes both the very old and the new. The buyer of a print does not think exclusively in terms of the age, but the artist, and (secondarily) the subject and, possibly, the medium. Simply because a print has survived 200 years does not rank it as a collectors' item — there are many old mediocre prints worth very little. However, a *tool* or *cooking utensil* 200 years old would automatically be a collectors' item, regardless of its physical attractiveness.

Nostalgia enters into the picture, too. An item could have been extremely ordinary, and really common in its time. But after 20 or 30 years, possibly even in less time, it could have disappeared from the American scene. The disappearance is so gradual that hardly anybody is aware of it at the time. Advertising symbols are a prime example. Do you really notice when they're changed? Do you remember the type of bottle your favorite shampoo was sold in 20 or 30 years ago? Do you remember how a chewing gum wrapper looked in 1945? Probably not — but when you see old everyday things again in the pages of a book or the window of an antique shop, you realize how much they've changed and how much the world has changed. Even though many of these items are really insignificant in themselves, they're appealing as "nostalgia" — little dynamite charges that rock your brain and unleash a flood of capped-up memories. Many of the objects made and sold today, and casually discarded, will be tomorrow's nostalgia items and antiques. The process never ends.

If it sounds as though the guidelines are extremely loose on establishing what IS and ISN'T a collector's item, that is exactly the case. There are no hard and fast rules in terms of age, beauty, rarity or material. The only criterion is whether people are collecting it. If collecting interest exists, then the object or group of objects is *collectible;* it develops established market values (as indicated in this book) and attracts networks of specialist dealers who cater to those collecting it.

Maybe you can't rank a Rembrandt painting and a box of Old Dutch cleanser in the same category. But before you draw the conclusion that some collectibles are second-class citizens, look at some of the well-established hobbies with long reputations. Postage stamps which now sell for thousands of dollars, and are acknowledged by everybody to be prime collectors' items, were *mass-produced,* and sold originally for a *very small price.* The U.S. 5¢ 1847 Franklin, our first postage stamp (for which most philatelists would gladly trade their entire collection) was just a nickel's worth of postage in its day. Look at the world of book rarities. Edgar Allen Poe paid out of his own pocket to publish *Tamerlane,* a collection of his poems. When the book failed to sell, a fit of frustration led Poe to destroy most of the copies. Today, *Tamerlane* is the most valuable first edition book by an American author. There's no reason to feel that TODAY'S ordinary things should be any less collectible than those of yesterday.

Another group of collectors' items is *limited editions,* which are receiving a great deal of publicity and hobbyist (not to mention investor) attention these days. The lure of limited editions is obvious. Scarcity or rarity is a factor in the appeal of many collectibles, and limited editions have an automatic, established scarcity. Only a certain number have been manufactured and there can be no more. Of this certain number, perhaps some are no longer in existence, so the actual scarcity becomes even greater. If a limited edition possesses, in addition to the appeal of scarcity, fine workmanship and originality, its standing as a collectible is assured.

Limited editions have a much longer history than you might think. We're living today in an era of a great number of limited editions, but the 20th century did not invent limited editions as a concept. Commemorative medals and special edition books have been issued as limited editions for hundreds of years. It was largely from the world of print publishing and book publishing that today's manufacturers got their ideas for limited editions. At the height of limited edition book publishing, some super-deluxe volumes were issued in editions as small as 10 copies — printed on vellum, bound in goatskin, and hand tooled. Few of today's limited editions, in books or anything else, exhibit *that* kind of quality.

Many limited editions are listed in this book. As you will note, some have a very substantial value. We would caution beginners, though, against becoming hypnotized by the words "limited edition." The mere fact that something is produced as a limited edition does not guarantee that it will rise in price, or that it will become a sought-after collectors' item, or even that it's well made. A certain amount of profiteering is occurring today in the limited editions market. Some manufacturers are issuing really second-rate merchandise, and charging inflated prices by creating them as "limited editions." With just a little experience you will easily be able to tell the difference between a worthwhile limited edition and one that merits only a furtive glance.

Odd as it may sound, some collectors' items started off as *imitations* of more expensive merchandise. The word "imitation" strikes a sour chord in the ears of hobbyists — but that's exactly how SOME collectibles came into the world. Louis C. Tiffany produced some of the world's finest Art Glass in the late 1800's and early 1900's. Other manufacturers were turning out Art Glass of their own, in various styles. Some of it was just as luxurious and costly as Tiffany's, or even more so. Eventually, it became apparent that middle class America, which could not afford Art Glass, would buy decently made imitations of it. So a number of glass factories started putting out a type of ware known as Carnival Glass. It wasn't as well designed or well made as Art Glass, but it was less expensive. And it sold! Today, Carnival Glass ranks as one of the most popular glass collectibles and some of the prices are just as high as for Art Glass.

Another *imitation* that ranks high with collectors is the "barbarous radiates" of the world of coins. In the later stages of the Roman Empire, the coin portraits of Rome's emperors showed them with beams of light (like halos) atop their heads, instead of the traditional laurel wreath. These coins were called "radiates," because the light beams "radiated." Barbarian tribes in other parts of Europe wanted to make their own coins. But since they knew nothing about art or coinage, they simply copied the Roman coins — thus, "barbarous radiates." Today, many of the barbarian copies of these coins are worth more than the originals, since they had a lower production.

The world of antiques is, without question, one of diversity and myriad collecting possibilities!

BUILDING A COLLECTION

Not everyone who buys collectors' items is interested in building a collection. Hobbyist buyers are in the majority, but there are also those who buy antiques for room decor or functional use (which many antiques do indeed have). There are investors who buy with the motive of turning a profit on their collectibles. And there are many individuals who *occasionally* buy collectibles, because certain items have a special appeal for them, without having the least intention of collecting. But usually, if someone is interested in a particular collectible or group of collectibles, he will become a collector sooner or later — whether he intends to or not.

Collecting has much to offer the hobbyist. It's estimated that about 70 million Americans are collectors, or nearly one out of every three people. Collecting can be exactly what you make of it: expensive or inexpensive, safe or risky, hectic or relaxing. For many of us, there are definite medical benefits in collecting. Just having a hobby to think about beats thinking of inflation, war, stiff joints or other negative things. Collecting opens up new worlds for the hobbyist, regardless of his age or level of education. Collect ancient coins and you're back in the days of Caesar and Cleopatra; collect folk art and you're transported (via that most powerful of all ingredients, imagination) to the simple life of early rural America. The term "food for thought" is certainly true in collecting. Collectors become — frequently — not only experts on the thing they collect, but amateur historians on the era in which it was made. And they immerse themselves so deeply in their hobby and everything involved with it that everyday problems just drift by unnoticed.

Virtually every type of collectors' item offers the possibility of building a collection, and adopting a hobby that can last a lifetime. All of those listed in this book, as obscure or remote as some may appear, fall into that category. And there are numerous others, hundreds in fact, which space limitations prevent us from covering. A visit to any antique shop will introduce you to many of them. So will a casual glance through the hobbyist periodicals, which are available at your public library.

If you THINK you might enjoy being a collector, chances are you will!

The collecting instinct exists in nearly everybody, but many people just don't give it a chance to flower and grow. Mankind has shown a predilection towards collecting since prehistoric days. Evidence of this is constantly found in archaeological sites, where the remains of our distant ancestors lay entombed with their "collections": colored beads, bits of jewelry, crudely chipped flint that passed for works of art. Hardly anyone can honestly say that he's NEVER collected anything. Did you have a stamp collection as a child? Did you look through pocket change for old coins, and gleefully put aside any specimens bearing obsolete designs? Or did you go prospecting for colorful rocks and minerals? Collecting tendencies show up early.

Collecting need not be expensive. And it needn't be time-consuming, if you don't want it to be. This depends on you, and on what you want from your hobby. The goals and motives of collectors are diverse. Some collectors receive most of their pleasure and satisfaction from seeing their collection grow. Others enjoy the hunt and chase: tracking down hard-to-find items, following their trail wherever it leads. To them, browsing for three hours in a crowded antique shop and leaving with dust-laden hands and clothing is a prime exhilaration. And still others enjoy collecting because it leads to meeting other collectors and widening out their circle of friends and social activities.

There are some things you ought to know about collecting — and the philosophy of collecting — before getting in too deeply.

If the prospect of never completing your collection disturbs you, just remember this: in most fields of collecting, no complete collection has ever been assembled. Count Ferrari, an Austrian railroad tycoon, owned the most valuable stamp collection of all time. But it wasn't complete. J. Pierpont Morgan, the banker, owned an art collection valued at $60,000,000 when he died in 1913 (the current value, if it was still intact, would be well up in the billions). But it was really a "miscellaneous" collection: a little of this and a little of that. It wasn't *complete* in any single area.

Working *toward* completion is fine, if your hobby lends itself to that kind of attack (some do, some don't).

WHAT SHOULD YOU COLLECT?

Your selection of a collecting topic depends on finances, space, and other considerations, but mainly on your own personal tastes and inclinations. It's largely a matter of what you'll be most comfortable with. Looking through this book will provide a kaleidoscope of suggestions. While you're thinking, here are some points to ponder. Most areas of collecting can be pursued inexpensively and adapted to fit just about any budget. But this is not, unfortunately, true of EVERY type of collectible. You cannot collect Tiffany lamps or Currier & Ives lithographs without spending rather substantial amounts for each acquisition. This has nothing to do with the size or scope of the particular hobby. Competition is a factor in price, but so is availability. There are millions of coin and stamp collectors — far more than for Tiffany lamps — yet the vast majority of stamps and coins are inexpensive. These are hobbies in which great rarities exist alongside pieces that can be bought for a few pennies. Book collecting is another pursuit in which prices run the scale from zero to lofty heights. Original art, antique furniture, and porcelain are others in that category (plenty to choose from, pricewise). And there are some collecting areas in which the MOST valuable existing items are not expensive at all.

One thing you may want to consider, in thinking about your choice of a collecting hobby, is whether you'd like to collect objects that bear a DIRECT relationship to each other — such as sets. Set collecting can be done with material which was originally issued as a set (as in silverware), or carries dates or numbers that permit set assembly (such as comic books or coins). A typical example of a "set collection" is a run of Lincoln cents, beginning with the earliest one for 1909 and continuing up to the present. With this sort of collection, you always have a clear direction and you don't lose sight of your purpose. But for many people, set collecting is not creative enough. Each component in the set is, in many instances, very similar to every OTHER component. A group of 70 Lincoln cents on which all the "heads" (obverse sides) are identical except for the dates is simply boring in the view of some hobbyists. They want more variety. If you fall into that category, set collecting is definitely not for you!

Another point to consider is whether you'd like to participate in a well-established hobby that's amply supplied with reference literature, clubs and periodicals, or get in on the "ground floor" of one that's just in the process of developing. There are pros and cons on both sides of the fence, so it becomes — as usual — a matter of personal preference. With a well-established hobby, you receive the benefit of all the work already done by experts in terms of research, classification, and inquiry into fakes and counterfeits. On the other hand, items in such a group all carry an equally well-established market value, so there is less chance of finding bargains or making any discoveries on your own. In a hobby which has not yet been well developed, you could get some really excellent buys (things that might be soaring skyward in values, next year or five years from now), but they'll be somewhat harder to find and possibly trickier to authenticate. In some instances, if the hobby is really new, the dealers may not have had the chance to accumulate much knowledge and will hesitate to proclaim an item "genuine" or "fake."

But what it really boils down to is: What do you like? What do you enjoy owning, looking at, handling, thinking about? Unless you get some true satisfaction out of owning the articles, the hobby isn't going to be very pleasurable for you — even if millions of other people are collecting that particular thing. Maybe you've never seriously collected anything as an adult, but you — and EVERYBODY — has inborn leanings in one direction or another. Just as there are foods and clothing styles you like better than others, there are hobbies you are sure to like better than others if you simply explore your own personality and your likes and dislikes in other fields. In other words, give yourself a hobby-aptitude test. The sort of books you read could be a clue. If you like adventure stories you might be a candidate for collecting Old West memorabilia or nautical gear or one of the many other hobbies revolving around relics of adventurous swashbuckling days.

Do you like detective shows on TV? You might be at home collecting first editions of detective novels; or police memorabilia; or old "wanted" posters.

Like pets? Many collections have been made of animal-motif items, such as porcelain dogs and cats, or mechanical banks in the shape of animals.

Are you a travel enthusiast? Stamps and coins take you to faraway places. So do foreign banknotes and many other collectibles.

Into cooking? There are old and scarce and VERY curious cookbooks to be collected, as well as the implements used by our forebears in cooking and eating.

In other words, just about anything that interests you in LIFE can be turned into a hobby, even if you never thought about it from the standpoint of "collecting." For the sports fan, there are baseball and football cards, autographs, team equipment, yearbooks and plenty of other collectibles. For the car buff, there are antique components rescued from vintage autos, as well as all kinds of automotive ephemera.

And how about your job? Love it or hate it, it occupies a good deal of your attention. Are you ever curious about the way your predecessors in THAT TYPE OF JOB worked 50 or 100 years ago? The implements they used? Quite a few collectors get curious enough to become historians of their profession. No matter what that profession happens to be, from clerk to sandhog, you CAN find relics of it in the antique shops. And you may, after reviewing some of them, be very pleased that you weren't in the profession 100 years ago.

More doctors and dentists build collections around their profession than anyone else. In the hobbyist publications, you will encounter many ads placed by doctors and dentists, seeking to buy medical or dental memorabilia of yesteryear. These are, of course, ideal fields for collecting, because the professions are very old, have a well-documented history, and have produced a vast quantity of collectible items of every description. Also, items in these groups have a strong historical interest. Such a collection would be welcomed by any museum if the hobbyist ever decided to part with it. Medical and dental tools dating all the way back to ancient Rome can be found on the market. They aren't cheap, but not terribly expensive either — you could buy most of them for LESS than the price of the first Beatles' 45 r.p.m. record!

Pharmacy is another field which offers a treasury of collectible professional items. We've all passed by pharmacies that featured displays of memorabilia in their windows: a 19th century mortar and pestle, a set of old vials,

8 / BUYING FROM DEALERS

possibly an alcohol-burning stove, and, of course, a stack of well-worn drug directory books. These displays come about because the proprietors are deeply interested in the history of pharmacy — what it was in the past, and how it became what it is today. Often, such displays represent a mere fraction of the owner's collection.

Even a profession in which the basic tools are IDEAS rather than OBJECTS can lend itself to collecting. Many excellent legal collections have been made, consisting of ancient legal doucuments (you can get specimens going back hundreds of years), books, court reports and the like.

Think about your job, and whether it might contain the spark for a collection.

Another consideration in matching yourself up with the right hobby for you is — the PAST. What hobbies did you have as a youngster? Even if your childhood occurred a LONG time ago, and you've collected nothing since then, your best bet in collecting might be to pick up where you left off 10, 20 or even 50 years ago! For one thing, you already have some knowledge of the hobby. (You've retained it, even if you don't think you have.) For another, the mere fact that you took an interest in it AT ONE TIME is a good indication that it will interest you today. Never think that your childhood hobby was "kid stuff," no matter what it was. Anything kids collect can be just as profitably collected and enjoyed by the grown-up generation, too.

BUYING FROM DEALERS

Chances are you will acquire some of your collectors' items by swapping and trading, by finding them in the attic, or even by getting a metal detector and doing your own archaeological exploration. But if you're serious about your hobby and want to build a good collection, you will rely mostly on purchases from dealers.

There may be occasional problems or drawbacks in buying from dealers, but on the whole they serve a vital prupose. Most of the collecting hobbies covered in this book could not exist without the professional dealers. They do the legwork for you, in finding the material and bringing a large selection of it together for your perusal. They serve as a kind of buffer between you and the counterfeiters and forgers who manufacture bogus collectibles. Sometimes fakes do get on dealers' shelves; but without the dealers as a line of defense, things would be far worse. Dealers can be helpful to you in many ways. They have contacts within the trade which would be hard for a private hobbyist to duplicate. If they know exactly what type of item you're looking for, even if it's something very offbeat or scarce, they can usually find it for you.

There are basically two types of dealers in collectors' items. The first is the general dealer. Most antique dealers fall into that category. They offer a broad variety of collectors' items, and possibly some objects which could not be called collectors' items, but are decorative or interesting. The second type is the specialist dealer. He sells primarily — or exclusively — collectors' items of a certain kind, such as stamps, comic books, or prints. Today there are specialist dealers for nearly every type of collectible. Naturally the bigger hobbies have the most specialist dealers; thousands of dealers specialize in coins, for example, while only a handful restrict themselves to something like firefighting memorabilia. This is governed strictly by the degree of hobbyist activity and the amount of money being spent in each field. But whatever your special interest in collectibles happens to be, you stand a 99% chance of finding dealers who have what you want. Quite likely you may need to hunt for them a bit, by checking the advertisements in hobby publications, and then do business with them by mail rather than visiting their shops. You will find that the majority put out price lists and are more than willing to sell by mail. Even the most delicate, fragile collectors' items are sold through the mails. Don't fret over this: the dealers are adept at packing their wares for a safe journey, even if you live 3,000 miles away. If something can't be mailed because of size or weight, arrangements can be made to transport it some other way. Even pianos are shipped.

What are the basic differences in buying from a general dealer as opposed to buying from a specialist?

In the shops of general antique dealers, you will find many of the identical items offered by specialist dealers. There IS a difference, though. The prices are usually a bit lower. When you buy from a general dealer, you will usually pay a lower price for the same item than if you had acquired it from a specialist. The savings might be only 5% or 10%, but it could be as much as 50% or even more.

The general dealer does not have as large a selection of specialist items. This may be fine if you're buying antiques for the purpose of decorating a room or giving one as a gift. But if you're a serious collector and your collecting interest runs in one particular direction (which is nearly always the case with antiques), you aren't likely to find much to choose from in a general dealer's shop. If you collect Depression Glass, for example, the general dealer might have a dozen pieces — or perhaps he might have none at all. A specialist dealer in glassware will be displaying HUNDREDS of examples of Depression Glass. If you collect nautical memorabilia, you could visit a dozen general antique shops without finding one single specimen. Paying higher sums charged by a specialist dealer might be MORE than compensated for by the savings in gas, not to mention the time wasted by hit-and-miss shopping.

There's something else to be considered, too. The general antique dealer does not, in most instances, profess to be an expert on everything in his stock. His wares represent a conglomeration of his purchases from many different sources, and he offers them "as they come." Not all general antique dealers fall into that category, as some deal in a higher grade of merchandise and have experts on their staff to appraise and identify incoming stock. In return for the opportunity to get a bargain, the onus falls upon you — the customer — to decide whether an item is exactly what it appears to be.

The specialist dealer goes to more trouble than the general dealer. He inspects his merchandise more carefully. He has expert knowledge of his pet subject and, usually, a reputation within the field. There is very little likelihood that fakes, counterfeits, or restorations can slip by him. Any item he contemplates buying is rigidly inspected. It goes under a magnifier or even a microscope, if necessary. It's tested in various ways, and it doesn't get into the dealers stock unless it can be pronounced "sound" without the shadow of a question mark. For this extra protection he offers to his customers, the specialist dealer feels justified in charging a higher price. Whether YOU feel like paying the higher price, or using your own skills and instincts to locate collectors' items, is for you to decide. Obviously, there are many differences of opinion on the subject, since both the general and specialist dealers are thriving — there are thousands of each of them spread across the country! Add the flea markets, garage sales, and charity bazaars, all of which are also doing splendidly, and it becomes apparent that America's collectors have no single favorite way to buy.

Displayed Prices. A beginning collector will probably be struck by the fact that some antique shops display prices on their merchandise while others do not. Traditionally, antique shops never showed their selling prices — it was mandatory to ask. This situation has changed greatly in the past decade or so. Nevertheless, you will still encounter many shops (mainly those run by dealers who got into the business many years ago) in which there are no price tags.

The natural assumption, when items are not priced, is that the dealer intends to change the prices — depending on how wealthy the interested party appears to be. This, of course, does happen, but it isn't really the MAIN reason for not showing prices. There has long been a belief in the antique trade that if merchandise is tagged, customers will go through the shop looking at the tags instead of the merchandise. By omitting tags, this rivets customer attention on the items. By the time a customer has developed sufficient interest in an item to ASK THE PRICE, the price may not seem as jolting.

In place of a price, you might find a PRICE CODE. The item will carry a tag or sticker, reading "Stock HDKK" or something of that nature. This is a price code. It reminds the dealer (or his salesman) of the price he paid for that item — which tells him just how low he can sell it, and still come out with a profit. The word "stock" is meaningless — only the letters or numerals following it comprise the code. Each one stands for a number, and when deciphered they spell out a price. There is no universal price code system in the antique business. Different codes are used by different dealers, for the purpose of originality and making their code unbreakable for OTHER DEALERS who might be browsing in their shops.

These days, most dealers know that their customers are able to recognize a price code when they see one, and, further, that quite a few customers will attempt to break the code. This can be worked to their advantage. All the dealer needs to do is PURPOSELY use a simple code, and code each item with a price 30% or 40% higher than he actually paid.

Price Variations. The question most often asked by beginners about buying in antique shops is: How firm are the prices? What will happen if I make a counter-offer? Will the dealer be offended? Do I stand much chance of getting an item for less than the named price?

Generally speaking, prices are not firm in MOST antique shops, the way they are at the supermarket or other places of business, but they aren't as flexible as many browsers seem to imagine.

The situation is generally this: the dealer has a price in mind (it may be tagged on the item, or truly "in mind") that he would LIKE to get — a price that would cover his cost and leave a favorable margin of profit. It may be double the sum he paid, or even triple: this varies depending on the item and its nature, and also his style and volume of business. But the dealer knows, from long experience, that he cannot get the price he'd LIKE to get on everything he handles. Of the thousands of objects in his shop, it is unthinkable that ALL will sell for the full price he believes they should fetch. For some he might have paid too much. For some, he may have overestimated collector interest in the item and bought too many of them. For any of various reasons, it is inevitable that some items will be sold for less than planned at the time of purchase. This is an inescapable fact of life in the collectible business, and it's counted in on the dealer's overall cost of operations, just like insurance and having the roof fixed.

A dealer will be more apt to show flexibility on a price if the item has been in stock for months or (in some cases) a year or more. When stock is relatively new, the dealer holds out, hoping that it will sell for the full price he wishes to get. As time passes and it fails to sell, it becomes evident that the price may need to be adjusted. With some dealers, the waiting period before price adjustment is very short, as they like to turn over their stock rapidly.

Also, if the dealer has a duplicate specimen in stock, he may be likely to reduce the price. When you find two (or more) of the same item in an antique shop, this is an opportunity for possibly getting a bargain. However, the more clever dealers will only display one at a time, keeping all duplicates out of sight.

The term "reducing the price" is apt to be misleading. To determine whether the reduction results in a favorable buy, you would need to know if the ORIGINAL price was in line with the true market value. If a dealer prices something at $300 when the average market price is $200, he can reduce it by 20% and still be charging more than most of his competitors.

With reductions in price, regardless of the dealer or the item, it's strictly a matter of HOW MUCH PROFIT the dealer is willing to settle for. A dealer may be prepared to settle for less profit than he had planned on. He may — if the item has been a real "white elephant" for him — settle for a very marginal profit. But a dealer will not sell for less than he paid. Nor will he even "break even" on a sale. His absolutely lowest price — which may take a good deal of dickering to reach — still involves some kind of profit for him. The only time a dealer will sell for cost or below cost is when he's going out of business or when some other very special circumstances are involved. No matter how good a "dickerer" you may be, you will not induce an antique dealer to part with something for a giveaway sum.

As far as the reaction you'll receive from dickering, this varies with the dealers. Some are insulted. Some pretend to be insulted, but aren't. Some welcome a no-holds-barred discussion about price, because it gets the customer talking and a talking customer is likely to end up buying. You're apt to get a more favorable reception by not drawing attention to flaws or taking a an overly casual approach. The skilled bargainer always takes a positive attitude about the item under discussion. He never asks for a discount because the item isn't EXACTLY what he really wants. Rather, he acknowledges his interest in it, and says something like, "If I could get this for $50, I wouldn't hesitate a minute," or words to that effect. If you have experience at all with antique shops and their proprietors, you can usually tell when dickering will be successful and when it won't. If you and the owner are TOO far apart in price, it's just a waste of your time to get into a bargaining session. Don't delude yourself into believing that you can work the price down to half the original sum. In most cases, a discount of 10% or 15% is the most you're going to get — because 10% off the PRICE means at least 20% off the PROFIT in most cases. And when you bargain, you're bargaining over the amount of profit the dealer is going to make.

There are many possible variations on approaches to bargaining — far too numerous to enter into here. One novel method is worth mentioning. There was a collector who would browse around an antique shop until he found something he wanted — say a tin pelican priced at $30. He would pretend he hadn't seen the item, then casually ask the dealer, "Do you happen to have any tin pelicans for around $20?" This is a very effective approach, because it establishes YOUR price range before the dealer has the chance to establish HIS price range. It's a way of bargaining without appearing to be bargaining.

BUYING AT AUCTION SALES

Antiques and most other collectibles are regularly sold at auctions. Auction buying is exciting, and offers more opportunities for bargains than in buying from dealers, but carries somewhat greater risks. As a rule, auction buying is more suitable for the experienced collector. But there is no reason why a beginner, using caution and common sense, cannot attend auctions and try his luck in the competition.

Some long-standing myths exist about auction sales.

One is that *everything* sold in an auction — whether it's jewelry, cars, or Tiffany lamps — invariably sells for less than a retail dealer charges. It's not hard to see how this notion got started. Antique dealers, and dealers in other collectibles, flock to the auctions and sometimes more than half the sales are made to them. (In European auctions, the figure is close to 100%.) If dealers are relying so heavily on auctions to replenish their stocks, they must be buying well under retail. So if *I* go to an auction, the believers in this myth conclude, then I can buy for wholesale just like the dealers!

It sounds good, but it doesn't work quite that way.

Dealers make many purchases for stock at auction — that is, items to put on the shelf, for which they have no immediate buyer. But it's untrue that EVERYTHING a dealer purchases at auction is being bought "at wholesale." A fair number of his auction acquisitions are made *on commission.* He enters the sale armed not only with his own bids, but those of his customers who would rather entrust their bids to him than do their own bidding. On an item for which the dealer is bidding for himself, he'll drop out of the contest when the price gets beyond wholesale. But those commission bids are sure to be far more than wholesale — much more in some instances. The dealer ends up buying quite a bit, but it would be a different story if he went to the auction to buy only for himself.

At almost any auction, some lots will sell for less than their fair market value. Some will sell right about at the market value, and others will actually fetch MORE than "average retail." You will see the prices in this book (which are "average retail") topped occasionally at auction, and you will probably witness some of these items selling for HALF the listed sums — or even less.

What causes such a wide divergence in auction prices?

Why would somebody pay more for something at an auction than he would need to pay a retail dealer?

Well, it's really all a matter of circumstances. Auction selling is totally different from retail selling, so the results just can't be expected to bear much resemblance. That's why, whenever anybody talks about the VALUE of a collectors' item, it's necessary to stop and add: *average market value.* No collectors' item has a standard value, like the things in a supermarket. The average market value is a balancing out of all the highs and lows.

Competition is the big factor at auctions. It exists in the retail trade, of course, in the sense that many potential buyers may want the same item. But on the retail level, competition is not as direct. The dealer, rather than his customers, sets the price. And the buyer is the individual who gets there first — not the one who's willing to pay the most. When something goes up for auction, there may be two or three collectors in attendance who want it, and to whom the price isn't as important as being the successful bidder. In the case of an extremely rare collectible, the chance to purchase a particular item might not occur for months or even years. A collector who "overpays" for such an item can, quite justifiably, argue that it may be selling for TWICE as much the next time around. This has happened with numerous rare coins, stamps, books, autographs, and (a phenomenon of the 1970's) Japanese arms and armor. There have been many cases, though, of auction bidders paying *more than retail* for items that aren't hard to get — for things that they could have walked right around the corner from the auction house and found in a dealer's shop. That, obviously, seems like something from Alice in Wonderland. Once again, it's the competition that does it. Some bidders are very determined. If they're engaged in a hot contest with another bidder, all logic vanishes. This is why SELLERS often get better prices by putting up their collections for auction, than selling them outright to a dealer. If they're lucky, some of these do-or-die bidders will compete for their treasures, and push the prices up far beyond a dealer's limit.

Hence, if you buy at auction, you are apt to be involved in bidding under a broad variety of circumstances. You will sometimes be bidding on a lot for which YOUR maximum bid represents one-tenth the sum another bidder is ready, willing, and able to pay. And you will, just as frequently or perhaps more so, come prepared to give a small fortune for an item that not a single other bidder wants. These things are very tough to predict in advance. Just HOW difficult they are to forecast can be readily seen by comparing the estimated presale prices (published by some auctioneers) against the sales results. The auctioneers are experts, but even they fall short of the mark REPEATEDLY in trying to foresee a sale's outcome. The price that something brings at an auction is not, therefore, an indication of its value, but only of its value to the bidders in that particular sale. If sold again the next day, with different bidders on the floor, it could go considerably higher or lower.

If it sounds as though auction buying entails a substantial measure of uncertainty, it does indeed. But if you know the mechanics of auctions, have a relatively cool head and sound judgment about collectors' items, you can do very well in the auction arena. The important thing is to keep a rein on your emotions and not overpay unless the item is something extra-special. Also important is to know what you're bidding on: if it's authentic, if it's in good condition, and whether it truly merits the size of the bid you intend to place. Yes, you need to take basically the same precautions in an antique shop, too. But the proportion of misjudged collectibles encountered at most auctions is a bit higher than in antique shops — things that have small components missing, are repainted or cemented back into one piece, or are out-and-out fakes. This is not because auctioneers are less reputable than retail dealers. It's just the nature of the business. Merchandise passes through the auction houses by the truckload. Only the largest, most prestigious auctioneers can afford to pay people to carefully inspect each and every item. All the rest of them sell "as is," or, as the expression is, "w.a.f.," which is auction lingo for "with all faults."

14 / BUYING AT AUCTION SALES

For the larger public auctions of antiques, stamps, coins and most other collectors' items, a catalogue is published in advance. If you're on the auctioneer's mailing list (this will require a subscription fee, unless you're a regular client of the house), you'll receive the catalogue several weeks before the sale. A good catalogue has MOST of the lots illustrated, and detailed descriptions with facts and figures for everything in the sale. More and more auctioneers are realizing the advantages of putting out good catalogues. You will still, however, encounter some in which there are descriptions like the following:

Lot 27. One table.
Lot 63. One box of books.

When a catalogue provides nothing more than descriptions of such brevity, you have to either attend the sale or forget about it. Absentee bidding is impossible with so little data to work from.

Postal bidding is nothing new at auctions; neither is bidding by phone or wire. If the auctioneer describes his wares carefully and accurately, there's no reason to worry at the prospect of an absentee bid. Of course, the nature of the merchandise plays some role. Certain kinds of collectors' items are easier to identify and appraise than others. Stamps and coins fall into that category. A stamp auctioneer need only state that he has a Scott #163 in VF used condition, and every potential bidder knows what he's talking about. It's quite a different matter to describe a 19th Century Dutch parlor cabinet, covering all its strong points and weak points. Unless a prospective bidder SEES the item, or a very sharp illustration of it, it will be just about impossible for him to draw an accurate mental image of it, or to decide how much it would be worth to him. So it should not be surprising to learn that a much larger percentage of sales, at coin and stamp auctions, are made to absent bidders than at general antique or art sales.

If you're going to attend the sale, don't fail to also attend the *presale exhibition.* By law, every *public auction* (this doesn't apply to mail-bid sales) must exhibit its merchandise for public inspection prior to the sale, regardless of whether or not the items have been pictured in the catalogue. The standard procedure is for the inspection to last two or three days, immediately before the sale date. This varies, though: check the auction catalogue or call the auctioneer to be sure.

You could (as many bidders do) wander around the presale exhibit and see what catches your fancy. This is time-consuming, though, and a better approach is to check off — in the catalogue — lots which SEEM as though they appeal to you. Then, at the presale exhibit, you can go directly to them and spend your time giving each a thorough examination. Don't be shy. Pick things up. Look at them from all angles. Use a magnifying glass. The auctioneers would rather have you settle your mind at the presale exhibit, then be dissatisfied about a purchase later.

As you make your inspections, mark your bid limit for each item in the catalogue. This is the time to think about price, not during the heat of competition. At the presale exhibit, you're not being influenced by the prices OTHER bidders are willing to pay. You can make a much sounder judgment of how much you want it and how much it's worth to you in dollars and cents. Once you've decided on the price, stick with it at the sale: be prepared to bow out when your limit is reached. Benjamin Franklin told a story in his memoirs about getting a scolding from his mother when he was very young. He had bought a whistle and was very happy with it; but his mother told him, in no uncertain terms, that he had paid too much for it, and shouldn't be happy with it. That happens with auction bidders, too. You're likely to end up scolding yourself if you pay too much. After you become a little experienced at the auction game, you'll find yourself not even giving a second thought to "the ones that got away." Most times — unless you're going for ultra-rarities — a dozen more chances to buy the same or a very similar item will arise before you even know it.

The sales themselves can be set up in various ways. You needn't be concerned about all the detailed inner workings of the auction business, but a few points definitely matter to bidders. One of these is *reserves*. Some auctions operate with reserves and some don't. At the major art and antique sales, EVERY SINGLE LOT will usually carry a reserve. If a sale is not advertised as "unreserved," you can be certain that reserves are attached to some — or all — of the merchandise. A reserve is a prearranged price agreed on by the auctioneer and the owner that represents the minimum selling figure. If the bidding fails to reach that level, the item is not sold. It goes back to the owner. Auctioneers have mixed feeling about reserves. When they permit reserves, it's a safeguard against the owner suffering a financial loss. Reserves are strictly to benefit the owners. They do nothing for the auctioneers, since the auctioneers have no investment in the merchandise. Bidders, of course, would like every item in every auction to be "unreserved." This would hold out the possibility of some really super bargains.

It is not usually possible to know WHICH lots in a sale are reserved, nor the reserve prices. Auctioneers will not publish or announce the reserve figures. This is considered harmful to the sale, as it plants the notion that the items are worth that much and no more. For auctions to be successful, bidders are supposed to get in the frame of mind that "the sky's the limit." If you're bidding on something and you know that the owner is content to take $100 for it, how enthusiastic would you be to bid $150?

As a general rule, the reserves are not very high. If an auctioneer estimates that a certain lot will sell at $200 to $300 in his sale, you can be fairly sure that the reserve price — if there is one on that lot — hovers somewhere in the $100-$125 zone. If you're willing to pay CLOSE to the retail value, you will ALWAYS be hitting higher than the reserve price. No auctioneer allows reserves to be set nearly that high. It would just be bad business for him — he'd end up with a sale in which half the lots didn't sell.

BUYING FROM OTHER SOURCES

One of the pleasures of being a collector is that collectors' items turn up in so many places — sometimes where (and when) least expected. Depending on the particular type of item or items you collect you MAY be able to do a considerable amount of buying outside the trade and save a great deal of money. To be really successful in buying from supplemental sources — such as flea markets, garage sales and thrift shops — you'll need a little more patience, a sharp eye, and at least a rudimentary knowledge of your field of collecting.

Nearly everybody who gets into collecting fancies himself making a really fabulous "find" in an out-of-the-way place: paying $2 for a grit-laden old canvas that proves to be a near-priceless portrait by Vermeer or VanDyke. Things

16 / BUYING FROM OTHER SOURCES

of this sort *have* happened, and there is nothing to prevent them from happening again. To make a spectacular find, though, the hopeful browser needs more than just a never-say-die attitude and a keen sense of what is and isn't valuable. Luck has to be on his side, because, when something like a Revere plate is nestled in a carton of basement discards, or a Tiffany lamp is mingled with miscellaneous crockery, it gets spotted almost immediately. This is true even of bargains of a somewhat lesser magnitude. Hoards of collectors — and dealers, too — hunt through these sources. The collector population is mushrooming, and EVERY outlet selling secondhand merchandise is combed more regularly and more thoroughly than it once was. YES, terrific buys are still to be found — but, unfortunately, your odds of getting them have diminished.

As a general piece of advice, we would say that confining your shopping EXCLUSIVELY to these secondary sources is unwise. There are disadvantages in trying to build up a collection wholly from purchases at the Salvation Army, garage sales and the like. The selection of these sources in any given field is just not diverse. You have very little to choose from, and you end up "backing into" a collection: building a collection of the objects you find, rather than the items which would make for a really good collection. If you make some great buys at carport sales, for example, it's tempting to stop and think, "Well, isn't it silly for me to pay an antique dealer $30 for something I can buy for $3?" True enough, but these are chance acquisitions. Many items that your local antique dealer offers will NEVER turn up at a carport sale, or in a charity bazaar, or anywhere they can be bought for even a FRACTION less than the full retail value. It's much more sensible to form the basis of your collection via purchases from the regular trade and possibly at auction sales, and supplement these acquisitions with your buys from secondary sources. This pays side dividends, too. By becoming a regular at the antique shops (and antique shows, where hundreds of dealers are exhibiting their wares), your level of expertise on COLLECTIBLES IN YOUR FIELD will become razor-sharp — thereby enabling you to ferret out bargains in an instant when you encounter them.

The type of collectibles that interest you will determine, to some degree, your ratio of success at flea markets, garage sales, and charity bazaars. There are certain classes or groups of items on which good buys occur more frequently than others. And there are some on which they hardly ever occur.

Your best bet, in terms of *availability* and *lower-than-retail prices,* are the newer areas of collecting interest. Material that has just recently become "collectible" is, usually, abundant at these sources, and nine sellers out of ten are NOT aware of its collector status. They have it priced simply as secondhand merchandise which means, most times, virtually a give-away price, but the sellers are not totally uninformed. After a while, they DO discover that their merchandise is being hunted down by collectors and dealers, and eventually the price goes up or they begin to sell it to dealers. This was the case with rock and roll records about ten years ago when rock record collecting was still very new and most people thought "an old record is an old record." If you shopped secondary sources in the early 1970's, you frequently came upon batches of 45 r.p.m. rock discs from the fifties, which obviously had been gathering dust in the upper reaches of somebody's closet for a decade or more. The sellers were not into record collecting. They charged LESS than the original retail prices for their records — usually 50¢, but sometimes as low as 25¢ or even 10¢. They priced them as used merchandise, figuring that if a

BUYING FROM OTHER SOURCES / 17

new record cost $1, these much-played discs should not command such a sum. For rock record collectors, it was paradise on earth. Yes, many of those dusty boxes contained nothing but records so badly scratched that they could hardly be played. But every once in a while a pristine Elvis on the Sun label appeared, or something equally eye-popping. You might still occasionally find a collectible rock record for 50¢ at a garage sale, but it isn't apt to be one worth $50 or $100. Just about everybody is now attuned to the potential value of scarce rock discs and won't let any of the "biggies" slip by.

Sports trading cards present alluring possibilities. If this is your hobby, you might do exceptionally well at flea markets and other secondary sources. Many of the sellers have cards, and VERY few of them keep in touch with the sports card market. They may have a vague notion that card collecting has become much bigger these days than it used to be. They might put aside a Babe Ruth or — say — a card from the forties or early fifties. But as far as being informed on the values of rookie cards from the sixties and seventies, Hall of Famers, and other cards of premium value — they simply aren't. Their cards are usually set forth in cigar boxes or trays, well mixed (it looks like a shambles, but don't let that dissuade you — just remember that pearls were once in oysters) — and anything is likely to turn up. In MANY cases, the cards have been lying around for a long while. They might represent the leftovers of a childhood accumulation, put together by the seller ten or twenty or even thirty years ago. A great rarity such as the 1952 Topps Mickey Mantle card could very well be included. If the seller was collecting cards back in 1952, he might have received that very card in a package of gum. And of course it was just a card to him, like any other — as it was to other card enthusiasts of the day. Since then it's acquired enormous cash value; but if the seller hasn't kept apprised of the baseball card market, he is blissfully unaware of that fact.

On the whole, sports trading cards present the BEST opportunity for making memorable buys at secondary sources. Even if this is not your chosen field of collecting, you may want to search out rare and valuable cards and then sell them to dealers (or hobbyists). All the current prices are contained in *The Official Price Guide to Baseball Cards* and *The Official Price Guide to Football Cards,* each available at $2.95 in your bookshop or from The House of Collectibles, 1900 Premier Row, Orlando, Florida 32809.

Printed matter on the whole yields more bargains than most other varieties of collectibles when mixed in with general secondhand merchandise. Just consider that nearly ALL old — and even a great deal of FAIRLY RECENT — paper material is in the "collectible" category. Then look at how much turns up at the flea markets, bazaars and other outlets! These sources are constantly selling items that people have had for years in their homes. Printed matter is saved by just about everyone, whether they're a collector or not. When any typical attic or basement gets cleaned out, it almost always yields at least one carton of vintage magazines, books, catalogues, pamphlets, repair manuals, or whatever. The owners, in most instances, are not collectors and are not aware that the items are collectible, or that they have any special value. Of course, much of it IS, indeed, junk. You will, in any trunkload or box of miscellaneous paper items, encounter magazines with covers missing, books badly mangled, and loose pages sprinkled around like sand on a beach. It looks disheartening — but the devoted flea marketeer and garage sale addict will always PERSEVERE. Even if just one good buy can be found amid a ton of rubbish, the rummaging is worthwhile. And there are few batches of paper

18 / BUYING FROM OTHER SOURCES

items in which you WON'T find something of at least mild collector appeal. Sheet music is one example out of many which could be cited. Anybody who's studied piano or another instrument bought sheet music. It was used, put away, and forgotten about. Like most other things that have acquired collector appeal today, it was thought of strictly in terms of its utilitarian value. When the individual gave up on his piano lessons, the sheet music — possibly sheaves and sheaves of it — had no further use, as far as he was concerned. If they include Jolson covers, or anything else of a memorable nature, the value can be $30, $40 or even more — and sometimes you'll have the chance to pick them up for little more than the original cover price (25¢ or 50¢).

The subject of paper items naturally brings us around to comic books. This SHOULD be an area of real opportunity for the browser among secondhand merchandise, junkshops, and out-of-the-way outlets for collectibles. Comic books have fallen into the hands of just about everybody. Since so many comics have acquired a collector value, the odds, it would seem, ought to be in the browser's favor for discovering scarce vintage comics. Comics fall into the BORDERLINE category, in terms of the success you're likely to enjoy in finding bargains. The problem here is simply that comic collecting has received widespread media exposure. Almost everyone knows by now (unless they've spent the last twenty years with Robinson Crusoe and Friday), that comics are potentially valuable. So the number of individuals who will place untouched arrays of comics on sale, without first ascertaining the contents and value, is virtually nil. What you WILL run across, of course, are comics worth $1 or $2 which the seller is letting go for 25¢ apiece. If luck is smiling upon you, you MIGHT do considerably better. At any rate it's worth checking through any accumulations of comics that you might encounter. You might want to take along *The Official Price Guide to Comic & Science Fiction Books,* published by the House of Collectibles and available in your local bookshop. Just one special word of advice: condition makes a considerable difference in the values of comics, because this hobby has grown EXTREMELY sophisticated over the years — to the point where comic enthusiasts even inspect a book's staples for signs of rusting. Just because you happen to unearth a scarce comic, which shows a listed market price of $60 or $70, is not a guarantee that this particular specimen is worth that much or even NEARLY that much. Make a careful examination of its condition, unless, of course, the price is so low that it would be worth buying at any rate.

Many other kinds of paper collectibles will turn up at bargain prices. If you go to enough flea markets, you're bound to encounter someone displaying a shoebox (or two) of postcards, offered for 10¢ or 25¢ each. Mostly they'll be common, recent, uninteresting cards — but who knows what might be buried amongst them? If you can find any OLDER card picturing a railroad train, airplane or auto, it's certainly worth more than ten cents or a quarter. There may even be some early *philatelic* postcards jumbled in — non-picture cards printed by the Post Office.

As far as postage stamps are concerned, these are definitely in the *difficult* category, in terms of your prospects for finding desirable specimens at well below market value. Stamp collecting is simply too well publicized. Even if someone is uninformed about the value potential in ALL other types of collectors' items, he usually will find out about the values of his stamps before selling them (if he doesn't know already). Most people who've collected stamps have a reference book lying around the house. Even if it's outdated, it still shows which stamps are worth more than others. Nevertheless, you should not give up without a fight on stamp collections: by all means investigate them when discovered at flea markets and elsewhere, ESPECIALLY when found in the form of an intact collection. There's always hope.

To be thoroughly informed on the subject of paper antiques, refer to *The Official Price Guide to Paper Collectibles,* published by The House of Collectibles. Thousands and thousands of items are listed, and if you're not too familiar with the values of paperana, there are sure to be some surprises in store for you.

CONDITION: A MAJOR INFLUENCE ON VALUE

The condition, or physical preservation of collectors' items, is receiving increasing attention. Collectors are becoming more demanding with regard to condition. For investors (those who plan to realize a profit from their collections), condition is of extreme importance, since it has been shown beyond a doubt that collectors' items in the best grades of condition rise sharpest in value.

Today's attentiveness to condition represents an almost diametric opposite to the situation of 100 or even of 50-60 years ago. In the earlier days of collecting, hobbyists were perfectly content just to OWN specimens of the things they collected, whether they were pristine "mint" or heavily worn. Coin buffs preferred taking old coins out of pocket change, even if the dates could barely be read, rather than pay dealers a slight premium for specimens in uncirculated condition. Stamp collectors committed a much worse sin in causing damage to their treasures after acquiring them. Instead of mounting them in a safe and sane fashion, they took glue and stuck them fast to the album pages.

A common feeling pervaded the world of collecting two and three generations ago. Antiques (and most other collectors' items) were old, so you had to have respect for age. That was a magical phrase, drummed by dealers into their customers. It meant you shouldn't worry about a bookcase with no shelves. Porcelain figures with hands and noses broken off? Books with loose bindings? The advice was always the same: have some respect for age! The collector was supposed to be thrilled that the item had merely survived, regardless of what shape it was in. And the sellers wove some interesting stories around their wares, too, to take your mind off the negative points: this coin was actually used at the time of Julius Caesar (so don't mind that big hole in it); this print might have hung in a prince's palace (so obviously you're going to overlook the staining and wrinkling).

Today's way of looking at things makes much more sense, and not only from a monetary point of view. Collectors' items in the higher grades of condition capture the ORIGINAL APPEARANCE much better. They show how the object looked when it was created, which can be VERY different than its appearance after decades of wear and tear. On a coin, for example, a worn specimen lacks much of the detailing. You may know that it's an 1862 quarter or an 1827 Large Cent, but the noble artistry of its design has long since vanished into a murky blur. Take an uncirculated specimen — or even a "near" uncirculated — and you have an artwork in miniature, sparkling with life and begging to be studied under a magnifier. A colonial silver teapot with corrosion would have been considered, in its day, fit only for the smelter's fire.

20 / CONDITION: A MAJOR INFLUENCE ON VALUE

There are other motives for being particular about condition, too.

One is that an object acquired in a good state of preservation is less apt to deteriorate more while in your possession. When something has already slipped into the mediocre class or worse, it may be just a matter of time before it falls totally apart.

Also, there is an interesting connection between condition and rarity, which apparently escaped our predecessors in the collecting sphere. The old-time collectors staunchly argued that rarity (which they held in lofty regard) was rarity, and condition was just icing on the cake. Actually it isn't that simple. Nearly ALL collectors' items in well-preserved condition have a higher rarity factor than the VERY SAME ITEMS in lesser condition. This is because the majority of existing specimens are, almost invariably, in less than outstanding condition. With some items, there may be one "mint" specimen in circulation for every ten showing signs of wear, use or abuse. With others, the ratio could be 1-to-100 or even 1-to-1000. It varies, of course, with the type of collectible, the age, and other factors. But the fact remains: when you have a collectors' item in mint or near-mint condition, its rarity factor is automatically increased.

Condition, therefore, is a prime influence in buying or selling collectors' items. Whether the beginning collector is really concerned about condition or not, he needs to learn something about it and its effect on prices. Otherwise he is likely to see bargains where they do not exist, or accuse a seller of overpricing when a premium is being charged because of noteworthy condition. If you're bidding at auction sales, you must be even MORE alert to condition and the difference it makes in values.

The prices listed in this book are not (for the vast majority of items) calculated for mint condition. "Mint" condition means absolutely no sign of wear, injury, or any alteration whatsoever from the original appearance. Truly mint specimens of some collectors' items do not exist, because of their age. There are a number of early U.S. coins, struck by the thousands, of which no mint specimens are known to exist. Mint is the ideal, but it cannot always be attained — for love or money. When it can be, it commands prices HIGHER THAN THOSE SHOWN IN THE LISTINGS.

The Official Price Guide to Antiques and Other Collectibles does not set its prices for mint condition because this would seriously reduce the book's usefulness. The prices given are for decently preserved specimens, which show some signs of wear but no serious injuries, repairs or alterations. Specimens in that class are sold much more frequently than "mint," and represent the type of merchandise you will find at better-class antique shops and other collectors' shops. *Defective* specimens will sell for less than these prices. It is not possible to give a blanket rule for figuring out "mint" premiums, based on the values in this book, or for making deductions for inferior condition. The nature of the particular collectible is the determining factor. Generally speaking, if an item is rather common on the whole, it will not command a huge premium in mint condition and may be worthless if defective. On the other hand, a hard-to-get item could carry a substantial premium in "mint," and still have a fairly strong sales potential when worn or slightly damaged.

No grading system fits all varieties of collectors' items. Each item has to be judged in terms of its material, age, the use for which it was intended, and other considerations. Something made as a household decoration to be hung on a wall and admired is in a far different category than a tool or cooking utensil. You would not expect a 19th century sledgehammer to be free of any nicks and scratches. This could only occur if someone took the trouble to put one away for posterity, or if a stray specimen got hidden in the recesses of a warehouse. Quite likely, every single one produced was USED, and in being used they were not handled gently. All you can reasonably demand of this type of antique is that the article be COMPLETE (no pieces missing or restored) and that the extent of wear not be TOO excessive.

In other words — common sense enters the grading picture. Don't expect the impossible, but don't settle for slipshod specimens of items that COULD have been preserved much better. Think twice before accepting the seller's claim that "you'll never see a finer one." You might — right around the corner.

FAKE!

Before an antique or some other collectors' item is purchased, the buyer should answer three basic questions about it. These are:
1. Does it appeal to me?
2. Is it genuine?
3. Is the price reasonable?

The first of these questions is never consciously asked, certainly not by the more experienced buyer. Anyone who has collected antiques, or even merely admired them in museums or the collections of friends, has an instinctive attraction to certain items. Browsing in an antique shop where hundreds or even thousands of items are displayed, he forms instant opinions of virtually everything on view: it is either love at first sight, or no love at all. This is a useful quality for the collector. In time it becomes even more useful. As one grows more and more skilled with antiques, this instinctive feeling becomes more refined; the shopper not only immediately spots what appeals to him, but what is genuine and fake. Many antique dealers can tell at a glance whether an item is what it appears to be, and veteran collectors can do the same. It either registers "good" or "bad," and this first visual impression in an experienced observer is right at least 90% of the time.

The beginner will not be able to trust his instincts quite so much. He has the handicap of being unfamiliar with the genuine article, as well as being unfamiliar with fakes. He is also unaware, usually, of the extent of faking, counterfeiting, and doctoring that occurs with collectors' items, and he thereby tends to keep his guard low. Hence the beginner is the chief target for those who manufacture fakes, and for those who knowingly sell them. If the deck seems to be stacked unalterably against him, it really isn't. There is no reason why a newcomer to the collector's market cannot buy safely, if he uses care and intelligence. The enormously successful traffic in bogus material occurs mainly because most beginners are not only new to antiques, but are quite careless in their buying habits. The old saw, *A fool and his money are soon parted,* goes double for collectors' items.

Fakes have always been on the antique market, coin market, art market, and in fact wherever collectors' items are sold. Pictures by Old Masters were being facsimilized 300 years ago. A brisk trade in faked Greek coins was thriving in Italy at the time of the Renaissance, and doctored or fabricated early American furniture has plagued antique lovers since the 1800's. Faking is not new, but the *extent* of fakery and the *clever methods* now used by fakers are recent phenomenons. For one thing, a much wider variety of items are now being counterfeited. For another, fakers now reproduce or doctor items of relatively small value, whereas they had traditionally concentrated on bigger game. Fakery has become a science. While many of those engaged in it are unskilled and produce easily recognizable products, the business (if we can call it that) likewise has its geniuses who know antiques as well as the best experts, and have devised very cunning ways of fooling the public. Some fakes of extremely high quality are being made today, which was not the case as recently as 10 years ago.

Why has faking mushroomed to such an unprecedented degree in the 1970's and '80's?

There is really no mystery about this. Collectors' items have become much more readily salable. Many types of articles now have value, sometimes substantial value, which once were considered worthless. Also, heavy investment buying of antiques has played its role in encouraging fakery. Investment activity began in earnest in the early seventies and grew torrid by the decade's close with BILLIONS of dollars spent annually by investors and speculators. The investment market was (and still is, to some extent) a paradise for fakers. The initial waves of antique investors were chiefly individuals who bought very impulsively and spent a great deal of money: an ideal combination for the makers and sellers of fakes. Things are now changing somewhat. Investors are becoming better educated as buyers of collectors' items. But there is still such ample opportunity for the sale of fakes that the counterfeiter prospers.

No one can become an expert overnight. And (if it's comforting at all), even the most expert collectors occasionally buy a faked or "improved" piece. Every great collection — of antiques, pictures, coins, stamps or other collectors' items — that has passed through the auction rooms contained at least several fakes, and sometimes an appalling number. Advanced collectors look upon the occasional acquisition of a fake as "the breaks of the game"; and there are some who firmly believe that initiation as a collector is not completed until the first fake is brought home. But this does not mean they take a lighthearted attitude in efforts to guard against fakes and the individuals who sell them.

This chapter gives some general advice for guarding against fakes, and specific advice on articles falling within some of the more widely counterfeited groups. Even if this chapter were the length of a book, however, it would be inadequate in fully protecting the shopper. The facts about fakery, when put on paper, serve only a limited purpose. One *must* supplement this knowledge by looking at, handling, and studying the collectors' items themselves. Explaining how to recognize a faked antique is almost like trying to explain love; one could write volumes and volumes, but the person who *feels* it is seldom in doubt about what it is. High on any beginning hobbyist's list of priorities should be visits to the local museums and historical societies. These may be superb or mediocre, depending on where one lives; but even a second-rate museum has enough displays to provide the basis of an education. Learn not only to *look,* but *how* to look. Study the workmanship, detailing, surface coloration, and other important details of an object; compare these features in one item with those in another. Also, visit the antique shops in your neighborhood and antique shows. At first, be a browser instead of a buyer. Study items in antique shops as IF you contemplated buying them.

Develop a critical sense, a vital quality which the bargain-hunter and casual shopper usually lack. You CAN, gradually, build yourself an armor-like defense against all but the most excellent fakes.

In nearly all cases, fakes fall into one of the following categories:

1. The outright fake. This is what most people think of as a fake, being unaware that other kinds exist. An outright fake is made wholly by the faker, "from scratch." He obtains materials and uses his own processes to create the object, and his goal is to defraud the eventual buyer.

2. The honest reproduction. These are multiplying in number. An honest reproduction is a facsimile of a collectors' item made as a decoration, souvenir, curio, or for some other legitimate purpose without the intent to defraud. They are, however, sometimes mistaken for originals.

3. The doctored item. This is a genuine collectors' item which the faker changes in some way or other to make it appear more valuable, such as a coin on which a mintmark is removed or a silver porringer to which an inscription and date are added.

4. The hybrid. These are objects made from components of two or more collectors' items. Hybrids occur most frequently in furniture. A faker will take two tables, one with good legs and the other with a good top, and marry together the well-preserved components.

Of these four categories of fakes, objects falling into the first (outright fakes) are automatically worthless, except for intrinsic value if they happen to contain a precious metal.

Honest reproductions can, and usually do, have some value, but the value is considerably less than that of the model. There are occasional exceptions to this rule. When a reproduction is made as a limited edition, in a deluxe manner using the best materials and workmanship, it can be a desirable collectors' item in itself and POSSIBLY of even greater value than the original. Some reproductions of antique firearms (for example) attain very high collector value.

Doctored items tend to be considered "spoiled" by collectors, even if they had a substantial value originally. As for the last category, hybrids, these are very commonplace on the antique market and are sold regularly. While the collector value or historical value of any hybrid is open to debate, there is definitely a good demand for them. They have the look of an antique and have a utilitarian value, if the object is a piece of furniture; and many noncollecting buyers will ask no further questions. So it is open to argument, really, whether the maker of hybrids can be called a faker.

Outright fakes are of two basic types: copies of existing pieces, and fantasies which the faker creates without a model. Copies of existing pieces are the more plentiful, as the faker has something to work with and (importantly) a potential buyer may recognize the item as something seen in a book or museum. With coins, stamps, furniture, silverware, glassware, pottery and nearly all other classes of material, duplicate specimens are the rule rather than the exception. Even if a manufactured object is recorded to exist in just a single specimen, this does not rule out the chance of a second being discovered: and that, of course, is incentive for the ambitious faker.

One of your chief weapons against buying fakes (of any variety) is to buy only from the more respected sources of supply. This advice makes obvious sense. Specialist dealers who handle just one type of collectors' item are likely to be expert on that type of collectors' item. A general antique dealer may know little about mechanical banks, and allow a reproduction to slip into his stock, but you would not likely find a reproduction in a shop specializing in old toys. The specialist dealers, because of their reputation for knowing their subject, are very seldom offered fakes for sale. Anyone who knowingly wants to sell a fake will, nine times in ten, take it to a general antique dealer. This may mean a little lower price, but the danger of detection is lower too, and this is what counts in such situations. The less careful and less expert the dealer is, the more careful and more expert his customers must be! You will naturally pay more when buying from a specialist, because his expertise and the fact that his stock is "hand picked" is counted in the price. Understandably, there are some collectors to whom paying the full market values on everything they buy is not appealing. They further point out that restricting oneself to specialist dealers eliminates the fun of poking about in out-of-the-way locations, flea markets, shows and the like. Probably the best general suggestion for the *beginner,* especially the beginner spending large sums of money, is to confine himself to dealers he can safely trust. Thereafter it becomes largely a matter of how well the buyer can rely on his own knowledge. If he has studied his chosen topic well, he can buy virtually anywhere.

The question naturally arises: do antique dealers knowingly sell fakes?

Here a distinction must be drawn between labeling a fake (knowingly) as an original and charging a price comparable to that of an original, and simply placing the item out for sale with a low price tag that should, in itself, warn of its nature. Professional antique dealers very seldom profess a fake to be a genuine item, if they know it to be fake. This of course is illegal and would be, if discovered, very damaging to them. But certain kinds of fakes (or reproductions) are knowingly sold by antique dealers, simply because they may be decorative, interesting, or have some collector appeal in themselves. The nature of the antique business is changing. Not many years ago, the average antique shop displayed a very limited variety of items, and everything in it was expected to be *old.* Today, hobbyists are collecting numerous things that are not old, but which have attraction for their artistry, nostalgia, etc. The antique shop has to flow with the tide. If a large percentage of its customers are not demanding that items be *old,* but merely interesting, this is what it will stock — and the sphere of "interesting" can include just about anything under the sun. There ARE buyers for reproductions of mechanical banks, and not just a few of them. There ARE buyers for facsimiles of many kinds of collectors' items, who admire the originals but either (a) cannot afford them, or (b) are not sufficiently indoctrinated to collecting that it makes any difference to them.

So many tricks are done with furniture, by fakers, that antique furniture ranks among the most difficult of collectors' items to buy safely. Furniture lends itself splendidly to faking: styles and workmanship varied, and so did the woods. Even if a piece does not fit the style of its purported time, it could still be a genuine example of backwoods or folk production (and it might even be worth a premium on that score!). In the days before factory-made furniture, which began around 1840 in the U.S., each cabinetmaker had his own way of doing things. Some were more elaborate than others, and some were simply more talented than others. This is why pieces of antique furniture are never quite alike, and it is also why authentication is no simple matter.

The style of a piece should give sufficient clue to the age, IF it is genuine. There are exceptions even to this, however. The more popular furniture styles have slipped in and out of vogue repeatedly over the years. During the

Victorian era, revivals occurred on many types of earlier furniture styles, including Louis XIV and Baroque. Many sculptured Renaissance-style pieces were made, too. Therefore an item might be perfectly genuine as an antique, and possibly worth a great deal of money, while really being much later in date than it appears. Actual Louis XIV, Baroque and Renaissance furniture are very seldom seen in antique shops, and sell for huge sums of money. When you find pieces that seem to date from these periods, they are nearly always Victorian or from another "revival" era. They can be extremely convincing. The impression they give is heightened by the fact that they have acquired an aged appearance.

The surface *patina* is the most reliable indicator of age in furniture woods. Patina can be faked, but not easily — the results are usually crude. Patina is the surface texture of the wood itself. Old wood is mellow, from generations of use and polishing. Layers of polish build up on the outside and also soak deeply into the wood, where they take the place of the wood's natural moisture. This gives the wood a kind of glow, almost a silkiness, which is never found on modern furniture. Look closely. If the piece is a genuine antique of 100 or more years old, you should find networks of barely visible scratches on the arms of chairs, the surfaces of tables, and on the legs of furniture right near the ground (these being the most vulnerable points). Many of the scratches will be so old that they've worn nearly smooth, and the color within them is identical to that of the surrounding wood. Or the color may be slightly DARKER in very old scratches, from the wax paste or other polishes which have lodged in them. When light scratches are found, lighter than the surrounding wood, this could be an indication that the piece is not antique.

Wormholes are common in colonial American furniture (and everything else made of wood from the colonial era), and in foreign furniture of an even later period. Their absence from any given piece is NOT an indication of fakery. Nor is their presence assurance of authenticity. Wormholes have been faked in various ways. The most popular method is to use a power drill and pinhead bit, with which the faker bores holes about a half an inch deep in strategic places. If a toothpick is inserted into genuine wormholes, it will usually break off at the tip, since worms did not bore in a straight line. In a faked wormhole, the toothpick will come to a stop at the end of the hole but will not break. The positions of wormholes might also be revealing. If they're mainly clustered at the front of the piece, where the prospective buyer is most apt to see them, they ought to be treated with greater suspicion. The worms themselves, 200 years ago, were not thinking about sales appeal.

Look critically at the proportions of a piece of furniture, and whether the style is uniform throughout. Some lowboys are actually floor chests that fakers have set atop a set of table legs. This is a clever deception and is often undetected, because the appearance of such a piece is so visually arresting that one often forgets to look closer. If the top is Queen Anne, the legs ought to be Queen Anne; and the top should neither be too large or small for the legs. On *gateleg tables* it is VERY common for one or more of the legs to be replaced, either with a refinished antique or (much more often) a modern copy. The same is true, though not to quite such an extent, of the leaves on drop-leaf tables. Whenever an antique piece of furniture had moveable parts, these parts were of course likely to wear out before the rest of the object — creating an irresistible lure for the faker. When buying an antique CHEST, see that all sides are original, and that the lid belongs to the base. Because chests are so simple and uniform in construction, it is relatively easy for a faker to interchange components from one to the next.

The method of construction is, of course, a clue to age; one looks for pegs rather than nails, and dovetailed joints rather than glue in antique furniture. The old cabinetmakers prided themselves on being able to join wood without nails or glue, though both existed at the time they worked; this pride evolved into the term "joiner" to mean "furnituremaker." Traces of old glue might indicate repair efforts rather than fakery or modern manufacturing. Nails in furniture are a bad sign, unless the piece is obviously an amateurish creation by someone who knew nothing about the rules of cabinetmaking. Some "folk art" furniture is nailed. This does not detract from the value, if the piece is genuine.

In terms of ornamentation, the turning of wood on hand lathes produced less uniform results than on later machine lathes. This is why, for example, the legs of an 18th century spool-turned table are not precisely alike. The cabinetmaker's goal was uniformity but this was impossible to achieve; and, in the opinion of collectors, this "variety" in antique furniture is one of its charms. Hand carving provides a very useful testament to authenticity. Even if a faker is very adept at hand carving, and can reproduce the old designs used on furniture, it is virtually impossible for him to capture the exact style of the carving. In other words, he may carve just as well as a furniture maker of the 1700's, but the results look a bit different. This is because the early carvers learned as apprentices and were taught certain techniques, which anyone who picks up carving "freehand" in the 20th century will not follow.

Silverware may be wholly faked, or a genuine antique specimen might be doctored in various ways. Fakes of silverware (of both types) have been increasing rapidly because of the focus of investor attention on silver. Antique silverware should carry appropriate markings, and the buyer is well advised to look for such markings before considering a purchase. While it is not commonplace, hallmarks and other silver markings can be faked, and we probably should be prepared to see more of this in coming years.

One method of faking silver antiques is to plate a pewter object in silver. This gives the item a very thin surface coating of silver. It really creates a "double fake": the object has virtually no bullion value, and has much less value as a collectors' item than if it were genuine silver. The weight, of course, is wrong. These plated fakes are lighter than if they were actually silver. But very few prospective buyers are able to recognize the difference. The truth can easily be told by testing (scratching the surface and applying nitric acid, or by specific gravity). If the pewter was marked, the markings will show through the plating — but will be rather indistinct. This in itself is a clue to plating.

Faked silverware is also made by taking a cast of a genuine piece and making reproductions from it. High-grade silver can be used for the fake, if the intention is to sell it for a substantial premium over the bullion value. Cast reproductions look very convincing at first glance: they're the exact size and design of the originals, and the weight is identical if the faker has used the same grade of silver. Usually they can be best distinguished by a close inspection of the surface, which in a cast fake is apt to show numerous tiny craters because of air bubbles in the cast. A clever faker tries to sand or scrape these out, but they will either remain detectable, or, if not, the sanding marks will be noticeable.

Another scam (of many) is the addition of bogus inscriptions, dates, or evidence of ownership, which may purport to link the piece with a celebrated historical character or family. The style of lettering in such inscriptions sometimes fails to suit the period. But an even better tip off is the fact that the silver showing through the inscription looks fresh and new — which indeed it is, having just been exposed. If the inscription were authentic, it would have an aged appearance just like the rest of the item.

Postage stamp faking is almost as old as the stamp hobby. In the dawning years of collecting, dealers (including the most respected) advertised reproductions of rarities for collectors who wanted to fill up their albums, but couldn't locate the real thing. Generally speaking, only the more valuable stamps are faked. A stamp fake may fall into the class of an outright fake, or a genuine specimen from which a cancel has been removed or added, or an overprint removed or added, or which has been tampered with in some other way to raise the value. Fakes of engraved stamps — which are the most plentiful, since nearly all the rare early stamps were engraved — are usually made by engraving a counterfeit plate, just as in making counterfeit currency. The alternative to this is for the faker to photograph a genuine specimen and print his counterfeits photomechanically. This is not as satisfactory because the stamp's surface can be felt with the fingertip in a genuine specimen, while a photomechanically printed stamp is absolutely flat. Some stamp fakes are of extremely high quality, to the degree that even the experts are confused by them. To identify a faked stamp, it is usually necessary to magnify it several times in a strong light, and compare every detail of its design to that of a specimen known to be genuine (also magnified several times). Scholarly books have been complied about stamp fakes. If the hobbyist intends getting into stamp collecting and adding rarities to his albums, he should consult these books. While stamp fakes are hard to detect, the buyer has a safeguard because stamp dealers automatically guarantee everything they sell to be genuine without a time limitation. It is only when buying at auction sales, or outside the ordinary stamp trade, that any real danger enters the picture.

Fakes abound in folk art. The field is inviting to fakers, because original specimens of folk art seldom follow any standard direction in style or execution. However, the burgeoning interest in folk art which arose in the 1960's and continues today is helping to limit fakes as much as possible, as the dealers are acquiring more expert knowledge than they possessed in the past. Some fakes still get through into the showrooms of reputable dealers, but the vast majority end up at flea markets or other secondary sources where they sell for a fraction of what an original would fetch. Nearly every type of folk art from furniture to samplers to watercolor paintings is faked, to one extent or another. Fakers are especially fond of doing furniture, since it can be painted (painted "folk" furniture is not at all unusual) and the painting tends to hide evidence of manufacturing methods. Of course, the paint job must look old to be successful. This is accomplished by using a flat paint (non-gloss), mixing in a little alcohol, and leaving the finished product outdoors for a few months to age. It may be further improved upon by scorching portions of the surface with a blowtorch, or in various other ways — including burying the whole object beneath the ground for a week or more. Sometimes the faker trips himself up by trying too hard. In his effort to captivate the prospective buyer, he may place a large prominent date on the piece, either carved or painted. While genuine pieces occasionally carry such

28 / FAKE!

dates, they are well in the minority, so a glaring date should invariably be cause for suspicion. Another blunder of folk art fakers is to use a picture in a book, of a genuine piece of folk art, as his line-for-line model. If he duplicates a famous piece too closely, he has at once exposed himself, since folk art is usually as different from one piece to another as snowflakes. This is particularly the case with decorations painted on furniture.

A folk art painting on a wooden panel may be very difficult to authenticate. The wood itself is sure to be old: the faker can easily get an old wooden board. He may have aged the painted surface to give it the appearance of being in an attic for two or three gererations. This is not hard to do. Therefore, the critical point will be the execution of the picture itself, whether it seems convincing as a piece of folk art, and very likely only an expert will be capable of making that determination.

On the subject of folk art, *tramp art* (considered a branch of folk art) has also come in for its share of fakery. With tramp art the materials are usually the best clue to authenticity or counterfeiting. If a faker is, for example, constructing a box from matchsticks, he will use modern matchsticks. While these are very similar in appearance to those of yesteryear, they are not quite identical. Likewise the toothpicks ot today — another common ingredient in tramp art — differ slightly from those of the late 1800's. If you choose to collect tramp art, these will be points for you to study.

Autographs from as early as 800 B.C. to those of current celebrities have been faked. However, autographs are one collecting area in which the number of fakes seems to be diminishing — probably because of greater expertise on the part of dealers and more caution by buyers. At one time, autograph faking was a flourishing profession. Some fakers specialized in a single celebrity; "Autograph" Smith, a Bowery derelict, created scores of bogus Abraham Lincoln documents. Though basically illiterate, he had a knack for duplicating Lincoln's handwriting. If you aren't really familiar with a genuine signature of Washington, Franklin, Lincoln, or other celebrities, you are not in a position to detect a fake — even a rather poor one. Leave this up to the experts and buy only from recognized autograph dealers, who will gladly refund the purchase price in the event of any problem. Autographs are one field in which very inexpensive fakes exist, going down even as low as $1 in price. This occurrs because a faked autograph takes just a few seconds to create.

Cast iron toys are reproduced by making molds from the originals and casting the copies in lead or iron. Such reproductions began to be made in large numbers in the early 1970's for sale in giftshops and through mail-order catalogues, inspired of course by the growing interest in the originals. They are identical in size to the originals, but the detailing is not quite as sharp because a little something is invariably lost in using these secondary molds — like making a xerox copy from a xerox copy. Also, the painting is too sharp and bright. As they were not intended to deceive anyone, the manufacturers took no pains to give the paint an aged look. You should not have much problem identifying reproductions of cast iron toys. However a bright paint job is not necessarily an indication of a reproduction. It could be a genuine original from which the paint was worn off, and which some owner decided to repaint.

Coins are high on the list of frequently counterfeited collectors' items. Yet the beginning hobbyist buys almost "blind," believing that the incidence of fakery with coins is low. The assumption that coins are difficult to fake is widespread, and of course fuels the counterfeiter's fire. Two types of coin fakes are in existence: circulation counterfeits and collector counterfeits.

The first group is much older, most of these "circulation counterfeits" having been made in the 1800's or early 1900's. They were produced simply for the purpose of spending the bogus coins as money. Circulation counterfeits are MOSTLY in the nature of gold U.S. coins, in which the gold content is much lower than the .900 government standard. They occur primarily on coins of $5 and $10 denominations (Half Eagles and Eagles). The $20 gold piece (Double Eagle) was not counterfeited as often for circulation, probably because the high face value caused it to be examined more closely. Circulation counterfeits are, on the whole, of very low quality and can be detected with no trouble at all if you have some knowledge of coins. Collector counterfeits include some work of a much higher caliber, as these coins (which are still being turned out today) are designed to be sold to collectors. All types of valuable coins, U.S. and foreign, modern and ancient, are being counterfeited. So long as a coin has substantial value, the faker is not concerned about the metal either — he will fake a valuable copper coin just as readily as one in gold or silver. There may be a slightly higher proportion of faked gold and silver coins on the market, but this is because some old fakes are still floating around. Take a magnifying glass and examine the fine areas of design, comparing them against those of a specimen known to be genuine (it need not, of course, be of the same date, so long as the design is the same). On a counterfeit, the fine detailing is not as distinct as on a genuine coin. This could occur through wear and handling, but with a little experience you will be able to tell the difference between a weak design and a worn one. Another potential problem with coins is the addition of a fake mintmark, or the removal of a genuine one. As the mintmark sometimes makes a vast difference in value, the faker can add several hundred dollars (or sometimes thousands) to the price by this operation. When a mintmark has been falsely applied, it will come loose if the coin is immersed in nailpolish remover for a few seconds and the mintmarked nudged with the fingertip. If a mintmark has been removed from a coin, there will be telltale evidence of grinding, either in the form of scrape marks or a depression where the mintmark should be, or a combination of both.

WHAT MAKES MARKET TRENDS

Those outside the sphere of collecting seldom realize that antiques and other collectibles are subject to trends, fads, and media influences. They assume that because most of the material is old, and familiar to the people buying it, it could not have the ability to set off bursts of excitement. This is utterly untrue, as the collectible markets show again and again. In fact, this is probably one of the most volatile of all international commercial markets, in that prices can soar without much warning and yesterday's ignored objects can be tomorrow's darlings.

Trends are caused in various ways, and the influencing factors can become quite complex. If someone is beginning a collection who has never before collected, the obvious question to ask is: what prompted him to begin? If we probe the various reasons for people beginning to collect, we have further insight into trends in the market.

A certain number of people take up collecting on the advice of a physician, as a weapon against stress; and others, in the old-fashioned sense of a "pastime," to occupy themselves in a harmless way. The ratio of *this type* of beginners remains fairly constant over the years, and so do their tastes. Anyone who begins by consciously attempting to "choose a hobby" will usually select one of the collecting areas that is traditional, popular, well supplied with reference books, and requires a minimum of personal initiative. Coins and stamps rank high on the list (which is not, by any means, to degrade them as hobbies, since any hobby is largely what you make of it). But these beginners do not always travel along like sheep herds. They might start out in basically the same way, buying a stamp kit in the variety store or something similar, but one thing can lead to another. It depends on the person. An individual with little personal creativity or motivation sees, for example, a stamp album as a book with blank spaces that must be filled. His goal is filling up the spaces, and to him that is a "hobby." He goes along filling the spaces, and when all are filled he buys another book and starts over again. Someone else, starting out exactly in the same way, becomes interested in the history and design of stamps. He soon chooses to specialize in one kind of stamp. His interest may then spread to other philatelic items, such as covers or postal cards. Or it could go elsewhere: perhaps the beauty of stamp engraving will lead him to collect engravings or other pictorial items. This is how, in a sense, "the men are separated from the boys." Some people just accumulate; others make a real sport of their hobbies.

But, as we have said, this comprises just one faction of beginning collectors — and they are distinctly in the minority. Those who *choose to start a collection* because *they would like to have a hobby* are far outnumbered by those who get into collecting in various other ways.

Many collections are begun without any decision to collect. They just "happen." The spark can be a chance purchase or reception of an exquisite gift, or discovery of something old and curious in the attic. At first the motive is to find a companion piece to it, not to build a collection. But the companion piece, after being located, fails to satisfy the subconscious collecting desire. More and more "companion pieces" are sought, and gradually the individual is building a collection and acting like a collector: going to antique shops and shows, reading the hobbyist publications, perhaps even joining local clubs. He has become a collector by degrees, and it may be a long while before he pauses to realize that he IS a bonafide collector. Collections begun in this way can, likewise, dart off into other directions. There may be love at first sight in collecting, but exposure brings new loves atop new loves. The average beginner is familiar with few collectors' items, aside from what he might have seen in museums. After becoming exposed to a wide range of collectibles, by way of visiting shops and shows, he often discovers that his passions run in more directions than one. You cannot very well be interested in collecting something if you've never seen it, and possibly not even known of its existence. MANY of the items covered in this book fall into that category. They may seem offbeat to collect; but if you see and handle them, and especially if you see a good collection of them properly labeled and displayed, your feelings are apt to be quite different.

Another way in which collections begin, and which influences the market, is through a desire to decorate one's home. Many people, seeking unusual or conversational decor, will browse in an antique store, even if they have never entered an antique store before in their lives. Quite a few of these individuals have no actual interest in antiques, and would recoil at the prospect of becoming a collector. But they know very well that the antique shop has decorative accessories of a much more singular nature than the department store or the mail-order catalogue. They will perhaps begin with something "safe" like a framed print or an anonymous Victorian oil painting in a gilt frame. Initially, they think of the home's color scheme and how well this new acquisition will suit the drapery or the carpet. If it draws favorable comment from the neighbors, they may go back for more; and, with each purchase, they give less and less thought to color scheme or room decor. The point is finally reached where they buy for the *item* and not for what it will add to the home, and they, too, have become collectors at that juncture. In fact with the majority of such persons, the interest in collecting becomes so extreme that the original purpose is lost entirely: what began as a careful approach to decorate the home turns, gradually, into a total disregard of the home's decor, and everything is rearranged to make ample space for the growing collection. It can happen to anyone. And if it happens to YOU, you won't be at all distrubed by having your living room lined with early American tools or porcelain owls. In fact, you will be firmly convinced that the room never looked better. To a collector, nothing makes a better decoration than his collection, even if it's rusty railroad spikes.

A collection may also be started for strictly financial reasons, for the purpose of building it up and selling it for profit. In this case it deserves to be called an investment, rather than a collection; but the effect on the market is, of course, the same. Whether someone is buying for investment, or for fascination with the item, or for any other reason, a sale is a sale. In recent years, investment buying has enormously increased, and has extended into many of the less traditional areas of collecting, which previously were unnoticed by investors. Investment buying has a very strong effect on the market; first, because investors usually spend rather substantial sums of money; second, because "bandwagoning" is common with investment buying. That is, when ten investors are buying something, ten others are likely to follow, and like ripples in a pool the buying activity widens outward. So extreme is the effect of investment buying, sometimes, that investors literally control the market on that particular type of collectors' item, at least for a period of time. This has happened with gold and silver U.S. coins, with classic (pre-1870) postage stamps, Old Master paintings, and a number of other classes of collectors' items.

INVESTING IN ANTIQUES

Antiques and other collectibles have become, in recent years, the focus of heavy investment attention. In some areas of collecting — coins, paintings, and a number of others — the dollar volume of sales made to investors exceeds that to hobbyists. Brokers are now in business to give advice to those investing in collectors' items and to act as agents in buying and selling. Publications are issued for the hobby-investor. At major auction sales, the majority of bidders are, often, investors.

This book is intended mainly for collectors. But it will obviously be read by many investors as well, and by many collectors who are curious about the investment angle in their hobby. Thus, we offer the following summary of facts and opinions on investing in collectors' items, prefaced by the statement that the publishers of this book neither *advocate* or *caution against* investing — it is for the reader to decide.

Investing in collectors' items is not a new phenomenon. The scale on which it is practiced today is, however, unprecedented. The origins of this current wave of investment can be dated roughly to 1964, when the U.S. government decided to remove the silver content from their dimes and quarters and reduce it drastically in their half dollars. This led immediately to hoarding silver coins then in circulation, and, what was more significant on the hobby market, a rush to purchase (for investment) scarce-date silver coins of all kinds.

Once investing had made itself felt in coin collecting, it gradually spread into other collectibles. Most of the silver coin investors profited, largely because they acted in unison and helped each other: with investors competing *against* collectors, prices went up faster than would otherwise have been the case. This drew in more and more investors. But some potential investors, at that time, believed that coins had already become overpriced (they were proven very wrong!), and looked for other collectors' items to invest in. They bought sculptures, Chinese jade, arms and armor, stamps and other things. And in each of these fields, the situation that prevailed with silver coins tended to replay itself. Activity on the part of investors shook the market, sent prices up faster than the usual rates of increase, and brought more investors into the picture. However this was still on a rather small scale compared to the chaotic investment activity which occurred in the following decade, and especially in the final few years of that decade (the 1970's). By then, all collectors' items had advanced strongly in value since the original dabblings by investors. They had more than demonstrated, over the years, that investment in them was just as sound or sounder than in the traditional forms of investment. What was needed, then, was simply a "push" to drive armies of traditional investors (in stocks, bonds, savings certificates, etc.) into the direction of antiques and other collectibles. Several "pushes" occurred during the 1970's. They included the devaluation of the U.S. dollar; rampaging inflation, not only in the U.S. but worldwide; the instability of the world monetary system; and — most significant — the failure of these traditional forms of investment to realize any worthwhile profit. With the exception of oil and real estate, nearly all investments performed disappointingly in the 1970's. Even those showing a profit turned so meager a profit that the rate of inflation wiped out all gain.

Investment in collectors items on a *grand scale* began overseas slightly before it began in the U.S. In Japan and Western Europe, where inflation was more drastic than in America, investors were turning to art and antiques in the early seventies. When prices for collectibles boomed abroad, as of course they did from the super-strong competition, the effect was dramatic on the U.S. market. Foreign investors by the score started buying from American dealers to take advantage of the savings. But the savings did not last long. Very shortly, U.S. prices for art, antiques and other collectibles were on a par with those of Japan and Western Europe. And the level of investor buying in all these far-flung regions of the globe was about the same — as it is today.

Of course, certain groups of collectors' items were targeted by investors (and their counsellors) more than others, while some received practically no attention whatever. At first, the chief logic of investors was to go with "blue chip" collectibles, things that had a long history of being collected and stood very little chance of going out of fashion. Thus they concentrated on Old Master paintings, prints, rare books and manuscripts, fine furniture, rare coins, stamps, and jewelry. They sought material which was ALREADY expensive, but which had plenty of popularity and the glamor of rarity behind it. And, as mentioned above in the case of early silver coin investors, they tended to benefit from the fact that most of the investors acted as a unit, competing for the same items in the same sales and thereby driving up the prices very, very high — often far out of proportion to the most recently recorded sales. When "investment fever" reached its height in the late 1970's, sales of art, coins and other collectibles broke their previous price records by 300%, 400%, and even 500%! And in some cases the previous record had been established only a few months earlier!

Naturally the reports of such sales, which always found their way into the media, encouraged more and more people to become investors in collectors' items. And that increased the competition and drove up the prices still further at the NEXT sales.

Today, as we approach the mid 1980's, antiques, art, coins and other "collectible investing" has been with us long enough to give us a fairly good perspective on its long-term potential, and to draw some conclusions which would have been impossible to arrive at (without a crystal ball) as recently as five years ago.

Collectible investment has proven itself more resilient than its critics believed. They were convinced that the first wave of heavy SELLING by investors — returning their purchases to the marketplace and taking their profit on them — would seriously reduce values and discourage any further investment. These collectibles would, they felt, be treated in the same manner as declining stocks.

Well, the first wave of heavy investment selling has come and gone — followed by more selling, in a rather balanced flow, since the late seventies. A VERY sizable amount of the merchandise bought by investors during the 1970's has gone back on the market, and some of it has passed through the hands of dealers and/or auctioneers half a dozen times since then. The disaster predicted by critics did not occur. Some slumps were evident in certain areas of collectibles, but these have occurred historically through the years without any influence from investors. In most cases, the slumps were not of long duration because new investors came in to snatch up bargains that resulted from falling prices.

Investing in collectors' items is here to stay. It is not a fad. Investors will be buying collectibles for as long as investment of any kind is engaged in. It can likewise be said that the dreams of HUGE PROFITS, held by many of those who invested in collectibles during the 1970's, were overly zealous. Some people thought they had found the secret road to riches — that investing in collectibles was like a legal form of chain letters. Succeeding events proved them to be wrong. You can make money by investing in collectors' items. You can also lose money. As in most other investments, some luck is involved, because the market is influenced by many things that cannot be easily predicted. But common sense and CAREFUL STUDY of the investment qualities of EACH COLLECTORS' ITEM are the most important factors — and that was where many, many "bandwagon" investment buyers totally missed the boat. They bought (and some are still buying) blindly, knowing nothing about collectibles, collectors, or what makes the various markets for collectibles "tick." They operated on the assumption that if one collectible goes up in value, all others will go up proportionately. Perhaps this is the case in some fields of investment, but in antiques, art, coins and other collectors' items it is definitely not the case. The first requirement for successful investing is that the buyer knows what he's purchasing: what sort of investment prospects it has, and whether the particular specimen merits investment.

In other words, you cannot simply "invest in collectibles." You choose your subject, analyze the field, and buy methodically.

Even then, you are not GUARANTEED success. But your chances of turning a profit, on a well-selected collectors' item bought for investment, are unquestionably in your favor.

So many subtle considerations are involved that we cannot detail them all here. For a much more thorough exploration of investing in collectors' items — with all the pros, cons, and professional strategy — the interested reader is advised to consult the series of books on that subject published by The House of Collectibles, 1900 Premier Row, Orlando, Florida 32809. These include *The Official Investors' Guide to Gold, Silver and Diamonds; The Official Investors' Guide to Gold Coins; The Official Investors Guide to Silver Coins;* and *The Official Investors Guide to Silver Dollars.* The basic methods outlined in these works can be applied to any types of collectors' items.

The person who contemplates investing is, often, misled by the changing values of collectors' items. This is one basic "hurdle" for a new investor to clear. For example, someone has purchased a certain antique five years ago for $100. He opens a magazine today and discovers an advertisement offering the item for $200. The instinctive reaction is that he could double his money, in five years, by purchasing additional specimens for investment. There ARE some collectors' items, in fact quite a few of them, on which the investor can profit in five years or even less. But in this example, he would be ill-advised to go out and put a great deal of money into the item that rose from $100 to $200. The simple fact is that you DON'T double your money on something which rises in value that gradually. You may actually end up taking a loss on it, depending on circumstances.

Let's explore things a bit further.

When that item is selling for $200, this represents the retail market value — such as is given in the listings section of this book for thousands and thousands of collectors' items. If YOU, as a private owner, sell the item to a dealer, you will not receive $200. You may get only 50% of the retail market value, which means getting back the $100 you paid for it five years ago. But you still aren't even "breaking even." In the meantime, inflation has reduced the buying power of money. One hundred dollars isn't worth as much, today, as it was five years ago. You would need to receive CLOSE TO $200 JUST TO BREAK EVEN, in terms of the actual value of the money. So what appears on paper or in your imagination to be an excellent investment is really not one at all.

To be a worthwhile investment, an item would need to recover the cost price (when sold); PLUS compensate for the declining value of the dollar; PLUS leave you a profit when BOTH OF THESE FACTORS have been taken into consideration. To accomplish this, the investment item needs to rise in value at a fast pace. In addition, YOU the investor must watch the market and be aware of developments occurring on collectibles at that time — so you can seize the proper moment to sell.

It is very common for investment buyers of collectors' items to use mistaken strategy. Two of the usual blunders are:
  1. **Looking for bargains.** This can work if you're extremely well informed on the market for collectibles of that type. Otherwise you may end up

discovering that your "bargain" was selling for a low price because of limited buyer interest.
2. **Buying items that are going up fastest in price.** This sounds logical but in collectibles it isn't usually the right approach. When an item is going up more rapidly in price than similar items in its group or series, this normally indicates a rush of investment buying — which in turn indicates that investors are in possession of a MAJORITY of the specimens in circulation. That presents a risky situation for any further investment. When the holders start selling, they may all sell at the same time (this happens), and the price could fall rapidly. It is much more sensible, in this kind of circumstance, to purchase a RELATED item whose price has been more stable in recent months. You will save some money, and, if things go true to form, other investors will very shortly be buying it — so you stand a much better chance of your investment going up in value. If two coins (different dates) of the same series are selling for about the same price, yet one had a mintage of twice as many specimens as the other, sound investor strategy is to buy the lower mintage piece REGARDLESS OF WHICH ONE HAS BEEN MOVING UPWARD THE QUICKEST IN PRICE. Of course, production figures are not available for most collectors' items. In that event, their scarcity ON THE MARKET has to be used as a yardstick in determining their investment quality — coupled with the sort of demand shown for them by collectors in the past and likely to be shown by collectors and investors in the future. An investor needs to be alert to price movements and how to interpret them. If a Royal Doulton figurine sells at auction for three times the normal retail price, this is apt to indicate an upward swing for other Royal Doultons of that type and possibly for ALL products manufactured by that company.

SELLING YOUR ANTIQUES

The Official Price Guide to Antiques & Other Collectibles is designed as a guide to *buying*. The first step in selling is to properly identify your merchandise and evaluate it. This can be easily accomplished with the information in this book. However, the price you receive in selling will depend on many factors. For some collectors' items you may be able to realize close to the full retail values as given in the listings. For the majority, sales will probably need to be made at a sharper discount, the amount of discount varying according to the item, its condition, current demand at the time you sell, where you sell (what part of the country), and what method of selling you select.

Many misconceptions prevail about selling collectors' items. Some people are automatically suspicious of dealers in collectibles. Mostly, these are individuals who have never been collectors, and therefore have not had personal contact with dealers. They've had collections willed to them, or found potentially valuable objects in the attic, and the thought immediately crosses their mind: "If I sell these things to a dealer, he'll take advantage of me." They have the notion that dealers get most of their stock by conning the public and buying for 5¢ on the dollar or some other ridiculous sum.

36 / SELLING YOUR ANTIQUES

Then — on the opposite end of the spectrum — you have people who think a dealer is cheating when he refuses to pay the full retail value or close to it. If a dealer is charging $30 for an item, this type of individual expects to be paid *at least* $25 for the same item. It just doesn't work that way, most of the time. Dealers cannot work on that narrow a margin, between their buying price and selling price. Remember that they aren't only turning over merchandise but at the same time are paying rent, utility bills, phone, employee salaries, advertising and all sorts of miscellaneous expenses — which add up to a huge amount of money. Yet the dealers have just one source of income, the sale of their goods. So there must be enough margin, between their cash investment in stock and its selling price, to cover these expenses AND leave the dealer a reasonable profit besides. Like anyone else, the antique dealer is in business to make money, and if he's a good businessman (which most of them are) he'll review each potential purchase coolly and unemotionally. All the alluring facets of a collectors' item which make it appealing to YOU and to collectors in general are meaningless to him. He can't allow himself to think like a collector and fall in love with fine workmanship, glowing patina, handsome carving, or historical connections. He has no choice but to think of prospective purchases in just one regard: What is the item worth to ME? How much can I safely put into it? Do I have any customers who might be interested in it? How long will it remain in stock before selling? Might I have to reduce the price BELOW THE ORDINARY RETAIL VALUE before making a sale? In short, is it worthwhile for me to buy the item at all?

If the item falls into the "popular" class and is in good physical condition, most dealers will be willing and even anxious to purchase it, so long as the seller is willing (in turn) to accept a reasonable price. When an item is in the borderline category — not really popular, but salable if the right customer comes along — the dealer would just as soon not buy it, unless he can buy it for a very favorable price. In this kind of situation, the item's retail market value is not the primary consideration.

It works this way:

Let's say a prospective seller comes into the shop with a "borderline" item. Just to give an example, we'll say it's an early typewriter. There are collectors for early typewriters and they DO have established market values (see the listings in this book). An old typewriter is certainly not a "white elephant." On the other hand, it does not fall into the fast-moving category for most antique shops. People do not buy old typewriters for decorative purposes. They do not buy them for investment. They do not buy them because "they'd like to start a hobby." For someone to buy an antique typewriter, he has to be a real dyed-in-the-wool, enthusiastic collector of antique typewriters, who's purposely going from shop to shop to seek them out. There are probably just a few dozen people in the whole country who roam about antique shops looking for old typewriters. Therefore, the dealer to whom such an item is offered has to stop and think. Possibly the item has an established retail value of $100. If he sells it to a collector who knows and appreciates the value, he can get $100 — or maybe even slightly more. But will such an individual ever enter his shop? The odds are, for most dealers, against it. If he could be reasonably sure of selling the item at its full retail value, he would not hesitate to pay at least 50% of that value for it ($50). But in this case, he would be taking a colossal gamble by giving $50. If the seller is intent on getting that kind of price, most dealers will politely decline the item. The only way this sort of merchandise is desirable to a dealer — even mildy — is if the price represents a minimal gamble. If a dealer can purchase an item with a retail value of $100 for $25 or $30, this is usually considered a worthwhile gamble — though, of course, if it fails to sell, *any* money paid for it is lost. In other words, the dealer is using mathematics and odds. The odds of him selling the item quickly are low; the odds of him selling it at all are medium; therefore he can be encouraged to take the gamble only by a very attractive price.

There are some classes of items for which you can get CLOSE to the retail value, in selling to a dealer. If you have bullion coins to sell, coins made of gold or silver which are in used condition and therefore of no numismatic (coin collector) appeal, a dealer in coins will pay you about 90% of his selling price for them. Oddly enough, you can get a better price, in relation to the dealer's selling price, on bullion coins than you can on mint condition coins of numismatic interest! This is one case where "junk" comes out on top! Why? Because the dealer's selling price on bullion coins is based on the daily market quotations for gold and silver. All dealers use the same market quotes, so nobody can undercut anyone else. Also, this material moves out at a rapid pace, and there is no argument about its condition because the buyers want it for bullion investment only. So the dealer can give you 90% of his selling price, and still handle such material profitably. He can't do that with the other merchandise in his shop. A rare coin in "mint" condition might be a very profitable item for him to buy and sell. But he will not pay 90% of the established market value, because a degree of uncertainty exists: the coin, even if a superb collectors' item, might not sell for months. And there is no guarantee, in these days of volatile price movements, that the value will hold steady. His buying price includes an EXTRA MARGIN to cover the possibility of a declining market. Still, you will do somewhat better selling coins OF GOOD QUALITY (that is, scarce dates in uncirculated condition) than selling many other kinds of collectors' items. You may receive 70% or 80% of the retail value for a really good coin, in other words $70 or $80 for a coin that the dealer can sell at $100.

As we said, many factors enter into the price you receive (or the price you're offered) when selling collectibles. Let's take a look at some of them:

1. Dealer's stock on hand. This, of course, varies from dealer to dealer, and even among the same dealers at different times of the year. You aren't in a position to know what kind of stock the dealer has on hand, or what he has coming in, yet this does play a role in determining (a) whether he'll be interested in purchasing your antiques, and (b) the extent of investment he cares to make in them. When a dealer says he's overstocked, this is not necessarily a ploy to induce you to accept a low price. All dealers in collectors' items DO become overstocked periodically — and they become *understocked,* too. It all hinges on the pace at which material moves in and out, and that's governed largely by circumstances over which the dealer has only partial control. Sometimes he'll go for weeks without anyone offering to sell him anything. Then armies of sellers all arrive at the same time. This works fine if the volume and flow of buying is comparable to that of selling. But if the dealer has been buying more than he's been selling, he has no choice but to slow down for a while. No dealer likes to bypass the opportunity to buy worthwhile merchandise, but he can't have more cash going out than coming in. Overstocking could occur in general (an overall slack period for selling), or the dealer might be overstocked on just certain types of items. At any given time, *specialist* dealers are usually overstocked on some items and "all out" of others. This is true of dealers in comic books, coins, stamps, baseball cards, and most fields in which the dealers TRY to keep a comprehensive stock of everything in the hobby. Naturally it is less true of the general antique dealer, because so much exists in the way of antiques that no dealer makes an attempt to stock it all. The matter of overstocking is confusing to some prospective sellers and it sometimes leads to friction between the dealers and public. In the case of comic books, for example, all the dealers buy new comics in wholesale batches as they come out, selling some immediately and putting the rest away for future "maturity" as collectors' items. When a recent comic shows a value of $2, this does not mean a dealer would pay $1 or even 50¢ for it. The comic's value at retail bears no relation to his degree of interest in buying it, which is virtually nil. He already has dozens of copies on hand, which he bought at the bare minimum wholesale price, right from the distributor. Unless a real stampede develops for that particular comic, he's not going to increase his stock until a goodly number have been sold. This holds true for baseball cards, too. Dealers stock themselves up on the new issues as they come out, and it's usually at least *two or three years* before they start buying these sets from the public.

You can sometimes induce an overstocked dealer to buy, by offering to accept a reduced price. But why should you do this, when another dealer might possibly be in need of that particular item, and be willing to pay more? If the opportunity exists to "shop around," by all means do so.

2. The Dealer's clientele. Every dealer — whether he sells antiques, militaria, dolls, or whatever — has his own special group of customers, who are the life and blood of his business. Some of them are sure to be general collectors, but others are specialists, and the specialties of these clients can be very exclusive in some cases. An antique dealer may have a customer who wants nothing but augers (old tools uses to bore holes in wood). You could survey 99 other antique dealers and find NONE who have customers for augers, but this particular dealer has one — and an avid one to boot. The customer possibly has one of the largest collections of augers in the country. He wants to buy any specimens and ALL specimens that he can find, regardless of size, shape or color. He never says "no" to an auger. Consequently, the dealer knows he can sell any augers that come into his stock. When an auger is offered to him, he automatically buys it, and he may pay a higher proportion of the retail value than he pays for other antiques. He has a sure sale at a sure price, so his degree of risk is just about zero. He wishes, in fact, he could buy a hundred augers or a thousand of them. Unfortunately, it is difficult to know what sort of clientele the dealer has, or what kind of objects they have a pet interest in. The only reliable indication of this is when the dealer runs buying ads. The pages of hobbyist periodicals are filled with buying ads placed by dealers, for all conceivable types of collectibles. You will note that some dealers are advertising to buy merchandise in which no other advertisers are expressing any interest. This is not because the dealer wants the items for stock. If they're offbeat and not of real interest to the trade in general, no dealer would be THAT anxious to stock them. You can be certain the advertiser has a special customer for them, and that every specimen he acquires is instantly turned over to that customer. It definitely pays to read the hobby periodicals — and also check the classified ads in your local daily newspaper.

The type of items that a dealer displays in his shop may be a clue to those in which he's most interested in buying. Certainly if you find an antique shop whose stock consists mainly of glass, this would be a more likely place to sell a collection of glassware than to a "general" antique shop. But it does not always work that way. In the example given above — of augers — you would not find a single auger in the shop, even though its proprietor would rather buy them than anything else. Why? Because every one he purchases is sold immediately to his special customer, without ever going out on display in the shop. This is the situation with many kinds of merchandise in many collectors' shops. What you see "out front" displayed to the public is the general stock. Articles that have been bought for special clients aren't around any longer.

3. Geographical location. With some types of collectors' items the PLACE of sale can be a factor in their price. Values given in this book are averages for the country as a whole. If an item has definite *regional interest,* it can be counted on to sell somewhat higher in that locality and, usually, a bit lower than the average elsewhere. More collectors' items have regional interest than you might imagine, though it is not usually strong enough to influence the value by more than 10% or at the most 15%. Items of STRONG regional interest (more than 10-15% difference in value, when sold in the locality of interest) include *early town and county directories, early city maps, city plans and views, vintage photographs of local interest (street scenes),* or anything dealing with a local celebrity or important historical event. Also of strong local interest, though the prices might vary somewhat, are early printed books from the southern and western states. A dealer in Arizona, for example, who specializes in rare books will pay MORE for an early Arizona imprint than will a rare book dealer in Maine or Michigan. Some rare book dealers slant their stock HEAVILY toward material of local interest — not only because there's abundant native collecting interest, but the fact that local libraries, museums and historical societies are potential customers.

The above are examples of added value placed on collectors' items for city, county or statewide local interest. There are classes of items on which the value differs in *different parts of the country.* Nautical memorabilia and gear has traditionally brought the best prices in New England. This is the nationwide center for nautical antiques and seafaring collectibles in general, largely because the old whaling industry of the 19th century was based there. The area has many nautically-oriented tourist attractions, and therefore draws numerous visitors who are interested in ships and the sea. The same is true of Old West memorabilia in the western states. It does better, pricewise, when sold from Texas to California, because this was its general place of origin and the area where MOST current collector interest prevails.

It also happens, sometimes, that certain collecting hobbies thrive a bit stronger in some parts of the country than others, for no really explainable reason. This has been the case with knife collecting, to name one; it has been more popular in the southern states than elsewhere. In the earlier days of *rock and roll record collecting,* nearly all collecting activity was confined to New York and California (this has since changed). Comic book collecting was a big hobby in New York before it surfaced anywhere else.

4. Condition. We have a chapter in this book on condition so there's no point going into it too deeply here. The inescapable fact is: when an item is worn, damaged, or otherwise not in the best of condition, it is not worth the full retail value. It may still be collectible and salable to a dealer, but it represents a kind of question mark for him. Maybe if the item was in "mint" condition he would not hesitate to purchase it. In inferior condition, he will automatically wonder how long it will take to sell, and whether it will sell at all. Some dealers do not care to stock damaged or defective items. Others will do so, in certain cases, but their buying offer will be CONSIDERABLY less than their offer for a mint or near-mint specimen. It may be just 10% of the retail value of a mint specimen or even less. If that seems unfair, you should stop to consider that the dealer is in a bind when he handles merchandise of that nature. He has to offer his customers a very healthy discount on it, possibly selling it for a third as much as a mint specimen. Therefore he can put very little money into it. Of course, you will want to be certain from your own examination, or that of a trusted friend, of the item's condition before offering it for sale.

Some types of items become worthless or almost worthless when defective, such as baseball cards and comic books (unless very rare). Porcelain or glass that is chipped or has any components missing is in the near-worthless category. However, there are other collectors' items — such as coins — for which a market exists on specimens in less than the best condition.

Even some relatively minor factors can make a difference in whether or not you're successful in selling your antiques, and the price obtained for them. There is usually a distinct difference between selling a single item and selling a collection. Dealers like to buy collections IF they've been put together with care and thought; IF the majority of items they contain are of more than minimal value; and IF the collection is not of a miscellaneous nature. A general antique collection, consisting of furnishings, household decorations and utensils, usually includes some items — sometimes many — that the dealer cannot use. He may offer to buy the collection, if there are enough items in it that he considers salable FOR HIM. But the prices you receive will be well below the sum total of every item's retail value. In calculating his buying price, he will figure about 50% of retail for the readily salable pieces and possibly 25% to 30% for the questionable ones. If the collection comprises about an equal number of pieces in both groups, you would then receive somewhere in the neighborhood of 35% to 40% of retail for it. Whenever a collection contains items of more than one type, it's considered "miscellaneous" and the buying price is usually not as high. Ideally the dealers would like to buy only specialized collections devoted to one type of item. This is why your collection will probably have more resale potential if you become a specialist collector — and especially if your chosen area of specialty happens to be something popular. In coins, for example, a coin dealer would rather buy a set of Walking Liberty Half Dollars than a collection of different types and denominations. There's the chance, on such a purchase, that he can sell the collection intact to a customer without going to the trouble of breaking it up and offering the pieces individually. When a dealer feels he can sell a collection intact, just as it comes, he will pay a very high proportion of the retail value for it. This is called a "low overhead" collection — one on which very little time and money need be spent in selling.

The method of presentation plays a role, too, and this is frequently overlooked by prospective sellers. If someone has been a collector, he usually does not make the mistake of poor presentation. He knows that stamps are supposed to be mounted on album pages, that coins should be enclosed in holders, that prints should be matted and so forth. But the non-collector selling family heirlooms may have no knowledge of proper presentation. Every antique dealer has had the experience of a seller coming in with a cloth sack, bulging with merchandise, and unceremoniously dumping its contents on the floor. If you take coins to a dealer in a tin coffee can, or jewelry in a manila envelope, you're seriously hurting the chances for a successful sale. This indicates to the dealer that YOU place very little value on the items. But a good presentation goes beyond this. It means cleaning up your items, if necessary, before taking them to sell. Anything found in an attic, garage, basement, or even something that's been hanging on the living room wall for years is sure to need a cleaning to get into presentable shape. Polishing may also be called for, depending on the nature of the item (do not polish coins). Don't get over-zealous and try to make an antique look brand new — that isn't the objective. The purpose is simply to make it look as though it hasn't been ignored for 50 or 60 years. Dust, dirt and grime do not add to the charm of antiques; they DETRACT. Surface patina (of wood, leather and other materials) is another story and it should not be tampered with. As far as REPAIRS are concerned, it is best NOT to attempt making repairs to any collectible for the purpose of enhancing its sales value, unless the repair is very elementary. You may do more harm than good. Chances are, if an item needs extensive repair work it will not be salable either BEFORE or AFTER the repair is made, as it will then fall into the category of a "restoration," and many dealers will not care to handle it. This however depends on the nature of the article and its rarity. An exception to the foregoing is ancient (Greek and Roman) statuary, pottery and glassware, which is nearly always restored.

If you have a collection which is mostly in good condition but contains some defective items, it may be best to REMOVE the defective items before offering it for sale. These sub-par components in a collection will always catch the dealer's eye and may give him a negative feeling toward the collection as a whole. Then, when you discuss price, the dealer is sure to point out the inferior condition of these items. Just like your garden, your collection may need weeding out before selling it. Put it in the best shape you can, and you'll stand an excellent chance of getting a satisfactory price for it.

SELLING BY AUCTION

Maybe you enjoy buying at auction. Have you considered the possibility of selling your collection in that fashion, when the time comes to sell?

Auction sales have become a much more popular method for selling all types of collectors' items. The chief attraction of selling by auction is that you have the chance — with a little luck — of realizing more than a dealer would pay for your collection. A dealer has to resell the material, so of course he takes a deduction from its retail market value in figuring up his purchase price. At auction, the sky is the limit. If two or three determined bidders lock horns on something YOU own, they could drive the price up far beyond the retail market value. Even after the auctioneer's "house commission" is deducted from the selling price, you would end up doing better than selling outright to a dealer.

Of course, it doesn't always work that way. Auctions are unpredictable. Just as you have the opportunity, at auction, of realizing more than a dealer

42 / SELLING BY AUCTIONS

would pay, the possibility also exists that your collection will bring LESS than a dealer would have given. Those are the breaks of the auction game.

Consider the type of collection you have for sale, its contents and value, and you may be able to judge fairly accurately which method of sale holds out the brighter prospects.

The best types of collections to sell by auction are those which are highly specialized and those containing a large proportion of investment items. But as you will see by attending auctions or just reading the reports of them, many collections are sold — thousands of them annually — which do not fall into either of these categories. Their owners chose the auction route, when they could have sold to a dealer and received quicker payment.

There are all types of auctions. They range from posh sales of art and jewels, accompanied by lavish catalogues which serve as reference books in themselves. At a sale of this type, bids totaling more than a million dollars might be recorded in less than a hour. At the other end of the scale are country auctions and state sales, at which anything under the sun is apt to turn up and where lots can go for as low as $1 each. (But do not underestimate the country or estate sale, either — when desirable collectors' items are included, as they sometimes are, dealers and collectors flock to them and the prices can get very, very strong.)

Some auctioneers are specialists while others handle whatever comes along, so long as it falls in the nature of secondhand property. The biggest groups of specialist auctioneers are those handling coins and stamps. Material of this nature requires specialist knowledge to appraise and classify, so it is very seldom sold by the general art or antique auctioneers. If you have a specialized collection, it is advisable (when selling by auction) to seek out an auctioneer whose sales are geared to that type of merchandise. Such an auctioneer has an established mailing list of active buyers for THAT PARTICULAR KIND OF COLLECTIBLE, and you're sure to do much better pricewise than if you select a local auctioneer just because of convenience.

The procedures vary among auction houses, in terms of the arrangements made with sellers and also the actual rules and regulations of their sales. The amount of their commissions varies, too, but this usually proves to be a rather minor detail. You should not automatically choose the auctioneer who offers the lowest commission rate (i.e., the percentage he deducts from the sale price of each lot before settling with the owner). When one house is operating on a 10% commission and another on 15%, it might seem as though the 10% house is the obvious choice. This just isn't so. Usually when an auctioneer is charging slightly higher commission rates than the competition, it's because he spends a great deal more in advertising and promoting his sales, and on the preparation of his catalogues. Therefore, the prices realized at his sales are likely to be MUCH higher — so you would do better selling through him, even though his commission rate might seem discouraging. A low commission rate is, often, an indication that the house has a hard time attracting property for sale. When an auction house has an established record of successful sales and satisfied clients, it has no problem getting material to sell. So do not allow yourself to be influenced by differences in commission rates.

If it's any comfort, look at things this way. The highest rate of commission in the auction business is around 25% — with MOST houses charging from 15% to 20%. With a 25% commission, you receive 75% of the sale price, on EVERYTHING that sells. This is quite a different story than selling outright to a dealer. It is not very often, in selling to a dealer, that you would receive 75% of the sum for which HE sells the item. This isn't because auctioneers are more generous or honest than retail dealers. They aren't either; it's just a matter or circumstances. When an auctioneer pays you, he's paying AFTER the sale has been made. He makes no investment in stock and therefore takes no risk of ending up with unsold or unsalable merchandise. So naturally he can afford to keep less for himself than the retail dealer. When a retail dealer buys from the public, he's buying with his own capital and without assurance that the item will sell or the price at which it will sell.

When you put material up for sale by auction, it is never sold immediately. It has to be lotted and catalogued and the catalogues have to be distributed. All of this takes time. It may be two to three months, between placing the merchandise in the auctioneer's hands and the actual date of sale. And, thereafter, it might be another 30 days before you receive settlement. Settlement is seldom made quickly. Each auction house works by contract. You and the auctioneer sign a sales contract at the time of placing the material in the auctioneer's care. The contract spells out all these details — the rate of commission, the sale date, and the length of waiting time between the sale date and receiving your payment.

CARE & STORAGE

Most collectors' items call for a minimum of attention in maintenance and storage. Here are some general suggestions:

ALMANACS. If you have runs or sets of the same title, don't get them bound into hard covers. While hard bindings offer an edge in preservation, their value is reduced by binding them. Have slipcases made instead, if you want to spend the money. An alternative is to store them in mylar envelopes, in boxes. Extremely rare, valuable almanacs or those in very fragile condition should always be kept in mylar.

AUTOGRAPHS. The traditional approach was to keep autographs in scrapbook-type albums with stiff pages, attached to the pages by means of philatelic hinges (for small items) or photo-corners (for larger ones). Today many hobbyists are using so-called *presentation books,* sold at stationary shops, which are ring binders containing clear vinyl pocket-pages into which the specimens can be inserted. These presentation books are made in various sizes up to a gigantic 18 x 24", so they will accommodate virtually any kind of autograph material. A drawback is that the pages are not made from chemically inert plastic. In a warm humid climate they could, over a period of time, become sticky and possibly cause damage to the contents. An alternative is to use philatelic *mint sheet albums* with mylar pocket-pages. These are very satisfactory, except that they're available ONLY in the size of mint sheets of postage stamps. Autographed material should *never be laminated.* Framing is another storage approach, and may be suitable for a small collection. Autographed items ought to be matted before framing, as the matt serves as a buffer between the autograph and the frame's glass cover.

BANKS, MECHANICAL. Never repaint the bank, or tamper with the mechanism. A small dab of oil on the joints of moving parts is permissible. Do not oil the whole bank. Washing is not recommended as it can cause removal of paint. Surface grime which is not ingrained can be removed with a dry artist's brush.

44 / CARE AND STORAGE

BARBED WIRE. The objective should be to preserve specimens in the condition in which they were discovered, within reasonable limits. Most collectors do not wash their specimens but clean them by brushing. Adhering mineral particles are considered attractive by some barbed wire hobbyists. If a specimen is badly rusted it can be treated by soaking for two or three days in kerosene, then boiling in ordinary water, and soaking again in kerosene for another two or three days. It is then brushed with a hard-bristle brush and, finally, coated with a thin layer of petroleum jelly. Whether this procedure should be performed on specimens with very little rusting, or only those heavily rusted, is for each collector to decide. No real difference will be made in the value. It's mostly a question of what pleases your eye. *Do not varnish or shellac* barbed wire.

BASEBALL CARDS. Albums with specially made mylar (chemically inert) pages are now available for keeping collections of baseball cards. This is the best storage approach for any collection containing valuable cards. Another method is to keep them in filing trays, of which there are special models for baseball cards on the market. Moisture, direct sunlight, dirt, and careless handling are the chief enemies of baseball cards. When handling a card, hold it by the edges to avoid fingerprints on the printed surface. Do not allow the front (glossy) sides of two cards to rub together. If stored in trays, always arrange cards so that all the front sides face forward.

BEER CANS. A just-emptied can should be thoroughly washed before adding it to your collection. A slight alcoholic residue, if allowed to remain, will create a noticeable odor and may also attract insects. Pour about one tablespoon of dish detergent into the can; fill the can one-half with hot (but not boiling) water. While holding your thumb over the can opening, shake vigorously for about ten seconds. Then rinse several times. After it's fully dry, some collectors will sprinkle a pinch of borax into the can before placing it on their display shelves. this serves as a further safeguard against invasion by insects.

BOOKS. Books are one class of collectors' items in which repairs, when expertly performed, enhance the value. Wonders can be done to damaged books, by rebinding, recasing (resewing the leaves and returning them to the present binding), mounting the leaves if fragile, closing tears in pages and replacing portions of missing pages. None of this work is, of course, inexpensive, and would hardly be worthwhile in a book of low value. If a book is very valuable, a bookbinder can make a special plush-line box to keep it in, with a lettering label on the back just like a book. In storing books, do not overcrowd shelves; and, by the same token, do not keep shelves half filled and thereby invite the books to tumble around. Use bookends when necessary (the "L" type, rather than the decorative but worthless kind sold in giftshops). If a book has penciled notations or underlinings, these can be removed with a pencil eraser. Ink notations cannot be removed. Books bound in genuine leather, whether calf, morocco or one of the other leathers, should be dressed from time to time. Use a good leather dressing such as British Museum Leather Dressing (readily available in the U.S.), and apply it with a cotton swab in a gentle circular motion. If leather bindings are not dressed, they dry out; the leather becomes brittle and eventually cracks or just crumbles into powder. Do not position bookcases so that they receive a great deal of direct sunlight, as this is sure to cause fading to the spines. When you see a book whose spine is paler than the covers, it's been stored by a sunny window.

CARE AND STORAGE / 45

BOTTLES. The approach to take in cleaning a bottle is determined by the amount of cleaning required, and whether or not the bottle has an applied label. In the case of bottles with applied labels, the label is of course a point of added interest and value, and should not be put to any danger in the cleaning process. For such bottles it is usually deemed wisest to do only a rudimentary cleaning, such as by whisking away surface dirt with an artist's brush. If the bottle has no applied label it can be subjected to a thorough cleaning. Any excavated bottle is sure to be in need of a good cleaning: with some the color cannot even be identified until cleaned. When bottle digging first became popular, the general feeling was that bottles should not be emptied of their contents, when found partially filled. Today the almost universal practice is to empty them, not only to accomplish a better cleaning but because the contents are apt to cause unpleasant odors or even damage the glass. When uncorking a bottle of undetermined contents, keep it well away from your face. As a general rule, gloves should be worn when handling newly excavated bottles or when cleaning bottles. An antique bottle that *looks* sturdy will sometimes shatter at the least provocation. Golf gloves are excellent for this purpose as they're thin enough to get the feel of what you're handling and are not slippery. The first step for excavated bottles should be to loosen chunks of adhering earth and mineral matter, using a brush or dental probe. Then soak the bottle for an hour or so in plain warm water. This will loosen much of the remaining grime, after which the bottle is soaked for another hour in a pot of warm soapy water. The water should not be hot, as excavated bottles react badly to sudden temperature changes. After removal from this second soaking, the bottle will have a greasy feel and still look quite grimy. If immersed in lukewarm plain water for a few minutes, most of the still-adhering earth and debris will come free. The bottle is still not entirely clean at this point, and you may or may not be satisfied to leave it that way. If not, the whole process can be repeated again. When an excavated bottle is in a really bad way, it can be soaked overnight in kerosene, then thoroughly washed in warm soapy water as above. It may be necessary to clean the inside with a wire-handle brush, while the bottle is filled with sudsy water. Bottles with narrow mouths usually require this treatment, as simply soaking does not get the inside clean. Finally, after all is done and the bottle has dried, it can be rubbed on the outside with mineral oil on a soft cloth. You have now brought back the color as much as possible to its original state.

CANES & WALKING STICKS. When made of wood, use commercial scratch remover and furniture polish to keep them looking their best. Use a paste polish rather than a liquid.

CHALKWARE. Wash in warm sudsy water. Don't scrub or brush — you'll probably remove some of the paint.

CLOCKS. Clock repairs and restorations should be performed only by a skilled professional *who specializes in antique clocks.* Just because someone is adept at repairing modern clocks is no assurance that their success with antiques will be any better than a layman's. Restoration of antique clocks can be a very time-consuming and costly process, depending on the size and complexity of the specimen and the number of parts which must be replaced. It is nearly always cheaper to buy a working specimen at the full retail value (as indicated in the listings section of this book), than a non-working "bargain" and have it repaired.

46 / CARE AND STORAGE

CLOTHING. Guidelines for the care and preservation of antique clothing are similar to those for clothing in general. Folding should be avoided if items are to be stored for a long period of time; they should be hung instead. Air circulation is very beneficial. Clothes should be taken out of the closets to air periodically, or, at least, the closet doors left open occasionally. Moths and other insect pests are more likely to attack antique clothing than that of today, because early clothing was not chemically treated in any way by the manufacturers and represents "raw food" for insects. Camphor crystals sprinkled about the closet floor and shelves should be helpful. Do not place them in the pockets of clothing or directly on clothing. Antique clothing should never be machine washed, or machine dried.

COINS. Many beginning collectors make the mistake of believing that coins, being made of metal, are almost invulnerable to harm and can be stored without any special care. This is certainly not the case! A poorly stored collection is sure to deteriorate in value. If you buy an "uncirculated" coin and fail to store it properly, it soon loses its "uncirculated" status and may be worth less than half the purchase price. Many types of coin storage equipment are on the market. The simplest is the cardboard folder, with diecut holes, for keeping sets of Lincoln cents, Mercury dimes and other U.S. coins. These are convenient for beginners, but in terms of storage protection they rank rather low. It is much better to get a three-ring binder and some vinyl pocket-pages, available at any coin shop. Coins are not placed loose into the pockets, but are first mounted in 2 x 2 cardboard "window" holders or 2 x 2 "flips," which are vinyl holders without cardboard frames. In recent years there has been a controversy regarding the "flips," since they contain a chemical known as PVC which can become sticky in hot weather and possibly damage the coins. Another means of storage is with 2 x 2 paper envelopes, which can be kept in a box. Information about the coin is written directly on the envelope. This is somewhat of an old-fashioned approach to the hobby, but it still has many adherents. Whatever method you choose, the important point is that coins should not be handled too much while unprotected. Pick them up by the edges. This is especially true of uncirculated specimens, in which the design is still very high and all details are present. Never allow two coins to bump or rub against each other. Do not attempt to clean or polish coins in any way. This invariably does more harm than good. The exception to this rule is ancient coins, which, when the surface is dull, can be lightly rubbed with olive oil. Some products are advertised which, it is claimed, bring out dates on worn coins. These are highly acidic solutions; they cause pitting to the coin's surface and should never be used.

COMIC BOOKS. Thanks largely to the high cash values attained by old comic books, collectors have become very alert to the question of storage and preservation. Comics are somewhat more difficult to preserve than regular books, first because they lack the protection of a hard binding and second because the interior pages are usually of a low-calibre paper stock. Even if a comic is acquired in "mint" condition, it can rapidly deteriorate while in the owner's possession if not carefully stored. Comics should be kept in mylar (chemically inert plastic) bags, sold by the comics dealers. The bags can either be filed in boxes, which is the more popular technique, or placed in albums. Comic books are vulnerable to damage or deterioration from heat, humidity, sunlight, rapid temperature changes, dry air, and mishandling. Restoration services are now offered by advanced specialists, which can accomplish a great deal in improving a comic's appearance and possibly in increasing the value somewhat.

DECOYS. If the wood looks very dry and whitish, rub the entire decoy with a mixture of one part castor oil to two parts linseed oil on a cloth. Pay more attention to the bottom than the top. Repeat this process every few months, or more often if the wood quickly becomes dry-looking again.

DOORSTOPS. If made of brass, use ordinary commercial brass polish.

FIREPLACE EQUIPMENT. Collectibles of this nature are often in abominable condition when found, having absorbed generations of smoke and soot. It is seldom possible to restore them to the original state, even if this were desirable; in the opinion of many collectors they should be left strictly "as is." If a cleaning attempt is made, the course to follow will depend on the object's construction. Ironware can be scrubbed with household ammonia, then dried and brushed with petroleum jelly.

FURNITURE. The care and preservation of antique furniture is somewhat more complex than that of most collectors' items. Mostly one is dealing, in antique furniture, with wood; but the woods are of vastly different types, and what is good for one is not necessarily good for all. However, some points of general advice can be given.

If an antique item is being purchased for utilitarian use, consider whether the use might injure its value as an antique. This would be a major consideration if the piece is very valuable. Some types of antiques, such as china cabinets, can be used without fear of deterioration. With chairs and gateleg or drop-leaf tables, one would need to think twice before placing the item through the rigors of daily use. SPECIAL CAUTION must be used with slant-front writing desks, as the fold-down writing board is NOT sturdy enough to support the weight of a typewriter — they were not made with typewriters in mind.

Metal hinges on doors or other components of antique furniture are likely to be rusty, unless they have already been treated or replaced. Remove them, soak in kerosene for several days, wash thoroughly with soap and water, and coat them with a thin film of petroleum jelly before replacing them. It is possible that some "squeaking" will still persist, but this is not usually considered objectionable in an antique.

If furniture is grimy when acquired, which is often the case, it should be washed with a mild cleanser. Do not use anything stronger than laundry detergent as a risk exists of disturbing the wood's patina. And do not make a really foamy lather, as this only adds more difficulty to the rinsing process. Avoid cleansers which contain ammonia or acetone. Getting into remote areas, especially on a piece with complex detailing, may require a toothbrush or other type of brush. Unfortunately the hardest to reach areas are invariably the most in need of cleaning, as they were apt to be neglected by former owners.

Antique furniture should be polished regularly (once a month in dry climates, or every two months where humidity is high). The results from polishing, in visual terms, will vary depending on the item. Factory made furniture, in which (usually) a thin veneer covers raw wood, does not absorb polish very well — but should still be polished nevertheless, simply to keep the surface from becoming dry and lifeless-looking. With older antiques you are sure to get more satisfaction from polishing. The wood is of better quality and has been building up layers of polish for many years — and layers of OLD polish are a perfect recipient for NEW polish. Always use a paste polish and apply it with a cloth. The liquid polishes may, in some cases, be satisfac-

48 / CARE AND STORAGE

tory for antiques, but paste polish is far more nourishing to the wood and NEARLY ALWAYS produces a better appearance.

If you do use liquid polish, avoid the spray-on types. These often contain a cleanser in addition to the polish, and invariably are harmful to the fine finish of antique furniture.

Old scratches in antique furniture, which give the impression of having received many coatings of polish over the years, ought to be left alone. Recent scratches in which the exposed wood is much lighter than the surrounding area can be treated in various ways. Ordinary commercial scratch remover may do the job: if it doesn't help, there's not much danger of it hurting. These preparations have an oil base, which is good for the wood. But you may get much better results with the following approach. Take a wax crayon of approximately the same color as the furniture wood. Crumble it into a cooking pan, and add several drops of castor oil. When the wax is thoroughly melted and mixed with the oil, pour it out and allow to dry and harden. After becoming hard, it can be shaped into a ball and rubbed into the scratch. The addition of castor oil helps the wax to adhere better to the wood. The area is then polished. This might need to be repeated a few times before hiding the scratch, depending on its severity. For a really bad gouge, wood filler is the answer (sold at hardware shops). You can make a better grade of wood filler — superior to the commercial product — if you want to take the trouble. You'll need sawdust (about half a cup), a coloring agent (commercial wood stain is fine), and a colorless wax candle. Melt the candle and pour the liquid wax into the sawdust, churning the mixture with a fork. Add enough of the coloring agent to make the mixture SLIGHTLY DARKER than the furniture wood — this is necessary because it will dry a little lighter than it looks when wet. When you have the ingredients thoroughly mixed, apply enough to fill up the gouge, wipe off any excess, and leave to dry overnight.

LABELS. Fruit-crate, matchbox and other labels can be kept in blank philatelic albums, using stamp hinges to mount them.

LOCKS AND KEYS. These are often heavily encrusted with rust or corrosion, from exposure to the elements; many have been buried beneath ground. Some collectors prefer to leave them as is. If you wish to remove the rust, follow the procedure outlined for Barbed Wire.

MAGAZINES. Runs or sets of magazines can be dealt with in various ways, to be governed by their value. Magazines of obvious rarity and value, such as pioneer issues of *National Geographic* or the first issue of *Playboy*, should be stored in mylar envelopes or bags, which can be kept in file boxes. Those of a more ordinary nature, but which still fall into the sphere of collectors' items, can (as one of the alternatives) be stored in slipcases. Inexpensive buckram-covered cardboard slipcases are available for magazines of various sizes, to hold one full volume or half a volume. These make a neat appearance on the bookcase shelves. Another possibility is to have them bound into hard covers, which is automatically done by libraries and by some collectors. This makes them easier to keep track of and gives them added protection. However, the binder should be given strict instructions not to remove the covers or advertisement pages, as this would seriously reduce their value as collectors' items. The least costly approach, though not the safest in terms of providing protection, is to file them unbound on shelving, just like books. This can lead to loosening or tearing of the covers, if the magazines are removed and replaced frequently on the shelf. Do not use scotch tape in mending torn magazine covers or pages. Magazines with deep

CARE AND STORAGE / 49

subscription folds down the center can be improved a bit by placing them under a heavy weight for several days. Sandwich them between sheets of waxed kitchen paper before doing this. A stack of books makes an acceptable weight if nothing better is available.

MEDAL (DECORATIONS). They will nearly always be in good condition when acquired, as past owners have usually given them careful attention. When a medal shows any evidence of surface grime, it can be cleaned by rubbing with a damp cloth. Following this, a rubbing with olive oil gives the surface a good protection and also enhances the appearance.

METAL — COPPER. Copper is subject to corrosion, which usually takes the form of a greenish crust that gradually spreads all over the item's surface. When an antique copper article shows mild corrosion, it may be considered attractive and desirable. Copper nautical gear and farm tools (to mention two groups) are always corroded to some extent when found, so the presence of corrosion on them cannot be considered a defect. It is only when corrosion reaches an excessive degree that it reduces the item's appeal. In such cases it is usually wisest to remove it, following the procedure given for Barbed Wire (above). If an item shows little or no corrosion when acquired, you may wish to coat it with a good oil, to guard against future development or corrosion — which can take place even without direct contact of moisture (normal humidity in the atmosphere is sufficient to promote corrosion).

MODEL SOLDIERS. They should not be washed as this is likely to remove the paint. Arms, legs or other components of *toy* soldiers (made of cast lead) will usually snap off if the model is dropped on a hard surface. They can be glued back in place with Duco cement. You will need to hold the pieces steady until the glue dries, a matter of only a few minutes. Do not paint over the joined area.

MUSIC — PHONOGRAPH RECORDS. The buyer should first of all realize that nothing can be done to improve the condition of a phono record — any wear or damage is irreversible. However, to accurately judge a record's condition it must be clean when played, and the tonearm needle must be free of dust. Old records, especially 78 r.p.m.'s, are usually in need of a cleaning when found. If played before cleaning, they will seem to be in a much worse condition than they actually are. Generally speaking, if the grooves of a 78 r.p.m. record are still dark and glossy (not whitish), there is a minimum of wear and the sound quality should be REASONABLY the same as it was originally. There is naturally some surface noise to be expected, even with MINT 78's, as the manufacturing process of 40 or 50 years ago was not as technically advanced as today's. The 78's can be wiped with a damp cloth, then with a record-cleaning cloth or brush as sold in record shops. 45's can be cleaned with alcohol on a rag (just damp — not soaking). Take care to leave the label alone as it could be damaged in the cleaning process. The best storage method for 78's is to place them in blank paper sleeves, also available at record shops, and then into storage albums. Glass-enclosed cabinets, or any cabinets with tight-fitting doors, are a help, as dust is one of the major enemies of phonograph records. Never allow the surfaces of two records to rub together.

PAPER MONEY. Albums are available with pocket vinyl pages, into which specimens of paper currency can be inserted. These are sold in two sizes, to accommodate the old-style "large size" U.S. currency and the standard currency of today. Nearly all collectors use these albums for the convenience and safety they offer. However, some prefer to insert their specimens into individual vinyl holders, before placing them in the album page, as an extra measure of protection. This makes it unnecessary to ever actually touch the notes, which, in the case of uncirculated specimens, is an important consideration. So much caution may not be necessary if your notes are in less than uncirculated condition to begin with. If you collect FOREIGN paper money, this will present somewhat more of a challenge as foreign currency varies greatly in size. Some foreign notes are tiny while others are larger than the largest ever issued by the U.S. government. One way of keeping them is in philatelic mint sheet albums.

Circulated currency notes which are badly soiled can be washed. Whether you SHOULD do this is a matter of disagreement, as some collectors (and authorities) feel that a washed note gives an undesirable appearance — limp and lifeless. The washing is done by floating the note, facedown, in a bowl of warm soapsuds for several minutes. The note is then turned over and floated with the reverse side down. Rinsing is accomplished by immersing it in a bowl of clear water. The note is then hung up to dry on a clothesline (indoors!), using a squeeze-type WOODEN clothespin. After drying, it is placed between two sheets of waxed kitchen paper and set beneath a heavy weight for two or three days, and finally returned to the collector's album. It will be much cleaner, but it will look different than a clean note which has not been washed.

Do not mend tears in currency with scotch tape or any other tape. A bit of glue brushed on with an artist's camel-hair brush does the trick. Always use a white glue such as Elmer's Glue-All, rather than a mucilage or cement.

Creases in currency can be lessened by ironing. This will improve their appearance, but it does not raise the cash value. To iron currency: dampen it with plain water, place between two sheets of waxed paper, then between two sheets of thin blotting paper. Set iron to about 300 degrees and move it back and forth across this little "sandwich" with gentle pressure for about ten seconds; turn over and repeat on the other side. Prolonged or too-hot ironing will cause the ink to fade.

PAPERWEIGHTS. Glass paperweights can be washed in soap and water, then dried and rubbed with a mild oil such as baby oil. This will minimize any small scratches they might have.

PENS. The writing nibs on old pens should be cleaned if caked with ink, as this will lead to corrosion. Acetone (nailpolish remover) on a cloth will do the job. Follow this up by washing in plain water, then drying and applying a bit of olive oil.

PLAYING CARDS. Though playing cards vary in size and shape, the majority can be housed in albums made for baseball trading cards. Both sides of the cards are visible in these albums. Valuable single cards can be kept in individual mylar holders. If a card has a glossy surface, it can be wiped with a damp cloth (plain water only) to remove grime. Cards with flat surfaces can, if soiled, be treated with an art gum eraser sold at stationary shops or art supply stores. Do not rub too vigorously or you may injure the paper. Better to live with some soiling than to damage the card.

POLITICAL BUTTONS. These have perennially been a problem for collectors in terms of storage. They seem to defy the usual storage devices made for every other type of collectible. If placed in the pockets of vinyl coin pages, they fall out. When their pins are thrust through paper pages, they likewise come free. The best approach is to pin them to fairly thick cardboard pages, and TAPE the protruding portion of the pin to the reverse side of the page.

Use adhesive tape. A dozen or more buttons of fairly large size can be kept on a single page with this technique. Of course, only one side of the page is used, and you can't crowd up an album with too many pages. SMALL buttons can be placed in coin holders, but there are many buttons for which coin holders aren't big enough. Also, the pin will usually break through the back of the holder sooner or later. Some hobbyists, annoyed after being pricked with these pins a few times, decide to remove them. That should never be done, as it greatly reduces the value of the button.

PORCELAIN & POTTERY. These attractive collectors' items seem to draw dirt like a magnet. They need to be frequently cleaned while in one's possession and, usually, very thoroughly cleaned when first acquired. One reason why old porcelain is so often grimy is, probably, the usual practice of displaying figurines on the mantlepiece — where soot from the fire attacks them. Porcelain figures of the 18th and 19th centuries often contained components, such as lace frills on costumes, that served as dust-catchers. These, while originally white, may be virtually black when the piece is acquired. Never scrub or brush a porcelain or pottery object, as the enameling could be disturbed. Cleaning is accomplished by soaking the object in warm sudsy water, and changing the water every ten or fifteen minutes until all traces of surface dirt have vanished. The item is then soaked in plain clear water and dried. It is best to let it dry by itself, rather than using a hair-drier to help things along, as the sudden change in temperature could be harmful. Display your collections of pottery and porcelain as far as possible from windows, to slow down the pace at which dust and grime accumulate. Displaying in a glass-fronted cabinet is the best approach.

POSTCARDS. Postcards can be kept in special albums made for collectors of philatelic postcards (those issued by the post office). However this will get rather expensive if you have many cards. Inexpensive cards — which comprise the vast majority — may be kept in shoeboxes, into which they fit very neatly. Reinforce the boxes at the corners with adhesive tape. You can index your collection by using indexing cards sold in stationary shops.

PRINTS. The best way to store prints is to frame them, placing them first into a matt and then into a glass-covered frame, hung so that it does not receive too much direct sunlight (especially if the print is colored, as the colors could be bleached out). For a large collection it is not usually possible to frame every item. Still, each print should be matted, if not acquired in that fashion. Use matts of a heavy stock. Once matted, they can be slipped into large manila envelopes and kept in drawers or filing cabinets. Cabinets specially made for storing prints, drawings and other works of art are available. They have very roomy shallow drawers and accommodate prints of nearly any size. While these cabinets are not inexpensive, the cost should not be prohibitive to anyone investing in fine prints. Smudges on prints can be removed or lightened with an ordinary art gum eraser. Do not trim down the margins of prints for any purpose, no matter how much blank area is involved. This applies even if damage has occurred in a blank margin, which could be removed by cutting. Instead, when the print is framed, use a matt with a small opening which reveals very little of the margin. Some old prints, especially of the 17th and 18th centuries, are "foxed." Foxing is a collector's term to indicate the presence of numerous small brownish-red blotches all over the paper, like rust spots. These are caused by lice, and will usually spread in time. Foxing is very difficult to eradicate, but the spots can be made somewhat lighter by dabbing them with a cotton wad moistened in alcohol. Afterwards, brush the spots with a bit of talcum powder or other chalk powder on an artist's brush. Do not buy a foxed print with the idea of raising its value by removing the foxing. You may improve the appearance but the value will not be increased. If a print has a hole in it, get a piece of paper of the same (or similar) grade and texture, and paste it on the reverse side under the hole.

REDWARE (pottery). When painted, the paint is very vulnerable to removal by any kind of cleaning effort. Proceed with caution.

ROGERS GROUPS. Their size and weight makes it inadvisable to immerse them in water for cleaning, which would otherwise be the best approach. The logical alternative is to clean them with a dry artist's brush, working your way into the various crevices and detailing. This is difficult, but the item will look much better. When picking up Rogers Groups, they should ideally be lifted from the BASE, not by grasping any of the component figures. It may require the help of a second party to move the larger ones.

SCRIMSHAW. Don't wash scrimshaw as you could dislodge some of the ink embedded in its design. It can be wiped with a damp cloth, then lightly oiled when dry, using olive oil. Nothing will remove the discoloration. Open cracks in scrimshaw can be hidden by melting the wax from a candle and working very small amounts of it into the crack. If the item is brownish or yellowish rather than pure white, which is often the case with scrimshaw, add a coloring agent to the wax. Finish this procedure by oiling the whole item. If a large piece is missing, it can be rebuilt with sculptor's clay (the kind that dries hard). Add a few drops of oil to the clay and, after the job is finished and the clay dried, paint over the area with colorless nailpolish.

SIGNS. The general feeling about the care and maintenance of antique signs is that they should be left in the acquired condition. But you may (at the least) want to remove protruding nails and sand down very rough edges, to the point where your sign will not pose physical dangers to anybody. In hanging an old sign, consider its weight and the strength of the wall. Consider, also, whether the wood (if the sign is made of wood) may be so rotted that a nail or screw used in hanging might pull free. In that event, it might be advisable to encircle each end of the sign with wire and hang it in that fashion. Bronze wire is better than the "rope" kind, as it will not scratch the sign. Do not repaint or touch up the paint on signs. Whenever something like this is done, although well intentioned, the value is virtually destroyed. And that advice goes for antiques in general.

STAMPS. The traditional method of keeping stamps is to hinge them to album pages, using commercially made philatelic hinges. This has been done prior the turn of the century. (Originally, collectors glued their stamps flat to the pages!) It is a very inexpensive approach and the stamps will not suffer by it. However, if you have MINT stamps, especially valuable ones which have never been hinged, you may not care to use hinges. In that case the best procedure is to encase them in vinyl mounts, which have sticky backs and will adhere — without moisture — to the album page. The mounts are sold in various sizes and will accommodate any stamps. They are naturally quite a bit more expensive than hinges, so you may want to use two approaches at the same time: hinges for your used stamps, mounts for your mints. Mounts are also available for blocks, covers and other philatelic items. For mint SHEETS, the only practical approach is to use a special mint sheet album, which has vinyl pocket pages. As you begin collecting, you may acquire some stamps on scraps of paper, torn from envelopes or parcels. These should not be mounted "as is," but removed from the adhering paper.

Devices are available which do this with a minimum of fuss. You can save some expense, however, by relying on the old-fashioned method of "soaking." For generations, philatelists soaked their stamps and the activity was — or so it seemed — an indispensable part of the hobby. Fill a small bowl with lukewarm water, and place in the scraps of paper face down (nothing will be accomplished if the stamps faces up). Don't overcrowd the bowl. Unsatisfactory results are nearly always caused by overcrowding. In about four or five minutes the stamps should float free. Do not help them along by peeling them off the paper; this makes thin spots on the stamps. When each stamp comes free, it still has some gum on the back. Place it FACE UP in a second bowl of lukewarm water, and leave it for five minutes at least. This will wash off the remaining gum. The stamp is now ready to be dried. If left simply on a sheet of paper to dry, the stamp will probably curl up. You can prevent curling by placing your just-soaked stamps between sheets of blotting paper and drying them under a weight. They should be left overnight or longer in humid weather. If they still appear damp when the drying time is up, transfer them to fresh blotting paper and leave them for another day. Don't omit the second step — removing the gum residue — as the stamps will be stuck fast to the blotting paper and require another soaking.

STOCK CERTIFICATES. The large sizes of some specimens make it necessary to use either an oversized *presentation album* (with vinyl pocket-pages), or a scrap album and mount them with photo-corners. The presentation album is much handier and makes a better appearance.

TOOLS. Most tools can be washed in soap and water, then greased with petroleum jelly on the metal portions. Wooden handles should be treated with linseed oil. This is not wise if the handles are painted, in which case a thorough cleaning alone is recommended. If a tool is really encrusted with grime when acquired, it can be soaked for two or three days in a mixture made of one part turpentine and three parts linseed oil, well mixed. Afterwards it should be washed in soap and water, then oiled as mentioned above. Hacksaw blades are likely to be VERY grimy and may require soaking in a stronger solution (equal parts of turpentine and linseed oil).

WOODENWARE. Old woodenware is subject to cracking, caused by the natural moisture of the wood drying out over the years. This is most noticeable in large objects made from single pieces of wood, such as carved bowls and buckets. It is not sufficient to merely oil the surfaces of these pieces, as the very small amount of oil imparted does not work its way to the interior. Such items should be immersed (totally covered) in basins of oil, for several days at the least. The best oil for this purpose is linseed oil, but olive oil could also be used. At the end of that time, take a dry cloth and wipe off all the excess oil. Leave the item out to "air" for another few days, before placing it in your collection. It will look darker than it did before, but stop and consider: that was the way it looked ORIGINALLY, before its moisture evaporated. What you have done is return it to its original appearance.

WHAT'S NEW IN ANTIQUES?

There used to be a joke about somebody walking into an antique shop and asking, "What's new?" You just *know* that's an old joke — because antique shops are hotbeds of activity these days. There IS plenty of new merchandise. Not necessarily new in the sense of recently made, but it's DIFFERENT, in some cases vastly different, than the items found in antique shops 20 or even 10 years ago.

Of course, the traditional antiques are still being collected, admired, and invested in. No matter how many new groups of items are added to the roster, interest invariably continues in porcelain, glass, fine furniture, and other "standard" collectibles. If any of these are your chosen field of collecting, you'll find them well represented in most antique shops. But if the standard and traditional doesn't appeal to you, you'll discover a wealth of other collectors' items in today's antique shops. You need only visit a few shops to see the eye-opening possibilities offered to hobbyists of the 1980's.

We've covered as many of the new fields of collecting as possible in this book, along with those of perennial attraction. Some of them might seem surprising to you. Not only are all of these things being actively collected, and fetching the prices stated in the listings, but new, fresh areas of collecting interest are popping up all the time, supported by throngs of dedicated hobbyists. This book is NOT designed to provide any guidelines on what IS or ISN'T being collected. Far more groups of items are being collected than any book could cover. There could never be guidelines on what merits collecting, and what doesn't. Public taste and attitudes dictate that — and they can change rapidly. Thirty years ago, hardly anybody would have thought of fruit crate labels, comic books, or MANY of the other items encompassed in this book as potential collectibles. Literally hundreds of new areas of collecting enthusiasm have been discovered, since the 1950's. Unless the world stops turning, hundreds more will be added in the NEXT thirty years. Or possibly thousands, at the rate at which interest in collecting — in itself — is booming.

The old rules of collecting have been broken down. Victorian attitudes prevailed in collecting long into the 20th century. Museums were partly responsible. Two or three generations of hobbyists operated on the assumption that museums provide direction in collecting. They kept seeing basically the same types of art, antiques and historical objects in museums — so they presumed this was the material acknowledged to be "collectible." If something was not found in museums, it was considered unworthy of the hobbyist's attention. Collectors tried to build their own museums. The wealthier ones — J. Pierpont Morgan, Benjamin Altman, Henry Huntington, and others — actually outdid most museums in the size and value of their collections. Hobbyists of modest means tried to emulate them, by collecting the same varieties of items but in lower price ranges.

Collecting ought to be enjoyable, and it is today. It shouldn't come saddled with stodgy traditions or unbendable precepts — and it doesn't anymore. Getting into collecting in the '80's can be just as creative as YOU want it to be.

The criterion for determining if objects were collectors' items was — in the uncreative past — whether the item was OLD, had ARTISTIC BEAUTY, and HISTORICAL SIGNIFICANCE. That was fine so far as it went. Obviously, anything meeting those guidelines deserves to be collected. But the staunch supporters of this theory failed to take a highly potent fourth quality into consideration: social impact. So many objects not created to be masterpieces or even works of art left permanent marks on society. Advertising items are one example (out of many). Everyone saw them every day. They shaped our culture in a way that real art could never do. And they have a very real claim on the hobbyist's attention. So it is with radio premiums, comic character merchandise, toys, and so much else from the past, even the very recent past.

COLLECTOR PUBLICATIONS

Periodical publications for collectors include those of a general and specialized nature — often highly specialized. Hundreds are issued and it is not possible to list them all here. The interested collector will have no trouble finding out about the others: almost every hobbyist newspaper and magazine carries ads from publishers of OTHER hobbyist newspapers and magazines.

As always, periodicals are prone to change ownership, change address, or cease publication. Therefore, the information below is not guaranteed for long-term accuracy.

Most of these publications accept advertising from the public (and of course from dealers). If interested in advertising or subscribing, a note to each publisher will bring information on current rates.

SOME publications will send a free sample copy (usually a back issue). This practice is, however, gradually being curtailed in the industry, because of widespread abuse by persons who request copies without any actual interest in subscribing or advertising. If you wish to obtain a copy of any of the following publications prior to subscribing or advertising, we would suggest that you write and ask how you may acquire a copy. The publisher will then either inform you of the single copy price, or possibly send a sample copy.

AMERICAN ART AND ANTIQUES
1515 Broadway, New York City, New York 10036

AMERICAN INDIAN ART
7045 Third Avenue, Scottsdale, Arizona 85251

ANTIQUE COLLECTING
P.O. Box 327, Ephrata, Pennsylvania 17522

ANTIQUE COLLECTOR
Chestergate House, Vauxhall Bridge Road, London SW1V 1HF, England

ANTIQUE MONTHLY
P.O. Drawer 2, Tuscaloosa, Alabama 35401

ANTIQUE TOY WORLD
3941 Belle Plaine, Chicago, Illinois 60618

56 / COLLECTOR PUBLICATIONS

ANTIQUE TRADER
Dubuque, Iowa 52001

ANTIQUES (The Magazine Antiques)
551 Fifth Avenue, New York City, New York 10017

ANTIQUES AND THE ARTS WEEKLY
Newtown Beem, Newtown, Connecticut 06470

ANTIQUES JOURNAL
P.O. Box 1046, Dubuque, Iowa 52001

ANTIQUES WORLD
P.O. Box 990, Farmingdale, L.I., New York 11737

ARMS GAZETTE
13222 Saticoy Street, North Hollywood, California 91605 *(firearms)*

BANKNOTE REPORTER
Iola, Wisconsin 54945 *(paper money)*

BIE NEWSLETTER
4601 NE Third Avenue, Ft. Lauderdale, Florida 33308 *(odd and error coins)*

BLUE RIDGE COIN NEWS
Banner Publishing Co., Camden, South Carolina 29020

CLARION, THE (America's Folk Art Magazine)
49 West 53rd Street, New York City, New York 10019

CLASSICS READER
Box 1191, Station Q, Toronto, Canada M4T 2P4 *(comics)*

COINage
16001 Ventura Boulevard, Encino, California 91316

COIN HOBBY NEWS
300 Booth Street, Anamosa, Iowa 52205

COIN PRICES
Iola, Wisconsin 54945

COINS MAGAZINE
Iola, Wisconsin 54945

COIN SLOT
P.O. Box 612, Wheatridge, Colorado 80033 *(coin-operated machines)*

COIN WHOLESALER
P.O. Box 893, Chattanooga, Tennessee 37401

COIN WORLD
P.O. Box 150, Sydney, Ohio 45367

COLLECTIBLES MONTHLY
P.O. Box 2023, York, Pennsylvania 17405

COLLECTOR'S DREAM
P.O. Box 127, Station T, Toronto, Canada M6B 3Z9

COLLECTOR PUBLICATIONS / 57

COLLECTOR EDITIONS QUARTERLY
170 Fifth Avenue, New York City, New York 10010

COLLECTOR'S PARADISE
P.O. Box 3658, Cranston, Rhode Island 02910

COLLECTORS UNITED
P.O. Box 1160, Chatsworth, Georgia 30705 *(dolls)*

COLONIAL NEWSLETTER
P.O. Box 4411, Huntsville, Alabama 35802 *(colonial coins)*

COMIC INFORMER
3131 West Alabama, Houston, Texas 77098

COMIC TIMES
305 Broad, New York City, New York 10007

COMIXINE
10 Geneva Drive, Redcar, Cleveland T510 1JP, United Kingdom

DEPRESSION GLASS DAZE
P.O. Box 57, Otisville, Michigan 48463

DYNAZINE
8 Palmer Drive, Canton, Massachusetts 02021 *(comics)*

ERB-DOM
Route 2, Box 119, Clinton, Louisiana 70722 *(Edgar Rice Burroughs)*

ERRORSCOPE
P.O. Box 695, Sidney, Ohio 45365 *(coin errors)*

ERROR TRENDS
P.O. Box 158, Oceanside, New York 11572 *(coin errors)*

ESSAY-PROOF JOURNAL
225 South Fischer Avenue, Jefferson, Wisconsin 53549 *(coins)*

FANTASY TRADER
34 Heworth Hall Drive, York, England *(comics)*

FANTASY UNLIMITED
47 Hesperus Crescent, Millwall, London, E.14, England *(comics)*

FUTURE GOLD
4146 Marlene Drive, Toledo, Ohio 43606 *(investment)*

GOBRECHT JOURNAL
5718 King Arthur Drive, Kettering, Ohio 45429 *(relating to life and work of Christian Gobrecht, 19th century coin designer)*

GRAPHIC TIMES
25 Cowles Street, Bridgeport, Connecticut 06607

GUN REPORT
P.O. Box 111, Aledo, Illinois 61231

HOBBIES
1006 South Michigan Avenue, Chicago, Illinois 60605

INDIAN TRADER
P.O. Box 31235, Billings, Montana 59107 *(Indian relics)*

58 / COLLECTOR PUBLICATIONS

JOEL SATER'S ANTIQUE NEWS
P.O. Box B, Marietta, Pennsylvania 17547

JOURNAL OF NUMISMATICS AND FINE ARTS
P.O. Box 777, Encino, California 91316 *(ancient coins and classical antiquities)*

JUKEBOX TRADER
P.O. Box 1081, Des Moines, Iowa 50311

LOOSE CHANGE
21176 South Alameda Street, Long Beach, California 90810 *(coin-operated machines)*

MAIN ANTIQUES DIGEST
P.O. Box 358, Waldoboro, Maine 04572

MEMORY LANE
P.O. Box 1627, Lubbock, Texas 79408

NATIONAL ANTIQUES COURIER
P.O. Box 500, Warwick, Maryland 21912

NEW YORK/PENNSYLVANIA COLLECTOR
Wolfe Publications, 4 South Main Street, Pittsford, New York 14534

NINETEENTH CENTURY (Forbes)
60 Fifth Avenue, New York City, New York 10011

NUMISMATIC NEWS
Iola, Wisconsin 54945

NUMISMATIST, THE
P.O. Box 2366, Colorado Springs, Colorado 80901

OHIO ANTIQUE REVIEW
72 North Street, Worthington, Ohio 43085

OLD TOY SOLDIER NEWSLETTER
209 North Lombard, Oak Park, Illinois 60302

OWL'S NEST
P.O. Box 5491, Fresno, California 93755 *(owl-motif items)*

PEN FANCIER
1169 Overcash, Dunedin, Florida 33528 *(writing instruments)*

POLITICAL COLLECTOR
503 Madison Avenue, York, Pennsylvania 17404

SPINNING WHEEL
Fame Avenue, Hanover, Pennsylvania 17331

TAMS JOURNAL
P.O. Box 127, Scandinavia, Wisconsin 54977 *(tokens and medals)*

WORLD COIN NEWS
Iola, Wisconsin 54945

WORLD WIDE AVON NEWS
44021 7th Street East, Lancaster, California 93534

BUILDING A REFERENCE LIBRARY

The hobbyist's most valuable possession, besides his collection, is his reference library. A great deal of published material exists on many collecting topics, some of it highly technical and (unfortunately) very expensive Just as in collectibles themselves, there are some books on collectibles which are much more desirable than others — from a standpoint of factuality, or the amount of useful knowledge provided on the subject vs. the book's price.

The publishers of *The Official Price Guide to Antiques and Other Collectibles* have specialized for many years in books for collectors. Some of them deal, in a very comprehensive fashion, with subjects that are only touched upon in this volume. If you choose to become a specialist in any given area of collecting, or just explore at greater length the possibilities offered by each collectible, the House of Collectibles offers a wide selection of books. The format in MOST of them is similar to that of this book, with listings and CURRENT market prices for thousands and thousands of items, each item described in full detail for positive identification. And of course ALL the books are well illustrated, and contain detailed collecting advice.

The OFFICIAL PRICE GUIDE SERIES is unique in that its books offer prices for thousands of objects as well as effective guidance on how to collect — they answer all the intricate questions that collectors have about where to buy, how to sell, how to bid at auctions, how to take care of collectibles properly, how to clean delicate items, how to restore them, how to display them imaginatively and safely, and how to learn more about different areas. After years of writing about all of the aspects of buying and selling, the House of Collectibles gathered all this information into *The Official Guide to Buying and Selling Collectors' Items*. Now the collector can discover all the nuances of buying and selling with special tips for hundreds of different collectibles in one volume. Collecting information on a wide range of objects with charts evaluating each area make this guide the ideal supplement to this general price guide.

After years of compiling numerous glossaries for the OFFICIAL PRICE GUIDE SERIES, the House of Collectibles developed and expanded this information into *The Official Encyclopedia of Antiques and Collectibles*. Thousands of terms for an extensive range of collectibles plus thorough appendices offer important statistics — information gleaned from dozens of books produced by the House of Collectibles. A treasury of facts, figures, and definition, this encyclopedia provides the hobbyist with a compendium of knowledge, a storehouse of pertinent information often only known to experts in each field.

For a description of each of these books, you may refer to the pages in the back of this volume. They are available at most bookstores, or can be ordered directly from the publisher, the House of Collectibles, Inc., 1900 Premier Row, Orlando, Florida 32809.

ABOUT THE PRICES IN THIS BOOK

There are no standard values for collectors' items. Values are not set by a manufacturer or wholesaler. They're determined exclusively by the sums collectors are willing to pay — which in turn hinges on popularity, scarcity and other factors (which you'll learn about in this book).

Therefore, the prices shown in this book are not given as fair values or standard values — simply as the *average* prices being charged at the time of publication. They were arrived at by reviewing dealers' catalogues, auction sale reports, and advertisements in hobbyist periodicals.

It is important to keep in mind that price is governed, in part, by the physical condition of the specimen. When the grade of condition is not stated in the listings, the price range is for well-preserved but NOT for mint specimens: for specimens which are not defective, but show some moderate signs of wear or use as is common to the great majority of antiques. The occasional MINT specimen, showing no signs of wear or use, is naturally scarcer and invariably sells at a higher price.

The price ranges reflect the *average* highs and lows that have occurred in numerous sales across the country, not the ultimate highs and lows. Some sales at MUCH HIGHER and MUCH LOWER prices than those shown were recorded for many of the listed items. These sharp deviations from the normal values were apparently the result of special circumstances, and did not affect the overall market values of the items. In the world of collectors' items, surprising prices are not uncommon and the collector should learn to anticipate them. They may be caused (on the high side) by local interest or excessive demand or possibly by superb condition; or (on the low side) by a sacrifice sale on the owner's part, or an owner's lack of knowledge of the real value.

All the values shown are RETAIL PRICES. That is, the prices charged by professional dealers in selling to the public. In selling TO A DEALER, the price received would be less. This is discussed at length in the chapter, "Selling Your Antiques."

You may, with the aid of this book, find bargains — items selling for less than their usual or normal price. Bargains do occur on collectors' items and anyone who regularly visits dealers' shops, shows or flea markets is certain to encounter some of them. However, do not be too quick to assume that something is a bargain just because its price is lower than that shown. Investigate the possibility that it may be defective, or a reproduction, or that it varies in some way from the specific item described in the listings. Items of a similar nature, but which are not identical to those listed, can be worth considerably more or less.

HOW TO USE THIS BOOK

The Official Price Guide to Antiques and Other Collectibles has been designed for the greatest possible ease in use. Its format is strictly alphabetical. All the collectors' items are grouped by subjects, and the subjects are arranged in alphabetical sequence.

Within each subject group, the listings are also alphabetical, as far as possible. Each listing provides all relevant information about the item, to avoid confusion in identification. In the great majority of cases, this includes the name of the item; material from which it is made; style of construction or design; place of manufacture (if known); manufacturer (if known); and the date or approximate date.

When dates are stated without qualification, this indicates that the item carries a date, or that the date it was manufactured is irrefutably known from historical records. When a date is being estimated, it is preceded by "c.," indicating "circa" (approximately). When a date is given as "circa," it can be assumed that the item was manufactured shortly before or after that date — for example, a range of 1850-1870 on an item stated to be "c. 1860."

Items that cannot be dated this precisely are shown as "first half of the 19th century," or "19th century," or (when very little information exists on which to base an estimate), "c. 19th century."

It is important to keep in mind that the prices shown are for the specific items listed. Items which are similar, but differ in one respect or another, are not necessarily of similar value.

Certain kinds of collectors' items are very easy to identify, and for these a minimum of description is given. Coins and comic books are in this class: the specimen is clearly marked with identifying data and no guesswork is involved.

Items which are difficult to identify have been described in greater detail. It is still possible, however, that similar items exist, which agree with those in the listings in every particular but differ in some detail not mentioned.

A price range is shown for each item. It represents a range of average retail sums, charged by dealers, for specimens in good collector condition. *(Note: Many collectibles fall into two or more areas of collecting interest. This is especially true of "motif" items, such as cats or dogs, which may appear on pottery, postcards, bottles, etc. Before concluding that an item is not listed, we advice you to CHECK THE INDEX at the back of the volume.)*

PRICE TREND INDICATOR

A third price column has been provided in the listings section of this book, showing the average value of each item *one year before the current listings were compiled*. This exclusive feature measures market performances and should be of special usefulness to investors as well as dealers and collectors.

ADVERTISING GIVEAWAYS

Left to Right: **Ceramic bank (removable lid)**, with reproduction of "Eight O'Clock Coffee" label; c. 1935, it sells for **$15.00-$20.00;** Ceramic bank used as a promotional giveaway by the Esso oil company. This one dates from the 1940's and has a value of .... **$35.00-$50.00**

Advertising giveaways were important sales tools for businesses in times preceding the inventions of radio and television. Manufacturers needed a way to publicize their products to a larger portion of the population than was covered by daily newspapers. Clever ad men came up with a wide variety of giveaways and gimmicks, including thermometers, clocks, calendars, trays, pin-back buttons, pocket mirrors, signs, etc., all carrying an advertising message from some manufacturer. Many items were graphically illustrated, colorful and entertaining. They are truly a good example of the ingenuity of the American business.

Giveaways may turn up in drawers or closets. Old stores and soda fountains are also good sources of supply as are many flea markets, garage sales and antique fairs. Prices range from a few cents for an imprinted pen or match folder to hundreds of dollars for a rare, desirable tip or serving tray. Most giveaways are appreciating rapidly although many may still be purchased at bargain basement prices.

Condition is an important consideration when determining the value of an advertising giveaway. A rare piece may be relatively valueless if in extremely poor condition, while a more common example may bring a premium price if it is in mint condition. Prices given are for specimens in excellent to mint condition. For more in-depth information and listings, you may refer to *The Official Price Guide to Paper Collectibles,* published by the House of Collectibles.

ADVERTISING GIVEAWAYS / 63

CALENDARS

	Current Price Range		Prior Year Average
☐ Alka Seltzer, c. 1942	3.30	5.50	4.00
☐ Ayers Cherry Pectoral, c. 1899	6.00	11.00	7.50
☐ Baker's Cocoa, c. 1909	42.00	62.00	50.00
☐ Blatz Beer, girl in light red, Victorian style, c. 1904	130.00	180.00	150.00
☐ Valley Brew Pale, girl in satin shorts talking on phone, c. 1940	31.00	36.00	32.50
☐ Camel Cigarettes, c. 1963	6.60	11.00	8.00
☐ Clark's Cotton Thread, c. 1889	11.00	16.00	12.50
☐ Columbia Stove, c. 1927	26.00	36.00	30.00
☐ Comford, mother and child, c. 1910	26.00	36.00	30.00
☐ Dr. Mile's Remedies, girl and boy, c. 1908	11.00	16.00	12.50
☐ Dr. Pepper, c. 1950	20.00	26.00	21.50
☐ Dr. Pierce's Cure, c. 1904	32.00	42.00	35.00
☐ Equitable Life Insurance, c. 1904	17.00	27.00	20.00
☐ Fairy Soap, officer in the Navy, c. 1899	12.50	18.50	14.50
☐ Farmer's Fire Insurance, c. 1888	22.00	33.00	25.00
☐ Firestone Tires, c. 1912	26.00	36.00	30.00
☐ Gordon R. Cloes Real Estate, girl and dog in car, c. 1946	11.00	16.00	12.50
☐ Gordon R. Cloes Real Estate, girl in sheer gown, c. 1946	11.00	16.00	12.50
☐ Harsford's, child in bobsled, framed under glass, c. 1893	42.00	54.00	45.00
☐ Hartford Fire Insurance, c. 1896	8.00	13.00	10.00
☐ Hood's Milk, c. 1933	6.00	11.00	8.00
☐ Hood's Sasparilla, c. 1896	27.00	37.00	30.00
☐ John Hancock Insurance, c. 1898	16.00	26.00	20.00
☐ Metropolitan Life Insurance, c. 1904	36.00	46.00	40.00
☐ Mrs. Dinsmore's Balsam, mother and child, c. 1901	32.00	44.00	35.00
☐ Nehi Soda Pop, c. 1904	36.00	46.00	40.00
☐ Pacific Mutual Insurance, c. 1909	11.00	16.00	12.50
☐ Panama Canal, c. 1915	20.00	28.00	21.50
☐ Prudential Insurance, c. 1897	5.50	11.00	7.50
☐ Richelieu Coffee, c. 1912	13.00	20.00	14.50
☐ Rolf Armstrong, girl in overalls and hat, distributed by Wyoming bottling firm, c. 1933	26.00	33.00	27.50
☐ Rolf Armstrong, "Encore," girl pulling up black nightgown, distributed by Baltimore food products company, c. 1943	32.00	37.00	32.50
☐ Ruppert Breweries, c. 1915	22.00	33.00	25.00
☐ Santa Fe R.R., "The Chief Is Still The Chief"	22.00	33.00	25.00
☐ Standard Oil, c. 1939	13.00	20.00	15.00
☐ Sunshine Biscuits, c. 1924	13.00	20.00	15.00
☐ Union Pacific Tea, c. 1892	27.00	37.00	30.00
☐ Wrigley's Gum, c. 1927	22.00	30.00	24.00

CLOCKS

☐ Anheuser Busch, wooden	24.00	30.00	26.00
☐ Bardahl Petroleum, square shape, electric	37.00	47.00	40.00
☐ Budweiser, 16" Dia	48.00	58.00	50.00
☐ Canada Dry Sport Cola, 13" x 18"	24.00	30.00	26.00
☐ Cat's Paw, 14" Dia.	44.00	66.00	50.00
☐ Coca-Cola, "Please Pay When Served"	58.00	86.00	70.00
☐ Coca-Cola, round metal	33.00	55.00	40.00

64 / ADVERTISING GIVEAWAYS

	Current Price Range		Prior Year Average
☐ Dr. Pepper, diamond shape	44.00	66.00	50.00
☐ Falstaff Beer, illuminated	48.00	54.00	47.00
☐ Florsheim Shoes, wooden, illuminated	33.00	44.00	35.00
☐ General Electric, refrigerator, metal	48.00	58.00	50.00
☐ Mr. Peanut, small alarm	24.00	30.00	26.00
☐ Pearl Beer, illuminated	28.00	38.00	30.00
☐ Pepsi, "The Light Refreshment", wrought-iron, 18" Dia.	32.00	47.00	38.00
☐ Pepsi, square with new logo	22.00	33.00	25.00
☐ Seven Up, round, brass color metal	28.00	38.00	30.00
☐ St. Joseph Aspirin for Children, 14" Dia.	54.00	64.00	55.00
☐ Vantage Cigarettes, battery, 12" Dia.	22.00	33.00	35.00

SIGNS

	Current Price Range		Prior Year Average
☐ Anheuser Busch, light up, plastic, picture of man and woman, 18" x 24"	22.00	33.00	25.00
☐ Bayer Aspirin, tin, 15" x 18"	22.00	33.00	25.00
☐ Beechnut Tobacco, rectangular shape	11.00	16.00	12.50
☐ Borden, ice cream advertisement, glass, 12" x 20"	60.00	70.00	65.00
☐ Budweiser, light up, plastic with bottle, 5" x 12"	11.00	16.00	12.50
☐ Budweiser, cardboard cutout of two black men riding a bicycle built for two	5.50	11.00	7.50
☐ Bull Durham, cardboard, 14" x 22"	33.00	44.00	35.00
☐ Burgermeister Burgie, light up, brunette lounging near pool, 12" x 15"	20.00	28.00	21.00
☐ Call Again, Cigars 5¢, cardboard fan hanger, 5" Dia.	3.50	5.50	4.00
☐ Camel Cigarettes, cardboard, blond woman, 20" x 11", c. 1941	11.00	16.00	12.50
☐ Carling Ale, scene of policemen drinking beer, tin, rectangular shape	60.00	80.00	65.00
☐ Carta Blanca Beer, light up bar sign	22.00	33.00	25.00
☐ Coca-Cola, "Drink Coca-Cola in Bottles", red tin disc, 15" Dia.	22.00	33.00	25.00
☐ Coca-Cola, "Join The Friendly Circle," c. 1954	22.00	33.00	25.00
☐ Columbian Beer, tin, 12" x 16"	33.00	44.00	35.00
☐ Coors Beer, light up, lake and mountain scene	22.00	33.00	25.00
☐ Dolly Madison Cakes, tin, 20" x 16"	16.00	26.00	17.50
☐ Dr. Meyer's Foot Soap, cardboard, many hands holding bars of soap, 7" x 10"	3.30	5.50	4.00
☐ Dr. Pepper, tin, 18" x 6"	27.00	37.00	30.00
☐ DuBois Budweiser, tin, 21" x 13"	16.00	21.00	17.50
☐ Dutch Masters Cigars, tin, oval with picture of six Dutch Masters, 11" x 9"	5.50	11.00	7.50
☐ Fairy Soap, 5¢, trolley car, rectangular shape	80.00	110.00	84.00
☐ Falstaff Beer, light up, logo in gold, 20" x 23"	26.00	32.00	27.00
☐ Fire Chief Gasoline, glass panel, 12" x 4"	5.50	11.00	7.50
☐ Goodyear Tires, oval shape	20.00	24.00	20.00
☐ Hires Root Beer, paper, 28" x 12"	38.00	48.00	40.00
☐ Hood Tires, tin, man wearing uniform and flag, 15" x 9"	9.00	13.00	10.00
☐ Hudepol Beer, beer bottle, tin, 12" x 8"	44.00	54.00	45.00
☐ Ivory Soap, bar of soap is held by small child, trolley car, 20" x 10"	65.00	85.00	70.00

ADVERTISING GIVEAWAYS / 65

	Current Price Range		Prior Year Average
☐ **Kelloggs Corn Flakes,** infant in basket of wicker, tin, rectangular shape	65.00	85.00	70.00
☐ **Kool Cigarettes,** tin, rectangular shape	11.00	16.00	12.50
☐ **L & N R.R.,** marked General Motors Locomotive, framed print, 16" x 14"	22.00	33.00	25.00
☐ **Lipton Tea,** copy on both sides, tin, 10" x 20"	30.00	38.00	31.50
☐ **Michelob Beer,** light up, cash register sign	20.00	28.00	21.50
☐ **Mobil Gas,** flying horse emblem, glass panel	38.00	48.00	40.00
☐ **Model Tobacco,** tin with colorful man, 4" x 12"	22.00	33.00	25.00
☐ **Narragansett Lager,** gold and silver letters on red, 20" x 10"	65.00	85.00	70.00
☐ **National Bohemian Beer,** light up, Mr. Boh and says "Exit", 12" Dia., c. 1940's	48.00	65.00	52.50
☐ **Nehi Soda Pop,** women, cardboard, 20" x 14"	13.00	20.00	14.00
☐ **Old Dutch Cleanser,** primary colors, cardboard, 10" x 13"	13.00	20.00	14.00
☐ **Old Milwaukee Beer,** plastic, Victorian style lady, 15" x 22"	15.00	22.00	17.00
☐ **Olympia Beer,** light up, sailboat scene, 41" x 15"	48.00	58.00	50.00
☐ **Olympia Gold,** cardboard, 12" x 10"	4.50	9.00	6.00
☐ **Pabst Blue Ribbon,** blackboard, bartender, c. 1950's	15.00	20.00	16.00
☐ **Parking 30 Minutes,** metal, 12" x 18"	6.50	11.00	8.00
☐ **Pepsi-Cola,** bottlecap, 9½" Dia.	27.00	37.00	30.00
☐ **Popsicle,** tin, rectangular, c. 1930	32.00	48.00	37.00
☐ **Rheingold Beer,** light up bar sign	15.00	20.00	16.00
☐ **Ritz Crackers,** cardboard, rectangular shape	27.00	37.00	30.00
☐ **Schaefer Beer,** wood barrel, 14" x 16"	20.00	28.00	21.50
☐ **Sherwin Williams Paint,** glass panel	24.00	30.00	25.00
☐ **Sky Chief Gasoline,** glass panel, 12" x 4"	4.50	9.00	6.00
☐ **Smith Brother Cough Drops,** 5¢, trolley car	80.00	110.00	86.00
☐ **Sprollins Odorless Mothproof,** cardboard, 14" x 16"	4.50	9.00	6.00
☐ **State Auto Insurance,** porcelain and enamel, 3" x 4"	15.00	20.00	16.00
☐ **Sun Maid Raisins,** trolley car	38.00	48.00	40.00
☐ **Texaco Gas,** fireman's hat and wings emblem, glass panel, rectangular shape	20.00	24.00	20.00
☐ **Uneeda Biscuits,** cardboard, 10" x 13"	22.00	33.00	35.00
☐ **Viceroy Cigarettes,** tin	22.00	33.00	35.00
☐ **Whitman's Chocolate Candy,** 13" x 18"	48.00	65.00	53.00
☐ **Woo Chong Import Co.,** paper, oriental women and art objects, 21" x 31", c. 1920	28.00	38.00	30.00

THERMOMETERS

☐ **Antifreeze,** 30"	28.00	38.00	30.00
☐ **Carstairs,** "Join The Carstairs Crowd," round	22.00	33.00	25.00
☐ **Coca-Cola,** bottle shape, 27"	48.00	58.00	50.00
☐ **Coca-Cola,** gold bottle shape, 7"	20.00	28.00	21.50
☐ **Coca-Cola,** oval bottle shape, 27"	55.00	65.00	55.00
☐ **Coca-Cola,** "Things Go Better With Coke," 17½"	20.00	27.00	21.50
☐ **Copenhagen Chewing Tobacco,** 12"	11.00	16.00	12.50
☐ **Dr. Pepper,** 17"	22.00	33.00	25.00
☐ **Gilbey's Gin,** 9"	44.00	54.00	45.00
☐ **Hires,** bottle shape, 27"	44.00	54.00	45.00

66 / ADVERTISING GIVEAWAYS

	Current Price Range		Prior Year Average
☐ **Mail Pouch Tobacco,** 39″	48.00	58.00	50.00
☐ **Nesbits,** bottle shape, 27″	38.00	48.00	40.00
☐ **Pabst Blue Ribbon Beer,** 20″	22.00	33.00	25.00
☐ **Pepsi,** "Have A Pepsi," 27″	30.00	40.00	32.00
☐ **Old Dutch Root Beer,** windmills, 26″	22.00	33.00	25.00
☐ **Royal Crown Cola,** 27″	20.00	28.00	21.50
☐ **Vernors Ginger Ale,** 12″ Dia.	40.00	50.00	42.00
☐ **Winston Cigarettes,** plastic, 10″	20.00	28.00	21.50

TRAYS

☐ **Beamer Shoes,** woman in Victorian dress, c. 1900	48.00	68.00	55.00
☐ **Beck's Brewing,** buffalo, 13″ Dia., c. 1950's	15.00	20.00	16.00
☐ **Billy Baxter,** big red bird, 12″ Dia., c. 1920's	33.00	44.00	35.00
☐ **Climax Furnaces and Stoves,** Roman soldier holding torch, c. 1910	70.00	82.00	72.00
☐ **Coca-Cola,** hostess, c. 1936	48.00	68.00	55.00
☐ **Coca-Cola,** springboard girl, c. 1939	44.00	65.00	50.00
☐ **Coca-Cola,** girl with menu, c. 1950	18.00	28.00	20.00
☐ **Coca-Cola,** Santa Claus, c. 1973	18.00	28.00	20.00
☐ **Cook's Beer,** young boy and bartender	9.00	14.00	10.00
☐ **Coors Beer,** glass and bottle of beer	22.00	28.00	22.50
☐ **Cracker Jack,** tin	9.00	14.00	10.00
☐ **Dobler Beer,** woman's portrait	16.00	22.00	17.50
☐ **DuBois Beer,** picture of brewery	28.00	38.00	30.00
☐ **Enterprise Beer,** c. 1900's	22.00	33.00	25.00
☐ **Eskimo Pie Ice Cream,** 5¢	18.00	22.00	17.50
☐ **Genessee 12 Horse Ale,** horse team, 13″ Dia.	33.00	44.00	35.00
☐ **Gunther's Beer,** c. 1933	40.00	48.00	41.50
☐ **Hamms Beer**	22.00	33.00	25.00
☐ **Hemmer's Ice Cream**	48.00	56.00	47.50
☐ **Hires Root Beer,** c. 1910	80.00	95.00	82.00
☐ **Imperial Ice Cream,** woman seated at table	48.00	58.00	50.00
☐ **Liberty Ice Cream,** c. 1900's	22.00	33.00	25.00
☐ **Miller High Life,** girl on moon, 13″ Dia., c. 1940's	33.00	58.00	40.00
☐ **Nu Grape Drink**	38.00	55.00	42.00
☐ **Olympia Beer,** "Good Luck"	14.00	20.00	14.00
☐ **Pepsi-Cola,** "Hits the Spot," children under tree	22.00	33.00	25.00
☐ **Piel's Beer,** N.Y., Bert and Harry Piel, 13″ Dia., c. 1957	16.00	22.00	17.00
☐ **Schmidt's Brewing,** Philadelphia, tiger's head and crest, 13″ Dia., c. 1950	9.00	16.00	11.50
☐ **Stroh's Beer,** c. 1901	33.00	44.00	35.00

TIP TRAYS

☐ **Baker's Cocoa**	68.00	78.00	70.00
☐ **Bromo Seltzer**	58.00	68.00	60.00
☐ **Camel Cigarettes**	9.00	14.00	10.00
☐ **Carnation Milk**	40.00	50.00	35.00
☐ **Corstair's White Seal**	9.00	14.00	10.00
☐ **Cortex Cigars**	27.00	37.00	32.00
☐ **DeLaval Cream Separator**	17.00	22.00	17.50
☐ **Dubbleware Overalls**	11.00	16.00	12.50
☐ **Fairy Soap**	32.00	42.00	38.00
☐ **Franklin Life Insurance**	22.00	28.00	22.50

ALMANACS / 67

	Current Price Range		Prior Year Average
☐ Garland Stoves	27.00	38.00	32.00
☐ Helvetia Condensed Milk	16.00	22.00	17.50
☐ Jenny Gasoline	38.00	48.00	40.00
☐ Kansas Gas and Electric	14.00	20.00	16.00
☐ Marilyn Monroe	22.00	28.00	22.50
☐ Miller High Life Beer	5.50	11.00	7.50
☐ Moxie	35.00	45.00	36.00
☐ Muriel Cigar, Gypsy girl	32.00	42.00	35.00
☐ Old Reliable Coffee	25.00	35.00	30.00
☐ Prudential Insurance	5.50	16.00	10.00
☐ Resinol Soap	38.00	48.00	40.00
☐ Roi-Tan Cigars	38.00	48.00	40.00
☐ Ruppert Beer	17.00	22.00	17.50
☐ Ryan's Beer	44.00	54.00	45.00
☐ Sears, Roebuck and Company	44.00	54.00	45.00
☐ Universal Stoves	27.00	32.00	27.50
☐ White Rock	35.00	45.00	40.00
☐ Wrigley's Gum	17.00	27.00	20.00

ALMANACS

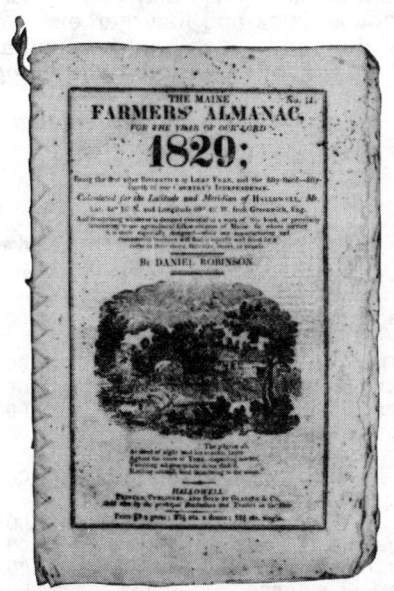

The Maine Farmers' Almanac, 1829 by Daniel Robinson **$24.00-$30.00**

ALMANACS

Almanacs were an important part of daily life for many Americans of the 18th and 19th centuries. They were used as guides and reference books for everyday occurrences. Crops were planted and harvested according to phases of the moon; weather and other natural events were predicted a year in advance often with more accuracy than one might expect. People planned social events and often took the homely advice given in these publications very seriously.

The publishing of almanacs in America dates back to the 17th century. For a very long time, collectors took no notice of almanacs, believing them to be unworthy articles for libraries of old and rare books. Gradually an interest in them developed, and today some early specimens carry handsome price valuations.

Almanacs may be found to carry a wide range of prices depending upon age, condition and desirability. It should not be presumed, however, that every old almanac is valuable. Collectors are primarily concerned with those published before 1880. Even then, quite a few are only modestly valued. The strongest prices are fetched by almanacs of extremely early date, those issued by famous printers, or those of territorial or literary interest.

Full market prices are achieved only by copies in the original wrappers, that are not badly worn or stained. A gilt morocco binding on an old almanac might make it more handsome, but detracts from the value. Prices have not risen dramatically and many almanacs may be purchased reasonably. Antiquarian bookstores, house sales and flea markets in rural areas are good sources for almanacs. For more in-depth information and listings, you may refer to *The Official Price Guide to Old Books and Autographs,* published by the House of Collectibles.

Note: *Prices stated are for issues of the years listed. Different issues of the same almanac — even if just a year different — can be worth considerably more or less.*

	Current Price Range		Prior Year Average
☐ 1714—The Farmer's Almanack, Whittemore. (No relation to the still-in existence "Old Farmer's Almanac".)	660.00	860.00	750.00
☐ 1717—An Almanack of the Coelestial Motions and Aspects, Travis	235.00	285.00	250.00
☐ 1724—The New-England Diary, Bowen	260.00	360.00	300.00
☐ 1725—The New-England Diary, Bowen	260.00	360.00	300.00
☐ 1738—The Rhode-Island Almanack, Stafford	775.00	1100.00	880.00
☐ 1753—Poor Job's Almanack, Shepherd, (James Franklin)	1100.00	1600.00	1250.00
☐ 1753—An Astronomical Diary; or, an Almanack, Ames	185.00	235.00	200.00
☐ 1764—An Astronomical Diary, Ames	55.00	75.00	60.00
☐ 1775—The New-England Almanack, West	185.00	235.00	200.00
☐ 1775—The North-American's Almanack, Stearns	70.00	90.00	75.00
☐ 1775—Bickerstaff's Boston Almanack	130.00	160.00	135.00
☐ 1776—North American Almanack, S. Sterns	38.00	48.00	40.00
☐ 1778—Bickerstaff's Boston Almanack	120.00	150.00	135.00
☐ 1782—American Almanack, Russell	75.00	95.00	80.00
☐ 1783—New England Almanack, Bickerstaff	35.00	45.00	35.00
☐ 1787—Webster's Connecticut Pocket Almanack, Nickerstaff	120.00	150.00	135.00

ALMANACS / 69

	Current Price Range	Prior Year Average
☐ 1788—An Astronomical Diary, Strong	85.00 140.00	110.00
☐ 1791—Hartford Almanack, Strong	30.00 40.00	30.00
☐ 1794—An Astronomical Diary, Sewall	85.00 125.00	100.00
☐ 1794—New England Almanack, Daboll	32.00 42.00	35.00
☐ 1796—Hartford Almanack, Strong	22.00 33.00	25.00
☐ 1796—Strong's Almanack	85.00 125.00	100.00
☐ 1797—Hagerstown Almanack, first edition	95.00 115.00	100.00
☐ 1799—Farmer's Almanack, Thomas	22.00 28.00	22.50
☐ 1799—Leapyear Issue Farmer's Almanack	28.00 38.00	30.00
☐ 1801—Greenleaf's New-York, Connecticut and New Jersey Almanack	75.00 85.00	80.00
☐ 1805—New England Almanack, Daboll	28.00 38.00	30.00
☐ 1808—New England Almanack, Daboll	28.00 38.00	30.00
☐ 1808—Farmer's Almanack, V. B. Bates	28.00 38.00	30.00
☐ 1810—New England Almanack, Daboll	28.00 38.00	30.00
☐ 1812—Law's Boston	11.00 22.00	15.00
☐ 1813—New England Almanack, Daboll	22.00 33.00	25.00
☐ 1815—New England Almanack, Daboll	22.00 33.00	25.00
☐ 1816—New England Almanack, Daboll	22.00 33.00	25.00
☐ 1818—New England Almanack, Daboll	22.00 33.00	25.00
☐ 1820—New England Almanack, Daboll	22.00 33.00	25.00
☐ 1828—Ontario Almanack, Abner Loud, Canandaiguq	18.00 28.00	17.50
☐ 1829—Western Almanack	18.00 28.00	17.50
☐ 1834—Poor Richard's Almanack	18.00 28.00	17.50
☐ 1837—Anti-Slavery Almanack	32.00 42.00	35.00
☐ 1843—Presbyterian Almanack	9.00 14.00	10.00
☐ 1848—Farmer's Almanack, Boston	9.00 14.00	10.00
☐ 1850—Town and Country Almanack	11.00 16.00	12.50
☐ 1851—National Comic Almanack	9.00 14.00	10.00
☐ 1852—The Gardener's Almanac	18.00 28.00	20.00
☐ 1853—Old Farmer's Almanack	22.00 33.00	25.00
☐ 1855—Ayer's American Almanack	14.00 20.00	15.00
☐ 1855—True Americans Almanack	40.00 50.00	42.00
☐ 1867—Western Almanack, Perkins	11.00 22.00	15.00
☐ 1869—Hagerstown Town and Country Almanack	5.50 12.00	8.00
☐ 1871—Farmer and Mechanics Almanack, Scovill	5.50 12.00	8.00
☐ 1871—Miners Almanack, Pittsburgh	5.50 12.00	8.00
☐ 1871—Morning, Noon and Night	18.00 22.00	17.50
☐ 1872—Tarrytown Almanack	5.50 12.00	8.00
☐ 1873—Miner's Almanac	12.00 18.00	15.00
☐ 1874—Centaur Almanac	12.00 18.00	15.00
☐ 1874—United States - Almanack, Hostetter	10.00 11.00	8.00
☐ 1886—Ayer's American Almanac	18.00 22.00	17.50
☐ 1879—Vinegar Bitters Almanac	11.00 16.00	12.50
☐ 1880—Hagerstown Almanack, Gruber	8.00 14.00	9.50
☐ 1881—Humans and Horses	6.00 11.00	7.50
☐ 1885—Presto-Fertilizer Co.	4.00 6.00	4.50
☐ 1886—Mandrahe Bitters Almanack	5.50 11.00	7.50
☐ 1887—Kendall Doctor at Home	8.00 13.00	11.00
☐ 1888—Williams and Clark Fertilizers, colored cover	5.50 11.00	7.50
☐ 1888—Wright's Pictorial Family Almanack	5.50 11.00	7.50
☐ 1889—Pocket Almanac and Account Book	11.00 16.00	12.50
☐ 1893—Leavitt's Farmer's Almanac	18.00 22.00	17.50
☐ 1895—"The Life Book", Boston D. Sarsaparilla .	10.50 11.00	10.00

70 / AMERICAN EAGLES

	Current Price Range		Prior Year Average
☐ 1895—Ayers American Almanack	5.50	8.00	6.00
☐ 1897—Home Almanack	5.50	8.00	6.00
☐ 1900—Baker's Guide/Cookbook	9.00	11.00	9.00
☐ 1902—Ladies Birthday Almanack	8.00	14.00	9.00
☐ 1902—Swamp Root	4.00	6.00	4.50
☐ 1908—Diamond Dye #6	8.00	14.00	11.00
☐ 1911—Dr. Ayer's, German	4.00	6.00	4.50
☐ 1912—Ranson's	4.00	6.00	4.50
☐ 1912—Royster's	4.00	6.00	4.50
☐ 1915—Dr. Ayer's, American Health	4.00	6.00	4.50
☐ 1917—Ladies Birthday Almanack	5.50	8.00	6.00
☐ 1919—Poor Richard's Almanack	4.00	6.00	4.50
☐ 1923—Hood Farm	4.00	6.00	4.50
☐ 1927—Rawleigh's Good Health Guide Almanac Cookbook	11.00	16.00	12.50
☐ 1937—Dr. Miles New Weather Almanac and Handbook	5.00	8.00	5.50
☐ 1939—Ford Home Almanac and Facts Book	7.00	10.00	5.50
☐ 1939—Watkins Almanac and Home Book	6.00	10.00	7.50

AMERICAN EAGLES

Bald Eagle, Watercolor Plate, by Ken Carlson, rel. 1975, ed. 580, s/n
....**$60.00-$75.00**

AMERICAN INDIAN ARTIFACTS / 71

The American Bald Eagle, with its fierce countenance and reputation for boldness and strength, was the symbol favored by the Founding Fathers as best representing the new nation called the United States. (Ben Franklin's favorite, the American Wild Turkey, was overruled.) As the symbol for America, countless designers and craftsmen have used the eagle, in one stylized version or another, for everything from coverlets to uniform buttons. No home furnished in the Early American style is complete without the American eagle. Many collectors are fascinated by the myriad uses of the eagle in American advertising, decorating and artwork. When combined with other American symbols, such as Miss Liberty and Uncle Sam, an interesting topical collection can be formed.

Prices for eagles are dependent on size, age, and construction materials. A dramatic increase in price has not been recorded, but examples documented to have been part of the decor of a famous or historical building, a decoration on a ship or some other unusual use, may command much higher prices. Price ranges given are for articles in excellent to mint condition. Items in good, average or worse condition should be priced accordingly.

	Current Price Range		Prior Year Average
☐ **Carved figure,** gilded plaster, wings upstretched, perched on green painted mound, 28″ x 39¼″ ...	210.00	260.00	225.00
☐ **Carved figure,** painted wood, legs painted orange-yellow, body and wings painted blue-green, 10″ x 18″	2550.00	3050.00	2750.00
☐ **Carved figure,** painted wood, grasping American shield, arrows in its talons, 14½″ x 44½″	520.00	720.00	600.00
☐ **Carved figure,** painted wood, upraised wings, wood stand, 6½″ H.	220.00	275.00	235.00
☐ **Carved figure,** pine, open beak, perched on an orb, 14″ x 22″	460.00	660.00	550.00
☐ **Carved figure,** wood, perched on an orb, 44½″ x 30″	910.00	1250.00	1050.00
☐ **Carved figure,** wood and gesso, perched on a rockwood, 29″ x 39″	2050.00	2650.00	2300.00
☐ **Carved head,** painted, yellow and red, 24″	910.00	1250.00	1050.00
☐ **Cast iron figure,** perched, grasping flowers, 30″ x 64″	1700.00	2100.00	1800.00
☐ **Cast iron figure,** snow eagle	14.00	22.00	16.00
☐ **Cast iron figure,** spread-winged, perched on an orb, J.I. Case, 47″ L.	610.00	710.00	650.00
☐ **Painted figure,** molded papier-mache, spread-winged, black, 19½″ x 44″	85.00	130.00	100.00
☐ **Painted sign,** 19th century, oil on metal, spread-winged, perched on U.S. shield	660.00	860.00	750.00
☐ **Tie pin,** eagle in globe advertising, J.I. Case	18.00	22.00	17.50

AMERICAN INDIAN ARTIFACTS

Until a few years ago, Indian art and artifacts were considered by most people to fall into a catagory somewhere between curiosities and handicrafts. As recently as 15 years ago, turquoise and silver jewelry along with Navaho rugs and blankets, were "tourist junk," classed only slightly above

72 / AMERICAN INDIAN ARTIFACTS

the rubber tomahawks and dyed chicken feather headresses people bought for their kids at the souvenir stand. Arrowheads and spearheads turned up by farmer's plows were more of a nuisance than an archeological find.

Civil rights movements of the 1960's brought the plight of America's native citizens into the spotlight and indirectly influenced a rebirth of interest in the culture and art of the Indian. Today, sales of Indian art and artifacts generate the same interest and enthusiasm as is provided by any display of valuable artwork from Europe or the Orient. Prices paid for items of Indian origin are now reaching unprecedented levels. High-quality turquoise jewelry, even that of recent manufacture, is rapidly becoming rare and expensive. Woven products, such as rugs and blankets made with natural materials and natural plants extracts for dyes, are scarce. Buckskin clothing decorated with beads or with exotic materials, such as porcupine quills, are increasingly in demand. Arrows and spearheads are graded and priced according to size, degree or workmanship and the geographical location in which they are found.

The magical ingredient which attracts collectors to these items can be summed up in one word: uniqueness. Every genuine Indian article, be it a clay pot, a squashblossom necklace, or a bone fishhook, was made by hand. No mass production techniques were used. Nothing was ever made of plastic or aluminum or any other manufactured material. Each item is painstakingly crafted — often with great skill and patience. There is evidence in a great many articles of a dedication to excellence and quality that far exceeds the criteria of merely making a serviceable product. The intrinsic qualities of pride in workmanship and simple beauty is what attracts collectors to these items.

There are several businesses that now specialize in supplying collectors with articles of Indian origin. Many have expanded their inventories to include trade items, such as beads, blankets, rifles, etc., which were manufactured by white settlers for use in bartering with the Indians. These articles are also rapidly appreciating due to their historical value. Nearly all Indian articles are appreciating at an astounding rate, particularly more recently produced items. Blankets, rugs and jewelry are among the best investments, but not for those on a limited budget. Chipped stone items may be purchased reasonably, or even still dug from the ground in some states.

AMERICAN INDIAN ARROWHEADS

Item	Current Price Range		Prior Year Average
☐ Agate Basin, 2-6″ L., 7000 BC	22.00	28.00	22.50
☐ Alba, 5⅝″ L., 700-1400 AD	25.00	30.00	25.00
☐ Aqua Plano, 3-6″ L., 7000 BC	27.00	32.00	27.50
☐ Avonlea, 1-2″ L., 220-660 AD	1.20	2.20	1.50
☐ Bakers Creek, 1½″ L., 200 BC-600 AD	4.50	7.00	5.20
☐ Bolen, 2″ L., age unknown	12.00	14.00	12.00
☐ Brewerton Eared, 1-2″ L., 4000 BC	2.00	3.00	1.75
☐ Calf Creek, 1½-3″ L., 4000 BC	12.00	16.00	13.00
☐ Candy Creek, 2-1½″ L., 1000 BC	7.00	10.00	8.00
☐ Carrolton, 2″ L., 1500 BC	14.00	16.00	13.00
☐ Castroville, 1⅞″ L., 4000 BC	10.00	12.00	10.00
☐ Coosa, 1-2″ L., 500 BC	2.00	3.00	1.75
☐ Cupp, 3¾″ L., 1100 AD	26.00	32.00	27.00
☐ Dalton, 3⅛″ L., 7000 BC	32.00	38.00	32.50
☐ Dalton, 1¾-3″ L., 6000 BC	20.00	24.00	20.00
☐ Damson, 2¼″ L.	8.50	11.00	9.00
☐ Darl, 3¼″ L., 1000 AD	15.00	18.00	15.00

AMERICAN INDIAN ARTIFACTS / 73

	Current Price Range		Prior Year Average
☐ Darl, 2⅜" L., 550 AD	8.00	12.00	10.00
☐ Delhi, 1½-3½" L., 1200 BC	3.00	5.00	4.00
☐ Duncan, 1" L., 850 BC	7.00	9.00	8.00
☐ Eden Valley, 3-6" L., 7000 BC	24.00	30.00	24.50
☐ Etley, 5-9" L., 2000 BC	23.00	28.00	23.00
☐ Etley, 6" L., 500 BC	100.00	120.00	105.00
☐ Flint Creek, 2⅜" L., 800 BC	13.00	15.00	13.00
☐ Fresno, 1¼" L.	10.00	12.00	10.00
☐ Gary, 1-4⅞" L., 500 BC	65.00	80.00	68.00
☐ Grand, 1-2" L., 500 BC	3.00	5.00	3.50
☐ Grand, 1¾" L., 200 AD	7.00	9.00	7.00
☐ Greenbriar, 2¾" L., 4000 BC	26.00	34.00	28.00
☐ Hardin, 3¼" L., 1500 BC	85.00	95.00	85.00
☐ Hardin, 2⅛" L., 1500 BC	28.00	32.00	27.00
☐ Hardin, 4½" L., 1000 BC	150.00	180.00	155.00
☐ Hell Gap, 2-5" L., 7000 BC	11.00	16.00	12.00
☐ Kent, 1½-3" L., 1000 BC	3.00	6.00	4.00
☐ Keota, ½-1½" L., 1200 AD	3.00	6.00	4.00
☐ Lange, 2⅜" L., 2000 BC	20.00	24.00	20.00
☐ Lerma, 1-2⅞" L., 50 AD	11.00	14.00	11.00
☐ Lost Lake, 2-3½" L., 6000 BC	9.00	11.00	10.00
☐ Madison, 1½" L., 1700-1832 AD	6.00	8.00	6.50
☐ Matamoros, ¾-1½" L., 500 AD	3.00	5.00	3.00
☐ Matanzas, 2¾" L., age unknown	32.00	38.00	32.50
☐ Moriss, 1⅛" L., 1200 AD	18.00	24.00	19.00
☐ Mountain Fork, 1-2" L., 3500 BC	2.00	3.00	2.00
☐ Palmer, 1-2½" L., 6000 BC	3.00	5.00	3.00
☐ Pandale, 3¾" L., 100 AD	20.00	26.00	19.00
☐ Pandora, 2⅝" L., 2000 BC	9.00	12.00	9.50
☐ Pedernales, 2⅜" L., 3500 BC	14.00	18.00	14.00
☐ Quad, 1½-4" L., 8000 BC	14.00	18.00	14.00
☐ Refugio, 3" L., 700 AD	10.00	14.00	11.00
☐ Scottsbluff, 4⅛" L., 7500 BC	260.00	330.00	285.00
☐ Searcy, 2¼-4" L., 5000 BC	16.00	26.00	18.00
☐ Starr, 1¼-2¼" L., 1600 AD	3.00	4.00	2.50
☐ Suwanee, 2-3" L., 7000 BC	9.00	11.00	10.00
☐ Swan Lake, 1-1½" L., 3000 BC	1.50	2.50	1.25

COLLECTIBLE BOOKS ON AMERICAN INDIANS

☐ **Abbott, C. C.,** Primitive Industry: or Illustrations of the handiwork of the native races of the Northern Atlantic Seaboard of America, Salem, 1881	55.00	80.00	68.00
☐ **Adair, James.** The History of the American Indians. London, 1775	920.00	1150.00	1000.00
☐ **Bancroft, H. H.** History of the Native Races of the Pacific Slope. San Francisco, 1882, five vols., maps	285.00	340.00	300.00
☐ **Biart, Lucien.** The Aztecs, Their History, Manners, and Customs. Chicago, 1887	65.00	85.00	75.00
☐ **Black Hawk.** The Great Indian Chief of the West. Cincinnati, 1849	85.00	130.00	100.00
☐ **Blair, E. H.** Indian Tribes of the Upper Mississippi Valley and Region of the Great Lakes. Cleveland, 1911, two vols.	65.00	90.00	80.00
☐ **Bloomfield, J. K.** The Oneidas. N.Y., 1907	22.00	33.00	25.00

74 / AMERICAN INDIAN ARTIFACTS

	Current Price Range		Prior Year Average
☐ **Bourke, John G.** The Snake-Dance of the Moquis of Arizona. N.Y., 1884, with colored and plain plates	285.00	345.00	300.00
☐ **Buchanan, James.** Sketches of the History, Manners and Customs of the North American Indians. N.Y., 1824, two vols. (sometimes bound together)	110.00	160.00	125.00
☐ **Carrington, Col. Henry B.** AB-SA-RA-KA, Land of Massacre. Philadelphia, 1879	44.00	64.00	50.00
☐ **Copway, G.** The traditional History and characteristic Sketches of the Ojibway Nation. Boston, 1851	55.00	80.00	62.00
☐ **Cotton, Josiah.** Vocabulary of the Massachusetts (or Ratick) Indian Language. Cambridge, 1829	28.00	38.00	30.00
☐ **Cushman, H. B.** History of the Choctaw, Chickasaw and Natchez Indians. Greenville, 1899	65.00	90.00	72.00
☐ **Davidson, J. N.** Muh-he-ka-ne-ok. A history of the Stockbridge Nation. Milwaukee, 1893	22.00	32.00	25.00
☐ **Dixon, Joseph K.** The Vanishing Race. N.Y., 1913	44.00	64.00	50.00
☐ **Dodge, Col. R. I.** Our Wild Indians. Hartford, 1882	65.00	90.00	72.00
☐ **Dorsey, George A.** Traditions of the Skidi Pawnee. Boston and N.Y., 1904	35.00	45.00	35.00
☐ **Douglas-Lithgow, R. A.** Dictionary of American-Indian Place and Proper Names in New England. Salem, 1909	32.00	42.00	35.00
☐ **Drake, Samuel G.** Biography and History of the Indians of North America. Boston, 1851, eleventh edition	80.00	130.00	100.00
☐ **Drake, Samuel G.** The Old Indian Chronicle. Boston, 1867, folding map	110.00	160.00	125.00
☐ **Eliot, John.** The Indian Primer; or, the Way of Training up of our Indian Youth in the good Knowledge of God. Edinburgh, 1880 (reprint of the 1669 edition)	30.00	40.00	30.00
☐ **Gookin, Daniel.** Historical Collections of the Indians in New England. Boston, 1792	760.00	860.00	810.00
☐ Grammar and Vocabulary of the Blackfoot Language. Ft. Benson, 1882	80.00	130.00	100.00
☐ **Hale, Horatio.** The Iroquois Book of Rites. Philadelphia, 1883, softbound	42.00	62.00	50.00
☐ **Heard, Isaac.** History of the Sioux War and Massacres of 1862 and 1863. Illustrated, N.Y., 1863	130.00	180.00	150.00
☐ **Heckewelder, John.** A Narrative of the Mission of the United Brethren among the Delaware and Mohegan Indians... Cleveland, 1907, large paper copy	130.00	180.00	150.00
☐ **Hoyt, E.** Antiquarian Researches: Comprising a History of the Indian Wars in the Country Bordering Connecticut River and parts adjacent... Greenfield, Mass, 1824, with engraved folding view	260.00	360.00	300.00
☐ **Hubbard, W.** A Narrative of the Troubles with the Indians in New England, from the first planting thereof in the year 1607, to this present year 1677. Boston, printed by John Foster in the year 1677, small quarto, with map of New England	35500.00	55000.00	37500.00

ANIMATION ART / 75

	Current Price Range		Prior Year Average

- ☐ **Indian Narratives.** Containing a Correct and Interesting History of the Indian Wars. Claremont, 1854 .... 55.00   80.00   62.00
- ☐ **James, George W.** What the White Race may learn from the Indian. Chicago, 1908 .... 22.00   33.00   25.00
- ☐ **Jones, Charles C.** Antiquities of the Southern Indians. N.Y., 1873 .... 110.00   160.00   125.00
- ☐ **Jones, David.** A Journal of two Visits made to some Nations of Indians on the West Side of the River Ohio. N.Y., 1865 .... 110.00   160.00   125.00
- ☐ **Kidder, Frederic.** The Abenaki Indians. Portland, 1859 .... 18.00   28.00   20.00
- ☐ **Lathrop, John.** The Speech of Caunonicus; or an Indian Tradition. Boston, 1803 .... 44.00   64.00   50.00
- ☐ Laws of the Cherokee Nation. St. Louis, 1868 ... 65.00   90.00   72.00
- ☐ **Lawson, Publius V.** Bravest of the Brave. Menasha, Wis., 1904 .... 22.00   32.00   25.00
- ☐ **Long, J.** Voyages and Travels of an Indian Interpreter and Trader. London, 1791, quarto, large paper copy 720.00   880.00   775.00
- ☐ **Morgan, Lewis H.** League of the Ho-de-no-sannee, or Iroquois. Rochester, 1851, with maps and plates 210.00   310.00   250.00
- ☐ **O'Mearea, Rev. F.** Report of a Mission to the Ottahways and Ojibwas, on Lake Huron. London, 1845-46, two vols. 35.00   55.00   40.00

ANIMATION ART

This field of collecting has boomed in recent years. Though the works themselves existed for more than a generation, they were not "discovered" by hobbyists until the 1970's.

Animation art is often referred to as "animation cels," because all are created on celluloid. These are the original pictures, IN FULL COLOR, used to produce color cartoons and full-length animated features. The word "animated" simply means (in this sense) a motion picture employing drawings rather than live actors. Some films, of course, use part animation/part live actors, and the cels from these films are equally collectible when they contain elements of drawing. Examples of such films are Disney's *Song of the South* and the Beatles' *Yellow Submarine*.

It was largely because of the Disney organization that interest arose in animation art. Disney had files of tens of thousands of animation cels from its films. It was decided in the 1960's to feature a selection of them (at prices which seem to be giveaways today) at the gift shops in Disneyland in California. They caught on, and soon Disney had arranged with art studios to sell them to collectors and investors. Gradually, collectors began seeking out animation cels from the work of other producers, too. But this remains largely a Disney hobby: MOST cels on the market are Disney animation art, and the majority of collectors specialize in them.

Naturally, a vast number of cels are required to produce even a 5-minute cartoon, since each frame in the filmstrip represents a different cel. To understand

76 / ANIMATION ART

Animation Celluloid, from Pinocchio, 1940, airbrush background showing Jiminy Cricket....................................$400.00-$500.00

the nature of cels, it is necessary to understand how cartoons and animated features are made. It would be far too time-consuming to create entirely original paintings for each cel. And this is not necessary, because the basic scene may remain the same for hundreds of frames. A character may just move his arm from one frame to the next; everything else is identical. So in the vast majority of cels, most of the cel is printed, and some details are added by an artist. Usually, the only cels that have no printing or very little printing are those representing a sudden change of scene. These are worth premium prices. But the price does not always depend on the amount of original artwork; the subject counts a good deal, too. For example, in a cel from *Cinderella,* the collector will be willing to pay a higher price for a specimen showing a good close-up of Cinderella rather than incidental characters or scenery.

Collectors of animation cels should be careful not to display them in direct sunlight. The colors could fade and the celluloid itself may darken and become brittle. They are best kept in mylar folders or in a display album with mylar pages.

CELLULOIDS	Current Price Range		Prior Year Average
☐ **Alice In Wonderland, 1951,** cut paper background, showing Alice holding the flamingo, 10" x 13" ...	120.00	130.00	125.00
☐ **Two Animations, c. 1955,** one of Chip 'n Dale, the chipmunks, one of two of Donald Duck's nephews, both were probably used in television productions, both 5½" x 7¼"	95.00	105.00	95.00

ANIMATION ART / 77

	Current Price Range		Prior Year Average

- ☐ **Two Animations, c. 1950's,** one of Donald Duck from television; the other of an owl schoolmaster from Toot, Whistle, Plunk and Boom, 1953, 9" x 6" 70.00 80.00 75.00
- ☐ **Two Animations, c. 1955,** both of Donald Duck and two penguins, label reads "One of the original hand-colored cels prepared for the animated cartoon sequences of Steel in America, a color film made by Walt Disney Productions for American Iron and Steel Institute," both 6" x 8" 140.00 160.00 142.00
- ☐ **The Art of Skiing, 1941,** airbrushed background, showing Goofy colliding with a tree, bears WDP stamp and Courvoisier label on reverse, 8¼" x 7½" 310.00 335.00 320.00
- ☐ **Bambi, 1942,** airbrushed and watercolor background, showing Bambi, Thumper and friends watching a butterfly, bears Courvoisier label on reverse, 7½" x 9¼" 1100.00 1300.00 1100.00
- ☐ **Bambi, 1942, and Chip 'n Dale, c. 1949,** the first of Bambi looking startled, significant paint loss, 10" x 12"; the second of a chipmunk, 10" x 12" .. 32.00 38.00 33.00
- ☐ **Cinderella, 1950,** showing the fairy waving her wand, bears Walt Disney Productions copyright on reverse, 6" x 9" 95.00 110.00 95.00
- ☐ **Cinderella, 1950,** showing the Grand Duke in grey and blue uniform, #2063-C. 14, 12½" x 15½" 70.00 80.00 70.00
- ☐ **The Country Cousin, 1936,** three trimmed cels, one of Monte; two of Abner, each approximately 3" high 54.00 68.00 58.00
- ☐ **A Coyote and Road Runner Story, c. 1960's,** *Warner Brothers Studio,* cut paper background, showing the two characters, probably used for promotional purposes, 9½" x 12" 77.00 88.00 75.00
- ☐ **Dumbo, 1941,** airbrushed background, showing Dumbo cradled in his mother's trunk, against a night sky, bears authentication label on reverse, minor cracking, 7" x 5¾" 1250.00 1450.00 1300.00
- ☐ **Fantasia, 1940,** showing a centaurette holding a flower from the Pastoral Symphony, #126, some fading and paint loss, 10" x 12" 110.00 135.00 112.00
- ☐ **Fantasia, 1940,** airbrushed background, showing a baby member of Pegasus's family attempting to stay airborne by yanking on its tail, bears Courvoisier label on reverse, 7" x 9¼" 235.00 260.00 238.00
- ☐ **Fantasia, 1940,** airbrushed background, showing nineteen Milkwood fairies against pine tree branches and a grey background, bears Courvoisier label on reverse, 10" x 19" 610.00 660.00 625.00
- ☐ **Fantasia, 1940,** airbrushed background, showing an ostrich in ballet dress against a colannade, 5" x 3¾" 200.00 225.00 192.00
- ☐ **Ferdinand, 1938,** airbrushed background, showing a matador, chest bared, facing Ferdinand in the ring, Ferdinand, far from being angered is enchanted by the flower tattooed on the matador's chest, bears Courvoisier label on reverse, 7" x 9" 520.00 620.00 550.00

78 / ANIMATION ART

	Current Price Range		Prior Year Average

- ☐ **Ferdinand The Bull, 1938,** airbrushed background, showing a picador riding his horse with some difficulty, bears Courvoisier label on reverse, 8½" x 7½" **170.00   185.00   168.00**
- ☐ **The Goddess of Spring, 1934,** a trimmed cel showing the Devil in red, 7" x 5" **68.00   78.00   70.00**
- ☐ **The Goddess of Spring, 1934 and Caballeros, 1945,** group of two, the first a trimmed cel of the Devil holding The Goddess of Spring, 4 inches high; the second of Pablo the Cold Blooded Penguin in a block of ice, significant paint loss, 10" x 12" **55.00   70.00   58.00**
- ☐ **Hockey Homocide, 1945, and one c. 1950's,** group of two, the first showing Goofy on skates, apparently running out of control on a turn, the second showing Goofy in riding coat and top hat, probably done for television, both 7½" x 9½" **130.00   160.00   140.00**
- ☐ **How To Sleep, 1953,** a cel with watercolor production background, showing Goofy carrying his mattress, rolled up under his arm, through the woods, 9" x 11½" **130.00   160.00   140.00**
- ☐ **Inside Donald, 1960's,** original watercolor background, showing Donald dropping sheets of paper on the floor of an analyst's office, 11½" x 15" **190.00   210.00   190.00**
- ☐ **The Jungle Book, 1967,** matching cel and animation drawing of the snake, cel #2179, drawing in colored pencils with animators margin directions, 12¼" x 15¼" **130.00   160.00   140.00**
- ☐ **Lady And The Tramp, 1955,** two cels showing Lady, some cracking and minor paint loss, both framed, 8" x 11" **110.00   135.00   115.00**
- ☐ **Make Mine Music, 1946,** Bumble Boogie sequence, showing a bumble bee with two flowers, 8" x 10" **100.00   110.00   95.00**
- ☐ **The Many Adventures of Winnie The Pooh, c. 1968,** Winnie the Pooh, bears Walt Disney Productions label, 10" x 13" **160.00   180.00   165.00**
- ☐ **Melody Time, 1948,** original gouache background, showing Pecos Bill and Widow Maker the horse, 8½" x 8½" **360.00   380.00   368.00**
- ☐ **The Pink Panther, c. 1965,** *Depatte-Freleng Studio,* with production, gouache background, showing the Pink Panther high above street on the side of a steel structure, 10" x 12½" **195.00   210.00   192.00**
- ☐ **Pinocchio, 1940,** airbrushed background showing Honest John, or Foulfellow, with cigar, bears Courvoisier label on reverse, 6½" x 7½" **440.00   520.00   465.00**
- ☐ **Pinocchio, 1940,** airbrushed background showing Jiminy Cricket stepping off a pipe, bears Courvoisier label on reverse, 3¼" x 3½" **385.00   410.00   385.00**
- ☐ **Pinocchio, 1940,** airbrushed background showing Jiminy Cricket on the sea floor startled by a fish, bears Courvoisier label on reverse, 5½" x 6½" .. **430.00   460.00   435.00**

ANIMATION ART / 79

	Current Price Range		Prior Year Average
☐ **Pinocchio, 1940,** showing the bust of Pinocchio against a blue background, bears Courvoisier label on reverse and is covered by the original cellophane over-wrap, 9" diameter	460.00	510.00	475.00
☐ **Pinocchio, 1940,** airbrushed background showing Jiminy Cricket standing beneath a shining star, bears Courvoisier label on reverse, 6¼" diameter	510.00	610.00	550.00
☐ **Pinocchio, 1940,** showing Honest John, the fox, picking up a cigar butt with his cane, 7½" x 9½"	110.00	135.00	118.00
☐ **Pinocchio, 1940,** showing Pinocchio from behind, his hands clasped behind his back looking up at something, 9¾" x 12¼"	200.00	230.00	210.00
☐ **Pinocchio, 1940,** original watercolor production background, showing Cleo in the fishbowl, being tempted by a piece of chocolate cake suspended from a floating cork; background shows a wooden chair, its arms around the fishbowl, standing in Geppetto's room, bears Courvoisier label on reverse authenticating it as "a master background," 10¼" x 14¼"	1150.00	1250.00	1150.00
☐ **Pluto, c. 1950's,** showing Pluto carrying a bone, probably used in a television cartoon, 13" x 14" .	95.00	105.00	95.00
☐ **The Pointer, 1939,** trimmed cel showing Mickey with gun startled by a bird, 4¼" high	240.00	280.00	255.00
☐ **Saludos Amigos, 1943,** group of two, one of Donald Duck in poncho from the Lake Titicaca sequence, some paint loss, 9½" x 11½"; second a trimmed cell of a native from the same sequence, 5½" high	38.00	48.00	40.00
☐ **Saludos Amigos, 1943,** group of two, one of Pedro, the mail plane; second of tropical fruit, both have significant paint loss, 10" x 12"	38.00	48.00	40.00
☐ **The Sinking of The Lusitania, c. 1918,** *Winsor McCay,* ink and gouache, showing the sinking of the Lusitania, 7½" x 9" .... (Note: Inscribed: "This is one of my original drawings. Winsor McCay.")	225.00	260.00	230.00
☐ **Sleeping Beauty, 1959,** two consecutive cels showing Sleeping Beauty on the arm of the Prince, released through Disneyland, both 5½" x 7¼"	95.00	110.00	100.00
☐ **Snoopy, c. 1970's,** *CBS Television,* matching cel and drawing showing Snoopy in tennis clothes and racket, probably used in a television cartoon, #SN44, 10¼" x 12½"	55.00	65.00	60.00
☐ **Snow White, 1937,** showing Happy against a star-patterned background, 6½" x 4½"	280.00	310.00	280.00
☐ **Snow White, 1937,** pencil and airbrushed background, showing bluebirds sitting in a nest, bears Walt Disney Enterprises copyright on reverse, 6" x 7"	210.00	235.00	215.00
☐ **Snow White, 1937,** showing Dopey standing with squirrels running past him, 8½" x 8½"	335.00	360.00	340.00
☐ **Snow White, 1937,** showing Bashful against a star-patterned background, 7" x 5"	260.00	280.00	262.00

80 / ANIMATION ART

	Current Price Range		Prior Year Average
☐ **Snow White, 1937,** airbrushed background, showing Dopey sitting on a seat, holding onto a cushion, bears Courvoisier label on reverse, 4½″ x 6″	360.00	410.00	375.00
☐ **Snow White, 1937,** airbrushed background, showing a fawn and bluebird in the woods, 8″ x 5¾″	135.00	165.00	140.00
☐ **Snow White, 1937,** showing a fawn and squirrels running, bears Walt Disney Enterprises copyright label, 5½″ x 5¼″	110.00	135.00	115.00
☐ **Snow White, 1937,** showing Bashful holding a mug, bears Walt Disney Enterprise copyright label on reverse, 7½″ x 8″	310.00	335.00	315.00
☐ **Society Dog Show, 1939; Pluto and The Armadillo, 1943,** group of three, one trimmed cel of Pluto with lady dog; one of Pluto running; one of an armadillo, the latter two with some paint loss, 3″ high; 10″ x 12″; 10″ x 12″	48.00	58.00	50.00
☐ **The Sword and The Stone, 1963,** Madame Medusa both as herself and as a cat, 9″ x 7″	68.00	82.00	72.00
☐ **You're An Education, 1938,** *Warner Brothers Studio,* production watercolor background of "Hep Cat" blowing a yellow trombone, 8″ x 11″	68.00	82.00	72.00

DRAWINGS

☐ **Andy Panda's Victory Garden, 1942,** *Walter Lantz Studio,* watercolor, production background showing vegetables in the garden, 9½″ x 13″ *(Note: Inscribed: "Walter Lantz" with Woody Woodpecker cartoon.)*	160.00	185.00	172.00
☐ **An Animation, c. 1924-26,** *Fleischer Studio,* black and white gouache drawing on board showing a comic man examining a pump through a magnifying glass, dates from the days of "follow-the-bouncing-ball." 10½″ x 13″	80.00	95.00	82.00
☐ **A Background, c. 1940's,** *studio unknown,* gouache on animation board, showing a spooky, Victorian room, 10½″ x 29″	62.00	72.00	65.00
☐ **For Better or Nurse, 1935, My Pop, My Pop, 1940,** *Fleischer Studio,* group of three, first two are rough character sketch sheets showing Bluto, apparently choking himself; third is a rough storyboard showing Popeye lifting something, 8½″ x 11″	52.00	68.00	58.00
☐ **Betty Boop, 1937,** *Fleischer Studio,* possibly from Housekeeping Blues, showing Betty Boop in apron with timing chart penciled in on the side of the sheet, 8½″ x 11″	95.00	105.00	95.00
☐ **Boat Builders, 1938,** group of three from the same sequence showing Mickey hoisted on the boat's mast and his pants gradually splitting, #58, 70, 102, 10″ x 12″	80.00	95.00	82.00

ANIMATION ART / 81

	Current Price Range		Prior Year Average

- **The Brave Little Taylor, 1938,** watercolor production background showing the throne, dated Feb. 18, 1938, bears several production stamps on reverse including the name of the animator, Thomas, 10" x 12¼" 520.00 620.00 550.00
- **The Country Cousin, 1936,** Four character sketch studies of Monte and Abner; two drawings, all done by Art Babbit, 10" x 12" 95.00 115.00 95.00
- **Country Cousin, 1936, and Musicland, 1935,** group of two, first showing The Country Cousin #164; second showing Prince Jasbo, 9½" x 12" . 42.00 52.00 45.00
- **Don Donald, 1937,** group of three, one of Donna Duck from Don Donald, #127; one rough sketch of Donald from Donald's Better Self, 1938; one of Mickey Mouse swinging a sledgehammer, c. 1940, 10" x 12" 68.00 78.00 70.00
- **Donald Duck, c. 1936,** eight rough sketches of Donald, most showing head-shots with various expressions, 10" x 12" 72.00 82.00 75.00
- **Donald and Donna Duck, c. 1936,** group of three, one is a character sketch sheet of Donald Duck from Moving Day, 1936; two drawings, one of Donald and sombrero, the other of Donna Duck from Don Donald, 1937 .... 98.00 120.00 97.50
- **Dumbo, 1941,** group of 11, first four are color-guides of Jim Crow; the crows Specks, Deacon, Fats and Dopey; the Stork; and an elephant in clown make-up; seven are sketches of some background drapes, 10" x 12" 165.00 185.00 165.00
- **Fantasia, 1940,** group of two, first, a "mood" drawing, or story sketch, in ink and wash, bears Courvoisier label inscribed "Landscape Moods from The Rite of Spring Sequence," 2¾" x 3¾"; second, a pastel abstract drawing, bears the Courvoisier label inscribed "Color Variations from Tocatta and Fugue," 5¼" x 7" 105.00 130.00 112.00
- **Farmer Tom Thumb, 1937,** *Fleischer Studio,* farmer bending over as if to pat something, artist Ub Iwerks, 10¼" x 12" 38.00 48.00 39.00
- **The Flying Mouse, 1934,** watercolor production background showing flowers against the sky, 15" x 12" 92.00 110.00 95.00
- **The Flying Mouse, 1934,** watercolor production background showing branches, leaves and flowers against the sky, 11½" x 49" 68.00 78.00 70.00
- **Hollywood Party, 1934,** *M.G.M. Studio,* watercolor background showing a wall decorated with hearts and "Lifesaver" candies, M.G.M. stamp bears animator's name, Ben Leonard, and note "Pan of last of troops-soldiers march in and melt down," refers to the hot chocolate soldiers, 8¾" x 30" 98.00 115.00 100.00
- **Lady and The Tramp, 1955,** sequence of animation drawings showing Lady walking, #106, 107, 110, 111, 113, 120, 12½" x 15½" 92.00 110.00 95.00

82 / ANIMATION ART

	Current Price Range		Prior Year Average
☐ **Magician Mickey, 1937,** group of four, three of Mickey Mouse; one of a walrus, 10″ x 12″	180.00	210.00	182.00
☐ **Mickey Mouse, c. 1935,** group of six, #67, 69, 712, 73, 75, 77; showing worried Mickey swinging, or flying through the air holding on to something, light water stains on two sheets, 8½″ x 10″	180.00	210.00	182.00
☐ **Mickey's Circus, 1936,** group of four, one of Mickey Mouse as MC of the circus; one of Mickey from The Worm Turns, 1937; two of Goofy, c. 1937, 10″ x 12″	52.00	62.00	55.00
☐ **Mickey's Circus, 1936,** group of 7, two of the spectators from Mickey's Circus; one early character sketch of Snow White; one from Water Babies, 1935; three from Fantasia of an ostrich, bubbles and flowers, all have some creasing and yellowing, 10″ x 12″	110.00	135.00	112.00
☐ **The Moose Hunters, 1937,** group of three, one showing Goofy's legs in different movements; two animation sheets, one showing Goofy and Donald in moose costume, one showing Goofy half in costume holding perfume atomizer, 10″ x 12″	52.00	62.00	55.00
☐ **Pinocchio, 1940,** charcoal drawing showing the coachman, Honest John and Gideon conspiring together, dated Oct., 1939, possibly a publicity drawing, bears the Good Housekeeping Magazine stamp on reverse, 7″ x 9″	92.00	115.00	100.00
☐ **Pinocchio, 1940,** charcoal drawing showing Jiminy Cricket delivering a speech, dated Oct., 1939, possibly a publicity drawing, bears the Good Housekeeping Magazine stamp on reverse, 7½″ x 5½″	105.00	125.00	110.00
☐ **Pinocchio, 1940,** two in red and blue pencil showing Jiminy Cricket with umbrella walking and talking, #117, 121, 10″ x 12″	130.00	160.00	138.00
☐ **Pinocchio, 1940,** group of two, one of Jiminy Cricket; one of Gideon, both framed and bearing authentication label on reverse, 4¼″ x 3¼″; 3¼″ x 3″	185.00	210.00	190.00
☐ **Pluto, c. 1935,** group of nine, odd #'s 43-59 (missing #55), showing Pluto running into frame and stopping, significant chipping and cracking on edges of most sheets, 9½″ x 12″	28.00	38.00	30.00
☐ **Pluto's Quin-Puplets, 1937,** group of two, one color-guide showing Pluto in mid-air with two paint buckets stuck on his feet; one, a vignette of Pluto's mouth carrying a piece of wood, both have pencil arrows from figure to margin numbers, both carry stamp "Model Drawing. Return to Dot Powers," 10″ x 12″	110.00	135.00	112.00
☐ **Snow White, 1937,** unused watercolor background showing a tree in the forest, 9½″ x 11½″	242.00	260.00	242.00
☐ **Snow White, 1937,** unused watercolor background showing the water trough outside the Dwarfs' cottage, 9″ x 8½″	195.00	210.00	195.00

	Current Price Range		Prior Year Average
☐ **Snow White, 1937,** group of three, one of Dopey, 4" x 3½"; another of Dopey, #410F; one of Doc holding a candle, #704, 10" x 12"	98.00	115.00	105.00
☐ **Snow White, 1937,** group of six, two of deer and rabbits; a sketch sheet of deer; an ink drawing of a tortoise; two of dwarfs, 10" x 12"	98.00	115.00	105.00

ART DECO

Art Deco Inkwell, glass, black amethyst, 2" x 3", 1930 . . **$12.00-$15.00**

Art Deco is essentially a design movement which was named for an important exhibition in Paris in 1925 called "l'Exposition Internationale des Arts Decoratifs." The show came, however, at least five years after the movement was underway.

Today, we call the 1920's and 1930's the period of Art Deco. Designers were inspired by Cubist art and artifacts from ancient Egypt and North and Central America. These are all characterized by strong color and abstract geometric design. There is some time overlap with the Art Nouveau period, but the major differences are characterized by the "modernist" look of Art Deco. The range of Art Deco collectibles is great — from plastic bracelets to custom-designed glass vases.

For more in-depth information on Art Deco jewelry, you may refer to *The Official Price Guide to Jewelry,* published by the House of Collectibles.

84 / ART DECO

	Current Price Range		Prior Year Average
☐ **Andirons,** brass, pair	235.00	280.00	250.00
☐ **Ashtray,** bronze and onyx figural, onyx bowl with flower head supporting a ballerina, inscribed Lorenzl, 12¾", c. 1925	820.00	1050.00	900.00
☐ **Bar pin,** platinum, diamond, jade and onyx with white gold clasp, c. 1925	820.00	1050.00	900.00
☐ **Bowl,** frosted birds and bowl, inscribed Lalique .	125.00	165.00	135.00
☐ **Brooch,** black onyx with 32 small diamonds and one large diamond	4300.00	4700.00	4400.00
☐ **Cabinet,** carved oak, glass paneled door, French, c. 1928	1250.00	1600.00	1350.00
☐ **Cabinet,** hardwood, nickel plated chrome, curved door with five shaped drawers, 3'11" x 13½", c. 1930	820.00	1050.00	900.00
☐ **Candelabra,** bronze, three receptacles	485.00	585.00	525.00
☐ **Candlesticks,** Jensen, pair, c. 1925	720.00	820.00	750.00
☐ **Centerpiece,** bronze and marble, dish and base made of marble with two bronze giraffes, 19" Dia.	335.00	435.00	375.00
☐ **Cigarette case,** gold and enamel, black enamel on the front, back and sides, green on top, 3" L. .	2700.00	3100.00	2800.00
☐ **Cigarette case,** silver and blue enamel	175.00	195.00	180.00
☐ **Clock,** desk, jade and enamel, square form, blue enamelled hands and black Roman numerals, Cartier, 1¼"	2300.00	3200.00	2600.00
☐ **Clock,** desk, rock crystal, gold, enamel and diamonds, Cartier, c. 1935	3100.00	3600.00	3250.00
☐ **Clock,** glass and chrome-plated bronze, chrome face, black glass and chrome base, 8¾", c. 1930	285.00	435.00	405.00
☐ **Compact,** black with diamond corners, black enamel link chain attached to finger ring	960.00	1200.00	1050.00
☐ **Compact,** rectangular, gold, enamel and diamonds, Cartier, c. 1930	3100.00	4200.00	3500.00
☐ **Desk,** drop front, English, c. 1935	1100.00	1600.00	1250.00
☐ **Figure,** dancer, exotic silvered figure, marble base, inscribed Fayral, c. 1925	560.00	760.00	650.00
☐ **Figure,** dancer, gilt-bronze nude figure with outstretched arms supporting a drapery, inscribed A. Kelety, 14½", c. 1930	720.00	1100.00	850.00
☐ **Figure,** dancer, swaying, inscribed CJR Colinet, 18½", c. 1925	620.00	720.00	650.00
☐ **Figure,** Pierette and Pierrot, bronze, green, marble base, inscribed Lorenzl, 16¾", c. 1925	1250.00	1700.00	1400.00
☐ **Figure,** young sailor, bronze and ivory, marked "BRONZE," plinth inscribed A. Jorel, 9", c. early 20th century	360.00	460.00	400.00
☐ **Figure,** young woman, bronze and tortoise shell .	760.00	920.00	825.00
☐ **Figure,** young woman, bronze and ivory, onyx base, Bessie Callender, 17", c. 1930	920.00	1300.00	1050.00
☐ **Figure,** young woman, silvered and gilt-bronze figure riding on elephant, onyx and marble base, French, 24", c. 1925	1500.00	1900.00	1600.00
☐ **Footstool,** upholstered and aluminum, designed by Deskey, c. 1931	420.00	620.00	500.00
☐ **Lapel watch,** black onyx panel, pin has rose-cut diamonds, platinum and gold watch, Dreicer & Co.	1350.00	1700.00	1450.00

ART NOUVEAU / 85

	Current Price Range		Prior Year Average
☐ **Rack,** hall, lacquer and brass, mirror plate, brass holders, black support, French, 5'1", c. 1930	385.00	485.00	425.00
☐ **Ring,** platinum, cabochon sapphire and six baguette diamonds	1650.00	2100.00	1800.00
☐ **Ring,** platinum, diamond and ruby, wide band ...	460.00	660.00	550.00
☐ **Ring,** ruby center panel, diamond sides, Van Cleef and Arpels, c. 1935	2700.00	3400.00	2900.00
☐ **Table,** glass top, three lucite legs, 26" x 36", c. 1940	460.00	660.00	550.00
☐ **Vanity,** with large mirror	1050.00	1300.00	1100.00
☐ **Vase,** cameo glass, frosted body, bulbous neck, straight rim overlaid in blue, 9"	170.00	230.00	190.00
☐ **Vase,** cameo glass, Le Verre Francais, trumpet form, yellow and orange overlaid in orange to deep purple with flowers and leafage, France, 18 1/8", c. 1925	235.00	335.00	375.00
☐ **Vase,** cameo glass, yellow, Galle, 5"	310.00	385.00	338.00
☐ **Vase,** pottery, band of flowers, Longwy, c. 1925 .	185.00	235.00	200.00
☐ **Vase,** Thuret, internally decorated glass, smokey grey and brown swirls, c. 1930	820.00	1250.00	1000.00

ART NOUVEAU

Art Nouveau Porcelain Vase, with portrait of Sarah Bernhardt, Amphora Teplitz Austria **$1500.00-2500.00**

86 / ART NOUVEAU

The period of Art Nouveau decorative and fine arts ranges from the last fifteen years or so of the 19th century to the second decade of the 20th century. The name derives from an 1895 opening of a design shop in Paris, the name of which was a L'Art Nouveau.

Two of the most important aspects of Art Nouveau are asymmetry and femininity. There is a wide use of maidens with flowing hair, flowers, scrolls, tendrils, snakes and anything else with sinuous curves. Art Nouveau objects, particularly fine jewelry, are in great demand today.

For more in-depth information on Art Nouveau jewelry, you may refer to *The Official Price Guide to Jewelry,* published by the House of Collectibles.

	Current Price Range		Prior Year Average
☐ **Basket,** silver, four flower molded feet, calla lily handles, Austrian, Maker's Mark R. O., 14″, c. 1900	520.00	620.00	550.00
☐ **Bell,** bronze, curtsying woman in gown, inscribed P. Tereszczuk, 2½″, c. 1900	235.00	310.00	270.00
☐ **Bookends,** reclining nude female figure on rocky base, inscribed S. Morani, 7½″, c. 1914	110.00	160.00	125.00
☐ **Bookends,** bronze busts, brown and green patinas, inscribed Gruber, pair, 5″, late 19th c.	510.00	610.00	550.00
☐ **Brooch,** flowers, ivory with opals, 3½″ Dia.	445.00	485.00	455.00
☐ **Brooch,** gold Egyptian goddess, outspread wings and serpent tail, Austrian, maker's mark M.L., 2⅛″ Dia., c. 1920	380.00	460.00	415.00
☐ **Brooch,** gold eagle with outstretched wings, open beak and curled talons, French, 2¼″ Dia., c. 1910	410.00	485.00	438.00
☐ **Clock,** desk type, nude nymph, metal case	52.00	82.00	65.00
☐ **Dining room suite,** buffet, table sideboard and five chairs, Belgian, c. 1900	2900.00	3600.00	3100.00
☐ **Dresser set,** sterling silver, Unger Brothers	245.00	275.00	250.00
☐ **Figure,** girl, gilt-bronze and ivory, playing musical instrument, black marble base, French, 9½″ H., c. 1910	785.00	885.00	825.00
☐ **Figure,** Justitia, bronze, figure in robe on marble base, inscribed Mausch/Paris, 11¼″ H.	460.00	560.00	500.00
☐ **Figurine,** woman, bronze and ivory bust of young Egyptian, dark brown patina, inscribed P. Tereszczuk, 5⅛″ H., 19th c.	310.00	410.00	350.00
☐ **Figure,** woman, bronze, dancer in classical costume, brown patina, German, 12″ H., c. 1900	285.00	385.00	325.00
☐ **Flask,** Lovers on the Beach, sterling silver, c. 1900	160.00	260.00	200.00
☐ **Knife,** paper, bronze, peacock with tail trailing into the body, bust portrait of a young woman and lily blossoms, inscribed HWH and 10CB, 12″ L., c. 1900	210.00	285.00	238.00
☐ **Knives and forks,** fruit, silver, whiplash motif, 18 of each, German, c. 1900	185.00	260.00	215.00
☐ **Lamp,** cameo glass, forest lake scene, shade signed Daum Nancy, 17″ H., c. 1900	3300.00	3700.00	3400.00
☐ **Lamp,** glass and wrought-iron, mustard, russet and deep blue, Muller Freres, 21¾″ H., c. 1900	520.00	620.00	550.00

	Current Price Range		Prior Year Average
☐ **Lamp,** bronze oil, maiden in robe on circular base, canister on swivel mount, inscribed Renaa, 11¼″ H., c. 1910	160.00	235.00	175.00
☐ **Lamp,** woman's head, bronze base, glass shade, amber on yellow ground, 16″ H.	310.00	385.00	338.00
☐ **Mirror,** hand, with woman's head and flowing hair, flowers and swans, sterling silver, Unger Bros., c. 1900	95.00	145.00	115.00
☐ **Mirror,** vanity, brass, c. 1900	55.00	80.00	62.00
☐ **Pendant and chain,** gold, opal and diamond, dragonfly with two diamonds at base, Alion and Co., 1¾″ Dia., c. 1910	1500.00	1900.00	1600.00
☐ **Pitcher,** pewter, signed	285.00	335.00	300.00
☐ **Pitcher,** silver-mounted glass, bulbous form, lip and handle decorated with flowers and tendrils, Gorham Co., 10⅜″ H., c. 1900	80.00	130.00	100.00
☐ **Plant stand,** hammered brass, wrought-iron and glass, straight legs, lower shelf, Viennese, 35½″ x 25¾″, c. 1910	180.00	280.00	225.00
☐ **Table,** writing, carved oak, inlaid leather top, inscribed L. Majorelle, 5′10⅜″ x 2′5″, c. 1900	1200.00	1700.00	1450.00
☐ **Tray,** bread, pewter with daisies and dragonfly, base inscribed Kayserzinn, 10⅜″ L.	120.00	170.00	135.00
☐ **Tray,** girl watching sunrise, bronze, inscribed Maxim, 5″ L.	160.00	210.00	175.00
☐ **Tray,** pin, female head, hair flowing into lily pads, inscribed J. Angles, 9¼″ Dia., c. 1900	785.00	910.00	830.00
☐ **Urn,** bust of woman on gold, Vienna, 8″ H.	85.00	125.00	100.00
☐ **Vase,** bronze with four beetles, brown patina, inscribed Ch. Thienot, 5¼″ H., c. 1900	160.00	210.00	175.00
☐ **Vase,** bronze, tapered cylindrical with four dragonflies forming handles, inscribed H.E.-T., 10″ H., c. 1900	185.00	280.00	225.00
☐ **Vase,** cameo glass, cranberry and mauve, inscribed Galle, 5¼″ H., c. 1900	385.00	485.00	425.00
☐ **Vase,** enamel cameo glass, russet, mustard and dark green on brown and mustard ground, Daum Nancy, 5″ H., c. 1900	285.00	385.00	325.00
☐ **Vase,** girl with doves, German, 12″ H., c. 1900	220.00	270.00	235.00
☐ **Vase,** pottery, cherry blossoms in shades of white, iron-red, tan and brown, sea blue at base, Rookwood, 9″ H., c. 1883	620.00	1100.00	800.00
☐ **Vase,** pottery, forest scene, dolphin handles enameled in gilt, Amphora, 7¼″ H., c. 1920	385.00	585.00	475.00
☐ **Vase,** pottery, iridescent with tendrils and leafage, amber, green and red glaze, French, 6½″ H., c. 1900	160.00	210.00	175.00

AUTOGRAPHS

Autograph collectors are usually thought of as a group of people who spend their lives dashing around after professional athletes and movie stars with a pen and notebook. This type of autograph is probably (in most cases)

88 / AUTOGRAPHS

Very respectfully &c.
Walt Whitman

S. L. Clemens
Mark

Top to Bottom: **Autograph** of the American poet who wrote *Leaves of Grass* **$300.00-$400.00**; Samuel L. Clemens' autograph with his pen name "Mark Twain" superimposed over the first signature.... **300.00-$400.00**

the easiest to get — signatures on napkins, scraps of paper and so on — and the least satisfying to most collectors in the long run.

While many autograph collectors begin this way, most who stay with the hobby soon change to less tiring and more fruitful methods of gathering signatures of the famous. (Signatures of United States presidents, usually cut from letters and documents, were popular during the 19th century as collectibles and many were pasted into scrapbooks and displayed in the parlor as a conversation piece. These "clipped signatures" became the basic commodity collected by autograph hounds at the stage door.)

The type of autograph preferred by most collectors is the "document signature," that is, an entire letter, note, or other document, often written in the celebrity's own hand and bearing the desired signature. Other valued examples of this type of autograph would be government documents, books bearing personal inscriptions by the author, contracts, and even checks bearing the signature of a famous person. Naturally, the fewer documents a person signed, the more valuable his signature.

A goal of many collectors may be collecting the signatures of an entire group of people important to a historical event such as the original signers of the Declaration of Independence. Others may prize having all the signatures of the 1975 Super Bowl winners.

Generally, the most valued autographs are those of political and military figures, literary personalities and other personalities influential in world events. Collecting autographs is not necessarily expensive. "Clipped signatures" of nearly every United States president can be purchased for $30-$75. Document signatures may, of course, be higher. Autograph prices tend to appreciate steadily, although the law of supply and demand may cause rapid increases for a suddenly favored signature. All autographs should be authentic. Analysis by an expert may be necessary in some cases as, unfortunately, good forgeries do exist. For more in-depth information and listings, you may refer to *The Official Price Guide to Old Books and Autographs,* published by the House of Collectibles.

ARTIST	Current Price Range		Prior Year Average
☐ Beardsley, Aubrey (1872-1898)	300.00	400.00	300.00
☐ Cellini, Benvenuto (1500-1571)	3300.00	4400.00	3500.00
☐ Cezanne, Paul (1839-1906)	250.00	350.00	250.00
☐ Chagall, Marc (1887-)	150.00	250.00	150.00
☐ Corot, Camille (1796-1875)	70.00	90.00	70.00
☐ DaVinci, Leonardo (1452-1519)	22000.00	55000.00	35000.00
☐ Degas, Edgar (1834-1917)	300.00	400.00	300.00
☐ Gainsborough, Thomas (1727-1788)	350.00	500.00	375.00
☐ Gauguin, Paul (1848-1903)	550.00	800.00	625.00
☐ Matisse, Henri (1869-1954)	90.00	130.00	100.00
☐ Michelangelo, Buonarroti (1475-1564)	11000.00	2200.00	1500.00
☐ Monet, Claude (1840-1926)	50.00	60.00	50.00
☐ Rembrandt, Van Rijn (1606-1669)	5500.00	8000.00	6250.00
☐ Renoir, Pierre A. (1841-1919)	200.00	300.00	200.00
☐ Rossetti, Dante G. (1828-1882)	200.00	300.00	200.00
☐ Whistler, James A. M. (1834-1903)	100.00	150.00	115.00
☐ Wyeth, N. C. (1882-1945)	35.00	85.00	50.00

AMERICAN — AUTHORS

☐ Alcott, Louisa M. (1832-1888)	200.00	300.00	200.00
☐ Aldrich, Thomas B. (1836-1907)	100.00	175.00	105.00
☐ Alger, Horatio (1834-1899)	50.00	130.00	75.00
☐ Austin, Jane (1775-1805)	1100.00	1600.00	1250.00
☐ Browne, Chas. F. ("Artemus Ward") (1834-1867)	35.00	55.00	38.00
☐ Bryant, William C. (1794-1878)	75.00	125.00	75.00
☐ Burroughs, John (1837-1921)	50.00	75.00	38.00
☐ Clemens, Samuel L. ("Mark Twain") (1835-1910)	850.00	1300.00	1000.00
☐ Cooper, James F. (1789-1851)	350.00	650.00	400.00
☐ Crane, Stephen (1871-1900)	350.00	650.00	400.00
☐ Dreiser, Theodore (1871-1945)	150.00	250.00	150.00
☐ Emerson, Ralph Waldo (1803-1882)	300.00	400.00	300.00
☐ Ferber, Edna (1887-1968)	45.00	85.00	55.00
☐ Field, Eugene (1850-1895)	75.00	125.00	75.00
☐ Frost, Robert (1874-1963)	400.00	550.00	425.00
☐ Hale, Edward E. (1822-1909)	20.00	30.00	20.00
☐ Hawthorne, Nathaniel (1804-1864)	850.00	1300.00	1000.00
☐ Hearn, Lafcadio (1850-1904)	200.00	300.00	200.00
☐ Hemingway, Ernest (1899-1961)	800.00	1350.00	1000.00
☐ Holmes, Oliver W. (1809-1894)	150.00	350.00	200.00
☐ Irving, Washington 1783-1859)	800.00	1100.00	900.00
☐ Lewis, Sinclair (1885-1951)	150.00	200.00	125.00
☐ London, Jack (1876-1916)	550.00	800.00	625.00
☐ Longfellow, H. W. (1807-1882)	150.00	250.00	150.00
☐ Lowell, Amy (1874-1925)	100.00	200.00	125.00
☐ Lowell, James R. (1819-1891)	45.00	75.00	50.00
☐ Melville, Herman (1819-1891)	1600.00	2600.00	2000.00
☐ Mencken, Henry L. (1880-1956)	75.00	125.00	75.00

	Current Price Range		Prior Year Average
☐ Nye, Edgar Wilson (1850-1896)	75.00	125.00	75.00
☐ O'Neill, Eugene (1888-1953)	800.00	1800.00	1300.00
☐ Porter, William Sydney ("O. Henry") (1862-1910)	450.00	800.00	575.00
☐ Riley, James Whitcomb (1849-1916)	100.00	225.00	125.00
☐ Stowe, Harriet Beecher (1811-1896)	100.00	225.00	125.00
☐ Tarkington, Booth (1869-1946)	200.00	300.00	200.00
☐ Thoreau, Henry D. (1817-1862)	800.00	1350.00	1000.00
☐ Wallace, Lew (1827-1905)	75.00	100.00	75.00
☐ Whitman, Walt (1819-1892)	550.00	1100.00	750.00
☐ Whittier, John Greenleaf (1807-1892)	150.00	250.00	150.00
☐ Wolfe, Thomas (1900-1938)	300.00	550.00	375.00

BRITISH — AUTHORS

	Current Price Range		Prior Year Average
☐ Addison, Joseph (1672-1719)	900.00	1300.00	1000.00
☐ Arnold, Edwin (1832-1904)	75.00	100.00	62.00
☐ Arnold, Matthew (1822-1888)	100.00	175.00	125.00
☐ Barrie, J. M. (1860-1937)	75.00	100.00	62.00
☐ Bennett, Arnold (1867-1931)	100.00	175.00	125.00
☐ Boswell, James (1740-1795)	1200.00	2200.00	1500.00
☐ Bronte, Charlotte (1816-1855)	1200.00	2200.00	1500.00
☐ Browning, Elizabeth (1806-1861)	1200.00	2200.00	1500.00
☐ Browning, Robert (1812-1889)	350.00	550.00	400.00
☐ Bulwer-Lytton, Edward (1803-1873)	75.00	100.00	62.00
☐ Byron, George G. (1788-1824)	1200.00	2200.00	1500.00
☐ Campbell, Thomas (1777-1844)	75.00	125.00	75.00
☐ Cibber, Colley (1671-1757)	800.00	1300.00	1000.00
☐ Coleridge, Samuel T. (1772-1834)	550.00	800.00	625.00
☐ Collins, Wilkie (1824-1889)	250.00	350.00	250.00
☐ Crabbe, George (1754-1832)	45.00	75.00	50.00
☐ DeQuincy, Thomas (1785-1859)	350.00	550.00	400.00
☐ Dickens, Charles (1812-1870)	250.00	550.00	350.00
☐ Disraeli, Benjamin (1804-1881)	75.00	125.00	75.00
☐ Dobson, Austin (1890-1921)	45.00	75.00	42.00
☐ Dodgson, Charles ("Lewis Carroll") (1832-1898)	250.00	550.00	350.00
☐ Doyle, Sir Arthur Conan (1859-1930)	100.00	275.00	175.00
☐ Edgeworth, Maria (1767-1849)	100.00	175.00	110.00
☐ Fitzgerald, Edward (1809-1883)	350.00	550.00	400.00
☐ Galsworthy, John (1867-1933)	45.00	60.00	42.00
☐ Gray, Thomas (1716-1771)	1200.00	2200.00	1500.00
☐ Hardy, Thomas (1840-1928)	200.00	400.00	250.00
☐ Henley, William Ernest (1849-1903)	100.00	175.00	115.00
☐ Herrick, Robert (1591-1674)	35.00	60.00	35.00
☐ Housman, Laurence (1859-1936)	45.00	60.00	42.00
☐ Hughes, Thomas (1822-1896)	250.00	350.00	275.00
☐ Johnson, Samuel (1709-1784)	3200.00	5200.00	4000.00
☐ Kingsley, Charles (1819-1875)	100.00	150.00	100.00
☐ Kipling, Rudyard (1865-1936)	200.00	350.00	225.00
☐ Lamb, Charles (1775-1834)	250.00	350.00	250.00
☐ Lang, Andrew (1844-1912)	45.00	60.00	42.00
☐ Lewes, Marian E. ("George Eliot") (1819-1880)	300.00	450.00	325.00
☐ Macaulay, Thomas B. (1800-1859)	100.00	150.00	100.00
☐ MacDonald, George (1824-1905)	75.00	125.00	62.00
☐ Masefield, John (1878-1967)	250.00	350.00	250.00
☐ Meredith, George (1828-1909)	200.00	300.00	200.00
☐ Moore, Thomas (1779-1852)	100.00	150.00	100.00
☐ Noyes, Alfred (1880-1958)	45.00	85.00	55.00

	Current Price Range		Prior Year Average
☐ Parker, Gilbert (1862-1932)	20.00	30.00	20.00
☐ Patmore, Coventry (1823-1896)	50.00	75.00	38.00
☐ Pope, Alexander (1688-1744)	1100.00	2100.00	1500.00
☐ Reade, Charles (1814-1884)	200.00	350.00	225.00
☐ Ruskin, John (1819-1900)	300.00	800.00	400.00
☐ Scott, Sir Walter (1771-1832)	250.00	400.00	275.00
☐ Seton, Ernest T. (1860-1946)	45.00	60.00	42.00
☐ Shaw, George B. (1856-1950)	200.00	450.00	300.00
☐ Shaw, H. W. ("Josh Billings") (1818-1885)	75.00	100.00	62.00
☐ Shelley, Percy B. (1792-1822)	2400.00	5400.00	3500.00
☐ Shelley, Mary (1797-1851)	800.00	1350.00	1000.00
☐ Southey, Robert (1774-1843)	250.00	400.00	275.00
☐ Sterne, Laurence (1713-1768)	550.00	1100.00	490.00
☐ Stevenson, Robert Louis (1850-1894)	400.00	600.00	400.00
☐ Swinburne, Algernon (1837-1909)	400.00	600.00	400.00
☐ Symonds, John A. (1840-1893)	250.00	450.00	300.00
☐ Tennyson, Alfred (1809-1892)	150.00	250.00	150.00
☐ Thackeray, William M. (1822-1863)	250.00	400.00	275.00
☐ Thomas, Dylan (1914-1953)	450.00	850.00	600.00
☐ Wilde, Oscar (1856-1900)	500.00	1100.00	650.00
☐ Wordsworth, William (1770-1850)	250.00	450.00	300.00

CIVIL WAR

	Current Price Range		Prior Year Average
☐ Beauregard, G. T. (1818-1893)	250.00	350.00	250.00
☐ Bragg, Braxton (1817-1876)	45.00	60.00	42.00
☐ Burnside, Ambrose (1824-1881)	100.00	125.00	82.00
☐ Custer, George A. (1839-1876)	350.00	550.00	400.00
☐ Davis, Jefferson (1808-1889)	800.00	1300.00	1000.00
☐ Farragut, Admiral David G. (1801-1870)	150.00	350.00	175.00
☐ Hooker, General Joseph (1814-1879)	35.00	60.00	28.00
☐ Jackson, Stonewall (1824-1863)	1200.00	3200.00	2000.00
☐ Johnston, Joseph E. (1807-1891)	45.00	60.00	42.00
☐ Kearny, Philip (1814-1862)	150.00	200.00	150.00
☐ Lee, Robert E. (1807-1870)	400.00	650.00	500.00
☐ McClellan, George B. (1826-1885)	45.00	60.00	42.00
☐ Meade, George G. (1815-1872)	40.00	55.00	38.00
☐ Miles, Nelson A. (1839-1925)	60.00	85.00	58.00
☐ Pickett, George E. (1825-1875)	250.00	350.00	250.00
☐ Porter, Admiral David D. (1813-1891)	70.00	100.00	68.00
☐ Rosecrans, William S. (1819-1898)	50.00	75.00	48.00
☐ Scott, Winfield (1786-1866)	150.00	250.00	175.00
☐ Seward, William H. (1801-1872)	100.00	150.00	100.00
☐ Sherman, William T. (1820-1891)	150.00	250.00	150.00
☐ Stanton, Edwin M. (1814-1869)	75.00	125.00	75.00
☐ Sumner, Charles (1811-1874)	50.00	75.00	65.00
☐ Thomas, Maj. Gen. George H. (1816-1870)	100.00	150.00	100.00
☐ Wheeler, Gen. Joseph (1836-1906)	45.00	60.00	42.00

COMPOSERS

	Current Price Range		Prior Year Average
☐ Bach, Johannes Sebastian (1685-1750)	11000.00	16000.00	12500.00
☐ Bartok, Bella (1881-1945)	200.00	300.00	200.00
☐ Berg, Alban (1885-1935)	200.00	300.00	200.00
☐ Borodin, Alexander (1833-1887)	350.00	550.00	400.00
☐ Brahms, Johannes (1833-1897)	300.00	400.00	300.00
☐ Bruch, Max (1838-1920)	70.00	100.00	68.00

92 / AUTOGRAPHS

	Current Price Range	Prior Year Average
☐ Elgar, Sir Edward (1857-1934)	150.00　250.00	150.00
☐ Foster, Stephen (1826-1864)	1600.00　2600.00	2000.00
☐ Franck, Cesar (1822-1890)	100.00　150.00	100.00
☐ Gershwin, George (1898-1937)	500.00　650.00	525.00
☐ Glazunov, Alexander (1865-1936)	100.00　150.00	100.00
☐ Grieg, Edvard (1843-1907)	150.00　250.00	200.00
☐ Handel, Georg F. (1685-1759)	6000.00　11000.00	7500.00
☐ Humperdinck, Engelbert (the composer) (1854-1921)	100.00　150.00	100.00
☐ Kern, Jerome (1885-1945)	40.00　60.00	40.00
☐ Kodaly, Zoltan (1882-1967)	75.00　100.00	72.00
☐ Leoncavallo, Ruggiero (1858-1919)	75.00　100.00	72.00
☐ MacDowell, Edward (1861-1908)	100.00　150.00	100.00
☐ Mahler, Gustav (1860-1911)	500.00　650.00	575.00
☐ Mascagni, Pietro (1863-1945)	60.00　75.00	52.00
☐ Massenet, Jules (1842-1912)	75.00　100.00	72.00
☐ Meyerbeer, Giacomo (1791-1864)	100.00　150.00	100.00
☐ Mozart, Wolfgang A. (1756-1791)	1600.00　2200.00	1750.00
☐ Offenbach, Jacques (1819-1880)	150.00　250.00	150.00
☐ Paderewski, Ignace (1860-1941)	75.00　100.00	72.00
☐ Paganini, Niccolo (1782-1840)	300.00　400.00	300.00
☐ Porter, Cole (1893-1964)	30.00　55.00	35.00
☐ Prokofieff, Serge (1891-1953)	300.00　400.00	300.00
☐ Rachmaninoff, Sergei (1873-1943)	150.00　200.00	150.00
☐ Rimsky-Korsakov, Nikolai (1844-1908)	500.00　650.00	525.00
☐ Rossini, Gioacchino (1792-1868)	175.00　275.00	200.00
☐ Rubinstein, Anton (1929-1894)	150.00　250.00	150.00
☐ Saint-Saens, Camille (1835-1921)	100.00　150.00	100.00

ENTERTAINMENT FIGURES

	Current Price Range	Prior Year Average
☐ Adams, Don	2.00　3.00	.82
☐ Akins, Claude	2.00　3.00	.82
☐ Allyson, June	2.00　3.00	.82
☐ Andrews, Julie	2.00　3.00	.82
☐ Arnaz, Desi	2.00　3.00	.82
☐ Bacall, Lauren	2.50　3.50	1.25
☐ Bailey, Pearl	2.50　3.50	1.25
☐ Ballard, Kaye	2.00　3.00	.82
☐ Bardot, Brigitte	3.00　4.00	2.00
☐ BelGeddes, Barbara	2.50　3.50	1.25
☐ Bergman, Ingmar	2.50　3.50	1.25
☐ Borgnine, Ernest	2.00　3.00	.82
☐ Bosley, Tom	2.00　3.00	.82
☐ Boyer, Charles	2.00　3.00	.82
☐ Burton, Richard	3.00　4.00	3.00
☐ Cagney, James	2.50　3.50	2.00
☐ Carney, Art	1.00　2.00	.82
☐ Carson, Johnny	1.00　2.00	.82
☐ Chamberlain, Richard	1.00　2.00	.82
☐ Christie, Julie	2.00　3.00	1.25
☐ Coco, James	1.00　2.00	.82
☐ Colbert, Claudette	2.00　3.00	1.25
☐ Connery, Sean	1.00　2.00	.82
☐ Crabbe, Buster	2.00　3.00	.82
☐ Dangerfield, Rodney	2.00　3.00	.82
☐ Davis, Bette	3.00　5.00	3.00
☐ DeHaviland, Olivia	2.50　3.50	2.00

	Current Price Range		Prior Year Average
☐ DeLuise, Dom	1.00	2.00	.82
☐ DeNiro, Robert	1.00	2.00	.82
☐ Dietrich, Marlene	6.00	10.00	5.50
☐ Douglas, Kirk	1.00	2.00	.82
☐ Dreyfuss, Richard	1.00	2.00	.82
☐ Duke, Patty	1.00	2.00	.82
☐ Dunaway, Faye	2.00	3.00	1.25
☐ Eastwood, Clint	1.00	2.00	.82
☐ Ekberg, Anita	1.00	2.00	.82
☐ Falk, Peter	1.00	2.00	.82
☐ Farrow, Mia	2.00	3.00	1.25
☐ Fawcett-Majors, Farrah	2.50	3.50	2.00
☐ Fellini, Federico	2.50	3.50	2.00
☐ Field, Sally	1.00	2.00	.82
☐ Fisher, Carrie	1.00	2.00	.82
☐ Fontanne, Lynn	3.00	4.00	3.00
☐ Gabor, Zsa Zsa	1.00	2.00	.82
☐ Garbo, Greta	10.00	15.00	8.50
☐ Garner, James	1.00	2.00	.82
☐ Garson, Greer	2.00	3.00	1.25
☐ Gleason, Jackie	1.00	2.00	.82
☐ Gobel, George	1.00	2.00	.82
☐ Godfrey, Arthur	1.00	2.00	.82
☐ Grant, Cary	2.50	3.50	1.25
☐ Griffin, Merv	1.00	2.00	.82
☐ Guinnes, Alec	2.00	3.00	1.25
☐ Hagman, Larry	2.00	3.00	1.25
☐ Harris, Richard	1.00	2.00	.82
☐ Harrison, Rex	1.00	2.00	.82
☐ Hawn, Goldie	1.00	2.00	.82
☐ Hayes, Helen	2.00	3.00	1.25
☐ Hepburn, Katherine	3.00	4.00	3.00
☐ Heston, Charlton	2.00	3.00	1.25
☐ Hitchcock, Alfred	2.00	3.00	1.25
☐ Hoffman, Dustin	1.00	2.00	.82
☐ Hope, Bob	2.00	3.00	1.25
☐ Hudson, Rock	1.00	2.00	.82
☐ Jackson, Glenda	1.00	2.00	.82
☐ Janssen, David	2.50	3.50	2.00
☐ Johnson, Van	1.00	2.00	.82
☐ Kahn, Madeline	2.00	3.00	1.25
☐ Kaplan, Gabe	1.00	2.00	.82
☐ Kazan, Elia	2.50	3.50	2.00
☐ Keaton, Diane	1.00	2.00	.82
☐ Kelly, Grace	10.00	15.00	5.50
☐ Klugman, Jack	1.00	2.00	.82
☐ Kristofferson, Kris	1.00	2.00	.82
☐ Kubrick, Stanley	2.00	3.00	1.50
☐ Lamarr, Hedy	10.00	15.00	5.50
☐ Lancaster, Burt	2.00	3.50	1.25
☐ Lawford, Peter	1.00	2.00	.82
☐ Learned, Michael	1.00	2.00	.82
☐ Lemmon, Jack	2.00	3.50	1.25
☐ Liberace	1.00	2.00	.82
☐ Linden, Hal	1.00	2.00	.82
☐ Lollobrigida, Gina	2.00	3.50	1.25

94 / AUTOGRAPHS

	Current Price Range		Prior Year Average
☐ Loren, Sophia	3.00	4.00	2.50
☐ MacGraw, Ali	2.00	3.50	1.25
☐ MacLaine, Shirley	2.00	3.50	1.25
☐ MacMurray, Fred	2.00	3.50	1.25
☐ Marceau, Marcel	3.00	4.00	2.50
☐ Marvin, Lee	1.00	2.00	.82
☐ McQueen, Steve	4.00	6.00	4.00
☐ Meredith, Burgess	2.00	3.50	1.25
☐ Midler, Bette	1.00	2.00	.82
☐ Montgomery, Elizabeth	1.00	2.00	.82
☐ Mostel, Zero	2.50	3.50	2.00
☐ Murray, Anne	1.00	2.00	.82
☐ Murray, Arthur	1.00	2.00	.82
☐ Neal, Patricia	2.00	3.50	1.25
☐ Newman, Paul	2.00	3.50	1.25
☐ Nicholson, Jack	2.00	3.50	1.25
☐ Nimoy, Leonard	2.50	4.00	2.15
☐ Olivier, Laurence	4.00	6.00	2.50
☐ O'Neal, Tatum	1.00	2.00	.82
☐ Pacino, Al	2.00	2.50	1.25
☐ Peck, Gregory	2.00	2.50	1.25
☐ Perrine, Valerie	1.00	2.00	.82
☐ Pickford, Mary	4.00	6.00	2.50
☐ Plummer, Christopher	1.00	2.00	.82
☐ Polanski, Roman	2.50	3.50	2.00
☐ Preminger, Otto	1.50	2.50	1.50
☐ Prentiss, Paula	1.00	2.00	.82
☐ Quinn, Anthony	2.00	3.50	1.25
☐ Raft, George	2.00	3.50	1.25
☐ Raye, Martha	2.00	3.00	1.25
☐ Redford, Robert	2.00	3.00	1.25
☐ Redgrave, Vanessa	4.00	6.00	2.50
☐ Reiner, Rob	1.00	2.00	.82
☐ Robards, Jason	1.00	2.00	.82
☐ Rogers, Ginger	2.00	3.50	1.25
☐ Savalas, Telly	1.00	2.00	.82
☐ Scott, George C.	2.00	3.50	1.25
☐ Sellers, Peter	2.00	3.50	1.25
☐ Sharif, Omar	1.00	2.00	.82
☐ Shearer, Norma	2.00	3.50	1.25
☐ Spacek, Cissy	1.00	2.00	.82
☐ Stallone, Sylvester	2.50	3.50	2.00
☐ Stanwick, Barbara	1.00	2.00	.82
☐ Steiger, Rod	1.00	2.00	.82
☐ Struthers, Sally	2.00	3.50	1.25
☐ Swanson, Gloria	6.00	10.00	4.00
☐ Swit, Loretta	2.50	4.00	2.15
☐ Taylor, Elizabeth	2.50	4.00	2.15
☐ Temple, Shirley	2.00	3.50	1.25
☐ Thomas, Richard	2.00	3.50	1.25
☐ Turner, Lana	2.50	4.00	2.15
☐ Ullman, Liv	2.00	3.50	1.25
☐ Ustinov, Peter	1.00	2.00	.82
☐ Vaughn, Robert	1.00	2.00	.82
☐ Voight, Jon	1.00	2.00	.82
☐ Walston, Ray	1.00	2.00	.82

AUTOGRAPHS / 95

	Current Price Range		Prior Year Average
☐ Wayne, John	4.00	10.00	4.00
☐ Weissmuller, Johnny	2.50	4.00	2.25
☐ Welch, Raquel	2.00	3.50	1.25
☐ West, Mae	1.00	2.00	.82
☐ Wilder, Billy	1.00	2.00	.82
☐ Winkler, Henry	4.00	6.00	2.75
☐ Winters, Shelley	1.00	2.00	.82
☐ Wood, Natalie	3.00	5.00	3.00
☐ Woodward, Joanne	1.00	2.00	.82
☐ Wray, Fay	1.00	2.00	.82
☐ Wyman, Jane	2.00	3.00	1.40
☐ York, Michael	1.00	2.00	.82
☐ York, Susannah	1.00	2.00	.82
☐ Young, Gig	2.00	3.00	1.25
☐ Young, Loretta	1.00	2.00	.82
☐ Young, Robert	1.00	2.00	.82
☐ Zanuck, Daryl	2.00	3.00	1.25

ENTERTAINMENT FIGURES — AUTOGRAPHS OF SPECIAL INTEREST

☐ **Allen, Woody,** motion picture still, "Take the Money and Run", signed	10.00	15.00	8.50
☐ **Andrews, Julie,** colored magazine cover with her as "Eliza Doolittle", signed and inscribed	8.00	12.00	7.00
☐ **Arnaz, Desi,** 8x10 color photo with Lucille Ball, signed by both, dated on back, 1954	45.00	45.00	40.00
☐ **Arness, James** 8x10 photo as "Matt Dillon", signed "Matt Dillon", then "James Arness"	12.00	16.00	10.50
☐ **Bacall, Lauren,** magazine photo with Humphrey Bogart, signed by both	70.00	90.00	70.00
☐ **Backus, Jim,** color cover, "Mr. Magoo Comics", signed	7.00	11.00	7.00
☐ **Baker, Carroll,** motion picture still, "Jean Harlow Story", signed	10.00	15.00	8.50
☐ **Bardot, Brigitte,** photo layout from "Cavalier" magazine, signed and inscribed, 1962	60.00	75.00	58.00
☐ **Beatty, Warren,** lobby card, "Shampoo", signed	30.00	40.00	25.00
☐ **Bellamy, Ralph,** photo as "Franklin Roosevelt", from theatrical production ("Sunrise at Campobello"), signed	8.00	12.00	7.00
☐ **Bergen, Candice,** photo at age two, on knee of father, Edgar Bergen, with puppet Charley McCarthy on other knee, unsigned	7.00	11.00	7.00
☐ **Bergman, Ingrid,** 8x10 photo as "Joan of Arc", signed	12.00	18.00	12.50
☐ **Berle, Milton,** "TV Guide" cover signed, 1951	8.00	12.00	9.00
☐ **Bernardi, Herschel,** photo with Zero Mostel and Paul Lipson, signed by all three (all played lead in "Fiddler on the Roof" at various times)	45.00	55.00	40.00
☐ **Bixby, Bill,** 8x10 photo with Lou Ferrigno of "Incredible Hulk", signed by Bixby only	9.00	13.00	8.50
☐ **Blair, Linda,** motion picture still, "The Exorcist", signed	10.00	15.00	10.50
☐ **Bloom, Claire,** motion picture still with Charles Chaplin, "Limelight", signed by both	85.00	115.00	85.00
☐ **Bogarde, Dirk,** English movie annual book, signed on dust jacket	11.00	16.00	10.50

96 / AUTOGRAPHS

	Current Price Range		Prior Year Average
☐ **Boone, Richard,** 8x10 photo as "Palladin", signed	8.00	12.00	8.00
☐ **Borgnine, Ernest,** motion picture still, "Marty", signed	8.00	12.00	8.00
☐ **Brando, Marlon,** Playbill, "Streetcar Named Desire", signed. Also signed by two others	30.00	40.00	22.50
☐ **Bridges, Beau,** photo with Lloyd Bridges, signed by both	8.00	12.00	8.50
☐ **Brynner, Yul,** photo from "King and I", signed	8.00	12.00	7.00
☐ **Burnett, Carol,** Magazine article, signed, 1959	6.00	8.00	6.00
☐ **Burton, Richard,** Theater poster, "Hamlet", signed; also signed by Hume Cronyn, William Redfield and three others	175.00	225.00	175.00
☐ **Caan, James,** motion picture still, "The Godfather", signed	12.00	18.00	12.50
☐ **Caesar, Sid,** 8x10 photo with Mel Brooks, signed by both, dated 1955	18.00	24.00	17.50
☐ **Cagney, James,** photo as "George M. Cohan" from motion picture, signed	12.00	18.00	12.50
☐ **Cantinflas,** motion picture still, "Around the World in 80 Days", signed. Also signed by David Niven and Michael Todd	45.00	60.00	40.00
☐ **Carlisle, Kitty,** 4x5 photo with Moss Hart, signed by both	18.00	24.00	17.50
☐ **Carney, Art,** 8x10 photo as "Norton", signed, 1956	8.00	12.00	8.50
☐ **Coburn, James,** newspaper ad for motion picture, signed	4.00	6.00	4.00
☐ **Colbert, Claudette,** motion picture still, "It Happened One Night", signed	12.00	18.00	12.50
☐ **Connery, Sean,** photo as "James Bond", signed	8.00	12.00	7.00
☐ **Connors, Chuck,** Brooklyn Dodger baseball yearbook, signed	10.00	15.00	12.50
☐ **Coogan, Jackie,** motion picture still with Charles Chaplin, signed by Coogan	10.00	15.00	12.50
☐ **Crabbe, Buster,** 8x10 photo as "Flash Gordon", signed	12.00	18.00	12.50
☐ **Davis, Ossie,** photo with Ruby Dee, signed by both	8.00	12.00	8.50
☐ **Day, Laraine,** photo with Leo Durocher, signed by both	18.00	24.00	17.50
☐ **Fellini, Federico,** motion picture still, "Satyricon", signed and with lengthy inscription	30.00	40.00	22.50
☐ **Field, Sally,** photo as "Flying Nun", signed	4.00	5.00	3.50
☐ **Fisher, Carrie,** motion picture still, "Star Wars", signed	18.00	24.00	17.50
☐ **Fonda, Henry,** motion picture still, "Jesse James", signed	8.00	12.00	7.00
☐ **Fonda, Peter,** motion picture still, "Easy Rider", signed	12.00	18.00	12.50
☐ **Fosse, Bob,** photo with Gwen Verdon, signed by both	12.00	18.00	12.50
☐ **Foxx, Redd,** LP record album cover, signed, no record, 1957	30.00	40.00	25.00
☐ **Gabor, Eva,** photo with Zsa Zsa and Magda Gabor, in jewelry shop, signed by all three, c. 1950's	14.00	18.00	13.50

AUTOGRAPHS / 97

	Current Price Range		Prior Year Average

☐ **Gardner, Ava,** motion picture still, "Barefoot Contessa", signed	14.00	18.00	13.50
☐ **Gaynor, Mitzi,** full-page color pin-up photo from magazine, signed, c. 1955	6.00	8.00	6.00
☐ **Gobel, George,** photo with guitar at age 12, signed	10.00	15.00	9.00
☐ **Gordon, Ruth,** copy of her autobiography, signed	12.00	18.00	12.50
☐ **Goulet, Robert,** photo with Carol Lawrence, signed by both	7.00	9.00	7.00
☐ **Greene, Lorne,** photo with Dan Blocker, Pernell Roberts and Michael Landon, signed by all	35.00	45.00	28.00
☐ **Grey, Joel,** motion picture still, "Cabaret", signed by him and Liza Minnelli	18.00	24.00	17.50
☐ **Harrison, Rex,** magazine cover with him as Henry Higgins ("My Fair Lady"), signed, 1956	7.00	11.00	7.00
☐ **Havoc, June,** 8x10 photo with Gypsy Rose Lee, signed by both, 1942	18.00	24.00	17.50
☐ **Hepburn, Audrey,** motion picture still, "Breakfast at Tiffany's", signed	8.00	12.00	7.00
☐ **Holbrook, Hal,** photo as Mark Twain, signed	8.00	12.00	7.00
☐ **Hope, Bob,** photo with Dwight D. Eisenhower, signed by Eisenhower	125.00	175.00	112.00
☐ **Ives, Burl,** LP record album cover, signed, record gone	30.00	40.00	25.00
☐ **Jones, Shirley,** photo with David Cassidy, signed by both	12.00	18.00	12.50
☐ **Kahn, Madeline,** motion picture still, "Paper Moon", signed	12.00	18.00	12.50
☐ **Kaye, Danny,** 8x10 color photo with Bing Crosby, signed by both	40.00	50.00	35.00
☐ **Keeler, Ruby,** photo with Dick Powell, signed by both	25.00	35.00	22.50
☐ **Kellerman, Sally,** 8x10 photo as "Hot Lips", signed	12.00	18.00	11.00
☐ **Kelly, Grace,** official Monaco wedding picture with Crown Prince Rainier, signed by both, matted and framed	250.00	325.00	230.00
☐ **Lancaster, Burt,** motion picture still, "Elmer Gantry", signed	12.00	18.00	12.50
☐ **Lavin, Linda,** photo as "Alice", signed by her, also signed by several others in cast	12.00	18.00	12.50
☐ **Lawford, Peter,** photo with Frank Sinatra, signed	7.00	11.00	7.00
☐ **Lewis, Jerry,** 8x10 photo with Dean Martin, signed by both, 1950	40.00	50.00	35.00
☐ **Linkletter, Art,** book, "Kids Say the Darndest Things", signed on front flyleaf	8.00	12.00	8.50
☐ **Lunt, Alfred,** photo with Lynn Fontanne, signed by both, 1947	35.00	45.00	35.00
☐ **MacLaine, Shirley,** book, "Don't Fall Off the Mountain", signed and inscribed	12.00	18.00	12.50
☐ **Majors, Lee,** photo with Farrah Fawcett-Majors, signed by both	18.00	24.00	17.50
☐ **Massey, Raymond.** photo as "Abe Lincoln", signed, c. 1952	12.00	18.00	12.50
☐ **Mature, Victor.** motion picture still, "One Billion B.C.", signed	7.00	11.00	7.00
☐ **May, Elaine.** photo with Mike Nichols, signed by both, 1960	18.00	24.00	17.50

98 / AUTOGRAPHS

	Current Price Range		Prior Year Average
☐ **Meadows, Audrey,** photo with Jackie Gleason, signed by both	10.00	15.00	11.00
☐ **Nicholson, Jack,** motion picture still, "One Flew Over the Cuckoo's Nest", signed	12.00	18.00	12.50
☐ **Nimoy, Leonard,** 8x10 color photo as "Spock", signed	18.00	24.00	17.50
☐ **O'Brian, Hugh,** photo as "Wyatt Earp", signed	6.00	8.00	6.00
☐ **Pacino, Al,** motion picture still, "Serpico", signed	12.00	18.00	11.00
☐ **Parker, Fess,** 8x10 photo as "Davy Crockett", signed	10.00	15.00	10.50
☐ **Poitier, Sidney,** motion picture still, "In the Heat of the Night", signed, also signed by Tony Curtis	12.00	18.00	12.50
☐ **Powell, Jane,** LP record album cover (10-inch), signed, record missing, c. 1949	35.00	45.00	30.00
☐ **Redford, Robert,** motion picture still, "Barefoot in the Park", signed	10.00	15.00	10.50
☐ **Redgrave, Vanessa,** photo as "Isadora Duncan", signed	18.00	24.00	17.50
☐ **Rooney, Mickey,** photo with Judy Garland, signed by both, 1943	275.00	325.00	250.00
☐ **Russell, Jane,** motion picture still, "The Outlaw", signed	12.00	18.00	12.50
☐ **Sellers, Peter,** motion picture still, "Pink Panther", signed	18.00	24.00	17.50
☐ **Stevens, Stella,** nude photo from "Playboy" magazine, signed	12.00	18.00	12.50
☐ **Swit, Loretta,** photo with "Mash" cast, signed by her, Alan Alda and several others, 1977	25.00	25.00	22.50
☐ **Tomlin, Lily,** LP record album cover, signed, record gone	18.00	24.00	17.50
☐ **Vaughn, Robert,** photo from "Man from U.N.C.L.E.", signed	6.00	8.00	6.00

UNITED STATES PRESIDENTS

☐ **Washington, George** (1732-1799)	4000.00	20000.00	11000.00
☐ **Adams, John** (1735-1826)	2800.00	7800.00	4000.00
☐ **Jefferson, Thomas** (1743-1826)	3500.00	18000.00	1100.00
☐ **Madison, James** (1751-1836)	1500.00	3200.00	2000.00
☐ **Monroe, James** (1758-1831)	1000.00	2200.00	9500.00
☐ **Adams, John Q.** (1767-1848)	1000.00	2200.00	9500.00
☐ **Jackson, Andrew** (1767-1845)	1200.00	2800.00	1700.00
☐ **Van Buren, Martin** (1782-1862)	600.00	800.00	625.00
☐ **Harrison, William H.** (1773-1841)	800.00	1200.00	800.00
☐ **Tyler, John** (1790-1862)	450.00	650.00	425.00
☐ **Polk, James K.** (1795-1849)	450.00	650.00	425.00
☐ **Taylor, Zachary** (1784-1850)	700.00	1600.00	1050.00
☐ **Fillmore, Millard** (1800-1874)	275.00	450.00	250.00
☐ **Pierce, Franklin** (1804-1869)	275.00	450.00	250.00
☐ **Buchanan, James** (1791-1868)	275.00	450.00	250.00
☐ **Lincoln, Abraham** (1809-1865)	4000.00	20000.00	11000.00
☐ **Johnson, Andrew** (1808-1875)	600.00	1600.00	900.00
☐ **Grant, U. S.** (1822-1885)	400.00	900.00	550.00
☐ **Hayes, Rutherford B.** (1822-1893)	250.00	350.00	230.00
☐ **Garfield, James** (1831-1881)	260.00	360.00	240.00
☐ **Arthur, Chester A.** (1830-1886)	200.00	300.00	170.00
☐ **Cleveland, Grover** (1837-1908)	100.00	175.00	100.00

AUTOS AND AUTOMOBILIA / 99

	Current Price Range		Prior Year Average
☐ Harrison, Benjamin (1833-1901)	275.00	425.00	300.00
☐ McKinley, William (1843-1901)	350.00	600.00	375.00
☐ Roosevelt, Theodore (1858-1919)	250.00	350.00	230.00
☐ Taft, William H. (1857-1930)	175.00	225.00	150.00
☐ Wilson, Woodrow (1856-1924)	400.00	650.00	375.00
☐ Harding, Warren G. (1865-1923)	500.00	800.00	550.00
☐ Coolidge, Calvin (1872-1933)	450.00	700.00	500.00
☐ Hoover, Herbert (1874-1964)	2000.00	3000.00	2400.00
☐ Roosevelt, Franklin (1882-1945)	500.00	900.00	600.00
☐ Truman, Harry (1884-1972)	800.00	1400.00	950.00
☐ Eisenhower, Dwight D. (1890-1969)	800.00	1400.00	950.00
☐ Kennedy, John F. (1917-1963)	1200.00	2600.00	1750.00
☐ Johnson, Lyndon B. (1908-1973)	700.00	1400.00	850.00
☐ Nixon, Richard M. (1913-)	2800.00	3800.00	2000.00
☐ Ford, Gerald (1913-)	450.00	700.00	500.00
☐ Carter, James E. (1924-)	400.00	650.00	385.00
☐ Reagan, Ronald W. (1911-)	350.00	500.00	325.00

AUTOS AND AUTOMOBILIA

Dogde, 1933 "Roadster".................$10000.00-$15000.00

The concept of self-powered vehicles which could run on cheap, easily obtainable fuel was the dream of many in the early and mid-19th century. It was not until the last 25 years of that century that the automobile came into existence. The man generally given credit for the first successful gasoline powered auto is Gottlieb Daimler. The first company to produce autos for sale to the public was Puegeot, still a highly respected manufacturer.

Despite these early successes, it took the ingenuity of an American, Henry Ford, to put the world on wheels. Although Ford is often mistakenly credited with inventing the automobile, his greatest idea was that of the assembly line. This technique of producing cars lowered the price-per-unit to a level that made it possible for nearly anyone to own an automobile. The

Ford "Model T" was sold for nearly two decades, and at one time was available for a few hundred dollars when new.

Car collecting was once limited to the very wealthy and consisted mostly of cars built before 1920. In recent years, however, many collectors have turned to cars of other eras and even to "modern classics" such as the two seater Thunderbirds of the 50's, the four-door Lincoln Continentals of the early 60's, and even the "muscle cars" of the 60's and 70's. Rising gasoline prices have some collectors investing in the less common imports of the 1950's such as Isetta, D.K.W. and the various English "Minis."

Strong gains in value are now being shown by many American cars of the late 50's and early 60's, particularly the high performance and/or sporty models. Corvairs, early Mustangs, the Ford Galaxie 500XL, the 1966 Olds Toronado and the Plymouth Barracuda are just a few examples of cars which can be purchased reasonably, but are expected to make dramatic increases in value in the future.

A related field of collecting is that of Automobilia items associated in some way to the automobile. This area encompasses a wide range of articles. Automotive insignias (manufacturers' symbols), decorative radiator caps, brass plated trim, original owner's manuals, early driving clothes (dusters, goggles, etc.) and early automotive advertising are just a few examples of the items collected.

Prices given for autos and automobilia are for specimens in excellent to mint condition and should be lower for objects needing repair or restoration. For more in-depth information and listings, you may refer to *The Official Price Guide to Collector Cars* by the Kruse Auctioneers, published by the House of Collectibles.

YEAR	MODEL	ENGINE	BODY	F	G	E
BUICK						
1941	Super	8 cyl.	Sedan	2300	6000	11900
1941	Roadmaster	8 cyl.	Sedan	2300	5100	12000
1941	Special (44-S)	8 cyl.	Coupe	2200	6100	11900
1942	Roadmaster	8 cyl.	Sedan	2200	6100	11900
1942	Special	8 cyl.	Sedan	2200	4600	10100
1942	Limited	8 cyl.	Limousine	3000	7500	15000
1942	Roadmaster	8 cyl.	Convertible	5000	12000	30800
1942	Roadmaster	8 cyl.	Sedanet	2400	4400	10400
1946	Super	8 cyl.	Convertible	4900	9900	19400
1946	Roadmaster	8 cyl.	Convertible	5100	11000	16000
1946	Roadmaster	8 cyl.	Sedanet	2200	4400	9900
1946	Super	8 cyl.	2 Door Sedan	2200	4600	9200
1947	Super	8 cyl.	Convertible	5000	7700	13400
1947	Roadmaster	8 cyl.	Sedanet	2200	4400	8800
1947	Roadmaster	8 cyl.	Convertible	5200	8000	13400
1947	Special	8 cyl.	2 Door Sedan	1100	3800	7700
1948	Roadmaster	8 cyl.	Convertible	5100	7900	12500
1948	Roadmaster	8 cyl.	Sedan	2300	4600	9700
1948	Super	8 cyl.	Convertible	5000	8500	13200
1949	Super	8 cyl.	Sedanet	1100	3500	8400
1949	Roadmaster	8 cyl.	Hardtop Coupe	2200	4900	8800

AUTOS AND AUTOMOBILIA / 101

YEAR	MODEL	ENGINE	BODY	F	G	E
1949	Roadmaster	8 cyl.	Convertible Coupe	3000	7100	13200
1949	Super	8 cyl.	Convertible	2900	7300	12600
1949	Super	8 cyl.	Estate Wagon	2200	5200	11500
1950	Special	8 cyl.	Sedan Fastback	1600	3400	7700
1950	Super	8 cyl.	Hardtop	1600	3900	6200
1950	Super	8 cyl.	Convertible	3400	6300	8200
1950	Roadmaster	8 cyl.	Hardtop	1300	3400	7200
1950	Roadmaster	8 cyl.	Convertible	2700	6400	9100
1950	Roadmaster	8 cyl.	Station Wagon	1100	3800	7900
1951	Special	8 cyl.	Hardtop	1100	2200	5900
1951	Super	8 cyl.	Hardtop	1100	2300	6000
1951	Super	8 cyl.	Convertible	1600	3900	7900
1951	Roadmaster	8 cyl.	Sedan	1100	2200	7200
1951	Roadmaster	8 cyl.	Convertible	2300	4200	7300
1951	Roadmaster	8 cyl.	Station Wagon	1300	3800	6800
1952	Special	8 cyl.	Sedan	1100	2200	6100
1952	Super	8 cyl.	Convertible	1600	3900	7900
1952	Super	8 cyl.	Hardtop	1200	3000	6000
1952	Roadmaster	8 cyl.	Hardtop	1300	3100	6200
1952	Roadmaster	8 cyl.	Convertible	1600	4700	9600
1952	Roadmaster	8 cyl.	Station Wagon	1400	2900	7100
1953	Special	8 cyl.	Hardtop	1100	2200	6300
1953	Super	8 cyl.	Sedan	1100	2200	4900
1953	Super	8 cyl.	Hardtop	1100	2200	5200
1953	Roadmaster	8 cyl.	Hardtop	1100	2500	5600
1953	Roadmaster	8 cyl.	Convertible	1300	3100	8800
1953	Skylark	8 cyl.	Convertible	2900	7400	15000
1954	Special	8 cyl.	Hardtop	1100	2700	6200
1954	Skylark	8 cyl.	Convertible	3100	7900	17600
1954	Super	8 cyl.	Sedan	1100	2400	5700
1954	Century	8 cyl.	Convertible	1600	3500	7700
1954	Century	8 cyl.	Station Wagon	1390	2700	8600
1954	Roadmaster	8 cyl.	Hardtop	1100	2500	5800
1954	Roadmaster	8 cyl.	Convertible	2300	4400	9200
1955	Special	8 cyl.	Convertible	1600	3000	7700
1955	Special	8 cyl.	4 Door Hardtop	1100	2300	5800
1955	Century	8 cyl.	Convertible	1600	3300	7000
1955	Century	8 cyl.	Hardtop	1100	2300	4700

CADILLAC

YEAR	MODEL	ENGINE	BODY	F	G	E
1941	61	(V) 8 cyl.	Convertible Coupe	6800	15200	31500
1941	60 Special	(V) 8 cyl.	Sedan	3150	7900	16800
1941	63	(V) 8 cyl.	Sedan	2900	5800	12800
1941	61	(V) 8 cyl.	Fast Back	3000	6100	13100
1942	75	(V) 8 cyl.	Formal Sedan	2600	6800	14500

102 / AUTOS AND AUTOMOBILIA

YEAR	MODEL	ENGINE	BODY	F	G	E
1942	75 Fleetwood	(V) 8 cyl.	Limousine	4000	9200	14700
1942	61	(V) 8 cyl.	Sedan	3300	5500	13100
1942	62	(V) 8 cyl.	Sedanet Fast Back	3400	6700	15700
1942	62	(V) 8 cyl.	Sedan Fast Back	3400	7800	15500

NOTE: 1943 to 1946 Cadillac and General Motors only produced Military Vehicles and Military Staff cars which used 1942 dies.

YEAR	MODEL	ENGINE	BODY	F	G	E
1946	61	(V) 8 cyl.	Fast Back Coupe	3400	7300	12800
1946	62	(V) 8 cyl.	Coupe	2600	4400	12000
1946	62	(V) 8 cyl.	Convertible	4200	12300	25600
1946	60 Special	(V) 8 cyl.	Sedan	3730	6300	11500
1947	62	(V) 8 cyl.	Sedan	2900	7100	11800
1947	62	(V) 8 cyl.	Sedanet	3150	7350	14000
1947	62	(V) 8 cyl.	Convertible	4400	12400	25200
1948	75 Fleetwood	(V) 8 cyl.	Limousine	3800	8400	15200
1948	62	(V) 8 cyl.	Convertible	5000	11800	27500
1948	61	(V) 8 cyl.	Sedan	3150	7000	13100
1948	60 Special	(V) 8 cyl.	Sedan	3400	7500	13200
1949	62	(V) 8 cyl.	Convertible	4500	11000	24000
1949	62	(V) 8 cyl.	Hardtop Coupe	2900	6300	12600
1949	75	(V) 8 cyl.	Limousine	2900	6700	14700
1950	62	(V) 8 cyl.	Convertible	4700	9450	23500
1950	Fleetwood 60 Special	(V) 8 cyl.	Sedan	2100	5400	11400
1950	62	(V) 8 cyl.	2 Door Hardtop	2100	5100	10700
1951	Fleetwood 60 Special	(V) 8 cyl.	Sedan	2100	5000	10500
1951	75 Fleetwood	(V) 8 cyl.	Limousine	2600	4800	13200

CHEVROLET

YEAR	MODEL	ENGINE	BODY	F	G	E
1940	Special Deluxe	6 cyl.	4 Door Sedan	1600	4000	8000
1941	Special Deluxe	6 cyl.	Convertible	4100	9600	16000
1941	Special Deluxe	6 cyl.	Sedan	1600	4000	8400
1941	Special Deluxe	6 cyl.	Club Coupe	1800	4200	8500
1941	Master Deluxe	6 cyl.	2 Passenger Coupe	1900	4400	9200
1942	Fleetline	6 cyl.	Aero Sedan	1800	4400	8800
1942	Master Deluxe	6 cyl.	Coupe	1600	3900	8200
1942	Special Deluxe	6 cyl.	4 Door Sedan	1600	3600	8100
1942	Special Deluxe	6 cyl.	Convertible	4200	8200	18000
1946	Fleetmaster	6 cyl.	Convertible	4100	7900	17000
1946	Fleetline	6 cyl.	Aero Sedan	1600	3300	8600
1946	Fleetline	6 cyl.	Town Sedan	1600	3100	8400
1946	Fleetline	6 cyl.	Sport Coupe	1600	2700	7500
1946	Stylemaster	6 cyl.	2 Door Sedan	1600	3900	8200

AUTOS AND AUTOMOBILIA / 103

YEAR	MODEL	ENGINE	BODY	F	G	E
1946	Stylemaster	6 cyl.	4 Door Sedan	1600	3850	8100
1946	Stylemaster	6 cyl.	Sport Coupe	2200	4900	9600
1947	Fleetmaster	6 cyl.	Convertible	4100	8300	17000
1947	Fleetmaster	6 cyl.	2 Door Sedan	1600	4200	8100
1947	Fleetline	6 cyl.	Town Sedan	1600	4100	9300
1948	Stylemaster	6 cyl.	Sedan	1600	3100	8600
1948	Fleetmaster	6 cyl.	Town Sedan	1600	4100	9300
1949	Styleline Deluxe	6 cyl.	Convertible	4100	8300	17900
1949	Styleline Deluxe	6 cyl.	Sedan	1600	3000	8500
1949	Styleline Deluxe	6 cyl.	Station Wagon	2200	5100	13000
1950	Bel Air	6 cyl.	Hardtop	1600	4100	9900
1950	Fleetline Deluxe	6 cyl.	2 Door Sedan	1600	3100	8500
1950	Fleetline Deluxe	6 cyl.	4 Door Sedan	1600	3100	8500
1950	Deluxe	6 cyl.	Convertible	4100	8500	17500
1951	Fleetline Deluxe	6 cyl.	4 Door Sedan	1600	3100	8400
1951	Styleline Deluxe	6 cyl.	Convertible	4200	9000	18000
1951	Styleline Deluxe	6 cyl.	Station Wagon	2200	5000	12000
1951	Bel Air	6 cyl.	Hardtop Coupe	1600	3900	9200
1952	Deluxe	6 cyl.	Convertible	4200	9600	18000
1952	Deluxe	6 cyl.	Hardtop Coupe	1600	3900	10200
1952	Fastback	6 cyl.	2 Door Sedan	1600	3100	7400
1953	Corvette	6 cyl.	Roadster	6600	15900	31000
1953	210	6 cyl.	Convertible	3800	8800	17900
1953	Bel Air	6 cyl.	Hardtop	2200	4100	10100
1953	Bel Air	6 cyl.	4 Door Sedan	1600	3800	8200
1953	Bel Air	6 cyl.	2 Door Sedan	2000	4600	8700
1953	Bel Air	6 cyl.	Convertible	3200	7800	15300
1954	Corvette	6 cyl.	Roadster	6600	15000	29000
1954	Bel Air	6 cyl.	Convertible	3800	9300	18000
1954	Bel Air	6 cyl.	Hardtop	2200	4200	13600
1954	Bel Air	6 cyl.	2 Door Sedan	1600	4100	11500
1954	Bel Air	6 cyl.	Station Wagon	1600	4100	11500
1955	210	6 cyl.	Hardtop	2200	4900	12700
1955	210 Del Rey	(V) 8 cyl.	2 Door Sedan	1900	3900	10500
1955	Bel Air	(V) 8 cyl.	2 Door Sedan	2200	4200	11900
1955	Bel Air	(V) 8 cyl.	Hardtop	3400	8500	14400
1955	Bel Air	(V) 8 cyl.	Station Wagon	1870	3900	8300

104 / AUTOS AND AUTOMOBILIA

YEAR	MODEL	ENGINE	BODY	F	G	E
1955	Bel Air	(V) 8 cyl.	Convertible	4950	9300	22000
1955	Nomad	(V) 8 cyl.	2 Door Wagon	2750	8000	13000
1955	Corvette	6 cyl.	Roadster	6600	17500	28500
1955	Corvette	(V) 8 cyl.	Roadster	6480	18500	29000
1956	210	(V) 8 cyl.	4 Door Hardtop	2750	6800	13000
1956	210	(V) 8 cyl.	Hardtop	3410	6800	12000
1956	Bel Air	(V) 8 cyl.	2 Door Sedan	2200	4400	10100
1956	Bel Air	(V) 8 cyl.	Hardtop	2420	5900	9500
1956	Bel Air	(V) 8 cyl.	Sedan	2200	3400	24000
1956	Bel Air	(V) 8 cyl.	Convertible	4840	11000	24000
1956	Nomad	(V) 8 cyl.	2 Door Wagon	2500	6600	12900
1956	Corvette	(V) 8 cyl.	Roadster	6000	14300	21400
1957	210	(V) 8 cyl.	Sedan	2200	5300	12900
1957	210	(V) 8 cyl.	Hardtop	3500	7100	14100
1957	Bel Air	(V) 8 cyl.	Sedan	2800	4900	11700
1957	Bel Air	(V)	2 Door Sedan	3500	7900	14000
1957	Bel Air	(V) 8 cyl.	Hardtop	4900	9700	18000
1957	Bel Air	(V) 8 cyl.	Convertible	6400	14000	22700
1957	Nomad	(V) 8 cyl.	2 Door Wagon	2400	7100	14800
1957	Corvette	(V) 8 cyl.	Roadster	7100	12000	20000
1957	Corvette	(V) 8 cyl. (Fuel Injection)	Roadster	7700	15400	29000
1957	Bel Air	(V) 8 cyl. (Fuel Injection)	Hardtop	4900	11000	19200
1957	El Morroco	(V) 8 cyl.	Hardtop	3800	7900	12600
1957	El Morroco	(V) 8 cyl.	4 Door Hardtop	4400	8800	13700
1958	Bel Air	(V) 8 cyl.	Hardtop Coupe	2200	4900	9300
1958	Impala	(V) 8 cyl.	Hardtop Coupe	3000	5500	11300
1958	Impala	(V) 8 cyl.	Convertible	4200	9200	22000
1958	Impala Nomad	(V) 8 cyl.	Station Wagon	2800	4900	10400
1958	Corvette	(V) 8 cyl.	Roadster	6600	13200	20900
1958	Corvette	(V) 8 cyl. (Fuel Injection)	Roadster	7700	15600	28000
1959	Bel Air	6 cyl.	2 Door Sedan	1600	3800	8500
1959	Impala	(V) 8 cyl.	Sport Coupe	2200	3700	11500
1959	Impala	(V) 8 cyl.	Convertible	4300	6700	12400
1959	Impala Nomad	(V) 8 cyl.	Station Wagon	2200	3500	8900
1959	Corvette	(V) 8 cyl.	Roadster	5500	12000	20000
1959	Corvette	(V) 8 cyl. (Fuel Injection)	Roadster	7700	15900	27000
1960	Bel Air	(V) 8 cyl.	Hardtop Coupe	1600	3500	7900
1960	Impala	(V) 8 cyl.	Sport Coupe	2200	4100	8600
1960	Impala	(V) 8 cyl.	Convertible	3100	6800	14700
1960	Corvette	(V) 8 cyl.	Roadster	5500	12000	19000

AUTOS AND AUTOMOBILIA / 105

YEAR	MODEL	ENGINE	BODY	F	G	E
1960	Corvette	(V) 8 cyl. (Fuel Injection)	Roadster	6600	14500	26000
1960	Corvair	6 cyl.	Coupe	1400	3000	6100
1960	Corvair Monza	6 cyl.	Coupe	1800	3500	7000
1960	Corvair	6 cyl.	Sedan	1400	2800	4900
1961	Impala	(V) 8 cyl.	2 Door Sedan	1700	3500	8100
1961	Bel Air	(V) 8 cyl.	Hardtop Coupe	1800	3700	8300
1961	Impala	(V) 8 cyl.	Sport Coupe	1900	3800	8400
1961	Impala SS	(V) 8 cyl. 409	Sport Coupe	2700	5500	10400
1961	Impala	(V) 8 cyl.	Convertible	3100	5200	9900
1961	Impala SS	(V) 8 cyl. 348	Convertible	3800	6600	12600
1961	Corvair Monza	6 cyl.	Coupe	1600	2700	4700
1961	Corvair	6 cyl.	Convertible	1900	3900	8800
1961	Corvair	6 cyl.	Sedan	1200	2400	4400
1961	Corvette	(V) 8 cyl.	Roadster	5200	7900	15700
1961	Corvette	(V) 8 cyl. (Fuel Injection)	Roadster	6300	10400	20300
1962	Bel Air	(V) 8 cyl.	Sport Coupe	1300	3000	5500
1962	Impala	(V) 8 cyl.	Sport Coupe	1500	3300	6000
1962	Impala SS	(V) 8 cyl. 327	Sport Coupe	1600	3800	7100
1962	Impala SS	(V) 8 cyl. 409	Convertible	2200	6000	8500
1962	Corvette	(V) 8 cyl.	Roadster	5500	8200	15900
1962	Corvette	(V) 8 cyl. (Fuel Injection)	Roadster	6400	10700	21000
1962	Corvair Monza	6 cyl.	Coupe	1300	2700	4700
1962	Corvair Monza	6 cyl.	Convertible	1800	3500	8200
1962	Corvair Lakewood	6 cyl.	Station Wagon	1400	2600	4600
1962	Nova	6 cyl.	Sport Coupe	1300	2600	4600
1963	Impala	(V) 8 cyl. 283	Sport Coupe	1700	3000	4900
1963	Impala SS	(V) 8 cyl. 409	Sport Coupe	2200	4600	7800
1963	Impala	(V) 8 cyl. 327	Convertible	2200	4600	8800
1963	Impala SS	(V) 8 cyl. 327	Convertible	2700	5700	10000
1963	Corvette	(V) 8 cyl. (Fuel Injection)	Coupe	4900	12600	19000
1963	Corvette	(V) 8 cyl.	Roadster	4400	10400	18000
1963	Corvair Monza	6 cyl.	Coupe	1300	2600	4700
1963	Corvair Monza	6 cyl.	Convertible	1800	3500	8200
1963	Corvair Spyder	6 cyl. (Turbo)	Convertible	2400	4000	8800
1963	Nova SS	6 cyl.	Sport Coupe	1600	2600	5800
1963	Nova SS	6 cyl.	Convertible	2200	3900	8400
1964	Impala	(V) 8 cyl.	Convertible	2200	4000	8500
1964	Impala SS	(V) 8 cyl. 327	Convertible	2500	4400	9100
1964	Impala SS	(V) 8 cyl. 409	Sport Coupe	2200	4000	8500
1964	Corvette	(V) 8 cyl.	Coupe	4900	10400	18100
1964	Corvette	(V) 8 cyl.	Roadster	5500	11500	19200
1964	Corvair Monza	6 cyl.	Coupe	1300	2600	4900
1964	Corvair Monza	6 cyl.	Convertible	1900	3700	6800
1964	Corvair Spyder	6 cyl. (Turbo)	Coupe	1400	3000	5500
1964	Corvair Spyder	6 cyl. (Turbo)	Convertible	2200	4400	8100
1964	Nova SS	(V) 8 cyl. 283	Sport Coupe	1600	3800	7200
1965	Impala SS	(V) 8 cyl. 327	Convertible	2700	4900	8400
1965	Impala SS	(V) 8 cyl. 327	Sport Coupe	2200	3500	6800
1965	Caprice	(V) 8 cyl. 286	Sport Sedan	1400	3400	6700
1965	Corvette	(V) 8 cyl.	Roadster	4400	9300	17000

106 / AUTOS AND AUTOMOBILIA

YEAR	MODEL	ENGINE	BODY	F	G	E
CHRYSLER						
1941	Newport	8 cyl.	Dual Cowl Phaeton	48000	113000	201600
1941	New Yorker	8 cyl.	Club Coupe	1800	3900	7700
1941	Saratoga	6 cyl.	Sedan	1400	2600	3900
1941	Royal	6 cyl.	Coupe	1400	2600	6400
1942	Royal	6 cyl.	Sedan	1400	2600	6450
1942	Saratoga	8 cyl.	Coupe	1450	2650	6500
1942	Imperial Crown	8 cyl.	Limousine	3200	7100	12600
1942	Town & Country	8 cyl.	Station Wagon	5100	9600	16800
1946	Royal	6 cyl.	Sedan	1400	2800	6500
1946	Town & Country	8 cyl.	Sedan	4800	8100	16800
1946	Crown Imperial	8 cyl.	8 Passenger Sedan	2400	5700	12000
1947	Windsor	6 cyl.	Convertible	4800	5400	7900
1947	Town & Country	8 cyl.	Sedan	3200	6900	14000
1947	New Yorker	8 cyl.	2 Passenger Coupe	1800	3600	8200
1947	Royal	6 cyl.	Sedan	1600	2800	6500
1947	Town & Country	8 cyl.	Convertible	4800	12900	35000
1948	Royal	6 cyl.	2 Passenger Coupe	1600	3100	7100
1948	Windsor	6 cyl.	Convertible	2400	7800	17000
1948	Windsor	6 cyl.	Sedan	1400	2600	6000
1948	New Yorker	8 cyl.	Sedan	1700	3500	7000
1949	Town & Country	(V) 8 cyl.	Convertible	4200	12000	34600
1949	New Yorker	(V) 8 cyl.	Convertible	3000	6000	17600
1949	New Yorker Highlander	(V) 8 cyl.	Sedan	1400	2900	6000
1949	New Yorker	(V) 8 cyl.	Club Coupe	1800	3700	8200
1949	Crown Imperial	(V) 8 cyl.	Limousine	2600	6000	14000
1950	Windsor	(V) 8 cyl.	Station Wagon	1300	3300	10000
1950	Windsor	(V) 8 cyl.	Club Coupe	1400	2800	6400
1950	New Yorker	(V) 8 cyl.	Convertible	3000	6000	14000
1950	Town & Country	(V)	Hardtop	3100	7500	14000
DODGE						
1930	DC	8 cyl.	Sedan	2300	4900	9200
1931	DG	8 cyl.	Sport Roadster	4000	9500	20000
1931	DG	8 cyl.	Rumble Seat Coupe	2700	5500	11200
1931	DH	6 cyl.	Sedan	1800	3000	8700
1932	DK	8 cyl.	Sedan	2300	4900	10200
1932	DL	6 cyl.	Sedan	1900	3200	7900
1932	DL	8 cyl.	Rumble Seat Coupe	2700	5500	9200
1932	DL	8 cyl.	Cabriolet	3600	8700	17000

AUTOS AND AUTOMOBILIA / 107

YEAR	MODEL	ENGINE	BODY	F	G	E
1933	Series DP	6 cyl.	Convertible	4000	8000	17000
1933	DO	8 cyl.	Sport Coupe	2500	4900	9800
1933	DO	8 cyl.	Sedan	1900	2700	7800
1934	DR	6 cyl.	Cabriolet	2200	5500	12000
1934	DR	6 cyl.	Coupe	1500	3000	7200
1934	DR	6 cyl.	Convertible	3500	8500	18000
1935	DU	6 cyl.	2 Door Sedan	1200	3100	8200
1935	DR	6 cyl.	Convertible	2200	6500	14500
1936	D2	6 cyl.	Convertible Sedan	3400	7800	15800
1936	D2	6 cyl.	Sedan	1000	3200	7000
1936	D2	6 cyl.	2 Door Sedan	1100	2500	7800
1937	D5	6 cyl.	Sedan	1000	2000	7500
1937	D5	6 cyl.	Coupe	1050	3600	8100
1938	D8	6 cyl.	Convertible	2800	5600	13800
1938	D8	6 cyl.	Sedan	1000	3600	6200
1938	D8	6 cyl.	Convertible Sedan	3200	7600	16300
1939	D13	6 cyl.	Victoria Coupe	1500	4300	9500
1939	D13	6 cyl.	Sedan	1000	2500	6000
1940	D17	6 cyl.	Sedan	1000	2300	5400
1940	D17	6 cyl.	Cabriolet	2500	4200	12000
1941	D19	6 cyl.	Sedan	1000	2400	5000
1941	D19	6 cyl.	2 Door Sedan	1000	2400	5000
1941	D19	6 cyl.	Convertible	2500	5200	13200
1941	D19	6 cyl.	Town Sedan	1500	3600	8300
1942	D22	6 cyl.	2 Door Sedan	1000	2400	6000
1942	D22	6 cyl.	Town Sedan	1250	3600	8300
1946		6 cyl.	Town Sedan	1250	3400	8000
1946	D24	6 cyl.	2 Passenger Coupe	1000	2200	6500
1946	D24	6 cyl.	Cabriolet	1300	3500	9800
1947	D24	6 cyl.	Sedan	1000	2100	6200
1948	D24	6 cyl.	Convertible Coupe	2500	4500	12800
1949	Wayfarer	6 cyl.	Roadster	2600	4700	13000
1950	Coronet	6 cyl.	Sedan	1000	2200	6200
1950	Wayfarer	6 cyl.	Roadster	2500	4500	12800
1951	Meadowbrook	6 cyl.	2 Door Sedan	1000	1900	5000
1952	Coronet	6 cyl.	Convertible	2000	3800	12400

FORD

YEAR	MODEL	ENGINE	BODY	F	G	E
1941	Super Deluxe	(V) 8 cyl.	Convertible Club	2100	7100	15800
1941	Super Deluxe	(V) 8 cyl.	Coupe	1700	4800	8600
1941	Super Deluxe	(V) 8 cyl.	Tudor	1500	4600	8200
1941	Super Deluxe	(V) 8 cyl.	Fordor	1500	4600	8200

108 / AUTOS AND AUTOMOBILIA

YEAR	MODEL	ENGINE	BODY	F	G	E
1941	Super Deluxe	(V) 8 cyl.	Station Wagon	2500	6500	14200
1941		(V) 8 cyl.	Pickup	1200	4000	8100
1942	Special	6 cyl.	Coupe	1800	3700	6900
1942	Deluxe	(V) 8 cyl.	Coupe	2000	2800	7100
1942	Deluxe	(V) 8 cyl.	Tudor	1100	2000	4100
1942	Super Deluxe	(V) 8 cyl.	Convertible	2000	6500	20500
1942	Super Deluxe	(V) 8 cyl.	Club Coupe	1200	2800	7300
1942	Super Deluxe	(V) 8 cyl.	Tudor	1100	2600	7000
1942	Super Deluxe	(V) 8 cyl.	Fordor	1200	2600	8200
1942	Super Deluxe	(V) 8 cyl.	Station Wagon	2100	6400	13400
1946	Deluxe	6 cyl.	Tudor	1700	3600	7800
1946	Super Deluxe	(V) 8 cyl.	Convertible	1900	6000	13100
1946	Super Deluxe	(V) 8 cyl.	Sportsman Convertible	3800	9300	19400
1946	Super Deluxe	(V) 8 cyl.	Club Coupe	1350	3800	7100
1946	Super Deluxe	(V) 8 cyl.	Tudor	1200	3700	7000
1946	Super Deluxe	(V) 8 cyl.	Fordor	1200	3800	7000
1946	Super Deluxe	(V) 8 cyl.	Station Wagon	1900	5900	20500
1947	Deluxe	6 cyl.	Sedan	1200	2500	6800
1947	Deluxe	(V) 8 cyl.	Coupe	1200	2600	7200
1947	Super Deluxe	(V) 8 cyl.	Convertible	2900	7100	16300
1947	Super Deluxe	(V) 8 cyl.	Club Coupe	1300	2800	6800
1947	Super Deluxe	(V) 8 cyl.	Sportsman Convertible	3800	9300	20500
1947	Super Deluxe	(V) 8 cyl.	Tudor	1250	2600	7200
1947	Super Deluxe	(V) 8 cyl.	Fordor	1200	2600	6800
1947	Super Deluxe	(V) 8 cyl.	Station Wagon	3000	7000	14200
1948	Deluxe	6 cyl.	Sedan	1200	2500	6800
1948	Super Deluxe	(V) 8 cyl.	Convertible	2900	7100	15200
1948	Super Deluxe	(V) 8 cyl.	Sportsman Convertible	3800	9300	20500
1948	Super Deluxe	(V) 8 cyl.	Club Coupe	1300	2700	7300
1948	Super Deluxe	(V) 8 cyl.	Coupe	1300	2700	7200
1948	Super Deluxe	(V) 8 cyl.	Tudor	1200	2500	6800
1948	Super Deluxe	(V) 8 cyl.	Fordor	1200	2500	7000

YEAR	MODEL	ENGINE	BODY	F	G	E
1948	Super Deluxe	(V) 8 cyl.	Station Wagon	2900	7000	14600
1949	Deluxe	(V) 8 cyl.	Sedan	1100	2300	7000
1949	Deluxe	(V) 8 cyl.	Coupe	1100	2600	6900
1949	Custom	(V) 8 cyl.	Convertible	2500	6300	14700
1949	Custom	(V) 8 cyl.	Club Coupe	1200	2500	7300
1949	Custom	(V) 8 cyl.	Sedan	1100	2400	7100
1949	Custom	(V) 8 cyl.	Station Wagon	1600	4900	12100
1950	Deluxe	(V) 8 cyl.	Business Coupe	1300	2600	7700
1950	Deluxe	(V) 8 cyl.	Sedan	1200	2400	7200
1950	Custom	(V) 8 cyl.	Convertible	2500	5200	13600
1950	Custom	(V) 8 cyl.	2 Door Sedan	1200	2500	6300
1950	Custom	(V) 8 cyl.	Crestliner	1600	3900	8900
1950	Custom	(V) 8 cyl.	Station Wagon	1100	3900	7900
1951	Deluxe	(V) 8 cyl.	Business Coupe	1200	2300	7100
1951	Deluxe	(V) 8 cyl.	Sedan	1100	2200	7000
1951	Custom	(V) 8 cyl.	Convertible	2500	5200	13600
1951	Custom	(V) 8 cyl.	Crestliner	1600	4000	9100
1951	Custom	(V) 8 cyl.	Club Coupe	1200	2300	6800
1951	Custom	(V) 8 cyl.	Victoria	1600	3600	8400
1951	Custom	(V) 8 cyl.	Station Wagon	1300	3600	7700
1952	Mainline	6 cyl.	Business Coupe	1200	2100	6500
1952	Customline	(V) 8 cyl.	Club Coupe	1200	2100	6500
1952	Customline	(V) 8 cyl.	Country Squire	1300	2300	8100
1952	Crestline	(V) 8 cyl.	Convertible	1950	5000	14200
1952	Crestline	(V) 8 cyl.	Victoria	1750	4000	8100
1952	Crestline	(V) 8 cyl.	Country Squire	1300	2900	8100
1953	Mainline	(V) 8 cyl.	Business Coupe	1200	2700	6700
1953	Mainline	(V) 8 cyl.	Sedan	1100	2300	7000
1953	Customline	(V) 8 cyl.	Sedan	1100	2400	7100
1953	Customline	(V) 8 cyl.	2 Door Sedan	1200	2600	6300
1953	Customline	(V) 8 cyl.	Club Coupe	1200	2600	6300
1953	Customline	(V) 8 cyl.	Sedan	1100	2400	7100
1953	Crestline	(V) 8 cyl.	Convertible	2300	5100	13400
1953	Crestline	(V) 8 cyl.	Victoria	1350	4100	8000
1953	Crestline	(V) 8 cyl.	Country Squire	1350	3900	7800
1954	Mainline	(V) 8 cyl.	Business Coupe	1200	2500	6300
1954	Mainline	6 cyl.	Station Wagon	1200	2300	7100
1954	Customline	(V) 8 cyl.	Sedan	1200	2300	7100

110 / AUTOS AND AUTOMOBILIA

YEAR	MODEL	ENGINE	BODY	F	G	E
1954	Customline	(V) 8 cyl.	Club Coupe	1200	2500	6800
1954	Customline	(V) 8 cyl.	Station Wagon	1200	2400	7100
1954	Crestline	(V) 8 cyl.	Convertible	2400	4200	12600
1954	Crestline	(V) 8 cyl.	Victoria	1600	3400	7200
1954	Crestline	(V) 8 cyl.	Skyliner	2300	5600	13700
1954	Crestline	(V) 8 cyl.	Sedan	1200	3000	7200
1954	Crestline	(V) 8 cyl.	Country Squire	1200	2800	7000
1955	Ranch Wagon	(V) 8 cyl.	Station Wagon	1200	2600	7100
1955	Country Squire	(V) 8 cyl.	Station Wagon	1200	2100	6700
1955	Mainline	6 cyl.	Business Sedan	1100	2000	6800
1955	Customline	(V) 8 cyl.	Sedan	1100	2200	7100
1955	Fairlane	(V) 8 cyl.	Convertible	2300	5200	14700
1955	Fairlane	(V) 8 cyl.	Victoria	1600	3000	7300
1955	Fairlane	(V) 8 cyl.	Crown Victoria	1700	3700	8400
1955	Fairlane	(V) 8 cyl.	Crown Victoria w/Glass Top	2200	4000	9100
1955	Fairlane	(V) 8 cyl.	Town Sedan	1300	3000	6100
1955	Fairlane	(V) 8 cyl.	Club Sedan	1100	3000	6100
1955	Thunderbird	(V) 8 cyl.	Roadster	5200	13100	29400
1956	Mainline	6 cyl.	2 Door Sedan	1300	3300	6500
1956	Country Squire	(V) 8 cyl.	Station Wagon	1400	3700	6600
1956	Customline	(V) 8 cyl.	2 Door Sedan	1300	2600	6500
1956	Customline	(V) 8 cyl.	Victoria	1500	2900	7900
1956	Fairlane	(V) 8 cyl.	Convertible	2500	5800	13600
1956	Fairlane	(V) 8 cyl.	Victoria	1450	3000	8000
1956	Fairlane	(V) 8 cyl.	Crown Victoria	1600	4200	11000
1956	Fairlane	(V) 8 cyl.	Crown Victoria w/Glass Top	1700	5200	12400
1956	Fairlane	(V) 8 cyl.	Victoria Sedan	1350	2900	7900
1956	Fairlane	(V) 8 cyl.	Club Sedan	1100	2600	7100
1956	Fairlane	(V) 8 cyl.	Town Sedan	1100	2600	6900
1956	Parklane	(V) 8 cyl.	2 Door Station Wagon	1300	3400	8000
1956	Thunderbird	(V) 8 cyl.	Roadster	4400	13100	30400
1957	Custom	6 cyl.	Sedan	1100	2000	6100
1957	Fairlane	(V) 8 cyl.	Club Sedan	1300	3700	6900
1957	Fairlane	(V) 8 cyl.	Victoria	1600	3900	7200

AUTOS AND AUTOMOBILIA / 111

YEAR	MODEL	ENGINE	BODY	F	G	E
1957	Fairlane 500	(V) 8 cyl.	Convertible	2100	3500	11700
1957	Fairlane 500	(V) 8 cyl.	Skyliner Convertible	2500	6200	14500
1957	Fairlane 500	(V) 8 cyl.	Town Sedan	1100	2300	5700
1957	Fairlane 500	(V) 8 cyl.	Victoria Sedan	1300	2400	5800
1957	Thunderbird	(V) 8 cyl.	Roadster	4900	12600	29400
1957	Thunderbird "F"	(V) 8 cyl. (Supercharged)	Roadster	6300	15200	33600
1957	Thunderbird "E"	(V) 8 cyl. (Supercharged)	Roadster	5500	14700	30600
1958	Fairlane	(V) 8 cyl. (Supercharged)	Town Sedan	1100	2100	5400
1958	Fairlane	(V) 8 cyl. (Supercharged)	Town Victoria	1300	2200	5500
1958	Fairlane 500	(V) 8 cyl. (Supercharged)	Convertible	2200	4000	8600
1958	Fairlane 500	(V) 8 cyl. Supercharged)	Club Victoria	1200	2200	5600
1958	Fairlane 500	(V) 8 cyl. (Supercharged)	Skyliner Convertible	2400	5800	10500
1958	Thunderbird	(V) 8 cyl. (Supercharged)	Hardtop	1600	3300	10300
1958	Thunderbird	(V) 8 cyl. (Supercharged)	Convertible	2200	5800	13100
1958	Country Square	(V) 8 cyl. (Supercharged)	Station Wagon	1300	3300	6800
1959	Fairlane 500	(V) 8 cyl. (Supercharged)	Club Sedan	1200	2200	5800
1959	Fairlane 500	(V) 8 cyl. (Supercharged)	Town Victoria	1300	2300	6300
1959	Galaxie	(V) 8 cyl. (Supercharged)	Convertible	2300	4200	10000
1959	Galaxie	(V) 8 cyl. (Supercharged)	Skyliner Convertible	2500	4300	11000
1959	Galaxie	(V) 8 cyl. (Supercharged)	Victoria	1200	2300	6000
1959	Thunderbird	(V) 8 cyl. (Supercharged)	Hardtop	1600	3200	9200
1959	Thunderbird	(V) 8 cyl. (Supercharged)	Convertible	2200	4700	12400
1960	Galaxie	(V) 8 cyl. (Supercharged)	Victoria	1400	2300	5900
1960	Starliner	(V) 8 cyl. (Supercharged)	Hardtop	1300	2400	6100
1960	Sunliner	(V) 8 cyl. (Supercharged)	Convertible	2100	4000	8500
1960	Country Squire	(V) 8 cyl. (Supercharged)	Station Wagon	1300	2100	5700
1960	Thunderbird	(V) 8 cyl. (Supercharged)	Convertible	2400	6100	13800
1960	Thunderbird	(V) 8 cyl. (Supercharged)	Hardtop	1600	4500	9500
1960	Thunderbird	(V) 8 cyl. (Supercharged)	Hardtop w/Sun Roof	1700	4900	10000

112 / AUTOS AND AUTOMOBILIA

YEAR	MODEL	ENGINE	BODY	F	G	E
1960	Falcon	6 cyl.	2 Door Sedan	1100	1900	4800
1961	Falcon Futura	6 cyl.	Coupe	1100	2000	5000
1961	Galaxie	(V) 8 cyl.	Victoria	1200	2000	5400
1961	Galaxie	(V) 8 cyl.	Skyliner Hardtop	1300	2200	6700
1961	Galaxie	(V) 8 cyl.	Convertible	1700	3800	8600
1961	Thunderbird	(V) 8 cyl.	Hardtop	1800	4400	10400
1961	Thunderbird	(V) 8 cyl.	Convertible	2300	5600	14400
1962	Falcon Futura	6 cyl.	Coupe	1100	2100	5600
1962	Galaxie 500	(V) 8 cyl.	Convertible	1800	4000	8800
1962	Galaxie 500	(V) 8 cyl.	Hardtop	1300	2500	5800
1962	Galaxie XL	(V) 8 cyl.	Hardtop	1400	2600	5900
1962	Galaxie XL	(V) 8 cyl. 406	Convertible	1900	3700	8900
1962	Thunderbird	(V) 8 cyl.	Hardtop	1600	3100	8700
1962	Thunderbird	(V) 8 cyl.	Hardtop Landau	1700	3500	9600
1962	Thunderbird	(V) 8 cyl.	Convertible	2300	5600	14400
1962	Thunderbird	(V) 8 cyl.	Sport Roadster	3700	7100	17300
1963	Falcon Futura	6 cyl.	Hardtop	1100	2400	4200
1963	Falcon Futura	6 cyl.	Convertible	1600	4200	8700
1963	Falcon Sprint	(V) 8 cyl. 260	Sport Coupe	1100	1900	3100
1963	Falcon Sprint	(V) 8 cyl. 260	Sport Convertible	1600	2900	6100
1963	Fairlane 500	(V) 8 cyl. 260	Sport Coupe	1100	1700	3100
1963	Galaxie 500	(V) 8 cyl. 390	Hardtop	1100	1800	3100
1963	Galaxie 500	(V) 8 cyl. 406	Convertible	1600	2900	6300
1963	Galaxie 500 XL	(V) 8 cyl. 390	Convertible	1600	2900	6300
1963	Galaxie 500 XL	(V) 8 cyl. 427	Sport Coupe	1100	2300	4300
1963	Thunderbird	(V) 8 cyl.	Hardtop	1100	2500	5800
1963	Thunderbird	(V) 8 cyl.	Landau Hardtop	1100	2600	6000
1963	Thunderbird	(V) 8 cyl.	Sport Roadster	2600	10000	16300
1963	Thunderbird	(V) 8 cyl.	Convertible	2000	4700	12000
1964	Falcon Sprint	(V) 8 cyl. 260	Hardtop	1100	2200	4000
1964	Falcon Sprint	(V) 8 cyl. 260	Convertible	1500	3700	7000
1964	Fairlane 500	(V) 8 cyl. 260	Sport Coupe	1100	2600	5700
1964	Galaxie 500 XL	(V) 8 cyl. 390	Convertible	1600	3500	7400
1964	Galaxie 500 XL	(V) 8 cyl. 352	Sport Coupe	1100	2700	6000
1964	Galaxie 500 XL	(V) 8 cyl. 427	Sport Coupe	1500	2900	6300
1964	Thunderbird	(V) 8 cyl.	Hardtop	1100	2600	6100

AUTOS AND AUTOMOBILIA / 113

YEAR	MODEL	ENGINE	BODY	F	G	E
1964	Thunderbird	(V) 8 cyl.	Landau Hardtop	1600	2900	17000
1964	Thunderbird	(V) 8 cyl.	Convertible	2400	4800	9400
1964½	Mustang	(V) 8 cyl. 260	Convertible	1600	6300	21000
1964½	Mustang	(V) 8 cyl. 260	Hardtop	1100	2700	5800
1965	Galaxie 500 XL	(V) 8 cyl. 390	Hardtop	1100	2500	4400
1965	Galaxie 500 XL	(V) 8 cyl. 390	Convertible	1600	3000	8100
1965	Mustang	6 cyl.	Hardtop	1100	2300	5700
1965	Mustang	(V) 8 cyl. 289	Convertible	1600	6100	21000
1965	Mustang	(V) 8 cyl. 289	Fastback 2 + 2	1600	4000	7900
1965	Shelby GT 350	(V) 8 cyl. 289	Fastback	2900	6800	12800
1965	LTD	(V) 8 cyl. 390	Hardtop Sedan	1100	2000	4900
1966	Fairlane 500 GTA	(V) 8 cyl. 390	Convertible	1500	3800	8300
1966	Galaxie 500 XL	(V) 8 cyl. 428	Convertible	1700	4000	8500
1966	Mustang	6 cyl.	Hardtop	1100	3400	5700
1966	Mustang GT	(V) 8 cyl. 289	Hardtop	1900	5900	9500
1966	Mustang GT	(V) 8 cyl. 289	Convertible	2900	8600	22600
1966	Mustang GT	(V) 8 cyl. 289	Fastback 2 + 2	1900	5000	9100

LINCOLN

YEAR	MODEL	ENGINE	BODY	F	G	E
1947	73	(V) 12 cyl.	Sedan	2600	6500	14200
1947	Continental	(V) 12 cyl.	Coupe	3100	6800	14200
1947	Continental	(V) 12 cyl.	Cabriolet	4950	9900	20500
1948	Continental	(V) 12 cyl.	Convertible	4100	13700	27800
1948	Continental	(V) 12 cyl.	Coupe	3500	7300	14700
1948	76	(V) 12 cyl.	Convertible	3900	12200	23900
1948	77	(V) 12 cyl.	Club Coupe	3500	7150	14400
1949	Cosmopolitan	(V) 8 cyl.	Fastback Sedan	1300	2800	6300
1949	Cosmopolitan	(V) 8 cyl.	Sedan	1200	7600	6100
1949	Cosmopolitan 76	(V) 8 cyl.	Convertible	1800	6800	13100
1949	72	(V) 8 cyl.	Club Coupe	1100	2850	6800
1949	74	(V) 8 cyl.	Sport Sedan	1200	3000	7100
1950	Cosmopolitan	(V) 8 cyl.	Convertible	2600	6150	12100
1950	Cosmopolitan	(V) 8 cyl.	Club Coupe	1300	3600	6800
1950	Cosmopolitan	(V) 8 cyl.	Sport Sedan	1700	2800	6300
1950	Cosmopolitan	(V) 8 cyl.	Capri Coupe	1200	2300	5700
1950	Lido	(V) 8 cyl.	Coupe	1250	2400	6150

114 / AUTOS AND AUTOMOBILIA

YEAR	MODEL	ENGINE	BODY	F	G	E
1951	Cosmopolitan	(V) 8 cyl.	Convertible	2300	4750	11000
1951	Lido	(V) 8 cyl.	Coupe	1200	3100	6200
1951	Cosmopolitan	(V) 8 cyl.	Sport Sedan	1100	2600	5850
1951	Cosmopolitan	(V) 8 cyl.	Coupe	1200	2400	4900
1951	Cosmopolitan	(V) 8 cyl.	Capri Coupe	1150	2300	4700

MERCEDES- BENZ

YEAR	MODEL	ENGINE	BODY	F	G	E
1948	190	6 cyl.	Sedan	2400	4350	8900
1949	170 D	6 cyl.	Limousine	2400	4300	8900
1949	170 D	4 cyl.	Sedan	1800	3300	7200
1949	170 V	4 cyl.	Coupe	2100	4200	8900
1950	170 V	4 cyl.	Sport	3000	6000	10800
1950	170 D	4 cyl.	Convertible Coupe	4200	13200	27600
1950	220	6 cyl.	Sedan	3000	5400	10700
1951	220	6 cyl.	Convertible	5100	15100	30000
1951	300	6 cyl.	Sedan	3600	7200	14400
1951	300	6 cyl.	Coupe	4200	8400	17800
1951	300	6 cyl.	Sport	4300	8500	18000
1952	300 C	6 cyl.	Cabriolet	8400	21600	28800
1952	300 S	6 cyl.	Sedan	3600	7200	14400
1952	300 S	6 cyl.	Coupe	4200	8400	17800
1952	170 V	4 cyl.	Coupe	3000	4300	8400
1952	170 D	4 cyl.	Cabriolet	3600	5700	13800
1952	170 S	4 cyl.	Limousine	2800	5200	10800
1953	170 SV	4 cyl.	Coupe	2500	4800	10800
1953	170 SD	4 cyl.	Sport	3600	5700	13800
1953	180	4 cyl.	Limousine	4600	6900	13800
1953	300	4 cyl.	Convertible Sedan	7300	19400	42400
1953	300 S	4 cyl.	Convertible Coupe	7300	19400	42400
1953	220	4 cyl.	Cabriolet	3600	13200	30100
1954	300 B	6 cyl.	Sedan	3600	7200	13400
1954	220	6 cyl.	Limousine	2400	7350	14600
1954	220A	6 cyl.	Coupe	7200	14400	30100
1954	300	6 cyl.	Limousine	4200	7300	15200
1954	300	8 cyl.	Convertible Coupe	7300	19400	38400
1955	190 SL	4 cyl.	Sport Roadster	2400	7400	17800
1955	300 C	6 cyl.	Sedan	3600	7200	14400

OLDSMOBILE

YEAR	MODEL	ENGINE	BODY	F	G	E
1946	66	6 cyl.	Coupe	1100	2700	5500
1946	66	6 cyl.	Station Wagon	1300	3700	7300
1946	78	8 cyl.	Club Sedan	1100	2700	6500
1946	98	8 cyl.	Convertible	2100	7200	15200
1946	98	8 cyl.	Sedan	1100	2900	5700
1947	66	6 cyl.	Club Sedan	1100	2700	5500
1947	66	6 cyl.	Convertible	2100	7000	14700

AUTOS AND AUTOMOBILIA / 115

YEAR	MODEL	ENGINE	BODY	F	G	E
1947	66	6 cyl.	Station Wagon	1300	3700	7300
1947	78	8 cyl.	Sedan	1100	2700	5500
1947	98	8 cyl.	Convertible	2100	7200	15200
1947	98	8 cyl.	Fastback Coupe	1300	2700	6900
1948	Dynamic	6 cyl.	Convertible	2600	6800	13100
1948	Dynamic	8 cyl.	Sedan	1100	2400	5900
1948	Dynamic	8 cyl.	Station Wagon	1300	3700	7300
1948	98	8 cyl.	Convertible	2100	8300	17300
1949	Futuramic	6 cyl.	Convertible	1900	7000	13100
1949	Futuramic	6 cyl.	Club Coupe	1200	2900	5900
1949	Futuramic	(V) 8 cyl.	Convertible	2300	7900	17100
1949	Futuramic	(V) 8 cyl.	Station Wagon	1300	3000	6500
1949	Futuramic	(V) 8 cyl.	Coupe	1100	2000	5000
1949	98	(V) 8 cyl.	Convertible	2100	7200	14200
1949	98	(V) 8 cyl.	Holiday Hardtop	1400	3500	6700
1950	88	(V) 8 cyl.	Convertible	2300	6800	14000
1950	88	(V) 8 cyl.	Holiday Hardtop	1400	3500	6100
1950	88	(V) 8 cyl.	2 Door Sedan	1100	2100	5400
1950	98	(V) 8 cyl.	Convertible	1900	7000	14000
1950	98	(V) 8 cyl.	Holiday Hardtop	1400	2900	5900
1950	88	(V) 8 cyl.	Station Wagon	1100	2700	4900
1951	S-88	(V) 8 cyl.	Club Coupe	1100	2800	4700
1951	S-88	(V) 8 cyl.	Convertible	2100	6300	14500
1951	98	(V) 8 cyl.	Convertible	2100	6300	14500
1951	98	(V) 8 cyl.	Holiday Coupe	1200	2900	5700
1951	98	(V) 8 cyl.	Sedan	1100	2700	5200
1952	S-88	(V) 8 cyl.	Convertible	1900	5000	13400
1952	S-88	(V) 8 cyl.	Coupe	1100	2900	5800
1952	98	(V) 8 cyl.	Convertible	2100	5000	13400
1953	S-88	(V) 8 cyl.	Convertible	1900	4200	13100
1953	S-88	(V) 8 cyl.	Holiday Coupe	1200	2800	5500
1953	S-88	(V) 8 cyl.	Sedan	1100	2300	4700
1953	98	(V) 8 cyl.	Convertible	2100	4700	12600
1953	98	(V) 8 cyl.	Holiday Coupe	1300	2900	5800
1953	Fiesta	(V) 8 cyl.	Convertible	2800	6300	14700
1954	S-88	(V) 8 cyl.	Convertible	2300	5400	11600
1954	S-88	(V) 8 cyl.	Holiday Coupe	1300	2700	5200

PACKARD

YEAR	MODEL	ENGINE	BODY	F	G	E
1934	1101	8 cyl.	Roadster	10600	23100	46700
1934	1101	8 cyl.	Convertible Sedan	14400	26400	49500

116 / AUTOS AND AUTOMOBILIA

YEAR	MODEL	ENGINE	BODY	F	G	E
1934	1102	8 cyl.	Limousine	6320	8200	18100
1934	1103	8 cyl.	Roadster	10600	22000	47400
1934	1103	8 cyl.	Victoria Convertible	12350	27500	62300
1935	120A	8 cyl.	Convertible Coupe	8800	16500	35200
1935	120A	8 cyl.	Sport Coupe	6100	8200	13400
1935	1200	8 cyl.	Sedan	4400	6600	12800
1935	1201	8 cyl.	Convertible Coupe	9300	17600	40000
1936	120B	8 cyl.	Touring Coupe	5750	9300	18100
1936	1400	8 cyl.	Victoria Convertible	15400	25800	60000
1936	1402	8 cyl.	Touring	11000	18700	47300
1936	1403	8 cyl.	Convertible Sedan	13200	22000	44000
1936	1407	(V) 12 cyl.	Roadster	14300	26400	63200
1937	115C	6 cyl.	Convertible Coupe	7300	12500	28000
1937	115C	6 cyl.	Touring Sedan	2200	6800	13700
1937	120C	6 cyl.	Convertible Sedan	5500	15400	31300
1937	120D	6 cyl.	Touring Coupe	6000	8200	15900
1937	1502	8 cyl.	Limousine	6600	9300	18100
1937	1508	(V) 12 cyl.	Touring Limousine	7700	18100	40700
1938	1600	6 cyl.	Convertible Coupe	7100	12100	25000
1938	1601	8 cyl.	Convertible Sedan	7700	15300	30200
1938	1603	8 cyl.	Touring Sedan	2200	6800	12600
1938	1608	(V) 12 cyl.	Touring Limousine	7950	15650	40300
1939	1700	6 cyl.	Club Coupe	6000	7400	14000
1939	1701	6 cyl.	Convertible Sedan	7800	14300	30000
1939	1703	8 cyl.	Limousine	7400	9300	17600
1939	1707	(V) 12 cyl.	Convertible Coupe	8200	23100	47800
1940	1800	6 cyl.	Convertible Sedan	7800	13700	29700
1940	1801	6 cyl.	Victoria Convertible	8100	16200	34600
1940	1806	8 cyl.	Club Sedan	3000	9500	17600
1940	Darrin	8 cyl.	Convertible Victoria	10500	29200	63800
1940	1807-Darrin	8 cyl.	Convertible Sedan	9700	27500	52800
1940	1807-Darrin	8 cyl.	Sport Sedan	4900	14300	30800
1941	1900	6 cyl.	Club Coupe	4700	7100	14000

AUTOMOBILIA

Item	Current Price Range		Prior Year Average
☐ **Advertisement**, Maxfield Parrish "Fisk Tire" king on throne, 8¼" x 12	24.00	30.00	25.00
☐ **Advertising Blotter**, Nash Auto. 5" x 9", illustration of sedan, 1928	2.50	4.50	3.00
☐ **Autograph**, Henry Ford I. Typed letter, signed, 1917	85.00	110.00	82.00
☐ **Bill of Sale**, H. J. Thompson, Inc., for "one Ford Roadster, delivered from factory." June 4, 1906	4.50	6.50	5.00
☐ **Bill of Sale**, for Bentley Auto (Birmingham, England, dealer), 1926	2.25	4.50	3.00
☐ **Book**, Audel's "Guide to Automobiles", 1915	45.00	55.00	45.00
☐ **Book**, "Blue Books," 1909-1915, each	28.00	38.00	30.00
☐ **Book** "Green Book of Automobiles," first volume, 1922	20.00	28.00	21.50
☐ **Book**, "How to Build Automobiles" by Bubler, 1914	55.00	65.00	55.00
☐ **Book**, "Putnam Automobile Handbook," c. 1918	20.00	28.00	21.50
☐ **Book**, "The Motor Manual," a practical handbook dealing with the working principles, construction and management of all types of motorcars, London, 1912	14.00	18.00	13.50
☐ **Books and Magazines**, "Automobile Engineers." Proceedings of the Incorporated Institution of Automobile Engineers. A series from 1908-9 to 1938-9, comprising volumes 3 to 33, some indexes lacking, bound in cloth, London, 1909-39	150.00	200.00	150.00
☐ **Bottone, S. R.**, "Magnetos for Automobilists," 4th edition, London, 1917	10.00	15.00	12.50
☐ **Buick**, Owner's Manual, 1947	10.00	15.00	9.00
☐ **Buick**, Owner's Manual, 1950	6.50	8.50	7.00
☐ **Buick**, Owner's Manual, 1955	6.50	8.50	7.00
☐ **Button**, Ford Motors, pin back, c. 1930's	11.00	14.00	11.00
☐ **Calendar**, Ford Motor Co., Norman Rockwell illustration, 1953	14.00	16.00	13.50
☐ **Chrysler**, Owner's Manual, 1936	12.00	16.00	12.50
☐ **Chrysler**, Owner's Manual, 1947	9.00	11.00	9.00
☐ **Clock**, key wind type, 8-day movement working condition	50.00	55.00	48.00
☐ **Coil**, Model T Ford	6.50	8.50	7.00
☐ **Collection**, 217 auto ads removed from magazines of the 1910-1920 period, for various American-made autos and trucks, mostly colored, mainly 11" x 14", housed in two leatherette folders	350.00	450.00	350.00
☐ **DeSoto**, Owner's Manual, 1948	6.50	8.50	7.00
☐ **Duster**, men's, silk	50.00	60.00	50.00
☐ **Duster**, ladies, silk	70.00	80.00	62.50
☐ **Fan**, used for defrosting, Dodge Bros., c. 1936	14.00	16.00	13.50
☐ **Fan**, Chevrolet paper advertising fan, motto "It's Wise to Choose a Six," 1920's	14.00	16.00	13.50
☐ **Farman, D.**, "Auto-Cars," London, 1896	200.00	250.00	175.00
☐ **Ford tire pump**, working condition	35.00	40.00	28.00
☐ **Gasoline pump globe**, Atlantic Gasoline, crossed arrows, milk glass	125.00	145.00	125.00
☐ **Gasoline pump globe**, Conoco, red and green triangle, metal frame	100.00	150.00	100.00

AUTOS AND AUTOMOBILIA / 117

118 / AUTOS AND AUTOMOBILIA

	Current Price Range		Prior Year Average
☐ **Gasoline pump globe,** Dino	70.00	100.00	75.00
☐ **Gasoline pump globe,** Gulf, orange and blue, milk glass	150.00	175.00	138.00
☐ **Gasoline pump globe,** Marathon, runner across center, metal frame	150.00	175.00	138.00
☐ **Gasoline pump globe,** Mobilgas, flying red horse, glass frame	100.00	150.00	100.00
☐ **Gasoline pump globe,** Phillips 66, shield, metal frame	155.00	185.00	150.00
☐ **Gasoline pump globe,** Richfield, yellow and gold, metal frame	155.00	185.00	150.00
☐ **Gasoline pump globe,** Shell, milk glass, no lettering	145.00	180.00	145.00
☐ **Gasoline pump globe,** Sinclair, green and white, glass frame	125.00	175.00	125.00
☐ **Gasoline pump globe,** Standard, red crown on blue, metal frame	145.00	175.00	150.00
☐ **Gasoline pump globe,** Sunoco, yellow diamond, blue lettering, metal frame	125.00	175.00	150.00
☐ **Gasoline pump globe,** Texaco, red star in center, milk glass	125.00	175.00	150.00
☐ **Gear shift,** amber glass in color	12.00	18.00	15.00
☐ **Headlamps,** Model T Ford, black enamel, pair	125.00	150.00	112.00
☐ **Headlamps,** 1916 Buick, pair	155.00	175.00	155.00
☐ **Headlamps,** 1915 Cadillac, brass, pair	200.00	250.00	185.00
☐ **Hood ornament,** Dodge, chrome ram	20.00	24.00	20.00
☐ **Hood ornament,** Lasalle, enameled	7.50	9.50	8.00
☐ **Hood ornament,** 1927 Mercury, brass	45.00	65.00	50.00
☐ **Hood ornament,** head with long hair, molded white glass	200.00	225.00	190.00
☐ **Horn,** brass, Klaxon, c. 1909	70.00	80.00	62.00
☐ **Horn,** bulb type, brass, single twist, c. 1916	130.00	180.00	120.00
☐ **Horn,** bulb type, brass, double twist	150.00	175.00	138.00
☐ **Horn,** hand model, "Klaxon" imprinted	30.00	40.00	28.00
☐ **Horn,** "Ooaga," electric auto lite	35.00	45.00	32.50
☐ **Hubcap,** Buick, brass, 3½" Dia.	20.00	26.00	20.00
☐ **Hubcap,** Model T Ford, pair	10.00	15.00	10.50
☐ **Hubcap,** Whippet, pair	15.00	20.00	14.50
☐ **Kennedy, R.,** "The Book of the Motor Car," three volumes, cloth binding. London, 1913	45.00	55.00	45.00
☐ **Lamp,** for driving, brass	125.00	175.00	105.00
☐ **Lamp,** Ford, brass and tin, electric, 10" x 15"	200.00	250.00	182.00
☐ **Letter,** Written from Roxbury, MA, to Hartford, CN., three pages, handwritten, about motor cars. Correspondent writes, in part, "I witnessed several days ago a demonstration of the motor-driven road carriage. A salesman here is taking orders and has received several tentatively. The price is extremely high, and I doubt if the machine would be suitable for most of the local roads," etc. Dated October 1, 1896.	10.00	15.00	10.00
☐ **Letterhead,** Chrysler Motors, Detroit, 1936	2.00	3.50	1.25
☐ **License plate,** Arkansas, 1932	18.00	24.00	17.50
☐ **License plate,** California, 1930	18.00	24.00	17.50
☐ **License plate,** Connecticut, 1915	75.00	85.00	70.00
☐ **License plate,** Iowa, 1932	25.00	35.00	22.50

AUTOS AND AUTOMOBILIA / 119

	Current Price Range		Prior Year Average
☐ **License plate,** Maine, 1920	8.00	12.00	7.50
☐ **License plate,** Kansas, 1933	14.00	18.00	13.50
☐ **License plate,** Massachusetts, 1915	25.00	35.00	22.50
☐ **License plate,** Rhode Island, 1926	10.00	15.00	12.50
☐ **License plate,** Wisconsin, 1925	10.00	15.00	12.50
☐ **License plate,** Michigan, good condition, 1916 ..	45.00	55.00	40.00
☐ **License plate,** Ohio, good condition, 1922	55.00	65.00	50.00
☐ **License plate,** Pennsylvania, 1908	50.00	60.00	45.00
☐ **Linenam, W.J.,** "The Modern Motor-Car." Parts 1-3. London	20.00	24.00	20.00
☐ **Motor meter,** 1915 Dodge	60.00	70.00	55.00
☐ **Motor meter,** 1916 Boyce	55.00	65.00	50.00
☐ **Newspaper ad,** American Weekly, 1939	10.00	15.00	10.00
☐ **Oil can,** "Ford" written in script	12.00	18.00	11.00
☐ **Packard,** handbook for Super Eight Sedan, c. 1948	35.00	45.00	32.50
☐ **Radiator cap,** Chevrolet, brass	8.00	12.00	8.00
☐ **Radiator cap,** Dodge, c. 1930-35	20.00	24.00	20.00
☐ **Radiator cap,** Ford, brass	8.00	12.00	8.00
☐ **Radiator cap,** Model T Ford, brass	14.00	18.00	13.50
☐ **Radiator cap,** Maxwell, brass	12.00	15.00	11.00
☐ **Radiator cap,** Pontiac, Indian Head, nickel plated over brass, c. 1930	50.00	60.00	45.00
☐ **Radiator emblem plate,** Buick.................	30.00	35.00	28.00
☐ **Radiator emblem plate,** Cadillac	35.00	45.00	32.50
☐ **Radiator emblem plate,** Flying Lady	35.00	45.00	32.50
☐ **Radiator emblem plate,** Packard	28.00	32.00	28.00
☐ **Radiator emblem plate,** Stutz	30.00	40.00	28.00
☐ **Radiator emblem plate,** Willy's-Overland, enameled	20.00	26.00	20.00
☐ **Radiator ornament,** Buick, blue glass	40.00	50.00	38.50
☐ **Shop manual,** Oldsmobile, 1933	20.00	30.00	25.00
☐ **Showroom banner,** reads: "Oakland Six — $875.00", wool, blue with yellow lettering, 48" x 8"	70.00	80.00	65.00
☐ **Spark plug,** Ford, c. 1911	25.00	35.00	22.50
☐ **Steering wheel,** Durant, wood and brass, c. 1920's	60.00	70.00	55.00
☐ **Steering wheel,** Model T Ford	50.00	60.00	45.00
☐ **Stock certificates,** Durant Motors, Inc., 1924	12.00	18.00	12.50
☐ **Stock certificates,** Hudson and Nash	10.00	15.00	9.00
☐ **Strickland, R.,** "A Manual of Petrol Motors and Motor Cars." London, 1914	12.00	15.00	11.00
☐ **Studebaker's,** Owner's manual, 1945	8.00	12.00	7.00
☐ **Studebaker's,** Owner's manual, 1951	4.50	5.50	4.50
☐ **Thompson, Sir H.,** "The Motor-Car." London, 1902	24.00	32.00	25.00
☐ **Tire pump,** "Ford" written in script, brass	24.00	32.00	25.00
☐ **Tire pump,** Model T Ford, brass	38.00	48.00	40.00
☐ **Vase,** Packard, clear glass, grapes and birds	35.00	38.00	32.50
☐ **Vase,** Rolls Royce, enameled	45.00	55.00	45.00
☐ **Waller-Taylor, A. L.,** "Motor Cars or Power-Carraiges for Common Roads." London, 1897 ...	225.00	325.00	250.00
☐ **White, T. H.,** "Petrol Motors and Motor Cars." London, 1905	20.00	26.00	20.00
☐ **Wrench,** imprinted with "Ford, U.S.A.," adjustable	12.00	16.00	11.00
☐ **Young, A. B.,** "The Complete Motorist." London, 1904	38.00	48.00	40.00

BANKS

Child's Safe, tin, 6"x4"x4" . . . . $25.00-$35.00

MECHANICAL BANKS

These banks were first produced in the 1860's by hardware and tool plants as new products after the Civil War and remain among the most popular and sought after memorabilia and collector items. They have been used for advertising promotion pieces by banks, insurance companies, investment firms, etc.

The best known manufacturers are Stevens of Cromwell, Connecticut; Ives Blaklee Co. of Bridgeport, Connecticut; and Hubley of Lancaster, Pennsylvania. They are generally made of iron, painted bright and attractive colors, and perform a mechanical movement on deposit of a coin.

These banks were designed for children to save their money by making it a playful experience. By depositing a coin, a child was entertained with the bank's intricate and fascinating mechanical action.

Banks in original mint condition are, of course, the most sought-after. Restored banks lose much of their value even if extreme care for authenticity has been exercised. Although it is difficult to buy a bank from a dealer for much less than retail, some bargains may be found at local flea markets and garage sales. A dealer who offers to buy banks at approximately 40% of the stated retail value is giving a very fair price for banks in good condition.

	Current Price Range		Prior Year Average
☐ **Bull Dog Savings Bank,** *dog crouched on top of bank facing man standing at end of bank*	450.00	550.00	500.00
☐ **Circus Elephant,** *with howdah, large stylized trunk*	100.00	200.00	150.00
☐ **Clown On Globe,** *straddles a globe with a design*	300.00	400.00	350.00
☐ **Confectionery Bank,** *woman stands behind circular counter in front of display of candies which are labeled*	500.00	600.00	550.00
☐ **Creedmore With William Tell,** *man stands pointing rifle*	175.00	225.00	100.00
☐ **Dancing Bear,** *organ grinder plays while bear dances in yard in front of house, two men lean on fence and watch*	450.00	550.00	500.00
☐ **Darktown Battery,** *three black boys play baseball, one pitches, one catches, and one bats*	275.00	375.00	325.00
☐ **Dog On Turn Table,** *goes in one door and out another, crank on the side*	100.00	150.00	125.00
☐ **Eagle And Eaglets,** *nonauthentic looking eagle perches on nest with wings partially spread*	125.00	175.00	150.00
☐ **Elephant With Swinging Trunk,** *carries elaborate howdah*	50.00	100.00	75.00
☐ **Football Bank,** *boy stands ready to kick football at bank*	400.00	500.00	450.00
☐ **Frog On Lattice,** *authentic frog perches on cylinder*	100.00	150.00	125.00
☐ **Frog On Rock,** *mouth opens*	150.00	200.00	175.00
☐ **Grenadier Bank,** *soldier stands aiming gun at tree*	175.00	275.00	225.00
☐ **Guessing Bank,** *man sits with arms folded over the top of a device with a dial*	400.00	500.00	450.00
☐ **Hall's Excelsior Bank,** *imposing building with dome and latticed windows, name of bank embossed on front*	75.00	125.00	100.00
☐ **Hoop-La Bank,** *English, clown holds hoop in front of barrow, dog prepares to jump through hoop*	300.00	400.00	350.00
☐ **Humpty Dumpty,** *bust of laughing clown*	100.00	150.00	125.00
☐ **Owl,** *stylized owl turns head*	100.00	150.00	125.00
☐ **Magic Bank,** *clown stands at entrance to house behind a Dutch door*	200.00	300.00	250.00
☐ **Mammy Feeding Baby,** *black woman holds baby on her lap with spoon hovering over child's open mouth*	350.00	450.00	400.00
☐ **Man In Howdah,** *lid on howdah folds back, man's head pops up out of howdah*	100.00	200.00	140.00
☐ **Mason Bank,** *one man lays bricks, other man props large shovel handle on his shoulder*	350.00	450.00	400.00
☐ **Merry Go Round,** *semi-mechanical, lattice work on roof and sides, on pedestal*	100.00	150.00	120.00
☐ **Money Moves The World,** *human figure with globe head sits on top of rectangular "Atlas Bank"*	250.00	350.00	300.00
☐ **Monkey And Parrot,** *tin, monkey reaches out with hand lifts coin to parrots mouth, parrot drops coin in dish*	100.00	200.00	140.00
☐ **Monkey Bank,** *organ grinder carries portable organ in front of him, faces dancing monkey*	175.00	275.00	225.00

122 / BANKS

	Current Price Range		Prior Year Average
☐ **Mule Entering Barn,** *mule prepares to jump into entrance area of barn*	250.00	350.00	300.00
☐ **Novelty Bank,** *door swings open, man stands in entrance of house with numerous gables and two chimneys*	100.00	150.00	125.00
☐ **Panorama,** *house with pastoral scene placed above the front door*	450.00	550.00	500.00
☐ **Peter Pan League,** *dog wearing hat and carrying garment in mouth stands on all four feet on top of rectangular chest*	200.00	300.00	240.00
☐ **Pig In High Chair,** *reaches out with dish begging for more*	300.00	400.00	340.00
☐ **Pistol,** *tin, decor on handle, length 5½"*	75.00	125.00	100.00
☐ **Punch And Judy Bank,** *two puppets on stage* ...	200.00	300.00	225.00
☐ **Rabbit With Rectangular Base,** *rabbit stands on rear feet, holds ball in front paws*	200.00	300.00	225.00
☐ **Two Frogs,** *one large frog, one small frog, authentic appearances*	250.00	350.00	300.00
☐ **Wireless Bank,** *iron, tin and wood, building*	150.00	250.00	200.00
☐ **Zoo Bank,** *small house with creatures staring out the windows*	250.00	350.00	300.00

STILL BANKS

Still banks were made of iron, white metal, tin, glass, pottery or plastic. A slot was provided in which to insert the coin and most have a trap door for retrieving coins.

These banks, while not scarce, are still difficult to locate in mint or fine condition. Good will mean no chips or breaks, paint bright but not shiny.

☐ **Building,** *hexagonal-shaped, elaborate scalloping around rim of roof, dome roof with Greek Orthodox designs cutaway*	25.00	35.00	30.00
☐ **Building,** *"Bank" embossed in semicircular over arched doorway*	45.00	55.00	50.00
☐ **Building,** *bank structure with arched doorway* ..	25.00	35.00	30.00
☐ **Building,** *fantasy design resembling Gothic structure, double-domed roof*	25.00	35.00	30.00
☐ **Building,** *bank structure, arched door flanked by two arched windows*	30.00	40.00	35.00
☐ **Building,** *castle structure, arched opening and stairs lead to front balcony*	30.00	40.00	35.00
☐ **Building,** *"Bank" printed on front, domed roof, turrets on top of dome and to the sides, height 5"*	50.00	100.00	75.00
☐ **Building With Belfry,** *school-house structure, height 8"*	75.00	125.00	100.00
☐ **Building With Bird,** *hexagonal shaped with design of bird on front side, height 6½"*	75.00	125.00	100.00
☐ **Building With Cupid,** *hexagonal shaped with bas relief design of Cupid on front side, height 7"* ...	75.00	125.00	100.00
☐ **Bull Dog,** *sits, wears collar, height 4¼"*	40.00	50.00	44.00
☐ **Bull Dog,** *English, height 3¼"*	75.00	125.00	100.00
☐ **Bull Dog,** *seated, height 3½"*	75.00	125.00	100.00
☐ **Bureaux Caisse,** *two-storied building, height 9"* .	125.00	175.00	150.00
☐ **Bust Of Man,** *height 5"*	100.00	200.00	150.00

BANKS / 123

	Current Price Range		Prior Year Average
☐ **Buster Brown And Tige Cashier,** *cashier box, height 5"*	100.00	150.00	125.00
☐ **Cabin,** *log cabin with two small windows and chimney stack*	30.00	40.00	35.00
☐ **Caisse,** *two-storied building, flat roof with turret, stairs lead up to front door*	50.00	100.00	75.00
☐ **Camel,** *authentic-looking except for extremely long neck, wears saddle, height 7¼"*	125.00	175.00	150.00
☐ **Camel,** *laying down with trunk on back, height 2½"*	125.00	175.00	150.00
☐ **Cannon,** *double barrel, mounted on a two-wheeled stand*	100.00	200.00	150.00
☐ **Captain Kidd,** *stands holding a shovel, height 5½"*	150.00	250.00	200.00
☐ **Carpet Bag,** *bronze, authentic-looking, height 3½"*	35.00	65.00	50.00
☐ **Car Garage,** *for one car, height 2½"*	20.00	30.00	23.00
☐ **Car Garage,** *for two cars, height 2½"*	20.00	30.00	25.00
☐ **Cash Register,** *height 3¾"*	50.00	100.00	75.00
☐ **Castle,** *four turrets, "Bank" embossed on front, height 4"*	50.00	100.00	75.00
☐ **Cat,** *black, with bow at neck, height 4½"*	50.00	100.00	75.00
☐ **Donkey,** *saddle and bridle, height 7"*	50.00	60.00	55.00
☐ **Duck On Tub,** *wears hat, umbrella tucked under wing, height 5¼"*	75.00	125.00	100.00
☐ **Duckling,** *wings spread, height 5"*	50.00	100.00	75.00
☐ **Dutch Boy,** *wears hat, scarf, hands in pocket, height 8½"*	75.00	125.00	100.00
☐ **Dutch Girl,** *traditional Dutch costume, carries tulips in one arm, height 5¼"*	60.00	70.00	65.00
☐ **Elephant,** *tin, sits on very low drum, height 5¼"*	20.00	30.00	25.00
☐ **Elephant,** *authentic-looking, height 4"*	30.00	40.00	35.00
☐ **Egg Man,** *Humpty Dumpty-type character with tall hat and small feet*	100.00	200.00	150.00
☐ **Egyptian Tomb,** *hieroglyphics design on the front, height 6¼"*	70.00	80.00	75.00
☐ **Eiffel Tower,** *authentic replica, height 8¾"*	75.00	125.00	100.00
☐ **Circus Elephant,** *sitting with legs to the front, wears polka-dot shirt, small hat with ribbon, height 4"*	50.00	100.00	75.00
☐ **Elephant With Drum,** *pot metal, sits with drum between legs, cymbal on trunk, height 4¼"*	15.00	25.00	18.00
☐ **Elephant,** *G.O.P., trunk lifted upwards, height 4"*	75.00	125.00	100.00
☐ **Elephant With Howdah,** *height 4¾"*	30.00	40.00	35.00
☐ **Elephant,** *"Jumbo Savings Bank" printed on drum, elephant sits on the drum*	20.00	30.00	25.00
☐ **Elephant,** *"Lucky Jumbo Bank" on lid, glass*	15.00	25.00	20.00
☐ **Elephant Seated,** *pot metal, tip of trunk held up to head, height 5¼"*	15.00	25.00	18.00
☐ **Elephant On Tub,** *elephant stands like a human, height 5¼"*	60.00	70.00	65.00
☐ **Elephant On Wheels,** *stands, with flat howdah, height 4"*	80.00	120.00	100.00
☐ **Elephant, Worcester Salt,** *pot metal, sits on square base, height 4½"*	15.00	25.00	20.00

124 / BANKS

	Current Price Range		Prior Year Average
☐ **Elmer Fudd,** *pot metal, stands next to tree trunk on rectangular base, height 5½"*	20.00	30.00	25.00
☐ **Every Copper Helps,** *bust of British policeman, height 6"*	100.00	200.00	150.00
☐ **Fat Man,** *Plochman and Harrison embossed on bottom, glass*	6.00	10.00	8.00
☐ **F.D. Roosevelt,** *bust, die cast, height 4½"*	20.00	30.00	25.00
☐ **Feed My Sheep,** *pot metal, lamb lying down, height 3"*	20.00	30.00	25.00
☐ **Ferry,** *paddle wheels, smoke stacks, length 7⅜"*	70.00	80.00	75.00
☐ **Fez,** *Shriner's hat with tassel, height 1½"*	100.00	200.00	150.00
☐ **Fireman,** *height 5½"*	75.00	125.00	100.00
☐ **Football Player,** *old fashioned uniform, height 5¾"*	100.00	200.00	140.00
☐ **Football Player With Ball Overhead,** *disproportionately, height 5"*	100.00	150.00	120.00
☐ **Fort Dearborn,** *three-storied, log building, height 6"*	50.00	100.00	75.00
☐ **Fortune Ship,** *small pole, one mast, "Marie" and "U.S.A." printed on the side*	75.00	125.00	100.00
☐ **French Artillery Hat,** *height 1¾"*	35.00	65.00	50.00
☐ **Galaxy Syrup Spaceman,** *orbit admiral, orange, glass*	3.00	5.00	4.00
☐ **Galaxy Syrup Spaceman,** *space commander, raspberry, glass*	3.00	5.00	4.00
☐ **Galaxy Syrup Spaceman,** *space scout, grape, glass*	3.00	5.00	4.00
☐ **Galaxy Syrup Spaceman,** *space sentry, black cherry, glass*	3.00	5.00	4.00
☐ **Gas Pump,** *old fashioned type, height 5¾"*	50.00	100.00	75.00
☐ **Gas Truck,** *tin, length 6¼"*	20.00	30.00	25.00
☐ **General Butler,** *comical-looking character, with large mustache, height 6½"*	150.00	250.00	200.00
☐ **General Sherman,** *rides rearing horse, height 5½"*	125.00	225.00	175.00
☐ **German Ship,** *length 7¼"*	75.00	125.00	100.00
☐ **Globe On Arc,** *on pedestal stand*	100.00	200.00	140.00
☐ **Globe With Eagle,** *pedestal food, small eagle on top*	150.00	250.00	200.00
☐ **Globe Savings Fund,** *height 7"*	75.00	125.00	100.00
☐ **Goose,** *authentic-looking, height 4"*	50.00	100.00	75.00
☐ **Goose,** *"Red Goose Shoes" printed on side, height 4½"*	40.00	50.00	45.00
☐ **Goose,** *height 5"*	60.00	70.00	65.00
☐ **Grapette Cat,** *with label, glass*	3.00	5.00	4.00
☐ **Grapette Cat,** *without label, glass*	4.00	6.00	5.00
☐ **Grapette Clown,** *glass*	4.00	6.00	5.00
☐ **Grapette Elephant,** *glass*	4.00	6.00	5.00
☐ **Grandpa Dukes,** *comical head with flat hat, height 2¼"*	20.00	30.00	25.00
☐ **Grandpa's Hat,** *upside down, top hat, height 2¼"*	50.00	100.00	75.00
☐ **Guardhourse,** *tin, soldier stands in archway, large striping on building, height 3½"*	30.00	40.00	35.00
☐ **Hand Grenade,** *height 3¾"*	60.00	70.00	65.00
☐ **Happy Fats,** *chubby figure stands on drum, candy container, height 4½"*	70.00	80.00	75.00

	Current Price Range		Prior Year Average
☐ **Hen On Nest**, *height 3"*	100.00	200.00	140.00
☐ **Hippo**, *authentic-looking, height 2½"*	100.00	200.00	150.00
☐ **Home Bank**, *tin, teller stands behind iron bar window, "Get Your Receipt Here" printed on counter*	45.00	65.00	55.00
☐ **Home Savings**, *"Time is Money, Save Both", printed on base, brass, height 4⅞"*	50.00	100.00	75.00
☐ **Horse**, *height 4¼"*	20.00	30.00	25.00
☐ **Horse With Saddle**, *bridle, height 4¼"*	45.00	55.00	50.00
☐ **Horse With Shoe**, *Buster Brown and Tige, stand next to horse, horseshoe arches over the horse, height 4¼"*	75.00	125.00	100.00
☐ **Horse Shoe Wire Bank**, *horse head in center of horseshoe with spokes behind, height 3½"*	40.00	50.00	45.00
☐ **Horse On Tub**, *horse stands with front feet on tub, height 5¼"*	60.00	70.00	65.00
☐ **Horse On Tub**, *horse stands with front feet on the tub, wears saddle and bridle, height 5¼"*	60.00	70.00	65.00
☐ **Horse On Wheels**, *prancing, height 5"*	80.00	120.00	100.00
☐ **Hound**, *sitting, disproportionately large head, height 3"*	100.00	200.00	140.00
☐ **House Of Knowledge**, *tin, height 6½"*	35.00	65.00	50.00
☐ **House With Dog**, *pot metal, height 2¾"*	15.00	25.00	20.00
☐ **Humpty Dumpty**, *tin, on pedestal stand, height 5½"*	15.00	25.00	18.00
☐ **Indian Chief**, *pot metal, bust with small headdress, height 3½"*	15.00	25.00	18.00
☐ **Indian Chief**, *pot metal, bust with headdress, with strung beads hanging at sides, height 4¼"*	20.00	30.00	24.00
☐ **Indian Family**, *combination busts of Indian, squaw, and papoose, height 3¾"*	70.00	80.00	75.00
☐ **Indian Maiden**, *pot metal, wears headband and one feather at the side, height 3½"*	15.00	25.00	20.00
☐ **Iron Maiden**, *canister shape with head on the top, height 4¾"*	100.00	200.00	150.00
☐ **Jarmulowsky Building**, *brick design, height 8"*	75.00	125.00	100.00
☐ **Keene Savings Bank**, *tin, replica of a bank, double doors*	65.00	95.00	80.00
☐ **Key**, *stands on end, height 5½"*	50.00	100.00	75.00
☐ **Koop's Mustard Barrel Bank**, *glass*	6.00	8.00	7.00
☐ **Kroger's Country Club Mustard Barrel Bank**, *glass*	6.00	8.00	7.00
☐ **Ladies Slipper**, *old-fashioned style, height 2½"*	45.00	55.00	50.00
☐ **Liberty Bell**, *amber, iridescent, glass*	8.00	12.00	10.00
☐ **Liberty Bell**, *embossed lettering, height 4"*	50.00	100.00	75.00
☐ **Lighthouse**, *keeper's house with tall tower, domed top, on rocky base*	100.00	200.00	175.00
☐ **Lion**, *not authentic-looking, stands on all fours, height 5¼"*	30.00	40.00	35.00
☐ **Lion On Tub**, *stands on rear legs, rope in mouth and around neck, height 5¼"*	60.00	70.00	65.00
☐ **Lion On Wheels**, *lion stands on all fours, on cart with wheels, height 5"*	80.00	120.00	100.00
☐ **Lindberg**, *bust, wearing pilot's gear, height 6½"*	45.00	55.00	50.00
☐ **Lincoln Bank Bottle**, *glass*	12.00	18.00	15.00
☐ **Little Red Riding Hood**, *with wolf standing next to her leaning head on her shoulder, height 5"*	125.00	175.00	150.00

126 / BANKS

	Current Price Range		Prior Year Average
☐ **Log Cabin Syrup,** *"Log Cabin" embossed on roof, glass*	12.00	18.00	15.00
☐ **Lost Dog,** *sitting on oval base, head lifted with mouth open as if howling, height 5½"*	75.00	125.00	100.00
☐ **Nickel Savings Bank,** *domed-shaped on square base with four feet, knob on top of dome, height 5½"*	100.00	200.00	150.00
☐ **Old Man,** *derby hat, vest, hands in pocket, height 5¾"*	75.00	125.00	100.00
☐ **Owl On Square Base,** *height 4¼"*	65.00	95.00	80.00
☐ **Owl On Stump,** *"Be Wise Save Money" embossed on stump, height 5"*	75.00	125.00	100.00
☐ **Our Empire Bank,** *elaborate garland surrounding embossed bust in profile, height 6½"*	65.00	95.00	80.00
☐ **Our Kitchen Bank,** *elaborate garland surrounding embossed bust, height 6½"*	65.00	95.00	50.00
☐ **Padlock,** *simple heart shape on pedestal stand, height 7"*	75.00	125.00	100.00
☐ **Pagoda,** *brass, height 7½"*	60.00	70.00	65.00
☐ **Peaceful Bill,** *bust set into oval background on circular base, height 4"*	150.00	250.00	200.00
☐ **Parlor Stove,** *tall, tin, decorative knob on top, height 7"*	50.00	100.00	75.00
☐ **Pig,** *"Brother can you spare a dime?" on lid, glass*	8.00	10.00	9.00
☐ **Pig,** *Fred Fear syrup with label, glass*	8.00	12.00	10.00
☐ **Pig Mustard Bank,** *Jas. H. Forbes, St. Louis, glass*	8.00	10.00	9.00
☐ **Pig With Bow Tie,** *sits on rear legs, height 3"*	75.00	125.00	100.00
☐ **Pinocchio,** *upper body protrudes out the top of a drum, height 5⅞"*	25.00	75.00	50.00
☐ **Pirate On Treasure Chest,** *sits, authentic-looking, height 6¼"*	100.00	200.00	150.00
☐ **Pittsburgh Corning Glass Block,** *no label*	8.00	12.00	10.00
☐ **Pittsburgh Paints,** *glass block with sun face*	8.00	12.00	10.00
☐ **Policeman,** *"Kennedy Clothing House" printed on the back, height 5½"*	75.00	125.00	100.00
☐ **Pony,** *wears saddle and bridle, height 2¾"*	50.00	100.00	75.00
☐ **Porky Pig With Tree Trunk,** *stands next to tree stump on rectangular stand, height 4"*	20.00	30.00	35.00
☐ **Rabbit,** *standing, ears standing straight up, height 6½"*	65.00	95.00	80.00
☐ **Radio,** *rectangular shape, height 3½"*	50.00	100.00	75.00
☐ **Radio,** *domed-shaped table radio, height 4¼"*	45.00	55.00	50.00
☐ **Radio,** *floor style, with four legs, height 4½"*	45.00	55.00	50.00
☐ **Railway Saloon Car,** *English, three windows each side, height 4½"*	60.00	70.00	65.00
☐ **Rearing Horse On Oval Base,** *height 5"*	60.00	70.00	65.00
☐ **Rearing Horse On Pebbled Base,** *height 7½"*	75.00	125.00	100.00
☐ **Reclining Man,** *pottery, fat, hands behind head, feet crossed*	25.00	75.00	40.00
☐ **Refrigerator,** *height 3¾"*	30.00	40.00	35.00
☐ **Reid Library,** *replica, height 5½"*	50.00	100.00	75.00
☐ **Rearing Horse On Oval Base,** *"Beauty" printed on side of horse, height 4¾"*	60.00	70.00	65.00

	Current Price Range		Prior Year Average
☐ **Red Goose Shoes,** *name printed on goose's wing, height 3¾"*	75.00	125.00	100.00
☐ **Rocking Chair,** *unusual design, openwork, height 6½"*	150.00	250.00	200.00
☐ **Roly Poly Monkey,** *tin, globe-shaped body with ovoid head, cone hat, height 6"*	20.00	30.00	25.00
☐ **Round Clown,** *spherical with nub feet, height 2¼"*	20.00	30.00	25.00
☐ **Safe,** *rectangular, free standing with four feet, height 3"*	10.00	20.00	12.00
☐ **Safe,** *free standing, double doors, height 6"*	35.00	65.00	50.00
☐ **Sailor,** *saluting with one hand, holds paddle at his side with other hand, height 5¾"*	75.00	125.00	100.00
☐ **Santa,** *holds a toy in each hand, height 5½"*	150.00	250.00	200.00
☐ **Santa With Pack,** *peaked hat, simplistic face*	125.00	175.00	150.00
☐ **Saving Sam,** *disproportionately short man, height 5¼"*	100.00	200.00	140.00
☐ **Scottie,** *height 5¼"*	15.00	25.00	20.00
☐ **Scotty Dog,** *sitting, height 5"*	45.00	55.00	50.00

BARBED WIRE

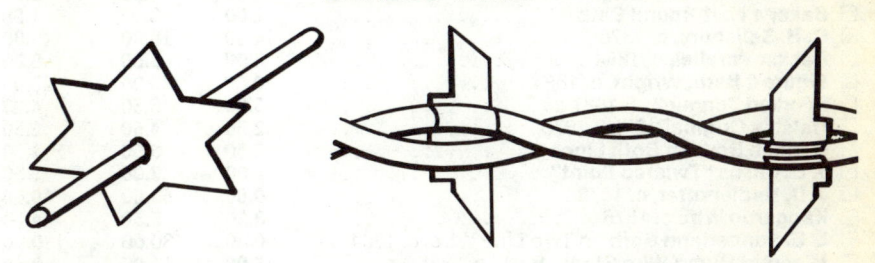

Left to Rigth: **Thomas H. Dogde "Star",** also called "Spur Barb", c. 1881 **$150.00-$200.00;** Early Stover, c. 1875... **$150.00-$200.00**

Barbed wire is widely collected because of its historical importance in the setting of the western territories. In their confrontation with cattlemen, farmers installed barbed wire instead of wooden or stone fences because it was quicker and less expensive. Railroads strung the wire along their rights-of-way to keep the trains from being delayed by cattle and buffalo who roamed nearby.

The first wire fencing was invented by W. H. Meriwether and patented in 1853. This was soon followed by a surge of competition. From 1868 to 1900 more than 750 patents were issued for bigger and better barbed wire styles, and at least 300 more were designed but never patented.

The best place to find examples of the many different types of wire is in the open range; however, wire cutting on private property is a felonious offense in most states. The collector must, therefore, beware of wire counterfeiting. It is very easy to alter a common, inexpensive wire into a very desirable and sought after collectible. It is imperative that the collector deal with trustworthy people and be apprised of the constant fluctuation in prices of a particular type of wire. Prices vary from less than $1 to more than $350 for a stick (18"). It is, therefore, a relatively inexpensive hobby than can be quite satisfying.

SINGLE ROUND WITH TWO POINTS

	Current Price Range		Prior Year Average
☐ Bakers Single Strand, c. 1883	2.00	4.00	2.50
☐ Charles D. Rogers, c. 1888	2.00	4.00	2.50
☐ Dobbs and Booth Single Line, c. 1875	4.00	6.00	4.00
☐ Gunderson, c. 1881	4.00	6.00	4.00
☐ Half-Hitch, c. 1877	2.25	5.50	3.50
☐ H. M. Rose Wrap Barb, c. 1877	2.00	4.00	2.50
☐ L. E. Sunderland No Kink, c. 1884	2.00	4.00	2.00
☐ Mack's Alternate, c. 1875	10.00	15.00	10.50
☐ Nelson Clip, c. 1876	75.00	90.00	77.00
☐ Putnams Flat Under Barb, c. 1877	14.00	16.00	13.50
☐ R. Emerson, c. 1876	150.00	175.00	138.00
☐ Rose Kink Line, c. 1877	2.50	4.50	2.50
☐ Single Line Wide Wrap Barb, c. 1878	75.00	90.00	77.00
☐ Sunderland Hammered Barb, c. 1884	2.50	3.50	2.00
☐ "Two Point Ripple Wire"	6.00	8.00	6.00

DOUBLE ROUND WITH TWO POINTS

	Current Price Range		Prior Year Average
☐ Australian Loose Wrap	2.50	4.50	2.50
☐ Baker's Half-Round Barb	2.00	3.00	1.50
☐ C. H. Salisbury, c. 1876	14.00	18.00	15.00
☐ Decker Parallel, c. 1884	6.00	8.00	5.00
☐ Figure 8 Barb, Wright, c. 1881	20.00	26.00	20.00
☐ "Forked Tongue", c. 1887	3.50	5.50	4.00
☐ Haish's Original "S", c. 1875	2.50	4.50	2.50
☐ Glidden Barb on Both Lines	3.50	6.50	4.50
☐ J. D. Curtis "Twisted Point"	2.00	3.00	1.50
☐ J. D. Nadlehoffer, c. 1878	40.00	50.00	40.00
☐ Kangaroo Wire c. 1876	3.50	5.50	4.00
☐ L. E. Sunderland Barb on Two Line Wire, c. 1884	100.00	130.00	110.00
☐ Missouri Hump Wire Staple Barb, c. 1876	8.00	11.00	9.50
☐ Peter P. Hill Parallel, c. 1876	150.00	175.00	138.00
☐ Rose Barb on Copper Lines, c. 1877	4.50	6.50	5.00
☐ W. Edenborn	3.50	5.50	4.00
☐ W. Edenborn's Locked in Barb, c. 1885	2.50	4.50	2.50

RIBBON WIRE

	Current Price Range		Prior Year Average
☐ Allis Barbless Ribbon and Single Wire, c. 1881	14.00	20.00	15.00
☐ Allis Flat Ribbon Barb, c. 1892	14.00	20.00	15.00
☐ Brinkerhoff's Ribbon Barb, c. 1881	3.50	5.50	4.00
☐ Cast Iron Buckthorn	5.50	9.00	7.50
☐ Factory Splice on Thin Barbed Ribbon, c. 1892	35.00	45.00	35.00
☐ F. D. Ford Flat Ribbon, c. 1885	3.50	5.50	4.00
☐ John Hallner's "Greenbriar", c. 1878	1.25	3.50	2.00
☐ Harbaugh's Torn Ribbon, c. 1881	5.50	9.00	7.50
☐ Kelly's Split Ribbon, c. 1868	20.00	32.00	22.00
☐ Kelmer Ornamental Fence, c. 1885	14.00	18.00	14.00
☐ "Open Face" by Brinkerhoff, c. 1881	7.00	10.00	7.50
☐ Scutt's Smooth Ribbon	12.00	18.00	12.50
☐ Scutt's Ridged Ribbon, c. 1883	50.00	60.00	50.00
☐ Three-Quarter Inch Ribbon	9.00	14.00	10.00
☐ Very Light and Narrow Ribbon, c. 1868	50.00	60.00	50.00

BASEBALL CARDS

The most valuable baseball card is a cigarette card picturing Pittsburgh Pirate shortstop Honus Wagner, issued around 1910. This was 24 years after the introduction of baseball cards so, obviously, age isn't the deciding factor. Wagner, a non-smoker, did not want his name associated with cigarettes. He threatened to sue the manufacturer if the card was not pulled off the market. It was, but not before a few had leaked into circulation. Only 19 specimens are known to exist at present. The value of a single card has been variably stated at between $15,000 and $17,000.

General guide to values:

PRE-1900. Usually $5 to $25. The most valuable pre-1900 cards are those issued by Gypsy Queen and Old Judge cigarettes (average $15-$25). The Old Judge are large in size and attractive. When these cards carry genuine signatures of the players their values are much higher.

1900-20. Enormous quantities of cards were issued in this period. In just one year, 1910, there were more than 500 "white border" cards, not only of major but minor league players. Most "white borders" bring under $1. Rarer cards of the era were those of Ramly, Turkey Reds and Hassan Triple Folders. Value of the Ramly is around $10 per card, the Hassan $4. Also valuable at $10 each are the Fatima "team cards," with team portraits rather than individual players. A complete set of 16, for the 16 big-league teams (there were fewer teams in those days), brings $300 in good condition. These date to 1913. "Gold Border" cards are common and cheap, usually under $1.

1920 to date. The values of post-1920 cards range from 1¢ (for current Topps bubblegum cards) to $30 or more for scarce specimens, such as the 1949 Bowman Pacific Coast League. Prior to the Dodgers and Giants moving to California in 1958, the Pacific Coast was an "open" league — that is, higher than Triple A — and had many star players. The Topps 1950 "Current Stars," fairly recent major league cards, bring $20. But this is the exception, not the rule, as a result of low printings. Most cards of this vintage are worth much less. For example, the regular Topps cards of 1955 have a value of 20¢ to 75¢. *Complete sets* of current Topps cards sell for around $20.

For more in-depth information and listings, you may refer to *The Official Price Guide to Baseball Cards*, published by the House of Collectibles.

Baseball Cards priced individually, not by sets	Current Price Range		Prior Year Average
☐ American caramel cards, c. 1908-1910	5.00	3.25	3.90
☐ Boucher's gold coin cigarette, "Triple Headers"	6.00	3.60	4.50
☐ Cracker Jack cards, c. 1914-1915	12.00	7.20	9.00
☐ Hassan Cigarette, "Triple Headers"	6.00	3.60	4.50
☐ Mecca Doublefolders, early 20th c.	6.00	3.60	4.50
☐ Old Judge cigarette sepia cards, 19th c.	20.00	12.00	15.00
☐ Tatoo-Orbit gum cards, 1933 Hall of Famers	10.00	6.00	7.50
☐ 1934-36 Batter-Up Series. These were gum cards issued by the National Circle Co. The complete set comprises 192 cards (there were only 16 major league teams then, and it was not usual for rookies or utility players to be pictured on cards, so a 1930's set will always run less than one from today). The complete set is worth, depending on condition	2000.00	1280.00	1600.00

130 / BASEBALL CARDS

		Current Price Range		Prior Year Average
☐	Prices of individual cards from the set:			
☐	3. Al Lopez	8.00	5.10	6.40
☐	14. Pie Traynor	10.00	6.40	8.00
☐	16. Chic Hafey	8.00	5.10	6.40
☐	21. Arky Vaughn	8.00	5.10	6.40
☐	57. Hank Greenberg	10.00	6.40	8.00
☐	64. Dizzy Dean	18.00	11.50	14.40
☐	101. Phil Cavaretta	18.00	11.50	14.40

(**NOTE:** All cards from this series are worth at least $4 in good condition, more in VF.)

BOWMAN — 1948 (2⅛" x 2½", Numbered 1-48. B&W)

☐	Complete Set	275.00	180.00	230.00
☐	1. Bob Elliot	6.00	4.50	5.00
☐	3. Ralph Kiner	10.00	6.00	8.25
☐	6. "Yogi" Berra	15.00	9.75	12.25
☐	8. Phil Rizzuto	20.00	13.00	16.50
☐	11. Johnny Lindell	3.00	2.00	2.50
☐	13. Willard Marshall	10.00	6.50	8.25
☐	18. Warren Spahn	10.00	6.50	8.25
☐	20. Buddy Kerr	10.00	6.50	8.25
☐	23. Larry Jansen	3.20	2.00	2.50
☐	25. Barney McCoskey	3.00	2.00	2.50
☐	29. Joe Page	10.00	6.50	8.25
☐	32. Bill Rigney	3.00	2.00	2.50
☐	36. Stan Musial	35.00	23.00	29.00
☐	39. Augie Galan	3.00	2.00	2.50
☐	48. "Dave" Koslo	3.00	2.00	2.50

BOWMAN — 1949 (2⅛" x 2½", Numbered 1-240. Color)
Bowman's first color set.

☐	Complete Set	2000.00	1300.00	1650.00
☐	1. Vernon Bickford	5.00	3.25	4.00
☐	24. Stan Musial	39.00	23.00	29.00
☐	45. Wally Westlake	3.00	2.00	2.50
☐	50. Jackie Robinson	40.00	26.00	33.00
☐	60. "Yogi" Berra	25.00	16.25	20.50
☐	84. Roy Campanella	25.00	16.25	20.50
☐	103. Joe Tipton	3.00	2.00	2.50
☐	140. Rae Scarborough	3.00	2.00	2.50
☐	155. "Mickey" Guerra	13.00	8.50	10.75
☐	175. Luke Appling	15.00	9.75	12.25
☐	226. "Duke" Snider	150.00	100.00	125.00
☐	238. Bob Lemon	50.00	32.50	42.00
☐	240. "Babe" Young	3.00	2.00	2.50

BOWMAN — 1950 (2⅛" x 2½", Numbered 1-252. Color)

☐	Complete Set	700.00	455.00	580.00
☐	1. Mel Parnell	12.50	8.00	10.00
☐	6. Bob Feller	15.00	9.75	8.00
☐	19. Warren Spahn	12.50	8.00	10.00
☐	22. Jackie Robinson	40.00	26.00	33.00
☐	28. Bobby Thomson	6.00	4.00	5.00
☐	46. "Yogi" Berra	20.00	13.00	16.50
☐	75. Roy Campanella	25.00	16.25	20.50

BASEBALL CARDS / 131

1949 Bowman,
#109 Ed Fitzgerald
$3.50-$4.50

1950 Bowman,
#235 Harold Gilbert
$2.50-$3.00

1951 Bowman,
#5 Dale Mitchell
$3.00-$3.50

132 / BASEBALL CARDS

		Current Price Range		Prior Year Average
☐	98. Ted Williams	50.00	32.50	42.00
☐	148. Early Wynn	8.00	5.20	6.50
☐	167. "Preacher" Roe	3.50	2.25	3.00
☐	179. Chuck Diering	1.75	1.25	1.50
☐	217. Casey Stengel	17.50	11.50	14.50
☐	232. Al Rosen	4.50	3.00	3.75

BOWMAN — 1951 (2⅛" x 2½", Numbered 1-324. Color)

☐	Complete Set	1250.00	800.00	1025.00
☐	1. Whitey Ford	40.00	26.00	33.00
☐	2. "Yogi" Berra	20.00	13.00	16.50
☐	31. Roy Campanella	20.00	13.00	16.50
☐	78. Early Wynn	7.50	5.00	6.25
☐	80. "Peewee" Reese	10.00	6.50	8.25
☐	165. Ted Williams	50.75	32.00	42.00
☐	181. Casey Stengel	15.00	9.75	12.25
☐	191. Billy Hitchcock	1.75	1.25	1.50
☐	203. Vernon Law	1.75	1.25	1.50
☐	230. Max Lanier	1.75	1.25	1.50
☐	253. Mickey Mantle	250.00	163.00	205.00
☐	282. Frank Frisch	12.50	8.00	10.00
☐	290. Billy Dickey	17.50	11.50	14.50
☐	305. Willie Mays	250.00	163.00	205.00
☐	324. Johnny Pramesa	10.00	6.50	8.25

BOWMAN — 1952 (2⅛" x 2½", Numbered 1-252. Color)

☐	Complete Set	650.00	423.00	535.00
☐	1. "Yogi" Berra	30.00	20.00	25.00
☐	18. Don Mueller	1.75	2.00	1.50
☐	44. Roy Campanella	20.00	13.00	16.50
☐	80. Gil Hodges	8.00	5.25	6.50
☐	101. Mickey Mantle	125.00	63.00	94.00
☐	116. Duke Snider	15.00	9.75	12.25
☐	142. Early Wynn	6.75	4.50	5.60
☐	146. Leo Durocher	4.00	2.50	3.25
☐	156. Warren Spahn	8.50	5.50	7.00
☐	159. "Dutch" Leonard	1.75	1.25	1.50
☐	180. Eddie Fitzgerald	1.75	1.25	1.50
☐	196. Stan Musial	45.00	30.00	37.50
☐	218. Willie Mays	100.00	65.00	80.00
☐	244. Lew Burdette	7.50	5.00	6.25
☐	252. Frank Crosetti	15.00	9.75	12.25

BOWMAN — 1953 (2½" x 3¼", Numbered 1-64. B&W)

☐	Complete Set	600.00	390.00	495.00
☐	1. Gus Bell	15.00	9.75	12.25
☐	2. Willard Nixon	7.50	5.00	6.25
☐	4. Pat Mullin	7.50	5.00	6.25
☐	15. Johnny Mize	20.00	13.00	16.50
☐	26. "Preacher" Roe	15.00	9.75	12.25
☐	27. Bob Lemon	20.00	13.00	16.50
☐	32. Rocky Bridges	7.50	5.00	6.25
☐	36. Jim Piersall	15.00	9.75	12.25
☐	39. Casey Stengel	80.00	52.00	66.00
☐	42. Howie Judson	3.75	2.50	3.25

BASEBALL CARDS / 133

		Current Price Range		Prior Year Average
☐	46. Bucky Harris	25.00	16.25	20.50
☐	51. Lou Burdette	6.50	4.25	5.25
☐	54. Billy Miller	3.75	2.50	3.25
☐	58. Jim Konstanty	3.75	2.50	3.25
☐	64. Andy Hansen	4.50	3.00	3.75

BOWMAN — 1953 (2½" x 3¼", Numbered 1-160. Color)

☐	Complete Set	1300.00	1105.00	885.00
☐	1. Dave Williams	7.50	5.00	6.25
☐	15. Jim Busby	3.75	2.50	3.25
☐	26. Roy McMillan	3.75	2.50	3.25
☐	32. Stan Musial	45.00	30.00	37.50
☐	44. Bauer, Berra, Mantle	30.00	19.50	25.00
☐	59. Mickey Mantle	125.00	82.00	105.00
☐	93. Rizzuto & Martin	20.00	13.00	16.50
☐	114. Bob Feller	45.00	30.00	37.50
☐	121. "Yogi" Berra	85.00	55.00	70.00
☐	130. Cass Michaels	6.50	4.25	5.25
☐	143. Al Lopez	12.00	7.75	9.75
☐	146. Early Wynn	20.00	13.00	16.50
☐	153. Whitey Ford	45.00	30.00	37.50
☐	160. Cal Abrams	10.00	6.50	8.25

BOWMAN — 1954 (2½" x 3¼", Numbered 1-224. Color)

NOTE: Because the Williams card (#66) is so scarce, it is worth more than the complete set which does not include it.

☐	Complete Set	450.00	293.00	370.00
☐	1. Phil Rizzuto	10.00	6.50	8.25
☐	43. Bob Friend	.75	.50	.60
☐	65. Mickey Mantle	50.00	33.00	42.00
☐	66. Ted Williams	450.00	293.00	375.00
☐	66. Jim Piersall	35.00	23.00	29.00
☐	89. Willy Mays	50.00	33.00	42.00
☐	90. Roy Campanella	20.00	13.00	16.50
☐	132. Bob Feller	12.50	9.00	10.00
☐	161. "Yogi" Berra	17.50	11.25	14.50
☐	164. Early Wynn	6.50	4.25	5.25
☐	170. Duke Snider	15.00	9.75	12.25
☐	177. "Whitey" Ford	10.00	6.50	8.25
☐	187. Vernon Law	1.00	.65	.85
☐	203. Vic Janowicz	1.00	.65	.85
☐	224. Bill Bruten	2.50	1.65	2.00

BOWMAN — 1955 (2½" x 3¼", Numbered 1-320. Color)

☐	Complete Set	375.00	245.00	310.00
☐	1. Hoyt Wilhelm	4.50	3.00	3.75
☐	22. Roy Campanella	10.00	6.50	8.25
☐	59. "Whitey" Ford	6.50	4.00	5.25
☐	134. Bob Feller	8.50	5.50	7.00
☐	179. Hank Aaron	24.00	15.60	20.00
☐	184. Willie Mays	24.00	15.00	20.00
☐	192. George Stickland	.50	.30	.40
☐	197. Ralph Kiner	6.40	4.25	5.25
☐	202. Mickey Mantle	30.00	19.50	25.00
☐	220. Jim Hearn	.50	.30	.40

134 / BASEBALL CARDS

		Current Price Range		Prior Year Average
☐ 242.	Ernie Banks	45.00	29.00	37.00
☐ 263.	Eddie Joost	2.00	1.25	2.50
☐ 296.	Bill Virdon	3.50	2.25	3.00
☐ 310.	Ken Lehman	2.00	1.25	1.50
☐ 320.	George Susce, Jr.	2.00	1.25	1.50

FLEER, Ted Williams — 1959 (2½" x 3½". Color)
Entire set devoted to the life of Ted Williams.

☐	Complete Set	80.00	52.00	66.00
☐ 1.	The Early Years	.50	.30	.40
☐ 2.	Ted's Idol-Babe Ruth	.50	.30	.40
☐ 4.	Learns Fine Points	.50	.30	.40
☐ 18.	1941-All Star Hero	.50	.30	.40
☐ 19.	Ted Wins Triple Crown	.50	.30	.40
☐ 28.	The Williams Shift	.50	.30	.40
☐ 32.	Most Valuable Player	.50	.30	.40
☐ 36.	Banner Year for Ted	.50	.30	.40
☐ 45.	Farewell to Baseball	.50	.30	.40
☐ 47.	Ted Crash Lands Jet	.50	.30	.40
☐ 49.	Smash Return	.50	.30	.40
☐ 56.	2,000th Hit	.50	.30	.40
☐ 68.	Ted Signs for 1959	50.00	32.00	41.00
☐ 78.	Honors for Williams	.50	.30	.40
☐ 80.	Ted's Goals for 1959	.50	.30	.40

FLEERS, Greats — 1960 (2½" x 3½", Numbered 1-79. Color)

☐	Complete Set	60.00	39.00	50.00
☐ 1.	Napoleon Lajoie	1.50	1.00	1.25
☐ 3.	George H. Ruth	5.00	3.25	4.00
☐ 6.	Walter P. Johnson	1.00	.65	.85
☐ 17.	Ernest Lombardi	.50	.25	.35
☐ 26.	Robert Feller	2.00	1.25	1.50
☐ 27.	Lucius Appling	.40	.25	.35
☐ 28.	Henry L. Gehring	3.00	2.00	2.50
☐ 31.	Anthony Larreri	.40	.25	.35
☐ 36.	Melvin Ott	.75	.50	.60
☐ 42.	Tyrus Cobb	3.00	2.00	2.50
☐ 47.	Denton Young	.40	.25	.35
☐ 53.	James Foxx	1.00	.65	.85
☐ 62.	John Wagner	1.00	.65	.85
☐ 72.	Theodore Williams	3.00	2.00	2.50
☐ 79.	Ralph Kiner	.75	.50	.60

FLEER, Greats — 1961 (2½" x 3½", Numbered 1-154. Color)

☐	Complete Set	125.00	82.00	105.00
☐ 1.	Baker, Cobb, Wheat	2.00	1.25	1.50
☐ 13.	Jack Chesbro	.40	.25	.35
☐ 28.	Jimmy Foxx	1.00	.65	.85
☐ 31.	Lou Gehrig	3.00	2.00	2.50
☐ 45.	Carl Hubbell	.40	.25	.35
☐ 66.	Hal Newhouser	.40	.25	.35
☐ 75.	Babe Ruth	5.00	3.25	4.00
☐ 94.	Lou Boudreau	1.50	1.00	1.25
☐ 120.	Napoleon Lajoie	1.50	1.00	1.25
☐ 138.	Luke Sewell	1.00	.65	.85

BASEBALL CARDS / 135

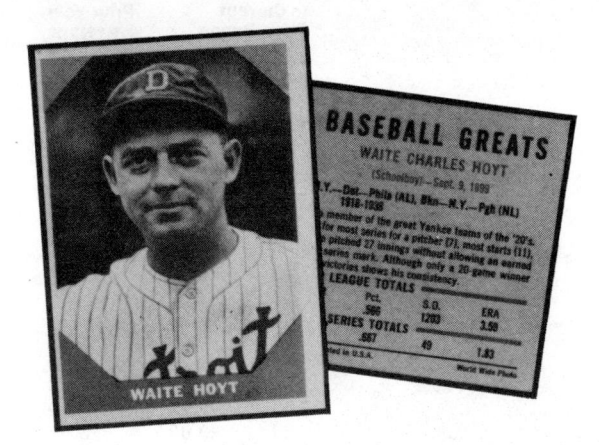

1960 Fleer,
#69 Waite Hoyt
$.50-$.60

1963 Fleer,
#15 Dick Howser
$.55-$.75

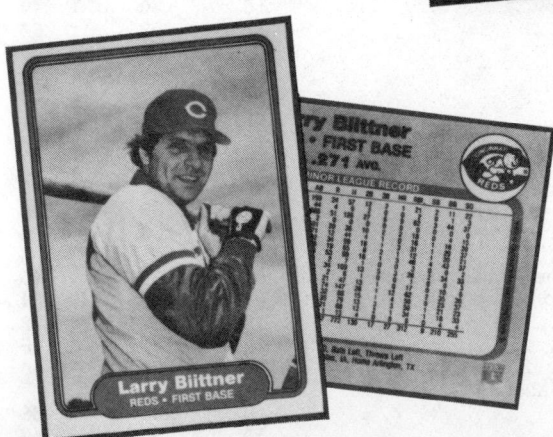

1982 Fleer,
#59 Larry Biittner
$.03-$.04

136 / BASEBALL CARDS

		Current Price Range		Prior Year Average
☐ 150.	Honus Wagner	3.50	2.25	3.00
☐ 152.	Ted Williams	6.00	4.00	5.00
☐ 153.	Cy Young	2.00	1.25	1.50
☐ 154.	Ross Young	1.00	.65	.85

FLEER — 1963 (2½" x 3½", Numbered 1-66. Color)

☐		Complete Set	100.00	65.00	83.00
☐	1.	Steve Barber	.75	.50	.60
☐	4.	Brooks Robinson	4.00	2.50	3.25
☐	5.	Willie Mays	7.00	5.60	4.50
☐	8.	Carl Yastrzemski	8.50	5.50	7.00
☐	32.	Ron Santo	.40	.25	.35
☐	36.	Jim Amalfitano	.40	.25	.35
☐	41.	Don Drysdale	3.50	2.25	3.00
☐	42.	Sandy Koufax	7.50	5.00	6.25
☐	43.	Maury Wills	5.00	3.25	4.00
☐	46.	Joe Adcock	30.00	20.00	25.00
☐	56.	Roberto Clemente	7.50	5.00	6.25
☐	58.	Vern Law	.40	.25	.35
☐	61.	Bob Gibson	3.50	2.25	3.00
☐	66.	Bill O'Dell	.40	.25	.35

FLEER — 1981 (2½" x 3½", Numbered 1-660. Color)

NOTE: There were two printings of this set. The first batch was produced in haste and numerous errors resulted. The second printing corrected many of them. Because the error cards which were later corrected had only a short production run, and were sent only through channels which served the general public, they are expected to continue to perform well on the market. The first and second printings of these error cards are noted.

☐		Complete Set (1st print)	30.00	16.25	23.00
☐		Complete Set (2nd print)	18.50	12.00	15.25
☐	1.	Pete Rose	.75	.50	.60
	87.	Graig Nettles			
☐		1st: "Craig"	10.00	6.50	8.25
☐		2nd: "Graig"	.25	.15	.20
	120.	Robert Welch			
☐		1st: "Bob" on back	.50	.30	.40
☐		2nd: "Robert" on back	.05	.03	.04
☐	153.	Chris Speier	.05	.03	.04
	480.	Stan Papi			
☐		1st: Pitcher on front	.50	.30	.40
☐		2nd: Shortstop on front	.05	.03	.04
☐	484.	Dave Winfield	.25	.15	.20
	493.	Tim Flannery			
☐		1st: Photo batting right	.50	.30	.40
☐		2nd: Photo batting left	.05	.03	.04
☐	533.	Bob Sykes	.05	.03	.04
	547.	Don Hood			
☐		1st: Pete Vuckovich name, front and back	.50	.30	.40
☐		2nd: Don Hood name, front and back	.05	.03	.04
☐	595.	Maury Wills	.10	.07	.08
☐	606.	Steve Garvey	.30	.20	.25
☐	638.	Carl Yastrzemski	.50	.30	.40
	650.	Reggie Jackson, "Mr. Baseball"			
☐		1st: No. 79 on back	1.00	.65	.85
☐		2nd: No. 650 on back	.50	.30	.40

BASEBALL CARDS / 137

		Current Price Range		Prior Year Average
	655. George Brett ".390 Average"			
☐	1st: No. 28 on back	1.00	.65	.85
☐	2nd: No. 655 on back	.10	.07	.4
	660. Steve Carlton, "Golden Arm"			
☐	1st: No. 6 on back	1.00	.65	.85
☐	2nd: No. 660 on back	.30	.20	.25

FLEERS — 1982 (2½" x 3½", Numbered 1-660. Color)

☐	Complete Set	13.50	8.75	11.25
☐	1. Dusty Baker	.10	.07	.08
☐	27. Fernando Valenzuela	.50	.30	.40
☐	39. Reggie Jackson	.50	.30	.40
☐	85. Tony Armas	.15	.10	.12
☐	185. Gary Carter	.25	.15	.20
☐	256. Pete Rose	.75	.50	.70
☐	312. Carl Yastrzemski	.35	.25	.30
☐	455. Rod Carew	.30	.20	.25
☐	641. Phillies Finest	.25	.15	.20
☐	660. Checklist	.03	.02	.02

TOPPS, Blue Backs — 1951 (2" x 2⅝", Numbered 1-52. B&W)

☐	Complete Set	375.00	240.00	320.00
☐	1. Eddie Yost	7.50	5.05	6.10
☐	3. Richie Ashburn	8.50	5.45	6.75
☐	6. "Red" Schoendinst	7.50	4.80	6.10
☐	10. Joe Page	7.50	4.80	6.10
☐	17. Roy Smalley	6.00	3.80	4.75
☐	20. Ralph Branca	7.50	4.80	6.10
☐	25. Sam Mele	6.00	3.80	4.75
☐	30. Enos Slaughter	8.50	5.40	6.75
☐	33. Don Lenhardt	6.00	3.80	5.60
☐	35. Tommy Byrne	6.00	3.80	5.60
☐	39. Ed Lopat	7.50	4.80	6.10
☐	42. Bruce Edwards	6.00	3.85	4.75
☐	45. Billy Pierce	7.50	4.80	6.10
☐	50. Johnny Mize	15.00	9.60	12.00
☐	52. Sam Chapman	6.00	3.85	4.75

TOPPS, Red Backs — 1951 (2" x 2⅝", Numbered 1-52. B&W)

☐	Complete Set	200.00	128.00	160.00
☐	1. Larry "Yogi" Berra	12.00	7.70	8.50
☐	5. Phil Rizzuto	8.00	5.10	6.20
☐	8. Early Wynn	6.00	3.85	4.75
☐	12. Jim Hegan	2.50	1.60	1.90
☐	15. Ralph Kiner	8.00	5.10	6.50
☐	19. Dick Kokos	2.50	1.60	2.10
☐	22. Bob Feller	12.50	7.90	9.20
☐	25. Cliff Chambers	2.50	1.60	2.10
☐	30. Warren Smith	8.50	5.40	6.80
☐	31. Gil Hodges	8.50	5.40	6.90
☐	36. Gus Zernial	4.00	2.55	3.25
☐	38. Duke Snider	12.50	7.90	9.20
☐	41. Whitey Lockman	2.50	1.60	2.10
☐	45. Andy Seminick	2.50	1.60	2.10
☐	52. Tommy Holmes	8.00	5.00	6.50

TOPPS — 1952
(2⅝" x 3⅝", Numbered 1-407. Color)

		Current Price Range		Prior Year Average
☐	Complete Set	7500.00	4780.00	6120.00
☐ 1.	Andy Palko	22.00	14.00	17.00
☐ 11.	Phil Rizzuto	15.00	9.55	12.00
☐ 37.	Duke Snider	20.00	12.75	16.00
☐ 52.	Don Mueller	3.00	1.70	2.25
☐ 88.	Bob Feller	18.00	11.50	15.00
☐ 126.	Fred Hutchison	3.00	1.70	2.40
☐ 150.	Ted Beard	2.50	1.60	2.10
☐ 157.	Bob Usher	2.50	1.60	2.10
☐ 175.	Billy Martin	15.00	9.50	12.00
☐ 191.	"Yogi" Berra	35.00	22.30	28.00
☐ 215.	Hank Bauer	4.50	2.85	3.75
☐ 219.	Bobby Shantz	3.50	2.20	2.75
☐ 227.	Joe Garagiola	10.00	6.40	8.25
☐ 239.	Rocky Bridges	2.50	1.60	2.10
☐ 253.	Johnny Berardino	12.00	7.65	9.50
☐ 261.	Willie Mays	225.00	144.00	180.00
☐ 268.	Bob Lemon	45.00	28.60	37.00
☐ 301.	Bob Porterfield	8.50	5.40	7.00
☐ 311.	Mickey Mantle	800.00	680.00	510.00
☐ 312.	Jackie Robinson	250.00	160.00	210.00
☐ 314.	Roy Campanella	250.00	160.00	210.00
☐ 315.	Leo Durocher	80.00	51.00	65.00
☐ 333.	"Peewee" Reese	150.00	95.00	125.00
☐ 344.	Ewell Blackwell	35.00	22.30	27.00
☐ 351.	Alvin Dark	45.00	29.25	37.00
☐ 357.	Smokey Burgess	35.00	21.50	27.00
☐ 369.	Dick Groat	65.00	41.50	53.00
☐ 372.	Gil McDougald	65.00	41.50	53.00
☐ 377.	Chuck Dressen	40.00	25.50	53.00
☐ 384.	Frank Crosetti	50.00	31.80	42.00
☐ 392.	Hoyt Wilhelm	85.00	54.00	70.00
☐ 394.	Billy Herman	50.00	31.80	43.00
☐ 400.	Bill Dickey	200.00	127.00	165.00
☐ 407.	Ed Mathews	300.00	191.25	260.00

TOPPS — 1953 (2⅝" x 3⅝", Numbered 1-280. Color)

☐	Complete Set	1300.00	828.00	1105.00
☐ 1.	Jackie Robinson	35.00	21.50	27.00
☐ 27.	Roy Campanella	27.50	17.50	22.00
☐ 54.	Bob Feller	18.00	11.40	15.00
☐ 61.	Early Wynn	8.50	5.40	7.00
☐ 76.	"Peewee" Reese	12.00	9.60	9.50
☐ 82.	Mickey Mantle	160.00	79.50	125.00
☐ 104.	"Yogi" Berra	18.00	14.00	22.00
☐ 120.	Davey Williams	1.75	1.10	1.40
☐ 147.	Warren Spahn	15.00	8.90	12.00
☐ 179.	Gene Hermanski	1.75	1.10	1.40
☐ 191.	Ralph Kiner	10.00	5.95	7.50
☐ 207.	Whitey Ford	12.00	7.15	9.50
☐ 220.	Satchel Paige	30.00	17.35	24.00
☐ 244.	Willie Mays	350.00	220.00	285.00
☐ 280.	Milt Bolling	15.00	8.90	11.50

1952 Topps,
#229 Gene Beardon
$2.50-$3.50

1954 Topps,
#20 Warren Spahn
$10.00-$15.00

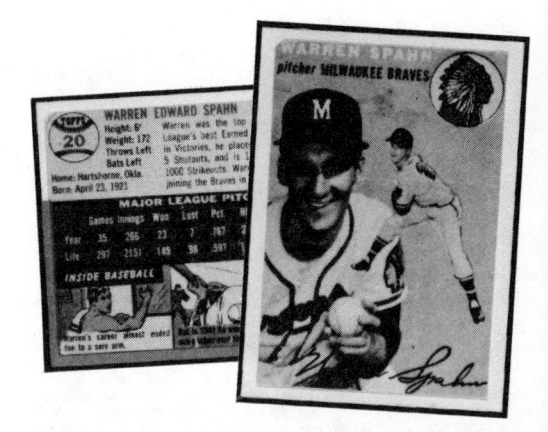

1955 Topps,
#121 Bill Renna
$.50-$.70

140 / BASEBALL CARDS

TOPPS — 1954
(2⅛" x 2⅝", Numbered 1-250. Color)

		Current Price Range		Prior Year Average
☐	Complete Set	650.00	385.00	525.00
☐	1. Ted Williams	45.00	26.75	35.00
☐	10. Jackie Robinson	25.00	14.80	20.00
☐	20. Warren Spahn	10.00	6.00	8.00
☐	32. Duke Snider	18.00	10.70	14.00
☐	37. Whitey Ford	12.00	7.15	9.50
☐	50. "Yogi" Berra	20.00	11.90	15.50
☐	90. Willie Mays	75.00	63.75	62.00
☐	94. Ernie Banks	45.00	25.20	35.00
☐	128. Hank Aaron	125.00	74.30	100.00
☐	169. Jim Hughes	1.00	.60	.80
☐	201. Al Kaline	45.00	25.20	35.00
☐	205. Johnny Sain	2.50	1.10	1.75
☐	231. Roy Smalley	.80	.60	.65
☐	250. Ted Williams	45.00	26.60	35.00

TOPPS — 1955 (2⅛" x 2⅝", Numbered 1-210, Color)

☐	Complete Set	525.00	312.00	430.00
☐	1. Dusty Rhodes	3.00	1.80	4.40
☐	2. Ted Williams	25.00	14.80	20.00
☐	28. Ernie Banks	10.00	6.00	8.00
☐	38. Bob Turley	.70	.45	.55
☐	50. Jackie Robinson	24.00	14.25	19.00
☐	70. Al Rosen	3.50	2.00	2.50
☐	89. Joe Frazier	.70	.40	.55
☐	105. Chuck Diering	.70	.40	.55
☐	123. Sandy Koufax	35.00	18.75	26.00
☐	124. Harmon Killebrew	16.00	7.15	11.50
☐	164. Roberto Clemente	80.00	47.60	113.00
☐	179. Joe Bolger	3.50	1.60	2.10
☐	187. Gil Hodges	25.00	14.10	20.00
☐	194. Willie Mays	125.00	74.80	205.00
☐	198. "Yogi" Berra	32.00	19.20	26.00
☐	210. Duke Snider	63.00	45.00	75.00

TOPPS — 1956 (2⅛" x 2⅝", Numbered 1-340. Color)

☐	Complete Set	530.00	304.00	415.00
☐	1. William Harridge	4.00	2.25	3.10
☐	5. Ted Williams	25.00	14.80	20.00
☐	30. Jackie Robinson	18.00	10.70	9.50
☐	31. Hank Aaron	26.00	15.40	20.00
☐	33. Roberto Clemente	18.00	10.70	14.00
☐	79. Sandy Koufax	15.00	9.75	12.25
☐	110. "Yogi" Berra	14.00	9.25	11.75
☐	113. Phil Rizzuto	8.50	5.50	7.00
☐	130. Willie Mays	28.00	19.25	20.00
☐	135. Mickey Mantle	55.00	35.75	45.25
☐	150. "Duke" Snider	12.00	7.75	9.75
☐	168. Sammy White	.65	.45	.55
☐	180. Robin Roberts	4.50	3.00	3.75
☐	200. Bob Feller	12.00	7.75	9.75
☐	340. "Mickey" McDermott	.65	.45	.55

TOPPS — 1957
(2½″ x 3½″, Numbered 1-407, Color)

		Current Price Range		Prior Year Average
☐	Complete Set	625.00	410.00	225.00
☐ 1.	Ted Williams	30.00	19.50	25.00
☐ 10.	Willie Mays	25.00	16.25	20.50
☐ 18.	Don Drysdale	12.00	7.75	9.75
☐ 20.	Hank Aaron	25.00	16.25	20.50
☐ 35.	Frank Robinson	25.00	16.25	20.50
☐ 57.	Jim Lemon	.60	.40	.50
☐ 75.	Jim Piersall	1.25	.80	1.00
☐ 76.	Roberto Clemente	15.00	9.75	12.25
☐ 95.	Mickey Mantle	40.00	26.00	33.00
☐ 170.	Duke Snider	11.00	7.00	9.00
☐ 210.	Roy Campanella	12.00	7.75	9.75
☐ 238.	Eddie Robinson	.60	.40	.50
☐ 302.	Sandy Koufax	50.00	32.00	41.00
☐ 328.	Brooks Robinson	50.00	32.00	41.00
☐ 338.	Jim Bunning	7.50	5.00	6.25
☐ 407.	Yankee Power Hitters	12.00	9.50	10.75

TOPPS — 1958 (2½″ x 3½″, Numbered 1-495. Color)

☐	Complete Set	350.00	230.00	300.00
☐ 1.	Ted Williams	25.00	16.50	21.00
☐ 5.	Willie Mays	18.50	12.00	15.25
☐ 30.	Hank Aaron	20.00	13.00	16.50
☐ 90.	Robin Roberts	4.00	2.50	3.25
☐ 127.	Tom Sturdivant	.35	.25	.30
☐ 150.	Mickey Mantle	28.00	18.25	23.00
☐ 173.	Eddie Yost	.35	.25	.30
☐ 187.	Sandy Koufax	10.00	6.50	8.25
☐ 270.	Warren Spahn	5.00	3.25	4.00
☐ 285.	Frank Robinson	7.50	5.00	6.25
☐ 288.	Harmon Killebrew	4.50	3.00	3.75
☐ 486.	Willie Mays	5.50	3.50	4.50
☐ 487.	Mickey Mantle	4.00	2.50	3.25
☐ 488.	Hank Aaron	5.50	3.50	4.50
☐ 495.	Herb Score	1.00	.65	.85

TOPPS — 1959 (2½″ x 3½″, Numbered 1-572. Color)

Some of the cards in this set have "option" or "traded" notes on the back which make them more valuable than the others.

☐	Complete Set	350.00	230.00	300.00
☐ 1.	Ford Frick	2.00	1.25	1.50
☐ 10.	Mickey Mantle	25.00	16.25	20.00
☐ 30.	Nellie Fox	2.50	1.65	2.00
☐ 50.	Willie Mays	15.00	9.75	12.00
☐ 150.	Stan Musial	9.50	6.25	8.00
☐ 163.	Sandy Koufax	9.00	5.00	7.25
☐ 180.	"Yogi" Berra	7.50	5.00	6.25
☐ 202.	Roger Maris	5.00	3.25	4.00
☐ 380.	Hank Aaron	15.00	9.75	12.25
☐ 387.	Don Drysdale	4.00	2.50	3.25
☐ 412.	Stan Lopata	.35	.25	.30
☐ 430.	Whitey Ford	5.00	3.25	4.00
☐ 439.	Brooks Robinson	5.50	3.50	4.50
☐ 478.	Bob Clemente	9.50	6.75	8.00
☐ 514.	Bob Robinson	20.00	13.00	16.50

142 / BASEBALL CARDS

		Current Price Range		Prior Year Average
☐ 536.	Danny Kravitz	1.25	.85	1.00
☐ 561.	Hank Aaron	10.00	6.50	9.25
☐ 563.	Willie Mays	10.00	6.50	8.25
☐ 564.	Mickey Mantle	12.00	7.75	9.75
☐ 572.	Billy Pierce	2.00	1.25	1.50

TOPPS — 1960 (2½″ x 3½″, Numbered 1-572. Color)

☐	Complete Set	350.00	250.00	300.00
☐ 1.	Early Wynn	2.50	1.65	2.00
☐ 92.	Whitey Herzog	.25	.15	.20
☐ 122.	Don Dillard	.25	.15	.20
☐ 148.	Carl Yastrzemski	45.00	30.00	45.00
☐ 250.	Stan Musial	8.50	5.50	7.00
☐ 300.	Hank Aaron	13.50	8.75	11.25
☐ 316.	W. McCovey	20.00	13.00	16.50
☐ 326.	Roberto Clemente	9.50	6.25	8.00
☐ 343.	Sandy Koufax	8.50	5.50	7.00
☐ 563.	Mickey Mantle	12.50	8.00	10.00
☐ 564.	Willie Mays	10.00	6.50	8.25
☐ 565.	Roger Maris	5.00	3.25	4.00
☐ 566.	Hank Aaron	16.50	8.00	10.00
☐ 570.	Don Drysdale	1.50	1.00	1.25
☐ 575.	J. Antonelli	1.50	1.00	1.25

TOPPS — 1961 (2½″ x 3½″, Numbered 1-589. Color)

☐	Complete Set	650.00	425.00	550.00
☐ 1.	Dick Groat	2.50	1.60	2.00
☐ 30.	Nellie Fox	1.50	1.00	1.25
☐ 80.	Harman Killebrew	3.00	2.00	2.50
☐ 92.	Hal Naragon	.25	.15	.20
☐ 132.	Al Lopez	1.00	.65	.85
☐ 150.	Willie Mays	12.00	7.75	9.75
☐ 160.	Whitey Ford	4.00	2.50	3.25
☐ 572.	Brooks Robinson	15.00	9.75	12.25
☐ 576.	Roger Maris	15.00	9.75	12.25
☐ 577.	Hank Aaron	40.00	26.00	33.00
☐ 578.	Mickey Mantle	50.00	32.00	41.00
☐ 579.	Willie Mays	40.00	26.00	33.00
☐ 581.	Frank Robinson	15.00	9.75	12.25
☐ 586.	Whitey Ford	15.00	9.75	13.00
☐ 589.	Warren Spahn	15.00	9.75	13.00

TOPPS — 1962 (2½″ x 3½″, Numbered 1-598. Color)

☐	Complete Set	350.00	230.00	305.00
☐ 1.	Roger Maris	9.00	5.75	7.25
☐ 5.	Sandy Koufax	8.50	5.50	7.00
☐ 28.	Minnie Minoso	1.00	.65	.85
☐ 38.	Gene Stephens	.25	.15	.20
☐ 70.	Harmon Killebrew	2.50	1.50	2.00
☐ 100.	Warren Spahn	3.50	2.25	3.00
☐ 125.	Gene Wooding	.25	.15	.20
☐ 152.	Mickey Vernon	.25	.15	.20
☐ 360.	Yogi Berra	5.00	3.25	4.00
☐ 387.	Lou Brock	18.00	11.75	15.00
☐ 425.	Carl Yastrzemski	25.00	16.25	20.50

BASEBALL CARDS / 143

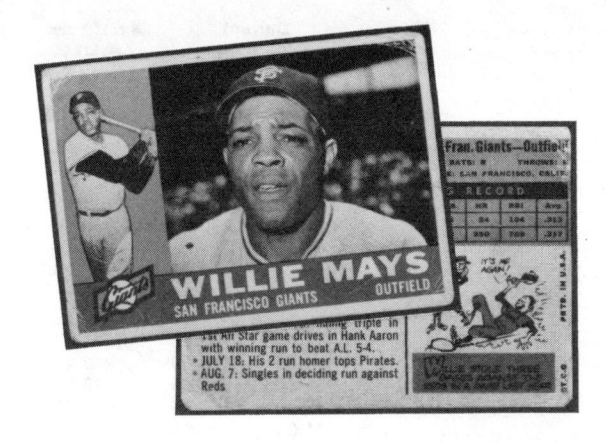

1960 Topps,
#200 Willie Mays
$25.00-$30.00

1961 Topps,
#547 Leon Wagner
$6.00-$7.00

1962 Topps,
#1 Roger Maris
$8.00-$8.50

144 / BASEBALL CARDS

		Current Price Range		Prior Year Average
☐ 530.	Bob Gibson	20.00	13.50	16.50
☐ 559.	Mike Higgins	1.25	.85	1.00
☐ 583.	Larry Osborne	1.25	.85	1.00
☐ 598.	Rookie Parade-8	3.00	2.00	2.50

TOPPS — 1963 (2½" x 3½", Numbered 1-576. Color)

☐	Complete Set	600.00	400.00	500.00
☐ 1.	Bat, Leaders, N.L.	.50	.35	.40
☐ 25.	Al Kaline	4.00	2.50	3.25
☐ 60.	Elston Howard	2.00	1.25	1.50
☐ 108.	Hoyt Wilhelm	.50	.35	.40
☐ 115.	Carl Yastrzemski	17.50	11.50	14.50
☐ 120.	Roger Maris	4.00	2.50	3.25
☐ 200.	Mickey Mantle	25.00	16.25	20.50
☐ 210.	Sandy Koufax	15.00	9.75	12.25
☐ 240.	Rocky Colavito	1.00	.65	.85
☐ 245.	Gil Hodges	3.00	2.00	2.50
☐ 268.	Don Demeter	.30	.20	.25
☐ 300.	Willie Mays	22.00	14.50	18.25
☐ 327.	Paul Foytack	.30	.20	.25
☐ 540.	Roberto Clemente	35.00	22.40	29.00
☐ 576.	Johnny Temple	1.00	.65	.75

TOPPS — 1964 (2½" x 3½", Numbered 1-587. Color)

☐	Complete Set	250.00	162.00	206.40
☐ 1.	E.R.A. Leader, N.L.	.75	.20	.60
☐ 13.	Hoyt Wilhelm	.75	.90	.75
☐ 21.	Yogi Berra	4.50	5.00	3.75
☐ 29.	Lou Brock	7.50	5.00	6.25
☐ 37.	Smokey Burgess	.20	.13	.17
☐ 50.	Mickey Mantle	15.00	9.75	13.25
☐ 55.	Ernie Banks	4.50	3.00	3.75
☐ 109.	Rusty Staub	.50	.35	.40
☐ 120.	Don Drysdale	3.00	2.00	2.50
☐ 125.	Pete Rose	35.00	22.75	29.00
☐ 134.	Don Zimmer	.20	.13	.17
☐ 560.	Dick Farrell	.50	.35	.40
☐ 567.	Jim Kaat	1.00	.65	.85
☐ 586.	Jim Piersall	.75	.30	.60
☐ 587.	Bennie Daniels	.50	.35	.40

TOPPS — 1965 (2½" x 3½", Numbered 1-598. Color)

☐	Complete Set	275.00	180.00	228.00
☐ 1.	Batting Leaders, A.L.	.75	.50	.60
☐ 15.	Robin Roberts	2.00	1.25	1.50
☐ 120.	Frank Robinson	3.50	2.25	3.00
☐ 130.	Al Kaline	4.00	2.50	3.25
☐ 155.	Roger Maris	3.50	2.25	3.00
☐ 170.	Hank Aaron	10.00	6.50	8.25
☐ 176.	Willie McCovey	3.50	2.25	3.00
☐ 187.	Casey Stengel	2.50	1.65	2.00
☐ 193.	Gaylord Perry	3.00	2.00	2.50
☐ 207.	Pete Rose	25.00	16.25	20.50
☐ 220.	Bill Williams	1.50	1.00	1.25
☐ 250.	Willie Mays	10.50	6.75	8.50

BASEBALL CARDS / 145

		Current Price Range		Prior Year Average
☐ 260.	Don Drysdale	3.00	2.00	2.50
☐ 276.	Hoyt Wilhelm	.75	.50	.60
☐ 280.	Dick Stuart	.20	.13	.17
☐ 300.	Sandy Koufax	8.50	5.50	7.00
☐ 313.	Jim Schaffer	.20	.13	.17
☐ 330.	Whitey Ford	4.50	3.00	3.75
☐ 346.	Bob Bragan	.20	.13	.17
☐ 598.	Al Downing	.50	.35	.40

TOPPS — 1966 (2½" x 3½", Numbered 1-598. Color)

☐		Complete Set	400.00	260.00	330.00
☐	1.	Willie Mays	5.00	3.00	4.00
☐	15.	Vern Law	.35	.25	.30
☐	30.	Pete Rose	12.50	8.00	10.00
☐	36.	Jim Hunter	2.00	1.25	1.50
☐	50.	Mickey Mantle	13.00	8.50	10.75
☐	70.	Carl Yastrzemski	12.50	8.00	10.00
☐	72.	Tony Perez	.75	.50	.60
☐	100.	Sandy Koufax	7.50	5.00	6.25
☐	106.	Rusty Staub	.50	.30	.40
☐	110.	Ernie Banks	3.50	2.25	3.00
☐	120.	Harmon Killebrew	2.50	1.65	3.00
☐	125.	Lou Brock	4.50	5.00	3.75
☐	132.	Orlando Cepeda	1.50	1.00	1.25
☐	535.	Willie Davis	3.00	2.00	2.50
☐	540.	Denny McLain	7.50	5.00	6.25
☐	550.	Willie McCovey	25.00	16.25	20.50
☐	565.	Jimmy Piersall	5.00	3.25	4.00
☐	570.	Art Mahaffey	2.00	1.25	1.50
☐	580.	Billy Williams	5.00	3.25	4.00
☐	598.	Gaylord Perry	35.00	23.60	30.00

TOPPS — 1967 (2½" x 3½", Numbered 1-609. Color)

☐		Complete Set	475.00	310.00	400.00
☐	1.	Champs	1.50	1.00	1.25
☐	5.	Whitey Ford	3.00	2.00	2.50
☐	45.	Roger Maris	3.00	2.00	2.50
☐	100.	Frank Robinson	3.00	2.00	2.50
☐	140.	Willie Stargell	2.50	1.65	2.00
☐	150.	Mickey Mantle	12.50	8.00	10.00
☐	166.	Ed Mathews	2.50	1.65	2.00
☐	200.	Willie Mays	10.00	6.50	8.25
☐	215.	Ernie Banks	3.00	2.00	2.50
☐	250.	Hank Aaron	10.00	6.50	8.25
☐	285.	Lou Brock	4.50	3.00	3.75
☐	295.	Sam McDowell	.15	.10	.12
☐	528.	Rico Petrocelli	.50	.30	.40
☐	534.	Hank Bauer	3.00	2.00	2.50
☐	540.	Norm Cash	.50	.30	.40
☐	570.	Maury Wills	55.00	36.00	45.00
☐	580.	Rocky Colavito	7.50	5.00	6.25
☐	593.	Wes Westrum	1.50	1.00	1.25
☐	600.	Brooks Robinson	75.00	48.00	62.00
☐	609.	Tommy John	15.00	9.75	12.25

146 / BASEBALL CARDS

TOPPS — 1968
(2½" x 3½", Numbered 1-598. Color)

		Current Price Range		Prior Year Average
☐	Complete Set	200.00	130.00	165.60
☐ 1.	Batting Leaders, N.L.	.50	.30	.40
☐ 45.	Tom Seaver	9.50	6.25	8.00
☐ 50.	Willie Mays	7.50	5.00	6.25
☐ 54.	Stan Williams	.15	.10	.12
☐ 80.	Rod Carew	8.50	5.50	7.00
☐ 150.	Bob Clemente	6.50	3.50	4.50
☐ 220.	Harmon Killebrew	2.25	1.50	1.75
☐ 230.	Pete Rose	14.00	9.25	11.50
☐ 240.	Al Kaline	2.75	1.75	2.25
☐ 250.	Carl Yastrzemski	8.00	5.25	6.50
☐ 280.	Mickey Mantle	12.00	7.75	9.75
☐ 500.	Frank Robinson	3.00	2.00	2.50
☐ 520.	Lou Brock	3.50	2.25	3.00
☐ 532.	Luis Tiant	.30	.20	.25
☐ 575.	Jim Palmer	4.00	2.50	3.25
☐ 598.	Jerry May	.30	.20	.25

TOPPS — 1969 (2½" x 3½", Numbered 1-664. Color)

☐	Complete Set	250.00	162.00	210.00
☐ 1.	Batting Leaders, A.L.	.50	.30	.40
☐ 20.	Ernie Banks	3.00	2.00	2.50
☐ 35.	Joe Morgan	1.50	1.00	1.25
☐ 45.	Maury Wills	.75	.50	.60
☐ 85.	Lou Brock	3.00	2.00	2.50
☐ 95.	Johnny Bench	8.50	5.50	7.00
☐ 100.	Hank Aaron	8.00	5.25	6.50
☐ 120.	Pete Rose	10.00	6.50	8.25
☐ 130.	Carl Yastrzemski	9.50	6.25	8.00
☐ 150.	Denny McLain	.50	.30	.40
☐ 175.	Jim Bunning	.50	.30	.40
☐ 190.	Willie Mays	7.50	5.00	6.25
☐ 220.	Sam McDowell	.25	.15	.20
☐ 235.	Jim Hunter	1.50	1.00	1.25
☐ 260.	Reggie Jackson	22.00	14.50	18.25
☐ 480.	Tom Seaver	9.00	5.75	7.25
☐ 485.	Gaylord Perry	2.50	1.65	2.00
☐ 500.	Mickey Mantle	16.00	10.50	13.25
☐ 510.	Rod Carew	7.50	5.00	6.25
☐ 533.	Nolan Ryan	5.00	3.25	4.00
☐ 545.	Willie Stargell	3.00	2.00	2.50
☐ 550.	Brooks Robinson	4.00	2.50	3.25
☐ 650.	Ted Williams	2.00	1.25	1.50
☐ 660.	Reggie Smith	.75	.50	.60
☐ 664.	Ron Hunt	.15	.10	.12

TOPPS — 1970 (2½" x 3½", Numbered 1-720. Color)

☐	Complete Set	250.00	163.00	210.00
☐ 1.	World Champs	1.00	.65	.85
☐ 10.	Carl Yastrzemski	7.50	5.00	6.25
☐ 50.	Tommie Agee	.15	.10	.12
☐ 140.	Reggie Jackson	5.50	3.50	4.50
☐ 150.	Harmon Killebrew	2.00	1.25	1.50
☐ 180.	Tommy John	1.00	.65	.85

BASEBALL CARDS / 147

1968 Topps,
#103 Don Sutton
$.60-$.75

1969 Topps,
#203 Dave Johnson
$.18-$.22

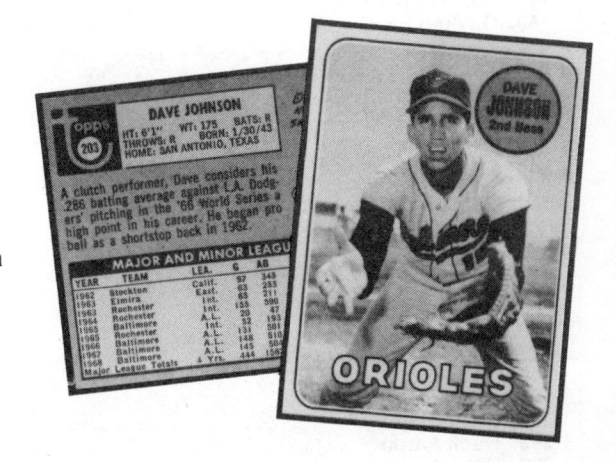

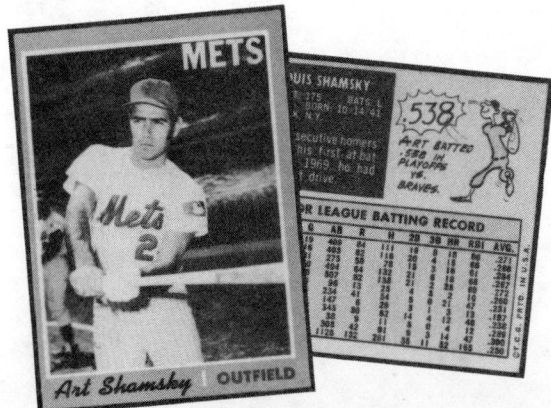

1970 Topps,
#137 Art Shamsky
$.18-$.22

148 / BASEBALL CARDS

		Current Price Range		Prior Year Average
☐ 595.	Maury Wills	.75	.50	.60
☐ 600.	Willie Mays	10.50	6.75	8.75
☐ 622.	Don Sutton	.75	.50	.60
☐ 640.	Al Kaline	6.50	4.25	5.25
☐ 660.	Johnny Bench	35.00	22.75	29.00
☐ 692.	Duffy Dyer	.50	.30	.40
☐ 700.	Frank Robinson	9.50	6.25	8.00
☐ 712.	Nolan Ryan	10.00	6.50	8.25
☐ 720.	Rick Reichardt	.50	.30	.40

TOPPS — 1971 (2½" x 3½", Numbered 1-752. Color)

☐	Complete Set	240.00	156.00	200.00
☐ 1.	World Champs	.75	.50	.60
☐ 5.	Thurman Munson	7.50	5.00	6.25
☐ 20.	Reggie Jackson	5.00	3.25	4.00
☐ 45.	Jim Hunter	1.50	1.00	1.25
☐ 91.	Bob Lemon	.75	.50	.60
☐ 117.	Ted Simmons	2.50	1.65	2.00
☐ 140.	Gaylord Perry	2.00	1.25	1.50
☐ 160.	Tom Seaver	5.50	3.50	4.50
☐ 210.	Rod Carew	6.00	4.00	5.00
☐ 230.	Willie Stargell	2.90	1.65	2.00
☐ 237.	Cesar Cedeno	1.00	.65	.85
☐ 244.	Bob Tillman	.15	.10	.12
☐ 250.	Johnny Bench	4.00	2.50	3.25
☐ 750.	Denny McLain	1.50	1.00	1.25
☐ 752.	Dick Drago	.50	.30	.40

TOPPS — 1972 (2½" x 3½", Numbered 1-787. Color)

☐	Complete Set	275.00	180.00	225.00
☐ 1.	Pittsburgh Pirates	.50	.30	.40
☐ 30.	Rico Petrocelli	.15	.10	.12
☐ 37.	Carl Yastrzemski	5.50	3.50	4.50
☐ 49.	Willie Mays	5.00	3.25	4.00
☐ 51.	Harmon Killebrew	1.50	1.00	1.25
☐ 285.	Gaylord Perry	2.00	1.25	1.50
☐ 299.	Hank Aaron	5.50	3.50	4.50
☐ 309.	Roberto Clemente	4.50	3.00	3.75
☐ 330.	Jim Hunter	1.00	.65	.85
☐ 420.	Steve Carlton	3.50	2.25	3.00
☐ 433.	Johnny Bench	4.00	2.50	3.25
☐ 435.	Reggie Jackson	5.00	3.25	4.00
☐ 441.	Thurman Munson	4.00	2.50	3.25
☐ 445.	Tom Seaver	4.50	3.00	3.75
☐ 447.	Willie Stargell	2.00	1.25	1.50
☐ 455.	Tommy Harper	.15	.10	.12
☐ 686.	Steve Garvey	30.00	19.50	25.00
☐ 695.	Rod Carew	30.00	20.00	25.00
☐ 719.	Cesar Geronimo	.50	.30	.40
☐ 730.	Rick Monday	.75	.50	.60
☐ 751.	Steve Carlton	8.50	5.50	7.00
☐ 752.	Joe Morgan	4.50	3.00	3.75
☐ 764.	Dusty Baker	.75	.50	.60
☐ 777.	Hoyt Williams	2.50	1.65	2.00
☐ 787.	Ron Reed	.50	.30	.40

BASEBALL CARDS / 149

TOPPS — 1973
(2½" x 3½", Numbered 1-660. Color)

		Current Price Range		Prior Year Average
☐	Complete Set	145.00	95.00	120.00
☐ 1.	All-Time Home Runs	3.50	2.25	3.00
☐ 50.	Roberto Clemente	4.50	3.00	3.75
☐ 280.	Al Kaline	3.00	2.00	2.50
☐ 305.	Willie Mays.............................	5.75	3.75	4.75
☐ 320.	Lou Brock	1.50	1.00	1.25
☐ 330.	Rod Carew	3.00	2.00	2.50
☐ 350.	Tom Seaver	4.50	3.00	3.75
☐ 358.	Jim Nettles	.12	.08	.10
☐ 370.	Willie Stargell	2.00	1.25	1.50
☐ 380.	Johnny Bench	3.00	2.00	2.50
☐ 400.	Gaylord Perry	1.50	1.00	1.25
☐ 410.	Willie McCovey	2.00	1.25	1.50
☐ 430.	Vida Blue	.50	.30	.40
☐ 436.	Jim McAndrew	.12	.08	.10
☐ 660.	Fred Scherman	.30	.20	.25

TOPPS — 1974 (2½" x 3½", Numbered 1-660. Color)

☐	Complete Set	125.00	81.00	100.00
☐ 1.	Hank Aaron, Henry	6.50	4.25	5.25
☐ 10.	Johnny Bench	2.50	1.65	2.00
☐ 35.	Gaylord Perry	1.00	.65	.85
☐ 50.	Rod Carew	3.00	2.00	2.50
☐ 60.	Lou Brock	2.00	1.25	1.50
☐ 80.	Tom Seaver	2.50	1.65	2.00
☐ 85.	Joe Morgan	1.00	.65	.85
☐ 95.	Steve Carlton	2.00	1.25	1.50
☐ 100.	Willie Stargell	1.00	.65	.85
☐ 130.	Reggie Jackson	4.00	2.50	3.25
☐ 160.	Brooks Robinson	2.00	1.25	1.50
☐ 179.	Yogi Berra	.75	.50	.60
☐ 251.	Graig Nestles	.50	.30	.40
☐ 280.	Carl Yastrzemski	3.50	2.25	3.00
☐ 300.	Pete Rose	6.50	4.25	5.25
☐ 340.	Thurman Munson	3.00	2.00	2.50
☐ 575.	Steve Garvey	2.50	1.65	2.00
☐ 634.	Ed Mathews	.75	.50	.60
☐ 646.	George Foster	2.00	1.25	1.50
☐ 660.	Larry Dierker	.12	.08	.10

TOPPS — 1975 (2½" x 3½", Numbered 1-660. Color)

Topps also issued a series of mini-cards 2¼" x 3⅛" that year. The mini set was an exact duplicate of the standard set only smaller. Relatively few mints were issued.

☐	Complete Set, Standard	120.00	78.00	100.00
☐	Complete Set, Mini	240.00	156.00	200.00
☐ 1.	Aaron: Record	4.50	3.00	3.75
☐ 20.	Thurman Munson	2.50	1.65	2.00
☐ 29.	Dave Parker	2.00	1.25	1.50
☐ 50.	Brooks Robinson	2.00	1.25	1.50
☐ 61.	Dave Winfield	2.00	1.25	1.50
☐ 70.	Mike Schmidt	6.00	4.00	5.00
☐ 93.	Dave Lopez.............................	.10	.07	.08
☐ 100.	Willie Stargell	.75	1.50	.60
☐ 140.	Steve Garvey	2.50	1.65	2.00

150 / BASEBALL CARDS

		Current Price Range		Prior Year Average
☐	170. Bert Campameris	.10	.07	.08
☐	228. George Brett	12.50	8.00	10.00
☐	260. Johnny Bench	2.00	1.25	1.50
☐	500. Nolan Ryan	2.00	1.25	1.50
☐	530. Gaylord Perry	1.00	.65	.85
☐	540. Lou Brock	1.50	1.00	1.25
☐	600. Rod Carew	2.00	1.25	1.50
☐	602. John Vukovich	.10	.07	.08
☐	628. Ron LeFlore	1.50	1.00	1.25
☐	640. Harmon Killebrew	.75	.50	.60
☐	660. Hank Aaron	5.50	3.50	4.50

TOPPS — 1976 *(2½" x 3½", Numbered 1-660, also issued set of 44 "traded" cards in the same manner as in 1974. Color)*

☐	Complete Set	65.00	42.00	53.00
☐	1. '75 Records: Aaron	3.00	2.00	2.50
☐	19. George Brett	3.50	2.25	3.00
☐	50. Fred Lynn	2.00	1.25	1.50
☐	95. Brooks Robinson	1.00	.65	.85
☐	113. Gary Sutherland	.08	.05	.07
☐	140. Vida Blue	.20	.13	.17
☐	150. Steve Garvey	2.00	1.25	1.50
☐	160. Dave Winfield	1.00	.65	.85
☐	169. Graig Nettles	.25	.15	.20
☐	185. Dave Parker	1.00	.65	.85
☐	400. Rod Carew	2.00	1.25	1.50
☐	453. Lou Piniella	.25	.15	.20
☐	480. Mike Schmidt	4.50	3.00	3.75
☐	500. Reggie Jackson	2.00	1.25	1.50
☐	530. Don Sutton	.30	.20	.25
☐	550. Hank Aaron	3.50	2.25	3.00
☐	580. Bert Campaneris	.20	.13	.17
☐	600. Tom Seaver	2.00	1.25	1.50
☐	650. Thurman Munson	2.00	1.25	1.50
☐	660. Dave Lopes	.15	.10	.12

TOPPS — 1977 *(2½" x 3½", Numbered 1-660.Color)*

☐	Complete Set	55.00	36.00	46.50
☐	1. '76 Batting Leaders	.50	.30	.40
☐	10. Reggie Jackson	2.00	1.25	1.50
☐	50. Ron Cey	.20	.13	.17
☐	60. Jim Rice	1.00	.65	.85
☐	80. Andy Messersmith	.07	.04	.06
☐	106. Mike Flanagan	.07	.04	.06
☐	120. Rod Carew	1.00	1.75	.65
☐	131. Orlando Ramirez	.07	.04	.06
☐	150. Tom Seaver	1.50	1.00	.25
☐	170. Thurman Munson	2.00	1.25	1.50
☐	210. Fred Lynn	1.00	.65	.85
☐	270. Dave Parker	1.00	.65	.85
☐	305. Mickey Rivers	.07	.04	.06
☐	535. Cesar Geronimo	.07	.04	.06
☐	580. George Brett	2.00	1.25	1.50
☐	598. Sparky Lyle	.15	.10	.12
☐	600. Jim Palmer	1.00	.65	.85
☐	630. Bert Blyleven	.15	.10	.12

BASEBALL CARDS / 151

1975 Topps,
#58 Chuck Taylor
$.08-$.12

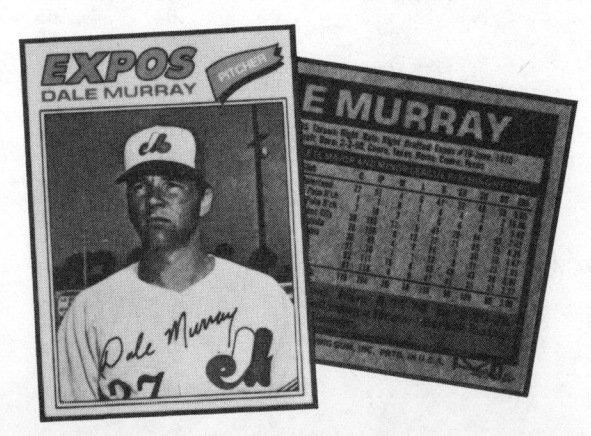

1976 Topps,
#84 Brent Strom
$.08-$.12

1977 Topps,
#252 Dale Murray
$.07-$.11

152 / BASEBALL CARDS

		Current Price Range		Prior Year Average
☐	656. Ron Guidry	1.00	.65	.85
☐	660. Willie Horton	.07	.04	.06

TOPPS — 1978 (2½″ x 3½″, Numbered 1-726. Color)

☐	Complete Set	35.00	23.00	30.00
☐	1. Brock (Record)	.50	.30	.40
☐	15. Tony Perez	.15	.10	.12
☐	20. Pete Rose	2.00	1.25	1.50
☐	32. Garry Templeton	.35	.25	.30
☐	40. Carl Yastrzemski	1.75	1.25	1.50
☐	48. Don Baylor	.20	.13	.17
☐	60. Thurman Munson	1.25	.85	1.00
☐	65. Ken Singleton	.20	.15	.20
☐	100. George Brett	1.50	1.00	1.25
☐	109. Joe Torre	.07	.04	.06
☐	143. Keith Hernandez	.20	.13	.17
☐	147. Lee Mazzilli	.15	.10	.12
☐	200. Reggie Jackson	1.50	1.00	1.25
☐	221. Chris Speier	.07	.04	.06
☐	630. Ron Cey	.15	.10	.12
☐	670. Jim Rice	1.00	.65	.85
☐	678. Tom Burgmeier	.07	.04	.06
☐	686. Gaylord Perry	.50	.30	.40
☐	691. Ross Grimsley	.07	.04	.06
☐	726. Wilbur Wood	.07	.04	.06

TOPPS — 1979 (2½″ x 3½″, Numbered 1-726. Color)

☐	Complete Set	32.00	21.00	26.80
☐	1. Batting Leaders	.25	.15	.20
☐	25. Steve Carlton	1.00	.65	.85
☐	30. Dave Winfield	1.00	.65	.85
☐	50. Steve Garvey	1.25	.85	1.00
☐	55. Willie Stargell	.50	.30	.40
☐	310. Thurman Munson	1.00	.65	.85
☐	320. Carl Yastrzemski	1.50	1.00	1.25
☐	321. Gaylord Perry	.50	.30	.40
☐	330. George Brett	1.25	.85	1.00
☐	340. Jim Palmer	.50	.30	.40
☐	365. Sparky Lyle	.06	.04	.05
☐	400. Jim Rice	.75	.50	.60
☐	409. Willie Wilson	2.50	1.65	2.00
☐	463. Steve Comer	.06	.04	.05
☐	489. Larry Cox	.06	.04	.05
☐	500. Ron Guidry	.25	.15	.20
☐	575. Luis Tiant	.10	.07	.08
☐	586. Bob Horner	.06	.04	.05
☐	650. Pete Rose	2.00	1.65	2.00
☐	726. Giants Prospects	.06	.04	.05

TOPPS — 1980 (2½″ x 3½″, Numbered 1-726. Color)

☐	Complete Set	25.00	16.00	21.40
☐	1. Highlights, 1979	.25	.15	.20
☐	17. Bruce Sutter	.10	.07	.08
☐	30. Vida Blue	.15	.10	.12
☐	35. Luis Tiant	.05	.03	.04

BASEBALL CARDS / 153

		Current Price Range		Prior Year Average
☐	110. Fred Lynn	.50	.30	.40
☐	135. Bill Buckner	.10	.07	.08
☐	157. Willie Wilson	.20	.13	.17
☐	210. Steve Carlton	.75	.50	.60
☐	220. Dave Concepcion	.10	.07	.08
☐	240. Dave Kingman	.25	.15	.20
☐	245. Phil Niekro	.10	.07	.08
☐	255. Dusty Baker	.10	.07	.08
☐	280. Gaylord Perry	.30	.20	.25
☐	290. Steve Garvey	.50	.30	.40
☐	300. Ron Guidry	.25	.15	.20
☐	321. Keith Hernandez	.15	.10	.12
☐	327. Ray Fosse	.05	.03	.04
☐	715. Sal Bando	.05	.03	.04
☐	720. Carl Yastrzemski	1.00	.65	.85
☐	726. Steve Yeager	.05	.03	.04

TOPPS — 1981 (2½" x 3½", Numbered 1-726. Color)

☐	Complete Set	23.00	15.00	19.00
☐	1. Brett/Buckner	.20	.13	.17
☐	13. Joe Charboneau	.15	.10	.12
☐	30. Jack Clark	.05	.03	.04
☐	50. Dave Lopes	.05	.03	.04
☐	75. Reggie Smith	.10	.07	.08
☐	80. Rusty Staub	.10	.07	.08
☐	100. Rod Carew	.50	.30	.40
☐	110. Carl Yastrzemski	.75	.50	.60
☐	116. Joe Simpson	.05	.03	.04
☐	132. Tommy Boggs	.05	.03	.04
☐	145. Mickey Rivers	.10	.07	.08
☐	580. Don Baylor	.10	.07	.08
☐	590. Bruce Sutter	.15	.07	.08
☐	605. Don Sutton	.25	.15	.20
☐	625. Bill Buckner	.10	.07	.08
☐	635. Bobby Bonds	.15	.10	.12
☐	640. Dave Parker	.40	.25	.35
☐	654. Ray Burris	.05	.03	.04
☐	700. George Brett	.75	.50	.60
☐	726. Rick Monday	.05	.03	.04

TOPPS — 1982 (2½" x 3½", Numbered 1-792. Color)

NOTE: The 1982 O-Pee-Chee set which includes 393 cards are identical to the Topps cards with asterisks.

☐	Complete Set	18.50	12.00	12.25
☐	1. '81 Highlight: Carlton	.25	.15	.20
☐	9. Ron Guidry*	.15	.10	.12
☐	44. Britt Burns	.15	.10	.12
☐	70. Tim Raines*	.35	.25	.30
☐	179. Steve Garvey*	.50	.30	.40
☐	337. N.L. All-Star: Rose*	.50	.30	.40
☐	410. Ron Cey*	.03	.02	.02
☐	460. Jack Clark	.40	.28	.34
☐	610. Rickey Henderson*	.30	.20	.25
☐	651. Super Action: Yastrzemski*	.50	.80	.60
☐	792. Frank Tanana*	.03	.02	.02

BASKETS

Hamper, natural finish, hinged lid, closely woven reed construction, c. 1910 . . . . **$75.00-$125.00**

The art of basketry is indeed a reflection of America's cultural past. Long before this nation's first colonization, the American Indian had achieved artistic excellence as a basket weaver. Indian baskets are said to be the world's finest. Each basket was woven for a specific purpose and with the utmost care. These baskets were not only used to hold food and water and for ceremonial purposes, but some were also used for cooking. Their works are unique because they used only materials from nature — pine needles, straw, leaves, willow, porcupine quills, vines, reeds and grass. Dyes were made from bark, roots or berries. Their distinctive designs have made them sought-after by most basket enthusiasts.

There are several types of basket construction. Wickerwork, the most common and widely used technique, is nothing more than an over and under pattern. Twining is similar except that two strands are twisted as they are woven over and under producing a finer weave. Plaiting gives a checkerboard effect and can be either a tight weave or left with some open spaces. Twillwork is much the same except that a diagonal effect is achieved by changing the number of strands over which the weaver passes. Coiling is the most desirable weave to the collector. This technique has been carefully refined since its conception around 7000 BC. Fibers are wrapped around and stitched together to form the basket's shape. Most of these pieces were either used for ceremonial purposes or for holding liquids, since the containers made in this fashion were tightly woven and leakproof.

BASKETS / 155

It is most difficult to find old baskets in mint condition, since they were made to be used. These may be more valuable than new ones, but the novice collector may wish to begin by purchasing new ones that have been crafted by traditional techniques and are historically authentic. An interesting collection can be assembled over a short period of time and with relatively few dollars invested.

	Current Price Range	Prior Year Average
☐ **American Indian,** 10″ Dia.	180.00 220.00	155.00
☐ **Apache burden basket,** 2½″ x 2½″	25.00 35.00	22.50
☐ **Apache burden basket,** rawhide bottom, plain, 11½″ H.	300.00 375.00	300.00
☐ **Apache burden basket,** geometric pattern, tin cones hanging from leather straps, 6½″ x 5″	60.00 75.00	62.00
☐ **Apache burden basket,** negative pattern, tin cones hanging from leather straps, 12″ x 10½″	225.00 300.00	238.00
☐ **Apache coiled storage basket,** round body, dark brown with geometric motifs, 12½″ H.	725.00 925.00	800.00
☐ **Apache coiled storage basket,** round body, flaring rim, dark brown with animals and human figures, 16¾″ H.	725.00 925.00	800.00
☐ **Apache coiled basket,** flat base, dark brown with snowflake motif, 8⅜″ Dia.	325.00 425.00	350.00
☐ **Apache grain barrel basket,** geometric design with human figures, 10″ x 11″	375.00 475.00	400.00
☐ **Apache plaque basket,** geometric design, 16″ x 5″	550.00 650.00	575.00
☐ **Apache miniature basket,** star design, 5½″ x 1″	145.00 210.00	160.00
☐ **Apache tray,** 10½″ Dia., c. 1890's	110.00 160.00	125.00
☐ **Apache wedding basket,** 13″ Dia., c. 1880	30.00 45.00	32.00
☐ **Bannock berry basket,** 8″ x 8½″	55.00 80.00	58.00
☐ **California,** tightly woven, light brown, diamond motif, 5¾″ Dia.	150.00 175.00	138.00
☐ **Caushatta effigy baskets,** pine cones and needles: Crawfish, 9″ x 6½″	25.00 35.00	22.50
☐ Crab, 6″ x 5″	25.00 35.00	22.50
☐ Alligator, 9″ x 2¾″	25.00 35.00	22.50
☐ Turtle, 6½″ x 3″	25.00 35.00	22.50
☐ **Cheese basket,** splint	125.00 175.00	100.00
☐ **Cheese shaker,** round, 12″ Dia.	250.00 275.00	225.00
☐ **Chehalis basket,** geometric and cross design, 4¼″ x 6¼″	200.00 250.00	160.00
☐ **Chemehuevi basket,** two concentric geometric bands, 11½″ x 2″	350.00 450.00	375.00
☐ **Clothes basket,** round with two handles	75.00 95.00	62.00
☐ **Cowlitz lidded basket,** 3″ x 4¼″	80.00 130.00	100.00
☐ **Havasupi coiled basket,** triangle design, 11¾″ Dia.	175.00 200.00	150.00
☐ **Hopi coiled basket,** rectangular body in brown, orange and yellow raincloud and thunder motif, 5⅝″ Dia.	110.00 160.00	125.00
☐ **Hopi corn sifter basket,** wicker with hoop around top, spiral design	80.00 110.00	82.00
☐ **Hopi coiled bowl basket,** floral design, 9¼″ Dia.	90.00 140.00	110.00
☐ **Hopi coiled plaque,** 14½″ Dia., c. 1930	110.00 160.00	125.00
☐ **Hopi tray,** mythological motif, 11″ Dia.	80.00 130.00	100.00

156 / BASKETS

Item	Current Price Range		Prior Year Average
☐ **Japanese,** tightly woven in brown and tan, circular, 7½" Dia.	55.00	80.00	62.00
☐ **Karok basket,** oval, bottom inverted, 10" x 7"	110.00	160.00	125.00
☐ **Klamath tray,** 14" Dia., c. 1900	210.00	260.00	225.00
☐ **Lilooet basket,** 12½" x 16"	160.00	210.00	175.00
☐ **Maidu basket tray,** 8½" Dia.	60.00	80.00	65.00
☐ **Makah basket,** zigzag designs, 7" Dia.	55.00	80.00	62.00
☐ **Mandan basket,** wood splint, circular	180.00	230.00	200.00
☐ **Mission basket tray,** 12" Dia.	330.00	410.00	360.00
☐ **Miwok basket,** 7" Dia., c. 1900	230.00	280.00	250.00
☐ **Modoc basketcap,** diamond design, 6" Dia.	120.00	140.00	125.00
☐ **Navajo wedding basket,** 10" Dia.	130.00	180.00	150.00
☐ **Nootka whaler's hat,** 10½" x 10½"	230.00	280.00	250.00
☐ **Paiute coiled basket,** exterior is beaded, 5" Dia.	180.00	210.00	182.00
☐ **Paiute lidded basket,** 10" H., c. 1900	90.00	125.00	100.00
☐ **Paiute water jar,** horse-hair handles, 5½" x 7½"	80.00	110.00	82.00
☐ **Panamint basket,** reverse diamond design, 10½" x 4"	310.00	410.00	350.00
☐ **Papago basket,** geometric design, 13" Dia.	80.00	110.00	82.00
☐ **Papago coiled basket,** body woven in dark brown with bands of swastikas, 11⅝" Dia.	230.00	280.00	250.00
☐ **Papago plaque,** concentric square design, 15" Dia.	130.00	180.00	150.00
☐ **Papago waste paper basket,** men and dogs motif, 10" Dia.	100.00	130.00	110.00
☐ **Pima basket bowl,** 16" Dia.	260.00	335.00	295.00
☐ **Pima coiled basket,** flat base, flaring body, dark brown with pattern of human figures, 11¼" Dia.	260.00	360.00	300.00
☐ **Pima coiled basket,** shallow, dark brown with crosses in the field, 9¼" Dia.	110.00	160.00	125.00
☐ **Pima grain barrel,** geometric design, 11" Dia.	430.00	530.00	475.00
☐ **Pima plaque,** 11" Dia.	180.00	230.00	200.00
☐ **Pomo basket,** decorated with feathers, 12" Dia.	180.00	230.00	200.00
☐ **Sewing basket,** wicker	55.00	80.00	58.00
☐ **Skokomish berry basket,** 7" x 8"	110.00	135.00	112.50
☐ **Southwest coiled storage basket,** flat base, dark brown with arrow motifs, 27" H.	730.00	830.00	775.00
☐ **Splint collecting basket,** tightly woven, 8" x 9"	55.00	85.00	62.00
☐ **Splint cradle,** hooded, c. early 19th century, 19" x 8"	100.00	130.00	110.00
☐ **Splint hickory basket,** open handles	55.00	80.00	58.00
☐ **Splint,** oval, with wooden handles	145.00	195.00	150.00
☐ **Splint,** back pack	65.00	165.00	90.00
☐ **Split,** oak buttocks	55.00	80.00	58.00
☐ **Split,** oak buttocks, large	80.00	160.00	120.00
☐ **Tlingit basket,** geometric design, 6" Dia.	330.00	380.00	350.00
☐ **Tlingit basket,** 5" Dia., c. 1880	330.00	380.00	350.00
☐ **Tlingit lidded basket,** 4½" x 6½"	430.00	510.00	460.00
☐ **Tlingit twined spruce root basket,** cylindrical body, pale yellow bands with orange zigzag decoration, 5" Dia.	360.00	460.00	400.00
☐ **Tulare basket,** step pattern, squaw stitch, 7½" Dia.	130.00	210.00	162.00
☐ **Tulare basket,** rattlesnake designs	110.00	135.00	112.50

	Current Price Range		Prior Year Average
☐ **Tulare coiled basket,** flat base, rounded sides, rattlesnake bands in black and reddish brown, 14½" Dia.	1250.00	1350.00	1150.00
☐ **Washo basket,** tightly woven, band design, 7" Dia.	85.00	115.00	80.00
☐ **Washo basket,** geometric design, 7"	65.00	95.00	75.00
☐ **Washo coiled trinket basket,** red, blue, black and green on white ground, 4¼" Dia.	110.00	160.00	125.00
☐ **Yokut coiled circular tray,** brown with rattlesnake band, 18¼" Dia.	425.00	525.00	450.00

BEER CANS

Left to Right: **Tally Ho Beer,** City Brewing Corp., New York City, NY **$1000.00+;** **Utica Club Beer,** West End Brewing, Utica, NY **$100.00-$125.00; Golden Gate Beer,** Maier Brewing Co., Los Angeles, CA **$65.00-$85.00; Wisconsin Gold Label,** Jos. Huber Brewing, Monroe, WI. . . . . **$5.00-$8.00**

  The world's first beer can was a flat-top design made by the American Can Company of Greenwich, Connecticut. It was used by the Krueger Brewing Company of New Jersey, in 1935. The variations in beer can design since that time have been tremendous due to the competition between breweries. Cans have been produced in every size from 4 oz. to one gallon. Shapes are generally either flat-top or cone-top. Pull tabs have added another subcategory for the flat-top collectors. Label designs have commemorated historical and sporting events, famous people, anniversaries of the individual breweries, etc. The list is nearly endless.

  Most advanced collectors and dealers consider the market to be undervalued except extremely rare specimens. In other words, there are many bargains on the market today.

  Beer cans are an interesting and colorful collectible for the person not wishing to initially invest a great deal of money in his hobby. Most can collectors will readily bargain or swap for a desirable specimen. Unopened cans may command a premium price for some collectors. Prices given are for cans in very good to mint condition — no dents, scrapes or rust; labels, markings, and designs should be clear. Flat-top cans should be punched from the bottom.

158 / BEER CANS

7 OZ. PUNCH TOP CANS	Current Price Range		Prior Year Average
☐ Ace Hi Malt Liquor, red, white and gold	22.00	32.00	25.00
☐ Coors, yellow, black, silver and red	2.25	3.25	2.50
☐ Lucky Lager, red, gold and white	7.00	8.50	6.75
☐ National Bohemian, red, white, blue and gold	9.00	14.00	10.00
☐ Ruppert Knickerbocker, red, white, blue and gold	4.00	5.50	4.20

8 OZ. PUNCH TOP CANS

☐ Ace Hi, red, white, black and gold	20.00	28.00	21.50
☐ Buccaneer Stout Malt Liquor	85.00	135.00	102.00
☐ Bull Dog Malt Liquor	14.00	18.00	13.50
☐ Country Club Malt Liquor	5.00	7.00	5.25
☐ Grace Brothers, brown, white, silver	28.00	34.00	28.00
☐ Mickey's Malt Liquor, black and white	20.00	28.00	22.00

12 OZ. PULL TAB CANS

☐ Al Light Pilsener, aluminum, red, off-white, brown and gold	.55	1.10	.75
☐ Alpen Glen, aluminum, red, white, green and silver	1.10	1.60	1.25
☐ Andeker, gold, black and red	1.10	1.60	1.25
☐ Arrow 77, red, white, black and gold	1.60	2.35	1.80
☐ Aspen Gold, blue, white, gold and silver	1.35	2.25	1.80
☐ Ballantine Premium, aluminum, gold, silver, red and black	1.10	1.60	1.25
☐ Becker's, red, white and blue	1.10	1.60	1.25
☐ Black Label, red, white and black	1.10	1.60	1.25
☐ Brewers Best Premium Bavarian, red, white, green and copper	2.25	3.25	2.50
☐ Budweiser Lager, red, white and blue	1.10	1.60	1.25
☐ Burger Premium, red, white and gold	1.60	2.35	1.65
☐ Busch Bavarian, aluminum, red, white, blue and black	1.10	1.60	1.25
☐ Canadian Ace Draft Premium, red, white, woodgrain, black and silver	1.10	1.60	1.25
☐ Circle Light Premium, red, white and black	1.10	1.60	1.25
☐ Colt 45 Malt Liquor, "1973/74 Warriors", red, white, blue, gold and silver	2.75	3.75	3.00
☐ Corona Extra, red, white, blue and gold	.55	1.10	.75
☐ Dawson Ale, aluminum, green, white and silver	.55	1.10	.75
☐ Dixie Light, white, green and gold	.55	1.10	.75
☐ Drewerys, red, white, gold and black	1.10	1.60	1.25
☐ Dubois, red, white, black and grey	2.25	3.25	2.50
☐ Dubois Budweiser Premium, gold, white and black	3.25	4.25	3.50
☐ Duke, red, white, black and gold	1.75	2.50	1.80
☐ El Rancho Light, yellow, red, green and gold	1.75	2.50	1.80
☐ Esslinger Premium, red, white and black	.55	1.10	.65
☐ Gamecock Ale, red, white, green and black	3.25	4.25	3.50
☐ Gettleman, white, brown and tan	1.10	1.60	1.25
☐ Genesee Light Cream Ale, green, white, black and silver	1.10	1.60	1.25
☐ Geyer's Lager, red, white, yellow, black and brown	1.10	1.60	1.25
☐ Gluck Pilsener, red, white, yellow, black gold and silver	.55	1.10	.75

	Current Price Range		Prior Year Average
☐ Golden Brew Premium, blue, white and gold	.55	1.10	.75
☐ Grand Union Premium, red, white, orange and blue	.55	1.10	.75
☐ Heibrau Premium, blue, white, black, green and gold	1.10	1.60	1.25
☐ Hi-En Brau, brown, white, gold, green and silver .	1.75	2.50	1.80
☐ Holihan's Pilsener, red, white, black and gold ...	1.10	1.75	1.25
☐ Hop'N Gator, white, brown, black and yellow	.55	1.10	1.25
☐ Hudepohl "14K", red, white, black and gold	1.10	1.75	1.25
☐ Imperial, red, white, gold and yellow	1.75	2.50	1.80
☐ Iron City, red, white, black and gray, 1960 World Series Pittsburgh	1.10	1.75	1.25
☐ Iron City, red, white, black and gray, 1971 World Series Pittsburgh	1.10	1.75	1.25
☐ Iron City, red, white, black and gray, Stanley Cup Champions Pittsburgh	1.10	1.75	1.25
☐ Iron City, red, white, black and gray, Baseball World Champions Pittsburgh	1.10	1.75	1.25
☐ Iron City, red, white, black and gray, Super Bowl Winners Pittsburgh	1.10	1.75	1.25
☐ Iron City, red, white, black and gray, NBA Champions Pittsburgh	1.10	1.75	1.25
☐ Iron City, red, white black and gray, Steelers	1.10	1.75	1.25
☐ Kingsbury Light, white, red and blue	1.10	1.75	1.25
☐ Koehler Lager, red, white and silver	.55	1.10	.75
☐ Light, white, blue, red and gold	.55	1.10	.75
☐ Lite, blue, white and gold	1.10	1.75	1.25
☐ Lucky Bock, white, gold and green	2.25	3.25	2.50
☐ Mein, multicolored	1.10	1.75	1.25
☐ Mickey's Malt Liquor, white, orange, green and silver	.55	1.10	.75
☐ Miller Ale, red, white, green and gold	.55	1.10	.75
☐ Milwaukee's Best, orange, brown and white	1.10	1.75	1.25
☐ Muhlheim Draft, red, white, black and gold	1.75	2.50	1.80
☐ Mustang, red, white, gold and black	2.25	3.25	2.50
☐ Narragansett Lager, red, white, gold and green ..	1.10	1.75	1.25
☐ National Bohemian Lager, aluminum, red, white, gold and silver	1.10	1.75	1.25
☐ National Bohemian Light, multicolored	5.50	7.50	6.00
☐ Oconto Premium, red, white, blue and gold	1.10	1.75	1.25
☐ Oertels '92, red and white	1.10	1.75	1.25
☐ Old Bohemian Light, red, white and gold	1.10	1.75	1.25
☐ Old Dutch, red, white and silver	1.75	2.50	1.80
☐ Old Dutch, red, white and gold	1.75	2.50	1.80
☐ Old German Premium Lager, red, white and blue .	1.10	1.75	1.25
☐ Old Heidel Brau Lager, red, white and blue	.55	1.10	.75
☐ Olde Frothingslosh, orange, white, black and gray	1.10	1.75	1.25
☐ Ortlieb's, red, white, black and silver	1.10	1.75	1.25
☐ Ortlieb's Draught, red, white and blue	1.75	2.50	1.80
☐ Pabst Bock, red, white, blue and silver	1.10	1.75	1.25
☐ Pearl Premium Light, multicolored	1.10	1.75	1.25
☐ Pfeiffer Premium, red, white, black and gold	1.10	1.75	1.25
☐ Pickett's Premium, red, white and blue	.55	1.10	.65
☐ Piels Light Lager, aluminum, red, white and silver	1.10	1.75	1.25
☐ Primo, blue, white, gold and black	.55	1.10	.65

160 / BEER CANS

	Current Price Range		Prior Year Average
☐ Prizer Extra Dry Premium, red, white, silver and brown	1.10	1.75	1.25
☐ Rahr's All Star, red, white and silver	2.75	3.75	2.95
☐ Raineir Light, red, white and gold	1.10	1.75	1.25
☐ Raineir Light, aluminum, red, white, gold, and silver	1.10	1.75	1.25
☐ Schaefer Draft, red, white and silver	.55	1.10	.75
☐ Schell's, black, orange and white	1.75	2.50	1.80
☐ Schlitz, aluminum, silver, white, blue and brown	.55	1.10	.75
☐ Schlitz Stout, aluminum, blue, white, black and silver	.55	1.10	.75
☐ Schmidt Draft, multicolored, black bear over strip mine	1.75	2.50	1.80
☐ Schmidt Draft, multicolored, collie with sheep	1.75	2.50	1.80
☐ Schmidt Draft, multicolored, elk	1.75	2.50	1.80
☐ Schmidt Draft, red, white, yellow and black	1.10	1.75	1.25
☐ Schmidt Light, red, white, black and gold	1.10	1.75	1.25
☐ Seven-Eleven Premium, copper, red, white, silver and black	1.10	1.75	1.25
☐ Silver Peak, blue, silver and white	1.50	2.25	1.42
☐ Spearman Ale, red, white and green	2.75	3.75	3.00
☐ Static Fair Premium, blue and silver	8.00	11.00	8.50
☐ Stoney's Pilsener, red, white, silver and gold	.55	1.10	.65
☐ Swinger Malt Liquor, red, white, blue and silver	3.25	4.25	3.50
☐ Tavern Pale Dry, red, gold, blue, silver and white	1.10	1.75	1.25
☐ Tudor Ale, red, white, gold and green	1.10	1.75	1.25
☐ Utica Club Cream Ale, aluminum, red, white, green and gold	.55	1.10	.65
☐ Velvet Glow Pale Dry, red, white and gold	1.10	1.75	1.25
☐ Walter's Light, red, white and black	1.10	1.75	1.25

12 OZ. PUNCH-TOP CANS

☐ ABC, red, white and blue	4.50	6.00	4.60
☐ ABC, red, white and silver	5.50	7.50	6.00
☐ Ace Pilsner, white, blue and gold	5.50	7.50	6.00
☐ Acme, red, silver and black	4.50	6.00	4.60
☐ Adler Brew, cream, gold, red and green	2.75	3.75	3.00
☐ All American, red, white, blue and silver	5.50	7.50	6.00
☐ Arrow 77, red, white, silver and black	2.75	3.75	3.00
☐ Atlantic, multicolored	6.50	8.50	7.00
☐ Augustines, red, white, blue and gold	2.75	3.75	3.00
☐ Ballantine's Ale, green, gold and black	2.75	3.75	3.00
☐ Ballantine's Light Lager Beer, copper, white and brown	2.75	3.75	3.00
☐ Banner Extra Dry, red, white and blue	3.25	4.25	3.50
☐ Best Premium, red, white, copper and brown	3.50	4.50	3.75
☐ Big State, brown, red and white	6.00	8.00	6.50
☐ Blatz Bock, tan, white, brown and gold	3.50	4.25	3.50
☐ Blatz Pilsner, red, white, black and gold	2.75	3.75	3.00
☐ Blue 'N Gold, blue, white and gold	4.75	6.50	5.25
☐ Brau Haus Premium Lager, multicolored	5.50	7.50	6.00
☐ Brew 52 Light Lager, red, white and black	5.50	7.50	6.00
☐ Brew 102 Pale Dry, red, white and yellow	4.50	6.00	4.80
☐ Budweiser Bock, red, gold, white and green	6.50	8.50	7.00
☐ Budweiser Lager, red, white and blue	3.25	4.25	6.50

BEER CANS / 161

	Current Price Range		Prior Year Average
☐ **Bull Dog,** red, white and green	4.25	5.75	4.80
☐ **Bull Dog Ale,** red, white and green	3.25	4.25	3.50
☐ **Bullfrog,** silver, white and green	5.50	7.50	6.00
☐ **Busch Lager,** red, white, green and gold	5.50	7.50	6.00
☐ **Busch Bavarian,** blue, white, green, black and brown	2.25	3.25	3.50
☐ **Canadian Ace Bock,** white, black, silver and woodgrain	5.50	7.50	6.00
☐ **Chief Oshkosh,** multicolored	2.75	3.75	3.00
☐ **Cold Brau,** red, white, blue and silver	3.25	4.25	3.50
☐ **Corona,** gold, white, red, black and yellow	3.25	4.25	3.50
☐ **Crystal Rock Pilsener,** blue, white and gold	3.75	4.75	4.00
☐ **Drewerys Extra Dry,** red, silver and black	4.75	6.50	5.25
☐ **Drewerys Old Stock Ale,** white, black and silver .	3.75	4.75	4.00
☐ **Dutch Lunch,** black, silver and gray	5.50	7.50	6.00
☐ **Eastside,** red, white, blue and gold	4.25	6.00	4.80
☐ **Edelweiss Bock,** brown, red, gold, white and yellow	6.00	8.00	6.50
☐ **Edelweiss Light,** red, white, black and tan	3.25	4.25	3.50
☐ **English Lad,** multicolored	6.50	8.50	7.00
☐ **Erin Brew,** gold, red, white and green	4.50	6.00	4.80
☐ **Falls City,** red, white, black and gold	3.75	4.75	4.00
☐ **Fehr's,** red, white, black and gold	3.75	4.75	4.00
☐ **Fisher Premium,** red, white, blue and gold	2.75	3.75	3.00
☐ **Fox Brew,** blue, white, green, yellow and purple .	3.75	4.75	4.00
☐ **Fox Deluxe,** red, white, black and gold	5.50	7.50	6.00
☐ **Fox Head 400,** gold, brown, red and tan	4.00	5.00	4.00
☐ **Fox Head Lager,** red, black, gold, tan and yellow	4.50	6.00	4.80
☐ **Fox Head Malt Liquor,** red, yellow, white, black and gold	5.00	6.50	5.25
☐ **Friars Ale,** brown, white and yellow	5.00	6.50	5.25
☐ **Pearl Lager,** multicolored	2.75	3.75	3.00
☐ **Peels Light Lager,** aluminum, red, white and silver	2.75	3.75	3.00
☐ **Prager,** red, white, black and gold	4.75	6.50	5.25
☐ **Prior Lager,** red, white, green and black	4.50	6.00	4.80
☐ **Rahr's,** red, white and silver	3.75	4.75	4.00
☐ **Raineir,** gold, red, silver, white and purple	3.75	4.75	4.00
☐ **Raineir Old Stock Ale,** gold, orange, black, green and white	3.75	4.75	4.00
☐ **Regal Pale,** red, white, blue and gold	2.75	3.75	3.00
☐ **Reserve,** blue, white, gold and black	3.25	4.25	3.50
☐ **Rheingold,** red, yellow, blue, green and woodgrain	3.25	4.25	3.50
☐ **Ruppert,** purple, white and woodgrain	3.75	4.75	4.00
☐ **Salzburg Eastern,** red, white and gray	3.25	4.25	3.50
☐ **Schaefer Lager,** red, black, gold and light woodgrain	3.75	4.75	4.00
☐ **Sheridan Premium,** red, white and gold	2.75	3.75	3.00
☐ **Southern Select,** gold, white and red	6.00	8.00	6.50
☐ **Special Brew,** red, silver and black	5.50	7.50	6.00
☐ **Star Model,** red, white, blue and silver	4.50	6.00	4.80
☐ **Sterling Ale,** green, red, brown, cream and silver .	6.50	8.50	7.00
☐ **Storz Gold Crest,** red, white, brown, gold and silver	4.50	6.00	4.80
☐ **Tahoe,** blue, green, yellow, white and red	6.50	8.50	7.00

162 / BEER CANS

	Current Price Range		Prior Year Average
☐ Tavern Pale, red, tan and gold	3.75	4.75	4.00
☐ Tivoli, red, white, black, gold and silver	3.75	4.75	4.00
☐ Tudor Ale, green, white and gold	3.25	4.25	3.50
☐ Tudor Bock, red, white, gold and green	5.75	7.75	6.50
☐ Tudor Premium, red, white and blue	3.25	4.25	3.50
☐ Utica Club Pale Ale, red, white, yellow and gold .	3.75	4.75	4.00
☐ Valley Forge, red, white and blue	3.75	4.75	4.00
☐ Viking, white, gold and red	6.50	8.50	7.00
☐ Walter's Bock, red, white, brown and green	3.75	4.75	4.00
☐ Walter's Pilsener, red, white, black and gold	3.75	4.75	4.00
☐ Western Gold Lager, purple, silver and white	4.50	6.00	4.80
☐ Weidemann Fine, red, white, black and gold	2.75	3.75	3.00
☐ Windsor Premium, blue, white and silver	3.25	4.25	3.50
☐ Wisconsin Gold Label, gold, white and silver	3.25	4.25	3.50
☐ Yusay Pilsen, red, white and blue	3.75	4.75	4.00

15 OZ. AND 16 OZ. CANS

☐ ABC Premium, pull-tab	1.00	1.10	.82
☐ Altes, pull-tab	1.10	2.75	1.75
☐ A-1 Pilsner, punch-top	38.00	52.00	42.00
☐ Ballantine, "125 Anniversary", punch top	20.00	28.00	21.00
☐ Blatz, pull-tab	1.00	1.10	.82
☐ Burgie, pull-tab	1.75	2.25	1.75
☐ Calgary Malt Liquor, pull-tab	48.00	62.00	52.00
☐ Cascade, pull-tab	4.50	6.50	5.00
☐ Falstaff, "Half-Quart", pull-tab	1.75	2.50	1.80
☐ Gablinger's, pull-tab	4.50	6.00	4.80
☐ Home, punch-top	14.00	18.00	16.00
☐ Jax, punch-top	14.00	18.00	16.00
☐ Jax, pull-tab	8.00	11.00	8.50
☐ King Snedley's	20.00	28.00	21.50
☐ Miller, pull-tab	1.00	1.75	1.25
☐ Miller, "Half-Quart, 16 OZ."	8.00	11.00	9.00
☐ Mule Malt Liquor	8.50	13.00	10.00
☐ Old Export, pull-tab	2.25	4.25	3.00
☐ Old Vienna, punch-top	40.00	52.00	44.00
☐ Olympia	.50	.55	.42
☐ Rainier	1.00	1.10	.82
☐ Ranier Malt Liquor	130.00	145.00	128.00
☐ Schaeffer, pull-tab	.55	1.00	.75
☐ Schmidt Draft, pull-tab	3.75	5.50	4.25
☐ Soul Mellow Yellow, pull-tab	160.00	185.00	162.00

STANDARD CONE-TOP CANS

☐ ABC, blue, gold, white and red	24.00	28.00	24.50
☐ Aero Club Pale Select Beer, gold, blue, white and red	28.00	34.00	30.00
☐ Altes Lager Beer, green, gold, black and red	32.00	38.00	32.50
☐ Apache Export Ale, copper, white and black	28.00	32.00	27.50
☐ Atlantis Ale, red, gold, white and black	30.00	34.00	29.50
☐ Augustines Beer, red, white, yellow, gold and blue	22.00	28.00	22.50
☐ Barbarossa, multicolored	28.00	32.00	27.50
☐ Berghoff 1887, black, orange, yellow and white ..	22.00	28.00	22.50
☐ Beverwyck Beer, green, white and gold	28.00	32.00	27.50

BEER CANS / 163

	Current Price Range		Prior Year Average
☐ **Blackhawk Topping Beer,** yellow, red, black and white	24.00	28.00	23.00
☐ **Blatz Ale,** yellow, brown, white and black	24.00	28.00	23.00
☐ **Blatz Milwaukee Beer,** blue and white	28.00	34.00	29.00
☐ **Bruck's Jubilee Beer,** blue, gray and red	24.00	30.00	24.50
☐ **Bubs Beer,** white, red, gold and black	22.00	28.00	22.50
☐ **Buckeye Beer,** multicolored	22.00	28.00	22.50
☐ **Canadian Ace Ale,** white, silver, red, black and woodgrain	22.00	28.00	22.50
☐ **Carling Red Cap Ale,** green, black and cream	24.00	30.00	24.50
☐ **Century Lager Beer,** red, white, blue, gray and black	30.00	34.00	29.50
☐ **Champagne Velvet,** red, white, cream, copper and red	18.00	24.00	19.50
☐ **Clyde Cream Ale,** cream, red and black	27.00	32.00	27.50
☐ **Copper Club Pilsner Beer,** green, white and copper	24.00	29.00	24.00
☐ **Cremo Beer,** blue, white, gold and black	27.00	32.00	27.50
☐ **Dawson's Master Ale,** yellow, orange, black and red	27.00	32.00	27.50
☐ **Diehl,** gold, black and white	18.00	22.00	17.50
☐ **Dubois Export,** white, red, gold and black	28.00	32.00	27.00
☐ **Duquesne Pilsner Beer,** white, gold, red and blue	24.00	30.00	24.00
☐ **Eastside,** red, white, blue and gold	18.00	22.00	17.50
☐ **Ebling,** silver, red and black	18.00	24.00	20.00
☐ **Ebling Ale,** silver, green and black	18.00	24.00	20.00
☐ **Edelweiss Light Beer,** red, white, black and gold	22.00	27.00	22.50
☐ **Falls,** red, white, yellow, gold and black	18.00	24.00	20.00
☐ **Falstaff,** brown, white, green yellow, black and red	12.00	15.00	11.50
☐ **Fehr's,** white, red, black and silver	18.00	22.00	17.50
☐ **Fort Pitt Pale Ale,** green, red, black, white and gold	27.00	32.00	27.50
☐ **Fort Pitt Special Beer,** red, white, gold and black	27.00	32.00	27.50
☐ **Fort Schuyler,** red, white, gold and black	18.00	22.00	17.50
☐ **Fountain Brew Beer,** green, yellow, white and black	24.00	28.00	24.00
☐ **Fox Deluxe Beer,** gold, white, brown and red	22.00	28.00	22.50
☐ **Free State,** red, white, blue and gold	17.00	22.00	17.50
☐ **Gam,** white, gold and black	28.00	32.00	27.50
☐ **Gettelman,** gold, brown, white and red	24.00	28.00	24.00
☐ **Gipps Amberlin Beer,** cream, red, white, green, gold and black	27.00	32.00	27.50
☐ **Glueck's,** red, white, silver and brown	18.00	22.00	17.50
☐ **Gold Medal Beer,** copper, brown and white	24.00	28.00	24.50
☐ **Gold Crest,** red, white, blue and gold	27.00	32.00	27.50
☐ **Gotham Fine Beer,** red, white, gray and gold	30.00	34.00	30.00
☐ **Grain Belt Beer,** red, black, white and gold	20.00	24.00	20.00
☐ **Gus' Premium Topper Beer,** black, red and white	28.00	32.00	27.50
☐ **Haas,** red, white, black and gold	28.00	32.00	27.50
☐ **Hanley's Extra Pale,** gold, white and purple	28.00	32.00	27.50
☐ **Hauenstein,** red, white, black, gray and gold	18.00	22.00	17.50
☐ **Heidel-Brau,** orange, green, white and gold	18.00	22.00	17.50
☐ **Hoosier Beer,** red, white, black and gold	28.00	32.00	27.50
☐ **Horton Old Stock Ale,** brown, black, gold and cream	28.00	32.00	27.50

164 / BEER CANS

	Current Price Range		Prior Year Average
☐ **Hudepohl,** red, white, blue and silver	18.00	22.00	17.50
☐ **Iron City Beer,** red, white and black	28.00	32.00	27.50
☐ **Iroquois,** multicolored	28.00	32.00	27.50
☐ **Jax Pilsner Style Beer,** blue, orange and white ..	28.00	32.00	27.50
☐ **Kato,** gold, black, red, yellow and white	18.00	24.00	20.00
☐ **Kato Lager Beer,** silver, black and red	22.00	28.00	22.50
☐ **Kessler,** red, white, blue, silver and black	18.00	24.00	20.00
☐ **Koehler Select,** blue, gold, black and white	28.00	32.00	27.50
☐ **Koehler's Beer,** red, white, black and gold	28.00	32.00	27.50
☐ **Koenig Brau Premium Beer,** red, white, gold and black	24.00	30.00	24.00
☐ **Kuebler Pale Beer,** red, black, white and silver ...	28.00	32.00	27.50
☐ **Leinemkugel's,** red, white, black and silver	18.00	22.00	17.50
☐ **Leisy's Light Beer,** blue, cream and gold	28.00	32.00	27.50
☐ **Life Staff Pale Lager Beer,** red, black and gold ..	28.00	32.00	27.50
☐ **Maier,** red, white and black	18.00	22.00	17.50
☐ **Maier Gold Label Ale,** green, gold and silver	28.00	32.00	27.00
☐ **Maier Export Beer,** red, blue and silver	28.00	32.00	27.00
☐ **Milwaukee Club Beer,** brown and cream	24.00	30.00	24.00
☐ **Milwaukee Club Beer,** gold, silver, black and yellow	24.00	30.00	24.00
☐ **Monarch Beer,** red, white, black and gold	28.00	32.00	27.00
☐ **Monterey Beer,** blue and white	30.00	34.00	30.00
☐ **Muehlebach's,** green, white, red and gold	20.00	24.00	20.00
☐ **Namar Premium Beer,** red, white, blue and gold .	27.00	32.00	27.00
☐ **National Bohemian Pale Beer,** black, yellow, red and white	24.00	30.00	24.00
☐ **Neuweiler's,** gray, tan, brown, black and silver ..	11.00	14.00	11.50
☐ **Neuweiler's Cream Ale,** blue, orange, white, gold and black	24.00	30.00	24.50
☐ **Northern Beer,** multicolored	22.00	28.00	22.50
☐ **Northern Beer,** brown, green and yellow	22.00	28.00	22.50
☐ **Oertels '92,** black, silver, red and blue	20.00	24.00	20.00
☐ **Old Dutch Brand,** black, brown, red, gold and white	28.00	32.00	27.00
☐ **Old Export,** red, white and purple	24.00	30.00	24.00
☐ **Old German,** red, white, blue and yellow	11.00	15.00	12.00
☐ **Old Shay,** cream, red, black and gold	28.00	32.00	27.50
☐ **Old Style Lager,** multicolored	18.00	22.00	17.50
☐ **Old Topper Golden Ale,** green, yellow, white and black	24.00	30.00	24.00
☐ **Old Topper Snappy Ale,** black, white, brown and yellow	22.00	28.00	22.50
☐ **Old Timer Premium Beer,** red, white, gold and black	28.00	32.00	27.00
☐ **Old Vienna,** red, white, black and gold	30.00	34.00	30.00
☐ **Olde Virginia,** red, white, blue, green and gold ...	18.00	22.00	17.50
☐ **Pacific Lager Beer,** blue, green, white and black .	30.00	35.00	30.00
☐ **Peel's Special Light Beer,** red, gold, black and cream	28.00	32.00	27.00
☐ **Peerless Beer,** red, white and gold	24.00	30.00	24.00
☐ **Peerless Extra Premium,** red, white, green and gold	22.00	28.00	22.50
☐ **Prima,** red, white, blue and gold	28.00	32.00	27.50
☐ **Rainier Old Stock Ale,** red, white, green and black	24.00	30.00	24.00
☐ **Rainier Special Export,** red, white and black	24.00	30.00	24.00

BEER CANS / 165

	Current Price Range		Prior Year Average
☐ **Rainier Club Extra Dry,** red, white, black and silver	24.00	30.00	24.00
☐ **Red Ribbon Beer,** red, white, silver and black	30.00	34.00	30.00
☐ **Red Top Ale,** red, black, gold and yellow	28.00	32.00	27.50
☐ **Red Top Extra Pale Beer,** red, white, gold and black	28.00	32.00	27.50
☐ **Regal,** brown, gold, red and white	22.00	28.00	22.50
☐ **Rhinelander,** green, white, black and gold	28.00	32.00	27.50
☐ **Rich Brau,** gold, black, red and white	28.00	32.00	27.50
☐ **Rocky Mountain,** red, white, black and silver	18.00	24.00	20.00
☐ **Royal,** red, white, black and yellow	30.00	34.00	30.00
☐ **Royal Bohemian,** red, white, blue and gold	20.00	24.00	20.00
☐ **Royal Pilsner Beer,** red, yellow and black	28.00	32.00	27.00
☐ **Schell's "Deer Brand",** red, blue, gold and cream	28.00	32.00	27.00
☐ **Schlitz,** white, brown, blue and copper	18.00	22.00	17.50
☐ **Schlitz Lager,** white, brown, cream and blue	24.00	30.00	24.00
☐ **Schmidt's,** red, white, gold and black	24.00	30.00	24.00
☐ **Schmidt's City Club,** red, white and yellow	18.00	22.00	17.50
☐ **Schmidt's First Premium,** red, white, blue, green, black and pink	18.00	22.00	17.50
☐ **Schmidt's of Philadelphia,** silver, cream, gold, red and black	32.00	38.00	32.50
☐ **Seven Eleven,** white, red, gold and black	32.00	38.00	32.50
☐ **'76 Ale,** red, black, green and cream	30.00	34.00	30.00
☐ **Sierra,** gold, yellow, white, blue and silver	18.00	22.00	17.50
☐ **Stag,** red, white, black and gold	18.00	22.00	17.50
☐ **Steinerbru,** red, gold, black and cream	32.00	38.00	32.50
☐ **Stock Ale by Croft,** red, gold and cream	30.00	34.00	30.00
☐ **Sun Valley,** blue, white and yellow	32.00	38.00	32.50
☐ **Tacoma Pale Beer,** blue, white and brown	32.00	38.00	32.50
☐ **Tavern Beer,** multicolored	28.00	32.00	27.50
☐ **Trophy,** red, white, gold and black	32.00	38.00	32.50
☐ **Tube City,** red, white, gold and black	30.00	34.00	30.00
☐ **Utica Club,** red, white and gold	30.00	34.00	30.00
☐ **Van Merritt,** green, white, red and black	32.00	38.00	32.50
☐ **V.R. Light Mellow,** red, white and black	32.00	38.00	32.50
☐ **Walter's Pilsner,** green, white, gold and black	28.00	32.00	27.50
☐ **Washington Pilsner,** red, white, blue and gold	32.00	38.00	32.50
☐ **W. Virginia Special Export Beer,** red, white, blue and gold	28.00	32.00	27.00
☐ **White Tap,** red, white, blue and gold	32.00	38.00	32.00
☐ **White Seal,** red, white, gold and black	30.00	34.00	30.00
☐ **Weidemann Bohemian,** red, white, gold and black	30.00	34.00	30.00
☐ **Wooden Shoe,** red, white and blue	30.00	34.00	30.00
☐ **Yuengling,** red, white and gold	30.00	34.00	30.00

ONE-QUART CONE-TOP CANS

☐ **Ballantine Ale,** "1840-1940 Centennial"	40.00	55.00	42.00
☐ **Blackhawk Pilsner**	70.00	85.00	72.00
☐ **Dawson Pale Ale**	38.00	55.00	42.00
☐ **Esslinger Little Man Ale**	48.00	68.00	55.00
☐ **Lion Sparkling Ale**	110.00	140.00	112.00
☐ **Old Reading**	100.00	135.00	110.00
☐ **Red Fox Ale**	65.00	90.00	72.00
☐ **Utica Club Pilsner**	50.00	65.00	52.00
☐ **White Horse**	90.00	110.00	90.00

166 / BELLS

	Current Price Range		Prior Year Average
☐ Wooden Shoe	100.00	135.00	110.00
☐ Yuengling Premium	80.00	110.00	82.00

ONE-GALLON BEER CANS

	Current Price Range		Prior Year Average
☐ Ballantine Draught Ale	65.00	90.00	72.00
☐ Ballantine Draught Beer	28.00	32.00	27.50
☐ Canadian Ace Premium	14.00	18.00	13.50
☐ Gettleman Draft Bock	90.00	110.00	90.00
☐ Grace Brothers Draft	110.00	135.00	112.00
☐ Hudepohl Draft	30.00	38.00	31.00
☐ Kegelbrau Draft	70.00	85.00	72.00
☐ Kingsbury Draft	22.00	30.00	24.00
☐ Koch's Draft	14.00	20.00	14.00
☐ Koch's Deer Run Ale	145.00	160.00	142.00
☐ National Draft	65.00	75.00	65.00
☐ Old Bohemian Light	14.00	18.00	14.50
☐ 102 Draft	110.00	145.00	118.00
☐ Pfeiffer Draught	70.00	85.00	72.00
☐ Regal Select Draft	70.00	85.00	72.00
☐ Standard Dry Ale	16.00	22.00	17.00
☐ Standard Draft	16.00	22.00	17.00
☐ Sterling Draught Ale	75.00	95.00	80.00
☐ Sterling Draught	55.00	65.00	55.00
☐ Topper Draught	14.00	20.00	15.00
☐ Walter	80.00	110.00	82.00

BELLS

Bells are known to have existed many thousands of years ago in the Far East and in South America. They were introduced in Europe over 1500 years ago.

Among the most prized bells are Swiss animal bells, valued for their beautiful tone, and porcelain bells from Austria and France, which are valued for their beauty. Most bell collectors pick up specimens merely because of personal whim — they just happen to like the appearance or tone.

Bells of all shapes, sizes and materials have been used for centuries to signal births, weddings, to summon or warn, and to record time. The inverted-tulip bell shape has been the most popular in Europe and the United States. The crotal bell is close-mouthed, much like modern jingle bells. The Oriental world prefers the gong shape which must be struck by an implement to sound. Bells are made of numerous materials including brass, iron, silver, gold, bronze, iron, wood, glass and porcelain. Glass and china bells are, for the most part, either decorative or part of the new wave edition of made-to-be-collected items.

Bells should be in good to excellent condition, with all parts present. Metal parts should not be rusted or corroded. Porcelain or other clay materials should not be cracked or chipped. The value of bells is primarily determined by age, construction material, size and the geographical location in which they were manufactured.

BELLS / 167

	Current Price Range		Prior Year Average
☐ **Alaska bell,** colored totem handle, original	42.00	58.00	48.00
☐ **Alexander's helmet bell,** no clapper, 5½" Dia.	13.00	18.00	14.00
☐ **Bayreuther bell,** hand painted porcelain, lilies of the valley	72.00	92.00	80.00
☐ **Brass bell,** stork	34.00	50.00	38.00
☐ **Brass clapper bell**	110.00	130.00	112.50
☐ **Brass dinner bell**	6.00	11.00	7.50
☐ **Brass hotel call bell,** 4" Dia.	50.00	65.00	52.00
☐ **Brass musical chime bell**	32.00	68.00	42.00
☐ **Brass school bell,** 4⅜" Dia., c. 1910	20.00	28.00	21.00
☐ **Brass bell,** wooden handle, 4"	12.00	18.00	12.50
☐ **Brass bell,** wooden handle, 6"	18.00	22.00	20.00
☐ **Brass bell,** wooden handle, 7"	28.00	38.00	30.00
☐ **Brass bell,** wooden handle, 8"	28.00	38.00	30.00
☐ **Bronze art figurine bells,** very detailed, rare	210.00	360.00	275.00
☐ **Bronze bell,** angel holder	95.00	115.00	100.00
☐ **Cast iron bell,** mechanical	130.00	160.00	138.00
☐ **Charlie Chaplin bell,** solid brass, cane and typical pose	18.00	22.00	17.50
☐ **China bell,** cobalt, 5"	48.00	62.00	52.00
☐ **China bell,** German, painted clown	68.00	82.00	72.00
☐ **Chinese brass gong bell,** 9"	45.00	60.00	48.00
☐ **Church bell,** solid brass, single tier	110.00	135.00	112.50
☐ **Church bell,** solid brass, triple tier	180.00	220.00	195.00
☐ **Church bell,** old, 1100 pounds	560.00	660.00	600.00
☐ **Church bell,** without wheel	130.00	160.00	138.00
☐ **Conestoga,** graduated on strap (4), brass	210.00	260.00	225.00
☐ **Cow bell,** iron ring with strap attachment	32.00	48.00	38.00
☐ **Cow bell,** leather collar	12.00	16.00	12.50
☐ **Cow bell,** clapper	28.00	38.00	30.00
☐ **Cow bells,** hand riveted	28.00	38.00	30.00
☐ **Crystal bell,** faceted drummer boy handle, Blair-Reubel	35.00	50.00	38.00
☐ **Cutter bells,** 4 bells, 2½" - 2¾" Dia.	45.00	60.00	48.00
☐ **Cutter-type bell,** iron strap	80.00	110.00	82.00
☐ **Damascus bell,** bronze, inlaid gold and green leaves with red berries	55.00	75.00	60.00
☐ **Dinner bell,** crystal	55.00	75.00	60.00
☐ **Dinner bell,** enamel on metal	55.00	75.00	60.00
☐ **Dinner bell,** nickel	12.00	18.00	12.50
☐ **Dinner bell,** ornate sterling silver	65.00	90.00	72.00
☐ **Dog bells,** sculptured handles, pair, 4"	80.00	110.00	87.50
☐ **Doorbell,** Abbe's patent double strike	35.00	50.00	38.00
☐ **Doorbell,** brass	55.00	75.00	60.00
☐ **Early American thumbprint bell,** design around skirt	50.00	65.00	48.00
☐ **Elephant bell,** brass	45.00	60.00	48.00
☐ **Elephant bell,** cloisonne	110.00	130.00	112.00
☐ **Fire Alarm bell**	45.00	60.00	48.00
☐ **French flint glass bell,** coordinated handle and clapper	420.00	495.00	430.00
☐ **Glass bell,** amber, glass	120.00	185.00	112.00
☐ **Glass bell,** bristol, 11½"	120.00	185.00	112.00
☐ **Glass bell,** bristol wedding bell, 14"	130.00	160.00	138.00
☐ **Glass bell,** carnival	18.00	22.00	17.50
☐ **Glass bell,** cranberry glass, clear handle	160.00	200.00	170.00

168 / BELLS

	Current Price Range		Prior Year Average
☐ **Glass bell,** clear dark green	90.00	115.00	90.00
☐ **Glass bell,** cut glass including handle	145.00	175.00	150.00
☐ **Glass bell,** nailsea bell, solid glass handle, loops and swirls in color	210.00	260.00	225.00
☐ **Venetian glass bell,** ruby red, enamel decoration	90.00	110.00	90.00
☐ **Venetian glass bell,** latticino, pink, 14"	160.00	195.00	165.00
☐ **Venetian glass bell,** goose bell	22.00	32.00	25.00
☐ **Hand bell,** brass	110.00	135.00	112.50
☐ **Hand bell,** brass with decorations	80.00	110.00	82.00
☐ **Hand bell,** brass with wooden handle	110.00	135.00	112.50
☐ **Iran bell,** bronze, lion and sun motif, bas relief	90.00	110.00	90.00
☐ **Iron bell,** cow	18.00	22.00	17.50
☐ **Iron bell,** dinner	110.00	135.00	112.50
☐ **Iron bell,** farm	230.00	280.00	250.00
☐ **Iron bell,** sleigh	55.00	75.00	60.00
☐ **Johannes Afine bell,** (Joseph Von Ende) bronze, wreath and cherub, bas relief	95.00	120.00	105.00
☐ **Lady sculptured bell,** 4"	160.00	190.00	170.00
☐ **Lennox-Imperial bell,** off-white porcelain, 18K gold, 6"	60.00	80.00	65.00
☐ **Majolica bell,** dog	40.00	55.00	42.00
☐ **Mass bell,** solid brass	80.00	110.00	82.00
☐ **Meissen bells,** decorated, antique	110.00	135.00	112.50
☐ **Meissen bells,** raised decorations	210.00	260.00	225.00
☐ **Mission bell,** min. clapper	80.00	110.00	82.00
☐ **Mission bell,** Spanish	110.00	135.00	112.50
☐ **Pewter sterling bell**	22.00	32.00	25.00
☐ **Pressed glass bell,** smokey	6.00	12.00	7.50
☐ **Quimper lady bell,** colored, 8"	75.00	95.00	80.00
☐ **Roeland Ghend,** bronze, sand cast, crusade handle	65.00	85.00	70.00
☐ **Saddle chimes,** set of 3 with pinwheel on each	145.00	175.00	150.00
☐ **School bell,** bronze, 20" iron yoke, Jones and Hitchcock, c. 1856	860.00	960.00	900.00
☐ **School bell,** metal, wooden handles, small	80.00	110.00	82.00
☐ **School bell,** metal, wooden handle, large	90.00	110.00	90.00
☐ **School bell,** 5"	50.00	65.00	52.00
☐ **School bell,** 6½"	72.00	92.00	80.00
☐ **School bell,** 8¼"	95.00	115.00	100.00
☐ **School bell,** 9½"	95.00	115.00	100.00
☐ **Sculptured bell,** lady 4"	55.00	75.00	60.00
☐ **Sculptured bell,** little boy on a coal pile, original clapper, detailed	155.00	190.00	170.00
☐ **Sculptured bell,** old woman on the green from "Canterbury Tales", detailed	110.00	160.00	125.00
☐ **Sheep bell**	55.00	75.00	60.00
☐ **Ship bell,** brass, c. 1845	210.00	260.00	225.00
☐ **Ship bell,** brass dolphin	210.00	260.00	225.00
☐ **Sleigh bells,** leather strap of 17 bells	210.00	260.00	225.00
☐ **Sleigh bells,** leather strap of 20 bells	260.00	285.00	262.00
☐ **Sleigh bells,** iron string of 25 bells	280.00	330.00	300.00
☐ **Sleigh bells,** brass string of 25 bells	230.00	280.00	250.00
☐ **Sleigh bells,** all brass, 29 bells mounted on a jointed brass strap, old	170.00	205.00	178.00
☐ **Soldier,** roman	55.00	75.00	60.00

	Current Price Range		Prior Year Average
☐ **Sterling silver bell,** woman	120.00	150.00	132.00
☐ **Swedish bell,** heavy brass, double throated, 2¾″ Dia.	20.00	26.00	20.50
☐ **Swedish bell,** heavy brass, triple throated, 3″ Dia.	22.00	32.00	25.00
☐ **Town Crier,** long with wooden handle	110.00	135.00	112.50
☐ **Trolley car,** 8″ Dia.	80.00	110.00	82.00
☐ **Turtle,** German mechanical	80.00	110.00	82.00
☐ **Waterford crystal bell**	60.00	80.00	65.00
☐ **Wedgwood,** porcelain, c. 1979	30.00	40.00	30.00

BICYCLES

Bicycle, Coaster Model by Hawthome Motorbike, 63 lbs . . . . **$70.00-$80.00**

From the earliest bicycle prototype—an unwieldy wooden two-wheeler which was operated by sitting on it straddle-legged, and propelling it with the feet touching the ground in giant strides—to some interesting streamlined 20th century types, most bicycles, tricycles and tandem cycles are collectible. The modern bicycle originated in 1818 with the invention of the Draisienne, a steerable wooden horse on wheels invented by a German baron. The first pedal-driven bike appeared in Scotland in 1839. These were followed by the velocipede, the high-wheeler and finally the safety bike, forerunner of modern bicycles.

The bicycle allowed people to propel themselves at a much faster pace than walking and with less effort — an idea still popular today. By the end of the 19th century, bicycling was very popular with adults on both sides of the ocean. Noted manufacturers of the day included names like Columbia and the Wright Brothers of Dayton, Ohio.

Bicycles were manufactured with two, three or four wheels, the most popular being the high-wheeler or "boneshaker". Despite the immense popularity of this model, most people welcomed the "safety bike" with its same-sized wheels, low seat and pedal brakes. Two-wheelers were quite expensive in those days, often costing $150.00 or more.

All bicycles built before 1900 and into the early 20th century are collectible. Most desirable are specimens that are milestones like the 1861 velocipede with front wheel pedals and the Rover of 1885, the first bicycle to resemble those of today. While safety bikes and even high-wheelers are not uncommon, tricycles and quadricycles are considered real finds. Any collectible bike should have all parts, including rubber and leather attachments, and should be in riding condition since bicycle collecting tends to be an active hobby as most collectors ride their antique bikes. The Wheelmen is a national organization of collectors and/or enthusiasts devoted to the preservation of antique bicycles.

		Current Price Range		Prior Year Average
☐ 1850,	Boneshaker	1650.00	2100.00	1750.00
☐ 1853,	Chainless	140.00	200.00	160.00
☐ 1856,	Columbia chainless	210.00	260.00	225.00
☐ 1862,	Spring fork	620.00	720.00	650.00
☐ 1865,	Eagle Hi-Wheeler with brake	3200.00	3800.00	3250.00
☐ 1866,	Buggy spoked triangle pedal hi-wheeler bicycle	580.00	680.00	600.00
☐ 1870,	Boneshaker	1100.00	1600.00	1250.00
☐ 1872,	Eagle 50 inch hi-wheeler	2100.00	2600.00	2250.00
☐ 1878,	Fifty inch hi-wheeler	1300.00	1700.00	1350.00
☐ 1885,	Adult tricycle	4600.00	5600.00	5000.00
☐ 1885,	Hi-wheeler bicycle	1100.00	1600.00	1250.00
☐ 1885,	Tandem adult tricycle	6100.00	7100.00	6500.00
☐ 1888,	Columbia, three-wheel tandem tricycle	3200.00	3800.00	3350.00
☐ 1890,	Solid tire safety	760.00	1100.00	820.00
☐ 1895,	Tandem bicycle	310.00	460.00	380.00
☐ 1896,	Two-wheeler	310.00	460.00	380.00
☐ 1898,	Fifty-six inch hi-wheeler	660.00	810.00	720.00
☐ 1900,	Chainless safety	210.00	260.00	225.00
☐ 1901,	Columbia hi-wheeler	1300.00	1800.00	1350.00
☐ 1914,	Tandem	260.00	310.00	275.00
☐ 1914,	Two-wheeler	130.00	180.00	150.00
☐ 1927,	Scooter, foot	210.00	260.00	225.00

BOOKPLATES

Bookplates, printed paper labels which identify the owner of a book, are very collectible. Bookplates are of much earlier origins than might be imagined, the first printed specimens dating from 15th century Germany, not too long after printing was invented. For the first 200 or so years of their existence, they were regarded more or less as novelties and few persons used them. They came into general use only in the 17th century, and even

Bookplate, with family crest . . . . . **$3.00-$6.00**

then they were largely restricted to use by noblemen or individuals who owned outstanding libraries. The 18th century saw bookplates in much greater favor.

The quantities of bookplates designed and printed over the years are beyond count. All are collectible, in the broad sense of the term, as there are some bookplate collectors who add any specimens to their collection regardless of age, design or rarity; however, the more discriminating collectors restrict themselves to plates of special interest, usually those with topical designs. Listed by artist first.

	Current Price Range		Prior Year Average
☐ **Eric Gill,** design for Scott Cunningham	7.00	9.00	7.00
☐ **Robert Bell,** design for Fanny Nicholson, c. 1900	7.00	9.00	7.00
☐ **Rockwell Kent,** design for Elmer Adler	6.00	8.00	6.00
☐ **Rockwell,** most designs	6.00	8.00	6.00
☐ **18th century armorials,** not done for famous people	4.00	7.00	6.00
☐ **18th century American bookplates,** except Revere or Hurd	5.00	7.00	5.00

Mixed Packets. They are seldom offered for sale in the United States, but in Europe, where bookplate collecting is a more popular hobby, dealers put up collections of common specimens in packets of 50 or 100 "all different" just as is done with postage stamps. The prices are generally as follows:

	Current Price Range		Prior Year Average
☐ 100 different 18th century	18.00	24.00	18.50
☐ 50 different 19th century	7.00	11.00	7.50
☐ 100 different 19th century	10.00	14.00	10.00

BOOKS

Title Page of the First Folio, Shakespeare's Comedies, Histories and Tragedies. London, Isaac Jaggard and Edward Blount, 1623, folio. The first collected edition of Shakespeare's writing . . . . **$50000.00-$75000.00**

Books have been among the most valued collectibles for many years. Until recently, they were the only method of storing man's accumulated knowledge. Libraries were the original storage places for books (actually their forerunners were scrolls) since Roman times. Early books were written entirely by hand. Copies also had to be reproduced by hand; therefore, books were only for the very wealthy. Ownership of books continued to be expensive even after Johann Gutenberg invented moveable type in the 15th century. The wealth and wisdom of a man were sometimes judged by the size of his library.

In more recent times, the reasons for collecting books have changed. Collectors may be after oversized books, by his favorite author, first editions or merely a group of beautifully bound volumes. Wealth is no longer a necessity for anyone wishing to possess books.

There are literally thousands of books written on almost every subject imaginable, so most collectors try to specialize in order to limit the size of their collection. Most book collectors concentrate their efforts on a certain author, period of time, subject or some area of interest. This approach permits the building of an interesting and coherent library rather than a very large and uncoordinated group of unrelated volumes. One of the advantages of book collecting is that it is not the type of hobby in which *completion* of a group of books is necessary to the success of the collector. Most collectors strive for quality rather than quantity and many would not trade their relatively small collections for a whole bookstore full of unrelated volumes. Because of the many areas of specialization, a fair-sized library can often be assembled at moderate cost. By patiently and carefully selecting only the best volumes affordable, the expense of compiling a good selection of books can usually be spread out over a long period of time. A collector should not be afraid of acquiring more than one copy of a certain volume. These can always be sold or traded for a book that has eluded the collector up to this point.

Obviously the cost-per-volume has a great effect on the size of most collections. While a novel by Bret Harte or Mark Twain can be purchased fairly reasonably in many cases, an original copy of the Bay Psalm Book (1640) may be priced in the neighborhood of $1 million.

Any book purchased should be in very good to mint condition. Bindings should not be broken, nor should any leaves be missing. These missing pages (even one or two) could lower the price of the book to half of its potential vlaue. Pages that have been cut down, books that are not in the original binding or are water or fire damaged, are worth much less than good copies.

Good sources of antiquarian and collector books are antique bookstores, garage and house sales and library or college book fairs. Most book experts advise against investing in books unless you have first acquired a great deal of knowledge about the subject, since most books tend to appreciate rather slowly but steadily. For more in-depth information and listings, you may refer to *The Official Price Guide to Old Books and Autographs*, published by The House Of Collectibles.

	Current Price Range		Prior Year Average
☐ **Allen, Col. Ethan,** *Reason, The Only Oracle of Man,* second edition, New York, 1836	80.00	90.00	75.00
☐ **Anderson, Sherwood,** Winesburg, Ohio, yellow cloth with paper label, NY, 1919	100.00	125.00	80.00
☐ **Austen, Jane,** *Sense and Sensibility,* second edition, three volumes, London, 1813	200.00	250.00	175.00
☐ **Austen, Jane,** *Pride and Prejudice,* third edition, two volumes, London, 1817	150.00	185.00	125.00
☐ **Beerbohm, Max,** *Zuleika Dobson,* London, 1911 .	65.00	85.00	60.00
☐ **Beerbohm, Max,** *Seven Men,* London, 1919	28.00	36.00	24.00
☐ **Bierce, Ambrose,** *Shapes of Clay,* San Francisco, 1903	165.00	190.00	138.00
☐ **Blake, William,** *The Book of Thel, Songs of Innocence and Songs of Experience,* Vale Press, 1897	90.00	120.00	80.00
☐ **Bronte, Charlotte,** *Jane Eyre,* three volumes, London, 1847	1000.00	1350.00	1150.00
☐ **Bronte, Charlotte,** The Professor, two volumes, London, 1857	150.00	185.00	125.00
☐ **Buchanan, James,** *Sketches of the History, Manners and Customs of the North American Indians,* New York, 1824	125.00	150.00	105.00

174 / BOOKS

	Current Price Range		Prior Year Average
☐ Burroughs, Edgar Rice, *Jungle Tales of Tarzan*, Chicago, 1919	75.00	85.00	70.00
☐ Chesteron, G. K., *Christiana and Her Children*, boards, London, 1914	22.00	28.00	20.00
☐ Clemens, Samuel Langhorne ("Mark Twain"), *The Innocents Abroad*, black cloth, Hartford, 1869	160.00	210.00	125.00
☐ Clemens, S. L., *The Gilded Age*, Hartford, 1873	500.00	650.00	350.00
☐ Clemens, S. L., *The Adventures of Tom Sawyer*, red cloth, London, 1876	375.00	475.00	225.00
☐ Clemens, S. L., *A Tramp Abroad*, black cloth or leather, Hartford, 1880	600.00	800.00	400.00
☐ Clemens, S. L., *The Prince and the Pauper*, red cloth, London, 1881	140.00	190.00	165.00
☐ Clemens, S. L., *A Connecticut Yankee in King Arthur's Court*, NY, 1889	400.00	500.00	300.00
☐ Collins, Wilkie, *The Queen of Hearts*, three volumes, London, 1859	120.00	150.00	100.00
☐ Collins, Wilkie, *The Woman in White*, NY, 1860	325.00	385.00	275.00
☐ Collins, Wilkie, *My Lady's Money*, Leipzig, 1877	100.00	130.00	85.00
☐ Conrad, Joseph, *Almayer's Folly*, NY, 1895	120.00	150.00	100.00
☐ Conrad, Joseph, *Typhoon*, black cloth, London, 1903	60.00	80.00	50.00
☐ Conrad, Joseph, *A Set of Six*, London, 1908	40.00	55.00	35.00
☐ Conrad, Joseph, *The Arrow of Gold*, London, 1919	40.00	55.00	35.00
☐ Conrad, Joseph, *One Day More*, limited edition, London, 1919	35.00	40.00	30.00
☐ Cooper, James F., *The Last of the Mohicans*, two volumes, Philadelphia, 1826	7500.00	10000.00	5000.00
☐ Cooper, James F., *The Pathfinder*, two volumes, Philadelphia, 1840	120.00	140.00	100.00
☐ Cooper, James F., *The Deerslayer*, purple cloth, two volumes, Philadelphia, 1841	160.00	190.00	150.00
☐ Corry, John, *The Life of George Washington*, New York, 1807	165.00	195.00	150.00
☐ Crane, Stephen, *The Red Badge of Courage*, first edition, NY, 1895	325.00	400.00	300.00
☐ Crane, Stephen, *Maggie a Girl of the Streets*, London, 1896	100.00	130.00	75.00
☐ Darwin, Charles, *Expression of Emotions in Man and Animals*, first edition, London, 1872	100.00	120.00	90.00
☐ Dickens, Charles, *Nicholas Nickleby*, first edition in book form, London, 1839	100.00	150.00	85.00
☐ Dickens, Charles, *A Christmas Carol*, New York, 1844	60.00	80.00	50.00
☐ Dickens, Charles, *Martin Chuzzlewit*, blue cloth, first edition in book form, London, 1844	150.00	175.00	125.00
☐ Dickens, Charles, *The Adventures of Oliver Twist*, third edition in book form, London, 1846	225.00	275.00	200.00
☐ Dickens, Charles, *David Copperfield*, dark green cloth, first edition in book form, London, 1850	500.00	600.00	450.00
☐ Dickens, Charles, *Bleak House*, green cloth, first edition in book form, London, 1853	325.00	425.00	275.00
☐ Dickens, Charles, *Hard Times For These Times*, green cloth, London, 1854	150.00	250.00	125.00

	Current Price Range		Prior Year Average
☐ Dickens, Charles, *A Tale of Two Cities*, red or green cloth, first edition in book form, London, 1859	2000.00	2400.00	1750.00
☐ Dickens, Charles, *Great Expectations*, plum cloth, first issue, London, 1861	5000.00	8000.00	4000.00
☐ Dickens, Charles, *Our Mutual Fund*, 19 parts, green wrappers, London, 1864-5	600.00	800.00	450.00
☐ Dickinson, Emily, *Poems*, third series, Boston, first issue has "Roberts Brothers" stamped on spine, 1896	250.00	300.00	238.00
☐ Dreiser, Theodore, *Sister Carrie*, NY, 1900	600.00	800.00	500.00
☐ Dreiser, Theodore, *A Hosier Holiday*, NY, 1916	85.00	115.00	75.00
☐ Eliot, George, *Silas Marner*, brown coarse-grained cloth, Edinburgh and London, 1861	70.00	95.00	50.00
☐ Eliot, George, *The Spanish Gypsy*, Edinburgh, 1868	45.00	60.00	40.00
☐ Eliot, George, *Brother and Sister*, softbound, London, 1869	350.00	400.00	300.00
☐ Ellsworth, H.W., *Teacher's Guide to Ellsworth's New System of Practical Penmanship*, New York, 1864	45.00	55.00	40.00
☐ Faulkner, William, *The Hamlet*, New York, black cloth cover, 1940	250.00	300.00	238.00
☐ Fitzgerald, F. Scott, *The Great Gatsby*, New York, green cloth cover, 1925	125.00	150.00	118.00
☐ Ford, Paul, *Bibliography of Benjamin Franklin*, Brooklyn, 1889	120.00	140.00	115.00
☐ Forster, E. M., *The Longest Journey*, London, 1907	60.00	80.00	50.00
☐ Frost, John, *History of the State of California*, Auburn, 1853	70.00	90.00	62.00
☐ Galsworthy, John, *The Man of Property*, NY, 1906	45.00	60.00	40.00
☐ Galsworthy, John, *The Dark Flower*, London, 1913	40.00	60.00	35.00
☐ Grey, Zane, *The Last of the Plainsmen*, Toronto, n.d. 1908	40.00	60.00	35.00
☐ Griffith, G.W.E., *My 96 Years in the Great West*, Los Angeles, 1929	45.00	65.00	38.00
☐ Haggard, H. Rider, *Allan Quaterman*, London, 1887	85.00	105.00	75.00
☐ Hart, Charles Henry, *A Biographical Sketch of His Excellency, Abraham Lincoln, Late President of The United States*, Albany, 1870	150.00	175.00	130.00
☐ Harte, Bret, *The Lost Galleon*, San Francisco, 1867	200.00	275.00	150.00
☐ Harte, Bret, *The Heathen Chinee*, Chicago, 1870	150.00	190.00	125.00
☐ Hawthorne, N., *The Scarlet Letter*, blind stamped cloth, Boston, 1850	200.00	250.00	225.00
☐ Hawthorne, N., *The House of the Seven Gables*, brown cloth, Boston, 1851	85.00	100.00	75.00
☐ Hawthorne, N., *The Marble Faun*, brown cloth, two volumes, Boston, 1860	60.00	80.00	50.00
☐ Hemingway, Ernest, *For Whom the Bell Tolls*, New York, 1940, light tan cloth cover	155.00	200.00	130.00
☐ Holmes, Oliver Wendell, *Dissertations*, Boston, 1836	80.00	105.00	90.00

176 / BOOKS

	Current Price Range		Prior Year Average
Irving, Washington, *The Rocky Mountains*, Philadelphia, 1837	160.00	290.00	148.00
James, Henry, *The American*, green cloth, Boston, 1877	125.00	160.00	100.00
James, Henry, *Daisy Miller*, blue cloth, London, 1880	18.00	24.00	15.00
James, Henry, *The Portrait of a Lady*, brown cloth, Boston, 1882	400.00	500.00	450.00
James, Henry, *What Maisie Knew*, Chicago and NY, 1897	175.00	225.00	150.00
James, Henry, *The Ambassadors*, NY, 1903	120.00	160.00	140.00
James, Henry, *The American Scene*, red cloth, London, 1907	60.00	80.00	50.00
James, Henry, *Traveling Companions*, New York, green cloth cover, 1919	130.00	160.00	100.00
Kipling, Rudyard, *Abaft the Funnell*, New York, 1909	45.00	55.00	40.00
Kipling, Rudyard, *The Jungle Book*, blue cloth, two volumes, London, 1894	200.00	250.00	175.00
Kipling, Rudyard, *Captains Courageous*, blue cloth, London, 1897	40.00	50.00	35.00
Kipling, Rudyard, *Just So Stories*, London, 1920	60.00	80.00	50.00
Lawrence, D. H., *Sons and Lovers*, dark blue cloth, London, 1913	250.00	300.00	225.00
Lawrence, D. H., *The Prussian Officer*, London, 1914	60.00	80.00	50.00
London, Jack, *The Faith of Men*, NY, 1904	115.00	135.00	100.00
London, Jack, *The Game*, green cloth, NY, 1905	35.00	45.00	30.00
London, Jack, *The Cruise of the Dazzler*, London, n.d. 1906	350.00	400.00	325.00
London, Jack, *Before Adam*, brown cloth, NY, 1907	60.00	80.00	50.00
London, Jack, *Revolution*, NY, 1910	85.00	115.00	75.00
London, Jack, *The Scarlet Plague*, NY, 1915	60.00	80.00	50.00
Longfellow, Henry Wadsworth, *Tales of a Wayside Inn*, Boston, 1858	55.00	65.00	50.00
Maugham, W. Somerset, *The Explorer*, London, 1909	60.00	80.00	50.00
Melville, Herman, *Typee*, softbound, two volumes, NY, 1846	1200.00	1675.00	1000.00
Mitchell, Margaret, *Gone With The Wind*, New York, 1936	170.00	200.00	150.00
Morris, William, *The Life and Death of Jason*, Kelmscott Press, 1895	400.00	450.00	375.00
Nebraska Ned, *Buffalo Bill and his Daring Adventures in the West*, Baltimore, 192 pp., soft bound, 1913	135.00	155.00	130.00
Newton, Isaac, *Universal Arithmetick, or, A Treatise of Arithmetical Composition and Resolution*, London, 1728	80.00	100.00	68.00
Nightingale, Florence, *Notes on Hospitals*, third edition, London, 1863	100.00	120.00	90.00
Reidesel, Madam, *Letters and Memoirs Relating to the War of American Independence*, 1827	125.00	150.00	118.00
Rodier, Paul, *The Romance of French Weaving*, New York, 1931	25.00	35.00	22.00

BOOKS / 177

	Current Price Range		Prior Year Average
☐ Scott, Sir Walter, *The Lady of the Lake*, London, 1863	125.00	150.00	118.00
☐ Seligman, G. S. and Hughes, E. T., *Domestic Needlework*, London, 1926	120.00	140.00	115.00
☐ Shakespeare, William, *Shakespeare's Comedies, Histories and Tragedies*, London, 1685	5000.00	7500.00	6250.00
☐ Sinclair, Upton, *The Jungle*, NY, 1906	22.00	26.00	20.00
☐ Siringo, Charles A., *A Texas Cowboy*, Chicago, 1885	400.00	600.00	400.00
☐ Standish, Burt L., *Frank Merriwell's Tact*, New York, 1910	15.00	25.00	13.50
☐ Steinbeck, John, *The Grapes of Wrath*, two volumes, New York, cloth with leather spine, 1940	175.00	200.00	168.00
☐ Stevenson, Robert Louis, *Treasure Island*, London 1883	450.00	550.00	425.00
☐ Stevenson, Robert Louis, *Kidnapped*, London, 1886	250.00	300.00	225.00
☐ Stevenson, Robert Louis, *The Strange Case of Dr. Jekyll and Mr. Hyde*, pink wrappers, London, 1886	250.00	300.00	225.00
☐ Stevenson, Robert Louis, *The Black Arrow*, red cloth, London, 1888	60.00	80.00	50.00
☐ Stevenson, Robert Louis, *The South Seas*, London, 1890	600.00	800.00	500.00
☐ Stowe, Harriett Beecher, *Uncle Tom's Cabin*, softbound, two volumes, Boston, 1852	17500.00	25000.00	12500.00
☐ Stowe, Harriett Beecher, *Uncle Sam's Emancipation*, Philadelphia, 1853	85.00	100.00	92.00
☐ Studen, J.H. and Jasper, T., *The Birds of North America*, two volumes, Columbus, Ohio, 1878	260.00	320.00	240.00
☐ Synge, John Millington, *The Tinker's Wedding*, Dublin, 1907	400.00	500.00	200.00
☐ Synge, John Millington, *The Playboy of the Western World*, Dublin, 1907	500.00	675.00	250.00
☐ Synge, John Millington, *Diedre of the Sorrows*, limited to 250 copies, Dundrum, 1910	350.00	475.00	150.00
☐ Tarkington, Booth, *Seventeen*, NY, n.d. 1916	40.00	50.00	35.00
☐ Thackeray, W. M., *Vanity Fair*, London, 1848	350.00	500.00	200.00
☐ Thackeray, W. M., *The History of Henry Esmond*, three volumes, London, 1852	450.00	600.00	300.00
☐ Thackeray, W. M., *The Virginians*, two volumes, London, 1858	100.00	135.00	80.00
☐ Thackeray, William M., *The Four Georges*, New York, 1860	130.00	170.00	112.00
☐ Thackeray, W. M., *The Adventures of Philip*, three volumes, London, 1862	80.00	100.00	50.00
☐ Thackeray, W. M., *The Orphan of Pimlico*, London, 1876	30.00	40.00	25.00
☐ Triplett, Frank, *The Life, Times and Treacherous Death of Jesse James*, Chicago, 1882	550.00	650.00	450.00
☐ Trollope, Anthony, *The Betrams*, three volumes, London, 1859	115.00	140.00	100.00
☐ Trollope, Anthony, *He Knew He Was Right*, two volumes, London, 1869	115.00	140.00	100.00
☐ Trollope, Anthony, *Lady Anna*, two volumes, London, 1873	120.00	175.00	140.00

178 / BOOKS

	Current Price Range		Prior Year Average
☐ **Trollope, Anthony,** *An Eye For an Eye,* two volumes, London, 1879	60.00	80.00	50.00
☐ **Trollope, Anthony,** *John Caldigate,* three volumes, London, 1879	90.00	110.00	75.00
☐ **Verne, Jules,** *Around the World in 80 Days,* Boston, 1873	140.00	190.00	160.00
☐ **Verne, Jules,** *From the Earth to the Moon,* NY, 1874	75.00	100.00	50.00
☐ **Walton, Izaak,** *The Complete Angler,* London, 1842	140.00	160.00	120.00
☐ **Wilde, Oscar,** *Lord Arthur Savile's Crime,* London, 1891	150.00	225.00	100.00
☐ **Wilde, Oscar,** *The Picture of Dorian Gray,* London, n.d., 1891	300.00	400.00	200.00
☐ **Wilder, Thornton,** *The Angel that Troubled the Waters,* New York, 1928	35.00	45.00	50.00
☐ **Wilkins, John,** *The Mathematical and Philosophical Works of the Right Reverend John Wilkins, Late Lord Bishop of Chester,* London, 1708	165.00	185.00	158.00
☐ **Williams, Tennessee,** *The Glass Menagerie,* New York, 1945	125.00	150.00	95.00
☐ **Zola, Emile,** *The Attack on the Mill,* London, 1892	18.00	23.00	15.00
☐ **Zola, Emile,** *Doctor Pascal,* London, 1893	18.00	23.00	15.00

BIBLES

	Current Price Range		Prior Year Average
☐ **American Bible,** Trenton, New Jersey, 1791	900.00	1250.00	750.00
☐ **American Bibles,** *The Holy Bible,* Philadelphia, two volumes, folio, 1798	1750.00	2250.00	1250.00
☐ **American Bibles,** Windsor, Vermont, 1812	750.00	1000.00	625.00
☐ **American Bibles,** NY, pocket size, 1822	75.00	100.00	62.00
☐ **American Bible,** Brooke County, Virginia, 1826	800.00	1000.00	675.00
☐ **American Bibles,** with Amendments of the Language by Noah Webster, New Haven, 1833	75.00	100.00	62.00
☐ **American Bibles,** Hartford, Connecticut, 1876	150.00	175.00	125.00
☐ **American Bibles,** Boston, Hinkley, 14 volumes, cloth, n.d., 1898-1900	100.00	125.00	82.00
☐ **Ashendene Press,** 20th c Book of Ecclasiasticus	400.00	600.00	400.00
☐ **Bible in English,** London, J. Daye, 1551	850.00	1600.00	1050.00
☐ **Bible in English,** London, Grafton, quarto, 478 leaves, 1553	600.00	1200.00	750.00
☐ **Bible in English,** London, E. Whytechurche, 1553	1400.00	1800.00	1050.00
☐ **Bible in English,** *Cranmer's Version,* London, R. Harrison, 1562	900.00	1200.00	620.00
☐ **Bible in English,** *Bishop's Bible,* London, R. Jugge, 1568	900.00	1250.00	620.00
☐ **Biblia Latina,** Venice, Reynaldus de Novimagio and Theodorus de Reynsburch, 1478	1200.00	1500.00	1000.00
☐ **Biblia Latina,** Venice, Nicolaus Jenson, 1479	900.00	1200.00	900.00
☐ **Biblia Latina,** Lyons, Jacques Maillet, 1490	800.00	1200.00	620.00
☐ **Biblia Latina,** Venice, Simon Bevilaqua, 1494	675.00	900.00	400.00
☐ **Biblia Latina,** Venice, Hieronymus de Paganinis, 1497	400.00	600.00	250.00
☐ **John Field's Bible,** woodcuts, mid-1600's	50.00	70.00	42.00
☐ **Nonesuch Press,** five volume Bible, 1924-1927	140.00	160.00	110.00
☐ **Miniature Bible,** 19th c.	55.00	65.00	50.00

BIG LITTLE BOOKS

Big Little Books, whose heyday was during the 1930's and early 1940's, were small but extremely thick hard-covered volumes for the juvenile market. An offshoot of comic strips, many featured the popular comic characters of their day. Others carried adventure stories or fables. Because of their sturdier coverings, the survival rate for Big Little Books was higher than for comic books. Nevertheless, some are scarce, as not all were printed in large quantities.

	Current Price Range		Prior Year Average
☐ Adventures of Scrappy	8.50	16.00	11.50
☐ Alice in Wonderland	16.00	26.00	20.00
☐ Alley Oop and Dinny	12.00	22.00	15.00
☐ Andy Panda	22.00	38.00	28.00
☐ Andy Panda's Vacation	8.50	16.00	11.50
☐ Bambi	16.00	26.00	20.00
☐ Barney Google	16.00	26.00	20.00
☐ Betty Boop in Miss Gulliver's Travels	8.50	16.00	11.50
☐ Big Little Mother Goose	16.00	26.00	20.00
☐ Blondie	16.00	26.00	20.00
☐ Blondie and Baby Dumpling, 1937	12.00	18.00	12.50
☐ Blondie and Dagwood in Hot Water	12.00	18.00	12.50
☐ Blondie — Cookie and Daisy's Pups	12.00	18.00	12.50
☐ Brer Rabbit, 1945	22.00	38.00	28.00
☐ Brer Rabbit, 1948	16.00	26.00	20.00
☐ Bringing Up Father	16.00	26.00	20.00
☐ Buck Jones and the Night Riders	22.00	38.00	28.00
☐ Buck Rogers in the 25th Century A.D., 1933	22.00	38.00	28.00
☐ Bugs Bunny	18.00	28.00	20.00
☐ Buz Sawyer and Bomber 13	18.00	28.00	20.00
☐ Captain Midnight and the Moon Woman	18.00	28.00	20.00
☐ Charlie Chan Solves a New Mystery	12.00	22.00	12.50
☐ Charlie McCarthy and Edgar Bergan	12.00	22.00	12.50
☐ Cinderella and the Magic Wand	12.00	22.00	12.50
☐ Clyde Beatty — Lions and Tigers	18.00	28.00	20.00
☐ Dan Dunn, Secret Operative 48, 1834	18.00	28.00	20.00
☐ Dick Tracy, Adventures of	35.00	55.00	40.00
☐ Dick Tracy Returns	18.00	28.00	20.00
☐ Donald Duck	18.00	28.00	20.00
☐ Donald Duck and the Ducklings	35.00	65.00	50.00
☐ Donald Duck Out of Luck	30.00	45.00	32.00
☐ Donald Duck Sees Stars	18.00	28.00	20.00
☐ Donald Duck Takes It On The Chin	30.00	45.00	32.00
☐ Dumbo	18.00	28.00	20.00
☐ Ellery Queen and the Adventure of the Murdered Millionaire	18.00	28.00	20.00
☐ Felix the Cat, 1935	9.00	16.00	12.00
☐ Flash Gordon and the Emperor of Mongo	35.00	60.00	42.50
☐ Flash Gordon in the Ice World of Mongo	40.00	65.00	48.00
☐ Flash Gordon and the Witch Queen of Mongo	45.00	65.00	50.00
☐ Gene Autry in Gunsmoke	30.00	45.00	32.00
☐ Gene Autry in Hawk of the Hills	18.00	28.00	20.00
☐ Green Hornet Returns	18.00	28.00	20.00
☐ Gumps in Radioland	18.00	28.00	20.00
☐ Joe Palooka, The Heavyweight Boxing Champ	25.00	35.00	25.00

180 / BOOKS

	Current Price Range		Prior Year Average
☐ John Carter of Mars	55.00	85.00	65.00
☐ Katzenjammer Kids	20.00	35.00	22.00
☐ Kayo and Moon Mullins	9.00	16.00	11.00
☐ Kit Carson	18.00	28.00	20.00
☐ Laurel and Hardy	12.00	22.00	15.00
☐ Li'l Abner in Sadie Hawkins Day	18.00	28.00	20.00
☐ Little Lulu, Alvin and Tubby	12.00	22.00	15.00
☐ Little Orphan Annie	35.00	50.00	38.00
☐ Little Orphan Annie and Sandy	18.00	28.00	20.00
☐ Little Orphan Annie in Rags to Riches	25.00	35.00	25.00
☐ Lone Ranger and His Horse Silver	30.00	45.00	32.00
☐ Lone Ranger and the Silver Bullets	18.00	28.00	20.00
☐ Mandrake the Magician and the Flame Pearls	25.00	35.00	25.00
☐ Mickey Mouse	45.00	75.00	55.00
☐ Mickey Mouse and the Magic Lamp	18.00	28.00	20.00
☐ Nancy and Sluggo	9.00	16.00	11.00
☐ Popeye and Castor Oyl the Detective	12.00	28.00	17.00
☐ Popeye in Choose Your Weppins	18.00	28.00	20.00
☐ Roy Rogers and the Deadly Treasure	12.00	22.00	15.00
☐ Tarzan and the Apes	35.00	55.00	40.00
☐ Tom Mix and the Hoard of Montezuma	25.00	35.00	25.00
☐ Woody Woodpecker, Big Game Hunter	9.00	16.00	11.00

CHILDREN'S BOOKS

	Current Price Range		Prior Year Average
☐ Abbott, Jacob, *Harper's Story Books*, engraved, NY, 1855	50.00	60.00	45.00
☐ Abbott, Jacob, *Marco Polo's Travels and Adventures*, Boston, 1848	35.00	45.00	30.00
☐ Abbott, Jacob, *Rollo's Travels*, Boston, 1840	450.00	550.00	400.00
☐ Alcott, Louisa M, *Little Women*, Boston, 1869	175.00	225.00	200.00
☐ Aldrich, Thomas Bailey, *The Story of a Bad Boy*, Boston, 1870	275.00	375.00	250.00
☐ Alger, Horatio, *Ragged Dick*, Boston, 1868	800.00	900.00	750.00
☐ Altsheler, Joseph A., *The Wilderness Road*, NY, 1901	20.00	30.00	17.50
☐ Andersen, H.C., *The Snow Queen*, London, Routledge, 1890	6.00	8.00	5.00
☐ Baldwin, James, *A Story of the Golden Age*, NY, 1887	35.00	45.00	30.00
☐ Barr, Amelia E., *The Bow of Orange Ribbon*, NY, n.d., reprint, 1907	10.00	12.00	8.00
☐ Barrie, Sir James M., *Peter and Wendy*, London, 1911	15.00	18.00	13.50
☐ Belson, Mary, *The Orphan Boy*, London, 1812	15.00	18.00	12.00
☐ Bennet, John, *Master Skylark*, NY, 1897	90.00	120.00	70.00
☐ Bouton, E. G., *Grandmother's Doll*, NY, 1931	20.00	30.00	17.50
☐ Burnett, Frances H., *Editha's Burglar*, Boston, 1888	10.00	15.00	8.00
☐ Burnett, Frances H., *Little Lord Fauntleroy*, NY, 1886	90.00	120.00	70.00
☐ Carroll, Lewis, *Alice's Adventures in Wonderland*, London, 1865	12000.00	14000.00	11000.00
☐ Carroll, Lewis, *Sylvia and Bruno*, London, 1889	100.00	125.00	82.00
☐ Carroll, Lewis, *Through the Looking-Glass and What Alice Found There*, London, 1872	250.00	350.00	250.00

BOOKS / 181

	Current Price Range		Prior Year Average
☐ Carroll, Lewis, *The Hunting of the Snark*, London, 1876	200.00	250.00	175.00
☐ *Child's Book About Whales*, softbound, Concord, NH, 1843	100.00	125.00	82.00
☐ *Cries of the Metropolis; or Humble Life in New York*, softbound, Rutland, VT, 1858	250.00	350.00	250.00
☐ Denslow, W. W., *Denslow's Animal Fair*, NY, n.d., 1904	65.00	75.00	60.00
☐ Disney, Walt, *The Adventures of Mickey Mouse, Book I*, Philadelphia, 1931	75.00	85.00	70.00
☐ Disney, Walt, *Who's Afraid of the Big Bad Wolf?* Philadelphia, 1933	550.00	650.00	550.00
☐ Field, Eugene, *Little Willie*	25.00	35.00	22.00
☐ Graham, Kenneth, *Fun o' the Friar*, London, 1929	30.00	40.00	28.00
☐ Graham, Kenneth, *The Golden Age*, London, 1900	45.00	55.00	40.00
☐ Greenaway, Kate, *Kate Greenaway's Book of Games*, London, 1889	140.00	160.00	120.00
☐ *Guess Again, A New Riddle Book, for the Entertainment of Children*, 22 pages, NY, 1834	30.00	40.00	25.00
☐ Harris, Joel Chandler, *The Story of Aaron*, New York, 1896	40.00	50.00	35.00
☐ Harris, Joel Chandler, *Uncle Remus, His Songs and His Sayings*, New York, 1881	325.00	375.00	325.00
☐ Headland, Isaac, *Chinese Mother Goose Rhymes*, NY, n.d. 1900	60.00	100.00	70.00
☐ Howells, William Dean, *A Boy's Town*, New York, 1890	30.00	40.00	25.00
☐ Lear, Edward, *A Book of Nonsense*, London, 1861	250.00	350.00	250.00
☐ Lofting, Hugh, *The Story of Dr. Doolittle*, New York, 1923	18.00	24.00	15.00
☐ Lofting, Hugh, *Dr. Dolittle's Circus*, NY, 1924	55.00	85.00	65.00
☐ Lofting, Hugh, *Dr. Dolittle's Garden*, NY, 1927	45.00	55.00	35.00
☐ Lofting, Hugh, *Dr. Dolittle and the Secret Lake*, Philadelphia and New York, 1958	35.00	45.00	30.00
☐ Milne, A. A., *Fourteen Songs From When We Were Very Young*, NY, 1925	25.00	35.00	20.00
☐ Milne, A. A. *The Ivory Door*, NY, 1938	20.00	30.00	15.00
☐ Milne, A. A., *Winnie-the-Pooh*, London, 1926	150.00	175.00	138.00
☐ *Night Before Christmas*, softbound, London, n.d., 1905	25.00	35.00	17.50
☐ Phillips, E. O., *Birdie and Her Dog*, London, 1885	25.00	35.00	17.50
☐ Porter, Eleanor H., *Pollyanna*, Boston, 1913	160.00	180.00	150.00
☐ Potter, Beatrix, *The Pie and The Patty-pan*, London, 1905	100.00	125.00	82.00
☐ Potter, Beatrix, *The Tale of Peter Rabbit*, London, 1901	500.00	575.00	500.00
☐ Potter, Beatrix, *The Tailor of Gloucester*, London, 1902	300.00	375.00	300.00
☐ Potter, Beatrix, *The Tale of Benjamin Bunny*, London, 1904	90.00	120.00	75.00
☐ Preston, D. R., *The Juvenile Instructor; or, a useful book for children*, Boston, John M. Dunham, 1800	30.00	40.00	25.00
☐ Ray, Joseph, *Ray's Arithmetic, First Book ... For Young Learners*, Cincinnati, 1857	25.00	35.00	20.00
☐ Richard, Laura E., *Captain January*, Boston, 1898	25.00	35.00	20.00

182 / BOOKS

	Current Price Range		Prior Year Average
☐ Schute, Henry A., *The Real Diary of a Real Boy*, first edition, Boston, 1902	80.00	120.00	70.00
☐ Sewell, Anna, *Black Beauty*, Boston, 1890	80.00	120.00	70.00
☐ Smith, E. Boyd, *The Story of Noah's Ark*, Boston, 1905	40.00	50.00	32.00
☐ Southey, Robert, *The Story of the Three Bears*, London, 1837	100.00	125.00	82.00
☐ Stockton, Frank R., *The Adventures of Captain Horn*, New York, 1895	15.00	25.00	12.50
☐ Goody Lovechild, *Stories for Children in familiar verse*, softbound, Colchester, 1814	40.00	50.00	35.00
☐ Watson, Henry C., *The Yankee Tea Party*, Philadelphia, 1851	20.00	30.00	17.50
☐ Webster, Jean, *Daddy Long Legs*, New York, 1912	70.00	90.00	60.00
☐ Wiggin, Kate Douglas, *The Story of Patsy*, Boston, 1890	15.00	20.00	12.50

COOKBOOKS

	Current Price Range		Prior Year Average
☐ Archdeacon's Kitchen Cabinet, Chicago, 1876	35.00	45.00	35.00
☐ Barrows, Anna, *Principles of Cookery*, Chicago, 1910	18.00	24.00	16.00
☐ Blot, Pierre, *What to Eat and How to Cook It*, New York, 1865	50.00	60.00	42.00
☐ Blot, Pierre, *Hand-Book of Practical Cookery*, New York, 1868	24.00	30.00	21.00
☐ Brooks, R. O., *Vinegars & Catsup*, New York, 1912	12.00	18.00	10.00
☐ Brown, Susan Anna, *The Invalid's Tea-Tray*, Boston, 1885	18.00	24.00	16.00
☐ Carson, Juliet, *The American Family Cookbook*, Chicago, 1898	50.00	60.00	40.00
☐ Clark, Imogen, *Rhymed Receipts for Any Occasion*, Boston, 1912	20.00	30.00	17.50
☐ Cornelius, Mrs., *The Young Housekeeper's Friend*, Boston and New York, 1846	150.00	175.00	138.00
☐ Croly, Mrs. J. C., *Jennie June's American Cookery Book*, New York, 1870	40.00	50.00	35.00
☐ Decker, John W., *Cheese Making*, Wisconsin, 1909	35.00	45.00	30.00
☐ Gillette, Mrs. F. L., *White House Cook Book*, Chicago, 1889	80.00	90.00	75.00
☐ Henderson, W. A., *Modern Domestic Cookery and Useful Receipt Book*, Boston, 1844	135.00	155.00	128.00
☐ Heug, H., *New Book of Designs for Cake-Bakers, etc.*, 1893	25.00	35.00	21.00
☐ Hilliard, Thomas M., *The Art of Carving*, Detroit, 1899	14.00	18.00	11.00
☐ Hitchcock, Nevada D., *The Record War-Time Cook Book*, Philadelphia, 1918	14.00	18.00	11.00
☐ Hurtzler, Victor, *The Hotel Francis Cook Book*, Chicago, 1919	12.00	18.00	12.50
☐ King, Chas. H., *Cakes, Cake Decorations and Desserts*, Philadelphia, 1896	30.00	40.00	27.50
☐ Kirwan, A. V., *Host and Guest*, London, 1864	25.00	35.00	21.50
☐ Kitchiner, Wm., *The Cook's Oracle*, Boston, 1822	100.00	125.00	82.00
☐ Lambert, Mrs. Almeda, *Guide for Nut Cookery*, Battle Creek, Michigan, 1899	100.00	120.00	95.00

BOOKS / 183

	Current Price Range		Prior Year Average
☐ **Langdon, Amelie,** *Just for Two,* Minneapolis, 1907	12.00	18.00	10.00
☐ **Lea, Elizabeth E.,** *Domestic Cookery,* Baltimore, 1853	65.00	75.00	58.00
☐ **Lehner, Joseph C.,** *World's Fair Menu and Recipe Book,* San Francisco, 1915	30.00	40.00	27.00
☐ **Leslie, Miss,** *Directions for Cookery,* 59th edition, Philadelphia, 1863	20.00	30.00	17.00
☐ **Leslie, Miss,** 75 Receipts For Pastry, Cakes and Sweetmeats By a Lady of Philadelpha, Boston, 1828	100.00	125.00	82.00
☐ **Lincoln, Mary,** *The Peerless Cook Book,* soft-bound, Boston, 1901	15.00	20.00	12.50
☐ **Lincoln, Mrs.,** *Boston Cook Book,* scarce, Boston, 1884	450.00	600.00	475.00
☐ **Lincoln, Mrs. D. A.,** *Boston School Kitchen Text-Book,* Boston, 1887	25.00	35.00	22.50
☐ **Lincoln, Mrs.,** *Carving and Serving,* Boston, 1915	15.00	18.00	13.00
☐ **Lippman, B. F.,** *Aunt Betty's Cook Book,* Cincinnati, 1918	15.00	18.00	13.00
☐ **Lockhart, Marion,** *Standard Cook Book for All Occasions,* New York, 1925	12.00	16.00	10.00
☐ **McCann, Alfred W.,** *Thirty Cent Bread,* NY, 1917	12.00	16.00	10.00
☐ **McKinney, E. and W.,** *Aunt Caroline's Dixie-Land Receipts,* Chicago, 1922	20.00	25.00	17.50
☐ **McLaren, L. L.,** *High Living,* San Francisco, 1904	60.00	70.00	55.00
☐ **MacDougall, A. F.,** *Coffee and Waffles,* New York, 1927	12.00	16.00	10.00
☐ **MacKenzie, Colin,** *MacKenzie's Five Thousand Recipes,* Philadelphia, 1825	150.00	175.00	138.00
☐ **Miller, Elizabeth S.,** *In the Kitchen,* Boston, 1875	25.00	35.00	22.00
☐ **Muckenstrum, Louis,** *Louis' Every Woman's Cook Book,* Boston and New York, 1910	15.00	25.00	13.00
☐ **Murrey, Thomas J.,** *Valuable Cooking Receipts,* NY, 1886	20.00	30.00	17.50
☐ **Neely, Flora,** *Hand-Book For the Kitchen and Housekeeper's Guide,* New Rochelle, NY, 1910	20.00	30.00	17.50
☐ **Neill, Miss E.,** *The Every-Day Cook-Book and Encyclopedia of Practical Recipes,* NY, 1888	25.00	35.00	22.50
☐ **Nelson, Harriet S.,** *Fruits and Their Cookery,* New York, 1921	15.00	20.00	12.50
☐ **Nicol, Mary E.,** *366 Dinners,* By "M.E.N." New York, 1892	20.00	30.00	17.50
☐ **Norton, Caroline T.,** *The Rocky Mountain Cook Book,* Denver, 1903	35.00	45.00	30.00
☐ **Owens, Mrs. F.,** *Cook Book and Useful Household Hints,* Chicago, 1883	25.00	35.00	22.50
☐ **Parloa, Maria,** *The Appledore Cook Book,* Boston, 1878	35.00	45.00	30.00
☐ **Paul, Mrs. Sara T.,** *Cookery from Experience,* Philadelphia, 1875	50.00	60.00	32.00
☐ **Pereira, J.,** *A Treatise on Food and Diet,* New York, 1843	40.00	50.00	35.00
☐ **Poindexter, Charlotte M.,** *Jane Hamilton's Recipes,* Chicago, 1909	20.00	30.00	17.50

184 / BOOKS

	Current Price Range		Prior Year Average
☐ Poole, H. M., *Fruits and How to Use Them*, New York, 1890	15.00	25.00	14.00
☐ Randolph, Mary, *The Virginia Housewife, or Methodical Cook*, Washington, D.C., 1830	400.00	550.00	425.00
☐ Ranholfer, Charles, *The Epicurean*, New York, 1900	50.00	60.00	42.00
☐ Rees, Mrs. Jennie Day, *The Complete Cook Book*, Philadelphia, 1900	12.00	18.00	10.00
☐ Rice, Louise, *Dainty Dishes from Foreign Lands*, Chicago, 1911	15.00	20.00	12.50
☐ Robinson, Mrs. H. M., *The Practical Cook Book*, New York, 1864	50.00	60.00	42.00
☐ Ronald, Mary, *Century Cook Book*, New York, 1895	35.00	45.00	30.00
☐ Rorer, Sarah Tyson, *Mrs. Rorer's Cakes, Icings and Fillings*, Philadelphia, 1905	20.00	30.00	17.50
☐ Rundell, Maria E., *A New System of Domestic Cookery*, Boston, 1807	175.00	225.00	175.00
☐ Sala, George A., *The Thorough Good Cook*, NY, 1896	75.00	100.00	82.00
☐ Scott, Mrs. Anna B., *Mrs. Scott's North American Seasonal Cook Book*, Philadelphia, 1921	20.00	30.00	17.50
☐ *Secrets of Meat Curing and Sausage Making*, Chicago, 1911	50.00	60.00	40.00
☐ Senn, C. Herman, *The Book of Sauces*, Chicago, 1915	12.00	18.00	10.00
☐ Shute, Miss T. S., *The American Housewife Cook Book*, Philadelphia, 1878	35.00	45.00	32.50
☐ Simonds. J., *The American Book of Recipes*, Boston, 1854	50.00	60.00	42.00
☐ Southworth, May E., *101 Chafing-Dish Recipes*, San Francisco, 1904	20.00	30.00	17.50
☐ Stanford, Martha P., *The Old and New Cook Book*, New Orleans, 1904	100.00	150.00	82.00
☐ Taylor, Jennie, *The Surprise Cook Book*, New York, 1889	12.00	18.00	10.00
☐ Tilden, Joe, *Joe Tilden's Recipes for Epicures*, San Francisco, 1907	35.00	45.00	30.00
☐ Tschirky, Oscar, *The Cook Book by "Oscar" of the Waldorf*, Chicago, 1896	50.00	60.00	42.00
☐ Tyree, Marion Cabell, *Housekeeping in Old Virginia*, Louisville, 1890	75.00	125.00	58.00
☐ Wallace, L. H., *The Modern Cook Book*, New York, 1912	15.00	25.00	12.50
☐ Ward, Artemas, *The Encyclopedia of Food*, New York, 1923	150.00	175.00	125.00
☐ *What Shall We Eat?* New York, 1868	25.00	35.00	22.50
☐ Wheeler, Eliza Ann, *The Frugal Housekeepers Kitchen Companion*, New York, 1848	35.00	45.00	30.00
☐ White, Mrs. Peter A., *The Kentucky Cookery Book*, Chicago, 1891	60.00	80.00	62.00
☐ Wilson, Mrs. Mary A., *Wilson's Cook Book*, Philadelphia, 1920	35.00	45.00	30.00
☐ Ysaguirre and LaMarca, *Cold Dishes for Hot Weather*, New York, 1896	12.00	18.00	10.00

DETECTIVE FICTION

	Current Price Range		Prior Year Average

- ☐ **Boothby, Guy,** *A Bid for Fortune,* first American edition, New York 30.00 40.00 25.00
- ☐ **Boothby, Guy,** *Curse of the Snake,* London, 1902 20.00 30.00 17.50
- ☐ **Chandler, Raymond,** *The Big Sleep,* London, 1939 30.00 40.00 27.50
- ☐ **Chandler, Raymond,** *The Little Sister,* London, 1949 .... 18.00 24.00 16.00
- ☐ **Chandler, Raymond,** *The Simple Art of Murder,* London, 1950 .... 15.00 25.00 12.50
- ☐ **Chandler, Raymond,** *Spanish Blood,* Cleveland/New York, 1946 .... 35.00 45.00 30.00
- ☐ **Christie, Agatha,** *Easy to Kill,* first American edition, New York, 1939 .... 18.00 24.00 16.00
- ☐ **Christie, Agatha,** *The Hollow,* London, 1946 ..... 18.00 24.00 16.00
- ☐ **Christie, Agatha,** *A Murder is Announced,* New York, 1950 .... 15.00 25.00 13.50
- ☐ **Christie, Agatha,** *The Mysterious Mr. Quinn,* London, 1930 .... 35.00 45.00 30.00
- ☐ **Christie, Agatha,** *Taken at the Flood,* London, 1948 .... 25.00 35.00 20.00
- ☐ **Collins, Wilkie,** *The Moonstone,* three volumes, London, violet cloth, the first detective story in the English language in book form, 1868 .... 1500.00 2000.00 1250.00
- ☐ **Doyle, Sir Arthur C.,** *The Adventures of Sherlock Holmes,* London, two volumes, blue cloth, 1892-94 .... 250.00 350.00 225.00
- ☐ **Doyle, Sir Arthur C.,** *The Adventures of Sherlock Holmes,* New York, blue cloth, not the first issue, 1892 .... 25.00 35.00 21.50
- ☐ **Doyle, Sir Arthur C.,** *My Friend the Murderer,* New York, 1893 .... 25.00 35.00 21.50
- ☐ **Doyle, Sir Arthur C.,** *The Memoirs of Sherlock Holmes,* London, dark blue cloth, 1894 .... 225.00 250.00 212.50
- ☐ **Doyle, Sir Arthur C.,** *The Hound of the Baskervilles,* London, red cloth, 1902 .... 450.00 550.00 450.00
- ☐ **Doyle, Sir Arthur C.,** *The Return of Sherlock Holmes,* London, dark blue cloth, 1904 .... 350.00 400.00 325.00
- ☐ **Doyle, Sir Arthur C.,** *Sir Nigel,* London, 1906 ..... 150.00 200.00 138.00
- ☐ **Doyle, Sir Arthur C.,** *The Croxley Master,* New York, 1907 .... 300.00 400.00 275.00
- ☐ **Doyle, Sir Arthur C.,** *The Poison Belt,* New York, 1913 .... 35.00 45.00 30.00
- ☐ **Doyle, Sir Arthur C.,** *The Case Book of Sherlock Holmes,* London, red cloth, 1927 .... 125.00 175.00 112.00
- ☐ **Fleming, Ian,** *Casino Royale,* London, 1950 ..... 30.00 40.00 25.00
- ☐ **Fleming, Ian,** *Diamonds are Forever,* London, 1956 .... 15.00 18.00 12.50
- ☐ **Fleming, Ian,** *Dr. No,* London, 1958 .... 15.00 18.00 12.50
- ☐ **Fleming, Ian,** *Goldfinger,* London, 1959 .... 15.00 18.00 12.50
- ☐ **Gardner, Earle Stanley,** *The Case of the Howling Dog,* New York, 1934 .... 15.00 18.00 12.50
- ☐ **Queen, Ellery,** *The Adventures of Ellery Queen,* London, 1935 .... 25.00 35.00 22.50
- ☐ **Sayers, Dorothy L.,** *Begin Here,* London, 1940 ... 15.00 18.00 12.50
- ☐ **Sayers, Dorothy L.,** *Busman's Honeymoon,* London, 1937 .... 15.00 18.00 12.50
- ☐ **Sayers, Dorothy L.,** *Gaudy Night,* London, 1935 .. 25.00 35.00 20.00

BOOKS / 185

186 / BOTTLES

BOTTLES

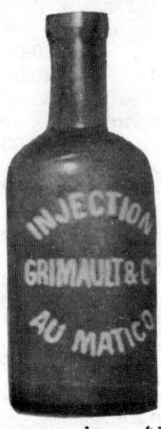

Left to Right: **L.M. Green**, clear, 4¼" **$3.00-$5.00; Grimault & Co.**, clear, 6½" **$3.00$4.00; Leon Hale**, clear, 5" **$3.00-$4.00; G.W. Hall**, aqua, 3½"
.... **$3.00-$5.00**

Bottle collecting is growing rapidly in popularity, largely because of the variety of bottles and the range of prices encompassed by the hobby. While some collectors prefer dealers and antique shops as a source of bottles, others would rather go on "digs" much in the same manner as that of archeologists. Old and new trash dumps are often full of interesting bottles, while other specimens are found under the porches of old houses, in barns, etc.

Presently, bitters bottles and flasks made in the mid- to late-1800's are highly favored by collectors. Other from the same era, used for patent medicines and other "snake oil" type remedies are also popular.

An interesting category, which is now generating a lot of interest, is the made-to-be-collected items produced by some companies. Avon Products, Inc. has marketed cosmetics in hundreds of fancy bottles, the shapes representing everything from animals to race cars. Figural bottles have been produced by many distilling companies including Jim Beam, Bols, Ezra Brooks, J. W. Dant and others. These are quite popular among some collectors and new designs come out yearly, usually around Christmas.

Bottles are valued for many reasons including size, shape, artistic merit, purpose and the presence of original contents and labels. Most bottles are considered to be undervalued, especially in light of their low survival rate. Prices quoted are for bottles in very good to excellent condition. Specimens with original closures, labels, etc. may be worth more. For more information and in-depth listings, you may refer to *The Official Price Guide to Bottles Old and New*, published by the House of Collectibles.

AVON BOTTLES

Avon began as the California Perfume Company (CPC) in 1886. In 1926 the name Avon was used, and in 1939 the company became Avon Products, Incorporated. The bottles were made in varied shapes and filled with cosmetic products.

BOTTLES / 187

	Current Price Range		Prior Year Average

☐ **Ballad Perfume,** (1945-53) Clear glass, small bottle, glass stopper, gold neck cord and label, 3 drams. Original price $3.50 .... 120.00 130.00 125.00
☐ **Bird Of Paradise Cologne Decanter,** (1970-72) Clear glass in shape of bird with gold head, 5 oz. 7.00 9.00 8.00
☐ **Bird Of Paradise Perfume Rollette,** (1970-76) Clear glass, gold cap ⅓ oz. Original price $3.00 .. 1.00 2.00 1.50
☐ **Blue Lotus After Bath Freshener,** (1967-72) Clear glass with blue cap, 6 oz. Original price $3.00 ... 4.00 6.00 5.00
☐ **Blue Lotus Cream Sachet,** (1968-72) Blue frosted glass, blue cap, .66 oz. Original price $2.50 ..... 1.00 3.00 2.00
☐ **Bright Night Cologne,** (1954-61) Clear glass, gold speckled cap, gold neck cord and white paper label, 4 oz. Original price $2.50 .... 16.00 20.00 18.00
☐ **Bright Night Cologne Mist,** (1958-61) Clear glass coated with white plastic, gold speckled gold cap, gold neck cord with white label, 3 oz. Original price $2.75 .... 16.00 22.00 20.00
☐ **Butterfly Cologne,** (1972-73) Clear glass, gold cap with two prongs for antenna, 1.5 oz. Original price $3.00 .... 2.00 4.00 3.00
☐ **Buttons 'N Bows Cologne,** (1960-63) Clear glass, white cap, pink lettering on front, pink ribbon around neck, 2 oz. Original price $1.35 .... 14.00 16.00 15.00
☐ **Charisma Cologne,** (1969-72) Red glass, red plastic cap trimmed in gold, 4 oz. Original price $6.00 .... 2.00 4.00 3.00
☐ **Charisma Cologne Mist,** (1968-76) Clear glass coated with red plastic, gold trimming, 3 oz. Original price $8.00 .... .50 3.00 1.50
☐ **Charisma Cologne Silk,** (1969) Frosted glass, red cap, 3 oz. Original price $4.50 .... 3.00 5.00 4.00
☐ **Charisma Cologne Silk,** (1970-71) Clear glass, red cap, 3 oz. Original price $4.50 .... 1.00 3.00 2.00
☐ **Charisma Perfume Rollette,** (1968-76) Red glass, gold trimming, .33 oz. Original price $4.50 ...... .50 3.00 1.50
☐ **Cologne Elegante,** (1971-72) Tall bottle with red rose on gold cap, clear glass painted gold, 4 oz. Original price $5.00 .... 2.00 4.00 3.00
☐ **Daisies Won't Tell Cologne,** (1958-62) Clear glass, white cap, painted lettering on front, lace bow around neck, 2 oz. Original price $1.19 .... 6.00 8.00 7.00
☐ **Daisies Won't Tell Cologne,** (1962-64) Clear glass, white cap, lettering painted on front, daisies on front, 2 oz. Original price $1.19 .... 5.00 7.00 6.00
☐ **Dew Kiss Decanter,** (1974-75) Clear glass painted, pink lid, 4 oz. Original price $3.00 .... 2.00 4.00 3.00
☐ **Elegante Cologne,** (1956-59) Clear glass, silver cap and neck tag, red ribbon, 4 oz. Original price $2.50 .... 35.00 45.00 40.00
☐ **Elegante Perfume,** (1956-59) Clear glass, silver cap and neck tag, red neck ribbon, ½ oz. Original price $7.50 .... 100.00 140.00 120.00
☐ **Elegante Toilet Water,** (1957-59) Clear glass, silver cap and neck tag, red neck ribbon, 2 oz. Original price $2.00 .... 30.00 40.00 35.00

188 / BOTTLES

	Current Price Range		Prior Year Average
☐ **Emerald Bud Vase Cologne,** (1971) Green glass, glass lid, 3 oz. Original price $5.00	2.00	4.00	3.00
☐ **Floral Bud Base,** (1973-75) White milk glass, 5 oz.	4.00	6.00	5.00
☐ **Flowertime Cologne,** (1949-53) Clear glass, pink cap, paper label on front, 4 oz. Original price $1.75	15.00	25.00	20.00
☐ **Forever Spring Cream,** (1956-59) Clear glass, yellow cap, lettering painted on front, 4 oz. Original price $.95	10.00	14.00	12.00
☐ **Forever Spring One Dram Perfume,** (1951-52) Clear glass, ribbed, gold cap, 1 dram. Original price $1.75	15.00	18.00	16.50
☐ **Flowertime Talc,** (1949-53) Clear glass, brass shaker lid, 5 oz. Original price $.89	15.00	25.00	20.00
☐ **Flowertime Toilet Water,** (1949-53) Clear glass, pink cap, paper label on front, 2 oz. Original price $1.25	18.00	25.00	21.50
☐ **Garden Of Love Swirl Perfume,** (1948) Clear glass, swirl design, glass stopper, gold neck tag, 3 drams. Original price $3.00	85.00	95.00	90.00
☐ **Golden Promise Cologne,** (1947-56) Clear glass, large gold dome shaped cap, lettering painted on front around shoulder, 4 oz. Original price $2.25 .	16.00	22.00	19.00
☐ **Here's My Heart Perfume,** (1948-49) clear glass, glass stopper, heart shaped bottle, pink satin ribbon around neck, lettering painted on front, ½ oz. Original price $7.50	110.00	140.00	125.00
☐ **Here's My Heart Perfume Oil,** (1964-68) clear glass, white plastic cap with scalloped rim and beading, lettering painted on front, ½ oz. Original price $3.50	5.00	8.00	6.50
☐ **Honeysuckle After Bath Freshener,** (1967-72) clear glass, orange cap, orange band around center of bottle, 8 oz. Original price $3.00	1.00	3.00	2.00
☐ **Honeysuckle Cologne Mist,** (1971-72) yellow glass, yellow cap, 2 oz. Original price $4.25	1.00	3.00	2.00
☐ **Honeysuckle Cologne Mist,** (1972-76) clear glass, clear plastic cap, inner cap of yellow and green, 2 oz. Original price $3.25	2.00	5.00	3.50
☐ **Honeysuckle Cream Sachet,** (1967-75) yellow glass, frosted, orange cap, .66 oz. Original price $2.50	.50	2.00	1.25
☐ **Jardin D'Amour Perfume,** (1929-33) clear stopper, black label at neck, 1 or 2 oz. Original price $3.50 or $6.10	90.00	120.00	105.00
☐ **Jardin D'Amour Perfume,** (1954) clear glass bottle that sits in a blue and gold bucket with gold cord that ties around the top of the bottle, clear plastic cap, gold label, 1 dram. Original price $15.00	160.00	195.00	178.00
☐ **Jasmine After Bath Freshener,** (1964-68) clear glass, tall shaped bottle, yellow cap, lettering painted on front, 8 oz. Original price $2.50	1.00	3.00	2.00
☐ **Jasmine Bath Salts,** (1945-52) clear glass, black cap and label, 9 oz. Original price $.75	25.00	35.00	30.00

Description	Current Price Range		Prior Year Average
☐ **Jasmine Powder Sachet,** (1949) clear glass, black cap and label, 1½ oz. Original price $1.25	35.00	45.00	40.00
☐ **Jasmine Toilet Water,** (1946-48) clear glass, gold cap, long narrow black label on front of bottle, 2 oz. Original price $1.19	25.00	35.00	30.00
☐ **Jasmine Toilet Water,** (1949) clear glass, black cap and label, 2 oz. Original price $1.25	35.00	45.00	40.00
☐ **Lemon Velvet Cologne Mist,** (1972-76) clear glass, clear plastic cap, yellow and green inner cap, 2 oz. Original price $4.25	1.00	3.00	2.00
☐ **Quaintance Perfume,** (1948-50) clear glass, with ribbed corners, large rose shaped cap, lettering and decorative borders painted on front, 1 dram. Original price $1.50	65.00	75.00	70.00
☐ **Quaintance Perfume,** (1950) clear glass, small dome shaped red cap with green leaf, 3 drams. ..	110.00	140.00	125.00
☐ **Quaintance Toilet Water,** (1953-56) clear glass, ribbed corners, rose shaped and colored cap, with green leaf neck band, green painted lettering on front, 2 oz. Original price $1.25	16.00	24.00	20.00
☐ **Rapture Half Ounce Cologne,** (1969-72) clear glass, bulbous shaped, large tulip shaped green cap, ½ oz. Original price $1.50	1.00	3.00	2.00
☐ **Rapture Perfumed Rollette,** (1965-69) blue glass, ribbed, large cylinder shaped/cap, ⅓ oz. Original price $2.50	5.00	7.00	6.00
☐ **Regence Perfume Rollette,** (1967-68) clear glass, ribbed, large cylinder shaped gold cap, .33 oz. Original price $3.00	2.00	4.00	3.00
☐ **Regence Perfume Rollette,** (1969-70) clear glass, ribbed, large cylinder green cap, .33 oz. Original price $3.00	1.00	3.00	2.00
☐ **Regence Bath Oil Skin So Soft,** (1967-71) clear glass, faceted bottle, large domed shaped gold cap, 6 oz. Original price $5.00	2.00	4.00	3.00
☐ **Regence Cologne,** (1967-69) clear glass, faceted, gold cap in dome shape, 2 oz. Original price $3.00	1.00	3.00	2.00
☐ **Regence Half Ounce Cologne,** (1970-71) clear glass, gold domed cap with decorative designs, ½ oz. Original price $1.75	2.00	4.00	3.00
☐ **Regence Perfume,** (1966-69) frosted glass, gold plastic cap, urn shaped bottle, gold band around shoulder, gold neck tag, ½ oz. Original price $15.00	12.00	18.00	15.00
☐ **Regence Perfume,** (1966-69) frosted glass, glass stopper, urn shaped bottle, gold and green trimmings around neck and shoulder, 1 oz. Original price $30.00	25.00	35.00	30.00
☐ **Somewhere Cologne,** (1966-71) clear glass, gold domed shaped cap, 2 oz. Original price $2.50	1.00	3.00	2.00
☐ **Somewhere Cologne,** (1961-66) clear glass, pink cap with jeweled trim, sculptured bottle, lettering painted around shoulder, 2 oz. Original price $2.00	4.00	6.00	5.00

190 / BOTTLES

	Current Price Range		Prior Year Average
☐ **Sonnet Toilet Water,** (1941) clear glass, purple cap and label, narrow paper label down the center, 2 oz. Original price $.20	30.00	40.00	35.00
☐ **Swan Lake Bath Oil,** (1947-49) clear glass, flat sid-ed bottle, pink cap, lettering and swan painted on front, 6 oz. Original price $1.25	50.00	60.00	55.00
☐ **Swan Lake Cologne,** (1947-50) clear glass, pink cap, lettering and decorative border painted on front, 4 oz. Original price $1.35	40.00	50.00	45.00
☐ **Sweet Honesty Cologne Mist,** (1973-74) clear glass, horizontal ribbing, inner and outer caps, 2 oz.	1.00	3.00	2.00
☐ **Topaz Four Ounces Cologne,** (1959-63) gold cap, faceted bottle, lettering painted on front, 4 oz.	8.00	12.00	10.00
☐ **Topaz Four Ounces Gift Cologne,** (1959-61) clear glass, gold cap, 4 oz.	10.00	15.00	12.50
☐ **Topaz Half Ounce Cologne,** (1970-71) clear glass, gold cap, lettering painted on front, ½ oz. Original price $1.50	2.00	4.00	3.00
☐ **Topaz Cream Lotion,** (1959-67) clear glass, tall narrow shaped bottle, yellow cap, 4 oz. Original price $1.50	6.00	10.00	8.00
☐ **Topaz Perfume,** (1959-63) amber glass, amber jeweled glass stopper, faceted bottle, 1 oz. Original price $20.00	90.00	120.00	105.00
☐ **Topaz Perfume Oil,** (1964-69) clear glass, gold cap, lettering painted on front, ½ oz. Original price $4.00	50.00	60.00	55.00

BEAM BOTTLES

In 1953 the James Beam Distilling Company designed a decanter for the Christmas season. This first issue was a fabulous success and was the start of the many variety "Beam" bottles. Most of the bottles are produced in fine Regal china.

☐ **Antioch,** (c. 1967) the Regal China Company is located in Antioch, Illinois, this decanter commemorates the Diamond Jubilee of Regal, large Indian head ("Sequoit") on one side, blue and gold diamond on reverse, Regal China, 10"	4.00	8.00	6.00
☐ With arrow package	4.00	8.00	6.00
☐ **Antique Coffee Grinder,** (1979) replica of a box coffee mill used in the mid 19th century, brown with black top and crank which moves, gold lettering	18.00	22.00	20.00
☐ **Antique Globe,** (1908) represents the Martin Behaim globe of 1492, the globe is blue and rotates on the wooden cradle stand	28.00	36.00	32.00
☐ **Antique Telephone 1897,** (1978) gold base with black speaker and ear phone, replica of an 1897 desk phone, the second in the series of antique telephones	16.00	22.00	19.00

	Current Price Range		Prior Year Average
☐ **Antique Trader,** (c. 1968-69) the widely read ANTIQUE TRADER weekly newspaper of the trade forms this bottle with the front page clearly shown in black and red, along side the "1968 NATIONAL DIRECTORY OF ANTIQUE DEALERS" both are on a black base, Regal China, 10½"...	4.00	8.00	6.00
☐ **Arizona,** (c. 1968-69) embossed scene of Canyon, river, and cactus in blue, yellow and brown, "THE GRAND CANYON STATE" "ARIZONA" in gold, map embossed on stopper, reverse has scenes of Arizona life, Regal China, 12"...............	4.00	8.00	6.00
☐ **Beam Pot,** (1980) shaped like a New England bean pot, a colonial scene is depicted on the front, on the back, there is a large map of the New England states, the stopper is a large gold dome, this is the club bottle for the New England Beam Bottle and Specialties Club.............	22.00	28.00	25.00
☐ **Beaver Valley Club,** (1977) figurine of a beaver sitting on a stump wearing blue pants, a white shirt, a red jacket, and black bow and hat, the beaver is saluting, a club bottle to honor the Beaver Valley Jim Beam Club of Rochester	18.00	24.00	22.00
☐ **Bell Scotch,** (c. 1970) tan center, gold base, brown top with coat-of-arms of Arthur Bell & Sons on front, bottle is in the shape of a large handbell, Regal China, 10½"........................	8.00	12.00	10.00
☐ **The Big Apple,** (1979) apple shaped bottle with embossed Statue of Liberty on the front with New York City in the background and the lettering "The Big Apple" over the top	10.00	15.00	12.50
☐ **Bing Crosby 36th,** (1976) same as the Floro de Oro except for the medallion below the neck, urn-shaped bottle with pastel wide band and flowers around the middle, remainder of bottle is shiny gold with fluting and designs	28.00	36.00	32.00
☐ **Black Katz,** (c. 1968) same Kitty different color: black cat, green eyes, red tongue, white base, both Katz are Regal China, 14½".............	8.00	14.00	11.00
☐ **Blue Cherub,** (c. 1960) blue and white decanter with heavily embossed figures of Cherubs with bow & arrows gold details, scrolls and chain holding Beam Label around neck, Regal China, 12½"..	125.00	175.00	150.00
☐ **Blue Daisy,** (c. 1967) also known as "ZIMMERMAN BLUE DAISY," light blue with embossed daisies and leaves around bottle, background resembles flower basket	4.00	8.00	6.00
☐ **Blue Jay,** (c. 1969) tones of sky blue on the birds body with black & white markings, black claws grip "oak tree stump" with acorns — leaves embossed	8.00	12.00	10.00
☐ **Cheyenne, Wyoming,** (c. 1967) circular decanter in shape of a wheel, spokes separate scenes of Cheyenne history, Regal China	4.00	8.00	6.00

192 / BOTTLES

	Current Price Range		Prior Year Average
☐ **Chicago Show Bottle,** (1977) stopper is a gold loving cup standing on a black pedestal, commemorates the 6th Annual Chicago Jim Beam Bottle Show	38.00	48.00	42.00
☐ **Churchill Downs—Pink Roses,** (c. 1969-70) same as below, pink embossed roses	4.00	8.00	6.00
☐ **Churchill Downs—Red Roses,** (c. 1969-70) "CHURCHILL DOWNS — HOME OF THE 95th KENTUCKY DERBY" is embossed in gold on the front, around the main paddock building, the shell-shaped bottle comes with both red roses framing the scene, reverse: "ARISTEDES", 1st Derby winner in 1875, on a decal, Regal China, 10¾"	8.00	12.00	10.00
☐ **Circus Wagon,** (1979) replica of a circus wagon from the late 19th century, blue with gold embossing, white wheels with red trim which are movable	26.00	36.00	31.00
☐ **Civil War North,** (c. 1961) blue and grey bottle depicting Civil War battle scenes, stopper has Lee's face on one side, Grant's on the other, Regal China, 10¾" (when sold as a pair)	35.00	45.00	40.00
☐ **Civil War South,** (c. 1961) one side portrays the meeting of Lee and Jackson at Chancellorville, on the other side a meeting of southern Generals, Regal China, 10¾" (when sold as a pair)	60.00	70.00	65.00
☐ **Clear Crystal Scotch,** (c. 1966) the original patterned embossed bottle, glass stopper ("DOORKNOB"), bottom is unpatterned and has number and date of issue, Clear Glass, 11½"	10.00	15.00	12.50
☐ **Clear Crystal Bourbon,** (c. 1967) patterned embossed glass bottle with "swirl" stopper, starburst design on base of the bottle, Clear Glass, 11½"	6.00	10.00	8.00
☐ **Clear Crystal Vodka,** (c. 1967) same as above	6.00	10.00	8.00
☐ **Cleopatra Rust,** (c. 1962) same as Cleo Yellow, scene with Mark Anthony and Cleopatra in white on rust-red background	4.00	6.00	5.00
☐ **Cleopatra Yellow,** (c. 1962) black purple, 2 handled, amphora-decanter, yellow figures of Mark Anthony in armor, & Cleopatra beside the Nile, Pyramid and Sphinx background, Egyptian border design circles bottles, white stopper, rarer than Cleopatra Rust, Glass, 13¼"	12.00	16.00	14.00
☐ **Convention Number-10 Norfolk,** (1980) the sailing ship the USS Beam passing between the spokes of a ship's helm, with a gold flag atop the mast, the USS Beam is located at the Norfolk Naval Base where the 10th convention was held	20.00	26.00	23.00
☐ **Cowboy,** (1979) either antique tan or multicolored, cowboy leaning on a fence with one hand on his belt buckle and the other holding a rifle, his cowboy hat is the stopper, awarded to collectors who attended the 1979 convention for the International Association of Beam Clubs	375.00	430.00	400.00

	Current Price Range		Prior Year Average

- **Crappie,** (1979) figure of a silver and black speckled crappie commemorates the National Fresh Water Fishing Hall of Fame 10.00 15.00 12.50
- **Dark Eyes Brown Jug,** (1978) also in beige; both flecked with color — the brown jug has red flecks; the beige jug has brown flecks, regular jug shape with small handle at neck with black stopper 5.00 8.00 6.50
- **Delaware Blue Hen Bottle,** (c. 1972) this diamond shaped bottle, fashioned of genuine hand crafted Regal China commemorates the state of Delaware, "The first state of the Union," front of the bottle depicts the act of ratification of the Federal Constitution on December 7, 1787, back shows the Delaware State House, a state map and the famous Twin Bridges 6.00 10.00 8.00
- **Delco Freedom Battery,** (1978) replica of a Delco battery, entire plastic top is removable 10.00 18.00 14.00
- **Delft Blue,** (c. 1963) "Windmill Bottles" — reverse has scene of embossed Dutch windmills, on grey-white bottle, Dutch fishing boats under sail on front in "Delft" (dark blue handle and stopper), Glass, 13" 3.00 6.00 4.50
- **Emmett Kelly,** (c. 1973) a delightful genuine Regal China creation, an exact likeness of the original Emmett Kelly, as sad-faced Willie the Clown, who has capitivated and won the hearts of millions of friends over the years from the Big Top to television 20.00 40.00 30.00
- **Ernie's Flower Cart,** (1976) replica of an old-fashioned flower cart used in San Francisco, wooden cart with movable wheels, in honor of Ernie's Wines and Liquors of Northern California 22.00 30.00 26.00
- **Falstaff,** (1979) replica of Sir John Falstaff with blue and yellow outfit holding a gold goblet, second in the Australian Opera Series, music box which plays "Va, vecchio, John," limited edition of 1000 bottles 250.00 350.00 300.00
- **Fantasia Bottle,** (c. 1971) this tall, delicately hand crafted Regal China decanter is embellished with 22 karat gold and comes packaged in a handsome midnight blue and gold presentation case lined with red velvet, 16¼" 12.00 18.00 15.00
- **Fiesta Bowl,** (c. 1973) the second bottle created for the Fiesta Bowl, this bottle is made of genuine Regal China, featuring a football player on the front side 10.00 16.00 13.00
- **Figaro,** (1978) figurine of the character Figaro from the opera "Barber of Seville, spanish costume in beige, rose, and yellow, holds a brown guitar on the ground in front of him, music box plays an air from the opera 325.00 425.00 375.00
- **Grecian,** (c. 1961) a pale blue glass, "CLUB SLOT MACHINE" in tones of grey and tan, gold pinwheel and black "H" on front, Regal China, 10". 5.00 8.00 6.50

194 / BOTTLES

	Current Price Range		Prior Year Average
☐ **Grey Cherub,** (c. 1958)) checkered design, bordered with scroll work, accented with 22 karat gold, 3 embossed cherubs on neck, Regal China, 12″	375.00	475.00	425.00
☐ **Grey Slot Machine,** (c. 1968-69) the famous "HAROLDS CLUB SLOT MACHINE" in tones of grey and tan, gold pinwheel and black "H" on front, Regal China, 10″	5.00	8.00	6.50
☐ **Hannah Duston,** (c. 1973) a beautiful Regal China creation designed after the granite monument erected in her memory on Contoocook Island, in the Merrimack River north of Concord, this was where in 1697 Hannah Duston, her nurse and a young boy made their famous frantic escape from Indians, who held them captive for two weeks	20.00	28.00	24.00
☐ **Hansel And Gretel Bottle,** (c. 1971) the forlorn, lost waifs from the Brothers Grimm's beloved fable "Hansel and Gretel" are depicted on the front of this charming and beautiful Regal China bottle, above them, the words "GERMANY . . . LAND OF HANSEL AND GRETEL" stand out in gold, 10¼″	4.00	8.00	6.00
☐ **King Kong,** (1976) three-quarters body of King Kong, commemorates the Paramount Picture movie release in December 1976	10.00	16.00	13.00
☐ **Koala Bear,** (c. 1973) the Koala Bear, the native animal of Australia, a genuine Regal China creation, the bottle features two Koala Bears on a tree stump, the top of the Stump is its pourer, with the name Australia across the front of the bottle	10.00	16.00	13.00
☐ **Laramie,** (c. 1968) "CENTENNIAL JUBILEE LARAMIE WYO. 1868-1968" embossed around cowboy on bucking bronco, locomotive of 1860's on reverse, 10½″	4.00	8.00	6.00
☐ **Las Vegas,** (c. 1969) this bottle was also used for CUSTOMER SPECIALS — CASINO SERIES, "almond" shaped with gold embossed "LAS VEGAS" in a banner, and scenes of Nevada, and a gambling montage, reverse: Hoover Dam and Lake Mead, Regal China, 12½″	4.00	8.00	6.00
☐ **Light Bulb,** (1979) regular bottle shape with replica of a light bulb for the stopper, picture of Thomas Edison in a oval, letter of tribute to Edison on the back	10.00	15.00	12.50
☐ **Lombard,** (c. 1969-70) a pear-shaped decanter, embossed with lilacs and leaves around a circular motto "VILLAGE OF LOMBARD, ILLINOIS — 1869 CENTENNIAL 1969" lilac shaped stopper, reverse has an embossed outline map of Illinois, colors are lavender and green	3.00	6.00	4.50
☐ **Louisville Downs Racing Derby,** (1978) short, oblong-shaped bottle, scene with horse, buggy and rider on the front framed by wide white band with gold lettering, medallion type stopper	10.00	15.00	12.50

BOTTLES / 195

	Current Price Range		Prior Year Average

☐ **Madame Butterfly,** (1978) figurine of Madame Butterfly character from the opera of the same name, female dressed in blue and black kimono holding a realistic fan made of paper and wood, music box plays "One Fine Day" from the opera ... 475.00 575.00 525.00

☐ **New York World's Fair,** (c. 1964) the emblem of the N.Y. World's Fair of 1964 — the Unisphere forms the shape of this bottle, blue tone oceans, grey continents crossed by space flight routes, emblem embossed in gold "1964 WORLD'S FAIR — 1965," stopper has Unisphere, Regal China, 11½" 18.00 24.00 21.00

☐ **North Dakota,** (c. 1964) embossed memorial picture of a pioneer family in NORTH DAKOTA—75" embossed in gold in banner, yellows, greens and browns, Regal China, 11¾" 90.00 110.00 100.00

"NORTH DAKOTA—(75)" embossed in gold in banner 30.00 38.00 34.00

☐ **Northern Pike,** (1978) replica of the Northern Pike, green and yellow with pointed head, the sixth in a series of bottles designed for the National Fresh Water Fishing Hall of Fame 10.00 18.00 14.00

☐ **Nutcracker Toy Soldier,** (1978) figurine based on the character the toy soldier in the ballet "The Nutcracker Suite," this is not part of the opera series, small man dressed in red, white uniform with blue suspenders and gold trim, the music box plays a selection from "The Parade of the Toy Soldiers" 275.00 375.00 325.00

☐ **Ohio,** (c. 1966) bottle in shape of State, one side bears State seal, other side has pictures of State industries, Regal China, 10" 10.00 16.00 13.00

☐ **Ohio,** (c. 1973) a handsome bottle made of genuine Regal China, created in honor of the 120th Ohio State Fair 8.00 12.00 10.00

☐ **Olympian,** (c. 1960) another Greek urn decanter, chariot horses, and warriors design in white on light blue bottle, white glass stopper, embossed base, Glass, 14" 3.00 6.00 4.50

☐ **One Hundred First Airborne Division,** (1978) honors the division known during World War II as "The Screaming Eagles," a gold flying eagles on top a white pedestal 10.00 15.00 12.50

☐ **Opaline Crystal,** (1969) milk glass bottle same pattern and embossing, and stopper, Milk glass, 11½" 4.00 8.00 6.00

☐ **Oregon,** (c. 1959) green-tone bottle to honor Centennial of the state, depicting famous scenery on both sides, two beavers on bottle neck, Regal China, 8¾" 40.00 50.00 45.00

196 / BOTTLES

	Current Price Range		Prior Year Average
☐ **Pearl Harbor Memorial,** (c. 1972) honoring the Pearl Harbor Survivors Association, this handsome genuine Regal China bottle is emblazoned with the motto: "REMEMBER PEARL HARBOR — KEEP AMERICA ALERT," the stopper features the official seal of the armed services that were present December 7, 1941 — Army, Navy, Marine Corps, and Coast Guard, the stopper is set off by an American eagle, 11½"	20.00	28.00	24.00
☐ **Royal Emperor,** (c. 1958) made in the shape of a Classic Greek urn, warrior figure with spear and helmet and fret design in white on purple-black glass, white glass stopper, Glass, 14"	4.00	8.00	6.00
☐ **Royal Gold Diamond,** (c. 1964) diamond-shaped decanter set on a flaring base, all in mottled gold, gold chain holds label, Regal China, 12"	50.00	60.00	55.00
☐ **Royal Gold Round,** (c. 1956) mottled with 22 karat gold, in classic round shape with graceful pouring spout, and curved handle, gold neck chain holds label, Regal China, 12"	125.00	175.00	150.00
☐ **Royal Opal,** (c. 1957) a round, handled bottle, of Opal glass, embossed geometric design on one side, white glass stopper, bottle made by Wheaton Glass of Millville, New Jersey, same bottle was used for Harolds Club, 25th Anniversary in silver, Glass, 10¾"	6.00	10.00	8.00
☐ **Royal Porcelain,** (c. 1955) gleaming black decanter, tapered with a large flared pouring lip, white stopper, gold cord & tassel, Regal China, 14½"	400.00	500.00	450.00
☐ **Royal Rose,** (c. 1963) decanter, gold embossed with hand painted roses on a background of soft blue, gold spout, stopper, base & handle, Regal China, 17"	45.00	55.00	50.00
☐ **Ruby Crystal,** (c. 1967) amethyst colored, patterned embossed bottle, "swirl" glass stopper, when bottle is filled with bourbon it's ruby red, sunburst pattern on bottom, Amethyst Glass, 11½"	10.00	16.00	13.00
☐ **Submarine Redfin,** (c. 1970) embossed submarine on ocean-blue background, "MANITOWOC SUBMARINE MEMORIAL ASSOCIATION" in black, round stopper, with map of Wisconsin, Regal China, 11½"	4.00	8.00	6.00
☐ **Superdome,** (1975) replica of the Louisiana Superdome which opened in August 1975, white and gold with black lettering around the top	6.00	10.00	8.00
☐ **Swagman,** (1979) replica of an Australian hobo — a Swagman — who roamed that country looking for work during the depression, he wears a greyish outfit with red kerchief around his neck, a brown dog and a sheep are curled around his feet	12.00	18.00	15.00
☐ **Sydney Opera House,** (1978) replica of the building housing the Sydney Opera in Sydney, Australia. music box is in the base	25.00	32.00	28.50

BOTTLES / 197

	Current Price Range		Prior Year Average

- **Tall Dancing Scot,** (c. 1964-70) a small Scotsman encased in a glass bubble in the base dances to the music of the base, a tall pylon shaped glass bottle with a tall stopper, no dates on these bottles, Glass, 17″ **12.00 18.00   15.00**
- **Tavern Scene,** (c. 1959) two "beer stein" tavern scenes are embossed on sides, framed in wide gold band on this round decanter, Regal China, 11½″ **65.00 75.00   70.00**
- **Telephone,** (1975) replica of a 1907 phone of the Magneto Wallset type which was used from 1890 until the 1930's **28.00 34.00   31.00**
- **U.S. Open,** (c. 1972) whimsically depicts Uncle Sam's traditional hat holding a full set of golf clubs, this charming Regal China creation honors the U.S. Open Golf Tourney at the famous Pebble Beach course in California, 10½″ **12.00 18.00   15.00**
- **Vendome Drummer's Wagon,** (1975) replica of a delivery wagon, green and cream wood with yellow wheels which are plastic, honored the Vendomes of Beverly Hills, California — a food chain store which was first established in 1937 .... **60.00 70.00   65.00**
- **V.F.W. Bottle,** (c. 1971) a handsome Regal China creation designed to commemorate the 50th Anniversary of the Department of Indiana V.F.W.,this proclamation is made on the neck of the bottle, in a plaque in the shape of the state of Indiana, over a striking reproduction of the medal insignia of the V.F.W., 9¾″ **4.00   8.00   6.00**
- **Volkswagen Commemorative Bottle (2) Colors,** commemorating the Volkswagen Beetle ... the largest selling single production model vehicle in automotive history, handcrafted of genuine Regal China, this unique and exciting bottle will long remain a memento for bottle collectors the world over **10.00 18.00   14.00**
- **Walleye Pike,** (1978) tall blue bottle with a large figurine of a yellow pike at the base, designed for the National Fresh Water Fishing Hall of Fame in Hayward, Wisconsin **8.00   12.00   10.00**
- **Washington,** (1975) shaped like the state of Washington, with border and lettering in gold and white embossing, an apple and a fir tree sit on the pedestal before the map **14.00 18.00   16.00**
- **Washington — The Evergreen State,** (c. 1974) a unique Regal China creation, honoring the state of Washington — The Evergreen State, contoured to the shape of the state of Washington, this bottle features a dimensional carving of an evergreen on the front **12.00 18.00   15.00**
- **Washington State Bicentennial,** (1976) patriot dressed in black and orange holding drum, liberty bell and plaque in front of drummer **12.00 20.00   16.00**
- **Waterman,** (1980) in pewter or glazed, boatman at helm of his boat wearing rain gear, glazed version in yellow and brown **175.00 225.00 200.00**

BITTERS BOTTLES

Bitters bottles are prized by collectors because they come in a range of sizes and shapes. They were generally filled with remedies for stomach and digestive disorders.

	Current Price Range		Prior Year Average
☐ **Aunt Charity's Bitters,** label, Geo. A. Jameson Druggist, Bridgeport, Conn., clear and amber, 8½"	18.00	23.00	20.50
☐ **Dr. Aurent IXL Stomach Bitters,** Barkers, Moore & Mein, Mfg. Wholesale Merch. Phila., clear, 8½"	27.00	35.00	31.00
☐ **Ayala Mexican Bitters,** on back M. Rothenberg & Co. San Francisco, Cal., long collar with ring, amber, 9½"	60.00	80.00	70.00
☐ **Dr. M. C. Ayers Restorative Bitters,** aqua, 8½"	65.00	85.00	75.00
☐ **E. L. Bailey's Kidney And Liver Bitters,** on back best blood purifier, amber, 7¾"	60.00	80.00	70.00
☐ **Baker's High Life Bitters,** The Great Nerve Tonic embossed on back, tapered top, machine made, pint	20.00	25.00	22.50
☐ **Bakers Orange Grove,** on back bitters, roped corners, tapered top, amber, 9½"	95.00	110.00	102.00
☐ **Same as above,** except yellow	175.00	225.00	200.00
☐ **Bakers Stomach Bitters,** label, lady's leg shape, amber, 11¼"	55.00	70.00	62.00
☐ **E. Bakers Premium Bitters,** Richmond, Va., aqua, 6¾"	50.00	65.00	58.00
☐ **Dr. Balls Veg. Stom. Bitters,** Pontil, aqua, 7"	75.00	95.00	85.00
☐ **Balsdons Golden Bitters,** 1856 N.Y. other side, amber, 10½"	100.00	125.00	112.00
☐ **Corn Juice Bitters,** flask-shaped bottle, quart, aqua, pint also	70.00	90.00	80.00
☐ **Corwitz Stomach Bitters,** Amber, 7½"	45.00	60.00	52.00
☐ **Crimean Bitters,** under it on base, patent 1863, on other side Romaines Crimean Bitters, amber, 10¼"	175.00	225.00	200.00
☐ **H.M. Crookess,** stomach bitters, letters separated from the mould seam, round big blob neck, long tapered top, small kick up olive green, 10½"	325.00	400.00	362.00
☐ **Cunderango Bitters,** same on back side, greenish amber, 7¾"	60.00	80.00	70.00
☐ **Curtis Cordial Calisaya, The Great Stomach Bitters,** tapered neck, amber, 11½"	140.00	190.00	165.00
☐ **Damiana Bitters,** Baja, Calif. on back, 8-pointed star under bottom, Lewis Hess Manufr. on shoulder, aqua, 11½"	70.00	90.00	80.00
☐ **Damiana,** same as above, except no Lewis Hess Manufr. on shoulder	35.00	48.00	42.00
☐ **Dandelion Bitters,** rectangular bottle, clear, amber, tapered top, 8"	35.00	48.00	42.00
☐ **Dandelion XXX Bitters,** aqua or clear, 7"	60.00	80.00	70.00
☐ **DeWitts Stomach Bitters,** Chicago, amber, 9¾"	55.00	75.00	65.00
☐ **Doc Dunning Old Home Bitters,** Greensboro, N. Carolina, dark red, amber, 13"	75.00	95.00	85.00

	Current Price Range		Prior Year Average
☐ **Doyle's Hop Bitters,** cabin shape, 1872 on roof, several shades of amber and many variants of colors	60.00	80.00	70.00
☐ **S.T. Drakes,** on top of roof panel, 1860 plantation on next panel, Bitters on next, reverse center panel Patented 1862 with six logs, front plain for label, other covered with logs, some have five logs and the earliest have four logs, amber the most common, others: citron, pale yellow, green, scarce in olive green, 10"	120.00	160.00	140.00
☐ **Eagle Aromatic Bitters,** round bottle, "Eagle Liquor Distilleries," yellow amber, 6¾"	18.00	23.00	20.50
☐ **East India Root Bitters,** Geo. P. Clapp, sole prop., gin shaped bottle, "Boston Mass," amber, 9⅝"	110.00	140.00	125.00
☐ **Emerson Excelsior Botanic Bitters,** rectangular bottle, "E.H. Burns-Augusta-Maine," amber, 9"	14.00	18.00	16.00
☐ **J. Grossman,** Old Celebrated Stomach Bitters on other side, amber, 8¼"	65.00	85.00	75.00
☐ **Dr. Gruessie Alther's Krauter Bitters,** label, B under bottom, amber, 10½"	80.00	100.00	90.00
☐ **Gunckels Eagle Bitters,** square bottle, labeled only, amber, 9⅜"	20.00	30.00	25.00
☐ **Hagans Bitters,** amber, 9½"	55.00	75.00	65.00
☐ **E. E. Hall, New Haven,** established 1842 on base, amber, 10¼"	70.00	90.00	80.00
☐ **Hall's Bitters,** E.E. Hall, New Haven, established 1842 on back, barrel shape, amber, 9¼"	170.00	220.00	195.00
☐ **Dr. T. Hall's, Calif. Pepsin Wine Bitters,** in three lines, amber, tapered top, 9¼"	85.00	105.00	95.00
☐ **Dr. Thos. Hall's / California / Pepsin Wine Bitters,** vertically on three lines on front, light amber, 9" tall, 2½" base	60.00	80.00	70.00
☐ **Hansard's Hop Bitters,** crock, tan and green, 8"	60.00	80.00	70.00
☐ **Dr. Manley Hardy's Genuine Jaundice Bitters,** Boston, Mass., long tapered neck, aqua, 7½"	90.00	115.00	102.50
☐ **A.H. Johnson & Co.,** other side Collingwood, Ont., on front Johnson's Tonic Bitters, clear or amethyst, double top, 8¾"	21.00	27.00	24.00
☐ **Jones Indian Specific Herb Bitters,** S. W. Jones -Prop. Phila; square, amber, "patent", 1868, tapered top, 9"	65.00	85.00	75.00
☐ **Dr. Herbert John's Indian Bitters,** Great indian Discoveries; amber, 8½"	70.00	90.00	80.00
☐ **Johnson's Calisaya Bitters,** reverse Burlington Vt.; tapered top, amber, 10"	35.00	48.00	42.00
☐ **Kaiser Wilhelm Bitters Co.,** Sandusky O.; bulged neck, ringed top, round bottle, amber, clear, 10"	175.00	225.00	200.00
☐ **Kelly's Old Cabin Bitters,** patd March 1863 on one side; green, 10"	275.00	350.00	312.00
☐ **Kelly's Old Cabin Bitters,** patented 1868 or 1870 on each side of roof, amber, 9¼"	275.00	350.00	312.00
☐ **Kennedy's East India Bitters,** clear, Omaha Neb., 6½"	55.00	70.00	62.00
☐ **Koehler & Henrich Red Star Stomach Bitters,** St. Paul Minn. in a circle; label in red, black and white circle; 1908, 11½"	175.00	225.00	200.00

200 / BOTTLES

	Current Price Range		Prior Year Average
☐ **Koehlers Stomach Bitters Co.**, amber, 12½ "	30.00	40.00	35.00
☐ **Landsberg's Century Bitters**, in three lines, over it a bird or eagle, in back The Ader Company, St. Louis also in three lines, 13 stars around shoulder, also 1776 & 1876, corner diamond effect, very decorative bottle, tapered top and ring, 11½ "	315.00	385.00	350.00
☐ **Lacour's Bitters**, Sarsopariper, round fancy bottle, amber, yellow-green, 9⅛"	90.00	115.00	102.00
☐ **Morning Star Bitters**, (with Iron Pontil), fancy triangular, amber, "Inceptum 5869", patented (curve) 5869, 13"	175.00	225.00	200.00
☐ **Same without pontil**	90.00	115.00	102.00
☐ **G. N. Morrison's**, invigorating - other side, G.N. Morrison, New Orleans, amber, tapered top, 9¼ "	190.00	235.00	212.00
☐ **Moultons Oloroso Bitters**, trade (pineapple) mark, round, aqua, ribbed bottle, 11½ "	80.00	100.00	90.00
☐ **Murray's Purifying Bitters**, rectangular bottle, labeled only, aqua, 8"	18.00	24.00	21.00
☐ **National Bitters, Ear Of Corn**, patent 1867 under bottom, amber, corn, 12¼ "	200.00	250.00	225.00
☐ **New York Hop Bitters Co.**, tapered top, aqua, 9 ".	115.00	140.00	128.00
☐ **Dr. Niskian's Stomach Bitters**, on one side, Morrin-Powers, Merc.-sole agents-Kansas City, Mo. on other side, other two plain, tapered top, clear, 8¼ "	150.00	190.00	170.00
☐ **Nightcap Bitters**, Schmidlopp & Co., distillers, Cincinnati, O., a good beverage, multi-sided bottle, tapered top with ring, clear, 9"	100.00	125.00	112.00
☐ **Saidschitser-Furstlich-Lobkowitz Bitter Wasser**, in circle, tan crock, four panels, round bottom, 9½ "	90.00	115.00	102.00
☐ **Sainsevins Wine Bitters**, label, ringed top, aqua, 12"	18.00	24.00	21.00
☐ **Salmon's Perfect Stomach Bitters**, tapered top, square beveled corners, amber, 9½ "	80.00	100.00	90.00
☐ **Sanborn's Kidney & Liver Vegetable Laxative Bitters**, on bottom B, tapered bottle to paneled shoulder with fluted neck, amber, 10"	90.00	115.00	102.00
☐ **San Joaquin Wine Bitters**, on back at bottom B. F. C. Co., deep kick-up in base, amber, 9¾ "	40.00	55.00	48.00
☐ **Sarsaparilla Bitters**, on side E. M. Rusha, back side Dr. De Andrews, amber, 10"	55.00	75.00	65.00

FLASKS

☐ **All Seeing Eye**, star and large eye in center, under it A.D., in back, six-pointed star with arms, Masonic emblem, under it G.R.J.A., pontil, sheared top, amber, pint	200.00	265.00	232.00
☐ **Baltimore Monument**, and under it Balto. door with step railing, in back sloop with pennant flying, sailing to right above it Fells below point, ½ pt. 3 ribbed on side, plain top, pontil, aqua, qt. (c. 1840)	115.00	145.00	130.00

	Current Price Range	Prior Year Average
☐ **Bridgeton, New Jersey,** around a man facing to left, in back a man facing to the left with Washington around it, ribbed sides, sheared top, pontil, aqua, pint	75.00 95.00	85.00
☐ **Byron & Scott,** one picture of each, Byron on front and Scott in back, ribbed sides, sheared top, pontil, 5½″ amber	165.00 200.00	188.00
☐ **Clasped Hands — Eagle Flask,** (c. 1860-75) Union 13 stars, clasped hands, eagle above banner mark, "E", Wormer & Co., Pittsburgh, aqua, quart .	90.00 120.00	105.00
☐ **Clasped Hands — Flask,** (c. 1860-75), one with eagle and banner, above oval marked Pittsburgh, Pa., other cannon to left, flag and cannonballs, aqua, pint	75.00 95.00	85.00
☐ **H. Frank, Pat. Aug. 6, 1872,** all on bottom, circular shaped flask, two circles in center on front, reverse side plain, wide rib on sides, ring neck, aqua, pint	40.00 55.00	48.00
☐ **Franklin & Franklin,** aqua, quart	120.00 160.00	135.00
☐ **Gen. MacArthur and God Bless America,** purple or green, ½ pint	10.00 15.00	12.50
☐ **G.H.A.,** Concord, N.Y. 1865, aqua, ½ pint	16.00 22.00	19.00
☐ **Girl For Joe,** girl on bicycle, aqua, pint	65.00 85.00	75.00
☐ **Granite Glass Co.,** in three lines, reverse Stoddard, N.H., sheared top, olive, pint	140.00 190.00	165.00
☐ **Isabella G.W.,** sheaf of wheat, pint	70.00 90.00	80.00
☐ **Jenny Lind Lyre,** aqua, pint	100.00 140.00	120.00
☐ **Keen — P & W — Sunburst Flask** (c. 1814-30), olive amber, ½ pint	175.00 260.00	218.00
☐ **Keene Masonic,** tooled lip, pontil, pint	180.00 230.00	205.00
☐ **Lowell R.R.,** olive, amber, ½ pint	120.00 150.00	135.00
☐ **Lyndeboro, L.G. CO.,** patent on shoulder, aqua, pint	18.00 25.00	21.50
☐ **Lyndeboro, L.G. Co.,** golden amber, quart	32.00 43.00	36.50
☐ **"New London Glasswork" — Anchor Eagle Flask,** golden amber, pint, (c. 1860-66)	375.00 500.00	420.00
☐ **For Pike's Peak,** old rye, aqua, pint	40.00 55.00	48.00
☐ **Pikes Peak,** traveler and hunter, olive, amber, pint	190.00 240.00	215.00
☐ **Pike's Peak Historical Flask — Penn. —** (c. 1859-70), ring top, Eagle - Prospector to right, under it "For Pike's Peak", yellow amber, pint ...	525.00 650.00	585.00
☐ **Pittsburgh,** double eagle, citron, pint	190.00 240.00	215.00
☐ **Ravenna,** in center, anchor with rope, under it Glass Company, ring top, aqua, pint	130.00 165.00	142.00
☐ **Ravenna Travelers Companion,** pontil, amber, quart	220.00 310.00	265.00
☐ **Rehm Bros.,** Bush & Buchanan Sts & O'Farrel & Mason Sts, in a sunken circle, ribbed bottom, two rings near shoulder, coffin type, metal and cork cap, clear or amethyst, ½ pint	90.00 125.00	107.00
☐ **Springfield G.W. And Cabin,** aqua, ½ pint	60.00 80.00	70.00
☐ **Spring Garden,** in center, anchor, under it Glass Works, reverse side, log cabin with a tree to the right, ring top, aqua, ½ pint	120.00 155.00	138.00
☐ **Spring Garden Glasswork Flask, Md.** yellow olive, pint	320.00 400.00	360.00

202 / BOTTLES

	Current Price Range		Prior Year Average
☐ **Taylor & Ringgold,** pontil, plaintop, aqua, pint (c. 1845)	110.00	140.00	125.00
☐ **Travelers,** in center a sunflower, under it Companion, in back Ravenna, in center sunflower, under it Glass Co., sheared top, amber, pint	110.00	145.00	125.00
☐ **Travelers Companion,** and sheaf, amber, quart	100.00	135.00	118.00
☐ **Union,** clasped hands in shield, eagle with banner on reverse side, pint	55.00	75.00	65.00
☐ **Vertically Ribbed Sunburst Flask** (c. 1810-50) light blue green, ½ pint	180.00	230.00	205.00
☐ **Warranted Flask,** clear or amethyst, 7½"	9.00	12.00	10.50
☐ **Washington,** above bust in ¾ circle, the father of his country in back I have endeavour, D. Do my duty above bust in ¾ circle, qt. plain edge, plain top, aqua	70.00	100.00	85.00
☐ **Washington Bust,** in back tree, Calabash flask, qt., aqua sloping collared with ring, vertical fluting, pontil, (c. 1850)	70.00	95.00	82.00
☐ **Washington Flask** (c. 1840-60) Father of His Country around bust, back plain, N.Y., plain top, light green, pint	90.00	120.00	105.00
☐ **Washington — Taylor** (c. 1833-60) Washington facing left, back, Taylor facing left, deep blue green, quart	350.00	450.00	400.00

MINERAL WATER BOTTLES

☐ **Allen Mineral Water,** horizontal letters placed vertically on bottle, blob top, golden amber, 11½"	12.00	16.00	14.00
☐ **American Kissinger Water,** in vertical lines, tapered top and ring, aqua, pint	55.00	70.00	62.00
☐ **Artesian Spring Co.,** in center an "S" superimposed over an "A". under it Ballston, N.Y., tapered top and ring pt. emerald green, (40.00)	36.00	48.00	43.00
☐ **Astorg Springs Mineral Water, S.F., Cal.,** blob top, green, 7"	11.00	15.00	13.00
☐ **Bartlett Spring Mineral Water, California,** in a slug plate, blob top, 11⅝"	15.00	22.00	18.50
☐ **Bauman, N., Pottsville, Pa.,** in 4 lines, slug plate, (c. 1860) ground pontil, tapered top and ring, green, 7½"	65.00	85.00	75.00
☐ **Blue Lick Water Co., Ky,** mineral water bottle, double ring top, pontil, pt. amber	110.00	135.00	128.00
☐ **Bowden Lithia Water,** under it a house and trees, under that Lithia Spring Ca., blob top, aqua	12.00	17.00	14.50
☐ **Buffalo Luthis' Water,** natures Materia Medica, lady sitting with pitcher in hand, under it, trade mark, round, aqua, 11½"	11.00	15.00	13.00
☐ **Bythinia Water,** tapered top, amber, 10¼"	6.00	9.00	7.50
☐ **California Natural Seltzer Water,** reverse side picture of a bear, H.&G., blob top, aqua, 7¼"	18.00	26.00	22.00
☐ **Campbell Mineral Water, C., Brulington, Vt.,** (c.1870), plain bottom, tapered top and ring, aqua, quart	120.00	170.00	150.00
☐ **Crystal Spring Water,** in horseshoe shape, under it, C.R. Brown Saratoga Spring, N.Y., quart, green, 9½"	90.00	125.00	107.00

	Current Price Range		Prior Year Average
☐ **Dearborn, J & A,** in ¼ moon letters under it New York, in back "D" tapered blob top, pontil, blue, 7½" (c.1857)................................	75.00	95.00	85.00
☐ **Deep Spring,** three-part mold, C in a diamond under bottom, amber, 12¾"...................	16.00	23.00	19.50
☐ **Eagle Spring Distillery Co.,** on front, rectangular, amethyst, 7".................................	5.00	7.00	6.00
☐ **Elk Spring Water Co., Buffalo, N.Y.,** on front in oval slug plate, blob top, ½ gallon, clear............	17.00	25.00	21.00
☐ **Empire Spring Co.,** E in center, Sarotoga, N.Y., back, Empire Water, green, tapered top and ring, 7½"..	27.00	36.00	31.50
☐ **The Excelsior Water,** on eight panels, blob top, graphite pontil, green, 7¼"...................	65.00	85.00	75.00
☐ **Farrel's Mineral Water, Evansville, Ind.,** graphite pontil, aqua, 7½".............................	47.00	60.00	52.00
☐ **Franklin Spring, Mineral Water,** Ballston, SPA Saratoga Co. N.Y., mineral water bottle, emerald green, pt.....................................	95.00	125.00	115.00
☐ **Geyser Spring, Saratoga Spring, State Of N.Y.,** light blue, 7¾"...............................	24.00	35.00	29.50
☐ **Gibley's Spey Royal,** label, three dots and number under bottom, golden amber, 8"..............	13.00	18.00	14.50
☐ **Glacier Spouting Spring,** glacier misspelled, In horseshoe shape, letters under it Saratoga Spring, N.Y., in back a fountain, green, pint............	130.00	165.00	148.00
☐ **Guilford Mineral Spring Water,** inside of a diamond in center, also G.M.S., under it Guilford, Vt., short neck, dark green, 10"....................	31.00	40.00	35.50
☐ **Harris Albany Mineral Waters,** graphite pontil, tapered top, aqua, 7¼"......................	24.00	33.00	28.50
☐ **Hathorn Spring,** in horseshoe shape, under this, Saratoga, N.Y., dark amber, under bottle a "drop" and a letter H, round, 7½"....................	31.00	42.00	36.50
☐ **Highrock Congress Spring,** rock, under it C&W, SAT, NY, green..............................	60.00	75.00	68.00
☐ **Holmes & Co. Mineral Water,** ground pontil, blue, 7½"..	40.00	60.00	50.00
☐ **Improved Mineral Water,** blob top, graphite pontil, blue, 6¼".....................................	31.00	40.00	34.50
☐ **Indian Spring,** in center, Indian head under bottom, aqua, 10½"............................	15.00	22.00	18.50
☐ **Jackson's NAPA Soda Spring,** on front, reverse side Natural Mineral Water, blob top, aqua, 7½".	8.00	12.00	10.00
☐ **Johnsotn & Co. Phila.,** in large block letters, on back large fancy 2" J., tapered top, sea green, 6¾"..	15.00	22.00	18.50
☐ **J. Kennedy, Mineral Water, Pittsburg,** in three lines on back, script letters J.K., graphite pontil, blob top, green, 7½"...............................	35.00	43.00	39.00
☐ **Kissinger Water,** dark olive, 6¼"..............	29.00	37.00	33.00
☐ **Lynch & Clark, New York Mineral Water,** tapered top & ring pontil, olive amber, pt...............	100.00	130.00	115.00
☐ **Lytton Spring,** in center a pelican, Sweet Drinks under it, in three lines P.M.H. Co., San Francisco, C.H.B., aqua, 6½"...........................	15.00	22.00	18.50

204 / BOTTLES

	Current Price Range		Prior Year Average
☐ **Magentic Spring, Henniker, N.H.,** tapered top & ring, qt. Go. amber plain bottom (c.1868)	80.00	100.00	90.00
☐ **J. Manke & Co, Savannah,** in two lines, in back mineral water, blob top, aqua, 7"	16.00	24.00	20.00
☐ **New Almaden Mineral Water, W&W,** on panels, ten panels, tapered top, blob top, graphite pontil, green, 7½"	40.00	60.00	50.00
☐ **Oak Orchard Acid Spring,** on shoulder H.W. BOSTWICK Agt., No. 574 Broadway, N.Y., on bottom From F. Hutchins Factory Glass, Lockport, N.Y., light amber, 9"	32.00	45.00	38.50
☐ **O.K. Bottling Co.,** O.K., in center 526, 528, 530, W. 38th St., N.Y., reverse side Indian holding a flag, aqua, 10¾"	16.00	23.00	19.50
☐ **Pablo & Co.,** Mineral Water Factory on back, aqua, 7½"	14.00	19.00	16.50
☐ **Pacific Congress Water,** on bottom, crown top, four-piece mold, aqua, 8¼"	7.00	10.00	8.50
☐ **Prist NAPA,** a natural mineral water recarbonated at St. Helena from the priest, Mineral Spring, Napa Co., Calif., applied crown, aqua, 7¼"	8.00	11.00	9.50
☐ **Pure Natural Waters Co., Pittsburg, Pa.,** inside fancy shield, with house embossed in center, crown top, ABM, aqua, 12¼"	5.00	8.00	6.50
☐ **The Puritan Water Co., N.Y.,** aqua, 12¼"	7.00	9.00	8.00
☐ **Rockbridge Alum Water,** aqua, 9½"	11.00	15.00	13.00
☐ **Round Lake Mineral Water,** Saratoga, N.Y., amber, 7¾"	80.00	100.00	90.00
☐ **Rutherfords Premium Mineral Water,** ground pontil, dark olive, 7½"	55.00	75.00	65.00
☐ **Shasta Water Co.,** Mineral Water Co., amber, 10½"	7.00	9.00	8.00
☐ **Shoco Lithia Spring Co., Lincoln, NEB.,** crown top, aqua, 7¾"	6.00	9.00	7.50
☐ **Steinike & Weinlig Schulz Marke,** embossed hand holding some tools, Seltzers in large letters on back, three-piece mold, blob top, emerald green, 9¾"	13.00	20.00	16.50
☐ **Tolenas Soda Springs,** reverse side Natural Mineral Water, tapered neck, blob top, aqua blue, 7"	15.00	21.00	18.00
☐ **Triton Spouting Spring,** in horseshoe shape, in center block letter T, under it, Saratoga, N.Y., in back Triton Water, pint, aqua	85.00	110.00	98.00
☐ **Union Spring,** Saratoga, N.Y. in a circle, green, 8"	75.00	100.00	82.00
☐ **Ute Chief Of Mineral Water,** Maniton, Colo., U.T. on base, crown top, clear or purple, 8"	5.00	8.00	6.50

POISON BOTTLES

☐ **The Clarke Fluid Co., Cincinnati,** poison on side, 8 to 64 oz. graduated measure on other side, clear or amethyst, quart size	20.00	30.00	25.00
☐ **Cocaine Hydrochlor Poison,** label, triangular, vertical ribs, ring top, amber, 5"	12.00	17.00	14.50

	Current Price Range		Prior Year Average
☐ **Depose**, on bottom, four-cornered, label reads Riodine Organic Iodine 50 capsules, 4 1/8" tall, 1 3/4" x 1/2" neck	6.00	9.00	7.50
☐ **Durfree Embalming Fluid Co.**, 8 to 64 oz. graduated measure, clear or amethyst, 1/2 gallon	16.00	23.00	19.50
☐ **Ecorc: Quinguina Pulv**, pontil, clear, painted brown, 5 3/4"	15.00	22.00	18.50
☐ **Evans Medical Ltd., Liverpool**, label, Chloroform B.A., Poison, number and U.Y.B. under bottom, ABM, amber, 6 1/2"	5.00	8.00	6.50
☐ **Ferris & Co., Ltd., Bristol**, near base, poison in center, vertical ribbing, wide ring top, aqua, 7 1/2"	11.00	15.00	13.00
☐ **Frederia**, vertical, flask type, hobnail clover, clear, 1/2 pint	50.00	70.00	60.00
☐ **Ikey Einstein, Poison**, on each side of it, rectangular, ring top, clear, 3 3/4"	18.00	25.00	21.50
☐ **Iodine Poison Tinct.**, machine made, amber, 2 1/4"	4.00	6.00	5.00
☐ **Lin Belladon**, label, under bottom Y.G. CO., green, 7"	18.00	25.00	21.50
☐ **McCormick & Co., Balto.**, in a circle, in center a fly or been under it, Patent Applied For, triangular, ring top, cobalt, 1 1/2" tall	6.00	9.00	7.50
☐ **Melvin & Badger, Apothecaries, Boston, Mass.**, ribbing on side, ring top, cobalt, 7 1/2"	100.00	130.00	115.00
☐ **The Norwick Pharmacy Co., Norwick, N.Y.**, label, M under bottom, ABM, cobalt, 3 1/2"	11.00	16.00	13.50
☐ **Orge Monde**, label, cut glass, blue	27.00	35.00	31.00
☐ **Owl Poison Ammonia**, label, three-cornered, cobalt, 5 1/4"	30.00	40.00	35.00
☐ **Pyrox Bowker Insecticide Co., Boston & Baltimore**, cream crock, glass top, 7 1/2"	10.00	15.00	12.50
☐ **Riddes**, 7073 under bottom, 6 1/2", *three-cornered with ribs or edges, ring top*, aqua	18.00	26.00	22.00
☐ **Reese Chemical Co., Cleveland, Ohio**, for external use only, etc., rectanglar, 5 1/2", *sides ribbed, flat and ring top*, cobalt, green, clear	16.00	24.00	20.00
☐ **S & D**, 173 under bottom, ABM, poison label, cobalt, 2 1/2"	17.00	25.00	21.00
☐ **Sharp & Dohme**, on one panel, Phila on other panel, label, X126-1 under bottom, three cornered, cobalt, 2"	9.00	12.00	10.50
☐ **Tincture: Senegae, Label**, under bottom number 6 U.G.B. ABM, amber, 6"	10.00	15.00	12.50
☐ **Trilets**, vertical, other side poison, triangular, cobalt, 3 1/2", ribbed corner, ABM	7.00	10.00	8.50

WHISKEY BOTTLES

Within the past decade modern, annual, and commemorative issues of many decorative and collectors items have been produced. This trend has moved into bottle collecting. Hundreds of new figurals have been produced to satisfy this demand.

EZRA BROOKS BOTTLES

☐ **American Legion**, (1971) distinguished embossed star emblem born out of WWI struggle, combination blue and gold, on blue base	25.00	34.00	29.50

206 / BOTTLES

	Current Price Range		Prior Year Average
☐ **Big Bertha,** Nugget Casino's very-own elephant with a raised trunk, gray, red, white and black, yellow & gold trim, "blanket" and stand	8.00	12.00	10.00
☐ **Busy Beaver,** this genuine Heritage China ceramic is a salute to the beaver, truly one of nature's wonders	6.00	10.00	8.00
☐ **Cabin Still,** hillbilly, papers from company, gallon	35.00	45.00	40.00
☐ **Conquistadors,** tribute to a great drum & bugle corps, silver colored trumpet attached to drum	6.00	12.00	9.00
☐ **English Setter—Bird Dog,** (c. 1971) happy hunting dog retrieving red pheasant, white flecked with black, yellow base	10.00	15.00	12.50
☐ **Gamecock,** (1970) all feathers and fury against rival birds, red with yellow base	10.00	15.00	12.50
☐ **Hopi Kachina,** (1973) genuine Heritage China ceramic reproduction of a Hummingbird Kachina Doll	60.00	70.00	65.00
☐ **Little Giant,** (1971) replica of the first horse-drawn steam engine to arrive at the Chicago fire in 1871, red, black with gold trim	11.00	16.00	13.50
☐ **Maine Lobster,** (1970) bottle in lobster shape, complete with claws, pinkish-red color, bottle is sold only in Maine	20.00	28.00	24.00
☐ **Oil Gusher,** bottle in shape of oil drilling rig, all silver, jet black stopper in shape of gushing oil	5.00	8.00	6.50
☐ **Pot-Bellied Stove,** (1968) "Old-Time" round coal burning stove with ornate legs and "Fire" in the grate, black and red	8.00	10.00	9.00
☐ **Red Fox,** (1979) wild life	40.00	46.00	43.00

GARNIER

☐ **Bahamas,** black policeman, white jacket, hat, black pants, red stripe, gold details	11.00	15.00	13.50
☐ **Canada,** "Mountie" in red jacket, black jodphur, brown boots	11.00	14.00	12.50
☐ **Coffee Mill,** (1966) white with blue flowers	11.00	15.00	13.00
☐ **Elephant Figural,** (1961) black with ivory white tusks, 6¾"	13.00	19.00	16.00
☐ **Ford, 1913,** (1970) green open body and wheels, black trim, 4" x 10¾"	5.00	8.00	6.50
☐ **Giraffe,** (1961) yellow "marble," modern animal figure, 18"	11.00	14.00	12.50
☐ **Hussar,** (1949) French Cavalry soldier of 1800's holding sword, maroon color, 13¾"	25.00	33.00	29.00
☐ **Lancer,** (1949) light green soldier holding drum, 13"	15.00	22.00	18.50
☐ **Loon,** (1970) sitting bird, white, brown, tan, blue base, 11"	7.00	10.00	8.50
☐ **Mockingbird,** (1970) black and white bird on "tree" stump, 11"	7.00	10.00	8.50
☐ **Packard, 1930,** (1970) orange body, cream roof and wheels, black trim, 4" x 10"	6.00	8.00	7.00
☐ **Rolls Royce, 1908,** (1970) open touring car in yellow, red seats and hubs, black trim, 4" x 10½"	8.00	11.00	9.50

	Current Price Range		Prior Year Average
☐ **Scarecrow,** (1960) yellow "straw" body and hat, green jacket, red stripe face and tie, bird on shoulder, 12"	11.00	14.00	12.50
☐ **Snail,** (1950) white and brown with spiral shell, 6½" x 10"	13.00	18.00	15.50

LUXARDO

	Current Price Range		Prior Year Average
☐ **Autumn Wine Pitcher,** (c. 1958) hand painted country scene, handled pitcher	19.00	26.00	22.50
☐ **Baby Amphoras,** (c. 1956) six hand painted miniature bottles set vari-colored	16.00	23.00	19.50
☐ **Cellini Vase,** (c. 1957) glass and silver handled decanter, fancy, with serpent handle	14.00	19.00	16.50
☐ **Diana—Decanter,** (c. 1956) white figure of Diana with deer on black single handled decanter	11.00	16.00	13.50
☐ **Duck-Green Glass Figural,** (c. 1960) green and amber duck, clear glass base	20.00	27.00	23.50
☐ **Fighting Cocks,** (c. 1962) combination decanter and ashtray, black and red fighting birds	14.00	19.00	16.50
☐ **Gondola,** (c. 1959) highly glazed "abstract" gondola and gondolier in black, orange and yellow, stopper on upper prow, 12¾"	21.00	27.00	24.00
☐ **Mayan,** (c. 1960) a Mayan temple God head mask, brown, yellow, black, white, 11"	14.00	19.00	16.50
☐ **Pheasant—Red And Gold Figural,** (c. 1960) red and gold glass bird on crystal base	23.00	35.00	29.00
☐ **Sir Lancelot,** (c. 1962) figure of English knight in full armor with embossed shield, tan-gray w/gold, 12"	14.00	19.00	16.50
☐ **Tower Of Fruit,** (c. 1968) various fruits in natural colors, 22¼"	14.00	19.00	16.50

BOXES

Boxes are among the most useful and fascinating collectibles. They come in a variety of shapes, sizes and materials and they can be used for storage of various articles. The artistic design of boxes reflects much of what is considered American today.

Once thought to be a woman's hobby, the collecting of boxes has begun to attract more males as more people become acquainted with various specialized uses for boxes. The perfume box and jewelry box are being supplemented with other special purpose designs, such as boxes for the storage of navigational or drafting equipment, surgical or pharmaceutical instruments, presentation boxes for pistols, bottles of wine or liquor, wine glasses, or silverware. The list is seemingly endless. Still other boxes were constructed to preserve perishable items such as tea, snuff, and cigars.

Prices for boxes are determined by size, shape, size, age, use, rarity and, of course, the material for which it is made and the degree of craftsmanship evident in its construction.

208 / BOXES

Box, shape #514, Lenox rose pattern .... $105.00-$120.00

	Current Price Range		Prior Year Average
☐ **Apple box,** footed, smoked finish	260.00	310.00	275.00
☐ **Apple box,** pine, painted, 11″ x 8½″	55.00	80.00	62.00
☐ **Ballot box,** maple, oblong, sliding top	105.00	135.00	120.00
☐ **Band box,** oval, painted, schoolhouse, flowers and trees on lid, 9″ x 6″	1400.00	1900.00	1600.00
☐ **Band box,** man and woman with flowers on lid, flowers on sides	1300.00	1800.00	1500.00
☐ **Band box,** hunter shooting deer	600.00	700.00	585.00
☐ **Bible box,** carved oak, English, mid 1600's	430.00	480.00	450.00
☐ **Book-shaped box,** inlaid, large	85.00	110.00	90.00
☐ **Book-shaped box,** with name and dated 1861 ...	325.00	375.00	350.00
☐ **Book-shaped box,** Pennsylvania German, painted wood	55.00	110.00	75.00
☐ **Book-shaped box,** inlaid colored wax hearts, stars	30.00	45.00	38.00
☐ **Box,** Wilcox, quadruple plate, scrolls, pointer dogs, lock lion's paw feet, 9″ x 5″	185.00	210.00	182.00
☐ **Brass box,** covered with leather, shape of coffin .	50.00	70.00	55.00
☐ **Bride's box,** painted flowers, dark green, c. 1817 .	275.00	325.00	275.00
☐ **Bride's box,** oval, painted bride and groom with floral motif, 18″	385.00	435.00	400.00
☐ **Bride's box,** German or Pennsylvania German, oval, 19th c.	210.00	260.00	225.00
☐ **Butter box,** six individual containers	110.00	145.00	118.00
☐ **Candle box,** cherry, carved, scalloped arch	410.00	460.00	425.00
☐ **Candle box,** geometric design, carved and inlaid, 8″	110.00	145.00	118.00

BOXES / 209

	Current Price Range	Prior Year Average
☐ **Candle box,** pine, sliding lid, red border, knob on lid, 14″	385.00 430.00	400.00
☐ **Candle box,** tin, hanging, round	180.00 230.00	200.00
☐ **Cheese box,** tree and leaf design, inlaid mahogany, 7″ Dia.	380.00 430.00	400.00
☐ **Cigar box,** coromandel with brass fittings, mid 19th c.	180.00 230.00	200.00
☐ **Cigarette box,** "Wavecrest," cream, blue, white, pink forget-me-nots, word "Cigarettes," 4″ H.	260.00 310.00	275.00
☐ **Cigarette box,** cloisonne, cylindrical, unmarked	65.00 110.00	80.00
☐ **Cigarette or chocolate box,** brass, Princess Mary, WW1, with Mary, and names of Allies around lid	38.00 48.00	40.00
☐ **Coin box,** oak, changer, c. 1823	260.00 310.00	275.00
☐ **Collar box,** man's, with drawer, black with red lining	9.00 13.00	10.00
☐ **Cookie box,** round with lid and handle, Pennsylvania Dutch design	280.00 330.00	300.00
☐ **Cutlery box,** triple compartments, walnut, 10″ x 16″	60.00 70.00	60.00
☐ **Deed box,** wood, carved	80.00 105.00	82.00
☐ **Desk box,** mahoghany, compartments for writing tools and ink, original hardware, 5″ x 4½″ x 14″.	280.00 330.00	300.00
☐ **Desk box,** painted red, slant lid, 17½″ W.	110.00 135.00	112.00
☐ **Dome top box,** bird motif, 10″ W.	460.00 510.00	475.00
☐ **Dresser box,** orange plush with molded celluloid trim, all tools intact	30.00 40.00	30.00
☐ **Glove box,** coromandel, gilt brass with green stones inlaid	65.00 95.00	75.00
☐ **Glove box,** covered with wallpaper	80.00 110.00	82.00
☐ **Hat box,** covered with bird motif wallpaper	135.00 160.00	138.00
☐ **Hat box,** wooden, original finish and hardware, c. 1874-90	110.00 135.00	112.00
☐ **Herb box,** oval, original paint and lid	280.00 330.00	300.00
☐ **Jewelry box,** plated silver (replated), cherubs playing, 8″ x 6″ x 3″	110.00 160.00	125.00
☐ **Jewel casket,** Simpson, Hall and Miller silverplate, round on pedestal with three cupids with wings, finial, another cherub	110.00 160.00	125.00
☐ **Jewel box,** Jenning Bros. ormolu, scenes of lovers, children in relief, pink plush lining, 2½″ H.	22.00 32.00	25.00
☐ **Jewel box,** Pairpont "Wavecrest," 9″ Dia.	725.00 825.00	750.00
☐ **Jewel box,** "Wavecrest," ormolu mounts, square shape, 7″ x 7″ x 5″	425.00 475.00	425.00
☐ **Knife box,** curly maple, dovetailed	55.00 70.00	58.00
☐ **Knife box,** pine, scalloped, dovetailed	160.00 185.00	162.00
☐ **Knife box,** walnut, carved handle	110.00 135.00	112.00
☐ **Lacquered box,** octagonal, yellow with Oriental designs, early 19th c.	280.00 330.00	300.00
☐ **Lap desk,** brass inlaid, walnut, 15″ W.	140.00 190.00	150.00
☐ **Leather box,** pressed design	14.00 20.00	15.00
☐ **Lectern box,** carved, painted, with carved book on top	17000.00 18000.00	17000.00
☐ **Lunch box,** oval, 19th c.	45.00 55.00	45.00
☐ **Lunch box,** tin, Art Deco design, nursery characters	45.00 55.00	45.00
☐ **Match box,** wooden, carved, 5″ H.	32.00 42.00	35.00

210 / BOXES

	Current Price Range		Prior Year Average
☐ **Pantry box,** Scandinavian Bentwood	110.00	150.00	125.00
☐ **Pantry box,** varnished, 10″	28.00	42.00	32.00
☐ **Pantry box,** two-fingered round, small size	110.00	150.00	120.00
☐ **Pantry box,** three-fingered oval, painted red (possibly Shaker)	135.00	180.00	150.00
☐ **Pantry box,** oval, two-fingered, c. 1820	135.00	180.00	150.00
☐ **Pantry boxes,** five graduated, round, painted ...	160.00	210.00	180.00
☐ **Patch box,** Royal Bayreuth tapestry, five sheep on lid, gray mark, 2½″ x 1½″	140.00	180.00	150.00
☐ **Pencil box,** sliding lid, dovetailed	22.00	32.00	25.00
☐ **Pipe box,** pine, drawer, dovetailed	330.00	360.00	338.00
☐ **Salt box,** curved front, flat black, painted red	55.00	70.00	62.00
☐ **Salt box,** maple and cherry, striped wood, hinged cover, hanging	110.00	135.00	112.00
☐ **Salt box,** pine, dovetailed, open, hanging	90.00	110.00	92.00
☐ **Salt box,** walnut, dovetailed, slant lid, hanging ..	140.00	170.00	150.00
☐ **Salt box,** Pennsylvania Dutch design, two compartments, open	180.00	210.00	182.00
☐ **Seed box,** compartments, sliding lid	135.00	160.00	138.00
☐ **Shaving box,** brush	45.00	55.00	45.00
☐ **Snuff box,** Mauchline ware, boxwood, 3½″ W. ..	55.00	80.00	62.00
☐ **Snuff box,** horn, acorn-shaped, screw-on top, 1¾″	28.00	38.00	30.00
☐ **Snuff box,** pewter	38.00	48.00	40.00
☐ **Snuff box,** treenware, 2¾″ Dia.	18.00	24.00	18.00
☐ **Spice box,** cherry, nine drawers, original, 13″ H. .	150.00	175.00	152.00
☐ **Spice box,** curly maple, twelve drawers, brass pulls	315.00	365.00	325.00
☐ **Spice box,** oak, eight drawers, wooden pulls, hanging	80.00	110.00	82.00
☐ **Spice box,** pine, eight drawers, porcelain pulls, hanging	100.00	130.00	102.00
☐ **Spice box,** tin, eight drawers, painted black	100.00	130.00	102.00
☐ **Spice box,** walnut, two drawers, carved back, dovetailed	280.00	330.00	300.00
☐ **Stamp box,** brass, footed, covered	45.00	55.00	45.00
☐ **Stamp box,** pewter, hinged top	65.00	85.00	70.00
☐ **Stamp box,** sterling with enameled lid, chair and finger ring	28.00	38.00	30.00
☐ **Stationery box,** walnut with brass and ivory decoration, 7″ H., late 19th c.	120.00	170.00	135.00
☐ **Tea caddy,** Marguetry, English, c. 1780	550.00	650.00	562.00
☐ **Tea caddy,** imitation tortoise shell, green, English, early 19th c.	230.00	280.00	250.00
☐ **Tobacco box,** Pennsylvania Dutch design, 19″ H.	55.00	70.00	62.00
☐ **Tool box,** oak	28.00	32.00	30.00
☐ **Tool box,** child's, with tools, c. 1930	45.00	55.00	45.00
☐ **Tramp Art box,** footed, geometic design, hinged top, 14″ x 15″	185.00	210.00	182.00
☐ **Tramp Art wall boxes,** small	32.00	48.00	38.00
☐ **Trinket box,** painted, one drawer	325.00	375.00	325.00
☐ **Trinket box,** wooden, carved, painted flowers, 6″ H.	325.00	375.00	325.00
☐ **Wall box,** open top, painted brown, 19th c.	160.00	210.00	175.00
☐ **Writing box,** oak, English, 13½″ W., 18th c.	135.00	185.00	150.00
☐ **Writing box,** Shaker, two drawers	135.00	185.00	150.00

BUTTONS

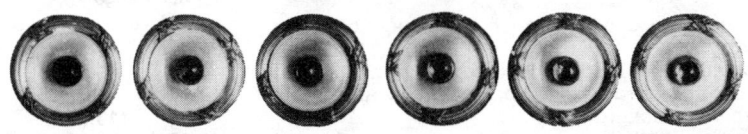

Mother-of-pearl, cabochon sapphires, platinum top, gold, fitted leather box, maker: Tiffany & Co., buttons, c. 1915 . . . . **$650.00-$750.00**

The invention of buttons dates back to the 13th century. They were used primarily as ornamentation on clothes that were fastened by some other means. As a form of jewelry, they were designed by notable jewelers and artisans for the wealthy and aristocratic.

Most surviving specimens are from the 18th to 20th centuries. They fall into more than 400 different categories. They are classified by subject, size or material of which they are made.

Buttons are, on the whole, a relatively inexpensive collectible. Even those of handsome or unusual design, or those proven to be quite old, are generally available for under $10. Many cost less than $1 and quite a few can be purchased for 25¢. Buttons made of exotic materials, exquisitely carved and detailed will, of course, be quite expensive.

A collector may want to start his collection by purchasing an assortment of buttons at a flea market or house sale. By sorting and classifying, he may find a few exciting specimens upon which to base his collection. Another method would be to purchase a collection from a former hobbyist. In this way the novice can learn from another's purchases and may be able to obtain specimens that are no longer easily accessible.

	Current Price Range		Prior Year Average
☐ **Black glass,** cameo head	12.00	18.00	12.50
☐ **Black glass,** elephant under palm tree	5.50	11.00	7.50
☐ **Black glass,** faceted ball, gold foil top	32.00	42.00	35.00
☐ **Black glass,** mountain with house scene, beaded gilt edge	32.00	42.00	35.00
☐ **Black glass,** shape of a slipper	9.00	13.00	10.00
☐ **Brass,** Aesop's Fable, frog and rabbit	20.00	28.00	21.50
☐ **Brass,** Aesop's Fable, two mice	32.00	42.00	35.00
☐ **Brass,** angry rooster	9.00	13.00	10.00
☐ **Brass,** cherubs with cornucopia and goat	3.25	6.50	4.50
☐ **Brass,** children playing game, Victorian era	20.00	28.00	21.50
☐ **Brass,** dancing gypsy girl with goat	42.00	58.00	48.00
☐ **Brass disc,** bridge and river scene, black and white	65.00	95.00	75.00
☐ **Brass,** Indian hunter	32.00	42.00	35.00
☐ **Brass,** mother feeding child, high relief	20.00	28.00	21.50
☐ **Brass,** rooster standing on wheat shaft	14.00	22.00	16.00
☐ **Celluloid,** angel head, gold background, gilt rims	32.00	42.00	35.00
☐ **Celluloid,** Count Fersen, floral brass frame	20.00	28.00	21.00
☐ **Celluloid,** Duchess of Devonshire, pastel colors .	38.00	52.00	42.00
☐ **Celluloid,** Marie Antonette	9.00	13.00	10.00
☐ **Ceramic,** bird, black and white	22.00	32.00	25.00

212 / BUTTONS

	Current Price Range		Prior Year Average
☐ **Ceramic,** bird with branch in beak, scalloped border	32.00	42.00	35.00
☐ **Ceramic,** cupid, scroll design on edge	45.00	55.00	45.00
☐ **Cloisonne,** birds flying, brass, black and white with red background	80.00	110.00	82.00
☐ **Enamel,** lighthouse with boat scene	45.00	55.00	45.00
☐ **Enamel,** lady riding bicycle, cut steel border	60.00	75.00	62.00
☐ **Enamel,** maiden, blue and white, diamond paste border	50.00	65.00	52.00
☐ **Enamel,** portrait of lady, black background, 18th c.	60.00	75.00	62.00
☐ **Enamel,** rose colored scene on white, embossed scroll border	185.00	235.00	200.00
☐ **Enamel,** shepherdess, light purple, diamond paste border	45.00	55.00	45.00
☐ **Enamel,** star shape decorated with cut steels	14.00	22.00	16.00
☐ **Enamel,** woman at fountain	50.00	70.00	55.00
☐ **Glass,** black liberty cap and flag, silver frame, 18th c.	50.00	70.00	55.00
☐ **Glass,** French Revolution motif, copper rim	65.00	85.00	70.00
☐ **Glass,** molded opaque, brown bird design	22.00	32.00	25.00
☐ **Gold plated,** dragon	6.00	11.00	7.50
☐ **Ivory,** carved Royal Salamander	28.00	38.00	30.00
☐ **Ivory,** cut-out girl and bird, blue background	145.00	175.00	150.00
☐ **Ivory,** painted cherub in chariot drawn by two horses	90.00	110.00	90.00
☐ **Ivory,** painted girl and dog chasing butterflies	90.00	110.00	90.00
☐ **Ivory,** painted lady and dog, silver rim	42.00	58.00	48.00
☐ **Ivory,** painted Oriental head	32.00	42.00	35.00
☐ **Oriental,** fan design, multicolored, scalloped border	28.00	38.00	30.00
☐ **Oriental,** floral motif, enameled	32.00	42.00	35.00
☐ **Pewter,** owl's head	4.00	7.00	4.50
☐ **Pierced brass,** Little Red Riding Hood	12.00	18.00	13.00
☐ **Porcelain,** cherub catching butterflies, pink, black and white	16.00	26.00	20.00
☐ **Porcelain,** cupid, scroll design on edge	44.00	60.00	48.00
☐ **Porcelain,** flowers and butterfly, 18th c.	18.00	28.00	17.50
☐ **Porcelain,** pasture scene with children	28.00	38.00	30.00
☐ **Silver,** Bacchus, God of Wine, etched design	22.00	32.00	25.00
☐ **Stamped brass,** two children fighting and pulling hair	20.00	28.00	21.00
☐ **Steel,** floral design	4.00	7.00	4.50
☐ **Victorian,** figure, black glass disc	8.00	12.00	8.50
☐ **Wedgewood,** classic figures, white relief on blue, cut steel border, 18th c.	235.00	285.00	250.00
☐ **Wedgewood,** classic figure, white on royal blue, gilt rim, 18th c.	210.00	260.00	235.00
☐ **Wedgewood,** classical figures, white relief on light blue	50.00	65.00	52.00
☐ **Wedgewood,** floral design, diamond paste border, silver frame	185.00	235.00	200.00
☐ **Wedgewood,** warrior, white relief on royal blue, copper border	210.00	260.00	225.00

CANES AND WALKING STICKS

The cane, or walking stick was as much a part of a 19th century man's wardrobe as are shoes to the modern male. Every man, no matter what his occupation or social status, had one. The construction materials, style and workmanship were indicitive of the person's degree of wealth, social status, or even his occupation.

"Gadget" canes concealed a wide variety of devices, such as folding music stands, tables, swords, daggers, pistols and even shotguns. While gadget canes generally are higher-priced, most cane prices are governed by materials, workmanship and age. Prices given are for examples in excellent and mint condition.

	Current Price Range		Prior Year Average
☐ **Amethyst,** cut glass handle	170.00	200.00	175.00
☐ **Bamboo,** curved handle	12.00	18.00	12.00
☐ **Blown glass,** green	65.00	80.00	72.00
☐ **Bottle cane,** glass liner holds liquor, 36″	145.00	175.00	150.00
☐ **Dog's head,** Fox Terrier, painted and carved wood	200.00	225.00	197.00
☐ **Dog's head,** wood with brown eyes, c. 1900	32.00	52.00	40.00
☐ **Dog's head,** glass eyes, c. 1900	45.00	55.00	45.00
☐ **Ivory,** carved hound's head	55.00	110.00	75.00
☐ **Ivory,** carved clenched hand	160.00	320.00	225.00
☐ **Monkey,** hand carved	85.00	110.00	90.00
☐ **Mother-of-pearl,** gold	55.00	75.00	60.00
☐ **Parade cane,** china clown head	30.00	40.00	30.00
☐ **Umbrella cane,** wood case, 34″	80.00	110.00	82.00
☐ **Walking stick,** gold head	100.00	125.00	105.00
☐ **Walking stick,** sterling	40.00	55.00	42.00

CARICATURES AND CARTOONS

This is an often overlooked but fascinating area of paper collecting. Cartoons and caricatures are closely related and, like many other art forms, originated in Italy. They did not become popular with the general public until the late 18th century in England. The demand for caricatures and cartoons of a political nature was so great that it supported over 80 shops in England and Ireland by 1790. These drawings satirized political and social personalities, events and evils of the day. They were so popular that people who could not afford to purchase the prints rented them to show to friends.

Cartoons are humorous drawings of people or events while caricatures satirize the subject's personality by distorting his physical characteristics. Editorial cartoons in newspapers provide a fascinating glimpse of history and the way in which the public perceived certain historical and social events of the day.

The popularity of this art form continued into the 19th century when weekly humor magazines began to appear. *La Caricature* in Paris and *Punch* which was published in Britain are two examples. Sir John Tenniel, a cartoonist for *Punch* was knighted for his contribution to British culture. Cartooning came to the United States in the late 19th Century in the pages of

Harper's, Thomas Nast being the primary contributor. Today's cartoons, particularly the political ones appearing on editorial pages of newspapers, are desirable if they are original drawings. Big names to look for are Gillray, Rowlandson, John Kay, Cruikshank, all early cartoonists, and Levine, Searles, and Herblock. Look also for items from *Judge* and *Vanity Fair.*

Cartoons and caricatures can be purchased for relatively reasonable sums. While some may run into the hundreds, most can be purchased for two or very low three-figure prices. Searching through "bargain" boxes at book fairs and antiquarian book stores may yield some real savings for those who have sharpened their knowledge of the subject and are willing to spend some time. Prices, which had been stable for many years, have shown a remarkable increase in the last 15 years and the trend appears to be continuing.

	Current Price Range		Prior Year Average
☐ **David Levine,** ink drawings, c. 1960's-70's	610.00	1100.00	800.00
☐ **Gillray,** "The Union Club", c. 1800	260.00	310.00	275.00
☐ *Harper's Weekly,* full spread cartoons, c. 1870's-80's	12.00	18.00	12.50
☐ **Kay,** "The Craft in Danger", (Dinosaur skeleton), b/w lithograph, second strike edition, c. 1837	18.00	32.00	22.00
☐ **Kay,** 329 portraits and caricatures in two volumes, c. 1837	135.00	160.00	138.00
☐ **Puck,** single page and cover cartoons, color lithographs, c. 1890's	18.00	28.00	20.00
☐ **Puck and Judge,** full-spread cartoons, color lithographs, c. 1890's	22.00	38.00	28.00
☐ **Robert Seymour,** "Going It by Steam", hand colored, c. 1829	135.00	160.00	138.00
☐ **Thomas Nast,** "The Tammany Tiger Loose," black and white, c. 1871	38.00	55.00	42.00
☐ **Rowlandson,** "Dr. Syntax", hand colored etchings, c. 1812	18.00	28.00	20.00
☐ **Vanity Fair,** caricatures, "Spy," "Ape," etc., color lithographs, c. 1870's	12.00	22.00	17.50

CAROUSEL ANIMALS

The collecting of carousel animals is one of the most unusual areas of collectibles. These beautiful, hand-carved and sculptured creations are true examples of a lost art.

The "golden age" of carousel animals in America began shortly after the Civil War. Circuses at that time were beginning to incorporate rides into their side-shows, and larger more elaborate rides were being set up at permanent amusement parks. By 1890 the carousel or "merry-go-round" had become a standard attraction at all amusement parks and many other places of entertainment. They became so popular that a number of public parks installed them, including New York's Central Park — whose 19th century carousel is still in operation. Outstanding quality in carousel animals called for expert wood carvers. Most of those who worked in America were Italians who had learned the art of wood carving in Italy.

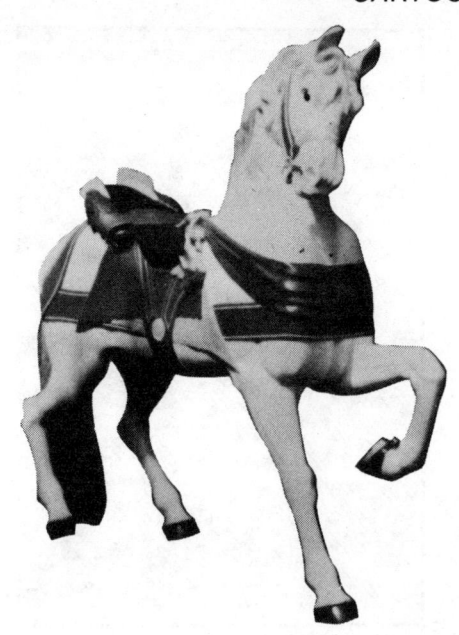

Carousel Horse, While this specimen isn't one of the earliest available to collectors (it dates from the 20th century), it's well designed and excellently preserved **$1200.00-1600.00**

	Current Price Range		Prior Year Average
☐ **Armitage Hershell Jumpers,** track type, no holes through horse, c. 1890	725.00	825.00	750.00
☐ **Carmel Borrelli,** 60" x 50"	2650.00	3250.00	2900.00
☐ **Carmel Borrelli,** 54" x 56"	3300.00	4100.00	3600.00
☐ **Carmel Borrelli,** 49" x 49"	2300.00	3100.00	2600.00
☐ **Carmel Borrelli,** stander	3200.00	4200.00	3500.00
☐ **Dentzel Jumping Mare,** Pittsburgh, PA Carrousel	2100.00	3100.00	2500.00
☐ **Metal Illions Jumper,** off kiddie machine, 36" ...	185.00	260.00	212.00
☐ **Muller,** medium stander, 71"	1850.00	2550.00	2100.00
☐ **Muller Dentzel,** parrots on back of saddle, 79" ...	3700.00	4100.00	3800.00
☐ **Parker,** large flowers with jewel centers	975.00	1350.00	1100.00
☐ **Parker Jumper,** super sweet horse	850.00	1100.00	900.00
☐ **Parker Style aluminum horse,** 52" x 29"	350.00	400.00	350.00
☐ **Spillman,** nice flowing mane, shield, 66"	900.00	1200.00	1050.00
☐ **Trojan Jumper,** 66"	650.00	750.00	650.00

CARTOON STRIPS

Cartoon art has a fascination all its own. Many early cartoons hold an interest for people of all ages. Listed below are a few of the famous and rare examples of cartoon art. Values given are for specimens in good condition, not badly soiled or torn, and mint.

216 / CARTOON STRIPS

Sunday Comic Page, Prince Valiant from "America's Greatest Comic Weekly," 1939. Full-page strips like this have added value 20"x15" **$15.00-$22.00**

	Current Price Range		Prior Year Average
☐ **Bode, Vaughn,** "Dr. Peeper" page	360.00	385.00	362.00
☐ **Bald, Ken,** "Dr. Kildare" daily	22.00	28.00	22.00
Sunday	38.00	44.00	37.50
☐ **Caniff, Milton.** "Steve Canyon" daily	110.00	160.00	125.00
☐ **Capp, Al,** "Lil'l Abner" daily	85.00	160.00	112.00
Sunday	210.00	310.00	250.00
☐ **Crane, Roy,** "Buz Sawyer" daily	160.00	185.00	162.00
☐ **Disney, Walt,** "Mickey Mouse" daily	90.00	110.00	92.00
☐ **Fisher, Bud,** "Mutt and Jeff" daily	310.00	360.00	325.00
☐ **Fisher, Ham,** "Joe Palooka" Sunday	210.00	260.00	225.00
☐ **Fredericks, Fred,** "Mandrake" daily	38.00	55.00	42.00
☐ **Gray, Harold,** "Little Orphan Annie" daily	320.00	420.00	350.00
☐ **Gould, Chester,** "Dick Tracy" Sunday	320.00	420.00	350.00
☐ **Hograth,** "Tarzan" Sunday	360.00	460.00	400.00
☐ **Kelly, Walt,** "Pogo" daily	285.00	360.00	312.00
☐ **Lehti, John,** "Tarzan" daily	55.00	80.00	62.00
☐ **Lank, Leonard,** "Mickey Finn" daily	210.00	260.00	225.00
☐ **Messmer, Otto,** "Felix the Cat" Sunday	235.00	260.00	238.00
☐ **Sagendorf, But,** "Popeye" daily	85.00	110.00	82.00
Sunday	135.00	160.00	138.00
☐ **Schulz, Charles,** "Peanuts" daily	220.00	260.00	230.00
Sunday	385.00	410.00	382.00
☐ **Smith, Al,** "Mutt and Jeff" daily	55.00	110.00	75.00
Sunday	95.00	125.00	115.00
☐ **Tobin, Don,** "Little Woman" daily	32.00	52.00	40.00

CASH REGISTERS / 217

	Current Price Range		Prior Year Average
☐ **Van Buren, Raeburn,** "Abbie an' Slats" daily	135.00	160.00	138.00
☐ **Wunder, George,** "Terry" daily	50.00	80.00	60.00
☐ **Young, Chic,** "Blondie" daily	220.00	320.00	250.00

CASH REGISTERS

Cash Register, 17" H., 1901, National #47 .... **$850.00-$1200.00**

    Probably one of the most interesting and decorative collectibles are old cash registers. The cash register was invented in Dayton, Ohio about 1879 by James Ritty who became weary of his bartenders stealing money from the cashbox. One of Ritty's early customers, John Patterson bought a controlling interest in what was to become the National Cash Register Company (N.C.R.).
    The vast majority of existing antique cash registers were manufactured by N.C.R. The collector may also occasionally find a machine built by the St. Louis, Ideal, or Michigan register companies; but other manufactures are rare, since N.C.R. quickly drove most of its competitors out of business.
    Registers were produced in various sizes for many types of businesses. Desirable models include those made in the 1890's, cast brass or bronze cases, machines with special keys or export models with the keys marked in foreign currency.
    Sources of antique registers include stores that sell secondhand business equipment and rural barbershops or general stores. Some proprietors will take a newer register as payment for the old one. Occasionally, a

218 / CATS

collector may come across a real prize — a multiple drawer model, such as those used in large department stores, or one from a famous store, such as Tiffany's or Marshall Field. Prices given are for machines in excellent physical and mechanical condition.

	Current Price Range		Prior Year Average
☐ **Hallwood,** Aluminum, 1890	685.00	760.00	712.00
☐ **Michigan,** nickel plated, 20th century	535.00	610.00	560.00
☐ **Monitor,** No. 1A, oak with decal, pat'd, 1900	360.00	435.00	380.00
☐ **National,** brass, side box	460.00	535.00	538.00
☐ **National,** brass, floor model with drawers, oak	2300.00	2800.00	2400.00
☐ **National,** brass, ornate	535.00	610.00	560.00
☐ **National,** brass and oak	860.00	960.00	900.00
☐ **National,** brass with marble	335.00	410.00	360.00
☐ **National,** brass and mahogany	385.00	460.00	412.00
☐ **National,** model 15, oak	210.00	260.00	225.00
☐ **National,** model 130	925.00	1100.00	950.00
☐ **National,** model 452, hand crank, brass, ornate	725.00	800.00	738.00
☐ **National,** double drawer, oak, brass inlaid, c. 1908	1400.00	1600.00	1350.00
☐ **National,** embossed nickel plated lockbox, 6″ x 6¾″ x 6¾″	210.00	285.00	238.00
☐ **Premier Junior**	320.00	370.00	325.00
☐ **St. Louis,** nickel plated	360.00	435.00	380.00
☐ **St. Louis,** brass	585.00	660.00	612.00

CATS

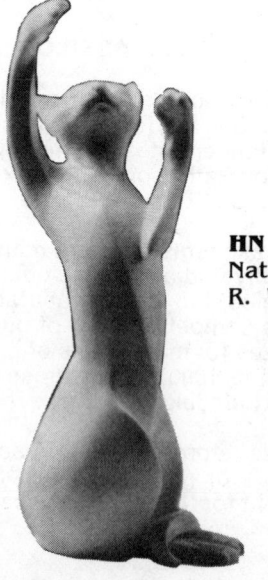

HN 3526–Shadowplay, Images of Nature by Royal Doulton, designer R. Wills . . . . **$75.00-$90.00**

Cats have long been a favorite subject for many American artists. They have even been personified as human beings engaged in all sorts of activities. Collectors of anything in the cat motif usually have secured hundreds of objects for their assemblage. Ceramics, precious metals, wood, glass, and cloth are all materials used by artisans for making cat figures. Price is, of course, dependent upon the age and construction of the piece rather than the subject which is depicted.

	Current Price Range		Prior Year Average
☐ **Bookend,** Art Deco, brass, copper and chrome, arched-back, heavy	14.00	18.00	13.50
☐ **Cookie jar,** stoneware, Chessie, 22″ H.	42.00	48.00	45.00
☐ **Fairy lamp,** gray and white kitten, blown green eyes, 3½″ H.	38.00	42.00	38.00
☐ **Mirror frame,** three cats playing around mirror ..	70.00	80.00	70.00
☐ **Painting,** oil, primitive of white cat, c. 1920's	22.00	28.00	22.50
☐ **Pillow,** needlepoint, folk art gray and white cat ..	22.00	28.00	22.50
☐ **Postcard,** animated cat, Arthur Thiele	6.00	12.00	8.00
☐ **Postcard,** embossed cat and dog on pillow	6.00	12.00	8.00
☐ **Still bank,** cat on tub, 4″ H.	85.00	110.00	82.00
☐ **Toy,** wind-up, cat and ball, Germany	22.00	42.00	30.00
☐ **Toy,** wind-up cat chasing rat, German, c. 1910 ...	85.00	95.00	85.00
☐ **Toy,** wind-up meowing cat, plush-covered, turn-of-the century, works but plush in poor condition	30.00	40.00	30.00

CHALKWARE

Chalkware is known as the "poor man's Staffordshire." Staffordshire sculptures of animals, people, buildings and birds were used as mantel ornaments throughout the 19th century. Chalkware was a cheap imitation in plaster of paris and sold for as little as 15¢. At these prices, these brightly colored figurines adorned most middle-class homes.

Chalkware is not to be confused with cast plaster figures given away as carnival prizes in the last 40 years. These were simple forms cast in molds and left hollow. More plaster or clay was added to weight the bottoms so they would not topple over. After drying, they were painted in bright, vivid colors, not necessarily in a realistic manner. Some pieces were molded in two parts and hooked together. These bobbing specimens are scarce and more valuable.

It is difficult to document age and determine exact value of a specimen since little is known about the craft's origin. Value is, therefore, determined by condition. Plaster tends to crack and chip easily and the paint flakes. Restoration is not advised and can lessen an item's worth if done poorly. The older the specimen, the more valuable. Age is authenticated by a change in the surface texture and how soiled a piece is, since chalkware cannot be cleaned.

☐ **Bank,** apple with red cheeks	28.00	32.00	27.50
☐ **Basket,** fruit filled	310.00	360.00	325.00
☐ **Bird,** nesting	260.00	310.00	280.00
☐ **Black boy with watermelon,** 4″	18.00	22.00	17.50

220 / CHESS SETS

	Current Price Range		Prior Year Average
☐ **Bookends,** pirates, painted, pair	42.00	48.00	42.00
☐ **Boy,** reading books, 10½"	90.00	110.00	92.00
☐ **Cat,** 4½"	160.00	185.00	162.00
☐ **Cat,** 10½"	185.00	235.00	200.00
☐ **Charley McCarthy,** 15"	22.00	28.00	22.50
☐ **Dancing Lady,** 14"	18.00	32.00	22.00
☐ **Deer,** 9½"	435.00	485.00	450.00
☐ **Dog,** 8½"	135.00	155.00	138.00
☐ **Dove,** green with blue wings, 12"	210.00	235.00	212.00
☐ **Dove,** green and yellow wings, 6"	260.00	310.00	275.00
☐ **Duck,**	140.00	165.00	142.00
☐ **Eagle,** spread, 9½"	285.00	335.00	300.00
☐ **Gnome,** German, 11", c. 1930's	22.00	28.00	22.50
☐ **Horn of Plenty,** 14"	18.00	32.00	22.00
☐ **Indian,** Cigar Store, reclining, 23"	210.00	235.00	212.00
☐ **Lamb,** grey body, 8½"	260.00	310.00	275.00
☐ **Lamb,** rectangular base, 6½"	135.00	160.00	138.00
☐ **Owl,** 12"	185.00	210.00	182.00
☐ **Parrot,** 10½"	1300.00	1600.00	1400.00
☐ **Pigeon,** 10"	135.00	160.00	138.00
☐ **Poodles,** 7¾"	185.00	235.00	200.00
☐ **Rabbit,** sitting, 8"	160.00	185.00	162.00
☐ **Rooster,** 6"	335.00	385.00	350.00
☐ **Santa Claus,** 24"	155.00	180.00	160.00
☐ **Sheep,** mother with babies, 7"	185.00	210.00	182.00
☐ **Shepherd,** German, 17½"	85.00	105.00	85.00
☐ **Squirrel,** 10"	185.00	210.00	182.00
☐ **Stag,** rectangular base, 15"	260.00	310.00	275.00

CHESS SETS

The earliest recorded version of chess dates back over 1300 years ago. In duplicating this war game, some playing pieces have evolved which represent actual people, while others are totally abstract works of art. The earliest collectible pieces date back to the 7th century; however, most sets collected were designed as decorative items in the 18th and 19th centuries.

Chess is the game of kings and paupers and can be collected by both, though many sets are extremely costly. The beginning collector is wise to examine those sets crafted by anonymous artists rather than those with notable reputations. Many fine and interesting specimens can be found for a relatively small investment.

Collections may be built around any complete sets, individual pieces such as kings, knights, etc., various styles (realistic or abstract), sets made of a particular material such as bone, wood or ivory, or method of manufacture such as hand carving or lathe turning. Missing pieces reduce the value of a complete set. While a king or queen would be almost impossible to replace, a pawn or bishop could be molded from an existing piece.

☐ **African,** carved white ivory, ebony stain	1550.00	1750.00	1600.00
☐ **American,** carved cedar wood, crude, c. 1862	135.00	185.00	150.00
☐ **American,** ceramic and wood, painted, modern	110.00	160.00	125.00
☐ **Chinese,** carved ivory, red stain, 19th c.	1250.00	1850.00	1500.00

CHRISTMAS TREE ORNAMENTS AND LIGHTS / 221

	Current Price Range		Prior Year Average
☐ **English,** wood, light and dark brown stain, 19th c.	460.00	560.00	500.00
☐ **English,** Staunton, ivory, red stain	1100.00	1900.00	1400.00
☐ **German,** cast metal, 19th c.	575.00	675.00	600.00
☐ **German,** carved bone, 19th c.	525.00	625.00	650.00
☐ **German,** iron, painted, 20th c.	750.00	850.00	750.00
☐ **German,** ivory and wood, late 18th c.	2600.00	3600.00	3000.00
☐ **Hungarian,** carved wood, blue and red polychrome	460.00	560.00	475.00
☐ **Hungarian,** porcelain, 20th c.	950.00	1250.00	1150.00
☐ **Indian,** carved white ivory, green stain	950.00	1250.00	1150.00
☐ **Indian,** carved white ivory, red stain	1100.00	1900.00	1400.00
☐ **Indian,** carved ivory, polychrome, 19th c.	1450.00	1850.00	1600.00
☐ **Italian,** coral and white ivory, 18th c.	1250.00	1850.00	1500.00
☐ **Italian,** ivory inlaid, hand carved, c. 1880's	500.00	575.00	500.00
☐ **Japanese,** carved ivory, gilded blank and red, 19th c.	2000.00	2300.00	2050.00
☐ **Polish,** white, red and brown costumes, carved, polychrome	450.00	550.00	450.00
☐ **Royal Dux porcelain,** Genghis Khan and entourage, white, cobalt, blue, gold	550.00	650.00	550.00
☐ **Scandinavian,** brushed steel	550.00	650.00	550.00
☐ **Spanish,** carved bone, light and dark brown stain	2600.00	3600.00	3000.00

CHRISTMAS TREE ORNAMENTS AND LIGHTS

Christmas Ornaments, Gorham, complete set of Snowflakes 1970 thru 1979 .... **$185.00-$200.00**

222 / CHRISTMAS TREE ORNAMENTS AND LIGHTS

Chances are you have at least one very old Christmas tree glass ornament in your decorating box. It has survived, amazingly, for at least 75 winters, and while the lacquer may be slightly chipped, and maybe a bent paperclip is now stuck in the neck, it still has a place of pride on the tree each year. Such an ornament might be worth as much as $25 or so, depending on subject and condition.

Christmas tree ornaments were first manufactured and sold to consumers in the 1870's. Replacing homemade decorations, most of these early ones were simple shapes made in small German villages. Dresden ornaments are the rarest and most valuable. Being made of embossed cardboard and covered with metalic paper, these intricate handcrafted specimens were soon superceded by easily produced blown glass items. It is estimated that by the 1920's, over 5,000 different designs were used for ornaments.

Age, rarity and, therefore, value are determined by the ornament's construction, design, patina and the material of which it is made. The best place to find old ornaments, at a reasonable price, is most likely in great-grandma's attic. Since they are in great demand at the moment, dealer prices are high, even for specimens in average condition.

Also quite collectible are Christmas tree lights dating from the 1920's and 1930's, even if they no longer work. The most collectible of these are the blown glass ones made in molds in Occupied Japan. A variety of shapes and sizes are available.

	Current Price Range		Prior Year Average
☐ Light, Andy Gump, milk glass	12.00	16.00	12.50
☐ Light, bear with guitar, milk glass	12.00	16.00	12.50
☐ Light, blue bird, milk glass	12.00	16.00	12.50
☐ Light, clock	12.00	16.00	12.50
☐ Light, clown, milk glass	18.00	22.00	17.50
☐ Light, elephant, milk glass	6.00	11.00	8.00
☐ Light, fish, milk glass	12.00	16.00	12.50
☐ Light, gingerbread man	12.00	16.00	12.50
☐ Light, grapes, milk glass	5.00	10.00	6.00
☐ Light, house, milk glass	12.00	16.00	12.50
☐ Light, Humpty Dumpty, milk glass	18.00	32.00	22.00
☐ Light, lantern	12.00	16.00	12.50
☐ Light, parrot, milk glass	6.00	11.00	7.50
☐ Light, Pinocchio	18.00	28.00	20.00
☐ Light, Puss N' Boots, milk glass	18.00	32.00	22.00
☐ Light, Santa, painted	18.00	32.00	22.00
☐ Light, snowman, milk glass	12.00	22.00	15.00
☐ Light, zeppelin with flag	18.00	32.00	22.00
☐ Ornament, ball, amber	22.00	28.00	22.50
☐ Ornament, ball, canary, blown glass	18.00	22.00	17.50
☐ Ornament, basket, fruit billed, blown glass	22.00	28.00	22.50
☐ Ornament, bear with muff, blown glass	45.00	55.00	45.00
☐ Ornament, camel, Dresden	28.00	38.00	30.00
☐ Ornament, child, milk glass	9.00	13.00	10.00
☐ Ornament, church, blown glass	28.00	38.00	30.00
☐ Ornament, clown head, blown glass	50.00	65.00	52.00
☐ Ornament, fence, wood	22.00	32.00	25.00
☐ Ornament, fish, blown glass	50.00	65.00	52.00
☐ Ornament, football player, milk glass	18.00	22.00	17.50
☐ Ornament, girl, blown glass	32.00	42.00	35.00

	Current Price Range		Prior Year Average
☐ **Ornament,** heart, blown glass, large	32.00	42.00	35.00
☐ **Ornament,** icicle, glass	18.00	22.00	17.50
☐ **Ornament,** lamp	50.00	65.00	52.00
☐ **Ornament,** lion, Dresden	28.00	38.00	30.00
☐ **Ornament,** musical instrument	18.00	22.00	17.50
☐ **Ornament,** peacock, blown glass, brush tail	18.00	22.00	17.50
☐ **Ornament,** pinecone, blown glass	6.00	11.00	7.50
☐ **Ornament,** pipe, blown glass	22.00	28.00	22.50
☐ **Ornament,** purse, blown glass	32.00	42.00	35.00
☐ **Ornament,** Santa, celluloid	32.00	42.00	35.00
☐ **Ornament,** Santa, with plaster face	22.00	28.00	22.50
☐ **Ornament,** star, Dresden	18.00	28.00	20.00
☐ **Ornament,** swan, blown glass	22.00	28.00	20.00
☐ **Ornament,** teapot	22.00	28.00	20.00
☐ **Ornament,** umbrella, tinsel	22.00	28.00	20.00

CIRCUS MEMORABILIA

Clown Rolly-Poly, Schoenhut,
9" .... **$20.00-$30.00**

If you always wanted to join the circus, but couldn't bring yourself to do it, perhaps a collection of circus memorabilia would suffice. The first American circus opened in Philadelphia in 1793. It became a major form of entertainment during the later part of the 19th century. Because promoters such as Barnum and Bailey and the Ringling Brothers spent so much time, effort and money on advertising, paper items are by far the most collectible area in this category. This does not mean that some people (with lots of room) will not collect circus wagons, carvings, costumes, props and even

224 / CIRCUS MEMORABILIA

"Big Top" tents. A few circus wagons have been discovered by diligent searchers.

It is possible to find circus items through dealers, but the vast majority of prized items come from sales in cities which served as "home" for the circus caravans. The circus' winter home, Sarasota, Florida now has a museum which sells duplicate items while displaying the real thing. Value of an item is not only dependent upon age, but also upon the number available.

	Current Price Range		Prior Year Average
☐ **Band wagon,** horse drawn	385.00	435.00	400.00
☐ **Book,** *Buffalo Bill's Wild West,* programme and descriptive booklet, 1885	110.00	160.00	125.00
☐ **Book,** *Burdett Twins,* Fanny and Major, age, 22 years, height 38 inches, New York, c. 1890	50.00	70.00	55.00
☐ **Book,** *Dr. Doolittle's Circus* by Hugh Loftring, New York, c. 1924	85.00	115.00	90.00
☐ **Book,** *Tom Thumb,* life of Charles S. Stratton, 28 inches high and 15 pounds, 24-page booklet published by Barnum, New York, 1847	160.00	260.00	200.00
☐ **Booklet,** Walter L. Main circus, 8pp, color, wraps	16.00	20.00	16.00
☐ **Broadside handbills,** illus., 10" x 28", c. 1920's	20.00	24.00	20.00
☐ **Courier,** "Illustrated News," P.T. Barnum, 16pp, c. 1897	40.00	55.00	42.00
☐ **Lithograph,** window card, "The Circus Kings of All Time," 14" x 22", mid 1930's	32.00	38.00	32.50
☐ **Herald or handbill,** Sparks Circus, c. 1921	16.00	20.00	16.00
☐ **Poster,** Adams Forepaugh Sells circus, pictures Aurora Zoaves	50.00	65.00	52.00
☐ **Poster,** Clyde Beatty, training lions and tigers, c. 1930	75.00	95.00	80.00
☐ **Poster,** Dale's animal three-ring circus	14.00	20.00	15.50
☐ **Poster,** "Lady Viola, the Most Beautiful Tattoed Woman in the World," painted in oils over large photo, 40" x 40", New York, c. 1925	435.00	485.00	450.00
☐ **Poster,** "Lilla," high-wire act, 34" x 45", c. 1895	230.00	250.00	230.00
☐ **Poster,** "Princess Topaze, Star of the Casino de Paris," female midget, 35" x 48"	300.00	340.00	300.00
☐ **Poster,** P.T. Barnum and Co., Lake Front, Chicago, Monday, July 19th	20.00	24.00	20.00
☐ **Poster,** "Terrell Jacobs the Lion King," 28" x 40", c. 1935	58.00	68.00	60.00
☐ **Poster,** Terrell Jacobs in Big Top, surrounded by lions, 28" x 40", c. 1934	72.00	82.00	75.00
☐ **Program,** Ringling Bros., Barnum and Bailey, c. 1948	14.00	20.00	15.00
☐ **Program,** Hagenbeck-Wallas	20.00	24.00	20.00
☐ **Sheet music,** Children At The Circus, c. 1909	22.00	32.00	25.00
☐ **Sheet music,** When It's Circus Day Back Home, c. 1917	22.00	32.00	25.00
☐ **Song book,** Barnum and London Musical Album, large size	22.00	32.00	25.00
☐ **Stationery,** Sparton Bros., ornate, unused	4.00	7.00	4.50
☐ **Tickets,** Barnum's Circus, c. 1890	14.00	20.00	15.00
☐ **Tickets,** Hunts Bros., illus. with clown, 100 large, c. 1940's	9.00	13.00	10.00
☐ **Toy,** circus train, tin, eight pieces, c. 1950's	110.00	135.00	112.00

CIVIL WAR MEMORABILIA / 225

	Current Price Range		Prior Year Average
☐ **Toy,** clown, wooden, hinged	65.00	95.00	75.00
☐ **Toy,** elephant pulling animals in cage, mechanical, c. 1935	170.00	200.00	170.00
☐ **Toy,** lion cage, driver and lions	120.00	180.00	130.00
☐ **Toy wagon,** wood and tin with scene of circus on wagon, 17½″ L.	100.00	150.00	115.00

CIVIL WAR MEMORABILIA

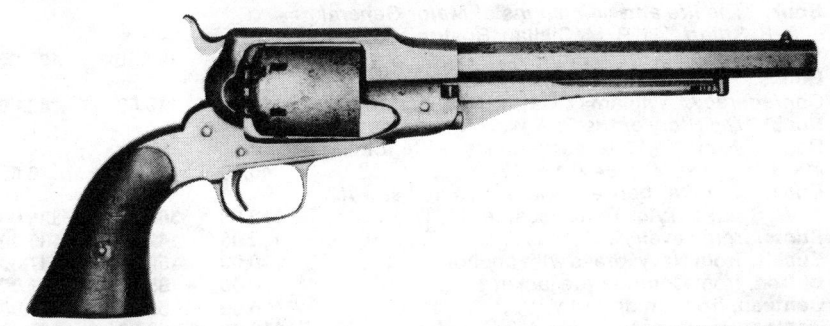

Remington-Beals Revolver, Navy model, .36 caliber.. **$325.00-$675.00**

The Civil War, which tore America apart for years, produced some of the most collectible antiques in today's marketplace. Items are available all over the world. Collecting Civil War memorabilia can be a most gratifying hobby for the collector as he delves into the history of each item and discovers the principles upon which this country has grown.

The most sought-after collectible in this category is that of firearms. This period in time marked a technological transition from a single shot gun to one that would shoot several times, including the first machine gun. Other collectible areas include uniforms, buttons, belt buckles, canteens, knapsacks, insignias and personal effects, such as diaries, letters, and photographs.

Auctions are a great place to pick up such items as well as dealer shops. Prices are as varied as the items so even the novice can afford to begin this type of collection. For more in-depth information and listings, you may refer to *The Official Price Guide to Military Collectibles* by Colonel Robert H. Rankin, published by the House of Collectibles.

☐ **Ammunition pouch,** black leather (U.S. Arsenal)	65.00	75.00	65.00
☐ **Badge,** for helmet, shield with eagle	24.00	29.00	22.00
☐ **Bayonet and Scabbard,** from .58 caliber rifle	68.00	78.00	70.00
☐ **Bayonet,** for U.S. 45-70 rifle	42.00	52.00	55.00
☐ **Bayonet,** with brass plate	70.00	80.00	70.00
☐ **Belt buckle,** with "U.S." insignia	28.00	38.00	30.00
☐ **Book,** "Military Reminiscences of the Civil War," Jacob D. Cox, New York, two volumes, 1900	80.00	110.00	82.00

226 / CIVIL WAR MEMORABILIA

	Current Price Range		Prior Year Average
☐ Book, "The Rise and Fall of the Confederate Government," Jefferson Davis, N.Y., two volumes, 1881	80.00	110.00	82.00
☐ Book, "Advance and Retreat," J. B. Hodd, New Orleans, 1880	30.00	42.00	32.00
☐ Book, "Recollections of a Maryland Confederate Soldier," McHenry Howar, Baltimore, scarce, 1914	110.00	160.00	125.00
☐ Book, "The Seige of Charleston," Samuel Jones, New York, 1911	55.00	80.00	62.00
☐ Book, "The life and campaigns of Major General J. E. B. Stuart," H. B. McClellan, Boston and New York, 1885	110.00	160.00	125.00
☐ Books, "The War between the Union and the Confederacy," William C. Oates, New York, 1905	85.00	110.00	82.00
☐ Book, "The Story of the Civil War," John Codman Ropes, New York, three volumes with folding maps in pockets, 1894-1913	40.00	55.00	42.00
☐ Book, "The War between the States as I saw it," A. W. Sparks, Tyler Texas, scarce, 1901	310.00	360.00	325.00
☐ Boots, from cavalry	132.00	142.00	135.00
☐ Buckle, from Navy, brass with anchor	140.00	150.00	137.00
☐ Button, from Confederate jacket	30.00	35.00	27.00
☐ Canteen, from Union Army	55.00	65.00	55.00
☐ Canteen, made of tin	150.00	160.00	145.00
☐ Cartridge box, brown leather	42.00	52.00	45.00
☐ Cavalry boots	150.00	160.00	147.00
☐ Chin straps, from officer's hat	22.00	28.00	22.50
☐ Doctor's bag, black leather	300.00	325.00	282.00
☐ Document, signed by Lincoln, July, 1863	1300.00	1550.00	1375.00
☐ Enlistment papers, fully endorsed, from Union Army	35.00	40.00	32.00
☐ Gloves, from officer's wardrobe, leather	85.00	95.00	80.00
☐ Holster, for rifle	85.00	95.00	80.00
☐ Horse bit	60.00	70.00	60.00
☐ Knife, bowie with ivory handles	110.00	120.00	105.00
☐ Knife, tool combination	25.00	30.00	22.00
☐ Leggings, black leather	130.00	140.00	127.00
☐ Mess kit, ivory handles, in case	42.00	52.00	45.00
☐ Print, "Battle of Atlanta," Chicago, Kurz and Allison, 1888, 17½" x 25"	135.00	185.00	150.00
☐ Print, "Battle of Bull Run, Virginia," New York, Currier and Ives, 1861, 9" x 12½"	135.00	185.00	150.00
☐ Print, "Battle of Gettysburg," Chicago, Milwaukee Litho. and Eng. Co., n.d., 25" x 35"	320.00	395.00	338.00
☐ Print, "Battle of Vicksburg, Mississippi," New York, Currier and Ives, 1863, 9" x 12½"	135.00	185.00	150.00
☐ Print, "Gallant Charge of the 54th Mass. Regiment," New York, Currier and Ives, 1863, 9" x 12½"	235.00	310.00	260.00
☐ Print, "Johnson Surrenders to Sherman," New York, Currier and Ives, 1865, 12½" x 9"	135.00	185.00	150.00
☐ Print, "Siege of Charleston," New York, Currier and Ives, 1863, 9" x 12½""	235.00	310.00	260.00
☐ Print, "Surrender of General Lee," New York, Currier and Ives, 1873, 9½" x 12½"	185.00	260.00	212.00

	Current Price Range	Prior Year Average
☐ **Recruiting poster,** Company F of the Wadsworth Guards, woodcut of an American Eagle standing on a shield	280.00 310.00	285.00
☐ **Revolver,** 44 cal., model 1860, Army Colt, fluted cylinder	560.00 1450.00	950.00
☐ **Revolver,** 44 cal., model 1860, Army Colt, plain round cylinder	335.00 825.00	500.00
☐ **Revolver,** 36 cal., model 1861, Navy Colt	750.00 1800.00	1200.00
☐ **Revolver,** 36 cal., model 1861, Navy Remington, government marked	260.00 560.00	400.00
☐ **Revolver,** 36 cal., Augusta Machine Works, rare .	1250.00 3650.00	1900.00
☐ **Revolver,** 36 cal., Columbus Fire Arms Manufacturing Company, only a few manufactured	3000.00 9100.00	6000.00
☐ **Revolver,** 36 cal., Leech and Ridgon	1300.00 3000.00	2000.00
☐ **Revolver,** 36 cal., figure 8 model, Savage and North, trigger in form of figure "8," limited production	1450.00 2250.00	1800.00
☐ **Revolver,** 36 cal., T. F. Cofer, rarest of all Civil War firearms, types I, II, III	6000.00 26000.00	15000.00
☐ **Revolver,** 36 cal., Whitney Navy, types I, II, III, IV .	300.00 910.00	600.00
☐ **Rifle,** 58 cal., Fayetteville Armory, fabricated from parts from the captured Harper's Ferry Armory, have lug for saber type bayonet, 3 types	520.00 2300.00	1500.00
☐ **Rifle,** 58 cal., H. C. Lamb Muzzle-Loading, lug for saber type bayonet	1100.00 3650.00	2300.00
☐ **Rifle,** 58 cal., Remington Percussion Contract, so-called Zouave rifle, government marked, c. 1863	520.00 820.00	650.00
☐ **Rifle,** 52 cal., Spencer, Navy model, lug for saber, limited production	485.00 975.00	700.00
☐ **Rifle,** 52 cal., Spencer, Army model, provision for socket type bayonet	410.00 835.00	600.00
☐ **Ribbon,** blue-gray in color with banner around Lincoln's head reading "With Malice Toward None With Charity For All", c. 1861-1865	62.00 72.00	65.00
☐ **Sword,** Confederate-made with ivory grip	360.00 385.00	362.00
☐ **Sword,** from Union Cavalry with shield	185.00 210.00	182.00
☐ **U.S. Musket,** Navy Colt, c. 1861	820.00 1100.00	900.00
☐ **U.S. Musket,** Morse Inside Lock, 71 cal., rare	1600.00 4100.00	2700.00

CLOCKS

    Clocks appear to be a very practical collectible until the collector looks around the room one day and realizes that he does not need 20 or 30 faces to tell the time. Fascination with sizes, shapes, mechanisms and cases is what attracts the clock collector.

    Early American clocks are generally "grandfather" or "grandmother" clocks and are seven to nine feet tall and three to five feet tall respectively. They were hand-crafted in a few Eastern cities and were too expensive, even when new, for anyone but the wealthy to afford. Near the end of the 18th century, Eli Terry, a Connecticut clockmaker, improved and miniaturized the movements of these tall clocks into models about two feet tall that were priced at about $15, well within the budget of many families. Terry was

Ansonia Regular-Figure Eight, Brooklyn, solid brass case and glass pendulum, height 34", dial 12", spring, c. 1910, 8 Day   **$2800.00-3000.00**

assisted by his apprentice, Seth Thomas, who later became the best known New England clockmaker. These clocks had internal movements which were mass produced of wood to keep the price low. In 1839, brass movements were first mass produced for clocks by Chauncey Jerome. Cheap, accurate shelf clocks were then available to nearly everyone.

Most of the appeal of the 19th century clocks can be attributed to their imaginative and sometimes elaborate cases. Engraved brass faces and scenes painted below the face are also attractive to some collectors. Other clocks may be decorated with fancy wooden scrolls, ornate arches, steeples or pillars made of wood, iron or even marble. Shapes and case materials are almost limitless.

Many clocks of the 19th century are extremely expensive when found in perfect condition. The same clocks needing some minor mechanical repair or case refinishing may be purchased much more reasonably. Some collectors run newspaper ads offering to buy any clock, regardless of condition. Unexpected bargains may be obtained in this manner, especially if the collector is able to do his own repairs.

Collectors with less space may wish to collect bedside alarms and novelty clocks manufactured during the 20th century. The prices paid for collectible clocks have shown increases in the past few years. As the demand for finely crafted items of past generations increases, this trend is likely to increase. All prices given are for timepieces in guaranteed working condition, assuming that cases, hands, labels, dials, decorated glass and hardware are original. Most clock or watch collectors can evaluate the extent of repair necessary to put a timepiece in proper working condition. For more in-depth information and listings, you may refer to *The Official Price Guide to Antique Clocks,* by Roy Ehrhardt, and published by the House of Collectibles.

ANSONIA CLOCK COMPANY

	Current Price Range	Prior Year Average

CABINET

- **Idaho**, oak, 15½" x 11¼", dial 6", spring, c. 1910, 8 Day, strike 120.00 140.00 130.00
- **Island**, oak, 13" x 9½", dial 6", spring, c. 1910, 8 Day, strike 115.00 135.00 125.00
- **Leeds**, oak, 11½" x 8⅓", dial 4¼", c. 1883, 8 Day, strike 140.00 160.00 150.00
- **Riverdale**, oak, 16½" x 11½", dial 6", c. 1910, 8 Day, strike 135.00 155.00 145.00
- **Summit**, oak, 14¾" x 10¾", dial 5", spring, c. 1883, 8 Day, strike 165.00 185.00 175.00
- **Toronto**, oak, 16¾" x 11¼", dial 5", spring, c. 1883, 8 Day, strike 155.00 175.00 165.00

CALENDAR

- **Adelaide**, walnut parlor, height 24", dial 6", spring, 8 Day, strike, simple calendar 250.00 275.00 262.00
- **Carlos**, walnut parlor, height 24½", dial 6", spring, 8 Day, strike, simple calendar 250.00 275.00 262.00
- **Novelty Calendar**, Ansonia Brass and Copper Co., Connecticut, height 26", dial 10½", spring, 8 Day 800.00 1000.00 900.00
- **Office Ink Stand**, height 13", dial 4", 1 Day, simple calendar 250.00 300.00 275.00
- **Planet**, round alarm, dial 4", spring, 1 Day, simple calendar 100.00 125.00 112.00
- **Rio Parlor**, wall regulator, height 39", dial 8", spring, 8 Day, strike, simple calendar 550.00 625.00 582.00

CRYSTAL REGULATOR

- **Admiral**, visible escapement, porcelain dial, white beveled plate glass front, back and sides, green onyx top and base, 18" x 10", dial 4", c. 1910, 8 Day, strike 950.00 1200.00 1100.00
- **Baronet**, polished brass, rich gold ornaments, visible escapement, porcelain dial, white beveled plate glass front, back and sides, 12½" x 7½", dial 4", c. 1910, 8 Day, strike 360.00 400.00 380.00
- **Cavalier**, visible escapement, porcelain dial, white beveled plate glass front, back and sides, green onyx top and base, 12" x 8", dial 4", c. 1910, 8 Day, strike 410.00 460.00 435.00
- **Colby**, porcelain dial, white beveled plate glass front, back and sides, 10¾" x 6¾", dial 4", c. 1910, 8 Day, strike, polished brass 195.00 225.00 210.00
- **Danube**, rich gold plate, beveled plate glass front, back and sides, porcelain dial, 9" x 7¾", dial 3", c. 1917, 8 Day, strike 190.00 210.00 200.00
- **Envoy**, polished brass, rich gold ornaments, visible escapement, porcelain dial, white beveled plate glass front, back and sides, 19" x 9¾", dial 4", c. 1910, 8 Day, strike 535.00 610.00 570.00
- **Griffin**, visible escapement, porcelain dial, white beveled plate glass front, back and sides, green onyx top and base, 13" x 8¾", dial 4", c. 1910, 8 Day, strike 450.00 500.00 475.00

230 / CLOCKS

	Current Price Range		Prior Year Average
☐ **Marquis,** polished brass, rich gold ornaments, visible escapement, porcelain dial, white beveled plate glass front, back and sides, 15½" x 7½", dial 4", c. 1910, 8 Day, strike	625.00	700.00	660.00
☐ **Provence,** visible escapement, porcelain dial, white beveled plate glass front, back and sides, 11" x 6½", dial 4", c. 1910, 8 Day, strike, polished brass	195.00	225.00	210.00
☐ **Radiant,** visible escapement, porcelain dial, white beveled plate glass front, back and sides, green onyx top and base, 17" x 9¼", dial 4", c. 1910, 8 Day, strike	645.00	720.00	680.00
☐ **Sirius,** visible escapement, porcelain dial, white beveled plate glass front, back and sides, 13" x 9", dial 4", polished brass, rich gold ornaments, c. 1910, 8 Day, strike	900.00	1000.00	950.00
☐ **Touraine,** rich gold plated, beveled white plate glass back door, pendulum visible through beveled white plate glass panel, 11" x 6¼", dial 4", c. 1917, 8 Day, strike	260.00	295.00	278.00
☐ **Vulcan,** porcelain dial, white beveled plate glass front, back and sides, 12¼" x 7½", dial 4", c. 1910, 8 Day, strike, rich gold	205.00	235.00	220.00

PARLOR WALL

☐ **Argentina,** walnut, height 33", dial 6", spring, c. 1910, 8 Day, strike	460.00	500.00	480.00
☐ **Bagdad,** ash, height 50½", dial 8", spring, c 1896, 8 Day	775.00	850.00	810.00
☐ **Barcelona,** walnut, 31½" x 14¼", dial 8", spring, c. 1920, 8 Day	370.00	400.00	385.00
☐ **Capital,** ash, height 54", dial 8", spring c. 1896, 8 Day	725.00	800.00	762.00
☐ **Dispatch,** wood, height 30", dial 8", spring, c. 1910, 8 Day, strike	425.00	475.00	450.00
☐ **Lisboa,** walnut, 37" x 18¾", dial 8", spring, c. 1920, 8 Day	370.00	400.00	385.00
☐ **Mississippi,** wood, 27" x 12", dial 6", spring, c. 1910, 8 Day	360.00	400.00	380.00
☐ **Prompt,** walnut, height 50", dial 8", spring, c. 1896, 8 Day	725.00	800.00	762.00
☐ **Queen Anne,** oak, height 40½", dial 8", spring, c. 1898, 8 Day	540.00	600.00	570.00
☐ **Queen Isabella,** dark wood or oak, height 38½", dial 8", spring, c. 1910, 8 Day	400.00	450.00	425.00
☐ **Rio,** oak, height 39", dial 8", spring, c. 1910, 8 Day	490.00	550.00	520.00
☐ **San Luis,** walnut, height 28", dial 6½", spring, c. 1910, 8 Day, strike	410.00	450.00	430.00

W.L. GILBERT CLOCK COMPANY
CALENDAR

☐ **Alpine,** gallery type, height 24", dial 12", 8 Day, strike, simple calendar	225.00	250.00	238.00
☐ **Benworth,** 27" x 15", dial 8", 8 Day, strike, simple calendar	700.00	800.00	750.00

CLOCKS / 231

	Current Price Range		Prior Year Average
☐ **Consort Octagon Top,** height 31″, dial 12″, 8 Day, strike, simple calendar	325.00	375.00	350.00
☐ **Longbranch,** 28″ x 16″, dial 8″, 8 Day, strike, simple calendar, spring	400.00	450.00	425.00
☐ **Mountauk Octagon Top,** short drop, height 26″, dial 12″, 8 Day, strike, simple calendar	325.00	375.00	350.00
☐ **National,** thermometer and barometer, 27½″ x 16″, dial 8″, 8 Day, strike, simple calendar, spring .	450.00	500.00	475.00
☐ **Octagon Top,** short drop gilt, height 25½″, dial 12″, 8 Day, strike, simple calendar	250.00	300.00	275.00
☐ **Riverside Octagon Top,** short drop, height 23″, dial 10″, 8 Day, strike, simple calendar	325.00	375.00	350.00
☐ **Star Octagon Top,** long drop, height 32½″, dial 12″, 8 Day, strike, simple calendar	450.00	500.00	475.00
☐ **Victorian Shelf No. 28,** 19½″ x 12″, 8 Day, strike, simple calendar	150.00	175.00	162.00

KITCHEN

☐ **Britannic No. 47,** oak, height 25″, dial 6″, c. 1900, 8 Day, strike, spring wound	155.00	180.00	168.00
☐ **Crius,** walnut, height 19½″, dial 6″, c. 1888, 1 Day, strike, spring wound	110.00	135.00	122.00
☐ **Dove,** oak, height 22″, dial 6″, c. 1896, 8 Day, strike, spring wound	145.00	170.00	158.00
☐ **Egypt,** oak, height 23″, dial 6″, c. 1905, 8 Day, strike, spring wound	150.00	175.00	162.00
☐ **Flora,** walnut with ash trimmings, height 17″, dial 5″, c. 1888, 1 Day, strike, spring wound	110.00	135.00	122.00
☐ **Geranium,** oak, height 24″, dial 6″, c. 1903, 8 Day, strike, spring wound	150.00	175.00	162.00
☐ **Huron,** oak, height 22½″, dial 6″, c. 1896, 8 Day, strike, spring wound	145.00	170.00	168.00
☐ **Iowa No. 23,** height 24″, dial 6″, c. 1900, 8 Day, strike, spring wound	155.00	180.00	168.00
☐ **Lincoln,** oak, height 23″, dial 6″, c. 1900, 8 Day, strike, spring wound	150.00	175.00	162.00
☐ **Mogul,** oak, height 23″, dial 6″, c. 1900, 8 Day, strike, spring wound	150.00	175.00	162.00
☐ **Owl,** oak, height 22″, dial 6″, c. 1896, 8 Day, strike, spring wound	145.00	170.00	158.00
☐ **Pharaoh,** oak, height 23″, dial 6″, c. 1905, 8 Day, strike, spring wound	150.00	175.00	162.00
☐ **Pyramid,** oak, height 23″, dial 6″, c. 1905, 8 Day, strike, spring wound	150.00	175.00	162.00
☐ **Swan,** oak, height 22″, dial 6″, C. 1896, 8 Day, strike, spring wound	145.00	170.00	158.00
☐ **Teutonic No. 46,** oak, height 25″, dial 6″, c. 1900, 8 Day, strike, spring wound	155.00	180.00	168.00
☐ **Washington,** oak, height 23″, dial 6″, c. 1900, 8 Day, strike, spring wound	150.00	175.00	162.00

NOVELTY GILTS

☐ **Arch Altar,** metal gold ormolu, plain sash, 8¼″ x 5″, dial 2″, c. 1910, 1 Day	85.00	105.00	95.00
☐ **Charlot No. 1,** metal gold ormolu, plain sash, 6¼″ x 9″, dial 2″, c. 1910, 1 Day	50.00	65.00	58.00

232 / CLOCKS

	Current Price Range		Prior Year Average
☐ **Comforter,** metal gold ormolu, plain gold or jeweled sash, 10½" x 5¼", dial 2", c. 1910, 1 Day	55.00	70.00	62.00
☐ **Darius,** metal gold ormolu, plain or jeweled sash, 9¾" x 5¼", dial 2", c. 1910, 1 Day	60.00	75.00	68.00
☐ **Father Time,** metal gold ormolu, 10¼" x 9¾", dial 2¾", c. 1910, 1 Day	65.00	80.00	72.00
☐ **Freedom,** metal gold ormolu, plain sash or Venetian green, 10" x 3¾", dial 2", c. 1910, 1 Day	85.00	105.00	95.00
☐ **Gold Pillar,** metal gold ormolu, plain sash, 9½" x 4½", dial 2", c. 1910, 1 Day	85.00	105.00	95.00
☐ **Hester,** ormolu gold, Venetian bronze and barbedienne, French sash, 13¾" x 7½", ivory dial 4", c. 1910, 8 Day, strike	105.00	130.00	127.00
☐ **Joy,** metal gold ormolu, plain or jeweled sash, 10" x 5", dial 2", c. 1910, 1 Day	55.00	70.00	62.00
☐ **Lasanada,** metal gold ormolu, plain or jeweled sash, 10" x 6", dial 2", c. 1910, 1 Day	55.00	70.00	62.00
☐ **Menes,** metal gold ormolu, plain or jeweled sash, 10" x 6½", dial 2", c. 1910, 1 Day	60.00	75.00	68.00
☐ **Nefer,** metal gold ormolu, plain or jeweled sash, 10¾" x 4", dial 2", c. 1910, 1 Day	65.00	80.00	72.00
☐ **Playful,** metal gold ormolu, plain sash, 9¾" x 5¼", dial 2", c. 1910, 1 Day	55.00	70.00	62.00
☐ **Restful,** metal gold ormolu, plain sash, 10" x 5", dial 2", c. 1910, 1 Day	60.00	75.00	68.00
☐ **Rococo No. 1,** gilt finish, enameled circle around dial in blue and pink, 9" x 7", dial 2¾", c. 1910, 1 Day	40.00	50.00	45.00
☐ **Tahar,** metal gold ormolu, plain or jeweled sash, onyx base, 9½" x 4", dial 2", c. 1910, 1 Day	50.00	65.00	58.00
☐ **Yawn,** metal gold ormolu, plain sash, 11¼" x 4½", dial 2", c. 1910, 1 Day	60.00	75.00	68.00

E. INGRAHAM CLOCK COMPANY
CABINET

☐ **Acme,** oak, height 17", dial 5", c. 1898, 8 Day, strike	115.00	140.00	128.00
☐ **Bismarck,** oak, fancy gilt, 15" x 10½", dial 6", 8 Day, strike	80.00	100.00	90.00
☐ **Cabinet No. 1,** oak, height 15½", dial 5", c. 1894, 8 Day, strike	80.00	100.00	90.00
☐ **Gladstone,** oak, fancy gilt, 15" x 10½", dial 6", 8 Day, strike	80.00	100.00	90.00
☐ **Tablet,** walnut, cathedral bell, patent regulator, height 15", dial 5", c. 1894, 8 Day, strike	80.00	100.00	90.00
☐ **Target,** walnut, cathedral bell, patent regulator, height 16", dial 5", c. 1894, 8 Day, strike	80.00	100.00	90.00
☐ **Thistle,** light wood, black ornaments, cathedral bell, patent regulator, height 16½", dial 5", c. 1894, 8 Day, strike	80.00	100.00	90.00
☐ **Thorn,** oak, cathedral bell, patent regulator, height 12", dial 5", c. 1894, 8 Day, strike	80.00	100.00	90.00
☐ **Verona,** oak, marbleized column, height 15¾", dial 5", 8 Day, strike	125.00	150.00	138.00

CALENDAR

	Current Price Range		Prior Year Average
☐ **Aurora,** Victorian kitchen, thermometer and barometer, height 25″, dial 6″, 8 Day, strike, simple calendar, spring wound	200.00	225.00	212.00
☐ **12″ Bristol Octagon Top,** short drop, oak, height 25″, 8 Day, strike, simple calendar	250.00	300.00	275.00
☐ **Chicago,** Victorian kitchen, thermometer and barometer, height 23″, dial 6″, 8 Day, strike, simple calendar, spring wound	200.00	225.00	212.00
☐ **Dew Drop Octagon,** 24″ x 16″, dial 11″, 8 Day, strike, simple calendar, spring wound	300.00	350.00	325.00
☐ **Gila,** barometer left of door, thermometer right of door, height 23″, dial 6″, 8 Day, strike, simple calendar, spring wound	225.00	250.00	238.00
☐ **Hartford 12″ Octagon Top,** long drop, oak, height 32″, 8 Day, strike, simple calendar	350.00	400.00	375.00
☐ **Lyric Octagon Top,** short drop, height 27″, dial 12″, 8 Day, strike, simple calendar	250.00	300.00	275.00
☐ **Minerva,** Victorian kitchen, thermometer and barometer, height 25″, dial 6″, 8 Day, strike, simple calendar	200.00	225.00	212.00
☐ **Ormond,** round top long drop regulator, height 35½″, dial 12″, 8 Day, simple calendar, spring wound	350.00	400.00	375.00
☐ **Parlor Shelf,** B.B. Lewis V calendar mechanism 22″ x 12″, 5″ time and 7″ calendar dial, 8″ Day, double dial	1400.00	1600.00	1500.00
☐ **Round Drop,** wall, 24″ x 16″, dial 11″, 8 Day, strike, simple calendar, spring wound	300.00	350.00	325.00
☐ **Trenton,** wall box regulator, oak, or mahogany, height 38″, dial 12″, 8 Day, strike, simple calendar	300.00	350.00	325.00
☐ **Urania,** Victorian kitchen, thermometer and barometer, height 25″, dial 6″, 8 Day, strike, simple calendar, spring wound	200.00	225.00	212.00
☐ **Western Union,** box wall regulator, oak, height 36″, dial 12″, 8 Day, strike, simple calendar	300.00	350.00	325.00

CONNECTICUT SHELF

☐ **Cottage Extra,** polished, veneered, height 12¾″, dial 6″, c. 1894, 1 Day, strike	70.00	85.00	78.00
☐ **Octagon Doric,** extra, wood, height 16″, c. 1880, 1 Day, strike	80.00	100.00	90.00
☐ **Octagon Doric,** mosaic, wood, height 16″, c. 1880, 1 Day, strike	80.00	100.00	90.00
☐ **O.G. Weight,** polished, veneered, height 26″, dial 8″, c. 1894, 1 Day, strike	130.00	155.00	142.00
☐ **Round Top Baltic,** wood, height 16″, c. 1880, 1 Day, strike	115.00	140.00	128.00
☐ **Round Top Empire,** wood, height 18″, c. 1880, 8 Day, strike	175.00	200.00	182.00
☐ **Round Top Idaho,** wood, gilt columns, height 18″, c. 1880, 8 Day, strike	140.00	165.00	152.00
☐ **Round Top Venetian No. 2,** extra, wood, gilt columns, height 18″, c. 1880, 8 Day, strike	155.00	180.00	168.00
☐ **Split Top Arctic,** wood, height 16″, c. 1880, 1 Day, strike	75.00	90.00	82.00
☐ **Doric,** gilt column, wood, height 16″, c. 1880, 1 Day, strike	80.00	100.00	90.00

ITHACA CALENDAR CLOCK COMPANY
CALENDAR

	Current Price Range		Prior Year Average
☐ **Bank Regulator No. 1,** sweep second, 72" x 19½", dial 12", 8 Day	7000.00	8000.00	7500.00
☐ **Chronometer,** spring, "Chronometer" in gold on glass, height 33", dial 7", 8 Day, strike	1250.00	1650.00	1450.00
☐ **Emerald Shelf No. 5,** spring 33" x 15", 6½" time and 8" calendar dial, 8 Day, strike	1750.00	1950.00	1850.00
☐ **Farmers With Pillars No. 10,** alarm, spring 21" x 12", dial 7", 8 Day, strike	890.00	950.00	920.00
☐ **Granger No. 14,** spring, 26" x 12", dial 7", 8 Day, strike	1000.00	1250.00	1125.00
☐ **Hanging Index No. 16,** spring, 30½" x 15", dial 7", 8 Day, strike	900.00	1000.00	950.00
☐ **Hanging Steeple,** spring, 32½" x 12", 7" time and 8" calendar dial, 8 Day, strike	1750.00	1950.00	1850.00
☐ **Index,** spring, "Index" in gold on glass, 33½" x 15", dial 7", 8 Day, strike	1500.00	1775.00	1625.00
☐ **Iron Case,** double spring, 21" x 9", 5" time and 7" calendar dial, 8 Day, strike	3100.00	3400.00	3250.00
☐ **Mantel Index No. 17,** spring, 28½" x 15½", dial 7", 8 Day, strike	900.00	1000.00	950.00
☐ **Parlor No. 3½,** 1st model, spring, black dials, silvered hands, 20" x 10", 5" time and 8" calendar dial, 8 Day, spring	2800.00	3400.00	3100.00
☐ **Regulator Hanging No. 1,** double weight, 49" x 19", both dials 12", 8 Day	3000.00	3500.00	3250.00
☐ **Reno,** "Reno" in gold on glass, 8 Day, time, strike	1100.00	1300.00	1200.00
☐ **Round Top Shelf No. 102A,** double spring, 22½" x 11", 7" time and 8" calendar dial, 8 Day	600.00	700.00	650.00
☐ **Shelf Library,** alarm, spring, 31½" x 11½", 6" time and 8" calendar dial, 8 Day, strike	900.00	1050.00	962.00
☐ **Shelf Steeple,** spring, 25½" x 12", 6½" time and 7½" calendar dial, 8 Day, strike	1600.00	1850.00	1750.00
☐ **Skeleton,** spring, nickel plated bell, silver cast iron dial and frame (walnut with ebony trim), 24" x 12", 4½" time and 6½" calendar dial, 8 Day, strike	7000.00	8000.00	7500.00
☐ **Vienna No. 3,** double spring, 52" x 16", dial 8", 30 Day	3250.00	3500.00	3375.00

JEROME AND COMPANY
COTTAGE

☐ **David Crocket,** mahogany and walnut, time piece, height 12", 30 hour	120.00	130.00	125.00
☐ **French Style,** marble, height 13", 8 Day	130.00	150.00	140.00
☐ **N.E. Company,** mahogany, walnut, zebra, time piece, height 11", 30 hour	110.00	125.00	118.00
☐ **Prince Albert,** mahogany, rosewood, height 15", 8 Day	155.00	175.00	165.00
☐ **S.B.T.,** time piece, height 10½", 30 hour	170.00	190.00	180.00
☐ **Union,** mahogany, rosewood, height 13", 8 Day, striking	120.00	140.00	130.00
☐ **Union,** rosewood with gilt moldings, height 13", 8 Day, striking	120.00	140.00	130.00
☐ **Victoria,** rosewood, height 15", 30 hour, striking .	130.00	150.00	140.00

GALLERY

	Current Price Range		Prior Year Average
☐ **Gallery,** gilt frames, mahogany, diameter 14", 8 Day	230.00	250.00	240.00
☐ **Gallery,** diameter 22", 8 Day	325.00	345.00	335.00
☐ **Gilt Gallery,** dial 15", 8 Day	240.00	260.00	250.00
☐ **Gilt Gallery,** dial 10", 8 Day, lever	180.00	200.00	190.00
☐ **Gilt Gallery,** dial 8", 8 Day, lever	160.00	180.00	170.00

OCTOGON TOP, SHORT DROP

☐ **Octagon,** mahogany, rosewood, dial 10", 8 Day	220.00	230.00	225.00
☐ **Octagon,** mahogany, rosewood, time piece 10", dial 12", 8 Day, striking	250.00	270.00	260.00
☐ **Octagon,** mahogany, rosewood, dial 12", 8 Day	245.00	265.00	255.00
☐ **Octagon,** mahogany, rosewood, time piece 12", dial 12", 8 Day	240.00	260.00	250.00

NEW HAVEN CLOCK COMPANY

CABINET

☐ **Angela,** oak, richly ornamented with cast brass trimmings, in antique finish, cathedral gong, height 21¾", dial 4½", c. 1900, 8 Day, strike	270.00	300.00	285.00
☐ **Argyle,** wood, height 17", c. 1894, 1 Day, strike	125.00	150.00	138.00
☐ **Arrow,** walnut, brass trimmings, height 16¼", dial 5", c. 1900, 8 Day, strike	140.00	165.00	152.00
☐ **Banshee,** cherry, brass ornaments, height 13½", dial 5", c. 1900, 1 Day, strike, alarm	165.00	190.00	178.00
☐ **Caliban,** oak, cathedral gong, 14¾" x 11", white, gilt or ivorine dial 6", c. 1910, 8 Day, strike	130.00	155.00	142.00
☐ **Cato,** oak, cathedral gong, 15" x 11½", fancy gilt or ivorine dial 5", c. 1910, 8 Day, strike	160.00	185.00	172.00
☐ **Funston,** oak cabinet, barometer, thermometer and spirit level, cathedral gong, 15½" x 11¾", white, gilt or ivorine dial 6", c. 1910, 8 Day, strike	165.00	190.00	178.00
☐ **Gallia,** antique oak, heavily gilt ornaments, cathedral gong, height 19", dial 5", c. 1900, 8 Day, strike	160.00	185.00	172.00
☐ **Hidalgo,** mahogany, solid wood, dead finish, height 17¾", dial 5", c. 1900, 8 Day, strike	150.00	175.00	162.00
☐ **Medea,** oak, cathedral gong, 15¼" x 11¾", fancy gilt or ivorine dial 5", c. 1910, 8 Day, strike	160.00	185.00	172.00
☐ **Nero,** polished oak 16" x 12", c. 1900, 8 Day, strike	125.00	150.00	138.00
☐ **Olga,** oak, height 13¾", dial 5", c. 1900, 8 Day, strike	135.00	160.00	148.00
☐ **Penobscot,** mahogany, solid wood, dead finish, height 16¼", dial 5", c. 1900, 8 Day, strike	165.00	190.00	178.00
☐ **Russia,** antique oak, heavily gilt ornaments, cathedral gong, height 18½", dial 5", c. 1900, 8 Day, strike	150.00	175.00	162.00
☐ **Servia,** antique oak, heavily gilt ornaments, cathedral gong, height 19", dial 5", c. 1900, 8 Day, strike	150.00	175.00	162.00
☐ **Trinidad,** oak, height 12", dial 4", c. 1894, 8 Day, strike	80.00	100.00	90.00
☐ **Umbria,** oak, heavily gilt ornaments, cathedral gong, 18" x 22½", dial 5", c. 1900, 8 Day, strike	195.00	220.00	207.00

236 / CLOCKS

CALENDAR

	Current Price Range		Prior Year Average
☐ **Austrian,** wall regulator, 49″ x 19″, dial 10″, 8 Day, strike, simple calendar	500.00	575.00	538.00
☐ **Barbara,** wall regulator, 47″ x 18½″, dial 10″, 8 Day strike, simple calendar	500.00	600.00	550.00
☐ **Conroy Victorian Shelf,** spring thermometer and barometer, 25″ x 15½″, dial 6″, 8 Day, strike, simple calendar	200.00	215.00	207.00
☐ **8″ Drop Octagon,** short, brass bands, height 19″	225.00	275.00	250.00
☐ **Emperor,** Square Top Short Drop, oak, height 25½″, dial 12″, 8 Day, strike, simple calendar	250.00	300.00	275.00
☐ **Globe,** round nickel, dial 4″, 1 Day, alarm, simple calendar	70.00	80.00	75.00
☐ **Hebe,** wall regulator, 49″ x 15½″, dial 10″, 8 Day, strike, simple calendar	500.00	575.00	538.00
☐ **Intrepid,** 49″ x 17″, dial 10″, 30 Day, simple calendar, double dial	900.00	1000.00	950.00
☐ **Louis Inkstand,** brass, height 11½″, dial 4″, 1 Day, simple calendar	300.00	350.00	325.00
☐ **Maywood Wall Regulator,** spring, 43½″ x 17″, dial 8″, 8 Day, simple calendar	650.00	750.00	700.00
☐ **Octagon Lever Wall,** spring, Mother-of-Pearl inlaid on wood dial 9¼″, diameter 13″, 1 Day, strike, simple calendar	250.00	275.00	262.00
☐ **Plush Manual,** height 7″, dial 2″, 1 Day, simple calendar	125.00	175.00	150.00
☐ **Register,** double dial wall, spring, also with Jerome label, height 31″, dial 8″, 8 Day	1200.00	1300.00	1250.00
☐ **Round Lever,** wall, spring, dial 8″, 8 Day, simple calendar	175.00	200.00	182.00
☐ **10″ Saxon,** figure 8, height 22″	325.00	375.00	350.00
☐ **Sprite,** round nickel, dial 4½″, 1 Day, alarm, simple calendar	65.00	85.00	75.00
☐ **Trojan Wall Regulator,** spring, 44″ x 13½″, dial 8″, 8 Day, simple calendar	650.00	700.00	675.00
☐ **Wood Lever Octagon,** veneered, width 12″, dial 8″, 1 Day, simple calendar	150.00	175.00	162.00

CONNECTICUT SHELF

☐ **Bee Hive Gothic,** wood, height 19¼″, c. 1900, 1 Day, strike	90.00	110.00	100.00
☐ **Bee Hive Round Gothic,** wood, height 19″, c. 1900, 1 Day, simple spring	90.00	110.00	100.00
☐ **Cottage,** wood, height 12″, c. 1900, 1 Day, strike	55.00	70.00	62.00
☐ **Cottage Extra,** zebra, height 14″, dial 6″, c. 1900, 1 Day, strike	110.00	125.00	118.00
☐ **Gem Cottage,** wood, height 9″, c. 1900, 1 Day	55.00	70.00	62.00
☐ **Octagon Top Alps,** wood, height 17″, c. 1900, 1 Day, strike	80.00	100.00	90.00
☐ **Octagon Top Dreadnaught,** mahogany, height 14″, dial 5″, c. 1900, 1 Day, strike	80.00	100.00	90.00
☐ **Octagon Prize,** wood, height 14½″, c. 1900, 1 day	70.00	85.00	78.00
☐ **Octagon Rocket,** imitation zebra, height 13″, dial 4″, c. 1900, 1 Day	75.00	90.00	82.00
☐ **O.G. (Weight No. 1 or No. 2),** mahogany, height 26″, dial 8″, c. 1900, 1 Day, strike, weight	140.00	165.00	152.00
☐ **O.O.G.,** mahogany, height 30″, c. 1900, 1 Day, strike, weight	175.00	200.00	182.00

CLOCKS / 237

	Current Price Range		Prior Year Average
☐ **Round Top Guide,** wood, height 17¼", c. 1900, 1 Day, strike	80.00	100.00	90.00
☐ **Round Top Gothic Extra,** wood, height 17¼", c. 1900, 1 Day, strike	95.00	115.00	105.00
☐ **Split Top Andes,** wood, height 17", c. 1900, 1 Day, strike	75.00	90.00	82.00
☐ **Split Top Eclipse,** rosewood, height 17", dial 6", c. 1900, 1 Day, strike	90.00	110.00	100.00
☐ **Split Top Gothic Gem,** wood, height 17¾", c. 1900, 1 Day, strike	80.00	100.00	90.00
☐ **Split Top Pyramid,** wood, height 17", c. 1900, 1 Day, strike	75.00	90.00	82.00
☐ **Split Top Rocket,** chestnut or imitation zebra, height 10¾", dial 4", c. 1900, 1 Day	60.00	75.00	68.00
☐ **Split Top Tuscan,** wood, height 17¾", c. 1900, 1 Day, strike	75.00	90.00	68.00
☐ **Steeple Derby,** wood, height 18½", dial 5½", c. 1900, 1 Day, strike	105.00	125.00	115.00
☐ **Steeple Dolphin,** zebra, veneered, height 17¾", dial 5", c. 1900, 1 Day	105.00	125.00	115.00

KITCHEN

	Current Price Range		Prior Year Average
☐ **Ambassador,** oak, height 23", dial 16", c. 1894, 1 Day, strike, spring wound	120.00	145.00	132.00
☐ **Bonita,** wood, height 17¾", dial 6", c. 1900, 1 Day, strike, spring wound	135.00	160.00	148.00
☐ **Carmen,** wood, height 21½", dial 6", c. 1900, 8 Day, strike, spring wound	140.00	165.00	152.00
☐ **Dora,** wood, height 20", dial 5", c. 1900, 8 Day, strike, spring wound	145.00	170.00	158.00
☐ **Electra,** walnut or mahogany veneered, brass ornaments, height 19½", dial 5", c. 1890, 8 Day, strike, spring wound	150.00	175.00	162.00
☐ **Festus,** oak, height 22", rococo dial 6", c. 1917, 8 Day, strike, spring wound	115.00	140.00	128.00
☐ **Grayling,** wood, height 19½", dial 5", c. 1900, 8 Day, strike, spring wound	135.00	160.00	148.00
☐ **Irex,** wood, height 23½", dial 6", c. 1900, 8 Day, strike, spring wound	150.00	175.00	162.00
☐ **Janitor,** oak, interchangeable tops, "Hustler Series", dial 6", c. 1896, 8 Day, strike, spring wound	145.00	170.00	158.00
☐ **Moselle,** wood, height 26", dial 6", c. 1900, 8 Day, strike, spring wound	190.00	220.00	205.00
☐ **Neva,** wood, height 19", dial 5½", c. 1900, 8 Day, strike, spring wound	145.00	170.00	158.00
☐ **Orient,** wood veneer, 18¾" x 10½", c. 1900, 1 Day, spring wound	115.00	140.00	128.00
☐ **Rhine,** wood, height 21", dial 6", c. 1900, 8 Day, strike, spring wound	135.00	160.00	148.00
☐ **Saline,** wood, height 21½", dial 6", c. 1900, 1 Day, strike, spring wound	105.00	130.00	117.00
☐ **Titania,** wood, height 24", dial 6", c. 1900, 8 Day, strike, spring wound	160.00	185.00	172.00
☐ **Volga,** wood, height 21½", dial 6", c. 1900, 8 Day, strike, spring wound	140.00	165.00	152.00

238 / CLOCKS

	Current Price Range		Prior Year Average
☐ **Walnut,** wood, height 20½", dial 5", c. 1900, 8 Day, strike, spring wound	145.00	170.00	158.00

MANTEL

	Current Price Range		Prior Year Average
☐ **Black Arno,** enameled iron, Empire sash with porcelain or pearl dial, visible escapement, c. 1900, 8 Day, strike	120.00	145.00	132.00
☐ **Black Chateau,** enameled iron, black or green marble, bronze or gilt trimmings, 9½" x 11½", dial 4", c. 1900, 8 Day, strike	100.00	120.00	110.00
☐ **Black Florence,** enameled iron, Empire sash with porcelain or pearl dial, visible escapement, c. 1900, 8 Day, strike	75.00	90.00	82.00
☐ **Black Harcourt,** enameled iron, Empire sash with porcelain or pearl dial, visible escapement, c. 1900, 8 Day, strike	105.00	130.00	117.00
☐ **Black Mona,** enameled iron, Empire sash, with porcelain or pearl dial, visible escapement, c. 1900, 8 Day, strike	80.00	100.00	90.00
☐ **Black Pocahontas,** enameled iron, Empire sash, porcelain or pearl dial, visible escapement, c. 1900, 8 Day, strike	115.00	140.00	128.00
☐ **Black Thetis,** enameled iron, Empire sash with porcelain or pearl dial, visible escapement, c. 1900, 8 Day Stirke	90.00	110.00	100.00
☐ **Wood Bancroft,** black enameled wood, white, gilt or pearl dial, bronze or gilt trimmings, 11" x 16", dial 6", c. 1900, 8 Day, strike	80.00	95.00	88.00
☐ **Wood Numa,** black enameled wood, white, gilt or pearl dial, 11" x 16", dial 6", c. 1900, 8 Day, strike	75.00	90.00	82.00
☐ **Wood Pembroke,** black enameled wood, white, gilt or pearl dial, 10⅞" x 16", dial 6", c. 1900, 8 Day, strike	70.00	85.00	78.00
☐ **Antique Brass No. 2,** visible escapement, height 13½", dial 4", c. 1900, 8 Day, strike	220.00	250.00	235.00

SETH THOMAS CLOCK COMPANY

CALENDAR

	Current Price Range		Prior Year Average
☐ **Office No. 1,** 40" x 19½", time dial 12", calendar dial 14", 8 Day	1600.00	1800.00	1700.00
☐ **Office Calendar No. 9,,** height 68", dials 14", 8 Day	2000.00	2500.00	2250.00
☐ **Office Calendar No. 11,** 68½" x 25", dials 14", 8 Day	4000.00	5000.00	4500.00
☐ **12" Octagon Top Short Drop,,** height 23½", 8 Day, strike, simple calendar	300.00	375.00	338.00
☐ **Parlor Calendar No. 6,** spring, 27" x 15", dials 7½", 8 Day, strike	900.00	1000.00	950.00
☐ **Parlor Shelf,** spring, 29½" x 18", dials 7½", 8 Day, strike	1750.00	2000.00	1880.00
☐ **8" Round Top Long Drop,** 8 Day, Strike, simple calendar	300.00	375.00	338.00
☐ **Shelf Double Dial,** Plymouth Hollow label, rosewood, octagon dial, openings in door, 30" x 18½" 8 Day, strike	1500.00	1650.00	1575.00

CLOCKS / 239

	Current Price Range		Prior Year Average

CONNECTICUT SHELF

- ☐ **Arch Top,** wood, height 16″, c. 1875, 8 Day, strike, spring ...... 160.00 / 185.00 / 172.00
- ☐ **Column,** wood, height 16″, c. 1875, 30 hour, strike, spring ...... 115.00 / 140.00 / 128.00
- ☐ **Column,** walnut veneer, polished rosewood shell or gilt columns, height 25″, dial 7½″, c. 1920, 1 Day, strike, weight ...... 105.00 / 125.00 / 118.00
- ☐ **Cottage,** wood, height 9″, c. 1880, 8 Day ...... 125.00 / 150.00 / 138.00
- ☐ **Empire Franklin,** mahogany, gold gilt columns, hand carved scroll at head, cathedral bell, dial 10″, c. 1912, 8 Day strike, weight ...... 400.00 / 450.00 / 425.00
- ☐ **Empire Large Rosewood,** gilt column, rosewood, height 32″, c. 1875, 8 Day, strike, weight ...... 310.00 / 350.00 / 330.00
- ☐ **Octagon Top Nashville,** V.P., wood, height 16″, c. 1875, 8 Day, strike, spring ...... 125.00 / 150.00 / 138.00
- ☐ **Octagon Top,** wood, height 9″, c. 1880, 1 Day ... 105.00 / 125.00 / 115.00
- ☐ **O.G.,** wood, height 25″, and 29½″, c. 1894, 1 Day, strike, weight ...... 130.00 / 155.00 / 142.00
- ☐ **O.G.,** wood, height 25″, c. 1875, 30 hour, strike, weight, Plymouth Hollow ...... 135.00 / 160.00 / 148.00
- ☐ **O.O.G.,** wood, height 25″, c. 1875, 8 Day, strike, weight, Thomaston ...... 105.00 / 130.00 / 118.00
- ☐ **Round Top Louisville,** V.P., wood, height 22″, c. 1875, 8 Day, strike, spring ...... 195.00 / 225.00 / 210.00
- ☐ **Round Top Tudor No. 1,** wood, height 16″, c. 1880, 8 Day, strike, spring ...... 125.00 / 150.00 / 138.00
- ☐ **Split Top New Orleans,** V.P., wood, height 16″, c. 1875, 8 Day, strike, spring ...... 150.00 / 175.00 / 162.00
- ☐ **Split Top Milan,** oak, cream porcelain dial, French sash, beveled glass, height 10¼″, base 9½″, dial 4″, c. 1900, 8 Day, strike ...... 135.00 / 160.00 / 148.00
- ☐ **Split Top Normandy,** walnut, height 15″, c. 1880, 15 Day, strike ...... 150.00 / 175.00 / 162.00
- ☐ **Split Top Selma,** walnut, height 16½″, dial 5″, c. 1920, 8 Day, strike ...... 115.00 / 120.00 / 117.50

WATERBURY CLOCK COMPANY

CALENDAR

- ☐ **Arion Octagon Top 10,** short drop, 22½″ x 15″, spring, 8 Day, strike, simple calendar ...... 275.00 / 325.00 / 300.00
- ☐ **Belden Victorian Shelf,** 22″ x 15″, dial 5″, spring, 8 Day, strike, simple calendar ...... 225.00 / 275.00 / 250.00
- ☐ **Dabney Shelf,** height 22″, dial 6″, with thermometer and barometer, 8 Day, strike, simple calendar ...... 225.00 / 275.00 / 250.00
- ☐ **Felix Shelf,** height 22″, dial 6″, spring, 8 Day, simple calendar ...... 225.00 / 275.00 / 250.00
- ☐ **Glenwood Figure 8,** height 25½″, dial 12″, 8 Day, strike, simple calendar ...... 450.00 / 550.00 / 500.00
- ☐ **Heron Octagon Top,** long drop, height 32″, dial 12″, 8 Day, strike, simple calendar ...... 350.00 / 425.00 / 385.00
- ☐ **Joliet Roller Type Wall,** spring, 8 Day ...... 1500.00 / 1750.00 / 1625.00
- ☐ **Natchez Wall,** 40″ x 13¾″, dial 8″, spring, 8 Day, simple calendar ...... 600.00 / 675.00 / 638.00
- ☐ **Octagon Top 12″,** short drop, height 24″, spring, 8 Day, strike, simple calendar ...... 300.00 / 375.00 / 338.00

240 / CLOTHING

	Current Price Range		Prior Year Average
☐ **Paris Parlor Shelf,** 23″ x 13″, dial 5″, spring, 8 Day, strike, simple calendar	300.00	400.00	350.00
☐ **Rochester Victorian Shelf,** 27″ x 17½″, dial 7″, spring, 8 Day, strike, simple calendar	300.00	375.00	338.00
☐ **Selborne Victorian Shelf,** height 23″, dial 6″, 8 Day, strike, simple calendar	200.00	300.00	250.00
☐ **Victorian Kitchen Shelf,** spring, dial 5″, with thermometer and barometer, 8 Day, strike, simple calendar	225.00	250.00	238.00

CRYSTAL REGULATORS

☐ **Aude,** rich gold plated, ivory center, visible escapement, cast gilt bezel, beveled glass front, sides and back, 10⅛″ x 7¾″, ivory dial 4¼″, c. 1910, 8 Day, strike	270.00	315.00	292.00
☐ **Brittany,** rich gold plated, ivory center, visible escapement, cast gilt bezel, beveled glass front, sides and back, 11⅞″ x 7″, ivory dial 4½″, c. 1910, 8 Day, strike	335.00	375.00	355.00
☐ **Calais,** rich gold plated, ivory center, visible escapement, cast gilt bezel, beveled glass front, sides and back, 11⅞″ x 7″, ivory dial 4¼″, c. 1910, 8 Day, strike	400.00	450.00	425.00
☐ **Gard,** rich gold plated, green onyx base and top, ivory center, visible escapement, cast gilt bezel, beveled glass front, sides and back, 16″ x 7½″, ivory dial 4½″, c. 1910, 8 Day, strike	540.00	600.00	570.00
☐ **Landes,** rich gold plated, polished mahogany columns, ivory center, visible escapement, cast gilt bezel, beveled glass front, sides and back, 10⅝″ x 7⅜″, ivory dial 4¼″, c. 1910, 8 Day, strike	285.00	325.00	310.00
☐ **Navaree,** rich gold plated, ivory center, visible escapement, cast gilt bezel, beveled glass front, sides and back, 8⅞″ x 6½″, ivory dial 3½″, c. 1910, 8 Day, strike	195.00	225.00	210.00
☐ **Ostend,** rich gold plated, ivory center, visible escapement, cast gilt bezel, beveled glass front, sides and back, 9⅞″ x 6⅛″, ivory dial 4¼″, c. 1910, 8 Day, strike	155.00	180.00	165.00
☐ **Savoy,** rich gold plated, ivory center, visible escapement, cast gilt bezel, beveled glass front, sides and back, 10⅝″ x 7″, ivory dial 3½″, c. 1910, 8 Day, strike	295.00	335.00	315.00
☐ **Toulon,** rich gold plated, ivory center, visible escapement, cast gilt bezel, beveled glass front, sides and back, 10⅝″ x 7″, ivory dial 4½″, c. 1910, 8 Day, strike	170.00	195.00	182.00

CLOTHING

Recently, collectors have come to view clothing in the same light as do museums. Clothing reflects not only stylistic preferences of each age, but the degree of workmanship expected, the knowledge of textile manufacture in evidence, and even indications of social customs of the time.

Satin Gown, Charles Williams Stores of New York, wedding or evening wear.. **$100.00-150.00**

The value of an item is usually determined by a combination of factors: age, condition, construction, type of fabric used and occasionally authentic documentation proving that the garment was worn by a famous person. (Recently, many Hollywood studios sold off movies costumes on this very premise.) A good way to determine the age of a garment is to inspect the consistency of stitching, as sewing machines were not perfected until the latter part of the 19th century. Many older garments may have been altered several times as the expense of new material far outweighed the cost, or trouble, of altering the existing article.

Old clothing is often quite fragile and must be handled carefully. Protection from light, moisture, insects, body oils and perspiration are usually essential as are proper techniques of storage (hanging or folding). Cleaning and repair work are risky and should be avoided if at all possible. Prices vary widely, even for the same article, so it is wise to research carefully before shopping. As with most other collectibles, prices are rising.

	Current Price Range		Prior Year Average
☐ **Apron,** long with lace	12.00	18.00	12.50
☐ **Apron,** ruffled bottom	7.00	12.00	8.00
☐ **Boa,** marabou	22.00	32.00	25.00
☐ **Bonnet,** lace with ribbon ties, Dutch style	28.00	38.00	30.00
☐ **Bonnet,** gingham with button	30.00	36.00	30.00
☐ **Camisole,** Victorian	22.00	28.00	22.50
☐ **Cape,** seal skin	38.00	42.00	37.00
☐ **Cape,** taffeta, c. 1900	18.00	22.00	17.50
☐ **Coat,** coonskin, c. 1920	220.00	280.00	210.00
☐ **Coat,** cutaway, c. 1880	44.00	55.00	45.00
☐ **Coat,** lady's sealskin, c. 1940	110.00	140.00	115.00
☐ **Coat,** man's morning with tails	28.00	32.00	27.00

242 / COCA-COLA COLLECTIBLES

	Current Price Range		Prior Year Average
☐ **Coat,** man's black velvet opera, c. 1910	110.00	130.00	110.00
☐ **Coat,** man's racoon	820.00	975.00	875.00
☐ **Dress,** black embroidered silk, c. 1890	80.00	110.00	82.00
☐ **Dress,** black and white, taffeta, c. 1870	30.00	35.00	27.50
☐ **Dress,** child's, embroidered white cotton, c. 1910	30.00	35.00	27.50
☐ **Dress,** early 1800's	32.00	38.00	37.00
☐ **Dress,** sheer wool stripe, c. 1850	32.00	38.00	37.00
☐ **Dress,** two-piece, black silk and brocade, c. 1880	360.00	410.00	375.00
☐ **Dress,** two-piece velveteen	38.00	48.00	40.00
☐ **Dress,** white, lace trim	85.00	105.00	90.00
☐ **Dress,** white silk wedding, c. 1880's	130.00	140.00	128.00
☐ **Dress,** wine velvet	28.00	32.00	27.50
☐ **Handbag,** alligator, envelope, c. 1930	55.00	70.00	57.00
☐ **Handbag,** beaded, drawstring, multicolor and black	26.00	32.00	27.00
☐ **Handbag,** beaded, black, top expands, c. 1900 ..	32.00	52.00	40.00
☐ **Handbag,** beaded, multicolored	60.00	80.00	65.00
☐ **Handbag,** crocheted, drawstring top, c. 1900	25.00	35.00	25.00
☐ **Handbag,** embroidered on velvet, c. 1880	85.00	105.00	90.00
☐ **Handbag,** embroidered on silk and gold, c. 1890 .	80.00	95.00	82.00
☐ **Handbag,** enameled clasp top, c. 1910	45.00	65.00	50.00
☐ **Handbag,** lucite, c. 1940-1950	15.00	42.00	25.00
☐ **Handbag,** mesh, gold, c. 1950	32.00	48.00	37.00
☐ **Handbag,** mesh, sterling silver	85.00	105.00	90.00
☐ **Handkerchief,** white silk	22.00	28.00	22.00
☐ **Hat,** black bonnet, silk, c. 1820	42.00	52.00	45.00
☐ **Hat,** bonnet, straw and silk bow, c. 1890	28.00	42.00	32.00
☐ **Hat,** felt, some with feathers, c. 1940	6.00	12.00	7.50
☐ **Hat,** flapper, felt	6.00	12.00	7.50
☐ **Hat,** ladies' pillbox, leopard	28.00	38.00	30.00
☐ **Hat,** ladies' straw with black plume, c. 1890	85.00	95.00	85.00
☐ **Hat,** ladies' straw cloche, c. 1920	22.00	32.00	25.00
☐ **Hat,** men's straw panama, c. 1890	32.00	42.00	35.00
☐ **Hat,** men's top, beaver gray silk band, c. 1870 ...	42.00	52.00	45.00
☐ **Hat,** men's top, wool felt, c. 1850	38.00	48.00	40.00
☐ **Hat,** men's top, collapsible, c. 1890	75.00	85.00	75.00
☐ **Hat,** opera, black silk	50.00	80.00	60.00
☐ **Pantaloons,** Victorian	18.00	22.00	17.50
☐ **Pantaloons,** Victorian	18.00	22.00	17.50
☐ **Parasol,** white linen	58.00	78.00	65.00
☐ **Parasol,** black taffeta	42.00	58.00	52.00
☐ **Petticoat,** white cotton with lace, long	22.00	32.00	25.00
☐ **Robe,** gold and black silk	18.00	22.00	17.50
☐ **Sailor suit,** boy's, three-piece wool	27.00	32.00	27.00
☐ **Shawl,** fringed design	58.00	78.00	65.00
☐ **Shawl,** Spanish silk, 51" square	78.00	88.00	80.00
☐ **Shawl,** tapestry, Czechoslovakia fringed, 64" x 64"	32.00	42.00	35.00
☐ **Shawl,** Turkish embroidered, 7' x 1'4"	175.00	250.00	180.00
☐ **Shoes,** childrens' button	32.00	40.00	38.00
☐ **Shoes,** ladies' high laced, black leather	48.00	58.00	50.00
☐ **Skirt,** hoop	22.00	28.00	22.00
☐ **Suit,** swallowtail, c. 1900's	80.00	100.00	85.00

COCA-COLA COLLECTIBLES

Coca-Cola Radio, c. 1949..................... **$120.00-$180.00**

The most popular soft drink in the world has another claim to fame. The Coca-Cola Company has always maintained an imaginative and successful campaign to promote its products, and over the years many of these items have become highly desirable collectibles. Coca-Cola collectibles continue to attract interest at an astonishing pace in the collector marketplace. Coke has managed to keep pace with the moods and events of our times. Many hobbyists feel the history of Coke advertising and promotions have directly mirrored the culture of America. The "duster girl" in her vintage auto represented Coca-Cola at the turn of the century on trays, bookmarks, and calendars. She was soon followed by the "flapper of the Roaring 20's," who in turn gave way to the United States Army Nurse Corps when both Coke and the United States knew that patriotism was the order of the day.

Although the older items in particular are the most valuable (especially pre-World War II), items continue to attract attention and are likely to increase in value. New Coca-Cola promotions are being conceived at this time. It's great fun collecting nostalgia pieces of yesterday, while at the same time keeping a sharp eye on the Coke collectibles of tomorrow.

	Current Price Range		Prior Year Average
☐ **Ashtray,** aluminum, c. 1955	3.00	6.00	3.00
☐ **Ashtray** and match holder. c. 1940	180.00	200.00	177.00
☐ **Ashtray,** metal, c. 1963	18.00	22.00	17.50
☐ **Ashtray,** Mexican, painted aluminum	3.00	4.00	2.50

244 / COCA-COLA COLLECTIBLES

	Current Price Range		Prior Year Average
☐ **Ashtray,** picture of Atlanta plant	18.00	22.00	20.00
☐ **Ashtray,** set of card suites, c. 1940	55.00	60.00	52.00
☐ **Bank,** pop bottle machine, tin	28.00	38.00	30.00
☐ **Bingo game**	55.00	65.00	55.00
☐ **Blackboard,** c. 1939	38.00	48.00	40.00
☐ **Blotter,** "Delicious and Refreshing", c. 1904	11.00	14.00	10.50
☐ **Blotter,** "Duster Girl" in auto, c. 1904	11.00	14.00	10.50
☐ **Blotter,** "Icy Style COLD Refreshment", c. 1939 .	7.00	9.00	7.00
☐ **Blotter,** "Restores Energy and Strengthens Nerves", c. 1906	9.00	11.00	9.00
☐ **Blotter,** Santa Claus with children, c. 1938	7.00	9.00	8.00
☐ **Blotter,** Sprite with bottle-top hat, c. 1953	3.25	4.25	3.50
☐ **Blotter,** Sprite with bottle-top hat, c. 1956	2.25	3.25	2.50
☐ **Book cover,** c. 1939	6.50	8.50	7.00
☐ **Book cover,** c. 1951	6.00	8.00	6.00
☐ **Bookmark,** Coke can, c. 1960	9.00	12.00	9.00
☐ **Bookmark,** Hilda Clark, c. 1899	140.00	160.00	142.00
☐ **Bookmark,** Hilda Clark, c. 1900	135.00	155.00	138.00
☐ **Bookmark,** little girl with bird house, c. 1904	160.00	180.00	160.00
☐ **Bookmark,** Lillian Russel, c. 1904	80.00	90.00	80.00
☐ **Bookmark,** owl on perch, c. 1906	105.00	115.00	100.00
☐ **Bookmark,** Valentine, c. 1899	110.00	130.00	110.00
☐ **Bookmark,** Victorian Lady	175.00	190.00	172.00
☐ **Bottle holder protector,** paper envelope, c. 1932 .	6.00	8.00	6.00
☐ **Bottle holder protector,** six bottle type, c. 1933 ..	38.00	45.00	37.50
☐ **Bottle,** "Best by a Dam Site", c. 1936	38.00	45.00	37.50
☐ **Bottle,** light green, c. 1905	12.00	16.00	11.00
☐ **Bottle,** applied paper label, c. 1915	38.00	42.00	37.50
☐ **Bottle,** display 20″ H., red or clear, c. 1923	125.00	235.00	120.00
☐ **Bottle,** Donald Duck, 7 oz., painted	5.00	10.00	6.00
☐ **Bottle,** double diamond, amber glass, c. 1905 ...	22.00	32.00	25.00
☐ **Bottle,** first throwaway, 9″	10.00	14.00	10.00
☐ **Bottle,** fountain syrup type, c. 1900-1920	68.00	88.00	75.00
☐ **Bottle,** gold dipped 50th Anniversary, 26 oz.	8.00	12.00	8.00
☐ **Bottle,** Israel Exposition, c. 1975	8.00	12.00	8.00
☐ **Bottle,** miniature perfume	28.00	42.00	32.00
☐ **Bottle,** 9″ H., c. 1902	18.00	22.00	17.50
☐ **Bottle,** Oklahoma Presentation 1903-1967	68.00	78.00	70.00
☐ **Bottle,** porcelain stopper	80.00	110.00	82.00
☐ **Bottle,** turkey, embossed four sides	18.00	28.00	17.50
☐ **Bottle,** Youngstown, Ohio, amber, c. 1905	22.00	28.00	22.50
☐ **Bottle,** WWI, c. 1915	18.00	22.00	20.00
☐ **Calendar,** American birds, c. 1959	12.00	18.00	12.50
☐ **Calendar,** Bathing Beauty, c. 1930	85.00	110.00	82.00
☐ **Calendar,** "Betty", c. 1914	260.00	310.00	275.00
☐ **Calendar,** boy with dog, c. 1931	110.00	135.00	112.00
☐ **Calendar,** boy with fishing pole, c. 1937	85.00	110.00	90.00
☐ **Calendar,** "Coca-Cola Girl", c. 1910	910.00	960.00	925.00
☐ **Calendar,** "Flapper Girl", glass in hand, c. 1926 .	560.00	610.00	575.00
☐ **Calendar,** "Garden Girl", c. 1920	75.00	95.00	80.00
☐ **Calendar,** girl at party, c. 1925	65.00	75.00	65.00
☐ **Calendar,** girl with record in hand, c. 1968	9.00	14.00	10.00
☐ **Calendar,** "Grisilda", c. 1905	260.00	310.00	275.00
☐ **Calendar,** Hilda Clark, c. 1900	460.00	510.00	475.00
☐ **Calendar,** knitting girl, c. 1919	110.00	140.00	115.00
☐ **Calendar,** lady at desk, c. 1899	760.00	810.00	820.00

	Current Price Range		Prior Year Average
☐ **Calendar,** lady with tennis racket, c. 1891	750.00	810.00	775.00
☐ **Calendar,** lady with roses, c. 1902	610.00	660.00	625.00
☐ **Calendar,** Lillian Nordica with bottle, c. 1904	860.00	900.00	862.00
☐ **Calendar,** modern image dancing, c. 1970	7.00	9.00	6.50
☐ **Calendar,** old man with boat, c. 1936	110.00	125.00	108.00
☐ **Calendar,** pearl white, c. 1916	240.00	260.00	235.00
☐ **Calendar,** snowman and girl, c. 1958	12.00	18.00	12.50
☐ **Calendar,** two models, c. 1912	285.00	310.00	382.00
☐ **Calendar,** U.S. Army Nurse Corp., c. 1943	28.00	32.00	27.50
☐ **Calendar,** Victorian lady cloth replica, c. 1972	9.00	13.00	10.00
☐ **Calendar,** World War I girl, c. 1917	210.00	230.00	210.00
☐ **Calendar,** 1973 reproduction of 1899 Valentine, c. 1973	12.00	18.00	12.50
☐ **Car bottle holder,** c. 1950	18.00	22.00	17.50
☐ **Cards,** set of 50, nature motif, c. 1930	38.00	58.00	45.00
☐ **Carrier,** first paper carton, c. 1924	28.00	32.00	27.50
☐ **Carrier,** foil-covered carton, c. 1941	18.00	22.00	17.50
☐ **Carrier,** July Fourth six-box wrapper, c. 1935	38.00	52.00	42.00
☐ **Carrier,** Santa Claus carton, c. 1931	22.00	28.00	22.50
☐ **Carrier,** vendor's holder, c. 1940	62.00	78.00	68.00
☐ **Carrier,** wooden take home type, c. 1940	20.00	26.00	20.00
☐ **Carrier,** yellow wooden, c. 1939	22.00	28.00	22.00
☐ **Case,** miniature, display type, 24 bottles	6.00	10.00	7.00
☐ **Case,** miniature, plastic bottles and case, c. 1973	6.00	10.00	7.00
☐ **Case,** miniature, 28 bottles, gold finish	32.00	42.00	35.00
☐ **Case,** shipping type, c. 1906	130.00	150.00	125.00
☐ **Case,** wooden, 24 bottle type, c. 1924	40.00	55.00	42.00
☐ **Change purse,** c. 1915	42.00	58.00	52.00
☐ **Cigar band,** c. 1931	150.00	170.00	152.00
☐ **Cigarette case,** frosted glass, 50th Anniversary c. 1936	100.00	120.00	100.00
☐ **Cigarette lighter,** aluminum, c. 1963	8.00	12.00	8.50
☐ **Cigarette lighter,** Coke bottle shape, c. 1940	9.00	14.00	10.00
☐ **Cigarette lighter,** Coke can, c. 1950	28.00	32.00	27.50
☐ **Cigarette lighter,** music box plays "Dixie"	20.00	28.00	22.00
☐ **Cigarette lighter,** musical, c. 1960	30.00	38.00	32.00
☐ **Clock,** brass mantle type, c. 1954	95.00	125.00	190.00
☐ **Clock,** dome style, c. 1950	185.00	200.00	192.00
☐ **Clock,** electric brass wall model, c. 1915	260.00	310.00	270.00
☐ **Clock,** Hilda Clark celluloid desk clock, c. 1901	2000.00	2100.00	1900.00
☐ **Clock,** "Ideal Brain Tonic", c. 1893	2050.00	2250.00	2100.00
☐ **Clock,** leather boudoir, c. 1919	220.00	260.00	230.00
☐ **Clock,** pendulum wall style, c. 1893	910.00	1100.00	950.00
☐ **Clock,** re-issue of Betty, c. 1974	55.00	75.00	65.00
☐ **Clock,** small boudoir style, c. 1915	250.00	270.00	250.00
☐ **Clock,** spring operated wall style, brass pendulum	310.00	360.00	325.00
☐ **Clock,** walnut wall model, c. 1960	225.00	250.00	225.00
☐ **Cooler,** c. 1930	310.00	385.00	340.00
☐ **Crock,** fountain dispenser, hand painted, c. 1890	1450.00	1700.00	1550.00
☐ **Cuff links,** bottle cap, c. 1954	8.00	12.00	9.00
☐ **Cuff links,** blue pearl	75.00	90.00	78.00
☐ **Cuff links,** gold burnish links and tie clip, c. 1952	14.00	18.00	14.00
☐ **Cuff links,** salesman's sterling silver links and tie tack, c. 1930	55.00	65.00	55.00
☐ **Cuff links,** sterling silver, c. 1923	50.00	60.00	48.00

246 / COCA-COLA COLLECTIBLES

	Current Price Range		Prior Year Average
☐ Cutouts, uncut, c. 1930	85.00	115.00	92.00
☐ Cutouts, uncut, c. 1932	55.00	80.00	62.00
☐ Door pull, bottle shape	48.00	58.00	50.00
☐ Flashlight, bottle shaped plastic	6.00	8.00	6.00
☐ Fountain dispenser	85.00	120.00	85.00
☐ Glass, 5¢ with arrow, c. 1905	130.00	155.00	132.00
☐ Glass, flair type, c. 1900	185.00	195.00	180.00
☐ Glass, flair lip, c. 1923	35.00	45.00	35.00
☐ Glass, fountain type with syrup line, c. 1900	52.00	62.00	55.00
☐ Glass, fountain type, no syrup line	8.00	12.00	8.50
☐ Glass, home promotion type, red and white	4.00	6.00	4.00
☐ Glass, pewter, c. 1930	72.00	82.00	75.00
☐ Glass globe, leaded, c. 1928	2900.00	3200.00	3000.00
☐ Ice pick and opener, c. 1940	8.00	12.00	8.50
☐ Key chain, amber replica bottle with brass chain, c. 1964	6.00	8.00	6.00
☐ Key chain, car key style, c. 1950	28.00	32.00	27.50
☐ Key chain, red with gold bottle, c. 1955	18.00	28.00	20.00
☐ Key chain, 50th Anniversary Celebration, c. 1936	12.00	18.00	12.50
☐ Knife, pocket, "Enjoy Coca-Cola"	80.00	110.00	82.00
☐ Knife, pocket, two blades	12.00	18.00	12.50
☐ Lamp, bottle shape, c. 1920	810.00	1000.00	875.00
☐ Lamp, leaded glass chandelier, Tiffany design, c. 1910	3850.00	4250.00	3900.00
☐ Menu board, tin, c. 1940	42.00	62.00	50.00
☐ Milk glass light fixture, c. 1920	760.00	860.00	800.00
☐ Milk glass light shade, c. 1920	385.00	410.00	382.00
☐ Mirror, cameo design, c. 1905	8100.00	8400.00	8150.00
☐ Mirror, fountain type, c. 1900	1500.00	1900.00	1550.00
☐ Mirror, trademark inscription, c. 1900	2900.00	3200.00	2950.00
☐ Mirror, pocket-size, "Bathing Beauty", c. 1918	285.00	300.00	282.00
☐ Mirror, pocket-size, "Betty", c. 1914	110.00	130.00	110.00
☐ Mirror, pocket-size, "Coca-Cola Girl", c. 1909	130.00	150.00	135.00
☐ Mirror, pocket-size, "Coca-Cola Girl", c. 1911	130.00	150.00	130.00
☐ Mirror, pocket-size, "Drink Coca-Cola 5¢", c. 1914	260.00	285.00	262.00
☐ Mirror, pocket-size, "Elaine", c. 1917	155.00	165.00	155.00
☐ Mirror, pocket-size, "Enjoy Thirst", c. 1930	80.00	95.00	82.00
☐ Mirror, pocket-size, "Garden Girl", c. 1920	260.00	285.00	262.00
☐ Mirror, pocket-size, "Juanita", oval, c. 1905	195.00	210.00	292.00
☐ Mirror, pocket-size, "Lillian Russel", round, c. 1904	72.00	82.00	75.00
☐ Mirror, pocket-size, oval, c. 1903	140.00	160.00	140.00
☐ Mirror, pocket-size, "Relieves Fatigue", c. 1906	160.00	190.00	170.00
☐ Mirror, pocket-size, "St. Louis Exposition", c. 1904	110.00	120.00	105.00
☐ Mirror, pocket-size, "St. Louis Fair", c. 1904	135.00	150.00	138.00
☐ Music box, cooler, c. 1951	55.00	80.00	62.00
☐ Note book, brown leather, embossed, c. 1903	280.00	360.00	372.00
☐ Note pad, celluloid covered, c. 1902	80.00	100.00	85.00
☐ Opener, bone handle knife, c. 1908	140.00	160.00	140.00
☐ Opener, Nashville Anniversary, c. 1952	55.00	70.00	58.00
☐ Opener, skate key style, c. 1935	38.00	48.00	40.00
☐ Opener, "Starr X", c. 1925	3.00	5.00	3.00
☐ Opener, stationary wall model, c. 1900	22.00	28.00	22.00
☐ Paperweight, Coca-Cola gum, c. 1916	80.00	90.00	80.00
☐ Paperweight, "Coke is Coca-Cola", c. 1948	75.00	95.00	80.00

COCA-COLA COLLECTIBLES / 247

	Current Price Range		Prior Year Average
☐ **Paperweight,** hollow glass, tin bottom, c. 1909 ..	260.00	285.00	262.00
☐ **Pen,** ball point with telephone dialer	6.00	8.00	6.00
☐ **Pen,** baseball bat, c. 1940	22.00	33.00	25.00
☐ **Pencil box,** c. 1930	40.00	55.00	42.00
☐ **Pencil holder,** celluloid, c. 1910	130.00	140.00	130.00
☐ **Pencil holder,** miniature ceramic, c. 1960	70.00	80.00	70.00
☐ **Pencil holder,** tin, c. 1925	4.50	7.00	5.00
☐ **Pencil sharpener,** plastic, c. 1960	6.00	12.00	7.50
☐ **Pencil sharpener,** red metal, c. 1933	14.00	18.00	13.50
☐ **Playing cards,** Airplane Spatter, (deck), c. 1942 ..	12.00	18.00	11.00
☐ **Playing cards,** Coca Cola Girls, (deck), c. 1909 ...	52.00	62.00	55.00
☐ **Plate,** glass and Coke bottle, c.1920	70.00	85.00	72.00
☐ **Pocket secretary,** leather bound, c. 1920	32.00	42.00	35.00
☐ **Postcard,** "All Over the World", c. 1913	115.00	125.00	112.00
☐ **Postcard,** "Duster Girl" driving car, c. 1906	95.00	105.00	95.00
☐ **Postcard,** girl with picture hat, c. 1909	28.00	38.00	30.00
☐ **Postcard,** horse and delivery wagon, c. 1900	130.00	150.00	130.00
☐ **Postcard,** men in speedboat, c. 1913	105.00	120.00	105.00
☐ **Postcard,** picture of bottling plant, c. 1905	120.00	140.00	120.00
☐ **Postcard,** school teacher at blackboard, c. 1913 .	88.00	98.00	90.00
☐ **Postcard,** truck carrying cases of Coke, c. 1913 .	135.00	155.00	135.00
☐ **Postcard set,** Dick Tracy series, c. 1942	140.00	160.00	145.00
☐ **Poster,** "Bathing Beauty", c. 1918	410.00	435.00	412.00
☐ **Poster,** "Betty". c. 1914	260.00	280.00	260.00
☐ **Poster,** "Early Display with Young Lovers", c. 1891	460.00	490.00	465.00
☐ **Poster,** "Flapper Girl", c. 1929	160.00	180.00	160.00
☐ **Poster,** "Florine McKinney", c. 1936	40.00	50.00	40.00
☐ **Poster,** "Girl in Hammock", c. 1900	435.00	460.00	438.00
☐ **Poster,** "Hilda Clark Cuban", c. 1901	310.00	335.00	312.00
☐ **Poster,** "Soldier and Girl", c. 1943	28.00	32.00	27.50
☐ **Pretzel bowl,** metal, c. 1935	50.00	62.00	52.00
☐ **Radio,** Coke bottle shaped, c. 1930	310.00	350.00	320.00
☐ **Radio,** Coke can shaped, c. 1971	14.00	20.00	15.00
☐ **Radio,** Coke cooler shaped, c. 1949	145.00	160.00	142.00
☐ **Radio,** crystal, c. 1950	100.00	110.00	100.00
☐ **Radio,** transistor, vending machine shaped, c. 1963	60.00	80.00	70.00
☐ **Sign,** "Betty", tin, c. 1914	550.00	750.00	600.00
☐ **Sign,** bottle tray, tin, c. 1900	310.00	350.00	320.00
☐ **Sign,** "Coca-Cola Girls", cardboard, c. 1922	80.00	90.00	80.00
☐ **Sign,** Coke bottle, tin	100.00	115.00	105.00
☐ **Sign,** "Drink Coca-Cola"	70.00	85.00	72.00
☐ **Sign,** "Elaine", tin, c. 1917	485.00	510.00	582.00
☐ **Sign,** "Hilda Clark", paper, c. 1900	260.00	290.00	262.00
☐ **Sign,** "Hilda Clark", tin, c. 1904	285.00	300.00	285.00
☐ **Sign,** "Lillian Russell", oval, tin, c. 1904	775.00	825.00	775.00
☐ **Sign,** "Please Pay Cashier," c. 1940	62.00	78.00	68.00
☐ **Shoe shine kit**	150.00	170.00	155.00
☐ **Thimble,** c. 1940	4.00	6.00	4.00
☐ **Toy,** bank, bottle cap, c. 1950	14.00	18.00	13.50
☐ **Toy,** bank, vending machine, c. 1948	22.00	28.00	22.00
☐ **Toy,** bean bag, c. 1971	22.00	28.00	22.00
☐ **Toy,** boomerang, c. 1940	40.00	48.00	42.00

248 / COCA-COLA COLLECTIBLES

	Current Price Range		Prior Year Average
☐ **Toy,** Coke truck, c. 1930	130.00	145.00	132.00
☐ **Toy,** Coke truck, c. 1945	62.00	82.00	70.00
☐ **Toy,** comic book, c. 1951	75.00	90.00	78.00
☐ **Toy,** darts, c. 1940	62.00	82.00	70.00
☐ **Toy,** hot rod, c. 1971	20.00	26.00	21.00
☐ **Toy,** kite, American Flyer, c. 1930	190.00	210.00	185.00
☐ **Toy,** train set (Lionel), c. 1974	105.00	115.00	100.00
☐ **Toy,** Volkswagen van, c. 1950	22.00	33.00	25.00
☐ **Toy,** whistle, c. 1945	5.50	8.50	6.50
☐ **Toy,** yo-yo, c. 1955	4.00	7.00	5.00
☐ **Tray,** "Autumn Girl", c. 1922	160.00	210.00	175.00
☐ **Tray,** "Bathing Beauty", c. 1930	105.00	125.00	115.00
☐ **Tray,** "Betty", c. 1912	85.00	110.00	88.00
☐ **Tray,** "Betty", oval, c. 1914	80.00	110.00	88.00
☐ **Tray,** ceramic "Change Receiver", c. 1900	485.00	560.00	512.00
☐ **Tray,** "Coca-Cola Girl", oval, c. 1909	105.00	125.00	105.00
☐ **Tray,** "Curb Service", c. 1927	85.00	180.00	125.00
☐ **Tray,** "Elaine", c. 1917	55.00	85.00	70.00
☐ **Tray,** "Farm Boy with Dog", c. 1931	100.00	120.00	100.00
☐ **Tray,** "Flapper Girl", c. 1923	80.00	110.00	82.00
☐ **Tray,** "Frances Dee", c. 1933	20.00	28.00	21.00
☐ **Tray,** "Girl at Party", c. 1925	80.00	110.00	82.00
☐ **Tray,** "Girl in the Afternoon", c. 1938	38.00	48.00	40.00
☐ **Tray,** "Girl with Fox Fur", c. 1925	70.00	90.00	75.00
☐ **Tray,** "Girl with French Menu", c. 1950	70.00	90.00	75.00
☐ **Tray,** "Girl with Umbrella", c. 1957	65.00	80.00	68.00
☐ **Tray,** "Hilda Clark", c. 1904	260.00	285.00	262.00
☐ **Tray,** "Juanita", round, c. 1905	150.00	175.00	158.00
☐ **Tray,** "Olympic Games", 15" x 11", c. 1976	12.00	18.00	12.50
☐ **Tray** (serving), plastic, c. 1971	50.00	60.00	52.00
☐ **Tray,** replica of "Duster Girl", c. 1972	28.00	42.00	32.00
☐ **Tray,** "Sailor Girl", c. 1940	28.00	42.00	32.00
☐ **Tray,** "Saint Louis Fair", oval, c. 1904	160.00	190.00	170.00
☐ **Tray,** "Santa Claus", 15" x 11", c. 1973	22.00	32.00	25.00
☐ **Tray,** "Soda Fountain Clerk", c. 1927	80.00	110.00	82.00
☐ **Tray,** "Springboard Girl", c. 1939	45.00	60.00	46.00
☐ **Tray,** "Summer Girl", c. 1921	185.00	235.00	200.00
☐ **Tray,** T.V., candle design, c. 1972	20.00	28.00	21.00
☐ **Tray,** T.V., picnic basket	28.00	38.00	30.00
☐ **Tray,** T.V., Thanksgiving motif, c. 1961	20.00	28.00	21.00
☐ **Tray,** "Topless", c. 1908	510.00	710.00	600.00
☐ **Tray,** "Two Girls at Car", c. 1942	32.00	42.00	35.00
☐ **Tray,** "Vienna Art Nude", c. 1905	210.00	285.00	238.00
☐ **Tray,** "Western Bottling Co.", c. 1905	110.00	160.00	125.00
☐ **Vendor's umbrella,** "Pause that Refreshes"	135.00	160.00	138.00
☐ **Wallet,** Coke bottle emblem, c. 1915	75.00	85.00	75.00
☐ **Wallet,** Coca-Cola script, c. 1922	88.00	98.00	90.00
☐ **Wallet,** embossed coin purse, c. 1906	150.00	165.00	148.00
☐ **Watch Fob,** bulldog, c. 1925	55.00	85.00	65.00
☐ **Watch Fob,** "Drink Coca-Cola in Bottles"	60.00	80.00	65.00

COINS

Indian Cent, Obverse / reverse . . . . $3000.00 - $5000.00

    A factor in determining the value of a coin is the condition or state of preservation. In almost all coins, and especially in rare or "key" coins, the better the condition or grade, the more desirable the coin. A "key" coin in strictly uncirculated (brand new) condition may bring a hundred times the price of the same date coin in poor condition.

    Coins, except in rare circumstances, are made not as collectors' items but to serve as money, to be released into public circulation and (presumably) remain in use a long period of time. Their intent is to be handled, and the average coin receives a great deal of handling — not to mention abuse. If the collector knew how roughly his treasured possessions were treated in the past, by persons to whom they were merely pieces of money, his blood would chill. The very specimens that he gingerly grasps with gloved fingers, and dares not breathe heavily upon, have probably been dropped into slot machines, tossed on countertops, played with by children, or even bitten to test the metallic content. Luckily, coins are made of metal and can survive most forms of maltreatment. To totally destroy a coin is not an easy task; if it were, piles of coins would not be unearthed from the rubble of Roman and Greek cities. But while a coin may live on, years of wear and tear take their toll.

    As soon as a coin begins to travel about in circulation, its condition starts deteriorating. The first indication of this is loss of surface lustre. Upon delivery from the Mint the coin is fresh, clean, bright and almost sparkling. It has the appearance of a proof, though not manufactured as one. To retain this quality it must remain virtually unhandled, which few coins getting into circulation do. You may receive coins in change that are bright and shiny and look like "proof state" or "proof like." But if these are compared to prooflike specimens of the same coins offered by dealers (at a premium over face value, of course) the difference will instantly be apparent. Your received-in-change coins have some lustre remaining but it has begun wearing away. This happens much quicker than may be imagined. Each contact with human fingers imparts a bit of grease to the coin, and the rubbing action — be it ever so gentle — eats away surface brilliance.

    Old coins are hard to get in outstanding condition not only because of their age. This of course is one factor and a significant one. Another, often overlooked, is the state of numismatics 100, 150 or 200 years ago. Two hundred years from now, it will probably not be difficult for collectors to obtain 20th

250 / COINS

century coins in the best grades of preservation. Millions of people are now putting them away and taking good care of them, as collectors' items. This was certainly not the situation in the past. Probably nobody in 1795 took examples of the then-current coins and placed them into collections. Every single one manufactured got into circulation and bounced around for a while, generally a very long while. Specimens of that era in uncirculated condition have pure chance to thank, not the loving attention of owners.

Historically, coins of past ages remained in circulation longer than those of the present. This is not because of the melting of coins now practiced, but the fact that any old coin in circulation today finds its way to the hands of a collector sooner or later. With 28 million numismatists in the population, a coin cannot travel too far without reaching someone who notices the date and removes it from circulation. On the rare occasions when a Lincoln cent from the teens, or a Buffalo nickel turns up in pocket change, it has *not been* idly circulating more than half a century. These oldies are cookie-jar coins, that somebody's grandmother was salting away ages ago. They finally got spent, after being out of circulation for decades — spent, obviously, by an individual with little awareness of coin values.

NOTE: *Silver is currently trading in the $8 to $12 per ounce range. The following prices will reflect this market value even through current levels fluctuate on a daily basis.*

Code abbreviations:
ABP — Average Buy Price   EX FINE — Extra Fine
V. FINE — Very Fine   UNC — Uncirculated

For more concise information on coin collecting, you may refer to *The Official Blackbook Price Guide of United States Coins* published annually by the House of Collectibles.

ANCIENT AND FOREIGN COINS

	Current Price Range		Prior Year Average
☐ 5th c. B.C. Persian gold coin	2750.00	3700.00	3000.00
☐ 220 B.C. Roman bronze coin, with double Janus head	900.00	1200.00	850.00
☐ 200 B.C. Greek drachma	175.00	225.00	175.00
☐ 170-117 B.C. Egyptian gold coin, with Arsinoe the First	1400.00	1900.00	1250.00
☐ 98 B.C. Tetradrachma, silver	500.00	700.00	500.00
☐ Roman denarius, silver, portrait of Roma	130.00	170.00	125.00
☐ 600 to 750 A.D. English sceat	300.00	375.00	300.00
☐ 12th c. India bronze coin	14.00	18.00	14.50
☐ 1658 English crown	1400.00	1700.00	1350.00
☐ 17th c. Chinese square-hole coin	70.00	90.00	75.00
☐ 1797 English Penny	45.00	60.00	42.00
☐ 1926 Greek drachma	6.00	9.00	5.00
☐ 1934 Australian 2-shilling, 1-florin piece	120.00	145.00	105.00
☐ 1973 Bangladesh square 5-poisha piece	.35	.45	.30
☐ 1976 Malaysian ringget	2.50	3.50	2.50
☐ 1965 Italian 500-lira	7.00	9.00	7.00

UNITED STATES
SMALL CENTS — INDIAN HEAD, 1859-1909

Probably the most famous of all United States coins (its only challenger for that honor being the Morgan Dollar), the Indian Head cent remained in production without change in design for half a century. After the disaster of the Flying Eagle Cent, rejected by the public because of its almost white color, the government knew that it must manufacture a cent with the appearance of being made of good metal. The question remained: would a small copper piece be accepted, when large cents, containing a much greater quantity of metal, were still widely circulating? The new cent had the same composition as its predecessor, 88% copper and 12% nickel. The first batch of Indian Heads, released in 1859, amounted to 36,400,000 pieces, more than had ever been coined of a single denomination in one year: $364,000 worth of pennies. Beginning in 1864 the copper content was increased to 95%, the nickel removed entirely and replaced with a 5% alloy of tin and zinc. This was so successfully absorbed into the copper that the resulting coin was hardly different in color than if copper alone were used. Finally, the problem was solved, and the Indian Head Cent was on the road to a long successful existence. Its designer was James Longacre. The weight was 4.67 grams and the diameter 19 mm. (These specifications were the same as the Flying Eagle Cent.) The portrait is that of an Indian maiden. As first designed, the reverse carried no shield but this was added in 1860, the second year of issue. The Indian Head became the first United States coin struck in a quantity of more than 100 million in a year, when 108 million specimens were turned out in 1907. This exceeded the country's population. It is interesting to note that the 1908 and 1909 editions, representing the last two years of this design, are the only dates to be found with mintmarks. The origin of the portrait has been for many years a matter of discussion. It was at one time thought that Longacre had taken it from life, using an Indian girl as his model. This was dismissed when the suggestion was advanced that the profile resembled Longacre's daughter. It is now generally believed that no live model sat for the likeness but that it was based upon classical statuary, of which Longacre was known to be a collector. The Indian Head Cent portrait is neither as realistic or impressive as that featured on the Buffalo Nickel, but this is nevertheless an important coin whose design represented a bold innovation.

Date	Mintages	ABP	G-4 Good	F-12 Fine	EF-40 Ex. Fine	MS-60 Unc.	PRF-65 Proof
☐ 1859 Copper-Nickel	36,400,000	3.50	5.00	9.00	60.00	325.00	5000.00
☐ 1860 Copper-Nickel	20,566,000	2.00	4.00	7.00	23.00	130.00	2500.00
☐ 1861 Copper-Nickel	10,100,000	4.50	8.00	17.00	42.00	215.00	2500.00
☐ 1862 Copper-Nickel	28,075,000	1.50	3.00	6.00	20.00	110.00	2500.00
☐ 1863 Copper-Nickel	49,840,000	1.50	2.75	5.00	17.50	110.00	2500.00
☐ 1864 Copper-Nickel	13,740,000	4.00	7.50	13.00	33.00	145.00	2500.00
☐ 1864 Bronze	39,233,714	1.50	3.00	7.00	26.00	100.00	2250.00

252 / COINS

	Date	Mintages	ABP	G-4 Good	F-12 Fine	EF-40 Ex.Fine	MS-60 Unc.	PRF-65 Proof
☐	1864 L on Ribbon...............		12.00	28.00	60.00	140.00	350.00	15000.00
☐	1865 35,429,286		1.25	2.75	7.00	25.00	75.00	1250.00
☐	1866 9,826,500		10.00	20.00	35.00	95.00	275.00	1250.00
☐	1867 9,821,000		10.00	20.00	35.00	95.00	275.00	1250.00
☐	1868 10,266,500		10.00	20.00	35.00	95.00	275.00	1250.00
☐	1869 6,420,000		15.00	32.00	70.00	170.00	400.00	1450.00
☐	1869 over 8 ..		45.00	85.00	220.00	500.00	1300.00	—
☐	1870 5,275,000		10.00	24.00	52.00	115.00	285.00	1500.00
☐	1871 3,929,500		17.00	32.00	65.00	125.00	320.00	1500.00
☐	1872 4,042,000		23.00	40.00	80.00	170.00	395.00	1500.00
☐	1873 11,676,500		3.50	7.50	17.00	45.00	150.00	1400.00
☐	1873 Doubled Liberty ..				EXTREMELY RARE			
☐	1874 14,187,500		3.50	7.00	16.00	57.00	150.00	1400.00
☐	1875 13,528,000		3.50	7.00	16.00	62.00	150.00	1400.00
☐	1876 7,944,000		4.50	11.00	23.00	50.00	175.00	1500.00
☐	1877..........852,500		150.00	285.00	475.00	900.00	1750.00	4750.00
☐	1878 5,799,850		4.50	11.00	26.00	55.00	200.00	1800.00
☐	1879 16,231,200		1.50	2.75	7.00	20.00	75.00	1200.00
☐	1880 38,964,955		.50	1.25	6.00	15.00	70.00	1200.00
☐	1881 39,211,575		.50	1.25	3.75	15.00	70.00	1200.00
☐	1882 38,581,100		.50	1.25	3.75	15.00	70.00	1200.00
☐	1883 45,598,109		.50	1.25	3.75	17.00	70.00	1200.00
☐	1884 23,261,742		.50	1.25	6.50	30.00	75.00	1200.00
☐	1885 11,765,384		1.25	3.25	9.00	32.00	95.00	1200.00
☐	1886 17,654,290		1.00	2.25	6.50	25.00	85.00	1200.00
☐	1887 45,226,483		.50	1.00	2.50	10.00	70.00	1200.00
☐	1888 37,494,414		.50	1.00	2.50	10.00	70.00	1200.00
☐	1889 48,868,361		.50	1.00	2.50	10.00	40.00	1200.00
☐	1890 57,182,854		.50	.90	2.40	10.00	35.00	1200.00
☐	1891 47,072,350		.50	.90	2.25	10.00	35.00	1200.00
☐	1892 37,649,832		.50	.90	2.25	10.00	35.00	1200.00
☐	1893 46,642,195		.50	.90	2.25	10.00	35.00	1200.00
☐	1894 16,752,132		1.50	1.90	7.25	20.00	75.00	1200.00
☐	1895 38,343,636		.50	.85	1.75	7.50	35.00	1200.00
☐	1896 39,057,293		.50	.85	1.75	7.50	35.00	1200.00
☐	1897 50,466,330		.50	.85	1.50	7.50	35.00	1200.00
☐	1898 49,923,079		.50	.85	1.50	7.50	35.00	1200.00
☐	1899 53,600,031		.50	.85	1.50	7.50	35.00	1200.00
☐	1900 66,833,764		.50	.85	1.50	7.00	32.00	1200.00
☐	1901 79,611,143		.50	.80	1.50	7.00	32.00	1200.00
☐	1902 87,376,722		.50	.75	1.50	7.00	32.00	1200.00
☐	1903 85,094,493		.50	.75	1.50	7.00	32.00	1200.00
☐	1904 61,328,015		.50	.75	1.50	7.00	32.00	1200.00
☐	1905 80,719,163		.50	.75	1.50	6.75	32.00	1200.00
☐	1906 96,022,255		.50	.75	1.50	6.75	32.00	1200.00
☐	1907 108,138,618		.50	.75	1.50	6.75	32.00	1200.00
☐	1908 32,327,987		.50	.75	1.50	6.75	32.00	1200.00
☐	1908S 1,115,000		12.00	23.00	28.00	48.00	175.00	
☐	1909 14,370,645		.75	1.50	3.00	8.00	60.00	1200.00
☐	1909S 309,000		60.00	120.00	150.00	240.00	400.00	

DIMES — LIBERTY HEAD OR BARBER, 1892-1916

After many years of using a seated figure of Liberty on the dime, it was decided in 1892 to return to a facial portrait. The designer was Charles E. Barber, resulting in the coin coming to be popularly known among collectors as the "Barber Dime." Liberty wears a wreath and is encircled by the inscription "UNITED STATES OF AMERICA," with the date appearing below the portrait. The reverse is unchanged from that used earlier, the words "ONE DIME" enclosed in a wreath. This coin's weight was set at 2½ grams. Its composition was nine parts silver to one part copper and its diameter 17.9 mm. It was struck at Philadelphia, Denver, San Francisco and New Orleans. The very rare 1894 San Francisco minting, of which only 24 were produced, is the stellar item of this series. In 1916 the Liberty Head design was replaced by the so-called Mercury Head.

Date	Mintages	ABP	G-4 Good	F-12 Fine	EF-40 Ex.Fine	MS-60 Unc.	PRF-65 Proof
1892	12,121,245	1.50	3.00	7.00	32.00	150.00	1850.00
1892O	3,841,700	2.00	4.00	12.00	37.00	200.00	
1892S	990,710	15.00	30.00	65.00	125.00	275.00	
1893	3,340,792	1.75	3.50	15.00	45.00	200.00	1850.00
1893, 3 over 2			EXTREMELY RARE				
1893O	1,760,000	5.00	10.00	30.00	85.00	250.00	
1893S	2,491,401	2.25	4.50	20.00	50.00	200.00	
1894	1,330,972	2.75	5.50	22.00	75.00	210.00	1850.00
1894O	720,000	12.00	25.00	80.00	200.00	1000.00	
1894S		EXTREMELY RARE PRIVATE SALE 1974 97,000.00					
1895	690,880	25.00	47.00	100.00	275.00	550.00	1850.00
1895O	440,000	100.00	140.00	235.00	500.00	900.00	
1895S	1,120,000	6.00	12.00	40.00	95.00	380.00	
1896	2,000,672	2.50	5.00	25.00	65.00	185.00	1850.00
1896O	610,000	18.00	39.00	100.00	225.00	625.00	
1896S	575,056	16.00	35.00	75.00	215.00	400.00	
1897	10,869,264	.60	2.00	9.00	40.00	150.00	1850.00
1897O	666,000	15.00	32.00	80.00	200.00	700.00	
1897S	1,342,844	2.50	5.00	25.00	90.00	250.00	
1898	16,320,735	.60	1.50	6.00	35.00	150.00	1850.00
1898O	2,130,000	2.00	3.50	22.00	80.00	325.00	
1898S	1,702,507	1.75	3.00	12.00	47.00	200.00	
1899	19,580,846	.60	1.50	6.00	35.00	150.00	1850.00
1899O	2,650,000	2.00	3.50	20.00	65.00	300.00	
1899S	1,867,493	1.50	3.00	15.00	42.00	220.00	
1900	17,600,912	.60	1.50	6.00	35.00	163.00	1850.00
1900O	2,010,000	2.50	5.00	23.00	80.00	325.00	
1900S	5,168,270	.60	2.00	7.00	32.00	165.00	
1901	18,860,478	.60	1.50	5.00	32.00	150.00	1850.00
1901O	5,620,000	.60	2.00	6.00	50.00	325.00	
1901S	593,022	18.00	38.00	95.00	275.00	750.00	
1902	21,380,777	.60	1.50	5.00	32.00	175.00	1850.00
1902O	4,500,000	.60	2.00	6.00	42.00	250.00	
1902S	2,070,000	1.75	3.50	17.00	65.00	290.00	
1903	19,500,755	.60	1.50	5.50	32.00	150.00	1850.00
1903O	8,180,000	.60	2.00	6.00	40.00	250.00	
1903S	613,300	15.00	30.00	67.00	200.00	600.00	
1904	14,601,027	.60	1.50	6.00	32.00	125.00	1850.00
1904S	800,000	11.00	23.00	65.00	190.00	600.00	

254 / COINS

Date	Mintages	ABP	G-4 Good	F-12 Fine	EF-40 Ex.Fine	MS-60 Unc.	PRF-65 Proof
☐ 1905	14,552,350	.50	1.75	6.50	32.00	150.00	1850.00
☐ 1905O	3,400,000	.50	2.75	15.00	65.00	200.00	
☐ 1905S	6,855,199	.50	1.75	7.00	40.00	220.00	
☐ 1906	19,958,406	.50	1.50	3.50	30.00	150.00	1850.00
☐ 1906D	4,060,000	.50	2.00	7.00	40.00	200.00	
☐ 1906O	2,610,000	.50	2.50	15.00	52.00	220.00	
☐ 1906S	3,136,640	.50	2.50	10.00	48.00	200.00	
☐ 1907	22,220,575	.50	1.50	3.50	30.00	150.00	1850.00
☐ 1907D	4,080,000	.50	1.75	7.00	42.00	190.00	
☐ 1907O	5,058,000	.50	1.75	7.00	40.00	150.00	
☐ 1907S	3,178,470	.50	1.75	7.00	45.00	240.00	
☐ 1908	10,600,545	.50	1.65	5.00	32.00	150.00	1850.00
☐ 1908D	7,490,000	.50	1.65	4.50	31.00	165.00	
☐ 1908O	1,789,000	1.25	2.50	15.00	52.00	240.00	
☐ 1908S	3,220,000	.50	2.00	7.00	42.00	200.00	
☐ 1909	10,240,650	.50	1.50	5.00	35.00	150.00	1850.00
☐ 1909D	954,000	.50	4.00	18.00	70.00	240.00	
☐ 1909O	2,287,000	.50	2.00	7.00	48.00	185.00	
☐ 1909S	2,000,000	2.00	4.00	22.00	85.00	250.00	
☐ 1910	11,520,551	.50	1.75	4.50	32.00	150.00	1850.00
☐ 1910D	3,490,000	.50	1.90	6.00	35.00	240.00	
☐ 1910S	1,240,000	1.50	3.00	12.00	50.00	200.00	
☐ 1911	18,870,543	.50	1.65	3.00	30.00	150.00	1850.00
☐ 1911D	11,209,000	.50	1.65	3.00	32.00	150.00	
☐ 1911S	3,530,000	.50	1.90	6.00	45.00	175.00	
☐ 1912	19,350,700	.50	1.65	3.00	27.00	150.00	1850.00
☐ 1912D	11,760,000	.50	1.65	3.00	27.00	150.00	
☐ 1912S	3,420,000	.50	1.85	5.00	36.00	175.00	
☐ 1913	19,760,000	.50	1.65	3.00	28.00	150.00	1850.00
☐ 1913S	510,000	3.50	7.00	30.00	175.00	325.00	
☐ 1914	17,360,655	.50	1.65	2.00	28.00	150.00	1850.00
☐ 1914D	11,908,000	.50	1.65	3.00	28.00	150.00	
☐ 1914S	2,100,000	.50	1.90	5.00	41.00	175.00	
☐ 1915	5,620,450	.50	1.90	5.50	36.00	300.00	1850.00
☐ 1915S	960,000	.50	2.25	10.00	50.00	190.00	
☐ 1916	18,490,000	.50	1.65	3.00	28.00	150.00	
☐ 1916S	5,820,000	.50	1.80	5.00	36.00	170.00	

QUARTERS — BARBER OR LIBERTY HEAD, 1892-1916

The Barber or Liberty Head Quarter with its classical portrait bust was introduced in 1892 after a design by Charles E. Barber. Liberty faces right and wears a cap and laurel wreath. On the reverse is a shield eagle holding arrows and branch, with (at long last) the words "QUARTER DOLLAR" spelled out without abbreviation. This was without doubt the handsomest design in the quarter dollar series and has become extremely popular with collectors. It was struck at Philadelphia, Denver, New Orleans and San Francisco. The Barber quarter has a composition of 90% silver and 10% copper with a weight of 6¼ grams and a diameter of 24.3 mm.

Date	Mintages	ABP	G-4 Good	F-12 Fine	EF-40 Ex.Fine	MS-60 Unc.	PRF-65 Proof
☐ 1892	8,237,245	1.50	3.75	12.00	65.00	285.00	2400.00
☐ 1892O	2,640,000	1.50	5.00	18.00	75.00	320.00	
☐ 1892S	964,079	5.00	12.00	40.00	140.00	375.00	

Date	Mintages	ABP	G-4 Good	F-12 Fine	EF-40 Ex.Fine	MS-60 Unc.	PRF-65 Proof
☐ 1893	5,444,815	1.25	4.00	15.00	70.00	275.00	2400.00
☐ 1893O	3,396,000	1.25	4.25	18.00	75.00	325.00	
☐ 1893S	1,454,535	1.25	6.50	26.00	100.00	325.00	
☐ 1894	3,432,972	1.25	4.00	13.00	65.00	275.00	2400.00
☐ 1894O	2,852,000	1.25	4.75	22.00	90.00	325.00	
☐ 1894S	2,648,821	1.25	4.25	16.00	75.00	325.00	
☐ 1895	4,440,880	1.25	3.75	12.00	65.00	275.00	2400.00
☐ 1895O	2,816,000	1.25	4.25	18.00	82.00	400.00	
☐ 1895S	1,764,681	1.25	5.50	26.00	100.00	375.00	
☐ 1896	3,874,762	1.25	3.75	14.00	65.00	300.00	2400.00
☐ 1896O	1,484,000	1.25	5.50	24.00	120.00	900.00	
☐ 1896S	188,039	100.00	225.00	450.00	1800.00	3875.00	
☐ 1897	8,140,731	1.25	3.75	10.00	65.00	300.00	2400.00
☐ 1897O	1,414,800	5.00	7.00	22.00	115.00	900.00	
☐ 1897S	542,229	5.50	10.00	37.00	140.00	425.00	
☐ 1898	11,100,735	1.25	3.50	9.00	65.00	300.00	2400.00
☐ 1898O	1,868,000	1.25	4.50	22.00	85.00	500.00	
☐ 1898S	1,020,592	1.25	4.00	16.00	70.00	380.00	
☐ 1899	12,624,846	1.25	3.50	10.00	65.00	300.00	2400.00
☐ 1899O	2,644,000	1.25	4.50	20.00	87.00	475.00	
☐ 1899S	708,000	3.50	7.00	30.00	100.00	380.00	
☐ 1900	10,016,912	1.25	3.75	10.00	65.00	300.00	2400.00
☐ 1900O	3,416,000	1.25	6.00	27.00	115.00	350.00	
☐ 1900S	1,858,585	1.25	3.75	15.00	65.00	425.00	
☐ 1901	8,892,813	1.25	3.75	12.00	65.00	300.00	2400.00
☐ 1901O	1,612,000	4.50	11.00	47.00	185.00	750.00	
☐ 1901S	72,664	450.00	950.00	2000.00	4500.00	15500.00	
☐ 1902	12,197,744	1.25	3.75	10.00	63.00	300.00	2400.00
☐ 1902O	4,748,000	1.25	4.25	15.00	77.00	400.00	
☐ 1902S	1,524,612	1.25	6.00	23.00	100.00	390.00	
☐ 1903	9,670,064	1.25	3.75	10.00	65.00	300.00	2400.00
☐ 1903O	3,500,000	1.25	5.00	17.00	75.00	350.00	
☐ 1903S	1,036,000	1.25	8.00	30.00	115.00	425.00	
☐ 1904	9,588,813	1.25	3.75	11.00	65.00	300.00	2400.00
☐ 1904O	2,456,000	2.00	4.25	23.00	115.00	800.00	
☐ 1905	4,968,250	1.25	4.00	13.00	65.00	325.00	2400.00
☐ 1905O	1,230,000	1.25	6.00	25.00	115.00	350.00	
☐ 1905S	1,884,000	1.25	4.75	17.00	77.00	350.00	
☐ 1906	3,656,435	1.25	4.75	14.00	77.00	300.00	2400.00
☐ 1906D	3,280,000	1.25	4.75	18.00	80.00	315.00	
☐ 1906O	2,056,000	1.25	5.50	21.00	90.00	315.00	
☐ 1907	7,192,575	1.25	3.75	10.00	63.00	300.00	2400.00
☐ 1907D	2,484,000	1.25	4.25	18.00	80.00	300.00	
☐ 1907O	4,560,000	1.25	4.50	12.00	70.00	300.00	
☐ 1907S	1,360,000	1.25	5.00	17.00	80.00	350.00	
☐ 1908	4,232,545	1.25	3.75	11.00	67.00	300.00	2400.00
☐ 1908D	5,788,000	1.25	3.50	9.00	62.00	300.00	
☐ 1908O	6,244,000	1.25	3.50	9.00	62.00	300.00	
☐ 1908S	784,000	2.50	5.00	23.00	100.00	450.00	
☐ 1909	9,268,650	2.00	4.00	9.00	62.00	300.00	2400.00
☐ 1909D	5,114,000	1.25	4.00	9.00	64.00	300.00	
☐ 1909O	712,000	3.00	7.00	40.00	175.00	775.00	
☐ 1909S	1,348,000	1.25	3.75	12.00	70.00	365.00	
☐ 1910	2,244,551	1.25	4.25	12.00	75.00	300.00	2400.00
☐ 1910D	1,500,000	1.25	4.75	20.00	85.00	325.00	
☐ 1911	3,270,543	1.25	3.75	12.00	70.00	300.00	2400.00

Date	Mintages	ABP	G-4 Good	F-12 Fine	EF-40 Ex.Fine	MS-60 Unc.	PRF-65 Proof
☐ 1911D	933,600	1.25	5.75	26.00	110.00	300.00	
☐ 1911S	988,000	1.25	5.00	22.00	95.00	340.00	
☐ 1912	4,400,700	1.25	4.00	10.00	70.00	300.00	2400.00
☐ 1912S	708,000	1.25	4.25	21.00	90.00	375.00	
☐ 1913	484,613	4.00	8.00	45.00	400.00	15000.00	2400.00
☐ 1913D	1,450,800	1.25	4.75	18.00	90.00	300.00	
☐ 1913S	40,000	210.00	330.00	800.00	1800.00	4250.00	
☐ 1914	6,244,610	1.25	4.00	9.00	60.00	300.00	2400.00
☐ 1914D	3,046,000	1.25	4.00	9.50	60.00	650.00	
☐ 1914S	264,000	5.00	9.00	38.00	225.00	1600.00	
☐ 1915	3,480,450	1.25	4.00	10.00	60.00	300.00	2400.00
☐ 1915D	3,694,000	1.25	4.00	10.00	60.00	300.00	
☐ 1915S	704,000	1.25	5.00	19.00	95.00	325.00	
☐ 1916	1,788,000	1.25	4.50	11.00	65.00	300.00	
☐ 1916D	6,540,000	1.25	4.00	10.00	62.00	300.00	

HALF DOLLARS — LIBERTY HEAD or BARBER, 1892-1915

These coins, which resemble the Morgan Dollar in portraiture, were prepared from designs by Charles E. Barber and really have no connection with the Morgan Dollar aside from the possibility that Barber may have been inspired by it. The face of Liberty, which faces right, is strong and classical, suggesting the portraiture of Greek coins of ancient time. The weight is somewhat greater than the final version of the Seated Liberty half, 12½ grams, but its composition is the same, 90% silver and an alloy of 10% copper. The reverse has an attractive eagle with shield and wings spread wide; it holds the traditional arrows and branch. The mintmark appears directly beneath the eagle's tail feathers. Without question this was artistically the finest coin of the half dollar series. It was struck at Philadelphia, New Orleans, Denver and San Francisco. Not a single rarity is to be found among the Barber halves, with the result that if offers splendid opportunities for completion — even if one wishes to include all the mintmarks.

Date	Mintages	ABP	G-4 Good	F-12 Fine	EF-40 Ex.Fine	MS-60 Unc.	PRF-65 Proof
☐ 1892	935,245	5.00	11.00	40.00	170.00	600.00	3600.00
☐ 1892O	390,000	32.00	75.00	180.00	420.00	1100.00	
☐ 1892S	1,029,028	27.00	70.00	170.00	400.00	1150.00	
☐ 1893	1,826,792	3.00	10.00	40.00	180.00	600.00	3600.00
☐ 1893O	1,389,000	6.00	12.00	50.00	250.00	850.00	
☐ 1893S	740,000	26.00	53.00	155.00	350.00	1075.00	
☐ 1894	1,148,972	3.00	10.00	45.00	200.00	1075.00	3600.00
☐ 1894O	2,138,000	3.00	9.50	40.00	225.00	700.00	
☐ 1894S	4,048,690	2.75	8.50	24.00	165.00	625.00	
☐ 1895	1,835,218	2.50	9.00	30.00	190.00	675.00	3600.00
☐ 1895O	1,766,000	3.00	11.00	45.00	200.00	725.00	
☐ 1895S	1,108,086	8.00	20.00	55.00	250.00	650.00	
☐ 1896	950,762	3.00	10.00	45.00	210.00	625.00	3600.00
☐ 1896O	924,000	5.00	10.00	50.00	315.00	1200.00	
☐ 1896S	1,140,948	20.00	45.00	110.00	365.00	1300.00	
☐ 1897	2,480,731	2.75	9.00	25.00	175.00	600.00	3600.00
☐ 1897O	632,000	25.00	45.00	110.00	390.00	1700.00	
☐ 1897S	933,900	30.00	75.00	165.00	400.00	1300.00	

Date	Mintages	ABP	G-4 Good	F-12 Fine	FF-40 Ex.Fine	MS-60 Unc.	PRF-65 Proof
1898	2,956,735	2.50	8.00	24.00	135.00	600.00	3600.00
1898O	874,000	5.00	12.00	80.00	350.00	775.00	
1898S	2,358,550	3.00	10.00	28.00	165.00	700.00	
1899	5,538,846	2.50	8.00	20.00	155.00	550.00	3600.00
1899O	1,724,000	2.50	8.00	30.00	185.00	725.00	
1899S	1,686,411	3.00	10.00	23.00	150.00	650.00	
1900	4,762,912	2.50	8.00	25.00	145.00	600.00	3600.00
1900O	2,744,000	2.50	8.00	26.00	160.00	900.00	
1900S	2,560,322	2.50	8.00	27.00	150.00	750.00	
1901	4,268,813	2.50	8.00	31.00	150.00	600.00	3600.00
1901O	1,124,000	2.50	8.00	35.00	275.00	1300.00	
1901S	847,044	3.00	12.00	60.00	400.00	1450.00	
1902	4,922,777	2.50	8.00	24.00	150.00	600.00	3600.00
1902O	2,526,000	2.50	8.00	30.00	155.00	800.00	
1902S	1,460,670	2.50	8.00	25.00	190.00	725.00	
1903	2,278,755	2.50	8.00	28.00	175.00	600.00	3600.00
1903O	2,100,000	2.50	8.00	30.00	185.00	725.00	
1903S	1,920,772	2.50	8.00	35.00	175.00	725.00	
1904	2,992,670	2.50	8.00	25.00	155.00	600.00	3600.00
1904O	1,117,600	3.00	8.50	43.00	275.00	1400.00	
1904S	553,038	3.50	9.50	62.00	325.00	1200.00	
1905	662,727	3.00	9.00	50.00	280.00	775.00	3600.00
1905O	505,000	4.00	11.00	60.00	300.00	900.00	
1905S	2,494,000	2.50	8.00	30.00	150.00	775.00	
1906	1,638,675	2.50	8.00	22.00	150.00	600.00	3600.00
1906D	4,028,000	2.50	8.00	23.00	145.00	625.00	
1906O	2,446,000	2.50	8.00	24.00	148.00	650.00	
1906S	1,740,154	2.50	8.00	32.00	175.00	750.00	
1907	2,598,575	2.50	8.00	22.00	150.00	600.00	3600.00
1907D	3,856,000	2.50	8.00	23.00	150.00	1000.00	
1907O	3,946,600	2.50	8.00	29.00	150.00	675.00	
1907S	1,250,000	2.50	8.00	30.00	170.00	800.00	
1908	1,354,545	3.00	9.00	28.00	200.00	600.00	3600.00
1908D	3,280,000	3.00	8.50	22.00	140.00	625.00	
1908O	5,360,000	3.00	8.50	22.00	140.00	625.00	
1908S	1,644,828	3.00	10.00	28.00	160.00	700.00	
1909	2,368,650	3.00	9.00	22.00	140.00	600.00	3600.00
1909O	925,400	3.50	11.00	25.00	225.00	900.00	
1909S	1,764,000	3.00	9.75	22.00	165.00	725.00	
1910	418,551	3.00	11.00	45.00	300.00	800.00	3600.00
1910S	1,948,000	3.00	9.00	23.00	150.00	725.00	
1911	1,406,543	3.00	9.00	24.00	150.00	600.00	3600.00
1911D	696,080	3.00	8.75	28.00	200.00	675.00	
1911S	1,272,000	3.00	8.75	23.00	165.00	700.00	
1912	1,550,700	3.00	8.75	22.00	145.00	600.00	3600.00
1912D	2,300,800	3.00	8.75	22.00	145.00	575.00	
1912S	1,370,000	3.00	8.50	22.00	150.00	650.00	
1913	188,627	10.00	25.00	75.00	350.00	1000.00	3600.00
1913D	534,000	3.00	12.00	30.00	200.00	650.00	
1913S	604,000	3.00	11.00	29.00	200.00	750.00	
1914	124,610	16.00	35.00	90.00	425.00	975.00	5000.00
1914S	992,000	3.00	9.00	25.00	175.00	650.00	
1915	138,450	13.00	30.00	80.00	385.00	1050.00	5000.00
1915D	1,170,400	3.00	9.00	22.00	140.00	600.00	
1915S	1,604,000	3.00	9.00	22.00	140.00	675.00	

COMBS

Flower Swirl Motif, tortoise hair comb, gold, c. 1890-1900
$365.00-$375.00

Since the 18th century, beautiful and decorative combs have adorned milady's hair. These ornate combs were originally designed to serve as jewelry pieces and were passed down in the family as prized possessions.

Combs are categorized by how they are used, back or side, and by the material of which they are made, such as silver, ivory, bone, tortoise shell, steel, pewter and celluloid. The collector must beware of celluloid that can be made to look like tortoise shell or ivory. Markings in genuine materials tend to be more irregular in comparison to the even and more regular patterns in celluloid.

Combs in good condition are rare since most are scratched, cracked, and have missing teeth. It is important to note, however, that a damaged comb may be worth more than an excellent one simply because of its design and workmanship.

	Current Price Range		Prior Year Average
☐ **Bakelite,** back comb with coral, 5″ L., c. 1880 . . .	82.00	92.00	85.00
☐ **Celluloid,** back comb, Art Deco, c. 1920	52.00	62.00	55.00
☐ **Celluloid,** back comb, Art Nouveau, c. 1900	42.00	52.00	45.00
☐ **Celluloid,** back comb, feather design, c. 1930 . . .	95.00	105.00	95.00
☐ **Celluloid,** back comb, rhinestones, c. 1940	65.00	80.00	68.00
☐ **Celluloid,** hairpins, rhinestones, c. 1930	18.00	22.00	17.50
☐ **Celluloid,** side comb, Victorian, c. 1880	22.00	28.00	22.50
☐ **Ivory,** carved	38.00	55.00	42.00
☐ **Ivory,** inlaid rhinestones	18.00	35.00	22.00
☐ **Russian,** amber	50.00	65.00	52.00
☐ **Silver,** back comb, rhinestones, 5″ L., c. 1890 . . .	135.00	160.00	138.00

	Current Price Range		Prior Year Average
☐ **Sterling silver,** elaborate carving	35.00	50.00	42.00
☐ **Tortoise,** back comb, coral, 6″ L., c. 1880	160.00	185.00	162.00
☐ **Tortoise,** back comb, 7½″ L., c. 1840	110.00	135.00	112.00
☐ **Tortoise,** back comb, English, rhinestones, c. 1890	130.00	155.00	138.00
☐ **Tortoise,** hairpin, Art Nouveau, c. 1910	32.00	42.00	35.00

COMIC ART

Original Comic Art, by Lou Fine .... $175.00-$200.00

    Hobbyists began collecting original comic art as an adjunct or sideline to comic book collecting. Since then it's increased enormously in popularity and become a recognized hobby in its own right.
    Original comic art encompasses drawings and paintings used in comic books, for the covers of comic books and for newspaper comic strips. It also covers the original artwork for magazine cartoons, but because these works are normally NOT created by comic book artists (but by full time cartoonists), they comprise a specialized area of collecting.
    Chiefly, collectors are interested in works by the leading comic artists, showing their foremost characters: and original drawing of Pogo by Walt Kelly, a Joe Palooka by Ham Fisher, a Flash Gordon by Alex Raymond and so on. In most cases, such works were created in huge numbers. If a daily strip ran in the newspaper for 10 years, more than 3,000 original artworks had to be

produced; a Sunday comics page running for 10 years yielded over 500 works. Nevertheless, some are still scarce on the market. This might be accounted for by the loss of large quantities by the original publishers, because the original art was considered nothing more than a model to print from. But even artwork that's relatively common on the market can fetch big prices. The drawings of Carl Barks of Disney Studios are far from scarce, but collector competition is fierce. Barks created Uncle Scrooge and for many years drew Donald Duck for the comic books.

There is usually a sharp difference in value between "penciled roughs" and "finished drawings." The penciled rough is the artist's original conception jof how the finished work will look. It is done in soft, easily-erased pencil. When such a work is framed and hung, it looks like blank paper unless one is standing quite close to it. This keeps the price for a penciled rough low: the lack of visual impact. A finished drawing is a penciled rough to which sharp outlines have been added in drawing ink, and it looks exactly the way the strip (or other work) will look in print. In many cases, the inking is done by an assistant, but finished drawings still normally outsell roughs by double or more.

Sunday pages were normally printed in black and white until about 1930. Therefore, you will seldom find original art of this type in color if it dates prior to that time. Very early Sunday pages, from before 1910, are quite difficult to find in the original artists' drawings. Some of these have gone into museums, which shows the level of apperciation for comic art.

Comic art collectors are also interested in "quikc sketches" done by top comic artists. These are turned out by the artists as souvenirs at cartoonists' conventions and benefits. In terms of cash value, they're not worth quite as much as published artwork.

	Current Price Range		Prior Year Average
☐ **Alley Oop,** Vincent T. Hamlin (b. 1900), pen and ink, signed, Newspaper Enterprise Association, 1/3/1939, 4½" x 20¼"	80.00	95.00	82.00
☐ **The Angler And The Signature,** Richard C. Taylor (1902-1970), group of two, pen and wash on paper, both signed, 7" x 13", and 7" x 13"	200.00	220.00	200.00
☐ **Archie,** Bob Montana (1920-1975), pen and ink with benday overlay, signed, King Features Syndicate, 4/4/1958, 5½" x 18"	75.00	85.00	75.00
☐ **Barney Google And Snuffy Smith,** Fred Lasswell (b. 1916), pen and ink, signed, King Features Syndicate, 10/3/1943, 11" x 17¼"	52.00	62.00	55.00
☐ **Baron Bean,** George Herriman (1880-1944), "This is Practical Astronomy," pen and ink, signed, c. 1917, 6½" x 26½"	225.00	275.00	230.00
☐ **Bringing Up Father,** George McManus (1884-1954), pen and ink with watercolor added as a color-guide, King Features Syndicate, c. 1920's 12" x 16½"	105.00	120.00	105.00
Note: This is the top half only of a Sunday strip, 6 panels)			
☐ **Bringing Up Father,** George McManus, pen and ink, signed, King Features Syndicate, 3/8/1943, 5" x 18"	55.00	70.00	62.00

	Current Price Range		Prior Year Average
☐ **Broom Hilda,** Russel Myers (b. 1938), pen and ink, signed, News-Tribune Syndicate, 2/2/1959, 6" x 21"	48.00	58.00	50.00
☐ **Broncho Bill,** Harry O'Neill, pen and ink, United Features Syndicate, Sunday, 7/12/1942, 14½" x 22½"	62.00	72.00	65.00
☐ **Buster Brown,** Richard Felton Outcault (1863-1928), pen and ink heightened with watercolor, signed, published by New York American, Sunday, 4/11/1915, bears engraving order form on reverse, dated 2/18/1915, 20" x 18½"	560.00	660.00	600.00
☐ **The Captain And The Kids,** Rudolph Dirks (1877-1968), pen and ink, signed, United Features Syndicate, Sunday, 11/13/1949, 16" x 24"	48.00	58.00	50.00
☐ **The Cisco Kid,** Jose-Luis Salinas, pen and ink, King Features Syndicate, 6/29/1951, 5½" x 18½"	105.00	120.00	105.00
☐ **Dennis The Menace,** Henry (Hank) Ketcham (b. 1920), pen and ink, signed, Publishers Hall Syndicate, Sunday, 7/29/1973, 18" x 25"	110.00	135.00	112.00
☐ **Dick Tracy,** Chester Gould, pen and ink, signed, Chicago Tribune Syndicate, Sunday, 9/28/1969, 25¾" x 23"	160.00	170.00	155.00
☐ **Donald Duck,** Charles Alfred Taliaferro (1905-1969), pen and ink with benday overlay, signed "Walt Disney," King Features Syndicate, 10/21/1952, 6" x 21"	55.00	70.00	58.00
☐ **Dream Of The Rarebit Fiend,** Winsor McCay, pen and ink, signed "Silas," New York Evening Telegram, 1906, 22½" x 14"	485.00	560.00	510.00
☐ **Felix The Cat,** Otto Messmer (b. 1894), pen and ink, King Features Syndicate, 1/26/1936, 16" x 20½"	110.00	130.00	110.00
Note: Lot accompanied by a copy of the Sunday newspaper page with a Bobby Dazzler topper.)			
☐ **Flash Gordon,** Emanuel (Mac) Raboy (1914-1967), pen and ink and pencil, signed, King Features Syndicate, Sunday, 2/1/1959, 14½" x 20½"	65.00	80.00	68.00
☐ **Gasoline Alley,** Frank O. King (1883-1969), pen and ink, signed, The Chicago Tribune, 9/25/1939, 6" x 20"	72.00	82.00	75.00
☐ **The Gumps,** Robert Sidney Smith (1877-1935), pen and ink, signed, The Chicago Tribune, 4/25/1925, 5¾" x 19¾"	52.00	62.00	55.00
☐ **Hagar The Horrible,** Richard (Dik) Browne, pen and ink, signed, King Features Syndicate, 9/10/1979, 3½" x 12¾"	72.00	82.00	75.00
☐ **Hi And Lois,** Mort Addison Walker and Richard (Dik) Browne, pen and ink, signed, King Features Syndicate, Sunday, 12/27/1964, 12½" x 18½" ...	110.00	135.00	112.00
☐ **Howdy Doody,** American, pen and ink, United Features Syndicate, 12/10/1950, 15" x 23½"	360.00	410.00	375.00
☐ **It's Only A Game,** Charles Monroe Schulz, pen and ink, United Features Syndicate, 5/28/1958, 8¼" x 17¾"	100.00	120.00	95.00

COMIC ART

	Current Price Range		Prior Year Average
☐ **The Katzenjammer Kids,** Harold Knerr (1883-1949), pen and ink, signed, King Features Syndicate, Sunday, 6/25/1933, 16½" x 20½"	110.00	220.00	150.00
☐ **Krazy Kat,** George Herriman, pen and ink, signed, c. 1915, 9¼" x 22½"	725.00	825.00	750.00
☐ **Krazy Kat,** George Herriman, pen and ink, signed, Sunday, 9/2/1917, 24½" x 19½"	1050.00	1250.00	1100.00
☐ **Li'l Abner,** Alfred Gerald Caplin (Al Capp), pen and ink, signed, United Features Syndicate, 5/23/1949, 6" x 22"	110.00	140.00	110.00
☐ **Little Iodine; Little Lulu; Nancy,** James Halto (1893-1963); Margie (Marjorie Henderson Buell); Ernest Bushmiller (b. 1905), group of three, all pen and ink and signed, first, King Features Syndicate 2/23/1958; second, Chicago Tribune-N.Y. News Syndicate 1/10/1956; third, United Features Syndicate 12/17/1947, 10" x 21¾", 6" x 19½", 5" x 18½"	72.00	82.00	75.00
☐ **A Mexican Snoopy And Charlie Brown On TV,** Charles Monroe Schulz (b. 1922), group of two, first of Snoopy with mustache standing in a desert landscape; second of Snoopy rolling in stitches watching Charlie Brown on TV, both felt-tipped pen, signed, first inscribed "copyright 1975 United Features Syndicate Inc.", second framed, 4½" x 6", and 6" x 5"	170.00	185.00	168.00
☐ **Mickey Mouse,** Floyd Gottfredson, pen and ink, signed by the artist and "Walt Disney," 1/4/1938, 5¾" x 25"	360.00	410.00	375.00
☐ **Moon Mullins,** Frank Henry Willard (1893-1958), pen and ink, signed, Chicago Tribune-N.Y. News Syndicate, 1935, 6" x 19½"	110.00	140.00	115.00
☐ **The Muppets,** Guy and Brad Gilchrist, pen and ink, signed, King Features Syndicate, 10/6/1981, 5½" x 19"	72.00	82.00	75.00
☐ **Mutt 'n Jeff,** Harry Conway (Bud) Fisher (1885-1954), pen and ink, signed, The World, 1926, 8¼" x 29"	95.00	115.00	100.00
☐ **Nancy: Blondie: Scamp,** Ernest Bushmiller (b. 1905); Lyman (Chic) Young (b. 1893); Walt Disney Studios, group of three, all pen and ink and signed, first, United Features Syndicate 12/11/1967; second King Features Syndicate 6/21/1969; third, signed "Walt Disney," King Features Syndicate 8/4/1958, 5¼" x 19¼", 5" x 17", 5½" x 19¼"	145.00	160.00	142.00
☐ **Peanuts,** Charles Monroe Schulz, pen and ink, signed, United Features Syndicate, 4/12/1967, 5½" x 27"	310.00	335.00	312.00
☐ **Peanuts,** Charles Monroe Schulz, pen and ink, signed and inscribed "For Judy with every best wish - Charles M. Schulz," United Features Syndicate, 6/8/1961, 5½" x 27"	235.00	260.00	238.00
☐ **Peanuts,** Charles Monroe Schulz, pen and ink, signed, United Features Syndicate, Sunday, 1953, 15½" x 23"	620.00	720.00	650.00

COMIC ART / 263

	Current Price Range		Prior Year Average

- **Pogo,** Walt Crawford Kelly Jr. (1913-1973), pen and ink, signed and inscribed "Best to Wayne De Wald... Walt Kelly," Publishers Hall Syndicate 8/8/1968, 6½" x 21" **335.00 360.00 338.00**
- **The Cavalier Cartoonist,** Hassman, pen and ink, signed, a cartoon showing an 18th Century artist drawing The Happy Holligan riding Maud, on a large canvas to the accompaniment of an orchestra, 19½" x 13" **62.00 72.00 65.00**
- **Snoopy The Pilot And Schroeder The Pianist,** Charles Monroe Schulz, group of two, first of Snoopy in helmet on top of doghouse with Charlie Brown looking bemused; second of Beethoven playing the piano with Lucy listening, both felt-tipped pen, signed, both copyright United Features Syndicate, 5" x 7½", and 5" x 7" **210.00 235.00 212.00**
- **Steve Canyon,** Milton Caniff, signed and inscribed "Steve Canyon," crayon on paper, 35" x 23½" **385.00 410.00 382.00**
- **Smokey Stover,** William Holman (b. 1903), pen and ink, signed, Chicago Tribune-N.Y. News Syndicate, Sunday, 1/15/1936, 13" x 19" **145.00 160.00 142.00**
  Note: One of the earliest appearances of the two-wheeled car.)
- **Tippie,** Edwina Frances Dumm (b. 1893), pen and ink, King Features Syndicate, 11/16/1947, 14" x 22" **100.00 120.00 95.00**
- **The Timid Soul (Mr. Milquetoast),** Harold T. Webster, pen and ink, signed, N.Y. Tribune Syndicate, Sunday, 6/11/1939, 28½" x 21½" **520.00 620.00 550.00**
- **Toonerville Trolley,** Fontaine Talbot Fox Jr. (1884-1964), pen and ink cartoon, signed, showing the infamous trolley and Toonerville folks, c. 1920, 9½" x 8½" **320.00 395.00 338.00**
- **Winnie The Pooh,** Walt Disney Studios, pen and ink with benday overlay, Walt Disney Productions, 10/10/1978, 5½" x 19" **110.00 130.00 110.00**
- **Yellow Kid: The Great Dog Show In Hogan's Alley,** George Benjamin Luks (1867-1933), original printed newspaper page, published in The World, Sunday, 2/21/1897, 20" x 16½" **310.00 335.00 312.00**
- **The Yellow Kid: Hoboken Handicap,** Richard Felton Outcault, pen and ink, signed, one panel cartoon of The Yellow Kid and friends in "The Spring Meeting of the Hogan's Alley Jockey Klub, de event will be de grate Hoboken Handikaps." c. 1896, 17" x 30" **6000.00 6300.00 5800.00**
  Note: This is one of four known surviving Yellow Kid panels by Outcault, the father of American comic art.)

COMIC BOOKS

World's Best Comic (#1), ©1940 DC Comics, Batman, Superman, Zatara
.... **$360.00-$1000.00**

The comic book evolved, obviously, from the newspaper comic strip. Indeed, all the early comic books were nothing but reprints of old newspaper strips collected and bound in soft covers. It was not until the appearance of *Detective Comics* in 1937 that any original material was used. A year later Superman made his debut in *Action #1,* and the comic book business was assured of success. *Detective #27* introduced Batman; *Timely* countered with The Human Torch, Captain America and The Submariner; *Fawcett* came up with Captain Marvel and his family; and the race for the most unique superhero was under way. It continues to this day.

AS AN INVESTMENT

Comic books, like any commodity, become valuable when the demand exceeds the supply. There are more comic book fans and collectors now than ever before, and a number of the Golden Age Comic books can be collected for speculation. If kept carefully preserved, and for a long enough period of time, certain select comic books can be very lucrative as long term investments.

"NUMBER ONES" FIRST ISSUES

On the following pages is a comprehensive listing of "Number Ones," the first issues of a given comic book series. They also serve as indicators to the values of other books in the series. When the No. 1 book is high in price,

COMIC BOOKS / 265

most of the other earlier editions are also in this category. Space does not permit a complete listing of each book and its value in this section. Those listed here give a good "outline" of the current comic book market. For more in-depth information and listings, you may refer to *The Official Price Guide to Comic and Science Fiction Books*, published by the House of Collectibles.

COMIC BOOKS (1933 TO DATE) "NUMBER ONES" FIRST ISSUES

	Current Price Range		Prior Year Average
☐ Abbott and Costello Comics	20.00	40.00	28.00
☐ Ace Comics	150.00	375.00	210.00
☐ Action Comics	4200.00	12500.00	8000.00
☐ Adventure Comics	20.00	70.00	40.00
☐ Adventure Comics, (#48, Hourman)	275.00	675.00	475.00
☐ Air Fighters	140.00	230.00	175.00
☐ Alice in Wonderland	4.50	6.50	5.00
☐ All American Comics, (Hop Harrigan and Scribbly)	130.00	250.00	180.00
☐ All Flash Comics	185.00	455.00	210.00
☐ All Funny Comics	18.00	38.00	25.00
☐ All Good Comics, (1949)	6.00	18.00	10.00
☐ All Hero Comics	125.00	250.00	162.00
☐ All Select Comics, (Vol. 1)	220.00	520.00	350.00
☐ All Surprise Comics	7.00	15.00	10.00
☐ All Winners Comics, (Vol. 1)	450.00	1100.00	600.00
☐ All Winners Comics, (Vol. 2)	185.00	420.00	275.00
☐ All Your Comics	14.00	30.00	20.00
☐ All Your Comics, (25¢ issue)	9.00	16.00	11.00
☐ Amazing Comics	95.00	210.00	145.00
☐ Amazing Fantasy, #15 (original Spiderman)	450.00	1250.00	800.00
☐ Amazing Man	200.00	520.00	320.00
☐ Amazing Spiderman	360.00	725.00	425.00
☐ American Air Forces	9.00	20.00	13.00
☐ America's Best Comics	80.00	170.00	120.00
☐ America's Greatest Comics	200.00	420.00	280.00
☐ Anarcho, Dictator of Death	18.00	32.00	22.00
☐ Animal Antics	14.00	26.00	18.50
☐ Animal Comics	320.00	670.00	425.00
☐ Animal Fables	39.00	85.00	55.00
☐ Animated Movie-Tunes	3.50	5.50	4.00
☐ Annie Oakley	18.00	42.00	28.00
☐ Aquaman	20.00	36.00	24.00
☐ Archie	320.00	820.00	550.00
☐ Archie Annual	12.00	22.00	15.00
☐ Archie's Joke Book Magazine	38.00	85.00	55.00
☐ Army and Navy Comics	26.00	50.00	35.00
☐ Arrow	70.00	145.00	100.00
☐ Astonishing	38.00	75.00	52.00
☐ Atoman	20.00	70.00	35.00
☐ Atomic Comics	16.00	40.00	22.00
☐ Atomic Thunderbolt	22.00	46.00	27.00
☐ Attack on Planet Mars	80.00	210.00	120.00
☐ The Avengers	140.00	360.00	220.00
☐ Aviation Cadets	6.00	8.00	6.00
☐ Baby Huey, The Baby Giant	32.00	92.00	60.00
☐ Bang-Up Comics	46.00	96.00	67.00
☐ The Barker	8.00	15.00	10.50
☐ Barney Google and Snuffy Smith	7.00	15.00	10.00

266 / COMIC BOOKS

	Current Price Range		Prior Year Average
☑ Batman	1650.00	4450.00	3000.00
☐ Beatles Life Story	38.00	70.00	47.00
☐ Bee-29 The Bombardier	5.50	11.00	7.00
☐ Big Shot Comics	110.00	190.00	135.00
☐ Bill Barnes Comics	28.00	70.00	50.00
☐ Bingo Comics	9.50	13.00	10.00
☐ Black Cat Comics	65.00	130.00	88.00
☐ Blackstone, Master Magician	12.00	28.00	17.50
☐ Black Swan Comics	13.50	28.50	18.00
☐ Black Terror	80.00	190.00	125.00
☐ Blazing Comics	11.50	28.00	18.00
☐ Blue Beetle	125.00	260.00	175.00
☐ Blue Bolt	160.00	320.00	225.00
☐ Blue Circle Comics	7.00	10.00	7.50
☐ Blue Ribbon Comics	105.00	270.00	210.00
☐ Bomber Comics	12.00	22.00	15.00
☐ Book of Comics, (25¢ issue)	20.00	36.00	24.00
☐ Boy Commandos	135.00	440.00	320.00
☐ Brave and The Bold	160.00	360.00	250.00
☐ Brer Rabbit	38.00	88.00	65.00
☐ Buck Rogers	165.00	340.00	220.00
☐ Bulletman	160.00	370.00	220.00
☐ Buster Brown, (1903)	75.00	160.00	105.00
☐ Buster Crabbe	25.00	55.00	35.00
☐ Buz Sawyer	12.00	22.00	15.00
☐ Buzzy	14.00	28.00	18.00
☐ Calling All Girls	6.00	12.00	7.50
☐ Calling All Kids	5.00	10.00	6.00
☐ Camera Comics	3.50	6.50	4.50
☐ Camp Comics	90.00	185.00	130.00
☐ Cannonball Comics	45.00	75.00	50.00
☐ Captain Aero	50.00	150.00	90.00
☐ Captain America	1850.00	4250.00	2800.00
☐ Captain America 100	6.00	12.00	7.50
☐ Captain Battle	60.00	110.00	75.00
☐ Captain Battle, Jr.	45.00	87.00	60.00
☐ Captain Fearless Comics	45.00	85.00	62.00
☑ Capt. Marvel Adventures	1650.00	4250.00	2800.00
☐ Capt. Marvel, Jr.	170.00	360.00	250.00
☑ Capt. Marvel, (Marvel Series)	6.00	12.00	7.50
☑ Captain Midnight	100.00	215.00	140.00
☐ Captain Steve Savage	35.00	80.00	50.00
☐ Captain Video	22.00	46.00	30.00
☐ Casper's Ghostland	14.00	30.00	20.00
☐ Casper, the Friendly Ghost	25.00	55.00	35.00
☐ Catman	70.00	160.00	105.00
☐ Cave Girl, (#11)	45.00	82.00	58.00
☐ Challengers of The Unknown	70.00	125.00	88.00
☐ Champion, (#2)	45.00	85.00	55.00
☐ Christmas Parade	70.00	110.00	80.00
☐ Circus	140.00	260.00	190.00
☐ Cisco Kid Comics	14.00	34.00	23.00
☐ Claire Voyant	60.00	110.00	75.00
☑ Classics Illustrated, (First Edition)	200.00	520.00	240.00
☐ Colossus	100.00	260.00	150.00
☐ Columbia, Gem of The Comics	14.00	30.00	20.00

COMIC BOOKS / 267

	Current Price Range		Prior Year Average
☐ Comedy	16.00	30.00	21.00
☐ Comic Capers	12.00	16.00	12.50
☐ Comic Cavalcade	160.00	430.00	270.00
☐ Comic Land	8.00	14.00	8.50
☐ Comics for Kids	3.50	6.50	4.50
☐ Comics On Parade, (Tarzan by Hal Foster)	140.00	275.00	185.00
☐ Coo Coo Comics	11.00	18.00	13.50
☐ Corliss Archer	28.00	42.00	32.00
☐ Crack Comics	260.00	575.00	455.00
☐ Crackajack Funnies	95.00	230.00	205.00
☐ Crash Comics	85.00	185.00	125.00
☐ Crime and Punishment	15.00	28.00	18.50
☐ Crime Does Not Pay	95.00	225.00	205.00
☐ Crime Exposed	9.00	18.00	13.00
☐ Crimefighters	9.00	18.00	13.00
☐ Crime Reporter	20.00	58.00	38.00
☐ Crime Smasher	16.00	30.00	25.00
☐ Crime Suspenstories	110.00	260.00	165.00
☐ Crimes by Women	38.00	75.00	52.00
☐ Crown Comics	18.00	42.00	27.00
☐ Cryin' Lion	2.50	4.50	3.00
☐ Crypt of Terror, (#17)	160.00	435.00	340.00
☐ Curly Kayoe	5.00	10.00	6.00
☐ Cyclone Comics	40.00	85.00	60.00
☐ Dale Evans, (#3)	8.00	14.00	10.00
☐ Dandy Comics	45.00	85.00	60.00
☐ Danger is Our Business	60.00	125.00	65.00
☐ Daredevil, (First Series)	420.00	820.00	600.00
☐ Daredevil, (Marvel)	65.00	70.00	85.00
☐ Daring Mystery	660.00	1450.00	1025.00
☐ Debbie Dean, Career Girl	9.00	15.00	10.50
☐ Dennis the Menace	32.00	80.00	50.00
☐ Detective Comics, (1937)	675.00	1850.00	1250.00
☐ Detective, (#27, 1st appearance of Batman)	2900.00	6700.00	4200.00
☐ Devil Dogs	16.00	30.00	21.00
☐ Dick Tracy, (Color)	110.00	185.00	138.00
☐ Dick Tracy, (Dell)	55.00	105.00	70.00
☐ Dime Comics	85.00	185.00	125.00
☐ Dixie Dugan	10.00	22.00	15.00
☐ Doc Savage	150.00	360.00	170.00
☐ Doctor Solar	4.00	8.50	5.50
☐ Doll Man	150.00	285.00	200.00
☐ Dolly Dill Comics	4.00	7.00	4.50
☐ Donald Duck, (Color #4)	1100.00	1600.00	1250.00
☐ Donald Duck, (Four Color #9, 1st appearance)	460.00	1500.00	950.00
☐ Don Fortune	12.00	22.00	15.00
☐ Don Winslow of The Navy	50.00	95.00	68.00
☐ Dotty Dripple	3.50	6.50	4.50
☐ Double Life of Private Strong	32.00	65.00	42.00
☐ Durango Kid	85.00	185.00	125.00
☐ Dynamic Comics	60.00	160.00	100.00
☐ The Eagle	70.00	135.00	92.00
☐ Earth Man on Venus	260.00	585.00	460.00
☐ Eerie	140.00	210.00	165.00
☐ Egbert	8.00	16.00	11.00
☐ Ella Cinders and Blackie	18.00	28.00	20.00

268 / COMIC BOOKS

	Current Price Range		Prior Year Average
☐ Ellery Queen	30.00	55.00	38.00
☐ Elmo	6.00	12.00	8.00
☐ Everybody's Comics	15.00	28.00	18.50
☐ Exciting Comics	80.00	180.00	125.00
☐ Exposed Comics	9.00	18.00	12.00
☐ The Face	28.00	50.00	40.00
☐ Fairy Tale Parade	250.00	475.00	330.00
☐ Famous Fairy Tales, (1942)	135.00	285.00	200.00
☐ Famous Funnies, (July 1934)	260.00	410.00	325.00
☐ Famous Stories	22.00	38.00	25.00
☐ Fantastic Comics	110.00	260.00	175.00
☐ Fantastic Four	550.00	1600.00	1000.00
☐ Fat and Slat	32.00	60.00	37.00
☐ Feature Books	85.00	190.00	120.00
☐ Felix The Cat	25.00	45.00	30.00
☐ Fight	90.00	210.00	140.00
☐ Fighting American	85.00	170.00	125.00
☐ Fighting Yank	75.00	160.00	105.00
☐ First Love Illustrated	12.00	22.00	15.00
☐ Flame	150.00	270.00	200.00
☐ Flash, (First Series)	600.00	1600.00	1025.00
☐ Flash, (Second Series, #105)	160.00	345.00	235.00
☐ The Fly	30.0	55.00	38.00
☐ Flying Saucers	75.00	185.00	125.00
☐ Forbidden Love	185.00	360.00	225.00
☐ Forever People	2.50	6.50	4.00
☐ Four Favorites	55.00	120.00	170.00
☐ The Fox and the Crow	85.00	160.00	105.00
☐ Frankenstein	28.00	55.00	38.00
☐ Frisky Fables	10.00	18.00	12.50
☐ Front Page	18.00	38.00	25.00
☐ Frontline Combat	90.00	200.00	135.00
☐ Funland Comics	5.00	9.00	6.50
☐ The Funnies, (1929)	100.00	155.00	120.00
☐ Funny Annual	45.00	90.00	62.00
☐ Funny Book	7.00	14.00	8.50
☐ Funny Folks	15.00	30.00	20.00
☐ Funny Frolics	6.50	10.50	6.50
☐ Funnyman, (Siegel & Schuster)	18.00	30.00	21.50
☐ Funny Picture Stories, (#1 - The Clock)	50.00	120.00	75.00
☐ Funny Stuff	30.00	55.00	40.00
☐ Future Comics	220.00	620.00	350.00
☐ Future World Comics	10.00	20.00	13.00
☐ Gang Busters	30.00	38.00	26.00
☐ Gangsters Can't Win	14.00	28.00	18.50
☐ Gay Comics	32.00	55.00	40.00
☐ Gem Comics	12.00	22.00	15.00
☐ Gene Autry Comics	150.00	400.00	250.00
☐ Georgie	12.00	22.00	15.00
☐ Ghost Rider, (First Series, A-1 Comics)	2.50	3.50	2.10
☐ Giant Comics Edition	20.00	38.00	26.00
☐ G.I. Combat	20.00	38.00	26.00
☐ Gift Comics	200.00	450.00	300.00
☐ Giggle Comics	4.50	8.50	6.00
☐ Golden Lad	40.00	75.00	52.00
☐ Goofy Comics	9.00	20.00	13.00

COMIC BOOKS / 269

	Current Price Range		Prior Year Average
☐ Great Comics, (1941)	30.00	55.00	38.00
☐ Great Comics, (1945)	16.00	55.00	31.00
☐ Green Giant Comics	600.00	1450.00	1000.00
☐ Green Lantern, (First Series)	340.00	845.00	550.00
☐ Green Lantern, (Second Series)	85.00	210.00	140.00
☐ Green Mask, (Vol. 1, #1)	85.00	190.00	125.00
☐ Grit Grady Comics	4.50	8.50	6.00
☐ Ha Ha Comics	9.00	18.00	12.50
☐ Hap Hazard Comics	3.50	6.50	4.50
☐ Happy Comics	10.00	20.00	13.00
☐ Happy Houlihans	40.00	90.00	65.00
☐ Harvey Comics Library	260.00	550.00	400.00
☐ Hawkman	18.00	30.00	21.00
☐ Henry	15.00	28.00	20.00
☐ Heroic	70.00	140.00	95.00
☐ Hi-Ho Comics	8.00	18.00	12.00
☐ Hi-Jinx	2.50	4.50	3.00
☐ Hi-Lite Comics	13.00	24.00	16.00
☐ Hit Comics	285.00	635.00	450.00
☐ Hollywood Confessions	25.00	45.00	30.00
☐ Hollywood Secrets	32.00	60.00	42.00
☐ Homer Cobb	20.00	35.00	22.00
☐ Hopalong Cassidy	60.00	110.00	75.00
☐ Hoppy the Marvel Bunny	14.00	28.00	18.50
☐ Horse Feathers Comics	18.00	35.00	24.00
☐ House of Mystery	38.00	84.00	58.00
☐ Howdy Doody	15.00	25.00	18.00
☐ Hulk	275.00	720.00	410.00
☐ Human Torch	750.00	1750.00	1200.00
☐ Humdinger	3.50	6.50	4.50
☐ Humor	9.00	14.00	10.00
☐ Humphrey Comics	12.00	22.00	15.00
☐ Hyper Mystery Comics	38.50	98.00	62.50
☐ Ibis The Invincible	100.00	225.00	150.00
☐ Ideal, A Classical Comic	25.00	40.00	28.00
☐ Incredible Hulk, (#102)	3.50	6.50	4.50
☐ Incredible Hulk Fiction, (#30)	38.00	42.00	37.50
☐ Iron Man	18.00	28.50	20.00
☐ It Really Happened	8.00	14.00	9.50
☐ Jackpot Comics	120.00	255.00	175.00
☐ Jaguar	11.00	18.00	13.50
☐ Jamboree Comics	2.50	4.50	3.00
☐ Jeep Comics	8.50	14.00	10.00
☐ Jesse James	30.00	55.00	38.00
☐ Jet	26.00	42.00	31.00
☐ Jim Hardy, (1944)	18.00	32.00	22.00
☐ Jimmy Olson	150.00	400.00	245.00
☐ Jimmy Wakely	30.00	55.00	38.00
☐ Jingle Jangle Comics	45.00	85.00	60.00
☐ Joe Palooka, (First Series)	42.00	72.00	52.00
☐ Joe Palooka, (Second Series)	30.00	55.00	38.00
☐ John Wayne Adventure Comics	28.00	55.00	37.00
☐ Jo-Jo Congo King	40.00	75.00	52.00
☐ Joker Comics	130.00	285.00	205.00
☐ Journey Into Mystery	100.00	215.00	140.00
☐ Jughead	100.00	275.00	140.00

270 / COMIC BOOKS

		Current Price Range		Prior Year Average
☐	Juke Box Comics	40.00	75.00	58.00
☐	Jumbo	320.00	770.00	512.00
☐	Jungle Comics	160.00	320.00	205.00
☐	Jungle Girl	75.00	135.00	95.00
☐	Jungle Tales of Tarzan, (Vol.5)	300.00	625.00	425.00
☐	Junie Prom Comics	8.00	14.00	9.50
☐	Junior Miss	14.00	26.00	18.00
☐	Justice League of America	85.00	220.00	135.00
☐	Justice Traps the Guilty	25.00	40.00	25.00
☐	Ka'A'nga Comics	30.00	55.00	38.00
☐	Kamandi, Last Boy on Earth	2.50	3.50	2.50
☐	Katy Keene	70.00	130.00	80.00
☐	Katzanjammer Kids	5.00	15.00	9.00
☐	Keen Detective Funnies	60.00	110.00	75.00
☐	Kewpies	35.00	60.00	38.00
☐	Key Comics	8.50	18.00	11.50
☐	Kid Eternity	85.00	160.00	125.00
☐	Kid Komics	210.00	435.00	312.00
☐	King Comics	285.00	560.00	365.00
☐	The Killers	125.00	300.00	200.00
☐	Kitty	2.50	4.50	3.00
☐	Koko and Kola	2.50	4.50	3.00
☐	Ko Komics	11.00	20.00	13.50
☐	Komic Kartoons	10.00	18.00	12.25
☐	Komik Pages, (#10)	5.50	8.50	6.50
☐	Krazy Komics, (First Series)	30.00	55.00	38.00
☐	Krazy Komics, (Second Series)	40.00	76.00	58.00
☐	Krazy Krow	2.50	4.50	3.00
☐	Krazylife Comics	2.50	4.50	3.00
☐	Laffy-Daffy Comics	2.50	4.50	3.00
☐	Lance O'Casey	12.00	22.00	15.00
☐	Land of The Lost Comics	30.00	55.00	38.00
☐	Large Feature Comics	70.00	160.00	105.00
☐	Lash Larue Western	36.00	65.00	46.00
☐	Latest Comics	2.50	4.50	3.00
☐	Lawbreakers Always Lose!	15.00	28.00	17.50
☐	Leading Comics	180.00	365.00	250.00
☐	Little Dot	65.00	120.00	80.00
☐	Little Max Comics	25.00	45.00	32.00
☐	Little Lulu, (Four Color, #74)	110.00	220.00	155.00
☐	Living Bible	15.00	30.00	18.00
☐	Lois Lane	120.00	260.00	160.00
☐	The Lone Ranger	60.00	110.00	78.00
☐	Looney Tunes, (First Series)	220.00	570.00	375.00
☐	Lucky "7" Comics	16.00	26.00	18.50
☐	Mad	150.00	285.00	205.00
☐	Mad Hatter	30.00	55.00	38.00
☐	Magic Comics	85.00	160.00	125.00
☐	Major Hoople Comics	20.00	35.00	22.00
☐	Major Victory Comics	30.00	52.00	34.00
☐	Manhunt!	40.00	75.00	52.00
☐	Man of War	60.00	160.00	100.00
☐	Marmaduke Mouse	10.00	18.00	13.00
☐	Marvel Family	95.00	220.00	150.00
☐	Mary Marvel	80.00	185.00	130.00
☐	Mask Comics	150.00	375.00	238.00

COMIC BOOKS / 271

		Current Price Range		Prior Year Average
☐	Master Comics	285.00	560.00	412.00
☐	Medal of Honor Comics	4.50	6.50	5.00
☐	Meet Miss Pepper, (#5, #6)	30.00	55.00	38.00
☐	Merry Comics, (1945)	3.50	7.50	5.00
☐	Merry-Go-Round Comics	7.00	10.00	7.50
☐	Mickey Mouse	285.00	550.00	375.00
☐	Mighty Mouse, (First Series)	40.00	80.00	50.00
☐	Military Comics	360.00	850.00	575.00
☐	Millie The Model	30.00	55.00	38.00
☐	Miracle Comics	40.00	75.00	50.00
☐	Miss America Comics	75.00	165.00	130.00
☐	Miss Fury Comics	350.00	725.00	512.00
☐	Mr. District Attorney	25.00	45.00	30.00
☐	Mister Miracle	3.00	6.00	4.00
☐	Mister Mystery	25.00	45.00	30.00
☐	Mr. Universe	15.00	28.00	20.00
☐	Modern Comics, (#44)	30.00	55.00	38.00
☐	Modern Love	70.00	190.00	135.00
☐	Molly O'Day	60.00	160.00	100.00
☐	Monkeyshines Comics	28.00	50.00	34.00
☐	Moon Girl	90.00	210.00	140.00
☐	Moon Mullins	40.00	70.00	50.00
☐	Mopsy	10.00	18.00	12.50
☐	More Fun Comics	360.00	860.00	600.00
☐	More Fun, (#52)	1900.00	4100.00	2900.00
☐	Movie Comics	32.00	56.00	39.00
☐	Murder, Inc.	30.00	55.00	38.00
☐	Mutt and Jeff	70.00	115.00	90.00
☐	Mystery Men Comics	145.00	335.00	225.00
☐	Mystic Comics, (First Series)	550.00	1250.00	850.00
☐	Mystic Comics, (#2)	300.00	575.00	460.00
☐	Namora	80.00	190.00	130.00
☐	Napoleon and Uncle Elby	20.00	40.00	24.00
☐	National Comics	285.00	725.00	500.00
☐	Navy Action	7.00	14.00	9.00
☐	Nellie The Nurse	16.00	28.00	21.00
☐	New Book of Comics	125.00	205.00	150.00
☐	New Funnies, (#76)	220.00	450.00	315.00
☐	New Gods	3.50	7.00	4.75
☐	Nickel Comics	150.00	325.00	200.00
☐	Northwest Mounties	24.00	44.00	31.50
☐	Nutty Comics	20.00	35.00	23.00
☐	Nyoka	70.00	130.00	95.00
☐	Oakey Doaks	25.00	42.00	31.00
☐	Okay Comics	25.00	48.00	32.00
☐	Our Army At War	50.00	90.00	65.00
☐	Our Fighting Forces	40.00	75.00	52.00
☐	Our Flag Comics	120.00	260.00	180.00
☐	Our Gang Comics	220.00	440.00	310.00
☐	Outlaws	22.00	40.00	26.00
☐	Out of the Night	40.00	75.00	52.00
☐	Ozzie and Harriet	20.00	36.00	24.00
☐	Pageant of Comics, (Mopsy)	10.00	18.00	10.50
☐	Panic	20.00	38.00	26.00
☐	Pat Boone	22.00	40.00	26.00
☐	Patches	11.00	20.00	13.50

272 / COMIC BOOKS

	Current Price Range		Prior Year Average
☐ Patsy Walker	32.00	58.00	40.00
☐ Penny	8.00	15.00	11.00
☐ Pep Comics	210.00	535.00	362.00
☐ Peter Panda	22.00	40.00	27.00
☐ Peter Pat	14.00	22.00	16.00
☐ Peter Rabbit	60.00	110.00	75.00
☐ Peter Wheat	50.00	95.00	68.00
☐ Phantom Lady, (#13)	220.00	540.00	355.00
☐ Phantom Witch Doctor	35.00	75.00	50.00
☐ Picture News	12.00	22.00	15.00
☐ Picture Stories From The Bible, (Old Testament)	10.00	14.00	10.00
☐ Picture Stories From The Bible, (New Testament)	10.00	14.00	10.00
☐ Planet Comics	320.00	845.00	562.00
☐ Plastic Man	200.00	360.00	265.00
☐ Pogo Possum	120.00	200.00	140.00
☐ Police Cases, Authentic	4.50	11.00	7.00
☐ Police Comics	460.00	1100.00	750.00
☐ Popeye Feature Book	950.00	1750.00	1300.00
☐ Pop-Pop Comics	3.50	6.50	4.50
☐ Popular Comics	130.00	190.00	150.00
☐ Power Comics	32.00	60.00	45.00
☐ Powerhouse Pepper Comics	80.00	210.00	135.00
☐ Prize Comics	70.00	198.00	125.00
☐ Public Enemies	12.00	22.00	16.00
☐ Punch and Judy	4.50	8.50	6.00
☐ Punch Comics	40.00	90.00	60.00
☐ Puppet Comics	3.50	6.50	4.50
☐ Puppetoons	20.00	40.00	24.00
☐ Puzzle-Fun Comics	12.00	22.00	15.00
☐ Raggedy Ann and Andy	32.00	55.00	39.00
☐ Rangers Comics	80.00	205.00	130.00
☐ Rawhide Kid	25.00	55.00	37.00
☐ Real Fact Comics	20.00	40.00	21.00
☐ Real Funnies	6.00	11.00	7.50
☐ Real Heroes Comics	7.00	14.00	10.00
☐ Real Screen Comics	90.00	180.00	135.00
☐ Real Sports Comics	10.00	18.00	13.00
☐ Red Band Comics	12.00	24.00	16.00
☐ Red Circle Comics	12.00	24.00	16.00
☐ Red Dragon	36.00	80.00	52.00
☐ Red Ryder Comics	150.00	270.00	180.00
☐ Remember Pearl Harbor	7.00	14.00	8.00
☐ Ribtickler	3.50	6.50	4.50
☐ Richie Rich	225.00	445.00	320.00
☐ Richie Rich Millions	26.00	56.00	37.00
☐ Robotmen of the Lost Planet	150.00	365.00	230.00
☐ Rocket Comics	75.00	160.00	110.00
☐ Romance Trail	7.00	14.00	8.00
☐ Romantic Adventures	3.50	6.50	4.50
☐ Romantic Picture Novelettes	12.00	18.00	12.00
☐ Roundup	4.50	8.50	6.00
☐ Roy Rogers Comics	35.00	75.00	52.00
☐ The Saint	60.00	120.00	75.00
☐ Samson, (First Series)	60.00	130.00	85.00
☐ Science Comics	110.00	270.00	180.00
☐ Scoop	30.00	60.00	51.00

COMIC BOOKS / 273

	Current Price Range		Prior Year Average
☐ Scream Comics	4.00	8.00	4.50
☐ Scribbly	45.00	90.00	62.00
☐ Sea Hound	8.00	16.00	10.50
☐ Secret Hearts	15.00	30.00	19.00
☐ Sensation Comics	335.00	920.00	610.00
☐ Seven Dead Men	4.50	8.50	6.00
☐ Seven Seas Comics	45.00	85.00	62.00
☐ Shadow	125.00	360.00	235.00
☐ Sharp Comics	16.00	30.00	21.00
☐ Shazam	2.00	3.00	2.50
☐ Sheena, Queen of the Jungle	110.00	285.00	180.00
☐ Shield-Wizard Comics	130.00	220.00	165.00
☐ Ship Ahoy	4.50	8.50	6.00
☐ Shock Illustrated, (#3)	485.00	925.00	720.00
☐ Showcase	140.00	370.00	245.00
☐ Silly Tunes	8.00	15.00	9.50
☐ Silver Streak Comics, (#1)	285.00	625.00	435.00
☐ Silver Streak Comics, (#6)	625.00	1450.00	1000.00
☐ Silver Surfer	35.00	65.00	47.00
☐ Single Series, (#1)	40.00	75.00	52.00
☐ Single Series, (#20)	225.00	500.00	400.00
☐ Skyman	40.00	70.00	52.00
☐ Sky Sheriff	5.50	11.00	7.50
☐ Smash Comics	100.00	200.00	130.00
☐ Smilin' Jack	60.00	90.00	90.00
☐ Snappy Comics	5.50	10.00	7.00
☐ Space Detective	120.00	360.00	235.00
☐ Sparkler Comics, (First Series)	20.00	60.00	35.00
☐ Sparkler Comics, (Second Series)	70.00	135.00	92.00
☐ Sparkling Stars	7.00	14.00	8.00
☐ Sparkman	15.00	30.00	20.00
☐ Sparky Watts	14.00	18.00	18.50
☐ Special Agent	3.50	6.50	4.50
☐ Special Comics	145.00	325.00	230.00
☐ Special Edition Comics, (Capt. Marvel)	650.00	1150.00	850.00
☐ Spectacular Adventures	20.00	35.00	22.00
☐ The Spectre	4.50	8.00	5.25
☐ The Speed Comics	100.00	200.00	135.00
☐ The Spirit, (First Series)	80.00	160.00	110.00
☐ Spitfire Comics	40.00	75.00	52.00
☐ Spook Comics	11.00	18.00	13.50
☐ Spooky	30.00	55.00	40.00
☐ Sport Comics	16.00	36.00	24.00
☐ Sport Stars	18.00	30.00	21.00
☐ Spotlight Comics	25.00	45.00	32.00
☐ Spunky	8.00	16.00	11.00
☐ Spy Smasher	150.00	330.00	200.00
☐ Star Comics	35.00	78.00	51.00
☐ Stars and Stripes Comics	65.00	170.00	110.00
☐ Star-Spangled Comics	140.00	325.00	205.00
☐ Star Studded	16.00	30.00	23.00
☐ Startling Comics	90.00	190.00	130.00
☐ Star Trek	22.00	40.00	28.00
☐ Star Wars	4.50	8.50	5.75
☐ Steve Canyon	40.00	75.00	58.00
☐ Steve Roper	4.50	8.50	6.00

274 / COMIC BOOKS

	Current Price Range		Prior Year Average
☐ Strange Adventures	90.00	210.00	140.00
☐ Strange Tales	120.00	300.00	185.00
☐ Strange Worlds	70.00	190.00	120.00
☐ Stuntman Comics	125.00	190.00	145.00
☐ Sub-Mariner, (First Series)	650.00	1400.00	1000.00
☐ Sub-Mariner, (Second Series)	8.00	16.00	11.00
☐ Superboy	350.00	975.00	625.00
☐ Super Comics	110.00	215.00	152.00
☐ Super Duck Comics	25.00	45.00	31.00
☐ Super Magic Comics	50.00	80.00	60.00
☑ Superman	3600.00	8300.00	6000.00
☐ Super—Mystery Comics	75.00	185.00	122.00
☐ Supermouse	5.50	11.00	7.50
☐ Super Rabbit	5.50	11.00	7.50
☐ Supersnipe	40.00	70.00	51.00
☐ Super Spy	45.00	110.00	70.00
☐ Super World Comics	55.00	130.00	82.00
☐ Suspense Comics	40.00	90.00	55.00
☐ Sweet Sixteen	10.00	20.00	12.50
☐ Taffy	10.00	20.00	12.50
☐ Tailspin Tommy, (1932)	40.00	70.00	52.00
☐ Tales of Suspense	70.00	170.00	110.00
☐ Tales of Terror Annual	550.00	1400.00	975.00
☐ Tales of the Unexpected	40.00	70.00	51.00
☐ Tales to Astonish	65.00	175.00	110.00
☐ Target Comics	115.00	360.00	170.00
☐ Tarzan, (1948)	90.00	190.00	140.00
☐ Tarzan, (Single Series, #20)	210.00	310.00	250.00
☐ Teen Titans	8.00	16.00	10.50
☐ Tegra, Jungle Empress	40.00	75.00	52.00
☐ Terrific Comics	10.00	45.00	20.00
☐ Terry Toons Comics	60.00	110.00	80.00
☐ Tessie The Typist	38.00	78.00	54.00
☐ The Texan	8.00	18.00	12.00
☐ Thimble Theatre Starring Popeye	150.00	275.00	180.00
☐ Three Ring Comics	3.50	6.50	4.50
☐ Three Stooges	50.00	100.00	67.00
☐ Thrilling Comics	75.00	195.00	115.00
☐ Thunder Agents	8.50	16.50	10.00
☐ Tick Tock Tales	8.50	16.50	10.00
☐ Tim Holt	45.00	85.00	62.00
☐ Tiny Tot Comics	25.00	50.00	33.00
☐ Tip Top Comics	140.00	325.00	215.00
☐ TNT Comics	14.00	20.00	15.00
☐ Tomahawk	35.00	85.00	56.00
☐ Tom Mix Western	38.00	88.00	55.00
☐ Top-Notch Comics	110.00	275.00	190.00
☐ Top Secrets of F.B.I.	4.50	6.50	5.00
☐ Top Spot Comics	5.50	11.00	4.50
☐ Topsy-Turvy Comics	2.50	6.50	4.50
☐ Tor, (1954)	48.00	88.00	64.00
☐ Torchy	270.00	585.00	400.00
☐ Tough Kid Squad	390.00	685.00	530.00
☐ Tower of Shadows	2.00	5.00	3.00
☐ Toyland Comics	15.00	28.00	19.00
☐ Toy Town Comics	3.50	6.50	4.50

COMIC BOOKS / 275

	Current Price Range		Prior Year Average
☐ Treasure Comics	14.00	24.00	17.00
☐ True Crime Comics, (#2)	220.00	590.00	400.00
☐ True Life Secrets	2.50	4.50	3.00
☐ Tubby, (Color #381)	18.00	28.00	20.00
☐ Uncle Sam	125.00	325.00	215.00
☐ Uncle Scrooge, (Color #386)	140.00	320.00	210.00
☐ Underworld	30.00	50.00	35.00
☐ United Comics, (Fritz Ritz)	10.00	14.00	10.00
☐ U.S. Agent	3.50	6.50	4.50
☐ U.S.A. Comics	600.00	1350.00	900.00
☐ US. Jones	75.00	135.00	95.00
☐ Variety Comics	14.00	22.00	16.00
☐ Vault of Horror, (#12)	220.00	500.00	400.00
☐ Venus	75.00	125.00	100.00
☐ V Comics	75.00	125.00	100.00
☐ Vic Flint	3.50	6.50	4.50
☐ Vic Jordan	3.50	6.50	4.50
☐ Victory Comics	85.00	180.00	130.00
☐ Vic Verity	4.50	8.50	6.00
☐ Walt Disney's Comics & Stories	1450.00	3150.00	2200.00
☐ War Comics	30.00	55.00	38.00
☐ War Heroes, (1942)	14.00	28.00	18.00
☐ Warlock	3.50	8.00	5.00
☐ War Victory Adventures	50.00	85.00	62.00
☐ Weird Comics	90.00	210.00	140.00
☐ Weird Fantasy, (#13)	200.00	465.00	285.00
☐ Weird Science, (#12)	210.00	500.00	340.00
☐ Weird Science Fantasy, (#23)	50.00	95.00	60.00
☐ Western Comics	30.00	55.00	38.00
☐ Wham	45.00	115.00	72.00
☐ Whirlwind Comics	35.00	85.00	55.00
☐ Whiz Comics, (#2)	2800.00	4600.00	3600.00
☐ Wilbur Comics	50.00	90.00	65.00
☐ Wild West	10.00	14.00	10.00
☐ Wings	75.00	155.00	110.00
☐ Winnie Winkle	22.00	38.00	28.00
☐ Witty Comics	4.50	8.50	6.00
☐ Wonder Comics	42.00	82.00	58.00
☐ Wonder Woman	285.00	640.00	495.00
☐ Wonderworld	165.00	425.00	340.00
☐ World Famous Heroes	12.00	18.00	12.50
☐ World's Best Comics	320.00	800.00	550.00
☐ Wow Comics, (1941)	1550.00	3950.00	2800.00
☐ X-Mas	210.00	610.00	400.00
☐ X-Men	85.00	210.00	140.00
☐ Yankee Comics	38.00	88.00	60.00
☐ Yellow Claw	30.00	60.00	41.00
☐ Yellowjacket	20.00	35.00	24.00
☐ Young Allies Comics	310.00	820.00	545.00
☐ Young King Cole	4.50	8.50	6.00
☐ Young Life	3.50	6.50	4.50
☐ Young Romance	12.00	22.00	15.00
☐ Ziggy Pig and Silly Seal	15.00	30.00	19.00
☐ Zip Comics	180.00	320.00	240.00
☐ Zoo Funnies	2.50	4.50	3.00
☐ Zoot, (#2)	15.00	30.00	19.00

COMIC CHARACTER SPINOFFS

Popeye and Olive Oil, Dakin, all plastic . . . . $17.00-$22.00

It is doubtful that there is any one who hasn't been charmed and delighted with the magic of Walt Disney's creativity. It may be that your favorite character is the spunky Mickey Mouse, the shy, gentle Bambi, or the loving Snow White and her mischievous Seven Dwarfs.

These and many other Disney-inspired superstars are among the most loved entertainers of our time. The great success of the Disney ventures led to an immense number of items that were marketed over the years. Such items now enjoy status as highly desirable collectibles.

The first comic character to become three dimensional was the Yellow Kid, who was produced as a plaster, hand-painted doll in 1897. Many of these toys were produced in the United States, but some came from Germany and Japan, as well. The most sought after are the early tin wind up toys of the 1930's.

Prices have shown the same dramatic increases as comic books for the same reason — low survival rates. A wind up, lithographed Popeye in a rowboat, sold for $2.50 when it was first released in 1935. Although considered worthless for years, a recent bid of $3000 failed to separate it from its owner. While this increase is not the rule, it is indicative of the general market in comic spinoffs.

The many figurines, dolls, toys, household items and Disney signature pieces of all varieties, continue to show marked gains in values. Increasing numbers of collectors are being drawn to the Disneyana and are establishing it as a stable and profitable collector area. Many of America's most popular comic characters have been taken off the printed page or the animated movie screen and made three-dimensional.

COMIC CHARACTER SPINOFFS / 277

For a more extensive listing of comic character, you may refer to *The Official Price Guide to Toys* published by the House of Collectibles.

	Current Price Range	Prior Year Average
☐ **Annie,** c. 1982, porcelain doll, "Applause", released to coincide with movie "Annie", velvet dress, height 10″	35.00 45.00	40.00
☐ **Archie,** Emenee, c. 1969, metal tambourine	6.00 8.00	7.00
☐ **Aristocats, The,** Schmid, Walt Disney Prod., set of five figural music boxes, all play different tunes, height 6″	100.00 125.00	112.00
☐ **Bambi, Thumper And Girlfriend,** c. 1940, triple "Marble" figurine, sculpted by "A. Santini," height 6¾″	40.00 50.00	45.00
☐ **Barney Google,** boxed set of eight G.E. textolite Christmas light covers	60.00 70.00	62.00
☐ **Batman,** ceramic figural bank, height 7″	30.00 45.00	37.50
☐ **Batman,** National Periodical Publications, c. 1966, metal license plate, shows him in full figure in center over city, 6″x12″	6.00 9.00	7.50
☐ **Batman And Robin,** c. 1966, ceramic figural banks	65.00 85.00	75.00
☐ **Bugs Bunny,** Shaw And Co., c. 1940, ceramic figurine, seated with hands holding his face, height 4″	32.00 43.00	37.50
☐ **Bugs Bunny,** Warner Brothers, c. 1975, ceramic figurine, eating a carrot, height 5½″	8.00 12.00	10.00
☐ **Bugs Bunny,** Warner Brothers, c. 1940, ceramic figural planter, seated on white picket fence, height 5″	38.50 47.00	43.50
☐ **Bugs Bunny,** Lafayette, c. 1978, wristwatch, in display box	24.00 32.00	28.00
☐ **Bulldog Drummond,** c. 1940, ceramic bulldog bank, promotional piece for radio show	28.00 37.00	32.50
☐ **Buster Brown,** c. 1930, bisque figural promotional piece, marked "Buster Brown Shoes", height 3″	10.00 16.00	14.00
☐ **Buster Brown,** c. 1910, demitasse china cup, shows him with Tige, who's balancing a tea pot on his nose, height 2″	20.00 29.00	25.00
☐ **Campbell Kids,** beautiful bisque dolls, jointed head, arms and legs, dressed in red and white, height 9″	100.00 200.00	150.00
☐ **Clarabelle,** F.B.A. Industries, c. 1950, musical wind up face of Howdy's favorite clown, in box	70.00 80.00	75.00
☐ **Clarabelle,** c. 1950, Terrycloth "Rag Doll," height 11″	13.50 18.50	16.00
☐ **Clutch Cargo And Space Angel,** c. 1950, pair of pin back buttons, early animated T.V. characters, diameter 1¼″	30.00 40.00	35.00
☐ **Coachman,** c. 1940, drinking glass, full figure in orange with poem on back, height 4⅜″	10.00 15.00	12.50
☐ **Conan The Conqueror,** c. 1974, pin back button, signed Caldwell	4.00 6.00	5.00
☐ **Crusader Rabbit,** T.A.P. Inc., c. 1950, ring toss game, cardboard figure and rings wood base	12.00 16.00	14.00

278 / COMIC CHARACTER SPINOFFS

	Current Price Range		Prior Year Average
☐ **Daddy Warbucks And Sandy,** c. 1930, pair of bisque figurines, Japan, height 1½″	30.00	39.00	35.00
☐ **Daffy Duck,** c. 1940, Shaw and Co., ceramic figurine, height 5¼″	58.00	65.00	62.50
☐ **Daffy Duck,** Brice, c. 1940, wooden paper lithographed pull, height 5½″	32.00	40.00	37.50
☐ **Dagwood,** Hazelle's, c. 1945, marionette, plastic head, hands and shoes, cloth over wood body, height 14″	20.00	25.00	22.50
☐ **Dagwood,** King Features, c. 1947, "The Dagwood Sandwich" tin musical kazoo	20.00	25.00	22.50
☐ **Daisy, Dagwood And Blondie's Dog,** Comic Toy MFG, Corp., c. 1940, rubber doll, collar and tag, swivels at neck, height 12″	50.00	70.00	65.00
☐ **Darth Vader,** California Originals, c. 1978, ceramic head tankard mug	20.00	30.00	25.00
☐ **Darth Vader,** Twenty Century Fox, c. 1977 metal figural face on silver chain necklace	12.50	4.00	3.00
☐ **Dennis The Menace,** battery operated toy, tin and vinyl plays xylophone, in original box	120.00	150.00	125.00
☐ **Dennis The Menace,** c. 1970, ceramic figurine, height 8″	10.00	15.00	12.50
☐ **Dennis The Menace,** Determined Productions, c. 1977, Christmas mug in original box	3.50	5.50	4.50
☐ **Dennis The Menace,** c. 1970, ceramic figurine, height 7″	10.00	15.00	12.50
☐ **Dennis The Menace And Ruff,** Determined Productions, c. 1977, pair, ceramic figural Christmas ornaments	8.00	12.00	10.00
☐ **Dennis The Menace And Ruff,** Determined Productions, c. 1979, pair of figural book ends, Dennis is sitting holding teddy bear, Ruff is standing with head tilted	30.00	40.00	35.00
☐ **Dick Tracy,** Seymour Products, c. 1940, camera, black bakelite with embossed metal plate with Tracy's picture on it	28.00	37.00	32.00
☐ **Dick Tracy,** Whitman, c. 1934, card game	5.00	9.00	7.00
☐ **Disney Band,** Schmid, six pewter figurines, set includes: Mickey The Bandleader, Minnie with piano, Donald with drums, Daisy with violin, Goofy with bass and Dumbo with sax	125.00	175.00	150.00
☐ **Disney Characters,** United China Co., miniature ceramic figurines, pie-eyed Mickey, pie-eyed Minnie, Donald Duck, Pluto, Dumbo, Mickey Bandleader, Mickey with tuba, Mickey with trumpet, Minnie with drum, Minnie with cymbals, Donald with guitar, Donald with trumpet, Goofy with bass and Goofy with drum, height 3¼″, all instruments	2.50	3.75	3.50
☐ **Disneyland,** 25th Anniversary coin, pictures Mickey, Minnie and Donald in relief, diameter 1⅝″	4.00	5.00	4.50
☐ **Disneyland,** crystal platter, has Mickey, Minnie, Donald, Goofy, Pluto and Winnie The Pooh dancing around perimeter with castle in center, diameter 12¾″	40.00	60.00	50.00

COMIC CHARACTER SPINOFFS / 279

	Current Price Range		Prior Year Average
☐ **Donald Duck,** c. 1935, bisque figurine, head to one side with long bill open wide, height 3¼" ...	30.00	40.00	35.00
☐ **Donald Duck,** Japan, c. 1930, bisque figurine, hands at side, with head turned to left and long bill wide open, height 3¼"	52.00	68.00	60.00
☐ **Donald Duck,** Japan, c. 1930, bisque figurine, riding three-wheel scooter	30.00	36.00	32.50
☐ **Donald Duck,** Royal Orleans, c. 1980, bisque figurine, in stocking cap with Christmas wreath ...	8.00	12.00	11.00
☐ **Donald Duck,** c. 1935, bisque figurine, long billed with hands on hips and head slightly turned, height 4½"	100.00	150.00	125.00
☐ **Donald Duck,** c. 1940, bisque figurine, on three-wheel scooter	15.00	20.00	18.00
☐ **Donald Duck,** c. 1939, Disney All Star Parade drinking glass, depicting Huey, Dewey and Louie and "Donna" Duck, forerunner of "Daisy," height 4⅜"	18.00	22.00	20.00
☐ **Donald Duck,** c. 1930, drinking glass, long billed Donald	15.00	17.00	16.00
☐ **Donald Duck And Jose Carioca,** c. 1942, "Brazil" song sheet music, from movie "Saludos Amigos"	14.00	19.00	17.50
☐ **Donald Duck And Ludwig Von Drake,** RCA, c. 1961, pair of ceramic drinking mugs, full figure of Donald in relief and Ludwig's head in relief, height 3½"	16.00	20.00	19.00
☐ **Donald Duck And Pluto,** Sun Rubber, c. 1940, rubber car, Donald driving and Pluto in rumble seat, length 6½"	16.00	28.00	18.00
☐ **Dopey,** Leeds, c. 1940, ceramic figurine, height 6½"	25.00	32.00	27.50
☐ **Dopey,** c. 1940, ceramic figural planter, height 6"	20.00	25.00	22.50
☐ **Dragnet,** Sherry T.V., c. 1955, brass plated tin "Badge 714" in original package with Jack Webb on it	11.00	15.00	13.00
☐ **Dr. Kildare,** MGM, c. 1962, game by Ideal	7.00	9.00	8.00
☐ **Dr. Seuss,** Mattel, c. 1970, "The Cat In The Hat" pop-up metal music box, plays a tune and he pops out	15.00	20.00	17.50
☐ **Dumbo,** c. 1950, ceramic bank marked "Disneyland," height 7"	40.00	47.50	45.00
☐ **Dumbo,** c. 1940, ceramic figural bank, incised "Dumbo," height 6½"	32.00	40.00	35.00
☐ **Dumbo,** California Originals, ceramic figural cookie jar, says "Dumbo's Greatest Cookies On Earth," height 12"	20.00	38.00	22.50
☐ **Flash Gordon,** c. 1951, Christmas card and original envelope, with his face in center of ornament surrounded by holly rocket ship inside, length 6"	7.00	10.00	9.50
☐ **Flash Gordon,** pin back button, signed Alex Raymond, shows full figure of Flash dueling Ming the Merciless, diameter 3"	5.50	7.50	6.50
☐ **Flash Gordon And The Martian,** King Features, c. 1965, plastic kit, "Revell," makes two figurines, unopened in box	22.00	27.00	25.00

280 / COMIC CHARACTER SPINOFFS

	Current Price Range		Prior Year Average
☐ **Flintstones, The,** Hanna Barbera, c. 1961, heavy ceramic bank, Fred and Wilma in relief on front and a heart "Fred Loves Wilma" on back, height 8"	40.00	50.00	45.00
☐ **Funnies, The,** c. 1940, Welch candy cards, complete set of all the famous comic strip characters of era	100.00	140.00	125.00
☐ **Gabby And Snitch,** Paramount Pictures, Inc., c. 1939, pair of figural tin sand molds, from Gulliver's Travels cartoon movie, height 4"	14.00	16.00	15.00
☐ **Garfield,** United Features Syndicate, c. 1978, cloisonne pins, set of nine	17.00	21.00	20.00
☐ **Garfield,** Enesco, c. 1981, ceramic figural bank, sitting with toothy grin, height 4¾"	18.00	22.00	20.00
☐ **Garfield,** Enesco, c. 1981, ceramic figural bank, sitting with arms crossed, height 6"	18.00	22.00	20.00
☐ **Garfield,** Enesco, c. 1981, ceramic figural "Chair Bank," Garfield is sitting in big green chair wearing Santa cap, height 6½"	22.00	30.00	27.50
☐ **Goofy,** California Originals, c. 1970, ceramic cannister lithographed cookie jar	12.00	17.00	15.00
☐ **Goofy,** California Originals, c. 1970, ceramic, figural cookie jar, wearing bakers hat standing up lifting cookie jar, "Goofy's Cookie Co.," height 12¾"	20.00	25.00	22.50
☐ **Goofy,** United China, Co., c. 1970, composition "Trailer" bank, sitting on log with fish by trailer, height 4½"	6.00	9.00	8.00
☐ **Gumby,** c. 1960, plush doll, googlie eyes, height 12"	8.00	10.00	9.00
☐ **Hairless Joe,** Capp Enterprises, Inc., c. 1968, tambourine from "Dog Patch USA," in box, diameter 6½"	8.00	12.00	10.00
☐ **Hanna Barbera,** c. 1979, "Cartoon Cards," boxed game	3.00	5.00	4.00
☐ **Happy,** c. 1930, drinking glass, full figure in green with poem on reverse, height 4¾"	14.00	18.00	16.00
☐ **Harold Teen,** Japan, c. 1930, bisque figurine, height 3¾"	34.00	43.00	37.50
☐ **Hopalong Cassidy... And Lucky At The Double X' Ranch,"** Doubleday And Co., c. 1950, pop-up book, length 11"	20.00	23.00	25.00
☐ **Horace Horsecollar,** c. 1930, drinking glass, full figure in red, bending over for coin, height 4¾"	20.00	25.00	22.50
☐ **Horace Horsecollar,** c. 1930, juice glass, full figure in black, bending over for coin, height 3½"	14.00	18.00	16.00
☐ **Hot Stuff,** c. 1960, ceramic figurine, Harvey famous cartoons, holding pitchfork, height 7"	35.00	41.00	37.50
☐ **Humphrey Pennyworth,** c. 1940, stuffed cloth doll, plastic face and rubber hands, height 18"	40.00	44.00	42.00
☐ **Howdy Doody,** Jolly Jumbo Inc., c. 1949, behavior chart	25.00	29.00	27.50
☐ **Howdy Doody,** Ideal, c. 1950, doll, moveable jaw, height 20"	43.00	52.00	48.00

COMIC CHARACTER SPINOFFS / 281

	Current Price Range		Prior Year Average
☐ **Jiggs And Maggie,** Borgfeldt, c. 1934, three bisque figures of Jiggs, Maggie and daughter, Rosie, height 4″	80.00	100.00	90.00
☐ **Joe Palooka,** Ham Fisher, c. 1947, sheet music, Joe being carried on shoulder of fans	18.00	22.00	20.00
☐ **Joe Palooka,** c. 1930, wood jointed doll, height 4″	34.00	43.00	37.50
☐ **Katnip,** c. 1950, vinyl and cloth hand puppet, in box	12.00	16.00	14.00
☐ **Kayo,** Germany, c. 1930, bisque "Nodder," "Moon Mullins" little brother, very good condition, height 2½″	42.00	48.00	46.00
☐ **Kayo,** c. 1930, cheesecloth doll, "Moon Mullins" comic strip, height 11½″	38.00	43.00	40.00
☐ **Kermit The Frog,** Sigma, c. 1980, ceramic floral arranger, seated on top playing banjo — C: Jim Henson	22.00	27.00	25.00
☐ **Kermit The Frog,** Henson, c. 1980, large figural ceramic round covered box, Muppet playing banjo	24.00	30.00	28.50
☐ **Kewpies,** L.F. Inc., c. 1979, set of four cloisonne pins, height 1″	11.00	16.00	15.00
☐ **King Features,** c. 1950, promotional glass dish ash tray, with character lithographed over it, Henry, Prince Valiant, Blondie and Dagwood, and Maggie and Jiggs, length 8″	40.00	48.00	45.00
☐ **Kitz 'N' Katz,** pin back button in black and red on white background, diameter 1½″	2.00	3.00	2.50
☐ **Kliban's Cat,** Sigma, c. 1975, ceramic figural music box, sitting on table listenin' to phonograph, height 7″	40.00	48.00	45.00
☐ **Lady And Tramp,** c. 1970, double bisque figurine, having spaghetti dinner over candlelight, height 7″	25.00	30.00	28.50
☐ **Lady And The Tramp,** c. 1980, Grolier bisque Christmas figurine in original box	38.00	42.00	40.00
☐ **Lady And the Tramp,** c. 1980, Grolier Christmas plate	18.00	22.00	20.00
☐ **Little Audrey,** Gund, c. 1950, vinyl and cloth puppet in box	12.00	19.00	14.00
☐ **Little Iodine,** c. 1960, ceramic figural bank, in sitting position	46.00	56.00	52.50
☐ **Little King,** K.F.S., c. 1949, Post Toasties tin ring, "giveaway" cereal premium	4.00	6.00	5.00
☐ **Little Lulu,** Schmid, c. 1970, ceramic figural revolving music box, playing accordion, plays "I'd Like To Teach The World To Sing," height 7″	38.00	46.00	42.40
☐ **Little Orphan Annie,** Bradley, c. 1927, boxed board game, length 17″	40.00	54.00	48.00
☐ **Little Orphan Annie,** N. Y. News Co., c. 1970, ceramic figural revolving music box, standing by Sandy waving, plays "I'd Like To Teach The World To Sing"	40.00	50.00	45.00
☐ **Looney Tunes,** c. 1975, pin back buttons, diameter 3½″.			
☐ Bugs Bunny, star spangled attire	6.00	8.00	7.00
☐ Tweety, skipping rope	5.00	7.00	6.00
☐ Daffy Duck	5.00	7.00	6.00

282 / COMIC CHARACTER SPINOFFS

	Current Price Range	Prior Year Average
☐ **Looney Tunes,** Warner Bros., c. 1979, set of ten bisque figural bells, Bugs, Elmer, Porky, Petunia, Daffy, Sylvester, Tweety, Yosemite Sam, Wile E. Coyote and Road Runner, height 4"	60.00 70.00	65.00
☐ **Looney Tunes,** Warner Bros., c. 1980, set of different pin back buttons, diameter 1¾"	5.00 7.00	6.00
☐ **Mr. Magoo,** UPA Pictures, c. 1960, double deck set of playing cards, advertising "G.E., Light Bulbs"	10.00 14.00	12.00
☐ **Main Street Parade,** triple bisque figurine, featuring Mickey Mouse with baton, Donald Duck with horn and Goofy on bass drum, height 6¾"	31.00 38.00	35.00
☐ **Mammy Yocum,** c. 1957, fabric and vinyl doll, "Baby Barry Toy," height 13½"	24.00 30.00	27.50
☐ **Man From U.N.C.L.E., The,** Gilbert, c. 1965, action figures, Napoleon Solo and Illya Kryakin	60.00 70.00	65.00
☐ **March Hare, The,** c. 1970, ceramic figurine, height 6"	12.00 16.00	14.00
☐ **Marx Bros.,** Arnart, porcelain art sculptures, Harpo, Chico, and Groucho, from the movie "Go West," height 10½"	70.00 80.00	75.00
☐ **Mary Poppins,** c. 1964, ceramic figural medicine spoon holder, she's holding medicine bottle and spoon, height 6"	15.00 20.00	17.50
☐ **Mickey McGuire, Himself,** Japan, c. 1930, bisque figurine, "Toonerville Trolley" character	35.00 42.00	38.00
☐ **Mickey Mouse,** Bradley, c. 1970, alarm clock, two big red bells on top, height 9½"	28.00 36.00	32.50
☐ **Mickey Mouse,** Modern Toys, wind-up vinyl figural walker, sold only in Japan, height 4"	6.00 7.00	6.50
☐ **Mickey Mouse,** c. 1930, wood figural door stop of "pie-eyed" Mickey, height 13"	33.00 42.00	37.50
☐ **Mickey Mouse,** Bradley, c. 1978, wristwatch, commemorating his 50th birthday.		
☐ Round dial, 1⅛"	25.00 35.00	30.00
☐ Round dial, 1¼"	35.00 45.00	40.00
☐ Rectangular dial, 1"x1⅛"	35.00 45.00	40.00
☐ **Mickey Mouse and Donald Duck,** J. Chein And Co., c. 1940, tin sand pail, also shows Daisy and nephews at the zoo, height 4½"	24.00 32.00	27.50
☐ **Mickey Mouse, Donald Duck And Goofy,** Masterwork, c. 1976, Bicentennial belt buckle, item laminated with colorful scene of the three of them marching and carrying flag as "Minutemen"	6.00 10.00	9.00
☐ **Mickey Mouse, Donald Duck And Goofy,** Schmid, ceramic Christmas ornament, height 3½"	13.00 17.00	15.00
☐ **Mickey Mouse, Donald Duck And Pluto,** c. 1930, "Patriot China" cup, shows them in a tug of war scene	6.00 8.00	7.00
☐ **Moon Mullins,** c. 1930, "Cracker Jack" tin comic stand up "Oval," height 2"	22.00 27.00	25.00
☐ **Moon Mullins,** c. 1930, wood jointed doll, he's got derby on and is smoking a cigar, height 5½"	50.00 60.00	55.00
☐ **Mork And Mindy,** Aviva, c. 1979, enamelled jewelry, six different styles on large colorful counter display	40.00 50.00	45.00

COMIC CHARACTER SPINOFFS / 283

	Current Price Range		Prior Year Average

- **Muppets, The,** Sigma, c. 1980, ceramic figural bookends, Kermit sitting on books and Fozzie leaning against books, by Jim Henson 40.00 50.00 45.00
- **Muppets, The,** Miss Piggy, Kermit, Fozzie and Animal Set of four cars, with each of these TV stars driving 26.00 32.00 28.00
- **Muppets, The,** Henson, c. 1980, set of four kilncraft mugs, includes: Kermit, Miss Piggy, Rowlf and Fozzie Bear 18.00 22.00 20.00
- **Mush,** pin back button, "Just Kids Safety Club," "The Globe," diameter 1¼" 18.00 22.00 20.00
- **Mutt, Jeff's Side-Kick,** Germany, c. 1930, bisque frozen action figurine, height 3¼" 38.00 46.00 42.50
- **Mutt And Jeff,** Bud Fischer, c. 1912, blotter, red, white and black, advertising "The Musical Comedy" 12.00 16.00 14.00
- **Nancy,** United Features, c. 1970, ceramic figural revolving music box, height 7" 38.00 46.00 42.50
- **Nautilus, The,** Sutcliffe Pressings Ltd., c. 1960, metal wind up toy submarine from Disney's "20,000 Leagues Under The Sea," length 10" 18.00 26.00 22.50
- **Nicodemus,** pin back button, "Just Kids Safety Club," "The San Diego Union," diameter 1¼" ... 18.00 22.00 20.00
- **Nipper,** RCA, c. 1940, seated ceramic figural salt and pepper shakers, promoting RCA's famous trademarked dog, height 3½" 20.00 24.00 22.00
- **Peanuts Gang,** United Features, c. 1970, composition figural banks, in baseball gear, height 7½".
  - Snoopy 10.00 15.00 12.50
  - Charlie Brown 10.00 15.00 12.50
  - Linus 10.00 15.00 12.50
  - Schroeder 10.00 15.00 12.50
  - Peppermint Patty 10.00 15.00 12.50
- **Peanuts Gang,** United Features, c. 1971, iron on patches, Weber's Bread premiums in original mailer, Charlie Brown, Lucy, and Frieda 5.00 7.00 6.00
- **Penguin Mobile, The, (From Batman)** Corgi –259 .. 5.00 9.00 7.50
- **Pepe Lew Pew,** Warner Bros., cloisonne pin, full figure with golf club, diameter 1¼" 3.00 5.00 4.00
- **Peter Pan,** Gare Mold Co., ceramic figure, height 11½" 28.00 36.00 32.50
- **Peter Pan,** Walt Disney Productions, c. 1950, seated vinyl figurine with cloth jacket 22.00 35.00 27.50
- **Peter Pan And Tinkerbell,** c. 1970, pair of ceramic figurines, seated on tree stump, she's kneeling, height 5" 10.00 14.00 12.00
- **Peter Weatherbird,** bisque "Nodder" figurine, Germany, height 3½" 80.00 90.00 85.00
- **Phanton, The, And The Voodoo Witch Doctor,** King Features, c. 1965, plastic figurine kit, Revell, height 8" 21.00 27.00 25.00
- **Pink Panther,** Royal Orleans, c. 1982, ceramic figural music box, dressed as Santa looking into big bag of presents, plays "Santa's Comin' To Town," height 5" 30.00 36.00 33.00

284 / COMIC CHARACTER SPINOFFS

	Current Price Range		Prior Year Average
☐ **Pinocchio,** c. 1938, bisque figurine, height 3¼" ..	27.00	33.00	30.00
☐ **Pinocchio,** Ceramica de Cuernavaca, c. 1960, ceramic figural bust cookie jar, height 12"	40.00	50.00	45.00
☐ **Pluto,** Marx, c. 1966, tin wind up toy, musical pluto, he goes around a track and his tail plays a tune	32.00	43.00	38.00
☐ **Pluto,** vinyl figural bank, moveable arm, drops coin into dog house, height 9"	6.50	8.50	7.50
☐ **Pluto And Goofy,** Radnor, c. 1970, set of two bone china thimbles, in box	13.00	16.00	15.00
☐ **Pluto And Mickey Mouse,** Patriot China, c. 1930, ceramic cup, seated Pluto	45.00	50.00	45.00
☐ **Popeye,** Saalfield, c. 1934, book, titled "Popeye," height 8"	24.00	32.00	28.00
☐ **Popeye,** King Features, c. 1929, set of eight G.E. textolite Christmas light covers, lithographed box	55.00	65.00	60.00
☐ **Popeye,** ED-U-CARDS, c. 1950, card game with 35 colorful cards, in original box	3.00	5.00	4.00
☐ **Popeye And Olive Oyl,** c. 1970, pair of two pewter figurines, spoontiques, valentines hearts marked "With Love," height 2½"	20.00	26.00	24.00
☐ **Popeye And Olive Oyl,** Schmid, c. 1970, set of two ceramic figural music boxes, height 8¼"	82.00	87.00	85.00
☐ **Popeye And Olive,** Vandor, set of two ceramic figural picture frames, figure of Olive holding her hands thinking "Hearts," figure of Popeye with flowers in one hand, height 6¾"	42.00	47.00	45.00
☐ **Popeye And Olive,** Vandor, c. 1980, ceramic figural salt and pepper shakers, he's holding can of spinach, she's holding her hands by her face, height 7½"	16.00	20.00	18.00
☐ **Popeye And Olive,** Vandor, c. 1980, ceramic heart shaped picture frame, pictures Popeye giving flowers to Olive on edges, height 6"	13.00	17.00	15.00
☐ **Popeye And Sweet Pea,** Vandor, ceramic figural salt and pepper shakers, they're sitting in a wooden boat, height 3"	16.00	20.00	18.00
☐ **Porky And Petunia,** Warner Bros., c. 1977, set of ceramic figurines, with chef's hat, she's pouring coffee, height 4½"	18.00	22.00	20.00
☐ **Porky And Petunia,** Shaw And Co., c. 1940, set of two ceramic figurines, height 5½"	72.00	82.00	78.50
☐ **Roy Rogers,** American Music Inc., c. 1942, song folio −1, 56 pages	14.00	18.00	16.00
☐ **Saint, The,** Corgi, −320, Jaguar XJS	7.00	9.00	8.50
☐ **Schmoo,** Al Capp, c. 1948, ceramic figural set of male and female salt and pepper shakers, character from Li'l' Abner comic strip, height 4"	23.00	33.00	27.50
☐ **Scrappy And Margy And Yippy,** Kirk Guild, c. 1930, set of three figural bars of soap, illustrated box	44.00	52.00	45.00
☐ **Sesame Street,** Gorham, c. 1971, set of ten composition figurines, plus lamppost, Big Bird, Ernie, Cookie Monster, Oscar, Bert, Grover, The Count, Inspector Snuffleupagus and Gonzo, height 7" ..	70.00	80.00	75.00

COMIC CHARACTER SPINOFFS / 285

	Current Price Range		Prior Year Average
☐ **Seven, Dwarfs, The,** c. 1930, bisque figurines, height 3⅛".			
☐ Doc	15.00	20.00	18.50
☐ Grumpy	15.00	20.00	18.50
☐ Sleepy	10.00	14.00	12.50
☐ **Skeezix,** King Features, c. 1930, tin figural hanging toothbrush holder "Listerine," toothpaste promotional item, height 6"	15.00	30.00	20.00
☐ **Sleeping Beauty,** c. 1958, drinking glasses, multicolored, height 5".			
☐ Sleeping Beauty Touching Spindle	4.00	7.00	6.00
☐ Prince Phillip To Rescue	4.00	6.00	5.00
☐ Samsom The Horse	4.00	6.00	5.00
☐ **Sluggo, Nancy's Boyfriend,** Schmid, c. 1970, ceramic figural revolving music box, walking with hands in pocket, plays "Who Can I Turn To"	50.00	60.00	55.00
☐ **Snoopy And The Peanuts Gang,** Anri, c. 1968, figural wooden music boxes.			
☐ **Charlie Brown** with baseball cap and bat, plays "Take Me Out To The Ball Game"	40.00	50.00	45.00
☐ **Linus And Snoopy,** Linus is clutching his blanket with Snoopy following closely, plays "Release Me"	45.00	55.00	50.00
☐ **Schroeder,** he's seated at piano, plays "Letmotiv Kaiserkonzert"	40.00	50.00	45.00
☐ **Snoopy,** playing hockey, plays "My Way"	30.00	40.00	35.00
☐ **Snoopy,** ice skating, plays "The Skater's Waltz"	30.00	40.00	35.00
☐ **Snoopy,** World War I, "Flying Ace" in battleground scene: plays "Pack Up Your Troubles," and "It's A Long Way To Tipperary"	40.00	50.00	45.00
☐ **Snoopy And Peanuts Gang,** United Features, composition "Bobbing Head" figurines:			
☐ **Snoopy,** sitting	5.00	7.00	6.00
☐ **Snoopy,** Joe Cool	5.00	7.00	6.00
☐ **Snoopy,** Flying Ace	5.00	7.00	6.00
☐ **Snoopy,** Santa Claus	5.00	7.00	6.00
☐ **Charlie Brown**	5.00	7.00	6.00
☐ **Lucy**	5.00	7.00	6.00
☐ **Woodstock**	5.00	7.00	6.00
☐ **Snow White,** Anri, c. 1971, wooden music box, figure of Snow White and Dopey revolve	90.00	100.00	95.00
☐ **Snow White And Dopey,** c. 1960, ceramic salt and pepper shakers, height 3¾"	20.00	28.00	24.00
☐ **Snow White And Dopey,** c. 1970, double bisque figurine, bending over him to kiss him on top of head, height 6½"	27.00	33.00	30.00
☐ **Snow White And Dopey,** Royal Orleans, porcelain figurine, she's bending down with hands folded and he's looking up at her showing her flowers, height 6½"	45.00	55.00	50.00
☐ **Snow White And Dopey,** Wedgewood plate, in relief, white on blue, diameter 6½"	65.00	75.00	60.00
☐ **Snow White And Seven Dwarfs,** Schmid, c. 1980, complete set of eight pewter figurines	150.00	200.00	175.00
☐ **Spiderman,** Corgi #266, Spiderbike, in box	7.00	9.00	8.50

286 / COMIC CHARACTER SPINOFFS

	Current Price Range		Prior Year Average
☐ **Spiderman,** Corgi #261, Spider Buggy with Green Goblin, in box	8.00	11.00	9.00
☐ **Star Wars,** Bradley, c. 1977, Darth Vader wristwatch, in box	20.00	27.00	25.00
☐ **Star Wars,** H. E. Harris And Co., c. 1977, postage stamp collecting kit	6.00	9.00	7.00
☐ **Superman,** pin back advertising button, showing full figure of him promoting "7-Up," diameter 1¾"	5.00	7.00	6.00
☐ **Tom And Jerry,** Gorham, c. 1980, ceramic figural bookends, Tom's on books reaching for Jerry	25.00	30.00	27.50
☐ **Tarzan,** c. 1930, ceramic figurine, Cheetah standing between his legs, height 4½"	31.00	39.00	35.00
☐ **Three Pigs, The,** Walt Disney Enterprises, tin sand pail, "Ohio Art," playing at beach with Big Bad Wolf lurking behind post, height 3"	40.00	45.00	42.50
☐ **Thumper,** c. 1960, "Soaky" figural plastic bottle, height 9½"	7.00	9.00	8.00
☐ **Tilda,** Germany, c. 1930, bisque "Nodder," from "The Gumps," height 3¾"	74.00	83.00	79.50
☐ **Tom And Jerry,** Gorham, c. 1980, ceramic figural mugs, brown Jerry face, gray Tom face	14.00	20.00	17.00
☐ **Tom And Jerry,** Gorham, c. 1980, ceramic figural mugs, figures are mug handles, height 4"	14.00	22.00	17.00
☐ **Tom And Jerry And Droopy,** MGM, c. 1975, wind up walking figures, in boxes	16.00	20.00	18.00
☐ **Uncle Walt And Skeezix,** King, c. 1930, pair of cheesecloth dolls, famous Gasoline Alley characters, height 12"	70.00	80.00	75.00
☐ **Uncle Walt And Skeezix,** c. 1945, set of two multicolored chalkware figurines, height 6"	45.00	55.00	50.00
☐ **Walt Disney,** Walt Disney Productions, c. 1956, "Cartooning Cards," set of 18 character cards with full figure in color on front, and instructions on how to draw that character on back	50.00	60.00	55.00
☐ **Walt Disney,** c. 1940, complete set of 100 World War II insignia stamps in albums, premiums of the New York Mirror	70.00	80.00	75.00
☐ **Wimpy,** King Features, c. 1940, rubber figural squeeze toy, height 8"	26.00	32.00	28.00
☐ **Windy Bear,** Walter Lantz, c. 1958, "Napco" ceramic planter, height 7"	40.00	46.00	42.50
☐ **Winnie The Pooh,** Schmid, set of nine pewter figurines, includes: Pooh, Tigger, Eeyore, S. J. Gopher, Piglet, Rabbit, Owl, Kanga and Roo, and Christopher Robin, height 2¼"	165.00	200.00	185.00
☐ **Yogi Bear And Friends,** Spoontiques, c. 1981, set of five pewter figurines, includes Yogi, Boo Boo, Huckleberry Hound, Quick Draw McGraw and Top Cat	35.00	45.00	40.00
☐ **Yosemite Sam,** Duncan, c. 1975, ceramic figurine, full figure of him with both guns raised in the air, height 11"	45.00	57.00	52.50
☐ **Ziggy,** Universal Press Syndicate, c. 1980, bisque Christmas bell, "Merry Christmas 1980," figural Ziggy holding on to end of chain which rings bell	8.00	13.00	11.00

CORKSCREWS

Kitchen Gadget, double lever corkscrew, #504, iron, c. 1870's **$175.00-225.00**

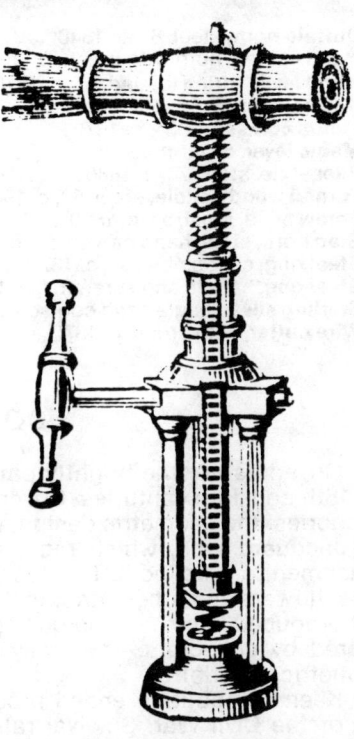

With the invention of corks in the 17th century came the invention of the corkscrew. Throughout the centuries, hundreds of various devices were made to extract corks from bottles. The most simple designs still remain the most efficient.

Corkscrews use various devices, such as gears, levers and screws, to produce enough force to remove the cork from its bottle. Some, however, are so intricate that they must have been designed to fascinate and amaze the user by their inability to do their job very well. Corkscrews can be collected according to their usefulness, material of which they were made, their decorative handles, or design.

Most specimens are marked with a manufacturer's name and patent date. These are clues to the age and rarity of a piece, as are workmanship and patina. Other than extremely rare corkscrews, most are moderately priced and prove to be a rather interesting collectible.

	Current Price Range		Prior Year Average
☐ **American,** folding corkscrew, 6″, c. 1900	18.00	22.00	17.50
☐ **Anheuser Busch,** brass plate, 3″, c. 1900	22.00	28.00	22.50
☐ **Animal design,** steel, 5″, c. 1880	12.00	18.00	12.50
☐ **Bone,** metal capped, 3¾″	42.00	52.00	45.00
☐ **Bone handle,** genuine steel, 6″, c. 1900	18.00	22.00	17.50

	Current Price Range		Prior Year Average
☐ **Buffalo horn,** steel, 8″, c. 1840	28.00	32.00	27.50
☐ **Hand carved,** horn with brush, 8″, c. 1870	52.00	62.00	55.00
☐ **Hand lever spring loaded,** 5″, c. 1910	18.00	22.00	17.50
☐ **Iron corkscrew,** 6″, c. 1900	28.00	32.00	27.50
☐ **Lunds corkscrew,** 5″, c. 1870	22.00	28.00	22.50
☐ **Magic lever,** 5″, c. 1840	52.00	62.00	55.00
☐ **Plier style,** steel, 7″, c. 1880	22.00	28.00	22.50
☐ **Turned wood handle,** steel, 6″, c. 1900	22.00	28.00	22.50
☐ **Screw style,** steel, 5″, c. 1870	42.00	52.00	45.00
☐ **Stag horn,** steel, hand carved, 6″, c. 1880	80.00	90.00	77.00
☐ **Steel ring,** collapsible, 3″, c. 1870	22.00	28.00	22.50
☐ **Steel ring,** handle and screw, 5″, c. 1880	22.00	28.00	22.50
☐ **Sterling silver,** eagle head corkscrew, 5″, c. 1870	110.00	130.00	110.00
☐ **Wire cutter,** with brush, c. 1870	32.00	38.00	32.50

COVERLETS

Coverlets are the brightly patterned spreads used to decorate beds in the 18th and 19th centuries. Coverlet designs generally fall into two distinct categories: the geometric design, which could be produced on any loom and the Jacquard type, which required the use of a special French-invented attachment on the loom. The Jacquard device permitted the weaving of pictures, flowers and other intricate designs into the coverlet. The Jacquard was first produced in the second quarter of the 19th century and is the type most favored by collectors. They may be worth up to 10 times the price of a geometric coverlet.

Keen competition ended production of the Jacquard coverlets by the end of the Civil War. Survival rates are fairly low, as many coverlets had second careers as horse blankets, etc. Finding one in like-new condition is a collector's dream come true.

☐ **Birds,** flowers, black and white	285.00	335.00	300.00
☐ **Butterflies,** blue, 6′ x 6′	52.00	72.00	60.00
☐ **Crewel pattern**	300.00	350.00	300.00
☐ **Crochet,** popcorn pattern	300.00	350.00	300.00
☐ **Double woven,** indigo and cream	260.00	280.00	255.00
☐ **Double woven,** blue and white, geometric design	110.00	135.00	112.00
☐ **Handloomed,** blue and white, c. 1840's	160.00	210.00	175.00
☐ **Jacquard woven,** blue, white, patriotic motif, signed, c. 1860	850.00	1350.00	1050.00
☐ **Jacquard woven,** red, eagle motif, signed	260.00	310.00	275.00
☐ **Jacquard woven,** red, eagle motif, unsigned	220.00	300.00	238.00
☐ **Jacquard woven,** red, green and white, single panel, oak-leaf and flower design	220.00	300.00	238.00
☐ **Jacquard woven,** red, tan, ivory, eagle motif, "Independence, Virtue, Liberty"	825.00	925.00	850.00
☐ **Jacquard woven,** red and white, single panel, floral motif	300.00	400.00	320.00
☐ **Jacquard woven,** red and white, single panel, lilies and floral sprays, signed	135.00	210.00	162.00
☐ **Jacquard woven,** red, white and blue, exotic birds feeding their young	650.00	850.00	725.00

COWBOY GEAR / 289

	Current Price Range		Prior Year Average
☐ **Jacquard woven,** red, white and blue, single panel, star and flower motif	200.00	220.00	190.00
☐ **Jacquard woven,** red, white and green, single panel, flowers, star, spread winged American eagle	210.00	230.00	195.00
☐ **Jacquard double woven,** blue and white, rosettes, leaves, snowflakes	360.00	410.00	375.00
☐ **Silk quilted,** "Pillar Stripe," yellow and white, vine with pink and white fruit	200.00	300.00	225.00
☐ **Tree of Life,** fringed, signed, c. 1848	450.00	550.00	475.00
☐ **Wool and cotton,** log cabin pattern, matching pillow	135.00	185.00	140.00

COWBOY GEAR

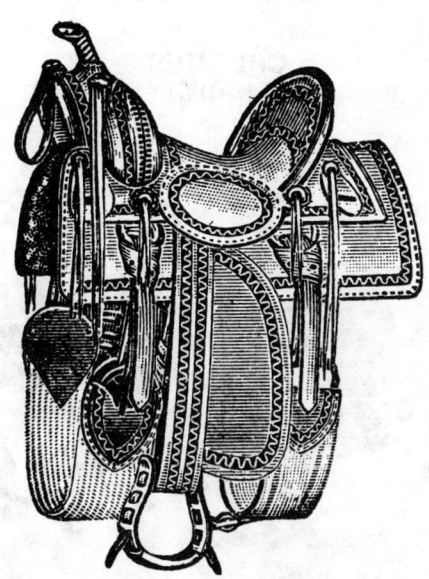

Monarch Stock Saddle, leather, equipped with Sampson Horn, 40" long .... **$100.00-$150.00**

Collectibles of the Old West are extremely popular. Everything from barbed wire to Colt revolvers is collected. A big segment of this field is cowboy gear—clothing, horse tack and other equipment used by the cowboy. Saddles are particularly important, and because they were made to be durable in the field, they have lasted as collectibles too.

☐ **Boots,** depending on condition	80.00	260.00	170.00
☐ **Chaps,** leather, good condition, c. 1880	160.00	260.00	200.00
☐ **Colt,** single action, Army revolver, .38 cal. to .45 cal., c. 1880	250.00	650.00	400.00

290 / CRECHES (MINIATURE NATIVITY SCENES)

	Current Price Range		Prior Year Average
☐ **Hat,** beaver fur, c. 1880	210.00	310.00	250.00
☐ **Holster and belt,** western style, c. 1880	110.00	260.00	175.00
☐ **Lariat,** rawhide, c. 1880	110.00	260.00	175.00
☐ **Lariat,** rope, c. 1890	70.00	160.00	105.00
☐ **Saddle,** early western style, c. 1840	210.00	410.00	300.00
☐ **Saddle,** cavalry style, c. 1860	175.00	325.00	225.00
☐ **Saddle,** Colorado, western, c. 1880	210.00	410.00	300.00
☐ **Saddle,** Texas, western, c. 1890	175.00	325.00	225.00
☐ **Spurs,** plain, iron small rowels, c. 1880	85.00	110.00	82.00
☐ **Spurs,** plain, army issue, c. 1880	70.00	110.00	80.00
☐ **Whip,** quirt, rawhide, c. 1880	60.00	110.00	75.00
☐ **Winchester,** 1876 model rifle, 40 to 50 cal., c. 1876	410.00	810.00	600.00
☐ **Winchester,** 1886 model rifle, 45 to 50 cal., c. 1886	320.00	720.00	500.00
☐ **Winchester,** 1894 model rifle, 25 to 38 cal., c. 1894"	175.00	425.00	275.00

CRECHES
(MINIATURE NATIVITY SCENES)

Creche Figures, Nativity scene, 9 pieces, detail work, 2" H., made in occupied Japan .... **$20.00-$30.00**

Creches are miniature manger scenes used at Christmas time to depict the birth of Christ. During the 18th century, craftsman from all over Europe produced as many kinds of creches as their own imagination would allow. Creches have been made in nearly every country of the world and of nearly every imaginable material. Figures may be free standing or the entire scene may be in one piece. Many have been mass produced in great numbers for one year and then discontinued, thus making them valuable collectibles.

	Current Price Range		Prior Year Average
☐ **American**, wood and painted plaster, six piece set, c. 1920	42.00	52.00	45.00
☐ **French**, hand painted, angel 12″ L., single piece, c. 1875	260.00	310.00	275.00
☐ **French**, hand painted, wooden, 12 piece set, c. 1890	210.00	260.00	225.00
☐ **German**, ceramic, 12 piece set, c. 1900	85.00	120.00	82.00
☐ **German**, hand carved, 14 piece set, c. 1880	110.00	135.00	112.00
☐ **Guatemalan**, hand carved, 15 piece set, c. 1900	85.00	100.00	82.00
☐ **Hummel**, nativity set #214, 11 china pieces	520.00	570.00	525.00
☐ **Hummel**, Ferrandiz creche set #375, 13 china pieces	480.00	520.00	490.00
☐ **Mexican**, hand painted clay, 18 piece set, c. 1920	80.00	95.00	82.00
☐ **Mexican**, red clay, 10 piece set, c. 1910	65.00	85.00	70.00
☐ **Polish**, hand carved, wood, nativity scene, one piece, c. 1890	110.00	135.00	112.0

DANCE MEMORABILIA

Dance memorabilia includes in many different types of collectibles. Programs, tickets, advertising bills and even moralistic pamphlets denouncing ballroom dancing as sinful are just a few examples. During the 19th century, lithographs of famous ballerinas were popular. Programs printed for the first performance of a new ballet are valued, particularly if the performance has become a standard part of the repertoire of a famous ballet company. Other landmark events could be such programs as Nureyev's first United States performance after defecting from the Soviet Union. Programs illustrated by noted artists, like Picasso, are always in demand.

Original sketches for costumes, or set designs are quite rare and desirable as are dancers' personal effects. Ballet shoes are generally used for only one performance. Costumes are a rare find on the market. Old books on dance instruction and choreography also occasionally turn up.

Dance memorabilia is a specialized field and the amount of existing collectible material is rather small when compared to other collectibles. Prices tend to be rather high and are on the increase.

☐ **Isadora Duncan**, holograph letter, signed, financial matters (17 lines)	175.00	200.00	162.00
☐ **Isadora Duncan**, b/w photo by Arnold Genthe, signed and inscribed, papier-mache molded frame, good condition, 8″ x 10″	400.00	450.00	400.00
☐ **Isadora Duncan**, b/w photo, dancing pose, wearing Greek-style costume, not signed, 8″ x 10″	52.00	62.00	55.00
☐ **Isadora Duncan**, b/w photo, full face, signed in purple ink, 8″ x 10″, c. 1924	260.00	310.00	275.00
☐ **Isadora Duncan**, photo, partially hand colored, signed, rare, 5″ x 4″	200.00	220.00	190.00
☐ **Isadora Duncan**, three pen-and-ink drawings, one signed by her, brief notes scribbled by her	460.00	560.00	400.00
☐ **Isadora Duncan**, b/w, photo by Arnold Genthe, reprinted from the original negative, unsigned	62.00	82.00	70.00
☐ **Isadora Duncan**, poster advertisement, large photographic illustration, 22″ x 30″	230.00	260.00	222.00

292 / DECOYS

	Current Price Range		Prior Year Average
☐ **Martha Graham,** holograph letter with original stamped envelope	130.00	140.00	125.00
☐ **Martha Graham,** program from dance recital, Los Angeles, signed by her, cover wrinkled, c. 1948	22.00	32.00	25.00
☐ **Martha Graham,** scrapbook containing 23 photos, four letters, numerous clippings	260.00	360.00	300.00
☐ **Souvenir programs,** most examples, 20th c.	12.00	22.00	15.00
☐ **Statuette of Russian dancer,** cast iron, 5" H.	70.00	85.00	72.00
☐ **Watercolor,** gouache costume designs, most examples, 20th c.	50.00	110.00	68.00
☐ **Watercolor or gouache set designs,** most examples	70.00	125.00	88.00

NOTE: designs by Braque, de Chirico or Picasso often are valued in the thousands of dollars.

POSTERS

The value of dance (ballet, classical etc.) posters representing major companies and/or noted stars can be guaged roughly as follows, except in the case of a great superstar such as Isadora Duncan:

☐ **American dance poster,** pre-1900	60.00	110.00	75.00
☐ **American dance poster,** 1901-1920	30.00	55.00	38.00
☐ **American dance poster,** 1921-1940	25.00	40.00	28.00
☐ **American dance poster,** after 1940	12.00	28.00	18.00

More colorful foreign posters tend to command higher prices. French posters are the most highly sought after and most expensive.

DECOYS

Most people think of ducks when they think of decoys, but there are also frog, fish, owl, goose and crow decoys, all of which are collectible. People collect by carver, type, species and flyway (the flying path taken by certain groups of species during migration).

Decoys are made of everything from woven reeds (ancient Amerind type) to painted canvas-over-wood, to combinations of naturally occurring roots and branches to well carved wood. Condition is important, particularly of those that are painted. Beware of decoys in mint condition, however, as they are often recent ornamental decoys meant for the den mantelpiece, not the reedy swamp.

☐ **Beach duck,** papier-mache, paper label, Mackey	145.00	175.00	150.00
☐ **Beach duck,** cork body, Thomas H. Gelston	80.00	130.00	100.00
☐ **Black duck,** August mock drake, c. 1900	175.00	200.00	162.00
☐ **Black duck,** Cobb Island, carved wing tips	150.00	175.00	138.00
☐ **Black duck,** Dan English	475.00	525.00	500.00
☐ **Black duck,** handcarved, c. 1900	65.00	85.00	70.00
☐ **Black duck,** hollow, carved, Ken Anger	300.00	350.00	300.00
☐ **Black duck,** hollow, carved, Stanley Grant	125.00	150.00	112.00
☐ **Black duck,** hollow, carved, John Heisler	300.00	375.00	205.00

	Item	Current Price Range		Prior Year Average
☐	**Black duck,** hollow, carved, K. Peck	250.00	275.00	238.00
☐	**Black duck,** hollow, carved, Harry V. Shourds	90.00	140.00	115.00
☐	**Black duck,** bird standing with wings spread, Ira Hudson	1250.00	1550.00	1350.00
☐	**Black duck,** sleeping, set of five, original paint	760.00	860.00	800.00
☐	**Black duck,** swimming, Down East Decoy Co.	125.00	155.00	130.00
☐	**Blue Jay,** signed, A. Elmer Crowell	1050.00	1350.00	1150.00
☐	**Brant,** carved cedar	210.00	310.00	250.00
☐	**Brant,** Cobb Island, carved wings	110.00	160.00	125.00
☐	**Brant,** hollow, carved, New Jersey, carved wings	235.00	310.00	260.00
☐	**Brant,** Long Island, cork body	145.00	175.00	150.00
☐	**Brant,** Mason's	160.00	185.00	162.00
☐	**Brant,** swimming, carved wings	165.00	195.00	175.00
☐	**Broadbill,** Chauncey Wheeler	250.00	300.00	250.00
☐	**Bufflehead,** drake, Doug Jester	80.00	110.00	82.00
☐	**Bufflehead,** drake, hollow, carved, Charles Parker	260.00	310.00	275.00
☐	**Bufflehead,** drake, primitive, Oscar Ayers	85.00	110.00	82.00
☐	**Canadian Goose,** Nathan Cobb	385.00	435.00	400.00
☐	**Canadian Goose,** Hurley Conklin	550.00	650.00	575.00
☐	**Canadian Goose,** John Furlow	220.00	270.00	225.00
☐	**Canadian Goose,** L. Parker	220.00	270.00	225.00
☐	**Canadian Goose,** Harvey V. Shourds	300.00	375.00	312.00
☐	**Canadian Goose,** swimming, signed, c. 1880	1600.00	1850.00	1700.00
☐	**Canvasback,** drake, balsa wood, Harry Megarry	60.00	90.00	70.00
☐	**Canvasback,** drake, feeding, A. Elmer Crowell	335.00	410.00	362.00
☐	**Canvasback,** drake, Michigan bobtail	135.00	185.00	150.00
☐	**Canvasback,** drake, Samuel Denny	200.00	240.00	200.00
☐	**Canvasback,** hen, Mason's	65.00	90.00	72.00
☐	**Coot,** Mason's	265.00	295.00	270.00
☐	**Coot,** Benjamin J. Schmidt	135.00	165.00	145.00
☐	**Crow,** hollow, carved, Charles H. Perdew Co.	270.00	320.00	280.00
☐	**Crow,** wooden, glass eyes, c. 1900	425.00	475.00	425.00
☐	**Curlew,** Barnegat	535.00	610.00	562.00
☐	**Curlew,** Cobb Island, running	685.00	760.00	705.00
☐	**Curlew,** Eskimo, carved wings, signed	660.00	735.00	690.00
☐	**Curlew,** Mason's	2500.00	2700.00	2550.00
☐	**Dowitcher,** Long Island	210.00	260.00	225.00
☐	**Duck,** J. H. Whitney	65.00	85.00	70.00
☐	**Duck,** Labrador	685.00	760.00	712.00
☐	**Duck,** Pacific Northwest	32.00	42.00	35.00
☐	**Duck,** papier-mache	22.00	32.00	25.00
☐	**Eider duck,** primitive	125.00	155.00	130.00
☐	**Fish,** carved and painted, pair, 19th c.	230.00	330.00	270.00
☐	**Gadwell,** hen, Ken Anger	235.00	260.00	238.00
☐	**Golden Eye,** drake, A. F. Bishop	100.0	130.00	105.00
☐	**Golden Eye,** drake, Mason's	260.00	285.00	262.00
☐	**Golden Eye,** drake, Steven's Decoy Factory	370.00	410.00	380.00
☐	**Golden Eye,** hen, Harry Shourds	130.00	155.00	132.00
☐	**Golden Eye,** hen, Bob White	280.00	320.00	290.00
☐	**Golden Plover**	60.00	70.00	60.00
☐	**Great Blue Heron,** sheet metal, painted	285.00	360.00	305.00
☐	**Gull,** with iron weight, J. W. Carter	1900.00	2500.00	2100.00
☐	**Heron,** primitive	585.00	660.00	605.00
☐	**Lesser Yellowlegs,** Bay Head	210.00	260.00	225.00
☐	**Lesser Yellowlegs,** Mason's	585.00	660.00	605.00
☐	**Lesser Yellowlegs,** William Matthews	265.00	310.00	280.00

294 / DECOYS

	Current Price Range		Prior Year Average
☐ Lesser Yellowlegs, c. 1896	210.00	310.00	250.00
☐ Mallard, drake, J. N. Dodge Decoy Factory	55.00	75.00	60.00
☐ Mallard, drake, Old Illinois River	335.00	385.00	350.00
☐ Mallard, drake, Charles H. Perdew Co.	485.00	560.00	525.00
☐ Mallard, hen, Mason's	55.00	75.00	60.00
☐ Mallard, hen, Ward Brothers, c. 1920	120.00	220.00	160.00
☐ Mallard, papier-mache	18.00	22.00	17.50
☐ Mallard, drake, cork body	22.00	28.00	22.50
☐ Merganser, drake, red-breasted, Hurley Conklin	145.00	175.00	150.00
☐ Merganser, hen, Doug Jester	440.00	490.00	445.00
☐ Merganser, Long Island	310.00	360.00	325.00
☐ Merganser, Harold Haertel	2250.00	2850.00	2500.00
☐ Old Squaw, drake, Mark English	710.00	860.00	775.00
☐ Owl, balsa wood, glass eyes	435.00	485.00	450.00
☐ Owl, 19th c.	200.00	225.00	182.00
☐ Pigeon, Lou Schifferell	250.00	275.00	238.00
☐ Pintail, drake, carved cedar	225.00	275.00	225.00
☐ Pintail, drake, carved wings and feathers	250.00	275.00	238.00
☐ Pintail, drake, A. Elmer Crowell	175.00	225.00	175.00
☐ Pintail, drake, Ira Hudson	760.00	860.00	800.00
☐ Pintail Duck, green beak	50.00	60.00	50.00
☐ Pintail, hen, Mason's	135.00	160.00	138.00
☐ Pintail, hen, Lem and Steve Ward	1400.00	1700.00	1500.00
☐ Pintail, hen and drake, L. T. Ward, pair	2300.00	3200.00	2600.00
☐ Plover, black-bellied, Cobb Island	285.00	385.00	325.00
☐ Plover, black-bellied, A. Elmer Crowell	1100.00	1600.00	1250.00
☐ Plover, black-bellied, William Matthews	285.00	335.00	300.00
☐ Plover, black-bellied, Charles E. Wheeler	1400.00	1700.00	1500.00
☐ Red-headed, cork body	170.00	190.00	170.00
☐ Red-headed, drake, Thomas Gelston	110.00	140.00	115.00
☐ Red-headed, drake, hollow, carved, signed	1100.00	1300.00	1100.00
☐ Red-headed, drake, sleeping, Mason's	285.00	335.00	300.00
☐ Red-headed, hen, Nate Quillen	450.00	525.00	462.00
☐ Ruddy Duck, hen, L. T. Ward	130.00	150.00	130.00
☐ Sanderling, A. Elmer Crowell	760.00	835.00	782.00
☐ Sanderling, Taylor Johnson	235.00	285.00	250.00
☐ Sandpiper, Cobb Island	200.00	275.00	212.00
☐ Sandpiper, primitive	55.00	70.00	58.00
☐ Scaup, drake, Bart Clayton	135.00	185.00	150.00
☐ Scaup, drake, Henry Grant	520.00	620.00	550.00
☐ Scaup, drake, hollow, carved feathers	1650.00	1900.00	1725.00
☐ Scaup, drake, Roland Horner	360.00	435.00	382.00
☐ Scaup, drake, Joe King, hollow, carved	62.00	82.00	70.00
☐ Scaup, hen, Mason's	485.00	560.00	512.00
☐ Scaup, hen, Chauncey Wheeler	210.00	260.00	225.00
☐ Shorebird, carved head, glass eyes	325.00	385.00	338.00
☐ Shorebird, Dodge Decoy Factory	75.00	100.00	82.00
☐ Snipe, robin, Cobb Island	150.00	225.00	175.00
☐ Snipe, robin, Dodge Decoy Factory	150.00	225.00	175.00
☐ Snipe, robin, Joe King	225.00	275.00	225.00
☐ Snipe, robin, primitive	85.00	125.00	100.00
☐ Swan, hollow, carved	835.00	910.00	845.00
☐ Swan, c. 1900	420.00	460.00	430.00
☐ Widgeon, A. Elmer Crowell	85.00	115.00	95.00
☐ Widgeon, c. 1880	145.00	175.00	150.00
☐ Willet, carved wings	350.00	450.00	375.00

DOGS

Sealyham, HN1030, large, discontinued 1937 **$500.00-600.00**

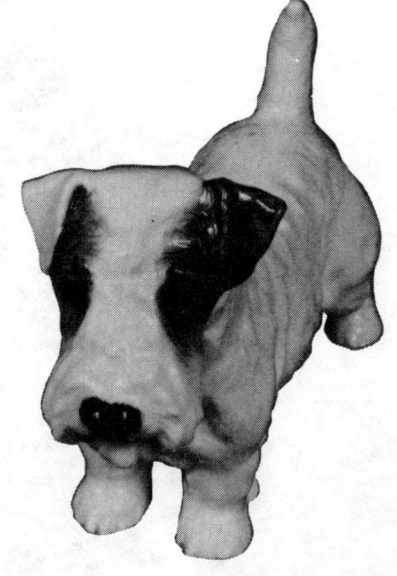

Dogs are probably even more popular among motif collectors than cats. The tendency is, however, for dog collectors to specialize by breed — be it Dachshunds, Dalmations, or whatever. Some of the most unique and interesting dog figures are not readily recognizable breeds. These are the folk art dog carvings and modelings of wood and clay.

	Current Price Range		Prior Year Average
☐ **Beagles,** painting, primitive contemporary folk artist	70.00	85.00	72.00
☐ **Bulldog,** cast iron, spotty paint	32.00	42.00	35.00
☐ **Cocker Spaniel,** cast iron, full body	22.00	32.00	25.00
☐ **Dachshund,** puppies in knapsack, Vienna bronze, 1″ H.	90.00	110.00	92.00
☐ **Dachshund,** terra cotta, glazed, 5½″ H.	42.00	52.00	45.00
☐ **English Pug,** cast iron, full figure, 6½″ x 9″	42.00	52.00	45.00
☐ **Great Dane,** porcelain, Hutschenreuther figurine, 7½″ H.	175.00	200.00	182.00
☐ **Greyhound,** paperweight, Belleek, third black mark, 7″ H.	580.00	640.00	600.00
☐ **Hunter and Dog,** porcelain, Czechoslovakian, 7½″ H.	150.00	190.00	160.00
☐ **Old English Sheep,** Royal Dux, c. 1945	40.00	50.00	40.00
☐ **Rose Quartz dog,** on base, 2″ H.	45.00	55.00	45.00
☐ **Spaniel,** sewer tile	185.00	235.00	200.00
☐ **Terriers,** in a basket, Royal Doulton	22.00	32.00	25.00
☐ **Wirehaired Terrier,** Vienna porcelain, show dog position, 4¾″ x 4½″	42.00	52.00	45.00

DOLLS

Sleeping Beauty, by Madam Alexander, gown and vail. **$220.00-$500.00**

Doll collecting has grown phenomenally in the last 25 years to become one of the top hobbies in the United States. People collect dolls for various reasons: to replace children who have grown up, or children they never had; they may represent children of certain ages, movie stars, comic strip characters, or, they may simply appeal to that little kid who is hidden somewhere inside all adults.

Individual appeal seems to be the magic ingredient in the world of doll collecting. Some dolls made of common materials show exquisite workmanship and detailing, while others made of fine porcelain bisque are crudely fashioned.

Doll costumes range from superbly crafted garments of silk, velvet, satin and lace to simple shifts made of printed cotton fabrics. Collectors agree that the costume original to the doll is most desirable. Replacement clothes of the period are less favored. Dresses made by the original owner or her mother and contemporary to the doll are acceptable.

Damaged body parts should be repaired or, if necessary, replaced, but only with exact duplicates. Heads, eyes, hair, etc., should all be present and in good condition. If the doll is soiled, some research should be done into cleaning, particularly if the owner is not certain about the material of which the doll is composed. Some surfaces which are resistant to solvents may be irreparably damaged by plain water and vice versa. The same care should be taken in the cleaning of doll clothing.

Germany dominated the commercial manufacture of dolls for many years, supplying the vast majority of dolls sold in Europe and the United States until the outbreak of World War I The German dolls were favored because of their fine detailing, life-like appearance and low prices. The French also produced fine fashion dolls, although they were unable to match the price of the German products.

More recently, dolls have been manufactured commercially in many countries and, of course, homemade dolls have been a part of every culture for centuries.

The prices of dolls cover such a wide range that the collector can find specimens to fit his budget. While the French and German fashion dolls are out of the financial reach of many collectors, most of the more recent composition dolls are relatively plentiful and inexpensive. Interesting and varied collections may be assembled by specializing in dolls of a certain era, a certain construction material, those dressed in similar nationalistic costumes, or all the various dolls made by a single manufacturer. Prices given are for dolls in excellent to mint original condition. Deductions must be made for any missing parts, worn-out or faded clothes, and broken or cracked heads.

For more extensive information, see *The Official Price Guide to Dolls*, published by the House of Collectibles.

ALEXANDER

	Current Price Range		Prior Year Average
☐ **Alexanderkin,** hard plastic, wears bathing suit, sandals, robe, square sunglasses, carries beach bag, 8″	70.00	90.00	65.00
☐ **Amy,** plastic sleep eyes, blonde looped curls, 14″	95.00	110.00	80.00
Note: Amy was a character in Louisa May Alcott's Little Women.			
☐ **Cissy,** hard plastic, jointed at knees and elbows, long flowing yellow cape-style coat, sleep eyes, high heel open dress shoes, 21″	90.00	115.00	85.00
☐ **Laurie,** vinyl head, sleep eyes, sad, long eyelashes, black hair, wears double-breasted jacket, plaid trousers, 12″	15.00	22.00	14.00
Note: Laurie was a character in Louisa May Alcott's Little Women.			
☐ **Lissy,** hard plastic, sleep eyes (straight-ahead staring), brown hair, long dress with waist sash, colonial style bonnet, 12″	230.00	280.00	200.00
Note: This is a scarce costume and accounts for much of the value. "Lissy" in one of the more common costumes sells in the $75.00 to $95.00 range.			
☐ **McGuffy Awake,** sleep eyes, braided hair	200.00	220.00	180.00
☐ **Pamela,** hard plastic, sleep eyes, dressed in national costume of Poland with multi-layered, boldly printed skirt, white ruffled blouse, 12″	140.00	170.00	125.00
☐ **Polly Pigtails,** hard plastic, sleep eyes, wide-brimmed straw hat, white dress with puff sleeves, white cotton stockings, black shoes, 13⅞″	110.00	140.00	100.00

298 / DOLLS

	Current Price Range		Prior Year Average

- ☐ **Scarlett O'Hara,** vinyl, sleep eyes, long black glossy hair, satin gown with trimming, satin bonnet, wears cameo on a chain at the neck, marked Alexander 1961, 21″ **110.00 140.00 90.00**
  Note: Scarlett O'Hara was a character in Margaret Mitchell's "Gone With The Wind," made into a motion picture in 1939.
- ☐ **Sleeping Beauty,** Disney special edition, 1959, 9″ **200.00 500.00 180.00**
- ☐ **M.I.B.** **450.00 500.00 400.00**
- ☐ **Wendy,** hard plastic, sleep eyes, dressed as tennis player with racquet, skirt, opentoe shoes, 8″. **90.00 115.00 80.00**
- ☐ **Wendy Ann,** hard plastic, sleep eyes, puffy cheeks, blond hair, wears jacket and skirt of matching style, two buttons on jacket, 8″ **70.00 90.00 62.00**

ARMAND MARSEILLE

- ☐ **Betsy Baby,** bisque, socket head, sleep eyes, open mouth with two teeth, chubby face with double chin, five-piece composition body, marked G.B. 329/A. 2 M., early 1920's. 13″ **130.00 170.00 125.00**
- ☐ **Bisque,** socket head, toddler body, sleep eyes with eyelashes, open mouth with two teeth, marked A.M. Koppelsdorf Germany/1330-A. 12 M., 21″ **190.00 235.00 180.00**
  Note: A large, impressive doll which would probably be more valuable, but for the fact that it seems to have been produced in rather large quantities.
- ☐ **Bisque,** socket head set on toddler body, fully jointed construction, open mouth showing two teeth, fixed eyes, marked Armand Marseille/Germany 996/A. 3 M., 16″ **180.00 225.00 170.00**
- ☐ **Bisque,** socket head, sleep eyes, open mouth with two teeth, five-piece body, marked G.B. 327/A. 12 M. Germany, 21″ **385.00 465.00 365.00**
- ☐ **Bisque,** five-piece composition body, set eyes, open mouth showing four teeth and traces of others, marked A.M. 560a/DRGM R 232/1, 14″ ... **330.00 380.00 315.00**
- ☐ **Bisque,** socket head, five-piece composition body, sleep eyes, open mouth with two teeth, marked Germany/971/A.4.M., 15″ **140.00 190.00 135.00**

ARRANBEE

- ☐ **Army Boy,** composition head and limbs, body stuffed with excelsior, molded hair, painted eyes, wears U.S. soldier's uniform of post-World War I era, featuring reproductions (in reduced size) of Lincoln cents for jacket buttons, 15″ **75.00 95.00 70.00**
  Note: The uniform style would suggest a dating of c. 1920-25, but it is believed Army Boy was made slightly later than this.
- ☐ **Baby Marie,** vinyl head, vinyl arms and legs, plastic body, sleep eyes, molded hair, partially open mouth, shaped for insertion of nursing bottle, wears diaper, quilt jacket, 8¼″ **5.00 7.00 5.00**

DOLLS / 299

	Current Price Range		Prior Year Average

- **Carolyn The Snow Queen** (sometimes spelled Caroline), composition head, composition arms, legs and body, sleep eyes, closed mouth, pursed lips, blonde hair with ribbon, long gown with waist sash, 20¼"................ 60.00 75.00 55.00
- **Composition head**, composition arms and legs, body stuffed with excelsior, molded hair, painted eyes, wears striped dress with stripes running horizontally on the upper portion and vertically on the lower portion, painted shoes, 15¼"..... 70.00 90.00 68.00
- **Debu-Teen**, composition head, cloth body, composition arms and legs, turnable head. Brunette wig, attached by adhesive, sleep eyes, marked R & B, made in 1940, 18"................ 43.00 52.00 40.00
- **Dream Bride**, plastic, sandy blonde wig attached by adhesive, sleep eyes (blue), wears bridal gown, marked R & B, also carrying the moldmark 210, made in 1954, 21"................ 43.00 55.00 40.00
- **Francine**, plastic, blonde hair attached by adhesive, sleep eyes (blue), marked R & B, made in 1955, 17"................ 48.00 59.00 44.00
- **Judy**, plastic, blonde wig attached by adhesive, the wig formed into an elaborate hairdo of tightly wound braids curled into a ram's-horn and pinned against the head, sleep eyes (blue), marked with the mold number 210 and the patent number 2,537,598, made in 1951, 19"................ 62.00 75.00 58.00
- **My Angel**, vinyl head, oilcloth body, vinyl arms and legs, blonde hair (rooted), sleep eyes (blue), open mouth with teeth, bright red lips, marked Arrabnee, made in 1959, 22"................ 45.00 56.00 42.00
- **Nancy**, doll plus trunk and accessories, marked Nancy, 12" Complete................ 40.00 50.00 38.00
  Doll only................ 24.00 29.00 23.00
  Note: Believed to have been sold around 1933 or 1934.
- **Nancy Lee**, composition head, composition arms, legs and body, sleep eyes with long eyelashes, long blond wig, wears brightly patterned short dress with squared white collar, carries matching handbag, white stockings, black shoes, 14"
  With handbag................ 50.00 65.00 45.00
  Without handbag................ 40.00 52.00 38.00
  Value of handbag alone................ 8.00 10.00 7.00
- **Nancy Lee**, hard plastic head, hard plastic arms, legs and body, saran wig, deep flesh toned skin, short silk dress with floral pattern, tied with waist ribbon, white shoes, silk stockings, 17"........ 50.00 65.00 47.00
- **Nanette**, plastic, brown wig, attached by adhesive, sleep eyes (blue), marked R & B, made in 1953, 14"................ 46.00 55.00 45.00
- **New Happytot**, vinyl head and body, sleep eyes (blue), marked Arranbee, made in 1955, 16"..... 24.00 30.00 23.00
- **Peachy**, plastic, molded hair (brown), painted eyes, unmarked, made c. 1950, 10"........ 11.00 14.00 10.00

300 / DOLLS

	Current Price Range		Prior Year Average

- ☐ **Scarlet,** composition head, composition arms, legs and body, sleep eyes (green), long eyelashes, closed mouth, wears long ball gown of U.S. Civil War era and large bonnet, gown is trimmed with silk ribbons, marked R & B, 15" 50.00 65.00 48.00

Note: Scarlet was inspired by the motion picture, "Gone With The Wind," released in 1939, and represents the character Scarlet O'Hara. It is believed that the doll went on sale in 1940. Public reaction to "Gone With The Wind" brought about a great deal of related merchandise — including quite a few Scarlet O'Hara dolls by various manufacturers.

- ☐ **Snuggle Doll,** composition head, stuffed body, stuffed arms and legs, blonde wig attached by adhesive, fixed eyes (blue), unmarked, made in 1941, 17" 53.00 65.00 50.00
- ☐ **Sonja Heinie,** composition head and body, brunette wig attached by adhesive, sleep eyes (brown), marked R & B, made in 1945, 21¼" 49.00 58.00 47.00

Note: Sonja Heinie was an Olympic ice-skating champion and, later, motion picture personality.

- ☐ **Taffy,** plastic, sleep eyes (green), marked R & B, made in 1954, 16½" 55.00 67.00 52.00

BAHR & PROSCHILD

- ☐ **Bisque,** composition body (five-piece), small sleep eyes, no upper lashes, tiny painted lower lashes, bearing the factory trademark (crossed bars with a B in the left field, a P in the right field, an O beneath, and a symbol above), 16½" 825.00 960.00 750.00
- ☐ **Bisque,** composition body (five-piece), sleep eyes with eyelashes, open mouth with two teeth (large space between them), bearing the factory trademark (crossed bars with a B in the left field, a P in the right field, an O beneath, and a symbol above); marked additionally with a mold number, 585/16, 25" 310.00 350.00 300.00
- ☐ **Bisque,** socket head, fixed eyes (dark, roundish), dark narrow brows, open mouth showing teeth, dark red lips, pug nose, almost spherical head, representing a toddler, marked BP within a heart, made in Germany and with the mold identification number 585-3/0, date of manufacture unknown, based on marking evidence this doll was apparently made somewhere between the later 1890's and 1910, 10¼" 380.00 440.00 350.00

FISHER PRICE

- ☐ **Audrey,** vinyl head, cloth body, rooted hair, painted eyes, blouse with small heart pattern, marked 168240, 1973, Fisher Price Toys, 14" 11.00 15.00 10.00

	Current Price Range		Prior Year Average

- **Baby Ann,** vinyl head, cloth body, rooted blond hair, painted eyes, floral print dress with large sash ribbon, marked 60, 188460, 1973, Fisher Price Toys, 13½" .... | 10.00 | 14.00 | 9.00
- **Elizabeth,** black, vinyl head, cloth body, rooted hair, closed mouth in semi-smile, painted eyes, marked 18, 168630, 1973, Fisher Price Toys, 13½" | 11.00 | 15.00 | 10.00
- **Mary,** vinyl head, cloth body, rooted hair, upturned eyes (painted), angelic facial expression, wears print dress and white apron, marked 168420, 1973, Fisher Price Toys, 14" .... | 10.00 | 14.00 | 9.00
- **Natalie,** vinyl head, cloth body, rooted hair, upturned eyes (painted), grinning smile, marked 168320, 1973, Fisher Price Toys, 13½" .... | 11.00 | 15.00 | 10.00

HASBRO

- **Baby Ruth,** vinyl head, stuffed body, vinyl hands, molded and painted features, blonde hair, rooted, sold originally with a tag reading Baby Ruth 1971, used as a premium by the Curtis Candy Co., 10". | 5.00 | 7.00 | 5.00
  Note: Baby Ruth candy bars were not named for baseball player Babe Ruth, as many people believe, but for Ruth Cleveland, daughter of President Grover Cleveland. She was born while Cleveland was President and the press referred to her as "baby Ruth."
- **Bonnie Breck,** plastic/vinyl, rooted hair, blond, painted eyes, jointed at the waist, two-piece matching outfit, made in Hong Kong, dated 1972, 9" .... | 7.00 | 9.00 | 6.00
  Note: There must have been some tie-in with Breck Shampoo, but the doll itself does not carry any indication of it.
- **Dahlia Darling,** vinyl head, vinyl arms, legs and body, rooted hair, painted eyes, surrounded by flowers, plastic, a doll-brooch designed to be worn on clothing, 2¼" .... | 3.00 | 4.00 | 3.00
- **Daisy Darling,** vinyl head, vinyl arms, legs and body, rooted hair, painted eyes, surrounded by flowers, plastic, a doll-brooch designed to be worn on clothing, 3" .... | 3.00 | 4.00 | 3.00
- **Flying Nun,** vinyl, brunette hair, rooted, molded and painted features, marked 1967 Hasbro, Hong Kong, 5" .... | 10.00 | 13.00 | 9.00
- **G.I. Joe,** Action Marine, plastic, molded hair, brown, brown eyes, painted, marked 7700, G.I. Joe TM Copyright by Hasbro Patent Pending, made in U.S.A., made in 1964, 11½" .... | 35.00 | 43.00 | 31.00
- **G.I. Joe,** Action Marine, plastic, molded hair, brown, brown eyes, painted, marked 7500, G.I. Joe, Copyright 1964 by Hasbro, Pat. No.3,277,602, made in U.S.A., no problem distinguishing this 1967 version from the previous: the patent is no longer pending, a patent number is shown, 11½" | 21.00 | 25.00 | 19.00

302 / DOLLS

	Current Price Range	Prior Year Average

Note: The G. I. Joe series by Hasbro is the second lengthiest in the world of modern dolls, in the number of issues encompassed, next only to Mattel's Barbie. It has not as yet attracted quite as much hobbyists interest as Barbies, but apparently it is only a matter of time before this occurs. The series was introduced in 1964 at the beginning of U.S. involvement in the Viet Nam war, long before the war became a major political issue. But even in the days of protest marches and sit-ins, G. I. Joe continued to sell. His young purchasers were simply not politically-minded.

☐ **G.I. Joe,** Action Marine, plastic, molded hair, brown, brown eyes, painted, marked 7700, G.I. Joe, Copyright 1964 by Hasbro Patent Pending, made in U.S.A., made in 1965, distinguished from the first issue, 1965, by the absence of the letters "TM" in the copyright notice, 11½ " 12.00 16.00 11.00

☐ **G.I. Joe,** Action Soldier, black, plastic, molded hair, black, brown eyes, painted, marked 7900, G.I. Joe, Copyright 1964 by Hasbro, Patent Pending, made in U.S.A., this is the 1966 version, distinguished by removal of the scar which had been on the faces of previous models, 11½ " 26.00 32.00 23.00

☐ **G.I. Joe,** Action Soldier, black, plastic, molded hair, black, brown eyes, painted, marked 7900, G.I. Joe, Copyright 1964 by Hasbro, Pat. No.3,277,602, made in U.S.A., no problem distinguishing this 1967 version from the previous: the patent is no longer pending, a patent number is shown, 11½ " 18.00 24.00 17.00

☐ **Goldilocks & The Three Bears,** vinyl, molded and painted features, blonde hair, rooted, sold with figures of Mama Bear, Papa Bear and Baby Bear, which must be present to command the indicated value, sold in 1967, height of Goldilocks, 3 " 6.00 8.00 5.00

☐ **Leggy Jill,** plastic/vinyl, rooted hair, painted eyes, represents a young woman with exaggerated Twiggy-type figure, inspired by fashion ads of the late 1960's and early 1970's, dated 1972, 10 " 5.00 7.00 4.00

☐ **Michelle,** vinyl, molded and painted features, blonde hair, rooted, represents a member of the vocal group "The Mamas and the Papas," made in 1967, 3 " 14.00 19.00 13.00

☐ **Mother Hubbard,** vinyl, marked 1967, Hasbro, Hong Kong, 3½ " 4.00 6.00 4.00

☐ **Music,** plastic/vinyl, rooted hair, painted eyes, closed mouth, wide-eyed expression, representing a young woman wearing boldly printed minidress, tall boots, marked Made in Hong Kong, Hasbro U.S. Pat. Pend., dated 1971, 9 " 10.00 13.00 9.00

☐ **Poodle-Oodle,** plastic/vinyl, wig attached by adhesive, painted features, a poodle's head with a human body, marked 1966 Hasbro, Japan, Patent Pending, 9½ " 6.00 8.00 5.00

	Current Price Range		Prior Year Average

- **Rumpelstilskin,** vinyl, molded and painted features including bulbous nose, rooted hair, cone-shaped hat, representing the storybook character from German folklore, marked Hasbro 1967, 3″ 6.00 8.00 5.00
- **Sunday,** vinyl, molded and painted features, molded and painted hair, partially open mouth, marked 1965 Hasbro, Japan, 4¼″ 5.00 7.00 5.00
- **Sweet Cookie,** plastic/vinyl, rooted hair, very pale platinum blond cut in bangs, wide painted eyes, open mouth, freckles and pug nose, wears print dress and apron, apron carries picture of strawberry and wording "Sweet Cookie," marked Hasbro Inc., Pat. Pend., 1972, made in U.S., 18¼″ 6.00 8.00 5.00

Note: The majority of Hasbro's dolls have not been made in the U.S. but in Hong Kong, even though this is, of course, an American company.

- **That Kid,** plastic/vinyl, rooted hair, large sleep eyes, short eyelashes, pug nose, freckled face, open mouth with two teeth, talker, activated by pulling singshot in back pocket, marked Hasbro 1967, 21¼″ 20.00 25.00 18.00
- **Violet Darling,** vinyl head, vinyl arms, legs and body, rooted hair, painted eyes, surrounded by flowers, plastic, a dollbrooch designed to be worn on clothing 3.00 4.00 3.00

HEINRICH HANDWERCK

- **Bisque,** head with bisque shoulder plate, fixed eyes, large, almond shaped, short painted lashes on top of eye socket, much longer painted lashes beneath, open mouth showing teeth, wide nose, thick prominent eyebrows, roundish jaw, prominent ears, marked with the letters HcH and the mold number 5/0, additionally marked with a device which resembles an airplane propeller or a flower with two petals, date of manufacture unknown, but the absence of the word "Germany" from the marking would suggest a dating of pre-1892, 17″ 230.00 280.00 210.00
- **Bisque,** head with bisque shoulder plate, fixed eyes, medium large, partially open mouth showing teeth, long face with prominent cheeks and jaw, moderately arched eyebrows, representing a girl of 4 or 5 years of age, marked with a four-petaled flower and the letters HcH, and also with the mold number 9/0, date of manufacture unknown, but the absence of the word "Germany" from the marking would suggest a dating of pre-1892, 14¾″ 160.00 190.00 150.00

304 / DOLLS

	Current Price Range		Prior Year Average

☐ **Bisque,** socket head, fixed eyes, almost circular, but not very large, applied lashes, medium-length eyebrows, open mouth showing four teeth, pastel lips, flattish nose, rounded jaw, facial expression of mild surprise, marked Germany, Heinrich Handwerck, Simon & Halbig, date of manufacture unknown, after 1892, probably around the turn of the century, this doll was assembled by Heinrich Handwerck using a head made by Simon & Halbig, the marking "Germany" means that a portion of the output, or all of it, was intended for export into America, 17½ " 220.00 265.00 205.00

HORSMAN

☐ **Athlete,** mechanical, plastic/vinyl, molded and painted hair, molded and painted features, stands on platform, operates by spring-driven motor, marked Horsman 1967, 5½ " 5.00 7.00 5.00

☐ **Babs,** composition, sleep eyes, blue, molded and painted hair, made in 1931, 10" 63.00 75.00 55.00

☐ **Baby Chubby,** composition head, cloth body, composition arms and legs, molded and painted hair, reddish blonde, sleep eyes, blue, marked A-Horsman, made in 1940, 23" 27.00 36.00 25.00

☐ **Bootsie,** black, plastic/vinyl, rooted hair, black, sleep eyes, brown, marked 1125-4-Horsman, made in 1969, 12" 26.00 34.00 23.00

☐ **Campbell Kid,** composition body and head, molded and painted hair, painted shoes and socks, 1948, 12" 90.00 110.00 85.00

☐ **Campbell Soup Kids,** plastic, boy in chef hat, girl with ribbon 25.00 32.00 22.00

☐ **Cindy,** plastic head, plastic arms, legs and body, swivel head, long blond rooted wig, sleep eyes, open mouth, bright red lips, puff sleeve dress with two buttons, walker, marked 170, 14½ " 22.00 27.00 20.00

Note: Cindy is dated 1953. For a Horsman doll this is considered "late" by collectors. The factory switched over to plastic, from composition, after World War II and its plastic dolls are not as valuable.

☐ **Cindy Kay,** plastic, blonde hair attached by adhesive, sleep eyes, blue, open mouth with teeth, has the appearance of an antique doll but this was probably accidental, marked Horsman, made in 1950, 15" 25.00 31.00 22.00

☐ **Dolly Dreamland,** plastic, red hair attached by adhesive, sleep eyes, blue, marked Made in U.S.A.-170, sold originally with a tag dated 1953, 15" 32.00 42.00 30.00

☐ **Fair Skin,** vinyl, blonde hair, rooted, sleep eyes, blue, marked Horsman H14, also bearing an additional mold number S16, made in 1960, 15" 15.00 20.00 13.00

DOLLS / 305

	Current Price Range	Prior Year Average
☐ **Love Me Baby,** plastic/vinyl, platinum blonde hair, rooted, sleep eyes, blue, nursing mouth, marked 2954-14Eye-1 Horsman, made in 1969, 16″	5.00 7.00	5.00
☐ **Lullabye Baby,** vinyl, blond hair, rooted, sleep eyes, blue, fitted with music box which plays rock-a-bye, marked M12 Horsman Doll, made in 1964, 12″	8.00 11.00	7.00
☐ **Mary Poppins,** walker, plastic/vinyl, sleep eyes, marked 5 Horsman Dolls, Inc., 1966, 66271, 25½″	36.00 45.00	32.00
Note: Strangely enough, this doll bears no markings connecting it with Disney Studios, though it almost certainly must have been made under license.		
☐ **Mary Poppins,** plastic/vinyl, black hair, rooted, molded and painted features, flowered hat, marked H, licensed from Walt Disney Studios, made in 1964, 12″	25.00 31.00	21.00
☐ **My Baby,** vinyl, blonde hair, rooted, sleep eyes, blue, marked Horsman O1, made in 1968, 9″	7.00 10.00	6.00
☐ **Pretty Betty,** vinyl, brunette hair attached by adhesive, sleep eyes, blue, closed mouth, bright red lips, marked Horsman, also bearing the mold number 1-S-5, made in 1954, ...	21.00 26.00	20.00
☐ **Princess,** plastic/vinyl, platinum blonde hair, rooted, sleep eyes, blue, puffy cheeks, marked 1963 Irene Szor, Horsman Doll Inc., 15½″	44.00 55.00	40.00
☐ **Renee Ballerina,** vinyl head, vinyl arms and legs, soft vinyl body, upswept hairdo, sleep eyes, closed mouth, jointed at the elbows, 18″	8.00 10.00	7.00
Note: Age uncertain, probably mid to late 1950's.		
☐ **Roberta,** composition head, composition arms, legs and body, molded and painted hair, painted eyes, wears puff sleeve dress, white stockings, 14″	41.00 47.00	38.00
☐ **Ruthie,** vinyl, black hair, rooted, with "widow's peak," sleep eyes, black, marked 12-6AA, made in 1958, 12½″	13.00 16.00	12.00
☐ **Softie Baby,** vinyl head, cloth body, vinyl arms and legs, brown hair, rooted, sleep eyes, blue, partially open mouth, marked 2515-10-Eye-S14-2, made in 1965, 14″	6.00 8.00	5.00
Note: The soft thing about Softie Baby was its cloth body — which, of course, was hardly an innovation by the year 1965. However, so many dolls on the market had plastic or vinyl bodies that a cloth-bodied doll almost SEEMED novel.		
☐ **Songster,** plastic/vinyl, platinum blonde hair, rooted, closed eyes with long lashes, mouth wide open, singing, marked Horsman Doll, 1967, 0712, ..	6.00 8.00	5.00
☐ **Sweet Memory,** vinyl head, cloth body, vinyl hands, brunette hair, rooted, sleep eyes, blue, marked Horsman Dolls, 1975, 14″	11.00 14.00	10.00
☐ **Teensie Baby,** plastic/vinyl, molded hair, painted eyes, nursing mouth, pug nose, dressed in overalls and striped short sleeve shirt, dated 1964, 12″	3.00 4.00	3.00

306 / DOLLS

	Current Price Range		Prior Year Average

IDEAL

- **Baby, Baby,** vinyl, rooted hair (blonde), fixed eyes (blue), nursing mouth, marked 115 Ideal, made in Hong Kong in 1974, 7″ 7.00   10.00   6.00
- **Baby Belly Button,** black, vinyl, black hair (rooted), painted features, brown eyes, smiling closed mouth, in the likeness of an infant, Baby Belly Button has a knob at its stomach which, when turned, makes the arms, legs and head move, dressed in a diaper and white lace-edged smock, marked Ideal Toy Corp., E9-2-H-165, made in Hong Kong in 1970, 9″ 5.50   7.00   5.00
- **Baby Big Eyes,** vinyl, blonde hair (rooted), sleep eyes (blue), closed mouth, marked Ideal Doll, made in 1954, 21″ 45.00   56.00   42.00
- **Busy Lizy,** plastic/vinyl, sleep eyes (blue), rooted hair (platinum blonde), pug nose, closed smiling mouth, wears dress with floral-printed cape, marked Ideal Toy Corp. HK-18, dated 1970 on the head and 1971 on the body, 17″ 26.00   32.00   25.00
- **Casey Flatsy,** vinyl, painted features, molded and painted hair (red), large eyes, smiling face, dressed as a railroad motorman, marked Ideal, 1969, Pat. Pending, made in Hong Kong 2.75   3.75   2.50
- **Carol Brent,** vinyl, marked Ideal Toy Corp., M-15-L, made in 1961 for the Montgomery Ward chain, "Carol Brent" was the name used by Ward's for one of its lines of female apparel, 15″ 28.00   35.00   25.00
- **Cinnamon,** plastic/vinyl, painted eyes (blue), open smiling mouth showing teeth, rooted hair (red), hair has "grow" feature (portion of wig is fitted inside head; when hair is gently pulled, it gives the appearance of "growing" out of the scalp), wears short lacy dress, ribbon at front, marked Ideal Toy Corp., GH-12-H-183, 12¼″ 8.00   10.00   7.00
- **Dracky, Mini Monster,** plastic/vinyl, molded and painted features, molded and painted hair, designed as a youthful Dracula, marked 1965 Ideal Toy Corp., made in Japan, 8½″ 14.00   19.00   12.00
- **Dr. Evil,** plastic, adult male model with various face changes (masks), sold in a box marked Ideal Toy Corp., and dated 1965, 11″ 9.00   12.00   8.00
  Note: The stated value is for the doll plus box and accessories.
- **Eric,** plastic/vinyl, molded and painted features, molded and painted hair, model of young adult, marked 1976 Ideal, made in Hong Kong, 12″ 13.00   17.00   12.00
- **Evel Knievel,** vinyl, posable, molded and painted hair, painted features, sold with three outfits and various props, representing the daredevil motorcycle stuntman, marked 1972 Ideal, made in Hong Kong
  Value with all original accessories 7.00   10.00   6.00
  Doll with one outfit, no props 4.00   6.00   4.00

DOLLS / 307

	Current Price Range		Prior Year Average

- ☐ **Flexy Soldier,** composition over wire (posable) with wooden feet, marked Ideal Doll, believed to have been made c. 1944, 13″ **50.00 62.00 48.00**
- ☐ **Giggle Toddler,** plastic/vinyl, blonde hair cut in bangs, painted eyes, giggles when arms are extended, marked Ideal Toy Corp., GG18-H77-1967, 18″ **36.00 45.00 35.00**
- ☐ **Ginger,** composition, rooted hair, sleep eyes (brown), open mouth with teeth, bright red lips, marked with an X inside a circle, made from a Shirley Temple mold, made in 1939, 15″ **65.00 80.00 60.00**
- ☐ **Goody Two-Shoes,** walker, plastic/vinyl, blonde hair (rooted), sleep eyes (blue), marked 1965 Ideal Toy Corp., WT18, Pat. Pending, 18″ **36.00 45.00 35.00**
- ☐ **Kerry,** plastic/vinyl, blonde hair (rooted), hair has "grow" feature (portion of wig is fitted inside head; when hair is pulled gently, it gives the appearance of "growing" out of the scalp), sleep eyes (blue), partially open mouth, marked 13 EYE, 1970, Ideal Toy Corp, NGH-18, 18″ **8.00 10.00 7.00**
Note: Kerry was patented in 1960 but did not get on the market until the following year.
- ☐ **Lemonade Flatsy (boy version),** vinyl, painted eyes (brown), molded and painted hair (blonde), dressed as a snack vendor, wearing a chef's hat reading "15¢," and a jacket picturing a frankfurter and reading "Dogs," bendable, 2½″ . **2.00 3.00 2.00**
- ☐ **Lindy,** plastic, molded and painted hair, sleep eyes, closed mouth, bright red lips, unmarked, made in 1956, 8″ **5.00 7.00 5.00**
- ☐ **Miss Revlon,** vinyl, brunette hair (rooted), sleep eyes (blue), wears high heels, representing the symbol of the Revlon Cosmetics Co., marked Ideal Doll VT-18, made in 1956, 17″ **29.00 37.00 26.00**
- ☐ **Mortimer Snerd,** composition, stuffed wire-encased body, composition hands and feet, molded and painted features, molded and painted hair, Mortimer Snerd was a character on the Edgar Bergen radio program; the original was a ventriloquist's dummy but this doll is a play-doll only, made in 1939, 13″ **140.00 170.00 130.00**
- ☐ **New Tiny Tears,** vinyl, fixed eyes (blue), long lashes, rooted hair (blonde), puckered lips with nursing mouth, comes with nursing bottle, doll is designed in such a manner that it drinks from the nursing bottle when held upright; when lying down, the water from the bottle enters the doll through its right arm and becomes "tears," flowing out at the eyes, dressed in a paper diaper, marked Ideal Toy Corp., TNT-14-B-34, made in 1971 .... **5.50 7.00 5.00**
- ☐ **Shirley Temple,** all vinyl, "flirty" eyes (eyes roll), rooted hair, open mouth, marked ST-19, dates to late 1930's or early 1940's, 19″ **42.00 53.00 40.00**

308 / DOLLS

	Current Price Range		Prior Year Average

- ☐ **Shirley Temple,** vinyl head, vinyl arms, legs and body, blonde wig, open mouth, dressed as Heidi from a motion picture role (but the doll is of considerably later date than the movie), marked Ideal Doll, ST17, 17″ 24.00 29.00 22.00
- ☐ **Shirley Temple,** vinyl head, vinyl arms, legs and body, open mouth (big smile), white stockings, patent leather shoes, marked Ideal Doll, ST-35-38-2, 35″ 110.00 135.00 100.00

Note: One of the finest Shirley Temple dolls in terms of realism.

- ☐ **Snow White,** composition head, arms and legs, cloth body, molded and painted hair, molded and painted features, open mouth, eyes turned to side, marked Ideal, made c. 1939, 17½″ 70.00 85.00 65.00
- ☐ **Sparkle Plenty,** plastic head, latex body, latex arms and legs, blonde hair attached by adhesive, sleep eyes (blue), Sparkle Plenty was a character in the comic strip "Dick Tracy," created by Chester Gould, marked made in U.S.A. Pat. No. 2252077, made in 1947, 15″ 50.00 65.00 45.00

Note: Competition from collectors of "comic character memorabilia" makes the price of this doll much higher than it would otherwise be.

- ☐ **Tonie,** plastic, black hair attached by adhesive, sleep eyes (blue), marked Ideal Doll, Made in U.S.A., and additionally marked with the mold number P-90, made in 1949, 14″ 28.00 36.00 25.00
- ☐ **Twins (girl),** vinyl head, cloth body, vinyl arms and legs, blue sleep eyes, marked Ideal Toy Corp., TW-14-2-U, date of manufacture not known, apparently 1960's, 15″ 28.00 35.00 25.00

Note: There was also a boy version of Twins, with the same value.

- ☐ **Tressy,** plastic/vinyl, black hair (rooted), sleep eyes (blue), pug nose, closed mouth, hair has "grow" feature (portion of wig is fitted inside head; when hair is pulled gently, it gives the appearance of "growing" out of the scalp), marked 1969, Ideal Toy Corp., GH-18, also marked (on hip) with Patent No. 3162976, made in Hong Kong ... 8.00 10.00 7.00

JUMEAU

- ☐ **Bebe Parle,** talker, bisque, sleep eyes (roundish), painted lashes on upper and lower lids, long arching brows, partially open mouth, narrow nose, joined at the elbows, talking mechanism operated by pullcord, says two words ("mama" — "papa"), date of manufacture unknown, probably c. 1895, 32″ 900.00 1100.00 850.00

Note: The value indicated is for a specimen in working condition. This is a really impressive doll, both for its size and the fact that it was one of the early foreign talkers. It would be even more expensive but apparently Jumeau turned it out in rather large quantities.

	Current Price Range		Prior Year Average

☑ **Cody,** bisque, fixed eyes (medium size, dark), lightly painted lashes on upper and lower lids, naturalistic brows (slightly arched), closed mouth, thin pale lips, narrow nose with well-defined nostrils, long thin face, found dressed as a child or adult, marked 13, date of manufacture unknown, c. 1887, one of the most famous and sought-after of the Jumeau dolls, 26″ 3200.00 3900.00 3175.00

Note: The Jumeau "Cody" doll got its name when Buffalo Bill Cody, the American showman, visited Paris in 1887 and bought a specimen of this doll. Buffalo Bill apparently had taste when it came to dolls: this long-face model represented a sharp departure from the usual mump-cheeked dolls of that era, and its facial features are very well presented.

☐ **Bisque,** fixed eyes (large, prominent, dark), painted lashes on the upper and lower lids, arching brows (rather bushy), partially open mouth (the lower lip much smaller than the upper), narrow nose, squarish jaw, conventional ears, representing a girl about 5 or 6 years of age, marked Depose E-3J, date of manufacture unknown, 10½″ 950.00 1100.00 900.00

☐ **Bisque,** socket head, walker, fixed eyes, open mouth showing teeth, head turns as doll walks, representing a young girl, marked with an X inside a circle, topped by a checkmark, date of manufacture unknown, presumed to have been made in the 1880's, 22½″ 600.00 750.00 575.00

☐ **Poupee Parisienne (Paris doll),** bisque head, wooden body, wooden arms and legs, fixed eyes (oval), painted lashes on upper and lower lids, thin brows, small closed mouth with lightly colored lips, narrow nose, squarish jaw, usually dressed to represent an adult woman, marked E, date of manufacture unknown, but probably 1890's, these are found in a variety of costumes and wearing a variety of wigs, 16″ 1375.00 1625.00 1325.00

Note: There is no doubt that the Poupee Parisienne was one of the standard Jumeau dolls for a number of years, however relatively few reached America as the firm was not (at least not at that time) export-oriented.

MATTEL
BARBIE AND BARBIE-RELATED

☐ **Barbie,** plastic, molded and painted features, bubble hairdo, wears red swimsuit (one piece), marked 850, made in 1962, 11½″ 320.00 400.00 300.00

310 / DOLLS

	Current Price Range		Prior Year Average

☐ **Barbie's Friend Christie,** black, plastic, molded and painted features, talker, brown hair (parted), wears knitted green shirt and red shorts, marked 1126, sold in 1968, 11½" 120.00 150.00 100.00

Note: The first black doll in the Barbie group. The second, introduced a year later, was modeled after a living person (singer/actress Diahann Carroll).

☐ **Bendable Ken,** plastic, molded and painted features, bendable legs, wears blue jacket and red trunks, marked 1020, sold in 1965, 12" 14.00 18.00 12.00

☐ **Busy Barbie,** plastic, molded and painted features, wears checked skirt and denim sunsuit, marked 3311, sold in 1972, 11½" 7.00 10.00 6.00

☐ **Chef Boy-Ar-Dee Barbie,** plastic, molded and painted features, painted lashes, wears green and red suit (one piece), marked 1190, sold in 1971, 11½" 8.00 11.00 7.00

☐ **Color Magic Barbie,** plastic, molded and painted features, posable legs, wears harlequin bathing suit, marked 1150, sold in 1966, 11½" 32.00 40.00 30.00

☐ **Color 'N' Curl Set Barbie,** special set with a Barbie head and a Midge head, plastic, molded and painted features, sold with four interchangeable wigs, hair coloring and hair dryer, marked 4035, sold in 1965 .... 45.00 60.00 40.00

☐ **Colored Twist 'N' Turn Francie,** plastic, molded and painted features, waist-length dark brown hair, marked 1100, sold in 1967, 11" 9.00 12.00 8.00

☐ **Cookin' Goodies Tutti,** plastic, molded and painted features, marked 3559, sold in 1967, 6¼" 5.00 7.00 4.00

GENERAL DOLLS

☐ **Big Jack,** black, plastic/vinyl, molded and painted hair, painted eyes, fully jointed, figure of an adult black male, marked 1971 Mattel Inc., US Patent Pending, made in Hong Kong, 9½" 7.00 10.00 7.00

☐ **Bouncy Baby,** vinyl head, plastic body, vinyl arms and legs, blonde hair (rooted), painted eyes, set with springs to make baby bounce, marked 1968 Mattel, Inc., 11₀ 5.00 7.00 5.00

☐ **Buffie,** plastic/vinyl, blonde hair (rooted), painted eyes, marked 1967 Mattel Inc., U.S. and For. Pats. Pend., 10" 16.00 21.00 15.00

☐ **Chester O'Chimp (a monkey),** vinyl head, plush body (stuffed), bendable fingers, molded and painted features, marked Mattel, Chester O'Chimp, 1964, 14½" 8.00 11.00 7.00

☐ **Gentle Ben (a bear),** talker, all plush (stuffed), plastic eyes and nose, marked Mattel, Gentle Ben, 1967, 18" 10.00 14.00 9.00

☐ **Lola Liddle,** vinyl, blonde hair (rooted), molded and painted features, marked Mattel 1965. 3" 6.00 8.00 6.00

☐ **Major Matt Mason,** vinyl, posable, molded and painted features, molded and painted hair, wears space suit, marked Mattel, Inc., 1967, made in Hong Kong, 6" 5.00 7.00 5.00

DOLLS / 311

	Current Price Range	Prior Year Average
☐ **Monkees,** talker, hand puppet representing all four members of this singing group, plastic, molded and painted features, molded and painted hair, made in 1967	40.00 55.00	32.00

Note: If this one wasn't collectible as "rock music memorabilia," its value would be much lower.

☐ **Platter Pal,** talker, printed cloth, marked Mattel, A Platter Pal, 1969, 15″	6.00 8.00	5.00
☐ **Randy Reader,** talker, plastic/vinyl, platinum blonde hair (rooted), operated by battery, eyes move as he reads, marked 1967 Mattel, Inc., 19″	38.00 49.00	35.00
☐ **Saucy,** plastic/vinyl, rooted hair, changing facial expressions, the left arm serves as a crank, by which the doll's face changes expression, marked 1972 Mattel, Inc., 16″	16.00 22.00	15.00

Note: One of the more imaginative novelty dolls sold by this firm.

PAPER DOLLS

They may not have three-dimensional substance, but children and collectors are as devoted to paper dolls as to more life-like dolls. They are the least expensive dolls to collect. The early ones from turn-of-the-century children's magazines, and even earlier ones made by such companies as Willimantic Thread are most desirable. Paper doll collectibles range from simple ones drawn on paper to more elaborate kinds. Most colorful and animated are those produced by Raphael Tuck and Sons of London, England and distributed all over the world. Those in uncut condition, are more select than cut items.

☐ Annie Oakley	9.00	11.00	8.50
☐ Beatles, Yellow Submarine	12.00	15.00	12.50
☐ Betty Grable	24.00	30.00	25.00
☐ Betsy McCall	1.25	1.75	1.25
☐ Betty Field	16.00	22.00	17.00
☐ Bremner's Biscuits, 6 dolls, c. 1895	40.00	55.00	42.00
☐ Captain Marvel	14.00	18.00	14.00
☐ Cleverest Fit Together Cutouts, 9 dolls, c. 1923	55.00	80.00	58.00
☐ Dolly Dimple	5.50	8.50	6.50
☐ Donna Reed	16.00	22.00	17.00
☐ Elizabeth Taylor	18.00	22.00	16.50
☐ Esther Williams	13.00	17.00	14.50
☐ Flying Captain Marvel	4.50	6.50	5.00
☐ F. W. Rueckheim Brothers, 4 dolls, c. 1895	18.00	24.00	19.00
☐ J. and P. Coats, 7 dolls, c. 1895	40.00	55.00	42.00
☐ Jane Russell	9.00	11.00	9.00
☐ Jolly Hane	9.00	11.00	9.00
☐ Katzenjammer Kids	8.00	11.00	8.50
☐ Linda Darnell	16.00	22.00	17.00
☐ Little Miss Sunbeam	20.00	24.00	20.00
☐ Mary Poppins	5.50	7.50	6.00
☐ Our Gang	50.00	60.00	52.00
☐ Palmer Cox, Brownies, Irishman, Scotsman, etc., c. 1888	40.00	55.00	42.00
☐ Princess Elizabeth	24.00	30.00	24.00
☐ Rabbit Family	7.50	11.00	8.50

312 / DOLLHOUSES

	Current Price Range		Prior Year Average
☐ Raggedy Ann	18.00	22.00	18.00
☐ Raphael Tuck and Sons, c. 1894	80.00	130.00	100.00
☐ Rosemary Clooney	16.00	22.00	17.00
☐ Sandra Dee	16.00	22.00	17.00
☐ Sandy and Candy	4.50	6.50	5.00
☐ Shirley Temple	12.00	32.00	20.00
☐ Teddy Bear	36.00	42.00	37.00
☐ Tricia Nixon	6.50	11.00	8.00
☐ Twiggy	6.50	11.00	8.00
☐ Wacs and Waves	16.00	20.00	16.00
☐ Willimantic Thread Co., uncut pair, boy and girl, with 28 articles of dress, 4″ L., c. 1885	60.00	70.00	60.00
☐ Winsome Winnie	40.00	48.00	41.50

DOLLHOUSES

Many dollhouses are actually miniatures of actual houses built during the late 19th century. The most expensive dollhouses are definitely those made by some identifiable company. Unfortunately, this tends to make people, at least new collectors, ignore the finely-crafted and exquisite handmade dollhouses, which grandfathers made for granddaughters, and have been passed down through generations. Prices for these handmade houses are quite low, usually under $100.00

	Current Price Range		Prior Year Average
☐ Dollhouse, Bliss, 13″	150.00	170.00	155.00
☐ Dollhouse, fireplaces in all rooms, simulated carved shingles, stucco exterior, late 1920's	720.00	820.00	750.00
☐ Dollhouse, lithographed, c. 1930	75.00	95.00	80.00
☐ Dollhouse, lithographed, wood, 2 wooden figures, 13″ L.	260.00	385.00	310.00
☐ Dollhouse, wood, faced with paper, painted, brick styled chimney, 17½″ L.	80.00	160.00	125.00
☐ Dutch Colonial, wood, accessories, c. 1925	450.00	550.00	475.00
☐ English, four rooms with staircase, two fireplaces, original, late 1800	825.00	925.00	850.00
☐ French chateau-style, windows on three sides, working door, c. 1890	625.00	725.00	650.00
☐ German, curtained windows, attic, steps leading to front door, c. 1890	1450.00	1550.00	1450.00
☐ German castle, ½″ to 1′ scale, molded after a late Gothic castle, c. 1875	2100.00	3100.00	2500.00
☐ German, small, embossed paper railing on second floor, unfurnished, c. 1900	300.00	375.00	325.00
☐ Nineteenth century style, roof shingled, clapboard sides, four rooms with hallways and staircase, two fireplaces, Victorian furnishings	2900.00	3900.00	3200.00
☐ Swiss chalet style, oak base on wheels, stenciled design on exterior, five rooms, Victorian furnishings, fourteen figures	2550.00	3550.00	3000.00
☐ Tootsietoy	30.00	40.00	30.00
☐ Tudor style, Schoenhut	290.00	325.00	300.00
☐ Twentieth century style, four rooms with hallways and staircase, conventional furnishings	260.00	385.00	310.00
☐ Walt Disney, six-room, metal	55.00	80.00	58.00

DOLLHOUSE FURNITURE

Small-scale furniture was made (and is still being made) for furnishing dollhouses. They are as skillfully designed and made as their full size counterparts. Everything from petite toilets to tiny candlesticks is available. The listings below are for old dollhouse furniture.

	Current Price Range		Prior Year Average
☐ **Bathtub,** tin, paint worn, 2½ ", late 19th c.	22.00	32.00	25.00
☐ **Bedroom suite,** four pieces: chairs, bureau	38.00	48.00	40.00
☐ **Bedroom suite,** three pieces, painted, c. 1920	45.00	70.00	48.00
☐ **Bowfront chest,** Tynietoy, scale	52.00	62.00	55.00
☐ **Broom holder,** tin, with brooms and dust pan	48.00	58.00	50.00
☐ **Dining table,** golden oak, scale 1" to 1'	65.00	80.00	68.00
☐ **Drum table,** rosewood, top tilts, edge lines in velvet, 3" Dia.	40.00	55.00	42.00
☐ **Fireplace,** open hearth, pine mantel	22.00	38.00	28.00
☐ **Hepplewhite sofa,** Tynietoy, scale	65.00	80.00	68.00
☐ **Ice cream parlor set,** 2 chairs with wire mesh seats, table 3½"	45.00	60.00	48.00
☐ **Rope bed,** ticking mattress and pillow, 15½" x 10½"	28.00	38.00	30.00
☐ **Rug,** needlepoint, 3½" Dia.	10.00	14.00	10.00
☐ **Shaving mirror,** mahogany frame and stand, mirror beveled glass, 4"	30.00	45.00	32.00
☐ **Stove,** cast iron	65.00	95.00	75.00
☐ **Stove,** tin kitchen, with utensils 11" H.	110.00	135.00	112.00
☐ **Teakettle,** brass with trivet	50.00	70.00	55.00
☐ **Victrola,** four-legs, painted wood, 4½"	50.00	70.00	55.00

FINE MINIATURE FURNITURE

☐ **Chest of drawers,** George III, mahogany, late 18th c., 14" H.	360.00	460.00	400.00
☐ **Chest of drawers,** George III style, mahogany, 10" H.	100.00	130.00	105.00
☐ **Longcase clock,** George III, 13½" H., early 19th c.	220.00	320.00	250.00
☐ **Tea caddy,** George III, 4½" H., 18th c.	100.00	140.00	100.00
☐ **Victorian dining room set,** walnut table and sideboard with marble tops, upholstered chairs	235.00	285.00	250.00
☐ **Wing chair,** Federal, upholstered in brocade, 8¼" H.	260.00	310.00	275.00

DOORSTOPS

Doorstops, also called door porters, were originally rocks, or other heavy but portable items used to hold doors open. The first manufactured doorstops appeared in England in the late 1700's. These doorstops were generally made of cast iron or cast brass and were round with a flat bottom and top. A long wooden shaft topped with a carrying loop was affixed to the device to facilitate moving it from room to room. Manufacture and use of doorstops continued until the early 1940's, giving the collector nearly 175 years of different shapes, styles and materials from which to choose.

DOORSTOPS

As the use of doorstops grew, the demand for more stylized pieces increased. Manufacturers responded by producing doorstops in a wide variety of fanciful shapes. Dogs, cats, monkeys and baskets of flowers were favored. The materials used included glass, wood, pottery and the most prevalent, cast iron. Iron was used extensively after the Civil War, as casting techniques had improved considerably by that time.

Cast iron doorstops were often painted and the combination of intricate casting and hand painting resulted in a real art form. Pottery and glass doorstops are less common as they were made of less durable materials. The most valued pieces, regardless of the material used, are those showing intricate casting, fine detailing and unusual subject matter, such as sporting figures or public personalities.

One of the areas in which the collector must be very cautious is that of authenticity. Production of doorstops generally ceased in the early 1940's. More recently, a large number of reproductions and fakes have appeared on the market. The collector should familiarize himself with the subtle differences that separate old from new.

Old cast iron is very smooth, almost silky, to the touch; newer pieces are coarser and feel "pebbled" in comparison. Older metal is less dense; therefore, a new piece of the same size would be heavier. Older pieces will show evidence of wear on the bottom and the back; and corrosion, if present, will be brown rather than the orange rust that appears on newer items. Additionally, older pieces show more intricate casting and better finishing as all sharp edges and "flashing" were filed smooth.

Since production of doorstops ceased in the early 1940's and many were discarded or sold for scrap, the doorstop is fast becoming a relatively rare collectible. They can be a good investment if purchased reasonably. Restoration, beyond the removal of surface dirt, is not recommended. Wire brushing to remove rust and repainting will detract from, rather than add to, the value.

	Current Price Range		Prior Year Average
☐ **Airedale,** iron	32.00	42.00	35.00
☐ **American Eagle,** iron	48.00	58.00	50.00
☐ **Aunt Jemima,** iron	62.00	72.00	65.00
☐ **Black Bear,** iron	38.00	48.00	40.00
☐ **Boxer,** iron	28.00	38.00	30.00
☐ **Bull,** iron	32.00	42.00	35.00
☐ **Bulldog,** iron	36.00	42.00	37.50
☐ **Cat,** black, iron	26.00	32.00	27.50
☐ **Cat,** black, iron, green eyes	38.00	48.00	40.00
☐ **Cockatoo,** iron	26.00	32.00	27.00
☐ **Cocker Spaniel,** iron	38.00	48.00	40.00
☐ **Conestoga Wagon,** iron	38.00	48.00	40.00
☐ **Court Jester,** with animal	48.00	58.00	50.00
☐ **Dogs,** large, iron	48.00	58.00	50.00
☐ **Doll,** with toy, iron	38.00	48.00	40.00
☐ **Elephant**	28.00	38.00	30.00
☐ **Fiddler,** with violin, iron	32.00	38.00	32.50
☐ **Flowers,** in basket, solid brass	60.00	70.00	60.00
☐ **Fox,** brass	68.00	78.00	70.00
☐ **Frog,** solid bronze	90.00	110.00	92.00
☐ **Fruit,** in bowl, iron	28.00	32.00	27.50
☐ **German Shepherd,** iron	42.00	52.00	45.00

	Current Price Range		Prior Year Average
☐ **Horses,** iron	42.00	52.00	45.00
☐ **Indian,** riding horse, iron	72.00	88.00	78.00
☐ **Irish Setter,** iron	42.00	52.00	45.00
☐ **Kitten,** iron	36.00	42.00	37.50
☐ **Lamb,** black, iron	48.00	52.00	47.50
☐ **Lighthouse,** iron	62.00	78.00	68.00
☐ **Lion,** iron	42.00	52.00	45.00
☐ **Little Red Riding Hood and the Wolf,** iron, pair	62.00	78.00	68.00
☐ **Mail Coach,** iron	48.00	58.00	50.00
☐ **Monkey,** iron	38.00	48.00	40.00
☐ **Parrot,** iron	27.00	32.00	27.50
☐ **Penguin,** iron	38.00	46.00	38.00
☐ **Pointer,** iron	38.00	46.00	38.00
☐ **Popeye,** iron	48.00	58.00	50.00
☐ **Punch,** with dog, iron	95.00	110.00	92.00
☐ **Rabbit,** iron	32.00	42.00	35.00
☐ **Rooster,** iron	48.00	58.00	50.00
☐ **Scottie Dog,** iron	38.00	48.00	40.00
☐ **Spanish Dancer,** iron	42.00	52.00	45.00
☐ **Squirrel,** iron	37.00	42.00	37.00
☐ **Stagecoach,** iron	42.00	52.00	45.00
☐ **St. Bernard,** iron	28.00	38.00	30.00
☐ **Terrier,** iron	38.00	48.00	40.00
☐ **Windmill,** iron	38.00	48.00	40.00
☐ **Wolf,** iron	32.00	42.00	35.00

EGGS

The egg has been admired as a symbol of eternal life beginning with the Greeks who decorated them for burial with the dead, possibly as early as the 17th century. Egg shapes have since been used for everything from religious ceremonies to wooden eggs for mending socks.

The collecting of real wild bird eggs is governed by Federal Law, so it is best to check with the United States Fish and Wildlife Service before entering this area of collecting.

Manmade eggs offer a wide variety of styles and prices to suit every collector's taste and budget. One of the favorite uses of the egg shape is for boxes. Small egg boxes can be carved from ostrich eggs or from the egg shaped coquilla nut. Egg shaped jewelry boxes can be made from mother-of-pearl or papier-mache. The rarest and most valuable of these egg boxes were made in the 19th century for the Russian Czars by Peter Faberge. Originally conceived to celebrate Easter, these eggs were fabulous creations of gold, jewels and other precious materials.

The most common collectible egg is the Easter egg which is thought to have originated in the 11th century Poland. The practice of decorating eggs became popular in other parts of Europe, each of which developed its own method of decoration. The technique of pysanky was brought to the U.S. from the Ukraine. It involves producing designs on an egg using wax and dyes and is usually in demand by collectors.

Minton Emperor's Garden, of the egg series, c. 1982 . . . . **$95.00**

	Current Price Range		Prior Year Average
☐ **Art Glass egg,** iridescent, large, Vanderbelt	32.00	42.00	35.00
☐ **Art Glass egg,** pink, gold flowers	135.00	160.00	138.00
☐ **Box,** china, painted with flowers and birds, hinged lid, brass fittings, 9½"	130.00	170.00	140.00
☐ **Easter candy container,** papier-mache, egg being drawn by rabbit, 4"	12.00	18.00	12.50
☐ **Easter egg,** baby chick, Goebel, c. 1978	18.00	22.00	17.50
☐ **Easter egg,** dove on cover, Wedgwood, c. 1977 . .	52.00	72.00	60.00
☐ **Easter egg,** glass, raised lettering	38.00	48.00	40.00
☐ **Easter egg,** glass, undecorated, large, set of four	38.00	48.00	40.00
☐ **Easter egg,** porcelain, Royal Bayreuth, c. 1979 . .	22.00	32.00	25.00
☐ **Easter egg,** porcelain, floral decoration, Furstenberg, c. 1974	18.00	28.00	20.00
☐ **Easter egg,** silver and enamel, lilies and forget-me-nots, Faberge, by Ruckert, c. 1900	11500.00	13000.00	11750.00
☐ **Jewel case,** mother-of-pearl, gilded metal, egg "wheelbarrow"	65.00	80.00	68.00
☐ **Mary Gregory Glass egg,** raised lettering and design	22.00	32.00	25.00
☐ **Milk Glass egg,** raised lettering and design	28.00	38.00	30.00
☐ **Wooden egg,** pine, hen, painted	5.50	11.00	7.50

EYEGLASSES

Eyeglasses have been available since the 13th century, but did not come into general use until the latter decades of the 18th century. Popular styles included the quizzing glass, which was a single hand held lense; and scissors glasses, which were two lenses joined in a single handle that was held under the nose. The modern temple glasses, those which are held in place by bars pressing against the temples, were unpopular as they were considered a mark of infirmity. The monocle went in and out of fashion many times. Wealthy women favored the lorgnette, while men and women generally wore the nose pinching pince-nez, a style that remained popular from 1840 until the 1920's when the modern version of glass became fashionable.

Eyeglasses of nearly every type are worth collecting, particularly old or discontinued styles. Naturally, very old glasses made in the 18th or 19th centuries are prized; but they may be costly, especially if made of precious ores, or even semi-precious materials. Some collectors specialize in the outrageous plastic styles of the 1950's, since most were unpopular and production runs were small.

Good sources of old eyeglasses include Lions and Rotary Clubs, who collect old frames for the needy, and old optometrist's offices. Prices for many specimens are still relatively reasonable.

	Current Price Range		Prior Year Average
☐ **Harold Lloyd,** bone frame, c. 1920	52.00	62.00	55.00
☐ **Lorgnette,** English, gilded, c. 1840	110.00	135.00	112.00
☐ **Lorgnette,** mother-of-pearl, c. 1800	62.00	72.00	65.00
☐ **Lorgnette,** sterling silver, c. 1840	135.00	160.00	138.00
☐ **Lorgnette,** tortoiseshell, c. 1800	110.00	135.00	112.00
☐ **Monocle,** gold frame, silk cord, c. 1800	42.00	52.00	45.00
☐ **Quizzing,** monocle, gold and silver, c. 1800	78.00	88.00	80.00
☐ **Scissor,** gold plated, ornate, c. 1880	78.00	88.00	80.00
☐ **Spectacles,** pinch, Art Deco, wire frame, c. 1930	42.00	62.00	50.00
☐ **Spectacles,** pinch, hard rubber, c. 1860	42.00	62.00	50.00
☐ **Spectacles,** pinch, wire frame, c. 1920	42.00	62.00	50.00
☐ **Spectacles,** steel framed with ties, c. 1800	92.00	110.00	95.00
☐ **Spectacles,** steel framed, wire temples, c. 1800	92.00	110.00	95.00

CASES

☐ **Engraved silver,** oval, clasp works, c. 1900	85.00	145.00	110.00
☐ **Papier-mache,** with mother-of-pearl inlay, c. 1850-1960	85.00	145.00	110.00

FANS

Folding fans were popular and fashionable accessories for women of means during the 18th, 19th and even into the early 20th centuries. Aside from the obvious function of being used to cool oneself, fans were used to show not only one's social position and wealth, but also for coquetry or flirting.

318 / FANS

Fan, pierced ivory sticks, cabochon rubies in pin, silver and gold foil, six miniatures portraits reverse is heavily embossed with gold and silver foil .... **$4500.00-$5000.00**

Folding fans were constructed in one of two ways. The more common method was the insertion of sticks into a pleated piece of material called a "leaf." Leaves were made of silk lace, paper, or even vellum (very thin goatskin). The other type of folding fan was called a "brise." The brise fan was made up of wide, overlapping sticks and joined by a ribbon. Nearly all fans of both types have scenes or designs painted on them.

Another type, considered quite stylish from the 1870's until about 1910, was the feather fan. Usually made of ostrich feathers, this type was quite perishable and is now relatively rare.

Because fans are not durable collectibles, their numbers tend to be rather low and prices accordingly high. Once a beautiful fan is acquired, the methods of display and preservation are vital factors. Special attention should be paid to store the item in an airtight container that screens out damaging ultraviolet rays. Most specimens do well when placed in a protective frame.

	Current Price Range		Prior Year Average
☐ **Advertising,** Hire's Root Beer, 6½", c. 1930	5.50	11.00	7.50
☐ **Advertising,** Homer's 5 Cigar, 7", c. 1910	5.50	11.00	7.50
☐ **Advertising,** lithographed, late 19th c.	5.50	11.00	7.50
☐ **Black net,** with sequins	18.00	22.00	17.50
☐ **Bride's,** lace, hand painted	18.00	22.00	17.50
☐ **Bride's,** lace, sequins, ivory sticks	32.00	42.00	35.00
☐ **Brise,** child's, painted, ribbon and floral design ..	55.00	70.00	58.00
☐ **Brise,** gilded, painted with three vignettes, loop .	125.00	145.00	125.00

	Current Price Range		Prior Year Average
☐ **Brise,** Regency, painted floral design, amber guards	105.00	125.00	105.00
☐ **Brise,** Regency, painted vase of flowers	35.00	55.00	40.00
☐ **Celluloid,** carved flower	35.00	55.00	40.00
☐ **Celluloid,** miniature	35.00	55.00	40.00
☐ **Celluloid,** Oriental design	18.00	28.00	20.00
☐ **Celluloid,** sequins, chiffon	38.00	48.00	40.00
☐ **Cockade,** silver and cut steel pique, middle quizzing glass	260.00	285.00	262.00
☐ **Feather,** celluloid sticks	42.00	52.00	45.00
☐ **Feather,** ivory sticks	80.00	100.00	85.00
☐ **Feather,** painted, c. 1870	75.00	95.00	80.00
☐ **Feather,** tortoiseshell sticks	65.00	80.00	68.00
☐ **Feather,** small, late 19th c.	110.00	135.00	112.00
☐ **Feather,** signed Duvelleroy, 19th c.	410.00	510.00	450.00
☐ **French,** painted, ivory sticks	125.00	145.00	125.00
☐ **French,** painted, tortoise sticks, sequins	105.00	120.00	102.00
☐ **French,** painted, signed Jolivet, 19th c.	410.00	510.00	450.00
☐ **French,** painted, carved, signed	52.00	62.00	55.00
☐ **Garrett Snuff,** advertising, paper, c. 1928	12.00	18.00	12.50
☐ **George Washington and Cherry Smash,** lithographed	18.00	22.00	17.50
☐ **Gold edge,** pink silk, ebony ribs	28.00	32.00	27.50
☐ **Hand painted,** floral design, wood	18.00	22.00	17.50
☐ **Horn,** carved, painted pansies, blue ribbon	75.00	95.00	80.00
☐ **Lacquered,** black, silver flower	50.00	65.00	52.00
☐ **Lacquered,** white, silver handle	45.00	60.00	48.00
☐ **Marabou feathers,** satin, hand painted, 20"	75.00	95.00	80.00
☐ **Oriental,** straw, lacquered handle	12.00	18.00	12.50
☐ **Oriental,** silk, Geisha figure	6.00	11.00	7.50
☐ **Ostrich plume,** tortoise shell sticks	18.00	28.00	20.00
☐ **Pearl sticks,** sequin design, 8"	28.00	38.00	30.00
☐ **Puzzle,** four scenes, two-way opening	110.00	120.00	107.00
☐ **Satin flower center,** carved, ivory sticks	55.00	80.00	58.00
☐ **Silk,** embroidered, ivory sticks	38.00	55.00	42.00
☐ **Silk,** hand painted animal figure and books	28.00	38.00	30.00
☐ **Silk,** hand painted figures and floral designs, original storage container	60.00	80.00	65.00
☐ **Silk,** Oriental design, ivory and bamboo	28.00	38.00	30.00
☐ **Souvenir Centennial,** historical buildings, 12"	55.00	90.00	72.00
☐ **Wedding,** ivory sticks, lace	55.00	70.00	58.00

FARM MACHINERY

This is a specialized area of collecting, but potentially enjoyable and even profitable for the collector who likes to tinker with machinery. Tractors, cultivators, reapers, plows and even manure spreaders have begun to generate enthusiasm among some collectors. Although a large storage and display area is needed, most farm machinery of the latter 19th and early 20th centuries can be obtained for the trouble of hauling it away.

Farm machinery is generally used and repaired constantly until it is useless. Then it is towed to an unused corner of the farm and left to rust. While nearly worthless in this condition, many items command surprisingly

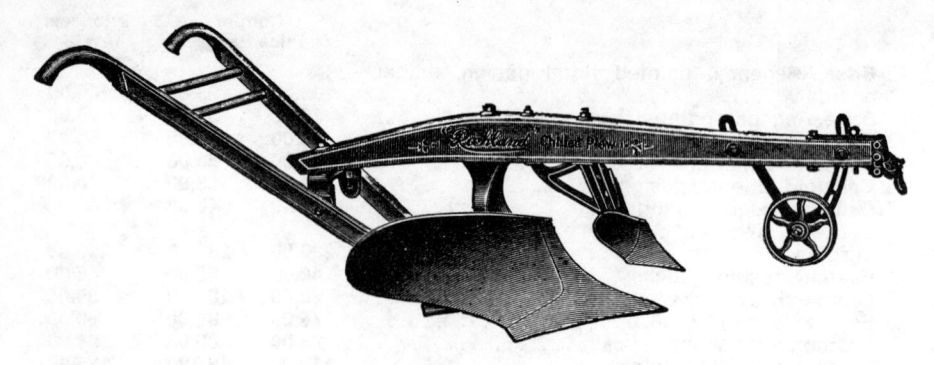

Chilled Plow, Richland Farm Implements, iron and oak, for two or three horses .... **$150.00-$250.00**

high prices when restored to operating condition. For those so inclined, restoration is not as complex as in many other antiques, such as automobiles. Most early farm machinery is simple in design so as to be easily repaired in the field.

Another related collectible is the cast iron implement seat with its cleverly cast, sometimes intricate, designs and manufacturer's name or trademark.

Hand tools are faily common items at flea markets. Although they require little or no restoration and occupy less space, they do tend to be somewhat overpriced.

	Current Price Range		Prior Year Average
☐ **Avery steam engine,** 40 hp. with full extension wheels, 1912	1650.00	1850.00	1700.00
☐ **Baker steam engine,** 20 hp. single cylinder side mount, 1920	3250.00	3550.00	3350.00
☐ **Case tractor,** model "C", 4 cylinder, rubber wheels, restored, good condition, c. 1927	800.00	1050.00	900.00
☐ **Case tractor,** VAC model, rubber wheels, restored, good condition, c. 1931	360.00	510.00	420.00
☐ **International Harvester tractor,** model "H", rubber wheels, restored, good condition, c. 1937	800.00	1050.00	900.00
☐ **John Deere tractor,** model "B", rubber wheels, restored, good condition, c. 1935	420.00	620.00	500.00
☐ **Russell traction steam machine,** 8 hp., restored ...	3550.00	4050.00	3750.00
☐ **Sattley's timber saw,** kerosene engine	1250.00	1450.00	1300.00

FIREARMS

The collecting of firearms is a popular and widespread hobby in the United States. Collectors usually fall into two groups: those who collect antique guns manufactured before 1898, and those whose primary interest is in weapons made from 1899 to the present. Classifying the guns is not as easily done as some models introduced in the mid 19th century were produced, largely unchanged, until well into the 20th century. A good example of this

Top to Bottom: **Singleshot Handgun,** Contender, various calibers, adjustable sights, super 14" barrel, (modern) **$155.00-$215.00; Percussion Handgun,** .45 Patriot, set trigger, octagon barrel, Reproduction, (antique) .... **$85.00-$130.00**

phenomenon is the Remington Double Derringer, which was produced from 1865 until 1935, with few major alterations to the original design.

Collectible guns need not be antiques, although many are. Nearly any gun of unusual design, low production, or historical interest may be termed collectible. Colt handguns and Winchester rifles of the late 1800's and early 1900's are not particularly rare, or costly, but are certainly considered collectible.

First models made by any company are also desirable, as are last models (if the company went out of business) and guns designed for special uses. Military firearms, particularly those used in wars fought by the United States, are also desirable.

The best route for the beginning collector to take is to first research his interest carefully, then to buy only from established dealers until his knowledge is such that he feels confident in making purchases without expert advice. There are many fakes and reproductions on the market. Many unscrupulous, but knowledgeable people alter existing weapons by changing dates, or other small features, to make common specimens appear to be rare ones. Altering serial numbers, nameplates, actions (the method in which the gun is fired) and other items are favored methods and are sometimes very difficult to spot.

As in all collecting, it is wise to narrow one's interest to a specialty so as to have a more coherent collection. A collector may wish to collect only first or last offerings of celebrated manufacturers, guns made by firms which ceased all production after a short time, weapons used during wars, or pistols of a certain period.

Due to the lack of space, the following listings offer only a sample selection of some of the major firearms manufacturers. For more in-depth information and listings, you may refer to *The Official Firearms Guide to Antique and Modern Firearms,* by David Byron, and published by the House of Collectibles.

322 / FIREARMS

BERETTA
HANDGUN, SEMI-AUTOMATIC

	Current Price Range		Prior Year Average
☐ 1915, .32 ACP, Clip Fed, Military, modern	175.00	265.00	220.00
☐ 1915, .380 ACP, Clip Fed, Military, modern	265.00	350.00	305.00
☐ 1915-19, .32 ACP, Clip Fed, Military, modern	200.00	275.00	238.00
☐ 1919 V P, .25 ACP, Clip Fed, modern	95.00	175.00	135.00
☐ Cougar, .380 ACP, Clip Fed, modern	125.00	200.00	162.00
☐ Jaguar, .22 L.R.R.F., Clip Fed, modern	95.00	175.00	238.00
☐ Jetfire, .25 ACP, Clip Fed, Blue, modern	75.00	125.00	100.00
☐ Jetfire, .25 ACP, Clip Fed, Nickel, modern	80.00	130.00	105.00
☐ Minx, Short, Clip Fed, Blue, modern	75.00	125.00	100.00
☐ Minx, .22 Short, Clip Fed, Nickel, modern	80.00	130.00	110.00
☐ Model 100, .32 ACP, Clip Fed, modern	95.00	160.00	128.00
☐ Model 101, .22 L.R.R.F., Clip Fed, Adjustable Sights, modern	110.00	175.00	140.00
☐ Model 1923, 9mm Luger, Clip Fed, Military, modern	225.00	350.00	285.00

SHOTGUN, DOUBLE BARREL, OVER-UNDER

☐ Golden Snipe, 12 and 20 Gauges, Single Trigger, Automatic Ejector, Engraved, Fancy Checkering, modern	350.00	450.00	400.00
☐ Golden Snipe, 12 and 20 Gauges, Single Selective Trigger, Automatic Ejector, Engraved, Fancy Checkering, modern	475.00	625.00	550.00
☐ Golden Snipe Deluxe, 12 and 20 Gauges, Single Selective Trigger, Automatic Ejector, Fancy Engraving, Fancy Checkering, modern	490.00	700.00	600.00
☐ Model ASEL, 12 and 20 Gauges, Single Trigger, Checkered Stock, modern	695.00	900.00	800.00
☐ Model BL 1, 12 Ga., Field Grade, Double Trigger, Checkered Stock, modern	275.00	365.00	300.00
☐ Model BL 2, 12 Ga., Field Grade, Single Selective Trigger, Checkered Stock, modern	325.00	445.00	385.00
☐ Model BL 3, 12 Ga., Trap Grade, Singe Selective Trigger, Checkered Stock, Light Engraving, Vent Rib, modern	400.00	515.00	455.00
☐ Model BL 3, Various Gauges, Skeet Grade, Single Selective Trigger, Checkered Stock, Light Engraving, Vent Rib, modern	400.00	510.00	455.00
☐ Model BL 3, Various Gauges, Field Grade, Single Selective Trigger, Checkered Stock, Light Engraving, Vent Rib, modern	400.00	510.00	455.00
☐ Model BL 4, 12 Ga., Trap Grade, Single Selective Trigger, Selective Ejector, Engraved, Vent Rib, modern	550.00	700.00	625.00
☐ Model BL 4, Various Gauges, Skeet Grade, Single Selective Trigger, Selective Ejector, Engraved, Vent Rib, modern	550.00	700.00	625.00
☐ Model BL 4, Various Gauges, Field Grade, Single Selective Trigger, Selective Ejector, Engraved, Vent Rib, modern	475.00	650.00	520.00

SHOTGUN, SEMI-AUTOMATIC

☐ Gold Lark, 12 Ga., Vent Rib, Light Engraving, Checkered Stock, modern	185.00	295.00	235.00

	Current Price Range		Prior Year Average
☐ **Model A301**, 12 Ga., Trap Grade, Vent Rib, modern	265.00	385.00	240.00
☐ **Model A301**, 12 and 20 Gauges, Field Grade, Vent Rib, modern	240.00	365.00	300.00
☐ **Model A301**, 12 and 20 Gauges, Skeet Grade, Vent Rib, modern	240.00	365.00	300.00
☐ **Model A301**, 12 Ga., Mag. 3", Field Grade, Vent Rib, modern	295.00	395.00	245.00
☐ **Model AL 1**, 12 and 20 Gauges, Checkered Stock, modern	170.00	280.00	225.00
☐ **Model AL 2**, 12 Ga., Vent Rib, Trap Grade, Checkered Stock, modern	225.00	295.00	255.00

BROWNING

HANDGUN, SEMI-AUTOMATIC

☐ **Various Calibers**, Baby-.380-Hi Power Set, Renaissance, Nickel Plated, Engraved, modern .	3250.00	4750.00	3800.00
☐ **380 Auto**, .380 ACP, Clip Fed, Renaissance, Nickel Plated, Engraved, modern	975.00	1450.00	1175.00
☐ **380 Auto**, .380 ACP, Clip Fed, Adjustable Sights, modern	185.00	325.00	270.00
☐ **380 Auto Standard**, .380 ACP, Clip Fed, Modern .	175.00	270.00	225.00
☐ **Baby**, .25 ACP, Clip Fed, Lightweight, Nickel Plated, modern	350.00	475.00	420.00
☐ **Baby**, .25 ACP, Clip Fed, Rennaissance, Nickel Plated, Engraved, modern	925.00	1400.00	1175.00
☐ **Baby Standard**, .25 ACP, Clip Fed, modern	175.00	275.00	225.00

SHOTGUN, DOUBLE BARREL, OVER-UNDER

☐ **Citori**, 12 Ga., Trap Grade, Vent Rib, Checkered Stock, modern	425.00	550.00	480.00
☐ **Citori**, 12 and 20 Gauges, Standard Grade, Vent Rib, Checkered Stock, modern	415.00	535.00	470.00
☐ **Citori**, 12 and 20 Gauges, Skeet Grade, Vent Rib, Checkered Stock, modern	425.00	550.00	480.00
☐ **Citori International**, 12 Ga., Skeet Grade, Vent Rib, Checkered Stock, modern	475.00	600.00	530.00
☐ **Citori Grade II**, Various Gauges, Hunting Model, Engraved, Checkered Stock, Single Selective Trigger, modern	650.00	850.00	750.00

SHOTGUN, SEMI-AUTOMATIC

☐ **Auto-5**, 12 Ga., Trap Grade, Vent Rib, Checkered Stock, modern	350.00	465.00	410.00
☐ **Auto-5**, 12 and 20 Gauges, Magnum, Checkered Stock, Light Engraving, Plain Barrel, modern ...	340.00	450.00	395.00
☐ **Auto-5**, 12 and 20 Gauges, Skeet Grade, Checkered Stock, Light Engraving, Vent Rib, modern	355.00	465.00	410.00
☐ **Auto-5**, 16 Ga. 2$9/_{16}$", Pre-WW2, Checkered Stock, Light Engraving, Plain Barrel, modern	400.00	550.00	475.00
☐ **Auto-5**, 16 Gauge, Sweet Sixteen, Lightweight, Checkered Stock, Light Engraving, Plain Barrel, modern	425.00	550.00	475.00

324 / FIREARMS

	Current Price Range		Prior Year Average
☐ **Auto-5,** Various Gauges, Lightweight, Checkered Stock, Light Engraving, Plain Barrel, modern	340.00	450.00	410.00

COLT

HANDGUN, PERCUSSION

☐ **.28 Model 1855 Root,** Round Cylinder, Side Hammer, Spur Trigger, Revolver, Round Barrel, antique	425.00	725.00	575.00
☐ **.28 Model Patterson (Baby),** 5 Shot, Various Barrel Lengths, Octagon Barrel, no Loading Lever, antique	2450.00	3750.00	3100.00
☐ **.28 Model Patterson (Baby),** 5 Shot, Various Barrel Lengths, Octagon Barrel, with Factory Loading Lever, antique	2850.00	4100.00	3600.00
☐ **.31 Model 1848 Revolver,** Baby Dragoon, 5 Shot, Various Barrels Lengths, no loading Lever, no Capping Groove, antique	1950.00	3000.00	2450.00

HANDGUN, REVOLVER

☐ **For Nickel Plating,** Add $20.00-$30.00			
☐ **.357 Magnum,** .357 Magnum, 6 Shot, Various Barrel Lengths, Adjustable Sights. Target Hammer, Target Grips, modern	275.00	425.00	325.00
☐ **.357 Magnum,** .357 Magnum, 6 Shot, Various Barrel Lengths, Adjustable Sights, modern	250.00	375.00	312.00
☐ **125th Anniversary,** .45 Colt, Single Action Army, Commemorative, Blue, with Gold Plating, cased, curio	450.00	700.00	575.00

HANDGUN, SEMI-AUTOMATIC

☐ **Ace 45-22 Conversion Unit,** .45 ACP, Clip Fed, Adjustable Sights, Tarket Pistol, curio	175.00	275.00	225.00
☐ **Ace Service Model,** .22 L.R.R.F., Clip Fed, Adjustable Sights, Target Pistol, curio	675.00	975.00	825.00
☐ **Combat Commander,** .38 Super, Clip Fed, Blue, modern	200.00	285.00	242.00
☐ **Combat Commander,** .45 ACP, Clip Fed, Blue, modern	200.00	285.00	242.00

HANDGUN, SINGLESHOT

☐ **#1 Deringer,** .41 Short R.F., all Metal, Spur Trigger, Light Engraving, antique	575.00	800.00	675.00
☐ **#2 Deringer,** .41 Short R.F., "Address Col. Colt", Wood Grips, Spur Trigger, Light Engraving, antique	600.00	950.00	775.00
☐ **#2 Deringer,** .41 Short R.F., Wood Grips, Spur Trigger, Light Engraving, antique	400.00	575.00	482.00
☐ **#3 Deringer Thuer,** .41 Short R.F., Wood Grips, Spur Trigger, 1st Issue, Contoured Swell at Pivot, High-Angled Hammer, antique	595.00	950.00	770.00

ITHACA GUN CO.

SHOTGUN, DOUBLE BARREL, OVER-UNDER

☐ **Model 500,** 12 and 20 Gauges, Field Grade, Selective Ejector, Vent Rib, modern	275.00	375.00	325.00

	Current Price Range		Prior Year Average
☐ **Model 500,** 12 and 20 Gauges, Field Grade, Selective Ejector, Vent Rib, modern	275.00	375.00	325.00
☐ **Model 500,** 12 Ga. Mag. 3″, Field Grade, Selective Ejector, Vent Rib, modern	285.00	390.00	340.00
☐ **Model 600,** 12 Ga., Trap Grade, Selective Ejector, Vent Rib, modern	375.00	500.00	430.00
☐ **Model 600,** 12 Ga., Trap Grade, Selective Ejector, Vent Rib, Monte Carlo Stock, modern	375.00	500.00	430.00

SHOTGUN, DOUBLE BARREL, SIDE-BY-SIDE

☐ **Outside Hammers,** Deduct 20%-30%

☐ **Various Gauges,** Field Grade, Hammerless, Magnum, Beavertail Forend, modern	600.00	775.00	680.00
☐ **Various Gauges,** Field Grade, Hammerless, Beavertail Forend, Double Trigger, modern	550.00	700.00	625.00
☐ **Various Gauges,** Field Grade, Hammerless, Double Trigger, Checkered Stock, modern	375.00	525.00	450.00
☐ **Various Gauges,** Field Grade, Hammerless, Magnum, Double Trigger, modern	425.00	575.00	500.00
☐ **#1 E Grade,** Various Gauges, Hammerless, Automatic Ejector, Bevertail Forend, Double Trigger, modern	725.00	975.00	850.00
☐ **#1 E Grade,** Various Gauges, Hammerless, Automatic Ejector, Magnum, Bevertail Forend, Double Trigger, modern	850.00	1200.00	1025.00

SHOTGUN, SEMI-AUTOMATIC

☐ **300 Standard,** 12 and 20 Gauges, modern	145.00	180.00	158.00
☐ **300 Standard,** 12 and 20 Gauges, Vent Rib, modern	150.00	190.00	170.00
☐ **300 XL Standard,** 12 and 20 Gauges, modern	155.00	195.00	175.00
☐ **300 XL Standard,** 12 and 20 Gauges, Vent Rib, modern	170.00	220.00	195.00
☐ **900 XL,** 12 Gauge, Trap Grade, modern	185.00	245.00	215.00
☐ **900 XL,** 12 Gauge, Trap Grade, Monte Carlo Stock, modern	185.00	250.00	222.00
☐ **900 XL,** 12 and 20 Gauges, Skeet Grade, modern .	180.00	235.00	205.00
☐ **900 XL Deluxe,** 12 and 20 Gauges, Vent Rib, modern	180.00	225.00	202.00
☐ **900 XL Slug,** 12 and 20 Gauges, Open Rear Sight, modern	170.00	220.00	195.00
☐ **Mag 10 Deluxe,** 10 Gauges, 3½″, Takedown, Vent Rib, Fancy Wood, Checkered Stock, modern	400.00	485.00	442.00
☐ **Mag 10 Standard,** 10 Gauge 3½″, Takedown, Vent Rib, Recoil Pad, Checkered Stock, Sling Swivels, modern	300.00	395.00	348.00
☐ **Mag 10 Standard,** 10 Gauge 3½″, Takedown, Recoil Pad, Checkered Stock, Sling Swivels, modern	260.00	340.00	300.00

SHOTGUN, SLIDE ACTION

☐ **Model 37,** 12 Gauge, Takedown, Bicentennial, Engraved, Fancy Wood, Checkered Stock, modern	450.00	550.00	500.00
☐ **Model 37,** Various Gauges, Takedown, Plain, modern	95.00	135.00	115.00

FIREARMS / 325

326 / FIREARMS

	Current Price Range		Prior Year Average

- ☐ **Model 37 Deerslayer,** Various Gauges, Takedown, Checkered Stock, Recoil Pad, Open Rear Sight, modern 140.00 175.00 158.00
- ☐ **Model 37 Deerslayer,** Various Gauges, Takedown, Fancy Wood, Checkered Stock Stock, Recoil Pad, Open Rear Sight, modern 150.00 200.00 175.00
- ☐ **Model 37 DSPS,** 12 Gauge, Takedown, Checkered Stock, 8 Shot, Open Rear Sight, modern 150.00 200.00 175.00
- ☐ **Model 37 DSPS,** 12 Gauge, Takedown, Checkered Stock, 5 Shot, Open Rear Sight, modern 145.00 190.00 162.00

IVER JOHNSON
HANDGUN, REVOLVER

- ☐ **.22 SLupershot,** .22 L.R.R.F., 7 Shot, Blue, Wood Grips, Top Break, Double Action, modern 50.00 85.00 65.00
- ☐ **Armsworth M855,** .22 L.R.R.F., 8 Shot, Single Action, Top Break, Adjustable Sights, Wood Grips, modern 60.00 100.00 80.00
- ☐ **Cadet,** .22 WMR, 8 Shot, Solid Frame, Double Action, Plastic Stock, Blue, modern 35.00 60.00 48.00
- ☐ **Cadet,** .32 S & W Long, 5 Shot, Solid Frame, Double Action, Plastic Stock, Nickel Plated, modern . 40.00 65.00 52.00
- ☐ **Cadet,** .32 S & W, 5 Shot, Solid Frame, Double Action, Plastic Stock, Blue, modern 35.00 60.00 48.00

SHOTGUN, DOUBLE BARREL, SIDE-BY-SIDE

- ☐ **Hercules,** Various Gauges, Double Trigger, Checkered Stock, Hammerless, modern 170.00 250.00 210.00
- ☐ **Hercules,** Various Gauges, Double Trigger, Automatic Ejector, Hammerless, Checkered Stock, modern 200.00 295.00 248.00
- ☐ **Hercules,** Various Gauges, Single Trigger, Hammerless, Checkered Stock, modern 235.00 345.00 285.00
- ☐ **Hercules,** Various Gauges, Single Trigger, Automatic Ejector, Hammerless, Checkered Stock, modern 275.00 385.00 330.00
- ☐ **Hercules,** Various Gauges, Single Selective Trigger, Hammerless, Checkered Stock, modern 275.00 400.00 335.00

MARLIN FIREARMS COMPANY
RIFLE, BOLT ACTION

- ☐ **Glenfield M10,** .22 L.R.R.F., Singleshot, modern .. 20.00 35.00 28.00
- ☐ **Glenfield M20,** .22 L.R.R.F., Clip Fed, modern 30.00 45.00 38.00
- ☐ **Model 100,** .22 L.R.R.F., Singleshot, Open Rear Sight, Takedown, modern 25.00 35.00 30.00
- ☐ **Model 100-S,** .22 L.R.R.F., Singleshot, Peep Sights, Takedown, modern 45.00 65.00 55.00
- ☐ **Model 100-SB,** .22 L.R.R.F., Singleshot, Smoothbore, Takedown, modern 25.00 35.00 30.00
- ☐ **Model 101,** .22 L.R.R.F., Singleshot, Open Rear Sight, Takedown, Bevertail Forend, modern 25.00 40.00 32.00

RIFLE, LEVER ACTION

- ☐ **Centennial Set 336-39,** Fancy Checkering, Fancy Wood, Engraved, Brass Furniture, modern 700.00 1100.00 900.00

FIREARMS / 327

	Current Price Range		Prior Year Average
☐ M1894 (Late), .357 Magnum, Tube Feed, Open Rear Sight, modern	130.00	165.00	148.00
☐ M1894 (Late), .44 Magnum, Tube Feed, Open Rear Sight, modern	95.00	145.00	120.00
☐ M1895 (Late), .45-70 Government, Tube Feed, Open Rear Sight, modern	140.00	180.00	160.00

RIFLE, SEMI-AUTOMATIC

☐ Glenfield M40, .22 L.R.R.F., Tube Feed, modern	40.00	55.00	48.00
☐ Glenfield M60, .22 L.R.R.F., Tube Feed, modern	30.00	45.00	38.00
☐ Model 49 DL, .22 L.R.R.F., Tube Feed, Open Rear Sight, modern	35.00	55.00	45.00
☐ Model 50, .22 L.R.R.F, Clip Fed, Open Rear Sight, Takedown, modern	35.00	55.00	45.00
☐ Model 50E, .22 L.R.R.F, Clip Fed, Peep Sights, Takedown, modern	35.00	55.00	45.00
☐ Model 88C, .22 L.R.R.F., Tube Feed, Takedown, Open Rear Sight, modern	40.00	55.00	48.00
☐ Model 88DL, .22 L.R.R.F., Tube Feed, Takedown, Peep Sights, modern	40.00	60.00	50.00

SHOTGUN, SLIDE ACTION

☐ Model 1898 Field, 12 Gauge, Hammer, Tube Feed, modern	145.00	300.00	220.00
☐ Model 1898 B, 12 Gauge, Hammer, Tube Feed, Checkered Stock, modern	165.00	350.00	260.00
☐ Model 1898 C, 12 Gauge, Hammer, Tube Feed, Checkered Stock, Fancy Wood, Light Engraving, modern	450.00	700.00	580.00
☐ Model 1898 D, 12 Gauge, Hammer, Tube Feed, Checkered Stock, Fancy Wood, Engraved, modern	850.00	1450.00	1150.00
☐ Model 19 Field, 12 Gauge, Hammer, Tube Feed, modern	120.00	245.00	182.00
☐ Model 19 B, 12 Gauge, Hammer, Tube Feed, Checkered Stock, modern	170.00	350.00	260.00
☐ Model 19 C, 12 Gauge, Hammer, Tube Feed, Checkered Stock, Fancy Wood, Light Engraving, modern	350.00	500.00	420.00
☐ Model 19 D, 12 Gauge, Hammer, Tube Feed, Checkered Stock, Fancy Wood, Engraved, modern	750.00	1100.00	975.00

MOSSBERG, O.F. AND SONS
RIFLE, BOLT ACTION

☐ Model 10, .22 L.R.R.F., Singleshot, Takedown, modern	40.00	55.00	48.00
☐ Model 14, .22 L.R.R.F., Singleshot, Takedown, Peep Sights, modern	45.00	60.00	52.00
☐ Model 140B, .22 L.R.R.F., Clip Fed, Peep Sights, Monte Carlo Stock, modern	45.00	70.00	58.00
☐ Model 140K, .22 L.R.R.F., Clip Fed, Open Rear Sight, Monte Carlo Stock, modern	40.00	65.00	52.00
☐ Model 142A, .22 L.R.R.F., Clip Fed, Peep Sights, modern	50.00	75.00	62.00

	Current Price Range		Prior Year Average
☐ **Model 142K,** .22 L.R.R.F., Clip Fed, Open Rear Sight, modern	50.00	75.00	62.00
☐ **Model 142K,** .22 L.R.R.F., Clip Fed, Carbine, Monte Carlo Stock, modern	40.00	60.00	50.00

SHOTGUN, BOLT ACTION

	Current Price Range		Prior Year Average
☐ **Model 173,** 410 Gauge, Takedown, Singleshot, modern	35.00	55.00	45.00
☐ **Model 173Y,** .410 Gauge, Clip Fed, Singleshot, modern	35.00	55.00	45.00
☐ **Model 183D,** .410 Gauge, Takedown, 3 Shot, modern	40.00	60.00	50.00
☐ **Model 183K,** 410 Gauge, Takedown, Adjustable Choke, Clip Fed, modern	40.00	60.00	50.00
☐ **Model 183T,** .410 Gauge, Clip Fed, modern	40.00	65.00	52.00
☐ **Model 184D,** .20 Gauge, Takedown, 3 Shot, modern	40.00	60.00	50.00
☐ **Model 185K,** 20 Gauge, Takedown, 3 Shot, Adjustable Choke, modern	40.00	60.00	50.00
☐ **Model 190D,** 16 Gauge, Takedown, Clip Fed, modern	40.00	60.00	50.00
☐ **Model 190K,** 16 Gauge, Takedown, Adjustable Choke, Clip Fed, modern	40.00	60.00	50.00

SHOTGUN, SLIDE ACTION

	Current Price Range		Prior Year Average
☐ **Cruiser,** 12 Gauge, One-Hand Grip, Nickel Plated, modern	140.00	190.00	165.00
☐ **Model 200D,** 12 Gauge, Clip Fed, Adjustable Choke, modern	55.00	85.00	70.00
☐ **Model 200K,** 12 Gauge, Clip Fed, Adjustable Choke, modern	60.00	90.00	75.00
☐ **Model 500 Super,** Checkered Stock, Vent Rib, modern	125.00	175.00	150.00
☐ **Model 500A,** 12 Gauge Mag. 3″, Field Grade, modern	110.00	150.00	130.00
☐ **Model 500AA,** 12 Gauge Mag. 3″, Trap Grade, modern	140.00	190.00	165.00
☐ **Model 500AK,** Field Grade, Adjustable Choke, modern	115.00	160.00	140.00

NAVY ARMS

HANDGUN, PERCUSSION

	Current Price Range		Prior Year Average
☐ **.36 M1851 New Navy,** Revolver, Reproduction, Brass Grip Frame, antique	65.00	85.00	75.00
☐ **.36 M1851 New Navy,** Revolver, Reproduction, Silver-Plated Grip Frame, antique	65.00	85.00	75.00
☐ **.36 M1853,** Revolver, Reproduction, Pocket Pistol, 4½″ Barrel, antique	65.00	85.00	75.00
☐ **.36 M1853,** Revolver, Reproduction, Pocket Pistol, 5½″ Barrel, antique	65.00	85.00	75.00
☐ **.36 M1853,** Revolver, Reproduction, Pocket Pistol, 6½″ Barrel, antique	65.00	85.00	75.00
☐ **.36 M1860 Reb,** Revolver, Reproduction, Brass Frame, antique	40.00	55.00	48.00

FIREARMS / 329

	Current Price Range		Prior Year Average

HANDGUN, REVOLVER
- ☐ **Froniter,** Various Calibers, Color Case Hardened Frame, Single Action, Western Style, modern ...   95.00   140.00   120.00
- ☐ **Frontier Target,** .357 Magnum, Color Case Hardened Frame, Single Action, Western Style, Adjustable Sights, with Detachable Shoulder Stock, modern 145.00   195.00   170.00
- ☐ **Frontier Target,** .45 Colt, Color Case Hardened Frame, Single Action, Western Style, Adjustable Sights, with Detachable Shoulder Stock, modern   150.00   170.00   170.00
- ☐ **Frontier Target,** Various Calibers, Color Case Hardened Frame, Single Action, Western Style, Adjustable Sights, modern 95.00   145.00   120.00
- ☐ **M1875 Remington,** .357 Magnum, Color Case Hardened Frame, Western Style, Single Action, modern 115.00   150.00   132.00

RIFLE, LEVER ACTION
- ☐ **M1873 1 Of 1000,** .44-40 WCF, Blue Tube, Octagon Barrel, Steel Buttplate, Engraved, modern 500.00   700.00   600.00
- ☐ **M1873-"101",** .22 L.R.R.F., Color Case Hardened Frame, Tube Feed, Round Barrel, Steel Buttplate, Carbine, modern 145.00   190.00   172.00
- ☐ **M1873-"101",** .44-40 WCF, Color Case Hardened Frame, Tube FEed, Octagon Barrel, Steel Buttplate, modern 165.00   215.00   185.00
- ☐ **M1873-"101",** .44-40 WCF, Color Case Hardened Frame, Tube Feed, Round Barrel, Steel Buttplate, Carbine, modern 145.00   190.00   172.00
- ☐ **M1873-"101",** Trapper, .22 L.R.R.F., Color Case Hardened Frame, Tube Feed, Round Barrel, Steel Buttplate, modern 145.00   190.00   172.00
- ☐ **M1873-"101",** Trapper, .44-40 WCF, Color Case Hardened Frame, Tube Feed, Round Barrel, Steel Buttplate, modern 145.00   190.00   172.00

RIFLE, PERCUSSION
- ☐ **.44 Remington,** Revolver, Reproduction, Carbine, Brass Furniture, antique 100.00   135.00   118.00
- ☐ **.45 "Kentucky",** Long Rifle, Reproduction, Brass Furniture, antique 110.00   150.00   130.00
- ☐ **.45 "Kentucky",** Carbine, Reproduction, Brass Furniture, antique 110.00   145.00   128.00
- ☐ **.45 "Kentucky",** Carbine, Reproduction, Brass Furniture, antique 110.00   150.00   130.00
- ☐ **.45 Hawken Hurricane,** Octagon Barrel, Brass Furniture, Reproduction, antique 130.00   165.00   148.00
- ☐ **.45 Morse,** Octagon Barrel, Brass Frame, Reproduction, antique 80.00   110.00   95.00
- ☐ **.50 Hawken Hurricane,** Octagon Barrel, Brass Furniture, Reproduction, antique 135.00   170.00   152.00
- ☐ **.50 Morse,** Octagon Barrel, Brass Frame, Reproduction, antique 80.00   115.00   98.00
- ☐ **.54 Gallagher,** Carbine, Reproduction, Military, Steel Furniture, antique 140.00   185.00   162.00

REMINGTON ARMS CO.
HANDGUN, DOUBLE BARREL, OVER-UNDER

	Current Price Range		Prior Year Average
☐ **Elliot Derringer,** 1st. Model, .41 Short R.F., Spur Trigger, Tip-Up, no Extractor, Markings on Sides of Barrel, E. Remington & Sons, antique	375.00	650.00	512.00
☐ **Elliot Derringer,** 2nd Model, .41 Short R.F., Spur Trigger, Tip-Up, with Extractor, Markings on Sides of Barrel, E. Remington & Sons, antique . .	325.00	600.00	462.00
☐ **Elliot Derringer,** 3rd Model, .41 Short R.F., Spur Trigger, Tip-Up, with Extractor, Markings on Top of Barrel, E. Remington & Sons, antique	225.00	400.00	312.00

HANDGUN, PERCUSSION

☐ **.31, Beals #1,** Revolver, Pocket Pistol, 5 Shot, Octagon Barrel, 3″ Barrel, antique	275.00	425.00	350.00
☐ **.31, Beals #2,** Revolver, Pocket Pistol, 5 Shot, Octagon Barrel, 3″ Barrel, Spur Trigger, antique .	975.00	1800.00	1425.00
☐ **.31, Beals #3,** Revolver, Octagon Barrel, 4″ Barrel, Spur Trigger, with Loading Lever, antique	600.00	1100.00	850.00
☐ **.31, New Model Pocket,** Revolver, Safety Notches on Cylinder, Spur Trigger, 5 Shot, Octagon Barrel, antique	275.00	525.00	425.00
☐ **.31, Rider Pocket,** Revolver, Double Action, 5 Shot, Octagon Barrel, 3″ Barrel	225.00	450.00	338.00
☐ **.36, Beals Navy,** Revolver, Single Action, Octagon Barrel, 7½″ Barrel, antique	375.00	650.00	512.00

HANDGUN, REVOLVER

☐ **Iroquois,** .22 L.R.R.F., 7 Shot, Solid Frame, Spur Trigger, Single Action, Fluted Cylinder, antique .	190.00	295.00	242.00
☐ **Iroquois,** .22 L.R.R.F., 7 Shot, Solid Frame, Spur Trigger, Single Action, Unfluted Cylinder, antique	270.00	395.00	322.00
☐ **Model 1875,** .44-40 WCF, Single Action, Western Style, Solid Frame, antique	550.00	950.00	750.00
☐ **Model 1875,** .45 Colt, Single Action, Western Style, Solid Frame, antique	500.00	900.00	700.00
☐ **Model 1890,** .44-40 WCF, Single Action, Western Style, Solid Frame, antique	850.00	1650.00	1250.00

HANDGUN, SINGLESHOT

☐ **#1 Vest Pocket,** .22 Short R.F., Iron Frame, no Breech Bolt, Spur Trigger, antique	225.00	350.00	282.00
☐ **#2 Vest Pocket,** .30 Short R.F., Iron Frame, "Split Breech" Model, Spur Trigger, antique	300.00	475.00	382.00
☐ **#2 Vest Pocket,** .41 Short R.F., Iron Frame, "Split Breech" Model, Spur Trigger, antique	275.00	425.00	350.00
☐ **Elliot Derringer,** .41 Short R.F., Iron Frame, Birdhead Grip, no Breech Bolt, antique	375.00	550.00	462.00
☐ **Mark III,** 10 Gauge, Signal Pistol, 9″ Barrel, Spur Trigger, Brass Frame, Curio	85.00	145.00	115.00
☐ **Model 1865 Navy,** .50 Rem. Navy R.F., Rolling Block, Spur Trigger, 8½″ Barrel, antique	800.00	1300.00	1050.00
☐ **Model 1867 Navy,** .50 Rem., Rolling Block, 7″ Barrel, antique	425.00	700.00	562.00

FIREARMS / 331

	Current Price Range		Prior Year Average

RIFLE, BOLT ACTION

- **Enfield 1914,** .303 British, Full-Stocked, Military, Curio 135.00 185.00 160.00
- **International (1961),** Various Calibers, Singleshot, Target Stock, no Sights, with Accessories, modern 250.00 375.00 312.00
- **Model 1907-15 French,** 8x50R Lebel, Military, Curio 95.00 160.00 132.00
- **Model 1907-15 French,** 8x50R Lebel, Carbine, Military, Curio 90.00 155.00 122.00
- **Model 1917 U.S.,** .30-06 Springfield, Full-Stocked, Military, Curio 145.00 225.00 190.00
- **Model 30A,** Various Calibers, Sporting Rifle, Plain, Open Rear Sight, modern 160.00 230.00 190.00
- **Model 30F Premier,** Various Calibers, Sporting Rifle, Fancy Checkering, Fancy Engraving, Fancy Wood, modern 475.00 625.00 550.00
- **Model 30R,** Various Calibers, Sporting Rifle, Plain, Carbine, Open Rear Sight, modern 160.00 220.00 190.00

RIFLE, SEMI-AUTOMATIC

- **Model Four,** Various Calibers, Clip Fed, Sporting Rifle, Open Rear Sight, Checkered Stock, Fancy Wood, modern 220.00 295.00 255.00
- **Model 10C Mohawk,** .22 L.R.R.F., Clip Fed, Plastic Stock, modern 45.00 65.00 55.00
- **Model 16,** .22 Rem. Automatic R.F., Takedown, Tube Feed, modern 135.00 200.00 172.00
- **Model 16D,** .22 Rem. Automatic R.F., Takedown, Tube Feed, Checkered Stock, Engraved, modern 285.00 375.00 312.00
- **Model 16F,** .22 Rem. Automatic R.F., Takedown, Tube Feed, Fancy Checkering, Fancy Engraving, modern 635.00 775.00 700.00
- **Model 241A,** .22 L.R.R.F., Tube Feed, Takedown, Open Rear Sight, modern 170.00 240.00 205.00

SHOTGUN, DOUBLE BARREL, SIDE-BY-SIDE

- **Model 1882,** Various Gauges, Hammer, Damascus Barrel, Checkered Stock, Double Trigger, antique 240.00 395.00 320.00
- **Model 1883,** Various Gauges, Hammer, Damascus Barrel, Checkered Stock, Double Trigger, antique .. 240.00 395.00 320.00
- **Model 1883,** Various Gauges, Hammer, Steel Barrel, Checkered Stock, Double Trigger, antique ... 275.00 425.00 350.00
- **Model 1894 A E,** Various Gauges, Hammerless, Damascus Barrel, Automatic Ejector, Checkered Stock, Double Trigger, Curio 175.00 300.00 342.00
- **Model 1894 A E O,** Various Gauges, Hammerless, Steel Barrel, Automatic Ejector, Checkered Stock, Double Trigger, Curio 375.00 500.00 420.00
- **Model 1894 A O,** Various Gauges, Hammerless, Steel Barrel, Plain, Checkered Stock, Double Trigger, Curio 325.00 450.00 382.00

SHOTGUN, SEMI-AUTOMATIC

- **Autoloading-0,** 12 Ga., Takedown, Riot Gun, Plain, modern 120.00 170.00 145.00

332 / FIREARMS

	Current Price Range		Prior Year Average
☐ **Autoloading-4,** 12 Ga., Takedown, Fancy Checkering, Fancy Wood, Engraved, modern ...	435.00	575.00	500.00
☐ **Autoloading-6,** 12 Ga., Takedown, Fancy Checkering, Fancy Wood, Fancy Engraving, modern	725.00	975.00	850.00
☐ **Model 11,** for Vent Rib, Add **$35.00-$45.00**			
☐ **Model 11,** Raised Solid Rib, Add **$15.00-$25.00**			
☐ **Model 11 Sportsman,** Various Gauges, Skeet Grade, Vent Rib, Light Engraving, Checkered Stock, modern	200.00	300.00	250.00

SHOTGUN, SLIDE ACTION

☐ **Model 10A,** 12 Ga., Takedown, Plain, modern	140.00	185.00	162.00
☐ **Model 108,** 12 Ga., Takedown, Checkered Stock, Fancy Wood, modern	165.00	225.00	190.00
☐ **Model 10C,** 12 Ga., Takedown, Fancy Wood, Checkered Stock, modern	180.00	215.00	250.00
☐ **Model 10D,** 12 Ga., Takedown, Fancy Checkering, Fancy Wood, Engraved, modern	425.00	575.00	500.00
☐ **Model 10E,** 12 Ga., Takedown, Fancy Checkering, Fancy Wood, Fancy Engraving, modern	575.00	750.00	640.00
☐ **Model 10F,** 12 Ga., Takedown, Fancy Checkering, Fancy Engraving, Fancy Wood, modern	725.00	975.00	850.00
☐ **Model 10R,** 12 Ga., Takedown, Riot Gun, Plain, modern	95.00	150.00	122.00

SAVAGE ARMS CO.
HANDGUN, SEMI-AUTOMATIC

☐ **Model 1970,** Factory Nickel, Add **$35.00-$45.00**			
☐ **Model 1907,** Grade A Engraving (Light), Add **$75.00-$95.00**			
☐ **Model 1907,** Grade C Engraving (Fancy), Add **$225.00-$300.00**			
☐ **Model 1907 (1908),** .32 ACP, Clip Fed, Burr Cocking Piece, (under #10,899), Curio	180.00	250.00	215.00
☐ **Model 1907 (1909),** .32 ACP, Clip Fed, Burr Cocking Piece, (#'s 10,900-70,499), Curio	150.00	190.00	170.00
☐ **Model 1907 (1912),** .32 ACP, Clip Fed, Burr Cocking Piece, (Higher # than 70500), Curio ....'	135.00	175.00	155.00
☐ **Model 1907 (1913),** .380 ACP, Clip Fed, Burr Cocking Piece, Curio	180.00	250.00	215.00
☐ **Model 1907 (1914),** .32 ACP, Spur Cocking Piece, Curio	135.00	170.00	152.00
☐ **Model 1907 (1914),** .380 ACP, Spur Cocking Piece, Curio	145.00	200.00	172.00
☐ **Model 1907 (1918),** .32 ACP, Clip Fed, no Cartridge Indicator, Burr Cocking Piece, (After # 175,000), Curio	120.00	155.00	138.00
☐ **Model 1907 (1918),** .32 ACP, Clip Fed, Spur Cocking Piece, (After # 195000), Curio	140.00	180.00	155.00

RIFLE, BOLT ACTION

☐ **Model 10,** .22 L.R.R.F., Target Sights, (Anschutz), modern	85.00	130.00	108.00

FIREARMS / 333

	Current Price Range		Prior Year Average
☐ **Model 110,** Magnum Calibers, Add $15.00			
☐ **Model 110,** Various Calibers, Open Rear Sight, Checkered Stock, modern	120.00	160.00	140.00
☐ **Model 110-B,** Various Calibers, Open Rear Sight, modern	135.00	180.00	158.00
☐ **Model 110-BL,** Various Calibers, Open Rear Sight, Left-Hand, modern	145.00	195.00	170.00
☐ **Model 110-C,** Various Calibers, Clip Fed, Open Rear Sight, modern	145.00	190.00	170.00
☐ **Model 110-CL,** Various Calibers, Clip Fed, Open Rear Sight, Left-Hand, modern	150.00	200.00	175.00
☐ **Model 110-E,** Various Calibers, Open Rear sight, modern	120.00	160.00	140.00
☐ **Model 110-EL,** Various Calibers, Open Rear Sight, Left-Hand, modern	130.00	170.00	150.00
☐ **Model 110-M,** Various Calibers, Open Rear Sight, Monte Carlo Stock, Checkered Stock, Magnum Action, modern	145.00	190.00	170.00
☐ **Model 110-MC,** Various Calibers, Open Rear Sight, Monte Carlo Stock, Checkered Stock, modern	120.00	160.00	140.00

SHOTGUN, DOUBLE BARREL, OVER-UNDER

☐ **Model 242,** .410 Ga., Hammer, Single Trigger, modern	85.00	125.00	105.00
☐ **Model 330,** 12 and 20 Gauges, Hammerless, Single Selective Trigger, modern	275.00	360.00	118.00
☐ **Model 330,** 12 and 20 Gauges, Hammerless, Extra Shotgun Barrel, Cased, modern	350.00	450.00	400.00
☐ **Model 333,** 12 and 20 Gauges, Hammerless, Vent Rib, Single Selective Trigger, modern	350.00	450.00	400.00
☐ **Model 333-T,** 12 Ga., Hammerless, Vent Rib, Trap Grade, Single Selective Trigger, modern	325.00	425.00	375.00

SHOTGUN, SEMI-AUTOMATIC

☐ **Model 720-P,** 12 Ga., Checkered Stock, Adjustable Choke, modern	120.00	155.00	138.00
☐ **Model 720-R,** 12 Ga., Riot Gun, modern	100.00	145.00	122.00
☐ **Model 721,** 12 Ga., Tube Feed, Checkered Stock, Raised Matted Rib, modern	140.00	175.00	158.00
☐ **Model 722,** 12 Ga., Tube Feed, Checkered Stock, Vent Rib, modern	155.00	195.00	175.00
☐ **Model 723,** 16 Ga., Tube Feed, Checkered Stock, Plain Barrel, modern	100.00	140.00	120.00

SHOTGUN, SLIDE ACTION

☐ **Model 21-A,** 12 Ga., Hammerless, Takedown, modern	110.00	140.00	125.00
☐ **Model 21-B,** 12 Ga., Hammerless, Takedown, Raised Matted Rib, modern	120.00	150.00	135.00
☐ **Model 21-C,** 12 Ga., Hammerless, Takedown, Riot Gun, modern	95.00	130.00	112.00
☐ **Model 21-D,** 12 Ga., Hammerless, Takedown, Trap Grade, modern	165.00	225.00	195.00
☐ **Model 21-E,** 12 Ga., Hammerless, Takedown, Fancy Wood, Fancy Checkering, Vent Rib, modern	200.00	275.00	238.00

SMITH & WESON
HANDGUN, REVOLVER

	Current Price Range		Prior Year Average
☐ **.32 Double Action**, .32 S & W, 1st Model, Top Break, 5 Shot, Straight-Cut Sideplate, Rocker Cylinder Stop, antique	800.00	1350.00	1100.00
☐ **.32 Double Action**, .32 S & W, 2nd model, Top Break, 5 Shot, Irregularly-Cut Sideplate, Rocker Cylinder Stop, antique	120.00	190.00	155.00
☐ **.32 Double Action**, .32 S & W, 3rd Model, Top Break, 5 Shot, Irregularly-Cut Sideplace, antique	110.00	175.00	142.00
☐ **.32 Double Action**, .32 S & W, 4th Model, Round-Back Trigger Guard, Top Break, 5 Shot, Irregularly-Cut Sideplate, modern	95.00	160.00	128.00
☐ **.32 Double Action**, .32 S & W, 5th Model, Round-Back Trigger Guard, Top Break, 5 Shot, Irregularly-Cut Sideplate, Front Sight Forged on Barrel, modern	95.00	165.00	130.00

WINCHESTER REPEATING ARMS CO.
RIFLE, BOLT ACTION

☐ **Hotchkiss**, .40-65 Win., Sporting Rifle, antique	750.00	1000.00	880.00
☐ **Hotchkiss 1st Model Fancy**, .45-70 Government, Sporting Rifle, antique	500.00	850.00	680.00
☐ **Hotchkiss 1st Model**, .45-70 Government, Military, Rifle, antique	300.00	600.00	450.00
☐ **Hotchkiss 1st Model**, .45-70 Government, Military, Carbine, antique	350.00	650.00	500.00
☐ **Hotchkiss 1st Model**, .45-70 Government, Sporting Rifle, antique	400.00	700.00	550.00

RIFLE, LEVER ACTION

☐ **Henry**, .44 Henry, Brass Frame, Rifle, antique	3500.00	6000.00	4800.00
☐ **Henry**, .44 Henry, Brass Frame, Military, Rifle, antique	4000.00	6750.00	5380.00
☐ **Henry**, .44 Henry, Iron Frame, Rifle, antique	5000.00	8000.00	6500.00
☐ **M 88**, Various Calibers, Clip Fed, Checkered Stock, Open Rear Sight, modern	175.00	275.00	225.00
☐ **M1866**, .44 Henry, Musket, antique	900.00	1750.00	1325.00
☐ **M1866**, .44 Henry, Rifle, antique	950.00	1950.00	1450.00
☐ **M1866**, .44 Henry, Carbine, antique	850.00	1600.00	1225.00
☐ **M1866 Improved Henry**, .44 Henry, Carbine, antique	850.00	1750.00	1325.00
☐ **M1866 Improved Henry**, .44 Henry, Rifle, antique	1100.00	2000.00	1550.00

SHOTGUN, DOUBLE BARREL, OVER-UNDER

☐ **Model 101**, 12 Ga., Trap Grade, Monte Carlo Stock, Single Trigger, Automatic Ejector, Engrave, modern	575.00	750.00	662.00
☐ **Model 101**, 12 Ga., Trap Grade, Single Trigger, Automatic Ejector, Checkered Stock, Engraved, modern	575.00	750.00	662.00
☐ **Model 101**, 12 Ga., Mag. 3″, Vent Rib, Single Trigger, Automatic Ejector, Checkered Stock, Engraved, modern	550.00	725.00	638.00
☐ **Model 101**, Various Gauges, Skeet Grade, Single Trigger, Automatic Ejector, Checkered Stock, Engraved, modern	575.00	750.00	662.00

FIREARMS / 335

	Current Price Range		Prior Year Average

- **Model 101,** Various Gauges, Featherweight, Single Trigger, Automatic Ejector, Checkered Stock, Engraved, modern 575.00 750.00 662.00

SHOTGUN, DOUBLE BARREL, SIDE-BY-SIDE

- **Model 21,** For Extra Barrels, Add 25%-30%
- **Model 21,** For Vent Rib, Add $350.00
- **Model 21,** .410 Ga., Checkered Stock, Fancy Wood, modern 4500.00 7500.00 6000.00
- **Model 21,** 12 Ga., Trap Grade, Hammerless, Single Selective Trigger, Selective Ejector, Vent Rib, modern 2900.00 4250.00 3600.00
- **Model 21,** 12 Ga., Trap Grade, Hammerless, Single Selective Trigger, Selective Ejector, Raised Matted Rib, modern 2700.00 4000.00 3650.00
- **Model 21,** 12 and 16 Ga., Skeet Grade, Hammerless, Single Selective Trigger, Selective Ejector, Vent Rib, modern 2800.00 4000.00 3600.00
- **Model 21,** 12 and 16 Gauges, Skeet Grade, Hammerless, Single Selective Trigger, Selective Ejector, Raised Matted Rib, modern 2900.00 4250.00 3625.00
- **Model 21,** 12 and 16 Gauges, Field Grade, Double Trigger, Automatic Ejector, Hammerless, modern 2250.00 3400.00 2850.00

SHOTGUN, SEMI-AUTOMATIC

- **Model 1400 Trap,** 12 Ga., Vent Rib, modern 180.00 250.00 215.00
- **Model 1400 Trap,** 12 Ga., Monte Carlo Stock, Vent Rib, modern 200.00 275.00 238.00
- **Model 1400 Trap,** 12 Ga., Vent Rib, Recoil Reducer, modern 220.00 300.00 260.00
- **Model 1400 Skeet,** 12 and 20 Gauges, Vent Rib, modern 180.00 250.00 215.00
- **Model 1400 Deer,** 12 Ga., Open Sights, Slug Gun, modern 165.00 225.00 195.00
- **Model 1400 Field,** 12 and 20 Gauges, Winchoke, modern 150.00 200.00 175.00
- **Model 1400 Field,** 12 and 20 Gauges, Winchoke, Vent Rib, ... 165.00 225.00 195.00

SHOTGUN, SLIDE ACTION

- **Model 12,** 12 Ga., Pre'64, Takedown, Trap Grade, Raised Matted Rib, modern 475.00 700.00 582.00
- **Model 12,** 12 Ga., Pre'64, Takedown, Trap Grade, Vent Rib, modern 525.00 775.00 650.00
- **Model 12,** 12 Ga., Pre'64, Takedown, Trap Grade, Vent Rib, Monte Carlo Stock, modern 575.00 825.00 700.00
- **Model 12,** 12 Ga., Pre-War, Takedown, Vent Rib, modern 475.00 525.00 500.00
- **Model 12,** 12 Ga., Pre-War, Takedown, Riot Gun, modern 250.00 375.00 312.00
- **Model 12,** 12 Ga., Post'64, Trap Grade, Checkered Stock, modern 425.00 525.00 475.00
- **Model 12,** 12 Ga., Post'64, Trap Grade, Monte Carlo Stock, modern 425.00 525.00 475.00

FIREFIGHTING EQUIPMENT

Fireman's Black Rubber Coat, made of heavy jean and coated with black rubber on each side
$60.00-$70.00

The collector of firefighting equipment can draw upon items from over 300 years of American history for his hobby. Organized firefighting in the United States began in the late 1650's, when the governor of New York (then the Dutch colony of New Amsterdam) asked citizens to keep leather buckets in their homes to assist in fighting nearby fires. Many were painted with the owner's name to ensure their return after the fires. Nearly everything having to do with firefighting and firemen from that time on has become collectible.

Fire engines, hand pumped, steam and the 20th century gasoline versions are all very glamorous, but also expensive and hard to find. Fire marks, made of cast iron, zinc, lead and other materials, were bolted to houses and buildings to signal rival firefighting companies that insurance premiums were paid. Although readily available at reasonable prices, these items are now being reproduced in lightweight aluminum. All other equipment from helmets and hose fittings to firemen's ball tickets are sought by collectors. Most items used by firemen are relatively scarce because of the hard wear they encountered in daily use. Thus, even the most insignificant piece of equipment is often more valuable than its appearance might indicate.

FIRE ENGINES	Current Price Range		Prior Year Average
☐ **American LaFrance,** Auburn V-12 engine with ladders, siren, bell unrestored, fair conditon, c. 1944	1050.00	1250.00	1100.00
☐ **American LaFrance,** 6 cyl., type 75 pumper, restored, good condition, c. 1924	2100.00	2500.00	2200.00
☐ **American LaFrance,** 6 cyl., type 40 pumper, restored, good condition, c. 1917	14500.00	16500.00	15000.00

FIREFIGHTING EQUIPMENT / 337

	Current Price Range		Prior Year Average
☐ American LaFrance, 6 cyl., pumper, restored, fair condition, c. 1948	1250.00	1550.00	1350.00
☐ Chevrolet, 4 cyl., one ton, restored, excellent condition, c. 1927	4050.00	4250.00	4100.00
☐ Ford, F-6, V-8, equipped, unrestored, excellent condition, c. 1948	1850.00	2050.00	1900.00
☐ Ford, unrestored, fair condition, c. 1947	1050.00	1250.00	1100.00
☐ Ford, 8 cyl., restored, good condition, c. 1941	1600.00	2100.00	1750.00
☐ Seagrave, Model "A", 4 cyl., restored, excellent condition, c. 1928	15500.00	18500.00	16500.00

FIRE MARKS

☐ Hands clasped, Germantown National Fire, c. 1843	135.00	160.00	138.00
☐ Hydrant, F. A., brass plaque, c. 1817	185.00	235.00	200.00
☐ Hydrant, F. A., brass plaque, c. 1843	85.00	110.00	92.00
☐ Insurance Co. of Florida, c. 1841	235.00	285.00	250.00
☐ Mutual Assurance Co., iron plaque	110.00	160.00	125.00
☐ Twentieth century fire marks	30.00	55.00	38.00
☐ United Firearms Insurance Co., iron plaque	80.00	130.00	100.00

HELMETS

☐ Aluminum, eagle finial	55.00	70.00	58.00
☐ Brass, eagle finial	210.00	260.00	225.00
☐ Firefighter parade helmet, spike top, army type	130.00	160.00	135.00
☐ Hand painted helmet shield, 19th c.	510.00	560.00	525.00
☐ Leather, black embossed with brass eagle, c. 1889	80.00	110.00	88.00
☐ Leather, ornamental parade helmet, 18th c.	660.00	710.00	675.00
☐ Leather, trumpet finial	125.00	150.00	127.00
☐ Leather, three cornered Gratacap, mid 19th c.	1050.00	1550.00	1350.00
☐ Leather, white, eagle, "Chairns Bros." mid 19th c.	110.00	135.00	112.00

MISCELLANEOUS

☐ Axe, nickel-plated head, c. 1850's	185.00	260.00	212.00
☐ Bell, brass, operated by hand crank	235.00	335.00	275.00
☐ Belt, leather, parade	50.00	90.00	65.00
☐ Belt Buckle, brass, fire engine engraved, c. 1870's	65.00	80.00	68.00
☐ Bucket, owner's name inscribed, early 19th c.	860.00	1050.00	920.00
☐ Bucket, leather, decorated with helmet and hatchet	210.00	235.00	212.00
☐ Bucket, leather, painted	180.00	210.00	185.00
☐ Bucket, painted, English	210.00	245.00	228.00
☐ Bucket, tin	28.00	38.00	30.00
☐ Extinguisher, brass	22.00	42.00	30.00
☐ Extinguisher, bulb shape	12.00	18.00	12.50
☐ Extinguisher, glass	50.00	65.00	52.00
☐ Extinguisher, tin	12.00	22.00	13.00
☐ Horn, brass	235.00	310.00	262.00
☐ Hose Nozzle, brass, 12"	50.00	80.00	60.00
☐ Hose Nozzle, brass, 15"	60.00	95.00	78.00
☐ Hose Nozzle, copper, 25"	70.00	110.00	82.00
☐ Lantern, brass	60.00	160.00	100.00
☐ Trumpet, brass, engraved	335.00	385.00	350.00

338 / FIREPLACE EQUIPMENT

	Current Price Range		Prior Year Average
☐ **Trumpet,** nickle plated, "working horn"	135.00	160.00	138.00
☐ **Trumpet,** silver plated with red tassel, engraved "Orig. 1877"	282.00	310.00	285.00
☐ **Trumpet,** sterling silver	410.00	485.00	438.00
☐ **Tickets,** fireman's benefits, 19th c.	5.50	9.00	6.25
☐ **Watercolor drawing,** pumpers, crowd, etc., 19th c.	382.00	410.00	385.00
☐ **Watercolor honor roll**	310.00	335.00	312.00

FIREPLACE EQUIPMENT

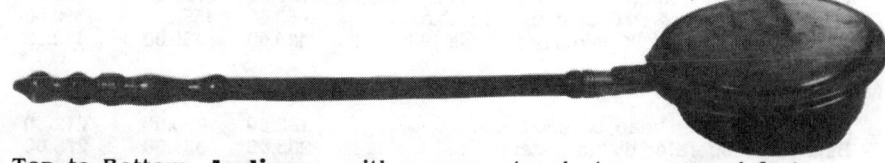

Top to Bottom: **Andirons,** with screen, steeple top, squared feet, brass, **$300.00-$400.00; Bed Warmer,** brass pan and wooden handle .... **$100.00-$150.00**

Tools for starting and tending fires include andirons, bellows, lighters, screens and trammel hooks. These accessories are made of many materials including brass, cast iron, leather, porcelain and wood. They may be finely made or crude according to the desires of the maker. Many are usable because of their sturdy construction and all add warmth and character to a home fireplace or heating stove.

ANDIRONS

☐ **Brass,** ball top, 15", c. 1800, pair	260.00	310.00	275.00
☐ **Brass,** dog, 19th c., pair	335.00	435.00	375.00
☐ **Brass,** faceted frontal piece, 23", 20th c., pair	210.00	240.00	210.00
☐ **Brass,** federal style, ball tops, spurred arch supports and snake feet, 13", pair	125.00	145.00	125.00

FIREPLACE EQUIPMENT / 339

	Current Price Range		Prior Year Average
☐ **Brass,** scroll footed base, 23, 17th c., pair	610.00	685.00	638.00
☐ **Brass,** solid, 30″, c.1850, pair	385.00	460.00	412.00
☐ **Cast iron,** carved ball on top, 7″, c. 1860, pair	150.00	190.00	160.00
☐ **Cast iron,** eagle, 12″, pair	80.00	125.00	95.00
☐ **Cast iron,** figures of Hessian soldiers, 20″, 20th c., pair	50.00	75.00	62.00
☐ **Wrought iron,** brass finial, late 16th c., pair	710.00	810.00	750.00
☐ **Wrought iron,** gooseneck, ball top, 18th c., pair	160.00	260.00	200.00
☐ **Wrought iron,** gooseneck, diamond top, 21″, pair	485.00	560.00	512.00
☐ **Wrought iron,** gooseneck, flattened finial, 17″, 18th c., pair	135.00	185.00	150.00
☐ **Wrought iron,** knife blade standard, brass urn finial, 23″, pair	235.00	310.00	265.00
☐ **Wrought iron,** knife blade standard, faceted ball on curved finial, 16″, pair	125.00	145.00	125.00
☐ **Wrought iron,** knife blade standard, hand forged, 18″, 18th c., pair	185.00	235.00	200.00
☐ **Wrought iron,** ring top, 17″, 18th c., pair	90.00	140.00	115.00

BELLOWS

☐ **Leather,** flowered panel, 16″	55.00	80.00	62.00
☐ **Leather,** flowered panel, brass tip, 16″	55.00	80.00	62.00
☐ **Wood,** brass nozzle, 18″	50.00	75.00	57.00
☐ **Wood,** hand carved mahogany, leather inset with brass nails, 18″	90.00	120.00	100.00
☐ **Wood,** hand painted design, 16th c.	185.00	210.00	182.00
☐ **Wood,** metal nozzle, 20″	55.00	80.00	62.00

MISCELLANEOUS

☐ **Coal box,** brass, hinged lid	210.00	285.00	238.00
☐ **Coal box,** cast iron, painted	150.00	175.00	152.00
☐ **Coal box,** copper trim, tin liner	210.00	285.00	238.00
☐ **Coal hod,** burnished brass, helmet type with scoop	160.00	210.00	175.00
☐ **Coal hod,** cast iron, green with floral decor, trimmed in gold	135.00	160.00	138.00
☐ **Coal hod,** copper with iron feet, handle and bail	70.00	100.00	80.00
☐ **Coal hod,** frog style porcelain covered lift top	80.00	110.00	82.00
☐ **Fender,** brass mesh with clowed feet, 50″	160.00	210.00	175.00
☐ **Fender,** brass, fan shape	535.00	610.00	562.00
☐ **Fender,** iron, with brass trim, 30″	235.00	310.00	262.00
☐ **Fender,** iron, with brass trim, 23″	185.00	260.00	212.00
☐ **Fender,** brass, 48″	385.00	460.00	412.00
☐ **Grate,** iron with legs, 9″ x 18″	55.00	75.00	60.00
☐ **Hearth broom,** birch splint, American	160.00	210.00	175.00
☐ **Hearth shovel,** wrought iron, 27″	25.00	45.00	30.00
☐ **Hearth shovel,** wrought iron, 33″	45.00	65.00	50.00
☐ **Lighter,** New England type, brass	60.00	80.00	65.00
☐ **Poker,** iron with tooled brass handle, 22½″	18.00	28.00	20.00
☐ **Poker,** iron, 59″	18.00	28.00	20.00
☐ **Screen,** classical Roman design, hinged three part	185.00	210.00	182.00
☐ **Screen,** lacquered, black with gold in Oriental design on stand	485.00	560.00	515.00
☐ **Screen,** wood, single panel, floral decor	70.00	100.00	80.00

340 / FISHING TACKLE

	Current Price Range		Prior Year Average
☐ **Tongs,** brass	22.00	38.00	28.00
☐ **Tongs,** wrought iron	55.00	75.00	60.00
☐ **Tools,** shovel, poker, tongs and holder, brass	210.00	260.00	225.00
☐ **Tool set,** signed, c. 1900	195.00	225.00	200.00
☐ **Tool set,** three pieces in holder	60.00	85.00	72.00
☐ **Trammel,** wrought iron with adjustable sawtooth, 48"	55.00	75.00	60.00
☐ **Trammel hook,** forged iron, holds pots, 39" to 60"	100.00	140.00	110.00

FISHING TACKLE

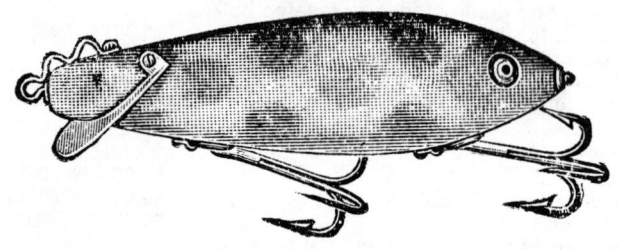

Lure, "Crab Wiggler" by Heddon, dives under water when retrieved, floats when not in motion.................................**$3.00-$4.00**

Rods, reels, flies and lures comprise the majority of collectible fishing tackle. The manufacture of fishing tackle did not begin in the United States until around 1810. Prior to that time, all fishing supplies were imported from Europe.

Reels made by J. F. and B. F. Meeks, B. Milam and Pfleuger are favored, as are rods made by Hiram Leonard. Flies, fake bait made by tying feathers, fur or other materials around the shaft of a hook, are also popular. There are over 5,000 patterns and sizes of flies, each with its own name. The manufacturer, or tier, of individual flies is very difficult to discern, unless the fly is in its original marked container.

☐ **Casting rod,** Heddon, split bamboo, 6', c. 1920	80.00	110.00	82.00
☐ **Casting rod,** split bamboo, straight handle, 5', c. 1800	42.00	52.00	45.00
☐ **Casting rod,** Tonkin. cane, 5½', c. 1900	52.00	62.00	55.00
☐ **Casting rod,** Union Hardware, 5', c. 1920	18.00	28.00	20.00
☐ **Casting rod,** Winchester, split bamboo, c. 1925	18.00	28.00	20.00
☐ **Creel fishing basket,** splint weave, pine lid, c.1900	80.00	130.00	100.00
☐ **Creel fishing basket,** wicker with leather straps, c. 1880	110.00	160.00	125.00
☐ **Fishhooks,** set of 50, c. 1910	18.00	22.00	17.50
☐ **Flies,** English, set of 12, c. 1880	410.00	435.00	412.00
☐ **Fly box,** metal, round, c. 1910	22.00	32.00	25.00
☐ **Fly box,** wooden, 6" x 10", c. 1900	52.00	62.00	55.00
☐ **Fly rod,** Heddon, split bamboo, 9½', c. 1922	62.00	72.00	65.00
☐ **Fly rod,** H. L. Leonard, 8½', c. 1890	160.00	185.00	162.00

	Current Price Range		Prior Year Average
☐ **Fly rod,** H. L. Leonard, 7′, c. 1885	310.00	335.00	312.00
☐ **Reel,** Billinghurst, fly, nickel plated, c. 1869	185.00	260.00	212.00
☐ **Reel,** Coxe, casting, aluminum, c. 1940	110.00	135.00	112.00
☐ **Reel,** English fly, silver, c. 1850	510.00	610.00	550.00
☐ **Reel,** Heddon, casting, silver, c. 1925	52.00	80.00	62.00
☐ **Reel,** Hendryx, fly, brass, c. 1890	22.00	32.00	25.00
☐ **Reel,** Leonard, fly, bronze, silver trim, c. 1878	460.00	560.00	500.00
☐ **Reel,** Leonard, fly, silver, c. 1925	260.00	310.00	275.00
☐ **Reel,** Meek, casting, brass, c. 1855	510.00	610.00	550.00
☐ **Reel,** Meek, casting, silver, c. 1930	135.00	185.00	150.00
☐ **Reel,** Meisselbach, casting, c. 1920	45.00	70.00	48.00
☐ **Reel,** Meisselbach, fly, nickel plated, c. 1895	40.00	55.00	42.00
☐ **Reel,** Meisselbach, trolling, wood, c. 1910	22.00	38.00	28.00
☐ **Reel,** Milam, casting, brass, c. 1865	410.00	510.00	450.00
☐ **Reel,** Milam, casting, silver, c. 1898	160.00	260.00	200.00
☐ **Reel,** Mills, fly, nickel, c. 1895	110.00	160.00	125.00
☐ **Reel,** Orvis, fly, nickel plated, c. 1874	110.00	160.00	125.00
☐ **Reel,** Orvis, fly, solid silver, c. 1874	610.00	710.00	650.00
☐ **Reel,** Pennell, casting, nickel plated, c. 1920	35.00	55.00	40.00
☐ **Reel,** Pfleuger, casting, brass, c. 1910	22.00	32.00	25.00
☐ **Reel,** Pfleuger, casting, silver, c. 1925	55.00	105.00	75.00
☐ **Reel,** Pfleuger, fly, rubber, c. 1905	110.00	160.00	125.00
☐ **Reel,** Pfleuger, trolling, brass, c. 1915	28.00	38.00	30.00
☐ **Reel,** Pfleuger, trolling, silver, c. 1890	35.00	55.00	40.00
☐ **Reel,** Sage, fly, solid silver, c. 1848	760.00	860.00	800.00
☐ **Reel,** Shakespeare, casting, plastic, c. 1940	40.00	60.00	45.00
☐ **Reel,** Shakespeare, casting, level wind, c. 1922	35.00	50.00	38.00
☐ **Reel,** Shakespeare, universal, take down, c. 1922	35.00	50.00	38.00
☐ **Reel,** Shipley, casting, brass, c. 1885	185.00	260.00	212.00
☐ **Reel,** Snyder, casting, brass, c. 1820	510.00	660.00	580.00
☐ **Reel,** South Bend, fly, aluminum, c. 1940	35.00	55.00	40.00
☐ **Reel,** Talbot, casting, silver, c. 1920	85.00	135.00	100.00
☐ **Reel,** Union Hardware, fly, nickel plated, c. 1920	30.00	45.00	32.00
☐ **Reel,** Vom Hofe, fly, nickel, small, c. 1890	135.00	185.00	150.00
☐ **Reel,** Vom Hofe, trolling, rubber, c. 1918	160.00	235.00	182.00
☐ **Reel,** Yawman and Erbe, fly, aluminum, c. 1889	110.00	160.00	125.00
☐ **Reel,** Zwarg, trolling, rubber, c. 1950	185.00	260.00	212.00
☐ **Rod case,** wood, brass trim, 5′, c. 1880	90.00	110.00	90.00
☐ **Steel casting rod,** Wards, telescopic, 9″, c. 1922	32.00	42.00	35.00
☐ **Steel casting rod,** Wards, with case, agate guides, 5½′, c. 1922	32.00	42.00	35.00
☐ **Tackle box,** wooden and brass trim, 14″, c. 1910	52.00	62.00	55.00
☐ **Tackle box,** metal and brass trim, 16″, c. 1925	52.00	62.00	55.00

FOLK ART

Folk art is painting and sculpture done by Americans with little or no formal training in art. Folk art is usually easy to recognize as most of the artists have little regard for the techniques of scale and perspective. The artist emphasizes what he feels to be the most important part of the individual work.

Folk art is not necessarily old, nor expensive. It can be found at flea markets, arts and crafts fairs, church bazaars and in country stores. This is truly an art form in which beauty and value are in the eye of the beholder. Folk art

FOLK ART

may be produced by ones' neighbor, barber, or the retired couple down the street. It may surprise the reader to know that the roster of American folk artists includes such famous names as Grandma Moses and Edward Hicks.

	Current Price Range		Prior Year Average
☐ **Banjo,** snake skin head, three strink, 31″	55.00	75.00	60.00
☐ **Barber's pole,** with hitching post	150.00	175.00	152.00
☐ **Bird,** cloth, Victorian	45.00	70.00	48.00
☐ **Boat,** model, wood, c. 1900	45.00	70.00	48.00
☐ **Bottlecap sculpture,** snake	160.00	185.00	162.00
☐ **Bottlecap sculpture,** carved heads of a man and woman, c. 1930	80.00	110.00	82.00
☐ **Carving,** bird, wood, painted, 6″	35.00	55.00	40.00
☐ **Cradle,** doll, pine, original paint, 18th c.	210.00	260.00	225.00
☐ **Cow,** felt, painted face, 9″	28.00	38.00	30.00
☐ **Doll,** dancer, jointed wood, hand operated, 14½″, 19th c.	185.00	235.00	200.00
☐ **Doll,** reversible face, dress and color, 14″	260.00	310.00	275.00
☐ **Face mask,** carved, man's face	125.00	145.00	125.00
☐ **Flute,** pine, 15″	55.00	75.00	60.00
☐ **Fraktur,** part printed, part hand-colored, Victorian frame	45.00	65.00	50.00
☐ **Game,** checkered game board, splined, signed, 19″ x 29″	80.00	110.00	82.00
☐ **Game,** ring toss, 5 rings, c. 1900	45.00	70.00	52.00
☐ **Game,** skittles, ornate steeple in center, 19th c.	185.00	235.00	200.00
☐ **Miniature,** bookcase on chest, accessories, 11¾″ x 9½″	150.00	190.00	160.00
☐ **Miniature,** furniture, set of 3 chairs, painted	55.00	75.00	60.00
☐ **Miniature,** windmill, wood, tin blades, 21″	70.00	90.00	75.00
☐ **Mourning picture,** embroidery on silk, 16″ x 20″	335.00	360.00	338.00
☐ **Oil on board,** little girl in hooded cape, 7″ x 9″, c. 1820	110.00	160.00	125.00
☐ **Oil on board,** rat terrior with rat, 19th c.	260.00	310.00	275.00
☐ **Oil on canvas,** apples and book, 8″ x 10″	385.00	410.00	382.00
☐ **Oil on canvas,** boy, girl, lamb, mid-19th c.	135.00	160.00	138.00
☐ **Oil on canvas,** fruit and bird, unframed, 24″ x 18″, c. 1835	510.00	610.00	550.00
☐ **Oil on canvas,** Irish Setter, 16″ x 19″, framed	310.00	360.00	325.00
☐ **Portraits,** oil, Ammi Phillips, man and woman (pair)	35500.00	40500.00	3750.00
☐ **Portraits,** man and woman (pair), unsigned, 19th c.	335.00	385.00	350.00
☐ **Portraits,** pair, signed, G. H. Blackburn, 30″ x 28″ framed, c. 1886	310.00	360.00	325.00
☐ **Toy,** baby rattle, hand carved, 9″	80.00	110.00	82.00
☐ **Toy,** monkey on pole, hand carved	65.00	90.00	72.00
☐ **Toy,** pecking chicken, hand carved	55.00	80.00	62.00
☐ **Toy,** rocking horse, handmade	55.00	80.00	62.00
☐ **Toy,** sheep on wheels, hand carved	135.00	160.00	138.00
☐ **Toy,** train, hand carved, painted, 23″, 19th c.	110.00	135.00	112.00
☐ **Whirligig,** cast iron, painted, man turning grind stone	435.00	535.00	475.00

FOOTBALL CARDS

Although the popularity of collecting football cards lags behind the longer-established baseball card hobby, football's tremendous popularity practically dictates the growth of football card collecting. Following in the footsteps of baseball fans, football fans eagerly snatch up any articles that relate to their favorite teams and players. The easiest items to attain are football cards produced by gum and food manufacturers. You don't have to live near a professional football stadium to buy cards — they are available through the mail either from the companies and dealers, and still with certain ones, at the stores.

The oldest sets, star cards (cards of famous players), and rookie cards (first-season cards of stars) are the most valuable. Except for the older cards, you should buy cards in excellent or mint condition, then keep them that way by storing them in maylar folders.

For more in-depth information, you may refer to *The Official Price Guide to Football Cards* published by the House of Collectibles.

BOWMAN — 1950
($2\frac{1}{16}$″ x $2\frac{1}{2}$″, Numbered 1-144. Color)

		Current Price Range		Prior Year Average
☐	Complete Set	270.50	185.00	220.00
☐	1 Doak Walker, Detroit Lions back	5.20	4.20	4.70
☐	5 Y.A. Tittle, Baltimore Colts, quarterback	8.80	7.00	6.15
☐	6 Lou Groza, Cleveland Browns, tackle	6.45	5.35	4.25
☐	16 Glenn Davis, Los Angeles Rams, back	5.10	4.10	4.60
☐	27 Sid Luckman, Chicago Bears, quarterback	6.75	4.30	5.50
☐	45 Otto Graham, Cleveland Browns, quarterback	13.75	10.20	11.75
☐	78 Dante Lavelli, Cleveland Browns, end	4.40	3.40	3.90
☐	100 Sammy Baugh, Washington Redskins, quarterback	14.00	9.50	11.75
☐	132 Chuck Bednarik, Philadelphia Eagles, center	5.50	4.40	4.90

BOWMAN — 1951 ($2\frac{1}{16}$″ x $3\frac{1}{8}$″, Numbered 1-144. Color)

☐	Complete Set	280.00	190.00	235.00
☐	2 Otto Graham, Cleveland Browns, quarterback	12.50	8.80	10.55
☐	4 Norm VanBrocklin, Los Angeles Rams, quarterback	7.50	5.70	6.60
☐	12 Chuck Bednarik, Philadelphia Eagles, center	5.60	4.50	4.05
☐	20 Tom Landry, New York Giants, back	12.50	8.80	11.70
☐	34 Sammy Baugh, Washington Redskins, quarterback	12.50	8.80	11.70
☐	75 Lou Groza, Cleveland Browns, tackle	5.75	4.60	5.15
☐	76 Elroy Hirsch, Los Angeles Rams, back	5.60	4.50	5.05
☐	102 Bobby Layne, Detroit Lions, quarterback	10.20	7.70	8.60
☐	105 Joe Perry, San Francisco 49ers, back	5.70	4.50	4.10

BOWMAN — 1952 ($2\frac{1}{16}$″ x $3\frac{1}{8}$″, Numbered 1-144. Color)

☐	Complete Set	300.00	200.00	250.00
☐	1 Norman Van Brocklin, Los Angeles Rams, quarterback	10.75	8.00	10.00
☐	2 Otto Graham, Cleveland Browns, quarterback	13.25	9.00	11.00
☐	14 Paul Brown, Cleveland Browns, coach	6.85	5.00	5.90

344 / FOOTBALL CARDS

		Current Price Range		Prior Year Average
☐ 30	**Sammy Baugh,** Washington Redskins, quarterback	15.00	10.75	12.75
☐ 48	**Geroge Halas,** Chicago Bears, coach	11.00	8.00	9.50
☐ 78	**Bobby Layne,** Detroit Lions, quarterback	10.25	8.00	9.55
☐ 137	**Bob Waterfield,** Los Angeles Rams, quarterback	7.45	5.50	6.50
☐ 142	**Tom Landry,** New York Giants, back	10.05	6.85	8.40

BOWMAN — 1952 (2½″ x 3¾″, Numbered 1-144. Color)

☐	Complete Set	400.00	275.00	325.00
☐ 1	**Norm Van Brocklin,** Los Angeles Rams, quarterback	11.50	8.45	10.00
☐ 2	**Otto Graham,** Cleveland Browns, quarterback	14.25	10.45	12.35
☐ 16	**Frank Gifford,** New York Giants, back	13.25	10.45	12.00
☐ 17	**Y.A. Tittle,** San Francisco 49ers, quarterback	8.20	6.25	7.25
☐ 30	**Sammy Baugh,** Washington Redskins, quarterback	13.75	9.90	11.00
☐ 78	**Bobby Layne,** detroit Lions, quarterback	12.75	9.00	11.00
☐ 127	**Ollie Matson,** Chicago Cardinals, back	6.60	4.75	5.65
☐ 137	**Bob Waterfield,** Los Angeles Rams, quarterback	10.50	8.00	9.25
☐ 142	**Tom Landry,** New York Giants, back	11.50	8.25	9.50

BOWMAN — 1953 (2½″ x 3¾″, Numbered 1-96. Color)

☐	Complete Set	250.00	162.00	295.00
☐ 9	**Marion Motley,** Cleveland Browns, back	4.25	3.25	3.75
☐ 11	**Norm Van Brocklin,** Los Angeles Rams, quarterback	7.70	5.75	6.75
☐ 21	**Bobby Layne,** Detroit Lions, quarterback	10.20	7.80	8.60
☐ 26	**Otto Graham,** Cleveland Browns, quarterback	12.50	8.80	9.60
☐ 32	**Hugh McElhenny,** San Francisco 49ers, back	5.70	4.55	5.10
☐ 43	**Frank Gifford,** New York Giants, back	12.50	8.80	10.60
☐ 53	**Emlen Tunnel,** New York Giants, back	4.25	3.25	3.75
☐ 88	**Leo Nomellini,** San Francisco 49ers, tackle	4.25	3.25	3.75
☐ 95	**Lou Groza,** Cleveland Browns, tackle	5.70	4.55	5.10

BOWMAN — 1954 (2½″ x 3¾″, Numbered 1-128. Color)

☐	Complete Set	138.50	96.00	118.00
☐ 6	**Joe Perry,** San Francisco 49ers, back	3.30	2.35	2.85
☐ 7	**Kyle Rote,** New York Giants, end	3.55	2.60	2.10
☐ 8	**Norm Van Brocklin,** Los Angeles Rams, quarterback	5.20	4.20	4.70
☐ 23	**George Blanda,** Chicago Bears, quarterback	7.40	5.50	6.45
☐ 40	**Otto Graham,** Cleveland Browns, quarterback	9.60	7.10	8.40
☐ 42	**Y.A. Tittle,** San Francisco 49ers, quarterback	5.50	4.40	4.90
☐ 53	**Bobby Layne,** Detroit Lions, quarterback	7.40	5.50	6.50
☐ 55	**Frank Gifford,** New York Giants, back	9.60	7.10	8.00
☐ 56	**Leon McLaughlin,** Los Angeles Rams, center	.66	.59	.63

BOWMAN — 1955 (2½″ x 3¾″, Numbered 1-160. Color)

☐	Complete Set	130.00	90.00	110.00

FOOTBALL CARDS / 345

1951 Bowman,
#140 Leo Nomellini
$3.00-$4.00

1952 Bowman,
#83 Joe Perry
$4.50-$5.50

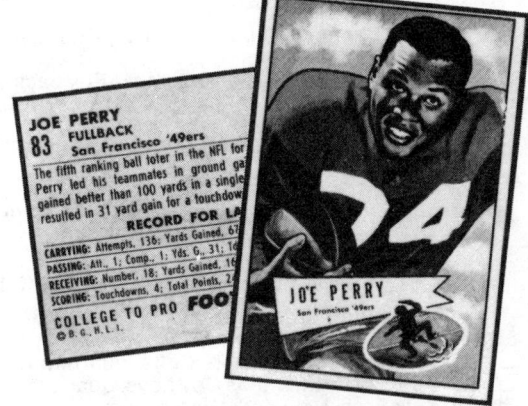

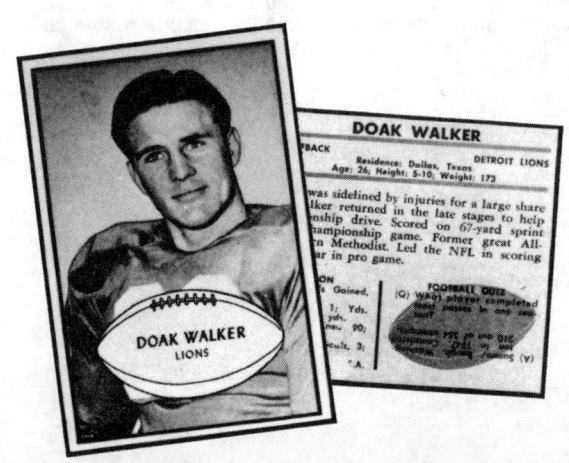

1953 Bowman,
#6 Doak Walker
$3.25-$4.25

346 / FOOTBALL CARDS

			Current Price Range		Prior Year Average
☐	7	**Frank Gifford,** New York Giants, back	9.10	6.85	8.10
☐	16	**Charley Conerly,** New York Giants, quarterback	2.05	1.45	1.70
☐	32	**Norm Van Brocklin,** Los Angeles Rams, quarterback	5.50	4.40	4.90
☐	37	**Lou Groza,** Cleveland Browns, tackle/kicker	5.10	4.10	4.60
☐	44	**Joe Perry,** San Francisco 49ers, back	2.95	2.15	2.55
☐	52	**Pat Summerall,** Chicago Cardinals, end ...	3.30	2.30	2.80
☐	62	**George Blanda,** Chicago Bears, quarterback	6.85	4.90	5.80
☐	71	**Bobby Layne,** Detroit Lions, end	9.30	7.00	7.65

FLEER — 1960 (2½" x 3½", Numbered 1-132. Color)

☐		Complete Set	65.00	50.00	58.00
☐	7	**Sid Gillman,** Los Angeles Chargers (AFL), coach	.77	.70	.73
☐	20	**Sammy Baugh,** New York Titans (AFL), coach	5.05	4.05	4.55
☐	58	**George Blanda,** Houston Oilers (AFL), quarterback/kicker	4.00	3.05	3.50
☐	66	**Billy Cannon,** Houston Oilers (AFL), back/end	2.20	1.60	1.90
☐	73	**Abner Haynes,** Dallas Texans (AFL), back ..	2.20	1.60	1.90
☐	76	**Paul Lowe,** Los Angeles Chargers (AFL), back	1.25	1.00	1.12
☐	116	**Hank Stram,** Los Angeles Chargers (AFL), back	2.20	1.60	1.90
☐	118	**Ron Mix,** Los Angeles Chargers (AFL), tackle	2.20	1.60	1.90
☐	124	**John Kemp,** Los Angeles Chargers (AFL), quarterback	5.05	4.05	4.55

FLEER — 1961 (2½" x 3½", Numbered 1-220. Color)

☐		Complete Set	130.00	96.00	115.00
☐	11	**Jim Brown,** Cleveland Browns, back	20.00	14.25	17.12
☐	30	**John Unitas,** Baltimore Colts, quarterback .	6.60	4.80	5.70
☐	41	**Don Meredith,** Dallas Cowboys, quarterback	7.50	5.00	6.20
☐	69	**Kyle Rote,** New York Giants, end	2.20	1.60	1.90
☐	88	**Bart Starr,** Green Bay Packers, quarterback	4.90	3.90	4.30
☐	90	**Paul Horning,** Green Bay Packers, back	3.55	2.60	3.10
☐	117	**Bobby Layne,** Pittsburg Steelers, quarterback	4.75	3.75	4.25
☐	155	**John Kemp,** San Diego Chargers (AFL), quarterback	7.20	5.25	6.25
☐	166	**George Blanda,** Houston Oilers (AFL), quarterback/kicker	5.50	4.40	4.95

FLEER — 1962 (2½" x 3½", Numbered 1-88. Color)

☐		Complete Set	50.00	37.50	43.00
☐	3	**Gino Cappelletti,** Boston Patriots (AFL), end/kicker	2.50	1.75	2.85
☐	25	**Abner Haynes,** Dallas Texans (AFL), back ..	1.45	1.05	1.25
☐	46	**George Blanda,** Houston Oilers (AFL), quarterback/kicker	5.05	4.05	4.55
☐	59	**Don Manynard,** New York Titans (AFL), end/back	1.45	1.05	1.25

FOOTBALL CARDS / 347

1960 Fleer,
#109 Doug Cline
$.30-$.40

1961 Fleer,
#216 Bob Mischak
$.35-$.45

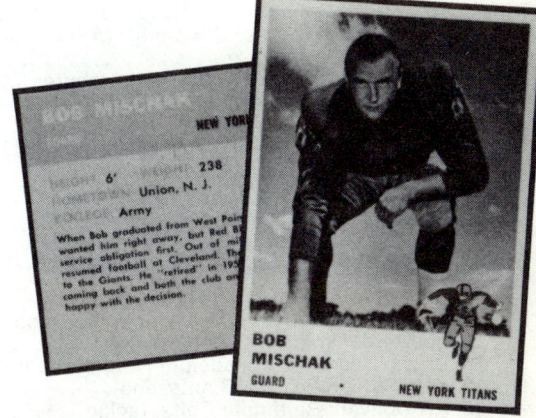

1962 Fleer,
#50 Al Jamison
$.35-$.45

348 / FOOTBALL CARDS

		Current Price Range		Prior Year Average
☐	72 Jim Otto, Oakland Raiders (AFL), center ...	1.45	1.05	1.25
☐	74 Fred Williamson, Oakland Raiders (AFL), back	1.45	1.05	1.25
☐	79 Jack Kemp, San Diego Chargers (AFL), quarterback	6.40	4.75	5.45
☐	82 Ron Mix, San Diego Chargers (AFL), tackle .	2.10	1.45	1.75

FLEER — 1963 (2½" x 3½", Numbered 1-88. Color)

☐	Complete Set	78.00	52.00	65.00
☐	5 Gino Cappelletti, Boston Patriots (AFL), end/kicker	1.90	1.35	1.62
☐	10 Nick Buoniconti, Boston Patriots (AFL), linebacker	3.80	2.80	3.30
☐	15 Don Maynard, New York Titans (AFL), end/back	1.90	1.35	1.62
☐	24 Jack Kemp, Buffalo Bills (AFL), quarterback	6.35	5.05	5.75
☐	36 George Blanda, Houston Oilers (AFL), quarterback/kicker	5.05	4.05	4.55
☐	47 Len Dawson, Kansas City Chiefs (AFL), quarterback	5.05	4.05	4.55
☐	62 Jim jOtto, Oakland Raiders (AFL), center ...	1.90	1.35	1.65
☐	64 Bob Dougherty, Oakland Raiders (AFL), linebacker	3.80	2.80	3.30
☐	72 Lance Alworth, San Diego Chargers (AFL), end	5.05	4.05	4.55
☐	76 Ernie Ladd, San Diego Chargers (AFL), tackle	1.90	1.35	1.62

TOPPS — 1956 (2⅝" x 3⅝", Numbered 1-120. Color)

☐	Complete Set	160.00	110.00	135.00
☐	6 Norm Van Brocklin, Los Angeles Rams, quarterback	4.75	3.75	4.25
☐	28 Chuch Bednarik, Philadelphia Eagles, center	3.30	2.35	2.80
☐	29 Kyle Rote, New York Giants, end	3.55	2.60	3.10
☐	36 Art Donvan, Baltimore Colts, tackle	2.20	1.60	1.90
☐	53 Frank Gifford, New York Giants, back	8.60	6.00	7.30
☐	60 Lenny Moore, Baltimore Colts, back	3.30	2.35	2.85
☐	78 Elroy Hirsch, Los Angeles Rams, end/back .	3.30	2.35	2.80
☐	87 Ernie Stautner, Pittsburgh Steelers, tackle .	1.90	1.35	1.62
☐	101 Roosevelt Grier, New York Giants, tackle ...	2.20	1.60	1.90
☐	110 Joe Perry, San Francisco 49ers, back	3.30	2.35	2.80

TOPPS — 1957 (2½" x 3½", Numbered 1-154. Color)

☐	Complete Set	180.00	132.00	155.00
☐	11 Roosevelt Brown, New York Giants, tackle .	2.20	1.60	1.90
☐	22 Norman Van Brocklin, Los Angeles Rams, quarterback	5.90	4.30	5.10
☐	28 Lou Groza, Cleveland Browns, tackle/kicker	3.15	2.20	2.70
☐	30 Y.A. Tittle, San Francisco 49ers, quarterback	5.70	4.40	5.10
☐	31 George Blanda, Chicago Bears, quarterback/kicker	8.20	6.20	7.20
☐	32 Bobby Layne, Detroit Lions, quarterback ...	8.50	6.40	7.45
☐	88 Frank Gifford, New York Giants, back	9.20	6.75	7.50
☐	119 Barr Starr, Green Bay Packers, quarterback	14.00	9.50	11.75

FOOTBALL CARDS / 349

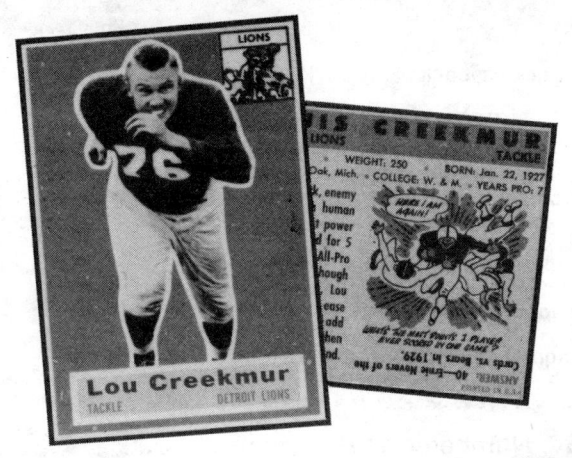

1956 Topps,
#8 Lou Creekmur
$.70-$.75

1957 Topps,
#59 Kyle Rote
$3.40-$4.40

1959 Topps,
#60 Lou Groza
$1.75-$2.75

350 / FOOTBALL CARDS

			Current Price Range		Prior Year Average
☐	151	Paul Horning, Green Bay Packers, back	13.75	9.85	11.75

TOPPS — 1958 (2½" x 3½", Numbered 1-132. Color)

☐		Complete Set	155.00	115.00	135.00
☐	2	Bobby Layne, Detroit Lions, quarterback ...	5.70	4.40	5.10
☐	22	John Unitas, Baltimore Colts, quarterback .	7.75	5.75	6.75
☐	62	Jim Brown, Cleveland Browns, back	50.00	35.00	42.00
☐	66	Bart Starr, Green Bay Packers, quarterback	5.70	4.40	5.10
☐	73	Frank Gifford, New York Giants, back	7.75	5.75	6.75
☐	86	Y.A. Tittle, San Francisco 49ers, quarterback	5.70	4.40	5.10
☐	90	Sonny Jurgensen, Philadelphia Eagles, quarterback	7.75	5.75	6.75
☐	122	Hugh McElhenny, San Francisco 49ers, back	2.95	2.15	2.55
☐	129	George Blanda, Chicago Bears, quarterback/kicker	5.70	4.40	5.10

TOPPS — 1959 (2½" x 3½". Numbered 1-176. Color)

☐		Complete Set	140.00	96.00	118.00
☐	1	Johnny Unitas, Baltimore Colts, quarterback	7.45	5.30	6.40
☐	5	Hugh McElhenny, San Francisco 49ers, back	2.65	1.85	1.25
☐	7	Kyle Rote, New York Giants, end	2.65	1.85	1.25
☐	10	Jim Brown, Cleveland Browns, back	21.50	14.50	18.00
☐	20	Frank Gifford, New York Giants, back	6.90	5.10	6.00
☐	23	Bart Starr, Green Bay Packers, quarterback	5.50	3.85	4.70
☐	40	Bobby Layne, Pittsburg Steelers, quarterback	6.05	4.00	5.00
☐	82	Paul Horning, Green Bay Packers, back	4.65	3.25	4.10
☐	130	Y.A. Tittle, San Francisco 49ers, quarterback	4.40	3.25	3.90

TOPPS — 1960 (2½" x 3½", Numbered 1-132. Color)

☐		Complete Set	95.00	72.00	84.00
☐	1	John Unitas, Baltimore Colts, quarterback .	6.35	4.70	5.50
☐	23	Jim Brown, Cleveland Browns, back	20.00	12.50	14.75
☐	51	Bart Starr, Green Bay Packers, quarterback	5.10	4.80	4.95
☐	74	Frank Gifford, New York Giants, back	6.35	4.70	6.00
☐	87	Chuck Bednarik, Philadelphia Eagles, center	2.60	1.80	2.20
☐	93	Bobby Layne, Pittsburgh Steelers, quarterback	5.10	3.80	4.25
☐	113	Y.A. Tittle, San Francisco 49ers, quarterback	3.80	2.70	3.25
☐	114	Joe Perry, San Francisco 49ers, back	2.60	1.80	2.20
☐	116	Hugh McElhenny, San Francisco 49ers, back	2.60	1.80	2.20

TOPPS — 1961 (2½" x 3½", Numbered 1-198. Color)

☐		Complete Set	122.00	85.00	105.00
☐	1	John Unitas, Baltimore Colts, quarterback .	6.90	4.40	5.60
☐	39	Bart Starr, Green Bay Packers, quarterback	5.50	4.20	4.85
☐	58	Y.A. Tittle, San Francisco 49ers, quarterback	4.10	2.65	3.45
☐	59	John Brodie, San Francixco 49ers, quarterback	3.20	2.25	2.75
☐	71	Jim Brown, Cleveland Browns, back	22.00	15.00	18.50
☐	77	Cleveland Browns Action Card, Jimmy Brown	8.85	5.80	7.30

FOOTBALL CARDS / 351

1960 Topps,
#54 Paul Hornung
$.25-$.30

1963 Topps,
#42 Frank Varrichione
$.25-$.30

1969 Topps,
#192 Nick Buoniconti
$.45-$.60

352 / FOOTBALL CARDS

		Current Price Range		Prior Year Average
☐	145 George Blanda, Houston Oilers (AFL), quarterback/kicker	5.50	3.85	4.60
☐	166 Jack Kemp, San Diego Chargers (AFL), end .	6.60	5.15	5.95

TOPPS — 1962 (2½″ x 3½″, Numbered 1-176. Color)

☐	Complete Set	115.50	88.00	102.00
☐	1 John Unitas, Baltimore Colts, quarterback .	6.35	4.70	5.50
☐	28 Jim Brown, Cleveland Browns, back	22.00	14.00	18.00
☐	36 Ernie Davis, Cleveland Browns, back	6.35	4.70	5.50
☐	39 Don Meredith, Dallas Cowboys, quarterback	6.35	4.70	5.50
☐	63 Bart STarr, Green Bay Packers, quarterback	6.35	4.70	5.50
☐	64 Paul Horning, Green Bay Packers, back	6.35	4.70	5.50
☐	66 Jim Taylor, Green Bay Packers, back	5.10	3.80	4.55
☐	88 Roman Gabriel, Los Angeles Rams, quarterback	5.10	3.80	4.55
☐	90 Fran Tarkenton, Minnesota Vikings, quarterback	14.00	8.85	10.85

TOPPS — 1963 (2½″ x 3½″, Numbered 1-170. Color)

☐	Complete Set	110.00	90.00	100.00
☐	14 Jim Brown, Cleveland Browns, back	22.00	14.00	18.00
☐	19 Lou Groza, Cleveland Browns, kicker/tackle	5.10	3.80	4.60
☐	49 Y.A. Tittle, New York Giants, quarterback ..	5.15	3.80	4.55
☐	74 Don Meredith, Dallas Cowboys, quarterback	6.35	4.70	5.50
☐	82 Bob Lilly, Dallas Cowboys, end	5.10	3.80	4.65
☐	86 Bart Starr, Green Bay Packers, quarterback	5.10	3.80	4.65
☐	98 Fran Tarkenton, Minnesota Vikings, quarterback	5.10	3.80	4.65
☐	110 Sonny Jurgensen, Philadelphia Eagles, quarterback	5.50	4.15	4.75
☐	129 Ernie Stautner, Pittsburg Steelers, end	5.00	3.60	4.30

TOPPS — 1964 (2½″ x 3½″, Numbered 1-176. Color)

☐	Complete Set	125	95	110
☐	30 Jack Kemp, Buffalo Bills (AFL), quarterback	6.30	4.50	5.40
☐	65 Denver Broncos Team	2.00	1.40	1.70
☐	68 Geroge Blanda, Houston Oilers (AFL), quarterback	6.65	4.75	5.75
☐	75 Charlie Henningan, Houston Oilers (AFL), end	2.20	1.40	1.80
☐	96 Len Dawson, Kansas City Chiefs (AFL), quarterback	4.70	3.40	4.10
☐	105 Johnny Robinson, Kansas City Chiefs (AFL), back	2.20	1.60	1.90
☐	155 Lance Alworth, San Diego Chargers (AFL), end	2.20	1.50	1.85
☐	159 John Hadl, San Diego Chargers (AFL), quarterback	2.45	1.60	2.00
☐	165 Paul Lowe, San Diego Chargers (AFL), back	2.75	1.80	2.00

TOPPS — 1965 (2½″ x 4¹¹/₁₆″, Numbered 1-176. Color)

☐	Complete Set	340.00	220.00	280.00
☐	28 Elbert Dubenion, Buffalo Bills (AFL), back ..	2.35	1.65	2.00

FOOTBALL CARDS / 353

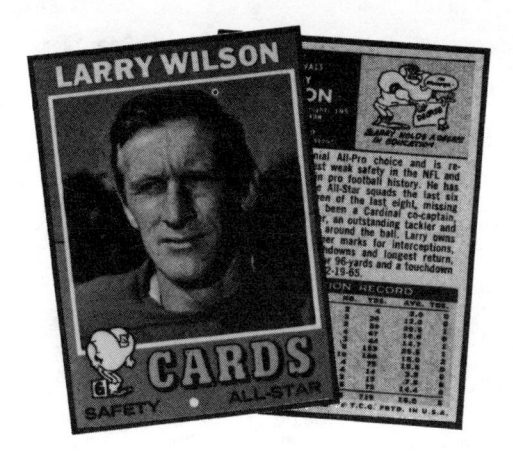

1971 Topps,
#20 Larry Wilson
$.35-$.45

1977 Topps,
#470 Cliff Branch
$.20-$.25

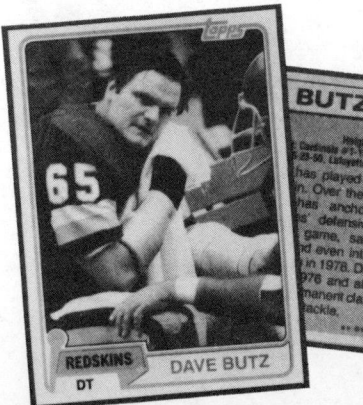

1981 Topps,
#276 Dave Butz
$.04-$.07

354 / FOOTBALL CARDS

		Current Price Range		Prior Year Average
☐ 69	Geroge Blanda, Houston Oilers (AFL), quarterback	6.30	3.80	5.00
☐ 99	Len Dawson, Kansas City Chiefs (AFL), quarterback	3.50	2.35	2.95
☐ 122	Joe Namath, New York Jets (AFL), quarterback	120.00	90.00	105.00
☐ 133	Fred Biletnikoff, Oakland Raiders (AFL), end	3.45	2.35	2.85
☐ 155	Lance Alworth, San Diego Chargers (AFL), back	2.30	1.75	2.00
☐ 161	John Hadl, San Diego Chargers (AFL), quarterback	3.50	2.40	2.95
☐ 166	Paul Lowe, San Diego Chargers (AFL), back	3.45	2.35	2.85

TOPPS — 1966 (2½″ x 3½″, Numbered 1-132. Color)

☐	Complete Set	90.00	65.00	78.00
☐ 4	Gino Cappelletti, Boston Patriots (AFL), end	1.35	1.05	1.20
☐ 26	Jack Kemp, Buffalo Bills (AFL), quarterback	4.40	2.80	3.10
☐ 48	George Blanda, Houston Oilers (AFL), quarterback	3.65	2.45	3.00
☐ 67	Len Dawson, Kansas City Chiefs (AFL), quarterback	1.90	1.40	1.65
☐ 96	Joe Namath, New York Jets (AFL), quarterback	11.00	8.00	9.50
☐ 104	Fred Biletnikoff, Oakland Raiders (AFL), end	1.65	1.25	1.45
☐ 119	Lance Alworth, San Diego Chargers (AFL), end	2.20	1.50	1.85
☐ 125	John Hadl, San Diego Chargers (AFL), quarterback	1.50	1.10	130.00
☐ 128	Ron Mix, San Diego Chargers (AFL), tackle	1.55	1.10	132.00

TOPPS — 1967 (2½″ x 3½″, Numbered 1-132. Color)

☐	Complete Set	68.00	50.00	59.00
☐ 13	Nick Buoniconti, Boston Patriots (AFL), linebacker	1.00	.92	.96
☐ 16	Tom Flores, Buffalo Bills, quarterback	1.00	.92	.96
☐ 24	Jack Kemp, Buffalo Bills (AFL), quarterback	3.85	2.75	3.25
☐ 58	Ernie Ladd, Houston Oilers (AFL), tackle	1.00	.92	.96
☐ 61	Len Dawson, Kansas City Chiefs (AFL), quarterback	2.70	1.85	1.30
☐ 82	Wahoo McDaniel, Miami Dolphins (AFL), linebacker	1.00	.92	.96
☐ 98	Joe Namath, New York Jets (AFL), quarterback	7.75	5.20	6.50
☐ 103	Daryle LaMonica, Oakland Raiders, quarterback	1.90	1.40	1.65
☐ 106	Fred Biletnikoff, Oakland Raiders, (AFL), end	1.85	1.35	1.60

TOPPS — 1968 (2½″ x 3½″, Numbered 1-219. Color)

☐	Complete Set	79.50	57.50	70.00
☐ 1	Bart Starr, Green Bay Packers, quarterback	3.05	2.05	2.55
☐ 25	Don Meredith, Dallas Cowboys, quarterback	3.15	2.10	2.65
☐ 65	Joe Namath, New York Jets, (AFL), quarterback	7.40	5.10	5.85
☐ 75	Gale Sayers, Chicago Bears, back	3.30	2.20	2.75

FOOTBALL CARDS / 355

		Current Price Range		Prior Year Average
☐ 100	John Unitas, Baltimore Colts, quarterback	4.45	3.00	3.75
☐ 127	Dick Butkus, Chicago Bears, linebacker	2.45	1.55	2.00
☐ 149	John Kemp, Buffalo Bills (AFL), quarterback	3.30	2.20	2.70
☐ 161	Fran Tarkenton, New York Giants, quarterback	4.10	2.80	3.45

TOPPS — 1969 (2½″ x 3½″, Numbered 1-263, Color)

☐	Complete Set	78.00	56.00	70.00
☐ 25	John Unitas, Baltimore Colts, quarterback	3.00	2.00	2.50
☐ 26	Brian Piccolo, Chicago Bears, back	13.00	8.75	11.00
☐ 51	Gale Sayers, Chicago Bears, back	3.00	2.00	2.50
☐ 76	Dick LeBeau, Detroit Lions, back	2.75	1.80	2.30
☐ 100	Joe Namath, New York Jets (AFL), quarterback	6.55	4.60	5.50
☐ 120	Larry Csonka, Miami Dolphins (AFL), back	5.20	3.75	4.50
☐ 150	Fran Tarkenton, New York Giants, quarterback	3.10	2.10	2.60
☐ 161	Bob Griese, Miami Dolphins (AFL), quarterback	2.65	1.70	2.15
☐ 232	George Blanda, Oakland Raiders (AFL), kicker	2.70	1.80	2.25

TOPPS — 1970 (2½″ x 3½″, Numbered 1-263. Color)

☐	Complete Set	65.00	47.00	56.00
☐ 1	Len Dawson, Kansas City Chiefs, quarterback	1.45	1.05	1.25
☐ 10	Bob Griese, Miami Dolphins, quarterback	2.20	1.80	2.00
☐ 30	Bart Starr, Green Bay Packers, quarterback	2.20	1.50	1.85
☐ 70	Gale Sayers, Chicago Bears, back	2.50	1.80	2.15
☐ 80	Fran Tarkenton, New York Giants, quarterback	2.80	2.00	2.40
☐ 90	O.J. Simpson, Buffalo Bills, back	9.55	6.80	7.35
☐ 150	Joe Namath, New York Jets, quarterback	5.50	4.15	4.85
☐ 162	Larry Csonka, Miami Dolphins, back	1.50	1.05	1.25
☐ 180	John Unitas, Baltimore Colts, quarterback	2.95	2.10	2.50
☐ 200	Sonny Jurgensen, Washington Redskins, quarterback	1.65	1.20	1.45

TOPPS — 1971 (2½″ x 3½″, Numbered 1-263. Color)

☐	Complete Set	48.50	34.00	41.00
☐ 1	John Unitas, Baltimore Colts, quarterback	3.25	1.80	2.50
☐ 39	George Blanda, Oakland Raiders, quarterback/kicker	1.82	1.34	1.60
☐ 120	Fran Tarkenton, New York Giants, quarterback	2.45	1.75	2.12
☐ 150	Gale Sayers, Chicago Bears, back	1.90	1.30	1.60
☐ 156	Terry Bradshaw, Pittsburg Steelers, quarterback	3.75	2.75	3.25
☐ 160	Bob Griese, Miami Dolphins, quarterback	2.00	1.50	1.75
☐ 200	Bart Starr, Green Bay Packers, quarterback	1.85	1.35	1.55
☐ 250	Joe Namath, New York Jets, quarterback	3.60	2.75	3.20
☐ 260	O.J. Simpson, Buffalo Bills, back	3.35	2.55	2.90

356 / FOOTBALL CARDS

TOPPS — 1972
(2½" x 3½", Numbered 1-351. Color)

		Current Price Range		Prior Year Average
☐	Complete Set	125.00	82.00	105.00
☐ 32	Donny Anderson, Green Bay Packers, back	1.05	.75	1.90
☐ 100	Joe Namath, New York Jets, quarterback	3.35	2.10	2.70
☐ 120	Terry Bradshaw, Pittsburgh Steelers, action	1.60	1.10	1.35
☐ 122	Roger Staubach, Dallas Cowboys, action	2.10	1.50	1.80
☐ 150	Terry Bradshaw, Pittsburgh Steelers, quarterback	2.10	1.50	1.80
☐ 160	O.J. Simpson, Buffalo Bills, back	2.75	2.00	2.38
☐ 165	John Unitas, Baltimore Colts, quarterback	2.10	1.50	1.80
☐ 200	Roger Staubach, Dallas Cowboys, quarterback	3.75	2.50	3.12
☐ 343	Joe Namath, New York Jets, pro action	5.20	3.60	4.40

TOPPS — 1973 (2½" x 3½", Numbered 1-528. Color)

☐	Complete Set	44.00	33.00	38.00
☐ 15	Terry Bradshaw, Pittsburgh Steelers, quarterback	1.35	1.00	1.18
☐ 25	George Blanda, Oakland Raiders, quarterback/kicker	1.20	.80	1.00
☐ 60	Fran Tarkenton, Minnesota Vikings, quarterback	1.35	1.10	1.22
☐ 89	Franco Harris, Pittsburgh Steelers, back	2.50	1.70	2.10
☐ 100	Larry Csonka, Miami Dolphins, back	1.10	.75	1.95
☐ 400	Joe Namath, New York Jets, quarterback	2.55	1.75	2.20
☐ 455	John Unitas, San Diego Chargers, quarterback	1.85	1.35	1.58
☐ 475	Roger Staubach, Dallas Cowboys, quarterback	1.85	1.35	1.55
☐ 500	O.J. Simpson, Buffalo Bills, back	2.50	1.75	2.20

TOPPS — 1974 (2½" x 3½", Numbered 1-528. Color)

☐	Complete Set	41	28.00	34.50
☐ 1	O.J. Simpson, Buffalo Bills, back	2.25	1.45	1.85
☐ 129	Fran Tarkenton, Minnesota Vikings, quarterback	1.75	1.20	1.25
☐ 130	O.J. Simpson, Buffalo Bills, back	1.75	1.25	1.50
☐ 131	Larry Csonka, Miami Dolphins, back	1.25	.85	1.05
☐ 150	John Unitas, San Diego Chargers, quarterback	1.85	1.30	1.55
☐ 200	Bob Griese, Miami Dolphins, quarterback	1.60	1.20	1.40
☐ 245	Geroge Blanda, Oakland Raiders, quarterback/kicker	1.55	1.10	1.35
☐ 435	Jim Plunkett, New England Patriots, quarterback	1.20	.75	.98
☐ 500	Roger Staubach, Dallas Cowboys, quarterback	2.10	1.50	1.80

FROGS

Although the collecting of frogs may seem a curious hobby, it should be noted that the frog motif has been used for Japanese netsuke (miniature decorations carved of ivory) for 300 years. Frogs have been made by such famous pottery works as Zsolnay in Hungary, and Staffordshire in England. The Zsolnay pieces are valued for their unusual glaze and intense colors. Staffordshire manufactured porcelain beer and ale mugs for British public houses. A frog leering from the inside of the mug informed the tippler when he was past his limit.

The Bergman Company of Vienna, Austria, also produced humorous frogs of cast bronze. The figures were hand painted and depicted frogs engaged in a variety of human activities, such as playing musical instruments.

Frogs have been used as the subjects for children's toys, clocks, paperweights and jewelry. Frogs have been made from many materials and in a wide variety of sizes. Artistic interpretations range from realistic to highly stylized. Prices may range from a few cents for a rubber frog to several thousand dollars for an antique netsuke frog.

	Current Price Range		Prior Year Average
☐ Cast iron, campaign souvenir, 19th c.	360.00	410.00	375.00
☐ Cybis frog	275.00	310.00	382.00
☐ Jadeite, frog on leaf, oriental, 2″ L.	110.00	135.00	112.00
☐ Mexican, wooden frog, painted and carved, contemporary	18.00	22.00	17.50
☐ Pewter, cast, 1″ H.	5.00	11.00	7.50
☐ Planter, large open-back frog, unmarked china	11.00	16.00	12.50
☐ Puerto Rican, clay frog, green glaze, 1½″ H.	3.50	5.50	4.00
☐ Ring, cast silver, finely detailed, garnet eyes	28.00	32.00	27.50
☐ Ring, cast silver, set with coral, Mexican	11.00	16.00	17.50
☐ Straw, Appalachia, woven like basket, 1930's	28.00	32.00	27.50
☐ Vienna, bronze frogs, seesaw	285.00	310.00	282.00
☐ Vienna, bronze, tiny frog on leaf, 1″ L.	22.00	28.00	22.50
☐ Zsolnay, signed, iridescent green	18.00	22.00	17.50

FURNITURE

Furniture has been a popular collectible for many years. People collected "antique" furniture in the 19th century. Much of what is called antique today is collectible, but is usually the furniture of two or three generations ago. True antiques are much older. It would be wise for the prospective collector to contact an established collectors' society or prominent antique dealer to obtain information about specific dates and classifications.

The variety offered the furniture collector is nearly unlimited. As many people use these collectibles to furnish at least some of the rooms in their homes, it may be wise to specialize in a certain period, style, or manufacturer in order to maintain an attractive and cohesive collection. Gaining insight into one's preferences is merely a matter of a few research trips to the library and some leisurely browsing through several antique stores which specialize

358 / FURNITURE

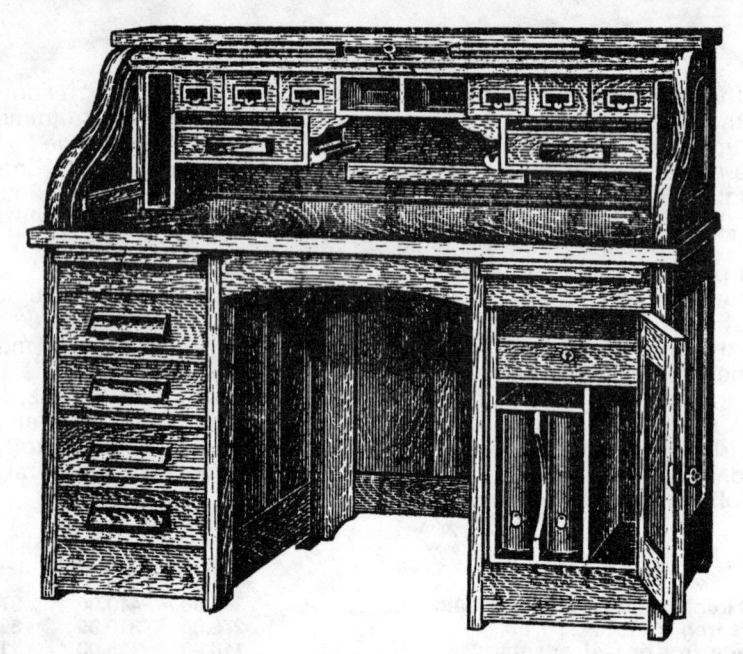

Roll Top Desk, seasoned oak, six wood filing boxes, private drawer, bookstall, two pigeonholes, etc. .... **$600.00-$1000.00**

in furniture. Do not go with the intention of buying. Spend a lot of time looking and deciding what is most appealing before spending any money. Have any furniture that is suspect examined by an expert.

Merely looking over the names of some famous furniture designers and different styles can be bewildering for the uninitiated; Chippendale, Hepplewhite, Sheraton, Duncan Phyfe, Queen Anne, William and Mary are just a few of names one encounters when dealing with antique and collectible furniture.

Many distinct types and styles of furniture are listed in this section. The differences between them are sometimes subtle and sometimes quite striking. All dates given are approximate.

PERIODS

AMERICAN EMPIRE	1815-1845	LATE FEDERAL	1835-1880
AMERICAN FEDERAL	1800-1815	LATE VICTORIAN	1870-1900
CHIPPENDALE	1745-1772	LOUIS XV	1720-1765
DIRECTOIRE	1795-1808	LOUIS XVI	1765-1789
DUNCAN PHYFE	1810-1827	QUEEN ANNE	1702-1714
EARLY VICTORIAN	1835-1870	REGENCY	1810-1830
FRENCH	1810-1875	RESTORATION	1665-1688
HEPPLEWHITE	1780-1790	SHERATON	1790-1810
JACOBEAN	1603-1665	WILLIAM AND MARY	1689-1702

BEDS

	Current Price Range		Prior Year Average
☐ Brass, American, bowed footboard, c. 1910	710.00	810.00	750.00
☐ Brass, canopy	950.00	1150.00	1025.00
☐ Brass, double, burnished, ornately decorated	385.00	510.00	420.00
☐ Brass, late Victorian period, English design	385.00	510.00	420.00
☐ Brass, double, ornate scrollwork	1050.00	1300.00	1125.00
☐ Brass, single, simple styling, round posts	460.00	510.00	475.00
☐ Cannonball, field bed	135.00	360.00	235.00
☐ Cannonball, scrolled headboard, original paint	210.00	285.00	238.00
☐ Cannonball, trundle, wooden wheels, original paint	335.00	435.00	375.00
☐ Canopy, birds-eye maple headboard, c. 1830	310.00	385.00	338.00
☐ Canopy, curly maple headboard	1500.00	1600.00	1500.00
☐ Canopy, spool, walnut, high poster	520.00	670.00	580.00
☐ Canopy, tiger maple, c. 1835	710.00	810.00	750.00
☐ Canopy, Victorian Renaissance, walnut, carved, c. 1850	1050.00	1350.00	1150.00
☐ Carved walnut, ornately decorated	235.00	410.00	312.00
☐ Day, Louis XVI, mahogany, ornamented	2550.00	3050.00	2750.00
☐ Day, pine, scrolled back rest, turned legs	610.00	710.00	650.00
☐ Four poster, American Empire, mahogany, pineapple tops	1750.00	2050.00	1850.00
☐ Four poster, bamboo-like head and foot pieces	310.00	460.00	380.00
☐ Four poster, maple, spool, early 18th c.	760.00	910.00	820.00
☐ Four poster, maple, spool, turned headboard and footboard, pine tree tops, c. 1830	460.00	610.00	520.00
☐ Four poster, maple with and without canopy, c. 19th c.	510.00	3550.00	1500.00
☐ Four poster, Sheraton, popular	585.00	660.00	612.00
☐ Four poster, tiger maple, walnut	435.00	510.00	462.00
☐ Iron, child's crib, painted, brass knobs	160.00	235.00	182.00
☐ Iron, double, painted, ornately decorated	260.00	460.00	350.00
☐ Iron, painted, ornately decorated, brass knobs and rods	160.00	285.00	212.50
☐ Jenny Lind, double, maple	310.00	360.00	325.00
☐ Jenny Lind, maple, field bed	235.00	360.00	285.00
☐ Jenny Lind, single, walnut	235.00	360.00	285.00
☐ Jenny Lind, spool, Victorian	110.00	185.00	138.00
☐ Rope, four poster, maple, urn finials, turned headboard	310.00	410.00	350.00
☐ Rope, four poster, pine	385.00	360.00	312.00
☐ Rope, fruitwood, c. 1830	335.00	435.00	375.00

BENCHES

☐ Bucket, pine, slant front, 19th c.	160.00	235.00	182.00
☐ Bucket, pine, three shelves	260.00	335.00	282.00
☐ Bucket, pine, three shelves, three drawers	560.00	660.00	600.00
☐ Bucket, scalloped shelves, cupboard with two doors	1250.00	1450.00	1300.00
☐ Church, pine, 48"	210.00	310.00	250.00
☐ Cobbler, pine, leather seat, one drawer, c. 1825	335.00	410.00	360.00
☐ Cobbler, pine, leather seat, six drawers, tools	485.00	610.00	530.00
☐ Cobbler, pine, ten drawers	360.00	460.00	400.00
☐ Cobbler, pine, upholstered seat	460.00	510.00	475.00
☐ Cobbler, walnut	260.00	310.00	275.00
☐ Deacon, spindle back, eight legs	460.00	510.00	475.00

360 / FURNITURE

	Current Price Range		Prior Year Average
☐ **Deacon,** Vermont style, original finish	110.00	210.00	150.00
☐ **Fireside,** pine, scalloped ends	360.00	435.00	382.00
☐ **Fireside,** pine, scroll design	510.00	610.00	550.00
☐ **Fireside,** walnut, scalloped edges	235.00	310.00	260.00
☐ **Mammy,** black, rocker, 6', c. 1830	485.00	585.00	525.00
☐ **Mammy,** green, 6', c. 19th c.	610.00	710.00	650.00
☐ **Porch,** pine, scalloped, refinished	110.00	185.00	138.00
☐ **Table,** poplar, original finish, c. 1820	385.00	460.00	412.00
☐ **Table,** scalloped legs, original finish	485.00	535.00	500.00
☐ **Water,** pine, three drawers, shelf, two doors	135.00	210.00	160.00
☐ **Water,** pine, two shelves, tapered front	210.00	260.00	225.00
☐ **Windsor,** bamboo turnings, 9"	360.00	410.00	375.00

BENTWOOD

The process of bending wood with steam was perfected by Michael Thonet in Vienna in 1856. Bentwood furniture is still being produced by the Thonet firm and several others including the Sheboygan Chair Company, Tidioute Chair Company, and Jacob and Joseph Kohn.

☐ **Arm,** cane seat	235.00	285.00	250.00
☐ **Arm,** wooden seat, signed Thonet	210.00	260.00	225.00
☐ **Chair,** caned seat	70.00	100.00	80.00
☐ **Child's,** highchair	160.00	210.00	175.00
☐ **Child's,** cane seat, nursing rocker	160.00	210.00	175.00
☐ **Child's,** rocker, cane seat, signed Thonet	260.00	360.00	300.00
☐ **Child's rocker,** wicker seat and back	160.00	210.00	175.00
☐ **Cradle,** on stand, with top	1350.00	1550.00	1400.00
☐ **Cradle,** signed Thonet	1100.00	1250.00	1175.00
☐ **Hat rack,** umbrella holder	285.00	310.00	282.00
☐ **Side,** caned seat	75.00	90.00	78.00
☐ **Side,** wood seat, signed Thonet	65.00	80.00	68.00
☐ **Stool,** caned seat	110.00	135.00	112.00

CANDLESTANDS

☐ **Chippendale,** carved and turned walnut, dish top	2050.00	3050.00	2500.00
☐ **Chippendale,** maple, snake feet	710.00	860.00	780.00
☐ **Chippendale,** tiger maple base, maple top	310.00	435.00	362.00
☐ **Chippendale,** turned and inlaid cherrywood	420.00	620.00	500.00
☐ **Chippendale,** turned maple and cherrywood	550.00	850.00	650.00
☐ **Federal,** birch, tilt-top	285.00	385.00	325.00
☐ **Federal,** carved mahogany, tilt-top	320.00	520.00	400.00
☐ **Federal,** inlaid mahogany, oval top	3050.00	5050.00	4000.00
☐ **Federal,** inlaid turned cherrywood	760.00	1050.00	840.00
☐ **Federal,** maple, octagonal	320.00	520.00	400.00
☐ **Federal,** mahogany, tilt-top, spider legs	620.00	770.00	680.00
☐ **Federal,** turned cherrywood	360.00	460.00	400.00
☐ **Hepplewhite,** birch and cherry	460.00	535.00	482.00
☐ **Hepplewhite,** smoked top, one drawer	1000.00	1150.00	1075.00
☐ **Hepplewhite,** tiger maple top, original finish	1100.00	1400.00	1150.00
☐ **Queen Anne,** scalloped cherrywood	560.00	710.00	620.00
☐ **Queen Anne,** turned maple, painted	420.00	620.00	500.00
☐ **Queen Anne,** turned cherrywood	420.00	620.00	500.00
☐ **Sheraton,** pine, original finish	420.00	495.00	438.00

	Current Price Range		Prior Year Average
☐ **William and Mary,** carved cherrywood, two light, trestle, base	2050.00	3050.00	2500.00
☐ **William and Mary,** turned walnut	4100.00	6100.00	5000.00
☐ **Wrought,** iron, walnut, adjustable	770.00	1050.00	820.00

CHAIRS

	Current Price Range		Prior Year Average
☐ **Bannister back,** maple, rush seat	410.00	485.00	438.00
☐ **Black lacquer,** cane, c. 19th c.	410.00	435.00	412.00
☐ **Boston,** rocker, rolled seat	210.00	285.00	238.00
☐ **Captain's,** child's	160.00	210.00	175.00
☐ **Captain's,** side, pine	260.00	285.00	262.00
☐ **Child's,** arrow back	160.00	210.00	175.00
☐ **Child's,** highchair, Windsor	160.00	210.00	175.00
☐ **Child's,** ladder-back, red paint	90.00	110.00	92.00
☐ **Chippendale,** carved walnut side, pair	15500.00	20500.00	17500.00
☐ **Chippendale,** corner	420.00	520.00	450.00
☐ **Chippendale,** corner, mahogany	320.00	420.00	350.00
☐ **Chippendale,** corner, rush seat	235.00	310.00	260.00
☐ **Chippendale,** country, 18th c.	520.00	620.00	550.00
☐ **Chippendale,** side, cherry	1300.00	1550.00	1375.00
☐ **Chippendale,** side, upholstered	760.00	1050.00	820.00
☐ **Chippendale,** side, walnut	335.00	410.00	362.00
☐ **Chippendale,** wing	9550.00	10500.00	9750.00
☐ **Eastlake,** Victorian, arm, walnut	160.00	210.00	175.00
☐ **Eastlake,** Victorian, side	110.00	160.00	125.00
☐ **Gentlemen's,** carved	360.00	410.00	375.00
☐ **Hepplewhite,** side	535.00	710.00	635.00
☐ **Hepplewhite,** side, upholstered	760.00	1050.00	900.00
☐ **Hitchcock,** maple, rush seat	185.00	235.00	200.00
☐ **Ladder-back,** arm, cherry	460.00	510.00	475.00
☐ **Ladder-back,** arm, hoopskirt	485.00	560.00	512.00
☐ **Ladder-back,** rocker, pine	185.00	260.00	212.00
☐ **Ladder-back,** side, maple	260.00	310.00	275.00
☐ **Ladder-back,** side, mahogany	360.00	410.00	375.00
☐ **Parlor,** walnut, upholstered seat and back	510.00	610.00	550.00
☐ **Pennsylvania,** arrow back	110.00	120.00	105.00
☐ **Queen Anne,** arm	2250.00	2550.00	2350.00
☐ **Queen Anne,** banister	420.00	520.00	450.00
☐ **Queen Anne,** corner, maple	720.00	820.00	750.00
☐ **Queen Anne,** country, round feet	360.00	410.00	375.00
☐ **Queen Anne,** side, cherry	385.00	485.00	425.00
☐ **Queen Anne,** side, walnut	1550.00	2050.00	1750.00
☐ **Queen Anne,** wing	9550.00	10050.00	9750.00
☐ **Salem,** rocker	360.00	435.00	382.00
☐ **Shaker,** ladder-back	260.00	310.00	275.00
☐ **Shaker,** side	460.00	510.00	475.00
☐ **Shaker,** straight	85.00	105.00	90.00
☐ **Sheraton,** arm	525.00	775.00	625.00
☐ **Sheraton,** corner, maple	510.00	585.00	538.00
☐ **Sheraton,** country	310.00	460.00	382.00
☐ **Sheraton,** side	385.00	510.00	435.00
☐ **Sheraton,** wing, fireside	460.00	560.00	500.00
☐ **Victorian,** arm	335.00	510.00	435.00
☐ **Victorian,** arm, gentleman's	510.00	760.00	625.00
☐ **Victorian,** arm, lady's	460.00	510.00	475.00
☐ **Victorian,** rosewood, upholster	1150.00	1450.00	1250.00

362 / FURNITURE

	Current Price Range		Prior Year Average
☐ **Victorian,** side	110.00	160.00	125.00
☐ **William and Mary,** bannister back	260.00	310.00	275.00
☐ **William and Mary,** walnut, carved	1550.00	1850.00	1650.00
☐ **Windsor,** arm, brace back	860.00	960.00	900.00
☐ **Windsor,** arrow back	260.00	360.00	300.00
☐ **Windsor,** child's, bamboo turned, bow back	410.00	560.00	480.00
☐ **Windsor,** side, fan back	210.00	310.00	250.00
☐ **Windsor,** side, bamboo turned, pair	360.00	385.00	362.00
☐ **Windsor,** side, bow back	210.00	260.00	225.00
☐ **Windsor,** side, brace back	420.00	720.00	550.00
☐ **Windsor,** side, comb back	260.00	510.00	438.00
☐ **Windsor,** side, hoop back	160.00	260.00	200.00

CHESTS

☐ **Apothecary,** with drawers	260.00	310.00	275.00

BLANKET

☐ **Chippendale,** walnut	950.00	1050.00	950.00
☐ **Curly maple**	960.00	1100.00	1000.00
☐ **Pine,** cannonball feet	260.00	285.00	262.00
☐ **Pennsylvania,** red	140.00	160.00	140.00
☐ **Tiger maple**	1050.00	1250.00	1100.00

CHIPPENDALE

☐ **Birch**	1800.00	2050.00	1850.00
☐ **Cherry**	3100.00	3600.00	3250.00
☐ **Commode,** bedside	510.00	760.00	620.00
☐ **Curly maple**	4600.00	5600.00	5000.00
☐ **Eastlake,** Victorian, drawers	235.00	510.00	438.00
☐ **Mahogany**	5100.00	6100.00	5500.00
☐ **Maple**	4050.00	4550.00	4250.00
☐ **Pine**	1050.00	1350.00	1150.00
☐ **Tiger maple**	2050.00	2550.00	2250.00
☐ **Walnut**	2200.00	3200.00	2500.00

HEPPLEWHITE

☐ **Cherry**	1050.00	1300.00	1100.00
☐ **Mahogany**	1050.00	1300.00	1100.00
☐ **Maple**	1300.00	1550.00	1400.00
☐ **Walnut**	1050.00	1300.00	1175.00

SHERATON

☐ **Cherry,** inlaid	760.00	1100.00	820.00
☐ **Curly maple**	1050.00	1350.00	1150.00
☐ **Mahogany,** four drawer	1100.00	1600.00	1250.00
☐ **Maple**	760.00	1100.00	840.00
☐ **Walnut**	510.00	760.00	620.00

CORNER CUPBOARDS

☐ **American,** mahogany	860.00	1050.00	925.00
☐ **Chippendale,** maple and cherrywood	1150.00	1550.00	1300.00
☐ **Chippendale,** pine	1600.00	2100.00	1750.00
☐ **Federal,** cherrywood, inlaid	2100.00	3100.00	2500.00
☐ **Primitive,** pine, carved, painted	620.00	820.00	700.00
☐ **Queen Anne,** pine, carved, barrel back	620.00	820.00	700.00

DESKS
AMERICAN

	Current Price Range		Prior Year Average
☐ **Cherry,** slant front	2100.00	2600.00	2250.00
☐ **Walnut,** carved, 72″	260.00	360.00	300.00

CHIPPENDALE

☐ **Flattop,** kneehole	4100.00	4600.00	4250.00
☐ **Slant front,** cherry	3300.00	3800.00	3450.00
☐ **Slant front,** mahogany	8600.00	9100.00	8750.00
☐ **Slant front,** maple	8600.00	9100.00	8750.00
☐ **Slant front,** platform	4100.00	4600.00	4250.00
☐ **Slant front,** walnut	2850.00	3050.00	2900.00

HEPPLEWHITE

☐ **Bureau style**	1600.00	2100.00	1750.00
☐ **Flattop,** kneehole	2300.00	2600.00	2370.00
☐ **Slant front,** mahogany	2300.00	2600.00	2370.00

LAP

☐ **Inlaid wood,** velvet lined	110.00	160.00	125.00
☐ **Mahogany,** brass hinged	160.00	210.00	175.00
☐ **Oak,** with inkwell	80.00	110.00	82.00
☐ **Walnut,** lined, secret compartment	80.00	110.00	82.00

ROLLTOP

☐ **Mahogany**	610.00	710.00	650.00
☐ **Oak,** brass	520.00	720.00	600.00
☐ **Oak,** S design, 50″	420.00	620.00	500.00
☐ **Oak,** waterfall	750.00	2050.00	1300.00
☐ **Walnut**	575.00	725.00	620.00

SCHOOLMASTER

☐ **Kneehole,** mahogany inlay	510.00	610.00	550.00
☐ **Pine and cherry**	310.00	360.00	325.00
☐ **Pine and maple**	260.00	285.00	262.00
☐ **Slant front**	210.00	310.00	250.00

SHERATON

☐ **Bureau style**	1050.00	1300.00	1125.00
☐ **Country,** pine, drawer	1050.00	1300.00	1125.00
☐ **Flattop,** kneehole	1050.00	1300.00	1125.00
☐ **Slant front**	1300.00	1600.00	1375.00

VICTORIAN

☐ **Flattop,** kneehole	675.00	825.00	725.00
☐ **Slant front**	675.00	825.00	725.00

DRY SINKS

☐ **Cherry,** refinished	285.00	385.00	325.00
☐ **Chestnut,** high back	660.00	710.00	675.00
☐ **Pine,** metal top	235.00	310.00	260.00
☐ **Pine,** painted	260.00	310.00	275.00
☐ **Pine,** primitive, rough condition	1250.00	1550.00	1350.00
☐ **Pine,** refinished	410.00	510.00	450.00
☐ **Walnut,** two shelves, zinc lined trough	760.00	910.00	820.00

HIGHBOYS AND LOWBOYS (American Made)

CHIPPENDALE

	Current Price Range	Prior Year Average
☐ **Cherry,** highboy	15500.00 18500.00	16500.00
☐ **Cherry,** lowboy	8050.00 1050.00	9000.00
☐ **Mahogany,** highboy	18500.00 20500.00	19000.00
☐ **Mahogany,** lowboy	10500.00 12500.00	11000.00
☐ **Maple,** highboy	25500.00 35500.00	30000.00
☐ **Maple,** lowboy	18000.00 20500.00	18750.00
☐ **Walnut,** highboy	15500.00 18500.00	16500.00
☐ **Walnut,** lowboy	5050.00 7050.00	6000.00

QUEEN ANNE

☐ **Cherry,** highboy	15500.00 18500.00	16500.00
☐ **Cherry,** lowboy	8550.00 10500.00	9200.00
☐ **Curly maple,** highboy, flattop	8050.00 10500.00	9000.00
☐ **Curly maple,** highboy, bonnet top	10500.00 15500.00	12500.00
☐ **Mahogany,** highboy	18500.00 20500.00	19000.00
☐ **Mahogany,** lowboy	10500.00 12500.00	11000.00
☐ **Maple,** highboy	18000.00 20500.00	18500.00
☐ **Maple,** lowboy	8550.00 10500.00	9200.00
☐ **Tiger maple,** highway	10500.00 12500.00	11000.00
☐ **Walnut,** highboy	15500.00 18500.00	16500.00
☐ **Walnut,** lowboy	5050.00 7050.00	6000.00

WILLIAM AND MARY

☐ **Burled walnut,** highboy, inlaid	3100.00 4600.00	3800.00
☐ **Mahogany,** highboy, bonnet top, inlaid	4600.00 6100.00	5200.00
☐ **Maple,** highboy, flattop	2600.00 3600.00	3000.00
☐ **Walnut,** highboy, flattop, inlaid	2600.00 3100.00	2750.00
☐ **Walnut,** highboy, bonnet top, carved	3600.00 4600.00	4000.00

KITCHEN UTILITY CUPBOARDS

☐ **Beveled glass,** four compartment storage	360.00 410.00	375.00
☐ **Hoosier,** original varnish	310.00 460.00	380.00
☐ **Hoosier,** painted	210.00 310.00	250.00
☐ **Hoosier,** porcelain surface	435.00 510.00	460.00
☐ **Oak,** wall type, oval	55.00 80.00	62.00

LOVE SEATS

☐ **Art Nouveau**	360.00 510.00	425.00
☐ **Eastlake,** Victorian, walnut	410.00 510.00	450.00
☐ **Empire,** Victorian, transitional	510.00 610.00	550.00
☐ **Hepplewhite,** walnut	1150.00 1350.00	1200.00
☐ **Louis XV,** wing back	2600.00 3100.00	2750.00
☐ **Queen Anne,** velvet	410.00 510.00	450.00
☐ **Rennaissance,** Victorian, upholstered	510.00 610.00	550.00
☐ **Rococo,** Victorian, upholstered	720.00 920.00	800.00
☐ **Sheraton,** upholstered	820.00 970.00	880.00
☐ **William and Mary,** upholstered	710.00 860.00	780.00

MIRRORS

☐ **Brass,** figural design	185.00 210.00	182.00
☐ **Chippendale,** Georgian	1600.00 2600.00	2000.00
☐ **Chippendale,** mahogany, English	820.00 1020.00	900.00
☐ **Chippendale,** mahogany, scrolled	160.00 210.00	175.00

	Current Price Range	Prior Year Average
☐ **Chippendale,** pine, shaving	110.00 160.00	125.00
☐ **Chippendale,** walnut and pine	235.00 285.00	250.00
☐ **Chippendale,** walnut	820.00 1020.00	900.00
☐ **Chippendale,** walnut, wall	520.00 620.00	550.00
☐ **Empire,** dressing table........................	410.00 460.00	425.00
☐ **Empire,** mahogany, wall	55.00 80.00	58.00
☐ **Empire,** standard	260.00 760.00	500.00
☐ **English,** dressing table	410.00 460.00	425.00
☐ **Federal,** Convex	1300.00 2300.00	1750.00
☐ **Federal,** dressing table	260.00 310.00	275.00
☐ **Federal,** gilt wood and gesso, eagle	710.00 860.00	780.00
☐ **Federal,** wall, ship	460.00 535.00	482.00
☐ **Floor,** oak, oval	285.00 310.00	282.00
☐ **Queen Anne,** curly maple, wall	485.00 585.00	525.00
☐ **Queen Anne,** mahogany, gilt wood.............	2600.00 3300.00	2800.00
☐ **Regency,** gilt wood	610.00 710.00	650.00
☐ **Regency,** standard	260.00 760.00	500.00
☐ **Rococo,** gilt wood...........................	260.00 360.00	300.00
☐ **Rococo,** wood, large	1050.00 1250.00	1100.00
☐ **Shaving,** carved	55.00 80.00	62.00
☐ **Shaving,** mahogany	160.00 185.00	162.00
☐ **Shaving,** tiger maple and cherry	160.00 210.00	175.00
☐ **Traveling,** wood inlay	30.00 55.00	38.00

MUSIC CABINETS

☐ **Serpentine,** legs, double door	160.00 185.00	162.00
☐ **Serpentine,** legs, single door	135.00 160.00	138.00
☐ **Victorian,** mahogany and rosewood, casters	410.00 510.00	450.00
☐ **Victorian,** rosewood, marble top	850.00 1250.00	1000.00
☐ **Victorian,** rosewood, ornate carving	1050.00 1350.00	1150.00

ROCKERS

☐ **Boston,** painted	510.00 660.00	580.00
☐ **Boston,** wicker seat	135.00 185.00	138.00
☐ **Cane,** back and seat refinished	110.00 135.00	112.00
☐ **Cherrywood,** American, yoke top, rail, scrolled armrests, mid 19th c.	160.00 260.00	200.00
☐ **Child's,** caned seat...........................	135.00 160.00	138.00
☐ **Child's,** turned and black painted wood platform .	110.00 160.00	125.00
☐ **Child's,** wood and wicker seat	55.00 75.00	60.00
☐ **Eastlake,** platform	80.00 95.00	82.00
☐ **Eastlake,** platform fabric seat	360.00 385.00	362.00
☐ **Federal,** arrow backs, painted, decorated	310.00 410.00	350.00
☐ **Federal,** painted and decorated	210.00 260.00	225.00
☐ **Hitchcock,** curly maple	210.00 260.00	225.00
☐ **Hunzinger,** walnut, platform	160.00 210.00	175.00
☐ **Ladder-back,** ornate	410.00 510.00	450.00
☐ **Shaker,** armless	385.00 435.00	400.00
☐ **Shaker,** arms	535.00 610.00	560.00
☐ **Victorian,** Grecian, restored	210.00 260.00	225.00
☐ **Victorian,** mahogany, 19th c.	85.00 125.00	100.00
☐ **Victorian,** sewing, wicker	80.00 110.00	85.00
☐ **Victorian,** side arms	135.00 160.00	138.00
☐ **Victorian,** walnut, leaf design	260.00 285.00	262.00

366 / FURNITURE

	Current Price Range		Prior Year Average
☐ **Walnut frame,** complete upholstery with tufted back	560.00	660.00	600.00
☐ **Windsor,** bamboo turned	410.00	610.00	500.00
☐ **Windsor,** bamboo turned, painted, hoop back	535.00	735.00	625.00
☐ **Windsor,** fanback, signed	460.00	610.00	520.00

SECRETARIES

☐ **Chippendale**	6600.00	8100.00	7200.00
☐ **Empire,** American	800.00	1800.00	1200.00
☐ **Federal**	2600.00	3600.00	3000.00
☐ **Hepplewhite**	3200.00	5200.00	4500.00
☐ **Regency**	1600.00	2600.00	2000.00
☐ **Sheraton**	1600.00	3100.00	1750.00
☐ **Victorian**	1100.00	3100.00	2000.00

SIDEBOARDS

☐ **Chippendale,** American	11000.00	16000.00	12500.00
☐ **Empire,** American	1600.00	2100.00	1750.00
☐ **Hepplewhite**	3600.00	4600.00	4000.00
☐ **Regency**	1600.00	2100.00	1750.00
☐ **Sheraton**	2600.00	4100.00	3250.00
☐ **Victorian**	1100.00	1600.00	1250.00
☐ **William and Mary**	2600.00	3600.00	3000.00

SOFAS AND SETTEES

☐ **American,** sofa, carved walnut	1850.00	2050.00	1900.00
☐ **Belter, sofa,** rosewood	3600.00	4600.00	4000.00
☐ **Chippendale,** settee	3600.00	4200.00	3750.00
☐ **Chippendale,** sofa, mahogany	3600.00	4200.00	3750.00
☐ **Chippendale,** sofa, six legs	7600.00	8200.00	7750.00
☐ **Directoire,** settee	950.00	1150.00	1000.00
☐ **Directoire,** sofa	1500.00	3200.00	2200.00
☐ **Eastlake,** settee	185.00	235.00	200.00
☐ **Eastlake,** sofa	235.00	285.00	250.00
☐ **Empire,** settee	210.00	310.00	250.00
☐ **Empire,** settee, French	460.00	610.00	520.00
☐ **Empire,** sofa	210.00	310.00	250.00
☐ **Empire,** sofa, mahogany, French	760.00	1050.00	1300.00
☐ **Federal,** settee, painted, decorated	1250.00	1450.00	1300.00
☐ **Federal,** sofa, mahogany, carved	650.00	800.00	680.00
☐ **Hepplewhite,** settee	1600.00	1800.00	1600.00
☐ **Hepplewhite,** sofa	3100.00	3600.00	3250.00
☐ **Queen Anne,** settee	4100.00	4600.00	4250.00
☐ **Queen Anne,** sofa	6200.00	6800.00	6250.00
☐ **Rococo,** settee, serpentine back	460.00	560.00	500.00
☐ **Rococo,** sofa, walnut, carved	2800.00	3100.00	2850.00
☐ **Sheraton,** settee	960.00	1150.00	1025.00
☐ **Sheraton,** sofa, mahogany	1800.00	2100.00	1900.00
☐ **Victorian,** sofa, Louis XV, walnut, carved	1250.00	1550.00	1350.00
☐ **Victorian,** sofa, Louis XV, walnut	625.00	725.00	650.00
☐ **Victorian,** settee, Louis XVI, French	1800.00	2100.00	1875.00
☐ **Victorian,** sofa, Louis XVI, French	3600.00	4100.00	3750.00
☐ **William and Mary,** settee, upholstered	725.00	825.00	750.00
☐ **Windsor,** settee	700.00	950.00	775.00
☐ **Windsor,** sofa, bamboo, spindle back	1850.00	2050.00	1900.00

STOOLS

	Current Price Range		Prior Year Average
☐ **Chippendale,** mahogany	420.00	620.00	500.00
☐ **George II,** mahogany oval	1600.00	2100.00	1750.00
☐ **George II,** walnut stool......................	2100.00	2600.00	2250.00
☐ **George III,** mahogany feet, carved	420.00	620.00	500.00
☐ **German Rococo,** gilt wood	850.00	1050.00	900.00
☐ **Louis XV,** painted, pair.....................	260.00	360.00	300.00
☐ **Queen Anne,** cherry	135.00	160.00	138.00
☐ **Queen Anne,** walnut........................	160.00	210.00	175.00
☐ **Regency,** rosewood, piano	210.00	310.00	250.00
☐ **Rush seat,** turned and painted	110.00	160.00	125.00
☐ **Sheraton,** walnut	110.00	160.00	125.00

TABLES

CARD AND GAME

☐ **Chippendale,** American	5600.00	6100.00	5750.00
☐ **Chippendale,** American, carved mahogany, turret-top	2600.00	3600.00	3000.00
☐ **Chippendale,** English........................	1800.00	2100.00	1900.00
☐ **Duncan Phyfe,** mahogany	760.00	1050.00	880.00
☐ **Federal,** maple inlay........................	850.00	1050.00	900.00
☐ **Federal,** marble inlay	2800.00	3200.00	2750.00
☐ **Hepplewhite,** American	860.00	1250.00	1000.00
☐ **Hepplewhite,** English	1300.00	1600.00	1425.00
☐ **Louis XVI,** French, backgammon	3100.00	3600.00	3250.00
☐ **Queen Anne,** English	2700.00	3100.00	2750.00
☐ **Regency,** rosewood	1600.00	2100.00	1750.00
☐ **Sheraton,** American	1300.00	1600.00	1375.00
☐ **Sheraton,** English...........................	775.00	1050.00	880.00

DROP LEAF

☐ **Birch,** gate leg, six legs, high drop leaf, American	1300.00	1600.00	1400.00
☐ **Birch,** gate leg, six legs, high drop leaf, English .	700.00	850.00	720.00
☐ **Chippendale,** American mahogany	5600.00	6100.00	5750.00
☐ **Chippendale,** English........................	1800.00	2100.00	1900.00
☐ **Empire,** Victorian, American	360.00	510.00	420.00
☐ **Empire,** Victorian, English...................	260.00	410.00	325.00
☐ **Hepplewhite,** American	1300.00	1600.00	1375.00
☐ **Hepplewhite,** English	550.00	800.00	620.00
☐ **Queen Anne,** American, swing legs	5600.00	6100.00	5750.00
☐ **Queen Anne,** English, swing legs	1800.00	2100.00	1875.000
☐ **Sheraton,** American	760.00	1100.00	880.00
☐ **Sheraton,** English...........................	520.00	775.00	620.00

OCCASIONAL TABLES

☐ **American,** pine	210.00	260.00	225.00
☐ **Hepplewhite,** American	660.00	810.00	725.00
☐ **Hepplewhite,** English	385.00	460.00	412.00
☐ **Sheraton,** American	460.00	510.00	475.00
☐ **Sheraton,** English...........................	360.00	410.00	275.00
☐ **Victorian,** American	260.00	410.00	275.00
☐ **Victorian,** English..........................	210.00	310.00	250.00

TILT-TOP

☐ **Chippendale,** American	2300.00	2600.00	2375.00
☐ **Chippendale,** English........................	1050.00	1300.00	1100.00

368 / FURNITURE

	Current Price Range		Prior Year Average
☐ **Federal,** American	1050.00	1300.00	1100.00
☐ **Federal,** English	485.00	610.00	535.00
☐ **Hepplewhite,** American	2300.00	2600.00	2400.00
☐ **Hepplewhite,** English	1300.00	1600.00	1400.00
☐ **Queen Anne,** American	1300.00	1600.00	1400.00
☐ **Queen Anne,** English	520.00	775.00	580.00
☐ **Regency,** American	1050.00	1300.00	1125.00
☐ **Regency,** English	485.00	610.00	530.00

WORK TABLES

☐ **Cherry,** with drawers	410.00	510.00	450.00
☐ **Empire,** cherry, sewing	460.00	510.00	475.00
☐ **Empire,** mahogany	360.00	460.00	400.00
☐ **Hepplewhite,** mahogany	460.00	560.00	500.00
☐ **Hepplewhite,** walnut	210.00	260.00	225.00
☐ **Mahogany,** English	1600.00	2100.00	1750.00
☐ **Maple,** American	950.00	1150.00	1000.00
☐ **Queen Anne,** painted	610.00	710.00	650.00
☐ **Regency,** English mahogany	1600.00	2100.00	1750.00
☐ **Victorian,** walnut, sewing	320.00	520.00	400.00

OAK FURNITURE

Oak, because of its durability, has been a favorite of furniture makers for centuries. Old pieces and European oak tend to be very dark in color. In the late 19th century, the refinement of steam powered equipment for working wood enabled the mass production of "golden oak" furniture. The vast majority of these pieces were made in Grand Rapids, Michigan, and were sold extensively throughout the United States by Sears and Roebuck through their catalogue. A plainer style, called Mission Oak, was preferred by many, but both types are considered collectible and are not particularly expensive.

BEDS

☐ **Cane,** headboard and footboard, plain style	235.00	260.00	238.00
☐ **Child's,** drop side	235.00	285.00	250.00
☐ **Eastlake style**	160.00	185.00	162.00
☐ **Folding style**	460.00	510.00	475.00
☐ **Folding style,** dresser	360.00	460.00	400.00
☐ **Folding style,** desk and bookcase	510.00	610.00	550.00
☐ **Lounge**	210.00	285.00	238.00
☐ **Murphy**	510.00	585.00	538.00
☐ **Open panel design**	200.00	235.00	215.00
☐ **Scrolled footboard**	310.00	360.00	325.00

BENCHES

☐ **Advertising**	285.00	360.00	312.00
☐ **Church,** 56″	310.00	410.00	350.00
☐ **Church pews,** decorated ends, 8′	60.00	75.00	62.00
☐ **Jacobean,** turned legs	285.00	360.00	312.00
☐ **Organ,** lift seat	80.00	110.00	88.00
☐ **Tinsmith's**	510.00	610.00	550.00

BOOKCASES

☐ **Desk,** adjustable shelves	350.00	750.00	500.00
☐ **Desk,** glass doors	435.00	510.00	462.00

	Current Price Range	Prior Year Average
☐ **Five horizontal adjustable shelves,** no glass	310.00　710.00	500.00
☐ **Four horizontal adjustable shelves,** glass	285.00　310.00	288.00
☐ **George II,** bureau	1150.00　1450.00	1250.00
☐ **Large library bookcase,** glass front	1350.00　1650.00	1450.00
☐ **Revolving style,** adjustable shelves	260.00　360.00	300.00
☐ **Side by side,** glass front	260.00　410.00	325.00
☐ **Six tiered stacking,** Gunn Furniture Co., c. 1901 ..	460.00　510.00	475.00

CHAIRS

☐ **Armless,** padded seat, no carving, set of four	210.00　260.00	225.00
☐ **Armless,** wood seat, very ornate, set of four	310.00　360.00	325.00
☐ **Barber shop,** pneumatic	1850.00　2250.00	2000.00
☐ **Office,** arms, tilt back........................	285.00　360.00	312.00
☐ **Ornate back**	360.00　410.00	375.00
☐ **Shaker style,** set of four.....................	235.00　310.00	260.00
☐ **Single upholstered seat,** with arms, square design, set of four	90.00　170.00	120.00
☐ **Upholstered seats,** four armchairs, two side	735.00　810.00	760.00
☐ **Windsor,** set of four	210.00　235.00	212.00

CHESTS

☐ **Apothecary**	820.00　970.00	880.00
☐ **Blanket**	260.00　360.00	300.00
☐ **Commode**	260.00　310.00	275.00
☐ **Ice,** paneled	460.00　560.00	500.00
☐ **Oak,** paneled	410.00　460.00	425.00

CHINA CABINETS

☐ **Bowed front,** curved sides	520.00　720.00	600.00
☐ **Claw legs,** ornate	620.00　820.00	700.00
☐ **Corner,** browed front	320.00　420.00	350.00
☐ **Hand carved,** swell shaped glass on ends, claw feet......................................	460.00　560.00	500.00
☐ **Leaded glass,** quartered oak, claw feet	560.00　610.00	575.00
☐ **Serpentine legs,** ornate	820.00　920.00	850.00

DESKS

☐ **Bombay style,** claw feet......................	235.00　310.00	260.00
☐ **C curve,** 36″...............................	460.00　560.00	500.00
☐ **Drop leaf**	135.00　185.00	150.00
☐ **Kneehole**	110.00　135.00	112.00
☐ **Lady's,** tall rolltop, glass doors on top shelves, matching chair	3300.00　3900.00	3500.00
☐ **Lady's,** flattop..............................	435.00　510.00	460.00
☐ **Lapdesk,** inkwell............................	80.00　110.00	88.00
☐ **Office type,** high curtain	460.00　610.00	520.00
☐ **Office type,** kneehole	260.00　310.00	275.00
☐ **Parlor type**.................................	110.00　185.00	138.00
☐ **Schoolmaster's,** flattop	135.00　185.00	150.00
☐ **S curve,** refinished, 42″	950.00　1150.00	1012.00
☐ **Secretary type,** with beveled glass	1250.00　1550.00	1350.00
☐ **S Design,** rolltop, 50″	410.00　610.00	500.00
☐ **Side by side**	110.00　160.00	125.00
☐ **Waterfall,** S curve, rolltop	750.00　2100.00	1350.00
☐ **Wooton,** simple to fancy	2400.00　15500.00	9000.00

370 / FURNITURE

	Current Price Range		Prior Year Average

DRESSERS
☐ **Bombay style,** ornately carved	210.00	310.00	250.00
☐ **Dressing table,** mirror	160.00	185.00	162.00
☐ **Square style,** three drawers, mirror	185.00	235.00	200.00

DRY SINK
☐ **High back**	210.00	260.00	225.00
☐ **Zinc lined top**	410.00	510.00	450.00

FERN OR PLANT STAND
☐ **Pedestal,** or legs, 28"-29"	60.00	110.00	75.00

HALL RACKS
☐ **Claw feet,** large mirror	610.00	660.00	625.00
☐ **Serpentine legs,** round mirror, one drawer	410.00	460.00	425.00
☐ **Square style,** ornately carved, paneled back	510.00	560.00	525.00
☐ **Two piece,** double seat bench, ornately carved	510.00	560.00	525.00
☐ **Umbrella holder,** large mirror	285.00	410.00	338.00

ICE BOXES
☐ **Double door,** refinished	210.00	310.00	250.00
☐ **Four door,** carved	1100.00	1200.00	1050.00
☐ **"Mascot",** brass hardware, refinished, 4' x 2'	385.00	460.00	412.00
☐ **Meat cooler,** walk-in, inlaid white glass panels, matching counter, 10' x 8' x 6', c. 1920	14500.00	15500.00	14500.00
☐ **Single door**	160.00	210.00	175.00
☐ **Six door,** mirror	410.00	460.00	425.00

MIRRORS
☐ **Oval,** floor type	235.00	285.00	250.00
☐ **Square,** floor type	210.00	235.00	215.00
☐ **Square,** wall type	55.00	80.00	62.00
☐ **Traveling,** wood inlay	30.00	55.00	38.00

MUSIC CABINETS
☐ **Quartered oak,** hand carved, single door	160.00	185.00	162.00

ROCKERS
☐ **Pressed back**	110.00	135.00	112.00
☐ **Spindled back**	80.00	110.00	88.00
☐ **Upholstered,** seat and back	320.00	420.00	350.00

SIDEBOARDS
☐ **Bowed front,** carved, claw feet	310.00	385.00	338.00
☐ **Four drawers,** cellavettes	235.00	310.00	260.00
☐ **Leaded glass,** doors and sides, mirror	510.00	560.00	525.00
☐ **Ornate,** drawers and mirrors	560.00	610.00	575.00
☐ **Plain,** drawers	260.00	310.00	275.00
☐ **Pressed design,** mirror	160.00	210.00	175.00

TABLES
☐ **Dining,** square, round pedestal	520.00	620.00	550.00
☐ **Drop leaf,** oval	110.00	135.00	112.00
☐ **Handkerchief,** 3-leg corner	360.00	435.00	382.00
☐ **Library**	70.00	210.00	130.00

	Current Price Range		Prior Year Average
☐ **Library,** carved lion head supports, claw feet, two drawers	900.00	975.00	912.00
☐ **Library,** golden oak, claw feet	320.00	420.00	350.00
☐ **Library,** large round legs, dark finish	135.00	185.00	150.00
☐ **Occasional**	60.00	210.00	130.00
☐ **Round,** claw feet	850.00	1050.00	900.00
☐ **Round,** egg and dart edges, octagonal base	760.00	835.00	780.00
☐ **Round,** large	320.00	470.00	375.00
☐ **Round,** ornate carvings	750.00	950.00	800.00
☐ **Round,** small	210.00	310.00	250.00
☐ **Side,** Queen Anne style	820.00	920.00	850.00
☐ **Square,** large	160.00	210.00	175.00
☐ **Square,** ornate	310.00	410.00	350.00
☐ **Square,** small	80.00	130.00	100.00
☐ **Tavern,** molded top	660.00	760.00	700.00

WARDROBES

☐ **Double door,** beveled glass	360.00	410.00	375.00
☐ **Double door,** without glass	235.00	310.00	350.00
☐ **Single door,** mirrored	335.00	385.00	350.00
☐ **Single door,** plain	160.00	210.00	175.00

MISSION OAK FURNITURE

☐ **G. Stickley,** signed, desk and chair, inlaid	15000.00	16000.00	1475.00
☐ **G. Stickley,** signed, sideboard	1350.00	1650.00	1450.00
☐ **G. Stickley,** signed, spindleback armchair and sidechair	3100.00	3600.00	3250.00
☐ **G. Stickley,** signed dowry chest	950.00	1250.00	1100.00
☐ **Limbert Arts and Crafts,** Grand Rapids, sideboard	135.00	185.00	150.00
☐ **Mission style,** recliner chair	160.00	210.00	175.00
☐ **Mission style,** unsigned library table, small	175.00	260.00	200.00
☐ **Morris,** chair and footstool	2600.00	3100.00	2750.00
☐ **Morris,** chair, lion's feet	185.00	260.00	212.00

PAINTED FURNITURE

Painted furniture was manufactured in America between 1790 and 1870. The various techniques used in finishing employed the use of brushes, steel and wooden combs, sponges, crinkled paper, even the sooty flame of a tallow candle. The decorations include plain painting, imitation wood graining, marbelizing, and decorative and imaginary painting (everything from flowers to mermaids). The larger early pieces command the highest prices. A good place for beginning collectors to start is with picture frames, small boxes, single side chairs, etc.

CHAIRS

☐ **Highchair,** English, Windsor, c. 1810	410.00	460.00	425.00
☐ **Highchair,** salmon, splay leg	285.00	310.00	282.00
☐ **Hitchcock,** set of four	310.00	360.00	325.00
☐ **Plank seat,** thumback, yellow, with stenciled flowers, set of four	920.00	1020.00	950.00
☐ **Side chair,** ladder-back, five slats, green over red, 49", 19th c.	360.00	410.00	375.00

372 / FURNITURE

	Current Price Range		Prior Year Average
☐ **Side chairs,** Federal, rush seats, six different townscapes or crest rails, Gregory Sale, c. 1895	14500.00	17500.00	15500.00
☐ **Side chairs,** shoulder back, Pennsylvania, set of six, c. 1830's	1600.00	2100.00	1750.00
☐ **Side chairs,** Pennsylvania, green with stenciled flowers, set of six, c. 1850's-1860's	760.00	1050.00	875.00
☐ **Side chairs,** Pennsylvania, balloon back, stenciled, set of four	335.00	360.00	338.00
☐ **Side chairs,** urn back, stenciled on green, set of six	1050.00	1150.00	1050

CHESTS

☐ **Blanket,** bracket base, green	310.00	360.00	325.00
☐ **Blanket,** Connecticut, carved and painted, lift top, top restored, 17th c.	17500.00	22500.00	19500.00
☐ **Blanket,** two drawers, red	460.00	510.00	475.00
☐ **Blanket,** paneled front and sides	560.00	710.00	620.00
☐ **Blanket,** scalloped base, green plaid, painted	135.00	160.00	138.00

CUPBOARDS

☐ **Corner,** glazed, turned feet, one drawer, original hardware, 84″	3100.00	3500.00	3200.00
☐ **Corner,** grained, Stewart Gregory Folk Art Auction	9050.00	10050.00	9050.00
☐ **Pantry,** red	160.00	210.00	175.00
☐ **Tabletop,** red	510.00	560.00	525.00

TABLES

☐ **Dressing,** Federal, yellow, reeded legs, Gregory Sale	4800.00	6100.00	5400.00
☐ **Dressing,** New England, grained	360.00	410.00	375.00
☐ **Drop leaf,** New England, black and red, small	1150.00	1250.00	1150.00
☐ **Tavern,** sawbuck style, scrub tops, pair, 19th c.	235.00	260.00	238.00
☐ **Tea,** Sheraton style, octagonal top, painted red	360.00	385.00	362.00

MISCELLANEOUS

☐ **Bed,** hired man's, red	60.00	110.00	75.00
☐ **Bench,** bucket, Pennsylvania, mustard graining over red, 41″ x 31″, early 1800's	335.00	360.00	338.00
☐ **Candlestand,** quatrefoil base, painted plain	235.00	260.00	238.00
☐ **Dry sink,** small, painted plain	435.00	460.00	438.00
☐ **Graining combs,** five, blued steel, c. 1890's	22.00	28.00	22.50
☐ **Graining combs,** 12, wooden handled in box	40.00	55.00	42.00
☐ **Hitchcock,** children's, settee with side chair and armchair	3800.00	4200.00	3750.00
☐ **Trunk,** Norwegian, rosemaling, c. 1871	385.00	410.00	382.00

WICKER FURNITURE

Wicker has been in use since the Egyptians used it for baskets and coffins as early as 4000 B.C. The American craze for wicker began in the 1840's and did not go out of fashion until the 1930's. During that time, nearly every type of furniture made in wood was copied in wicker; bedroom pieces, bookcases, etageres and living room sets were all made of this material.

FURNITURE / 373

Many reproductions of early wicker exist, but the early versions are generally more ornate, heavier (they were built on a wood frame instead of bamboo) and the reed used is much smoother than that in modern wicker. Older pieces that have not been painted are valued by collectors, as are complete living, dining, or bedroom sets. Do not pass over slightly damaged items as most are not difficult to repair. Prices may vary depending on locality and availability.

For more in-depth information and listings, you may refer to *The Official Price Guide to Wicker Furniture,* published by, the House of Collectibles.

VICTORIAN

	Current Price Range		Prior Year Average
☐ **Armchair,** natural finish, circular reed seat, c. 1890's	275.00	375.00	300.00
☐ **Armchair,** white, odd combination of several styles, c. 1880's	350.00	450.00	380.00
☐ **Armchair,** white, serpentine back and arms, elaborate fancywork, set-in cane seat, c. 1880's	275.00	395.00	315.00
☐ **Baby Carriage,** natural finish, serpentine edges, original velveteen upholstery, c. 1890's	550.00	700.00	600.00
☐ **Baby Carriage,** white, rare use of wooden beadwork set into closely woven side panels and front, Heywood Brothers and Company, c. 1890's	600.00	725.00	650.00
☐ **Child's Rocker,** white, spider-web caned back panel, wooden beadwork under arms, c. 1890's	200.00	275.00	220.00
☐ **Corner Chair,** natural finish, fancy scrollwork, Heywood Brothers and Company, c. 1890's	600.00	750.00	650.00
☐ **Corner Chair,** white, triangular back panel, rosette arm tip, c. 1890's	450.00	600.00	500.00
☐ **High Chair,** natural finish, serpentine back and arms, footrest, c. 1890's	275.00	375.00	300.00
☐ **Ottoman,** white, closely woven top and birdcage legs, c. 1890's	135.00	190.00	155.00
☐ **Oblong Table,** white, woven top and bottom shelf, wooden beadwork, c. 1890's	300.00	400.00	340.00
☐ **Oval Table,** natural finish, oak top and bottom shelf, serpentine design, wooden beadwork, c. 1890's	475.00	600.00	515.00
☐ **Platform Rocker,** natural finish, fine example of fan motif set into back panel, Wakefield Rattan Company, c. 1870's	600.00	750.00	650.00
☐ **Rocker,** natural finish, chevron-shaped back panel, serpentine back and arms, turned wood legs, c. 1890's	325.00	450.00	375.00
☐ **Rocker,** natural finish, leaf motif set into back panel, hand-caned seat, c. 1880's	475.00	575.00	500.00
☐ **Round Table,** white, top is 28" in diameter, cabriole legs, wooden beadwork frames top and bottom shelf, c. 1890's	450.00	600.00	500.00
☐ **Settee,** natural finish, serpentine arms, Whitney Reed Chair Company, c. 1880's	900.00	1250.00	1000.00
☐ **Settee,** white, serpentine design, c. 1890's	750.00	950.00	820.00
☐ **Settee,** white, very ornate scrollwork, Heywood Brothers and Company, c. 1880's	900.00	1250.00	1000.00
☐ **Sewing Basket,** natural finish, Wakefield Rattan Company, c. 1890's	165.00	225.00	185.00

374 / FURNITURE

	Current Price Range	Prior Year Average
☐ **Side Chair,** natural finish, rare mixture of curlicues and closely woven back panel, c. 1890's	175.00 250.00	200.00
☐ **Side Chair,** white, spiderweb hand caning set into circular backrest, c. 1890's	235.00 350.00	285.00
☐ **Square Table,** white, closely woven top, beadwork set into skirting, c. 1880's	300.00 400.00	340.00
☐ **Turkish Chair,** white, sometimes called a "fireside bench," rolled serpentine arms, c. 1890's	250.00 350.00	205.00
☐ **Whatnot,** white, elongated bridcage design decorates legs, four tiers, c. 1890's	500.00 650.00	550.00
☐ **Whatnot,** white, pineaple motif in back is the symbol of hospitality, four oak shelves, c. 1890's	285.00 395.00	310.00
☐ **Wood Basket,** white, 12" x 18", closely woven reed bottom, c. 1890's	125.00 165.00	145.00

TURN-OF-THE-CENTURY

	Current Price Range	Prior Year Average
☐ **Armchair,** natural finish, serpentine edges, c. 1900's	400.00 550.00	450.00
☐ **Armchair,** white, crisscross effect woven into back makes use of three reeds, c. 1910's	265.00 350.00	285.00
☐ **Armchair,** white, willow, classic Bar Harbor design, closely woven seat, ball feet, c. 1910's	250.00 350.00	290.00
☐ **Child's Rocker,** white, closely woven back, arms and seat, c. 1900's	175.00 235.00	200.00
☐ **Corner Chair,** natural finish, ball feet, c. 1900's	550.00 700.00	600.00
☐ **Dining Set,** natural finish, octagon-shaped table, oak top, chairs have set-in cane seat, c. 1910's	1250.00 1750.00	1400.00
☐ **High Chair,** natural finish, willow, Bar Harbor design, oak shelf lifts off, ball feet, c. 1915's	185.00 250.00	210.00
☐ **Lounge,** white, Bar Harbor design, closely woven seat, c. 1915's	475.00 600.00	430.00
☐ **Lounge,** white, Bar Harbor design, closely woven seat, c. 1915's	475.00 600.00	430.00
☐ **Lounge,** white, closely woven flat back and arms, upholstered back and seat, springs attached to framework, c. 1910's	600.00 800.00	680.00
☐ **Oil Lantern,** natural finish, closely woven base, c. 1900's	100.00 150.00	115.00
☐ **Ottoman,** natural finish, closely woven design, wooden beadwork, c. 1900's	125.00 175.00	140.00
☐ **Oval Table,** white, Bar Harbor design, unique magazine pockets on inside of bottom shelf, c. 1910's	325.00 425.00	360.00
☐ **Plant Stand,** white, Bar Harbor design, need loop motif under planter, c. 1910's	125.00 175.00	140.00
☐ **Platform Rocker,** rare, natural finish, closely woven reed seat, turned wood framework, Heywood Brothers and Wakefield Company, c. 1910's	385.00 525.00	430.00
☐ **Rocker,** natural finish, wingback design, Paines Furniture Company, c. 1910's	300.00 425.00	345.00
☐ **Rocker,** white, serpentine back and arms, set-in cane seat, c. 1900's	300.00 400.00	330.00
☐ **Rocker,** white, wingback design, closely woven wickerwork, magazine holders under both arms rests, c. 1915's	375.00 475.00	410.00

	Current Price Range		Prior Year Average
☐ **Round Table,** white, Bar Harbor design, circular woven top and bottom shelf employs wooden center piece, c. 1910's	225.00	300.00	255.00
☐ **Settee,** natural finish, serpentine back and arms, figure eight design worked into back and skirting, ball feet wrapped with twisted reed, Heywood Brothers and Wakefield Company, c. 1900's	1000.00	1600.00	1250.00
☐ **Settee,** natural finish, set-in cane seat, braidwork on back and arms, c. 1910's	650.00	850.00	720.00
☐ **Sewing Basket,** natural finish, closely woven, birdcage legs, c. 1900's	250.00	325.00	270.00
☐ **Sewing Basket,** natural finish, oval design with wrapped handle, c. 1910's	185.00	250.00	210.00
☐ **Side Chair,** white, closely woven reed seat, framed by braidwork, c. 1910's	125.00	200.00	165.00
☐ **Square Table,** white, closely woven top, ball design at top of legs wrapped with Oriental sea grass, round bottom shelf, c. 1910's	350.00	450.00	385.00
☐ **Table Lamp,** white, wooden ball feet, double bulb style, silk lined shade, c. 1915's	250.00	350.00	290.00
☐ **Turkish Chair,** closely woven reed seat, ball feet, Heywood Brothers and Wakefield Company, c. 1900's	300.00	400.00	330.00
☐ **Wood Basket,** natural finish, closely woven Oriental sea grass, reed braidwork, c. 1910's	65.00	95.00	78.00

1920's

	Current Price Range		Prior Year Average
☐ **Armchair,** white, handmade of fiber, upholstered backrest and inner-spring cushion, c. 1920's	325.00	425.00	360.00
☐ **Child's Armchair,** white, made of Oriental sea grass and reed trim, c. 1920's	140.00	180.00	150.00
☐ **Coat Rack-Umbrella Stand,** white, bentwood hooks, wrapped center post, fiber, c. 1920's	250.00	350.00	290.00
☐ **End Table,** white, made of fiber by the LLoyd loom, Heywood-Wakefield Company, c. 1920's	150.00	225.00	165.00
☐ **Floor Lamp,** white, "Eiffel tower" design, unique braidwork adorns neck, c. 1920's	400.00	550.00	455.00
☐ **Four Piece Set,** white, made of fiber, unupholstered lounge, upholstered settee, armchair and matching ottoman, springs attached to frame, c. 1920's	1500.00	1850.00	1625.00
☐ **Lounge,** white, upholstered back and seat, closely woven fiber design, footrest, diamond design woven into lower back, openwork on skirting, c. 1920's	600.00	775.00	660.00
☐ **Lounge,** white, made of fiber, diamond design woven into back, upholstered, c. 1920's	700.00	850.00	765.00
☐ **Night Stand,** white, square oak top and three painted shelves, handmade of fiber, c. 1920's	200.00	275.00	225.00
☐ **Oval Table,** natural finish, oak top is 26″ long, c. 1920's	300.00	400.00	340.00
☐ **Plant Stand,** white, closely woven design, scalloped reedwork, turned wood frame, c. 1920's	135.00	180.00	145.00
☐ **Rocker,** white, Bar Harbor design made of thick reed, springs attached to frame, c. 1920's	235.00	345.00	270.00
☐ **Rocker,** white, made of fiber, quality upholstery job covers backrest and seat, c. 1920's	275.00	375.00	300.00

376 / GAMES

	Current Price Range		Prior Year Average
☐ **Round Table,** white, willow, circular-woven two tier design, twisted willow ball feet, c. 1920's	160.00	200.00	170.00
☐ **Settee,** white, Bar Harbor design, closely woven reed seat, ball legs wrapped with twisted reed, c. 1920's	500.00	625.00	550.00
☐ **Sofa,** white, inner-spring mattress, ball feet, made of fiber, c. 1920's	500.00	750.00	600.00
☐ **Side Chair,** natural finish, made of reed, closely woven seat, c. 1920's	100.00	145.00	120.00
☐ **Table Lamp,** white, intricate wickerwork on base and neck, brass finial, c. 1920's	260.00	350.00	290.00
☐ **Tea Cart,** brown, lift-off glass tray, bottom shelf, two drawers, c. 1920's	425.00	550.00	470.00
☐ **Three Piece Set,** white, unupholstered, made of fiber, unique design woven into back, c. 1920's	1000.00	1500.00	1200.00
☐ **Vanity and Matching Chair,** white, closely waven oval shaped desk, c. 1920's	550.00	675.00	600.00

GAMES

Table Or Parlor Games, These came into a big vouge in the years following our Civil War. Those pictured here date from c. 1870 to 1900. For collector values of old table or parlor games, see listings.

GAMES / 377

Games have been manufactured in the United States since the mid-1800's. Over the years, this form of entertainment has mirrored the changing thoughts and concerns of a growing nation. As a collectible, games are truly a piece of Americana.

Early board games were printed on cardboard and colored by hand. These items are rare and command a steep price of $100 or more. Lithography replaced this painstaking process in the latter part of the 19th century. The most prized specimens are those manufactured by the McLoughlin Brothers of New York.

It is important to examine a prospective purchase carefully. Playing pieces and the game's instructions should be complete and intact. The condition of the game's box is critical, especially the cover. Surface dirt is not a major concern as it can be washed off by using a mild soap and water.

A game does not have to be old to be collectible. Those no longer in production or from a manufacturer out of business are desirable and a potential investment. The games reflecting society today will be the prized specimens of future generations.

	Current Price Range		Prior Year Average
☐ **Alley Oop,** c. 1937	10.00	15.00	12.00
☐ **Anagrams,** Milton Bradley	10.00	20.00	14.00
☐ **Around The World With Nellie Bly,** lithograph	70.00	90.00	80.00
☐ **Authors,** Milton Bradley	10.00	20.00	14.00
☐ **Babe Ruth,** Baseball Game	35.00	50.00	40.00
☐ **Backgammon,** black and red, c. 1880	75.00	95.00	82.00
☐ **Bet Your Life,** Groucho Marx, c. 1955	18.00	22.00	19.00
☐ **Baseball,** marble, pinch hitter	25.00	30.00	26.00
☐ **Blacks,** wood with pictures, c. 1900	35.00	50.00	40.00
☐ **Bonanza**	8.00	12.00	9.00
☐ **Calling All Cars**	12.00	17.00	14.00
☐ **Captain Video**	20.00	30.00	23.00
☐ **Cards,** original box, c. 1896	25.00	35.00	30.00
☐ **Careers,** Parker Bros., c. 1958	7.00	12.00	9.00
☐ **Chinese Checkers,** akro agate marbles	20.00	30.00	24.00
☐ **Cinderella,** Selchow and Righter, c. 1896	45.00	60.00	50.00
☐ **Corn and Beans,** Selchow and Righter, c. 1875	20.00	30.00	24.00
☐ **Cows in the Corn,** Parker Bros., c. 1930	20.00	30.00	24.00
☐ **Cribbage Board,** carved ivory	55.00	70.00	60.00
☐ **Cribbage Board,** cast iron	60.00	75.00	65.00
☐ **Dominos,** ebony and ivory, brass pegs	35.00	50.00	40.00
☐ **Dominos,** miniature, ivory	25.00	30.00	26.00
☐ **Donkey Party,** Whitman	12.00	17.00	15.00
☐ **Fibber McGee,** c. 1940	15.00	25.00	19.00
☐ **Fish Pond,** McLoughlin Bros.	55.00	70.00	60.00
☐ **Fishing Party,** Saalfield, c. 1916	35.00	50.00	40.00
☐ **Flip Your Wig,** Beatles, Milton Bradley, c. 1964	25.00	35.00	29.00
☐ **Fortune's Wheel,** Parker Bros., c. 1903	40.00	55.00	46.00
☐ **Fortune Teller,** Milton Bradley, c. 1905	25.00	35.00	29.00
☐ **Game of Auction,** Milton Bradley, c. 1900	15.00	20.00	16.00
☐ **Game of Boy Scouts,** Parker Bros., c. 1912	25.00	35.00	29.00
☐ **Game of Snaps,** West and Lee, c. 1873	10.00	20.00	14.00
☐ **Game of Tri-Bang,** McLoughlin Bros., c. 1898	25.00	35.00	29.00
☐ **Hearts,** Parker Bros., c. 1916	5.00	10.00	7.00
☐ **Honeymooners,** Jackie Gleason	15.00	20.00	17.00
☐ **Humpty Dumpty,** Parker Bros., c. 1924	30.00	45.00	35.00

378 / GAMES

	Current Price Range		Prior Year Average
☐ I've Got a Secret, c. 1956	12.00	17.00	14.00
☐ Jack Straws, Milton Bradley, c. 1910	15.00	20.00	17.00
☐ Keno, Milton Bradley	8.00	12.00	9.00
☐ Little Red Riding Hood, Milton Bradley, c. 1900	25.00	35.00	30.00
☐ Lotto, McLoughlin Bros., c. 1880	20.00	30.00	24.00
☐ Mah-Jong Set, bone tiles, boxed	45.00	60.00	50.00
☐ Mah-Jong Set, ivory and bamboo tiles in black lacquered box, c. 1923	75.00	95.00	80.00
☐ Mah-Jong Set, ivory tiles	275.00	325.00	290.00
☐ Mah-Jong Set, plastic tiles, boxed	25.00	35.00	28.00
☐ Mah-Jong Set, wooden tiles, boxed	30.00	45.00	35.00
☐ Meet the Presidents, Selchow and Righter, c. 1953	15.00	25.00	18.00
☐ Monopoly, Parker Bros., c. 1935	25.00	35.00	28.00
☐ Mother Goose, Milton Bradley, c. 1910	20.00	30.00	24.00
☐ Parcheesi	10.00	20.00	13.00
☐ Pick-Up-Sticks, wooden, c. 1937	5.00	10.00	7.00
☐ Pinball, Bagatelle, c. 1950	8.00	12.00	9.00
☐ Pollyanna, c. 1940	12.00	17.00	14.00
☐ Ring My Nose, c. 1925	20.00	30.00	24.00
☐ Sinking of the Titanic	10.00	15.00	12.00
☐ Sleeping Beauty, c. 1958	12.00	17.00	14.00
☐ Tell It To The Judge, Eddie Cantor, c. 1936	18.00	22.00	19.00
☐ Tiddly Winks, Milton Bradley	12.00	17.00	14.00
☐ Touring Game, Parker Bros., c. 1926	12.00	17.00	14.00
☐ Toy Money, Milton Bradley	10.00	15.00	11.00
☐ Uncle Wiggily	10.00	20.00	14.00
☐ Waterloo, Parker Bros.	30.00	45.00	35.00
☐ What's My Line, c. 1950	10.00	15.00	12.00
☐ Who Am I, Pinky Lee	18.00	22.00	19.00

MARBLES

Marble collecting has become very popular since most common types can be purchased at relatively low prices at flea markets, garage sales and the like. It is also nice to know that some specimens are quite unique and are worth as much as $100.

Early marbles, especially those handmade prior to World War I, are made not only of stone, porcelain, steel, glass and clay, but also of semiprecious stones such as onyx, quartz and agate. A desireable piece depends on its beauty and design as much as on the material of which it is composed. Most range in size from one-half to two inches, but some are as large as five inches.

While some marbles are solid opaque colors or speckled, others are transparent or swirled. An opaque sphere may show the face of a comic character. A transparent sulfide may house a clay animal, person or object. A porcelain or china marble may be decorated with a floral or geometric design. No matter what the collector's preference, he is sure to find something desireable and reasonably priced.

☐ Agate, ½ "	15.00	20.00	17.00
☐ Agate, ¾ "	10.00	20.00	14.00
☐ Agate, ⅞ "	15.00	25.00	19.00
☐ Bennington, box of 50	75.00	125.00	95.00

	Current Price Range		Prior Year Average
☐ **Bennington,** light to dark blue, 1½"	8.00	12.00	9.00
☐ **China,** bull's eye, ⅝"	5.00	10.00	7.00
☐ **China,** bull's eye, 1⅛"	15.00	20.00	17.00
☐ **Comic Strip,** various characters	25.00	45.00	30.00
☐ **Goldstone,** ⅝"	20.00	30.00	24.00
☐ **Limestone,** ⅝"	5.00	10.00	7.00
☐ **Spatterglass,** 2"	65.00	80.00	70.00
☐ **Sulfide,** anteater, 1"	45.00	60.00	50.00
☐ **Sulfide,** baby	75.00	100.00	80.00
☐ **Sulfide,** bear, ⅞"	55.00	70.00	60.00
☐ **Sulfide,** bird, 1¼"	50.00	65.00	55.00
☐ **Sulfide,** boar	75.00	100.00	82.00
☐ **Sulfide,** camel	45.00	60.00	50.00
☐ **Sulfide,** cat, sitting, 1¼"	75.00	100.00	82.00
☐ **Sulfide,** chicken	45.00	60.00	50.00
☐ **Sulfide,** cougar, standing	55.00	70.00	60.00
☐ **Sulfide,** cow, 1⅝"	55.00	70.00	60.00
☐ **Sulfide,** dog, large	60.00	75.00	65.00
☐ **Sulfide,** dog, Shaggy, 1¼"	55.00	70.00	60.00
☐ **Sulfide,** fish, 1¾"	125.00	150.00	130.00
☐ **Sulfide,** frog	50.00	100.00	70.00
☐ **Sulfide,** goat	65.00	80.00	72.00
☐ **Sulfide,** horse, running, 1½"	60.00	75.00	65.00
☐ **Sulfide,** lamb, 1¾"	50.00	75.00	60.00
☐ **Sulfide,** monkey, sitting, 2"	65.00	80.00	70.00
☐ **Sulfide,** monkey, standing, 2"	135.00	170.00	150.00
☐ **Sulfide,** pigeon	75.00	100.00	82.00
☐ **Sulfide,** rabbit, running	60.00	75.00	65.00
☐ **Sulfide,** ram	75.00	100.00	82.00
☐ **Sulfide,** rooster, running, 2"	65.00	80.00	70.00
☐ **Sulfide,** rooster, standing, 2"	50.00	65.00	55.00
☐ **Sulfide,** sheep	75.00	125.00	98.00
☐ **Sulfide,** squirrel, 1½"	65.00	80.00	70.00
☐ **Sulfide,** swan	70.00	85.00	75.00
☐ **Sulfide,** woodpecker	60.00	75.00	65.00
☐ **Swirl,** blue, red, white, 2"	45.00	60.00	50.00
☐ **Swirl,** blue, green, yellow, 1½"	45.00	60.00	50.00
☐ **Swirl,** cane, 1½"	60.00	75.00	50.00
☐ **Swirl,** green, yellow, red, 1½"	60.00	75.00	50.00
☐ **Swirl,** onionskin, 1¾"	40.00	55.00	45.00
☐ **Swirl,** red, green, white, 1¾"	65.00	80.00	70.00

GLASSWARE

ART GLASS

One of the most beautiful art forms to develop from the Art Nouveau era was art glass. While many European artists were giving birth to Art Nouveau, American art glass craftsmen were developing their own techniques and designs. It was not long until the quality of American art glass surpassed that of European glass makers. Although the Art Nouveau period lasted only about 20 years, examples like those listed below will be treasured and will last forever.

	Current Price Range		Prior Year Average
☐ **Atomizer,** blue, Aurene	210.00	260.00	225.00
☐ **Atomizer,** Despres, 5"	260.00	310.00	275.00
☐ **Atomizer,** ebony colored, Mueller Freres	260.00	310.00	275.00
☐ **Bottle,** cologne, floral design, Daum Nancy	520.00	620.00	550.00
☐ **Bottle,** cologne, iridescent gold, with stopper, Quezal	335.00	410.00	368.00
☐ **Bottle,** cologne, silver tip, red and white, Webb	1450.00	1650.00	1500.00
☐ **Bottle,** cologne, silver stopper, Webb	820.00	920.00	850.00
☐ **Bowl,** centerpiece, Schneider, 10"	285.00	335.00	300.00
☐ **Bowl,** snow scene, Daum Nancy	1050.00	1350.00	1150.00
☐ **Bowl,** two handles, Aurene, 9½" x 3¼"	760.00	910.00	820.00
☐ **Box,** carved flower on lid, Daum Nancy	435.00	485.00	450.00
☐ **Candlestick,** gold, twisted stem, Aurene, pair, 8"	560.00	660.00	600.00
☐ **Compote,** footed, Daum Nancy, 8"	385.00	435.00	400.00
☐ **Compote,** footed, multicolor, Schneider	185.00	235.00	200.00
☐ **Compote,** iridescent gold, Quezal, 8"	460.00	560.00	500.00
☐ **Compote,** mottled blue, metal frame, Schneider, 8¾"	335.00	410.00	368.00
☐ **Dresser jar,** leaves and vines, Gres	320.00	420.00	350.00
☐ **Finger bowl,** butterfly design, Webb	110.00	135.00	112.00
☐ **Finger bowl,** with plate, smoked glass, Schneider	170.00	200.00	175.00
☐ **Goblet,** blue, twisted stem, Aurene	235.00	310.00	260.00
☐ **Goblet,** enameled, floral design, Daum Nancy	185.00	235.00	200.00
☐ **Inkwell,** two color, foil lined, Daum Nancy	860.00	945.00	890.00
☐ **Inkwell,** three color, Schneider, 6"	335.00	435.00	375.00
☐ **Jar,** crackle design, Marinot	1350.00	1450.00	1350.00
☐ **Lamp,** enameled, floral design, Daum Nancy	1050.00	1350.00	1200.00
☐ **Lamp,** wall, white and red shade, Schneider	185.00	235.00	200.00
☐ **Pitcher,** enamel, bowl on layered glass, unsigned	435.00	460.00	438.00
☐ **Pitcher,** frosted green, Daum Nancy, 9½"	435.00	485.00	450.00
☐ **Pitcher,** Gres, 8"	410.00	460.00	425.00
☐ **Pitcher,** Marinot, 4"	1350.00	1450.00	1350.00
☐ **Pitcher,** mottled yellow, amethsy handle, Schneider, 11"	335.00	410.00	362.00
☐ **Pitcher,** salt, Aurene	185.00	210.00	182.00
☐ **Rose bowl,** flowers, unsigned	360.00	410.00	375.00
☐ **Rose bowl,** iridescent blue, Quezal	460.00	560.00	500.00
☐ **Rose bowl,** yellow, multicolor, Daum Nancy	310.00	360.00	325.00
☐ **Toothpick holder,** dark flowers, Daum Nancy	185.00	210.00	182.00
☐ **Tumbler,** gold, Aurene	335.00	410.00	360.00
☐ **Tumbler,** iridescent gold, Quezal	185.00	235.00	200.00
☐ **Tumbler,** white, multicolor, Daum Nancy	385.00	460.00	412.00
☐ **Vase,** blue and white, Webb, 6"	1500.00	1600.00	1500.00

GLASSWARE / 381

	Current Price Range		Prior Year Average
☐ **Vase,** cameo and enamel, crackled amber background, Daum Nancy, 8″	950.00	1150.00	1100.00
☐ **Vase,** cameo, white flowers on red, Webb, 4½″	950.00	1150.00	1000.00
☐ **Vase,** Citron, carved floral, Webb, 5″	1400.00	1500.00	1412.00
☐ **Vase,** floral pattern on yellow background, unsigned, 12″	800.00	925.00	830.00
☐ **Vase,** footed, elaborate three colors, 4½″	1100.00	1400.00	1150.00
☐ **Vase,** frosted white to green, Quezal, 10″	820.00	920.00	850.00
☐ **Vase,** lake scene, gold, brown, Daum Nancy, 11″	1250.00	1400.00	1275.00
☐ **Vase,** miniature, three color, Marinot	1250.00	1400.00	1275.00
☐ **Vase,** mother-of-pearl, white on red, Webb, 16″	2200.00	2600.00	2300.00
☐ **Vase,** purple with butterfly, Webb, 7″	1850.00	2050.00	1900.00
☐ **Vase,** ruby, flowers, Patte De Verre, G. Argy — Rousseau	360.00	510.00	425.00
☐ **Vase,** scene, amber, unsigned, 18″	910.00	960.00	925.00
☐ **Vase,** scenic view, Decourchemont, 5″	410.00	460.00	425.00
☐ **Vase,** scenic view, 5″	420.00	520.00	450.00
☐ **Vase,** small, blue and white, signed Webb	1500.00	1600.00	1460.00
☐ **Vase,** white cameo leaves on citron, butterfly, Webb, 7¼″	2000.00	3000.00	2300.00
☐ **Vase,** white on deep yellow, Marinot	1600.00	1900.00	1600.00
☐ **Vase,** white on raisin, deeply carved, 4½″	975.00	1050.00	975.00
☐ **Vase,** yellow glass with applied iris decoration, 8″	635.00	735.00	660.00

AGATA

This art glass was made by Joseph Locke of the New England Glass Company in Cambridge, Massachusetts. It is characterized by a single layer opaque glass, with shades of color ranging from deep raspberry at the top to a rich cream at the bottom. The most important characteristics of this type of art glass is the mottled effect created by the spattering of alcohol, causing it to blur and run.

☐ **Bowl,** finger	950.00	1050.00	950.00
☐ **Bowl,** handle, 4″	1900.00	2000.00	1850.00
☐ **Bowl,** raspberry	750.00	850.00	760.00
☐ **Celery**	1650.00	1800.00	1550.00
☐ **Cruet**	1350.00	1850.00	1550.00
☐ **Pitcher,** milk, akro agate handle	3100.00	3600.00	3250.00
☐ **Pitcher,** water	2600.00	3100.00	2750.00
☐ **Punch cup,** pink	620.00	770.00	680.00
☐ **Sugar bowl**	1650.00	1850.00	1700.00
☐ **Toothpick holder**	650.00	1050.00	800.00
☐ **Toothpick holder,** square top	360.00	510.00	420.00
☐ **Tumbler,** water	720.00	820.00	850.00
☐ **Tumbler,** water, deep color, good mottling	850.00	1050.00	900.00
☐ **Vase,** fluted rim, 8″	1600.00	1900.00	1650.00
☐ **Vase,** lily shape, 8″	1400.00	1800.00	1500.00
☐ **Vase,** pinched top, 4½″	1050.00	1250.00	1100.00
☐ **Vase,** square top, two handle, 4½″	1450.00	1650.00	1500.00
☐ **Whiskey**	820.00	970.00	880.00

AMBERINA

This art glass was another of Locke's revolutionary inventions. It is distinguished by a beautiful amber shading to a deep red, fuchsia or bluish purple. The process of reheating the glass and adding a small amount of gold to achieve the desired effect was used, under license, by many companies.

	Current Price Range		Prior Year Average
☐ Basket, diamond, handle	285.00	360.00	312.00
☐ Basket, fluted rim, handle	410.00	485.00	438.00
☐ Basket, green and red	310.00	385.00	338.00
☐ Bottle, perfume, automizer	210.00	260.00	225.00
☐ Bottle, water, inverted thumbprint, 8″	185.00	235.00	200.00
☐ Bowl, daisy and button, square, 9″	260.00	310.00	275.00
☐ Bowl, diamond quilted, 4½″	135.00	210.00	160.00
☐ Bowl, diamond quilted, 8″	235.00	260.00	238.00
☐ Bowl, diamond quilted, 9½″	260.00	310.00	275.00
☐ Bowl, finger, ruffled	160.00	185.00	162.00
☐ Bowl, fluted rim, two handles, 5″	210.00	310.00	275.00
☐ Bowl, inverted diamond, 4¼″	260.00	310.00	275.00
☐ Bowl, square, 5″	80.00	110.00	88.00
☐ Bowl, thumbprint, footed	185.00	260.00	212.00
☐ Butter, covered	335.00	385.00	350.00
☐ Candlestick, pair, 10″	210.00	260.00	225.00
☐ Candlestick, pair, 14″	235.00	285.00	250.00
☐ Carafe, 6″	410.00	510.00	450.00
☐ Castor, pickle, enameled design	385.00	460.00	412.00
☐ Castor, pickle, inverted thumbprint	485.00	585.00	425.00
☐ Celery, diamond quilted, 5½″	210.00	285.00	238.00
☐ Celery, diamond quilted, 6½″	285.00	360.00	312.00
☐ Celery, invert thumbprint, 6½″	320.00	385.00	338.00
☐ Compote, fuchsia, 7″	320.00	385.00	338.00
☐ Compote, signed, 8″	460.00	560.00	500.00
☐ Creamer, amber, applied handle, 4½″	160.00	210.00	175.00
☐ Creamer, daisy and button, 6″	185.00	235.00	200.00
☐ Creamer, diamond quilted, applied handle	160.00	175.00	158.00
☐ Creamer, inverted thumbprint, 4½″	260.00	335.00	280.00
☐ Cruet, diamond quilted, handle	210.00	260.00	225.00
☐ Cruet, inverted thumbprint, handle	310.00	385.00	338.00
☐ Cup, diamond quilted, reeded amber handle	110.00	135.00	112.00
☐ Decanter, inverted thumbprint	435.00	510.00	460.00
☐ Decanter, thumbprint	385.00	460.00	412.00
☐ Ice bucket, 6½″	360.00	435.00	382.00
☐ Mug, amber handle	110.00	160.00	125.00
☐ Mug, baby thumbprint	160.00	210.00	175.00
☐ Pitcher, daisy and button, 5″	260.00	300.00	275.00
☐ Pitcher, diamond quilted, applied handle	285.00	335.00	300.00
☐ Pitcher, inverted thumbprint, 7″	260.00	335.00	300.00
☐ Pitcher, milk, inverted thumbprint, 10″	260.00	310.00	275.00
☐ Pitcher, thumbprint, enameled design	360.00	435.00	380.00
☐ Pitcher, water, enameled design, 11″	285.00	360.00	312.00
☐ Pitcher, water, square, 10″	285.00	335.00	300.00
☐ Pitcher, water, swirled, 9″	260.00	310.00	275.00
☐ Plate, daisy and button, 7″	110.00	135.00	112.00
☐ Plate, diamond quilted, 7¼″	135.00	160.00	138.00

GLASSWARE / 383

	Current Price Range	Prior Year Average
☐ **Punch cup,** baby thumbprint	110.00 135.00	112.00
☐ **Punch cup,** diamond quilted, amber handle	135.00 160.00	138.00
☐ **Punch cup,** inverted thumbprint	110.00 135.00	112.00
☐ **Salt and pepper,** inverted thumbprint	210.00 260.00	225.00
☐ **Sauce,** daisy and button, 4¼"	80.00 135.00	100.00
☐ **Sauce,** diamond quilted, 4¼"	90.00 140.00	110.00
☐ **Sugar and creamer,** daisy and button	435.00 510.00	480.00
☐ **Sugar shaker,** inverted thumbprint	185.00 235.00	200.00
☐ **Toothpick holder,** daisy and button	185.00 235.00	200.00
☐ **Toothpick holder,** diamond quilted	160.00 210.00	175.00
☐ **Toothpick holder,** inverted thumbprint	185.00 235.00	200.00
☐ **Tumbler,** diamond quilted	135.00 160.00	138.00
☐ **Tumbler,** enameled design	75.00 120.00	90.00
☐ **Tumbler,** expanded diamond	80.00 135.00	100.00
☐ **Tumbler,** inverted baby thumbprint	80.00 135.00	100.00
☐ **Vase,** diamond quilted, 6½"	185.00 235.00	220.00
☐ **Vase,** hobnail	260.00 335.00	280.00
☐ **Vase,** inverted thumbprint, 6½"	210.00 260.00	225.00
☐ **Vase,** Jack-in-the-Pulpit, signed	435.00 535.00	475.00
☐ **Vase,** ribbed, fluted rim	210.00 260.00	225.00
☐ **Vase,** swirled, 11"	185.00 260.00	212.00
☐ **Whiskey,** diamond quilted	90.00 140.00	110.00

BACCARAT

French craftsmen have made Baccarat glass since 1765. It is characterized by its heavy weight, caused by the addition of lead, and its beautiful form and finish. All Baccarat, even the newest, is very desirable to lovers of glass.

☐ **Bottle,** atomizer, signed	110.00 135.00	112.00
☐ **Bottle,** cologne, gold and blue, stopper, 4", c. 1880	160.00 185.00	162.00
☐ **Bottle,** perfume, black, signed	90.00 125.00	100.00
☐ **Bottle,** perfume, cut crystal, c. 1900	260.00 285.00	262.00
☐ **Bottle,** perfume, gold design, signed	70.00 100.00	80.00
☐ **Bowl,** centerpiece, signed	435.00 510.00	460.00
☐ **Bowl,** cut crystal, ruby, 10"	360.00 435.00	380.00
☐ **Box,** oval, green opalene multicolored floral	100.00 130.00	110.00
☐ **Box,** covered, gold etched floral design, 4" x 6", c. 1890	160.00 185.00	162.00
☐ **Butter,** covered, blue animal design, c. 1890	42.00 52.00	45.00
☐ **Candlestick,** cobalt blue, gold trim, pair	335.00 410.00	360.00
☐ **Candlestick,** single swirl pattern, gold etched, pair, c. 1890	135.00 160.00	138.00
☐ **Cake stand,** rose tiente swirl, covered, c. 1900	110.00 130.00	110.00
☐ **Compote,** amber, signed, c. 1890	185.00 235.00	200.00
☐ **Compote,** emerald green, swirled	160.00 185.00	162.00
☐ **Cruet,** amberina swirl	110.00 135.00	112.00
☐ **Decanter,** bronze, scrollwork	135.00 160.00	138.00
☐ **Decanter,** cut crystal, signed	80.00 110.00	88.00
☐ **Decanter,** perfume, rose swirl, stopper, c. 1890	60.00 85.00	62.00
☐ **Decanter,** rose tiente swirl, 10", c. 1900	110.00 135.00	112.00
☐ **Decanter set,** six glasses, blue floral pattern, c. 1880	210.00 260.00	225.00
☐ **Dish,** flat, blue, 6", c. 1890	55.00 80.00	62.00
☐ **Figure,** dolphin, crystal	35.00 55.00	40.00
☐ **Figure,** turtle, crystal	45.00 70.00	52.00
☐ **Goblet,** signed, c. 1850	80.00 130.00	100.00

384 / GLASSWARE

	Current Price Range	Prior Year Average
☐ **Inkwell,** covered, clear swirl, c. 1900	160.00 210.00	175.00
☐ **Pitcher,** diamond quilted, applied handle	135.00 185.00	150.00
☐ **Pitcher,** water, six glasses	435.00 535.00	475.00
☐ **Powder jar,** covered, rose swirl, c. 1890	55.00 80.00	62.00
☐ **Relish,** rose tiente swirl, signed	70.00 100.00	80.00
☐ **Toothpick holder,** crystal	32.00 48.00	38.00
☐ **Toothpick holder,** rose swirl, c. 1890	30.00 45.00	32.00
☐ **Tray,** oval, rose tiente swirl, 12″, c. 1890	80.00 110.00	88.00
☐ **Tumbler,** swirl	28.00 38.00	30.00
☐ **Vase,** amerina swirl, 7″	80.00 110.00	82.00
☐ **Vase,** cameo cut, floral design, 11″	260.00 310.00	275.00
☐ **Vase,** cobalt blue and gold, signed, 12″, c. 1890	160.00 210.00	175.00
☐ **Vase,** rose tiente swirl, floral design, 10″, c. 1890	70.00 95.00	72.00

BOHEMIAN GLASS

Bohemian glass is named for the location of origin, which is now a part of Czechoslovakia. It was extremely popular with the Victorians who loved its brilliant colors. Bohemian glass is "flashed" that is, coated with a thin, translucent layer of colored glass. Often a design is etched or cut through the flashing.

	Current Price Range	Prior Year Average
☐ **Basket,** ruby, clear floral design, oval	70.00 95.00	80.00
☐ **Bell,** ruby, Deer and Castle	80.00 110.00	88.00
☐ **Bottle,** cologne, green, Deer and Castle, 6″	80.00 110.00	88.00
☐ **Bottle,** perfume, amber, etched, 8″	105.00 125.00	105.00
☐ **Bottle,** perfume, ruby, Vintage, 5″	50.00 70.00	55.00
☐ **Bowl,** amber, Deer and Pine Tree, 9″	70.00 95.00	80.00
☐ **Bowl,** berry, ruby, Vintage, 8½″	52.00 70.00	58.00
☐ **Bowl,** finger, ruby, Vintage	50.00 65.00	52.00
☐ **Box, powder,** ruby, bird and butterfly	95.00 115.00	100.00
☐ **Butter,** covered, ruby, Deer and Castle	150.00 175.00	152.00
☐ **Candy dish,** covered, amber	75.00 95.00	80.00
☐ **Castor set,** ruby, with stoppers	170.00 205.00	175.00
☐ **Celery,** ruby, Deer and Castle	75.00 100.00	80.00
☐ **Compote,** ruby, Deer and Castle, 8″ x 7″	75.00 100.00	80.00
☐ **Compote,** ruby, Deer and Pine Tree	160.00 210.00	175.00
☐ **Compote,** ruby, Vintage, 9″	45.00 65.00	50.00
☐ **Cordial set,** amber, Deer and Pine Tree	185.00 235.00	200.00
☐ **Cordial set,** green to clear, six pieces	185.00 235.00	200.00
☐ **Cordial set,** green, seven pieces	160.00 210.00	175.00
☐ **Cruet,** ruby, Deer and Pine Tree	85.00 110.00	88.00
☐ **Decanter,** ruby, Deer and Castle, 15″	145.00 180.00	150.00
☐ **Decanter,** ruby, Vintage, fluted stopper, 10″	45.00 65.00	50.00
☐ **Decanter,** ruby, Vintage, 12″	65.00 95.00	75.00
☐ **Door knobs,** ruby, set	65.00 95.00	75.00
☐ **Dresser set,** animal design, five pieces	235.00 260.00	238.00
☐ **Dresser set,** leaf pattern, three pieces	80.00 135.00	100.00
☐ **Goblet,** amber feet, knob stem, intaglio cut	65.00 90.00	72.00
☐ **Goblet,** cut and fluted, birds in flight, 6″	42.00 52.00	45.00
☐ **Goblet,** ruby, Vintage, knob stem	85.00 110.00	88.00
☐ **Jar,** amethyst, with lid	55.00 80.00	62.00
☐ **Lamp,** cobalt overlay, 12″	170.00 200.00	180.00
☐ **Liqueur set,** ruby, cut florals, seven pieces	135.00 185.00	150.00
☐ **Lustres,** ruby, enamel flowers, pair	235.00 260.00	238.00
☐ **Mug,** ruby, clear handle, 4½″	48.00 58.00	50.00

GLASSWARE

	Current Price Range		Prior Year Average
☐ Pitcher, ruby, Deer and Castle	110.00	145.00	118.00
☐ Pitcher, ruby, Vintage	150.00	180.00	155.00
☐ Plate, ruby, Deer and Castle	65.00	90.00	72.00
☐ Salt and pepper, ruby, Deer and Castle	80.00	135.00	100.00
☐ Sugar shaker, ruby cut to clear roses, original top	55.00	70.00	58.00
☐ Tankard, deep cut panels, applied clear handle, 5⅝"	90.00	120.00	100.00
☐ Toothpick holder, ruby, Deer and Pine Tree	32.00	42.00	35.00
☐ Tray, amber etched design	110.00	135.00	112.00
☐ Tumbler, amber, Flowers and Birds	42.00	62.00	50.00
☐ Tumbler, green, Deer and Pine Tree	40.00	60.00	45.00
☐ Tumbler, ruby, Bird and Castle	28.00	38.00	30.00
☐ Tumbler, ruby, Vintage	32.00	42.00	35.00
☐ Tumbler, ruby, Vintage, footed	52.00	62.00	55.00
☐ Urn, covered, large, deers	175.00	200.00	178.00
☐ Urn, cover, ruby, Deer and Pine Tree, 14"	155.00	180.00	158.00
☐ Vase, amber, Deer and Pine Tree, 12"	160.00	190.00	165.00
☐ Vase, blue, Deer and Castle, 10"	80.00	110.00	88.00
☐ Vase, green, enameled grapes, 13½"	110.00	135.00	112.00
☐ Vase, green, with white overlay, pair	185.00	235.00	200.00
☐ Vase, ruby, Bird and Castle, 10¼"	135.00	160.00	138.00
☐ Vase, ruby, Deer and Castle, 5"	80.00	110.00	88.00
☐ Vase, ruby, Deer and Castle, 19½"	170.00	205.00	180.00
☐ Vase, ruby, Flower and Birds, 12½"	120.00	145.00	122.00
☐ Whiskey set, apricot, Deer and Castle, decanter with four shot glasses	160.00	210.00	175.00
☐ Wine set, ruby, Deer and Castle, decanter with six glasses	285.00	335.00	300.00

BRISTOL

The broad term Bristol is given to various types of semiopaque glass. It is brightly decorated with enamel and gold. Several glassmakers in England produced this glass from the mid-1700's until 1900.

☐ Bottle, barber	28.00	38.00	30.00
☐ Bottle, dresser, blue, gold trim, stopper	90.00	120.00	98.00
☐ Bottle, dresser, green and gold, blue trim, stopper	60.00	80.00	65.00
☐ Bottle, dresser, pink, black trim, stopper	40.00	55.00	42.00
☐ Bowl, punch, covered, enameled design	175.00	200.00	178.00
☐ Bottle, white, blue overlay, enameled design	110.00	135.00	112.00
☐ Box, dark blue, covered, 3½"	65.00	90.00	72.00
☐ Box, powder, covered	80.00	100.00	85.00
☐ Candlestick, green, duck, pair, 10"	110.00	135.00	112.00
☐ Cookie jar, enameled design, silver plate trim	110.00	135.00	112.00
☐ Decanter, blue, shield labeled "Rum"	100.00	125.00	102.00
☐ Dresser set, three pieces, black, white floral design	125.00	155.00	130.00
☐ Lamp, blue, enameled design	135.00	160.00	138.00
☐ Mug, "I Love You", 3½"	38.00	48.00	40.00
☐ Mug, "Remember Me", 3¼"	48.00	58.00	50.00
☐ Mug, "Think of Me", 4"	42.00	52.00	45.00
☐ Pitcher, "Remember Me", 4"	55.00	75.00	60.00
☐ Smoke bell, 7"	28.00	38.00	30.00
☐ Ring tree, blue, 3"	42.00	52.00	45.00

386 / GLASSWARE

	Current Price Range		Prior Year Average
☐ Sugar and creamer, white	150.00	170.00	150.00
☐ Toothpick holder, blue	32.00	42.00	35.00
☐ Tumbler, peasant scene	22.00	32.00	25.00
☐ Urn, covered, enamel cupids, 19"	190.00	220.00	190.00
☐ Vase, bird on branch, 5"	40.00	55.00	42.00
☐ Vase, flying ducks, 6", pair	80.00	110.00	88.00
☐ Vase, green with enameled florals, pair, 10"	80.00	110.00	88.00
☐ Vase, pink, enameled design, pair, 13"	135.00	185.00	150.00
☐ Vase, pink, hand holding vase	70.00	85.00	72.00
☐ Vase, smokey opaline, 7"	45.00	60.00	48.00

BURMESE

The process used in making Burmese art glass was accidently discovered by Fredrick S. Shirley, an employee of the Mt. Washington Glass Works, New Bedford, Massachusetts. The glass was patented in 1885. Most items have no particular pattern, although some have a ribbed, hobnail or diamond quilted design.

	Current Price Range		Prior Year Average
☐ Basket, Mt. Washington, 8¼"	950.00	1150.00	1000.00
☐ Bell, glossy finish, 6"	435.00	485.00	450.00
☐ Bell, ivy design	410.00	460.00	425.00
☐ Biscuit jar, handpainted	860.00	960.00	900.00
☐ Bowl, filigree around neck, 4"	335.00	385.00	350.00
☐ Bowl, finger, Mt. Washington	210.00	260.00	225.00
☐ Bowl, fluted rim, signed, 5"	610.00	660.00	625.00
☐ Bowl, footed, decoration, 8"	410.00	460.00	425.00
☐ Candlestick, diamond, four feet	585.00	660.00	612.00
☐ Condiment set, Mt. Washington	435.00	485.00	450.00
☐ Creamer, acid finish, unsigned, Webb	285.00	335.00	300.00
☐ Creamer, Mt. Washington, 3½"	360.00	410.00	375.00
☐ Cruet, vinegar, dull finish, light coloring, 7"	485.00	535.00	500.00
☐ Cup, custard	260.00	310.00	275.00
☐ Epergne, single lily in sculptured brass on brown, marble base	360.00	410.00	375.00
☐ Lamp fairy, clear base	385.00	460.00	412.00
☐ Lamp fairy, , Clarke, patent, signed, 5"	485.00	560.00	512.00
☐ Mug, lemonade, handle	235.00	285.00	250.00
☐ Nut dish, three feet	360.00	385.00	362.00
☐ Pitcher, blue and white floral design	385.00	435.00	400.00
☐ Pitcher, Mt. Washington	1050.00	1350.00	1150.00
☐ Plate, 5"	285.00	335.00	300.00
☐ Plate, Mt. Washington, 7"	260.00	310.00	275.00
☐ Plate, 8"	410.00	460.00	425.00
☐ Punch cup, Mt. Washington	310.00	360.00	325.00
☐ Rose bowl, acid finish, unsigned, Webb	310.00	360.00	325.00
☐ Rose bowl, Mt. Washington, 5"	735.00	810.00	760.00
☐ Salt and pepper, ribbed	460.00	560.00	500.00
☐ Sherbet, footed	375.00	415.00	380.00
☐ Sugar and creamer, wishbone handles	685.00	760.00	712.00
☐ Toothpick holder, acid finish, floral decoration	310.00	360.00	325.00
☐ Toothpick holder, acid finish, Mt. Washington	260.00	335.00	280.00
☐ Toothpick holder, original label, tricorn	360.00	435.00	380.00
☐ Tumbler, fine coloring, Queen's design, 4"	485.00	535.00	500.00
☐ Tumbler, glossy finish, Mt. Washington	310.00	360.00	325.00
☐ Tumbler, water, good color, 4"	285.00	335.00	300.00

	Current Price Range		Prior Year Average
☐ **Vase,** acid finish, 8″	210.00	260.00	225.00
☐ **Vase,** double gourd shape, 12½″	610.00	650.00	615.00
☐ **Vase,** dull finish, 4″	285.00	285.00	238.00
☐ **Vase,** Grecian decoration, two handles, 18″	3200.00	3800.00	3400.00
☐ **Vase,** ruffled rim, acid finish, 4″	175.00	205.00	180.00
☐ **Vase,** swirled ribs, average color, 4″	280.00	335.00	298.00

CAMBRIDGE

Named for its maker, Cambridge Glass was manufactured in Cambridge, Ohio. Noted for their production of Crown Tuscan, Cambridge Glass also manufactured tableware, black satin, etched crystal and stemware. Not all pieces are marked with a **c** impressed in the glass. Other trademarks were employed, while some pieces were never signed.

	Current Price Range		Prior Year Average
☐ **Ashtray,** crystal, Cambridge Square	5.50	11.00	7.50
☐ **Ashtray,** Ebon, 3½″	8.00	13.00	9.00
☐ **Ashtray,** sea shell, milk glass	18.00	28.00	20.00
☐ **Ashtray,** silver on ebony	28.00	38.00	30.00
☐ **Ashtray,** swan, amber, 3″	52.00	62.00	55.00
☐ **Basket,** crystal, cut	65.00	80.00	68.00
☐ **Basket,** crystal, engraved, 11″	18.00	28.00	20.00
☐ **Basket,** crystal, ram's head, Gadroon	70.00	85.00	72.00
☐ **Basket,** deep blue, handle, 6″	38.00	48.00	40.00
☐ **Basket,** ebony, 8½″	80.00	110.00	88.00
☐ **Basket,** emerald, Cleo	25.00	40.00	28.00
☐ **Basket,** handle, Rose Point	28.00	38.00	30.00
☐ **Bonbon,** crystal, etched, amber, Gloria	18.00	28.00	20.00
☐ **Bonbon,** pedestal, Rose Point	18.00	28.00	20.00
☐ **Bonbon,** pink, Apple Blossom	16.00	22.00	17.50
☐ **Bonbon,** rock crystal, engraved	8.00	13.00	9.00
☐ **Bonbon,** rock crystal, Lucia	16.00	21.00	17.50
☐ **Bonbon,** scalloped edge, emerald, Decagon	8.00	16.00	11.00
☐ **Bonbon,** square, two handles, blue, Caprice	18.00	28.00	20.00
☐ **Bonbon,** two handles, pedestal, Cascade	12.00	16.00	12.50
☐ **Bowl,** belled edge, Mt. Vernon	12.00	16.00	12.50
☐ **Bowl,** centerpiece, blue, 10″	40.00	55.00	42.00
☐ **Bowl,** Crown Tuscan, 11″	55.00	80.00	62.00
☐ **Bowl,** oval, etched, Cleo, 9½″	12.00	22.00	15.00
☐ **Bowl,** oval, three feet, Rose Point, 12″	55.00	75.00	60.00
☐ **Bowl,** rock crystal, engraved, 13″	16.00	21.00	17.50
☐ **Bowl,** sea shell, three feet, Crown Tuscan	80.00	110.00	88.00
☐ **Bowl,** silver deposit on back, 9″	45.00	70.00	52.00
☐ **Bowl,** two handles, carmen, Tally-Ho, 10½″	32.00	42.00	35.00
☐ **Candelabra,** bird design, 10″	50.00	65.00	52.00
☐ **Candelabra,** dolphin, milk glass, 9″	95.00	110.00	92.00
☐ **Candelabra,** silver on ebony	45.00	60.00	48.00
☐ **Candelabra,** sea shell, 7″	16.00	21.00	17.50
☐ **Candlestick,** ball with nappy, Majestic	18.00	28.00	20.00
☐ **Candlestick,** Crown Tuscan, 4″	38.00	48.00	40.00
☐ **Candlestick,** crystal, figure stem, 9″	50.00	65.00	52.00
☐ **Candlestick,** crystal, Gadroon, 6½″	22.00	32.00	25.00
☐ **Candlestick,** dark blue, Mount Vernon, 8″	40.00	55.00	42.00
☐ **Candlestick,** etched, engraved, pair, 3½″	12.00	22.00	15.00
☐ **Candlestick,** frosted, emerald, Sprintime, pair, 5″	22.00	32.00	25.00
☐ **Candlestick,** Helio, pair, 10″	110.00	140.00	110.00

388 / GLASSWARE

	Current Price Range		Prior Year Average
☐ **Candlestick,** rock crystal, engraved, 4″	8.00	14.00	9.00
☐ **Candlestick,** rock crystal, lily, Silver Maple	18.00	28.00	20.00
☐ **Candy dish,** covered, Candelight	22.00	32.00	25.00
☐ **Candy dish,** covered, Ebon	28.00	38.00	30.00
☐ **Candy dish,** covered, gold decoration, Woodlily	32.00	42.00	35.00
☐ **Candy dish,** covered, etched, pink, Gloria	32.00	42.00	35.00
☐ **Candy dish,** covered, milk glass	55.00	70.00	58.00
☐ **Candy dish,** covered, Roselyn, 6″	28.00	38.00	30.00
☐ **Champagne,** figure stem	55.00	70.00	58.00
☐ **Champagne,** hollow stem, etched, Bacchus	12.00	16.00	12.50
☐ **Champagne,** saucer, etched, Vichy	16.00	21.00	17.50
☐ **Compote,** carmen, Mount Vernon, 6″	32.00	42.00	35.00
☐ **Compote,** crystal, Caprice	18.00	28.00	20.00
☐ **Compote,** ebony base, Crown Tuscan	65.00	85.00	70.00
☐ **Compote,** Everglade, 6″	16.00	20.00	17.50
☐ **Compote,** rock crystal, Rondo	18.00	28.00	20.00
☐ **Decanter,** Ball Shaped	20.00	45.00	28.00
☐ **Decanter,** crystal, Mount Vernon	32.00	42.00	35.00
☐ **Decanter,** footed, Crown Tuscan	120.00	145.00	122.00
☐ **Flower holder,** figure, amber, 8½″	70.00	90.00	75.00
☐ **Flower holder,** figure, crystal, 13″	60.00	75.00	62.00
☐ **Goblet,** carmen, Gadroon	18.00	28.00	20.00
☐ **Goblet,** etched crystal, Marlene	11.00	16.00	12.50
☐ **Goblet,** figure stem, etched crystal, Apple Blossom	110.00	135.00	112.00
☐ **Goblet,** gold decoration, Talisman Rose	18.00	28.00	20.00
☐ **Goblet,** milk glass	18.00	28.00	20.00
☐ **Goblet,** Rose Point	18.00	28.00	20.00
☐ **Ice bucket,** ebony	35.00	50.00	38.00
☐ **Ice bucket,** etched, chrome handle, blue, Chintz	28.00	38.00	30.00
☐ **Ice bucket,** etched, handle, Tulip	18.00	28.00	20.00
☐ **Ice bucket,** rock crystal, Elaine	45.00	60.00	48.00
☐ **Ice bucket,** rock crystal, Norwood	22.00	32.00	25.00
☐ **Ivy ball,** Carmen, 7″	45.00	60.00	48.00
☐ **Ivy ball,** Crown Tuscan	50.00	70.00	55.00
☐ **Ivy ball,** two tone, 8″	35.00	55.00	40.00
☐ **Marmalade,** gold decoration, three piece, Woodlily	28.00	38.00	30.00
☐ **Marmalade,** deep blue, Ball Shaped	35.00	50.00	38.00
☐ **Mayonnaise,** two piece, Chantilly	22.00	32.00	25.00
☐ **Mayonnaise,** three piece, Magnolia	28.00	38.00	30.00
☐ **Mayonnaise,** rock crystal, three piece, Silver Maple	22.00	32.00	25.00
☐ **Pitcher,** ball shape, deep blue, Caprice	55.00	70.00	58.00
☐ **Pitcher,** etched, yellow	40.00	55.00	38.00
☐ **Pitcher,** Heirloom	28.00	38.00	30.00
☐ **Pitcher,** milk glass	60.00	75.00	62.00
☐ **Pitcher,** Nautilus	22.00	32.00	25.00
☐ **Pitcher,** pink, Mount Vernon	35.00	50.00	38.00
☐ **Pitcher,** rock crystal, engraved, round shape	32.00	42.00	35.00
☐ **Plate,** cake, handle, amber, 10″	22.00	28.00	22.50
☐ **Plate,** cake, square, pedestal base, yellow	22.00	27.00	22.50
☐ **Plate,** dinner, Rose Point	31.00	36.00	32.50
☐ **Plate,** dinner, square etched, Apple Blossom	12.00	22.00	15.00
☐ **Plate,** dinner, Wildflower	22.00	32.00	25.00
☐ **Plate,** sandwich, deep blue, Tally-Ho, 11½″	40.00	55.00	42.00

GLASSWARE / 389

	Current Price Range		Prior Year Average
☐ **Plate,** sandwich, pedestal, two piece, Pristine, 13½"	28.00	38.00	30.00
☐ **Plate,** sandwich, rock crystal, engraved, center handle	18.00	28.00	20.00
☐ **Plate,** sandwich, four feet, carmen, Everglades, 13"	65.00	85.00	70.00
☐ **Relish,** carmen, divided, Gadroon	75.00	90.00	78.00
☐ **Relish,** center handle, Crown Tuscan, 5½"	55.00	70.00	58.00
☐ **Relish,** center handle, divided, silver on ebony	38.00	48.00	40.00
☐ **Relish,** oval, divided, Magnolia	18.00	28.00	20.00
☐ **Relish,** rock crystal, engraved, irregular shape	22.00	32.00	25.00
☐ **Salt,** Decagon	12.00	22.00	15.00
☐ **Salt,** oval, carmen, Mount Vernon	25.00	40.00	28.00
☐ **Salt and pepper,** blue, tray, Caprice	45.00	60.00	48.00
☐ **Salt and pepper,** chrome tops, Daffodil	16.00	21.00	17.50
☐ **Salt and pepper,** deep blue, tray, Nautilus	40.00	55.00	42.00
☐ **Salt and pepper,** ebony, tray, Pristine	28.00	38.00	30.00
☐ **Salt and pepper,** glass tops, tray, amber	25.00	40.00	28.00
☐ **Salt and pepper,** milk glass	22.00	32.00	25.00
☐ **Sherbet,** Chantilly	20.00	28.00	22.00
☐ **Sherbet,** Decagon	9.00	13.00	10.00
☐ **Sherbet,** green, Chantilly	18.00	28.00	20.00
☐ **Sherbet,** Rose Point	16.00	24.00	18.00
☐ **Sugar and creamer,** Cambridge Square	16.00	21.00	17.50
☐ **Sugar and creamer,** deep blue, Martha Washington	35.00	50.00	38.00
☐ **Sugar and creamer,** silver on ebony	52.00	62.00	55.00
☐ **Sugar and creamer,** rock crystal, engraved, Ball Shaped	22.00	32.00	25.00
☐ **Sugar and creamer,** tray, Magnolia	28.00	38.00	30.00
☐ **Sugar and creamer,** tray, Rose Point	40.00	55.00	42.00
☐ **Sugar basket,** handle, tongs, Gadroon	25.00	40.00	28.00
☐ **Sugar basket,** handle, tongs, pink	18.00	28.00	20.00
☐ **Sugar shaker,** etched, glass top, Gloria	25.00	45.00	30.00
☐ **Sugar shaker,** silver top, amber	20.00	35.00	22.00
☐ **Swan,** amber, 3½"	35.00	85.00	55.00
☐ **Swan,** Crown Tuscan, 2½"	28.00	38.00	30.00
☐ **Swan,** Crown Tuscan, 3"	40.00	55.00	42.00
☐ **Swan,** crystal, signed, 3"	32.00	42.00	35.00
☐ **Swan,** crystal, signed, 5"	60.00	75.00	62.00
☐ **Swan,** ebony, 3½"	55.00	70.00	58.00
☐ **Swan,** emerald, 3½"	50.00	65.00	52.00
☐ **Swan,** milk glass, 6½"	105.00	130.00	108.00
☐ **Swan,** pink, 4½"	30.00	55.00	38.00
☐ **Tray,** blue, Caprice, 6"	12.00	22.00	15.00
☐ **Tray,** silver on ebony	65.00	90.00	72.00
☐ **Tray,** etched, oval, blue, 12½"	18.00	28.00	20.00
☐ **Tumbler,** blue, Caprice	20.00	28.00	22.00
☐ **Tumbler,** carmen, Victorian	21.00	26.00	22.50
☐ **Tumbler,** etched, Chantilly	16.00	21.00	17.50
☐ **Tumbler,** gold decoration, Talisman Rose	21.00	26.00	22.50
☐ **Tumbler,** Rose Point	20.00	30.00	23.00
☐ **Urn,** cover, Gadroon, 10"	38.00	48.00	40.00
☐ **Urn,** deep blue with cover, Martha Washington	85.00	100.00	88.00
☐ **Vase,** bud, gold decoration, Woodlily, 8"	21.00	26.00	22.50
☐ **Vase,** bud, Rose Point	26.00	31.00	27.50

390 / GLASSWARE

	Current Price Range		Prior Year Average
☐ Vase, cornucopia, Ebony, 10″	50.00	65.00	52.00
☐ Vase, deep blue, pedestal, Nautilus, 7″	32.00	42.00	35.00
☐ Vase, ebony, pedestal, Crown Tuscan, 6″	45.00	60.00	48.00
☐ Vase, etched, yellow, bird design, 8″	55.00	70.00	58.00
☐ Vase, Everglade, 7½″	28.00	38.00	30.00
☐ Vase, globe shape, Crown Tuscan, 5″	100.00	120.00	100.00
☐ Vase, milk glass, 4½″	28.00	38.00	30.00
☐ Vase, open stem, emerald, Apple Blossom, 12″	50.00	65.00	52.00
☐ Vase, oval, silver on ebony, 9″	160.00	185.00	162.00

CORALENE

One of the many types of art glass, Coralene takes its name from its appearance, not its color. The tiny beads affixed to the surface make it look rather like coral from the sea. These beads can be affixed to any kind of glass.

☐ Basket, on peachblow, coral design in blue m.o.p.	385.00	410.00	382.00
☐ Bottle, perfume, multicolor, stopper	260.00	285.00	262.00
☐ Bowl, blue m.o.p.	410.00	460.00	425.00
☐ Pitcher, green, bird design, signed	460.00	510.00	475.00
☐ Pitcher, satin glass, wheat motif, 8″	285.00	335.00	300.00
☐ Toothpick holder, peachblow, seaweed design	335.00	385.00	350.00
☐ Toothpick holder, satin glass	335.00	385.00	350.00
☐ Tumbler, pink, gold design	235.00	260.00	238.00
☐ Tumbler, water, blue to white m.o.p., coral design	260.00	310.00	275.00
☐ Vase, apricot satin glass, seaweed design, 5½″	385.00	435.00	400.00
☐ Vase, blue satin glass, floral design, 6¼″	460.00	510.00	475.00
☐ Vase, pink, gold design	185.00	235.00	200.00
☐ Vase, satin glass, yellow to white, seaweed design	360.00	410.00	375.00
☐ Vase, white m.o.p., zigzag design in yellow beads	410.00	485.00	438.00

*m.o.p — mother-of-pearl

DURAND

Victor Durand, a descendant of the family which made Baccarat glass, headed the Durand Art Glass Company in Vineland, New Jersey, which produced this glass in the 1920's. This glass was of similar quality and beauty to that made by Tiffany.

☐ Bottle, perfume, iridescent orange, signed	135.00	160.00	138.00
☐ Bowl, blue, signed	360.00	410.00	375.00
☐ Bowl, gold, signed, 4¾″	260.00	310.00	275.00
☐ Bowl, vase, blue with white heart, 6½″	385.00	435.00	400.00
☐ Candleholder, amber base, 3″	160.00	210.00	175.00
☐ Candleholder, blue, signed, 10″	285.00	335.00	300.00
☐ Candleholder, gold, signed, 6″	210.00	235.00	212.00
☐ Compote, cranberry, 5½″	485.00	560.00	512.00
☐ Decanter, blue, signed, 8″	360.00	410.00	375.00
☐ Goblet, red, gold trim	335.00	385.00	350.00
☐ Inkwell, iridescent blue	185.00	210.00	188.00
☐ Lamp, umbrella shape shade, 30″	1550.00	1650.00	1550.00
☐ Liqueur, blue and white, canary yellow stem	210.00	260.00	225.00
☐ Plate, feather pattern, 8″	335.00	385.00	350.00

	Current Price Range	Prior Year Average
☐ **Vase,** iridescent blue, signed, 7″	510.00 560.00	525.00
☐ **Vase,** iridescent emerald green, 5″	135.00 160.00	138.00
☐ **Vase,** iridescent orange, 8½″	335.00 385.00	350.00
☐ **Vase,** iridescent peach, 7½″	460.00 560.00	500.00
☐ **Vase,** red and clear "Crackle", signed, 12″	760.00 810.00	775.00
☐ **Wine,** feather pattern, 5¾″	185.00 235.00	200.00

GALLE

Emile Galle (1846-1905), the most renowned of the French art glass masters, was born in Nancy, the glass center of France. He began his first glass factory in 1879 and in 1884 gained recognition at an art exposition. This led to his appointment as the headmaster of the glass school at Nancy.

Galle was able to obtain fascinating artistic effects with the use of colored glass "casings," or applied layers, over a base of translucent or transparent glass. Detail was engraved on a wheel.

	Current Price Range	Prior Year Average
☐ **Atomizer,** sable with honey tones, 5¾″	260.00 310.00	275.00
☐ **Bottle,** perfume, frosted gold with violets, 4⅛″	260.00 285.00	262.00
☐ **Bowl,** blue, white, frosted, purple flowers and leaves, 4″	210.00 260.00	225.00
☐ **Bowl,** green, blue, frosted, boat shape, 9½″	285.00 360.00	312.00
☐ **Bowl,** red leaves, yellow ground, acorns, 3″ x 4¼″	385.00 410.00	382.00
☐ **Box,** cameo, covered, gold with purple flowers, 4¼″	435.00 485.00	450.00
☐ **Box,** green floral, frosted, diamond shape, 8½″ x 5½″	510.00 560.00	525.00
☐ **Box,** powder, cameo, carved, signed with star, square, 4½″	460.00 510.00	475.00
☐ **Cruet,** dragon, beetle and butterfly, signed	330.00 360.00	335.00
☐ **Cup and saucer,** enameled	110.00 135.00	112.00
☐ **Dish,** covered, clear with enameled grey, red, black and pink, 5″, c. 1900	360.00 385.00	362.00
☐ **Lamp,** base, amber, deep maroon leaves, 13½″	535.00 610.00	560.00
☐ **Lamp,** night light, fuchsia, lemon ground, brass fitting	510.00 585.00	538.00
☐ **Pitcher,** bird in flight, 3″	160.00 210.00	175.00
☐ **Pitcher,** yellow with grapes, 8″	385.00 410.00	382.00
☐ **Shot glass,** cameo, green thistle, 2½″	210.00 260.00	225.00
☐ **Toothpick holder,** enameled, multicolor, signed, 2″	135.00 160.00	138.00
☐ **Tumbler,** deep amber, enameled dragon, 2½″	2650.00 3250.00	2900.00
☐ **Vase,** cameo, carved amber iris, frosted dark ground, signed	460.00 510.00	475.00
☐ **Vase,** cameo, carved brown florals against pink ground, signed, 5½″	385.00 435.00	400.00
☐ **Vase,** cameo, carved deep purple design, signed, 3¼″	385.00 435.00	400.00
☐ **Vase,** cameo, carved gold, blue and brown trees and mountain, 10″	585.00 635.00	600.00
☐ **Vase,** cameo, carved green river with trees, pink sky, signed, 6½″	560.00 610.00	575.00
☐ **Vase,** cameo, carved green vines, gold and white frosted ground, signed, 26″	1050.00 1150.00	1050.00

392 / GLASSWARE

	Current Price Range		Prior Year Average
☐ **Vase,** cameo, carved purple and green pendant, pink and grey ground, signed, c. 1900	385.00	410.00	388.00
☐ **Vase,** cameo, carved pink flowers, beige and green leaves, blue sky, signed, 13½"	685.00	760.00	712.00
☐ **Vase,** cameo, carved red berries and leaves, frosted ground, signed, 3½"	310.00	335.00	312.00
☐ **Vase,** cameo, carved scene, four colors, signed, 14"	1350.00	1450.00	1350.00
☐ **Vase,** cameo, fruit, leaves and flowers, 10"	1050.00	1250.00	1100.00
☐ **Vase,** cameo, tapered cylinder, carved scene, signed, 14"	1450.00	1550.00	1450.00
☐ **Vase,** cameo overlay, ovoid, iris on white, original label, signed, 7½"	1300.00	1700.00	1400.00
☐ **Vase,** dragonfly, four colors, 17¼"	1300.00	1400.00	1325.00
☐ **Vase,** forest on pink, ferns, tri-petal top, 11½" . . .	1050.00	1150.00	1050.00
☐ **Vase,** gray and amber floral, green foot, frosted, signed, 4½"	510.00	560.00	525.00
☐ **Vase,** praying mantis, crystal and enamel, 5½" . .	610.00	660.00	625.00
☐ **Vase,** triple overlay cameo, landscape, pedestal, 7"	1300.00	1700.00	1400.00
☐ **Vase,** white/green wisteria, pink base and top, 17½"	410.00	460.00	425.00

HEISEY

Heisey Glass was made in Newark, Ohio, by the A. H. Heisey Company, from the late 1890's to 1957 when the factory closed. Molds of animal figures were obtained by the Imperial Glass Company of Bellaire, Ohio, and reproduced between 1964 and 1967.

Heisey is probably the most sought after of all tableware, and prices are constantly increasing. Most Heisey Glass was marked with a H impressed in glass. Some pieces can still be found in thrift shops and garage sales and can be bought cheaply.

☐ **Ashtray,** Crystolite, 5"	22.00	32.00	25.00
☐ **Ashtray,** duck	40.00	55.00	42.00
☐ **Ashtray,** Empress	22.00	32.00	25.00
☐ **Ashtray,** Old Sandwich	18.00	38.00	25.00
☐ **Basket,** bow tie, Flamingo	65.00	90.00	72.00
☐ **Basket,** etched butterfly	110.00	135.00	112.00
☐ **Basket,** flute and panel 10½"	100.00	125.00	102.00
☐ **Basket,** Lariat	65.00	90.00	72.00
☐ **Basket,** panels, ribbed, Flamingo	65.00	90.00	72.00
☐ **Bonbon,** Crystolite	16.00	21.00	17.50
☐ **Bonbon,** pink, 5½" x 7"	42.00	52.00	45.00
☐ **Bonbon,** Ridgeleigh	11.00	16.00	12.50
☐ **Bonbon,** Waverly	28.00	38.00	30.00
☐ **Bookends,** figural horses, pair	160.00	210.00	175.00
☐ **Bookends,** fish	80.00	110.00	88.00
☐ **Bottle,** cologne, Crystolite	22.00	32.00	25.00
☐ **Bottle,** cologne, pink, swirl	28.00	38.00	30.00
☐ **Bottle,** perfume, blue band, gold trim	50.00	65.00	52.00
☐ **Bottle,** perfume, silver overlay, 8"	160.00	185.00	162.00
☐ **Bottle,** water, Old Williamsburg	22.00	32.00	25.00
☐ **Bowl,** berry, butterfly design	50.00	80.00	60.00

GLASSWARE / 393

	Current Price Range		Prior Year Average
☐ **Bowl,** berry, Empress	32.00	42.00	35.00
☐ **Bowl,** berry, Greek Key	90.00	130.00	105.00
☐ **Bowl,** berry, Pied Piper	38.00	48.00	40.00
☐ **Bowl,** berry, Provincial	70.00	85.00	72.00
☐ **Bowl,** centerpiece, Orchid	40.00	55.00	42.00
☐ **Bowl,** Colonial, 12″	55.00	70.00	58.00
☐ **Bowl,** Crystolite, 8″	32.00	42.00	35.00
☐ **Bowl,** Crystolite, two handles	38.00	48.00	40.00
☐ **Bowl,** Empress, three feet, 11″	55.00	70.00	58.00
☐ **Bowl,** Fandango, 9″	28.00	38.00	30.00
☐ **Bowl,** finger, Diana	16.00	21.00	17.50
☐ **Bowl,** finger, Pied Piper	11.00	16.00	12.50
☐ **Bowl,** finger, with underplate, Ipswich	22.00	32.00	25.00
☐ **Bowl,** finger, with underplate, Victorian	28.00	38.00	30.00
☐ **Bowl,** Flamingo, three feet, 11″	45.00	60.00	48.00
☐ **Bowl,** Lariat, 12″	35.00	50.00	38.00
☐ **Bowl,** Orchid, 12″	50.00	65.00	52.00
☐ **Bowl,** Plantation, 5½″	22.00	32.00	25.00
☐ **Bowl,** punch, pedestal, Greek Key, 15″	285.00	335.00	300.00
☐ **Bowl,** punch, Prince of Wales, Plumes, two pieces	185.00	235.00	200.00
☐ **Bowl,** punch, Victorian	80.00	160.00	112.00
☐ **Bowl,** Queen Anne, 11″	45.00	60.00	48.00
☐ **Bowl,** silver overlay, Ridgeleigh, 12″	35.00	50.00	38.00
☐ **Bowl,** waverly, 12″	22.00	32.00	25.00
☐ **Candelabra,** three light, 10″	110.00	160.00	125.00
☐ **Candlestick,** crystal etched, pair, 4″	50.00	70.00	55.00
☐ **Candlestick,** Crystolite, pair	35.00	50.00	38.00
☐ **Candlestick,** Empress, Sahara, pair	135.00	185.00	150.00
☐ **Candlestick,** Flamingo, three feet, pair	170.00	200.00	175.00
☐ **Candlestick,** Lariat, pair	45.00	60.00	48.00
☐ **Candlestick,** Old Sandwich, pair, 6½″	110.00	135.00	112.00
☐ **Candlestick,** Orchid, two light, pair	55.00	80.00	62.00
☐ **Candlestick,** Queen Anne, pair	85.00	135.00	100.00
☐ **Candlestick,** Ridgeleigh, pair, 10½″	85.00	135.00	100.00
☐ **Candy dish,** Colonial	28.00	38.00	30.00
☐ **Candy dish,** Crystolite, two handles	50.00	65.00	52.00
☐ **Candy dish,** Empress, three feet	50.00	65.00	52.00
☐ **Candy dish,** Lariat	45.00	70.00	48.00
☐ **Candy dish,** Orchid	65.00	85.00	70.00
☐ **Candy dish,** pierced silver rim, Greek Key	45.00	60.00	48.00
☐ **Candy dish,** Ridgeleigh, two handles	40.00	55.00	42.00
☐ **Celery,** Empress	40.00	55.00	42.00
☐ **Celery,** Greek Key, 12″	35.00	50.00	38.00
☐ **Celery,** Queen Anne, Sahara	50.00	65.00	52.00
☐ **Celery,** vase, Colonial	40.00	55.00	42.00
☐ **Champagne,** Flamingo	22.00	32.00	25.00
☐ **Champagne,** Ipswich	18.00	28.00	20.00
☐ **Champagne,** Minuet	22.00	32.00	25.00
☐ **Champagne,** Orchid	22.00	32.00	25.00
☐ **Champagne,** Pied Piper	18.00	28.00	20.00
☐ **Champagne,** Sahara	22.00	32.00	25.00
☐ **Champagne,** Trojan	18.00	28.00	20.00
☐ **Cigarette box,** Crystolite	32.00	42.00	35.00
☐ **Cigarette box,** Orchid	80.00	110.00	88.00
☐ **Cigarette box,** Ridgeleigh	28.00	38.00	30.00

394 / GLASSWARE

	Current Price Range		Prior Year Average
☐ **Cigarette urn,** gold border	42.00	52.00	45.00
☐ **Cigarette urn,** Ridgeleigh	28.00	38.00	30.00
☐ **Cocktail shaker,** seahorse	110.00	135.00	112.00
☐ **Cocktail shaker,** rooster head	135.00	185.00	150.00
☐ **Compote,** Colonial	28.00	38.00	30.00
☐ **Compote,** green, diamond optic, 8″	55.00	80.00	62.00
☐ **Compote,** Plantation	50.00	65.00	52.00
☐ **Compote,** Orchid	45.00	70.00	52.00
☐ **Compote,** Waverly	28.00	38.00	30.00
☐ **Creamer,** Fandango	28.00	38.00	30.00
☐ **Creamer,** Flamingo	30.00	35.00	29.50
☐ **Creamer,** Greek Key	32.00	42.00	35.00
☐ **Creamer,** Prince of Wales	35.00	50.00	38.00
☐ **Creamer,** Waverly	40.0	55.00	42.00
☐ **Creamer,** Winged Scroll	80.00	110.00	88.00
☐ **Cruet,** Diamond Optic	45.00	70.00	52.00
☐ **Cruet,** Flamingo	35.00	50.00	38.00
☐ **Cruet,** Greek Key	40.00	55.00	42.00
☐ **Cruet,** Old Sandwich	80.00	110.00	88.00
☐ **Cruet,** Pineapple and Fan	50.00	65.00	52.00
☐ **Cup and saucer,** Empress, Sahara	28.00	38.00	30.00
☐ **Cup and saucer,** Orchid	28.00	38.00	30.00
☐ **Cup and saucer,** pink, Queen Anne	32.00	42.00	35.00
☐ **Custard dish,** Waverly	21.00	26.00	22.50
☐ **Dish,** cheese and cracker, Colonial	40.00	55.00	42.00
☐ **Dish,** cheese and cracker, Saturn	70.00	95.00	78.00
☐ **Dish,** lemon, Ridgeleigh	28.00	38.00	30.00
☐ **Figurine,** donkey	160.00	210.00	175.00
☐ **Figurine,** giraffe	85.00	110.00	88.00
☐ **Figurine,** horse	110.00	160.00	125.00
☐ **Goblet,** Colonial	12.00	22.00	15.00
☐ **Goblet,** Greek Key	55.00	80.00	62.00
☐ **Goblet,** Ipswich	18.00	28.00	20.00
☐ **Goblet,** Minuet	35.00	50.00	42.00
☐ **Goblet,** Old Sandwich	16.00	21.00	17.50
☐ **Goblet,** Orchid	22.00	32.00	25.00
☐ **Goblet,** Princess Anne, Sahara	22.00	32.00	25.00
☐ **Goblet,** Saturn, Sahara	22.00	32.00	25.00
☐ **Ice bucket,** Colonial	40.00	55.00	42.00
☐ **Ice bucket,** Greek Key	80.00	110.00	88.00
☐ **Ice bucket,** Moongleam	65.00	95.00	80.00
☐ **Jar,** candy, covered, Greek Key	80.00	130.00	100.00
☐ **Jar,** candy, covered, Ipswich	35.00	50.00	38.00
☐ **Lemonade set,** pitcher and six glasses	135.00	185.00	150.00
☐ **Mug,** Old Sandwich	28.00	38.00	30.00
☐ **Mug,** Pineapple and Fan	32.00	42.00	35.00
☐ **Mug,** Wedding Band	40.00	55.00	42.00
☐ **Nut dish,** Crystolite	12.00	22.00	15.00
☐ **Nut dish,** Empress, Sahara	18.00	28.00	20.00
☐ **Nut dish,** Queen Anne, Sahara	18.00	28.00	20.00
☐ **Pitcher,** Colonial, 7¾″	50.00	70.00	55.00
☐ **Pitcher,** Flamingo	65.00	95.00	80.00
☐ **Pitcher,** Greek Key, 6¼″	65.00	95.00	80.00
☐ **Pitcher,** milk, Wedding Band	55.00	80.00	62.00
☐ **Pitcher,** Pied Piper	80.00	110.00	88.00
☐ **Pitcher,** water, Crystolite	55.00	80.00	62.00

	Current Price Range		Prior Year Average
☐ **Pitcher,** water, emerald green	160.00	210.00	175.00
☐ **Pitcher,** water, eight panels	100.00	130.00	110.00
☐ **Pitcher,** water, Greek Key	110.00	135.00	112.00
☐ **Plate,** Beehive, 14″	80.00	110.00	88.00
☐ **Plate,** Colonial, 6″	28.00	38.00	30.00
☐ **Plate,** Crystolite, 10½″	40.00	55.00	42.00
☐ **Plate,** fancy loop, 8″	28.00	38.00	30.00
☐ **Plate,** Fandango, 8″	12.00	22.00	15.00
☐ **Plate,** Flamingo, Empress, 8″	18.00	28.00	20.00
☐ **Plate,** Greek Key, 7″	18.00	28.00	20.00
☐ **Plate,** Ipswich, 8″	18.00	28.00	20.00
☐ **Plate,** Moongleam, 8″	25.00	40.00	28.00
☐ **Plate,** Pied Piper, 7″	22.00	32.00	25.00
☐ **Plate,** Queen Anne, 7″	32.00	42.00	35.00
☐ **Plate,** Waverly, 14″	32.00	42.00	35.00
☐ **Powder jar,** covered, sterling silver top, colonial .	80.00	110.00	88.00
☐ **Relish,** divided, Crystolite	20.00	35.00	22.00
☐ **Relish,** divided, Empress	28.00	38.00	30.00
☐ **Relish,** divided, Lariat	28.00	38.00	30.00
☐ **Relish,** divided, Orchid	35.00	50.00	38.00
☐ **Relish,** divided, Ridgeleigh	32.00	42.00	35.00
☐ **Relish,** divided, Whirlpool	22.00	32.00	25.00
☐ **Salt and pepper,** etched, floral design, pair	45.00	65.00	50.00
☐ **Salt and pepper,** Greek Key	65.00	95.00	75.00
☐ **Salt and pepper,** Plantation	55.00	80.00	62.00
☐ **Sherbet,** Colonial	16.00	21.00	17.50
☐ **Sherbet,** fluted	16.00	21.00	17.50
☐ **Sherbet,** Flamingo	21.00	26.00	22.50
☐ **Sherbet,** Greek Key	16.00	21.00	17.50
☐ **Sherbet,** Minuet	16.00	21.00	17.50
☐ **Sherbet,** Old Sandwich	22.00	32.00	25.00
☐ **Spooner,** Beaded Swag, milk white	55.00	80.00	62.00
☐ **Spooner,** Crystolite	28.00	38.00	30.00
☐ **Sugar,** Colonial	35.00	50.00	38.00
☐ **Sugar,** Plantation	12.00	22.00	15.00
☐ **Sugar and creamer,** Empress, Sahara	45.00	60.00	48.00
☐ **Sugar and creamer,** Fandango	55.00	70.00	58.00
☐ **Sugar and creamer,** green, Pineapple and Fan ..	80.00	110.00	88.00
☐ **Sugar and creamer,** Moonglo	40.00	55.00	42.00
☐ **Sugar and creamer,** Ridgeleigh	35.00	50.00	38.00
☐ **Syrup,** etched, floral design	28.00	38.00	30.00
☐ **Syrup,** Fandango	80.00	110.00	88.00
☐ **Syrup,** Plantation	50.00	65.00	52.00
☐ **Toothpick holder,** Beaded Swag	50.00	55.00	48.00
☐ **Toothpick holder,** Crystolite	35.00	50.00	38.00
☐ **Toothpick holder,** Fancy Loop	45.00	70.00	52.00
☐ **Toothpick holder,** green, Pineapple and Fan	135.00	185.00	150.00
☐ **Toothpick holder,** Prince of Wales	65.00	95.00	75.00
☐ **Toothpick holder,** Winged Scroll	110.00	135.00	112.00
☐ **Tumbler,** Beaded Swag	55.00	80.00	62.00
☐ **Tumbler,** Colonial	18.00	28.00	20.00
☐ **Tumbler,** Fancy Loop	18.00	28.00	20.00
☐ **Tumbler,** green, Pineapple and Fan	50.00	65.00	52.00
☐ **Tumbler,** juice, Ipswich	18.00	28.00	20.00
☐ **Tumbler,** Old Sandwich	11.00	16.00	12.50
☐ **Tumbler,** Prince of Wales	25.00	38.00	30.00

396 / GLASSWARE

	Current Price Range		Prior Year Average
☐ **Tumbler,** Winged Scroll	50.00	65.00	52.00
☐ **Vase,** Colonial, 8″	45.00	60.00	48.00
☐ **Vase,** crystal, 21″	160.00	185.00	162.00
☐ **Vase,** etched vine design, 10″	85.00	110.00	88.00
☐ **Vase,** green, Pineapple and Fan, 10″	65.00	95.00	75.00
☐ **Vase,** Lariat, 7½″	18.00	22.00	17.50
☐ **Vase,** Ridgeleigh, 8″	22.00	32.00	25.00
☐ **Vase,** Whirpool, 5″	28.00	38.00	30.00
☐ **Whiskey,** Coronation, 2½ oz.	22.00	32.00	25.00
☐ **Wine,** Colonial, 3 oz.	22.00	32.00	25.00
☐ **Wine,** Minuet	28.00	38.00	30.00
☐ **Wine,** Tally Ho	45.00	60.00	48.00

LALIQUE, RENE

Rene Lalique produced art glass in Paris from the 1890's until his death in 1945. Each piece was marked "R. Lalique." Present pieces simply bear the name "Lalique." It is a very high quality glass designed in the Art Deco and Art Noveau styles. Those pieces signed "R. Lalique," of course, command much higher prices and are more sought-after by collectors than those produced since 1945.

	Current Price Range		Prior Year Average
☐ **Ashtray,** frosted and clear, lovebirds	50.00	65.00	52.00
☐ **Ashtray,** frosted, sun	110.00	135.00	112.00
☐ **Ashtray,** swan	45.00	60.00	48.00
☐ **Atomizer,** daisy, 3½″	185.00	210.00	188.00
☐ **Atomizer,** frosted, chrome top, 4″	135.00	160.00	138.00
☐ **Atomizer,** metal top, six nude figures on frosted ground, 5″	310.00	460.00	375.00
☐ **Bell,** frosted and clear, 5½″	110.00	135.00	112.00
☐ **Bookends,** frosted and clear	185.00	135.00	200.00
☐ **Bottle,** perfume, apple shape	55.00	80.00	58.00
☐ **Bottle,** perfume, brown frosted ground, elegant ladies in several positions, 6″	260.00	310.00	275.00
☐ **Bottle,** perfume, butterflies, 2″	235.00	285.00	250.00
☐ **Bottle,** perfume, emerald green, stopper	160.00	185.00	162.00
☐ **Bottle,** perfume, floral design, 4″	285.00	335.00	300.00
☐ **Bottle,** perfume, frosted and clear, tulips	80.00	110.00	80.00
☐ **Bottle,** perfume, heart shape	80.00	110.00	80.00
☐ **Bottle,** perfume, inclined toward middle with woman's profile, square	110.00	135.00	112.00
☐ **Bottle,** perfume, leaf design, 4½″	160.00	185.00	162.00
☐ **Bottle,** perfume, monkey, signed	285.00	335.00	300.00
☐ **Bottle,** perfume, nudes, Art Nouveau, 4½″	385.00	435.00	400.00
☐ **Bottle,** perfume, seashell shape	160.00	185.00	162.00
☐ **Bottle,** perfume, shaped like two flowers	260.00	310.00	275.00
☐ **Bottle,** perfume, square with dome shaped stopper	90.00	120.00	90.00
☐ **Bottle,** perfume, swirl design, signed, 6½″	285.00	335.00	300.00
☐ **Bowl,** cupids and roses, 9½″	285.00	335.00	300.00
☐ **Bowl,** dragonfly on the lid, 3″ x 2″	85.00	110.00	88.00
☐ **Bowl,** green, leaf design, 5″	85.00	110.00	88.00
☐ **Bowl,** intaglio, foliage and birds, 9″	135.00	160.00	138.00
☐ **Bowl,** iridescent green, signed, 3″	235.00	285.00	225.00
☐ **Bowl,** molded berry design, 10″	235.00	285.00	225.00
☐ **Bowl,** six lovebirds in middle, signed, 8½″	210.00	260.00	225.00

GLASSWARE / 397

	Current Price Range		Prior Year Average
☐ **Bowl,** starfish, signed, 9½"	385.00	460.00	412.00
☐ **Bowl,** swirl design, 8"	235.00	260.00	238.00
☐ **Box,** cupid and flowers, frosted	185.00	210.00	188.00
☐ **Box,** Grecian women in frosted beige, signed	210.00	260.00	225.00
☐ **Box,** powder, cactus	135.00	160.00	138.00
☐ **Box,** powder, satin finish, three dancing nudes, 3½"	260.00	310.00	275.00
☐ **Box,** swan design, covered	160.00	185.00	162.00
☐ **Clock,** love birds on blue ground, square, 4½"	460.00	560.00	500.00
☐ **Clock,** wrens on black enameled clock face, Omega, 8"	975.00	1075.00	975.00
☐ **Decanter,** square with bubble design, signature	210.00	260.00	225.00
☐ **Figurine,** bear, standing, signed, 4"	160.00	210.00	175.00
☐ **Figurine,** dove with turned head, 2½"	45.00	65.00	50.00
☐ **Figurine,** frosted, bird, 3½"	45.00	65.00	50.00
☐ **Figurine,** lion, 4"	160.00	210.00	175.00
☐ **Figurine,** frosted, nude man on a clear base, 8"	260.00	310.00	275.00
☐ **Figurine,** opalescent, squirrel, 4¾"	210.00	260.00	225.00
☐ **Glass,** roosters on raised band, 3"	30.00	60.00	40.00
☐ **Knife rest,** baby head on each end, 4"	45.00	65.00	50.00
☐ **Lamp,** clear model of a fish on a wave, shaped bronze stand	1350.00	1850.00	1550.00
☐ **Paperweight,** beehive, 3"	185.00	210.00	188.00
☐ **Pitcher,** berries and leaves, applied handle, 10"	260.00	310.00	275.00
☐ **Plaque,** flowers and lovebirds on green ground, 7" x 10"	510.00	585.00	538.00
☐ **Plate,** bordered with frosted grapes, 8½"	85.00	110.00	88.00
☐ **Plate,** bordered with frosted pansies, 4"	45.00	70.00	52.00
☐ **Plate,** chrysanthemums engraved on clear glass, 15"	235.00	285.00	250.00
☐ **Plate,** opalescent fish design, 12"	285.00	335.00	300.00
☐ **Plate,** opalescent swirl, 11"	185.00	210.00	188.00
☐ **Plate,** shell design, 6½"	65.00	95.00	75.00
☐ **Plate,** 1966 Annual, 8½"	310.00	385.00	338.00
☐ **Plate,** 1967 Annual, 8½"	210.00	285.00	238.00
☐ **Plate,** 1968 Annual, 8½"	135.00	185.00	150.00
☐ **Plate,** 1969 Annual, 8½"	80.00	130.00	100.00
☐ **Plate,** 1970 Annual, 8½"	90.00	115.00	98.00
☐ **Plate,** 1976 Annual, 8½"	120.00	150.00	125.00
☐ **Sugar shaker,** Egyptians on orange frosted ground, signed, 5¼"	185.00	235.00	200.00
☐ **Tray,** nudes in relief, 4½"	80.00	110.00	88.00
☐ **Tumbler,** berries in relief on base	65.00	90.00	72.00
☐ **Tumbler,** fish in relief, footed	70.00	95.00	78.00
☐ **Tumbler,** rooster in relief, footed	55.00	75.00	60.00
☐ **Vase,** Art Nouveau, two cranes on frosted blue ground, 7¼"	335.00	385.00	350.00
☐ **Vase,** "Coqs et Plumes"	610.00	960.00	725.00
☐ **Vase,** fan design in frosted, signed	235.00	285.00	250.00
☐ **Vase,** frosted and clear, floral design, 6½"	185.00	210.00	188.00
☐ **Vase,** frosted and clear, fruit design, 6½"	385.00	435.00	400.00
☐ **Vase,** leaf design in gray, 6½"	535.00	585.00	550.00
☐ **Vase,** nudes on panels, 7½"	1100.00	1500.00	1200.00
☐ **Vase,** roosters on turquoise, Art Deco, 4½"	310.00	360.00	325.00
☐ **Vase,** rose handles with thorns, brown satin, 7½"	260.00	310.00	275.00

398 / GLASSWARE

	Current Price Range		Prior Year Average
☐ **Vase,** sea horses on handles, fish and seaweed design, signed	260.00	310.00	275.00
☐ **Vase,** snails on frosted ground, 6½"	285.00	335.00	300.00
☐ **Vase,** squirrels on gray glass, signed, 7"	435.00	485.00	450.00
☐ **Wine,** Art Deco stem, 6"	65.00	90.00	72.00
☐ **Wine,** nude figure stem, 5½"	110.00	135.00	112.00
☐ **Wine,** rooster stem	50.00	70.00	55.00

LEGRAS

Legras was a contemporary of Galle, Daum and the other great French masters in the art of Cameo glass. Although a lesser known artist among the collectors of Cameo glass, his work is starting to command prices as high as some of the more familiar designers.

☐ **Bowl,** acid finish, etched bleeding hearts, 6½"	335.00	385.00	350.00
☐ **Bowl,** centerpiece, morning glories, signed, 14"	460.00	510.00	475.00
☐ **Dish,** carved harbor scene with boats, 5" x 5"	310.00	360.00	325.00
☐ **Rose bowl,** carved, enamel gold flowers, 4"x 4½"	335.00	385.00	350.00
☐ **Tray,** frosted, orange cameo cuttings, 4¾" x 2¾"	210.00	235.00	212.00
☐ **Vase,** cameo, bud, carved fuchsia blossoms and foliage, signed, 11½"	335.00	385.00	350.00
☐ **Vase,** cameo, carved and enameled landscape scene, signed, 6¼"	285.00	310.00	288.00
☐ **Vase,** cameo, carved and enameled hounds and trees, signed, 9"	385.00	435.00	400.00
☐ **Vase,** cameo, carved scene of trees and water, signed, 5¾"	285.00	335.00	300.00

LIBBEY

Successor of the New England Glass Co., Libbey Glass Company in Toledo, Ohio, produced not only fine cut and intaglio glass, but also fine art glass. Amberina and animal stemware designed by Nash are perhaps the best known.

☐ **Banana dish,** mitre cut glass, 5"	245.00	275.00	250.00
☐ **Basket,** cut glass with florals and geometrics, signed, 7"	285.00	335.00	300.00
☐ **Basket,** intaglio cut, signed	460.00	560.00	500.00
☐ **Bowl,** cobalt blue design, footed, 10"	235.00	285.00	250.00
☐ **Bowl,** cream colored satin, decorated, signed 2½"	560.00	660.00	600.00
☐ **Bowl,** cut glass, signed	130.00	185.00	148.00
☐ **Bowl,** frosted and clear, lovebirds, 8"	660.00	760.00	700.00
☐ **Bowl,** richly cut, signed, 9"	285.00	335.00	300.00
☐ **Candlestick,** crystal stem, red feather top, signed pair, 6"	385.00	435.00	400.00
☐ **Candlestick,** floral design on stem and base, 10"	110.00	135.00	112.00
☐ **Champagne,** bear stem	110.00	160.00	125.00
☐ **Champagne,** squirrel stem	85.00	135.00	100.00
☐ **Compote,** floral design, intaglio cut	90.00	115.00	102.00
☐ **Cordial,** "Vista," Nash series	55.00	80.00	62.00
☐ **Goblet,** kangaroo stem	110.00	160.00	125.00
☐ **Goblet,** squirrel stem	65.00	90.00	72.00

GLASSWARE / 399

	Current Price Range		Prior Year Average
☐ **Pitcher**, inverted baby thumbprint	235.00	285.00	250.00
☐ **Pitcher**, 14 tumblers, signed	1050.00	1250.00	1100.00
☐ **Plate**, "Gloria," 8"	160.00	210.00	175.00
☐ **Plate**, "Santa Maria", signed, 7¾"	210.00	260.00	225.00
☐ **Punch cup**, 1893 World's Fair	285.00	360.00	312.00
☐ **Salt and pepper**, "Columbian Expo" 1893	210.00	260.00	225.00
☐ **Sugar shaker**, pewter top, 5½"	235.00	310.00	260.00
☐ **Syrup**, original top, 6"	260.00	335.00	280.00
☐ **Tazza bowl**, crystal and shades of blue, signed, 6"	460.00	510.00	475.00
☐ **Tumbler**, opaque white, green and rust husks, 4"	80.00	110.00	88.00
☐ **Tumbler**, richly cut, star base	55.00	80.00	62.00
☐ **Vase**, corset shape, amethyst overlay cut to clear, signed, 12"	340.00	380.00	350.00
☐ **Vase**, floral and leaf design, footed	185.00	210.00	188.00
☐ **Vase**, loving cup, two handles, footed, signed	560.00	660.00	600.00
☐ **Vase**, opaque white, green and rust husks, 4"	80.00	110.00	88.00
☐ **Vase**, peacock, intaglio cut, 10"	135.00	160.00	138.00
☐ **Water carafe**, blue husks with gold	310.00	385.00	338.00
☐ **Wine**, bear stem	110.00	160.00	125.00
☐ **Wine**, "Diana," Nash series	55.00	80.00	62.00
☐ **Wine**, monkey stem	80.00	110.00	88.00

LOETZ

Loetz is an Austrian art glass which was made just before the turn of the century. Similar in appearance to Tiffany glass, Loetz is characterized by an iridescence on the outside of the glass. His most popular iridescent blue peacock feather design is highly prized. Loetz was a contemporary of Tiffany and worked in his factory. Most pieces were not signed, thus signed pieces command higher prices.

☐ **Atomizer**, blue, green and brown design, signed	260.00	285.00	262.00
☐ **Basket**, blue, looped handle, 7"	190.00	230.00	200.00
☐ **Basket**, brides, red with enamel decoration, silver holder	310.00	360.00	325.00
☐ **Bonbon dish**, signed, 5½"	310.00	360.00	325.00
☐ **Bowl**, iridescent blue, snail design, 8"	385.00	460.00	412.00
☐ **Bowl**, iridescent gold, pinched sides, 4"	360.00	435.00	382.00
☐ **Bowl**, iridescent green, 8"	160.00	210.00	175.00
☐ **Bowl**, lavender, aqua, signed, 3"	285.00	335.00	300.00
☐ **Cameo box**, covered, carved blue florals	460.00	510.00	475.00
☐ **Candlestick**, red, green fern decoration, pair, 10"	120.00	160.00	130.00
☐ **Compote**, iridescent green and blue	185.00	235.00	200.00
☐ **Cruet**, multicolor	160.00	210.00	175.00
☐ **Epergne**, four green trumpet lilies and small baskets	260.00	310.00	275.00
☐ **Inkwell**, Art Nouveau, iridescent blue	235.00	285.00	250.00
☐ **Inkwell**, brass lid, iridescent blue	185.00	235.00	200.00
☐ **Inkwell**, feather design, iridescent blue	260.00	310.00	275.00
☐ **Paperweight**, feather design, iridescent blue	260.00	310.00	275.00
☐ **Rose bowl**, applied lily pads, 3¾"	285.00	335.00	300.00
☐ **Syrup**, blue and green	185.00	235.00	200.00
☐ **Tumbler**, ornate	80.00	110.00	88.00
☐ **Vase**, Art Nouveau, 5½"	160.00	260.00	200.00

400 / GLASSWARE

	Current Price Range		Prior Year Average
☐ **Vase,** blue, Austria, signed, 3½"	285.00	335.00	300.00
☐ **Vase,** feather design, signed, 7"	310.00	360.00	325.00
☐ **Vase,** fine iridescence, heavy silver overlay, signed, 10"	875.00	975.00	900.00
☐ **Vase,** iridescent blue, pinched sides, signed, 4¼"	285.00	360.00	312.00
☐ **Vase,** iridescent bronze, pedestal base, 8"	85.00	110.00	88.00
☐ **Vase,** iridescent, dark and light blue, 12"	875.00	975.00	900.00
☐ **Vase,** iridescent green and blue, signed, 6½" ...	360.00	385.00	362.00
☐ **Vase,** iridescent green and blue, signed, 7"	160.00	185.00	162.00
☐ **Vase,** iridescent teal blue on red, 9"	335.00	385.00	350.00
☐ **Vase,** multicolor, fan shape	235.00	285.00	250.00
☐ **Vase,** multicolored iridescent, signed, 8¾"	335.00	385.00	350.00
☐ **Vase,** olive, silver overlay, signed, 9½"	460.00	610.00	520.00

LUTZ

This term is usually applied to any piece of finely threaded or striped glass and named after its designer, Nicholas Lutz. Lutz was employed by the Boston and Sandwich Glass Company, where the glass was manufactured in the late 1870's.

☐ **Basket,** candy cane stripes, 6"	135.00	160.00	138.00
☐ **Bottle,** blue, green and red, 5"	80.00	110.00	88.00
☐ **Bowl,** clear with red, white and green threads, 6¼"	160.00	210.00	175.00
☐ **Bowl,** finger, underplate, red and white filigree striping	135.00	160.00	138.00
☐ **Bowl,** finger, rose colored threading, 5"	55.00	80.00	62.00
☐ **Bowl,** finger, and underplate, clear with ruffled edges, pink and white goldstone stripes	110.00	135.00	112.00
☐ **Compote,** sterling with ring handle, 14"	460.00	510.00	475.00
☐ **Creamer,** Latticinio, blue threads, miniature	135.00	185.00	150.00
☐ **Cup and saucer,** filigree white and light blue, 4" Dia.	135.00	185.00	150.00
☐ **Cup and saucer,** Latticino	160.00	185.00	162.00
☐ **Ewer,** pink ribbons with goldstone, applied handle	310.00	360.00	325.00
☐ **Liqueur,** stripes on clear crystal	85.00	125.00	100.00
☐ **Pitcher,** water, gold threading	335.00	385.00	350.00
☐ **Plate,** spiral green design, 7"	110.00	160.00	125.00
☐ **Sugar and creamer,** blue	235.00	285.00	250.00
☐ **Tumbler,** blue threading	80.00	110.00	88.00
☐ **Tumbler,** lavender stripes	260.00	310.00	275.00
☐ **Tumbler,** water, twisted blue and white threading, 4"	160.00	210.00	175.00
☐ **Vase,** clear with white threads, 3½"	90.00	120.00	98.00
☐ **Vase,** Latticino	90.00	120.00	85.00
☐ **Vase,** pink threads, 8½"	135.00	160.00	138.00
☐ **Vase,** white and applied bosses, filigree handles, 12"	310.00	360.00	325.00
☐ **Whiskey,** Latticinio, pink, gold and white, 2½" ..	80.00	110.00	88.00

MARY GREGORY

Mary Gregory was an artist hired by the Boston and Sandwich Glass Company, and was responsible for many delightful "children playing" motifs. Clear or colored glass decorated with white enamel silhouette type figures is labeled Mary Gregory glass. Since her popularity in the late 1800's and early 1900's, many manufacturers have employed this method of production; therefore, many reproductions are in the market place.

	Current Price Range		Prior Year Average
☐ **Ale glass,** white enameled girl, 6"	55.00	80.00	62.00
☐ **Ale mug,** hand painted, girl	70.00	95.00	82.00
☐ **Atomizer,** barefoot boy in knee pants	135.00	160.00	138.00
☐ **Bottle,** barber, cobalt blue, white enamel girl	160.00	210.00	175.00
☐ **Bottle,** barber, pale green, white enamel decorations, hand painted boy on side	110.00	135.00	112.00
☐ **Bottle,** cologne, cranberry, white enamel boy, 7"	160.00	210.00	175.00
☐ **Bottle,** perfume, cream, white enamel boy, 4"	110.00	135.00	112.00
☐ **Bottle,** perfume, green, white enamel boy	135.00	185.00	150.00
☐ **Bowl,** light blue, white enamel decorations, 10"	235.00	285.00	250.00
☐ **Box,** cobalt blue, white enamel girl	185.00	210.00	188.00
☐ **Box,** cranberry, hinged lid	185.00	235.00	200.00
☐ **Box,** powder, hinged lid, cream and red decorations, 4"	160.00	210.00	175.00
☐ **Butter,** white enamel decorations	135.00	145.00	125.00
☐ **Creamer,** white enamel boy	125.00	145.00	125.00
☐ **Cruet,** cranberry, white enamel girl	200.00	225.00	200.00
☐ **Cruet,** green, white enamel girl	160.00	185.00	162.00
☐ **Decanter,** blue crystal stopper, 10"	120.00	150.00	125.00
☐ **Decanter,** blue, white enamel decorations	110.00	135.00	112.00
☐ **Decanter,** green, white enamel girl, 9½"	135.00	185.00	150.00
☐ **Inkwell,** black swirl pattern, square	80.00	110.00	88.00
☐ **Mug,** white enamel boy holding flowers	90.00	120.00	98.00
☐ **Pitcher,** cobalt blue, white enamel girl, 9"	210.00	235.00	212.00
☐ **Pitcher,** cranberry, white enamel boy, 9"	160.00	185.00	162.00
☐ **Pitcher,** green, white enamel boy, 6"	135.00	160.00	138.00
☐ **Pitcher,** water, cranberry, 6¾"	210.00	260.00	225.00
☐ **Plaque,** young girl in woodland scene, 10½"	235.00	310.00	362.00
☐ **Stein,** pale amber glass, tall pewter lid, hand painted girl, 15"	95.00	145.00	110.00
☐ **Sugar bowl,** clear, white enamel girl	120.00	150.00	125.00
☐ **Tumbler,** amber, white enamel girl, 5"	110.00	135.00	112.00
☐ **Tumbler,** green, white enamel boy, 5"	70.00	100.00	75.00
☐ **Tumbler,** cranberry, white enamel girl	55.00	80.00	62.00
☐ **Vase,** bud, white enamel boy, 11"	285.00	360.00	312.00
☐ **Vase,** bud, cranberry, 4"	95.00	115.00	100.00
☐ **Vase,** cranberry, 8¼"	175.00	205.00	180.00
☐ **Vase,** green, filigree, white enamel decorations, 10"	135.00	160.00	138.00
☐ **Vase,** light blue, white enamel girl, 12"	235.00	285.00	250.00
☐ **Vase,** light green, white enamel girl, 6"	135.00	160.00	138.00
☐ **Vase,** red, white enamel girl	110.00	160.00	125.00

MILLEFIORI

The name literally means "thousand flowers." Millefiori glass is made by joining colored glass rods or canes before blowing. The rods are rather like an icebox cookie roll, meant to be sliced before baking so that the contrasting inside would show. The Millefiori technique was known to Egyptians in 100 B.C.

	Current Price Range		Prior Year Average
☐ Bowl, two handles, 3½"	110.00	135.00	112.00
☐ Box, covered, 3"	160.00	210.00	175.00
☐ Box, covered, 4"	170.00	220.00	185.00
☐ Creamer	160.00	210.00	175.00
☐ Cruet, applied clear handle, cut glass stopper, 6"	285.00	335.00	300.00
☐ Cruet, with complete millefiori, handle and stopper, 5"	160.00	210.00	175.00
☐ Goblet, colored canes in bows, stem and base clear, 7½"	185.00	210.00	188.00
☐ Jug, 2½"	105.00	130.00	110.00
☐ Lamp, miniature with dome shade and base in millefiore, 12"	560.00	660.00	600.00
☐ Lamp, with matching shade, 14"	235.00	310.00	262.00
☐ Paperweight, crowned all over design, modern, 3"	35.00	55.00	40.00
☐ Pitcher, applied handle, 2¾"	110.00	160.00	125.00
☐ Pitcher, cream, scattered millefiori on white ground, 4"	235.00	285.00	250.00
☐ Punch set, seven pieces	410.00	510.00	450.00
☐ Rose bowl, ruffled, 6"	135.00	185.00	150.00
☐ Salt	80.00	130.00	100.00
☐ Toothpick holder, four pinched sides	135.00	185.00	150.00
☐ Toothpick holder, flared rim with flowers	110.00	160.00	125.00
☐ Tumbler, 4"	160.00	185.00	162.00
☐ Tumbler, overall millefiori in blues and greens 4"	110.00	160.00	125.00
☐ Tumbler, clear, 3½"	80.00	130.00	100.00
☐ Vase, blue and green paperweight canes, 5"	95.00	120.00	100.00
☐ Vase, double handled, millefiori laid in rows, 8"	210.00	260.00	225.00
☐ Vase, double handled, lavender background, Venetian, 8"	50.00	70.00	55.00
☐ Vase, fluted rim, 2¾"	65.00	95.00	75.00
☐ Vase, multicolor canes, red background, 3½"	110.00	135.00	112.00
☐ Vase, random millefiori, blue background, 8"	335.00	385.00	350.00
☐ Vase, two handles, 7¾"	80.00	110.00	88.00
☐ Vase, unusual dragonfly design with netting, signed	435.00	510.00	460.00
☐ Vase, urn shaped, regular pattern, 10"	260.00	310.00	275.00

PEACHBLOW

Somewhat of a universal term, "Peachblow" is used by collectors to describe several varieties produced by more than a half dozen glass companies. Shadings will vary from rose to yellow, blue or white, depending on its maker, and will also vary in layers. Sandwich Peachblow is one layer and the English is two layer. A relative newcomer is a single layer called Martinsville Peachblow.

GLASSWARE / 403

	Current Price Range		Prior Year Average
☐ **Bisque jar,** enameled and jeweled decor, Mt. Washington, signed	610.00	660.00	625.00
☐ **Bowl,** black-eyed Susans and stems, Mt. Washington	3200.00	3500.00	3250.00
☐ **Bowl,** bride's, New Martinsville, 10″	135.00	160.00	138.00
☐ **Bowl,** ruffled edge, New England, 5″ x 2½″	360.00	435.00	382.00
☐ **Bowl,** ruffled edge, Sandwich, 7″ x 3½″	210.00	260.00	225.00
☐ **Bowl,** sunburst, ruffled edge, New Martinsville	135.00	160.00	138.00
☐ **Bowl,** three feet, Gunderson, 7″	635.00	710.00	660.00
☐ **Carafe,** glossy finish, Wheeling	685.00	785.00	625.00
☐ **Compote,** Gunderson, 6″	225.00	270.00	245.00
☐ **Creamer,** acid finish, New England, 4″	460.00	510.00	475.00
☐ **Cruet,** glossy finish, Wheeling	510.00	610.00	550.00
☐ **Cup and saucer,** raspberry color with white handle, Gunderson	360.00	435.00	382.00
☐ **Darner,** open end, New England	135.00	185.00	150.00
☐ **Darner,** glossy finish, New England	210.00	285.00	238.00
☐ **Decanter,** amber, Wheeling, 9½″	2600.00	3100.00	2750.00
☐ **Hat,** diamond quilted, 3″	130.00	170.00	140.00
☐ **Lamp base,** ornate, yellow to cranberry, Wheeling, 9″	950.00	1150.00	1000.00
☐ **Muffineer,** original metal top, Wheeling, 5½″	735.00	810.00	760.00
☐ **Pear,** glossy finish, New England	185.00	235.00	200.00
☐ **Pitcher,** gold enameling of branches and butterfly, Webb, 9½″	435.00	535.00	475.00
☐ **Pitcher,** water, Wheeling	1300.00	1600.00	1350.00
☐ **Rose bowl,** New England	385.00	435.00	400.00
☐ **Rose bowl,** Wheeling	310.00	385.00	338.00
☐ **Salt,** dip, New Martinsville	55.00	80.00	62.00
☐ **Salt,** glossy finish, Wheeling	235.00	285.00	250.00
☐ **Toothpick holder,** Gunderson	160.00	210.00	175.00
☐ **Toothpick holder,** square, New England	260.00	335.00	280.00
☐ **Tumbler,** acid finish, New England	310.00	410.00	350.00
☐ **Tumbler,** acid finish, Wheeling	335.00	460.00	382.00
☐ **Tumbler,** glossy finish, New England	360.00	410.00	375.00
☐ **Tumbler,** Gunderson	95.00	120.00	98.00
☐ **Vase,** enameled dragonfly, branches and blossoms, Webb, 5″	335.00	385.00	350.00
☐ **Vase,** glossy finish, Wheeling, 7″	900.00	1050.00	925.00
☐ **Vase,** lily with three petals, New England, 7¾″	735.00	810.00	762.00
☐ **Vase,** replica of Morgan Vase, glossy finish, Wheeling, 10″	1800.00	2300.00	1900.00
☐ **Vase,** ruffled, Sandwich, 5½″	130.00	170.00	140.00
☐ **Vase,** scalloped rim, Gunderson, 8½″	235.00	285.00	250.00
☐ **Vase,** trumpet shape, glossy finish, New England, 15″	1150.00	1350.00	1200.00

RUBENA VERDE

Rubena Verde, a Victorian glass made by Hobbs, Brockunier and Company of Wheeling, West Virginia around 1890, is now considered an art glass. It varies in colors from yellow green to red.

☐ **Basket,** pointed handle and applied cranberry petals, 6″ x 6¼″	80.00	110.00	88.00

404 / GLASSWARE

	Current Price Range		Prior Year Average
☐ **Bottle,** cologne bottle, applied decorations around base	80.00	110.00	88.00
☐ **Bottle,** cologne, blue and white enameled flowers, 3" x 7¾"	120.00	150.00	125.00
☐ **Bowl,** finger, ruffled rim, 4"	75.00	95.00	80.00
☐ **Butter dish,** daisy and button, clear base	285.00	310.00	288.00
☐ **Creamer,** cranberry to green, applied handle	135.00	160.00	138.00
☐ **Cruet,** shades of red to green	160.00	185.00	162.00
☐ **Epergnes,** ruffled with clear glass edges, three horns, and hanging basket, 13" x 8½"	360.00	385.00	362.00
☐ **Mustard pot,** spoon, 3"	120.00	150.00	125.00
☐ **Pitcher,** canary handle, 7"	260.00	310.00	275.00
☐ **Pitcher,** inverted thumbprint, 5½"	260.00	310.00	275.00
☐ **Punch cup,** enamel decor	85.00	110.00	88.00
☐ **Rose bowl,** "Crackle", 5⅛" x 4¼"	110.00	135.00	112.00
☐ **Tray,** butterfly, 8"	190.00	210.00	192.00
☐ **Tieback,** opalescent, pewter mounts, pair, 4¼"	70.00	95.00	78.00
☐ **Tieback,** Rosette, pewter mounts, pair, 4"	45.00	65.00	50.00
☐ **Vase,** bird, enameled design, pair, 8½"	410.00	485.00	438.00
☐ **Vase,** yellow, pair, 11"	820.00	920.00	950.00
☐ **Vase,** lavender, loop, pair, 9"	1350.00	1550.00	1400.00

SATIN

Articles made of opaque glass, in white or colors, that have been treated with acid to form a smooth, dull surface are referred to as "Satin Glass." Many of these pieces are shaded from a darker tone at the top to a lighter shade at the bottom. Blue, orange and red are some of the colors.

Mother-of-pearl is a special two layer satin glass. A pattern, such as diamond quilting, thumbprint, raindrop is impressed in the first layer. The second layer traps air in the low places, which shows through the finished piece as a pearly iridescence. Usually called Mother-of-Pearl Satin Glass, this process was perfected in 1886 by Joseph Webb, an Englishman.

	Current Price Range		Prior Year Average
☐ **Basket,** m.o.p. looped handle, 6½"	135.00	185.00	150.00
☐ **Basket,** white and purple, 8"	185.00	235.00	200.00
☐ **Bobeche,** yellow, ruffled rim, pair	70.00	100.00	80.00
☐ **Bottle,** perfume, ruffled edge, stopper	135.00	185.00	150.00
☐ **Bowl,** black with gold trim	235.00	260.00	215.00
☐ **Bowl,** cloverleaf m.o.p. swirl, cased in blue, ribbon crimped edge, 5"	435.00	510.00	462.00
☐ **Bowl,** blue, m.o.p., crystal, feet, 6"	510.00	585.00	538.00
☐ **Bowl,** finger, pink and blue	160.00	185.00	162.00
☐ **Bowl,** three flowers, ribbed, baby blue, 3"	80.00	130.00	100.00
☐ **Box,** covered, diamond quilted, 5"	160.00	210.00	175.00
☐ **Box,** collar and cuff box, diamond quilted, pink, signed, 6" x 6"	510.00	585.00	538.00
☐ **Butter,** pink, diamond quilted, frosted underplate	260.00	310.00	275.00
☐ **Cracker jar,** green with pink floral design	210.00	235.00	212.00
☐ **Ewer,** applied handle, blue m.o.p., Herringbone	510.00	560.00	525.00
☐ **Ewer,** blue, overlay, with frosted handle, 10"	280.00	310.00	282.00
☐ **Jar,** powder, covered, green	135.00	160.00	138.00
☐ **Lamp,** amber, peacocks, 13¼"	450.00	490.00	460.00
☐ **Lamp,** "Gone with the Wind," m.o.p. with brass frame	610.00	685.00	640.00

	Current Price Range		Prior Year Average
☐ **Lamp,** hanging, red, Regal iris	260.00	310.00	275.00
☐ **Lamp,** peg, blue, m.o.p., swirl	560.00	635.00	582.00
☐ **Mustard pot,** white ribbed satin with blue enamel flowers, 3″	125.00	145.00	130.00
☐ **Pitcher,** raindrop, soft pink and blues, frosted handle, m.o.p., 10½″	760.00	860.00	800.00
☐ **Pitcher,** rose to pink, applied camphor handle, 5″	235.00	260.00	238.00
☐ **Plate,** painted strawberries, 12″	135.00	160.00	138.00
☐ **Rose bowl,** blue overlay, flowers, 4½″	135.00	160.00	138.00
☐ **Rose bowl,** pink to white, rough pontil, 6″	160.00	210.00	175.00
☐ **Rose bowl,** white m.o.p. Venetian Diamond, applied camphor thorn feet, 5½″	285.00	360.00	312.00
☐ **Rose bowl,** wine to white, ruffled top, 4″	60.00	80.00	65.00
☐ **Salt and pepper,** apples	125.00	145.00	130.00
☐ **Salt and pepper,** enamel floral design	145.00	165.00	150.00
☐ **Sugar and creamer,** red with silver trim	310.00	360.00	325.00
☐ **Sugar shaker,** blue	150.00	170.00	150.00
☐ **Sugar shaker,** cream shading to blue, silver top .	160.00	185.00	162.00
☐ **Tumbler,** apricot, diamond quilted	150.00	200.00	165.00
☐ **Tumbler,** raspberry, diamond quilted	110.00	135.00	112.00
☐ **Tumbler,** blue, Herringbone	120.00	150.00	125.00
☐ **Tumbler,** blue, swirl	130.00	170.00	140.00
☐ **Vase,** bud, blue, clear overlay, violets, 3¾″	185.00	235.00	200.00
☐ **Vase,** diamond quilted, blue, ruffled top	260.00	285.00	262.00
☐ **Vase,** diamond quilted, pink, signed Webb	435.00	510.00	462.00
☐ **Vase,** diamond quilted, rainbow, 5⅛″	735.00	810.00	762.00
☐ **Vase,** pink to deep rose m.o.p., signed Webb, 4½″ x 3¾″	185.00	235.00	200.00
☐ **Vase,** raindrop, rainbow, 6″	835.00	910.00	862.00

TIFFANY

Louis Comfort Tiffany (1848-1933), scion of the most important family of jewelers in America during the 19th century, began his career as a painter under the noted American landscape master, George Inness (1825-1894), in New York, and later with the French Orientalist, Lem Belly, in Paris.

After many visits to North Africa, Tiffany's imagination was fired by the exotic colors, fascinating forms and textures which combined Roman, Etruscan, Byzantine and medieval works of art. His interests turned toward the decorative in 1879.

Tiffany's Favrile (a name which was derived from the Old English word "fabrile," meaning a craft or craftsman) resulted from his fascination with the iridescence that ancient glass developed after being buried for centuries in damp soil. The Tiffany furnaces opened in Corona, Long Island in 1893. There, Favrile pieces were produced both in the classical, as well as the Art Nouveau style of plant-like shapes with their affinity for natural forms.

After 1895, Tiffany and his associates began experimenting with enamel and repousse copper. Apples and leaves, dragonflies, flowers and lily pads were the motifs combining iridescent glass and copper boxes. These smaller items signed "L.C.T." are usually accompanied by an identifying number.

☐ **Bottle,** perfume, iridescent blue, 3¾″	660.00	735.00	682.00
☐ **Bottle,** rock crystal, 18K gold stopper	385.00	460.00	412.00
☐ **Bowl,** blue, scalloped, 5″	360.00	410.00	375.00
☐ **Bowl,** etched leaves on bronze base, 5″	2000.00	2300.00	2100.00

406 / GLASSWARE

	Current Price Range		Prior Year Average
☐ **Bowl,** finger, with underplate, iridescent gold ...	360.00	410.00	375.00
☐ **Bowl,** gold intaglio cut, 6″	635.00	710.00	660.00
☐ **Bowl,** iridescent gold, ribbed, 2¼″	210.00	260.00	225.00
☐ **Bowl,** iridescent gold, ruffled rim, 4½″	235.00	285.00	250.00
☐ **Bowl,** lavender, opalescent, 8″	460.00	510.00	475.00
☐ **Box,** cigar, lined with cedar, copper with green glass	285.00	360.00	312.00
☐ **Candlestick,** iridescent blue, 10″	385.00	435.00	400.00
☐ **Candlestick,** iridescent gold, twisted stems, pair, 7″	785.00	860.00	812.00
☐ **Candy dish,** peacock blue, flower form	660.00	735.00	680.00
☐ **Champagne,** gold, flower design	210.00	260.00	225.00
☐ **Champagne,** hollow stem, 7″	510.00	660.00	575.00
☐ **Compote,** iridescent blue, 6″	560.00	635.00	582.00
☐ **Compote,** iridescent gold, 6½″ x 9½″	760.00	835.00	782.00
☐ **Cordial,** iridescent gold	235.00	285.00	250.00
☐ **Goblet,** iridescent gold, twisted stem, 7″	285.00	335.00	300.00
☐ **Goblet,** pink and white, flower form, 9″	285.00	335.00	300.00
☐ **Lamp,** acorn, base and shade, 10″ x 19″	3150.00	3350.00	3200.00
☐ **Nut dish,** iridescent blue, ruffled rim	360.00	435.00	382.00
☐ **Nut dish,** iridescent gold with blue highlights, ruffled rim	185.00	235.00	200.00
☐ **Paperweight,** owl	1700.00	2200.00	1850.00
☐ **Pitcher,** deep blue, 4¼″	560.00	635.00	580.00
☐ **Plate,** iridescent gold, 6″	310.00	385.00	338.00
☐ **Plate,** lavender, 9″	285.00	335.00	300.00
☐ **Plate,** pink, white feather ribbing, 10¼″	385.00	460.00	382.00
☐ **Salt,** iridescent gold, ruffled edge	135.00	160.00	138.00
☐ **Salt,** iridescent gold, ruffled edge, footed	235.00	285.00	250.00
☐ **Salt,** multicolor	135.00	160.00	138.00
☐ **Shade,** green feather design, on opalescent, 6″ .	335.00	385.00	350.00
☐ **Sherbet,** iridescent gold	285.00	335.00	300.00
☐ **Toothpick holder,** iridescent gold, feather design, 3″	610.00	660.00	625.00
☐ **Toothpick holder,** iridescent gold, pinched sides, 1½″	285.00	335.00	300.00
☐ **Tumbler,** green feathering on clear, numbered, 5″	135.00	185.00	150.00
☐ **Tumbler,** vintage	460.00	535.00	482.00
☐ **Urn,** iridescent gold, handle, 10½″	1050.00	1250.00	1100.00
☐ **Urn,** iridescent gold, numbered, 3¼″	335.00	410.00	362.00
☐ **Vase,** flower form, gold, green, L.C. Tiffany, Favrile, 6″	785.00	885.00	825.00
☐ **Vase,** iridescent blue, 7¼″	910.00	1050.00	950.00
☐ **Vase,** iridescent gold, green leaf and vine, trumpet, 12″	1300.00	1400.00	1325.00
☐ **Vase,** iridescent gold, bronze base, pair, 13″ ...	880.00	980.00	920.00
☐ **Vase,** iridescent green, L.T.C., 7″	1350.00	1550.00	1400.00
☐ **Vase,** lotus leaf decor, metal base, 12″	2650.00	2850.00	2700.00
☐ **Vase,** molded flowers, 10″	1700.00	2000.00	1750.00
☐ **Wine,** engraved vintage, 6″	285.00	335.00	300.00
☐ **Wine,** iridescent gold, L.C.T., 4″	235.00	285.00	250.00
☐ **Wine,** Royal design, gold, numbered, 7″	335.00	410.00	362.00

VENETIAN

Venetian Glass has been made on the island of Murano in Italy since about 1350. Typical of the work of the 19th and 20th centuries is the fine filigree white and colored twisted spirals. The use of gold and bronze powder in the glass is also characteristic of this art glass. It is still being made in a wide range of qualities affordable to most.

	Current Price Range		Prior Year Average
☐ Basket, clear glass, green leaves and flowers ...	195.00	225.00	200.00
☐ Bottle, lavender, flowers, goldstone	90.00	110.00	90.00
☐ Bottle, white ribbons, gold stone, 4″	75.00	95.00	80.00
☐ Bowl, amber to cranberry, applied flowers, crystal base	160.00	185.00	162.00
☐ Bowl, clear, gold foot and edge	75.00	95.00	80.00
☐ Bowl, finger, with underplate, pink, red, white floral	40.00	55.00	42.00
☐ Candlestick, dolphin, clear glass with gold, 5″ ..	60.00	80.00	65.00
☐ Candlestick, fruits, applied, 10″	30.00	40.00	32.00
☐ Candlestick, dolphin, blue fluted top, pair, 6¼″ .	155.00	185.00	155.00
☐ Candy dish, enamel pink roses and green leaves, 6″	60.00	80.00	65.00
☐ Candy dish, orchid and blue, enamel pink flowers, 10½″	95.00	120.00	98.00
☐ Card holder, swans on both sides	42.00	52.00	45.00
☐ Champagne, dolphin stem	80.00	110.00	88.00
☐ Champagne, fruit and cherubs	80.00	110.00	88.00
☐ Compote, two dolphins, gold, ruby with gold flecks	150.00	175.00	152.00
☐ Compote, red with twisted stem	55.00	75.00	60.00
☐ Compote, blue with gold overlay, 10″	185.00	210.00	188.00
☐ Cordial set, gold and enamel on clear, decanter, tray, eight glasses	210.00	235.00	212.00
☐ Cup and saucer, pink, demitasse	55.00	75.00	60.00
☐ Goblet, dolphin stem, yellow eyes, 8″	45.00	60.00	48.00
☐ Pitcher, water, blue enamel, bulbous shape flowers	105.00	125.00	105.00
☐ Plate, pink, gold sprayed, 7½″	28.00	38.00	30.00
☐ Plate, pink, diamond optic, 8½″	20.00	28.00	21.50
☐ Salt, swan, pink, gold trim	22.00	32.00	25.00
☐ Sherbet, green, gold trim	80.00	110.00	88.00
☐ Vase, gold, green and white, 6″	65.00	85.00	70.00
☐ Vase, pale rose bottom, applied green leaves, 9½″	160.00	185.00	162.00
☐ Vase, ruby with applied clear ring, 10½″	95.00	120.00	95.00
☐ Vase, dolphin stem, pale rose, 12″	55.00	75.00	60.00
☐ Vase, pink and gold flowers with green vines, inlaid amethyst	155.00	175.00	155.00
☐ Wine, cherubs and grapevine, cranberry	60.00	80.00	65.00
☐ Wine set, amber decanter, 11″, six wine glasses, 5½″	235.00	285.00	250.00

VERRE DE SOIE

Verre De Soie was manufactured by the Steuben Glass Company under the direction of Frederic Carder during the early 1900's. This iridescent type glass was among the finest glassware produced in America. Production was discontinued in the 1930's.

	Current Price Range		Prior Year Average
☐ **Basket,** blue handle	160.00	185.00	162.00
☐ **Bottle,** cologne, Steuben, 7"	260.00	310.00	275.00
☐ **Box,** powder, sterling lid, engraved flowers	110.00	160.00	125.00
☐ **Candlestick,** stem twisted, pair, 10"	310.00	360.00	325.00
☐ **Compote,** engraved, signed Hawkes, 5" x 8"	260.00	310.00	275.00
☐ **Glass,** portrait, etched, signed Hawkes, 6"	80.00	110.00	88.00
☐ **Goblet,** Steuben	160.00	210.00	175.00
☐ **Pitcher,** 9¾"	235.00	285.00	250.00
☐ **Salt,** pedestal, Steuben	60.00	110.00	75.00
☐ **Sherbet,** with underplate, set of eight	460.00	510.00	475.00
☐ **Sugar and Cream,** engraved, signed Hawkes, set	360.00	410.00	375.00
☐ **Vase,** bulbous base, short neck, 7"	285.00	335.00	300.00
☐ **Vase,** Fleur-de-Lis, Steuben, 3½" x 6"	460.00	510.00	475.00
☐ **Vase,** floral decor with crimped top, 7½"	185.00	210.00	188.00
☐ **Water set,** decanter, lavender orchids, six matching tumblers, 12½"	460.00	560.00	500.00
☐ **Wine,** etched flowers and leaves	110.00	160.00	125.00

CARNIVAL GLASS

The term "Taffeta Glass" was the original name for what is now known as Carnival Glass. Made from 1900 to 1925, this iridescent glass was inexpensively produced in an attempt to imitate more expensive art glass designers, such as Tiffany.

ACORN BURRS — NORTHWOOD

☐ **Berry set,** master bowl and four sauce dishes, purple	260.00	285.00	262.00
☐ **Berry set,** master bowl and six sauce dishes, marigold	160.00	185.00	162.00
☐ **Bowl,** berry, purple, 9½"	100.00	140.00	110.00
☐ **Bowl,** blue	38.00	48.00	40.00
☐ **Bowl,** red	135.00	155.00	140.00
☐ **Butter,** covered, green	185.00	235.00	200.00
☐ **Butter,** covered, purple	235.00	310.00	262.00
☐ **Butter,** covered, marigold	135.00	160.00	138.00
☐ **Creamer and sugar bowl,** marigold	210.00	260.00	225.00
☐ **Pitcher,** water, purple	435.00	510.00	462.00
☐ **Punch bowl** and base, ice green	935.00	1050.00	962.00
☐ **Punch cup,** ice green	50.00	60.00	50.00
☐ **Punch cup,** marigold	28.00	38.00	30.00
☐ **Sauce dish,** purple	16.00	21.00	17.50
☐ **Spooner,** marigold	80.00	120.00	95.00
☐ **Spooner,** purple	110.00	135.00	112.00
☐ **Tumbler,** green	55.00	80.00	62.00
☐ **Water set,** six pieces, green	535.00	585.00	550.00

GLASSWARE / 409

	Current Price Range		Prior Year Average

APPLE BLOSSOM TWIGS
- ☐ **Bowl,** marigold, 6" 16.00 21.00 17.50
- ☐ **Bowl,** frosty white, 6¾" 35.00 50.00 38.00
- ☐ **Bowl,** white, 8" 55.00 80.00 62.00
- ☐ **Bowl,** peach opalescent, 9" 60.00 75.00 62.00
- ☐ **Bowl,** purple, 9" 60.00 75.00 62.00
- ☐ **Creamer and sugar bowl,** marigold 38.00 48.00 40.00
- ☐ **Plate,** cobalt blue, 9" 140.00 165.00 142.00
- ☐ **Plate,** peach opalescent, 9" 125.00 145.00 125.00
- ☐ **Plate,** purple, 9" 185.00 210.00 188.00

BASKET — NORTHWOOD
- ☐ **Aqua** 155.00 185.00 160.00
- ☐ **Aqua Opalescent** 285.00 335.00 300.00
- ☐ **Cobalt Blue** 65.00 90.00 72.00
- ☐ **Green** 80.00 110.00 88.00
- ☐ **Ice Blue** 120.00 160.00 130.00
- ☐ **Ice Green** 110.00 160.00 125.00
- ☐ **Marigold** 45.00 75.00 55.00
- ☐ **Purple** 70.00 100.00 80.00
- ☐ **Teal Blue** 140.00 170.00 145.00
- ☐ **White** 95.00 125.00 100.00

BIRDS AND CHERRIES
- ☐ **Bonbon dish,** marigold 42.00 52.00 45.00
- ☐ **Bonbon dish,** purple 55.00 80.00 62.00
- ☐ **Bonbon dish,** white 65.00 95.00 75.00
- ☐ **Bowl,** purple, 8" 65.00 90.00 72.00
- ☐ **Bowl,** green, 9" 235.00 310.00 262.00
- ☐ **Butter,** covered, clear 65.00 90.00 72.00
- ☐ **Compote,** ice blue 95.00 125.00 100.00
- ☐ **Compote,** marigold 36.00 42.00 37.50
- ☐ **Compote,** purple 48.00 68.00 55.00

BUTTERFLY AND BERRY
- ☐ **Bowl,** deep, marigold, 8" 45.00 65.00 50.00
- ☐ **Bowl,** footed, marigold, 5" 18.00 32.00 22.00
- ☐ **Bowl,** three feet, green, 9¾" 80.00 130.00 100.00
- ☐ **Butter,** covered, blue 160.00 185.00 162.00
- ☐ **Creamer,** covered, marigold 55.00 80.00 62.00
- ☐ **Creamer,** covered, purple 110.00 135.00 112.00
- ☐ **Hatpin holder,** marigold 735.00 1050.00 850.00
- ☐ **Spooner,** marigold 70.00 95.00 82.00
- ☐ **Spooner,** cobalt blue 110.00 135.00 112.00
- ☐ **Sauce dish,** blue 22.00 28.00 22.50
- ☐ **Sugar bowl,** covered, green 110.00 135.00 112.00
- ☐ **Sugar bowl,** covered, marigold 70.00 95.00 82.00
- ☐ **Tumbler,** green 65.00 90.00 72.00
- ☐ **Vase,** marigold, 9" 35.00 50.00 38.00
- ☐ **Vase,** red 260.00 385.00 312.00
- ☐ **Water set,** seven pieces, blue 435.00 510.00 462.00

COIN DOT
- ☐ **Bowl,** blue, 7" 40.00 55.00 42.00
- ☐ **Bowl,** aqua opalescent, 8½" 75.00 110.00 85.00
- ☐ **Bowl,** purple, 8½" 40.00 55.00 42.00
- ☐ **Bowl,** marigold, 9" 35.00 50.00 38.00

410 / GLASSWARE

	Current Price Range		Prior Year Average
☐ Bowl, red	410.00	510.00	450.00
☐ Compote, peach opalescent, 6¾" x 4½"	40.00	55.00	42.00
☐ Pitcher, water, marigold	235.00	310.00	262.00
☐ Rose bowl, green	55.00	80.00	62.00
☐ Rose bowl, purple	55.00	80.00	62.00
☐ Tumbler, blue	120.00	145.00	125.00
☐ Tumbler, marigold	70.00	95.00	77.50
☐ Water set, seven pieces, marigold	385.00	485.00	425.00

GRAPE AND CABLE

☐ Banana boat, blue	235.00	310.00	262.00
☐ Banana boat, ice blue	335.00	410.00	362.00
☐ Banana boat, marigold	135.00	185.00	150.00
☐ Banana boat, purple	160.00	210.00	175.00
☐ Banana boat, white	260.00	310.00	275.00
☐ Berry set, seven pieces, purple	235.00	285.00	250.00
☐ Bonbon, two handled, blue	50.00	65.00	52.00
☐ Bonbon, two handled, ice green	65.00	90.00	72.00
☐ Bonbon, two handled, marigold	35.00	50.00	38.00
☐ Bowl, marigold, 5"	22.00	32.00	25.00
☐ Bowl, red, 5"	210.00	260.00	225.00
☐ Bowl, ice blue, 6½"	65.00	90.00	72.00
☐ Bowl, purple, 7"	45.00	70.00	52.00
☐ Bowl, marigold, 7½"	40.00	55.00	42.00
☐ Bowl, footed, green, 8½"	40.00	55.00	42.00
☐ Bowl, ice cream, amethyst	160.00	235.00	182.00
☐ Bowl, ice cream, white, 11"	210.00	310.00	250.00
☐ Butter, covered, green	185.00	210.00	182.00
☐ Butter, covered, marigold	110.00	135.00	112.00
☐ Butter, covered, purple	160.00	210.00	175.00
☐ Candle lamp, marigold	535.00	585.00	550.00
☐ Candlestick, blue, one	80.00	130.00	100.00
☐ Candlestick, marigold, pair	135.00	185.00	150.00
☐ Card tray, green	80.00	110.00	88.00
☐ Centerpiece bowl, cobalt blue	310.00	360.00	325.00
☐ Centerpiece bowl, ice green	560.00	610.00	575.00
☐ Centerpiece bowl, marigold	260.00	335.00	285.00
☐ Cologne bottle, with stopper, green	160.00	210.00	175.00
☐ Cologne bottle, with stopper, purple	210.00	260.00	225.00
☐ Compote, covered, purple	285.00	360.00	312.00
☐ Compote, open, marigold	335.00	410.00	362.00
☐ Cookie jar, marigold	185.00	210.00	188.00
☐ Cookie jar, white	410.00	460.00	425.00
☐ Creamer, marigold	65.00	90.00	72.00
☐ Creamer, individual size, purple	80.00	110.00	88.00
☐ Creamer and sugar bowl, individual size, green	160.00	185.00	162.00
☐ Cup and saucer, amethyst	80.00	110.00	88.00
☐ Cup and saucer, ice blue	335.00	385.00	350.00
☐ Cup and saucer, purple	185.00	235.00	200.00
☐ Decanter, with stopper, marigold	410.00	460.00	425.00
☐ Decanter, with stopper, purple	710.00	785.00	738.00
☐ Dresser set, six pieces, purple	1050.00	1150.00	1050.00
☐ Dresser set, ice blue	310.00	360.00	325.00
☐ Dresser set, marigold	135.00	160.00	138.00
☐ Dresser tray, marigold	125.00	145.00	125.00
☐ Dresser tray, purple	175.00	210.00	182.00

	Current Price Range		Prior Year Average
☐ **Dresser tray,** white	335.00	385.00	350.00
☐ **Fernery,** amethyst	660.00	810.00	720.00
☐ **Fernery,** marigold	1200.00	1350.00	1225.00
☐ **Fernery,** purple	1000.00	1200.00	1075.00
☐ **Hat,** marigold	32.00	42.00	35.00
☐ **Hat,** ice green	80.00	105.00	85.00
☐ **Hatpin holder,** amethyst	160.00	210.00	175.00
☐ **Hatpin holder,** ice blue	335.00	410.00	362.00
☐ **Hatpin holder,** ice green	710.00	810.00	750.00
☐ **Hatpin holder,** marigold	160.00	210.00	175.00
☐ **Nappy,** handle, marigold	50.00	65.00	52.00
☐ **Nappy,** handle, purple	70.00	95.00	78.00
☐ **Orange bowl,** footed, green	160.00	210.00	175.00
☐ **Orange bowl,** footed, marigold	135.00	160.00	138.00
☐ **Pin tray,** marigold	110.00	135.00	112.00
☐ **Pin tray,** purple	170.00	210.00	180.00
☐ **Pin tray,** white	235.00	285.00	250.00
☐ **Pitcher,** water, purple, 8½″	185.00	235.00	200.00
☐ **Pitcher,** tankard, marigold, 9¾″	435.00	485.00	450.00
☐ **Pitcher,** tankard, purple, 9¾″	635.00	735.00	675.00
☐ **Plate,** footed, green, 9″	75.00	105.00	82.00
☐ **Plate,** footed, ice blue, 9″	95.00	135.00	105.00
☐ **Plate,** hand grip, green, 7½″	65.00	90.00	72.00
☐ **Plate,** marigold, 9½″	62.00	72.00	65.00
☐ **Powder jar,** covered, green	85.00	105.00	90.00
☐ **Powder jar,** covered, purple	65.00	85.00	70.00
☐ **Punch bowl,** base, green, 11″	410.00	460.00	425.00
☐ **Punch bowl,** base, white, 11″	835.00	885.00	850.00
☐ **Punch bowl,** base, marigold, 14″	535.00	585.00	550.00
☐ **Punch bowl,** base, purple, 17″	1650.00	1750.00	1650.00
☐ **Punch cup,** amethyst	22.00	32.00	25.00
☐ **Punch cup,** aqua opalescent	210.00	260.00	225.00
☐ **Punch cup,** green	28.00	38.00	30.00
☐ **Punch cup,** ice green	60.00	80.00	65.00
☐ **Punch cup,** purple	22.00	32.00	25.00
☐ **Punch cup,** white	55.00	80.00	62.00
☐ **Punch set,** base and six cups, green, bowl, 14″	660.00	710.00	675.00
☐ **Punch set,** base and eight cups, marigold, bowl, 14″	635.00	685.00	650.00
☐ **Sauce dish,** ice blue	60.00	80.00	65.00
☐ **Sauce dish,** white	50.00	65.00	52.00
☐ **Spooner,** marigold	65.00	90.00	72.00
☐ **Spooner,** purple	110.00	135.00	112.00
☐ **Sugar bowl,** covered plate	170.00	190.00	170.00
☐ **Sugar bowl,** individual size, marigold	75.00	100.00	82.00
☐ **Sweetmeat jar,** covered, marigold	560.00	660.00	600.00
☐ **Sweetmeat jar,** covered, purple	235.00	285.00	250.00
☐ **Tobacco humidor,** marigold	185.00	235.00	200.00
☐ **Tobacco humidor,** purple	335.00	410.00	362.00
☐ **Tumbler,** six pieces, marigold	135.00	185.00	150.00
☐ **Tumbler,** six pieces, purple	185.00	235.00	200.00

GRAPE AND GOTHIC ARCHES

☐ **Berry set,** seven pieces, blue	160.00	210.00	175.00
☐ **Bowl,** large, green	55.00	75.00	60.00
☐ **Bowl,** large, marigold	50.00	65.00	52.00

412 / GLASSWARE

	Current Price Range		Prior Year Average
☐ Bowl, small, green	28.00	38.00	30.00
☐ Bowl, small, marigold	22.00	32.00	25.00
☐ Butter, covered, marigold	85.00	105.00	90.00
☐ Creamer, blue	45.00	85.00	60.00
☐ Creamer and sugar bowl, marigold	80.00	110.00	88.00
☐ Pitcher, water, blue	235.00	310.00	262.00
☐ Spooner, marigold	45.00	70.00	52.00
☐ Sugar bowl, covered, blue	45.00	85.00	60.00
☐ Table set, four pieces, blue	360.00	385.00	362.00
☐ Tumbler, blue	40.00	55.00	42.00
☐ Tumbler, green	35.00	50.00	38.00
☐ Water set, seven pieces, blue	360.00	410.00	375.00

MAPLE LEAF

☐ Berry set, seven pieces, marigold	55.00	90.00	68.00
☐ Bowl, berry, footed, marigold	32.00	42.00	35.00
☐ Bowl, berry, footed, purple	38.00	48.00	40.00
☐ Bowl, large, footed, marigold	65.00	90.00	72.00
☐ Bowl, large, footed, purple	110.00	135.00	112.00
☐ Butter, covered, blue	120.00	150.00	125.00
☐ Butter, covered, marigold	90.00	115.00	105.00
☐ Creamer, marigold	50.00	65.00	52.00
☐ Creamer, purple	60.00	75.00	62.00
☐ Dish, ice cream, marigold, 4"	16.00	21.00	17.50
☐ Pitcher, water, blue	135.00	185.00	150.00
☐ Pitcher, water, marigold	135.00	185.00	150.00
☐ Pitcher, water, purple	235.00	285.00	250.00
☐ Sauce dish, blue	28.00	38.00	30.00
☐ Spooner, blue	55.00	80.00	62.00
☐ Spooner, marigold	42.00	52.00	45.00
☐ Sugar bowl, covered, green	70.00	85.00	72.00
☐ Sugar bowl, covered, purple	55.00	70.00	58.00
☐ Table set, four pieces, purple	250.00	280.00	255.00
☐ Tumbler, blue	65.00	90.00	72.00
☐ Tumbler, purple	45.00	60.00	48.00
☐ Water set, seven pieces, purple	410.00	485.00	438.00

ORIENTAL POPPY

☐ Pitcher, water, green	435.00	485.00	450.00
☐ Pitcher, water, purple	660.00	710.00	675.00
☐ Pitcher, water, white	485.00	560.00	512.00
☐ Tumbler, green	55.00	65.00	55.00
☐ Tumbler, ice blue	135.00	160.00	138.00
☐ Tumbler, ice green	190.00	210.00	190.00
☐ Tumbler, marigold	32.00	42.00	35.00
☐ Tumbler, white	90.00	105.00	90.00
☐ Water set, five pieces, white	860.00	910.00	875.00
☐ Water set, seven pieces, blue	1400.00	1500.00	1400.00
☐ Water set, seven pieces, ice blue	585.00	660.00	612.00
☐ Water set, seven pieces, purple	785.00	835.00	800.00

RASPBERRY

☐ Bowl, green, 5"	32.00	42.00	35.00
☐ Bowl, marigold, 9"	45.00	60.00	48.00
☐ Bowl, purple, 9"	60.00	75.00	62.00
☐ Compote, blue	58.00	68.00	60.00
☐ Pitcher, milk, ice blue	885.00	935.00	900.00

April, artist: Rudy Escalera, producer: Hackett American Collectors . . . . . .
. . . . $40.00 $45.00

Daisy Dreamer, artist: Frances Hook, producer: Roman $22.50 $27.50

1942 Ford Deluxe Woodie Station Wagon
$2100-6400-13400
Photographer Bob Lichty, courtesy OLD CARS Weekly

Forehand & Wadsworth, British Bulldog, .38 S & W, 6 shot, double action, solid frame, antique . . . . . . **$55.00 - 95.00**

Kolb, Henry M., Baby Hammerless, .22 short R.F., folding trigger, nickel plated, round butt, curio . . . . . **$90.00 - 150.00**

Red Jacket, .32 Short R.F., 5 shot, single action, solid frame, spur trigger, antique **$95.00 - 165.00**

Kolb, Henry M, Baby Hammerless, .22 short R.F., folding trigger, nickel plated, square butt, curio . . . . . **$90.00 - 150.00**

Wandering Minsteral, HN1224..$1350.00-1500.00

Sunshine Girl HN1344..........$1400.00-1500.00

Regent, Ansonia, Syrian bronze gilt finish, cathedral gong, half hour strike, height 20½", dial 5", 8 day. **$1050.00-1250.00**

Apex, Crystal Regulator, Ansonia, visible escapement, white beveled plate glass, 4" porcelain dial, c. 1920 completely restored, 18½" x 10½", 8 day, spring, hour and half hour gong strike. **$2350.00-2500.00**

Roseville Pottery *(top to bottom)*, Row #1, "Blended" 21½" Umbrella Stand, *early 1900's*, $290.00-$325.00; "Blended" 24" Umbrella Stand, *early 1900's*, $375.00-$400.00; Row #2, "Gardinia" Vase, *c. 1940*, $85.00-$100.00; "Dogwood II" 12" Jardiniere, *c. 1918*, $150.00-$175.00; Row #3, "Freesia" Cookie Jar, *c. 1945*, $110.00-$125.00.

SUPERMAN • BATMAN AND **ROBIN**
RED, WHITE AND **BLUE • ZATARA**

© 1941, 1968 DC Comics Inc.
WORLD'S BEST *(#1)* . . . . $360.00 - 1000.00

LOG CABIN EXTRACT. *Medicine, amber, 8"* 100.00   125.00

GLASSWARE / 413

	Current Price Range		Prior Year Average
☐ **Pitcher,** milk, marigold	85.00	135.00	102.00
☐ **Pitcher,** milk, purple	160.00	185.00	162.00
☐ **Pitcher,** water, green	185.00	235.00	200.00
☐ **Pitcher,** water, purple	160.00	210.00	175.00
☐ **Sauce boat,** green	90.00	120.00	100.00
☐ **Sauce boat,** marigold	70.00	85.00	72.00
☐ **Sauce boat,** peach opalescent	100.00	135.00	110.00
☐ **Tumbler,** ice blue	140.00	170.00	145.00
☐ **Tumbler,** ice green	485.00	535.00	500.00
☐ **Tumbler,** marigold	32.00	42.00	35.00
☐ **Tumbler,** purple	45.00	60.00	48.00
☐ **Water set,** seven pieces, green	460.00	435.00	480.00
☐ **Water set,** seven pieces, purple	485.00	560.00	512.00

STAG AND HOLLY

☐ **Bowl,** footed, blue, 7"	55.00	70.00	58.00
☐ **Bowl,** footed, green, 8"	70.00	85.00	72.00
☐ **Bowl,** footed, purple, 8"	70.00	85.00	72.00
☐ **Bowl,** footed, marigold, 9"	55.00	70.00	58.00
☐ **Bowl,** blue, 10"	235.00	260.00	238.00
☐ **Bowl,** purple, 10½"	160.00	185.00	162.00
☐ **Bowl,** three feet, aqua, 11"	235.00	285.00	250.00
☐ **Bowl,** nut, marigold	28.00	38.00	30.00
☐ **Plate,** footed, marigold, 9"	160.00	185.00	162.00
☐ **Plate,** footed, marigold, 13"	235.00	285.00	250.00
☐ **Rose bowl,** footed, green	185.00	235.00	200.00
☐ **Rose bowl,** footed, marigold	160.00	185.00	162.00
☐ **Wine,** marigold	22.00	32.00	25.00

STRAWBERRY

☐ **Berry set,** seven pieces, purple	135.00	160.00	138.00
☐ **Bonbon,** two handles, blue	50.00	65.00	52.00
☐ **Bowl,** marigold, 8"	135.00	160.00	138.00
☐ **Bowl,** purple, 8½"	60.00	75.00	62.00
☐ **Bowl,** green, 9"	65.00	80.00	68.00
☐ **Bowl,** fluted, white, 10"	80.00	110.00	88.00
☐ **Epergne,** purple	70.00	85.00	72.00
☐ **Nappy,** two handles, red	285.00	310.00	288.00
☐ **Plate,** hand grip, marigold, 6"	55.00	70.00	58.00
☐ **Plate,** hand grip, green, 7½"	80.00	110.00	88.00
☐ **Plate,** marigold, 9"	65.00	90.00	72.00
☐ **Plate,** purple, 9"	80.00	110.00	88.00
☐ **Powder jar,** covered, green	80.00	110.00	88.00

THREE FRUITS

☐ **Berry set,** seven pieces	185.00	210.00	188.00
☐ **Bonbon,** pedestal, aqua opalescent	210.00	235.00	212.00
☐ **Bonbon,** pedestal, blue	45.00	70.00	52.00
☐ **Bonbon,** pedestal, white	60.00	75.00	62.00
☐ **Bowl,** marigold, 7"	40.00	55.00	42.00
☐ **Bowl,** green, 7½"	40.00	55.00	42.00
☐ **Bowl,** purple, 8½"	50.00	65.00	52.00
☐ **Bowl,** white, 8½"	65.00	80.00	72.00
☐ **Bowl,** fluted, purple, 9"	75.00	100.00	88.00
☐ **Bowl,** aqua opalescent, 9"	260.00	335.00	280.00
☐ **Bowl,** green, 9"	45.00	60.00	48.00
☐ **Bowl,** marigold, 9"	30.00	45.00	32.00

414 / GLASSWARE

	Current Price Range	Prior Year Average
☐ Bowl, dome footed, white, 9"	80.00 95.00	82.00
☐ Bowl, purple, 10"	90.00 110.00	92.00
☐ Card tray, green, hand grip, 7½"	70.00 85.00	72.00
☐ Plate, amethyst, 9"	80.00 110.00	88.00
☐ Plate, aqua opalescent, 9"	335.00 385.00	350.00
☐ Plate, green, 9"	80.00 110.00	88.00
☐ Plate, ice blue	485.00 535.00	500.00
☐ Plate, marigold, 9"	70.00 85.00	72.00
☐ Plate, purple, 9"	75.00 90.00	78.00

VINEYARD

☐ Bowl, purple	45.00 60.00	48.00
☐ Pitcher, water, marigold	55.00 80.00	62.00
☐ Pitcher, water, peach opalescent	435.00 485.00	450.00
☐ Pitcher, water, purple	260.00 310.00	275.00
☐ Tumbler, green	40.00 55.00	42.00
☐ Tumbler, marigold	18.00 28.00	20.00
☐ Tumbler, white	135.00 160.00	138.00
☐ Water set, five pieces, marigold	160.00 210.00	175.00
☐ Water set, seven pieces, purple	385.00 460.00	412.00

WINDMILL MEDALLION

☐ Bowl, marigold, 7"	22.00 32.00	25.00
☐ Bowl, footed, marigold, 9"	32.00 42.00	35.00
☐ Bowl, ruffled, marigold, 8"	38.00 48.00	40.00
☐ Bowl, white, 7½"	48.00 58.00	50.00
☐ Dresser tray, oval, green	135.00 160.00	138.00
☐ Pickle dish, marigold	18.00 28.00	20.00
☐ Pitcher, milk, purple	210.00 235.00	212.00
☐ Tumbler, marigold	22.00 32.00	25.00
☐ Tumbler, purple	50.00 65.00	52.00
☐ Water set, five pieces, marigold	110.00 160.00	125.00
☐ Water set, seven pieces, purple	385.00 460.00	412.00

WINE AND ROSES

☐ Pitcher, marigold	160.00 210.00	175.00
☐ Water set, six pieces, marigold	285.00 335.00	300.00
☐ Wine, blue	50.00 65.00	52.00
☐ Wine, marigold	38.00 48.00	40.00

ZIGZAG

☐ Bowl, marigold, 9¼"	65.00 90.00	72.00
☐ Bowl, ruffled rim, purple, 10"	80.00 100.00	88.00
☐ Pitcher, water, blue with enamel decor	160.00 235.00	188.00
☐ Pitcher, water, ice green with enamel decor .	285.00 335.00	300.00
☐ Pitcher, water, white with enamel decor	185.00 260.00	212.00
☐ Tumbler, ice green with enamel decor	65.00 90.00	72.00
☐ Tumbler, purple with enamel decor	45.00 60.00	48.00

CUSTARD GLASS

Custard glass was named for its similarity to the color of baked custard. Most major glass companies produced over twenty patterns. Some were decorated with gold enamel or painted on some part of the embossed design.

☐ Banana dish, Chrysanthemum Sprig	260.00 285.00	262.00
☐ Banana dish, Louis XV	160.00 175.00	158.00

GLASSWARE / 415

	Current Price Range		Prior Year Average
☐ **Banana dish,** oval, 10″	210.00	235.00	212.00
☐ **Bonbon,** Winged Scroll	42.00	52.00	45.00
☐ **Berry bowl,** Diamond Peg	42.00	52.00	45.00
☐ **Berry bowl,** Fan and Feather	48.00	58.00	50.00
☐ **Berry bowl,** Grape	48.00	58.00	47.50
☐ **Berry bowl,** Winged Scroll	47.00	52.00	47.50
☐ **Berry bowl,** Victoria	52.00	62.00	55.00
☐ **Berry bowl,** master, Argonaut Shell	210.00	250.00	220.00
☐ **Berry bowl,** master, Beaded Circle	185.00	205.00	185.00
☐ **Berry bowl,** master, Chrysanthemum Sprig	160.00	205.00	172.00
☐ **Berry bowl,** master, Everglades	210.00	245.00	218.00
☐ **Berry bowl,** master, Grape	180.00	195.00	178.00
☐ **Butter,** covered, Cherry and Scale	235.00	285.00	250.00
☐ **Butter,** covered, Chrysanthemum Sprig	220.00	260.00	230.00
☐ **Butter,** covered, Geneva	145.00	170.00	150.00
☐ **Butter,** covered, Grape and Gothic Arches	175.00	190.00	172.00
☐ **Butter,** covered, Intaglio	220.00	250.00	225.00
☐ **Butter,** covered, Louis XV	175.00	195.00	185.00
☐ **Butter,** covered, Vermont	180.00	200.00	180.00
☐ **Celery,** Chrysanthemum Sprig	260.00	310.00	275.00
☐ **Celery,** Victoria	190.00	235.00	112.00
☐ **Celery,** Winged Scroll	210.00	285.00	238.00
☐ **Compote,** Argonaut Shell	95.00	110.00	95.00
☐ **Compote,** Chrysanthemum Sprig	105.00	125.00	105.00
☐ **Compote,** Geneva	75.00	95.00	80.00
☐ **Compote,** Intaglio	85.00	105.00	90.00
☐ **Compote,** Ring Band	140.00	160.00	140.00
☐ **Creamer,** Chrysanthemum Sprig	100.00	120.00	100.00
☐ **Creamer,** Everglades	105.00	120.00	102.00
☐ **Creamer,** Grape	85.00	100.00	88.00
☐ **Creamer,** Grape and Gothic Arches	70.00	90.00	75.00
☐ **Creamer,** Heart with Thumbprint	90.00	110.00	92.00
☐ **Creamer,** Inverted Fan and Feather	95.00	115.00	100.00
☐ **Creamer,** Maple Leaf	95.00	130.00	107.00
☐ **Creamer,** souvenir, Diamond Peg	48.00	58.00	50.00
☐ **Cruet,** Chrysanthemum Sprig	185.00	210.00	188.00
☐ **Cruet,** Intaglio	200.00	220.00	200.00
☐ **Cruet,** Louis XV	170.00	210.00	175.00
☐ **Cruet,** Ring Band	185.00	210.00	188.00
☐ **Goblet,** Beaded Swag	70.00	95.00	78.00
☐ **Goblet,** Grape and Gothic Arches	55.00	70.00	58.00
☐ **Mug,** Chrysanthemum Sprig	38.00	42.00	37.50
☐ **Mug,** Geneva	55.00	70.00	58.00
☐ **Mug,** Shield	22.00	28.00	22.50
☐ **Pitcher,** Argonaut Shell	260.00	285.00	262.00
☐ **Pitcher,** Everglades	335.00	385.00	350.00
☐ **Pitcher,** Inverted Fan and Feather	310.00	360.00	325.00
☐ **Pitcher,** Maple Leaf	235.00	260.00	238.00
☐ **Pitcher,** Ring Band	210.00	245.00	218.00
☐ **Pitcher,** Vermont	210.00	245.00	218.00
☐ **Salt and pepper,** Argonaut Shell	310.00	360.00	325.00
☐ **Salt and pepper,** Chrysanthemum Sprig	260.00	310.00	275.00
☐ **Salt and pepper,** Everglades	210.00	235.00	212.00
☐ **Salt and pepper,** Intaglio	135.00	160.00	138.00
☐ **Salt and pepper,** Louis XV	145.00	170.00	150.00
☐ **Sauce dish,** Beaded Swag	48.00	58.00	50.00

416 / GLASSWARE

	Current Price Range	Prior Year Average
☐ Sauce dish, Chrysanthemum Sprig	80.00 100.00	85.00
☐ Sauce dish, Diamond Peg	80.00 95.00	82.00
☐ Spooner, Argonaut Shell	110.00 135.00	112.00
☐ Spooner, Chrysanthemum Sprig	110.00 135.00	112.00
☐ Spooner, Diamond Peg	80.00 95.00	82.00
☐ Spooner, Grape and Gothic Arches	65.00 80.00	68.00
☐ Spooner, Louis XV	85.00 100.00	88.00
☐ Sugar, covered, Argonaut Shell	140.00 165.00	142.00
☐ Sugar, covered, Beaded Circle	160.00 180.00	160.00
☐ Sugar, covered, Geneva	100.00 120.00	100.00
☐ Sugar, covered, Intaglio	130.00 160.00	135.00
☐ Sugar, covered, Louis XV	120.00 140.00	120.00
☐ Sugar, covered, Vermont	100.00 125.00	107.00
☐ Sugar, covered, Victoria	100.00 140.00	110.00
☐ Sugar, covered, Winged Scroll	90.00 110.00	92.00
☐ Toothpick holder, Diamond Peg	45.00 65.00	50.00
☐ Toothpick holder, Geneva	70.00 85.00	78.00
☐ Toothpick holder, Ring Band	58.00 68.00	60.00
☐ Toothpick holder, Vermont	65.00 80.00	68.00
☐ Tumbler, Argonaut, Shell	75.00 90.00	78.00
☐ Tumbler, Cherry and Scale	42.00 52.00	45.00
☐ Tumbler, Chrysanthemum Sprig	55.00 70.00	58.00
☐ Tumbler, Diamond Peg	40.00 55.00	42.00
☐ Tumbler, Grape and Gothic Arches	45.00 60.00	48.00
☐ Tumbler, Intaglio	58.00 68.00	60.00
☐ Tumbler, Louis XV	55.00 65.00	60.00
☐ Tumbler, Winged Scroll	50.00 65.00	52.00
☐ Vase, bud, souvenir	28.00 32.00	27.50
☐ Vase, Vermont	65.00 80.00	68.00
☐ Vase, Winged Scroll	70.00 90.00	75.00

CUT GLASS

Cut glass is deeply cut on a wheel in all over patterns. The edges are very sharp, thus allowing light to be refracted easily. Its high lead content makes it heavier than most blown glass. It also has a distinct bell tone when struck.

Most collectors seek pieces made from 1871 to 1905 during the "Brilliant Period." Cut glass was made in many factories such as Hawkes, Libbey and Dorflinger, some of which marked their pieces with a trademark.

☐ Ashtray, rectangular	55.00 80.00	62.00
☐ Ashtry, richly cut, signed	80.00 110.00	88.00
☐ Basket, floral design, handle, 10″	210.00 260.00	225.00
☐ Basket, scalloped edge, handle, 6″	160.00 210.00	175.00
☐ Basket, floral and miter cut, twisted handle, 8″	170.00 195.00	172.00
☐ Bell, diamond and fan	110.00 135.00	112.00
☐ Bell, star design	135.00 160.00	138.00
☐ Bonbon, diamond shape, 6″	70.00 95.00	78.00
☐ Bonbon, heart shape, 6″	80.00 110.00	88.00
☐ Bonbon, oval, 5¼″	28.00 38.00	30.00
☐ Bonbon, pedestal, pair	460.00 510.00	475.00
☐ Bonbon, Plymouth, 5″	50.00 65.00	52.00
☐ Bonbon, Royal, square	80.00 110.00	88.00
☐ Bonbon, scalloped edge	38.00 48.00	40.00
☐ Bottle, bitters, silver plate stopper	160.00 185.00	162.00
☐ Bottle, cologne, butterfly design, 8 oz.	80.00 110.00	88.00

GLASSWARE / 417

	Current Price Range	Prior Year Average
☐ **Bottle,** cologne, diamond and fan, 4 oz.	50.00　65.00	52.00
☐ **Bottle,** cologne, globe shape, pinwheel, 2 oz.	38.00　48.00	40.00
☐ **Bottle,** cologne, hobstar, 6 oz.	28.00　38.00	30.00
☐ **Bottle,** cordial, bell shape, pinwheel stopper	110.00　135.00	112.00
☐ **Bottle,** dresser, Middlesex, signed Hawkes	80.00　110.00	88.00
☐ **Bottle,** whiskey, strawberry, diamond and fan, cut stopper, 9½″	70.00　100.00	80.00
☐ **Bottle,** whiskey, blue to clear, bull's eye, notched prism	460.00　510.00	475.00
☐ **Bowl,** diamond and fan, footed, 8″	135.00　160.00	138.00
☐ **Bowl,** fern, metal liner, floral design, 9″	80.00　110.00	88.00
☐ **Bowl,** finger with underplate, rayed star	40.00　55.00	42.00
☐ **Bowl,** floral and star design, 8″	105.00　125.00	105.00
☐ **Bowl,** floral design, three feet, 6″	80.00　110.00	88.00
☐ **Bowl,** fruit, pinwheel and feathered fan c. 1900's	210.00　260.00	225.00
☐ **Bowl,** Harvard 8″	135.00　160.00	138.00
☐ **Bowl,** hobnail, 9″	160.00　210.00	175.00
☐ **Bowl,** hobstar and fan, Hawkes, 8″	160.00　185.00	162.00
☐ **Bowl,** hobstar and strawberry	185.00　235.00	200.00
☐ **Bowl,** heavily cut, signed Libbey	260.00　310.00	275.00
☐ **Bowl,** hobstar, large with stand, 14″	660.00　860.00	750.00
☐ **Bowl,** Middlesex, 10″	210.00　260.00	225.00
☐ **Bowl,** oval, richly cut	185.00　235.00	200.00
☐ **Bowl,** oval, French, c. 1890	310.00　360.00	325.00
☐ **Bowl,** pinwheel, 8″	50.00　65.00	52.00
☐ **Box,** Art Nouveau brass and leather trim	460.00　535.00	482.00
☐ **Box,** cigarette, ashtray lid	80.00　110.00	88.00
☐ **Box,** dresser, Harvard, intaglio corn flower	70.00　95.00	78.00
☐ **Box,** dresser, Russian, cut buttons on lid, three applied feet, 5½″ x 3½″	185.00　235.00	200.00
☐ **Box,** hairpin, sterling silver cover	70.00　95.00	78.00
☐ **Box,** jewelry, floral design	65.00　90.00	72.00
☐ **Box,** jewelry, Florence, sterling silver rims, 6½″ x 3	260.00　310.00	275.00
☐ **Box,** jewelry, hobstar on cover, cut base, 5¾″ ...	160.00　185.00	162.00
☐ **Box,** powder, diamond and star, hinged, 6″	185.00　210.00	188.00
☐ **Box,** powder, hobstar, 4½″	70.00　95.00	78.00
☐ **Box,** powder, signed Hawkes	260.00　310.00	275.00
☐ **Bracelet,** heart locket	460.00　535.00	480.00
☐ **Butter,** covered, American crystal, c. 1900's	285.00　385.00	325.00
☐ **Butter,** covered, English, c. 1900's	160.00　235.00	180.00
☐ **Butter,** dome cover, diamond and fan, 5″	310.00　360.00	325.00
☐ **Butter,** dome cover, pinwheel	335.00　385.00	350.00
☐ **Candelabra,** Art Deco, four branch glass	235.00　285.00	250.00
☐ **Candelabra,** rayed star, three branch glass	335.00　385.00	350.00
☐ **Candlestick,** panels, bull's eye, pair, 10½″	210.00　260.00	225.00
☐ **Candlestick,** prism cut, hobstar, 10″	110.00　135.00	112.00
☐ **Candlestick,** strawberry and diamond, rayed star base, pair, 9″	185.00　235.00	200.00
☐ **Candy dish,** English, c. 1890's	135.00　160.00	138.00
☐ **Candy dish,** American, Clarke	90.00　140.00	110.00
☐ **Candy dish,** sterling and crystal, Hawkes	160.00　210.00	175.00
☐ **Carafe,** block and fan	32.00　42.00	35.00
☐ **Carafe,** diamond and strawberry	185.00　210.00	188.00
☐ **Carafe,** hobstar and clover	55.00　80.00	62.00
☐ **Carafe,** prism and fan	80.00　110.00	88.00

418 / GLASSWARE

	Current Price Range		Prior Year Average
☐ **Carafe**, Russian, starred buttons	235.00	335.00	275.00
☐ **Carafe**, water, Harvard, prism stem	110.00	135.00	112.00
☐ **Carafe**, water, hobstar and notched prism	80.00	110.00	88.00
☐ **Carafe**, water, pinwheel, crosscut diamond and flasked fan	90.00	120.00	98.00
☐ **Carafe**, water, pinwheel cut flowers	80.00	110.00	88.00
☐ **Carafe**, wine, hobstar and fan, sterling collar ...	135.00	160.00	138.00
☐ **Celery**, Harvard, Libbey	260.00	310.00	275.00
☐ **Celery**, hobstar and fan, signed Hawkes	135.00	160.00	138.00
☐ **Celery**, strawberry, diamond and fan, Hawkes ...	185.00	210.00	188.00
☐ **Champagne**, Russian, rayed star base	80.00	110.00	88.00
☐ **Compote**, Harvard, hobstar base, intaglio cut, 9″	310.00	360.00	325.00
☐ **Compote**, hobstar, strawberry, diamond and fan, 8″	360.00	410.00	375.00
☐ **Compote**, pinwheel, hobstar, prism cut, 7½ ″ ...	135.00	160.00	138.00
☐ **Compote**, square, signed Hoare	510.00	585.00	538.00
☐ **Cordial**, crystal and silver, pair	760.00	835.00	780.00
☐ **Cordial**, Russian	80.00	110.00	88.00
☐ **Cordial**, sterling, blown glass	135.00	185.00	150.00
☐ **Creamer**, hobstar	80.00	95.00	82.00
☐ **Creamer**, pinwheel	55.00	70.00	58.00
☐ **Creamer**, Waterford, c. 1930's	45.00	65.00	50.00
☐ **Cruet**, Harvard, signed Hoare	160.00	185.00	162.00
☐ **Cruet**, Middlesex	75.00	95.00	80.00
☐ **Cruet**, prism, signed Libbey	155.00	175.00	155.00
☐ **Cruet**, pyramid shape, 7½ ″	55.00	80.00	62.00
☐ **Decanter**, Art Deco, pressed pattern of Chrysler Building	110.00	160.00	125.00
☐ **Decanter**, Harvard, 8″	95.00	140.00	110.00
☐ **Decanter**, hobstar, diamond and fan, cut stopper	160.00	185.00	162.00
☐ **Decanter**, original stopper, numbered	185.00	210.00	188.00
☐ **Decanter**, pineapple cut	110.00	135.00	112.00
☐ **Decanter**, pineapple fan, brilliant cut	80.00	130.00	100.00
☐ **Decanter**, pinwheel	185.00	210.00	188.00
☐ **Dish**, cheese and cracker, signed Hoare	310.00	410.00	350.00
☐ **Dish**, cheese and cracker, hobstar, strawberry and diamond	100.00	125.00	105.00
☐ **Dish**, cheese, pinwheel	285.00	335.00	300.00
☐ **Dish**, cheese, diamond and fan, covered	385.00	460.00	412.00
☐ **Dish**, ice cream, hobstar	385.00	435.00	400.00
☐ **Dish**, lemon, signed Hawkes	40.00	55.00	42.00
☐ **Dish**, nut, signed Libbey, pair	285.00	335.00	300.00
☐ **Dish**, olive, hobstar and comet	40.00	55.00	42.00
☐ **Dish**, shell, signed Hoare	110.00	135.00	112.00
☐ **Dish**, signed Omega	50.00	65.00	52.00
☐ **Dish**, square, Imperial, signed Libbey	185.00	235.00	200.00
☐ **Dish**, four sections, strawberry, and diamond point	160.00	210.00	175.00
☐ **Dish**, condiment, heavily cut, c. 1900's	135.00	185.00	150.00
☐ **Dish**, pedestal	285.00	335.00	300.00
☐ **Glass**, etched, signed Libbey, pair	110.00	160.00	125.00
☐ **Glass**, magnifying, Art Nouveau, sterling	135.00	185.00	150.00
☐ **Glass**, magnifying, ivory handles	1250.00	1450.00	1300.00
☐ **Glass**, magnifying, mother-of-pearl	135.00	185.00	150.00
☐ **Goblet**, panel, prism cut	55.00	80.00	62.00
☐ **Goblet**, prism cut, signed Hawkes	60.00	85.00	68.00

GLASSWARE / 419

	Current Price Range	Prior Year Average
☐ Goblet, Russian	110.00 135.00	112.00
☐ Goblet, spiral pinwheel	40.00 55.00	42.00
☐ Goblet, Vintage	55.00 80.00	62.00
☐ Inkwell, crystal	235.00 310.00	262.00
☐ Inkwell, silver and crystal	535.00 610.00	562.00
☐ Inkwell, sterling lid, 2″	40.00 55.00	42.00
☐ Jar, Art Nouveau, sterling lid	45.00 65.00	50.00
☐ Jar, candy, Hawkes, 11″	210.00 260.00	225.00
☐ Jar, mustard, signed Webb	55.00 80.00	62.00
☐ Jar, powder, Art Nouveau, hobstar and fan	110.00 135.00	112.00
☐ Jar, powder, Reine Des Fleurs	80.00 110.00	88.00
☐ Jar, powder, sterling lid, 3″ x 3″	80.00 110.00	88.00
☐ Jar, tobacco, sterling top, 7″	135.00 160.00	138.00
☐ Jug, whiskey, Clarke	285.00 335.00	300.00
☐ Knife rest, c. 1920's	22.00 32.00	25.00
☐ Knife rest, ball ends, diamond cut	28.00 38.00	30.00
☐ Knife rest, signed Hawkes	45.00 65.00	50.00
☐ Lamp, diamond cut, 17″	385.00 485.00	425.00
☐ Lamp, table, mushroom shade, 18″	485.00 585.00	525.00
☐ Matchstrikes, antique, pair	210.00 260.00	225.00
☐ Muffineer, sterling, cone shaped	80.00 130.00	100.00
☐ Nappy, hobstar and fan, signed Clarke	65.00 80.00	68.00
☐ Nappy, pinwheel	50.00 65.00	52.00
☐ Nappy, strawberry and diamond	45.00 60.00	48.00
☐ Pitcher, cider, prism and bull's eye, hobstar base, 8″	160.00 185.00	162.00
☐ Pitcher, claret, Encore by Strauss, 12″	260.00 310.00	275.00
☐ Pitcher, Harvard, signed Libbey, 8″	160.00 210.00	175.00
☐ Pitcher, hobstar and fan, 8″	160.00 210.00	175.00
☐ Pitcher, milk, Russian, starred buttons, 5″	360.00 435.00	380.00
☐ Pitcher, milk, deep cutting, twelve point star base, signed Hawkes, 5½″	185.00 235.00	200.00
☐ Pitcher, pinwheel, strawberry and diamond, 9″ ..	135.00 160.00	138.00
☐ Pitcher, tankard, Florence, hobstar base, 11″ ...	235.00 270.00	242.00
☐ Pitcher, tankard, hobstar, strawberry, diamond and fan, 16 point base, 11½″	185.00 210.00	188.00
☐ Pitcher, tankard, pinwheel	210.00 260.00	225.00
☐ Pitcher, water, daisy, button and pinwheel, 9″ ...	160.00 185.00	162.00
☐ Pitcher, water, Harvard, double faceted, handle .	210.00 260.00	225.00
☐ Pitcher, water, Irving's white rose, 9″	185.00 235.00	200.00
☐ Pitcher, water, Maple City Glass Co., signed	185.00 235.00	200.00
☐ Pitcher, water, Millicent, signed Hawkes, 8½″ ..	185.00 235.00	200.00
☐ Plate, floral design, signed Hawkes, 7″	135.00 160.00	138.00
☐ Plate, Harvard, signed Liberty, 12″	260.00 310.00	275.00
☐ Plate, hobstar center, signed Hawkes, 6½″	55.00 80.00	62.00
☐ Plate, hobstar, signed Hoare, 7″	110.00 135.00	112.00
☐ Plate, Hunt's Royal, 7″	55.00 85.00	62.00
☐ Plate, Middlesex, 6½″	55.00 85.00	62.00
☐ Plate, Russian, square, 7″	135.00 185.00	150.00
☐ Plate, twelve panels, frosted stars and hobstars, 10″	195.00 220.00	198.00
☐ Platter, ice cream, hobster, 17″	435.00 510.00	462.00
☐ Platter, ice cream, oval, Russian	310.00 370.00	330.00
☐ Punch bowl, two pieces, flower with star, box pattern	1250.00 1450.00	1300.00
☐ Punch bowl, two pieces, signed Tuthill, 10½″ ...	660.00 760.00	700.00

420 / GLASSWARE

	Current Price Range	Prior Year Average
☐ **Relish dish**, Harvard	95.00 125.00	100.00
☐ **Relish dish**, hobstar, strawberry and diamond, 11½"	185.00 235.00	200.00
☐ **Relish dish**, Royal, 7"	95.00 125.00	100.00
☐ **Rose bowl**, Harvard, signed Libbey	310.00 360.00	325.00
☐ **Rose bowl**, hobstar and fan, footed, 4"	185.00 235.00	200.00
☐ **Rose bowl**, hobstar, diamond and fan	210.00 260.00	225.00
☐ **Salt and pepper shakers**, 6"	25.00 35.00	30.00
☐ **Stickpin**, antique cameo	160.00 185.00	162.00
☐ **Stickpin**, cameo	145.00 185.00	155.00
☐ **Stickpin**, horseshoe	80.00 110.00	88.00
☐ **Stickpin**, opal	100.00 130.00	110.00
☐ **Sugar**, Harvard, fan, rayed star	45.00 60.00	48.00
☐ **Sugar**, hobstar and pinwheel	45.00 60.00	48.00
☐ **Sugar**, signed Hoare	85.00 115.00	95.00
☐ **Syrup**, silver plate, strawberry, diamond and fan	70.00 95.00	78.00
☐ **Syrup**, sterling, Hawkes	160.00 210.00	175.00
☐ **Toothpick holder**, diamond and fan	55.00 80.00	62.00
☐ **Toothpick holder**, pinwheel	40.00 60.00	45.00
☐ **Tray**, bread, cane, intaglio florals	80.00 100.00	88.00
☐ **Tray**, card, Russian, starred buttons	75.00 95.00	80.00
☐ **Tray**, Harvard, floral and leaves, 11" x 6¼"	95.00 130.00	110.00
☐ **Tray**, hobstar and fan, signed Clarke, 14" x 7½"	235.00 285.00	250.00
☐ **Tray**, ice cream, Brazilian, signed Hawkes, 12¼" x 8½"	185.00 235.00	200.00
☐ **Tray**, ice cream, Corinthian, 14" x 8½"	235.00 285.00	250.00
☐ **Tray**, ice cream, cane, prism cut, signed Hoare, cane, prism 9" x 2½"	185.00 210.00	188.00
☐ **Tray**, ice cream, Russian, intaglio, 14" x 7"	110.00 135.00	112.00
☐ **Tray**, Noels, Libbey signed	510.00 610.00	550.00
☐ **Tray**, Royal, heart shape	185.00 235.00	200.00
☐ **Tumbler**, diamond and fan, signed Libbey	42.00 52.00	45.00
☐ **Tumbler**, hobstar, signed Hoare	28.00 38.00	30.00
☐ **Tumbler**, Middlesex, signed Hawkes	45.00 70.00	52.00
☐ **Tumbler**, pinwheel and pineapple	32.00 42.00	35.00
☐ **Tumbler**, Russian, starred buttons	80.00 110.00	88.00
☐ **Vase**, Art Deco	80.00 130.00	100.00
☐ **Vase**, bud, English	55.00 80.00	62.00
☐ **Vase**, corset style, ribbed etchings	50.00 65.00	52.00
☐ **Vase**, double handle, 4"	55.00 80.00	62.00
☐ **Vase**, dahlias and leaves, 8"	135.00 160.00	138.00
☐ **Vase**, English, graceful shape, 16"	285.00 385.00	325.00
☐ **Vase**, floral and leaf, intaglio cut, Libbey 9½"	260.00 310.00	275.00
☐ **Vase**, flower, signed Hawkes, 16"	260.00 335.00	280.00
☐ **Vase**, grapes and leaves, Libbey, 12"	160.00 185.00	162.00
☐ **Vase**, Hawkes, 18"	160.00 185.00	162.00
☐ **Vase**, pedestal, notched and cross cut, 16"	110.00 160.00	125.00
☐ **Vase**, pinwheel, strawberry, diamond and fan, 8"	55.00 80.00	62.00
☐ **Vase**, sterling and crystal vase, signed Hawkes	310.00 410.00	350.00
☐ **Vase**, sunburst	685.00 735.00	700.00
☐ **Vase**, trumpet, 16"	200.00 285.00	238.00
☐ **Vase**, trumpet, fluted, signed Hawkes	210.00 260.00	225.00
☐ **Vase**, trumpet, pinwheel, ruffled rim	160.00 210.00	175.00
☐ **Vase**, Verre De Soie, signed Hawkes	235.00 285.00	250.00
☐ **Vase**, wide mouth, flower, signed Webb, c. 1900's	210.00 260.00	225.00
☐ **Wine**, rose, Libbey	45.00 60.00	48.00

GLASSWARE / 421

DEPRESSION GLASS

Colored glassware was machine made during the Depression years of the late 1920's and early 1930's. The glass was available in ten cent stores, and given away at filling stations, and theatres, and used for promotional purposes. There are approximately 150,000 collectors and the popularity is steadily increasing each year. There are over 80 Depression Glass clubs which sponsor shows with attendance in the thousands.

Of the approximately 100 different patterns and colors produced, rose pink remains the favorite color. Luncheon sets of 16 pieces sold new for as low as $1.29. Today a dinner service, depending on the scarcity of the pattern, may cost from $100.00 to $1000.00.

	Current Price Range		Prior Year Average

ADAM (Pink, Green — Jeannette Glass Co.)

☐ **Ashtray**, 4½"	14.00	18.00	14.00
☐ **Bowl**, 5¾"	14.00	18.00	14.00
☐ **Bowl**, covered, 9"	30.00	55.00	38.00
☐ **Bowl**, oval, 10"	11.00	16.00	12.50
☐ **Butter**, covered	60.00	210.00	78.00
☐ **Candlesticks**, pair, 4"	40.00	65.00	48.00
☐ **Candy dish**, covered, 2½"	45.00	60.00	48.00
☐ **Creamer**	8.00	11.00	8.50
☐ **Cup and saucer**	13.00	17.00	14.00
☐ **Pitcher**, 8"	22.00	27.00	23.50
☐ **Plate**, 6"	2.50	4.50	3.00
☐ **Plate**, 9"	10.00	14.00	12.00
☐ **Plate**, cake, footed, 10"	11.00	16.00	12.50
☐ **Platter**, 11¾"	9.00	13.00	10.00
☐ **Relish**, divided, 8"	6.00	10.00	7.00
☐ **Salt and pepper**, 4"	35.00	65.00	47.00
☐ **Sherbet**, 3"	10.00	15.00	11.50
☐ **Sugar**	8.00	11.00	8.50
☐ **Tumbler**, 4½"	11.00	16.00	12.50
☐ **Tumbler**, 5½"	18.00	28.00	20.00
☐ **Vase**, 7½"	35.00	95.00	60.00

AKRO AGATE (Solid and Marbleized Colors — Akro Agate Co.)

☐ **Ashtray**, leaf, marbleized	6.00	11.00	7.50
☐ **Ashtray**, rectangular, marbleized, 4"	11.00	16.00	12.50
☐ **Ashtray**, shell, marbleized	7.00	13.00	8.00
☐ **Basket**, two handles, marbleized	18.00	28.00	20.00
☐ **Bell**, white	30.00	45.00	32.00
☐ **Bowl**, tab handles, marbleized, 7¼"	18.00	28.00	20.00
☐ **Child's cup and saucer**, jade	11.00	16.00	12.50
☐ **Child's cup and saucer**, marbleized	14.00	22.00	16.00
☐ **Child's plate**, marbleized	9.00	13.00	10.00
☐ **Child's sugar and creamer**, blue	27.00	32.00	27.50
☐ **Child's sugar and creamer**, white	32.00	42.00	35.00
☐ **Child's tea set**, marbleized, 16 piece	135.00	155.00	140.00
☐ **Child's tea set**, solid color, octagon, 21 piece	145.00	165.00	150.00
☐ **Child's water set**, green, 7 piece	55.00	70.00	58.00
☐ **Cup and saucer**, marbleized	11.00	16.00	12.50
☐ **Flower pot**, fluted edge, 5½"	9.00	16.00	11.50
☐ **Flower pot**, ribbed top, marbleized, 3½"	8.00	13.00	9.00
☐ **Flower pot**, with stand, solid color, 4"	14.00	20.00	16.00

	Current Price Range		Prior Year Average
☐ **Jardinier,** square	8.00	13.00	11.00
☐ **Lamp,** without shade, marbleized	55.00	80.00	62.00
☐ **Planter,** decorated, oval, 6″	20.00	30.00	23.00
☐ **Planter,** rectangular, marbleized	8.00	16.00	11.00
☐ **Powder box,** dog on dome lid, white	45.00	60.00	48.00
☐ **Powder box,** lady on dome lid, blue	40.00	55.00	42.00
☐ **Vase,** cornucopia, marbleized, 3¼″	11.00	16.00	12.50
☐ **Vase,** lily, solid color, 4½″	20.00	28.00	22.00
☐ **Vase,** scalloped top, marbleized, 6¼″	22.00	32.00	25.00
☐ **Vase,** tab handles, 6¼″	18.00	28.00	20.00

AMERICAN PIONEER (Crystal, Pink, Green — Liberty Works)

☐ **Bowl,** handled, 5″	6.50	8.50	7.00
☐ **Bowl,** handled, 9″	9.00	13.00	10.00
☐ **Candy dish,** covered	35.00	65.00	45.00
☐ **Creamer,** 3½″	4.50	7.50	5.50
☐ **Cup and saucer**	7.00	10.00	7.50
☐ **Goblet,** 6″	15.00	20.00	16.00
☐ **Pitcher,** covered, 5″	75.00	115.00	90.00
☐ **Plate,** 8″	3.50	5.50	4.00
☐ **Plate,** handled, 11½″	8.00	13.00	9.00
☐ **Sugar,** 3½″	4.50	7.50	5.50
☐ **Sherbet**	7.00	13.00	9.00
☐ **Tumbler,** 4″	12.00	18.00	13.50
☐ **Vase,** 7″	35.00	65.00	45.00

AMERICAN SWEETHEART (Pink, Monax — MacBeth-Evans Glass Co.)

☐ **Bowl,** 4½″	18.00	32.00	22.00
☐ **Bowl,** 6″	7.00	10.00	7.50
☐ **Bowl,** 9″	15.00	35.00	20.00
☐ **Bowl,** oval, 11″	20.00	38.00	27.00
☐ **Creamer**	4.50	7.50	5.50
☐ **Cup and saucer**	10.00	13.00	11.00
☐ **Plate,** 6″	2.50	4.50	3.00
☐ **Plate,** 8″	4.50	6.50	5.00
☐ **Plate,** 9¾″	11.00	14.00	11.50
☐ **Platter,** oval, 13″	15.00	35.00	22.00
☐ **Sherbet,** footed, 4¼″	7.00	14.00	9.00
☐ **Sugar,** footed	5.50	7.50	6.00
☐ **Tumbler,** 3½″ (pink only)	21.00	26.00	22.00
☐ **Tumbler,** 4½″ (pink only)	24.00	30.00	24.50

AUNT POLLY (Green, Blue — U.S. Glass Co.)

☐ **Bowl,** 4¾″	8.00	12.00	9.00
☐ **Bowl,** 7⅞″	10.00	15.00	11.50
☐ **Bowl,** oval, 7¼″	8.00	12.00	9.00
☐ **Bowl,** oval, 8⅜″	16.00	21.00	17.50
☐ **Butter,** covered	100.00	140.00	115.00
☐ **Candy dish,** covered	20.00	32.00	24.00
☐ **Creamer**	15.00	21.00	16.00
☐ **Plate,** 6″	2.50	4.50	3.00
☐ **Plate,** 8″	4.50	7.50	5.50
☐ **Pitcher,** 8″	95.00	105.00	92.00
☐ **Salt and pepper**	130.00	145.00	128.00
☐ **Sugar**	10.00	14.00	11.00
☐ **Tumbler,** 3⅝″	10.00	13.00	10.50
☐ **Vase,** 6½″	20.00	26.00	22.00

GLASSWARE / 423

	Current Price Range		Prior Year Average
BLOCK OPTIC (Pink, Green — Hocking Glass Co.)			
☐ Bowl, 4¼″	3.50	5.50	4.00
☐ Bowl, 7″	8.00	11.00	8.50
☐ Butter, covered	20.00	28.00	22.00
☐ Candy dish, covered	20.00	28.00	22.00
☐ Creamer	4.50	7.50	5.50
☐ Cup and saucer	6.00	10.00	7.00
☐ Goblet, 5¾″	10.00	13.00	10.50
☐ Goblet, 7¼″	12.00	18.00	14.00
☐ Pitcher, 8″	26.00	31.00	27.50
☐ Plate, 8″	2.50	4.50	3.00
☐ Plate, 9″	7.00	15.00	9.00
☐ Salt and pepper	20.00	40.00	28.00
☐ Sherbet	4.00	9.00	5.50
☐ Sugar	4.00	9.00	5.50
☐ Tumbler, 5 oz.	4.50	12.00	7.50
☐ Tumbler, 9 oz.	5.50	11.00	7.50
☐ Tumbler, 10 oz.	7.00	13.00	9.00
BUBBLE (Crystal, Light Blue, Dark Green — Hocking Glass Co.)			
☐ Bowl, 4″	2.50	7.50	4.50
☐ Bowl, 5¼″	2.50	5.50	3.50
☐ Bowl, 7¾″	5.00	9.00	6.00
☐ Bowl, 8⅜″	5.00	9.00	6.00
☐ Creamer	6.00	18.00	11.00
☐ Cup and saucer	3.50	6.50	4.50
☐ Plate, 6¾″	2.50	7.50	4.50
☐ Plate, 9⅜″	2.50	7.50	4.50
☐ Platter, oval, 12″	4.00	9.00	5.50
☐ Sugar	4.00	11.00	6.50
CAMEO (Green — Hocking Glass Co.)			
☐ Bowl, 5½″	10.00	12.00	10.00
☐ Bowl, 8¼″	20.00	24.00	20.00
☐ Bowl, oval, 10″	9.00	11.00	9.00
☐ Bowl, three feet	32.00	42.00	35.00
☐ Butter, covered	120.00	135.00	112.00
☐ Candlesticks, pair, 4″	52.00	62.00	55.00
☐ Candy dish, covered	34.00	40.00	35.00
☐ Cookie jar	25.00	34.00	27.00
☐ Creamer	14.00	18.00	14.00
☐ Cup and saucer	38.00	58.00	45.00
☐ Decanter	52.00	62.00	55.00
☐ Goblet, 4″	36.00	42.00	37.50
☐ Goblet, 6″	26.00	31.00	27.50
☐ Pitcher, 6″	31.00	36.00	32.50
☐ Pitcher, 8½″	26.00	32.00	27.00
☐ Plate, 8″	4.50	6.50	5.00
☐ Plate, 9½	12.00	22.00	15.00
☐ Plate, 10½″	7.00	9.00	7.00
☐ Plate, cake, three feet	11.00	13.00	11.00
☐ Platter, 12″	10.00	12.00	10.00
☐ Salt and pepper	38.00	48.00	40.00
☐ Sugar	12.00	22.00	15.00
☐ Tumbler, 3¾″	13.00	17.00	14.00
☐ Tumbler, 4¾″	14.00	18.00	15.00
☐ Tumbler, 5″	13.00	17.00	14.00
☐ Vase, 8″	15.00	19.00	16.00

424 / GLASSWARE

CHERRY BLOSSOM
(Pink, Green — Jeannette Glass Co.)

	Current Price Range		Prior Year Average
☐ Bowl, 4¾"	7.00	10.00	7.50
☐ Bowl, 7¾"	28.00	35.00	28.00
☐ Bowl, 8½"	12.00	16.00	12.00
☐ Bowl, handled, 9"	13.00	17.00	14.00
☐ Bowl, oval, 9"	13.00	17.00	14.00
☐ Bowl, three feet, 10½"	30.00	38.00	32.00
☐ Butter, covered	55.00	75.00	60.00
☐ Creamer	9.00	12.00	9.50
☐ Cup and saucer	11.00	17.00	13.00
☐ Pitcher, 6¾"	28.00	38.00	30.00
☐ Pitcher, 8"	30.00	45.00	32.00
☐ Plate, 7"	11.00	15.00	12.00
☐ Plate, 9"	10.00	14.00	11.00
☐ Plate, cake, three feet, 10¼"	13.00	17.00	14.00
☐ Platter, oval, 11"	14.00	20.00	16.00
☐ Sherbet	8.00	11.00	8.50
☐ Sugar	8.00	11.00	8.50
☐ Tumbler, 3¾"	11.00	15.00	12.00
☐ Tumbler, 4½"	20.00	26.00	22.00

COLONIAL, (Pink, Green — Hocking Glass Co.)

☐ Bowl, 4½"	5.00	8.00	5.50
☐ Bowl, 5½"	18.00	32.00	22.00
☐ Bowl, 7"	20.00	30.00	22.00
☐ Bowl, 9"	9.00	13.00	10.00
☐ Bowl, oval, 10"	10.00	15.00	12.50
☐ Creamer	10.00	14.00	11.00
☐ Cup and saucer	6.00	12.00	8.00
☐ Goblet, 5¾"	15.00	18.00	14.50
☐ Pitcher, 7"	22.00	32.00	25.00
☐ Plate, 8½"	3.50	5.50	4.00
☐ Plate, 10"	12.00	22.00	15.00
☐ Platter, oval, 12"	9.00	13.00	10.00
☐ Salt and pepper	85.00	100.00	88.00
☐ Sherbet	5.00	9.00	6.00
☐ Sugar	8.00	12.00	9.00
☐ Tumbler, 3"	6.50	12.00	8.50
☐ Tumbler, 10 oz.	10.00	16.00	12.00
☐ Tumbler, 12 oz.	14.00	24.00	17.00

DOGWOOD (Pink — MacBeth Evans Glass Co.)

☐ Bowl, 5½"	10.00	13.00	10.50
☐ Bowl, 8½"	22.00	32.00	25.00
☐ Creamer	7.00	13.00	9.00
☐ Cup and saucer	9.00	13.00	10.00
☐ Plate, 8"	2.50	4.50	3.00
☐ Plate, 9¼"	12.00	14.00	12.00
☐ Plate, 10½"	12.00	16.00	12.50
☐ Sherbet	12.00	16.00	12.50
☐ Sugar	6.00	9.00	7.00
☐ Tumbler, 4"	18.00	20.00	16.50
☐ Tumbler, 5"	21.00	26.00	22.50

DORIC (Pink, Green — Jeannette Glass Co.)

☐ Bowl, 4½"	3.50	6.50	4.50
☐ Bowl, 5½"	11.00	17.00	13.00

GLASSWARE / 425

	Current Price Range		Prior Year Average
☐ Bowl, 8¼"	8.00	11.00	8.50
☐ Bowl, oval, 9"	9.00	11.00	9.00
☐ Butter, covered	50.00	60.00	53.00
☐ Candy dish, covered, 8"	20.00	25.00	20.50
☐ Creamer	6.00	9.00	6.50
☐ Cup and saucer	7.00	10.00	7.50
☐ Pitcher, 6"	21.00	26.00	22.50
☐ Plate, 7"	9.00	13.00	10.00
☐ Plate, 9"	6.00	10.00	7.00
☐ Plate, cake, three feet, 10"	9.00	14.00	10.50
☐ Platter, oval, 12"	9.00	11.00	9.00
☐ Relish	3.50	8.50	6.50
☐ Salt and pepper	21.00	26.00	22.50
☐ Sherbet	4.50	7.50	5.50
☐ Sugar	7.00	9.00	7.00
☐ Tray, 10"	6.00	11.00	7.50
☐ Tumbler, 4"	14.00	20.00	14.50
☐ Tumbler, 5"	15.00	19.00	15.00

ENGLISH HOBNAIL (Pink, Green — Westmoreland Glass Co.)

	Current Price Range		Prior Year Average
☐ Bowl, 6"	9.00	11.00	9.00
☐ Bowl, 8"	14.00	17.00	14.50
☐ Bowl, footed and handled, 8"	34.00	40.00	34.00
☐ Bowl, square, 5"	7.50	9.50	8.00
☐ Candlesticks, pair, 3½"	25.00	30.00	25.50
☐ Candy dish, covered, three feet	50.00	60.00	51.50
☐ Celery dish	16.00	20.00	16.00
☐ Creamer	12.00	14.00	12.00
☐ Cup and saucer	14.00	16.00	14.00
☐ Goblet, 2 oz.	12.00	14.00	12.00
☐ Goblet, 8 oz.	14.00	16.00	14.00
☐ Pitcher, 23 oz.	72.00	82.00	75.00
☐ Plate, 6½"	2.50	4.50	3.00
☐ Plate, 8"	5.50	7.50	6.00
☐ Relish, oval, 12"	16.00	19.00	15.50
☐ Salt and pepper	50.00	60.00	50.00
☐ Sherbet	9.00	13.00	9.50
☐ Sugar	13.00	15.00	13.00
☐ Tumbler, 3¾"	11.00	13.00	11.00
☐ Tumbler, 5"	15.00	18.00	15.50

FLORAL-POINSETTA (Pink, Green — Jeannette Glass Co.)

	Current Price Range		Prior Year Average
☐ Bowl, 4"	7.00	10.00	8.00
☐ Bowl, 7½"	8.00	11.00	8.50
☐ Bowl, oval, 9"	9.00	12.00	9.50
☐ Butter, covered	55.00	60.00	58.00
☐ Candlesticks, 4", pair	40.00	60.00	50.00
☐ Candy dish, covered	23.00	29.00	22.50
☐ Creamer	7.00	10.00	7.50
☐ Cup and saucer	10.00	13.00	10.50
☐ Pitcher, 8"	18.00	24.00	19.00
☐ Pitcher, 10¼"	130.00	165.00	138.00
☐ Plate, 6"	3.00	5.00	3.00
☐ Plate, 9"	9.00	12.00	9.50
☐ Platter, oval, 10¾"	8.00	11.00	8.50
☐ Refrigerator dish, covered, 5"	32.00	42.00	35.00
☐ Salt and pepper	26.00	34.00	28.00

426 / GLASSWARE

	Current Price Range		Prior Year Average
☐ Sherbet	7.00	10.00	7.50
☐ Sugar	6.00	9.00	7.50
☐ Tumbler, 4"	10.00	13.00	10.50
☐ Tumbler, 4¾"	9.00	12.00	9.50
☐ Tumbler, 5¼"	23.00	28.00	22.00

FLORENTINE II-POPPY (Crystal, Green, Yellow — Hazel Atlas Glass Co.)

☐ Bowl, 4½"	7.00	13.00	9.00
☐ Bowl, 4¾"	8.00	14.00	10.00
☐ Bowl, 6"	12.00	22.00	15.00
☐ Bowl, 8"	13.00	18.00	13.00
☐ Bowl, oval, 9"	28.00	38.00	30.00
☐ Butter, covered	75.00	125.00	95.00
☐ Candy dish, covered	65.00	125.00	90.00
☐ Creamer	5.00	8.00	5.50
☐ Cup and saucer	7.00	10.00	7.50
☐ Pitcher, 8"	60.00	130.00	90.00
☐ Plate, 6"	3.00	5.00	3.00
☐ Plate, 8½"	5.00	8.00	5.50
☐ Plate, 10"	7.00	10.00	7.50
☐ Platter, oval, 11"	9.00	13.00	9.50
☐ Relish	8.00	14.00	10.00
☐ Salt and pepper	30.00	37.00	31.00
☐ Sherbet	6.00	9.00	6.50
☐ Sugar	5.00	8.00	5.50
☐ Tumbler, 3½"	6.00	14.00	9.00
☐ Tumbler, 4"	8.00	14.00	10.00
☐ Tumbler, 5"	12.00	22.00	16.00
☐ Vase, 6"	18.00	38.00	25.00

HOLIDAY (Pink — Jeannette Glass Co.)

☐ Bowl, 5⅛"	4.50	6.50	5.00
☐ Bowl, 8½"	12.00	14.00	12.00
☐ Bowl, oval, 9½"	8.00	11.00	8.50
☐ Bowl, 10¾"	45.00	60.00	48.00
☐ Butter, covered	26.00	32.00	27.50
☐ Candlesticks, pair, 3"	35.00	45.00	40.00
☐ Creamer	4.50	6.50	5.00
☐ Cup and saucer	5.50	7.50	6.00
☐ Pitcher, 4¾"	35.00	42.00	34.50
☐ Pitcher, 6¾"	22.00	25.00	21.00
☐ Plate, 6"	2.50	4.50	3.00
☐ Plate, 9"	6.50	8.50	7.00
☐ Plate, 13¾"	50.00	60.00	50.00
☐ Platter, oval, 11⅜"	6.50	9.50	7.50
☐ Sherbet	4.00	6.00	4.00
☐ Sugar	4.00	6.00	4.00
☐ Tumbler, 4"	12.00	22.00	15.00
☐ Tumbler, 6"	40.00	46.00	41.00

IRIS AND HERRINGBONE (Crystal — Jeannette Glass Co.)

☐ Bowl, 5"	4.00	6.00	4.00
☐ Bowl, 8"	9.00	11.00	9.00
☐ Bowl, 11"	8.00	10.00	8.00
☐ Butter, covered	22.00	29.00	23.50
☐ Candlesticks, pair	14.00	19.00	14.50
☐ Candy dish, covered	45.00	50.00	45.50

GLASSWARE / 427

	Current Price Range	Prior Year Average
☐ Creamer	4.00 6.00	4.00
☐ Cup and saucer	8.00 12.00	9.00
☐ Cup and saucer, demitasse	30.00 38.00	32.00
☐ Goblet, 4"	10.00 12.00	10.00
☐ Goblet, 5¾"	9.00 13.00	10.00
☐ Pitcher, 9½"	15.00 20.00	16.50
☐ Plate, 8"	25.00 30.00	25.50
☐ Plate, 11¾"	8.00 11.00	8.50
☐ Sherbet	7.00 11.00	8.00
☐ Sugar	5.00 7.00	5.00
☐ Tumbler, 4"	22.00 32.00	25.00
☐ Tumbler, footed, 7"	11.00 14.00	11.50
☐ Vase, 9"	10.00 14.00	11.00

LACE EDGE (Pink — Hocking Glass Co.)

	Current Price Range	Prior Year Average
☐ Bowl, 6⅜"	7.00 9.00	7.00
☐ Bowl, 9½"	9.00 11.00	9.00
☐ Bowl, three feet, 10½"	85.00 95.00	88.00
☐ Butter, covered	38.00 48.00	40.00
☐ Candlesticks, pair	80.00 95.00	82.00
☐ Candy dish, covered	20.00 28.00	21.50
☐ Compote, 7"	9.00 12.00	9.50
☐ Cookie jar	30.00 38.00	31.00
☐ Creamer	9.00 12.00	9.50
☐ Cup and saucer	14.00 18.00	15.00
☐ Plate, 7¼"	8.00 12.00	9.00
☐ Plate, 10½"	8.00 16.00	11.00
☐ Platter, 13¾"	11.00 16.00	12.50
☐ Relish, divided	22.00 29.00	23.50
☐ Sherbet	30.00 35.00	20.50
☐ Sugar	9.00 12.00	9.50
☐ Tumbler, 5"	22.00 29.00	23.50

MADRID (Amber, Green — Federal Glass Co.)

	Current Price Range	Prior Year Average
☐ Ashtray, 6"	77.00 115.00	90.00
☐ Bowl, 5"	4.00 6.00	4.00
☐ Bowl, 7"	7.00 11.00	8.00
☐ Bowl, 9⅜"	12.00 18.00	13.50
☐ Bowl, oval, 10"	10.00 14.00	11.00
☐ Butter, covered	50.00 65.00	55.00
☐ Candlesticks, pair, 2½"	12.00 15.00	12.50
☐ Cookie jar	22.00 29.00	23.50
☐ Creamer	5.00 9.00	6.00
☐ Cup and saucer	6.00 10.00	7.00
☐ Gelatin mold	6.00 8.00	6.00
☐ Pitcher, 5½"	21.00 26.00	22.50
☐ Pitcher, 8"	30.00 100.00	60.00
☐ Plate, 7½"	7.00 9.00	7.00
☐ Plate, 10½"	21.00 26.00	22.00
☐ Platter, oval, 11½"	8.00 13.00	9.50
☐ Salt and pepper, footed, 3½"	50.00 75.00	58.00
☐ Sherbet	5.00 9.00	6.00
☐ Sugar	5.00 9.00	6.00
☐ Tumbler, 4"	18.00 38.00	25.00
☐ Tumbler, 5½"	18.00 28.00	20.00

428 / GLASSWARE

	Current Price Range		Prior Year Average

MAYFAIR — OPEN ROSE
(Pink — Hocking Glass Co.)

	Current Price Range		Prior Year Average
☐ Bowl, 5½"	10.00	13.00	10.50
☐ Bowl, 7"	12.00	15.00	12.50
☐ Bowl, covered, 10"	40.00	50.00	43.00
☐ Bowl, oval, 9½"	12.00	15.00	12.50
☐ Bowl, 12"	25.00	35.00	28.00
☐ Butter, covered	40.00	47.00	38.50
☐ Candy dish, covered	26.00	31.00	27.50
☐ Celery dish, 10"	12.00	15.00	12.50
☐ Cookie jar	21.00	26.00	22.50
☐ Creamer	10.00	13.00	10.50
☐ Cup and saucer	22.00	29.00	23.50
☐ Decanter	68.00	78.00	70.00
☐ Goblet, 4"	38.00	48.00	40.00
☐ Goblet, 5¾"	25.00	35.00	27.00
☐ Goblet, 7¼"	72.00	82.00	75.00
☐ Pitcher, 8"	26.00	34.00	28.00
☐ Plate, 8½"	10.00	13.00	10.50
☐ Plate, 9½"	18.00	32.00	22.00
☐ Plate, cake, 12"	20.00	24.00	20.00
☐ Platter, oval, 12"	10.00	14.00	11.00
☐ Relish, 8⅜"	12.00	14.00	13.50
☐ Salt and pepper	30.00	38.00	32.00
☐ Sherbet, 3"	9.00	12.00	10.50
☐ Sherbet, 4¾"	38.00	45.00	38.50
☐ Sugar	12.00	15.00	12.50
☐ Tumbler, 3½"	18.00	24.00	20.00
☐ Tumbler, 4¾"	38.00	48.00	40.00
☐ Tumbler, 5¼"	20.00	26.00	21.00
☐ Tumbler, 6½"	21.00	27.00	22.00

MISS AMERICA (Crystal, Pink — Hocking Glass Co.)

	Current Price Range		Prior Year Average
☐ Bowl, 6¼"	5.00	11.00	7.00
☐ Bowl, 8"	22.00	42.00	35.00
☐ Bowl, oval, 10"	8.00	15.00	10.50
☐ Butter, covered	190.00	370.00	270.00
☐ Candy dish, covered	45.00	80.00	58.00
☐ Celery dish, oval, 10½"	7.00	13.00	9.00
☐ Compote, 5"	7.00	13.00	9.00
☐ Creamer	6.00	11.00	7.50
☐ Cup and saucer	8.00	17.00	11.50
☐ Goblet, 3¾"	20.00	45.00	28.00
☐ Goblet, 5½"	20.00	35.00	22.00
☐ Pitcher, 8"	45.00	80.00	58.00
☐ Plate, 8½"	5.00	11.00	7.00
☐ Plate, 10¼"	7.00	16.00	10.50
☐ Platter, oval, 12"	9.00	13.00	10.00
☐ Relish, 8¾"	8.00	13.00	9.00
☐ Salt and pepper	18.00	38.00	27.00
☐ Sherbet	6.00	11.00	7.50
☐ Sugar	6.00	11.00	7.50
☐ Tumbler, 4"	15.00	35.00	20.00
☐ Tumbler, 6¾"	20.00	40.00	27.00

NO. 612 — HORSESHOE (Green, Yellow — Indiana Glass Co.)

	Current Price Range		Prior Year Average
☐ Bowl, 4½"	12.00	18.00	14.00
☐ Bowl, 7½"	12.00	16.00	13.50

	Current Price Range		Prior Year Average
☐ Bowl, 9½"	20.00	26.00	22.00
☐ Bowl, oval, 10½"	12.00	16.00	13.50
☐ Creamer	9.00	13.00	10.00
☐ Cup and saucer	8.00	12.00	9.00
☐ Pitcher, 8½"	185.00	210.00	188.00
☐ Plate, 8⅜"	4.00	7.50	4.50
☐ Plate, 10⅜"	12.00	18.00	13.00
☐ Platter, oval, 10¾"	12.00	18.00	13.00
☐ Sherbet	8.00	12.00	9.00
☐ Sugar	8.00	12.00	9.00
☐ Tumbler, 9 oz."	10.00	14.00	11.00
☐ Tumbler, 12 oz."	50.00	65.00	52.00

NORMANDIE (Amber, Pink — Federal Glass Co.)

	Current Price Range		Prior Year Average
☐ Bowl, 5"	3.50	5.50	4.00
☐ Bowl, 6½"	5.50	7.50	6.00
☐ Bowl, 8½"	7.00	11.00	8.00
☐ Bowl, oval, 10"	10.00	17.00	12.50
☐ Creamer	4.00	7.00	4.50
☐ Cup and saucer	6.00	7.00	6.50
☐ Pitcher, 8"	48.00	58.00	50.00
☐ Plate, 8"	4.50	6.50	5.00
☐ Plate, 9¼"	4.00	7.00	4.50
☐ Platter, 11¾"	8.00	12.00	9.00
☐ Salt and pepper	30.00	40.00	33.00
☐ Sherbet	4.50	6.50	5.00
☐ Sugar	3.00	5.00	3.00
☐ Tumbler, 4½"	11.00	17.00	13.00
☐ Tumbler, 5"	14.00	22.00	16.00

PATRICIAN-SPOKE (Amber, Pink, Green — Federal Glass Co.)

	Current Price Range		Prior Year Average
☐ Bowl, 5"	6.00	11.00	7.50
☐ Bowl, 6"	11.00	16.00	12.50
☐ Bowl, 8½"	14.00	29.00	17.00
☐ Creamer	5.00	9.00	6.00
☐ Cup and saucer	9.00	13.00	9.50
☐ Pitcher, 8"	60.00	100.00	75.00
☐ Plate, 7½"	7.00	14.00	9.50
☐ Plate, 9"	5.00	8.00	5.50
☐ Plate, 10½"	6.00	16.00	10.00
☐ Platter, oval, 11½"	8.00	13.00	9.50
☐ Salt and pepper	35.00	70.00	48.00
☐ Sherbet	6.00	11.00	7.50
☐ Sugar	5.00	8.00	5.50
☐ Tumbler, 4"	14.00	18.00	15.00
☐ Tumbler, 5½"	22.00	32.00	25.00

PRINCESS (Pink, Green — Hocking Glass Co.)

	Current Price Range		Prior Year Average
☐ Bowl, 4½"	7.00	15.00	10.00
☐ Bowl, 9"	15.00	20.00	16.50
☐ Bowl, oval, 10"	9.00	13.00	10.00
☐ Butter, covered	58.00	68.00	60.00
☐ Candy dish, covered	22.00	32.00	25.00
☐ Cookie jar	28.00	38.00	30.00
☐ Creamer	5.00	9.00	6.00
☐ Cup and saucer	6.00	11.00	7.50
☐ Pitcher, 6"	18.00	26.00	21.00

430 / GLASSWARE

	Current Price Range		Prior Year Average
☐ Pitcher, 8"	26.00	36.00	29.00
☐ Plate, 8"	5.00	9.00	6.00
☐ Plate, 11½"	5.00	7.00	5.00
☐ Platter, 12"	9.00	11.00	9.00
☐ Relish, divided, 7½"	10.00	15.00	11.50
☐ Salt and pepper	22.00	32.00	25.00
☐ Sherbet	8.00	13.00	9.00
☐ Sugar	4.00	6.00	4.00
☐ Tumbler, 3"	11.00	16.00	12.50
☐ Tumbler, 4"	10.00	17.00	12.50
☐ Tumbler, 6½"	20.00	40.00	23.00
☐ Vase, 8"	14.00	20.00	16.00

SHARON (Amber, Pink — Federal Glass Co.)

☐ Bowl, 6"	8.00	14.00	10.00
☐ Bowl, 8½"	4.00	10.00	6.00
☐ Bowl, oval, 9½"	7.00	13.00	9.00
☐ Butter, covered	32.00	42.00	35.00
☐ Candy dish	28.00	38.00	30.00
☐ Creamer	6.00	11.00	7.50
☐ Cup and saucer	11.00	15.00	12.00
☐ Pitcher, 80 oz.	75.00	95.00	80.00
☐ Plate, 7½"	7.00	15.00	10.00
☐ Plate, 9½"	7.00	11.00	8.00
☐ Platter, oval, 12½"	8.00	13.00	9.50
☐ Salt and pepper	28.00	38.00	30.00
☐ Sherbet	6.00	10.00	7.00
☐ Sugar	5.00	9.00	6.00
☐ Tumbler, 5¼"	21.00	26.00	22.50
☐ Tumbler, 6½"	28.00	38.00	31.00

SWIRL (Pink, Teal Blue — Jeannette Glass Co.)

☐ Bowl, 5¼"	4.00	8.00	5.00
☐ Bowl, 9"	9.00	14.00	10.50
☐ Bowl, 10½"	12.00	17.00	13.50
☐ Candy dish, covered	45.00	65.00	50.00
☐ Creamer	5.00	9.00	6.50
☐ Cup and saucer	6.00	10.00	7.00
☐ Plate, 7¼"	4.00	7.00	4.50
☐ Plate, 8"	4.00	10.00	6.00
☐ Plate, 9¼"	5.00	10.00	7.50
☐ Plate, 12½"	6.00	12.00	8.00
☐ Sherbet	5.00	9.00	6.00
☐ Sugar	5.00	8.00	5.50
☐ Tumbler, 4"	7.00	11.00	8.00
☐ Tumbler, 4¾"	12.00	24.00	17.00
☐ Vase, 6½"	9.00	15.00	11.00

SYLVN (Green, Amber — Federal Glass Co.)

☐ Bowl, 5"	8.00	11.00	8.50
☐ Bowl, 7"	16.00	21.00	17.50
☐ Bowl, 8"	38.00	48.00	40.00
☐ Bowl, oval, 10"	28.00	38.00	30.00
☐ Creamer	12.00	17.00	13.50
☐ Cup and saucer	20.00	28.00	22.00
☐ Plate, 9"	16.00	18.00	15.50
☐ Plate, 10¼"	17.00	21.00	18.00

	Current Price Range		Prior Year Average
☐ **Platter,** 11¼"	25.00	40.00	28.00
☐ **Sherbet**	9.00	13.00	10.00
☐ **Sugar**	11.00	15.00	12.00
☐ **Tumbler,** 5½"	58.00	68.00	60.00

TEA ROOM (Green, Pink — Indiana Glass Co.)

	Current Price Range		Prior Year Average
☐ **Bowl,** 8½"	10.00	14.00	11.00
☐ **Bowl,** oval, 9½"	28.00	38.00	30.00
☐ **Candlesticks,** pair	24.00	32.00	26.00
☐ **Creamer**	9.00	11.00	9.00
☐ **Cup and saucer**	20.00	24.00	20.00
☐ **Goblet,** 9 oz.	14.00	24.00	17.00
☐ **Parfait**	9.00	16.00	11.50
☐ **Pitcher,** 64 oz.	75.00	90.00	78.00
☐ **Plate,** 8¼"	16.00	20.00	16.50
☐ **Plate,** handled, 10½"	20.00	35.00	22.00
☐ **Relish**	8.00	10.00	8.00
☐ **Salt and pepper**	28.00	38.00	30.00
☐ **Sherbet**	10.00	13.00	10.50
☐ **Sugar**	10.00	13.00	10.50
☐ **Tumbler,** 8½ oz.	15.00	19.00	16.00
☐ **Tumbler,** 11 oz.	13.00	17.00	14.00
☐ **Vase,** 9"	21.00	27.00	23.00

WINDSOR (Crystal, Pink — Jeannette Glass Co.)

	Current Price Range		Prior Year Average
☐ **Bowl,** 5"	4.00	11.00	6.50
☐ **Bowl,** 8½"	5.00	9.00	6.00
☐ **Bowl,** boat shape	10.00	17.00	12.50
☐ **Bowl,** oval, 9½"	6.00	11.00	7.50
☐ **Butter,** covered	25.00	40.00	28.00
☐ **Candy dish,** covered	9.00	17.00	12.00
☐ **Creamer**	3.00	7.00	4.00
☐ **Cup and saucer**	4.00	8.00	5.00
☐ **Pitcher,** 6¾"	9.00	17.00	12.00
☐ **Plate,** 7"	3.00	8.00	5.50
☐ **Plate,** 13⅝"	7.00	12.00	8.50
☐ **Plate,** cake, 13½"	5.00	11.00	7.00
☐ **Platter,** oval, 11½"	3.00	8.00	4.50
☐ **Salt and pepper**	10.00	23.00	15.00
☐ **Sherbet**	3.00	5.00	3.00
☐ **Sugar**	6.00	14.00	9.00
☐ **Tumbler,** 3¼"	4.00	9.00	5.50
☐ **Tumbler,** 5"	5.00	12.00	7.50

MILK GLASS

Created to resemble fine porcelain, this white opaque glass dates back to the ancients. Milk glass gained prominence in England during the 18th century. By the mid-1820's American glassmakers were able to produce excellent quality milk glass in a variety of tints and patterns.

	Current Price Range		Prior Year Average
☐ **Basket,** basket weave, twisted handle, 4"	28.00	38.00	30.00
☐ **Bell,** smoke, fluted rim, 7"	18.00	28.00	20.00
☐ **Bottle,** cologne, Portraite Medallion, 5½"	60.00	85.00	68.00
☐ **Bottle,** dresser, Actress, 11"	48.00	68.00	50.00
☐ **Bottle,** perfume, Germany, 1¾"	35.00	50.00	38.00

432 / GLASSWARE

	Current Price Range	Prior Year Average
☐ Bowl, Acanthus leaf, 10″	80.00　110.00	88.00
☐ Bowl, hobnail, fluted edge, 10″	48.00　68.00	55.00
☐ Bowl, lacy edge, 12″	80.00　100.00	88.00
☐ Bowl, lattice, 8½″	100.00　135.00	112.00
☐ Bowl, scalloped edge, 8″	60.00　75.00	62.00
☐ Box, glove, covered 10″ x 4″	38.00　48.00	40.00
☐ Box, powder, covered	35.00　55.00	40.00
☐ Butter, apple blossom	48.00　68.00	55.00
☐ Butter, covered, rectangle	42.00　52.00	45.00
☐ Cake stand, star in center, 11″	105.00　135.00	110.00
☐ Candlestick, crucifix, round base, pair, 10″	80.00　100.00	88.00
☐ Celery, maize	80.00　100.00	88.00
☐ Compote, Atterbury	45.00　65.00	50.00
☐ Compote, raised grapes, pink	18.00　28.00	20.00
☐ Compote, scrollwork, 8″	52.00　62.00	55.00
☐ Creamer, owl	41.00　46.00	42.50
☐ Creamer, prism	30.00　45.00	32.00
☐ Creamer, sawtooth	28.00　38.00	30.00
☐ Creamer, scrollwork	55.00　70.00	58.00
☐ Creamer, swan	55.00　80.00	62.00
☐ Dish, covered, cat, blue and white, 5½″	58.00　78.00	65.00
☐ Dish, covered, chicken on nest, Atterbury	135.00　175.00	145.00
☐ Dish, covered, Dewey on battleship, marked	85.00　110.00	88.00
☐ Dish, covered, dog, 5″	95.00　105.00	90.00
☐ Dish, covered, duck, Atterbury	185.00　235.00	200.00
☐ Dish, covered, eagle	120.00　140.00	120.00
☐ Dish, covered, hand and dove, Atterbury	160.00　210.00	175.00
☐ Dish, covered, hen, blue with white head	38.00　48.00	40.00
☐ Dish, covered, lamb, McKee	160.00　210.00	175.00
☐ Dish, covered, quail	65.00　85.00	70.00
☐ Dish, covered, rabbit	70.00　90.00	75.00
☐ Dish, covered, Santa on sleigh	55.00　80.00	62.00
☐ Dish, covered, swan, closed neck	78.00　88.00	80.00
☐ Dish, covered, turkey	22.00　32.00	25.00
☐ Egg cup, birch leaf	22.00　32.00	25.00
☐ Egg cup, chicken	16.00　21.00	17.50
☐ Figurine, chicken	31.00　36.00	32.50
☐ Figurine, owl	26.00　31.00	27.50
☐ Figurine, swan	31.00　36.00	32.50
☐ Goblet, blackberry	35.00　55.00	40.00
☐ Goblet, cane	50.00　80.00	60.00
☐ Goblet, strawberry	28.00　38.00	30.00
☐ Hat, Uncle Sam	45.00　60.00	48.00
☐ Lamp, blue, 6½″	110.00　135.00	112.00
☐ Lamp, owl	210.00　260.00	225.00
☐ Lamp, painted	55.00　80.00	62.00
☐ Lamp, panels, floral design, 4″	110.00　160.00	125.00
☐ Match holder, hen and rabbit	22.00　32.00	25.00
☐ Mug, hobnail	28.00　38.00	30.00
☐ Mustard jar, Dutch figures, 4″	40.00　60.00	45.00
☐ Pitcher, blackberry	160.00　185.00	162.00
☐ Pitcher, hobnail	110.00　135.00	112.00
☐ Pitcher, little boy	80.00　110.00	88.00
☐ Pitcher, owl, 7½″	185.00　235.00	200.00
☐ Pitcher, tankard, scrollwork	135.00　160.00	138.00
☐ Pitcher, water, pink	50.00　80.00	60.00

GLASSWARE / 433

	Current Price Range	Prior Year Average
☐ **Plate,** angel	28.00 38.00	30.00
☐ **Plate,** Battleship Maine	38.00 48.00	40.00
☐ **Plate,** chicken and eggs	32.00 42.00	35.00
☐ **Plate,** Columbus	32.00 42.00	35.00
☐ **Plate,** dogs and squirrel	45.00 65.00	50.00
☐ **Plate,** eagle	22.00 32.00	25.00
☐ **Plate,** Easter bunnies	28.00 38.00	30.00
☐ **Plate,** Easter duck	35.00 50.00	38.00
☐ **Plate,** Fleur-de-Lis	28.00 38.00	30.00
☐ **Plate,** heart shape	42.00 52.00	45.00
☐ **Plate,** Lincoln	32.00 42.00	35.00
☐ **Plate,** Niagara Falls	22.00 32.00	25.00
☐ **Plate,** rooster	48.00 58.00	50.00
☐ **Plate,** scrollwork	32.00 42.00	35.00
☐ **Plate,** three kittens, square	42.00 52.00	45.00
☐ **Plate,** three owls	40.00 60.00	45.00
☐ **Plate,** Washington	55.00 80.00	62.00
☐ **Platter,** Liberty Bell	260.00 310.00	275.00
☐ **Platter,** Rock of Ages	135.00 185.00	150.00
☐ **Reamer,** Sunkist	12.00 22.00	15.00
☐ **Rolling pin,** wooden handles	42.00 62.00	45.00
☐ **Salt and pepper,** acorn	65.00 90.00	72.00
☐ **Salt and pepper,** beehive	40.00 55.00	42.00
☐ **Salt and pepper,** flowers	50.00 65.00	52.00
☐ **Salt and pepper,** grape	25.00 45.00	30.00
☐ **Salt and pepper,** owls	110.00 135.00	112.00
☐ **Salt and pepper,** rabbits	65.00 90.00	72.00
☐ **Salt and pepper,** scrollwork	40.00 55.00	42.00
☐ **Spooner,** blackberry	65.00 80.00	68.00
☐ **Spooner,** rose	35.00 50.00	38.00
☐ **Spooner,** strawberry	45.00 60.00	48.00
☐ **Spooner,** swan	30.00 55.00	38.00
☐ **Sugar,** blackberry	38.00 48.00	40.00
☐ **Sugar,** rose	45.00 60.00	48.00
☐ **Sugar,** scrollwork	65.00 90.00	72.00
☐ **Sugar,** strawberry	60.00 75.00	62.00
☐ **Sugar,** swan	25.00 40.00	28.00
☐ **Sugar shaker,** acorn	40.00 55.00	42.00
☐ **Sugar shaker,** flowers	30.00 55.00	38.00
☐ **Sugar shaker,** poppy	45.00 70.00	52.00
☐ **Sugar shaker,** swirl	50.00 65.00	52.00
☐ **Syrup,** butterfly	55.00 70.00	58.00
☐ **Syrup,** flowers	45.00 60.00	48.00
☐ **Syrup,** scrollwork	55.00 70.00	58.00
☐ **Syrup,** Tree of Life, blue, pewter top	140.00 175.00	148.00
☐ **Toothpick,** monkey and stump	32.00 42.00	35.00
☐ **Toothpick holder,** acorn	38.00 48.00	40.00
☐ **Toothpick holder,** blue, hat shape	50.00 65.00	52.00
☐ **Toothpick holder,** blue, signed	65.00 90.00	72.00
☐ **Toothpick holder,** heart design	28.00 38.00	30.00
☐ **Toothpick holder,** square, Fostoria	40.00 55.00	42.00
☐ **Toothpick holder,** swirl	45.00 60.00	48.00
☐ **Tray, cake,** Atterbury	40.00 55.00	42.00
☐ **Tray,** dresser, Art Nouveau, lady	55.00 70.00	58.00
☐ **Tray,** dresser, blue	28.00 38.00	30.00
☐ **Tray,** dresser, flower	22.00 32.00	25.00

434 / GLASSWARE

	Current Price Range		Prior Year Average
☐ **Tray,** pin, blue, flower	28.00	38.00	30.00
☐ **Tray,** pin, heart shape	11.00	16.00	12.50
☐ **Tray,** World's Fair, St. Louis, 1904	35.00	50.00	38.00
☐ **Tumbler,** black trim	11.00	16.00	12.50
☐ **Tumbler,** blue, hobnail	16.00	21.00	17.50
☐ **Tumbler,** cuff with button	28.00	38.00	30.00
☐ **Tumbler,** Louisiana Purchase	28.00	38.00	30.00
☐ **Tumbler,** rose	22.00	32.00	25.00
☐ **Tumbler,** scrollwork	32.00	42.00	35.00
☐ **Tumbler,** St. Louis Exposition	18.00	28.00	20.00
☐ **Vase,** gargoyle 8½"	22.00	32.00	25.00
☐ **Vase,** grapes and vines, 10"	65.00	90.00	72.00
☐ **Vase,** roses, 7"	32.00	42.00	35.00
☐ **Vase,** ruffled top, 9½"	35.00	50.00	38.00
☐ **Vase,** swans, 6½"	16.00	21.00	17.50

PRESSED AND PATTERN GLASS

During the 1800's, a machine was invented to press glass into a mold; thereby creating mass production of Victorian tableware at a lesser expense than art glass creations. Lacy pressed glass was the earliest type to become popular in France, as it imitated the delicate effect of lace. Produced from the mid-1820's until the 1850's, Lacy was sold as individually designed and decorated pieces. From the 1850's until 1900, pattern glass was produced. Contrary to the earlier Lacy designs, this glass consisted of various dinnerware pieces all pressed into the same pattern. They were then sold as matched sets.

The most collectible glass in this category dates from the 1820's to the 1890's. Desirability of a piece is contigent upon the rarity of the design and or form. Generally older, covered, larger or colored pieces command a premium.

Some collectors specialize by manufacturer, such as Boston and Sandwich or New England; however, this can be difficult since most factories rarely signed their products.

ACTRESS (c. 1872)

☐ Butter dish, CVD	70.00	85.00	72.00
☐ Cake stand	100.00	125.00	108.00
☐ Cheese dish, CVD	175.00	185.00	205.00
☐ Compote, CVD	130.00	160.00	135.00
☐ Creamer	70.00	85.00	72.00
☐ Goblet, FTD	75.00	90.00	78.00
☐ Honey dish, CVD	65.00	80.00	68.00
☐ Marmalade dish, CVD	72.00	92.00	80.00
☐ Pitcher, Pinafore	145.00	180.00	152.00
☐ Relish dish, CVD	70.00	85.00	72.00
☐ Sauce dish, flat	18.00	28.00	20.00
☐ Sauce dish, FTD	25.00	40.00	28.00
☐ Shakers, S/P	80.00	110.00	88.00
☐ Spoon holder	60.00	75.00	88.00
☐ Sugar bowl, CVD	80.00	110.00	88.00
☐ Tray	65.00	85.00	70.00

ALABAMA (c. 1898)

☐ Bottle, mustard	17.00	24.00	18.00
☐ Butter dish, CVD	40.00	55.00	42.00
☐ Cake stand	42.00	62.00	45.00

	Current Price Range		Prior Year Average
☐ Celery	25.00	40.00	29.00
☐ Compote	30.00	45.00	32.00
☐ Creamer	25.00	40.00	32.00
☐ Goblet	30.00	45.00	32.00
☐ Honey dish, CVD	16.00	24.00	18.00
☐ Mustard dish	18.00	28.00	20.00
☐ Pickle dish	14.00	22.00	16.00
☐ Pitcher, M	60.00	75.00	62.00
☐ Spoon holder	30.00	40.00	30.00
☐ Sugar, bowl, CVD	40.00	55.00	42.00
☐ Syrup jar	30.00	50.00	34.00
☐ Tumbler	18.00	28.00	20.00

ALMOND THUMBPRINT (c. 1890)

☐ Ale tumbler	64.00	80.00	69.00
☐ Butter dish, CVD	85.00	105.00	88.00
☐ Celery vase	65.00	80.00	68.00
☐ Champagne glass	65.00	80.00	68.00
☐ Compote, CVD	55.00	80.00	62.00
☐ Cordial glass	65.00	80.00	68.00
☐ Creamer	65.00	80.00	68.00
☐ Cruet, FTD	65.00	80.00	68.00
☐ Decanter	60.00	75.00	62.00
☐ Egg cup	25.00	40.00	28.00
☐ Goblet	40.00	55.00	42.00
☐ Pitcher	90.00	110.00	95.00
☐ Punch bowl	150.00	185.00	158.00
☐ Salt, individual	12.00	20.00	14.00
☐ Salt, large, flat	16.00	24.00	18.50
☐ Sugar bowl, CVD	65.00	80.00	68.00
☐ Tumbler	40.00	55.00	42.00

AMAZON (c. 1870)

☐ Bowl	20.00	35.00	24.00
☐ Butter dish, CVD	32.00	48.00	38.00
☐ Cake stand	35.00	50.00	38.00
☐ Celery	22.00	32.00	25.00
☐ Champagne glass	20.00	35.00	24.00
☐ Claret glass	14.00	22.00	16.00
☐ Compote	40.00	55.00	42.00
☐ Cordial, ruby	20.00	28.00	22.00
☐ Creamer	25.00	40.00	28.00
☐ Goblet	25.00	40.00	28.00
☐ Mug	9.00	16.00	11.50
☐ Pitcher, syrup	30.00	45.00	32.00
☐ Pitcher, W	50.00	65.00	52.00
☐ Sauce dish	10.00	18.00	11.50
☐ Shakers, S/P	30.00	45.00	32.00
☐ Spoon holder	22.00	32.00	25.00
☐ Sugar bowl, CVD	30.00	45.00	32.00
☐ Table set, child's	90.00	110.00	92.00
☐ Tumbler	20.00	30.00	20.00
☐ Vase	20.00	28.00	22.00
☐ Wine glass	20.00	30.00	20.00

436 / GLASSWARE

	Current Price Range		Prior Year Average
APOLLO (c. 1875)			
☐ Butter dish, CVD	35.00	50.00	38.00
☐ Cake stand	35.00	50.00	38.00
☐ Celery, etched	30.00	45.00	34.00
☐ Compote, CVD	55.00	75.00	60.00
☐ Creamer	40.00	55.00	42.00
☐ Egg cup	12.00	22.00	15.00
☐ Goblet	30.00	45.00	32.00
☐ Muffineer, etched	40.00	55.00	42.00
☐ Pickle dish	14.00	22.00	16.00
☐ Pitcher, M	40.00	55.00	42.00
☐ Sauce, dish, flat	11.00	16.00	12.50
☐ Sauce, dish, FTD	16.00	28.00	18.00
☐ Spoon holder	20.00	36.00	42.00
☐ Sugar bowl, CVD	35.00	50.00	38.00
☐ Tray, W	40.00	55.00	42.00
☐ Tumbler	20.00	28.00	22.00
☐ Whiskey	20.00	28.00	22.00
☐ Wine glass	14.00	22.00	16.00
ARCHED GRAPE (c. 1870)			
☐ Butter dish, CVD	52.00	62.00	55.00
☐ Celery vase	40.00	55.00	44.00
☐ Compote, CVD	60.00	75.00	62.00
☐ Cordial	22.00	32.00	35.00
☐ Creamer	40.00	55.00	44.00
☐ Goblet	30.00	45.00	32.00
☐ Pitcher, W	60.00	75.00	64.00
☐ Sauce dish	12.00	20.00	14.00
☐ Spoon holder	35.00	50.00	38.00
☐ Sugar bowl, CVD	60.00	75.00	62.00
☐ Tumbler	20.00	28.00	22.00
☐ Wine glass	23.00	28.00	23.50
ARGUS (c. 1870)			
☐ Butter dish, CVD	75.00	90.00	78.00
☐ Cake stand	85.00	100.00	88.00
☐ Celery vase	65.00	90.00	72.00
☐ Champagne glass	60.00	75.00	62.00
☐ Cordial glass	25.00	40.00	29.00
☐ Creamer	60.00	75.00	62.00
☐ Decanter, qt.	70.00	95.00	78.00
☐ Goblet	45.00	60.00	50.00
☐ Lamp, FTD	65.00	80.00	68.00
☐ Mug	80.00	95.00	82.00
☐ Pitcher, W applied handle	185.00	220.00	192.00
☐ Sauce dish	25.00	40.00	28.00
☐ Shakers, S/P	55.00	70.00	58.00
☐ Spoon holder	50.00	65.00	52.00
☐ Sugar bowl, CVD	75.00	90.00	72.00
☐ Tumbler, jelly	40.00	55.00	42.00
☐ Tumbler, W	30.00	45.00	34.00
☐ Wine glass	50.00	65.00	52.00
ART (c. 1890)			
☐ Banana dish	100.00	130.00	105.00
☐ Basket, fruit	65.00	90.00	72.00
☐ Bowl	26.00	42.00	31.00

GLASSWARE / 437

	Current Price Range		Prior Year Average
☐ Butter dish, CVD	40.00	55.00	34.00
☐ Cake stand	45.00	60.00	48.00
☐ Celery	35.00	50.00	38.00
☐ Compote, CVD, FTD	55.00	70.00	58.00
☐ Cracker jar	30.00	45.00	34.00
☐ Creamer	40.00	55.00	42.00
☐ Cruet	25.00	40.00	34.00
☐ Goblet	50.00	65.00	52.00
☐ Mug	20.00	28.00	22.00
☐ Pickle dish	18.00	28.00	20.00
☐ Pitcher, W	65.00	80.00	68.00
☐ Plate	35.00	60.00	46.00
☐ Relish dish	18.00	28.00	20.00
☐ Sauce, flat	18.00	28.00	20.00
☐ Spoon holder	28.00	38.00	30.00
☐ Sugar bowl, CVD	36.00	52.00	42.00
☐ Tumbler	22.00	32.00	25.00
☐ Wine glass	22.00	32.00	25.00

ASHBURTON (c. 1855)

☐ Ale glass	60.00	75.00	62.00
☐ Bitters bottle	50.00	65.00	52.00
☐ Butter dish, CVD	120.00	155.00	125.00
☐ Celery, plain top	75.00	90.00	78.00
☐ Celery, scalloped top	130.00	160.00	135.00
☐ Champagne glass	60.00	75.00	64.00
☐ Creamer	165.00	200.00	172.00
☐ Decanter, quart	85.00	100.00	88.00
☐ Egg cup, two styles	40.00	55.00	42.00
☐ Goblet, straight	60.00	75.00	62.00
☐ Jug, three pints	125.00	160.00	135.00
☐ Lamp	90.00	105.00	92.00
☐ Mug	60.00	75.00	62.00
☐ Sauce dish	22.00	32.00	25.00
☐ Spoon holder	45.00	60.00	49.00
☐ Sugar bowl, CVD	110.00	145.00	118.00
☐ Toddy jar, two sizes	250.00	285.00	268.00
☐ Tumbler, jelly	25.00	40.00	30.00
☐ Tumbler, W	40.00	55.00	42.00
☐ Whiskey	50.00	65.00	52.00
☐ Wine bottle, tumble-up	150.00	185.00	168.00

BABY FACE (c. 1870)

☐ Butter dish, CVD	160.00	180.00	160.00
☐ Cake stand, sm./lg.	95.00	125.00	110.00
☐ Celery vase	75.00	90.00	78.00
☐ Compote, sm./lg.	125.00	160.00	138.00
☐ Cordial	80.00	100.00	82.00
☐ Creamer	115.00	150.00	130.00
☐ Lamp	100.00	135.00	108.00
☐ Pitcher	190.00	230.00	200.00
☐ Salt	35.00	50.00	38.00
☐ Sauce dish, flat	25.00	40.00	29.00
☐ Spoon holder	70.00	85.00	74.00
☐ Wine glass	60.00	75.00	62.00

BALL AND SWIRL (c. 1890)

	Current Price Range		Prior Year Average
☐ Bowl, finger	16.00	28.00	20.00
☐ Butter dish, CVD	45.00	60.00	48.00
☐ Cake stand	25.00	40.00	30.00
☐ Celery	20.00	28.00	22.00
☐ Compote, open, CVD	40.00	55.00	44.00
☐ Cordial glass	25.00	40.00	29.00
☐ Creamer	26.00	42.00	31.00
☐ Decanter	26.00	42.00	30.00
☐ Goblet	20.00	28.00	22.00
☐ Mug, large	14.00	22.00	16.00
☐ Pitcher, plain	50.00	65.00	52.00
☐ Pitcher, etched	55.00	70.00	60.00
☐ Sauce dish, flat	9.00	16.00	11.00
☐ Spoon holder	18.00	25.00	18.50
☐ Sugar bowl	40.00	55.00	44.00
☐ Tumbler	12.00	20.00	14.00
☐ Whiskey, flint	32.00	46.00	36.00
☐ Wine glass	18.00	24.00	18.50

BALTIMORE PEAR (c. 1880)

☐ Bowl	25.00	40.00	28.00
☐ Celery	40.00	55.00	42.00
☐ Plate	45.00	60.00	48.00
☐ Sauce dish, flat	9.00	15.00	12.00
☐ Sauce dish, FTD, sm./lg.	12.00	20.00	14.00
☐ Pitcher, W	60.00	75.00	62.00
☐ Spoon holder	30.00	45.00	34.00
☐ Sugar bowl, CVD	45.00	60.00	50.00

BAMBOO (c. 1800)

☐ Celery	35.00	50.00	38.00
☐ Compote, CVD	50.00	65.00	52.00
☐ Creamer	22.00	32.00	25.00
☐ Dish, oblong	20.00	28.00	22.00
☐ Pitcher, M	35.00	50.00	38.00
☐ Sauce dish, flat	12.00	20.00	14.00
☐ Shaker, S/P	28.00	38.00	30.00
☐ Spoon holder	18.00	28.00	20.00
☐ Sugar bowl, CVD	35.00	50.00	38.00
☐ Tumbler	18.00	24.00	18.50

BARBERRY (c. 1880)

☐ Bowl	30.00	45.00	34.00
☐ Butter dish, CVD	50.00	65.00	52.00
☐ Celery	35.00	50.00	38.00
☐ Compote, L/H	65.00	80.00	68.00
☐ Cordial glass	38.00	48.00	40.00
☐ Creamer	45.00	60.00	48.00
☐ Egg cup	40.00	55.00	42.00
☐ Goblet	23.00	38.00	28.00
☐ Pickle dish	22.00	32.00	25.00
☐ Pitcher, syrup, pewter top	65.00	80.00	68.00
☐ Pitcher, W	70.00	85.00	72.00
☐ Plate	35.00	50.00	38.00
☐ Salt, FTD	28.00	38.00	30.00
☐ Sauce dish, flat, FTD	20.00	28.00	22.00
☐ Spoon holder	55.00	70.00	58.00

GLASSWARE / 439

	Current Price Range		Prior Year Average

BARLEY (c. 1870)
- ☐ Butter dish, CVD 35.00 50.00 40.00
- ☐ Cake stand 35.00 50.00 38.00
- ☐ Celery 30.00 45.00 32.00
- ☐ Compote, open, CVD 44.00 60.00 50.00
- ☐ Cordial glass 28.00 38.00 30.00
- ☐ Creamer 35.00 50.00 38.00
- ☐ Goblet 30.00 45.00 34.00
- ☐ Jam jar 40.00 55.00 42.00
- ☐ Pickle dish, handled 20.00 28.00 22.00
- ☐ Pitcher, M 40.00 55.00 42.00
- ☐ Plate, bread 35.00 50.00 38.00
- ☐ Platter 40.00 55.00 42.00
- ☐ Sauce dish, flat, FTD 18.00 28.00 20.00
- ☐ Spoon holder, CVD 40.00 55.00 42.00
- ☐ Sugar bowl 40.00 55.00 34.00
- ☐ Wine glass 28.00 38.00 30.00

BARRED FORGET-ME-NOT (c. 1883)
Butter dish
- ☐ Clear 35.00 50.00 38.00
- ☐ Yellow 44.00 60.00 58.00
- ☐ Blue 52.00 66.00 56.00
- ☐ Green 60.00 75.00 64.00

Cake, md/lg
- ☐ Clear 45.00 60.00 48.00
- ☐ Yellow 55.00 70.00 58.00
- ☐ Blue 65.00 80.00 68.00
- ☐ Green 75.00 90.00 78.00

Celery
- ☐ Clear 35.00 50.00 38.00
- ☐ Yellow 40.00 55.00 45.00
- ☐ Blue 44.00 60.00 48.00
- ☐ Green 56.00 72.00 62.00

Compote, L
- ☐ Clear 50.00 65.00 52.00
- ☐ Yellow 70.00 85.00 72.00
- ☐ Blue 80.00 95.00 82.00
- ☐ Green 90.00 105.00 92.00

Cordial glass
- ☐ Clear 18.00 25.00 18.50
- ☐ Yellow 22.00 32.00 35.00
- ☐ Blue 35.00 50.00 40.00
- ☐ Green 40.00 55.00 44.00

Creamer
- ☐ Clear 30.00 45.00 32.00
- ☐ Yellow 35.00 50.00 38.00
- ☐ Blue 40.00 55.00 42.00
- ☐ Green 50.00 65.00 52.00

Goblet
- ☐ Clear 30.00 45.00 32.00
- ☐ Yellow 35.00 50.00 38.00
- ☐ Blue 45.00 60.00 48.00
- ☐ Green 55.00 70.00 58.00

440 / GLASSWARE

	Current Price Range		Prior Year Average
Pickle dish			
☐ Clear	18.00	28.00	20.00
☐ Yellow	28.00	38.00	30.00
☐ Blue	30.00	45.00	41.00
☐ Green	38.00	55.00	38.00
Pitcher, M			
☐ Clear	45.00	60.00	48.00
☐ Yellow	55.00	70.00	58.00
☐ Blue	60.00	75.00	62.00
☐ Green	75.00	90.00	77.00
Plate			
☐ Clear	22.00	32.00	25.00
☐ Yellow	40.00	55.00	42.00
☐ Blue	45.00	60.00	48.00
☐ Green	55.00	70.00	58.00
Sauce dish			
☐ Clear	12.00	22.00	15.00
☐ Yellow	16.00	28.00	20.00
☐ Blue	18.00	30.00	22.00
☐ Green	22.00	32.00	25.00
Spoon holder			
☐ Clear	38.00	40.00	40.00
☐ Yellow	45.00	60.00	50.00
☐ Blue	50.00	65.00	44.00
☐ Green	60.00	75.00	64.00
Sugar bowl, CVD			
☐ Clear	38.00	55.00	42.00
☐ Yellow	60.00	75.00	62.00
☐ Blue	65.00	90.00	78.00
☐ Green	75.00	100.00	82.00
Wine glass			
☐ Clear	22.00	32.00	25.00
☐ Yellow	38.00	48.00	40.00
☐ Blue	45.00	60.00	48.00
☐ Green	50.00	70.00	58.00
BASKET WEAVE (c. 1883)			
Butter dish			
☐ Clear	35.00	50.00	38.00
☐ Yellow	45.00	60.00	48.00
☐ Blue	55.00	70.00	58.00
☐ Green	65.00	80.00	68.00
Compote			
☐ Clear	40.00	55.00	42.00
☐ Yellow	55.00	70.00	60.00
☐ Blue	70.00	85.00	72.00
☐ Green	90.00	110.00	92.00
Cordial Glass			
☐ Clear	25.00	40.00	30.00
☐ Yellow	40.00	55.00	38.50
☐ Blue	45.00	60.00	50.00
☐ Green	60.00	75.00	62.00
Creamer			
☐ Clear	35.00	50.00	38.00
☐ Yellow	55.00	70.00	60.00

	Current Price Range		Prior Year Average
☐ Blue	60.00	75.00	65.00
☐ Green	75.00	90.00	77.00

Cup and saucer

☐ Clear	30.00	45.00	32.00
☐ Yellow	40.00	55.00	42.00
☐ Blue	40.00	55.00	44.00
☐ Green	50.00	70.00	55.00

Egg cup

☐ Clear	18.00	28.00	20.00
☐ Yellow	35.00	50.00	38.00
☐ Blue	35.00	50.00	40.00
☐ Green	50.00	65.00	52.00

Lamp

☐ Clear	30.00	45.00	32.00
☐ Yellow	40.00	55.00	42.00
☐ Blue	45.00	60.00	47.00
☐ Green	60.00	75.00	62.00

Mug

☐ Clear	22.00	38.00	28.00
☐ Yellow	35.00	50.00	38.00
☐ Blue	40.00	55.00	44.00
☐ Green	55.00	70.00	58.00

Pickle dish

☐ Clear	16.00	22.00	17.00
☐ Yellow	25.00	32.00	26.00
☐ Blue	26.00	62.00	31.00
☐ Green	40.00	55.00	45.00

Pitcher

☐ Clear	40.00	55.00	42.00
☐ Yellow	50.00	65.00	52.00
☐ Blue	55.00	70.00	58.00
☐ Green	65.00	80.00	56.00

Plate

☐ Clear	20.00	28.00	22.00
☐ Yellow	25.00	40.00	30.00
☐ Blue	40.00	55.00	42.00
☐ Green	50.00	65.00	52.00

Sugar bowl, CVD

☐ Clear	35.00	50.00	40.00
☐ Yellow	45.00	60.00	49.00
☐ Blue	55.00	70.00	60.00
☐ Green	65.00	80.00	70.00

Tray, bread

☐ Clear	40.00	55.00	42.00
☐ Yellow	50.00	65.00	52.00
☐ Blue	65.00	90.00	72.00
☐ Green	75.00	100.00	82.00

Tray, W

☐ Clear	25.00	40.00	28.00
☐ Yellow	35.00	50.00	38.00
☐ Blue	45.00	60.00	48.00
☐ Green	50.00	65.00	52.00

442 / GLASSWARE

Tumbler	Current Price Range		Prior Year Average
☐ Clear	25.00	40.00	30.00
☐ Yellow	32.00	42.00	35.00
☐ Blue	35.00	50.00	38.00
☐ Green	45.00	60.00	48.00

BEADED ACORN MEDALLION (c. 1869)

☐ Butter dish, CVD	45.00	60.00	48.00
☐ Champagne glass	35.00	50.00	38.00
☐ Compote, L/H	45.00	60.00	50.00
☐ Creamer	52.00	68.00	58.00
☐ Egg cup	30.00	45.00	44.00
☐ Goblet	35.00	50.00	40.00
☐ Honey dish	22.00	38.00	28.00
☐ Pickle dish	22.00	38.00	28.00
☐ Pitcher, W	55.00	70.00	58.00
☐ Plate	25.00	40.00	30.00
☐ Salt, FTD	20.00	28.00	22.00
☐ Sauce dish	14.00	22.00	16.00
☐ Spoon holder	40.00	55.00	42.00
☐ Sugar bowl, CVD	55.00	65.00	52.00
☐ Wine glass	20.00	28.00	22.00

BEADED BAND (c. 1884)

☐ Butter dish	35.00	50.00	38.00
☐ Cake stand	30.00	45.00	32.00
☐ Compote	40.00	55.00	44.00
☐ Creamer	25.00	60.00	30.00
☐ Goblet	28.00	38.00	30.00
☐ Jam jar	22.00	32.00	25.00
☐ Pickle dish, CVD	45.00	60.00	48.00
☐ Pitcher, W	50.00	65.00	52.00
☐ Sauce dish	14.00	22.00	16.00
☐ Spoon holder	22.00	38.00	28.00
☐ Sugar bowl	25.00	40.00	30.00
☐ Wine glass	22.00	32.00	25.00

BEADED DEWDROP (c. 1898)

☐ Butter dish, CVD	60.00	75.00	62.00
☐ Cake stand	45.00	60.00	48.00
☐ Celery tray	40.00	55.00	44.00
☐ Celery vase	50.00	65.00	52.00
☐ Condiment, four pc.	75.00	90.00	78.00
☐ Creamer, sm./lg.	50.00	70.00	54.00
☐ Cruet	22.00	38.00	28.00
☐ Cup and saucer	38.00	55.00	42.00
☐ Goblet	50.00	65.00	52.00
☐ Mug	42.00	58.00	48.00
☐ Pitcher, W	65.00	80.00	68.00
☐ Sauce dish, flat, handled	12.00	20.00	14.00
☐ Shakers, S/P	30.00	45.00	35.00
☐ Spoon holder	22.00	38.00	28.00
☐ Sugar bowl, sm./lg.	55.00	70.00	58.00
☐ Toothpick holder	35.00	50.00	38.00
☐ Tumbler	40.00	55.00	44.00
☐ Wine glass	36.00	52.00	42.00

GLASSWARE / 443

	Current Price Range		Prior Year Average

BEADED GRAPE (c. 1880)
Bowl
- ☐ Clear 20.00 28.00 22.00
- ☐ Green 26.00 42.00 32.00

Butter dish
- ☐ Clear 55.00 70.00 58.00
- ☐ Green 80.00 95.00 82.00

Cake stand
- ☐ Clear 50.00 65.00 54.00
- ☐ Green 70.00 85.00 74.00

Celery
- ☐ Clear 35.00 50.00 44.00
- ☐ Green 55.00 70.00 58.00

Compote
- ☐ Clear 55.00 70.00 58.00
- ☐ Green 75.00 90.00 78.00

Cordial glass
- ☐ Clear 45.00 60.00 50.00
- ☐ Green 60.00 75.00 62.00

Creamer
- ☐ Clear 50.00 65.00 52.00
- ☐ Green 80.00 95.00 82.00

Cruet
- ☐ Clear 45.00 60.00 48.00
- ☐ Green 65.00 80.00 68.00

Dish
- ☐ Clear 40.00 55.00 42.00
- ☐ Green 60.00 80.00 62.00

Pickle dish
- ☐ Clear 22.00 38.00 28.00
- ☐ Green 40.00 55.00 44.00

Pitcher
- ☐ Clear 50.00 65.00 52.00
- ☐ Green 90.00 110.00 92.00

Platter
- ☐ Clear 65.00 85.00 70.00
- ☐ Green 90.00 115.00 95.00

Shakers, S/P
- ☐ Clear 40.00 55.00 42.00
- ☐ Green 65.00 80.00 68.00

Spoon holder
- ☐ Clear 45.00 60.00 48.00
- ☐ Green 40.00 55.00 42.00

Sugar bowl, CVD
- ☐ Clear 50.00 65.00 52.00
- ☐ Green 68.00 72.00 67.50

BEADED GRAPE MEDALLION (c. 1867)
- ☐ Butter dish, CVD 55.00 70.00 58.00
- ☐ Celery vase 60.00 75.00 62.00
- ☐ Compote, CVD 70.00 85.00 72.00
- ☐ Cordial glass 40.00 55.00 44.00
- ☐ Creamer 90.00 105.00 92.00
- ☐ Egg cup 40.00 55.00 42.00

444 / GLASSWARE

	Current Price Range		Prior Year Average
☐ Goblet	35.00	50.00	40.00
☐ Honey dish	28.00	38.00	30.00
☐ Pickle dish	28.00	38.00	30.00
☐ Pitcher, W	110.00	140.00	120.00
☐ Plate	30.00	45.00	34.00
☐ Salt and pepper	25.00	40.00	28.00
☐ Sauce dish	18.00	28.00	20.00
☐ Spoon holder	40.00	55.00	44.00
☐ Sugar bowl, CVD	60.00	75.00	64.00

BEADED LOOP (c. 1906)

☐ Bowl, berry, CVD	35.00	50.00	38.00
☐ Butter dish	30.00	45.00	34.00
☐ Cake stand	45.00	60.00	48.00
☐ Celery	45.00	60.00	50.00
☐ Compote	30.00	45.00	32.00
☐ Cordial glass	22.00	32.00	25.00
☐ Creamer	30.00	45.00	34.00
☐ Goblet	32.00	42.00	35.00
☐ Mug	22.00	32.00	25.00
☐ Pickle dish	22.00	32.00	25.00
☐ Pitcher, W	45.00	50.00	48.00
☐ Sauce dish	18.00	28.00	20.00
☐ Salt and pepper	30.00	45.00	34.00
☐ Spoon holder	45.00	60.00	48.00
☐ Sugar bowl, CVD	40.00	55.00	42.00
☐ Sugar shaker	32.00	42.00	35.00
☐ Toothpick holder	20.00	28.00	22.00
☐ Tray, bread	36.00	52.00	42.00
☐ Tumbler	38.00	48.00	40.00
☐ Wine glass	32.00	42.00	35.00

BEADED TULIP (c. 1894)

☐ Butter dish, CVD	45.00	60.00	48.00
☐ Compote, H	45.00	60.00	50.00
☐ Cake stand	45.00	60.00	50.00
☐ Cordial glass	26.00	42.00	31.00
☐ Creamer	32.00	42.00	35.00
☐ Dish, oval	28.00	38.00	30.00
☐ Goblet	40.00	55.00	42.00
☐ Jam jar	35.00	50.00	40.00
☐ Lamp	45.00	60.00	48.00
☐ Pickle dish	26.00	42.00	31.00
☐ Pitcher, M	40.00	55.00	42.00
☐ Pitcher, W	60.00	75.00	62.00
☐ Plate	25.00	40.00	28.00
☐ Sauce dish, flat	18.00	24.00	17.50
☐ Spoon holder	26.00	42.00	31.00
☐ Sugar bowl, CVD	36.00	50.00	41.00
☐ Tray, W	40.00	55.00	42.00
☐ Wine glass	35.00	50.00	40.00

BELLFLOWER (c. 1850)

☐ Bowl, berry and flat	120.00	145.00	122.00
☐ Butter dish, CVD	85.00	115.00	95.00
☐ Castor bottle	65.00	80.00	68.00
☐ Celery, banded and ribbed top	140.00	180.00	155.00

GLASSWARE / 445

	Current Price Range		Prior Year Average
☐ Champagne glass	65.00	125.00	90.00
☐ Compote, open, CVD	110.00	210.00	150.00
☐ Cordial glass	80.00	95.00	52.00
☐ Creamer	150.00	185.00	158.00
☐ Decanter, qt.	150.00	185.00	158.00
☐ Egg cup	35.00	60.00	42.00
☐ Goblet	25.00	65.00	35.00
☐ Honey dish	15.00	35.00	20.00
☐ Lamp, marble base	135.00	185.00	150.00
☐ Mug, applied handle	135.00	210.00	162.00
☐ Pickle dish	100.00	120.00	102.00
☐ Pitcher, M	410.00	510.00	450.00
☐ Pitcher, syrup	235.00	285.00	250.00
☐ Pitcher, W	200.00	260.00	215.00
☐ Plate	65.00	100.00	77.00
☐ Salt, CVD	140.00	175.00	160.00
☐ Sauce dish	20.00	35.00	26.00
☐ Spoon holder	45.00	60.00	50.00
☐ Sugar bowl, CVD	75.00	105.00	85.00
☐ Tumbler	75.00	200.00	120.00
☐ Wine glass	65.00	80.00	72.00

BLACKBERRY (c. 1870)
Bowl
☐ Clear	37.00	52.00	44.00
☐ Milk Glass	65.00	70.00	67.00

Champagne glass
☐ Clear	45.00	60.00	50.00
☐ Milk Glass	67.00	82.00	74.00

Compote
☐ Clear	75.00	90.00	80.00
☐ Milk Glass	155.00	190.00	170.00

Creamer
☐ Clear	60.00	75.00	66.00
☐ Milk Glass	90.00	120.00	100.00

Dish
☐ Clear	55.00	70.00	62.00
☐ Milk Glass	105.00	135.00	118.00

Egg cup
☐ Clear	42.00	57.00	48.00
☐ Milk Glass	105.00	135.00	118.00

Goblet
☐ Clear	45.00	60.00	52.00
☐ Milk Glass	80.00	95.00	86.00

Honey dish
☐ Clear	20.00	30.00	24.00
☐ Milk Glass	45.00	60.00	52.00

Salt
☐ Clear	30.00	45.00	37.00
☐ Milk Glass	67.00	82.00	74.00

Sauce dish
☐ Clear	15.00	25.00	20.00
☐ Milk Glass	30.00	45.00	37.00

446 / GLASSWARE

	Current Price Range		Prior Year Average
Spoon holder			
☐ Clear	50.00	65.00	58.00
☐ Milk Glass	80.00	95.00	87.00
Tumbler			
☐ Clear	25.00	40.00	32.00
☐ Milk Glass	38.00	53.00	44.00
BLOCK AND FAN (c. 1880)			
☐ Butter dish	35.00	50.00	42.00
☐ Cake stand	35.00	45.00	40.00
☐ Carafe	40.00	55.00	47.00
☐ Celery	30.00	45.00	37.00
☐ Compote	45.00	60.00	52.00
☐ Cordial glass	20.00	35.00	27.00
☐ Creamer	30.00	45.00	37.00
☐ Cruet, sm./lg.	22.00	37.00	29.00
☐ Goblet	27.00	42.00	33.00
☐ Jam jar	22.00	37.00	29.00
☐ Lamp	25.00	40.00	32.00
☐ Pickle dish	18.00	26.00	21.00
☐ Pitcher, W	30.00	45.00	37.00
☐ Plate	25.00	40.00	32.00
☐ Sauce dish	12.00	20.00	16.00
☐ Salt and pepper	22.00	37.00	29.00
☐ Spoon holder	23.00	38.00	30.00
☐ Sugar bowl, CVD	27.00	42.00	34.00
☐ Tumbler	15.00	25.00	20.00
☐ Wine glass	25.00	40.00	32.00
BOW TIE (c. 1888)			
☐ Bowl	45.00	60.00	52.00
☐ Butter dish, CVD	70.00	85.00	77.00
☐ Cake stand	47.00	62.00	54.00
☐ Compote	50.00	65.00	57.00
☐ Creamer	52.00	67.00	59.00
☐ Goblet	47.00	62.00	54.00
☐ Honey dish, CVD	50.00	65.00	57.00
☐ Jam jar	40.00	55.00	47.00
☐ Pitcher, W	67.00	82.00	74.00
☐ Relish dish	27.00	42.00	34.00
☐ Sauce dish	18.00	26.00	21.00
☐ Spoon holder	30.00	45.00	37.00
☐ Sugar bowl, CVD	65.00	80.00	72.00
BUDDED IVY (1870)			
☐ Butter dish, CVD	40.00	55.00	47.00
☐ Compote, L/H	50.00	65.00	57.00
☐ Creamer	43.00	58.00	49.00
☐ Goblet	35.00	50.00	42.00
☐ Mug	25.00	40.00	32.00
☐ Pickle dish	10.00	25.00	16.00
☐ Pitcher, W	45.00	60.00	52.00
☐ Salt	25.00	35.00	30.00

	Current Price Range		Prior Year Average
☐ Sauce dish	8.00	14.00	10.00
☐ Spoon holder	30.00	45.00	36.00
☐ Sugar bowl, CVD	40.00	55.00	47.00

BULL'S EYE (c. 1850)

☐ Butter dish	90.00	105.00	96.00
☐ Celery vase	60.00	75.00	67.00
☐ Champagne glass	70.00	85.00	76.00
☐ Cologne bottle	60.00	75.00	67.00
☐ Compote, L/H	75.00	100.00	82.00
☐ Cordial glass	40.00	55.00	47.00
☐ Creamer	80.00	120.00	100.00
☐ Cruet, small	45.00	60.00	52.00
☐ Decanter, pt. and qt.	52.00	67.00	59.00
☐ Egg cup, DBL	49.00	55.00	42.00
☐ Goblet	50.00	65.00	57.00
☐ Jar, CVD	55.00	70.00	62.00
☐ Lamp	60.00	80.00	70.00
☐ Pickle dish	30.00	45.00	37.00
☐ Salt	35.00	50.00	42.00
☐ Spoon holder	40.00	55.00	47.00
☐ Sugar bowl, CVD	90.00	110.00	100.00
☐ Tumbler	75.00	100.00	82.00
☐ Water bottle	55.00	70.00	62.00
☐ Wine	40.00	55.00	47.00

BULL'S EYE WITH FLEUR-DE-LIS (c. 1850)

☐ Bowl, berry	80.00	95.00	87.00
☐ Butter dish, CVD	95.00	110.00	100.00
☐ Celery	130.00	165.00	140.00
☐ Compote, L/H	95.00	110.00	100.00
☐ Cordial glass	65.00	80.00	72.00
☐ Creamer	110.00	145.00	120.00
☐ Decanter, pt. and qt.	75.00	100.00	82.00
☐ Goblet	65.00	80.00	72.00
☐ Lamp	110.00	145.00	120.00
☐ Pitcher, W	265.00	300.00	280.00
☐ Plate	70.00	85.00	77.00
☐ Salt, FTD	50.00	65.00	57.00
☐ Sugar bowl, CVD	105.00	140.00	115.00

CABBAGE ROSE (c. 1870)

☐ Butter dish	75.00	90.00	82.00
☐ Cake stand	70.00	85.00	77.00
☐ Celery vase	45.00	60.00	50.00
☐ Compote	60.00	75.00	67.00
☐ Cordial glass	29.00	44.00	35.00
☐ Creamer	52.00	67.00	59.00
☐ Egg cup, DBL	27.00	42.00	34.00
☐ Pickle dish	20.00	30.00	24.00
☐ Pitcher	75.00	90.00	82.00
☐ Salt	20.00	35.00	27.00
☐ Sauce dish	15.00	22.00	19.00
☐ Spoon holder	40.00	55.00	47.00
☐ Sugar bowl, CVD	52.00	67.00	59.00
☐ Tumbler	47.00	62.00	54.00
☐ Wine glass	40.00	55.00	47.00

448 / GLASSWARE

	Current Price Range		Prior Year Average
CACTUS (c. 1903)			
☐ Bowl	75.00	95.00	85.00
☐ Butter dish	105.00	130.00	110.00
☐ Celery	45.00	65.00	54.00
☐ Creamer	70.00	85.00	76.00
☐ Cruet	90.00	105.00	95.00
☐ Mug	52.00	68.00	59.00
☐ Pitcher, W	160.00	185.00	172.00
☐ Relish dish	65.00	80.00	72.00
☐ Shakers, S/P	55.00	70.00	62.00
☐ Spoon holder	60.00	75.00	66.00
☐ Sugar bowl	75.00	90.00	82.00
☐ Toothpick holder	45.00	60.00	52.00
☐ Tumbler	55.00	70.00	62.00
CANADIAN (c. 1870)			
☐ Butter dish, CVD	50.00	65.00	57.00
☐ Celery	37.00	52.00	44.00
☐ Compote, CVD	55.00	70.00	62.00
☐ Cordial glass	27.00	42.00	34.00
☐ Creamer	45.00	60.00	52.00
☐ Goblet	40.00	55.00	47.00
☐ Jam jar	30.00	40.00	34.00
☐ Pitcher, sm./lg.	60.00	75.00	67.00
☐ Plate	30.00	45.00	37.00
☐ Sauce dish	10.00	20.00	14.00
☐ Spoon holder	37.00	52.00	44.00
☐ Sugar bowl, CVD	50.00	60.00	54.00
☐ Wine glass	30.00	40.00	34.00
CAPE COD (c. 1870)			
☐ Bowl	26.00	42.00	33.00
☐ Butter dish, CVD	52.00	67.00	59.00
☐ Celery	35.00	45.00	40.00
☐ Compote, open, CVD	40.00	65.00	52.00
☐ Creamer	40.00	55.00	47.00
☐ Cup and saucer	30.00	45.00	37.00
☐ Goblet	42.00	57.00	49.00
☐ Jam jar	50.00	65.00	57.00
☐ Pickle dish	22.00	30.00	26.00
☐ Pitcher, W	55.00	75.00	65.00
☐ Plate	27.00	42.00	34.00
☐ Spoon holder	26.00	41.00	33.00
☐ Sugar bowl, CVD	55.00	70.00	60.00
☐ Wine glass	32.00	47.00	39.00
CATHEDRAL (c. 1880)			
☐ Bowl	27.00	42.00	33.00
☐ Butter dish	45.00	60.00	52.00
☐ Cake stand	47.00	62.00	54.00
☐ Compote, CVD	62.00	77.00	69.00
☐ Creamer	37.00	52.00	34.00
☐ Egg cup	25.00	40.00	32.00
☐ Goblet	30.00	45.00	37.00
☐ Pitcher, W	60.00	70.00	64.00
☐ Relish dish	20.00	35.00	27.00
☐ Spoon holder	27.00	42.00	34.00

GLASSWARE / 449

	Current Price Range		Prior Year Average
☐ Sugar bowl, CVD	45.00	60.00	52.00
☐ Tumbler	25.00	40.00	32.00
☐ Wine glass	30.00	45.00	37.00

CHAIN WITH STAR (c. 1880)

☐ Butter dish, CVD	35.00	50.00	42.00
☐ Cake stand	25.00	35.00	30.00
☐ Compote, L/H	32.00	47.00	39.00
☐ Cordial glass	20.00	30.00	24.00
☐ Creamer	35.00	50.00	42.00
☐ Dish	18.00	26.00	21.00
☐ Goblet	20.00	35.00	27.00
☐ Pickle dish	15.00	25.00	20.00
☐ Pitcher, W	37.00	52.00	43.00
☐ Plate	20.00	35.00	27.00
☐ Sauce dish	18.00	26.00	22.00
☐ Shakers, S/P	20.00	35.00	27.00
☐ Spoon holder	30.00	45.00	37.00
☐ Sugar bowl, CVD	40.00	55.00	46.00
☐ Wine glass	20.00	30.00	24.00

CHECKERBOARD (c. 1900)

☐ Bowl, sm./lg.	23.00	38.00	30.00
☐ Butter dish, CVD	25.00	40.00	32.00
☐ Celery	10.00	18.00	13.00
☐ Celery vase	18.00	26.00	21.00
☐ Cheese dish	20.00	30.00	24.00
☐ Creamer	18.00	26.00	22.00
☐ Cruet, small	20.00	35.00	27.00
☐ Goblet	15.00	25.00	20.00
☐ Pickle dish	12.00	20.00	16.00
☐ Pitcher, M/W	25.00	40.00	32.00
☐ Plate	15.00	23.00	18.00
☐ Punch cup	8.00	14.00	11.00
☐ Sauce dish	6.00	12.00	8.00
☐ Shakers, S/P	15.00	22.00	18.00
☐ Sherbet	10.00	15.00	12.00
☐ Spoon holder	23.00	30.00	25.00
☐ Sugar bowl, CVD	20.00	35.00	27.00
☐ Tumbler	10.00	18.00	16.00
☐ Wine glass	16.00	24.00	20.00

CLASSIC (c. 1880)

☐ Bowl, FTD	50.00	65.00	57.00
☐ Butter dish, CVD	135.00	165.00	145.00
☐ Celery	105.00	140.00	118.00
☐ Compote, open, CVD	110.00	185.00	150.00
☐ Creamer	110.00	145.00	115.00
☐ Goblet	160.00	185.00	170.00
☐ Plate, Warrior	125.00	160.00	140.00
☐ Sauce dish	30.00	45.00	37.00
☐ Spoon holder, CVD	100.00	135.00	118.00
☐ Sugar bowl, CVD	125.00	160.00	135.00

CLEAR RIBBON (c. 1880)

☐ Butter dish, CVD	42.00	57.00	48.00
☐ Cake stand	55.00	70.00	62.00

450 / GLASSWARE

	Current Price Range		Prior Year Average
☐ Celery	20.00	35.00	27.00
☐ Compote, CVD	60.00	75.00	67.00
☐ Creamer	32.00	47.00	39.00
☐ Dish	32.00	47.00	39.00
☐ Goblet	30.00	45.00	37.00
☐ Mug	15.00	30.00	21.00
☐ Pickle dish	21.00	36.00	28.00
☐ Pitcher	57.00	72.00	64.00
☐ Platter	30.00	45.00	37.00
☐ Sauce dish	8.00	16.00	10.00
☐ Spoon holder	30.00	45.00	37.00
☐ Sugar bowl, CVD	40.00	55.00	47.00

CLEMANTIS (c. 1876)

☐ Bowl, berry	15.00	22.00	18.00
☐ Butter dish	34.00	49.00	41.00
☐ Creamer	30.00	45.00	37.00
☐ Goblet	22.00	37.00	29.00
☐ Lamp	30.00	40.00	34.00
☐ Pickle dish	12.00	20.00	16.00
☐ Pitcher, W	37.00	42.00	39.00
☐ Sauce dish	15.00	22.00	18.00
☐ Spoon holder	20.00	30.00	24.00
☐ Sugar bowl, CVD	35.00	50.00	42.00

COLUMBIAN-COIN (c. 1890)

☐ Bowl, finger	80.00	95.00	87.00
☐ Butter dish, CVD	110.00	145.00	120.00
☐ Cake stand	95.00	110.00	100.00
☐ Celery	70.00	85.00	77.00
☐ Compote, open	130.00	165.00	145.00
☐ Creamer	80.00	120.00	100.00
☐ Cruet	95.00	110.00	100.00
☐ Goblet	75.00	90.00	82.00
☐ Lamp	100.00	135.00	118.00
☐ Pickle dish	42.00	57.00	49.00
☐ Pitcher, M/W	140.00	175.00	155.00
☐ Sauce dish	23.00	38.00	29.00
☐ Shakers, S/P	100.00	135.00	118.00
☐ Spoon holder	57.00	72.00	63.00
☐ Sugar bowl, CVD	105.00	140.00	125.00
☐ Toothpick holder	70.00	85.00	77.00
☐ Tray, W	90.00	105.00	95.00
☐ Tumbler	80.00	95.00	87.00

CORDOVA (c. 1890)

☐ Bottle, perfume	27.00	42.00	33.00
☐ Bowl, finger, CVD	20.00	30.00	24.00
☐ Butter dish	20.00	35.00	27.00
☐ Cake stand	25.00	40.00	32.00
☐ Celery	32.00	47.00	39.00
☐ Compote, open, CVD	22.00	37.00	29.00
☐ Creamer	20.00	35.00	27.00
☐ Cruet, small	18.00	26.00	21.00
☐ Pitcher, W/M	33.00	48.00	40.00
☐ Cup	12.00	20.00	15.00
☐ Sauce dish	8.00	14.00	10.00

	Current Price Range		Prior Year Average
☐ Spoon holder	15.00	22.00	18.00
☐ Sugar bowl, CVD	22.00	37.00	28.00
☐ Toothpick holder	10.00	18.00	13.00
☐ Tumbler	15.00	25.00	20.00

CROESUS (c. 1897)

☐ Bowl	60.00	75.00	67.00
☐ Butter dish	80.00	95.00	87.00
☐ Celery	55.00	70.00	62.00
☐ Compote	70.00	85.00	77.00
☐ Creamer	60.00	75.00	67.00
☐ Cruet, small	55.00	70.00	62.00
☐ Pickle dish	30.00	45.00	37.00
☐ Pitcher, W	95.00	110.00	100.00
☐ Plate	67.00	82.00	73.00
☐ Relish dish	30.00	45.00	37.00
☐ Sauce dish	22.00	37.00	28.00
☐ Shakers, S/P	45.00	60.00	52.00
☐ Spoon holder	37.00	52.00	43.00
☐ Sugar bowl, CVD	90.00	105.00	95.00
☐ Toothpick holder	35.00	45.00	40.00
☐ Tumbler	27.00	42.00	33.00

CRYSTAL (c. 1860)

☐ Ale glass	25.00	40.00	32.00
☐ Bowl	50.00	65.00	56.00
☐ Butter dish, CVD	55.00	70.00	60.00
☐ Celery	47.00	62.00	54.00
☐ Champagne glass	27.00	42.00	34.00
☐ Compote	50.00	65.00	57.00
☐ Cordial glass	30.00	40.00	34.00
☐ Creamer	60.00	75.00	67.00
☐ Decanter, pt. and qt.	55.00	70.00	62.00
☐ Egg cup	27.00	42.00	33.00
☐ Goblet	27.00	42.00	33.00
☐ Mug	25.00	40.00	32.00
☐ Pitcher, W	80.00	95.00	87.00
☐ Sauce dish	12.00	20.00	16.00
☐ Spoon holder	27.00	42.00	33.00
☐ Sugar bowl, CVD	70.00	85.00	76.00
☐ Tumbler	35.00	50.00	42.00
☐ Wine glass	30.00	45.00	37.00

CRYSTAL WEDDING (c. 1880)

☐ Banana dish	50.00	65.00	56.00
☐ Bowl, berry	34.00	49.00	40.00
☐ Butter dish	34.00	49.00	40.00
☐ Cake stand	45.00	60.00	52.00
☐ Celery vase	29.00	44.00	34.00
☐ Creamer	30.00	45.00	37.00
☐ Dish, CVD	50.00	65.00	57.00
☐ Lamp	27.00	42.00	33.00
☐ Mug	25.00	40.00	32.00
☐ Pitcher, W	45.00	60.00	52.00
☐ Sauce dish	8.00	14.00	11.00
☐ Shakers, S/P	20.00	35.00	27.00

452 / GLASSWARE

	Current Price Range		Prior Year Average
☐ Spoon holder	20.00	35.00	27.00
☐ Sugar bowl, CVD	37.00	52.00	43.00
☐ Tumbler	20.00	35.00	26.00

CURRANT (c. 1870)

☐ Butter dish, CVD	57.00	67.00	61.00
☐ Cake stand	60.00	75.00	67.00
☐ Celery vase	40.00	55.00	47.00
☐ Compote, L/H	52.00	67.00	59.00
☐ Cordial glass	34.00	49.00	41.00
☐ Creamer	49.00	64.00	56.00
☐ Egg cup	26.00	37.00	30.00
☐ Goblet	32.00	47.00	39.00
☐ Pitcher, W	60.00	75.00	66.00
☐ Plate	26.00	36.00	30.00
☐ Salt	22.00	32.00	26.00
☐ Spoon holder	35.00	55.00	45.00
☐ Sugar bowl, CVD	47.00	62.00	53.00
☐ Tumbler	30.00	45.00	37.00
☐ Wine glass	34.00	49.00	40.00

CURTAIN (c. 1880)

☐ Bowl, berry	10.00	15.00	12.00
☐ Bowl	18.00	26.00	21.00
☐ Butter dish, CVD	45.00	60.00	52.00
☐ Cake stand	27.00	42.00	33.00
☐ Celery	22.00	37.00	29.00
☐ Compote	40.00	60.00	50.00
☐ Creamer	30.00	45.00	37.00
☐ Goblet	25.00	40.00	32.00
☐ Mug	20.00	30.00	24.00
☐ Pickle dish	18.00	26.00	22.00
☐ Pitcher, W/M	50.00	65.00	57.00
☐ Plate, square	18.00	26.00	22.00
☐ Sauce dish, FTD	12.00	20.00	16.00
☐ Shakers, S/P	23.00	38.00	30.00
☐ Spoon holder	30.00	45.00	36.00
☐ Sugar bowl, CVD	45.00	60.00	52.00
☐ Tray, bread	34.00	47.00	39.00
☐ Tumbler	22.00	37.00	29.00

CUT LOG (c. 1880)

☐ Butter dish, CVD	40.00	55.00	48.00
☐ Cake stand	65.00	80.00	72.00
☐ Celery	42.00	57.00	49.00
☐ Compote, open, CVD	25.00	50.00	35.00
☐ Cracker jar	32.00	47.00	39.00
☐ Creamer	37.00	52.00	43.00
☐ Cruet	30.00	45.00	36.00
☐ Goblet	35.00	45.00	40.00
☐ Honey dish	27.00	42.00	33.00
☐ Mug	18.00	26.00	22.00
☐ Mustard dish	23.00	38.00	29.00
☐ Pickle dish	18.00	26.00	21.00
☐ Pitcher, W	65.00	80.00	72.00
☐ Sauce dish	12.00	20.00	16.00
☐ Shakers, S/P	50.00	65.00	56.00

	Current Price Range		Prior Year Average
☐ Spoon holder	27.00	42.00	33.00
☐ Sugar bowl, CVD	47.00	62.00	53.00
☐ Tumbler	23.00	40.00	32.00
☐ Wine glass	30.00	45.00	37.00

DAISY AND BUTTON WITH CROSS BARS (c. 1888)

Bowl

☐ Clear	18.00	26.00	22.00
☐ Vaseline	30.00	45.00	36.00

Butter dish, CVD

☐ Clear	65.00	95.00	80.00
☐ Vaseline	90.00	120.00	100.00

Celery

☐ Clear	30.00	45.00	35.00
☐ Vaseline	35.00	50.00	40.00

Compote

☐ Clear	40.00	55.00	46.00
☐ Vaseline	60.00	75.00	66.00

Creamer

☐ Clear	21.00	36.00	26.00
☐ Vaseline	33.00	48.00	40.00

Cruet

☐ Clear	27.00	42.00	33.00
☐ Vaseline	47.00	62.00	53.00

Goblet

☐ Clear	20.00	30.00	24.00
☐ Vaseline	31.00	46.00	37.00

Mug

☐ Clear	18.00	26.00	21.00
☐ Vaseline	22.00	37.00	30.00

Pickle dish

☐ Clear	10.00	18.00	14.00
☐ Vaseline	20.00	30.00	24.00

Pitcher

☐ Clear	30.00	45.00	36.00
☐ Vaseline	47.00	62.00	52.00

Sauce dish

☐ Clear	10.00	20.00	14.00
☐ Vaseline	15.00	25.00	20.00

Shakers, S/P

☐ Clear	20.00	30.00	24.00
☐ Vaseline	33.00	48.00	39.00

Spoon holder

☐ Clear	18.00	26.00	21.00
☐ Vaseline	30.00	45.00	36.00

Sugar bowl, CVD

☐ Clear	35.00	50.00	42.00
☐ Vaseline	47.00	62.00	53.00

Toothpick holder

☐ Clear	12.00	20.00	16.00
☐ Vaseline	20.00	30.00	24.00

454 / GLASSWARE

	Current Price Range		Prior Year Average
Tray			
☐ Clear	33.00	48.00	39.00
☐ Vaseline	47.00	62.00	53.00
Tray, bread			
☐ Clear	47.00	62.00	53.00
☐ Vaseline	60.00	85.00	66.00
Tumbler			
☐ Clear	12.00	20.00	15.00
☐ Vaseline	20.00	30.00	25.00
DAKOTA (c. 1890)			
☐ Basket	50.00	65.00	56.00
☐ Bowl, berry	30.00	40.00	34.00
☐ Bowl, finger	20.00	30.00	25.00
☐ Butter dish, CVD	40.00	60.00	44.00
☐ Celery	35.00	50.00	40.00
☐ Compote, CVD	50.00	75.00	62.00
☐ Creamer	30.00	40.00	34.00
☐ Goblet	30.00	45.00	37.00
☐ Jam jar	18.00	26.00	22.00
☐ Mug	25.00	40.00	32.00
☐ Pitcher, W	70.00	85.00	76.00
☐ Plate	18.00	26.00	21.00
☐ Shakers, S/P	22.00	37.00	29.00
☐ Spoon holder	25.00	40.00	32.00
☐ Sugar bowl, CVD	50.00	70.00	60.00
☐ Sugar bowl, etched	40.00	55.00	47.00
☐ Tumbler	30.00	50.00	40.00
☐ Wine glass	28.00	43.00	33.00
DEER AND PINE TREE (c. 1860)			
☐ Butter dish, CVD	60.00	85.00	72.00
☐ Cake stand	65.00	90.00	80.00
☐ Celery	50.00	65.00	56.00
☐ Compote, CVD	80.00	00.00	90.00
☐ Creamer	43.00	58.00	49.00
☐ Jam jar	40.00	55.00	46.00
☐ Mug, sm./lg.	30.00	45.00	35.00
☐ Pickle dish	20.00	30.00	24.00
☐ Pitcher	60.00	80.00	70.00
☐ Platter	45.00	60.00	52.00
☐ Salt	12.00	20.00	15.00
☐ Sauce dish, FTD	18.00	26.00	22.00
☐ Spoon holder	40.00	65.00	52.00
☐ Sugar bowl, CVD	55.00	70.00	62.00
☐ Tray, bread	67.00	82.00	73.00
DELAWARE (c. 1899)			
Banana dish			
☐ Clear	33.00	48.00	39.00
☐ Cranberry	48.00	63.00	54.00
☐ Green	42.00	57.00	48.00
Bowl, berry			
☐ Clear	20.00	35.00	26.00
☐ Cranberry	55.00	70.00	62.00
☐ Green	45.00	60.00	52.00

Butter dish, CVD

	Current Price Range		Prior Year Average
☐ Clear	70.00	85.00	77.00
☐ Cranberry	110.00	135.00	120.00
☐ Green	95.00	110.00	100.00

Celery

☐ Clear	50.00	65.00	56.00
☐ Cranberry	90.00	105.00	95.00
☐ Green	70.00	85.00	75.00

Creamer

☐ Clear	30.00	45.00	36.00
☐ Cranberry	45.00	60.00	52.00
☐ Green	35.00	50.00	42.00

Cruet

☐ Clear	37.00	52.00	43.00
☐ Cranberry	52.00	67.00	59.00
☐ Green	45.00	60.00	52.00

Pitcher, W

☐ Clear	55.00	70.00	62.00
☐ Cranberry	95.00	110.00	100.00
☐ Green	75.00	90.00	82.00

Punch

☐ Clear	12.00	20.00	16.00
☐ Cranberry	35.00	50.00	42.00
☐ Green	22.00	37.00	29.00

Sauce dish

☐ Clear	18.00	26.00	21.00
☐ Cranberry	35.00	50.00	42.00
☐ Green	30.00	45.00	37.00

Spoon holder

☐ Clear	45.00	60.00	52.00
☐ Cranberry	70.00	85.00	77.00
☐ Green	60.00	75.00	67.00

Sugar bowl, CVD

☐ Clear	60.00	75.00	67.00
☐ Cranberry	95.00	110.00	100.00
☐ Green	80.00	95.00	87.00

Toothpick holder

☐ Clear	18.00	26.00	22.00
☐ Cranberry	40.00	55.00	47.00
☐ Green	30.00	45.00	37.00

Tray

☐ Clear	30.00	45.00	37.00
☐ Cranberry	60.00	75.00	66.00
☐ Green	50.00	65.00	57.00

Tumbler

☐ Clear	25.00	40.00	32.00
☐ Cranberry	40.00	55.00	47.00
☐ Green	30.00	45.00	35.00

DIAGONAL BAND AND FAN (c. 1880)

☐ Butter dish	30.00	45.00	37.00
☐ Celery vase	34.00	49.00	40.0
☐ Champagne glass	23.00	38.00	29.00
☐ Compote, L/H	35.00	50.00	42.00
☐ Creamer	27.00	42.00	33.00

456 / GLASSWARE

	Current Price Range		Prior Year Average
☐ Goblet	22.00	37.00	29.00
☐ Pitcher	30.00	45.00	37.00
☐ Plate	15.00	25.00	20.00
☐ Shakers, S/P	20.00	30.00	23.00
☐ Spoon holder	24.00	39.00	31.00
☐ Sugar bowl	35.00	50.00	42.00
☐ Wine glass	20.00	30.00	24.00

DIAMOND BAND (c. 1870)

☐ Butter dish, CVD	35.00	50.00	42.00
☐ Celery	15.00	25.00	20.00
☐ Compote	33.00	48.00	40.00
☐ Creamer	30.00	45.00	36.00
☐ Goblet	18.00	26.00	21.00
☐ Pitcher, W	27.00	42.00	33.00
☐ Plate	12.00	20.00	16.00
☐ Spoon holder	15.00	25.00	20.00
☐ Sugar bowl, CVD	35.00	50.00	42.00
☐ Wine glass	20.00	30.00	23.00

DIAMOND MEDALLION (c. 1880)

☐ Butter dish, CVD	25.00	40.00	32.00
☐ Cake stand	18.00	26.00	21.00
☐ Celery	20.00	30.00	23.00
☐ Compote	12.00	20.00	16.00
☐ Creamer	18.00	26.00	21.00
☐ Goblet	22.00	27.00	24.00
☐ Pitcher, M/W	23.00	38.00	29.00
☐ Plate	20.00	30.00	23.00
☐ Shakers, S/P	20.00	35.00	27.00
☐ Spoon holder	18.00	26.00	21.00
☐ Sugar bowl, CVD	20.00	30.00	23.00
☐ Toothpick holder	32.00	37.00	34.00
☐ Wine glass	20.00	30.00	23.00

DIAMOND QUILTED (c. 1880)

☐ Bowl	15.00	22.00	18.00
☐ Bowl, waste	10.00	18.00	13.00
☐ Butter dish, CVD	30.00	45.00	36.00
☐ Celery	22.00	37.00	29.00
☐ Champagne glass	20.00	30.00	23.00
☐ Compote, CVD	40.00	55.00	47.00
☐ Compote, open	23.00	38.00	29.00
☐ Cordial glass	10.00	18.00	13.00
☐ Creamer	20.00	35.00	27.00
☐ Pickle dish	12.00	20.00	16.00
☐ Pitcher, W	37.00	52.00	43.00
☐ Sauce dish, round	12.00	20.00	15.00
☐ Sauce dish, FTD	15.00	22.00	18.00
☐ Spoon holder	20.00	35.00	26.00
☐ Sugar bowl, CVD	30.00	45.00	37.00
☐ Tray	23.00	38.00	30.00
☐ Tumbler	12.00	20.00	16.00
☐ Whiskey	18.00	26.00	22.00
☐ Wine glass	20.00	35.00	27.00

	Current Price Range		Prior Year Average

DIAMOND ROSETTES (c. 1870)
☐ Bowl	12.00	20.00	15.00
☐ Butter dish, CVD	25.00	40.00	32.00
☐ Celery	15.00	25.00	20.00
☐ Compote, CVD	40.00	55.00	47.00
☐ Creamer	21.00	36.00	28.00
☐ Goblet	18.00	26.00	21.00
☐ Pitcher, W	32.00	47.00	39.00
☐ Spoon holder	15.00	20.00	17.00
☐ Sugar bowl, CVD	23.00	38.00	28.00
☐ Tumbler	15.00	22.00	18.00

DIAMOND THUMBPRINT (c. 1850)
☐ Bottle	95.00	110.00	100.00
☐ Bowl	95.00	110.00	100.00
☐ Butter dish, CVD	135.00	170.00	150.00
☐ Celery	175.00	250.00	210.00
☐ Cordial glass	185.00	220.00	200.00
☐ Creamer	140.00	175.00	160.00
☐ Decanter, pt. and qt.	110.00	150.00	120.00
☐ Honey dish	35.00	50.00	42.00
☐ Mug, handle	95.00	110.00	100.00
☐ Sauce dish	20.00	35.00	26.00
☐ Spoon holder	70.00	85.00	76.00
☐ Sugar bowl	150.00	185.00	165.00
☐ Tumbler	95.00	110.00	100.00
☐ Vase	120.00	155.00	132.00
☐ Wine glass	175.00	250.00	210.00

DOUBLE SPEAR (c. 1880)
☐ Celery	25.00	40.00	32.00
☐ Compote, H	40.00	55.00	47.00
☐ Creamer	30.00	45.00	36.00
☐ Dish, deep	22.00	37.00	29.00
☐ Egg cup, DBL	12.00	20.00	15.00
☐ Goblet	30.00	45.00	37.00
☐ Pickle dish	20.00	35.00	27.00
☐ Pitcher, W	40.00	65.00	47.00
☐ Sauce dish	15.00	30.00	21.00
☐ Spoon holder	22.00	37.00	28.00
☐ Sugar bowl	45.00	60.00	52.00

DRAPERY (c. 1870)
☐ Bowl, CVD	25.00	40.00	30.00
☐ Butter dish, CVD	45.00	60.00	52.00
☐ Compote	45.00	60.00	52.00
☐ Creamer	40.00	55.00	46.00
☐ Dish	20.00	35.00	26.00
☐ Egg cup, DBL	20.00	30.00	24.00
☐ Goblet	35.00	50.00	41.00
☐ Pitcher, W	34.00	49.00	40.00
☐ Plate	22.00	37.00	29.00
☐ Sauce dish	15.00	25.00	20.00
☐ Spoon holder	30.00	45.00	36.00
☐ Sugar bowl, CVD	40.00	55.00	46.00
☐ Tumbler	20.00	35.00	26.00

EGYPTIAN (c. 1870)

	Current Price Range		Prior Year Average
☐ Butter dish, CVD	50.00	65.00	56.00
☐ Celery vase	32.00	47.00	39.00
☐ Compote	50.00	75.00	62.00
☐ Creamer	35.00	50.00	42.00
☐ Goblet	35.00	50.00	42.00
☐ Honey dish	12.00	20.00	15.00
☐ Pickle dish	22.00	37.00	29.00
☐ Pitcher, W	95.00	110.00	100.00
☐ Plate, cake	33.00	48.00	40.00
☐ Platter	45.00	60.00	52.00
☐ Relish dish	18.00	26.00	21.00
☐ Spoon holder	29.00	44.00	34.00
☐ Sugar bowl, CVD	40.00	55.00	46.00

EUREKA (c. 1860)

☐ Butter dish, CVD	60.00	85.00	70.00
☐ Champagne glass	25.00	40.00	32.00
☐ Compote	50.00	85.00	65.00
☐ Cordial glass	30.00	45.00	37.00
☐ Creamer	60.00	75.00	67.00
☐ Dish, oval	25.00	40.00	32.00
☐ Egg cup	30.00	45.00	37.00
☐ Goblet	25.00	40.00	32.00
☐ Plate	30.00	45.00	37.00
☐ Salt	18.00	26.00	22.00
☐ Sauce dish	10.00	18.00	13.00
☐ Spoon holder	24.00	39.00	30.00
☐ Sugar bowl, CVD	50.00	65.00	57.00
☐ Tumbler	20.00	35.00	26.00
☐ Wine glass	30.00	45.00	37.00

EYEWINKER (c. 1890)

☐ Bowl	40.00	55.00	47.00
☐ Butter dish, CVD	47.00	62.00	53.00
☐ Cake stand	55.00	70.00	62.00
☐ Celery	45.00	60.00	52.00
☐ Compote	29.00	44.00	34.00
☐ Creamer	37.00	52.00	43.00
☐ Cruet	30.00	45.00	37.00
☐ Lamp	49.00	64.00	55.00
☐ Pitcher, syrup	60.00	75.00	67.00
☐ Plate	24.00	39.00	30.00
☐ Sauce dish	20.00	30.00	24.00
☐ Shakers, S/P	40.00	55.00	47.00
☐ Spoon holder	18.00	26.00	22.00
☐ Sugar bowl, CVD	50.00	65.00	57.00
☐ Toothpick holder	15.00	22.00	18.00
☐ Tumbler	18.00	26.00	22.00

FAN WITH DIAMOND (c. 1870)

☐ Butter dish	35.00	50.00	42.00
☐ Compote, L/H	37.00	52.00	43.00
☐ Cordial glass	18.00	26.00	22.00
☐ Creamer	27.00	37.00	32.00
☐ Dish, oval	10.00	20.00	15.00
☐ Egg cup	12.00	27.00	19.00
☐ Goblet	30.00	40.00	34.00

GLASSWARE / 459

	Current Price Range		Prior Year Average
☐ Pitcher, W	35.00	50.00	42.00
☐ Relish dish	10.00	20.00	14.00
☐ Sauce dish	10.00	20.00	14.00
☐ Spoon holder	15.00	30.00	21.00
☐ Sugar bowl	20.00	35.00	26.00
☐ Wine glass	22.00	37.00	29.00

FEATHER (c. 1896)

☐ Banana dish	50.00	65.00	58.00
☐ Bowl	20.00	30.00	24.00
☐ Butter dish, CVD	40.00	55.00	46.00
☐ Cake stand	30.00	45.00	36.00
☐ Celery vase	27.00	42.00	33.00
☐ Compote, open	35.00	45.00	40.00
☐ Cordial glass	35.00	50.00	42.00
☐ Creamer	25.00	40.00	32.00
☐ Cruet	32.00	47.00	39.00
☐ Goblet	45.00	60.00	52.00
☐ Pitcher, W	40.00	55.00	47.00
☐ Sauce dish, flat, FTD	12.00	20.00	15.00
☐ Spoon holder	18.00	26.00	21.00
☐ Sugar bowl, CVD	25.00	40.00	32.00
☐ Toothpick holder	35.00	50.00	42.00
☐ Tumbler	35.00	50.00	42.00
☐ Wine glass	25.00	40.00	32.00

FINE CUT (c. 1870)

☐ Bowl, finger	22.00	37.00	28.00
☐ Bowl, waste	24.00	39.00	29.00
☐ Butter dish, CVD	35.00	50.00	42.00
☐ Celery	22.00	37.00	28.00
☐ Compote	45.00	60.00	52.00
☐ Creamer	22.00	37.00	29.00
☐ Cruet, small	16.00	24.00	20.00
☐ Goblet	20.00	35.00	27.00
☐ Mustard jar	12.00	20.00	15.00
☐ Pickle dish	14.00	20.00	16.00
☐ Pitcher, W	30.00	45.00	36.00
☐ Plate	18.00	33.00	24.00
☐ Sauce dish	10.00	20.00	15.00
☐ Shakers, S/P	22.00	37.00	28.00
☐ Spoon holder	20.00	30.00	25.00
☐ Sugar bowl, CVD	26.00	41.00	32.00
☐ Tray, bread	22.00	37.00	29.00

FINE CUT MEDALLION (c. 1897)

☐ Bowl, berry	25.00	40.00	32.00
☐ Butter dish	52.00	67.00	60.00
☐ Compote	35.00	50.00	42.00
☐ Creamer	22.00	37.00	28.00
☐ Goblet	25.00	40.00	32.00
☐ Pitcher	55.00	70.00	62.00
☐ Punch cup	12.00	27.00	19.00
☐ Spoon holder	30.00	40.00	34.00
☐ Tumbler	30.00	45.00	36.00

460 / GLASSWARE

FINE RIB (c. 1860)

	Current Price Range		Prior Year Average
☐ Bitters bottle	60.00	75.00	67.00
☐ Bowl, CVD	80.00	95.00	87.00
☐ Butter dish, CVD	95.00	110.00	100.00
☐ Castor bottle	20.00	35.00	26.00
☐ Celery	60.00	75.00	66.00
☐ Champagne glass	45.00	60.00	52.00
☐ Cordial glass	55.00	70.00	62.00
☐ Creamer	110.00	135.00	118.00
☐ Cup	35.00	50.00	42.00
☐ Decanter, bar, pt. and qt.	55.00	70.00	62.00
☐ Dish	50.00	65.00	56.00
☐ Egg cup, CVD	60.00	75.00	67.00
☐ Goblet	45.00	60.00	52.00
☐ Honey dish	18.00	33.00	24.00
☐ Jug, W	60.00	75.00	67.00
☐ Lamp	135.00	170.00	150.00
☐ Mug	50.00	65.00	57.00
☐ Pitcher, W	160.00	195.00	175.00
☐ Plate	45.00	60.00	52.00
☐ Salt	18.00	26.00	22.00
☐ Sauce dish	15.00	22.00	18.00
☐ Spoon holder	55.00	70.00	62.00
☐ Sugar bowl, CVD	75.00	100.00	80.00
☐ Tumbler, lemonade, water, whiskey	40.00	55.00	46.00
☐ Wine glass	38.00	53.00	42.00

FLATTENED SAWTOOTH (c. 1880)

☐ Bowl	60.00	75.00	67.00
☐ Bowl, finger	30.00	45.00	37.00
☐ Celery	50.00	65.00	58.00
☐ Compote, CVD	55.00	70.00	62.00
☐ Cordial glass	40.00	55.00	46.00
☐ Creamer	35.00	50.00	41.00
☐ Decanter, qt	45.00	60.00	50.00
☐ Egg cup	24.00	39.00	30.00
☐ Goblet	29.00	44.00	34.00
☐ Ice bucket	60.00	75.00	67.00
☐ Pitcher, W	75.00	90.00	81.00
☐ Plate	31.00	46.00	39.00
☐ Salt, CVD, FTD, round, flat	40.00	70.00	54.00
☐ Spoon holder	50.00	65.00	56.00
☐ Sugar bowl, CVD	45.00	60.00	50.00
☐ Tumbler	35.00	50.00	40.00
☐ Butter dish, CVD	60.00	75.00	67.00
☐ Celery	30.00	45.00	37.00
☐ Compote	65.00	80.00	72.00
☐ Creamer	40.00	55.00	47.00
☐ Goblet	45.00	60.00	52.00
☐ Jam jar	50.00	65.00	57.00
☐ Ptitcher	70.00	85.00	77.00
☐ Sauce dish	18.00	26.00	22.00
☐ Spoon holder	30.00	45.00	36.00
☐ Sugar bowl, CVD	65.00	80.00	71.00

	Current Price Range		Prior Year Average

FLUTE (c. 1850)
☐ Bitters bottle	30.00	45.00	37.00
☐ Candlesticks, pr.	45.00	60.00	52.00
☐ Champagne glass	21.00	36.00	28.00
☐ Creamer	30.00	45.00	37.00
☐ Cup, FTD	18.00	26.00	21.00
☐ Decanter, qt.	50.00	70.00	60.00
☐ Egg cup, DBL	20.00	35.00	26.00
☐ Goblet	20.00	30.00	24.00
☐ Lamp	45.00	60.00	50.00
☐ Mug	30.00	45.00	37.00
☐ Pitcher, M/W	35.00	50.00	42.00
☐ Spoon holder	15.00	22.00	18.00
☐ Sugar bowl	20.00	35.00	26.00
☐ Tumbler	25.00	40.00	30.00
☐ Wine glass	25.00	45.00	35.00

FROSTED LEAF (c. 1850)
☐ Bottle	115.00	150.00	130.00
☐ Butter dish, CVD	125.00	160.00	140.00
☐ Celery vase	125.00	160.00	140.00
☐ Champagne glass	165.00	200.00	180.00
☐ Compote, CVD and open	150.00	250.00	200.00
☐ Cordial glass	140.00	175.00	160.00
☐ Creamer	110.00	145.00	125.00
☐ Decanter, qt.	225.00	275.00	250.00
☐ Egg cup	80.00	105.00	90.00
☐ Salt, FTD	45.00	60.00	50.00
☐ Sauce dish	20.00	35.00	27.00
☐ Spoon holder	70.00	85.00	76.00
☐ Sugar bowl, CVD	95.00	110.00	100.00
☐ Tumbler	115.00	150.00	130.00
☐ Wine glass	125.00	160.00	140.00

FROSTED STORK (c. 1880)
☐ Bowl, waste	45.00	60.00	52.00
☐ Butter dish, CVD	65.00	80.00	72.00
☐ Creamer	70.00	85.00	77.00
☐ Goblet	55.00	75.00	62.00
☐ Jam jar	45.00	60.00	52.00
☐ Pitcher, W	95.00	120.00	105.00
☐ Platter	50.00	65.00	57.00
☐ Sauce dish	20.00	35.00	27.00
☐ Spoon holder	55.00	70.00	62.00
☐ Sugar bowl, CVD	80.00	95.00	87.00
☐ Tray, W	75.00	90.00	82.00

GOOSEBERRY (c. 1880)
☐ Butter dish, CVD	35.00	50.00	42.00
☐ Cake stand	45.00	60.00	52.00
☐ Compote, CVD	50.00	65.00	57.00
☐ Creamer	30.00	45.00	37.00
☐ Goblet	42.00	57.00	49.00
☐ Honey dish	18.00	26.00	22.00
☐ Mug	15.00	25.00	18.00
☐ Pickle dish	12.00	20.00	14.00
☐ Pitcher	50.00	65.00	56.00
☐ Sauce dish	15.00	22.00	18.00

462 / GLASSWARE

	Current Price Range		Prior Year Average
☐ Spoon holder	27.00	42.00	34.00
☐ Sugar bowl, CVD	37.00	52.00	43.00
☐ Tumbler	30.00	40.00	34.00

GRAPE BAND (c. 1850)

☐ Butter dish, CVD	35.00	50.00	42.00
☐ Compote, L/H	55.00	70.00	62.00
☐ Cordial glass	30.00	45.00	37.00
☐ Egg cup, DBL	12.00	20.00	16.00
☐ Goblet	18.00	33.00	24.00
☐ Pickle dish	10.00	16.00	13.00
☐ Pitcher, W	45.00	60.00	52.00
☐ Plate	20.00	30.00	24.00
☐ Salt, FTD	10.00	16.00	13.00
☐ Sauce dish	8.00	16.00	12.00
☐ Spoon holder	18.00	26.00	21.00
☐ Sugar bowl, CVD	35.00	50.00	42.00
☐ Tumbler	18.00	26.00	22.00
☐ Wine glass	22.00	37.00	29.00

GRASSHOPPER (c. 1880)

☐ Bowl, CVD	43.00	58.00	48.00
☐ Butter dish, CVD	50.00	75.00	60.00
☐ Celery vase	27.00	52.00	39.00
☐ Compote	55.00	70.00	60.00
☐ Creamer	35.00	50.00	42.00
☐ Pickle dish	20.00	35.00	27.00
☐ Pitcher, W/M	55.00	80.00	65.00
☐ Sauce dish	18.00	26.00	21.00
☐ Spoon holder	60.00	75.00	67.00
☐ Sugar bowl, CVD	65.00	80.00	72.00

HAMILTON WITH LEAF (c. 1870)

☐ Butter dish	110.00	135.00	120.00
☐ Celery vase	95.00	120.00	105.00
☐ Compote, L/H, open	80.00	95.00	85.00
☐ Cordial glass	85.00	110.00	95.00
☐ Creamer	70.00	85.00	77.00
☐ Egg cup	35.00	50.00	42.00
☐ Goblet	55.00	70.00	62.00
☐ Lamp	115.00	145.00	125.00
☐ Salt	45.00	60.00	52.00
☐ Sauce dish	12.00	20.00	16.00
☐ Spoon holder	60.00	75.00	67.00
☐ Sugar bowl	75.00	90.00	82.00
☐ Tumbler	55.00	70.00	62.00

HANOVER (c. 1888)

☐ Butter dish, CVD	35.00	50.00	42.00
☐ Cake stand	34.00	49.00	40.00
☐ Celery	33.00	48.00	40.00
☐ Compote, CVD, open	27.00	42.00	33.00
☐ Creamer	25.00	35.00	30.00
☐ Goblet	20.00	30.00	24.00
☐ Pitcher	35.00	50.00	40.00
☐ Spoon holder	18.00	26.00	21.00

	Current Price Range		Prior Year Average
☐ Sugar bowl, CVD	40.00	50.00	43.00
☐ Tumbler	24.00	39.00	31.00
☐ Wine glass	27.00	42.00	33.00

HEART WITH THUMBPRINT (c. 1898)

☐ Banana dish	28.00	43.00	33.00
☐ Bowl	30.00	45.00	37.00
☐ Butter dish, CVD	45.00	60.00	52.00
☐ Carafe	43.00	58.00	50.00
☐ Celery	21.00	36.00	28.00
☐ Compote, H	43.00	58.00	50.00
☐ Cordial glass	25.00	40.00	32.00
☐ Creamer	45.00	60.00	52.00
☐ Goblet	40.00	55.00	48.00
☐ Ice bucket	60.00	75.00	67.00
☐ Pitcher, W	45.00	60.00	52.00
☐ Plate	31.00	46.00	38.00
☐ Punch cup	14.00	20.00	17.00
☐ Sauce dish	20.00	35.00	25.00
☐ Sugar bowl, CVD	44.00	59.00	48.00
☐ Tumbler	30.00	45.00	37.00
☐ Vase	18.00	26.00	21.00
☐ Wine glass	30.00	45.00	37.00

HOBNAIL FAN TOP (c. 1880)

☐ Bowl, berry	25.00	40.00	32.00
☐ Butter dish, CVD	40.00	55.00	47.00
☐ Celery	23.00	38.00	30.00
☐ Creamer	23.00	38.00	30.00
☐ Goblet	20.00	30.00	23.00
☐ Salt, individual	6.00	12.00	9.00
☐ Sauce dish	10.00	16.00	12.00
☐ Sugar bowl, CVD	31.00	46.00	38.00
☐ Tray	16.00	24.00	19.00

HOBNAIL PANELLED (c. 1880)

☐ Bowl	22.00	32.00	26.00
☐ Butter dish, CVD	33.00	48.00	40.00
☐ Celery vase	25.00	40.00	32.00
☐ Compote	30.00	45.00	36.00
☐ Creamer	22.00	32.00	26.00
☐ Goblet	18.00	33.00	24.00
☐ Plate	16.00	24.00	22.00
☐ Sauce dish	6.00	12.00	9.00
☐ Spoon holder	18.00	26.00	21.00
☐ Sugar bowl, CVD	30.00	45.00	37.00
☐ Wine glass	16.00	24.00	22.00

HONEYCOMB (c. 1870)

☐ Barber bottle	18.00	26.00	23.00
☐ Bowl, CVD, FTD	16.00	24.00	21.00
☐ Butter dish, CVD	30.00	45.00	36.00
☐ Celery vase	23.00	38.00	30.00
☐ Champagne glass	20.00	35.00	26.00
☐ Compote, L/H, CVD	40.00	55.00	47.00
☐ Cordial glass	12.00	20.00	16.00
☐ Creamer	20.00	35.00	27.00

464 / GLASSWARE

	Current Price Range		Prior Year Average
☐ Cup, custard	12.00	20.00	15.00
☐ Decanter, pt. and qt.	25.00	40.00	32.00
☐ Dish	8.00	16.00	12.00
☐ Egg cup	14.00	20.00	17.00
☐ Goblet	18.00	26.00	21.00
☐ Honey dish	20.00	35.00	27.00
☐ Jug, three pts.	34.00	49.00	41.00
☐ Mug	12.00	20.00	15.00
☐ Pitcher, W	35.00	50.00	40.00
☐ Plate	12.00	20.00	14.00
☐ Pomade jar	12.00	20.00	14.00
☐ Salt, FTD	18.00	26.00	22.00
☐ Sauce dish	8.00	16.00	12.00
☐ Shakers, S/P	18.00	26.00	22.00
☐ Spoon holder	12.00	20.00	14.00
☐ Sugar bowl, CVD	22.00	37.00	30.00
☐ Tumbler, FTD	12.00	20.00	15.00
☐ Wine glass	10.00	18.00	14.00

HORSESHOE (c. 1880)

☐ Bowl	25.00	40.00	32.00
☐ Butter dish, CVD	60.00	75.00	67.00
☐ Cake stand	45.00	60.00	52.00
☐ Celery, FTD	35.00	50.00	42.00
☐ Compote, open, CVD	40.00	65.00	47.00
☐ Cordial glass	33.00	48.00	40.00
☐ Creamer	30.00	45.00	37.00
☐ Goblet	30.00	45.00	36.00
☐ Jam jar	45.00	60.00	52.00
☐ Muffineer	50.00	65.00	57.00
☐ Pickle, oval	14.00	22.00	18.00
☐ Pitcher, W	55.00	70.00	62.00
☐ Plate	45.00	60.00	52.00
☐ Relish dish	18.00	26.00	22.00
☐ Salt, individual	18.00	26.00	22.00
☐ Spoon holder	50.00	65.00	57.00
☐ Sugar bowl, CVD	45.00	60.00	52.00
☐ Tray	45.00	60.00	52.00

HUMMINGBIRD (c. 1880)

☐ Bowl, finger	18.00	26.00	21.00
☐ Butter dish, CVD	50.00	65.00	57.00
☐ Celery	35.00	50.00	42.00
☐ Creamer, FTD	35.00	50.00	42.00
☐ Goblet	22.00	37.00	28.00
☐ Pickle dish	14.00	22.00	18.00
☐ Pitcher, W/M	50.00	70.00	60.00
☐ Sauce dish	18.00	33.00	24.00
☐ Spoon holder	25.00	40.00	30.00
☐ Sugar bowl, CVD	40.00	55.00	46.00
☐ Tray	35.00	50.00	40.00
☐ Tumbler	26.00	41.00	32.00
☐ Wine glass	23.00	38.00	29.00

INVERTED FERN (c. 1860)

☐ Butter dish, CVD	70.00	85.00	77.00
☐ Compote	50.00	65.00	57.00

GLASSWARE / 465

	Current Price Range		Prior Year Average
☐ Cordial glass	35.00	50.00	42.00
☐ Creamer	80.00	95.00	87.00
☐ Egg cup	23.00	38.00	29.00
☐ Goblet	32.00	47.00	39.00
☐ Honey dish	10.00	18.00	13.00
☐ Pitcher, W	215.00	250.00	230.00
☐ Plate	115.00	150.00	130.00
☐ Salt, FTD	23.00	38.00	29.00
☐ Sauce dish	8.00	16.00	10.00
☐ Spoon holder	32.00	47.00	40.00
☐ Sugar bowl, CVD	60.00	75.00	67.00
☐ Tumbler	55.00	70.00	62.00
☐ Wine glass	60.00	75.00	67.00

JACOB'S LADDER (c. 1870)

☐ Bowl	30.00	45.00	36.00
☐ Butter dish, CVD	55.00	70.00	62.00
☐ Cake stand	35.00	50.00	42.00
☐ Celery	45.00	60.00	52.00
☐ Compote, CVD	50.00	65.00	57.00
☐ Cordial glass	35.00	50.00	42.00
☐ Creamer, FTD	45.00	60.00	52.00
☐ Cruet	55.00	70.00	62.00
☐ Dish, oval	20.00	35.00	25.00
☐ Goblet	45.00	60.00	50.00
☐ Honey dish	18.00	26.00	21.00
☐ Jam jar	45.00	60.00	52.00
☐ Mug	35.00	50.00	42.00
☐ Pickle	20.00	35.00	26.00
☐ Pitcher, W	50.00	75.00	62.00
☐ Plate	20.00	30.00	23.00
☐ Relish dish	12.00	20.00	15.00
☐ Sauce dish, FTD	20.00	35.00	27.00
☐ Spoon holder	45.00	60.00	52.00
☐ Sugar bowl, CVD	60.00	75.00	67.00
☐ Tumbler	40.00	55.00	47.00
☐ Wine glass	20.00	35.00	35.00

JERSEY SWIRL (c. 1887)

☐ Butter dish, CVD	45.00	60.00	52.00
☐ Compote, open, CVD	25.00	50.00	35.00
☐ Creamer	30.00	45.00	36.00
☐ Goblet	25.00	40.00	32.00
☐ Pitcher	45.00	55.00	50.00
☐ Plate	20.00	35.00	26.00
☐ Sauce dish	15.00	25.00	20.00
☐ Sugar bowl, CVD	35.00	50.00	42.00
☐ Tumbler	25.00	40.00	32.00
☐ Wine glass	20.00	35.00	26.00

KING'S CROWN (c. 1890)

☐ Banana dish	55.00	70.00	62.00
☐ Bowl	30.00	45.00	37.00
☐ Bowl, oval	50.00	65.00	57.00
☐ Bowl, punch	140.00	175.00	160.00
☐ Butter dish	45.00	60.00	52.00
☐ Cake stand	35.00	50.00	42.00

466 / GLASSWARE

	Current Price Range		Prior Year Average
☐ Castor jug	10.00	18.00	14.00
☐ Celery	35.00	50.00	42.00
☐ Champagne glass	18.00	26.00	22.00
☐ Compote	50.00	65.00	57.00
☐ Cordial glass	12.00	0.00	16.00
☐ Creamer	40.00	55.00	47.00
☐ Dish, cheese	43.00	58.00	50.00
☐ Goblet	25.00	40.00	32.00
☐ Jar, CVD	18.00	26.00	22.00
☐ Pitcher, W	110.00	135.00	120.00
☐ Plate	20.00	35.00	27.00
☐ Sauce dish	22.00	37.00	29.00
☐ Shakers, S/P	30.00	45.00	37.00
☐ Spoon holder	35.00	50.00	42.00
☐ Sugar bowl, CVD	40.00	55.00	47.00
☐ Toothpick holder	20.00	35.00	26.00
☐ Tumbler	23.00	38.00	29.00
☐ Wine glass	18.00	33.00	24.00

LIBERTY BELL (c. 1876)

☐ Bowl, FTD	70.00	85.00	77.00
☐ Butter dish, CVD	125.00	160.00	145.00
☐ Celery	85.00	110.00	95.00
☐ Compote	85.00	110.00	95.00
☐ Creamer	80.00	105.00	90.00
☐ Goblet	50.00	65.00	56.00
☐ Pickle dish	34.00	49.00	40.00
☐ Plate	65.00	80.00	72.00
☐ Platter	100.00	135.00	120.00
☐ Relish dish	25.00	40.00	32.00
☐ Sauce, dish, FTD	23.00	38.00	29.00
☐ Shakers, S/P	35.00	50.00	40.00
☐ Spoon holder	80.00	95.00	87.00
☐ Sugar bowl	85.00	100.00	90.00

LINCOLN DRAPE (c. 1860)

☐ Bowl	35.00	50.00	42.00
☐ Butter dish	80.00	105.00	90.00
☐ Celery	80.00	105.00	90.00
☐ Compote open, CVD	60.00	75.00	67.00
☐ Cordial glass	27.00	42.00	33.00
☐ Creamer	110.00	135.00	120.00
☐ Decanter	90.00	110.00	100.00
☐ Egg cup	45.00	60.00	52.00
☐ Goblet	70.00	85.00	77.00
☐ Honey dish	18.00	26.00	21.00
☐ Pitcher, W	165.00	195.00	175.00
☐ Plate	55.00	70.00	62.00
☐ Salt, FTD	23.00	38.00	29.00
☐ Sauce dish	18.00	26.00	21.00
☐ Spoon holder	60.00	75.00	67.00
☐ Sugar bowl	80.00	105.00	90.00
☐ Tumbler	35.00	50.00	42.00
☐ Wine glass	40.00	55.00	46.00

GLASSWARE / 467

	Current Price Range		Prior Year Average

LOOP (c. 1860)

☐ Bowl	45.00	60.00	52.00
☐ Butter dish, CVD	50.00	65.00	57.00
☐ Cake stand	55.00	70.00	62.00
☐ Celery	30.00	45.00	37.00
☐ Champagne glass	25.00	35.00	30.00
☐ Compote, CVD	50.00	65.00	57.00
☐ Creamer	45.00	60.00	52.00
☐ Egg cup	22.00	37.00	29.00
☐ Goblet	18.00	33.00	23.00
☐ Pitcher, W	60.00	75.00	67.00
☐ Spoon holder	22.00	37.00	28.00
☐ Sugar bowl, CVD	40.00	55.00	45.00
☐ Wine glass	30.00	40.00	33.00

MAGNET AND GRAPE FROSTED LEAF (c. 1860)

☐ Butter dish	95.00	110.00	100.00
☐ Celery	105.00	140.00	125.00
☐ Champagne glass	95.00	120.00	110.00
☐ Compote	95.00	120.00	110.00
☐ Cordial glass	80.00	105.00	90.00
☐ Creamer	80.00	105.00	90.00
☐ Decanter, pt. and qt.	70.00	100.00	80.00
☐ Egg cup	42.00	57.00	48.00
☐ Salt, FTD	45.00	60.00	52.00
☐ Sauce dish	25.00	40.00	32.00
☐ Spoon holder	42.00	57.00	48.00
☐ Tumbler	55.00	70.00	62.00
☐ Wine jug	65.00	90.00	75.00

MAPLE LEAF (c. 1890)

Bowl
☐ Clear	20.00	30.00	24.00
☐ Canary	27.00	43.00	33.00

Bowl, FTD
☐ Clear	20.00	35.00	27.00
☐ Canary	33.00	48.00	39.00

Butter dish, CVD
☐ Clear	40.00	55.00	46.00
☐ Canary	60.00	75.00	66.00

Cake stand
☐ Clear	35.00	50.00	42.00
☐ Canary	55.00	7.00	62.00

Celery vase
☐ Clear	35.00	50.00	42.00
☐ Canary	45.00	60.00	52.00

Compote, CVD
☐ Clear	70.00	85.00	77.00
☐ Canary	110.00	135.00	125.00

Creamer
☐ Clear	30.00	45.00	36.00
☐ Canary	45.00	60.00	52.00

Goblet
☐ Clear	35.00	50.00	42.00
☐ Canary	60.00	75.00	60.00

468 / GLASSWARE

	Current Price Range		Prior Year Average
Pitcher, W/M			
☐ Clear	40.00	65.00	46.00
☐ Canary	60.00	85.00	66.00
Plate			
☐ Clear	35.00	50.00	42.00
☐ Canary	50.00	65.00	57.00
Platter			
☐ Clear	25.00	40.00	32.00
☐ Canary	40.00	55.00	47.00
Sauce dish, FTD			
☐ Clear	18.00	33.00	24.00
☐ Canary	22.00	37.00	29.00
Spoonholder			
☐ Clear	25.00	40.00	32.00
☐ Canary	30.00	45.00	37.00
Sugar bowl, CVD			
☐ Clear	35.00	50.00	42.00
☐ Canary	45.00	60.00	52.00
Tumbler			
☐ Clear	22.00	37.00	29.00
☐ Canary	28.00	43.00	3.00

MASCOTTE (c. 1890)

☐ Basket, cake	70.00	85.00	72.00
☐ Bowl	18.00	26.00	22.00
☐ Butter dish	34.00	49.00	42.00
☐ Celery	27.00	42.00	33.00
☐ Compote, CVD	42.00	57.00	48.00
☐ Creamer	23.00	48.00	33.00
☐ Dish	20.00	30.00	24.00
☐ Goblet	25.00	40.00	32.00
☐ Jar, CVD	40.00	55.00	46.00
☐ Plate	32.00	47.00	38.00
☐ Sauce dish	8.00	14.00	11.00
☐ Spoon holder	20.00	30.00	24.00
☐ Sugar bowl, CVD	50.00	65.00	56.00
☐ Tray	33.00	48.00	39.00
☐ Tumbler	25.00	40.00	32.00
☐ Wine glass	18.00	33.00	23.00

MINERVA (c. 1870)

☐ Butter dish, CVD	75.00	90.00	82.00
☐ Cake stand	80.00	95.00	87.00
☐ Celery vase	35.00	50.00	42.00
☐ Compote, CVD	65.00	80.00	72.00
☐ Cordial glass	20.00	30.00	23.00
☐ Creamer	50.00	65.00	57.00
☐ Dish	25.00	40.00	32.00
☐ Goblet	50.00	65.00	56.00
☐ Jam jar, CVD	40.00	55.00	46.00
☐ Pickle dish	40.00	55.00	46.00
☐ Pitcher, W	70.00	85.00	77.00
☐ Plate	45.00	60.00	52.00
☐ Platter	65.00	80.00	72.00
☐ Sauce dish, FTD	23.00	38.00	29.00
☐ Spoon holder	45.00	60.00	52.00

NAILHEAD (c. 1885)

	Current Price Range		Prior Year Average
☐ Butter dish, CVD	50.00	65.00	57.00
☐ Cake stand	55.00	70.00	62.00
☐ Celery	50.00	65.00	57.00
☐ Compote, CVD	50.00	65.00	57.00
☐ Cordial glass	25.00	40.00	32.00
☐ Creamer	40.00	55.00	46.00
☐ Goblet	30.00	45.00	37.00
☐ Pitcher, W	55.00	70.00	62.00
☐ Plate	40.00	55.00	47.00
☐ Sauce dish	20.00	30.00	25.00
☐ Shakers, S/P	30.00	45.00	37.00
☐ Spoon holder	40.00	55.00	47.00
☐ Sugar bowl, CVD	55.00	70.00	62.00
☐ Tumbler	30.00	45.00	37.00
☐ Wine glass	22.00	37.00	28.00

NEW HAMPSHIRE (c. 1863)

☐ Bowl, berry	25.00	40.00	32.00
☐ Butter dish	25.00	40.00	32.00
☐ Celery vase	23.00	38.00	29.00
☐ Champagne glass	18.00	26.00	21.00
☐ Creamer	12.00	27.00	18.00
☐ Goblet	12.00	20.00	16.00
☐ Mug	10.00	18.00	14.00
☐ Pitcher, W	30.00	50.00	44.00
☐ Punch cup	10.00	18.00	13.00
☐ Sauce dish	6.00	12.00	9.00
☐ Sugar bowl, CVD	20.00	35.00	26.00
☐ Toothpick holder	18.00	26.00	22.00
☐ Tumbler	10.00	18.00	13.00
☐ Wine glass	18.00	26.00	22.00

ONE HUNDRED ONE (c. 1870)

☐ Butter dish, CVD	60.00	75.00	67.00
☐ Cake stand	45.00	60.00	52.00
☐ Celery	50.00	65.00	57.00
☐ Compote, CVD	55.00	70.00	62.00
☐ Creamer	43.00	58.00	50.00
☐ Goblet	40.00	55.00	46.00
☐ Lamp	60.00	80.00	70.00
☐ Pickle dish	25.00	35.00	30.00
☐ Pitcher, W	90.00	110.00	100.00
☐ Plate	25.00	40.00	32.00
☐ Relish dish	18.00	26.00	21.00
☐ Sauce dish, flat, FTD	18.00	26.00	21.00
☐ Shakers, S/P	35.00	50.00	42.00
☐ Spoon holder	40.00	55.00	47.00
☐ Sugar bowl, CVD	45.00	60.00	52.00

OVAL LOOP (c. 1880)

☐ Bowl	18.00	26.00	21.00
☐ Butter dish, CVD	35.00	45.00	40.00
☐ Celery	30.00	40.00	35.00
☐ Compote	45.00	55.00	50.00
☐ Creamer	18.00	26.00	22.00
☐ Goblet	25.00	35.00	30.00
☐ Pitcher	30.00	45.00	37.00

470 / GLASSWARE

	Current Price Range		Prior Year Average
☐ Spoon holder	20.00	30.00	24.00
☐ Sugar bowl, CVD	30.00	40.00	33.00
☐ Tumbler	25.00	35.00	30.00
☐ Wine glass	20.00	30.00	23.00

PANELLED CHERRY (c. 1888)
☐ Bowl	20.00	35.00	27.00
☐ Butter dish, CVD	60.00	85.00	72.00
☐ Compote, CVD	65.00	90.00	75.00
☐ Creamer	45.00	60.00	52.00
☐ Goblet	30.00	45.00	37.00
☐ Pitcher, W	50.00	75.00	62.00
☐ Sauce dish, FTD	18.00	26.00	21.00
☐ Spoon holder	27.00	42.00	34.00
☐ Sugar bowl, CVD	45.00	65.00	55.00
☐ Toothpick holder	12.00	20.00	15.00
☐ Tumbler	25.00	40.00	32.00

PANELLED DEWDROP (c. 1878)
☐ Butter dish, CVD	30.00	45.00	37.00
☐ Celery	31.00	46.00	38.00
☐ Compote, CVD	50.00	65.00	57.00
☐ Cordial glass	25.00	40.00	32.00
☐ Creamer	20.00	35.00	27.00
☐ Goblet	27.00	42.00	33.00
☐ Jam jar	23.00	38.00	29.00
☐ Pickle dish	20.00	30.00	25.00
☐ Pitcher, M	34.00	49.00	40.00
☐ Platter	37.00	52.00	34.00
☐ Sauce dish	14.00	22.00	17.00
☐ Spoon holder	20.00	35.00	27.00
☐ Sugar bowl, CVD	25.00	40.00	32.00
☐ Tumbler	25.00	40.00	32.00
☐ Wine glass	18.00	26.00	21.00

PANELLED THISTLE (c. 1910)
☐ Banana dish	50.00	65.00	57.00
☐ Bowl berry, FTD	25.00	40.00	32.00
☐ Butter dish, CVD	40.00	55.00	47.00
☐ Cake stand	40.00	55.00	47.00
☐ Celery	45.00	60.00	52.00
☐ Compote	35.00	50.00	20.00
☐ Cordial glass	20.00	35.00	27.00
☐ Creamer	35.00	50.00	42.00
☐ Cruet	50.00	65.00	57.00
☐ Egg cup	17.00	32.00	23.00
☐ Goblet	35.00	50.00	42.00
☐ Pitcher, sm./lg.	45.00	60.00	54.00
☐ Relish dish	20.00	30.00	25.00
☐ Salt, FTD	18.00	26.00	21.00
☐ Sauce dish, FTD	10.00	18.00	14.00
☐ Shakers, S/P	40.00	55.00	45.00
☐ Spoon holder	35.00	50.00	42.00
☐ Sugar bowl, CVD	40.00	55.00	46.00
☐ Toothpick holder	12.00	20.00	16.00
☐ Tumbler	30.00	45.00	37.00
☐ Wine glass	27.00	42.00	33.00

GLASSWARE / 471

	Current Price Range		Prior Year Average

PAVONIA (c. 1885)
- ☐ Bowl 12.00 20.00 16.00
- ☐ Butter dish, CVD 45.00 60.00 52.00
- ☐ Cake stand 35.00 50.00 42.00
- ☐ Celery 35.00 50.00 42.00
- ☐ Compote, CVD 55.00 70.00 62.00
- ☐ Creamer 35.00 50.00 42.00
- ☐ Goblet 30.00 45.00 37.00
- ☐ Pitcher, W 45.00 60.00 52.00
- ☐ Shakers, S/P 14.00 22.00 18.00
- ☐ Spoon holder 25.00 40.00 30.00
- ☐ Sugar bowl, CVD 40.00 55.00 46.00
- ☐ Tumbler 18.00 33.00 23.00
- ☐ Wine glass 35.00 50.00 41.00

PICKET (c. 1880)
- ☐ Butter dish, CVD 45.00 60.00 52.00
- ☐ Celery vase 34.00 49.00 41.00
- ☐ Compote, CVD 42.00 57.00 50.00
- ☐ Creamer 37.00 52.00 42.00
- ☐ Goblet 30.00 45.00 36.00
- ☐ Marmalade jar 25.00 40.00 32.00
- ☐ Pitcher, W 50.00 65.00 55.00
- ☐ Salt 18.00 26.00 21.00
- ☐ Sauce dish, flat, FTD 12.00 20.00 16.00
- ☐ Spoon holder 20.00 35.00 26.00
- ☐ Sugar bowl, CVD 45.00 60.00 52.00
- ☐ Toothpick holder 25.00 40.00 32.00
- ☐ Tray 50.00 60.00 55.00

PINEAPPLE AND FAN (c. 1891)
- ☐ Bowl, berry 25.00 40.00 32.00
- ☐ Bowl, punch 60.00 75.00 67.00
- ☐ Butter dish, CVD 40.00 55.00 47.00
- ☐ Cake stand 25.00 40.00 32.00
- ☐ Celery vase 25.00 40.00 32.00
- ☐ Creamer, sm./lg. 30.00 45.00 37.00
- ☐ Cup, custard 12.00 20.00 16.00
- ☐ Goblet 18.00 26.00 21.00
- ☐ Mug 25.00 40.00 32.00
- ☐ Pitcher, W 45.00 60.00 52.00
- ☐ Plate 12.00 20.00 16.00
- ☐ Sauce dish 15.00 25.00 20.00
- ☐ Spoon holder 25.00 40.00 30.00
- ☐ Sugar bowl, CVD 30.00 45.00 36.00
- ☐ Tumbler 20.00 35.00 26.00

PORTLAND (c. 1880)
- ☐ Butter dish, CVD 35.00 50.00 42.00
- ☐ Celery 27.00 42.00 33.00
- ☐ Compote 35.00 45.00 40.00
- ☐ Creamer 37.00 52.00 33.00
- ☐ Cruet 22.00 37.00 29.00
- ☐ Goblet 23.00 38.00 30.00
- ☐ Jam jar 25.00 35.00 30.00
- ☐ Pitcher, W 37.00 52.00 43.00
- ☐ Spoon holder 22.00 37.00 28.00
- ☐ Sugar bowl 30.00 45.00 37.00

472 / GLASSWARE

	Current Price Range		Prior Year Average
☐ Toothpick holder	18.00	26.00	26.00
☐ Tumbler	25.00	40.00	32.00
☐ Wine glass	25.00	35.00	30.00

PRESSED LEAF (c. 1881)

☐ Butter dish, CVD	40.00	55.00	47.00
☐ Cake stand	55.00	70.00	62.00
☐ Champagne glass	37.00	52.00	43.00
☐ Cordial glass	25.00	40.00	32.00
☐ Creamer	50.00	65.00	57.00
☐ Egg cup	25.00	40.00	32.00
☐ Goblet	25.00	40.00	32.00
☐ Pickle dish	12.00	20.00	16.00
☐ Pitcher, W	95.00	110.00	100.00
☐ Sauce dish	25.00	40.00	110.00
☐ Shakers, S/P	35.00	50.00	32.00
☐ Spoon holder	30.00	45.00	42.00
☐ Sugar bowl, CVD	50.00	65.00	57.00
☐ Wine glass	50.00	65.00	57.00

PRISCILLA (c. 1890)

☐ Biscuilt jar, CVD	45.00	60.00	52.00
☐ Bowl	35.00	50.00	42.00
☐ Butter dish, CVD	40.00	55.00	47.00
☐ Cake stand	27.00	42.00	33.00
☐ Celery	20.00	35.00	27.00
☐ Creamer	23.00	38.00	28.00
☐ Cruet	30.00	45.00	37.00
☐ Cup and saucer	27.00	42.00	33.00
☐ Goblet	20.00	30.00	24.00
☐ Mug	12.00	20.00	16.00
☐ Pickle dish	20.00	30.00	23.00
☐ Plate	30.00	45.00	37.00
☐ Spoon holder	18.00	26.00	21.00
☐ Sugar bowl, CVD	30.00	45.00	37.00
☐ Syrup pitcher	45.00	60.00	52.00
☐ Tumbler	14.00	22.00	18.00

RED BLOCK (c. 1892)

☐ Bowl	60.00	75.00	67.00
☐ Butter dish, CVD	70.00	85.00	76.00
☐ Celery	50.00	65.00	57.00
☐ Cordial glass	23.00	38.00	28.00
☐ Creamer, sm./lg.	50.00	65.00	57.00
☐ Dish	33.00	48.00	39.00
☐ Pitcher, W	90.00	110.00	100.00
☐ Sauce dish	25.00	35.00	30.00
☐ Shaker, S/P	80.00	100.00	90.00
☐ Spoon holder	30.00	45.00	35.00
☐ Sugar bowl, CVD	55.00	70.00	60.00
☐ Sugar, shaker	37.00	52.00	43.00
☐ Tumbler	25.00	40.00	30.00
☐ Wine glass	35.00	50.00	42.00
☐ Wine jug	50.00	65.00	57.00

GLASSWARE / 473

	Current Price Range	Prior Year Average

RIBBED IVY (c. 1858)
- ☐ Butter, CVD 90.00 105.00 95.00
- ☐ Castor bottle 30.00 45.00 37.00
- ☐ Compote, CVD 115.00 150.00 130.00
- ☐ Cordial glass 57.00 72.00 63.00
- ☐ Creamer 115.00 150.00 130.00
- ☐ Egg cup 30.00 45.00 37.00
- ☐ Goblet 45.00 60.00 52.00
- ☐ Honey dish 12.00 20.00 16.00
- ☐ Salt, CVD 105.00 140.00 120.00
- ☐ Sauce dish 20.00 35.00 27.00
- ☐ Spoon holder 25.00 40.00 32.00
- ☐ Sugar bowl, CVD 80.00 100.00 90.00
- ☐ Tumbler 70.00 85.00 75.00
- ☐ Wine glass 90.00 110.00 95.00

RIBBED PALM (c. 1868)
- ☐ Bowl 40.00 65.00 52.00
- ☐ Butter dish, CVD 80.00 100.00 90.00
- ☐ Celery vase 75.00 90.00 88.00
- ☐ Champagne glass 80.00 100.00 90.00
- ☐ Compote, open 60.00 85.00 72.00
- ☐ Cordial glass 32.00 47.00 38.00
- ☐ Creamer 95.00 115.00 100.00
- ☐ Egg cup 33.00 48.00 39.00
- ☐ Goblet 42.00 57.00 48.00
- ☐ Lamp 80.00 100.00 90.00
- ☐ Pickle dish 25.00 40.00 32.00
- ☐ Pitcher, W 165.00 200.00 180.00
- ☐ Plate 45.00 60.00 52.00
- ☐ Salt, FTD 20.00 35.00 26.00
- ☐ Sauce dish 15.00 22.00 18.00
- ☐ Spoon holder 40.00 55.00 46.00
- ☐ Sugar bowl, CVD 60.00 75.00 65.00
- ☐ Toothpick holder 35.00 50.00 42.00
- ☐ Tumbler 70.00 85.00 77.00
- ☐ Wine glass 50.00 65.00 55.00

RIBBON (c. 1867)
- ☐ Bottle 20.00 35.00 25.00
- ☐ Butter dish, CVD 60.00 75.00 66.00
- ☐ Cake stand 25.00 40.00 32.00
- ☐ Celery 37.00 52.00 43.00
- ☐ Cheese dish, CVD 80.00 100.00 90.00
- ☐ Compote, L/H, CVD 40.00 55.00 45.00
- ☐ Cordial glass 32.00 47.00 38.00
- ☐ Creamer 50.00 65.00 56.00
- ☐ Pitcher, W 75.00 90.00 80.00
- ☐ Platter 60.00 75.00 67.00
- ☐ Sauce dish, FTD 20.00 35.00 27.00
- ☐ Spoon holder 22.00 37.00 29.00
- ☐ Sugar bowl, CVD 60.00 75.00 67.00
- ☐ Tray 95.00 110.00 100.00
- ☐ Waste bowl 30.00 45.00 37.00

ROMAN ROSETTE (c. 1875)
- ☐ Bowl 25.00 40.00 32.00
- ☐ Butter dish, CVD 37.00 52.00 43.00

474 / GLASSWARE

	Current Price Range		Prior Year Average
☐ Cake	47.00	62.00	53.00
☐ Celery	27.00	42.00	34.00
☐ Compote, CVD	60.00	75.00	67.00
☐ Cordial glass	40.00	55.00	47.00
☐ Creamer	30.00	45.00	37.00
☐ Dish	18.00	26.00	21.00
☐ Mug	15.00	22.00	18.00
☐ Pickle dish	20.00	30.00	24.00
☐ Plate	40.00	55.00	47.00
☐ Shakers, S/P	30.00	45.00	37.00
☐ Spoon holder	20.00	35.00	27.00
☐ Sugar bowl, CVD	35.00	50.00	42.00
☐ Tray	30.00	45.00	37.00
☐ Tumbler	23.00	38.00	28.00
☐ Wine glass	30.00	45.00	36.00

ROSE SPRIG (c. 1886)

☐ Butter	45.00	60.00	52.00
☐ Cake stand	40.00	50.00	46.00
☐ Celery vase	35.00	50.00	42.00
☐ Compote, CVD	32.00	47.00	39.00
☐ Creamer	40.00	55.00	47.00
☐ Goblet	30.00	45.00	37.00
☐ Mug	35.00	50.00	42.00
☐ Pickle dish	14.00	26.00	20.00
☐ Pitcher, sm./lg.	45.00	60.00	52.00
☐ Plate	25.00	40.00	32.00
☐ Platter	30.00	45.00	37.00
☐ Relish dish	18.00	33.00	24.00
☐ Salt	35.00	50.00	42.00
☐ Sauce dish, FTD	10.00	18.00	14.00
☐ Spoon holder	25.00	40.00	30.00
☐ Sugar bowl, CVD	40.00	55.00	47.00
☐ Tray	30.00	45.00	37.00
☐ Tumbler	30.00	45.00	37.00
☐ Wine glass	35.00	50.00	42.00

SAWTOOTH (c. 1860)

☐ Bottle	20.00	35.00	27.00
☐ Bowl	60.00	75.00	67.00
☐ Butter dish, CVD	80.00	95.00	87.00
☐ Cake stand	50.00	65.00	58.00
☐ Celery vase	75.00	90.00	82.00
☐ Champagne glass	60.00	75.00	67.00
☐ Compote, CVD	95.00	110.00	100.00
☐ Cordial glass	47.00	62.00	52.00
☐ Creamer	80.00	100.00	90.00
☐ Decanter	60.00	75.00	67.00
☐ Goblet	50.00	65.00	57.00
☐ Honey dish	14.00	26.00	20.00
☐ Egg cup	45.00	60.00	52.00
☐ Pitcher, M/W	75.00	90.00	82.00
☐ Salt, CVD	55.00	70.00	62.00
☐ Sauce dish	20.00	30.00	23.00
☐ Spoon holder	55.00	70.00	62.00
☐ Sugar bowl, CVD	75.00	90.00	82.00

	Current Price Range		Prior Year Average
☐ Tray	60.00	75.00	67.00
☐ Tumbler, FTD	45.00	60.00	52.00
☐ Wine	50.00	65.00	57.00

SHELL AND TASSEL (c. 1890)

☐ Bowl	40.00	55.00	46.00
☐ Butter dish, CVD	45.00	60.00	52.00
☐ Cake stand	60.00	75.00	67.00
☐ Celery vase	40.00	55.00	46.00
☐ Compote, CVD	55.00	70.00	62.00
☐ Creamer	40.00	55.00	47.00
☐ Jam jar	45.00	60.00	52.00
☐ Pickle dish	14.00	26.00	20.00
☐ Pitcher, W	50.00	65.00	56.00
☐ Salt shaker	25.00	40.00	32.00
☐ Sauce dish, FTD	12.00	20.00	16.00
☐ Shakers, S/P	95.00	110.00	100.00
☐ Spoon holder	35.00	50.00	42.00
☐ Sugar bowl, CVD	70.00	85.00	76.00
☐ Tray	40.00	55.00	46.00

SPRIG (c. 1880)

☐ Bowl, FTD	30.00	45.00	37.00
☐ Butter plate, CVD	40.00	55.00	46.00
☐ Cake stand	35.00	50.00	42.00
☐ Celery	23.00	38.00	29.00
☐ Compote, CVD	40.00	55.00	45.00
☐ Creamer	35.00	50.00	42.00
☐ Goblet	30.00	45.00	35.00
☐ Pickle dish	12.00	20.00	16.00
☐ Pitcher, W	45.00	60.00	52.00
☐ Platter	35.00	50.00	40.00
☐ Sauce dish, FTD	12.00	20.00	16.00
☐ Spoon holder	20.00	35.00	26.00
☐ Sugar bowl, CVD	30.00	45.00	36.00
☐ Tumbler	18.00	26.00	21.00
☐ Wine glass	25.00	35.00	30.00

STATES, THE (c. 1905)

☐ Bowl	30.00	45.00	37.00
☐ Butter dish, CVD	35.00	50.00	42.00
☐ Celery vase	18.00	26.00	21.00
☐ Compote, open	25.00	35.00	30.00
☐ Creamer	18.00	26.00	21.00
☐ Goblet	20.00	30.00	23.00
☐ Plate	25.00	40.00	30.00
☐ Punch cup	8.00	14.00	11.00
☐ Relish dish	20.00	30.00	23.00
☐ Shakers, S/P	12.00	20.00	16.00
☐ Sugar bowl, CVD	30.00	45.00	36.00
☐ Toothpick holder	25.00	35.00	30.00
☐ Tray	10.00	18.00	14.00
☐ Tumbler	18.00	26.00	21.00
☐ Wine glass	15.00	22.00	18.00

STRAWBERRY (c. 1860)

	Current Price Range		Prior Year Average
☐ Butter dish, CVD	50.00	65.00	55.00
☐ Compote, L/H, CVD	65.00	95.00	80.00
☐ Creamer	40.00	55.00	46.00
☐ Egg cup	20.00	35.00	25.00
☐ Goblet	25.00	40.00	32.00
☐ Honey dish	14.00	26.00	20.00
☐ Pickle dish	12.00	20.00	16.00
☐ Pitcher, syrup	35.00	50.00	42.00
☐ Pitcher, W	65.00	80.00	70.00
☐ Relish dish	20.00	30.00	23.00
☐ Salt, FTD	20.00	35.00	25.00
☐ Sauce dish	12.00	20.00	16.00
☐ Spoon holder	20.00	35.00	25.00

SUNBURST (c. 1898)

☐ Bowl	18.00	26.00	20.00
☐ Butter dish, CVD	40.00	55.00	45.00
☐ Cake stand	30.00	45.00	35.00
☐ Celery	25.00	40.00	32.00
☐ Compote, CVD	35.00	50.00	40.00
☐ Cordial glass	18.00	26.00	20.00
☐ Creamer	25.00	40.00	32.00
☐ Cruet	20.00	35.00	27.00
☐ Egg cup	15.00	22.00	18.00
☐ Goblet	22.00	37.00	29.00
☐ Jam jar, CVD	25.00	40.00	32.00
☐ Pickle dish	15.00	22.00	18.00
☐ Pitcher, W/M	35.00	50.00	42.00
☐ Plate	20.00	30.00	23.00
☐ Salt	16.00	24.00	20.00
☐ Sauce dish, handled	10.00	18.00	13.00
☐ Spoon holder	22.00	37.00	29.00
☐ Sugar bowl, CVD	30.00	45.00	36.00
☐ Tumbler	15.00	22.00	18.00
☐ Wine glass	20.00	30.00	23.00

TEARDROP AND TASSEL (c. 1890)

☐ Bowl	40.00	55.00	45.00
☐ Butter dish, CVD	50.00	65.00	55.00
☐ Compote, CVD	70.00	85.00	77.00
☐ Creamer	35.00	50.00	42.00
☐ Goblet	55.00	70.00	62.00
☐ Pickle dish	18.00	26.00	21.00
☐ Pitcher, W	65.00	80.00	72.00
☐ Sauce dish	10.00	16.00	13.00
☐ Shakers, S/P	95.00	110.00	100.00
☐ Spoon holder	35.00	50.00	40.00
☐ Sugar bowl, CVD	50.00	65.00	57.00
☐ Tumbler	25.00	40.00	32.00
☐ Wine glass	60.00	75.00	67.00

TEXAS (c. 1900)

☐ Bowl	20.00	35.00	27.00
☐ Butter dish, CVD	40.00	55.00	45.00
☐ Cake stand	45.00	60.00	50.00
☐ Celery	12.00	20.00	16.00
☐ Celery vase	25.00	40.00	32.00

GLASSWARE / 477

	Current Price Range		Prior Year Average
☐ Compote, CVD	50.00	65.00	56.00
☐ Cruet	25.00	40.00	32.00
☐ Goblet	25.00	40.00	32.00
☐ Jar	14.00	26.00	20.00
☐ Pickle dish	20.00	30.00	23.00
☐ Pitcher, W	40.00	55.00	47.00
☐ Plate	18.00	26.00	21.00
☐ Relish dish	15.00	22.00	18.00
☐ Sauce dish	10.00	18.00	13.00
☐ Shakers, S/P	30.00	45.00	37.00
☐ Spoon holder	18.00	26.00	21.00
☐ Toothpick holder	14.00	26.00	20.00
☐ Tumbler	25.00	35.00	30.00
☐ Wine glass	30.00	40.00	34.00

THISTLE (c. 1875)

☐ Bowl, CVD	40.00	55.00	47.00
☐ Butter dish, CVD	60.00	75.00	65.00
☐ Cake stand	55.00	70.00	62.00
☐ Compote, L/H, CVD	45.00	60.00	52.00
☐ Cordial glass	40.00	55.00	47.00
☐ Creamer	50.00	65.00	56.00
☐ Decanter	60.00	75.00	67.00
☐ Egg cup	25.00	40.00	32.00
☐ Goblet	30.00	45.00	37.00
☐ Pickle dish	18.00	33.00	23.00
☐ Pitcher, W	55.00	70.00	62.00
☐ Relish dish	20.00	35.00	27.00
☐ Salt, FTD	18.00	33.00	23.00
☐ Spoon holder	35.00	50.00	42.00
☐ Sugar bowl, CVD	55.00	70.00	62.00
☐ Tumbler, FTD	35.00	50.00	40.00
☐ Wine glass	35.00	50.00	40.00

THUMBPRINT (c. 1860)

☐ Bitters bottle	90.00	105.00	95.00
☐ Celery vase	90.00	125.00	110.00
☐ Champagne glass	60.00	75.00	65.00
☐ Compote, CVD	80.00	100.00	90.00
☐ Cordial glass	30.00	45.00	36.00
☐ Creamer	60.00	75.00	66.00
☐ Decanter	90.00	110.00	100.00
☐ Egg cup	35.00	50.00	42.00
☐ Goblet	55.00	70.00	60.00
☐ Honey dish	18.00	33.00	23.00
☐ Mug	23.00	38.00	28.00
☐ Pickle dish	25.00	40.00	30.00
☐ Pitcher, W	95.00	120.00	105.00
☐ Sauce dish	18.00	26.00	21.00
☐ Shakers, S/P	40.00	55.00	45.00
☐ Spoon holder	30.00	45.00	36.00
☐ Sugar bowl, CVD	90.00	110.00	100.00
☐ Tumbler, FTD	50.00	65.00	57.00
☐ Wine glass	45.00	60.00	52.00

478 / GLASSWARE

TREE OF LIFE (c. 1867)

	Current Price Range		Prior Year Average
☐ Bowl	25.00	35.00	30.00
☐ Butter dish, CVD	55.00	70.00	62.00
☐ Cake stand	65.00	80.00	70.00
☐ Celery vase	45.00	60.00	52.00
☐ Compote, CVD	80.00	100.00	90.00
☐ Creamer	55.00	70.00	62.00
☐ Goblet	45.00	60.00	50.00
☐ Mug	25.00	40.00	30.00
☐ Pitcher, W	70.00	85.00	77.00
☐ Plate	18.00	26.00	22.00
☐ Punch cup	14.00	26.00	20.00
☐ Sauce dish, FTD	14.00	26.00	20.00
☐ Spoon holder	35.00	50.00	40.00
☐ Sugar bowl, CVD	60.00	75.00	66.00
☐ Tray	35.00	50.00	40.00
☐ Tumbler, FTD	30.00	45.00	36.00
☐ Wine glass	35.00	50.00	36.00

TULIP WITH SAWTOOTH (c. 1854)

☐ Butter dish, CVD	110.00	145.00	125.00
☐ Celery vase	55.00	70.00	60.00
☐ Champagne glass	70.00	85.00	77.00
☐ Compote, L/H, CVD	75.00	100.00	82.00
☐ Cordial galss	25.00	40.00	30.00
☐ Creamer	95.00	115.00	100.00
☐ Cruet	60.00	75.00	66.00
☐ Decanter, qt.	145.00	180.00	160.00
☐ Goblet	45.00	60.00	50.00
☐ Honey dish	20.00	30.00	23.00
☐ Pitcher, W	150.00	185.00	165.00
☐ Plate	50.00	65.00	55.00
☐ Pomade jar	45.00	60.00	50.00
☐ Salt	22.00	37.00	25.00
☐ Sauce dish	15.00	22.00	18.00
☐ Spoon holder	30.00	45.00	36.00
☐ Sugar bowl, CVD	90.00	110.00	95.00
☐ Tumbler, FTD	43.00	58.00	48.00
☐ Wine glass	40.00	55.00	45.00

UTAH (c. 1901)

☐ Bowl	18.00	26.00	21.00
☐ Butter dish, CVD	35.00	45.00	40.00
☐ Cake stand	22.00	37.00	28.00
☐ Celery	20.00	30.00	23.00
☐ Compote, CVD	25.00	35.00	30.00
☐ Goblet	18.00	26.00	21.00
☐ Pickle dish	15.00	22.00	18.00
☐ Pitcher, W	30.00	45.00	35.00
☐ Plate	22.00	37.00	29.00
☐ Sauce dish	10.00	15.00	12.00
☐ Shakers, S/P	25.00	35.00	30.00
☐ Spoon holder	18.00	26.00	20.00
☐ Sugar bowl, CVD	25.00	35.00	30.00
☐ Tumbler	18.00	26.00	22.00

GLASSWARE / 479

	Current Price Range		Prior Year Average

VIKING (c. 1880)

☐ Bowl	25.00	40.00	30.00
☐ Butter dish, CVD	60.00	75.00	65.00
☐ Candleholder	14.00	26.00	20.00
☐ Cake plate, FTD	45.00	60.00	52.00
☐ Celery vase	40.00	55.00	46.00
☐ Compote, CVD	60.00	75.00	66.00
☐ Creamer	32.00	47.00	38.00
☐ Eagg cup	35.00	50.00	40.00
☐ Goblet	30.00	45.00	36.00
☐ Mug	45.00	60.00	50.00
☐ Pickle dish	22.00	37.00	28.00
☐ Pitcher, W	70.00	85.00	77.00
☐ Platter	35.00	50.00	40.00
☐ Salt	22.00	37.00	28.00
☐ Sauce dish, FTD	12.00	20.00	16.00
☐ Spoon holder	25.00	40.00	30.00
☐ Sugar bowl, CVD	40.00	55.00	46.00
☐ Tray	45.00	60.00	52.00
☐ Tumbler	35.00	50.00	42.00

WAFFLE AND THUMBPRINT (c. 1860)

☐ Bowl	37.00	52.00	42.00
☐ Butter dish, CVD	115.00	150.00	125.00
☐ Celery	77.00	92.00	84.00
☐ Champagne glass	80.00	95.00	85.00
☐ Claret	75.00	90.00	82.00
☐ Compote, open	90.00	120.00	100.00
☐ Creamer	115.00	150.00	130.00
☐ Decanter, pt. and qt.	80.00	145.00	110.00
☐ Egg cup	40.00	55.00	45.00
☐ Goblet	65.00	80.00	72.00
☐ Relish dish	18.00	26.00	22.00
☐ Salt	35.00	50.00	40.00
☐ Spoon holder	60.00	75.00	67.00
☐ Sugar bowl, CVD	110.00	145.00	125.00
☐ Tumbler, FTD	70.00	85.00	77.00
☐ Wine glass	55.00	70.00	62.00

WHEAT AND BARLEY (c. 1878)

☐ Bowl, CVD	30.00	45.00	37.00
☐ Butter dish, CVD	40.00	55.00	47.00
☐ Cake stand	35.00	50.00	42.00
☐ Compote, CVD	45.00	60.00	52.00
☐ Creamer	30.00	45.00	36.00
☐ Goblet	25.00	40.00	32.00
☐ Mug	18.00	26.00	21.00
☐ Pitcher, M/W	30.00	45.00	37.00
☐ Plate	22.00	37.00	28.00
☐ Sauce dish, FTD	14.00	26.00	20.00
☐ Shakers, S/P	25.00	40.00	32.00
☐ Spoon holder	25.00	40.00	32.00
☐ Sugar bowl, CVD	30.00	45.00	35.00
☐ Toothpick holder	15.00	22.00	18.00
☐ Tumbler, FTD	30.00	45.00	37.00
☐ Wine glass	25.00	40.00	32.00

480 / GREETING CARDS

WINDFLOWER (c. 1870)

	Current Price Range		Prior Year Average
☐ Butter dish	60.00	75.00	66.00
☐ Celery	38.00	52.00	43.00
☐ Compote	62.00	77.00	68.00
☐ Cordial glass	32.00	47.00	38.00
☐ Creamer	40.00	55.00	48.00
☐ Egg cup	27.00	42.00	33.00
☐ Goblet	35.00	50.00	43.00
☐ Pickle dish	20.00	30.00	24.00
☐ Pitcher, W	62.00	77.00	68.00
☐ Sauce dish	18.00	26.00	21.00
☐ Spoon holder	25.00	40.00	30.00
☐ Sugar bowl, CVD	50.00	65.00	55.00
☐ Tumbler	35.00	45.00	39.00
☐ Wine glass	37.00	52.00	42.00

GREETING CARDS

Cartoon Valentine, mechanical, c. 1915 .... **$30.00-$40.00**

The collecting of greeting cards has been, until recently, limited mostly to valentines. In the past few years, many other types of cards have won favor with card collectors.

The first greeting card was a Christmas card published in England in 1843. Only about 1000 were printed and the idea did not gain public acceptance for about twenty years. In 1860, the English publishing firm of Charles Goodall & Son began printing "visiting cards", small decorative cards one would leave with friends after a formal visit. Soon it became popular to send a card bearing seasonal greetings ahead of one's visit to a friend or relative.

Other publishers quickly joined in with their own greeting cards: Marcus Ward & Co., DeLaRue & Co., and Raphael Tuck & Co. were all successful in England and popular in America. L. Prang & Co. produced cards in the United States.

Cards printed in the 19th century are the most popular and beautiful because of the lithography process used to print them. The favorite card designer of this period is Kate Greenaway, an illustrator of children's books.

Old greeting cards are widely available, as a popular turn-of-the-century pastime was the preservation of greeting cards in scrapbooks. The collector should check house sales, garage sales and flea markets. Many good examples are priced under one dollar.

Additional listings may be found in *'The Official Price Guide to Paper Collectibles,'* published by the House of Collectibles.

CHRISTMAS

	Current Price Range		Prior Year Average
☐ "A Merry Christmas and Happy New Year," children playing under Christmas tree, c. 1870's	3.00	5.00	3.75
☐ "A Merry Christmas to you All," family strolling through snow-blanketed woodland, c. 1880	4.00	7.00	5.00
☐ Fold out Christmas card, Santa Claus	9.00	14.00	11.00
☐ Fold out Christmas card, Nativity scene, c. 1820	5.00	10.00	7.00
☐ "Hail, Day of Joy," card by L. Prang and Co., angel kneeling with dove on finger, c. 1870's	12.00	17.00	14.00
☐ "Here Comes the New Year with Lots of Good Cheer," child with Christmas tree and toys, c. 1870	9.00	14.00	10.00
☐ "Here, Open the Door," card by Kate Greenaway, young messenger boy knocking on door, c. 1880	35.00	50.00	40.00
☐ "Merry Christmas and Happy New Year," children romping in snow, church in background, c. 1860	3.00	5.00	3.75
☐ "Merry Christmas to You All," card by L. Prang and Co., brown suited Santa in chimney, square, c. 1880's	18.00	24.00	21.00
☐ "My Lips May Give a Message," card by Kate Greenaway, young girl holding letter, c. 1880	35.00	50.00	40.00
☐ Pop up Christmas card, ice skating scene, England, c. 1890	20.00	25.00	22.00
☐ Prang's American Third Prize Christmas Card, designed by C. C. Coleman, oriental scene	15.00	20.00	17.00
☐ Victorian Christmas card, paper lace border surrounds season's greeting, c. 1800's	7.00	12.00	9.00
☐ "Wishing You a Happy New Year," card by L. Prang and Co., folded, young girl on front, old man on back, fringed, tied with tasseled cord, c. 1884	20.00	30.00	24.00

482 / GREETING CARDS

	Current Price Range		Prior Year Average
☐ "Wishing You a Merry Christmas," card by L. Prang and Co., fireplace scene, cat and kittens looking up chimney, square, c. 1880's	18.00	24.00	21.00
☐ "With Best Christmas Wishes," card by Raphael Tuck and Sons, young girl holding spray of flowers, c. late 1800's	10.00	15.00	12.00
☐ "With the Season's Greetings," card by W. S. Coleman, girl on swing (back view), c. 1890	5.00	10.00	7.00

VALENTINES

	Current Price Range		Prior Year Average
☐ Comic Valentine, the "Hat Trimmer," Elton and Co., New York, illustration of glum-looking woman sewing hat, with verse, c. 1860	20.00	25.00	22.00
☐ "Dainty Dimples" series, per card	2.00	5.00	3.00
☐ Easel Valentine, fold back, free standing, c. early 1900's	30.00	40.00	34.00
☐ "Hearts Are Ripe," children picking heart shaped apples from tree	2.00	5.00	3.00
☐ H. Dobbs and Co., "Pillar Post," illustration of mailbox, c. 1800	20.00	25.00	22.00
☐ "It Must Be Fine, To Have a Valentine," from "Valentine Wishes" series	5.00	10.00	7.00
☐ "Lady Killer," comic valentine by A.J. Fisher, N.Y., c. 1850	25.00	35.00	29.00
☐ Mansell, lace paper, lovers in a park, heavily ornamented, white with silver, c. 1855	40.00	50.00	44.00
☐ Mansell, cameo embossing, two lovers walking along woodland path, c. 1845	35.00	45.00	39.00
☐ Mechanical, set of fifteen, c. 1920	30.00	40.00	34.00
☐ Mechanical, "Such is Married Life," c. 1850	35.00	45.00	39.00
☐ Mechanical, various animals, c. 1930	7.00	12.00	10.00
☐ Mechanical, Walt Disney character, c. 1930's	15.00	20.00	17.00
☐ Meek & Son., Gibson Girl (from photo), surrounded by lace in various ornamental patterns, cherub heads, c. 1890	50.00	60.00	54.00
☐ "Temple of Love," mother-of-pearl on satin background	50.00	60.00	54.00
☐ "To My Valentine," from Raphael Tuck's "Betsy Beauties" series, young girl chasing butterfly	4.00	7.00	5.00
☐ "To My Valentine," from Raphael Tuck's "Good Luck" series, country maid with baskets	3.00	6.00	4.00
☐ "To My Valentine," fron Raphael Tuck's "Innocence Abroad" series, two young children, brief verse	4.00	7.00	5.00
☐ "To My Wife," embossed woman, hearts and flowers, cutout flowers tied with satin ribbon, real lace surrounds cutout heart, c. 1936	9.00	14.00	11.00
☐ Victorian Valentine, fold out, paper lace	18.00	23.00	20.00
☐ Whitney, embossed paper in pattern, a child delivering a note to a young lady, with original embossed envelope, c. 1870	35.00	45.00	39.00

HORSE-DRAWN CARRIAGES

Horse Drawn Carriage, piano style body, 23"x56"... **$2000.00-2800.00**

    Horse-drawn carriages were used for public and private transportation from about 1800 until 1910. Before 1800, the roads and streets in the United States were so poor that people had to travel on horseback or foot. After 1910, the popularity of the automobile and the need to clean up city streets led to the quick demise of horse-drawn vehicles.

    Carriages were made mostly of wood; metal was used only for bolts, tires, springs and other suspension parts. Mass production methods were perfected by Cincinnati carriage makers in the 1870's. In 1900 over 900,000 carriages were manufactured in the United States. This figure does not include utility vehicles such as farm wagons, delivery vans, etc.

    Collectible carriages are classified in four general groups; two or four-wheeled light vehicles with room for two or three people; four-wheeled with room for four or more; heavy elegant carriages driven by a coachman (rather like modern limousines); and commercial vehicles.

    The finest coachbuilder in the United States was James Brewster and Co. of Connecticut. Brewster's products were and still are, the finest available. Prices for a new Brewster carriage were often 20 times the price of a competitor's similar model. Other famous builders were C. B. Kimball, James Cunningham & Son and Studebaker.

484 / HORSE-DRAWN CARRIAGES

	Current Price Range		Prior Year Average
☐ **Ambulance,** restored with bob runners, 18′, c. 1900's	6000.00	7000.00	6400.00
☐ **Bobsleigh,** four-passenger, slat sides, restored, c. 1905	900.00	1200.00	1000.00
☐ **Bobsleigh,** original wool upholstery, mfg. in Boston, Massachusetts, c. late 1800's	1000.00	1300.00	1100.00
☐ **Buggy,** Amish, c. early 1900's	800.00	1000.00	875.00
☐ **Buggy,** Jenny Lind, nonconvertible top, c. 1880's	2200.00	2500.00	23.00
☐ **Buggy,** Thomas Goddard, convertible leather top, mfg. in Boston, Massachusetts, c. late 1800's	1500.00	1800.00	1600.00
☐ **Buggy lantern,** reflector	75.00	100.00	80.00
☐ **Buggy seat,** original velvet upholstery, trestle base	325.00	425.00	360.00
☐ **Carriage candle lamps,** three lights, inscribed Wm. R. Cannon, pair	450.00	550.00	480.00
☐ **Carriage foot warmer,** portable	65.00	85.00	72.00
☐ **Carriage jack**	60.00	80.00	68.00
☐ **Carriage lamp,** brass, eagle finial	135.00	175.00	150.00
☐ **Carriage lamps,** beveled glass, reflectors, pair	275.00	350.00	310.00
☐ **Carriage lamps,** brass, pair	350.00	450.00	385.00
☐ **Carriage step,** cast iron	25.00	40.00	30.00
☐ **Coach,** brougham, unrestored, mfg. in New York, c. 1900	2000.00	2500.00	2200.00
☐ **Coach lamps,** candle, restored, pair, 17″	500.00	600.00	540.00
☐ **Coach,** large Victorian, unrestored	1800.00	2200.00	1900.00
☐ **Farm wagon,** wooden wheels	850.00	1000.00	920.00
☐ **Governess cart,** basket weave, mfg. in New England, c. 1920	2000.00	2500.00	2200.00
☐ **Hearse,** bowed doors, fringed drapery, silver and brass fittings, c. 1880's	6500.00	7500.00	6800.00
☐ **Hearse,** silver coach lamps, black lacquered, mfg. in Cincinnati, Ohio, c. 1885	12000.00	15000.00	1300.00
☐ **Horse-drawn two level pumper,** Pawtucket, Rhode Island, c. 1850	2400.00	2800.00	2500.00
☐ **Horse tether,** iron	30.00	40.00	34.00
☐ **Milk trolley,** restored, c. early 1900's	4800.00	5500.00	5000.00
☐ **Open carriage,** canoe Victoria, with jump seat	7000.00	9000.00	7900.00
☐ **Peddler's wagon,** divided sections and drawers, c. mid 1800's	1400.00	1600.00	1480.00
☐ **Phaeton,** basket, wicker and wood, restored, mfg. by Brewster and Co., c. 1905	7000.00	10000.00	8250.00
☐ **Phaeton,** restored, elegant, drop front, mfg. by Brewster and Co., c. 1898	3500.00	4500.00	4000.00
☐ **Sleigh cutter,** Victorian style, unrestored, two-passenger	300.00	500.00	390.00
☐ **Speeding cutter,** mfg. in Massachusetts, c. 1886	800.00	1200.00	900.00
☐ **Spring wagon,** yellow and black, mfg. in Chester, Pennsylvania	625.00	725.00	660.00
☐ **Sulky racer,** high wheel, restored	1400.00	1700.00	1525.00
☐ **Surrey,** four-passenger with fringe canopy, mfg. in Syracuse, New York, restored, c. 1896	2500.00	3000.00	2700.00
☐ **Surrey,** two-passenger, fringe canopy	2400.00	2800.00	2500.00
☐ **Town carriage,** brougham, closed, lacquered and upholstered, mfg. by Brewster and Co., c. 1895	5500.00	6500.00	5900.00
☐ **U.S. Mail wagon**	1100.00	1400.00	1225.00

HUMMELS

The Photographer #178, statuette in current production, the camera used has the likeness of an 1850's design . . . . **$90.00-$425.00**

Hummel figures have attained worldwide popularity, as decorations and collector's items. They have now been issued for 50 years and many of the earlier editions, as well as even some later ones, have become scarce. Since the overall total of Hummel figures is quite large, we cannot list every product here. The following is an alphabetical listing of the specimens most likely to be found on today's market. Variations exist of these figures, which, again, space prohibits us from listing. For more in-depth information and listings, you may refer to *The Official Price Guide to Hummel Figurines and Plates* published by the House of Collectibles.

ACCORDION BOY

	Current Price Range		Prior Year Average
☐ 185, Full Bee trademark, 5-6"	125.00	175.00	150.00
☐ 185, 3-line trademark, 5-6"	75.00	85.00	80.00
☐ 185, Goebel trademark, 5-6"	55.00	75.00	60.00

ADORATION

☐ 23/I, Goebel/V trademark, 6¼-7"	120.00	160.00	140.00
☐ 23III, Stylized Bee trademark, 8¾-9"	250.00	375.00	315.00
☐ 23/III, Goebel/V trademark, 8¾-9"	190.00	230.00	185.00

ANGEL SERENADE WITH LAMB

	Current Price Range		Prior Year Average
☐ 83, Full Bee trademark, 5½-5¾"	350.00	450.00	400.00
☐ 83, 3-line trademark, 5½-5¾"	175.00	225.00	200.00
☐ 83, Goebel trademark, 5½-5¾"	70.00	90.00	70.00

ANGELIC SONG

☐ 144, CM trademark, 4-4½"	225.00	300.00	235.00
☐ 144, Stylized Bee trademark, 4-4½"	80.00	120.00	90.00
☐ 144, Goebel/V trademark, 4-4½"	62.00	70.00	52.00

APPLE TREE BOY

☐ 142/3/0, Stylized Bee trademark, 4-4¼"	60.00	95.00	78.00
☐ 142/3/0, Goebel trademark, 4-4¼"	42.00	58.00	48.00
☐ 142/I, Goebel trademark, 6-6¾"	85.00	110.00	88.00

APPLE TREE GIRL

☐ 141/3/0, Stylized Bee trademark, 4-4¼"	60.00	95.00	82.00
☐ 141/3/0, Goebel/V trademark, 4.4¼"	60.00	70.00	48.00
☐ 141/I, 3-line trademark, 6-6¾"	100.00	135.00	105.00

AUF WIEDERSEHEN

☐ 153/0, Goebel/V trademark, 5½-6"	85.00	110.00	80.00
☐ 153/I, Stylized Bee trademark, 6¾-7"	425.00	500.00	475.00
☐ 153/I, Goebel/V trademark, 6¾-7"	115.00	140.00	110.00

BAKER

☐ 128, CM trademark, 4¾-5"	200.00	300.00	235.00
☐ 128, Stylized Bee trademark, 4¾-5"	80.00	125.00	100.00
☐ 128, Goebel/V trademark, 4¾-5"	60.00	78.00	62.00

BAND LEADER

☐ 129, Full Bee trademark, 5-5⅞"	150.00	200.00	175.00
☐ 129, 3-line trademark, 5-5⅞"	95.00	110.00	90.00
☐ 129, Goebel trademark, 5-5⅞"	72.00	86.00	78.00

BARNYARD HERO

☐ 195/2/O, Goebel/V trademark, 3¾-4"	68.00	78.00	62.00
☐ 195/I, 3-line trademark, 5½"	110.00	140.00	125.00
☐ 195/I, Goebel/V trademark, 5½"	100.00	130.00	110.00

BE PATIENT

☐ 197/2/O, Goebel/V trademark, 4¼-4½"	60.00	75.00	68.00
☐ 197/I, Full Bee trademark, 6-6¼"	210.00	275.00	250.00
☐ 197/I, Goebel/V trademark, 6-6¼"	80.00	100.00	90.00

BEGGING HIS SHARE

☐ 9, CM trademark, 5¼-5¾"	400.00	500.00	525.00
☐ 9, Full Bee trademark, 5¼-5¾"	200.00	300.00	225.00
☐ 9, 3-line trademark, 5¼-5¾"	90.00	120.00	105.00

BIRD DUET

	Current Price Range		Prior Year Average
☐ **169,** 3-line trademark, 3¾-4"	65.00	85.00	70.00
☐ **169,** Goebel/V trademark, 3¾-4"	56.00	72.00	58.00
☐ **169,** Goebel trademark, 3¾-4"	52.00	68.00	58.00

BIRTHDAY SERENADE

☐ **218/2/O,** Goebel trademark, 4¼-4½"	64.00	78.00	68.00
☐ **218/O,** Goebel/V trademark, 5¼"	110.00	136.00	105.00
☐ **218,** Full Bee trademark, 5¼"	425.00	725.00	550.00

BLESSED EVENT

☐ **333,** Sytlized Bee trademark, 5¼-5½"	350.00	500.00	335.00
☐ **333,** 3-line trademark, 5¼-5½"	185.00	250.00	195.00
☐ **333,** Goebel trademark, 5¼-5½"	120.00	150.00	130.00

BOOTS

☐ **143/O,** Goebel/V trademark, 5-5½"	65.00	80.00	62.00
☐ **143/I,** Goebel/V trademark, 6½-6¾"	100.00	145.00	95.00
☐ **143,** Stylized Bee trademark, 6¾"	300.00	390.00	345.00

BOY WITH TOOTHACHE

☐ **217,** Full Bee trademark, 5¼-5½"	140.00	190.00	165.00
☐ **217,** 3-line trademark, 5¼-5½"	75.00	95.00	85.00
☐ **217,** Goebel trademark, 5¼-5½"	64.00	78.00	68.00

BROTHER

☐ **95,** CM trademark, 5¼-5¾"	225.00	300.00	220.00
☐ **95,** Stylized Bee trademark, 5¼-5¾"	80.00	120.00	100.00
☐ **95,** Goebel/V trademark, 5¼-5¾"	55.00	72.00	58.00

THE BUILDER

☐ **305,** Stylized Bee trademark, 5½"	150.00	200.00	175.00
☐ **305,** Goebel/V trademark, 5½"	80.00	110.00	80.00
☐ **305,** Goebel trademark, 5½"	75.00	95.00	80.00

BUSY STUDENT

☐ **367,** Stylized Bee trademark, 4¼"	150.00	250.00	175.00
☐ **367,** 3-line trademark, 4¼"	75.00	100.00	88.00
☐ **367,** Goebel trademark, 4¼"	60.00	75.00	62.00

CARNIVAL

☐ **328,** Full Bee trademark, 6"	1000.00	2200.00	1300.00
☐ **328,** 3-line trademark, 6"	90.00	130.00	100.00
☐ **328,** Goebel trademark, 6"	64.00	78.00	68.00

CELESTIAL MUSICIAN

☐ **188,** CM trademark, 7"	350.00	475.00	412.00
☐ **188,** Stylized Bee trademark, 7"	160.00	220.00	170.00
☐ **188,** Goebel/V trademark, 7"	110.00	130.00	100.00

488 / HUMMELS

	Current Price Range		Prior Year Average

CHICK GIRL
- ☐ **57/0**, Stylized Bee trademark, 3½" 80.00 110.00 85.00
- ☐ **57/0**, Goebel/V trademark, 3½" 50.00 70.00 55.00
- ☐ **57/I**, 3-line trademark, 4¼" 90.00 125.00 105.00

CHIMNEY SWEEP
- ☐ **12/2/0**, Goebel/V trademark, 4-4¼" 34.00 44.00 35.00
- ☐ **12/I**, Stylized Bee trademark, 5½-6½" 75.00 125.00 100.00
- ☐ **12/I**, Goebel/V trademark, 5½-6½" 55.00 70.00 62.00

CLOSE HARMONY
- ☐ **336**, 3-line trademark, 5¼-5½" 130.00 325.00 235.00
- ☐ **336**, Goebel/V trademark, 5¼-5½" 130.00 150.00 110.00
- ☐ **336**, Goebel trademark, 5¼-5½" 110.00 130.00 110.00

CONFIDENTIALLY
- ☐ **314**, 3-line trademark, 5¾" 150.00 400.00 275.00
- ☐ **314**, Goebel/V trademark, 5¾" 80.00 110.00 80.00
- ☐ **314**, Goebel trademark, 5¾" 80.00 100.00 80.00

COQUETTES
- ☐ **179**, Full Bee trademark, 5-5¼" 200.00 275.00 238.00
- ☐ **179**, 3-line trademark, 5-5¼" 110.00 135.00 112.00
- ☐ **179**, Goebel trademark, 5-5¼" 90.00 110.00 90.00

DOCTOR
- ☐ **127**, CM trademark, 4¾-5¼" 200.00 290.00 230.00
- ☐ **127**, Stylized Bee trademark, 4¾-5¼" 80.00 115.00 195.00
- ☐ **127**, Goebel/V trademark, 4¾-5¼" 55.00 70.00 54.00

DOLL BATH
- ☐ **319**, Stylized Bee trademark, 5" 175.00 300.00 200.00
- ☐ **319**, 3-line trademark, 5" 100.00 135.00 120.00
- ☐ **319**, Goebel/V trademark, 5" 90.00 110.00 80.00

DUET
- ☐ **130**, CM trademark, 5-5½" 300.00 400.00 350.00
- ☐ **130**, Stylized Bee trademark, 5-5½" 110.00 165.00 135.00
- ☐ **130**, Goebel/V trademark, 5-5½" 100.00 120.00 90.00

EVENTIDE
- ☐ **99**, CM trademark, 4¼ x 5" 350.00 450.00 400.00
- ☐ **99**, Stylized Bee trademark, 4¼ x 5" 150.00 200.00 175.00
- ☐ **99**, Goebel/V trademark, 4¼ x 5" 115.00 148.00 105.00

FAREWELL
- ☐ **65**, Geobel/V trademark, 4¾-5" 90.00 120.00 92.00
- ☐ **65/I**, Full Bell trademark, 4½-4⅞" 200.00 350.00 275.00
- ☐ **65/1**, 3-line trademark, 4½-4⅞" 115.00 140.00 120.00

FARM BOY

	Current Price Range		Prior Year Average
☐ 66, CM trademark, 5-5¾"	225.00	350.00	287.00
☐ 66, Stylized Bee trademark, 5-5¾"	120.00	160.00	112.00
☐ 66, Geobel/V trademark, 5-5¾"	75.00	95.00	75.00

FAVORITE PET

☐ 361, 3-line trademark, 4½"	105.00	130.00	107.00
☐ 361, Goebel/V trademark, 4½"	95.00	110.00	85.00
☐ 361, Goebel trademark, 4½"	85.00	105.00	85.00

FEATHERED FRIENDS

☐ 344, 3-line trademark, 4¾"	125.00	250.00	185.00
☐ 344, Goebel/V trademark, 4¾"	115.00	135.00	98.00
☐ 344, Goebel trademark, 4¾"	105.00	120.00	98.00

FEEDING TIME

☐ 199/0, Goebel trademark, 4¼-4½"	70.00	90.00	75.00
☐ 199/I, Goebel/V trademark, 5½-5¾"	80.00	110.00	80.00
☐ 199, CM trademark, 5¾"	375.00	475.00	400.00

FESTIVAL HARMONY WITH FLUTE

☐ 173/0, Goebel/V trademark, 8"	110.00	130.00	100.00
☐ 173/II, Stylized Bee trademark, 10¼-11"	300.00	400.00	350.00
☐ 173/II, Goebel/V trademark, 10¼-11"	200.00	260.00	195.00

FESTIVAL HARMONY WITH MANDOLIN

☐ 172/0, Goebel trademark, 8"	90.00	110.00	100.00
☐ 172/II, 3-line trademark, 10¼-10¾"	220.00	275.00	225.00
☐ 172, CM trademark, 10¾"	1200.00	2200.00	1700.00

FLOWER VENDOR

☐ 381, 3-line trademark, 5¼"	175.00	300.00	240.00
☐ 381, Goebel/V trademark, 5¼"	95.00	115.00	85.00
☐ 381, Goebel trademark, 5¼"	85.00	105.00	85.00

FOR FATHER

☐ 87, CM trademark, 5½"	250.00	350.00	270.00
☐ 87, Stylized Bee trademark, 5½"	110.00	160.00	115.00
☐ 87, Goebel/V trademark, 5½"	85.00	100.00	72.00

FOR MOTHER

☐ 257, 3-line trademark, 5-5¼"	65.00	90.00	77.00
☐ 257, Goebel/V trademark, 5-5¼"	60.00	75.00	52.00
☐ 257, Goebel trademark, 5-5¼"	55.00	70.00	52.00

FRIENDS

☐ 136/I, Goebel/V trademark, 5"	80.00	100.00	75.00
☐ 136/V, Stylized Bee trademark, 10¾-11"	600.00	800.00	700.00
☐ 136/V, Goebel/V trademark, 10¾-11"	450.00	575.00	450.00

490 / HUMMELS

	Current Price Range		Prior Year Average

GLOBE TROTTER
- ☐ **79,** CM trademark, 5-5¼" 200.00 350.00 262.00
- ☐ **79,** Stylized Bee trademark, 5-5¼" 90.00 140.00 105.00
- ☐ **79,** Goebel/V trademark, 5-5¼" 65.00 80.00 62.00

GOOD FRIENDS
- ☐ **182,** Full Bee trademark, 4-4¼" 150.00 225.00 185.00
- ☐ **182,** 3-line trademark, 4-4¼" 80.00 100.00 85.00
- ☐ **182,** Goebel trademark, 4-4¼" 65.00 85.00 70.00

GOOD HUNTING
- ☐ **307,** Stylized Bee trademark, 5" 150.00 225.00 185.00
- ☐ **307,** 3-line trademark, 5" 130.00 160.00 122.00
- ☐ **307,** Goebel trademark, 5" 75.00 95.00 80.00

GOOSE GIRL
- ☐ **47/3/O,** Stylized Bee trademark, 4-4¼" 70.00 120.00 105.00
- ☐ **47/O,** CM trademark, 4¾-5¼" 260.00 375.00 317.00
- ☐ **47/II,** 3-line trademark, 7-7½" 200.00 275.00 220.00

HAPPINESS
- ☐ **86,** CM trademark, 4½-5" 160.00 220.00 165.00
- ☐ **86,** Stylized Bee trademark, 4½-5" 60.00 85.00 68.00
- ☐ **86,** Goebel/V trademark, 4½-5" 50.00 60.00 48.00

HAPPY BIRTHDAY
- ☐ **176/O,** Stylized Bee trademark, 5-5¼" 120.00 160.00 140.00
- ☐ **176/O,** Goebel trademark, 5-5¼" 80.00 100.00 80.00
- ☐ **176/1,** 3-line trademark, 5¾-6" 175.00 225.00 200.00

HAPPY DAYS
- ☐ **150/2/O,** 3-line trademark, 4¼" 80.00 110.00 82.00
- ☐ **150/O,** Full Bee trademark, 5-5¼" 225.00 325.00 312.00
- ☐ **150/I,** CM trademark, 6-6½" 650.00 850.00 825.00

HAPPY TRAVELER
- ☐ **109/O,** 3-line trademark, 4¾-5" 65.00 85.00 62.00
- ☐ **109,** Goebel trademark, 5" 45.00 55.00 50.00
- ☐ **109/II,** 3-line trademark, 7½" 200.00 255.00 175.00

HEAR YE, HEAR YE
- ☐ **15/O,** Stylized Bee trademark, 5-5¼" 115.00 150.00 132.00
- ☐ **15/O,** Goebel/V trademark, 5-5¼" 75.00 100.00 75.00
- ☐ **15/I,** 3-line trademark, 6-6¼" 95.00 125.00 110.00

HEAVENLY ANGEL
- ☐ **21/O,** 3-line trademark, 4-4¾" 40.00 60.00 55.00
- ☐ **21/O½,** 3-line trademark, 5¾-6½" 75.00 100.00 70.00
- ☐ **21/I,** Stylized Bee trademark, 6¾-7¼" 100.00 175.00 150.00

HEAVENLY PROTECTION

	Current Price Range		Prior Year Average
☐ 88/I, Goebel/V trademark, 6¼-6¾"	135.00	165.00	142.00
☐ 88/II, Stylized Bee trademark, 8¾-9"	300.00	475.00	310.00
☐ 88/II, Goebel/V trademark, 8¾-9"	220.00	265.00	200.00

HELLO

☐ 124/0, Stylized Bee trademark, 5¾-6¼"	100.00	150.00	125.00
☐ 124/0, Goebel/V trademark, 5¾-6¼"	80.00	95.00	68.00
☐ 124/I, Goebel/V trademark, 6¾-7"	100.00	120.00	92.00

THE HOLY CHILD

☐ 70, Full Bee trademark, 6¾-7"	135.00	200.00	165.00
☐ 70, Stylized Bee trademark, 6¾-7½"	75.00	125.00	95.00
☐ 70, Goebel/V trademark, 6¾-7½"	55.00	75.00	52.00

HOME FROM MARKET

☐ 198/2/0, Goebel/V trademark, 4½-4¾"	50.00	65.00	48.00
☐ 198/I, Stylized Bee trademark, 4½-4¾"	100.00	160.00	130.00
☐ 198/I, Goebel/V trademark, 4½-4¾"	90.00	110.00	70.00

INFANT OF KRUMBAD

☐ 78/0, Full Bee trademark, 2¼"	100.00	175.00	138.00
☐ 78/II, Full Bee trademark, 3½"	75.00	125.00	100.00
☐ 78/V, 3-line trademark, 7½-7¾"	55.00	75.00	75.00

IN TUNE

☐ 414, Goebel trademark, 3¾"	100.00	120.00	110.00

JOYFUL

☐ 53, CM trademark, 3½-4¼"	160.00	275.00	225.00
☐ 53, Stylized Bee trademark, 3½-4¼"	68.00	78.00	68.00
☐ 53, Goebel/V trademark, 3½-4¼"	45.00	55.00	40.00

JUST RESTING

☐ 112/3/0, Stylized Bee trademark, 3¾-4"	75.00	115.00	95.00
☐ 112/3/0, Goebel/V trademark, 3¾-4"	55.00	70.00	52.00
☐ 112/I, Goebel/V trademark, 4¾-5½"	90.00	110.00	80.00

KISS ME

☐ 311, 3-line trademark, 6-6¼"	150.00	400.00	275.00
☐ 311, Goebel/V trademark, 6-6¼"	90.00	110.00	80.00
☐ 311, Goebel trademark, 6-6¼"	80.00	100.00	80.00

KNITTING LESSON

☐ 256, 3-line trademark, 7½"	235.00	285.00	250.00
☐ 256, Goebel/V trademark, 7½"	200.00	250.00	190.00
☐ 256, Goebel trademark, 7½"	185.00	225.00	190.00

LATEST NEWS

☐ 184, 3-line trademark, 5-5¼"	130.00	160.00	135.00
☐ 184, Goebel/V trademark, 5-5¼"	110.00	130.00	100.00
☐ 184, Goebel trademark, 5-5¼"	100.00	120.00	100.00

492 / HUMMELS

	Current Price Range	Prior Year Average

LET'S SING
- ☐ **110/O**, Stylized Bee trademark, 3-3¼″ 70.00 120.00 100.00
- ☐ **110/O**, Goebel/V trademark, 3-3¼″ 50.00 60.00 45.00
- ☐ **110/I**, Stylized Bee trademark, 3½-4″ 100.00 150.00 125.00

LITTLE CELLIST
- ☐ **89/I**, 3-line trademark, 5¼-6¼″ 90.00 110.00 92.00
- ☐ **89/II**, Full Bee trademark, 7½-7¾″ 325.00 450.00 365.00
- ☐ **89/II**, 3-line trademark, 7½-7¾″ 200.00 250.00 200.00

LITTLE DRUMMER
- ☐ **240**, Stylized Bee trademark, 4-4¼″ 70.00 95.00 82.00
- ☐ **240**, Goebel/V trademark, 4-4¼″ 55.00 75.00 65.00
- ☐ **240**, Goebel/V trademark, 4-4¼″ 48.00 62.00 48.00

LITTLE FIDDLER
- ☐ **2/O**, 3-line trademark, 5¾-6″ 95.00 120.00 105.00
- ☐ **2/II**, Goebel/V trademark, 10¾-11″ 550.00 650.00 550.00
- ☐ **2/III**, Goebel/V trademark, 12¼″ 600.00 700.00 600.00

LITTLE GOAT HERDER
- ☐ **200/O**, 3-line trademark, 4½-4¾″ 90.00 110.00 82.00
- ☐ **200/I**, Stylized Bee trademark, 5-5½″ 120.00 160.00 130.00
- ☐ **200**, CM trademark, 5½-5¾″ 350.00 450.00 375.00

LITTLE HELPER
- ☐ **73**, CM trademark, 4-4½″ 175.00 250.00 212.00
- ☐ **73**, Stylized Bee trademark, 4-4½″ 75.00 115.00 105.00
- ☐ **73**, Goebel/V trademark, 4-4½″ 50.00 60.00 48.00

LITTLE SCHOLAR
- ☐ **80**, CM trademark, 5¼-5¾″ 200.00 300.00 250.00
- ☐ **80**, Stylized Bee trademark, 5¼-5¾″ 85.00 135.00 100.00
- ☐ **80**, Goebel/V trademark, 5¼-5¾″ 65.00 80.00 62.00

LITTLE SHOPPER
- ☐ **96**, CM trademark, 4½-5″ 140.00 220.00 180.00
- ☐ **96**, Stylized Bee trademark, 4½-5″ 80.00 100.00 90.00
- ☐ **96**, Goebel/V trademark, 4½-5″ 50.00 65.00 48.00

LITTLE SWEEPER
- ☐ **171**, CM trademark, 4¼-4½″ 175.00 235.00 205.00
- ☐ **171**, Stylized Bee trademark, 4¼-4½″ 65.00 95.00 80.00
- ☐ **171**, Goebel/V trademark, 4¼-4½″ 50.00 65.00 48.00

LOST SHEEP
- ☐ **68/2/O**, Stylized Bee trademark, 4¼-4½″ 75.00 95.00 85.00
- ☐ **68/2/O**, Goebel/V trademark, 4¼-4½″ 50.00 65.00 48.00
- ☐ **68/O**, 3-line trademark, 5½″ 80.00 100.00 85.00

	Current Price Range		Prior Year Average

MADONNA WITHOUT HALO
- ☐ **46/O**, 3-line trademark, 10¼-10½" **40.00** **80.00** **48.00**
- ☐ **46/I**, 3-line trademark, 11¼-12" **55.00** **75.00** **70.00**
- ☐ **46/III**, 3-line trademark, 16¼-16¾" **125.00** **150.00** **137.00**

MADONNA WITH HALO
- ☐ **45/O**, Stylized Bee trademark, 10¼-10½" **45.00** **80.00** **62.00**
- ☐ **45/O**, Goebel/V trademark, 10¼-10½" **30.00** **40.00** **35.00**
- ☐ **45/I**, 3-line trademark, 11¼-12" **55.00** **85.00** **70.00**

MAIL IS HERE
- ☐ **226**, Full Bee trademark, 4¼-6" **425.00** **625.00** **560.00**
- ☐ **226**, Stylized Bee trademark, 4¼-6" **325.00** **450.00** **380.00**
- ☐ **226**, Goebel/V trademark, 4¼-6" **250.00** **300.00** **225.00**

MAX AND MORITZ
- ☐ **123**, CM trademark, 5-5½" **240.00** **340.00** **300.00**
- ☐ **123**, Stylized Bee trademark, 5-5½" **100.00** **150.00** **125.00**
- ☐ **123**, Goebel/V trademark, 5-5½" **65.00** **85.00** **68.00**

MEDITATION
- ☐ **12/2/O**, 3-line trademark, 4¼" **55.00** **80.00** **68.00**
- ☐ **13/O**, 3-line trademark, 5¼-5¾" **75.0** **100.00** **88.00**
- ☐ **13/II**, Goebel trademark, 7" **175.00** **225.00** **175.00**

MOTHER'S DARLING
- ☐ **175**, CM trademark, 5½" **225.00** **325.00** **235.00**
- ☐ **175**, Stylized Bee trademark, 5½" **100.00** **150.00** **125.00**
- ☐ **175**, Goebel/V trademark, 5½" **70.00** **90.00** **75.00**

MOTHER'S HELPER
- ☐ **133**, CM trademark, 4¾-5" **260.00** **340.00** **280.00**
- ☐ **133**, Stylized Bee trademark, 4¾-5" **100.00** **140.00** **115.00**
- ☐ **133**, Goebel/V trademark, 4¾-5" **80.00** **100.00** **75.00**

THE PHOTOGRAPHER
- ☐ **178**, CM trademark, 4¾-5¼" **275.00** **425.00** **375.00**
- ☐ **178**, Stylized Bee trademark, 4¾-5¼" **125.00** **175.00** **150.00**
- ☐ **178**, Goebel/V trademark, 4¾-5¾" **100.00** **120.00** **90.00**

PLAYMATES
- ☐ **58/O**, Stylized Bee trademark, 4" **80.00** **120.00** **90.00**
- ☐ **58/O**, Goebel/V trademark, 4" **60.00** **75.00** **58.00**
- ☐ **58/I**, Goebel/V trademark, 4¼" **85.00** **110.00** **82.00**

POSTMAN
- ☐ **119**, CM trademark, 5-5½" **275.00** **350.00** **312.00**
- ☐ **119**, Stylized Bee trademark, 5-5½" **115.00** **135.00** **135.00**
- ☐ **119**, Goebel/V trademark, 5-5½" **75.00** **95.00** **70.00**

PRAYER BEFORE BATTLE

	Current Price Range		Prior Year Average
☐ 20, CM trademark, 4-4½"	225.00	325.00	275.00
☐ 20, Stylized Bee trademark, 4-4½"	100.00	135.00	130.00
☐ 20, Goebel/V trademark, 4-4½"	65.00	80.00	62.00

PUPPY LOVE

☐ 1, CM trademark, 5-5¼"	250.00	350.00	275.00
☐ 1, Stylized Bee trademark, 5-5¼"	90.00	130.00	120.00
☐ 1, Goebel/V trademark, 5-5¼"	70.00	85.00	68.00

RETREAT TO SAFETY

☐ 201/2/O, Stylized Bee trademark, 3¾-4"	80.00	120.00	100.00
☐ 201/2/O, Goebel/V trademark, 3¾-4"	60.00	80.00	60.00
☐ 201/I, Goebel/V trademark, 5½-5¾"	120.00	140.00	110.00

RIDE INTO CHRISTMAS

☐ 396/O, Goebel trademark, 4½"	90.00	100.00	95.00
☐ 396, Goebel/V trademark, 5¾"	175.00	225.00	150.00
☐ 396, Goebel trademark, 5¾"	155.00	185.00	150.00

RING AROUND THE ROSIE

☐ 348, 3-line trademark, 6¾"	1400.00	1750.00	1625.00
☐ 348, Goebel/V trademark, 6¾"	1300.00	1500.00	1125.00
☐ 348, Goebel trademark, 6¾"	1100.00	1350.00	1125.00

SCHOOL BOY

☐ 82/2/O, 3-line trademark, 4-4½"	50.00	70.00	52.00
☐ 82/O, Stylized Bee trademark, 4¾-6"	70.00	125.00	95.00
☐ 82/II, Stylized Bee trademark, 7½"	300.00	400.00	350.00

SCHOOL BOYS

☐ 170/I, Goebel/V trademark, 7¼-7½"	450.00	550.00	450.00
☐ 170/III, Full Bee trademark, 10-10¼"	1750.00	2000.00	1825.00
☐ 170/III, Goebel/V trademark, 10-10¼"	1200.00	1400.00	1125.00

SCHOOL GIRL

☐ 81/2/O, 3-line trademark, 4¼-4¾"	60.00	80.00	65.00
☐ 81/2/O, Goebel trademark, 4¼-4¾"	45.00	60.00	48.00
☐ 81/O, 3-line trademark, 4¾-5¼"	70.00	90.00	75.00

SCHOOL GIRLS

☐ 177/I, Stylized Bee trademark, 7½"	625.00	725.00	650.00
☐ 177/I, 3-line trademark, 7½"	475.00	625.00	525.00
☐ 177/III, Full Bee trademark, 9½"	1700.00	2200.00	1950.00

SENSITIVE HUNTER

☐ 6/O, 3-line trademark, 4¾"	70.00	85.00	72.00
☐ 6/I, Stylized Bee trademark, 5½"	120.00	175.00	120.00
☐ 6/II, 3-line trademark, 7½"	195.00	250.00	200.00

SHE LOVES ME, SHE LOVES ME NOT

	Current Price Range		Prior Year Average
☐ 174, Full Bee trademark, 4¼"	175.00	250.00	180.00
☐ 174, 3-line trademark, 4¼"	90.00	150.00	80.00
☐ 174, Goebel trademark, 4¼"	60.00	75.00	62.00

SHEPHERD'S BOY

☐ 64, CM trademark, 5½-6¼"	225.00	350.00	300.00
☐ 64, Stylized Bee trademark, 5½-6¼"	95.00	150.00	125.00
☐ 64, Goebel/V trademark, 5½-6¼"	80.00	100.00	75.00

SIGNS OF SPRING

☐ 203/2/0, Stylized Bee trademark, 4"	90.00	120.00	98.00
☐ 203/2/0, Goebel/V trademark, 4"	65.00	85.00	60.00
☐ 203/I, 3-line trademark, 5-5½"	95.00	125.00	100.00

SINGING LESSON

☐ 63, Full Bee trademark, 2¾-3"	110.00	150.00	130.00
☐ 63, 3-line trademark, 2¾-3"	65.00	80.00	68.00
☐ 63, Goebel trademark, 2¾-3"	45.00	60.00	48.00

SISTER

☐ 98/2/0, Stylized Bee trademark, 4½-4¾"	75.00	100.00	88.00
☐ 98/2/0, Goebel/V trademark, 4½-4¾"	40.00	55.00	48.00
☐ 98/0, 3-line trademark, 5¼-5½"	65.00	95.00	80.00

SKIER

☐ 59, CM trademark, 5-6"	250.00	350.00	300.00
☐ 59, Stylized Bee trademark, 5-6"	100.00	150.00	125.00
☐ 59, Goebel/V trademark, 5-6"	85.00	105.00	75.00

SOLOIST

☐ 135, CM trademark, 4½-5"	175.00	250.00	180.00
☐ 135, Stylized Bee trademark, 4½-5"	65.00	95.00	78.00
☐ 135, Goebel/V trademark, 4½-5"	50.00	65.00	48.00

SPRING CHEER

☐ 72, Full Bee trademark, 5-5½"	125.00	225.00	175.00
☐ 72, 3-line trademark, 5-5½"	60.00	80.00	60.00
☐ 72, Goebel trademark, 5-5½"	45.00	60.00	48.00

STAR GAZER

☐ 132, Full Bee trademark, 4¾"	175.00	225.00	175.00
☐ 132, 3-line trademark, 4¾"	10.00	125.00	105.00
☐ 132, Goebel trademark, 4¾"	75.00	90.00	78.00

STREET SINGER

☐ 131, CM trademark, 5-5½"	200.00	275.00	220.00
☐ 131, Stylized Bee trademark, 5-5½"	80.00	100.00	88.00
☐ 131, Goebel/V trademark, 5-5½"	60.00	75.00	58.00

496 / HUMMELS

	Current Price Range		Prior Year Average

SURPRISE
☐ 94/3/O, Stylized Bee trademark, 4-4½"	80.00	120.00	100.00
☐ 94/3/O, Goebel/V trademark, 4-4½"	60.00	70.00	58.00
☐ 94/I, Stylized Bee trademark, 5¼-5½"	100.00	130.00	125.00

SWEET GREETINGS
☐ 352, Goebel, 4"	75.00	95.00	85.00

SWEET MUSIC
☐ 186, Full Bee trademark, 5-5½"	140.00	210.00	195.00
☐ 186, 3-line trademark, 5-5½"	80.00	100.00	85.00
☐ 186, Goebel trademark, 5-5½"	65.00	85.00	70.00

TELLING HER SECRET
☐ 196/O, Stylized Bee trademark, 5-5½"	150.00	225.00	165.00
☐ 196/O, Goebel/V trademark, 5-5½"	120.00	145.00	110.00
☐ 196/I, Stylized Bee trademark, 6½-6¾"	250.00	350.00	285.00

THOUGHTFUL
☐ 415, Goebel trademark, 4¼"	95.00	115.00	100.00

TIMID LITTLE SISTER
☐ 394, Goebel trademark, 6¾"	180.00	200.00	190.00

TO MARKET
☐ 49/3/O, Stylized Bee trademark, 4"	90.00	140.00	100.00
☐ 49/3/O, Goebel/V trademark, 4"	70.00	85.00	68.00
☐ 49/O, Goebel/V trademark, 5-5½"	100.00	120.00	100.00

TRUMPET BOY
☐ 97, Full Bee trademark, 4½-4¾"	100.00	155.00	127.00
☐ 97, Stylized Bee trademark, 4½-4¾"	65.00	100.00	88.00
☐ 97, Goebel/V trademark, 4½-4¾"	55.00	70.00	48.00

VILLAGE BOY
☐ 51/3/O, Goebel/V trademark, 4"	40.00	50.00	35.00
☐ 51/2/O, Stylized Bee trademark, 5"	60.00	80.00	82.00
☐ 51/2/O, Goebel/V trademark, 5"	40.00	60.00	48.00

VOLUNTEERS
☐ 50/2/O, Stylized Bee trademark, 4¾-5"	130.00	170.00	150.00
☐ 50/2/O, Goebel/V trademark, 4¾-5"	100.00	130.00	90.00
☐ 50/O, Goebel/V trademark, 5½-6"	120.00	150.00	115.00

WAITER
☐ 154/O, 3-line trademark, 6-6¼"	80.00	105.00	92.00
☐ 154/O, Goebel trademark, 6-6¼"	65.00	85.00	75.00
☐ 154/I, Goebel trademark, 6½-7"	95.00	115.00	95.00

INKWELLS AND INK STANDS / 497

	Current Price Range		Prior Year Average
WATCHFUL ANGEL			
☐ **194,** Full Bee trademark, 6¼-6¾"	225.00	375.00	287.00
☐ **194,** 3-line trademark, 6¼-6¾"	140.00	175.00	168.00
☐ **194,** Goebel trademark, 6¼-6¾"	110.00	140.00	115.00
WAYSIDE HARMONY			
☐ **111/3/O,** 3-line trademark, 3¾-4"	65.00	80.00	68.00
☐ **111/I,** Full Bee trademark, 5-5½"	175.00	250.00	212.00
☐ **111/I,** 3-line trademark, 5-5½"	100.00	135.00	95.00
WEARY WANDERER			
☐ **204,** CM trademark, 5½-6"	275.00	400.00	337.00
☐ **204,** Stylized Bee trademark, 5½-6"	100.00	145.00	122.00
☐ **204,** Goebel/V trademark, 5½-6"	75.00	100.00	75.00

INKWELLS AND INKSTANDS

Inkwell, Lenox, shape #313, 4" high . . . . **$195.00-$235.00**

    Inkwells were a feature of everyday life all over the world for nearly 4500 years. Inkwells have been made of pottery, porcelain, stone, shells, wood and of metals including brass, silver and gold. The most common material since the early 1800's is glass. Examples from the 19th and early 20th centuries are considered the most collectible. Glass inkwells complete with a non-attached lid are relatively rare and considerably more valuable than those without lids.

498 / INKWELLS AND INK STANDS

Two or more inkwells combined are called an inkstand. Inkstands often include other writing accessories such as a pounce pot (powdered sand to dry ink); adhesive wafers to seal letters; a candle, sealing wax and metal seal for sealing letters; or a bell for summoning servants to post the letter. Some inkstands had more than a dozen accessories and an intact set would be valuable indeed.

Other related collectibles are pen stands, pen wipers (a small ring of tightly packed bristles) and small decorative glue pots, with matching brush lids, used for sealing letters.

	Current Price Range		Prior Year Average
☐ **Brass,** Art Deco, glass insert	40.00	55.00	45.00
☐ **Brass,** crab, glass insert, hinged lid	75.00	100.00	82.00
☐ **Brass,** cups on brass, tray, 6″ x 9″, c. 1900's	200.00	250.00	220.00
☐ **Brass,** devil, German, c. 1900	75.00	100.00	85.00
☐ **Brass,** horse, two milk glass inserts, 5½″ x 9½″	100.00	125.00	112.00
☐ **Brass,** scrollwork, porcelain insert, square	65.00	90.00	78.00
☐ **Brass,** shape of kettle, Japanese, 2½″, 19th c. ..	200.00	250.00	220.00
☐ **Brass,** Victorian, two glass inserts	70.00	95.00	80.00
☐ **Bronze,** Art Deco, glass insert, silver inlay	65.00	90.00	75.00
☐ **Bronze,** Art Nouveau, ornate sailing vessel	125.00	150.00	130.00
☐ **Bronze,** Art Nouveau, woman's head with flowing hair for lid	125.00	150.00	130.00
☐ **Bronze,** clay pot of natural flowers	130.00	165.00	145.00
☐ **Cast iron,** car, two glass inserts, 5½″ x 10″	150.00	175.00	160.00
☐ **Cast iron,** cat's head, 4″, c. 1800's	200.00	250.00	220.00
☐ **Cast iron,** globe, Columbian Exposition	50.00	75.00	60.00
☐ **Cloisonne,** stone wall and tray, 7″, c. 1900's	100.00	125.00	112.00
☐ **Cut glass,** eagle finial on brass lid, 19th c.	150.00	200.00	170.00
☐ **Cut glass,** hinged crystal lid	90.00	120.00	100.00
☐ **Cut glass,** sterling silver lid, 2″	90.00	120.00	100.00
☐ **Delft,** lion, Germany, 7½″ x 9″	165.00	190.00	175.00
☐ **Delft,** windmill, Germany, 3″ x 3½″, c. 1800's ...	90.00	120.00	100.00
☐ **Enameled metal,** camel, glass insert, c. 1900's ..	175.00	225.00	195.00
☐ **Enameled metal,** floral designs, mottled colors, Chinese, c. 1800's	100.00	140.00	118.00
☐ **Enameled metal,** gold and brass trim, glass insert	50.00	75.00	60.00
☐ **Glass,** blue, hinged brass lid, 2½″	150.00	175.00	162.00
☐ **Glass,** sterling silver overlay	85.00	115.00	95.00
☐ **Glass,** umbrella shape, c. 1800's	200.00	250.00	220.00
☐ **Marble,** blue and gray, cherubs, French, 4″	145.00	180.00	165.00
☐ **Milk glass,** cat on iron base, 5″	125.00	150.00	135.00
☐ **Milk glass,** dogs on iron base, 4″	100.00	135.00	115.00
☐ **Pewter,** blue pottery insert, 9″, c. 1820	150.00	175.00	162.00
☐ **Pewter,** dome rolltop, 5″	75.00	100.00	82.00
☐ **Pewter,** pear with bees on tray, Kayserzinn	200.00	250.00	212.00
☐ **Pewter,** round, 6½″	90.00	120.00	100.00
☐ **Porcelain,** boy wearing hat, French, 12″, c. 1880's	140.00	180.00	155.00
☐ **Porcelain,** hinged lid, painted flowers	60.00	95.00	80.00
☐ **Porcelain,** Victorian woman, 4″	50.00	75.00	60.00
☐ **Pressed glass,** chair with cat on cushion, 4″, 19th c.	140.00	180.00	155.00
☐ **Soapstone,** carved dog on stand, Italian, 8″, 18th c.	100.00	135.00	115.00

INSULATORS / 499

	Current Price Range		Prior Year Average
☐ **Stand,** bronze, crab and shell, pen tray, signed Tiffany Studios, New York, 7″, c. 1899-1920	1900.00	2400.00	2100.00
☐ **Stand,** Georgian silver, complete	800.00	1200.00	975.00
☐ **Stand,** iron horse, brass cap, pen holder, 5″	40.00	60.00	44.00
☐ **Stand,** silver, engraved, by Paul de Lamerie	5000.00	6000.00	5400.00
☐ **Stand,** wooden, signed J. R. Chappell, 3¾″	50.00	75.00	60.00
☐ **Stoneware,** dark red glaze, roped edge, four pen holes, signed, 5″	125.00	150.00	135.00
☐ **Stoneware,** round, chiseled edge	45.00	60.00	50.00
☐ **Wooden,** carved, Black Forest deer	125.00	150.00	130.00
☐ **Wooden,** glass insert, four pen holes, 4″	50.00	75.00	60.00
☐ **Wooden,** porcelain insert, 3″	45.00	60.00	50.00

INSULATORS

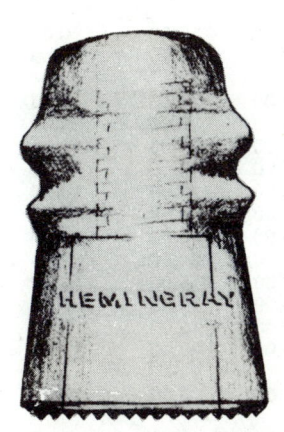

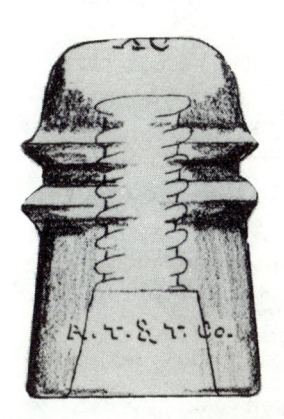

Left to Right: **Hemingray #16,** green single skirt, 2⅞″x4″ **$1.25-$3.35; A. T. & T. Co.,** aqua, single skirt, 2½″x3¾″ **$5.75-$10.00; Star,** aqua, single skirt, pony, 2⅜″x3½″ .... **$5.75-$9.50**

Electrical insulators are the nonconducting glass objects used to attach wires to supporting poles. The inventor was apparently Ezra Cornell, who was the chief construction engineer for Samuel Morse and later became the founder of Western Union Telegraph.

Insulators fall into two general catagories; threadless, which were merely slipped over wood or metal pins, and threaded insulators, which screwed onto the pin by means of a molded internal thread and were permanently attached.

Age and shape are two of the determining factors in the valuation of old insulators. The nonthreaded type was used exclusively until the 1860's. The threaded version was invented in France in 1865. Nonthreaded insulators usually bear no date nor manufacturer's mark.

Color is what attracts most collectors to insulators. Clear glass is the most common followed by green. Much less common, and correspondingly

500 / INSULATORS

more valuable, are milk white, amber, iridescent, amethyst, cobalt blue and (very rare) red. The different colors were created either by design or, as in the amethyst color, by long exposure to sunlight.

Insulators can occasionally be found around construction sites. Old railroad tracks, intercity tracks and some rural roads are other sources of insulators. Never climb poles to collect insulators; some "polecats" have been electrocuted.

	Current Price Range		Prior Year Average
☐ A.G.M., amber, 3¾" x 2¾"	10.00	15.00	12.00
☐ A.T.& T. Co., aqua, single skirt, 2⅛" x 3¾", c. 1900	6.00	10.00	7.00
☐ A.T.& T. Co., aqua, 3⅜"	6.00	10.00	7.00
☐ A.T.& T. Co., aqua, two-piece, 2¾" x 3⅝"	4.00	7.00	5.00
☐ A.T.& T. Co., green, single skirt, 2½" x 3¾"	4.00	7.00	5.00
☐ Agee, clear amethyst, 3⅝" x 2¾"	10.00	15.00	12.00
☐ American Insulator Co., aqua, double petticoat, 4⅛" x 3⅛"	9.00	12.00	10.00
☐ Armstrong, amber 4" x 3¼"	9.00	12.00	10.00
☐ Armstrong, No. 5, clear, double petticoat, 3⅛" x 3¾"	4.00	7.00	5.00
☐ A.U. Patent, green, 4⅜" x 2¾"	25.00	35.00	29.00
☐ B. & O., aqua, 3⅞ x 3¼"	28.00	35.00	29.00
☐ B.F.G. Co., aqua, 4" x 3½"	35.00	45.00	39.00
☐ B.G.M. Co., clear amethyst, 3⅜" x 2¼"	15.00	20.00	17.00
☐ Barclay, aqua, double petticoat, 3" x 2¼"	15.00	20.00	17.00
☐ Boston Bottle Works, aqua, 4⅛" x 3"	40.00	50.00	44.00
☐ Brookes, Homer, aqua, 3¾" x 2¾"	18.00	24.00	21.00
☐ Brookfield, No. 36, aqua, green, 3⅞" x 3⅛"	10.00	15.00	12.00
☐ Brookfield, No. 45, aqua, green, 4⅛" x 3⅛"	6.00	10.00	7.00
☐ Brookfield, No. 55, aqua, green, 4" x 2½"	10.00	15.00	12.00
☐ Brookfield, No. 83, aqua, green, 4" x 3⅛"	15.00	20.00	17.00
☐ Brookfield, dark olive green, double petticoat, 3¾" x 4"	6.00	10.00	7.00
☐ Brookfield, green, double petticoat, 3³⁄₁₆" x 3⅝", c. 1865	6.00	10.00	7.00
☐ B.T. Co. of Canada, clear, amethyst, 3½" x 2⅛"	12.00	17.00	14.50
☐ B.T. Co. of Canada, aqua, green, 3¼" x 2⅜"	10.00	15.00	12.00
☐ C. & P. Tel Col., aqua, green, 3½" x 2⅞"	9.00	12.00	10.00
☐ C.E.L., amethyst, 4⅛" x 2¾"	10.00	15.00	12.00
☐ C.E.N., amethyst, 3¼" x 2½"	30.00	40.00	34.00
☐ C.G.I., clear, amethyst, 3½" x 2⅛"	18.00	24.00	21.00
☐ Cable, aqua, green, 4½" x 3¼"	20.00	27.00	23.00
☐ California, aqua, green, 3½" x 2⅛"	20.00	27.00	23.00
☐ California, clear, amethyst, 4⅜" x 3½"	28.00	35.00	32.00
☐ California, clear, amethyst, 4⅛" x 3¼"	4.00	7.00	5.00
☐ California, CK-162, purple, double petticoat, 3¾" x 4"	6.00	10.00	7.00
☐ Canadian Pacific, blue, green, aqua, 3⅝" x 2¾"	40.00	50.00	44.00
☐ Canadian Pacific, clear, amethyst, 3½" x 2¾"	12.00	17.00	15.00
☐ Castle, aqua, 3⅞" x 2½"	40.00	50.00	44.00
☐ Chester, aqua, 4" x 2⅜"	45.00	55.00	48.00
☐ Columbia, aqua, green, 3¾" x 4"	35.00	45.00	38.00
☐ Derflinger, T.N.I., aqua, green, 4" x 3½"	15.00	20.00	17.00
☐ Dominion No. 9, amber, aqua and clear, 3¾" x 2½"	2.00	5.00	3.00

INSULATORS / 501

	Current Price Range	Prior Year Average
☐ **Duquesne,** aqua, green, 3 3/8" x 2 3/8"	28.00 35.00	30.00
☐ **Dwight,** aqua, 4" x 3"	28.00 35.00	30.00
☐ **E.C. & M. Co.,** green, 4" x 2 1/2"	20.00 27.00	23.00
☐ **Electrical Supply Co.,** aqua, green, 3 5/8" x 2 5/8" ...	28.00 35.00	30.00
☐ **Folembray,** No. 221, olive green, 2 5/8" x 3 3/8"	35.00 45.00	38.00
☐ **Gayner,** 36-190, aqua, 3 3/4" x 3 1/4"	9.00 12.00	10.00
☐ **Gayner,** green, double petticoat, 3 3/16" x 3 7/8"	20.00 27.00	23.00
☐ **H.G. Co.,** amber, double petticoat, 3 1/4" x 3 3/4" ..	10.00 15.00	12.00
☐ **H.G. Co. Petticoat,** aqua, green, 3 3/4" x 3 3/4"	4.00 7.00	5.00
☐ **H.G. Co. Petticoat,** clear, 4 1/8" x 3 1/4"	9.00 12.00	10.00
☐ **Hawley,** aqua, 3 1/4" x 2 1/4"	12.00 17.00	15.00
☐ **Hemingray,** No. 2 Cable, aqua, green, 4" x 3 5/8" ..	20.00 27.00	23.00
☐ **Hemingray,** No. 7, aqua, green, 3 1/2" x 2 1/2"	2.00 5.00	3.00
☐ **Hemingray,** No. 8, aqua, green, 3 3/8" x 2 3/8"	12.00 17.00	14.00
☐ **Hemingray,** No. 9, aqua, single skirt, 2 1/4" x 3 1/2"	15.00 20.00	17.00
☐ **Hemingray,** No. 10, clear, single skirt, 2 5/8" x 3 1/2"	10.00 15.00	12.00
☐ **Hemingray,** No. 16, green, single skirt, 2 7/8" x 4" ..	2.00 5.00	3.00
☐ **Hemingray,** No. 19, aqua, double petticoat, 3 1/4" x 3"	25.00 35.00	28.00
☐ **Hemingray,** No. 25, aqua, green, 4" x 3 1/4"	12.00 17.00	14.00
☐ **Hemingray,** No. 95, aqua, green, 3 5/8" x 2 7/8"	30.00 40.00	34.00
☐ **Hemingray Beehive,** green, double petticoat, 3 1/8" x 4 3/4"	15.00 20.00	17.00
☐ **Hemingray Petticoat,** cobalt blue, 4" x 3 1/4"	28.00 35.00	30.00
☐ **Hemingray Transportation,** green, 4 1/2" x 3 1/4" ..	20.00 27.00	23.00
☐ **Isorex,** clear, black, green, blue, 5 1/2" x 3 1/2"	4.00 7.00	5.00
☐ **Jeffery Mfg. Co.,** aqua, 3 5/8" x 2 3/4"	28.00 35.00	30.00
☐ **Jumbo,** aqua, 7 1/4" x 5 1/4"	18.00 24.00	21.00
☐ **Knowles Cable,** aqua, green, 4" x 3 5/8"	28.00 35.00	32.00
☐ **Fred M. Locke,** No. 14, aqua, 4 3/8" x 3 1/8"	18.00 24.00	21.00
☐ **Fred M. Locke,** No. 21, aqua, green, 4" x 4"	4.00 7.00	5.00
☐ **Lynchburg,** No. 10, aqua, green, 3 3/8" x 2 1/4"	6.00 10.00	7.00
☐ **Lynchburg,** No. 31, aqua, green, 3 1/2" x 2 3/8"	6.00 10.00	7.00
☐ **Lynchburg,** No. 44, aqua, single skirt, 2 1/4" x 3 5/8"	9.00 12.00	10.00
☐ **Lynchburg,** No. 44, 4" x 3 5/8"	4.00 7.00	5.00
☐ **Maydwell** No. 9, clear, aqua, 3 5/8" x 2 1/8"	4.00 7.00	5.00
☐ **Maydwell,** No. 9, clear, single skirt, 2 1/8" x 3 1/2" ..	4.00 7.00	5.00
☐ **Maydwell,** No. 16, amber, 3 7/8" x 2 3/4"	4.00 7.00	5.00
☐ **Maydwell,** No. 20, white milk glass, 3 5/8" x 3 1/8" ...	18.00 24.00	21.00
☐ **McLaughlin,** No. 9, green, single skirt, 2 1/4" x 3 5/8".	10.00 15.00	12.00
☐ **McLaughlin,** No. 16, amber, aqua, green, 3 5/8" x 2 5/8"	4.00 7.00	5.00
☐ **McLaughlin,** No. 19, aqua, 3 3/4" x 3 1/4"	2.00 5.00	3.00
☐ **McLaughlin,** No. 42, aqua, 4" x 3 5/8"	4.00 7.00	5.00
☐ **McLaughlin,** No. 62, aqua, 3 5/8" x 3 5/8"	6.00 10.00	7.00
☐ **Mershon,** aqua, 5" x 5 1/2"	28.00 35.00	31.00
☐ **Monogram H.I. Co.,** aqua, 4 1/2" x 3 1/8"	18.00 24.00	21.00
☐ **Mulford & Biddle,** aqua, 3 1/4" x 2 5/8"	30.00 40.00	34.00
☐ **N.E.G.M. Co.,** aqua, green, 3 1/2" x 2 1/8"	12.00 17.00	14.00
☐ **N.E.G.M. Co.,** aqua, 3 1/2" x 3 1/4"	15.00 20.00	17.00
☐ **N.E.T. & T. Co.,** aqua, green, 3 5/8" x 2 3/8"	4.00 7.00	5.00
☐ **N.E.T. & T. Co.,** blue, 3 1/2" x 3"	10.00 15.00	12.00
☐ **Noleak,** aqua, green, 4" x 4"	28.00 35.00	31.00
☐ **O.V.G. Co.,** aqua, 3 1/2" x 2 1/4"	6.00 10.00	7.00
☐ **O.V.G. Co.,** aqua, green, 3 1/2" x 2 1/4"	10.00 15.00	12.00
☐ **Pettingel Anderson Co.,** aqua, 4" x 2 3/4"	15.00 20.00	17.00

	Current Price Range		Prior Year Average
☐ **Pony,** blue, 3⅛" x 2⅜"	18.00	24.00	21.00
☐ **Postal,** aqua, green, 4⅛" x 3½"	12.00	17.00	15.00
☐ **Pyrex,** carnival glass, 3⅛" x 3¾"	15.00	20.00	17.00
☐ **Pyrex,** carnival glass, 3" x 3¾"	10.00	15.00	12.00
☐ **Pyrex,** double threads, carnival glass, 2⅝" x 4¼"	12.00	17.00	14.00
☐ **S.B.T. & T. Co.,** aqua, green, 3½" x 2¼"	12.00	17.00	14.00
☐ **Santa Ana,** aqua, green, 4¼" x 4¾"	28.00	35.00	28.00
☐ **Standard,** clear, amethyst, 3⅝" x 2¾"	10.00	15.00	12.00
☐ **Star,** aqua, single skirt, pony, 2⅜" x 3½"	6.00	10.00	7.00
☐ **Sterling,** aqua, 3¼" x 2¼"	12.00	17.00	14.00
☐ **T.C.R.,** aqua, 4" x 3¾"	10.00	15.00	12.00
☐ **T.H.E. Co.,** aqua, 4" x 3⅛"	28.00	35.00	29.00
☐ **Thomas,** brown pottery, 2½" x 1⅛"	4.00	7.00	5.00
☐ **Transportation,** No. 2, aqua, 4¼" x 2⅞"	18.00	24.00	21.00
☐ **U.S. Tel. Co.,** aqua, 3¾" x 2⅜"	12.00	17.00	14.00
☐ **V.M.R. Napoli,** aqua, green, 4" x 2¾"	10.00	15.00	12.00
☐ **W.F.G. Co.,** clear, amethyst, 3½" x 2⅛"	12.00	17.00	14.00
☐ **W.G.M. Co.,** clear, amethyst, 3½" x 2¼"	20.00	27.00	23.00
☐ **W.G.M. Co.,** clear, amethyst, 3⅞" x 3⅛"	15.00	20.00	17.00
☐ **W.V.,** No. 5, aqua, 4¼" x 2¾"	15.00	20.00	17.00
☐ **Westinghouse,** aqua, green, 3⅛" x 2⅜"	25.00	30.00	27.00
☐ **Whitall Tatum,** amber, 3⅞" x 3¼"	10.00	15.00	12.00
☐ **Whitall Tatum,** 512-A, amber, red, 3½" x 3⅝"	4.00	7.00	5.00

IRONS

Electric Iron, Montgomery Ward, nickel-plated .... **$30.00-$40.00**

Irons are interesting collectibles because of the tremendous variety of shapes, sizes and methods of testing.

Although pans heated with charcoal have been used to press clothing in Asia since 100 BC, heated irons were not used in the West until the 17th century. Two of the most popular, the box iron and the sadiron were used into the 20th century.

The box iron was a hollow metal box with a handle into which a heated slug was placed. A spare slug was kept heating on the stove. The sadiron (from an old word meaning "solid") was a solid metal device which was heated on the stove. The biggest improvement in sadirons came in 1871 when Mary Potts invented a sadiron with a detachable handle. The Potts iron gave way to self-heating irons fueled with gasoline or cooking gas, which were both dangerous and unsatisfactory.

The first electric iron was patented in 1882 and did not become popular until electric utility companies agreed to supply power to homes during the daytime hours.

Most collectible irons are still fairly inexpensive. The collector should look for odd shapes, unusually large or small irons, and unusual methods of self-heating.

Another related collectible is the laundry stove, a large stove used to heat from four to several dozen irons.

	Current Price Range		Prior Year Average
☐ **Alcohol iron,** wooden handle, c. 1880	60.00	75.00	65.00
☐ **Box iron,** heated slug, c. 1890	40.00	55.00	45.00
☐ **Box iron,** English, heated slugs, c. 1800	75.00	100.00	82.00
☐ **Charcoal iron,** brass fittings, chimney vent	65.00	80.00	70.00
☐ **Charcoal iron,** twisted handle, chimney vent	70.00	85.00	75.00
☐ **Charcoal iron,** wooden handle, c. 1890	40.00	55.00	45.00
☐ **Charcoal iron,** wooden iron, with trivet	60.00	75.00	65.00
☐ **Flat iron,** charcoal, chimney vent, c. 1860	25.00	35.00	29.00
☐ **Flat iron,** hollow handle	25.00	35.00	29.00
☐ **Flat iron,** metal handle, c. 1860	25.00	35.00	29.00
☐ **Flat iron,** red, small, c. 1877	40.00	55.00	45.00
☐ **Flat iron,** removable handle, c. 1870	25.00	35.00	29.00
☐ **Flat iron,** rope handle	20.00	30.00	28.00
☐ **Flat iron,** stone body, metal handle, c. 1850	40.00	55.00	45.00
☐ **Flat iron,** wooden handle, child's, c. 1860	25.00	35.00	29.00
☐ **Flat iron,** wooden handle, large	30.00	40.00	34.00
☐ **Fluting iron,** double, with holder	60.00	75.00	65.00
☐ **Fluting iron,** Geneva, c. 1870's	45.00	60.00	50.00
☐ **Gasoline iron,** Coleman	25.00	35.00	28.00
☐ **Gasoline iron,** wooden handle, c. 1910	50.00	65.00	55.00
☐ **G.E. electric iron,** c. 1905	35.00	45.00	39.00
☐ **G.E. electric iron,** c. 1920	30.00	40.00	34.00
☐ **Laundry stove,** cast iron, double burner	150.00	200.00	170.00
☐ **Laundry stove,** cast iron, single burner	100.00	150.00	120.00
☐ **Laundry stove,** fancy cast iron, c. 1895	475.00	550.00	500.00
☐ **Nickel plated iron**	20.00	30.00	24.00
☐ **Tailor's iron**	30.00	40.00	34.00
☐ **Travel iron,** asbestos	25.00	35.00	29.00

JARS

Jars were perfected for use in food preservation by the French in 1795. Food was placed in glass containers, then corked and boiled to sterilize the contents. This is still the basic method of canning. These early jars are called wax sealers and were covered with metal or cork lids, then sealed with melted wax. This method was awkward to use and home canning did not become popular until 1858, when a great improvement in jar sealing was made.

John L. Mason patented a system of jar sealing in 1858 which used a zinc screw cap and rubber ring. His system was so successful that after his patent expired many companies brought out copies, some even bearing his name.

Another successful design, introduced in 1882, was the Lightning jar, which used a glass lid and rubber ring held in place by a wire spring clip. The third type is the style used today, a metal lid precoated on the underside with a material that self-seals when heated and cooled.

As might be expected, the successful jars are not the most collectible ones. Items that didn't work, or were impractical, were produced for only a short time and are, therefore, comparatively rare. Unusual closures and colors are what the jar collector desires. Earlier jars have lips that were finished by grinding and often contain many imperfections. Many reproductions have been made. The prospective jar collector should study his subject, then buy carefully.

	Current Price Range		Prior Year Average
Acme, clear, half gal.	12.00	18.00	14.00
Adams, Allison & Co., redware, c. 1860	100.00	130.00	118.00
Atlas E-Z Seal, amber, qt.	25.00	35.00	29.00
Atlas E-Z Seal, green, half gal.	8.00	15.00	11.00
Atlas Improved Mason, qt.	3.00	6.00	4.00
Atlas Mason, Patent 11/30/1858, green, zinc top, half gal.	10.00	20.00	14.00
Automatic Sealer, aqua, glass top, qt.	18.00	24.00	21.00
Ball Ideal, clear, half pt.	10.00	15.00	12.00
Ball Improved, aqua, qt.	5.00	12.00	8.00
Ball Mason, Patent 1858, handmade	30.00	40.00	34.00
Ball Perfect Mason, amber, qt.	30.00	40.00	34.00
Banner, Patent 2/9/1864; reinstated 1/22/1867	45.00	55.00	48.00
Beaver, zinc band with glass insert, qt.	30.00	45.00	35.00
Best Wide Mouth, clear, qt.	5.00	12.00	8.00
Bold, aqua, qt.	18.00	24.00	21.00
G. D. Brown, clear, pt.	55.00	75.00	62.00
Champion, Patent 8/31/1869, aqua, qt.	90.00	120.00	100.00
Clarke Fruit Jar Co., aqua, glass top, qt., c. 1886	45.00	60.00	50.00
Cohansey Glass Co., Patent 2/12/1868	35.00	50.00	40.00
Dandy Trademark, amber, qt.	65.00	85.00	72.00
Darling Imperial, blue, qt.	25.00	40.00	30.00
Electroglass Mason, amber, qt.	8.00	12.00	9.00
Eureka, Patent 12/27/1864, aqua, qt.	60.00	85.00	70.00
Gayner Mason, clear, qt.	8.00	15.00	10.00
Glenshaw Mason, screw band	8.00	15.00	10.00
Globe, amber, qt.	45.00	60.00	50.00
Griffin's, Patent 1862	85.00	100.00	90.00
Hazel, aqua, qt.	18.00	24.00	21.00

	Current Price Range		Prior Year Average
☐ Hazel-Atlas Lightning Seal & E-Z Seal	12.00	18.00	14.00
☐ J & B, Patent 6/14/1869, aqua, pt.	40.00	55.00	45.00
☐ Keystone Mason, aqua, qt.	8.00	15.00	11.00
☐ Knowlton Vacuum Fruit Jar, blue	30.00	40.00	34.00
☐ Lamb Mason, amber, qt.	8.00	15.00	11.00
☐ Lightning, amber	30.00	45.00	35.00
☐ Lightning, aqua, pt.	5.00	12.00	8.00
☐ Lightning, aqua, qt.	8.00	15.00	11.00
☐ Leotric, clear, qt.	4.00	8.00	5.00
☐ Lorillard, Patent 1872	18.00	24.00	21.00
☐ Lynchburg Standard Mason, aqua, qt, ...	12.00	20.00	15.00
☐ Macomb Pottery Co., beige with brown trim, zinc top, qt.	35.00	50.00	40.00
☐ Mason's, CF-J Co. emblem, improved "Trademark"	15.00	25.00	18.00
☐ Mason's Improved Maltese Cross, two types	8.00	15.00	11.00
☐ Mason's Maltese Cross, Patent 11/30/1858	15.00	25.00	18.00
☐ Milville Improved, aqua, qt.	25.00	35.00	29.00
☐ New Gem, clear, qt.	8.00	15.00	11.00
☐ Pacific Mason, zinc top, clear, qt.	15.00	25.00	19.00
☐ Premium Coffeyville, Kansas, handmade	25.00	35.00	29.00
☐ Presto, screw on top, clear	4.00	8.00	5.00
☐ Putnam Glass Works, amber, qt.	30.00	40.00	34.00
☐ Putnam Lightning, blue, pt.	12.00	20.00	15.00
☐ Queen, zinc band, aqua, qt., c. 1875	18.00	24.00	21.00
☐ Ramsey, glass top, aqua, qt.	45.00	60.00	50.00
☐ Red Key Mason, clear or amethyst	25.00	35.00	29.00
☐ Reid Murdock & Co., zinc top, clear, qt.	5.00	12.00	8.00
☐ Reliance Brand Mason, Wide Mouth	5.00	12.00	8.00
☐ Rockingham, mottled, tin top, wax sealer	65.00	85.00	70.00
☐ Royal, clear, qt.	8.00	15.00	11.00
☐ Scranton Jar, glass stopper, aqua, qt.	40.00	55.00	45.00
☐ Selco Surity Seal, glass top, green or blue	8.00	15.00	11.00
☐ Silicon Glass, qt., c. 1930	8.00	15.00	11.00
☐ Smalley Self Sealer, wide mouth	5.00	12.00	8.00
☐ C.F. Spencer, Patent Rochester, New York, qt. ...	35.00	60.00	45.00
☐ C.F. Spencer's Improved, Patent 1868	35.00	60.00	45.00
☐ Star, zinc band with glass insert, clear, qt.	18.00	24.00	21.00
☐ Sun Trademark, green, half gal.	45.00	55.00	48.00
☐ Sun Trademark J.P. Barstow	25.00	35.00	28.00
☐ Swayzee's Improved Mason, dark green, half qt. ..	30.00	40.00	34.00
☐ T & Co., paneled, orange, qt.	30.00	40.00	34.00
☐ Trademark Lightning, amber, half gal.	35.00	50.00	40.00
☐ Tropical T.F. Canners	4.00	8.00	5.00
☐ True Fruit, JHS Co. emblem, Trademark Reb. ...	15.00	25.00	18.00
☐ True Seal, glass top, clear	12.00	18.00	15.00
☐ United Drug Co., clear, qt.	4.00	8.00	5.00
☐ Universal, screw top, clear, qt.	5.00	12.00	8.00
☐ Valne Jar, screw top, aqua, qt.	25.00	35.00	28.00
☐ Van Vliet, green, pt., c. 1881	375.00	425.00	390.00
☐ Victor, Patent, c. 1899	8.00	15.00	11.00
☐ Victor, Patent, 2/20/1900	12.00	20.00	15.00
☐ Victory, green with clear lid, qt., c. 1864	120.00	150.00	130.00
☐ Wallaceburg Gem	5.00	12.00	8.00
☐ Wears Improved	12.00	20.00	15.00
☐ Weir, qt., c. 1892	25.00	35.00	29.00

506 / JEWELRY

	Current Price Range		Prior Year Average
☐ **Weir Seal,** white stoneware lid, qt.	8.00	12.00	9.00
☐ **Whitall-Tatum,** pt.	30.00	40.00	34.00
☐ **Winslow,** Patent 1870	75.00	100.00	82.00

CANNING TOOLS

☐ **Canning booklets,** c. 1890-1930	3.00	6.00	4.00
☐ **Canning kettle,** enameled tinware, lid, two handles	25.00	35.00	29.00
☐ **Canning processor,** Mudge patent, c. 1880's-1900 .	15.00	25.00	19.00
☐ **Jar filler,** funnel, tin, 5" Dia., c. 1890-1910	2.00	5.00	3.00
☐ **Jar lifter,** wire, holds two jars, c. 1910	5.00	8.00	6.00
☐ **Jar lifter,** wire and wood, finger ring release, c. 1895	5.00	8.00	6.00
☐ **Jar wrench,** A.C. Williams, nickeled iron, c. 1910 ..	3.00	6.00	4.00

JEWELRY

Brooche, hardstone onyx portrait cameo of a lady, rose diamonds, pearls, gold, c. 1880............................... **$1400.00-$1600.00**

The jewelry collector is a multifaceted person; part detective, historian, artist, even chemist and geologist. He must have a broad knowledge of cultures, styles, metals and minerals. He must also have the patience to sift through a lot of relatively worthless jewelry to find that special buy.

Jewelry, much more than other antiques and collectibles, is dependent upon materials for its value. Diamonds, rubies, gold and silver make jewelry

JEWELRY / 507

expensive, even though artistic value may be lacking. In some cases, however, jewelry made of rather ordinary materials may be valued for workmanship alone, or simply because they were made by a certain artist.

Most of the styles of jewelry sought by collectors falls into historical stylistic periods: Georgian (1700's), Victorian (1800's), Art Nouveau (turn of the century) and Art Deco (1920's). Asian and American Indian jewelry are also very collectible. Each has its own charactertistics and reflects the style of the era during which it was made.

Beauty may be in the eye of the beholder, but, particularly in the case of antique jewelry. The beholder should arm himself with a good knowledge of gem cutting and setting techniques, a touchstone and a jewelers' loupe before parting with any hard-earned cash.

For more in-depth information and listings, you may refer to *The Official Price Guide to Antique Jewelry*, by Arthur Guy Kaplan, published by the House of Collectibles.

BRACELETS / BANGLE – GOLD

	Current Price Range		Prior Year Average
☐ **Beaded Edge Flat Bangle,** five round diamonds in front, gold, English, c. 1903-04	450.00	475.00	460.00
☐ **Cultured Pearl Bangle,** 17 pearls in straight row in center, gold, English, c. 1903-04	280.00	320.00	300.00
☐ **Cultured Pearl Hollow Tubular Bangle,** 45 pearls in flower and leaf motif, gold, English, c. 1903-04	375.00	425.00	385.00
☐ **Diamond Bangle,** five old mine diamonds approx. 1.0 ct., engraved bangle, gold	1250.00	1450.00	1350.00
☐ **Diamonds and Pearls,** 20 round diamonds approx. 1.50 cts., two rows of cultured pearls, 14K gold	2000.00	2400.00	2150.00
☐ **Etruscan Granulation Wide Bangle,** gold, c. 1840	600.00	700.00	675.00
☐ **Flat Bangle,** two round diamonds and one round ruby in center, Etruscan granulation, engraved, gold, English, c. late 19th	250.00	325.00	260.00
☐ **Hollow Oval and Ball Design Links,** gold, English, c. 1903-04	350.00	375.00	375.00
☐ **Loveknot Hollow Tubular Motif,** engraved scrolls, gold, English, c. 1903-04	175.00	225.00	200.00
☐ **Opals and Diamonds,** nine oval cabochon opals, 28 round diamonds, gold, c. 1890	2000.00	2400.00	2000.00
☐ **Oval Openwork Center Motif,** rose and round diamonds, engraved bangle, gold, c. 1845	1250.00	1500.00	1350.00
☐ **Plaited Bangle,** Etruscan granulation ends, gold, c. 1870	1100.00	1250.00	1100.00
☐ **Seed Pearl Hollow Tubular Bangle,** one round diamond, gold, c. 1900	750.00	850.00	700.00
☐ **Straight Row Motif,** one row of round rubies, two rows of rose diamonds, gold, c. 1920	1150.00	1400.00	1100.00
☐ **Wide Bangle,** floral motif, champleve opaque black enamel, gold, c. 1860	650.00	800.00	650.00

BRACELETS / DIAMOND LINK

☐ **Box Oval Link,** 13 old mine diamonds approx. 9 cts., two square-cut sapphires between each link, platinum, American, c. 1930	14000.00	16000.00	13500.00

508 / JEWELRY

	Current Price Range		Prior Year Average
☐ **Scroll Links,** rose diamonds, gold topped platinum, French, c. 1890	700.00	900.00	850.00
☐ **Square Cluster Center,** four genuine oriental seed pearls, 11 diamonds, oblong openwork links, platinum topped gold, French, c. 1890-1900	1000.00	1400.00	1000.00

BRACELETS / FLEXIBLE

	Current Price Range		Prior Year Average
☐ **Animal Gold Silhouettes on Green Glass,** Indian Pitch, engraved floral reverse, 22K gold, Indian, c. 19th	1200.00	1500.00	1100.00
☐ **Button Motif,** repousse links, three round diamonds, gold, c. 1920	800.00	900.00	700.00
☐ **Coral,** three branch coral chains, seed pearls, surrounding glass locket with woven hair clasp, gold, c. 1870	250.00	375.00	275.00
☐ **Flower Motif,** robin's egg blue and white champleve enamel, gold, c. 1830	600.00	650.00	600.00
☐ **Geometric Motif Flat Links,** one round emerald, one round ruby, one round sapphire, two round diamonds, 14K gold, c. 1930	1000.00	1250.00	1050.00
☐ **Heart Lock Motif,** curb links, 9K gold, English, c. 20th	125.00	150.00	100.00
☐ **Jade Carved Circular Motif,** seed pearls, gold, c. 20th	600.00	700.00	650.00
☐ **Mesh Woven,** Greek key motif on oval slide, black enamel, gold, c. 1860	800.00	900.00	760.00
☐ **Oval Link Motif,** three round peridots and two cushion-cut peridots alternating with chain links, gold, American, c. 1900	500.00	550.00	500.00
☐ **Ribbon and Flower Motif,** center panel on wide band, 17 rose diamonds in flowers, gold, maker G. Ehnl, c. 1871	3000.00	3250.00	3000.00
☐ **Scroll Motif Links,** alternating with light green cabochon emeralds, gold	2500.00	3000.00	2200.00
☐ **Snake,** woven flexible band, engraved head, gemstone eyes, gold, c. 1840	1200.00	1400.00	1100.00
☐ **Turquoise Pave Set,** in three clusters, old mine diamond centers, snake link bracelet, gold, c. 1840	3250.00	3650.00	3200.00

BROOCHES / ANIMAL AND BUG

	Current Price Range		Prior Year Average
☐ **Bird,** pave diamonds, center emerald-cut, emerald in closed back mounting, silver, c. 1800-10	700.00	900.00	700.00
☐ **Cat,** pave rose diamond body, ruby eyes, pearl ball, white gold, French, c. 1935	1000.00	1200.00	900.00
☐ **Dragonfly,** colored stones, silver, c. mid 19th	200.00	225.00	175.00
☐ **Fly,** cabochon ruby eyes and body, old mine diamond body and wings, pearl, gold, c. 1860	1800.00	2000.00	1750.00
☐ **Rams' Head,** Etruscan granulation, rope motif, gold, c. 1860	1200.00	1400.00	1100.00
☐ **Snake,** one cabochon turquoise, gold, English, c. early 20th	250.00	275.00	225.00
☐ **Turtle,** six rose diamonds, 36 demantoid garnets, gold, c. early 20th	450.00	650.00	300.00

JEWELRY / 509

BROOCHES / BAR

	Current Price Range		Prior Year Average
☐ **Bird Motif,** seed pearls, 14K gold, American, c. 1894-95	250.00	275.00	230.00
☐ **Crown Motif,** round diamonds, square sapphires, platinum topped gold, c. early 20th	450.00	500.00	425.00
☐ **Half Pearl,** round and rose diamonds, gold, silver, c. mid 19th	800.00	900.00	750.00
☐ **Lily-Of-The-Valley Flower Motif,** 11 seed pearls, 14K gold, American, c. 1894-95	145.00	165.00	140.00
☐ **Pearls,** knife-edge bar, 14K, American, c. 1894-95	100.00	120.00	75.00
☐ **Rubies,** three cabochon, rose diamonds, silver topped gold, c. 1880	1200.00	1400.00	1200.00
☐ **Sword with Removable Scabbard,** seed pearls, 14K gold, American, c. 1894-95	275.00	300.00	266.00

BROOCHES / CAMEO

☐ **Coral,** *Cameo of a Lady,* engraved frame, gold, c. late 19th	500.00	600.00	500.00
☐ **Hardstone Cameo,** three gentlemen and a ram, gold, c. 19th	950.00	1150.00	900.00
☐ **Mother-Of-Pearl,** scenic cameo with oriental figures, gold, c. 19th	425.00	475.00	425.00
☐ **Opal,** matrix cameo of the Sphinx, gold, c. 1920	2600.00	3000.00	2750.00
☐ **Sardonyx,** cameo of a lady, four round diamonds, eight seed pearls, gold, c. 1880	1100.00	1250.00	1000.00
☐ **Wedgewood,** cameo of a Muse, c. 1840, blue enameled 10K gold frame, c. 1900	450.00	550.00	425.00

BROOCHES / DIAMOND

☐ **Bow Openwork Motif,** round diamonds, platinum, c. 1920	2400.00	2600.00	2350.00
☐ **Cluster and Bow Motif,** rose diamonds, gold pendant or brooch, c. 1860	1300.00	1500.00	1300.00
☐ **Flower Bow Motif,** rose diamonds, platinum topped gold, c. late 19th	1000.00	1150.00	950.00
☐ **Leaf Motif,** one round diamonds approx. 1.20 cts., 14 round diamonds, approx. 5.0cts, platinum, gold, c. 1910	6250.00	6750.00	6200.00
☐ **Rectangular Geometric Motif,** three round diamonds, rose diamonds, gold topped platinum, c. 1900	1650.00	2000.00	1600.00
☐ **Thistle Motif,** round demantoid garnets in body of thistle, rose diamonds, platinum, gold, Scottish, c. 1890	1200.00	1400.00	1200.00

BROOCHES / GEMSTONE

☐ **Art Nouveau Motif,** rose diamonds, one round pearl, emerald bead, platinum, gold, c. 1890-1900	2400.00	2600.00	2350.00
☐ **Crescent Motif,** nine round rubies, old mine diamonds, gold, c. 19th	2750.00	3200.00	2700.00
☐ **Flower Motif,** one oval sapphire, gold, c. 1890	1400.00	1600.00	1400.00
☐ **Heart Dangle Motif,** four almandine garnets, six pearls, gold, c. 1860	400.00	475.00	425.00
☐ **Mosaic of St. Peter's Basilica of Rome,** malachite background, gold, c. 1870	1200.00	1350.00	1150.00

510 / JEWELRY

	Current Price Range		Prior Year Average

BROOCHES / SILVER

- ☐ **Angel Motif,** sterling, American, c. 1896 .... 135.00 · 145.00 · 125.00
- ☐ **Flower Motif,** enameled, sterling silver, American, c. 1935 .... 65.00 · 85.00 · 70.00
- ☐ **Heart Motif,** sterling, American, c. 1896 .... 40.00 · 50.00 · 45.00
- ☐ **Madonna and Child Motif,** bas-relief panel, blue enamel, four half-pearls, silver, c. 1905 .... 185.00 · 200.00 · 185.00
- ☐ **Swirl and Dangle Motif,** engraved, maker: Ellis & Son, Exeter, England, silver, c. 1869 .... 125.00 · 150.00 · 115.00
- ☐ **Wreath Motif,** enamel, sterling, American, c. 1896 65.00 · 75.00 · 57.50

EARRINGS / DIAMOND

- ☐ **Bird Motif,** rose diamonds, ruby eyes, silver gilt, c. 1820 .... 650.00 · 750.00 · 650.00
- ☐ **Dangle Flower Motif,** rose diamonds, closet-set, silver topped gold, c. early 19th .... 700.00 · 900.00 · 700.00
- ☐ **Leaf and Flower Motif,** two pear-shape rose diamonds, round rose diamonds, silver back gold, c. 1790 .... 3750.00 · 4200.00 · 3750.00
- ☐ **Single Stone Motif,** old mine diamonds, 14K gold, c. 1900 .... 275.00 · 325.00 · 275.00
- ☐ **Wreath Motif,** two old mine diamonds, rose diamonds, silver, c. 18th .... 1200.00 · 1300.00 · 1200.00

EARRINGS / DIAMOND AND GEMSTONE

- ☐ **Bell and Bow,** openwork motif, seed pearls, diamonds, gold, c. early 20th .... 2800.00 · 3200.00 · 2750.00
- ☐ **Emerald Beads,** rose diamonds, gold, c. 1920-30 . 1350.00 · 1450.00 · 1300.00
- ☐ **Geometric Motif,** 14 round diamonds, four pearls, approx. 9MM to 9.5MM, platinum, c. 1915-30 .... 750.00 · 950.00 · 750.00

EARRINGS / GEMSTONE

- ☐ **Black Onyx Ball and Bar Motif,** seed pearls, gold, c. 1860-80 .... 500.00 · 550.00 · 500.00
- ☐ **Circle Dangle Motif,** marcasites, sterling silver, c. 1920-30 .... 75.00 · 95.00 · 75.00
- ☐ **Hoop Motif,** sead pearls, gold, c. 1860-80 .... 400.00 · 450.00 · 400.00
- ☐ **Lava Cameos,** openwork frames, silver gilt, c. 1870-80 .... 375.00 · 475.00 · 375.00
- ☐ **Mosaic Butterfly Dangle Motif,** gold, c. 1860 .... 1650.00 · 1750.00 · 1600.00
- ☐ **Snake Motif,** pear-shape diamond in head, gold, c. 19th .... 1000.00 · 1200.00 · 1100.00
- ☐ **Teardrop Motif,** lapis lazuli, seed pearls, gold, c. 1890 .... 400.00 · 450.00 · 400.00

LOCKETS

- ☐ **Butterfly and Grape Vine Motif,** enameled, rose diamonds, gold, c. late 19th .... 2600.00 · 2800.00 · 2600.00
- ☐ **Enameled Oval Locket,** slides open, brass, c. late 19th .... 100.00 · 150.00 · 110.00
- ☐ **Floral And Scenic Engraved Motif,** 14K gold, American, c. 1896 .... 225.00 · 275.00 · 225.00
- ☐ **Horseshoe Motif,** pearls, turquoise, gold, c. 1870 375.00 · 475.00 · 375.00

	Current Price Range		Prior Year Average
☐ **Leaf Motif,** cabochon turquoise in center, gold, c. mid 19th	1150.00	1250.00	1100.00
☐ **Medallion Portrait of a Lady,** 14K gold, Art Nouveau, c. 1890-1910	275.00	325.00	275.00
☐ **Oval Motif,** Etruscan granulation, one seed pearl, gold, c. 1880	1200.00	1400.00	1150.00
☐ **Pique,** tortoise shell with gold rose, reverse: glass locket, 9K gold, maker C & Co., Edinburgh, Scotland, c. 1947	175.00	225.00	170.00
☐ **Round Floral Motif,** 14K gold, American, c. 1896	100.00	120.00	100.00
☐ **Shield Motif,** Etruscan granulation, one old mine diamond, link chain, gold, c. 1860	1500.00	1600.00	1475.00

NECKLACES

☐ **Art Deco,** triple pendant necklace, 14K gold, American, c. 1930	700.00	900.00	700.00
☐ **Bog Oak Motif,** ovals carved with scenes of Irish castles, c. 1850-70	275.00	375.00	270.00
☐ **Cherubs with Leaf Feet,** on scroll motif, silver, designed by A. Ortwein, Germany, c. 1873	1800.00	2200.00	1750.00
☐ **Egyptian Motif,** carved lapis lazuli scarab, turquoise, gold, c. 1920	900.00	1100.00	850.00
☐ **Festoon Motif,** four cabochon carbuncles, gold link chain, c. 1890	1300.00	1500.00	1300.00
☐ **Flower Motif,** oval cabochon opals, demantoid garnets, Art Nouveau, c. 1900	4200.00	4400.00	4200.00
☐ **Geometric Hinged Pendant Motif,** 14 teardrops on link chain, gold, c. late 19th	650.00	2400.00	650.00
☐ **Ivory Medallion and Curved Links,** silver, Chinese, c. 1900-20	275.00	400.00	275.00
☐ **Japanese Motif Locket,** book link chain, silver, maker S. Bros., Birmingham, England, c. 1883	375.00	425.00	370.00
☐ **Leaf Motif,** two faceted coral beads, 15K gold, English, c. 1850	1000.00	1200.00	950.00
☐ **Mosaic Motif,** oval and pear-shape pendants, foxtail chain, gold-plated metal, Italian, c. mid 20th	175.00	300.00	175.00
☐ **Pink Topaz Necklace,** fancy scroll motif links, each with one oval foil-back pink topaz, c. 1810	2000.00	2400.00	1850.00
☐ **Scotch Agate,** various colors, 15K gold mounts, English, c. 1860	725.00	825.00	700.00
☐ **Turquoise Baroque Beads,** 9K gold, English, c. 20th	275.00	325.00	250.00

PENDANTS

☐ **Bell Motif,** round diamond, seed pearls, 14K gold, American, c. 1920	100.00	145.00	100.00
☐ **Cameo,** mythological figure, carved snake frame, gold, c. 19th	2500.00	2700.00	2500.00
☐ **Crescent and Star Motif,** one turquoise, six seed pearls, 12 in. chain, 14K gold, American, c. 1894-95	135.00	165.00	130.00
☐ **Cutout Swirl Motif,** marcasites, sterling silver, American, c. 1920	35.00	45.00	35.00
☐ **Fire Opal,** cabochon, rose diamonds, silver, gold, c. mid 19th	1650.00	1850.00	1650.00

512 / JEWELRY

	Current Price Range		Prior Year Average
☐ **Flower Motif,** translucent colored enamel, one round diamond, 12 in. chain, 14K gold, American, c. 1894-95	225.00	265.00	225.00
☐ **Hardstone,** cameo of a lady, half seed pearl border, gold, pendant or brooch, c. 1880	1300.00	1600.00	1250.00
☐ **Heart Motif,** heart-shaped moonstone, rose diamonds, silver topped gold, c. 1870	450.00	475.00	450.00
☐ **Lady and Child Motif,** cutout ivory, gold, c. 1925 .	75.00	100.00	75.00
☐ **Maltese Cross Motif,** engraved, gold, c. 1800	750.00	850.00	740.00
☐ **Oval Center of Frosted Crystal,** marcasites, sterling silver, American, c. 1920	65.00	85.00	65.00
☐ **Snowflake Motif,** one seed pearl, 12 in. chain, 14K gold, American, c. 1894-95	85.00	95.00	90.00
☐ **Tassel Motif,** seed pearls, diamonds in cap, 14K white gold, c. 1920	650.00	675.00	650.00

RINGS / DIAMOND

☐ **Belt Motif,** three old mine diamonds, 18K gold, c. 1860	650.00	750.00	625.00
☐ **Geometric Motif,** one round diamond approx. .90 ct., round diamonds, platinum, c. 1920	2400.00	3000.00	2400.00
☐ **Marquis Motif,** 15 old mine diamonds, 18K gold, c. late 1850	800.00	1000.00	800.00
☐ **Oval Motif,** old mine diamonds, white gold, c. 1890	3650.00	4650.00	3650.00
☐ **Pierced Motif,** round diamonds, calibre sapphires, platinum, c. 1920	400.00	500.00	400.00
☐ **Rosette Motif,** seven old mine diamonds, white gold, c. 1880	1400.00	1600.00	1400.00
☐ **Shield Motif,** one marquise-shape diamond approx. .50 ct., round diamonds, square emeralds, platinum, c. 1925	2400.00	2600.00	2400.00

RINGS / DIAMOND AND GEMSTONE

☐ **Amethyst,** rose diamonds, silver topped 18K gold, c. 1850	450.00	550.00	425.00
☐ **Black Opal,** eight baguette and round yellow diamonds approx. 1. ct., c. 1910	3750.00	4750.00	3750.00
☐ **Carved Amethyst Quartz,** seed pearl border, carved leaf motif shank, 14K gold, c. late 19th ...	375.00	475.00	375.00
☐ **Olivines,** two almondine garnets, 14K gold, American, c. 1896	120.00	145.00	120.00
☐ **Opal,** 14K gold, c. 1886	100.00	120.00	100.00
☐ **Pearls,** natural, round diamonds, gold, platinum, c. 1900	900.00	1100.00	900.00
☐ **Sapphire,** two pearls, rose diamonds, gold, c. 1860	650.00	750.00	650.00
☐ **Sapphire,** cabochon, round diamonds, silver topped gold, c. 1925	3200.00	3400.00	3200.00
☐ **Straight Row Motif,** five cabochon turquoise, rose diamonds, gold, c. 1850	750.00	950.00	750.00
☐ **Turquoise,** four pearls, 14K gold, American, c. 1896	110.00	140.00	110.00

WATCHES / GENTLEMEN'S POCKET

	Current Price Range		Prior Year Average
☐ **Bicycle with Rider Motif,** engraved, HC, 14K gold, American, c. 1896	600.00	800.00	600.00
☐ **Initial Shield Motif,** with deep wavy engraving, 21 jewel, model 993, white porcelain dial, HC, 14K gold, 16 size, maker: Hamilton, c. 1900	800.00	1000.00	800.00
☐ **Miniature Enamel,** of an angel and a putti, pink base taille enamel background, engraved case, HC, 18K gold, Swiss, c. 19th	1200.00	1400.00	1200.00
☐ **Repeater,** quarter hour, Jaquemar, standard better grade movement, gold hands, OF, gold, maker, Vacheron, Swiss, c. 1900	3700.00	4200.00	3700.00
☐ **Sead Pearls Pave,** high grade lever movement, fusee, jeweled, OF, gold, English, c. 1830-60	14000.00	16000.00	14000.00
☐ **Train and Flower Engraved Motif,** HC, 14K gold, American, c. 1896	800.00	1000.00	775.00

WATCHES / LADIES – PENDANT

☐ **Art Deco Motif,** blue and green enamel, white matte dial, Arabic numeral, 18K gold, Swiss, c. 1930	1100.00	1200.00	1100.00
☐ **Bird and Twig Motif,** one round ruby in eye, nine round emeralds, 27 round diamonds, HC, 14K gold, American, c. 1896	1500.00	1700.00	1500.00
☐ **Crescent and Star Motif,** six round diamonds, HC, 14K gold, American, c. 1896	800.00	900.00	775.00
☐ **Flower Motif,** multi-colored enamel, OF, 18K gold, maker: Henri Capt, c. late 19th	1400.00	1600.00	1400.00
☐ **Guilloche,** blue enamel face and case, OF, gold, Swiss, c. 1880	650.00	700.00	650.00
☐ **Key Wind Watch,** white enamel dial, Roman numerals, black enamel on case reverse, OF, 18K gold, Swiss, c. 19th	300.00	400.00	300.00
☐ **Oval,** round and rose diamond motif center, guilloche translucent steel grey and opaque white enamel, rose diamond bow, OF, gold, maker: Tiffany & Co., matching brooch with watch loop, gold, c. early 20th	1500.00	1700.00	1500.00

JUKEBOXES

Jukeboxes first appeared in cafes in the rural South as replacements for live jazz bands. The word "juke" came from a similar sounding Black dialect word meaning "wicked." Jazz was frowned upon by many religious people of the time. The popularity of the jukebox spread quickly despite this disapproval. It is estimated that by 1942 there were over 350,000 jukeboxes in operation in the United States. The most collectible jukeboxes were manufactured from 1938 until 1948. Although jukeboxes are still made, they are generally unobtrusive and unimaginative appliances.

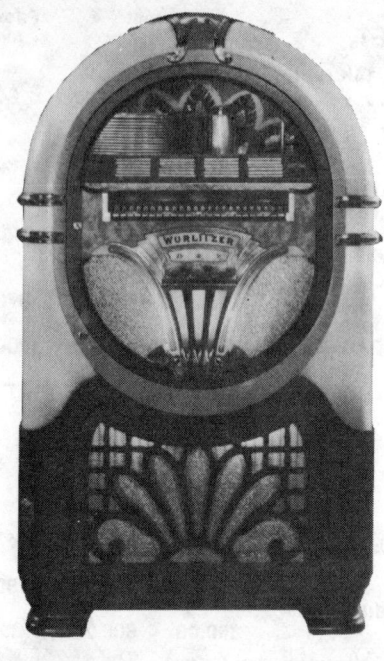

Wurlitzer model 750, classic style with 24 tune selections, c. 1937-40's **$2000.00-3000.00**

The most popular machines were manufactured by Wurlitzer. They are prized for their imaginative cabinetry and see through mechanisms. Favored models are the 850, 950 and 1015. Other contemporary machines were built by J. P. Seeburg, Rock-Ola, and AMI. Although valued by some collectors, none of these models have achieved the popularity of the Wurlitzers.

Taverns in small towns are the best sources of old jukeboxes. Local distributors may have some old models stored away in a warehouse, but usually these dealers have a good idea of prices and the cost may be high. Make sure that the record changing mechanism and selection buttons are operable as they may be difficult to repair.

For more information, the avid collector should refer to the House of Collectibles publication entited *The Official Price Guide to Music Machines and Instruments,* by Susan Gould.

	Current Price Range		Prior Year Average
☐ **AMI Model A,** 40 tune selections, called "Mother of Plastic," lights up, "jewels" on front of case, c. 1948	1600.00	2600.00	2000.00
☐ **AMI Model FR,** 20 tune selections, simple wood case in an Art Deco style, top glass panel is record mechanism and tune cards, c. 1932	320.00	520.00	400.00
☐ **AMI "Singing Tower,** 10 tunes, looks like an Art Deco skyscraper, 6' H., c. 1941	2600.00	3100.00	2750.00

JUKEBOXES / 515

	Current Price Range		Prior Year Average
☐ **AMI "Top Flight,"** 20 tune selections, straight rectangular case, metal trim, rounded speaker opening, lights up, c. 1936	420.00	620.00	500.00
☐ **Capehart Jukebox,** early example, simple rectangular oak case, glass panels to view mechanism, decorative grill, c. 1930's	525.00	775.00	620.00
☐ **Filben "Maestro,"** 30 tune selections, very space age design, plastic top section, c. 1940's	1100.00	1600.00	1250.00
☐ **Gabel's Charme,** 18 tune selections, all wood rectangular case, selection dial, some case decoration, tune cards inside clear glass window	320.00	520.00	400.00
☐ **Mills "Empress" Model 910,** 20 tune selections, rounded wood case, large plastic panels, small window to view tune cards, lights up	1300.00	1800.00	1500.00
☐ **Mills Jukebox,** 12 tune selections (78rpm), arranged in a "Ferris Wheel" effect, wood case, some decoration, dial tune selector, volume control, doors open on front top of case, speaker grill in bottom, c. 1930's	550.00	1100.00	750.00
☐ **Mills "Throne of Music,"** 20 tune selections, plastic panels, very similar in appearance to "Empress"	1100.00	1600.00	1250.00
☐ **Packard Pla-Mor (Capehart),** 24 tune selections, plastic and wood, large viewing window in top front, decorative grill in base, tune selection cards on wheel, coin mechanism in top center ..	800.00	1300.00	1000.00
☐ **Rock-Ola "Luxury Light-Up,"** 20 tune selections, large rounded corners case, orange and green plastic panels, push button tune selector in center, tune cards under plastic panel, decorative grill panel and trim	2100.00	2600.00	2250.00
☐ **Rock-Ola "Multi-Selector,"** 12 tune selections, clear glass, top front panel to view mechanism, push button tune selection, simple walnut case and front grill, c. 1935	525.00	725.00	600.00
☐ **Rock-Ola "Rocket" Model 1434,** 50 tune selections, push button, simple grill, colored panels, dome, top covers record mechanism, colored corner panels, c. 1950's	550.00	1100.00	750.00
☐ **Rock-Ola "Rhythm King,"** 12 tune selections, wood base, plain case, viewing window to see mechanism, c. 1938	800.00	1300.00	1000.00
☐ **Rock-Ola Style 1426,** 20 tune, "Classic" style, push buttons, revolving lights, plastic, viewing window, c. 1947	2100.00	2600.00	2250.00
☐ **Seeburg Audiophone,** 8 disc records, plain rectangular case, oval glass opening on top front, "Ferris Wheel" type mechanism with 8 turntables, speaker on door in front, c. 1928	525.00	725.00	600.00
☐ **Seeburg "Commander,"** 20 tune selections, "Space Age" 1930s look, plastic front, sides, top, decorative trim mouldings, button next to each tune card, c. 1940	800.00	1300.00	1000.00
☐ **Seeburg P147 (P148),** 20 tune selections, "washing machine" case style, plastic panels, c. 1947 .	1100.00	1600.00	1250.00

516 / JUKEBOXES

	Current Price Range		Prior Year Average
☐ **Seeburg "Symphonola,"** 12 tune selections, rectangular plain case style, window to view mechanism, selector dial, c. 1936	525.00	725.00	600.00
☐ **Seeburg "Symphonola Classic,"** 20 tune selections, push button, mainly wood and red plastic panels in front and top corners, decorative trim, lights up, c. 1938	525.00	775.00	620.00
☐ **Seeburg "Symphonola Regal,"** 20 tune selections, plastic panels, tune cards in top section (no viewing of mechanism), c. 1940	1100.00	1600.00	1250.00
☐ **Wurlitzer Model P 10,** 10 tune selections, rectangular wooden case, simple lines, glass window, tune selector dial, simple front grill on bottom, early version of "Simplex," c. 1934	325.00	525.00	400.00
☐ **Wurlitzer Model 35,** 12 tune selections, more elaborate walnut case, art deco style, clear glass front window to view mechanism, c. 1930's	425.00	625.00	500.00
☐ **Wurlitzer Counter Model 61,** 12 tune selection, wood base and sides, some plastic (comes with floor stand), c. 1938-39	1300.00	2600.00	2800.00
☐ **Wurlitzer Counter Model 81,** 12 tune selections, wood base and sides, curving plastic panels, graceful front grill, small viewing window with tune selection cards, push buttons, c. 1940's	625.00	825.00	700.00
☐ **Wurlitzer Model 416,** 16 tune selections, simple wood case, tune selector dial, rounded front corner columns, decorative front grill over speaker, c. 1930's	325.00	425.00	350.00
☐ **Wurlitzer Model 616 Simplex,** 16 tune selections, wood case, rounded rectangular style, simple lines, clear glass top front viewing panel, tune selector dial, decorative grill, c. 1930's	425.00	625.00	500.00
☐ **Wurlitzer Model 700,** 24 tune selections, wood case, plastic panels on front corners and top, push button tune selections, decorative metal grill, c. 1940	800.00	1100.00	880.00
☐ **Wurlitzer Model 750,** 24 tune selections, "Classic" style, plastic panels, viewing window, push buttons, c. 1937-40	2100.00	3100.00	2500.00
☐ **Wurlitzer Model 800,** 24 tune selections, wood trim and base, large orange and red plastic corner side and top panels, decorative grill, clear glass panel to view mechanism and tune selections, lights up, c. 1940	800.00	1300.00	1000.00
☐ **Wurlitzer "Victory,"** 24 tune selections, distinctive design, wood case, multicolored glass panels along front with musical instruments, harlequins, etc., small half circle viewing window, push buttons, decorative grill with colored panels behind, c. 1942-43	2100.00	3100.00	2500.00
☐ **Wurlitzer Model 1015,** 24 tune selections, "Classic" style, revolving lights in plastic bubble tubes, viewing window, c. 1946-47	3600.00	5600.00	4500.00
☐ **Wurlitzer Model 1050,** 100 tune selections, similar in style to the 1014 "Classic" style, c. 1947	1600.00	3100.00	2200.00

KITCHEN COLLECTIBLES / 517

	Current Price Range		Prior Year Average
☐ **Wurlitzer Model 1080,** 24 tune selections, "Classic" style, curving contours with decorated mirrored panels, viewing window, c. 1946-49	3100.00	5100.00	4000.00
☐ **Wurlitzer Model 1100,** 24 tune selections, space age case style, large pointed dome-like top, roller mechanism for tune cards, push buttons, c. 1948-49	1600.00	3600.00	2500.00
☐ **Wurlitzer Model 1250,** 48 tune selections, wood case, rounded top clear plastic dome, multi-colored panels along front sides of speaker, metal grill, push buttons, c. 1950	1300.00	1800.00	1500.00
☐ **Wurlitzer Model 1500,** 104 tune selections, wood case, rounded top to view mechanism, colored corner front panels, push buttons, twin stacks of discs, either 78, 45 or 33⅓ rpm, c. 1952	525.00	725.00	600.00

KITCHEN COLLECTIBLES

Coffee Perculator, aluminum, c. 1915-25............ $20.00-$25.00

  During the 19th century, most of America was rural, and the people were, by necessity, self-sufficient. Processed food was unknown until nearly the end of the century; therefore, the growing, processing, preparing and preserving of food was a daily chore in most households. The vast array of simple, yet ingenious tools that were invented to ease this drudgery is what collecting kitchen equipment is all about.

518 / KITCHEN COLLECTIBLES

Favorite items are the handmade objects used from the 1600's to the early 1800's when cooking was done in the home fireplace. Such items include cast iron Dutch ovens, iron or copper kettles, brass ladles, wire chimney cleaners and other items used for "hearth" cooking.

Other popular items are those that were mass-produced for use on wood and coal burning iron stoves. Many items such as waffle irons, were designed specifically to fit in the fire holes of these stoves. Other equipment appears in the form of apple parers, egg beaters, ice cream scoops — the list is endless.

One of the main problems encountered with old kitchen utensils is over restoration, a practice which may ruin the articles by completely stripping away the original finish.

Flea markets are good sources of kitchen items and most can be purchased reasonably.

BRASS

	Current Price Range		Prior Year Average
☐ **Bowl,** hammered, iron and brass, 17½"	55.00	65.00	58.00
☐ **Bowl,** mixing, side handles applied with rivets	35.00	45.00	37.00
☐ **Bucket,** iron bail handle, 1850's	100.00	125.00	105.00
☐ **Candlelabra,** brass, alabaster urn and base	510.00	565.00	540.00
☐ **Candleholders,** French, silvered brass, with crest and crown, 1700's, pair	375.00	425.00	395.00
☐ **Candleholder,** lions at base, goat heads and grapes at top	125.00	135.00	127.00
☐ **Candlesticks,** a pair, brass, 9½" high, c. 1840	55.00	75.00	55.00
☐ **Candlesticks,** English, brass, almost petal based, seamed column, 7" high, c. 1740	125.00	175.00	140.00
☐ **Candlesticks,** French, brass, 5" high, c. 1766, pair	250.00	300.00	270.00
☐ **Candlesticks,** a pair of George I, brass, 7" high, c. 1720	450.00	600.00	500.00
☐ **Candlesticks,** a pair of brass George III, 8½" high, c. 1810	200.00	250.00	220.00
☐ **Coal Bucket,** iron bail handle	58.00	70.00	60.25
☐ **Coffee Grinder,** lap, brass plate signed Kenrick, porcelain-lined cup, iron drawer	69.00	75.00	72.25
☐ **Coffee Pot,** covered, nickel plated, copper with brass trim, wooden handle	32.00	50.00	40.00
☐ **Coffee Pot,** brass, 10" high	32.00	47.00	33.60
☐ **Coffee Pot,** Turkish, tin lined, single handle, 2 cup	12.00	15.00	12.60
☐ **Colander,** long handle, brass	45.00	55.00	47.50
☐ **Corkscrew,** early 19th century, brass, Farrow and Jackson wingnut, 6" long	100.00	125.00	105.00
☐ **Corkscrew,** early 20th century, brass, 5½" long	45.00	65.00	47.50
☐ **Dipper,** 12½" long, brass	47.00	57.00	49.45
☐ **Egg Cup Stand,** English, rare, brass, 8", c. 1790	1500.00	2000.00	1575.00
☐ **Flagon,** 18th century, brass, 11" high	400.00	500.00	420.00
☐ **Flour Dredger,** 18th century, brass, 4" high	125.00	175.00	131.00
☐ **Flour Sifter,** wood frame and teeth, crank handle, brass label O Bond, c. 1875	85.00	105.00	89.00
☐ **Ice Cream Server,** nickeled brass c. 1930	22.00	30.00	23.00
☐ **Ice Tongs,** heavy brass	62.00	72.00	65.00
☐ **Iron Stand,** late 18th century, miniature, brass, 4" long	40.00	50.00	42.35
☐ **Iron Stand,** late 18th century, brass, 7½" long	35.00	55.00	36.50
☐ **Kettle,** brass and copper, early 19th century, 11" high	100.00	150.00	115.00

KITCHEN COLLECTIBLES / 519

	Current Price Range		Prior Year Average
☐ **Kettle,** open, brass tin lined, iron bail handles ...	65.00	87.00	69.00
☐ **Ladle,** brass, early	55.00	70.00	57.50
☐ **Match Holder,** brass, with eagle and arch border, schooner on pocket, hanging type	30.00	42.00	31.50
☐ **Match Holder,** sheet brass, knight's glove on pallette shaped back piece	15.00	37.00	21.95
☐ **Match Safe,** package, nickeled brass, tied in four sections with cord	95.00	115.00	99.50
☐ **Match Safe,** silver plate over brass, ornate, old ..	32.00	48.00	33.50
☐ **Mortar and Pestle,** approximately 4″ high	30.00	55.00	31.50
☐ **Mortar and Pestle,** brass, early 1800's	120.00	130.00	127.00
☐ **Muffineer,** 18th century, brass, 3″ high	200.00	250.00	210.00
☐ **Nutcracker,** alligator, brass, 13″ long	63.00	70.00	66.00
☐ **Nutcracker,** squirrel, brass, 8½″ long, same operation	45.00	55.00	47.00
☐ **Nutcracker,** 18th century, brass, simple wing nut and screw type, 4″	125.00	175.00	131.00
☐ **Pail,** spun, E. Miller and Co., pat. 1870, 13″x9″ ...	75.00	105.00	78.00
☐ **Pastry Jigger,** 19th century, brass	20.00	30.00	22.00
☐ **Pepperpot,** an 18th century, brass, 3½″ high	125.00	175.00	126.00
☐ **Pot,** hand engraved all over design, 6½″	200.00	275.00	235.00
☐ **Scale,** fishtail, flat tray, original paint, brass arm	135.00	175.00	142.00
☐ **Skimmer,** fancy cut out handle, 20″	75.00	95.00	82.00
☐ **Strainer,** small woven brass tea strainer	5.00	15.00	5.50
☐ **Teakette,** dovetailed joints, swan spout, handles of iron or copper, pre-1880	55.00	105.00	58.00
☐ **Teakettle and Stand,** alcohol burner	110.00	125.00	116.00
☐ **Toaster,** English, one slice, scissor action handle, 13″	50.00	165.00	53.75
☐ **Tongs,** hanging ring, claw ends, 11″	15.00	28.00	17.50
☐ **Trivet,** a 19th century, brass, 9″ long, c. 1870	55.00	75.00	68.00
☐ **Trivet,** a 19th century, brass, 10½″x6″	45.00	65.00	57.00
☐ **Trivet,** brass and iron, hooks over edge of fireplace fender	55.00	65.00	58.00
☐ **Trivet,** horse shoe, Good Luck to All Who Use This Stand	45.00	80.00	72.00
☐ **Trivet,** brass, early 18th century, turtle	85.00	95.00	89.00
☐ **Waffle Iron,** wire with spiral handle, brass ferrule, 8½″	19.00	38.00	28.00
☐ **Warning Pan,** brass and copper, floral design, 42″	165.00	205.00	167.00
☐ **Washboard,** brass and wood, Made-Rite, large ..	22.00	42.00	25.00

COPPER

☐ **Ale Warmer,** Georgian copper, with iron handle, 4″ high	85.00	110.00	92.00
☐ **Bowl,** hand hammered, silver lined, Novick, 3″x8″	165.00	195.00	167.00
☐ **Bucket,** brass spout, handles and decor, 14″	95.00	110.00	99.00
☐ **Candle Snuffer,** cone shape with handle, eagle and shield mark	68.00	72.00	70.00
☐ **Candy Kettle,** early 1800's, 19″	220.00	240.00	230.00
☐ **Canner,** stovetop, tin with copper base, 2 door, Conservo	25.00	45.00	32.00
☐ **Chafing Dish,** complete, 1920's	120.00	130.00	121.50

520 / KITCHEN COLLECTIBLES

	Current Price Range		Prior Year Average
☐ **Chesnut Roaster,** pierced cover, twisted wrought shaft	135.00	175.00	138.00
☐ **Coffee Pot,** brass finial, 8½"	15.00	30.00	16.00
☐ **Coffee Pot,** covered, nickel-plated trim, wooden handle	32.00	42.00	33.00
☐ **Coffee Urn,** antique, copper	225.00	275.00	228.00
☐ **Dipper,** burnished	59.00	72.00	63.00
☐ **Evaporating Pan,** dovetail, rolled trim, iron handle and rings	80.00	95.00	84.00
☐ **Funnel,** hanging rim, 10" diameter	30.00	45.00	32.00
☐ **Hot Water Urn,** antique	250.00	300.00	255.00
☐ **Kettle,** for apple butter, copper, dovetail bottom, 25" diameter, mid 1800's	450.00	500.00	459.00
☐ **Kettle,** copper, early 20th century	50.00	60.00	51.00
☐ **Kettle,** late 19th century, copper, kitchen, with brass knop, 12" high	85.00	110.00	92.00
☐ **Kettle,** Victorian, copper, 9½"x13"	125.00	175.00	132.00
☐ **Measures,** three copper rum measures, the largest 12" high, late 19th century	550.00	750.00	615.00
☐ **Milk Churn,** early 19th century, Dutch, copper with brass ring handles, rim and urn finial, 30" high	800.00	1200.00	848.00
☐ **Milk Jug,** strap handle, dovetail	75.00	95.00	82.00
☐ **Mixing Bowl,** round bottom, single handle, 12"x6"	35.00	65.00	48.00
☐ **Mold,** jelly or pudding, copper	50.00	70.00	53.00
☐ **Pan,** dovetail bottom	135.00	155.00	129.00
☐ **Pitcher,** dovetail, ½ gal.	35.00	55.00	41.00
☐ **Saucepan,** matching lid, single long brass handle, tinlined, 1 qt.	45.00	65.00	52.00
☐ **Saucepot,** matching lid, tin lined, brass side handles	51.00	75.00	56.00
☐ **Skimmer,** wrought iron handle	25.00	45.00	27.00
☐ **Soup Pot,** with cover, both have iron handles, 13"	110.00	160.00	45.00
☐ **Spatula,** wrought iron handle, signed	170.00	195.00	176.00
☐ **Tasting Spoon,** tapered tubular handle, 1830's, 8½"	65.00	82.00	68.00
☐ **Tea Kettle,** George I, copper, 13" high, c. 1720	550.00	750.00	575.00
☐ **Tea Pot,** brass handle, marked Majestic in large letters	185.00	203.00	195.00
☐ **Washer,** copper, to dash clothes up and down in tub	75.00	95.00	78.00

IRON

	Current Price Range		Prior Year Average
☐ **Apple Parer,** cast, clamp-on type, pares, marked "Simplex"	20.00	35.00	25.00
☐ **Apple Parer,** cores, and slices, marked "Vermont Apple Parer"	20.00	25.00	21.00
☐ **Apple Segmenter,** bolt type, cast iron, patented 1809	20.00	28.00	23.00
☐ **Basket,** a 20th century, iron grate, 20"x10"x14"	120.00	180.00	126.00
☐ **Broiler,** also called gridiron or hearth broiler, hand wrought, 13" diameter, 4 legs, revolving	60.00	75.00	68.00
☐ **Butter Tester,** narrow borer for testing butter and cheese, 15"x18"	8.00	16.00	8.50
☐ **Charcoal Iron,** a mid 19th century, 7" high	120.00	180.00	126.00

KITCHEN COLLECTIBLES / 521

	Current Price Range	Prior Year Average
☐ **Cheese Cutter,** iron on round wood base, counter used	100.00 125.00	105.00
☐ **Cherry Pitter,** enterprise 1870, iron, 4 spider legs with bolts	40.00 50.00	42.00
☐ **Cherry Seeder,** also called cherry stoner, table model type	25.00 50.00	26.00
☐ **Chopper,** Blacksmith made, all iron, oblong shape, hanging loop	18.00 32.00	20.00
☐ **Choppers,** early, all iron, hand wrought, crescent-shaped	18.00 32.00	19.00
☐ **Coal Tongs,** for handling hot coals, hand wrought	18.00 36.00	19.00
☐ **Coffee Mill,** iron, wheel turn, c. 1898	15.00 35.00	26.00
☐ **Coffee Roaster,** iron, wood, crank handle	30.00 40.00	32.00
☐ **Corkscrew,** magic patent, c. 1900	40.00 50.00	42.00
☐ **Corn Dryer,** iron branch-like rod for holding ears of corn to dry, handwrought	18.00 36.00	19.00
☐ **Cornstick Pan,** cast iron, 7 sticks with kernels, marked "Krusty Korn Kobs, Wagner ware, patented July 6, 1920"	18.00 36.00	19.00
☐ **Cracker Stamp,** iron, early 19th century	8.00 12.00	8.50
☐ **Cranberry,** picker, tinned handle, 45 teeth, 4½″ 14½″x10″	75.00 95.00	79.00
☐ **Dipper,** applebutter, iron, wood handle, 9″ diameter, 1700's	110.00 130.00	115.00
☐ **Doughbowl,** fine ironstone, 10″x14″ diameter	95.00 115.00	99.00
☐ **Dough Scraper,** hoe shaped, for scraping dough from mixing bowl or dough box, all wrought iron	12.00 24.00	13.00
☐ **Dutch Oven,** three legs, bail handle, deep lid for setting coals on top	50.00 60.00	53.00
☐ **Eggbeaters,** crank handle, marked "Dover, patented 1878", 10½″ family size	15.00 30.00	16.00
☐ **Fish Broiler,** c. 1700's	225.00 250.00	236.00
☐ **Fish Roaster,** 18th century, wrought iron, wood	25.00 35.00	26.00
☐ **Flat Iron Saw Tooth Blade,** with wooden handle	3.00 6.00	3.50
☐ **Flat Iron,** gas, late 19th century, heated by gas jet	15.00 30.00	16.00
☐ **Flat Iron,** gasoline	15.00 30.00	16.00
☐ **Flat Iron,** hand forged, has door for coals, 1700's	85.00 95.00	89.00
☐ **Fork,** lifting plain, 2 tined, 18″ long with hanging hole, hand forged	12.00 24.00	13.00
☐ **Fork,** toasting 2 or 3 tined long handled fork, long, flat prongs, hand wrought	20.00 30.00	21.00
☐ **Fruit Press,** combination fruit, wine and jelly press, heavy iron, clamp-on type, crank handle	18.00 36.00	19.00
☐ **Gophering Iron,** iron poker-like stick with sheath-like holder, footed	100.00 135.00	110.00
☐ **Griddle,** solid oblong piece of wrought or cast iron for grilling food, also called grill, with grease catching trough all around edge and end handles, oblong	20.00 30.00	21.00
☐ **Ice Crusher,** marked "Chandler's Ice Cutting Machine", crank handle, 4 legs	35.00 45.00	37.00
☐ **Ice Pick,** all iron, hand wrought	6.00 12.00	6.50
☐ **Ice Shaver,** rectangular hand shaver, hinged cover with advertising of ice company or iron works	8.00 16.00	8.50
☐ **Ice Tongs,** 22″ long, hand forged	25.00 50.00	26.00

522 / KITCHEN COLLECTIBLES

	Current Price Range		Prior Year Average
☐ **Kettle,** Gypsy, 3 footed, 1 gallon, bail handle	40.00	50.00	42.00
☐ **Ladle,** hand wrought, 5¼″ bowl, 15″ handle	28.00	38.00	30.00
☐ **Ladle,** soup ladle with twisted shank and hanging loop	25.00	50.00	30.00
☐ **Lemon Squeezer,** hinged cast iron, handle holes for hanging, plain solid cup part, pouring lip	10.00	15.00	11.00
☐ **Matchholder,** mechanical, cast iron, Phoenix Bird picks up matches with beak	95.00	110.00	99.00
☐ **Meat Chopper,** Russwin No.0, patented 1901-02, crank handle, clamp-on type	12.00	15.00	13.00
☐ **Mortar,** urn shaped, 5½″, with pestle	35.00	49.00	37.00
☐ **Muffins Pans,** plain nine hold muffin mold, hanging hole, no maker	12.00	24.00	13.00
☐ **Nutcraker,** crank handle, clamps on table, marked "Home Nut Cracker, St. Louis, U.S.A.", patented August 24, 1915	14.00	26.00	15.00
☐ **Nutmeg Grater,** Victorian, with compartment for spare nutmeg in the handle, 7½″ long	20.00	30.00	21.00
☐ **Olive Forks,** 8″ long double tines, open ring end marked "Olive & Pickle Fork"	2.50	5.00	3.00
☐ **Pancake Turner,** opener combo, advertising, pat. 1914	8.00	12.00	8.50
☐ **Paring Knife,** marked "C. W. Dunlap", steel blade, wood handle	2.50	5.00	3.00
☐ **Pea Sheller,** clamp on type	16.00	26.00	17.00
☐ **Pie Crimper,** also called pastry jagger, pie edger, pie cutter, revolving cast iron cutter, wood handle, factory made	9.00	15.00	9.50
☐ **Porringer,** about 5″ diameter, marked with maker's name, double or single eared	75.00	95.00	79.00
☐ **Potato Basket,** potato or vegetable boiler, to set in cookpot in fireplace	25.00	50.00	27.00
☐ **Potato Parer,** cast iron, clamp on type, crank handle, marked "Vermon Potato Parer"	18.00	22.00	19.00
☐ **Potato Ricer,** cast iron frame and handles, tinplate, strainer	10.00	18.00	11.00
☐ **Pot Hook,** for lifting pots from fireplace or oven, also called pot lifter, hand wrought, wood handle	12.00	24.00	13.00
☐ **Raisin and Grape Seeder,** clamp on type, made by Enterprise	25.00	35.00	26.00
☐ **Range,** cast iron, finished in blue vitreous enamel, each of the five access doors decorated, 40″ wide	500.00	700.00	525.00
☐ **Range,** cast iron, marked L. Blton Perinster, finished in black-leading and ceramic tiles, Belgian, 35½″x31″, c. 1910	600.00	800.00	630.00
☐ **Rug Beater,** many different wire patterns with wood handles	12.00	24.00	13.00
☐ **Rushlight,** English, 18th century, on oak base, 10″ high	300.00	400.00	315.00
☐ **Saratoga Potato Chipper,** clamp on type, crank handle	18.00	22.00	19.00
☐ **Sardine Shears,** narrow, pointed spring, action shears, marked "C. W. Dunlap"	8.00	16.00	9.00
☐ **Scales,** brass and cast iron salter, spring balance kitchen, 17″ high, c. 1940	150.00	200.00	156.00

KITCHEN COLLECTIBLES / 523

	Current Price Range		Prior Year Average
☐ **Skewer Set,** wrought skewer holder with various length skewers	100.00	150.00	105.00
☐ **Skillet,** 3 legs, 12″ handle, for fireplace cookery, also called spider	50.00	60.00	52.00
☐ **Stove,** Art Grand, #12, coal heating, round, Utica, New York	310.00	350.00	326.00
☐ **Stove,** Charter Oak #580, cook, missing reservoir	1100.00	1600.00	1250.00
☐ **Sugar Devil,** iron, to loosen hardened chunks of sugar, brown	80.00	95.00	84.00
☐ **Toaster,** wrought iron, jointed head which flipped to allow toast to be browned on both sides, footed for hearth use	130.00	160.00	136.00
☐ **Tongs,** pair of late 18th century, goffering, 10½″ long	20.00	30.00	21.00
☐ **Trivet,** Mrs. Potts Co. Philadelphia, Pa., ftd, for sadiron	14.00	18.00	15.00
☐ **Trivet,** musical lyre, brass and iron, handles and feet	35.00	75.00	37.00
☐ **Turner-Fork,** hand-wrought, fork on one end, flat turner on other, 16″ long	25.00	50.00	26.00
☐ **Twine Holder,** also called string holder, hanging or sitting holder for ball of twine or string, lacey design	35.00	65.00	37.00
☐ **Wafer Iron,** oval or round 6″ diameter heads, 3′ long handle	75.00	95.00	79.00
☐ **Waffle Iron,** cast iron for coal stove, ball bearing joint, pie shaped design on grid, marked "Fanner Mfg. Co., Cleveland, O., Crescent Waffles No.7"	25.00	50.00	26.00

TIN

☐ **Apple Corers,** all tin, 19th century	5.00	8.00	5.50
☐ **Apple Roaster,** tin reflecting oven, c. 1850's	85.00	100.00	89.00
☐ **Bee Smoker,** tin, leather bellows	35.00	45.00	39.00
☐ **Biscuit Cutler,** Victorian tin pig-shaped	10.00	20.00	10.50
☐ **Boiler,** fish, pierced tin, two parts, c. 1890	8.00	15.00	8.50
☐ **Bread Cake Boxes,** tin, brown, No.1, 13½″x10½″ x9¾″	29.00	39.00	31.00
☐ **Bread Mixer,** White House Bread Mixer and Kneader, tin bucket and cover, crank handle, clamp on table type, awarded gold medal, St. Louis Exposition 1904, made by Landers, Frary, and Clark, New Britain, Conn.	35.00	45.00	37.00
☐ **Bread Pan,** round, two halves fastened together with wire hoop at one end	10.00	20.00	10.50
☐ **Broom Holder,** embossed blue jays, Marcos Blue Jay, 1910	75.00	95.00	78.00
☐ **Cake Maker,** tin, 3 gears, wood handle, Universal, 8″, c. 1905	50.00	60.00	53.00
☐ **Cake Mold,** 10″x3″	18.00	25.00	19.00
☐ **Cake Pan,** six pointed star tube pan	8.00	12.00	8.50
☐ **Cake Pan,** tube, fluted, 8″	10.00	15.00	10.50
☐ **Candle Box,** with loop for hanging	220.00	260.00	231.00
☐ **Candle Maker,** Pat Drummond, 8″, c. 1846	385.00	435.00	404.00
☐ **Candle Molds,** one hole	12.00	24.00	13.00
☐ **Candle Mold,** good handle, 12 tube, 10″	38.00	48.00	40.00

524 / KITCHEN COLLECTIBLES

	Current Price Range		Prior Year Average
☐ **Candy Molds,** tin, 6½" overall	25.00	50.00	35.00
☐ **Cheese Drainer,** punched tin	175.00	210.00	180.00
☐ **Cheese Strainer,** heart shaped punched tin on three legs	25.00	50.00	30.00
☐ **Churn,** tin, tin handles, wooden, dasher	230.00	300.00	260.00
☐ **Coffepot,** black, orange, red, green decor, 12" high	270.00	285.00	279.00
☐ **Coffeepot,** 8-10 cup size, crook spout	80.00	95.00	84.00
☐ **Coffee Roaster,** cylindrical hearth type, sliding door	30.00	40.00	32.00
☐ **Cream Ladle,** marked "Cream Top, Pat. Sept. 2nd 1924, Mar. 3rd 1925"	3.50	5.00	4.00
☐ **Crumb Set,** black wooden handle, embossed metal, decorated	8.00	12.00	8.50
☐ **Dish Pan,** heavy tin, side handles	15.00	25.00	16.00
☐ **Dispenser,** handmade, soldered, 5"x3" dia.	14.00	28.00	15.00
☐ **Doughnut Cutter,** all tin, with handle, c. 1915	3.00	5.00	3.50
☐ **Eclair Pan,** makes 12 eclairs	12.00	16.00	13.00
☐ **Eggbeater,** cream whipper combination, also called whip or syllabub churn, two parts, marked "Patented 1868"	35.00	45.00	37.00
☐ **Eggbeaters,** crank handle, marked "Duplex Cream & Egg Whipper", patented Nov. 25, 1919	8.00	12.00	8.50
☐ **Egg Boiler,** wire holder for boiling six eggs, folds up	9.00	12.00	9.50
☐ **Egg Poacher,** tinware, wire handle, for single egg, old	12.00	15.50	13.00
☐ **Flour Bin and Sifter,** tin bin holds 25, 50, or 100 pounds	35.00	45.00	37.00
☐ **Flour Sifter,** Blood's 1861 patent, mesh and wood	80.00	100.00	84.00
☐ **Fly Sprayer,** quick loader	7.50	14.00	8.00
☐ **Food Warmer,** stenciled flowers	188.00	198.00	193.00
☐ **Fruit Press,** Henis fruit and vegetable press and strainer, tinned iron	8.00	12.00	8.50
☐ **Funnel,** 2" diameter with hanging ring	3.00	6.00	3.50
☐ **Grater,** fruit and vegetable hand pierced, attached to wooden back with handle	12.00	18.00	13.00
☐ **Grater,** nutmeg marked "The Edgar", patented 1896, sliding type, two wood knobs	18.00	26.00	19.00
☐ **Hot Water Bottle,** with screw cap, oval with oval top lid, 7"x10"	15.00	20.00	16.00
☐ **Ice Cream Scoops,** tinned steel, cone shaped cup, turn knob on top of cone releases ice cream from cup, various sizes, numbers on handle or cup indicate number of dips to the quart, 20 dip size	10.00	18.00	10.50
☐ **Ice Shaver,** round open cup, double toothed shaver, advertising on wooden handle	8.00	13.00	8.50
☐ **Lamp,** stove shape, red glass in fire box door, marked "Pollite Bijou", 6½"	55.00	65.00	58.00
☐ **Lard Lamp Font,** blk, 4½"	145.00	165.00	149.00
☐ **Loaf Pan,** lid, 4 section, 22"x13"	25.00	50.00	26.00
☐ **Lunch Box,** complete with cup and trays	30.00	60.00	32.00
☐ **Matchsafe,** tin, painted, "Matches", c. 1910	8.00	14.00	9.00
☐ **Meal Funnel,** mapel, dovetail 4 corners, c. 1860	45.00	55.00	47.00
☐ **Measure,** handle, mug shape, 4¼"x5¾"	35.00	45.00	37.00

KITCHEN COLLECTIBLES / 525

	Current Price Range		Prior Year Average
☐ **Milk Can,** two quart, lid, spout, spout cover attached to can with chain	18.00	26.00	19.00
☐ **Mixing Spoons,** slotted bowl, hanging hole	4.00	8.00	5.00
☐ **Mold,** bread or pudding, hinged, 9"x11"	35.00	45.00	37.00
☐ **Muffin or Cupcake Pan,** 6 or 12 cups, marked "Patd. Nov. 3. 74"	20.00	40.00	21.00
☐ **Muffin Tin,** shell and maple designs, 12½"x9½", early 1900's	18.00	21.00	19.00
☐ **Nutmeg Grater,** tin, turned wood handles, pat., 4"	40.00	50.00	42.00
☐ **Nutmeg Grater,** circular handmade drum type	16.00	22.00	17.00
☐ **Oven,** open on fireplace side, top handle, back legs, one shelf	100.00	135.00	105.00
☐ **Pastry Board,** tin, rolling pin cradle, hanging ring, 22"x18½"	135.00	165.00	142.00
☐ **Pastry Board,** with rolling pin cradle, 22"x18½"	140.00	150.00	146.00
☐ **Pie Lifter,** all heavy tinned wire, pitch fork shaped	8.00	12.00	8.50
☐ **Pie Pan,** marked "Crisco", patented Jan. 5, 1926	8.00	12.00	8.50
☐ **Plate Warmer,** dome-shaped top, four splayed legs, side handles	85.00	100.00	90.00
☐ **Popcorn Popper,** fancy pierced hinged lid, rectangular, wooden handle, handmade, 18th century	40.00	50.00	42.00
☐ **Pot,** oval with handle with hanging ring, lid with hanging ring	20.00	30.00	21.00
☐ **Press,** meat loaf wood frame, oblong tin press, top turn handle	35.00	45.00	37.00
☐ **Rolling Pin,** tin body, wooden handles, rare	35.00	45.00	37.00
☐ **Sausage Gun,** tubular tin, snout on one end, hanging ring on other, with wood plunge	25.00	30.00	26.00
☐ **Sifter,** marked "Kewpie", 3½" high	20.00	30.00	21.00
☐ **Skimmer,** 6" round with short finger grip handle	6.00	12.00	6.50
☐ **Spice Boxes,** set of 6 miniature tin spice canisters in matching tray with handle, contents stencilled on lids	50.00	60.00	52.00
☐ **Steam Cooker,** tin, handled top, pat. date 1879, 12½" dia.	28.00	38.00	29.00
☐ **Strainer,** simple tin-sided tea strainer, wooden handle strainer marked "C.D. Kenny Co." a find for Kenny collectors	20.00	30.00	21.00
☐ **Sugar Scoop,** tin, small with strap handle, kitchen container type	12.50	16.50	13.00
☐ **Syrup Pitcher,** green, black, red flowers, 5½" high	188.00	200.00	192.00
☐ **Toaster,** steel toaster for gas, gasoline, or oil stove, no markings	5.00	12.00	5.50
☐ **Tongs,** for lifting hot foods, marked "Ritz's 'Tasty' Bread"	4.00	8.00	4.50
☐ **Wash Boiler,** heavy tin, copper bottom, side handles, handled lid	35.00	40.00	36.00
☐ **Water Cooler,** metal, two gallon capacity nickle plated faucets	40.00	50.00	42.00

526 / KITCHEN COLLECTIBLES

WOOD

	Current Price Range		Prior Year Average
☐ **Biscuit Roller,** wood board with grooved roller, side handturn, c. 1860's	90.00	110.00	95.00
☐ **Bootjack,** primitive wood forked bootjack	10.00	15.00	10.50
☐ **Bottle Corker,** all wood two part gadget for inserting corks into bottles	16.00	21.00	17.00
☐ **Bowl,** burl, 5"x13", c. 1800's	500.00	650.00	520.00
☐ **Bowl,** burl, oblong 22" handmade	350.00	400.00	368.00
☐ **Bowls,** mixing, round, 14"	15.00	30.00	18.00
☐ **Bowl,** yellow, No.6, 1 gal.	11.00	15.00	13.00
☐ **Box,** cheese-aging box, ventilated, old red paint	30.00	40.00	32.00
☐ **Box,** quartered oak, inset hinges, 29"x15½"x7½" deep	350.00	375.00	368.00
☐ **Bread Boards,** maple, "Bread" carved on border, 9½"	40.00	50.00	42.00
☐ **Breadboard,** pine, hanging eye cut in 1 piece wood, 12"x10"	75.00	85.00	79.00
☐ **Breadboards,** round, c. 1918	5.00	10.00	5.50
☐ **Bread Peel,** poplar, long handle, 54", mid 1800's	75.00	85.00	79.00
☐ **Bucket,** tin top, walnut, serpentine legs, 19"x24"x17"	135.00	165.00	141.00
☐ **Bung Pusher,** barrel bung pusher for placing bung into barrel, all wood	12.00	17.00	13.00
☐ **Butcher's Block,** sycamore, Amish 'shonk' carved inside	650.00	725.00	685.00
☐ **Butter Churn,** large Maine wooden, c. 1866	285.00	325.00	294.00
☐ **Butter Churn,** strap hinges, old red paint	350.00	375.00	368.00
☐ **Butter Churns,** 25½", wood with bandings, with lid and dasher	195.00	220.00	205.00
☐ **Butter Molds,** box with flower and leaf, hoop type, machine made	30.00	58.00	32.00
☐ **Butter Paddles,** flat	10.00	15.00	10.50
☐ **Butter Roller,** hand carved birch, in wooden pinned yoke	150.00	155.00	151.00
☐ **Cabbage Cutting Board,** three blades and sliding hopper box, 7¼"x20"	45.00	55.00	47.00
☐ **Candle Box,** pine, sliding top, 16" long	80.00	90.00	84.00
☐ **Candle Dipping Rack,** wooden, mid 1700's	325.00	350.00	336.00
☐ **Candle Stand,** Harvard, Mass., cherry and birch, adjustable	3750.00	4100.00	3925.00
☐ **Candlesticks,** 19th century, oak treen, 10" high, pair	200.00	250.00	210.00
☐ **Candlesticks,** 18th century, yew wood, c. 1780, 12" high, pair	600.00	800.00	630.00
☐ **Candy Scoop,** poplar, 5" long	32.00	42.00	34.00
☐ **Canteen,** oak, handmade	65.00	70.00	68.00
☐ **Canteen,** Shaker, buttonhole or eyelet loops, wood, 1st half of 19th century	175.00	225.00	184.00
☐ **Cheese Drainer,** Windsor style, arrow shaped slats, 19½"	450.00	475.00	463.00
☐ **Cheese Ladder,** wild cherry	80.00	85.00	84.00
☐ **Chopping Knife,** factory made, maple handle, c. 1880-1900	35.00	45.00	37.00
☐ **Chopping Bowl,** turned wood, old mustard paint, early 19th century	88.00	95.00	89.00
☐ **Churn,** barrel, with crank	80.00	90.00	84.00
☐ **Churn,** bucket type	90.00	100.00	95.00

KITCHEN COLLECTIBLES / 527

	Current Price Range		Prior Year Average
☐ **Clothes Wringer,** marked "Rival, The American Wringer Co., New York"	12.00	18.00	13.00
☐ **Coaster,** 18th century, Treen eight-sided	200.00	250.00	210.00
☐ **Coffee Grinder,** 19th century, wooden Peugeot	60.00	80.00	63.00
☐ **Cookie Board,** carved daisy pattern, walnut, 6"x8"	58.00	68.00	61.00
☐ **Cookie Mold,** musketeer on a saddle strapped to a chicken, large	95.00	105.00	98.00
☐ **Cookie Roller,** handcut from one piece birdseye maple	30.00	35.00	31.00
☐ **Cracker Pricker and Biscuit Stamp,** oval with turned handle, 1½"x2½"	140.00	165.00	146.00
☐ **Cranberry Picker,** a toothed rack-like tool for removing cranberries from the bushes, 14" across	60.00	75.00	63.00
☐ **Cream Skimmer,** pine, handled	60.00	70.00	63.00
☐ **Crock,** pine, stop shelf, deep lower shelf, base bar, 27"x37"x12"	275.00	300.00	289.00
☐ **Cupboard,** softwood, c. 1800's	600.00	625.00	606.00
☐ **Cutting Board,** walnut	32.00	40.00	34.00
☐ **Dipper,** turned bowl attached by wooden pin, 7"	35.00	40.00	37.00
☐ **Dipper,** honey, maple, wide ridges on one end, 13" long, 8"	40.00	45.00	41.00
☐ **Dough Bowl,** maple, hand-carved	120.00	140.00	126.00
☐ **Dough Box,** cherry, 4 leg frame, one piece lid, self handles, 30"x14", c. 1860	250.00	275.00	263.00
☐ **Doughnut Cutter,** all wood with handle	12.00	18.00	13.00
☐ **Dough Trough,** cherry, no lid, slanted sides, 26"x12½", c. 1830	225.00	295.00	236.00
☐ **Flour Sifter,** duplex, 5 cup, wood handle works sideways, c. 1922	20.00	30.00	21.00
☐ **Food Stomper,** handcarved poplar	19.00	28.00	20.00
☐ **Fruit Press,** cherry, woodpinned, drainage spout, c. 1800's	225.00	250.00	229.00
☐ **Funnel,** small, factory made in 1880's	12.00	17.00	13.00
☐ **Grain Storage Bin,** pine, with roll top, five section	1400.00	1600.00	1470.00
☐ **Ice Tongs,** wood handles, large icehouse size, latter 1800's	60.00	75.00	63.00
☐ **Ladle,** hand carved, bowl, 3½" dia. 9" long	55.00	65.00	58.00
☐ **Lemon Squeezer,** maple, early factory period, c. 1850-75	55.00	70.00	58.00
☐ **Mash Agitator,** handfashioned wood, 8" handle	75.00	85.00	79.00
☐ **Mashers,** Beetle, maple, early	19.00	26.00	20.00
☐ **Masher,** hickory, pestle on one end, bulbous center turning, 12" long	25.00	30.00	26.00
☐ **Matchsafe,** tiger maple, turned ped, heavy uniform stripes, table model, 3½"	75.00	95.00	79.00
☐ **Measure,** ½ pint, wooden carved from the solid, 5" high	40.00	60.00	42.00
☐ **Mortar and Pestle,** hickory, maple pestle, c. 1700's	75.00	85.00	79.00
☐ **Mortar and Pestle,** maple, mid 19th century	90.00	110.00	95.00
☐ **Noodle Roller,** maple, corrugations good condition, 20" long, c. 1850	58.00	67.00	61.00
☐ **Oak Keg,** staved and hooped with hickory bands	90.00	110.00	94.00

528 / KITCHEN COLLECTIBLES

	Current Price Range		Prior Year Average
☐ **Paddles,** butter, handcut variations in maple and hickory, 10″	35.00	45.00	37.00
☐ **Paper Roll Holder,** wood and iron, double	28.00	38.00	30.00
☐ **Peel,** all wood peel for removing baked goods from fireplace oven	55.00	60.00	58.00
☐ **Peel,** all wood peel for removing baked goods from fireplace oven	55.00	60.00	58.00
☐ **Pie Crimper,** wood handle, The Dandy, Gold Medal, April 28, 1925	5.00	8.00	5.50
☐ **Piggin,** replaced iron band, c. late 19th century	55.00	75.00	58.00
☐ **Potato Grater,** resembles later metal meat grinders, used for grating potatoes to make starch and yeast, scarce	45.00	52.00	47.00
☐ **Potato Masher,** maple	17.00	28.00	18.00
☐ **Potato Masher,** simple lathe turned, 2 pieces, all wood	8.00	12.00	8.50
☐ **Rolling Pin,** birdseye maple, 1 piece carved wood, c. 1800's	35.00	45.00	37.00
☐ **Rolling Pins,** handleless, same diameter throughout	6.00	12.00	6.50
☐ **Rolling Pin,** shaped handles, all one solid piece	8.00	14.00	8.50
☐ **Salt Box,** wooden wall hanging salt box, rectangular box, sloping lid	55.00	75.00	58.00
☐ **Scouring Box,** rectangular wood frame, approximately one foot long, complete with scouring brick for polishing steel bladed knives	30.00	35.00	31.00
☐ **Scrubbing Stick,** c. 1830, 24″ long	100.00	120.00	105.00
☐ **Shaker Cheese Boxes,** eyelet or button hoops, 19th century	275.00	350.00	281.00
☐ **Shaker Keeler,** pine, staved construction, mid-19th century	500.00	600.00	525.00
☐ **Slaw Cutter and Spice Box,** factory made, early 20th century	100.00	120.00	105.00
☐ **Spatula,** cherry, heart carved center, c. 1700's	65.00	75.00	68.00
☐ **Spice Boxes,** round wooden box, with 8 smaller round spice containers stencilled with contents, 10″	45.00	60.00	47.00
☐ **Spinning Wheel,** common type, flax wheel about 42″ high 33″ long, all pieces intact	200.00	220.00	205.00
☐ **Spoonholder,** handcarved walnut wall hanger, early, 36″ long	145.00	170.00	152.00
☐ **Spoon Rack,** pine, 8 carved slots, 16″ high	220.00	260.00	231.00
☐ **Stocking Drier Forms,** hand whittled, pair	16.00	32.00	17.00
☐ **Storage Cupboard,** 19th century	450.00	550.00	473.00
☐ **Sugar Bowl,** lathe turned sugar bowl with lid	35.00	45.00	37.00
☐ **Sugar Bucket,** button hole or eyelet hoops, bail handle, c. 1850-70	185.00	215.00	194.00
☐ **Sweater Stretcher,** large, pegged, folding sweater stretcher	25.00	32.00	26.00
☐ **Tea Caddy,** wooden, apple form body, with cover, late 18th century	475.00	525.00	495.00
☐ **Tobacco Cutters,** counter type, smithy made, wood handled	50.00	58.00	52.00
☐ **Trencher,** hard carved, small	55.00	65.00	58.00
☐ **Vegetable Cutter,** maple board, corrugated tin, c. 1880's	20.00	35.00	21.00

	Current Price Range		Prior Year Average
☐ **Vegetable Slicer,** wood, dated 1890, 20″	30.00	40.00	32.00
☐ **Vinegar Pump,** with spigot	52.00	62.00	55.00
☐ **Vise,** used for holding leather, wood	120.00	130.00	125.00
☐ **Washboard,** handcarved wood, small rolls	65.00	75.00	68.00
☐ **Wash or Scrubbing Board,** c. 1850-85	85.00	115.00	89.00
☐ **Washtub,** oak slats, deep stain, 22″x13″x51″ ...	65.00	75.00	68.00
☐ **Wooden Box,** Shaker type, T.F. initials in top	185.00	230.00	194.00
☐ **Wooden Grain or Gunpowder Shovel**	270.00	280.00	275.00
☐ **Wooden Wash Bowl,** chesnut, c. 1800	100.00	150.00	105.00

KNIVES

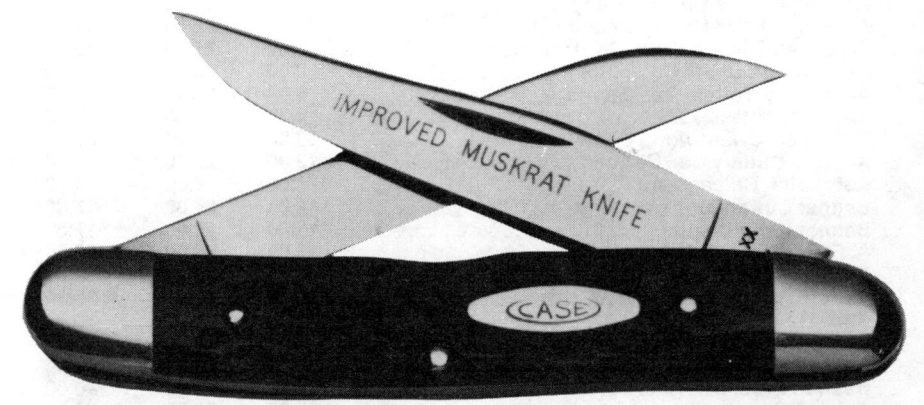

Muskrat Hawbaker Special, 3⅞″, c. 1950-60 .... **$150.00-$200.00**

Knife collecting started in the southern states. It's now spread throughout the country with club shows, meetings and numerous dealers from coast to coast. The popular types of interest to hobbyists are case knives and pocket knives, both of which have a long history. Precision-made, high-grade knives are sought by serious collectors, and these can often bring very high prices. The condition of the knife is very important. When the blades are rusted or resharpened or the handle is cracked, this decreases the value sharply.

Many of these manufacturers made a wide variety of different patterns of knives. This is the reason this section lists a low and high value. **Example:** A-1 NOVELTY CUTLERY (1st listing) made small penknives that sell for $10 but their folding hunters sell for $120. The following prices are listed in dollars only for knives in Mint condition. For lesser grades: near Mint-75% of Mint price, Excellent-50% of Mint price, Good-Very Good-25% of Mint price.

For the most comprehensive list of U.S. and foreign knife manufacturers refer to *The Official Price Guide to Collector Knives* by James Parker and Bruce Volyles, published by the House of Collectibles.

530 / KNIVES

	Current Price Range		Prior Year Average
☐ **A-1 Novelty Cutlery** Canton, OH	10.00	120.00	60.00
☐ **Ack Cutlery Co.** Freemont, OH	25.00	60.00	40.00
☐ **Adams & Bros.**	30.00	90.00	55.00
☐ **Adams & Sons**	30.00	90.00	55.00
☐ **Adolph Blaich,** San Francisco, CA	15.00	165.00	80.00
☐ **Adolphuis Cutlery Co.,** Sheffield, England	7.00	65.00	30.00
☐ **Aerial Mfg. Co.,** Marionette, WI	4.00	110.00	50.00
☐ **Akron Cutlery Co.,** Akron, OH	25.00	65.00	40.00
☐ **Alamo,** Japan	2.00	6.00	4.00
☐ **American Cutlery Co.,** U.S.A.	15.00	35.00	22.00
☐ **American Cutlery Co.,** Germany	8.00	20.00	13.00
☐ **American Knife Co.,** Plymouth, MA	65.00	95.00	75.00
☐ **American Knife Co.,** Winstead, CT	20.00	45.00	32.00
☐ **American Knife Co.,** Germany	12.00	20.00	15.00
☐ **American Knife Co.,** Thomaston, CT	20.00	60.00	35.00
☐ **American Shear & Knife Co.,** U.S.A.	25.00	75.00	45.00
☐ **Armstrong Cutlery Co.,** U.S.A.	8.00	15.00	11.00
☐ **Armstrong Cutlery Co.,** Germany	6.00	12.00	8.00
☐ **Arnex (stainless),** Solingen, Germany	4.00	10.00	7.00
☐ **Atenback,** Swanswork, Germany	10.00	50.00	28.00
☐ **Atlantic Cutlery Co.,** Germany	12.00	25.00	16.00
☐ **Autopoint,** Chicago, IL	3.00	8.00	5.00
☐ **Banner Cutlery Co.,** Germany	12.00	25.00	17.00
☐ **Banner Knife Co.**	12.00	25.00	17.00
☐ **A. F. Bannister & Co.,** New Jersey	3.00	45.00	23.00
☐ **Barhep,** Solingen, Germany	6.00	10.00	8.00
☐ **Barlett Tool Co.,** Newark, NY	15.00	65.00	35.00
☐ **Barrett & Sons**	6.00	65.00	30.00
☐ **Barton Bros.,** Sheffield, England	15.00	95.00	50.00
☐ **Bassett,** Derby, CT	8.00	25.00	15.00
☐ **Bastian Bros. Co.,** Rochester, NY	25.00	65.00	40.00
☐ **Bates & Bacon**	25.00	150.00	80.00
☐ **Battle Ax Cutlery Co.**	45.00	75.00	60.00
☐ **Bayonne Cutlery,** Bayonne, NJ	10.00	75.00	45.00
☐ **Bay Ridge Works,** Solingen, Germany	10.00	20.00	14.00
☐ **Bayridge Works,** Germany	5.00	30.00	16.00
☐ **Bay State,** Worcester, MA	30.00	175.00	95.00
☐ **Blish, Mize & Stillman Hdwe. Co.**	20.00	150.00	80.00
☐ **Blue Grass Belknap Hdwe.,** Louisville, KY	15.00	100.00	55.00
☐ **Blue Ribbon**	15.00	25.00	20.00
☐ **Bohler Stahl**	8.00	15.00	11.00
☐ **Bohler Star**	8.00	15.00	11.00
☐ **Boker,** U.S.A.	10.00	100.00	50.00
☐ **Boker,** Solingen, Germany	10.00	175.00	90.00
☐ **Bon Knife Co.**	3.00	15.00	9.00
☐ **Borneff,** Germany	3.00	10.00	6.00
☐ **Bostwick Braun Co.,** Toledo, OH	25.00	150.00	85.00
☐ **Bowen Knife Co.** Atlanta, GA	20.00	110.00	65.00
☐ **J. Bunger & Sons Celebrated Cutlery**	30.00	150.00	90.00
☐ **Bridge Cutlery Co.** St. Louis, MO	65.00	200.00	135.00
☐ **Buck Creek,** Solingen	10.00	25.00	16.00
☐ **Buck,** El-Cajon, CA	7.00	45.00	28.00
☐ **Buffalo Cutlery Co.**	35.00	160.00	65.00
☐ **Buhl & Sons Co.** Detroit, MI	15.00	65.00	35.00
☐ **R. Bunting & Sons** Sheffield	75.00	500.00	280.00
☐ **Burkinshaw Knife Co.** Pepperell, MA	35.00	300.00	100.00

KNIVES / 531

	Current Price Range		Prior Year Average
☐ Frank Buster Cutlery Co.	10.00	1000.00	460.00
☐ Butler Bros. Chicago, IL	15.00	85.00	45.00
☐ Camden Cutlery Co., Germany	25.00	100.00	60.00
☐ Camillus Cutlery Co. Camillus, NY	8.00	110.00	50.00
☐ Camillus, New York, NY	5.00	25.00	15.00
☐ Camp Buddy, USA	8.00	25.00	16.00
☐ Camp King	8.00	25.00	16.00
☐ Case MFG.	50.00	800.00	325.00
☐ Case Cutlery Co.	50.00	500.00	260.00
☐ Catskill Knife Co., New York	12.00	85.00	42.00
☐ Clements Cutlery Sheffield, England	8.00	60.00	30.00
☐ Cleveland Cutlery Germany	35.00	60.00	45.00
☐ Colt (Imperial), U.S.A.	4.00	12.00	8.00
☐ Columbia Knife Co., New York	45.00	60.00	52.00
☐ Commander Little Valley, NY	65.00	95.00	80.00
☐ Conn Cutlery Co. Contents, Germany	15.00	65.00	35.00
☐ Continental Cutlery Co. New York	15.00	60.00	35.00
☐ Continental Cutlery Co. Sheffield, England	12.00	60.00	32.00
☐ Continental Cutlery Co. Kansas City, MO.	25.00	65.00	45.00
☐ Cook Bros.	75.00	125.00	100.00
☐ Copper Bros.	8.00	18.00	13.00
☐ Delux	6.00	15.00	10.00
☐ Depend-on-me-Cutlery Co., New York	7.00	35.00	20.00
☐ E.A.A. Solingen, Germany	5.00	10.00	7.00
☐ E. F. & Co.	65.00	90.00	75.00
☐ Eagle	20.00	35.00	26.00
☐ Eagle Cutlery Co.	65.00	300.00	180.00
☐ Eagle Knife Co., U.S.A.	30.00	300.00	160.00
☐ Eagle Pencil Co.	5.00	15.00	10.00
☐ Eagleton Knife Co.	20.00	125.00	70.00
☐ Emmon Hawkins Hardware	15.00	100.00	55.00
☐ Empire Knife Co. Winsted, CT	30.00	300.00	160.00
☐ Empire, Winsted, CT	30.00	300.00	160.00
☐ Emrod Co., Germany	4.00	15.00	9.00
☐ Wm. Enders Mfg. Co., U.S.A.	15.00	125.00	68.00
☐ Faulkhiner & Co. Germany	10.00	20.00	14.00
☐ Favorite Knife Co. Germany	4.00	25.00	14.00
☐ A Field & Co. (Criterion) Germany	15.00	45.00	30.00
☐ Alfred Field & Co. Germany	15.00	30.00	25.00
☐ Marshall Field & Co. Germany	15.00	60.00	35.00
☐ Fife Cutlery Co. (Hen & Rooster), Germany	40.00	150.00	70.00
☐ Fightin' Rooster Cutlery Co. Solingen, Germany .	10.00	1000.00	500.00
☐ Gerber, U.S.A.	20.00	150.00	80.00
☐ Gerbr Hopre, Germany	10.00	15.00	12.00
☐ Gerlach, Poland	8.00	20.00	14.00
☐ Ernst Gerleg, Germany	15.00	50.00	35.00
☐ Germania Cutlery Co.	10.00	25.00	17.00
☐ Hermitage Cutlery	8.00	25.00	15.00
☐ Herms, Germany	10.00	35.00	22.00
☐ T. Hessen Bruch & Co.	15.00	35.00	25.00
☐ Hibbard, Spencer, & Bartlett Chicago, IL	10.00	350.00	170.00
☐ Hickory	4.00	200.00	100.00
☐ Highcarbon Steel, U.S.A.	10.00	150.00	90.00
☐ Higler & Sons	15.00	75.00	45.00
☐ Hike Cutlery Co. Solingen, Germany	10.00	35.00	22.00
☐ Hill Bros.	20.00	60.00	40.00

532 / KNIVES

	Current Price Range		Prior Year Average
☐ **Honk Falls** Napanoch, NY	35.00	900.00	450.00
☐ **Imperial Knife Co.** Providence, RI	2.00	75.00	38.00
☐ **Imperial,** Mexico	1.00	3.00	2.00
☐ **Imperial,** Germany	6.00	26.00	15.00
☐ **Indiana Cutlery Co.**	36.00	75.00	50.00
☐ **Iroquois,** U.S.A.	2.00	12.00	7.00
☐ **Iroquois Cutlery Co.** Utica, NY	3.00	25.00	12.00
☐ **Iros,** Keen, NY	8.00	45.00	25.00
☐ **Irving Cutlery Co.** Germany	4.00	15.00	9.00
☐ **Issac Milner,** Sheffield	25.00	60.00	40.00
☐ **Ivy,** Germany	5.00	15.00	10.00
☐ **Jim Bowie (German Eye)**	12.00	65.00	24.00
☐ **Jim Dandy**	20.00	150.00	80.00
☐ **John Wilton,** Sheffield	45.00	125.00	80.00
☐ **Jonathan Crooks,** England	10.00	200.00	100.00
☐ **Jones & Son,** Germany	5.00	15.00	10.00
☐ **Jordan,** St. Louis, MO	10.00	65.00	35.00
☐ **Joseph Allen & Sons**	10.00	250.00	120.00
☐ **K.I.E.,** Sweden	3.00	15.00	9.00
☐ **Ka-Bar,** U.S.A.	10.00	600.00	300.00
☐ **Kabar,** U.S.A.	10.00	300.00	160.00
☐ **Kamp Cutlery Co.** Germany	5.00	15.00	10.00
☐ **Kamp Huaser** Plumacher, Germany	15.00	60.00	35.00
☐ **Kampfe Bros.,** New York	10.00	20.00	14.00
☐ **Kamphaus**	10.00	20.00	14.00
☐ **Kan-Der,** Germany	15.00	35.00	25.00
☐ **Keystone Cutlery**	35.00	200.00	100.00
☐ **Kinfolks** Little Valley, NY	40.00	300.00	160.00
☐ **King Cutlery Co.** Germany	15.00	30.00	22.00
☐ **Kings Quality,** U.S.A.	4.00	10.00	6.00
☐ **Mantua Cutlery**	5.00	15.00	10.00
☐ **Mappin Bros.,** Sheffield	65.00	200.00	125.00
☐ **Marbles,** Gladstone, MI	75.00	2000.00	1000.00
☐ **Murcott,** Germany	5.00	25.00	20.00
☐ **R. Murphy,** Boston, MD	15.00	25.00	20.00
☐ **New Port Cutlery Company** Germany	12.00	18.00	15.00
☐ **Newton Premier** Sheffield	10.00	25.00	16.00
☐ **New York Knife Company** Walden, NY	25.00	1000.00	500.00
☐ **Norsharp**	10.00	35.00	22.00
☐ **N. American,** Wichita, KS	10.00	55.00	30.00
☐ **Olcut,** Olean, NY	45.00	300.00	200.00
☐ **Old Cutlery** Olean, NY	15.00	125.00	65.00
☐ **Old American Knife,** U.S.A.	10.00	35.00	22.00
☐ **Old Hickory (Ontario Knife Company)**	4.00	12.00	8.00
☐ **Old Timer (Schrade Walden)**	5.00	100.00	50.00
☐ **Olscut,** Germany	6.00	15.00	10.00
☐ **Olsen Knife Co.** Howard City, MI	6.00	45.00	25.00
☐ **Pal Cutlery** Plattsburg, NY	15.00	90.00	50.00
☐ **Palace Cutlery Co.**	25.00	30.00	32.00
☐ **Palalto Cutlery Co.** Germany	5.00	15.00	10.00
☐ **Palmett Cutlery Co.**	20.00	35.00	27.00
☐ **Papes Thiebes Cutlery Co.**	10.00	200.00	100.00
☐ **Parker Cutlery Co.**	10.00	900.00	450.00
☐ **Parker-Frost**	10.00	200.00	100.00
☐ **Wm. & J. Parker**	100.00	400.00	250.00
☐ **Petters Cutlery Company** Chicago, IL	25.00	85.00	55.00

KNIVES / 533

	Current Price Range		Prior Year Average
☐ Phoenix Knife Co. Phoenix, NY	10.00	135.00	70.00
☐ Pic, Germany	3.00	8.00	5.00
☐ PIC, Japan	2.00	5.00	3.00
☐ Pine Knot, U.S.A.	35.00	300.00	250.00
☐ Pine Knot James W. Price	45.00	400.00	160.00
☐ C. Platts & Sons Andover, NY	40.00	800.00	400.00
☐ Platts Bros. Andover, NY	40.00	800.00	400.00
☐ Platts Bros., Union, NY	75.00	800.00	420.00
☐ Poor Boy	5.00	100.00	50.00
☐ Pop Cutlery Co. Camillus, NY	5.00	20.00	12.00
☐ Pottery Hoy Hardware Co.	35.00	65.00	50.00
☐ Powell Bros.	15.00	60.00	35.00
☐ Power Kraft	5.00	10.00	7.00
☐ C. Pradel	15.00	60.00	30.00
☐ Pradel, France	15.00	60.00	30.00
☐ Pratt & Co., London	70.00	110.00	90.00
☐ Providence Cutlery Co.	15.00	65.00	40.00
☐ Puma, Germany	25.00	900.00	450.00
☐ Queen City Titusville, PA	10.00	250.00	125.00
☐ Queen Steel Titusville, PA	10.00	110.00	60.00
☐ Quick-Kut, Inc. Freemont, OH	10.00	35.00	22.00
☐ Quick Point St. Louis, MO	25.00	75.00	50.00
☐ Quick Point (Winchester stamped on back of tang)	50.00	75.00	62.00
☐ R. J. Richter, Germany	4.00	15.00	9.00
☐ Ring Cutlery, Japan	1.00	5.00	3.00
☐ Rivington Works	15.00	65.00	30.00
☐ Rizzaro Estilato, Milan, Italy	35.00	75.00	55.00
☐ Roberts & Johnson & Rand St. Louis, MO	15.00	75.00	45.00
☐ Robertson Bros. & Co. Louisville, KY	15.00	300.00	150.00
☐ Robeson, Germany	25.00	75.00	50.00
☐ Robeson, Rochester, NY	15.00	400.00	200.00
☐ Robeson, Suredge	10.00	125.00	60.00
☐ Robeson, Socketeze	25.00	400.00	250.00
☐ Robeson Cutlery Rochester, NY	10.00	400.00	250.00
☐ Robinson Bros. & Co. Louisville, KY.	15.00	300.00	150.00
☐ Rodgers Cutlery Sheffield	40.00	1000.00	500.00
☐ Rodgers Cutlery Hartford, CT	15.00	30.00	22.00
☐ Romo, Germany	5.00	15.00	10.00
☐ Romo, Japan	1.00	6.00	3.00
☐ J. Rosenbaulm	15.00	35.00	25.00
☐ I. H. S. Rose & Co.	15.00	60.00	35.00
☐ T. Ross & Son	30.00	60.00	45.00
☐ Royce Brand, U.S.A	5.00	10.00	7.00
☐ Sheffield Steel	5.00	15.00	10.00
☐ F. W. Sheldon & Co. Germany	4.00	25.00	14.00
☐ Sheldon, Sheffield	15.00	35.00	25.00
☐ Shumatic Cutlery Co.	20.00	75.00	32.00
☐ Shur Snap (Colonial)	15.00	20.00	17.00
☐ Sizeker Manstealed, Germany	10.00	15.00	12.00
☐ Sliberstein Laporte & Co.	35.00	65.00	45.00
☐ Simmons Hardware Co. Germany	20.00	300.00	150.00
☐ Simmons Hardware St. Louis, MO	25.00	300.00	150.00
☐ Simmons Warden White Co. Dayton, OH	15.00	75.00	45.00
☐ Spartts, England	35.00	90.00	65.00
☐ Spear Cutlery Co., Germany	10.00	25.00	17.00

534 / KNIVES

	Current Price Range		Prior Year Average
☐ Spring Cutlery Co. Sheffield	15.00	125.00	65.00
☐ Springer, Japan	4.00	15.00	9.00
☐ Standard Cutlery Co. Germany	5.00	25.00	15.00
☐ Standard Cutlery Co. Division of Case	65.00	400.00	200.00
☐ Sta-Sharp	20.00	150.00	80.00
☐ Steelton Cutlery Works Germany	15.00	25.00	20.00
☐ F. Sterling	5.00	25.00	15.00
☐ Trinton Cutlery Co.	15.00	30.00	22.00
☐ Trout Hardward Co. Chicago, IL	25.00	50.00	35.00
☐ Trout Hardware Co. Chicago, IL	5.00	20.00	12.00
☐ Thomas Turner & Co. Sheffield, England	15.00	175.00	90.00
☐ United, Germany	3.00	10.00	6.00
☐ Universal Knife Co. New Britain, CT	15.00	35.00	25.00
☐ Utica Co., Czechoslovakia	12.00	35.00	22.00
☐ Utica Cutlery Co. Utica, NY	10.00	150.00	80.00
☐ Utica Knife Co., U.S.A.	10.00	150.00	80.00
☐ V. K. Cutlery Co., Germany	5.00	15.00	10.00
☐ Valley Falls Cutlery Co.	15.00	75.00	45.00
☐ Valley Forge Cutlery Co.	20.00	95.00	55.00
☐ Valor, Germany	3.00	15.00	9.00
☐ Valor, Japan	3.00	15.00	9.00
☐ Van Camp, U.S.A.	3.00	100.00	50.00
☐ Van Camp H & I Co., U.S.A.	15.00	300.00	150.00
☐ Van Camp Indianapolis, IN	15.00	300.00	150.00
☐ Van Camp, Germany	10.00	30.00	15.00
☐ Vanco, Indianapolis, IN	5.00	35.00	20.00
☐ Vernider, St. Paul, MN	5.00	25.00	15.00
☐ Volort Cutlery Co., Sheffield	5.00	15.00	10.00
☐ Vom Cleff & Co., Germany	10.00	135.00	70.00
☐ Voos, U.S.A.	25.00	40.00	40.00
☐ Voos Cutlery Co., Germany	5.00	25.00	15.00
☐ Waltham Cutlery, U.S.A.	5.00	25.00	15.00
☐ Waltham Cutlery, Germany	5.00	15.00	10.00
☐ Wandy, Italy	4.00	10.00	7.00
☐ Ward Bros.	5.00	35.00	20.00
☐ Wardlon Cutlery Co. Walden, NY	25.00	85.00	55.00
☐ Wards, U.S.A.	5.00	35.00	20.00
☐ W & W Walter Warrington Sheffield	15.00	65.00	30.00
☐ Warren, Baker, OR	5.00	25.00	15.00
☐ Warren Bros., Soffolk Works, England	35.00	150.00	80.00
☐ Warwick Knife Co., NY	151.00	200.00	170.00
☐ John Watts, Sheffield	15.00	30.00	21.00
☐ Webster, Sycamore Works U.S.A.	10.00	35.00	22.00
☐ Webster Cutlery Co., Germany	5.00	15.00	10.00
☐ Weck, N.Y.	15.00	65.00	27.00
☐ Wedgeway Cutlery Co.	14.00	35.00	22.00
☐ Weed & Co., Buffalo	35.00	75.00	55.00
☐ G. Weiland, New York	5.00	25.00	15.00
☐ Marshall Wells Hardware Co.	35.00	125.00	55.00
☐ H. C. Wentworth & Son Germany	5.00	35.00	20.00
☐ Weske Cutlery Co. Sandusky, OH	15.00	35.00	25.00
☐ Westaco, Boulder, CO	30.00	60.00	45.00
☐ Wester, B. C.	5.00	35.00	20.00
☐ Wester Bros., Germany	35.00	250.00	120.00
☐ Wester Stone, Inc., U.S.A.	15.00	115.00	65.00
☐ Western, Boulder, CO	50.00	500.00	225.00

	Current Price Range	Prior Year Average
☐ Western Cutlery Co., Germany	5.00 30.00	17.00
☐ Western Shear Co.	15.00 65.00	27.00
☐ Wilbert Cutlery Co. Chicago, IL	15.00 75.00	45.00
☐ E. Wilds & Sons	15.00 75.00	45.00

LABELS

Though merchandise labels will probably always be with us, in one form or other, it seems that this art form has declined a good deal. Older labels, from the late 1800's and early 1900's, are highly pictorial, often topical, and much more eye-catching than their modern counterparts. They first caught the notice of collectors when store cartons and other containers began to be collected. Then, gradually, collecting interest developed for the labels themselves, which often can be found loose — and, when loose, are less expensive than on the original cartons. Label collecting has much to offer, not the least of which is the storage convenience; labels can be kept in albums just like stamps, and in fact, can be mounted in place with standard philatelic hinges. A large collection therefore takes up very little space. Specialization in one direction or another is probably wisest, because so much is available. *Fruit crate* labels have become the favorite of many label hobbyists. These are the labels originally attached to wooden crates of oranges, melons and other fruits as they traveled from wholesaler to retailer. Each company, and there were many, had its distinctive label. The individual values depend very much on the topical interest, if any, of the subject matter. Labels picturing Indians, railroad trains, and sporting events are among the favorites of collectors. But rarity also enters the question, and (you might be surprised to learn) label historians have already completed a great deal of research into the rarity of different labels. Some labels are known to exist in only a few specimens.

For further information, readers are advised to consult *The Official Price Guide to Paper Collectibles,* published by the House of Collectibles.

FRUIT CRATE LABELS

☐ **America's Delight,** apples, orchard scene	1.25 2.00	1.60
☐ **Azalea,** oranges, azalea blossoms, Florida	1.25 2.00	1.60
☐ **Basketball,** lemons, girls playing basketball	6.00 9.00	7.00
☐ **Black Hawk,** oranges, Indian Riverside	20.00 30.00	25.00
☐ **Blue Goose,** oranges, large goose, Los Angeles	3.00 4.75	3.60
☐ **Corona Beauty,** lemons, blossoms, Corona	1.25 2.00	1.65
☐ **Florigold,** oranges, Indian head, Florida	1.75 3.00	1.30
☐ **Hiawatha,** oranges, Indian brave face	8.00 12.00	10.00
☐ **Indian Belle,** grapefruit, chief and squaw, Porterville	37.00 48.00	42.00
☐ **Mission,** lemons, Santa Barbara Mission	8.00 12.00	10.00
☐ **Rising Sun,** oranges, sun scene, Chicago	3.00 4.50	3.60
☐ **San Francisco,** oranges, bird, Golden Gate Bridge	35.00 45.00	40.00
☐ **Sea Gull,** lemons, gulls flying	3.00 4.50	3.60
☐ **Sunkist,** apples, Sunkist emblem	22.00 32.00	26.00
☐ **50 labels,** Western packing houses, 8″ x 10″	12.00 18.00	15.00

MATCH BOX LABELS

This is one of those hobbies that for years received a kind of casual interest from collectors — and then, in a coming-of-age, really excited intent collecting. We know that people were saving pretty match box labels at the turn-of-the-century, because specimens are continually found in the catch-all scrapbooks of that era, along with cigar bands, photos, news cuttings, dried flowers and what-not. Anything appealing enough to have been saved has the potential to become a collectible, and this is what happened to match box labels. While the hobby is still not large, compared to some, match box labels have now been studied, catalogued, and evaluated to the point of eliminating all guesswork. The favorites are the older ones, especially ones going back before 1900. Few are dated; the ages are known from investigations into early advertising. Also popular are those picturing highly topical subjects. Whenever mixed batches are offered for sale and you have the opportunity to rummage, the best to look for are those picturing airplanes or autos. Also worthwhile are labels showing Indians or blacks. The old term "Lucifer match," by which sulphur matches were known in the 1800's, led to frequent depictions of devils on labels — more than enough to permit a whole specialized collection of them. Keep your match box labels on philatelic pages (the blank kind) in a standard three-ring binder. Mount them with hinges — don't glue them down to the page, as this destroys the value. If you vacation in Europe, visit a hobby shop and you will probably find packets of "100 different" match box labels being sold just like stamps.

	Current Price Range		Prior Year Average
☐ Ciclista Safety Matches, man riding bicycle	2.25	3.50	2.80
☐ Ed Booher (Germany), photo of man reading book by Vladimir Nabokov	.65	1.15	1.85
☐ Favorite Yacht, J.M. Shaska, Manchester, Arabic writing on lower portion	2.50	3.50	3.00
☐ Fosforos Hercules, Hercules fighting lion	1.25	2.25	1.75
☐ Gulnar Jan Safety Match, made in Sweden, girl in lace mantilla	1.25	2.75	2.00
☐ The Kookaburra or Laughing Jackass (Sweden), "Damp proof," illustration of birds	1.75	3.00	2.30
☐ Phonograph Match, engraving of old phonograph with megaphone, no name, three dice on label, made in Sweden	.75	1.25	1.00
☐ Radja Stamboel, man in military dress, wearing fez	1.50	2.75	2.15
☐ Sorbia Safety Matches, Negro head in profile ...	3.50	5.00	4.25
☐ The Automobile Safety Match, four riders in car, c. 1910	5.75	8.00	6.80
☐ Three Globes Safety Match	.75	1.25	1.00
☐ Three Steamers, "Do Not Glow"	2.50	3.75	3.12

MISCELLANEOUS LABELS

☐ 50 beverage labels, Art Deco	6.00	10.00	8.00
☐ 100 Beer labels, c. 1930-1960	12.00	18.00	15.00
☐ 1000 Food and cosmetic labels, 80 different types	20.00	30.00	24.00
☐ 100 Whiskey labels, assorted	6.00	9.00	7.00

LAMPS AND LIGHTING DEVICES

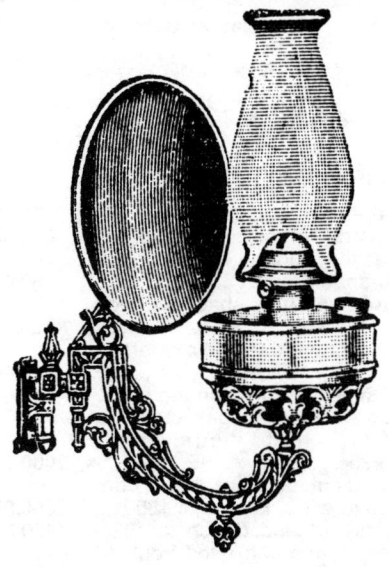

Bracket Oil Lamp, with adjustable reflector, #2 sun burner, chimney and wick . . . . **$175.00-$275.00**

    Not many individuals collect lamps and lighting devices, but specimens are eagerly sought for room decor or as accent items. Lighting devices also serve, too, as adjuncts to other collections: the Tiffany collector certainly wishes to own at least one Tiffany lamp, and the enthusiast of whaling relics wants to have one or more whale oil lamps in his collection. The available variety is immense. In terms of age, the oldest lighting devices on the market are the clay oil lamps of ancient times, going back about 2,000 years. These are teardrop-shaped, usually quite small, and sometimes, they carry very appealing decoration either in painting or molding. Despite their acknowledged status as museum pieces, small plain ones can be found for no more than $100. The common "lighting device" of Colonial America was, of course, the tallow candle. Candle holders are abundant on the antique market. Not so numerous, but very intriguing and historical, are the pierced tin lanterns in which candles were often carried out-of-doors at night. Because of wind, it was useless to carry an unshielded candle, so some kind of container was necessary. The crudest lanterns merely have holes punched randomly in the sides, for light to escape. Later, glass panels were used. Whale oil lamps are usually attractive, but scarcer than you might imagine. They were replaced after a relatively short time, by the kerosene lamp in the 1860's. Kerosene lamps were being made well into the 1900's to serve rural communities not supplied with electrical power.

538 / LAMPS AND LIGHTING DEVICES

	Current Price Range		Prior Year Average

BULBS

- [ ] **Edison Single Curl,** 5" x 2¼", plaster base, c. 1901 .... 75.00 100.00 85.00
- [ ] **Thomson-Houston,** single curl, 6" x 2¾", plaster base, c. 1900 .... 35.00 50.00 42.00
- [ ] **Westinghouse Single Curl,** 6" x 2½", plaster base, c. 1893 .... 80.00 110.00 95.00

LAMPS AND LIGHTING DEVICES

- [ ] **Angle lamps,** brass, double lacquered 175.00 275.00 225.00
- [ ] **Art Deco chandelier,** leaded glass, signed Quezal 650.00 850.00 750.00
- [ ] **Art Deco globe,** opalescent, signed Verlys 400.00 550.00 460.00
- [ ] **Betty lamp,** tin with hanger 80.00 110.00 95.00
- [ ] **Bradley and Hubbard,** caramel shade, signed base, 24" H. 525.00 700.00 600.00
- [ ] **Carriage lamps,** brass, clear glass and red reflector lenses 260.00 340.00 340.00
- [ ] **Chandelier,** Louis XV style, cut glass shade 950.00 1150.00 1050.00
- [ ] **Chandelier,** pewter, converted from gas, c. 1870 . 800.00 1000.00 900.00
- [ ] **Crystal chandelier,** hand cut lead, Czechoslovakia, c. 1925 .... 2000.00 2500.00 2200.00
- [ ] **Crystal chandelier,** hand cut, unusual shape, converted from candles to electric, French, c.1800 .. 2600.00 3200.00 28.00
- [ ] **Crystal chandelier,** hand cut lead, Czech., c. 1920 1400.00 1900.00 1600.00
- [ ] **Courting lamp,** pewter, clear and frosted front, 4" H. 85.00 110.00 95.00
- [ ] **Gas chandelier,** handwrought, French, turn of century 800.00 1100.00 950.00
- [ ] **Gas, sconces,** pair, handwrought, French 280.00 350.00 315.00
- [ ] **"Gone With the Wind" lamp,** umbrella shade with cupids and foliage, brass foot, 20" H 260.00 325.00 290.00
- [ ] **"Gone With the Wind" lamp,** grape pattern with green leaves, 22" H 480.00 600.00 530.00
- [ ] **"Gone With the Wind"** lamp, magnolia blossoms handpainted, 24" H 525.00 650.00 610.00
- [ ] **"Gone With the Wind"** lamp, red glass with red bull's eye, 28½" H 625.00 750.00 680.00
- [ ] **Greentown lamp,** chocolate glass, 10" H 450.00 535.00 480.00
- [ ] **Hand lamp,** tin drum shape 65.0 90.00 75.00
- [ ] **Handel lamps,** all signed, Boudoir-reverse painted scene, 14" H. 480.00 565.00 520.00
- [ ] **Hanging lamp,** brass with chocolate glass panels, 14" H. 60.00 80.00 70.00
- [ ] **Hanging lamp,** cranberry with prisms 675.00 800.00 735.00
- [ ] **Hanging lamp,** striped with canopy, 13" H. 150.00 200.00 200.00
- [ ] **Hurricane lamp,** pair 11" H. 35.00 45.00 40.00
- [ ] **Iron chandelier,** handwrought, floral vines, c. 1920 .... 725.00 900.00 800.00
- [ ] **Iron fixture,** handwrought, Moorish influence, early 20th c. 340.00 410.00 370.00
- [ ] **Jefferson,** boudoir trees 200.00 250.00 225.00
- [ ] **Kerosene lamp,** cabbage case pattern 55.00 75.00 65.00
- [ ] **Kerosene lamp,** country store fixture, brass front 130.00 160.00 145.00
- [ ] **Kerosene lamp,** green pattern, milk glass base .. 75.00 95.00 85.00
- [ ] **Kerosene lamp,** hanging fixture, cranberry glass with brass frame 160.00 200.00 180.00

LAMPS AND LIGHTING DEVICES / 539

	Current Price Range		Prior Year Average
☐ **Kerosene lamp,** hobnail pattern	30.00	40.00	35.00
☐ **Kerosene lamp,** table, Lincoln Drape pattern, amber	100.00	140.00	120.00
☐ **Kerosene lamp,** table, overlay glass, 13″ H.	625.00	750.00	685.00
☐ **Kerosene lamp,** table, "Ripley Marriage Lamp"	400.00	500.00	450.00
☐ **Kerosene lamp,** wall, cast iron bracket, 12″ H.	50.00	65.00	56.00
☐ **Lily,** amber shades, three lights, bronze base	2000.00	2500.00	2200.00
☐ **Mac-Beth "Nite Glow,"** ruby shade	28.00	37.00	32.00
☐ **Pairpoint,** Boudoir, "Puffy" rose shade with metal base, 8″ Dia.	725.00	875.00	800.00
☐ **Pairpoint,** butterflies and roses, signed base and shade, 10″ Dia.	1000.00	1250.00	1100.00
☐ **Peg lamps,** brass burner, 6″ H.	65.00	85.00	75.00
☐ **Peg lamps,** ribbed glass with brass candlesticks, pair	325.00	400.00	368.00
☐ **Student lamp,** double brass, green glass shade with original chimney	490.00	565.00	528.00
☐ **Student lamp,** hanging double, burnished, green shade	650.00	775.00	712.00
☐ **Student lamp,** single brass front, milk glass shade	300.00	375.00	338.00
☐ **Table,** "Arrow Root," leaded glass shade with bronze base, 25½″ H	8000.00	10000.00	900.00
☐ **Table,** "Dragonfly," leaded glass shade with dragonfly bodies, bronze base, 10½″ H	6500.00	8000.00	7200.00
☐ **Table,** hibiscus, leaded shade in red, yellow, white and pink	2000.00	2500.00	2200.00
☐ **Table,** leaded-glass shade with green leaves and dogwood blossoms, 27″ H	3200.00	3900.00	3500.00
☐ **Table,** nasturtium, amber chisled ground, signed in triplicate	700.00	900.00	800.00
☐ **Table,** stained-glass shade with tulip bronzed copper base, 23½″ H	825.00	1000.00	900.00
☐ **Tiffany,** acorn, green with orange acorns shade, signed, 19″ H	2850.00	3500.00	3150.00
☐ **Tiffany,** floor lamp, "Damascene" shade, bronze base and lily pad feet	2300.00	2700.00	2500.00
☐ **Tiffany,** table lamp, bronze base with leaded glass shade, acorn pattern, both pieces signed, Tiffany Studios	4000.00	6000.00	5000.00
☐ **Tiffany,** table lamp, Kapa shell, bronze base, 12¾″ H	1000.00	1350.00	1150.00
☐ **Tiffany type,** glass fixture, leaded fruit pattern, c. 1910	1300.00	1700.00	1500.00
☐ **Tole sconces,** wall, French, set of six, early 20th c.	180.00	250.00	215.00
☐ **Venetian mirror,** hand cut and etched, carved backing, 5′ x 3′	2000.00	2500.00	2200.00
☐ **Whale oil,** amethyst paneled front with marble base, 10″ H	300.00	375.00	338.00
☐ **Whale oil,** giant sawtooth, 9″ H	100.00	135.00	118.00
☐ **Whale oil,** paneled front, blue with marble base, 10″ H	280.00	330.00	305.00

540 / LAMPS AND LIGHTING DEVICES

	Current Price Range		Prior Year Average

LANTERNS

☐ **Auto lamp,** brass, oil burning, 14½″ H.	90.00	130.00	110.00
☐ **Barn,** Peter Gray, Boston	95.00	140.00	115.00
☐ **Buggy dashboard,** kerosene	20.00	30.00	24.00
☐ **Candle lantern,** sheet metal painted black, 16¼″ H.	60.00	80.00	70.00
☐ **Carriage lamp,** brass trim, pair	325.00	395.00	355.00
☐ **Chinese junk lantern,** brass, oil	40.00	60.00	50.00
☐ **Coach,** pierced, 17½″ H.	160.00	200.00	180.00
☐ **Dietz driving lamp,** red glass in rear, 7½″ H.	115.00	150.00	130.00
☐ **Kerosene lantern,** brass base and top engraved "Joseph Gavett, Roxbury," 17″ H.	240.00	300.00	270.00
☐ **Kerosene lantern,** Dietz red reflector	22.00	30.00	26.00
☐ **Miner's lantern,** tin and brass, 5½″ H., Jan. 10, 1882	23.00	33.00	27.00
☐ **Paul Revere lantern,** tin with swirled punched holes	150.00	200.00	175.00
☐ **Skater's lantern,** brass with glass globe	65.00	90.00	75.00
☐ **Ship's lantern,** copper, pair, 16″ H.	260.00	315.00	285.00
☐ **Wagon lantern,** clamp-on type with rear red reflector	23.00	29.00	26.00
☐ **Wood lantern,** rare second material	150.00	190.00	170.00

MINIATURE LIGHTING DEVICES

☐ **Brass acorn burner,** 6″ H.	60.00	85.00	72.00
☐ **Blue banquet lamp,** jewels on base, glass with blue and white wildflowers and tendrils, 10″ H. ...	250.00	350.00	300.00
☐ **Brass saucer,** nutmeg burner, 2″ H.	65.00	90.00	75.00
☐ **Brass skating lamp,** complete with link chain, 8″ H.	55.00	80.00	65.00
☐ **Bristol,** blue enameled flowers, 6½″ H.	75.00	100.00	82.00
☐ **Bristol type,** decorative figures on sides, hexagonal base	110.00	160.00	135.00
☐ **Bull's eye,** red	65.00	90.00	85.00
☐ **Clear glass base,** nutmeg, clear glass chimney ..	35.00	50.00	42.00
☐ **Cosmos lamp,** multicolored floral decorations, 8″ H.	250.00	450.00	350.00
☐ **Cranberry glass,** beaded swirl, 8¾″ H.	300.00	375.00	338.00
☐ **Glow night lamp,** ribbed base and shade with original wicker holder	50.00	65.00	57.00
☐ **Golden eagle,** orange body with gold and yellow trim	140.00	190.00	160.00
☐ **Green glass,** bull's eye pattern, nutmeg burner, clear chimney	45.00	60.00	52.00
☐ **Milk glass,** blue enameled lilies, pair, 8½″ H. ...	225.00	350.00	280.00
☐ **Milk glass,** chimney top with fluted stem and footed base, 5½″ H.	160.00	240.00	200.00
☐ **Milk glass,** night light, long neck and metal tank .	35.00	45.00	40.00
☐ **Milk glass,** white, embossed with iris, acorn burner, clear glass chimney	170.00	220.00	195.00
☐ **Opalescent glass,** applied feet, 8½″ H.	420.00	500.00	460.00
☐ **Opaline glass base and chimney,** house scene in green acorn burner	180.00	235.00	205.00
☐ **Pink milk glass,** house, clear glass chimney, four original burners	200.00	260.00	230.00
☐ **Pressed glass,** daisy, kerosene	30.00	40.00	34.00

LIGHTNING ROD ORNAMENTS / 541

	Current Price Range		Prior Year Average
☐ **Pressed glass,** pineapple basket	325.00	400.00	362.00
☐ **Satin glass,** petal with beading, embossed base, nutmeg burner, 9" H.	335.00	415.00	375.00
☐ **Tin acorn burner**	15.00	25.00	20.00
☐ **Vapo-cresolene,** original box	65.00	85.00	75.00

LIGHTNING ROD ORNAMENTS

Arrow Vane, five foot upright, ornamented glass ball . . **$175.00-$225.00**

These are glass balls that were placed onto lightning rods and served strictly to decorate them. Glass, being a non-conductor of electricity, was ideal for such a purpose. Though lightning rods had earlier origins, they began to be mass produced just before the middle of the 19th century. They instantly became one of the foremost items of the traveling salesman, who packed up his buggy with lightning rods and went from farmhouse to farmhouse telling of the perils of lightning. If the prospect of his home being reduced to a pile of cinders did not induce the farmer to buy lightning rods, there was yet another ace up the saleman's sleeve: install a lightning rod and you'll *beautify* the house, since it comes with a little glass ornament that reflects the sun and will bedazzle neighbors for miles around. The average size is from four to five inches in diameter (bigger than it sounds — about the size of a fortune-teller's crystal ball). Some are clear, but the majority are tinted in handsome pastel colors. Most of those on the antique market date from about 1880 to 1910. They can be cleaned with a mild soapsuds solution. After cleaning, a rubbing with olive oil on a rag gives them a good "sparkle."

☐ **Diddie Blitzer,** mercury glass ball	75.00	95.00	85.00
☐ **Electra ball,** amber/brown	37.00	45.00	42.00
☐ **Hawkeye,** brick red	115.00	140.00	125.00
☐ **Mercury glass,** gold-toned, 4½" Dia.	26.00	33.00	29.00
☐ **Milk glass,** doorknob ball, orange	230.00	270.00	250.00
☐ **Moon and star ball,** red	50.00	65.00	55.00

LINDBERGH MEMORABILIA

Top to Bottom: **Newspaper Headlines**, the sinking of the Titanic in the *New York American* **$75.00-$100.00;** the defeat of the Germans in the *San Francisco Examiner* **$25.00-$30.00;** Lindbergh's crossing of the Atlantic in *The Seattle Daily News*........................ **$100.00-$160.00**

When the Spirit of St. Louis touched down in France, following the first trans-Atlantic aircraft crossing, its pilot was assured of eternal immortality. He was the hero of the day, and the media toasted him as it had toasted few celebrities up to that time. Books were rushed to press and there was a barrage of souvenirs and commemorative items of all kinds produced: badges, medals, banners, tokens, postcards, pictures, and pins. They continued to be produced for several years after the epochal 1927 flight; even as late as the 1940's and 1950's, a trickle of Lindbergh memorabilia was entering the market. Of course, the collector will be interested first and foremost in personal articles, such as letters written by Lindbergh or anything owned or used by him, if it can be reliably authenticated. The next step is to build a file of original newspapers carrying the story of his historical flight — this in itself could become an immense collection. Another desirable item for the collector is a first edition of Lindbergh's book, *Spirit of St. Louis,* autographed by the author. There are no specialist dealers in Lindbergh memorabilia, but the hobbyist will have no trouble finding plenty for sale in the antique and paper collectible markets.

	Current Price Range		Prior Year Average
☐ **Book**, "Lone Eagle"	18.00	27.00	22.00
☐ **Button**, "Welcome Lindy"	14.00	19.00	16.00
☐ **McCormick bottles**, "American Portraits," Lindbergh	16.00	22.00	19.00

LOCKS AND KEYS / 543

	Current Price Range		Prior Year Average
☐ **Medal,** bronze Congressional, c. 1928	32.00	40.00	35.00
☐ **Pencil box**	18.00	23.00	20.00
☐ **Portrait banner,** "Welcome Lindbergh," cloth, 56½″ x 33½″	250.00	325.00	280.00
☐ **Postcard,** photo of Lindbergh and plane	5.00	9.00	7.00
☐ **Tapestry,** New York to Paris	120.00	170.00	150.00
☐ **Wheaton/Nuline decanters,** Lindbergh, c. 1968 ..	6.00	9.00	7.00

OTHER AIRPLANE COLLECTIBLES

☐ **Airplane,** French, chromolith, early 20th c.	500.00	650.00	560.00
☐ **1926 Ford Tri-motor,** "Tin Goose"	175000.00	225000.00	195000.00
☐ **Luftwaffe fighter pilot pressurized goggles,** in original case, marked with eagle and swastika, c. 1940	17.00	25.00	21.00
☐ **Lockheed Vega**	235000.00	285000.00	255000.00
☐ **North American DeHaviland,** "Tiger Moth," 1931-1945	18000.00	27000.00	22000.00
☐ **North American P-51,** "Mustang," 1944	225000.00	265000.00	245000.00
☐ **North American Trainer,** AT-6-SNJ, 1945	14000.00	18000.00	16000.00
☐ **World War I Curtiss JN4-D,** "Jenny"	24000.00	29000.00	26000.00

Courtesy: Yesterday's Wings, Pottstown, PA, 1964

LOCKS AND KEYS

Lock, solid steel, brass plated, spring shackle, 2½″x3½″, with key **$20.00-25.00**

Collecting locks and keys is a thoroughly fascinating hobby, and one which has gone from "small time" to "big time". Lock collecting will never, perhaps, boast as many followers as stamp or coin hobbies, but there are extremely dedicated individuals who compete with a passion for the better specimens and drive up values strikingly high (as these listings show!). Early and unusual locks and keys, are genuinely scarce and, in some instances, truly rare. Nearly all late-medieval locks that pass through the market are one-of-a-kind, in terms of overall form and decoration if not in originality of mechanism. The large castle and gate locks were obviously not made in

544 / LOCKS AND KEYS

large numbers — how great a use could have existed for them? Padlocks and smaller door locks were produced in larger quantities, but, not in wholesale lots until about the 18th century. A lock was definitely not just a lock 200 to 400 years ago. Decorative forms were often used in which the whole lock was cast into the likeness of a fish, Satan's head, bear, pumpkin, etc. The most collectible keys are those from the larger doorlocks of the 16th, 17th and 18th centuries. Most of those found on the U.S. antique market are not American but have been imported by antique wholesalers from such places as Portugal, Spain and Italy. This does not make them any less collectible, but do not delude yourself into believing you're buying an item of vintage Americana. As far as finding antique locks accompanied by the original key is concerned, this is a slim chance; but many old keys will fit many different antique locks, because of the simplicity of the mechanisms. Because of their impressive value climbs, antique locks have now come to the attention of investors.

	Current Price Range		Prior Year Average
☐ **American combination padlock,** working condition, 3" L., c. 1895	50.00	70.00	60.00
☐ **American padlock,** cover over keyhole, good condition (non-working), approx. 5" x 4", mid 19th c.	120.00	150.00	135.00
☐ **American padlock,** crudely wrought iron, "cigar" design, probably New England, 13" L., c. late 18th c.	750.00	1000.00	880.00
☐ **American padlock,** heart-shaped, keyhole at front, late 19th c.	75.00	100.00	88.00
☐ **European door or padlock key,** well preserved, 7½", c. 1600	80.00	110.00	95.00
☐ **German (probably) chest lock,** iron and steel, one key throws ten bolts size with bolts extended 34½" x 25", weight 62 pounds	2500.00	3500.00	3000.00
☐ **German or English castle door key,** brass, heavy shank, 14" L., c. 1200-1300	300.00	375.00	338.00
☐ **German padlock,** V-shaped barrel, decorative design, non-working, 5" H., c. 1680	350.00	450.00	400.00
☐ **Iron castle lock,** heavy iron resembling steel, thick iron bolts on a sliding frame, key present, in working condition, somewhat rusted, 17" x 11½", c. 1450-1500	4000.00	6000.00	5000.00
☐ **Italian palace key,** iron, late Renaissance, 9¼"	325.00	400.00	360.00
☐ **Spanish door key,** heavy iron, ornamental, c. 1500-1550	350.00	400.00	375.00
☐ **Medieval castle or church door lock,** German or Flemish, heavy hammered iron, some surface damage, no key, 13½" x 8¾", 12th or 13th c.	1800.00	2300.00	2000.00
☐ **Medieval gate lock,** "large," iron, decorated with heads of gargoyles and griffins, other decoration, some damage but an unusual and fine specimen. (Sold at auction in England)	2000.00	2500.00	2200.00
☐ **Nuremberg (Germany) padlock,** polished steel, decorated with incised hunting scene, perfect outward condition, non-working mechanism, no key, 7" L., barrel 5½" L., c. 1590	1800.00	2300.00	2000.00
☐ **Nuremberg padlock,** the barrel in the likeness of a skull, very rare, 5" x 4", c. 1620	3750.00	4500.00	4150.00

	Current Price Range		Prior Year Average
☐ **Portion of a Roman doorlock,** pitted, green patina, VG, 5⅜", first or second c. A.D.	400.00	600.00	500.00
☐ **Roman key,** simple design, green patina, 2¼" L., first or second c. A.D.	175.00	225.00	200.00
☐ **Roman padlock,** brass, slightly twisted, green patina, average to good condition, 3¼" L	500.00	700.00	600.00
☐ **Roman ring key,** copper with light patina, well preserved, second c. A.D.	200.00	250.00	225.00
☐ **Spanish doorlock,** black iron, iron studs or nailheads, some incised decoration on thin plate attached to the lock, 8" x 4½", c. 1400.	1000.00	1500.00	1200.00

MAGAZINES

Magazine Look, Vol. 4, No.1, January 2, 1940. This issues features Judy Garland on the cover............................. **$11.00-$16.00**

It isn't usually a collecting interest that induces anyone to save magazines, but simply a feeling that they will, in time, be worth reading again. But there ARE collectors of vintage magazines, who take a serious approach to the hobby, and there are likewise many old (and not-too-old) magazines with a fairly substantial cash value. A number of factors influence the value of old magazines, aside from condition. Some magazines are just more popular than others, because of the topics they cover or their style or for other reasons, and random copies will be worth more than random copies of other magazines. *National Geographic* is an example of such a magazine. There is very little scarcity factor with National Geographics except the extremely early issues, but they sell well because many people are interested in them. Highly specialized magazines on popular subjects can be VERY valuable, such as photography magazines of the 1800's and early 1900's. The early issues of *Camera Work* each sell for hundreds of dollars. Another way in which old magazines acquire value is via special articles, or illustrations, in a given issue. Issues of the *Saturday Evening Post* from the 1920's with covers by Norman Rockwell sell considerably higher than other issues. An example of a rather recent magazine whose early issues have acquired high value is Hugh Hefner's *Playboy,* begun in 1953. Its chief rival, *Penthouse,* has so far not attracted nearly as much collecting interest.

For more in-depth information, you may refer to *The Official Price Guide to Paperbacks and Magazines* published by the House of Collectibles.

ATLANTIC MONTHLY

	Current Price Range		Prior Year Average
☐ Vol. 1, #1, November, 1857	30.00	50.00	38.00
☐ complete year, 1858	220.00	290.00	250.00
☐ April, 1880	5.50	8.25	6.00
☐ complete year, 1886 or 1887	75.00	95.00	85.00
☐ complete year, 1900	60.00	87.50	72.00
☐ complete year, 1912	55.00	75.00	64.00
☐ complete year, 1917	70.00	95.00	82.00
☐ June, 1923	3.75	5.25	4.25
☐ complete year, 1929	38.00	52.00	45.00
☐ most issues, 1951-60	2.00	3.00	2.40

COLLIER'S

☐ Vol. 99, #10, March 6, 1937	45.00	65.00	53.00
☐ complete year, 1938	750.00	970.00	850.00
☐ complete year, 1939	635.00	810.00	720.00
☐ complete year, 1941	635.00	810.00	720.00
☐ most issues, 1947	8.75	12.25	10.00
☐ most issues, 1950	8.00	11.00	9.50
☐ complete year, 1953	390.00	520.00	450.00
☐ most issues, 1955	6.75	9.25	8.50
☐ January 4, 1957 (final issue)	10.00	14.50	12.00

COSMOPOLITAN

☐ Vol. 1, #1, 1886	18.00	24.00	20.00
☐ January, 1896	9.00	14.00	11.00
☐ most issues, 1900	9.00	14.00	11.00
☐ November, 1904	7.00	10.50	8.50
☐ complete year, 1911	100.00	135.00	115.00
☐ most issues, 1922	6.00	9.00	7.50
☐ February, 1925	5.75	8.75	7.00
☐ complete year, 1927	85.00	110.00	92.00
☐ most issues, 1931	4.50	6.75	5.25
☐ most issues, 1938	4.00	5.75	4.80
☐ most issues, 1951-55	3.00	4.50	3.60

FIELD AND STREAM

☐ most issues, 1897	3.00	5.00	4.00
☐ most issues, 1905	2.25	3.50	2.80

	Current Price Range		Prior Year Average
☐ complete year, 1916	38.00	52.00	44.00
☐ most issues, 1922	2.50	4.50	3.50
☐ complete year, 1830	36.00	50.00	42.00
☐ complete year, 1941	27.00	38.00	32.00
☐ complete year, 1939	635.00	810.00	720.00
☐ most issues, 1956-57	4.00	5.50	4.00
☐ most issues, 1962-63	3.25	4.50	3.80

GODEY'S LADY'S BOOK

☐ bound volume, 1842	30.00	35.00	32.00
☐ bound volumes, half roan, 1841, 1845, 1846, 1851-57	250.00	300.00	270.00
☐ single issues, 1844-53	4.00	6.00	5.00
☐ single issues, late 1860's	2.00	3.00	2.50
☐ bound volumes, complete, three-quarters green leather, scuffed, some covers extracted, 1881-97	225.00	275.00	250.00

GOOD HOUSEKEEPING

☐ Vol. 1, #1, May, 1885	22.00	30.00	25.00
☐ any issue, 1889	8.00	11.50	9.50
☐ September, 1900	6.50	9.00	8.00
☐ complete year, 1910	65.00	87.50	75.00
☐ complete year, 1916	65.00	87.50	75.00
☐ June, 1922	5.00	7.00	6.00
☐ September, 1932	3.75	5.50	4.50

HARPER'S BAZAAR

☐ Vol. 1, #1, November, 1867	13.00	19.00	16.00
☐ most issues, 1872	7.00	10.00	8.00
☐ complete year, 1883 or 1884	90.00	135.00	115.00
☐ complete year, 1892	100.00	150.00	120.00
☐ complete year, 1900	120.00	170.00	140.00
☐ complete year, 1914	70.00	105.00	82.00
☐ complete year, 1925	90.00	130.00	110.00
☐ most issues, 1929	6.75	9.50	7.75
☐ complete year, 1943	50.00	70.00	60.00
☐ most issues, 1966-70	1.50	2.25	1.80

LIFE

☐ Vol. 19, #1, November 23, 1936	175.00	250.00	210.00
☐ most issues, 1937	22.00	30.00	25.00
☐ most issues, 1940	17.00	27.00	22.00
☐ complete year, 1948	440.00	525.00	480.00
☐ most issues, 1950-51	7.00	10.00	8.50
☐ most issues, 1961-65	3.75	5.25	4.25
☐ complete year, 1968 or 1969	130.00	170.00	150.00

LOOK

☐ Vol. 1, #2, February, 1937 (first issue distributed)	22.00	30.00	26.00
☐ other issues, 1937	14.00	22.00	18.00
☐ most issues, 1938	12.00	18.00	15.00
☐ complete year, 1938	150.00	210.00	180.00
☐ most issues, 1940	11.00	16.00	13.00

548 / MAGAZINES

	Current Price Range		Prior Year Average
☐ most issues, 1941-45	14.00	22.00	18.00
☐ most issues, 1947	6.00	9.00	7.50
☐ complete year, 1974	56.00	77.00	62.00
☐ complete year, 1975	51.00	70.00	62.00
☐ complete year, 1976	46.00	63.00	52.00
☐ complete year, 1977	42.00	58.00	50.00
☐ most issues, 1978-80	.75	1.00	.85

NATIONAL GEOGRAPHIC

☐ Vol. 1, #1, 1888, rare	500.00	700.00	600.00
☐ Vol. 1, #2, 1888	175.00	275.00	225.00
☐ most issues, 1889	125.00	175.00	150.00
☐ most issues, 1896	35.00	50.00	42.00
☐ most issues, 1906-07	26.00	33.00	28.00
☐ most issues, 1913	21.00	30.00	25.00
☐ complete year, 1927	130.00	170.00	145.00
☐ complete year, 1935	105.00	135.00	120.00
☐ complete year, 1940	80.00	105.00	90.00
☐ most issues, 1947	3.50	5.25	4.25
☐ most issues, 1952	2.25	3.25	2.75
☐ most issues, 1966-70	1.00	2.00	1.50

NEW YORKER

☐ Vol. 1, #1, February 21, 1925	16.00	27.00	21.00
☐ most issues, 1930-33	8.00	11.00	9.00
☐ most issues, 1950	4.00	5.75	4.50
☐ most issues, 1961-65	2.50	3.50	3.00
☐ most issues, 1976-80	1.00	1.50	1.25

PLAYBOY

☐ Vol. 1, #1, 1953	375.00	500.00	420.00
☐ most issues, 1954	42.00	65.00	52.00
☐ February, 1956 — Jayne Mansfield	44.00	68.00	55.00
☐ March, 1958 — Brigette Bardot	28.00	35.00	31.00
☐ April, 1959 — Tina Louise	19.00	26.75	22.00
☐ October, 1960 — "Girls of Hollywwod"	10.00	15.00	12.00
☐ December, 1960 — Marilyn Monroe	37.00	50.00	42.00
☐ October, 1962 — "Girls of London"	10.00	15.00	12.00
☐ January, 1963 — Elizabeth Taylor	20.00	30.00	24.00
☐ February, 1964 — Mamie Van Doren	10.00	15.00	11.00
☐ May, 1964 — Playmates of the year	11.00	16.00	12.00
☐ February, 1965 — Beatles, interview	20.00	27.00	23.00
☐ June, 1965 — Ursula Andress	9.00	12.00	10.50
☐ January, 1966 — "Playmates Review"	7.00	10.00	8.50
☐ June, 1966 — "Girls of Texas"	7.00	10.00	8.00
☐ December, 1967 — Johnny Carson, interview	7.00	10.00	8.00
☐ December, 1968 — "Girls of the Orient"	7.00	10.00	8.50
☐ April, 1969 — Brigette Bardot	9.00	12.00	10.50
☐ December, 1969 — Joe Namath, interview	8.00	11.00	9.00
☐ September, 1970 — Peter Fonda, interview	8.00	11.00	9.00
☐ May, 1972 — Barbi Benton, Valerie Perrine	6.00	9.00	7.50
☐ January, 1973 — "Playmate Review"	7.00	10.00	8.00
☐ July 1973 — "James Bond's Girls"	7.00	10.00	8.00
☐ February, 1974 — Clint Eastwood, interview	5.00	8.00	6.50

	Current Price Range		Prior Year Average
☐ December, 1974 — Robert Redford, interview ...	5.00	8.00	6.50
☐ June, 1975 — "Playmate of the Year"	5.00	8.00	6.50
☐ January, 1976 — Elton John, interview	5.00	8.00	6.50
☐ September, 1976 — David Bowie, interview	5.00	7.50	6.50
☐ February, 1977 — "Playmate Review"	4.00	6.25	5.10
☐ December, 1977 — John Denver, interview	5.00	7.50	6.00
☐ May, 1978 — Anita Bryant, interview	3.50	5.00	4.25
☐ October, 1978 — Dolly Parton	4.00	6.00	5.00
☐ December, 1978 — Farrah Fawcett	4.50	6.75	5.25

POPULAR MECHANICS

☐ Vol. 1, #1, 1902	32.00	48.00	40.00
☐ December, 1907	16.00	25.00	20.00
☐ September, 1909	14.00	20.00	18.00
☐ complete year, 1915 or 1916	190.00	280.00	230.00
☐ complete year, 1924 or 1925	150.00	200.00	175.00
☐ complete year, 1932	120.00	160.00	140.00
☐ complete year, 1943	115.00	155.00	135.00
☐ most issues, 1961-65	3.00	4.75	3.80

PUNCH

☐ Vol. 1, #1, July 17, 1841	16.00	29.00	23.00
☐ most issues, 1847	10.00	14.50	12.00
☐ most issues, 1855	8.00	12.00	10.00
☐ most issues, 1864	8.00	12.00	10.00
☐ most issues, 1881	6.00	9.00	7.50
☐ most issues, 1892	4.00	6.00	5.00
☐ most issues, 1911-13	2.50	3.75	3.25
☐ most issues, 1922	2.00	3.00	2.50
☐ most issues, 1931-33	1.25	2.00	1.00

REDBOOK

☐ Vol. 1, #1, May, 1903	7.00	10.00	8.50
☐ complete year, 1911	42.00	65.00	48.00
☐ complete year, 1927 or 1928	40.00	60.00	50.00
☐ complete year, 1935	27.00	40.00	32.00
☐ most issues, 1942-44	1.50	2.25	1.80
☐ most issues, 1958	1.00	1.75	1.38

SATURDAY EVENING POST

☐ most issues, 1872	8.00	11.00	9.00
☐ complete year, 1899	580.00	725.00	640.00
☐ most issues, 1911	10.00	16.00	13.00
☐ complete year, 1922	320.00	400.00	350.00
☐ most issues, 1931	4.00	6.00	5.00

TIME

☐ complete year, 1924	320.00	450.00	380.00
☐ complete year, 1930	260.00	325.00	290.00
☐ complete year, 1943	365.00	550.00	510.00
☐ complete year, 1947	220.00	270.00	280.00

550 / MAGICIANS' MEMORABILIA

	Current Price Range		Prior Year Average
☐ JFK Assassination issue, 1963	12.00	18.00	15.00
☐ Nixon resignation issue, 1974	4.00	6.00	5.00

TV GUIDE

☐ most issues, 1953	14.00	20.00	17.00
☐ complete year, 1955	610.00	770.00	680.00
☐ most issues, 1957	9.00	12.75	11.00
☐ most issues, 1959	7.00	10.00	8.00
☐ most issues, 1961	5.25	8.00	6.50
☐ complete year, 1963	215.00	260.00	235.00

MAGICIANS' MEMORABILIA

Magicians' memorabilia is collected by amateur professional magicians as well as enthusiasts of theatrical collectibles. Some collectors make a science of the history of magic, an extremely intriguing topic, and collect — in addition to memorabilia — books and other research material. Basically, the field of magicians' memorabilia encompasses posters, photographs, personal items (which may be difficult to authenticate), and actual trick devices. The avid hobbyist is also likely to be interested in magic catalogues, some of which were large and lavish around the turn of the century and are now quite valuable. Many of the old trick devices, going back to the 1800's, are still in use, with modifications, today. Although much of this material is not really scarce, it can be difficult to find because the average antique and collectible dealers do not handle it. You may do better checking the classified ad sections of hobbyist newspapers for offerings by specialist dealers or from other collectors who have duplicates to dispose of.

☐ "Chung Lung Soo," colored poster, early 1900's	325.00	375.00	345.00
☐ Harry Houdini, 8" x 10" b/w photo, signed and inscribed, c. 1920	90.00	120.00	102.00
☐ Harry Houdini, small card printed with address of Houdini in holograph	28.00	35.00	31.00
☐ Harry Houdini, "challenge" poster, to be carried out on a London stage, c. 1910	45.00	55.00	50.00
☐ Kellar, 8" x 10" photo of Kellar, dressed in tophat, signed with lengthy description, c. 1910	95.00	120.00	105.00
☐ Kellar, silk hat in velvet-lined box	60.00	85.00	70.00
☐ "Lorenz the Miraculous Magician," letterhead, with holograph letter	45.00	60.00	52.00
☐ Matinka & Co., magic catalogue, New York, c. 1898	90.00	120.00	100.00
☐ "Bosco" the magician, poster, color, c. 1900	110.00	145.00	125.00
☐ "The Headless Countryman," c. 1910	320.00	390.00	350.00
☐ "The Second Advent of Rip Van Winkle," trick sold originally for 30 pounds, c. 1910	170.00	210.00	190.00
☐ "Thurston the Great Magician," full color poster, four sections, rare, 9' x 7', c. 1914	1250.00	1750.00	1450.00
☐ Thurston, 8" x 10" b/w photo, performing trick, signed, painted, glazed wooden frame	70.00	90.00	80.00

MAPS

World Map, Antwerp, 1545, from Apianus Cosmographia **$600.00-650.00**

Old maps have both historical and artistic appeal — and can have a considerable cash value as well. Maps as old as the 1400's are on the market, and in terms of size you'll find miniature maps — smaller than a playing card — all the way to sectioned wall maps that cover nearly 100 square feet. The value of an old map is determined largely by the age, the area depicted, the mapmaker if known, ornateness, scarcity, and physical condition. Though age is important, "old" for one type of map might not be old for another. For example, a map of Oklahoma Territory printed in 1850 would definitely qualify as early, but a map of England from that same year would hardly arouse interest because of its age. Also, the *specialization* of a map affects the value. Large territories — such as whole continents — were so often shown in maps that a specimen would need to be very early or unusual in some way to have special appeal. Individual *towns, counties and villages* were much less frequently depicted, and any map of fairly early origin of a locality is sure to be of interest. The majority of old maps found on the market were published originally as part of atlases, even those of immense size. (Some old atlases were of gargantuan proportions.) Folds are not considered a defect in maps, so long as the paper is not separating at the fold. Many maps, including some of those in books, were issued folded and cannot be found any other way. The best way of storing maps is to have them matted and framed, but if you have a large collection and framing is not practical, the alternative is to keep them between sheets of stiff paper in large folders. They can even be indexed in this way if you choose.

552 / MEDALS

	Current Price Range		Prior Year Average
☐ **America,** new map, by John Cary, colored outline, 20″ x 23″, c. 1806	24.00	33.00	28.00
☐ **America,** by J. D'Anville, colored, mounted on linen, 21¼″ x 31¾″, c. 1797	130.00	170.00	150.00
☐ **Central America** by W. R. Palmer, Washington, D.C., undated, outline colored, 45″ x 42″	80.00	110.00	90.00
☐ **East Indian,** chart by Aaron Arrowsmith, engraved, tinted, mounted on linen, c. 1800	75.00	100.00	85.00
☐ **England, Surrey,** by Joannus Blaeu, partly colored, no date (1600's)	190.00	240.00	210.00
☐ **Greece,** by Aaron Arrowsmith, colored, outlined, c. 1824	19.00	28.00	23.00
☐ **Louisiana,** by J. D'Anville, 16″ x 21″, c. 1788	110.00	140.00	125.00
☐ **New York,** colored, 17½″ x 21½″, c. 1836	36.00	44.00	40.00
☐ **North America,** by J. D'Anville, colored outline, 17″ x 22½″, c. 1752	110.00	145.00	130.00
☐ **North America and the West Indies,** by Sayer and Bennett, colored outline, 21″ x 26½″, c. 1783	210.00	270.00	240.00
☐ **North Carolina,** new and accurate, 10½″ x 24″, c. 1779	58.00	67.00	62.00
☐ **Oxford County,** by John Cary, c. 1797	400.00	500.00	440.00
☐ **South Carolina,** by William DeBrahm, two sheets, colored, total size 26½″ x 48″, c. 1757	420.00	530.00	470.00
☐ **United States,** by Amos Lay, colored, mounted on linen, 52″ x 61″, c. 1834	285.00	330.00	305.00
☐ **United States of North America,** by Aaron Arrowsmith, engraved and hand colored, c. 1796	310.00	360.00	320.00
☐ **Venezuela,** by Wilhelm Blaeu, colored, 14¾″ x 19″, c. 1740	32.00	40.00	36.00

MEDALS

These are *decorations,* not to be confused with numismatic medals. Military and other official decorations and awards have been issued by most governments since the 19th century, and from a much earlier time in some cases. They have strong collecting appeal, because they generally carry high-grade artwork, are cast in an intrinsically valuable metal and always bear some kind of history behind them whether great or small. The most celebrated decorations, the Victoria Cross and Purple Heart, are rare, and rarer still in circulation as they tend normally to pass from one generation to the next of a family without getting on the market. Within recent years, investors have competed strongly for the few specimens being sold. This has driven prices up to extraordinary levels. If you cannot afford medals in this class, there are many others of a less expensive variety, such as those awarded to victors in sporting contests.

Medal of Honnor, Navy.......................... **$425.00-$475.00**

	Current Price Range		Prior Year Average
☐ American Presidential Life Saving Medal, c. 1857	1600.00	1900.00	1700.00
☐ Award medal, bicycling, nickel-plated, c. 1900 ...	30.00	40.00	34.00
☐ Award medal, tug-of-war, nickel-plated, c. 1900 ..	30.00	40.00	34.00
☐ Breast Staff of the Most Noble Order of the Garter, second quarter of the 19th c.	3200.00	3700.00	3400.00
☐ England Seven Bar Naval General Service Medal (Napoleonic Wars), only one specimen of this medal is believed to exist	5750.00	6500.00	6100.00
☐ Ireland, James I, gold and enamel badge for the London Society, c. 1620	4100.00	4600.00	4300.00
☐ Italy, Sicily, order of St. Januarius, gold and enamel, mid 19th c.	2700.00	3200.00	2900.00
☐ Knight's Badge of the Order of St. Patrick, gold, c. 1809	3300.00	3900.00	3600.00
☐ Naval General Service Medal, two bars, c. 1793-1840	1900.00	2300.00	2100.00
☐ Peninsular War, Military General Service Medal (English), with eleven battle clasps	1100.00	1500.00	1300.00
☐ Royal National Lifeboat Institute, gold medal (saving a life)	1000.00	1400.00	1200.00
☐ Star of the Most Noble Order of the Garter	2100.00	2500.00	2250.00
☐ Victoria Cross, lion and crown with motto, "For Valour"	8000.00	10000.00	9000.00

MENUS

The value of old menus depends upon their age, size, decorative appeal and whether or not they bear autographs of famous persons. This is still a small hobby, and has not yet reached the point where values are set depending on the restaurant from which the menu originates. However, most collectors are anxious to have menus from famous restaurants and will usually pay a premium price for them — say $5 for a New York "Stork Club" or (with some sports interest added) a "Jack Dempsey's." In the case of restaurants still in operation (the two just mentioned aren't), older specimens are more desirable, the older the better. Menus from still-active restaurants bring only $1 or $2 if current or fairly recent. In fact, most menus sell for no more than $5.00.

Valuable menus. Among the most valuable menus are those written by hand on wooden boards, which adorned the walls of early American and foreign taverns. The fare was simple and the prices ridiculously low by modern standards. All during the 18th century and well into the 19th, it was the custom of taverns to post menus rather than distribute printed copies to each diner. A few dishes would be listed along with beverages. Often the menu carried the establishment's name and symbol (bull and bear, etc.), along with "rules of the house" if there happened to be rooms for rent. They can be large, sometimes a yard or more in height, and can be quite decorative. The board might be carved and the lettering handsomely painted. The *values* of board menus depend on the age, place of origin, visual appeal and, of course, physical condition. Since these factors are so variable, it is almost impossible to set price guidelines. A very rough idea of prices is as follows:

	Current Price Range		Prior Year Average
☐ **California,** 1850-1880 (most)	1200.00	2500.00	1800.00
☐ **California,** 1880-1910 (most)	400.00	700.00	550.00
☐ **Midwestern U.S.,** 1860-1890 (most)	600.00	1000.00	800.00
☐ **Midwestern U.S.,** 1890-1910 (most)	200.00	350.00	270.00
☐ **New England,** pre-1800	800.00	1200.00	1000.00
☐ **New England,** large size, 1800-1859	600.00	1000.00	800.00
☐ **New York City,** pre-1800	1200.00	1700.00	1400.00
☐ **New York City,** depending on size, 1800-1850	700.00	1200.00	900.00
☐ **Old West,** to 1890	800.00	7500.00	3500.00
☐ **Southern States,** with listing of many dishes, 1800-1850	2500.00	3500.00	3000.00
☐ **Southwestern U.S.,** 1890-1910 (most)	350.00	600.00	460.00

Printed Wall menus. Printed wall menus, while not as valuable as those written by hand, are nevertheless very collectible and can run into several hundred dollars if early, decorative, etc. Specimens in the original frames, even if broken, are much preferred over modern frames.

A problem with some early menus of the "wall" type is that they do not state the place of origin — merely the establishment's name, and sometimes not even that. The collector must then search through old town directories or other records.

White House menus. The single most popular group of menus among collectors is that of special White House dinners, balls and other affairs. Menus for Presidential inaugural ball dinners are worth $30 and up, depending on the president. Their scarcity is, however, difficult to calculate. Presumably, there should be in existence just one menu for each person attending, but one never knows whether the printer ran off extra copies to sell to collectors.

Signed menus. The value of signed menus depends on the value of the signature. These are more common than you might think; restaurants are good hunting-grounds for collectors seeking celebrity autographs, and often the only available paper is a menu. Among the most creative signed menus are those of the opera star Caruso, who often drew caricatures on them. A good caricature menu by Caruso is worth $200 to $250.

	Current Price Range		Prior Year Average
☐ **Hand-painted bill of fare,** unnamed tavern, believed to be Midwest. Flat-cut wooden board with decorative top (spindles at either side), the board painted cream color, lettering in black ink applied with a thin brush, more than 100 items listed, overall size 22″ x 31″, c. 1875	1500.00	2250.00	1800.00
☐ **Silver Star Cafe** (location unknown, thought to be southwestern U.S.), hand-lettered bill of fare on wooden board. The board shellacked and painted over in various colors with decorations, artistic lettering, etc. Few dishes listed, along with house rules. 18½″ x 33⅔″, c. 1910	500.00	700.00	600.00
☐ **Washington Inn** (probably New Hampshire or Vermont), hand-lettered bill of fare on thick wooden board. The board is whitewashed, with list of dishes and prices lettered in dark brown paint. Corners worn down, some of the painted surface cracked, 13″ x 18½″ x 1½″, c. 1835	475.00	650.00	550.00

METALS

BRASS

Brass, an alloy of copper and zinc, has been used since ancient times. The brassware collector literally has the world at his feet, as there have been cultures which did not, at one time or other, make objects of brass. It has been used in artwork, but mainly in utilitarian household objects and such things as uniform buttons, toys and novelties. Coins have occasionally been made of brass, especially in the ancient Roman Empire. While the listing provided here is very general, in an effort to be comprehensive in the small available space, it is advisable for collectors to narrow their interest down a bit. There is just too much available for indiscriminate general collecting. Choose doorknockers, candlesticks, inkwells or whatever suits you — and you'll find an ample supply in the antiques shops. Brass can usually be distinguished rather easily from copper because the color is lighter and more yellowish. When an item is very old and has some corrosion the distinction may be more difficult to draw.

556 / METALS

		Current Price Range		Prior Year Average
☐	**Anvil,** 5″ x 2¼″	24.00	38.00	31.00
☐	**Ashtray,** Art Nouveau maiden, outstretched arms, 7″ x 3½″	30.00	45.00	37.50
☐	**Ashtray,** shape of bulldog's head, 4½″ H.	17.00	25.00	21.00
☐	**Bell,** gong-shaped alarm with trip hammer, 14″ H.	72.00	100.00	83.00
☐	**Bird cage,** three singing birds, movable heads, 18″ H.	650.00	850.00	750.00
☐	**Bookends,** pair of sailing ships, 4″ L.	17.00	25.00	21.00
☐	**Book rack,** Art Nouveau lady and flowers	35.00	45.00	40.00
☐	**Bowl,** dragons on teak stand, 10″ Dia.	20.00	28.00	24.00
☐	**Bowl,** etched cow, trees and men, W. Wettemberg	13.50	20.00	16.50
☐	**Bowl,** rice, figures, 5″ H.	65.00	85.00	75.00
☐	**Box,** butterfly on dome lid, inlaid, 2¾″ H	50.00	65.00	57.50
☐	**Box,** Chinese dragon on lid, 4″ x 3¼″	11.00	16.50	13.50
☐	**Box,** Lincoln Memorial, Jacoby-Benz, 5″ x 2″	55.00	78.00	66.00
☐	**Box,** Oriental with jade trim, 2½″ x 4″	27.50	40.00	33.50
☐	**Box,** stamped, shape of fly, 3″ x 2″ x 1½″	9.00	13.00	11.00
☐	**Calling card holder,** ornate	38.00	50.00	44.00
☐	**Candelabrum,** Chinese, five arms, 9″ x 8″	13.00	20.00	16.50
☐	**Candelabrum,** scrolls, three arms, 6¾″ H.	8.00	11.00	9.50
☐	**Candelabrum,** seven candles, 18″ H.	240.00	330.00	265.00
☐	**Candelabrum,** supported by two lions, three arms, 11½″ H.	35.00	50.00	42.50
☐	**Candlesticks,** beehive and diamond pattern, pair, 12″ H.	155.00	210.00	180.00
☐	**Candlesticks,** engraved bases, floral design, pair, 7½″ H.	38.00	52.00	45.00
☐	**Candlesticks,** English, 4½″ H., c. 1890	38.00	52.00	45.00
☐	**Candlesticks,** Chlinese flowers and medallions, 8¼″ H.	13.00	20.00	16.50
☐	**Candlesticks,** Louis XVI, pair, 10½″ H.	175.00	225.00	200.00
☐	**Candlesticks,** push-up, 11½″ H., c. 1901	210.00	265.00	235.00
☐	**Candlesticks,** Russian, footed, 10″ H.	45.00	60.00	52.00
☐	**Candlesticks,** Storrar's Chester, push-up, pair, 10″ H.	60.00	80.00	70.00
☐	**Candlesticks,** turtle, holder on turtle's back, pair, 3″ H.	20.00	25.00	22.50
☐	**Chestnut roaster,** brass handles, 18″ L.	95.00	125.00	110.00
☐	**Coal box,** ornate coal scoop, ball feet, 12″ x 16″ x 17″	265.00	330.00	285.00
☐	**Coffeepot,** Russian, long spout, 9″ H.	100.00	150.00	125.00
☐	**Compote,** three-footed base, 6″ x 4″	70.00	95.00	82.00
☐	**Cup,** nickel-plated, folds in, 1½″ H.	9.00	13.00	11.00
☐	**Cuspidor,** 12″ H.	95.00	125.00	110.00
☐	**Desk set,** Chinese, four piece	90.00	120.00	105.00
☐	**Doorbell,** fire gong, 7″ H.	55.00	78.00	66.00
☐	**Doorknocker,** anchor, c. 1920	13.00	20.00	16.50
☐	**Doorknocker,** Oriental deer, 4¼″ H.	20.00	27.00	23.00
☐	**Doorknocker,** lady's hand	20.00	26.00	23.00
☐	**Doorknocker,** William Wordsworth bust, 2½″ H.	45.00	65.00	55.00
☐	**Ewer,** Russian, turned lip, 17″ H.	85.00	125.00	105.00
☐	**Figurine,** cigarette holder in shape of a camel	6.50	10.00	8.50
☐	**Fire hose nozzle**	100.00	125.00	112.50
☐	**Foot warmer,** oval, pierced, wood handle	100.00	145.00	123.00
☐	**Frame** (easel), 6½″ x 5″	6.50	11.00	9.00

METALS / 557

	Current Price Range		Prior Year Average
☐ **Frame,** heart-shaped, 2⅛″ H.	33.00	50.00	42.00
☐ **Gong,** engraved, flowers with animals	42.00	57.00	49.50
☐ **Hatpin,** head of Indian	16.50	24.00	20.00
☐ **Heel plate,** heart-shaped cutouts	30.00	43.00	36.00
☐ **Horse head,** circled by horseshoe, 3″ H.	25.00	32.00	29.00
☐ **Humidor,** china, painted cover, enameled bands	95.00	120.00	107.00
☐ **Incense burner,** Chinese, small	13.00	20.00	16.50
☐ **Inkwell,** crab, pewter inside well, 6″ x 5″	60.00	85.00	72.00
☐ **Inkwell,** German devil figure	100.00	125.00	112.50
☐ **Inkwell,** double, Harvard cut glass, pen rest	150.00	175.00	162.00
☐ **Inkwell,** heart-shaped, 3½″ H.	200.00	255.00	228.00
☐ **Inkwell,** lid with owl's head, 11″ H.	210.00	260.00	235.00
☐ **Inkwell,** ornate, glass insert	88.00	125.00	115.00
☐ **Jardiniere,** ball feet, 8″ H., 10″ Dia.	82.00	120.00	99.00
☐ **Jardiniere,** deer head handle, 10″ H.	178.00	230.00	200.00
☐ **Jardiniere,** 5″ x 5″	65.00	90.00	77.00
☐ **Lamp and heater,** nautical design	95.00	135.00	115.00
☐ **Lamp,** candlestick style, pair, 19″ H.	55.00	70.00	82.00
☐ **Letter opener,** dog's head, 10¼″ H.	13.00	20.00	16.50
☐ **Mailbox,** combination lock	6.00	8.00	7.00
☐ **Match holder,** caricature of man	45.00	55.00	50.00
☐ **Match safe,** horseback rider	35.00	42.00	38.50
☐ **Mold,** spoon, tapered wavy handle, 8″ L.	305.00	385.00	340.00
☐ **Mold,** spoon, c. 1790	355.00	440.00	395.00
☐ **Nutcracker,** parrot figure, 5½″ H.	34.00	47.00	41.50
☐ **Nutcracker,** rooster figure	13.00	20.00	16.50
☐ **Opener,** bottle, elephant figure	6.50	10.00	8.00
☐ **Opener,** letter, bust of devil	4.50	6.50	5.50
☐ **Opener,** letter, stork figure	5.00	7.00	6.00
☐ **Pan,** iron handle, 6″ x 3″ x 7″	95.00	125.00	110.00
☐ **Pan,** iron handle, 8″ x 4″ x 9″	110.00	150.00	130.00
☐ **Pancake flipper,** decorative handle	35.00	50.00	42.00
☐ **Paperclip,** English, man reading book, 3¾″ L.	25.00	33.00	29.00
☐ **Paperclip,** Palmer Cox brownie, 2½″ H.	30.00	40.00	35.00
☐ **Paperweight,** dragon design, 5″ L.	45.00	60.00	52.00
☐ **Paperweight,** embossed foliage design, 4″ L.	13.50	19.00	15.00
☐ **Pitcher,** 23″ H.	305.00	385.00	345.00
☐ **Pot,** three legs, 8½″ x 7″	45.00	60.00	52.50
☐ **Powder box,** painted scene, 2½″ H.	100.00	125.00	112.50
☐ **Sconce,** wall hanging, pair	105.00	125.00	115.00
☐ **Sconce,** wall hanging, two-arm Victorian, pair	110.00	135.00	122.50
☐ **Sconce,** wall hanging, three-arm, pair, 15½″ H.	355.00	495.00	355.00
☐ **Screen,** fireplace, scene of town	175.00	220.00	198.00
☐ **Seal,** figure of girl, 5″ H.	110.00	150.00	130.00
☐ **Silent butler,** embossed floral lid	20.00	28.00	24.00
☐ **Snuff box,** decorative	190.00	228.00	205.00
☐ **Spittoon,** 11″ H.	145.00	200.00	175.00
☐ **Strainer,** tea, cupid handle	20.00	25.00	22.50
☐ **Tea caddy,** decorative, 5¼″ x 4¼″	78.00	100.00	89.00
☐ **Tea caddy,** octagon shape, 5½″	25.00	32.00	29.00
☐ **Teakettle,** Chinese motif	45.00	60.00	52.00
☐ **Teakettle,** on stand	65.00	82.00	71.00
☐ **Teapot,** decorative, 8″ H.	35.00	50.00	42.00
☐ **Teaspoon,** Chinese floral	6.50	10.00	8.50
☐ **Telescope,** small, extends to 7″ L.	36.00	50.00	41.00
☐ **Tieback,** decorative, pair	5.50	9.00	7.50

558 / METALS

	Current Price Range	Prior Year Average
☐ Tray, folk art, sports award, c. 1880	100.00 130.00	115.00
☐ Tray, floral design, 10½″ L.	30.00 38.00	34.00
☐ Tray, raised design of an elk, 5″ x 6″	55.00 72.00	64.00
☐ Tray, oval shaped, hammered, 9½″ x 15″	122.00 145.00	133.00
☐ Vase, enamel, painted, Japanese	20.00 25.00	22.50
☐ Vase, engraved symbols, 8″ H.	19.00 25.00	22.00
☐ Warmer, bed, 15″ L.	190.00 230.00	210.00
☐ Whistle, conductor's, two-barrel	13.00 19.00	16.00
☐ Whistle, steam, 13½″ L.	50.00 65.00	57.00

COPPER

Copper is a natural ore, not made (as is brass) by alloying two or more metals. In manufacturing it is sometimes used as is, and sometimes combined with other metals depending on the circumstances. Copper is handsome, fairly durable, heavy in weight (but not as heavy as gold or silver), and takes decoration very well in a variety of mediums. Perhaps the most pleasing quality of old copper is the manner in which it tones, or changes surface color with age. Old copper is sometimes a deep reddish brown. It can also tone to a strong mahogany, burgundy, orange, or other colors, even though all copper is originally the same color (pale brown). The degree and color of toning is caused by atmospheric conditions. An item kept near a fireplace will tone differently than one in an attic. Differences in toning are most strikingly noticeable on old copper coins, such as the U.S. Large Cent. When an encrustation appears on the surface of old copper (usually greenish), this is known as patina. It is usually advisable not to remove it.

NOTE: Reproductions are made.

	Current Price Range	Prior Year Average
☐ Bed warmer, wooden handle, perforated design	155.00 200.00	188.00
☐ Boiler, wash, brass and copper with bail and handle	65.00 95.00	80.00
☐ Burnished copper pan, two iron handles, 8″ deep, 23″ Dia.	80.00 110.00	98.00
☐ Candlesnuffer	5.50 9.00	6.75
☐ Candy kettle, circular, two handles, three iron feet, 5½″ deep, 12″ Dia.	150.00 200.00	175.00
☐ Coal hod, helmet type, lacquered and polished, 16″ H.	205.00 260.00	232.00
☐ Coffeepot, pewter trim, copper body, straight spout	100.00 135.00	117.50
☐ Coffeepot, lacquered, 10″ H.	95.00 120.00	107.00
☐ Compote, pierced open-work design	65.00 90.00	78.00
☐ Cooking pan, cast, heavy iron handle, 6″ deep, 12½″ Dia.	55.00 78.00	66.00
☐ Dipper, polished and lacquered	90.00 120.00	105.00
☐ Dow pot, Dutch-type, large and heavy	210.00 255.00	235.00
☐ Funnel, with handle	50.00 65.00	57.00
☐ Jug, for water, with hinged cover, 8″ H.	745.00 880.00	815.00
☐ Kettle, 18″ H.	175.00 230.00	210.00
☐ Kettle, 24″ H.	200.00 260.00	230.00
☐ Milk tank, 10-gallon capacity, handles, spout and lid	180.00 225.00	105.00
☐ Megaphone, from sailing ship, 36″ H.	125.00 155.00	140.00
☐ Mold, 2¼″ L.	30.00 40.00	35.00

	Current Price Range		Prior Year Average
☐ **Mug,** beer	30.00	38.00	34.00
☐ **Pan,** iron handle, 10″ Dia., 7½″ L.	100.00	128.00	114.00
☐ **Pail,** 11″ Dia.	82.00	110.00	96.00
☐ **Pail,** 16″ Dia.	100.00	130.00	115.00
☐ **Pitcher,** small	18.00	25.00	22.00
☐ **Saucepan,** covered and lacquered, iron handle, 12″ L.	95.00	120.00	107.00
☐ **Skillet,** iron handle, 9¾″ Dia.	100.00	125.00	112.00
☐ **Sap bucket,** large with iron handles	275.00	360.00	320.00
☐ **Teakettle,** early American, gooseneck spout, 12″ H.*	240.00	320.00	240.00
☐ **Teapot,** lacquered, tin-lined, hinged spout	90.00	120.00	105.00
☐ **Tray,** oval-shaped, embossed handles	95.00	125.00	110.00
☐ **Umbrella stand,** lion head handles	75.00	95.00	85.00
☐ **Vase,** sterling silver inlay in floral design, c. 1900's	110.00	150.00	130.00
☐ **Wash basin,** burnished, 6″ deep, 14″ Dia.	78.00	100.00	90.00
☐ **Watercan,** 15″ H.	90.00	120.00	105.00

Early American hallmarked teakettles — $400.00-$550.00

IRONWARE

Ironware is the most basic and probably the most plentiful of all collectible metalwares. In early times the village blacksmith provided his community with most of their cooking utensils, tools, and farming implements. Because he customarily worked in iron, he chose this material automatically for most of the things he crafted, even if it was not especially decorative. Iron had strength and durability on its side, and for most of the original buyers that was recommendation enough. Ironware began to be produced in America very soon after the establishment of colonist villages, and continued until well past the Revolution. Items dating to the colonial era are of course the most highly prized but are scarce. Most of the ancient-looking pieces found on the antiques market are not colonial, but of later origin; they appear early because the style of workmanship is crude. It really requires the knowledge of an expert to accurately tell the age of antique ironware. A good suggestion for the beginner is to make a careful inspection of specimens in museums, and get to know the look of ironware of various ages. Modern reproductions are quite plentiful, but on the whole are not especially troublesome to detect.

☐ **Ashtray and pipe rest,** black and white Scottie dog	20.00	25.00	22.00
☐ **Ashtray,** bowling symbols	22.00	30.00	26.00
☐ **Anvil,** small	10.00	13.50	11.70
☐ **Bathtub,** miniature, 5½″ L.	50.00	70.00	60.00
☐ **Bedwarmer,** wooden handle, 36″ L.	110.00	155.00	132.00
☐ **Bootjack,** bug design	4.50	6.50	5.50
☐ **Bootjack,** cricket design	35.00	45.00	40.00
☐ **Bootjack,** double-ended for men's and ladies' boots	13.00	20.00	16.50
☐ **Box,** treasure chest, with dividers, brass finish	22.00	35.00	28.00
☐ **Bracket** (shelf), decorative, pair, 17″ x 13½″	20.00	25.00	22.00
☐ **Broiler,** three feet, early, 12″ Dia.	210.00	255.00	232.00
☐ **Burner,** incense	8.00	11.00	9.50

560 / METALS

	Current Price Range		Prior Year Average
☐ **Candelbra,** curved, painted holders for five candles	60.00	85.00	72.00
☐ **Candle snuffer,** tong type	28.00	36.00	32.00
☐ **Christmas tree stand,** three legs, two-piece, North Brothers Manufacturing Co.	22.00	30.00	26.00
☐ **Doorknocker,** basket of flowers	15.00	22.00	18.00
☐ **Doorknocker,** parrot	18.00	24.00	22.00
☐ **Doorknocker,** rose	8.00	11.00	9.50
☐ **Doorlatch,** leaf design, 9½" L.	78.00	100.00	87.00
☐ **Doorlatch,** Suffolk, 10⅞" L.	130.00	180.00	155.00
☐ **Doorstop,** Aunt Jemima	25.00	35.00	30.00
☐ **Doorstop,** bird	23.00	29.00	26.00
☐ **Doorstop,** Boston terrier	25.00	35.00	30.00
☐ **Doorstop,** coach and horses, pair	22.00	32.00	27.00
☐ **Doorstop,** elephant	52.00	72.00	62.00
☐ **Doorstop,** sailing ship, 11" L.	28.00	38.00	32.00
☐ **Doorstop,** sitting cat, 7" L.	22.00	32.00	27.00
☐ **Eagle,** wings spread, 40 lbs., 31" x 10"	255.00	320.00	290.00
☐ **Figurine,** buffalo, 9" L.	28.00	36.00	32.00
☐ **Figurine,** dog, pair, 1" H.	28.00	36.00	32.00
☐ **Figurine,** monkey, 3½" H.	20.00	27.00	23.50
☐ **Flowerpot holder,** wall hanging, 30" L.	28.00	36.00	32.00
☐ **Griddle,** 24" W.	10.00	13.00	11.50
☐ **Grinder,** table or counter type	15.00	22.00	18.50
☐ **Haircurling iron**	13.00	20.00	16.50
☐ **Hat rack,** six curved arms	60.00	80.00	70.00
☐ **Hinge,** for barn door, 42"	200.00	250.00	225.00
☐ **Hinges,** pair, 15" x 17"	145.00	190.00	168.00
☐ **Holder,** rush, spring, 20" L.	155.00	200.00	178.00
☐ **Hook,** boot, cast iron, U.S. Cavalry	4.50	6.50	5.50
☐ **Hook,** meat, 8¼" L.	40.00	50.00	45.00
☐ **Hook,** screw-in style, wall bracket, 8" L.	6.50	9.00	8.00
☐ **Horseshoe,** large	6.50	8.50	7.50
☐ **Irons,** box, cast iron with wooden handles	38.00	52.00	45.00
☐ **Irons,** charcoal, wooden handle with trivet, 10" L.	55.00	75.00	65.00
☐ **Irons,** fluting, three pieces	45.00	60.00	52.00
☐ **Irons,** sad, engraved floral design, hollow handle	13.00	20.00	16.50
☐ **Irons,** Taylors, embossed #12	20.00	28.00	24.00
☐ **Juicer,** Landers, Frary and Clar, New Britain, Ct.	35.00	50.00	42.00
☐ **Kettle,** arch handle, three-legged, 10-quart	28.00	40.00	34.00
☐ **Kettle,** round, on legs, 11" H., c. 1813	155.00	210.00	182.00
☐ **Key,** 6" L.	8.00	11.00	9.50
☐ **Ladle,** pouring cup	5.00	6.50	5.75
☐ **Latch,** Suffolk	45.00	60.00	52.00
☐ **Match holder,** two holders, animal design	30.00	40.00	35.00
☐ **Match holder,** wall hanging, floral	20.00	28.00	24.00
☐ **Match holder,** wall hanging with lid, 4¼" L.	25.00	35.00	30.00
☐ **Milk warmer,** long handle, footed, quart-size	36.00	50.00	42.00
☐ **Muffin pan,** eight cups	30.00	42.00	36.00
☐ **Nutcracker,** alligator	20.00	28.00	24.00
☐ **Nutcracker,** St. Bernard	32.00	40.00	36.00
☐ **Nutcracker,** marked Nestorm, England	25.00	32.00	28.00
☐ **Paperclip,** dog's head	55.00	72.00	62.00
☐ **Paperweight,** lady's figurine, 5" H.	42.00	55.00	48.00
☐ **Paperweight,** steam engine	22.00	30.00	26.00

	Current Price Range		Prior Year Average
☐ **Peeler,** apple	20.00	28.00	24.00
☐ **Pot,** hinged lid, curved handle, 3½" L.	16.00	22.00	19.00
☐ **Press,** meat	15.00	21.00	18.00
☐ **Pump,** cast iron	78.00	100.00	90.00
☐ **Rushlight holder,** 8" L.	120.00	155.00	138.00
☐ **Sausage stuffer,** 13" L.	55.00	75.00	65.00
☐ **Scraper,** shoe, dog, 12½" L.	100.00	130.00	115.00
☐ **Shoe,** oxen, patent, pair, c. 1880	17.00	25.00	21.00
☐ **Snow eagle,** 5" H.	35.00	45.00	40.00
☐ **Snuffer,** wick, scissors style	28.00	35.00	32.00
☐ **Spittoon,** turtle, 14" H.	110.00	135.00	122.00
☐ **Teakettle**	35.00	50.00	42.00
☐ **Teapot,** Japanese motif, signed, brass lid	120.00	150.00	135.00
☐ **Trivet,** triangular, 26" x 12"	78.00	100.00	90.00
☐ **Waffle iron,** decorative, 5" Dia., 10" L. handle	82.00	110.00	96.00
☐ **Warmer,** bed, cut-out tin cover, Vermont	140.00	175.00	158.00
☐ **Warmer,** bed, wooden handle, 36" L.	100.00	130.00	115.00

PEWTER

Pewter has a special attraction for American antiques collectors because the pewter industry was really more consequential, in early America, than in most other countries. A mixture of tin and lead, sometimes further combined with other metals, pewter has a resemblance to silver — and this is largely what brought it into popularity in early times. The well-to-do naturally wanted silver tableware and other household articles (if they were not well-to-do enough to have gold), and pewter served as a reasonable facsimile for the middle classes at a price they could afford. Originally, most pewterware carried a retail price of less than half as much as the same article in high-grade silver. Interestingly enough, the enthusiasm for old pewter among collectors has boosted up the values to a point where fine pewter is almost, though not quite, on a level with silver in price. The value of any individual piece will hinge on its maker (if known, which quite often it is not, because pewter was not usually under control of the hallmarking regulations), the time and place of manufacture, the style, the scarcity or unusualness of objects of that type, and any such considerations that are pertinent to the specimen. The most desirable American pewter is of course from the colonial era. This can be found in the higher grade antiques shops and at auction sales, but it brings almost uniformly high prices and may be "too much" for the beginner. Very fine pewter objects of the 19th century are more common and somewhat more easily affordable. Since pewter is rather soft, because of the lead content, surface scratches are almost inevitable.

☐ **Basin,** Austin, R., 8" Dia.	355.00	440.00	398.00
☐ **Basin,** Boardman, 8" Dia.	355.00	465.00	405.00
☐ **Basin,** Pierse, 8" Dia.	440.00	525.00	480.00
☐ **Basin,** unmarked, 6½" Dia.	242.00	320.00	286.00
☐ **Basin,** unmarked, 10½" Dia.	310.00	400.00	355.00
☐ **Beaker,** Dixon and Son, pint size	310.00	400.00	355.00
☐ **Beaker,** Griswold A.	525.00	745.00	620.00
☐ **Bedpan,** Boardman.	275.00	355.00	315.00
☐ **Bowl,** Compton and Leonard, 8" Dia.	220.00	300.00	260.00
☐ **Bowl,** Danforth S. Boardman T., 8" Dia.	500.00	650.00	575.00
☐ **Candlestick,** Dunham, 6" H.	230.00	310.00	270.00

562 / METALS

	Current Price Range		Prior Year Average
☐ **Candlestick,** J. B., 6″ H.	210.00	265.00	235.00
☐ **Candlesticks,** unmarked pair, 9″ H.	365.00	430.00	395.00
☐ **Candlesticks,** unmarked pair, 10″ H.	240.00	300.00	270.00
☐ **Candlesticks,** saucer-type, Gleason, pair, 8″	400.00	550.00	475.00
☐ **Chalice,** Boardman, 7½″ H.	368.00	500.00	440.00
☐ **Charger,** English, 17″ Dia.	310.00	400.00	355.00
☐ **Charger,** English, 18″ Dia.	385.00	500.00	440.00
☐ **Charger,** English, hallmarked, 20″ Dia.	450.00	575.00	515.00
☐ **Charger,** rose mark, 13½″ Dia,	220.00	300.00	260.00
☐ **Charger,** unmarked, 12″ Dia.	210.00	265.00	240.00
☐ **Chocolate pot,** Swiss manufacturer, 18th c.	230.00	310.00	270.00
☐ **Coffeepot,** Boardman	310.00	400.00	355.00
☐ **Coffeepot,** Dixon, I.	60.00	90.00	75.00
☐ **Coffeepot,** Dixon & Son, wooden handle, 10½″ H.	245.00	385.00	365.00
☐ **Coffeepot,** Dunham & Sons	330.00	440.00	385.00
☐ **Coffeepot,** Gleason	330.00	440.00	385.00
☐ **Coffeepot,** Leonard, Reed, & Barton, 9″ H., c. 1830	525.00	735.00	630.00
☐ **Coffeepot,** Porter, A., 6″ H.	550.00	735.00	640.00
☐ **Coffeepot,** Trask, I	635.00	800.00	715.00
☐ **Coffee urn,** footed base, Reed & Barton, 14″ H.	340.00	420.00	380.00
☐ **Communion set,** two chalices and two plates, 11″ H.	1750.00	2200.00	1950.00
☐ **Creamers,** Sheldon & Feltman, 5½″ H.	195.00	275.00	235.00
☐ **Cuspidor,** oval-shaped	210.00	280.00	245.00
☐ **Decanter funnel**	120.00	155.00	148.00
☐ **Deep dish,** Calder, Danforth or Barns	525.00	650.00	585.00
☐ **Flagon,** unmarked	460.00	550.00	505.00
☐ **Flagon,** Gleason, 10″ H.	1350.00	2000.00	1680.00
☐ **Foot warmer,** oval-shaped	155.00	245.00	200.00
☐ **Inkwell,** Whitcomb	110.00	155.00	135.00
☐ **Inkwell,** "Fish on Leaf"	355.00	465.00	405.00
☐ **Ladle** with wooden handle, unmarked, 13″ L.	110.00	155.00	135.00
☐ **Lamp,** Porter Co., burns whale oil	230.00	300.00	265.00
☐ **Mug,** curved handle, English, 19th c.	145.00	200.00	175.00
☐ **Mug,** with handle, Merey and Smith, 6″ H.	210.00	265.00	240.00
☐ **Pewter molds,** ice cream, apple, small to large	28.00	35.00	32.00
☐ **Pewter molds,** ice cream, boxer, small to large	30.00	38.00	34.00
☐ **Pewter molds,** ice cream, carrot, small to large	17.00	25.00	21.00
☐ **Pewter molds,** ice cream, daisy, small to large	38.00	60.00	50.00
☐ **Pewter molds,** ice cream, heart, small to large	18.50	27.50	23.00
☐ **Pewter molds,** ice cream, morning glory, small to large	35.00	44.00	40.00
☐ **Pewter molds,** ice cream, orange, small to large	32.00	42.00	37.00
☐ **Pewter molds,** ice cream, pear, small to large	30.00	40.00	35.00
☐ **Pewter molds,** ice cream, pig, small to large	45.00	75.00	60.00
☐ **Pewter molds,** ice cream, Santa, small to large	50.00	65.00	58.00
☐ **Pewter molds,** ice cream, swan, small to large	33.00	48.00	40.00
☐ **Pewter molds,** ice cream, turkey, small to large	35.00	50.00	42.00
☐ **Plates,** Austin, N., 8″ Dia.	330.00	440.00	375.00
☐ **Plates,** Austin Richard, 8″ Dia.	275.00	350.00	315.00
☐ **Plates,** Badger, T., 7½″ Dia.	320.00	410.00	365.00
☐ **Plates,** Badger, T., 8½″ Dia.	395.00	495.00	445.00
☐ **Plates,** Basset, Fred, 9″ Dia.	650.00	855.00	765.00
☐ **Plates,** Boardman, T., 7¾″ Dia.	420.00	525.00	475.00
☐ **Plate,** Wm. Calder, 8″ Dia.	330.00	440.00	385.00

	Current Price Range		Prior Year Average
☐ Plate, Wm. Calder, 11″ Dia.	365.00	460.00	410.00
☐ Plate, E. Danforth and S. Danforth, 8″ Dia.	520.00	770.00	615.00
☐ Plate, Thomas Danforth, 8″ Dia.	330.00	415.00	375.00
☐ Plate, Wm. Danforth, 13¼″ Dia.	550.00	740.00	645.00
☐ Plate, T.S. Derby, 8⅞″ Dia.	880.00	1100.00	985.00
☐ Plate, Gleason, Roswell, 9″ Dia.	220.00	300.00	260.00
☐ Plate, Kayserzinn, 7″ Dia.	65.00	95.00	80.00
☐ Plate, Kayserzinn, 10″ Dia.	100.00	125.00	112.00
☐ Plate, S. Killorne, 7¾″ Dia.	440.00	600.00	520.00
☐ Plate, flat with eagle mark, 13½″ Dia.	690.00	825.00	750.00
☐ Plate, unmarked, 8″ Dia.	190.00	240.00	215.00
☐ Plate, unmarked, 7½″ Dia.	90.00	125.00	110.00
☐ Plate, unmarked, 9¾″ Dia.	135.00	210.00	175.00
☐ Plate, unmarked, 12″ Dia.	175.00	255.00	215.00
☐ Platter, T. Badger, 12″ Dia.	465.00	550.00	500.00
☐ Platter, Kayserzinn, 11″ x 14″	72.00	92.00	82.00
☐ Platter, Kayserzinn, 12½″ x 20″	180.00	240.00	210.00
☐ Platter, Nekrassof, 17″ Dia.	45.00	75.00	60.00
☐ Porringer, heart handle, marked I.C., 4½″ Dia.	365.00	440.00	400.00
☐ Porringer, Boardman, 5″ Dia.	300.00	410.00	355.00
☐ Porringer, Hamlin, 5½″ Dia.	580.00	715.00	640.00
☐ Porringer, R. Lee, 2¹/₁₆″ Dia.	660.00	880.00	780.00
☐ Porringer, unmarked, R. Lee type handle, 3″ Dia.	250.00	330.00	290.00
☐ Shaving mug, Richardson	110.00	145.00	128.00
☐ Spoon, crown and rose, made in Holland	90.00	120.00	105.00
☐ Spoon, Dutch	14.00	20.00	17.00
☐ Spoon, Yates tablespoon	45.00	65.00	55.00
☐ Sugar and creamer, Kayserzinn, trumpet flower	50.00	70.00	60.00
☐ Sugar and creamer, four feet, Winthrop	60.00	80.00	70.00
☐ Tankard, with hinge cover, "P. Boyd," 16″ H.	3850.00	4950.00	4300.00
☐ Teapot, Boardman and Hart, 7½″ H.	350.00	420.00	385.00
☐ Teapot, Palethorp and Connell, 9″H., c. 1835	190.00	240.00	215.00
☐ Teapot, R. Dunham, 7½″ H.	340.00	460.00	400.00
☐ Teapot, G. Richardson, 11″ H.	660.00	825.00	745.00
☐ Teapot, Savage, hallmark, 10″ H.	350.00	450.00	400.00
☐ Teapot, Shaw and Fisher, England, 5¾″ H.	220.00	305.00	265.00
☐ Teapot, Wilcox	260.00	345.00	305.00
☐ Trays, Kayserzinn, 12¼″ x 6″	88.00	125.00	105.00
☐ Tureen, Kayserzinn, poppy decoration, 11½″ H.	155.00	210.00	190.00
☐ Vases, Liberty and Co., 11″ H.	110.00	150.00	130.00
☐ Vases, Kayserzinn, 12½″ H.	125.00	165.00	145.00
☐ Wine taster, Taunton, 2⅛″ H.	60.00	85.00	72.00

SILVER

The meteoric rise in bullion prices during 1979 and early 1980 focused unprecedented attention on silver collectibles of all kinds, coins as well as antiques, jewelry, etc. Not only did collecting activity increase, but investment became a feverish rush. Since mid-1980 the bullion market has greatly stabilized, but silver collectibles are unquestionably drawing more buying attention than before the 1979/80 "stampede." The beginner should realize that in the case of all silver collectors' items, the price charged by dealers exceeds the actual value of the silver, usually by a wide margin. These articles all possess a twofold value. First is the bullion value, which is simply the market price of the silver contained and no consideration of age,

564 / METALS

workmanship, rarity or any other factor. Second is the collector value. While the silver value can be easily computed, by taking the object's weight and silver fineness and figuring this against the current "spot" value of silver, the collector value is more indefinable. If the item falls within a popular collecting category and is deemed a good example of its kind, it may have ten times as much collector value as silver value, or even considerably more. The more collector value a piece has, the less it will be influenced in overall value by the ups and downs of silver bullion. Early silver table services, for example, are collectibles of long standing which have gained almost continuously in value despite bullion fluctuations. To be entirely safe in purchasing you should confine yourself to marked pieces.

A necessary reference book for the silver collector or investor is *The Official Price Guide to American Silver and Silver Plate*, published by the House of Collectibles.

CREAM SOUP SPOONS	Current Price Range		Prior Year Average
☐ **Rogers "Gracious"**, cream soup spoon, silver-plated, no monogram, excellent condition	8.00	11.00	9.50
☐ **Rogers "Inspiration"**, cream soup spoon, silver-plated, no monogram, excellent condition	8.00	11.00	9.50
☐ **Rogers "Inspiration"**, cream soup spoon, silver-plated, no monogram, fair condition	2.50	3.50	3.00
☐ **Rogers "Navarre"**, cream soup spoon, silver-plated, no monogram, excellent condition	8.00	11.00	9.50
☐ **Rogers "Navarre"**, cream soup spoon, silver-plated, no monogram, good condition	6.50	8.75	7.50
☐ **Rogers "Victorian Rose"**, cream soup spoon, silver-plated, no monogram, excellent condition	6.00	8.00	7.00
☐ **Rogers & Bro. "Daybreak"**, cream soup spoon, silver-plated, no monogram, excellent condition	7.75	11.00	9.50
☐ **Rogers & Bro. "Daybreak"**, cream soup spoon, silver-plated, no monogram, fair condition	1.75	3.55	2.50
☐ **Rogers & Bro. "Flemish"**, cream soup spoon, silver-plated, no monogram, excellent condition	7.75	11.00	9.50
☐ **Rogers & Bro. "Flemish"**, cream soup spoon, silver-plated, no monogram, fair condition	1.75	3.55	2.50
☐ **Rogers & Bro. "Thistle"**, cream soup spoon, silver-plated, no monogram, good condition	6.50	8.75	7.50
☐ **Rogers & Bro. "Thistle"**, cream soup spoon, silver-plated, no monogram, excellent condition	10.00	14.00	12.00
☐ **Rogers & Hamilton "Alhambra"**, cream soup spoon, silver-plated, no monogram, mint condition	15.00	19.00	17.00
☐ **Rogers & Hamilton "Alhambra"**, cream soup spoon, silver-plated, no monogram, good condition	6.50	8.75	7.50
☐ **Rogers & Hamilton "Alhambra"**, cream soup spoon, silver-plated, no monogram, fair condition	4.00	6.25	5.15
☐ **Sears "Rose"**, cream soup spoon, silver-plated, monogram, good condition	4.50	6.50	5.50
☐ **S.L. & G.H. Rogers "Minerva"**, cream soup spoon, silver-plated, no monogram, excellent condition	6.50	8.75	7.50
☐ **S.L. & G.H. Rogers "Minerva"**, cream soup spoon, silver-plated, no monogram, good condition	6.50	8.75	7.50

	Current Price Range		Prior Year Average
☐ **S.L. & G.H. Rogers "Thor"**, cream soup spoon, silver-plated, no monogram, good condition	6.50	8.75	7.50
☐ **S.L. & G.H. Rogers "Thor"**, cream soup spoon, silver-plated, no monogram, excellent condition ...	7.75	11.00	9.50
☐ **S.L. & G.H. Rogers "Violet"**, cream soup spoon, silver-plated, no monogram, good condition	8.00	11.00	9.50
☐ **S.L. & G.H. Rogers "Violet"**, cream soup spoon, silver-plated, no monogram, excellent condition .	9.00	13.00	11.00
☐ **Towle "Byfield"**, cream soup spoon, silver-plated, no monogram, mint condition	5.50	7.50	6.50
☐ **Towle "Byfield"**, cream soup spoon, silver-plated, no monogram, fair condition	1.75	3.50	2.50
☐ **Towle "Londonderry"**, cream soup spoon, silver-plated, no monogram, mint condition	5.50	7.50	6.50
☐ **Towle "Londonderry"**, cream soup spoon, silver-plated, no monogram, good condition	5.50	7.50	6.50
☐ **Tudor "Queen Bess II"**, cream soup spoon, silver-plated, no monogram, excellent condition	8.00	11.00	9.50

DINNER FORKS

	Current Price Range		Prior Year Average
☐ **Community "Louis XVI"**, dinner fork, silver-plated, no monogram, good condition	5.50	7.50	6.50
☐ **Community "Louis XVI"**, dinner fork, silver-plated, monogram, excellent condition	3.50	5.50	4.50
☐ **Community "Milady"**, dinner fork, silver-plated, no monogram, good condition	5.50	7.50	6.50
☐ **Community "Milady"**, dinner fork, silver-plated, no monogram, fair condition	2.25	3.25	2.75
☐ **Community "Morning Rose"**, dinner fork, silver-plated, no monogram, excellent condition	6.50	8.75	7.50
☐ **Community "Morning Rose"**, dinner fork, silver-plated, no monogram, good condition	5.50	7.50	6.50
☐ **Community "Morning Star"**, dinner fork, silver-plated, no monogram, good condition	3.50	5.50	4.50
☐ **Community "Morning Star"**, dinner fork, silver-plated, no monogram, fair condition	1.75	2.75	2.25
☐ **Community "Morning Star"**, dinner fork, silver-plated, viande style, no monogram, good condition	5.50	7.50	6.50
☐ **Community "Noblesse"**, dinner fork, silver-plated, viande style, no monogram, good condition	5.50	7.50	6.50
☐ **Community "Noblesse"**, dinner fork, silver-plated, viande style, monogram, excellent condition	2.25	3.25	2.75
☐ **Community "Noblesse"**, dinner fork, silver-plated, no monogram, excellent condition	4.50	6.50	5.50
☐ **Community "Patrician"**, dinner fork, silver-plated, monogram, excellent condition	1.75	2.75	2.25
☐ **Community "Patrician"**, dinner fork, silver-plated, no monogram, excellent condition	4.50	6.50	5.50
☐ **Community "Patrician"**, dinner fork, silver-plated, no monogram, excellent condition	6.50	8.75	7.50
☐ **Community "Patrician"**, dinner fork, silver-plated, no monogram, good condition	5.50	7.50	6.50

566 / METALS

	Current Price Range		Prior Year Average
☐ Community "Paul Revere", dinner fork, silver-plated, no monogram, excellent condition	6.50	8.75	7.50
☐ Community "Paul Revere", dinner fork, silver-plated, no monogram, good condition	5.50	7.50	6.50
☐ Community "Paul Revere", dinner fork, silver-plated, no monogram, fair condition	1.75	3.50	2.25
☐ Community "Sheraton", dinner fork, silver-plated, hollow-handled, no monogram, excellent condition	9.00	13.00	11.00
☐ Community "Sheraton", dinner fork, silver-plated, hollow-handled, no monogram, good condition	6.50	10.00	8.25
☐ Community "Sheraton", dinner fork, silver-plated, no monogram, excellent condition	6.50	10.00	8.25
☐ Community "Sheraton", dinner fork, silver-plated, no monogram, good condition	5.50	7.50	6.50
☐ Community "Silver Sands", dinner fork, silver-plated, no monogram, excellent condition	8.00	11.00	9.50
☐ Community "Silver Sands", dinner fork, silver-plated, no monogram, good condition	5.50	7.50	6.50
☐ Community "Silver Sands", dinner fork, silver-plated, monogram, excellent condition	3.50	4.75	4.25
☐ Community "South Seas", dinner fork, silver-plated, no monogram, mint condition	5.50	7.50	6.50
☐ Community "South Seas", dinner fork, silver-plated, no monogram, good condition	5.50	7.50	6.50

DINNER KNIVES

☐ Rogers & Hamilton "Alhambra", dinner knife, silver-plated, flat-handled, no monogram, good condition	8.00	11.00	9.50
☐ Rogers & Hamilton "Raphael", dinner knife, silver-plated, no monogram, excellent condition	15.00	19.00	17.00
☐ Rogers & Hamilton "Raphael", dinner knife, silver-plated, no monogram, good condition	8.00	13.00	10.50
☐ Rogers & Hamilton "Raphael", dinner knife, silver-plated, no monogram, fair condition	3.50	6.50	5.00
☐ S.L. & G.H. Rogers "Countess II", dinner knife, silver-plated, no monogram, excellent condition	8.00	11.00	9.50
☐ S.L. & G.H. Rogers "Countess II", dinner knife, silver-plated, no monogram, good condition	4.50	6.50	5.50
☐ S.L. & G.H. Rogers "English Garden", dinner knife, silver-plated, no monogram, excellent condition	8.00	11.00	9.50
☐ S.L. & G.H. Rogers "Jasmine", dinner knife, silver-plated, no monogram, fair condition	1.75	3.50	2.25
☐ S.L. & G.H. Rogers "Minerva", dinner knife, silver-plated, no monogram, good condition	8.00	11.00	9.50
☐ S.L. & G.H. Rogers "Minerva", dinner knife, silver-plated, no monogram, fair condition	4.25	6.00	5.20
☐ S.L. & G.H. Rogers "Silver Rose", dinner knife, silver-plated, viande style, no monogram, fair condition	2.25	3.25	2.75
☐ S.L. & G.H. Rogers "Silver Rose", dinner knife, silver-plated, viande style, no monogram, good condition	4.50	6.50	5.50

	Current Price Range		Prior Year Average
☐ Towle "Grenoble", dinner knife, silver-plated, no monogram, excellent condition	9.00	13.00	11.00
☐ Towle "Grenoble", dinner knife, silver-plated, no monogram, good condition	5.25	7.00	6.00
☐ Tudor "Bridal Wreath", dinner knife, silver-plated, no monogram, excellent condition	8.00	10.00	9.00
☐ Tudor "Bridal Wreath", dinner knife, silver-plated, no monogram, good condition	4.50	6.50	5.50
☐ Tudor "Bridal Wreath", dinner knife, silver-plated, no monogram, mint condition	4.50	6.50	5.50
☐ Tudor "Duchess", dinner knife, silver-plated, flat-handled, no monogram, excellent condition	3.50	5.50	4.50
☐ Tudor "Duchess", dinner knife, silver-plated, flat-handled, no monogram, fair condition	1.75	2.50	2.25
☐ Tudor "Elaine", dinner knife, silver-plated, no monogram, excellent condition	8.00	11.00	9.50
☐ Tudor "Elaine", dinner knife, silver-plated, no monogram, fair condition	2.25	3.75	3.00
☐ Tudor "Enchantment", dinner knife, silver-plated, no monogram, excellent condition	6.50	8.75	7.50
☐ Tudor "Enchantment", dinner knife, silver-plated, no monogram, good condition	4.50	6.50	5.50
☐ Tudor "Queen Bess II", dinner knife, silver-plated, flat-handled, no monogram, good condition	2.25	3.25	2.75
☐ Tudor "Queen Bess II", dinner knife, silver-plated, no monogram, good condition	6.50	8.75	7.50
☐ Tudor "Queen Bess II", dinner knife, silver-plated, no monogram, fair condition	2.25	3.25	3.00

FLATWARE

☐ International "Frontenac", flatware set, sterling silver, total 90 items, includes 12 dinner forks, 12 dinner knives, 12 flat handled butter spreaders, 12 salad forks, 12 cream soup spoons, 24 teaspoons, cocktail forks, no monogram	3300.00	4400.00	3850.00
☐ International "Silver Rhythm", flatware set, sterling silver, total 20 items, six three-piece place settings (place fork, place knife and teaspoon) plus butter knife and sugar shell, no monogram	500.00	600.00	550.00
☐ National "Overture", flatware set, sterling silver, total 61 pieces, includes 12 five-piece place settings (place fork, place knife, teaspoon, salad fork, round soup spoon) plus sugar shell, no monogram	1200.00	1550.00	1380.00
☐ Reed & Barton "Francis I", flatware set, sterling silver, total 167 pieces, includes 24 cream soup spoons, 12 place knives, 12 luncheon knives, 24 teaspoons, 12 place forks, 12 luncheon forks, 12 hollow-handled butter spreaders, 12 salad forks, 12 demitasse spoons, 12 fruit spoons, 12 seafood forks, salad serving fork and spoon, punch ladle, three-piece carving set, cake server, three vegetable serving spoons, berry spoon, no monogram	6300.00	7150.00	6725.00

568 / METALS

	Current Price Range		Prior Year Average
☐ **Royal Crest "Castle Rose"**, flatware set, sterling silver, 40 items, includes eight five-piece place settings (dinner fork, dinner knife, teaspoon, salad fork, oval soup spoon), no monogram	400.00	500.00	450.00
☐ **Stieff "Rose"**, flatware set, sterling silver, total 82 items, includes eight nine-piece place settings (dinner fork, dinner knife, teaspoon, oval soup spoon, salad fork, iced teaspoon, butter spreader, demitasse spoon and cocktail fork), plus 10 serving pieces (gravy ladle, sugar shell, butter knife, pickle fork, cold meat fork, salad serving set, and three vegetable serving spoons), monogram	3600.00	4400.00	4000.00
☐ **Towle "Georgian"**, flatware set, sterling silver, total 73 pieces, includes 12 each teaspoons, dinner forks, dinner knives, salad forks, cream soup spoons, flat-handled butter readers, plus a cake server, no monogram	3000.00	3400.00	3200.00
☐ **Towle "Louis XIV"**, flatware set, sterling silver, total 180 includes 16 hollow handled dinner knives (old style blades), 15 dinner forks, 12 salad forks, 23 teaspoons, eight oval soup spoons, six cream soup spoons, six cocktail forks, six flat-handled butter spreaders, four melon spoons, three tablespoons, one cold meat fork, one sugar shell, four iced teaspoons, one master butter knife, one large roast carving set, monogram . . .	1500.00	1700.00	1600.00
☐ **Wallace "Evening Mist"**, flatware set, sterling silver, total 24 pieces, includes seven hollow-handled dinner knives, five dinner forks, six salad forks, six teaspoons, one sugar shell and one butter knife, no monogram	180.00	200.00	190.00
☐ **Westmoreland "Lady Hilton"**, flatware set, sterling silver, total 41 pieces, includes eight four-piece place settings (dinner knife, dinner fork, teaspoon, cream soup spoon), plus six salad forks and three serving pieces (gravy ladle, sugar shell, butter knife), no monogram	1000.00	1350.00	1175.00
☐ **Whiting "Louis XV"**, flatware set, sterling silver, total 23 pieces, includes seven luncheon forks, four cream soup spoons, four ice cream forks, and eight teaspoons, monogram	900.00	1100.00	1000.00

LUNCHEON FORKS

☐ **1847 Rogers "Arcadian"**, luncheon fork, silver-plated, no monogram, resilvered	10.00	14.00	12.00
☐ **1847 Rogers "Arcadian"**, luncheon fork, silver-plated, no monogram, excellent condition	10.00	14.00	12.00
☐ **1847 Rogers "Arcadian"**, luncheon fork, silver-plated, no monogram, good condition	6.50	8.75	7.50
☐ **1847 Rogers "Armenian"**, luncheon fork, silver-plated, monogram, excellent condition	4.00	5.50	4.75
☐ **1847 Rogers "Avon"**, luncheon fork, silver-plated, no monogram, good condition	2.50	3.50	3.00
☐ **1847 Rogers "Berkshire"**, luncheon fork, silver-plated, monogram, fair condition	4.00	5.50	4.75

METALS / 569

	Current Price Range		Prior Year Average
☐ **1847 Rogers "Berkshire",** luncheon fork, silverplated, no monogram, good condition	8.00	11.00	9.50
☐ **1847 Rogers "Charter Oak",** luncheon fork, silverplated, no monogram, good silver condition, tines worn	7.00	9.50	8.25
☐ **1847 Rogers "Charter Oak",** luncheon fork, silverplated, no monogram, good condition	8.75	13.00	11.50
☐ **1847 Rogers "Charter Oak",** luncheon fork, silverplated, no monogram, resilvered	10.00	13.75	11.75
☐ **1847 Rogers "Charter Oak",** luncheon fork, silverplated, no monogram	8.75	13.00	11.50
☐ **1847 Rogers "Charter Oak",** luncheon fork, silverplated, no monogram, fair condition	5.50	7.75	6.50
☐ **1847 Rogers "Charter Oak",** luncheon fork, silverplated, monogram, fair condition	2.75	4.00	3.25
☐ **1847 Rogers "Columbia",** luncheon fork, silverplated, no monogram, excellent condition	8.75	13.00	11.50
☐ **1847 Rogers "Columbia",** luncheon fork, silverplated, no monogram, fair condition	5.50	7.75	6.50
☐ **1847 Rogers "Cromwell",** luncheon fork, silverplated, no monogram, excellent condition	5.00	7.00	6.00
☐ **1847 Rogers "Crown",** luncheon fork, silverplated, no monogram, poor condition	3.50	5.50	4.50
☐ **1847 Rogers "First Love",** luncheon fork, silverplated, viande style, no monogram, excellent condition	6.50	8.75	7.50
☐ **1847 Rogers "Floral",** luncheon fork, silverplated, monogram, mint condition	12.00	15.50	13.75
☐ **1847 Rogers "Grecian",** luncheon fork, silverplated, no monogram, good condition	2.00	3.00	2.50
☐ **1847 Rogers "Heritage",** luncheon fork, silverplated, viande style, no monogram, mint condition	5.50	7.75	6.50
☐ **1847 Rogers "Heritage",** luncheon fork, silverplated, viande style, no monogram, mint condition	8.75	12.00	10.50
☐ **1847 Rogers "Lorne",** luncheon fork, silverplated, no monogram, good condition	2.25	3.25	3.00
☐ **1847 Rogers "Louvain",** luncheon fork, silverplated, no monogram, good condition	5.25	7.75	6.50
☐ **1847 Rogers "Magic Rose",** luncheon fork, silverplated, no monogram, excellent condition	3.50	5.50	4.50
☐ **1847 Rogers "Moselle",** luncheon fork, silverplated, no monogram, mint condition	24.00	29.75	26.50
☐ **1847 Rogers "Moselle",** luncheon fork, silverplated, no monogram, good condition	14.00	18.75	16.50
☐ **1847 Rogers "Moselle",** luncheon fork, silverplated, no monogram, fair condition	7.75	11.00	8.50

SALAD FORKS

☐ **Community "South Seas",** salad fork, silverplated, no monogram, fair condition	2.00	2.75	2.50
☐ **Community "Tangier",** salad fork, silver-plated, no monogram, excellent condition	5.50	7.75	6.50
☐ **Community "Tangier",** salad fork, silver-plated, no monogram, good condition	6.50	8.75	7.50

570 / METALS

	Current Price Range		Prior Year Average
☐ **Community "Tangier"**, salad fork, silver-plated, no monogram, fair condition	2.25	3.75	3.00
☐ **Community "Tangier"**, salad fork, silver-plated, no monogram, poor condition	1.10	1.65	1.40
☐ **Community "Tangier"**, salad fork, silver-plated, monogram, fair condition	1.10	1.65	1.40
☐ **Community "White Orchid"**, salad fork, silver-plated, no monogram, excellent condition	7.75	11.00	8.50
☐ **Community "White Orchid"**, salad fork, silver-plated, no monogram, good condition	6.50	8.75	7.50
☐ **Community "White Orchid"**, salad fork, silver-plated, no monogram, poor condition	1.10	1.65	1.40
☐ **Community "White Orchid"**, salad fork, silver-plated, no monogram, silver in excellent condition but tines bent	1.10	1.65	1.40
☐ **DeepSilver "Laurel Mist"**, salad fork, silver-plated, no monogram, excellent condition	7.75	10.00	8.75
☐ **DeepSilver "Laurel Mist"**, salad fork, silver-plated, no monogram, good condition	6.50	8.75	7.50
☐ **DeepSilver "Laurel Mist"**, salad fork, silver-plated, no monogram, fair condition	2.00	2.75	2.50
☐ **DeepSilver "Triumph"**, salad fork, silver-plated, no monogram, excellent condition	7.75	11.00	8.50
☐ **DeepSilver "Triumph"**, salad fork, silver-plated, no monogram, good condition	6.50	8.75	7.50
☐ **DeepSilver "Triumph"**, salad fork, silver-plated, no monogram, fair condition	2.25	3.75	3.00
☐ **DeepSilver "Triumph"**, salad fork, silver-plated, no monogram, poor condition	1.10	1.65	1.40
☐ **Embassy "Bouquet"**, salad fork, silver-plated, no monogram, excellent condition	7.75	11.00	8.50
☐ **Embassy "Bouquet"**, salad fork, silver-plated, no monogram, good condition	6.50	8.75	7.50
☐ **Embassy "Bouquet"**, salad fork, silver-plated, fair condition	1.65	2.50	2.00
☐ **Fortune "Fortune"**, salad fork, silver-plated, no monogram, excellent condition	7.75	10.00	8.75
☐ **Fortune "Fortune"**, salad fork, silver-plated, no monogram, good condition	6.50	8.75	7.50
☐ **Fortune "Fortune"**, salad fork, silver-plated, no monogram, fair condition	1.65	2.50	2.00
☐ **Gorham "Empire"**, salad fork, silver-plated, no monogram, excellent condition	6.50	8.75	7.50
☐ **Gorham "Empire"**, salad fork, silver-plated, monogram, fair condition	1.65	2.75	2.00
☐ **Gorham "New Elegance"**, salad fork, silver-plated, no monogram, excellent condition	7.75	10.00	8.75
☐ **Gorham "New Elegance"**, salad fork, silver-plated, no monogram, good condition	6.50	8.75	7.50

SERVING SPOONS

☐ **Community "South Seas"**, serving spoon, silver-plated, no monogram, excellent condition	8.75	12.00	9.50
☐ **Fortune "Fortune"**, serving spoon, silver-plated, no monogram, excellent condition	8.75	12.00	9.50

METALS / 571

	Current Price Range		Prior Year Average
☐ Gorham "Kings", serving spoon, silver-plated, no monogram, excellent condition	8.75	12.00	9.50
☐ Gorham "Kings", serving spoon, silver-plated, no monogram, good condition	7.75	11.00	8.50
☐ Gorham "New Elegance", serving spoon, silver-plated, no monogram, excellent condition	8.75	12.00	9.50
☐ Gorham "New Elegance", serving spoon, silver-plated, no monogram, good condition	7.75	11.00	8.50
☐ Holmes & Edwards "Century", serving spoon, silver-plated, no monogram, good condition	7.75	11.00	8.50
☐ Holmes & Edwards "Danish Princess", serving spoon, silver-plated, no monogram, excellent condition	8.75	12.00	9.50
☐ Holmes & Edwards "Danish Princess", serving spoon, silver-plated, no monogram, good condition	7.75	11.00	8.50
☐ Holmes & Edwards "Lovely Lady", serving spoon, silver-plated, no monogram, excellent condition	8.75	12.00	9.50
☐ Holmes & Edwards "Lovely Lady", serving spoon, silver-plated, no monogram, good condition	7.75	11.00	8.50
☐ Holmes & Edwards "May Queen", serving spoon, silver-plated, no monogram, excellent condition .	8.75	12.00	9.50
☐ Holmes & Edwards "May Queen", serving spoon, silver-plated, no monogram, good condition	7.75	11.00	8.50
☐ Holmes & Edwards "Spring Garden", serving spoon, silver-plated, no monogram, excellent condition	7.75	11.00	8.50
☐ Holmes & Edwards "Spring Garden", serving spoon, silver-plated, no monogram, good condition	5.50	7.75	6.50
☐ Holmes & Edwards "Youth", serving spoon, silver-plated, no monogram, excellent condition ...	8.75	12.00	9.50
☐ Holmes & Edwards "Youth", serving spoon, silver-plated, no monogram, good condition	7.75	11.00	8.50
☐ International "Silver Tulip", serving spoon, silver-plated, no monogram, excellent condition	7.75	11.00	8.50
☐ International "Silver Tulip", serving spoon, silver-plated, no monogram, good condition	6.50	8.75	7.50
☐ International "Silver Tulip", serving spoon, silver-plated, pierced, no monogram, excellent condition	7.75	11.00	8.50
☐ International "Silver Tulip", serving spoon, silver-plated, pierced, no monogram, good condition ..	6.50	8.75	7.50
☐ King Edward "Cavalcade", serving spoon, silver-plated, no monogram, excellent condition	8.75	12.00	9.50
☐ King Edward "Cavalcade", serving spoon, silver-plated, no monogram, good condition	6.50	8.75	7.50

TABLESPOONS

☐ Oneida "Flower de Luce", tablespoon, silver-plated, no monogram, excellent condition	10.00	13.00	11.50
☐ Oneida "Flower de Luce", tablespoon, silver-plated, no monogram, good condition	6.50	10.00	9.25

572 / METALS

	Current Price Range		Prior Year Average
☐ **Oneida "Flower de Luce",** tablespoon, silver-plated, no monogram, fair condition	2.25	3.25	2.75
☐ **Oneida "Jamestown",** tablespoon, silver-plated, no monogram, excellent condition	7.75	16.50	11.50
☐ **Oneida "Jamestown",** tablespoon, silver-plated, no monogram, fair condition	3.50	5.50	4.50
☐ **Oneida "Louis XVI",** tablespoon, silver-plated, no monogram, excellent condition	7.75	11.00	8.50
☐ **Oneida "Louis XVI",** tablespoon, silver-plated, no monogram, good condition	6.50	8.75	7.50
☐ **Oneida "Louis XVI",** tablespoon, silver-plated, no monogram, good condition except for slight bend in handle	2.25	3.25	2.75
☐ **Oneida "Wildwood",** tablespoon, silver-plated, no monogram, excellent condition	5.50	7.75	6.50
☐ **Oneida "Wildwood",** tablespoon, silver-plated, no monogram, excellent condition	6.50	8.75	7.50
☐ **Oneida "Wildwood",** tablespoon, silver-plated, no monogram, excellent condition	5.50	7.75	6.50
☐ **Oneida "Wildwood",** tablespoon, silver-plated, no monogram, fair condition	2.25	3.25	2.75
☐ **Paragon "Sweet Pea",** tablespoon, silver-plated, no monogram, excellent condition	6.50	8.75	7.50
☐ **Paragon "Sweet Pea",** tablespoon, silver-plated, no monogram, good condition	4.50	6.50	5.50
☐ **Paragon "Sweet Pea",** tablespoon, silver-plated, no monogram, fair condition	2.25	3.25	2.75
☐ **Reed & Barton "Carlton",** tablespoon, silver-plated, no monogram, excellent condition	5.50	7.75	6.50
☐ **Reed & Barton "Carlton",** tablespoon, silver-plated, no monogram, good condition	4.50	6.50	5.50
☐ **Reed & Barton "Oxford",** tablespoon, silver-plated, no monogram, excellent condition	7.75	11.00	8.50
☐ **Reed & Barton "Oxford",** tablespoon, silver-plated, no monogram, good condition	5.50	7.75	6.50
☐ **Reed & Barton "Oxford",** tablespoon, silver-plated, no monogram, fair condition	1.65	2.75	2.00
☐ **Reed & Barton "Oxford",** tablespoon, silver-plated, no monogram, good condition	10.00	13.00	11.50
☐ **Reed & Barton "Oxford",** tablespoon, silver-plated, no monogram, poor condition	1.50	2.25	2.00
☐ **Rockford "Louvre",** tablespoon, silver-plated, no monogram, excellent condition	11.00	20.00	15.50
☐ **Rockford "Louvre",** tablespoon, silver-plated, no monomonogram, fair condition	3.00	7.75	5.50
☐ **Rockford "Louvre",** tablespoon, silver-plated, no monogram, poor condition	2.50	4.00	3.25
☐ **Rogers "Alhambra",** tablespoon, silver-plated, no monogram, excellent condition	8.75	12.00	9.50
☐ **Rogers "Alhambra",** tablespoon, silver-plated, no monogram, excellent condition	6.50	10.00	8.25
☐ **Rogers "Alhambra",** tablespoon, silver-plated, no monogram, poor condition	2.75	3.50	3.00

TEASPOONS

	Current Price Range		Prior Year Average
☐ **Derby "Lily"**, teaspoon, silver-plated, no monogram, excellent condition	5.50	7.75	6.50
☐ **Derby "Lily"**, teaspoon, silver-plated, monogram, fair condition	1.10	2.25	1.75
☐ **Embassy "Bouquet"**, teaspoon, silver-plated, no monogram, excellent condition	5.50	7.75	6.50
☐ **Embassy "Bouquet"**, teaspoon, silver-plated, no monogram, good condition	4.50	6.50	5.50
☐ **Fortune "Fortune"**, teaspoon, silver-plated, no monogram, excellent condition	5.50	7.75	6.50
☐ **Fortune "Fortune"**, teaspoon, silver-plated, no monogram, good condition	5.00	7.50	6.50
☐ **Fortune "Fortune"**, teaspoon, silver-plated, no monogram, fair condition	1.10	2.25	1.75
☐ **Gorham "Cavalier"**, teaspoon, silver-plated, no monogram, excellent condition	4.50	6.50	5.50
☐ **Gorham "Cavalier"**, teaspoon, silver-plated, no monogram, excellent condition	5.50	7.75	6.50
☐ **Gorham "Cavalier"**, teaspoon, silver-plated, no monogram, good condition	4.50	6.50	5.50
☐ **Gorham "Cavalier"**, teaspoon, silver-plated, no monogram, fair condition	1.10	2.25	1.75
☐ **Gorham "Empire"**, teaspoon, silver-plated, no monogram, good condition	4.50	6.50	5.50
☐ **Gorham "Empire"**, teaspoon, silver-plated, no monogram, fair condition	1.10	2.25	1.75
☐ **Gorham "Empire"**, teaspoon, silver-plated, monogram, good condition	2.25	3.75	3.00
☐ **Gorham "Kings"**, teaspoon, silver-plated, no monogram, excellent condition	5.50	7.75	6.50
☐ **Gorham "Kings"**, teaspoon, silver-plated, no monogram, good condition	4.50	6.50	5.50
☐ **Gorham "Kings"**, teaspoon, silver-plated, U.S. Navy marks, good condition	4.50	6.50	5.50
☐ **Gorham "Roman"**, teaspoon, silver-plated, monogram, excellent condition	6.50	10.00	8.25
☐ **Gorham "Roman"**, teaspoon, silver-plated, monogram, good condition	5.50	7.75	6.50
☐ **Hall, Elton & Co. "Lyonnaise"**, teaspoon, silver-plated, no monogram, excellent condition	6.00	8.50	7.25
☐ **Hall, Elton & Co. "Lyonnaise"**, teaspoon, silver-plated, no monogram, fair condition	1.10	2.25	1.75
☐ **Harmony House "Maytime"**, teaspoon, silver-plated, no monogram, excellent condition	3.50	5.50	4.50
☐ **Harmony House "Maytime"**, teaspoon, silver-plated, no monogram, good condition	2.75	4.00	3.50
☐ **Harmony House "Maytime"**, teaspoon, silver-plated, no monogram, fair condition	1.10	2.25	1.75
☐ **Harmony House "Serenade"**, teaspoon, silver-plated, no monogram, excellent condition	3.50	5.50	4.50
☐ **Harmony House "Serenade"**, teaspoon, silver-plated, no monogram, good condition	3.50	5.50	4.50
☐ **Heirloom "Cardinal"**, teaspoon, silver-plated, no monogram, excellent condition	5.50	7.75	6.50
☐ **Heirloom "Cardinal"**, teaspoon, silver-plated, no monogram, good condition	4.50	6.50	5.50

TIN & TOLEWARE

These bright, colorful items were inexpensive originally and designed for the ordinary working classes of the past. The material itself — tin — was very cheap for manufacturers to use, could be shaped and worked without great difficulty, which left only one problem: in its natural state it was simply too raw looking. The answer was to coat such items with enamel paint, and to further apply designs on the base coat. Thus with a minimum of effort and expense they were given a cheery appearance and sales appeal. Another means of decoration was by lacquering the surface. When paint was used, the item falls into the category of Toleware; otherwise collectors designate it as tin. The centers of production were Pennsylvania, New England, Ohio, and Kentucky. Value depends on the item's nature and quality of decoration, if any. Small rural antiques shops have traditionally been the favorite hunting grounds for Toleware. They aren't quite as fruitful as a decade or two ago, because of continual assualts by collectors; but they still occasionally receive consignments from the attics of local residents and anything could turn up. Beware of reproductions and (more confusing) repaintings of old pieces. When you find a DATE on an item of toleware, painted in large figures, this is cause for extreme suspicion. Genuine Toleware is seldom dated, but fakers often apply dates for the sake of adding more sales appeal.

	Current Price Range		Prior Year Average
☐ **Biscuit tin,** English, eight volumes of books, 6¼" H.	100.00	130.00	115.00
☐ **Candy tin,** simulated wood, 5¾" Dia.	25.00	35.00	30.00
☐ **Cigarette tin,** jewel box shape, State Express brand, 3½" H.	31.00	40.00	35.50
☐ **Comb case,** tin, eagle in relief	20.00	27.00	24.00
☐ **Cradle,** tin, painted green, yellow, red	635.00	740.00	685.00
☐ **Foot warmer,** rectangular, heart-piercing	125.00	150.00	140.00
☐ **Spice set,** round, eight pieces, nutmeg rasp, brown	110.00	145.00	128.00
☐ **Tin bed warmer,** wooden handle	140.00	165.00	150.00
☐ **Tin tea caddies,** simulated inlaid wood, pair, 5" H.	85.00	105.00	95.00
☐ **Tole canister,** cylindrical	205.00	260.00	225.00
☐ **Tole Eeling lamp,** three-wick, 19th c.	55.00	80.00	65.00
☐ **Tole spice set,** six pieces, brass-handled, tin box	55.00	80.00	65.00
☐ **Tole potpourri container** (pierced lid)	150.00	195.00	170.00
☐ **Tole store canister,** "mustard," porcelain knob, 9" H.	140.00	175.00	160.00
☐ **Tole sugar bowl,** with lid	200.00	260.00	230.00
☐ **Tole snuff box,** painted shell decoration	100.00	130.00	115.00

MILITARIA

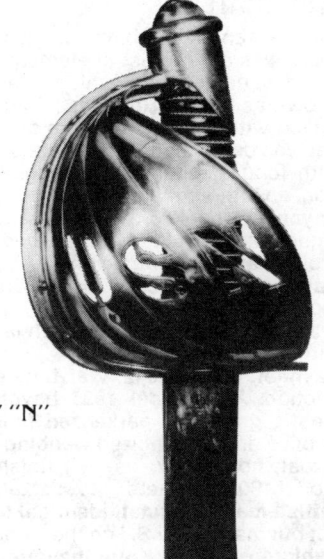

U.S. Non Regulation 1860 Pattern Cutlass, gilted haf basket guard with a swirl pattern with large letters "U" "S" "N" cut out. . **$1090.00-$1200.00**

The relics of war were being collected and preserved by museums before hobbyists took an interest in them. Private collectors have, however, broadened out the field quite a bit, studying and collecting many items that are not really in the "museum piece" class. To most collectors, militaria encompasses everything relating to the military. First and foremost are equipment of military issue, such as firearms, uniforms, mess kits, etc., which carry distinctive markings in most cases. Ranking behind, but still of considerable interest, are items dealing with military history: books, documents, newspapers, etc., and this can be extended all the way into commemorative medals marking anniversaries of important battles. For United States collectors, militaria from the Civil War (both sides) has long been the most popular, being both strongly historic and very readily available on the market. Much of this material is a good deal LESS expensive than the uninformed public might believe. Relics of the much earlier Revolutionary War are also on the market but tend to run higher in price. There is no line of demarcation in what is and isn't collectible: items from the Vietnam war are very enthusiastically sought, but are too recent, as yet, to bring really strong sums. If your interest extends to Nazi relics of World War II, it is well to keep in mind that REPRODUCTIONS ARE ABUNDANT and are coming into the market regularly at all times. Another area in which you are likely to encounter fakes is Japanese arms and armor.

For more in-depth information and listings, you may refer to *The Official Price Guide to Military Collectibles,* by Colonel Rankin and published by the House of Collectibles.

BAYONETS
UNITED STATES

	Current Price Range		Prior Year Average

- **Bannerman Cadet bayonet.** In the early 1900's there was an interest in elementary drill in some boy's schools and local organizations usually known as "Boy's Brigades." These units usually drilled with dummy muskets or rifles. This bayonet was designed for these guns. Socket bayonet with long slender blade, roughly made of cast iron, an interesting oddity 56.00 62.00 57.00
- **Bayonet. Model 55.** Long bright fullered modified yataghan-type blade. Brass one piece hilt and crossguard with muzzle ring 75.00 82.00 76.00
- **Bayonet. Model 1860.** For the Sharps rifle. Long recurved fullered blade of bright finish steel, brass hilt and crossguard with large muzzle ring, without scabbard 110.00 125.00 110.00
- **Bayonet. Model 1942.** War time expediency production. The model 1905 bayonet with ribbed plastic grips and parkerized finished, scabbard of olive drab plasticized webbing with parkerized throat, not nearly as well finished as previous model 1905 bayonets 56.00 62.00 57.00
- **British-made bayonet.** Identical to the U.S. bayonet but marked "U.S." on the wood grips 34.00 38.00 33.50
- **Dahlgren Bowie Knife bayonet.** For the Plymouth/Whitneyville .69-mm. muzzle loading Navy rifle. Bowie profile knife blade with hilt and crossguard fashion from a single brass casting. Wood grips inset into the hilt, muzzle ring on crossguard with reverse gullions, black leather scabbard with bright brass mounts. This bayonet will not fit the rifle for which it was intended without some alteration of the muzzle ring and slot in hilt. There is considerable conjecture as to the reason for this. Apparently this bayonet was *primarily* intended for use as a hand weapon. It is one of the rarest of U.S. bayonets. 470.00 520.00 475.00

FIGHTING KNIVES AND STILETTOS
BRITISH

- **Commando fighting knife.** Single edge stabbing blade with fuller, flat plain brass "knuckle duster" hilt. Identified as a Middle East Commando Knife, c. World War II 125.00 140.00 127.00
- **Commando stiletto.** Sykes-Fairborn pattern made by Wilkinson Sword. Blade is 6½" long, white metal oval crossguard and crosshatch pattern aluminum grips, complete with metal tipped leather sheath, c. World War II 70.00 78.00 71.00
- **Trench knife.** Curved 8½" saber-like blade, has sword pattern hilt with handguard, greatly resembles a naval dirk, complete with scabbard, odd and interesting. Marked to Robbins Dudley 210.00 235.00 212.00

MILITARIA / 577

	Current Price Range		Prior Year Average

- **Trench knife.** Short double edge stabbing blade with median line on each side, brass hilt in form of "knuckle duster" rivetted to blade. Similar in general appearance to the Mark I U.S. Army trench knife, complete with leather scabbard. Made by Robert Kelley and Sons, Liverpool and so marked, c. World War I **165.00 185.00 171.00**

FRANCE

- **World War I trench knife.** Double edge stabbing 8" blade with median line, has etched inscription "Le Nettoyeur de Tranchees Campagne 1914-15-16" (The Trench Cleaner Campaigns of 1914-15-16.) Metal bulb pattern hilt with rugged metal crossguard, has its original leather scabbard, unusual **72.00 82.00 75.00**

GERMANY

- **Luftwaffe fighting/utility knife.** 8½" modified Bowie pattern blade which folds back into staghorn handle, locking lugs, complete with brown leather sheath, c. Third Reich **70.00 78.00 71.00**
- **Trench knife.** 8" broad, sharply pointed blade attached to off-set leather covered hilt with brass pommel and reverse brass quillion on one side opposite the off-set. Has two inscriptions, one in German reads "I was forged in the Iron Age from France's ravaged fields," this on the obverse side. On the reverse side in Flemish an inscription reads "I come from the fires of the sun, 1916." Complete with brass-mounted leather scabbard. It has been suggested that this knife originally belonged to a German soldier who was captured and the second inscription added. Mosting interesting, one of kind, c. World War I . **72.00 82.00 75.00**
- **Trench knife.** Straight 9" blade with sawtooth back, odd sharp pointed beak, small steel crossguard, horn grips with steel pommel. Marked "Kriegshead." c. World War I **70.00 78.00 71.00**

FIREARMS (GENERAL) United States

- **Aston and Johnson Percussion pistol,** model 1842, .54 cal. In connection with percussion pistols it should be noted that many flintlock weapons, both hand guns and shoulder weapons were converted to the percussion system. The conversion was neither difficult nor expensive and the U.S. Government for reasons of economy favored the conversion. This particular pistol, however, was designed as a percussion weapon, brass mounted, U.S. proof marks, some specimens marked "US" and "H. ASTON" in two lines plus date of manufacture **320.00 645.00 460.00**
- **As above,** but marked "US" "H.ASTON AND CO." **385.00 735.00 450.00**

578 / MILITARIA

	Current Price Range		Prior Year Average

- ☐ **Colt Army and Navy revolver,** new model, all in .38 cal., 6" barrel, with Colt and Navy markings 160.00 335.00 220.00
- ☐ **As above,** but with Army markings 135.00 285.00 200.00
- ☐ **Colt Army Automatic pistol,** model 1900. As above but with Army markings 420.00 760.00 540.00
- ☐ **Colt Army revolver,** model 1917, .45 cal. Improved version of the model 1919, much used during World War I and to some extent in World War II. Some officers preferred the revolver over the automatic, claiming it was more reliable and accurate 160.00 335.00 230.00
- ☐ **Colt Automatic pistol,** model 1905, .45 cal. A very limited number of these were made. It was the first Colt automatic pistol in .45 caliber, a caliber much desired by the U.S. Army. Of a total production of slightly over 6000, only around 200 were purchased by the Army. These bear the Colt markings plus government inspector's marks, Lanyard loop on frame 425.00 850.00 610.00
- ☐ **Colt Hammerless Pocket Automatic pistol,** model 1903, .32 cal. 8 shot magazine, Colt markings plus "U.S. PROPERTY" 160.00 425.00 275.00
- ☐ **Colt Marine Corps D.A. revolver,** model 1905, .38 cal. 6 shot in Colt .38 and Smith & Wesson .38 calibers, Colt and USMC markings. An interesting model but not at all rare 285.00 510.00 385.00
- ☐ **Colt Military Automatic pistol,** model 1902, .38 cal. 8 shot magazine, Browning, Colt and Army markings 425.00 825.00 600.00
- ☐ **Colt Navy Automatic pistol,** model 1900, .38 cal. 7 shot magazine, first Colt production automatic, designed by John Moses Browning, Browning, Colt and Navy markings 450.00 850.00 625.00
- ☐ **Colt Navy Double Action revolver,** model 1889, .38 cal. Swingout cylinder, with Colt and Navy markings 220.00 420.00 300.00
- ☐ **Colt U.S. Services revolver,** model 1909, .45 cal. 5½" barrel, lanyard ring on butt, a heavy, reliable, rugged piece.
- ☐ **Army model,** with Colt and Army markings ... 220.00 420.00 300.00
- ☐ **Navy model,** with Colt and Navy markings 260.00 435.00 320.00
- ☐ **Marine Corps model,** with Colt and USMC markings 320.00 600.00 438.00
- ☐ **Colt Walker Model revolver,** .44 cal. 6 shot, percussion type, marked "ADDRESS SAMI COLT NEW YORK CITY" and "US" "1847" in two lines. Government inspection marks, cylinder engraved with Indian vs Ranger fight 5500.00 14500.00 9000.00
- ☐ **Harpers Ferry Flintlock pistol,** model 1805, .54 cal. brass furniture, first pistol made in a national arsenal. Partially marked with eagle and shield with "US," also marked "HARPERS FERRY," serial number and date of manufacture. Prices vary according to year of manufacture, as well as to condition.
- ☐ **1806** 4500.00 8500.00 6000.00

	Current Price Range		Prior Year Average
☐ **Navy Elgin Cutlass pistol**, .54 cal. This is an excellent example of one of the multitude of freak combination weapons produced through the years. Since the introduction of firearms, men have tinkered with the idea of combining them with edged weapons. Firearms have appeared in combination with shields, swords, daggers, spears, halberds and just about every other type of weapon with a blade. They have been universally unsuccessful. In combining the two entirely dissimilar weapons, the better characteristics of each has been sadly modified or even lost. These weapons proved to be of much greater value to present day collectors than they ever were in the hands of their original users. Several versions of this so-called cutlass pistol appeared, in both military and civilian models. The U.S. Navy version, of which only a very limited number was ever bought by the service, is a percussion pistol in .54 caliber with a cutlass blade 11½" long, 2" wide, attached to the under side of the barrel. The weapon is 15¾" long overall. It was carried in a brass and leather holster. (This holster which is more of a sheath for the blade is worth $750.00 by itself in good condition.) Frame marked "C.B. ALLEN" "SPRINGFIELD" "MASS." in three lines. The serial number appears on various parts. A total of 150 of these pistols were made for the Navy	4500.00	8500.00	6000.00

CIVIL WAR HANDGUNS

☐ **Remington-Beals revolver**, Army model, .44 cal. Government marked	750.00	1450.00	1000.00
☐ **Remington-Beals revolver**, Navy model, .33 cal. similar to the above but smaller, Government marked	320.00	670.00	420.00
☐ **Remington Navy revolver**, model 1861, .36 cal. Government marked	320.00	600.00	438.00
☐ **Remington Navy revolver**, new model, .36 cal. Reported to have been popular with Navy personnel, government marked	600.00	1200.00	800.00
☐ **Savage and North revolver**, figure 8 model, .36 cal. So-called because trigger is in the form of an "8," limited production for the U.S. Government, martially marked. This specimen is the second variation of the first production model, very limited production	1450.00	2250.00	1800.00
☐ **Savage and North revolver**, third figure 8 model. Extremely limited production for Navy	1600.00	2500.00	2050.00
☐ **Savage Revolving Firearms Co.**, Navy model, .36 cal. Produced in some numbers for Navy, Government marked	325.00	525.00	400.00

580 / MILITARIA

	Current Price Range	Prior Year Average

- ☐ **Whitney Navy revolver**, .36 cal. Extremely popular with both the U.S. Army and Navy, as well as with many state militia units. Along with the Colt model 1851 revolver, it often served as the pattern for Confederate made revolvers. For some unexplained reason the legend "EAGLE CO" appears on some of the first models instead of the Whitney markings.
- ☐ **First model.**

	Current		Prior Year
☐ Type I, very limited number made	375.00	925.00	660.00
☐ Type II, very limited number made	275.00	660.00	450.00
☐ Type III	275.00	660.00	450.00
☐ Type IV	300.00	725.00	500.00

- ☐ **Second model,** made in considerable numbers.

☐ Type I, heavy frame, Whitney markings	225.00	525.00	350.00

LONGARMS

- ☐ **Gwyn and Campbell Carbine**, .52 cal. Sometimes known as the Union Carbide' or the Grapevine Carbine.

☐ Type I	350.00	575.00	430.00
☐ Type II	320.00	520.00	400.00

- ☐ **Jenks "Mule Ear" carbine**, .54 cal. So-called because of the side hammer action, percussion, made by N. P. Ames, marked to the U.S. Navy ... 360.00 660.00 500.00
- ☐ **Jenks "Mule Ear" carbine.** As above but marked to the U.S. Revenue Cutter Service 650.00 1200.00 850.00
- ☐ **Jenks "Mule Ear" carbine.** As above but with tape primer instead of percussion, made by E. Remington and Son 450.00 825.00 600.00
- ☐ **Jenks "Mule Ear" Navy rifle**, .54 cal. A few were made in .55 cal. made by N. P. Ames 450.00 950.00 625.00
- ☐ **Joslyn carbines**, model 1862 and 1864, .55 cal. rimfire, much used by Union cavalry, Government marked 350.00 600.00 420.00
- ☐ **Remington 1863 Percussion Contract rifle**, .58 cal. So-called Zouave rifle, for saber type bayonet, extremely well made. Because so many are found in excellent condition it is believed that they were never issued, Government marked 550.00 850.00 650.00
- ☐ **Rifled Musket,** .58 cal. Made by any of the above contractors or by the Springfield Armory 350.00 750.00 500.00
- ☐ **Rifled Musket,** .58 cal. as above but made by either C. H. Funk or Union Arms Co. 475.00 875.00 650.00
- ☐ **Sharps Carbines and Rifles,** new model 1859, 1863, and 1865, .52 cal. Well over 100,000 of these delivered to the Army and the Navy.

☐ 1859 carbine, brass furniture with patchbox ...	475.00	725.00	575.00
☐ 1859 carbine, iron furniture with patchbox	350.00	550.00	400.00
☐ 1863 carbine, iron furniture with patchbox	325.00	425.00	400.00
☐ 1863 carbine, iron furniture without patchbox .	325.00	425.00	400.00
☐ 1865 carbine, iron furniture without patchbox .	400.00	725.00	520.00
☐ 1859 rifle, lug for saber type bayonet	425.00	725.00	550.00
☐ 1859 rifle, as above but longer barrel	525.00	875.00	625.00
☐ 1863 rifle, no bayonet lug	450.00	725.00	510.00
☐ 1865 rifle, no bayonet lug	560.00	1150.00	850.00

	Current Price Range	Prior Year Average

☐ **Sharps "Coffee Mill" Carbine.** In the days before instant or ready ground coffee it was necessary for the user to grind coffee beans before he could prepare his brew. This could be a major problem in campaigning in the field. Experiments were made to build a coffee mill or grinder into the buttstock of a longarm. Condemned Sharps new model 1859 and 1863 carbines were used for these experiments. The special coffee mill was designed, built and installed by a private firm by the name of McMurphy. The mill was turned by a removable handle. Trials determined the idea to be impracticable and the idea was never put to use. The few trial weapons bring a premium price. Collectors are warned that fake coffee mill carbines are being offered for sale.

☐ **Sharps "Coffee Mill" carbine.** Authentic 3400.00 6400.00 4800.00
☐ **Sharps and Hankins Carbine,** model 1862, .55 cal.
  ☐ **Army Model.** Similar to Navy model but never fitted with leather cover, although screw holes for retaining cover are present 320.00 550.00 400.00
  ☐ **Cavalry Model.** Similar to Navy model but barrel is shorter and coated with tin. Of the limited number made, some went to the 11th New York Volunteer Cavalry and some went to the Navy. It was believed that the tinned barrel would prevent corrosion 400.00 700.00 525.00
  ☐ **Navy Model.** Leather covered barrel. Leather resisted corrosive effect of salt air at sea. It also prevented heated barrel from burning hand of user after continual firing. An interesting offering 300.00 550.00 450.00
  ☐ **Navy Model.** As above but with leather missing 160.00 235.00 188.00

CONFEDERATE
HANDGUNS
☐ **Augusta Machine Works Revolver,** .36 cal. Patterned on the Colt, Navy Model 1851. Very well made for a Confederate piece. Very few made, very rare 1300.00 3700.00 2400.00
☐ **Columbus Fire Arms Manufacturing Co. Revolver,** .36 cal. Patterned on the Colt, Navy Model 1851. Only a very few manufactured and fewer offered for sale 2800.00 9500.00 5800.00
☐ **Leech and Ridgon Revolver,** .36 cal. Patterned on the Colt, Navy Model 1851. Made upon contract from the Confederate Government, rather highly regarded 1350.00 2900.00 2050.00
☐ **Spiller and Burr Revolver,** .36 cal. Less than a thousand made on a government contract for 15,000. The company was purchased by the government and some 700 were made at the Government's Macon Armory 1550.00 3100.00 1700.00

582 / MILITARIA

	Current Price Range	Prior Year Average

- **T. F. Cofer Revolver,** .36 cal. Patterned on the Whitney, Navy model. Total production not known but only a very few have ever been offered. The rarest of all Confederate firearms and priced accordingly, unique spur type trigger. Three types have been offered for sale at various times.
  - **Type I,** with so-called split cylinder which could use the percussion type cartridges of the period or the metallic cartridge with nipple ... 9000.00 26000.00   16000.00
  - **Type II,** for percussion cartridges only........ 6000.00 18000.00   11000.00
  - **Type III,** a shoulder where the barrel breech joins the cylinder precludes rifling being seen . 6000.00 18000.00   11000.00

LONGARMS
- **Fayetteville Armory Rifles,** .58 cal. Production believed limited to no more than a few thousand. Interesting piece inasmuch as many were fabricated from parts from the captured Harper's Ferry Armory. Usually have lug for saber type bayonet.
  - **Early Production Examples,** Harpers Ferry parts.. 925.00   2300.00   1550.00
  - **Second Production Type,** also Harpers Ferry parts.. 700.00   1850.00   1200.00
  - **Standard Type,** most common although still rare... 550.00   2050.00   1200.00
- **H. C. Lamb Muzzle-Loading Rifle,** .58 cal. Lug for saber type bayonet, probably patterned on the U.S. Model 1841 rifle, sometimes known as the Mississippi rifle 1100.00   3700.00   1800.00
- **Morse Carbine,** .50 cal. Designed by George Morse and manufactured on captured machinery from the Harpers Ferry Armory at the factory of H. Marshall and Company. Some delivered to the Confederate Army but the majority to the S. C. State Militia. Production later moved from Atlanta, Ga. to Greenville, S.C.
  - **Atlanta Production Specimens,** limited 1700.00   3700.00   2000.00
  - **Greenville Production.**
    - **Type I**................................. 1400.00   3300.00   2100.00
    - **Type II** 950.00   2050.00   1450.00
    - **Type III** 950.00   2050.00   1450.00
- **Morse Inside Lock Musket,** .71 cal. Manufactured by George Morse in his shop in Greenville, S.C., reputed to be the simplest made of all Confederate longarms. Rare 1500.00   4300.00   2800.00
- **Richmond Armory Carbine,** .58 cal. Also made on macherinery captured at Harpers Ferry. Musketoons and rifle-muskets were produced in greater quantity than all other Confederate manufactured firearms combined. Several fakes, made from parts picked up following the Civil War, are being offered for sale. These are cleverly made and the collector should be wary!
  - **Carbine** 700.00   1900.00   1200.00
  - **Musketoon,** for both naval and artillery use ... 900.00   2400.00   1520.00
  - **Rifled Musket,** for socket bayonet 500.00   1350.00   850.00

HELMETS

	Current Price Range		Prior Year Average

- **Air Crew Helmet,** World War II. Very similar to standard World War II helmet but with cut-outs over the ears which are covered by hinged semi-cupped ear pieces with provision for radio headset 20.00 22.00 19.00
- **Experimental Model 2,** This is the so-called "deep salade" model. It was patterned after the medieval salade. Fairly deep skull flaring out sharply in front to form a visor. The flare was not so sharp on the sides and back. Helmet came down low over the eyes and dipped sharply to provide protection for the sides and back of the head. Rough khaki finish, only a few thousand made 235.00 260.00 238.00
- **Experimental Model 8,** Deep shell with well-rounded dome. Medium flare to sides and back. Sides of skull dipped sharply to protect sides and back of head. Has metal visor with eye slots which may be pulled down to cover the entire face to below the chin. Provided limited vision, was clumsy to wear, rough khaki finish, less than 2,000 made 300.00 3100.00 1700.00
- **"Liberty Bell" Model,** This was another experimental model. This helmet is something of an absurdity. Fairly deep skull flaring sharply out in the front and only slightly to the rear. Medium brim, khaki color. This helmet is not well-balanced and is too heavy. Only a few thousand were ever made. Troops testing it gave it an extremely low morale aspect, suggesting that it looked like a Chinese fisherman's hat 280.00 310.00 285.00
- **Navy "Talker" or Antiaircraft Gun Crew Helmet,** Extremely large shell with well-rounded dome and slight flare to front, sides and back. Skull had pronounced dip to cover ears and back of head. Helmet large enough to permit comfortable wearing of communication earphones. Extremely heavy padding, painted blue 20.00 22.00 19.00
- **World War I Helmet.** Shallow, basin-like skull with wide brim, rough "sand" khaki color. Either British or American manufacture 15.00 18.00 14.50
- **Model 30,** As above but with improved liner and suspension 10.00 12.00 9.50
- **World War II Helmet,** The standard helmet of the war and after, including Korea and Vietnam. Deep, well-rounded skull with nearly straight sides, small brim (visor) in front and narrow brim to sides and back, fits snugly over a plastic liner of the same shape. This liner is fitted with the suspension, olive drab color, helmet is rather well-designed 20.00 22.00 19.00

584 / MILITARIA

SWORDS — United States

	Current Price Range		Prior Year Average
☐ **Army Cavalry Sword,** Model 1913, Patterned after the British Army Model 1905 Cavalry Trooper's sword. So-called Patton saber, having been recommended for adoption by then Colonel George S. Patton. Heavy steel half basket guard reinforced longitudinally by ribs, steel grips incised with a diamond pattern, plain pommel, long tapering straight blade marked on the obverse of the ricasso with "U.S." and the serial number of the sword. Additional markings show its manufacture at the Springfield Armory and the date of manufacture. The steel scabbard is covered with khaki webbing and the throat and tip are blackened. On each side of the throat is a ring to permit the scabbard to be easily attached to the saddle. This weapon was intended for use only when mounted and was not designed for personal wear. This weapon was also issued to members of the Mounted Detachment of the U.S. Marines in the Legation guard at Peiping, China, the so-called "Horse Marines"	130.00	150.00	122.00
☐ **Army Foot Artillery Sword,** Model 1833, During the middle 1800's the U.S. Army issued this type of short bladed sword, of the so-called Roman pattern. Brass scaled grip cast in one piece with a short cross guard with plain disk finials, blade marked with the American Eagle and "N.P. AMES SPRINGFIELD." An American Eagle appears on the pommel. Hilt attached to the tang of the blade by three iron traverse rivets. Similar swords with a variety of hilts were used in England and Europe. The value of these as a weapon is questionable	148.00	165.00	152.00
☐ **Army Officer's Sword,** Model 1850. Based on French army model, half basket hilt in gilt with gilt wire wrapped leather covered grips. Phrygian helmet pattern pommel, blade single edge and slightly curved, polished black leather scabbard with gilt/brass fittings. These may be found with several slight variations	185.00	205.00	190.00
☐ **Army Officer's Sword,** Model 1902, Generally similar to above except that the grips are notched on the inside for the fingers. Full back strap, simple rounded semicap pommel with small caspan top, "D" shape knuckle guard divides into three parts as it becomes the guard, turned down tear shape finial, nickled scabbard. This is the last model Army sword authorized. Examples will appear in several qualities. Some will have elaborately etched blades and may be named. These will cost more. Blade slightly curved, good quality specimen	136.00	150.00	133.00
☐ **Army Officer's Sword,** Model 1902, Recently made copy manufactured in Spain, blade etched with American Eagle and "US"	75.00	82.00	76.00

	Current Price Range		Prior Year Average
☐ **Cavalry Saber,** American Revolutionary War, another example of an American-made weapon of the period but of rougher workmanship than the above. All iron hilt, leather grips wrapped with iron wire, guard cut from sheet iron with pierced slots on each side of grips. This is part of the narrow knuckle bow which joins a flat cap pommel, slightly curved heavy blade, no scabbard	475.00	525.00	475.00
☐ **Cavalry Saber,** American Revolutionary War. Large size all brass hilt and two branch knuckle guard, large semioval quillon, large ball pommel, black leather covered grips with brass ferrules at each end, long and fairly wide single edge blade. This is an excellent example of an American made weapon of the period, no scabbard	755.00	835.00	785.00
☐ **Cavalry Saber,** Long hilt with divided type guard, roughly carved one piece wood grips, iron hand guard and pommel, long single edge blade, metal parts of iron, all roughly forged by some local blacksmith, much paint to all parts, an excellent example of a colonial-made weapon, no scabbard, rare, c. 1776	505.00	560.00	525.00
☐ **Confederate Foot Artillery Sword,** These may vary somewhat in pattern, some may have almost Bowie knife-like blades and vary in price. The average	210.00	230.00	215.00
☐ **"Grenadier Sword,"** European sword made for issue and use in the infant United States, all brass hilt with heavily ribbed grips, fairly long curved single edge blade. Obverse is heavily engraved with lightning bolts and the legend "Grenadier of Virginia" in three lines. Obverse bears the motto "Victory or Death" in three lines. Back of blade stamped with the name of the maker "Klingenthal" together with proof marks. This is a very rare specimen and is considered of great importance to a collector of early American swords	2800.00	3100.00	2850.00
☐ **Heavy Cavalry Saber,** Model 1840, Brass semi-basket guar joining the Phrygian helmet pattern pommel, slightly curved blade, metal scabbard .	165.00	180.00	167.00

MODEL SOLDIERS

These are individually made craft models, as opposed to the cast lead (and other material) toy soldiers sold commerically from about 1890 to the present. Model soldiers have been manufactured largely as a pastime in the same way as model ships, though not apparently by as many people. It is conceivable that some were made to be sold, possibly as playthings for children of the wealthy in early times. Some could likewise have originated as novel playing pieces for deluxe chess sets. Whatever their intended purpose, the value is judged by quality of execution, and faithfulness of the costuming (which can be checked against histories of military dress).

586 / MOVIE MEMORABILIA

	Current Price Range		Prior Year Average
☐ **American Revolutionary Soldier,** Carved wood, mounted on a wooden stand, original paint, repaired, probably New England, 14" H., c. 1830 .	1000.00	1200.00	1025.00
☐ **British Dragoon Trumpeter,** Single, Georg Heyde	28.00	35.00	28.00
☐ **Coldstream Guards,** Set, W. Britain's Ltd., c. 1930's	120.00	150.00	125.00
☐ **National Guard and Horse,** Single, McLaughlin Bros.	16.00	22.00	17.00
☐ **Six Prussian Infantry with Wall,** Post-World War I, Gebruder Schneider	70.00	90.00	75.00
☐ **Soldier in British Army Dress,** Napoleonic period, body with carved and painted face and hands, holding a rifle made of brass or copper, probably American, 9½" H., c. 1870	475.00	625.00	520.00
☐ **United States Cavalry Soldier,** Mexican war period, sculptured wood, size not given, arms move, head turns, apparently contemporary	1700.00	2100.00	1800.00
☐ **World War I French Soldiers,** German flats, c. 1930's	32.00	40.00	34.00
☐ **World War I United States Radioman,** Barclay Mfg.	16.00	22.00	17.00

MOVIE MEMORABILIA

America's romance with the movies goes on and on, and each new innovation on the screen seems to bring more collecting interest for the classics of movie heritage. Fan magazines, posters, lobby cards, stills, publicity photos and personal mementos all rate high. So strong is collector interest that some of the most prestigeous auction companies, which normally restrict themselves to artworks and the more traditional collectibles, have been holding "movie" sales. There are also many specialist dealers, who keep stocks of movie memorabilia and sell through lists and catalogues. Another excellent hunting ground for the collector is comic and science-fiction conventions, as these hobbies tend to overlap and the exhibitors at such shows always display a great deal of movie items. Values are getting quite high on the more desirable, older, and scarcer pieces — and naturally anything signed by, or personally owned by a major star will sell high, if it can be authenticated.

FAN MAGAZINES

"The older the better" is usually the view of collectors with regard to motion picture fan magazines. The earlier magazines are scarcer because of (a) smaller printings and (b) loss over the years. However, the value of any *individual issue* depends to some extent on the articles it contains and the star or stars pictured on its cover, there being a much greater demand for material on some stars than on others.

	Current Price Range		Prior Year Average
☐ **Fan magazines 1930,** per issue................	10.00	25.00	17.00
☐ **Fan magazines 1931-1935,** per issue...........	7.00	12.00	9.50
☐ **Fan magazines 1936-1940,** per issue...........	6.00	10.00	6.00
☐ **Fan magazines 1941-1945,** per issue...........	4.00	8.00	6.00
☐ **Fan magazines 1946-1950,** per issue...........	3.00	6.00	4.50
☐ **Fan magazines 1951-1955,** per issue...........	1.50	4.00	2.75

Fan magazines published after 1955 have little collector appeal (most can be obtained from dealers in backdate magazines for around $1) except those carrying articles on Elvis Presley, Marilyn Monroe or other "cult" figure stars. By the same token, a magazine of the 1930's that would normally fetch $4 or $5 will bring $20 or more with a Jean Harlow or Judy Garland cover.

MISCELLANEOUS

☐ **Helmets,** Worn by "extras" in Biblical movies of the 1950's	45.00	65.00	54.00
☐ **Library Table,** Gold-leaf motif used in a number of Warner Bros. productions	525.00	600.00	550.00
☐ **Lobby Card,** Film "The Tall Men" starring Jane Russell	55.00	70.00	62.00
☐ **Lobby Card,** Film, "This is Cinerama,"	90.00	120.00	105.00
☐ **Review,** Movie "The Wizard of Oz," clipped from the Chicago Tribune, 1939	7.00	10.00	8.50
☐ **Scrapbook,** 300 items pertaining to Vivien Leigh, including six autographed pieces	295.00	350.00	320.00
☐ **Scrapbook,** 175 pieces pertaining to Tab Hunter, with one 8" x 10" color photo inscribed and signed	175.00	225.00	200.00
☐ **Seat,** Roxy Theater, New York, plush covered	400.00	475.00	438.00
☐ **Shoes,** Worn by Gene Kelly in "An American in Paris," pair	225.00	275.00	250.00
☐ **Special Eyeglasses,** Distributed to patrons of 3-D movies, plastic or cello lenses with cardboard frames, c. 1950's	8.00	12.00	10.00
☐ **Ticket Stub,** Radio City Music Hall, c. 1940's	400.00	600.00	500.00
☐ **Wig,** Worn by Debbie Reynolds	160.00	190.00	170.00

MUSIC

COUNTRY MUSIC

Country music has produced many a legendary artist, and for collectors the original recordings of country greats are gold indeed. Usually, the earliest recordings of any artist made when he or she was struggling for recognition are the most valuable. Condition counts. When a record has been played a great deal, it no longer qualifies as "mint" and the value is lower. To rank as mint, a record must have no surface noise or scratches — it gives the impression, when played, of coming straight from the factory. Generally speaking, records in "mint" condition sell for nearly twice as much, and sometimes more than twice as much, as those showing even slight evidence of wear or

Roy Orbison, doesn't sing the blues; however, if anybody were born to sing them, it is during the late 1960's, Roy's string of hits subsided.

imperfection. Prices given here are for prices that range from very good to mint specimens. In the case of LPs, the sleeve must be present and well preserved.

For more in-depth information and listings, you may refer to *The Official Price Guide to Collectible Rock Records,* published by the House of Collectibles.

RECORDING (45 records)	Current Price Range		Prior Year Average
☐ **Big Memphis Marainey,** *Call Me Anything,* Sun #184	3.50	5.00	4.20
☐ **Charlie Rich,** *Big Man/Rebound,* Phillips Inter. #3542	3.50	6.00	5.20
☐ **Charlie Rich,** *There's Another Place I Can't Go/I Need Your Love,* Phillips Inter. #3584	2.50	4.00	3.20
☐ **Conway Twitty,** *I Need Your Lovin'/Born to Sing the Blues,* Mercury #71086	7.00	12.50	9.50
☐ **Conway Twitty,** *Double Talk Baby/Why Can't I Get Through To You,* Mercury #71384	9.00	16.00	11.50
☐ **G. L. Crockett,** *Did U Ever Love Somebody,* Checker #1121	4.00	5.50	4.20
☐ **Harmonica Frank,** *Howlin Tomcat,* Chess #1494	4.00	5.50	4.20
☐ **Harmonica Frank,** *Rockin Chair Boogie,* Sun #205	4.00	5.50	4.20
☐ **Roy Orbison,** *Sweet and Innocent/Seems to Me,* RCA #7381	7.00	11.00	8.00
☐ **Roy Orbison,** *Almost Eighteen/Jolie,* RCA #7447	7.00	11.00	8.00

LP's

	Current Price Range		Prior Year Average
☐ Ira and Charles, *The Louvin Brothers*, MGM	70.00	85.00	72.00
☐ Merle Travis, *Back Home*, Capitol	50.00	65.00	52.00
☐ Bob Wills and His Texas Playboys, *Ranch House Favorites*, 10", MGM	52.00	62.00	55.00

MEMORABILIA

☐ Roy Acuff, Necktie, c. 1940	130.00	160.00	135.00
☐ Eddie Arnold, Autograph on program of "The Grand Old Opry," c. 1955	14.00	18.00	15.00
☐ Chet Atkins, 8" x 10" b/w photo signed	8.00	11.00	8.50
☐ Gene Autry, Spurs, silver-plated, pair	150.00	190.00	160.00
☐ Grandpa Jones, 8" x 10" b/w photo, signed, c. 1970	8.00	11.00	8.50
☐ Bradley Kincaid, 4" x 5" b/w photo, signed	12.00	16.00	13.00
☐ W. Lee O'Daniel, Typed letter, signed to Lyndon Johnson	130.00	160.00	130.00
☐ W. Lee O'Daniel, 3' pen used to sign legislation as U.S. Senator from Texas	235.00	260.00	262.00
☐ W. Lee O'Daniel, Typed letter, signed, to Sam Rayburn, mentioning President Roosevelt, with framed photo of O'Daniel	285.00	360.00	312.00
☐ Dolly Parton, 8" x 10" b/w photo, signed	10.00	13.00	10.50
☐ Carson Robeson, Guitar, c. 1945	620.00	920.00	750.00
☐ Carson Robeson, 8" x 10" b/w photo, signed, and a holograph letter	16.00	21.00	16.50
☐ Jimmie Rodgers, 8" x 10" b/w photo, sepia, unsigned	40.00	52.00	41.00
☐ Roy Rogers, Scrapbook of 200 photos, unsigned clippings, etc.	145.00	185.00	155.00
☐ Ernest Tubb, Guitar and original leather strap	155.00	195.00	165.00
☐ Hank Williams, Magazine article signed and inscribed	75.00	95.00	80.00

MISCELLANEOUS

☐ Book, *"Stars of Country Music,"* autographed by Johnny Cash, Porter Waggoner, Dolly Parton and several others	175.00	210.00	180.00
☐ Cassette Tape, Perry Como television program featuring Hank Snow as guest star, c. 1950	20.00	28.00	21.00
☐ Collection, 300 pieces of sheet music, c. 1950-1965	95.00	125.00	105.00
☐ Poster, "The Grand Old Opry," advertising, late 1940's	50.00	65.00	52.00
☐ Scrapbook, Leather bound, 600 clippings, photos and other miscellaneous items including 30 autographed pieces on country music stars of the pre-1950 era, 14" x 17"	1100.00	1600.00	1250.00

JAZZ RECORDS AND MEMORABILIA

Jazz recordings have been scoring big successes on the popularity charts since the 1920's. These early 78 rpm's have strong collector appeal, as do important jazz recordings from later eras. Most of the jazz greats were prolific artists who cut hundreds and hundreds of records; putting together a

590 / MUSIC

complete collection can be a rewarding challenge. If you have certain favorite artists, memorabila will very likely appeal to you as well, to supplement you collection of recordings. While memorabilia — such as autographed photos — may be somewhat harder to find, it is not usually too expensive. The value depends on the nature of the item, and on the overall scarcity of memorabilia of that particular artist. Memorabilia of jazz immortals from the earlier days, such as Bessie Smith and Bix Beiderbecke, can be quite costly because of the rarity factor and the strong demand from hobbyists.

For more in-depth information and listings, you may refer to *'The Official Price Guide to Music Collectibles,'* published by the House of Collectibles.

RECORDINGS (78 Records)

	Current Price Range		Prior Year Average
☐ **Benny Goodman,** with Ben Pollack and his orchestra, *Waitin' for Katie,* Victor, c. 1927	10.00	13.00	10.50
☐ **Benny Goodman,** with Ted Lewis and his band, *Dip Your Brush in Sunshine,* Columbia, c. 1931	20.00	27.00	21.50
☐ **Benny Goodman,** with the Charleston Chasers, *Basin Street Blues,* Columbia, c. 1931	26.00	32.00	27.00
☐ **Benny Goodman,** with the Benny Goodman Quintet, *Pick-a-Rib,* Victor, c. 1938	9.00	13.00	10.00
☐ **Billie Holiday,** with Benny Goodman and his orchestra, *Your Mother's Son-In-Law,* Columbia, c. 1933	40.00	50.00	42.00
☐ **Billie Holiday,** with Teddy Wilson and his orchestra, *What a Little Moonlight Can Do,* Brunswick, c. 1935	16.00	22.00	17.00
☐ **Billie Holiday,** with Teddy Wilson and his orchestra, *Miss Brown to You,* Brunswick, c. 1935	17.00	24.00	18.50
☐ **Billie Holiday,** and her orchestra, *God Bless the Child,* Okeh, c. 1941	9.00	13.00	10.00
☐ **Bix Beiderbecke,** with the Wolverines, *Copenhagen,* Gennett, c. 1924	120.00	150.00	125.00
☐ **Bix Beiderbecke,** with Jean Goldkette, *Clementine (from New Orleans),* Victor, c. 1927	16.00	22.00	17.00
☐ **Bix Beiderbecke,** with Frankie Trumbauer and his orchestra, *Riverboat Shuffle,* Okeh, c. 1927	60.00	80.00	65.00
☐ **Bix Beiderbecke,** with Paul Whiteman and his orchestra, *Because My Baby Don't Mean "Maybe" Now,* Okeh, c. 1928	20.00	27.00	21.50
☐ **Coleman Hawkins,** with the Mound City Blue Blowers, *Hello Lola,* Victor, c. 1929	26.00	35.00	28.00
☐ **Coleman Hawkins,** with Fletcher Henderson and his orchestra, *Underneath the Harlem Moon,* Columbia, c. 1932	21.00	28.00	22.50
☐ **Coleman Hawkins,** with Lionel Hampton and his orchestra, *Dinah,* Victor, c. 1939	9.00	13.00	10.00
☐ **Duke Ellington,** with his orchestra, *Creole Love Call,* Victor, c. 1927	16.00	21.00	16.50
☐ **Duke Ellington,** with the Jungle Band, *Mood Indigo,* Brunswick, c. 1930	16.00	21.00	16.50
☐ **Duke Ellington,** with his orchestra, *Rockabye River,* Victor, c. 1946	4.50	6.50	5.00
☐ **Earl Hines,** *Chicago Rhythm,* Victor, c. 1929	30.00	40.00	32.50
☐ **Jelly Roll Morton,** *Muddy Water Blues,* Paramount, c. 1923	200.00	250.00	215.00

MUSIC / 591

LP's	Current Price Range		Prior Year Average
☐ Dave Bailey Sextet, *Gettin' Into Somethin'*, Epic .	25.00	35.00	27.50
☐ James Clay and David "Fathead" Newman, *The Sound of the Wide Open Spaces*, Riverside	20.00	27.00	20.50
☐ Stan Getz Quintet, *Jazz at Storyville*, Roost, 10" .	26.00	35.00	28.50
☐ Paul Nero, *Jam Session*, Skylark, 10"	72.00	90.00	76.00
MEMORABILIA			
☐ **Bessie Smith,** signed photos, rare	100.00	125.00	102.00
☐ **Buddy Rich,** set of drumsticks, said to have been used by him	60.00	80.00	65.00
☐ **Charlie Parker,** signed photo, rare	75.00	95.00	80.00
☐ **Coleman Hawkins,** front page of *Billboard* magazine, signed by him	16.00	21.00	16.50
☐ **Count Basie,** inscribed photograph	6.00	8.00	6.00
☐ **Count Basie,** piano stool, said to have been used by him, mahogany covered in green leatherette, sold with autographed photo	140.00	180.00	150.00
☐ **Duke Ellington,** signed photograph	21.00	27.00	22.00
☐ **Duke Ellington,** signed hotel menu, c. 1940	10.00	13.00	10.50
☐ **Harry James,** trumpet, original velvet-lined wooden box, good condition	475.00	625.00	520.00
☐ **Harry James,** signed photograph	9.00	13.50	10.00
☐ **Harry James,** signature on record sleeve	5.00	6.50	5.20
☐ **Jimmie Dorsey,** signed photograph	14.00	19.00	15.50
☐ **Jimmie Dorsey,** cancelled check endorsed by him (from a recording company)	20.00	27.00	21.50
☐ **Jimmie Dorsey,** two scrapbooks, containing 700 (approx.) clippings from newspapers, some signed photos, 16" x 12"	400.00	475.00	412.00
☐ **Jimmie and Tommie Dorsey,** photo of both signed by both	34.00	42.00	36.00
☐ **Louis Armstrong,** signed photo	16.00	22.00	17.00
☐ **Louis Armstrong,** 11" x 13" color photo from newspaper, signed	300.00	375.00	312.00
☐ **Louis Armstrong,** ceramic statuette, modern ...	16.00	21.00	16.50

ROCK 'N' ROLL

Since its birth in the '50's, rock has revolutionized the entertainment world — and brought about one of the most popular fields of collecting. Rock fans and hobbyists seek out the "oldies" and find interest in discs by obscure artists as well as the big stars. Many "flop" rock records from the '50's have value because of small pressings and regional distribution. Compilings have been made of the names of thousands of rock artists and song titles, but it is still believed that SOME early rock 45's exist that collectors are not yet aware of. This is a hobby where persistence and a detective spirit can pay off. As far as memorabilia goes, it's more abundant for Rock than any other form of music. Without any doubt, rock fans have traditionally been the most meticulous in gathering and preserving the souvenirs of their favorites. Little could they have known, originally, that it would someday have a big cash value as well as a sentimental value! If you were a teenager in the sixties and put away Beatles mementos, they can easily be turned into cash today — as can the memorabilia of nearly all rock performers. Naturally, collectors have the keenest interest in items that are unusual and might be "one of a kind."

592 / MUSIC

For more in-depth information and listings, you may refer to *The Official Price Guide to Collectible Rock Records*, and *The Official Price Guide to Music Collectibles*, both published by the House of Collectibles.

	Current Price Range		Prior Year Average
ELVIS PRESLEY (45 records)			
☐ Mystery Train/I Forgot to Remember to Forget, RCA #6357	12.00	20.00	13.00
☐ That's All Right/Blue Moon of Kentucky, RCA #6380	12.00	20.00	13.00
☐ Good Rockin' Tonight/I Don't Care If The Sun Don't Shine, RCA #6381	12.00	20.00	13.00
☐ Milkcow Blues Boogie/You're a Heartbreaker, RCA #6382	12.00	20.00	13.00
☐ Baby Let's Play House/I'm Left, You're Right, She's Gone, RCA #6383	12.00	20.00	13.00
☐ Heartbreak Hotel/I Was The One (1), RCA #6420	4.00	6.50	5.00
☐ I Want You, I Need You, I Love You/My Baby Left Me (3), RCA #6540	4.00	6.50	5.00
LP's			
☐ Elvis Presley (double-pocket), RCA #1254	80.00	135.00	95.00
☐ Elvis Presley, RCA #747	10.00	18.00	11.50
☐ Heartbreak Hotel, RCA #821	12.00	18.00	13.50
☐ Elvis Presley, RCA #830	12.00	18.00	13.50
☐ The Real Elvis, RCA #940	12.00	18.00	13.50
☐ Anyway You Want Me, RCA #965	12.00	18.00	13.50
☐ Love Me Tender, RCA #4006	10.00	18.00	11.50
☐ Elvis, Vol. 1, RCA #992	10.00	18.00	11.50
☐ Elvis, Vol. 2, RCA #993	12.00	18.00	13.50
☐ Strictly Elvis, RCA #994	12.00	18.00	13.50
☐ Loving You, Vol. 1, RCA #1-1515	12.00	18.00	13.50
☐ Loving You, Vol. 2, RCA #2-1515	12.00	18.00	13.50
BUDDY HOLLY (45 records)			
☐ Love Me/Blue Days, Black Nights, Decca #29854	22.00	38.00	27.00
☐ Modern Don Juan/You Are My One Desire, Decca #30166	20.00	32.00	23.50
☐ That'll Be The Day/Rock Around With Ollie Vee, Decca #30534	30.00	45.00	32.00
☐ Love Me/You Are My One Desire, Decca #30543	18.00	28.00	20.00
☐ Girl On My Mind/Ting-A-Ling, Decca #30650	20.00	32.00	23.50
☐ Worlds of Love/Mailman Bring Me No More Blues, Coral #61852	45.00	80.00	58.00
☐ Peggy Sue/Everyday, Coral #61885	4.00	6.00	5.20
☐ I'm Gonna Love You Too/Listen To Me, Coral #61947	6.00	10.00	7.00
☐ Rave On/Take Your Time, Coral #61985	4.00	6.50	5.20
☐ Early In The Morning/Now We're One, Coral #62006	4.00	6.50	5.20
☐ Heartbeat/Well... All Right, Coral #62051	4.00	6.50	5.20
☐ It Doesn't Matter Anymore/Raining In My Heart, Coral #62074	4.00	6.50	5.20
☐ Peggy Sue Got Married/Crying, Waiting, Hoping, Coral #62134	14.00	22.00	15.50
☐ True Love Ways/That Makes It Tough, Coral #62210	14.00	22.00	15.50

MEMORABILIA

	Current Price Range		Prior Year Average
☐ **Chuck Berry,** three signed photos, two unsigned photos, one signed in purple ink	26.00	34.00	28.00
☐ **Pat Boone,** signed 8″ x 10″ b/w photos	3.00	3.75	3.12
☐ **Pat Boone,** signed phonograph records, Dot label	13.00	17.00	13.00
☐ **Bobby Darin,** scrapbook of his career items, few signed colored photos, c. 1950's	150.00	190.00	165.00
☐ **The Diamonds,** 8″ x 10″ b/w photo, signed by all members, notes on back	20.00	25.00	20.50
☐ **Fats Domino,** collection of 36 original phonograph records along with 16 signed photos/other items, in leather-bound albums, soiled	475.00	625.00	520.00
☐ **Fats Domino,** signed 8″ x 10″ b/w photo, seated at piano	5.00	7.00	5.50
☐ **Connie Francis,** autographed magazine article	10.00	14.00	10.00
☐ **Connie Francis,** holograph postcard, six lines	10.00	14.00	11.00
☐ **Connie Francis,** signed LP album cover	10.50	16.00	12.00
☐ **Bill Haley,** autographed sheet music, *Shake, Rattle and Roll*	15.00	20.00	15.50
☐ **Buddy Holly** (all items scarce because of his early death), autographed photographs	25.00	33.00	27.00
☐ **Buddy Knox,** signed tear sheet, *Cashbox* magazine showing his recording, *Party Doll*, c. 1956	25.00	32.00	26.00
☐ **Lloyd Price,** signed 5″ x 7″ b/w photo	4.00	5.50	4.20
☐ **Bobby Sherman,** coloring book, pub. in 1971 for 59¢	8.00	11.00	8.50

SHEET MUSIC

The collector of sheet music should first of all understand that values depend not only on composer and composition but the cover illustration, and in many cases the cover illustration proves the most influential factor. Many collectors buy these items for framing and are interested only in the artwork. Thus, the best hunting ground for them is print galleries where they can be found both framed and unframed.

☐ *Dundreary's Brother Sam,* by J. E. Carpenter, cover by Concanen and Lee, published by Metzler, c. 1865	175.00	230.00	195.00
☐ *I'm a Ship Without a Rudder,* composed by Frank Vernon, published by Hopwood	130.00	175.00	150.00
☐ *Many a Time,* written and composed by Arthur West, sung by Harry Freeman	55.00	80.00	68.00
☐ *Oh, Come With Me,* written by Richard Ryan, published by R. Cocks and Co.	11.00	15.00	13.00
☐ *Prince Albert's Marching Band,* as performed by the Military Bands, rider in military dress on cover	9.00	12.00	10.50
☐ *See-Saw Waltz,* composed by A. G. Crowe, published by Metzler	11.00	15.00	13.00
☐ *The Calendar Polka,* D. Smith, c. 1884	11.00	15.00	13.00
☐ *The Crystal Palace Quadrille,* published by G.H. Davidson	9.00	12.00	10.50
☐ *The Excursion Train,* sung by E. Marshall, published by J. Williams	95.00	120.00	108.00
☐ *The Great Eastern Polka* (about an ocean liner)	14.00	19.00	16.50

594 / MUSIC BOXES

	Current Price Range		Prior Year Average
☐ *Two in the Morning*, sung with the Greatest Applause by Mr. W. Randall, published by Duff and Stewart	90.00	115.00	102.00
☐ *Wait for the Turn of the Tide*, written and sung by Mr. Harry Clifton, c. 1860's	14.00	19.00	16.50
☐ *Who's That Tapping at the Garden Gate?*, composed by S. W. New, published by Hutchings and Romer	9.00	12.00	10.50

MUSIC BOXES
(Cylinder and Disc)

Reginaphone Disc Table Model Music Box, disc phonograph combination, inside horn, simple case style.

Music boxes were the forerunners of the phonograph. They brought music into the home and were hailed as the invention of the age. From about 1870 to 1890 they enjoyed enormous popularity, and this is the era to which most specimens on the market date. Some date a bit later, as they continued to be brought out by optimistic manufacturers who believed the Edison Phonograph to be a passing fancy. Alas for the music box industry, it was a lost cause. The phonograph, though not nearly as good-looking as the music box, could do something the latter was incapable of: capturing the human voice. Music boxes could produce music, but not vocals. There are two types of music boxes, disc and cylinder, just as there are disc and cylinder phonographs. Selections played by the disc type looked like records, except that they were metal. The principal was the same with both: the selection rotated, and little bumps on its surface engaged pins in the machine, which produced music. Despite this very simplistic mechanism, music of rather good quality could be achieved by the better music boxes. They were considered good enough to install in places of amusement, fitted with slots to take coins, and thus became the first jukeboxes.

Test a music box thoroughly before purchase to make certain it's in operating condition. Don't crank it too tightly or you could break the spring. The mere fact that a specimen runs after cranking is not assurance that it's in good working order: the pins may be out of line, and some of them might not be working at all. Play a disc (or cylinder) on the machine and listen to it carefully. If you buy a machine that needs restoration this can be quite expensive. Most of the specialist dealers restore their music boxes before placing them on sale.

CYLINDER MUSIC BOXES

	Current Price Range		Prior Year Average
☐ **Carved mahogany case,** three round bells with hammer strikers, plays 10 separate tunes	700.00	850.00	720.00
☐ **Double-cylinder box,** multiple carvings on polished mahogany case, wide, flared legs, plays six tunes on each of two fat cylinders, over one hour playing time	950.00	1250.00	1025.00
☐ **Double Dawkins cylinder box,** seven separate cylinders. Each cylinder is brass and over 11″ long, hand-polished golden wood box has container for storage of spare cylinders	2600.00	3400.00	2850.00
☐ **Drum and bell box,** polished inlaid rosewood case with drum and six fine-tuned bells with manual controls, 14″ cylinder, Swiss made, plays 12 tunes	800.00	1000.00	850.00
☐ **Mermod Freres,** 10-tune orchestral box, outside crank wind, 13½″ cylinder, bells, drums, castanets and mandolin, oak case with some carving, brass handles, coin operated, c. 1896	2350.00	2900.00	2500.00
☐ **Mermod Freres box,** two 8″ brass cylinders, plays twelve tunes, originally coin operated	1400.00	1900.00	1550.00
☐ **Mermod Freres double-cylinder box,** beautifully polished and matched rosewood, walnut and ebony woods, complete with dial, tune-selector and safety lock, contains six separate tunes on each 13″ cylinder	800.00	1100.00	850.00
☐ **Organ music box,** plays 13″ cylinder, eight tunes, has bellows, unusual	1200.00	1450.00	1250.00
☐ **Paillard Vaucher Fils,** 13″ cylinder, six bells with bird strikers, inlaid box, lever wind	1700.00	2000.00	1750.00
☐ **Twenty-tune cylinder box,** large, polished mahogany box contains two 10″ brass cylinders, each with 10 separate tunes, finest Swiss manufacturer	900.00	1100.00	900.00

DISC MUSIC BOXES

	Current Price Range		Prior Year Average
☐ **Adler disc music box,** scrolled Victorian case, 18¾" disc, coin-operated	2100.00	2600.00	2250.00
☐ **Britannia music box,** lever-wound machine with 9¼" discs, table model	500.00	625.00	530.00
☐ **Monopol disc music box,** double-comb machine .	750.00	950.00	800.00
☐ **Olympia disc music box,** single-comb table machine with 15½" discs, contained in hand-carved mahogany grained case	1300.00	1600.00	1350.00
☐ **Same as above** except with double comp	1500.00	1900.00	1600.00
☐ **Polyphone deluxe bell box,** 12-tuned saucer bells, 18½" x 17" x 25", c. 1900	2000.00	2400.00	2100.00
☐ **Polyphone disc music box,** takes 19⅝" discs, coin-operated, upright walnut case, glass front .	3700.00	4200.00	3850.00
☐ **Polyphone upright music box,** German, glass front, walnut case, plays 35 discs, 20" diameter, coin-operated, 64" H.	2900.00	3500.00	3000.00
☐ **Regina floor model,** bow front, glass door, oak or mahogany, 15" discs, automatic changer, coin-operated with 12 discs	6000.00	7200.00	6100.00
☐ **Stella disc music box,** mahogany-cased table model, uses 9½" discs	500.00	575.00	512.00
☐ **Symphonion floor model,** 25¼" discs, storage case in bottom, burled walnut, carved case, c. 1880	3300.00	3850.00	3475.00
☐ **Symphonion disc music box,** small decorated case, plays 6" discs, c. 1880	400.00	475.00	412.00
☐ **Symphonion disc music box,** top-mounted, plays 4½" discs, unusual	600.00	750.00	620.00
☐ **Symphonion table model,** case slightly carved, plays 15½" discs, c. 1880	1200.00	1500.00	1250.0

NOVELTY MUSIC BOXES

☐ **Cake plate,** plays "Happy Birthday," revolving, c. 1940	18.00	24.00	18.50
☐ **Cigar holder,** wood and brass, 15" H.	75.00	105.00	88.00
☐ **Plush elephant toy,** tail winds music box, c. 1950	8.00	13.00	9.50
☐ **Salt and pepper holder,** chromed white metal, Occupied Japan, Oriental music	42.00	54.00	44.00

MUSICAL INSTRUMENTS

Musical instruments have been made for thousands of years, and collecting them is, to hobbyists, even more rewarding than listening to them. Early specimens of all instruments are preserved (except, of course, those of modern invention) and can be found on the market. Some show extraordinary workmanship and are decorative enough simply to display. The value of an old instrument depends on factors which differ, somewhat, from the usual considerations for collectors' items. An important point is whether the instrument could be used today for concert play and, if so, whether it could be deemed superior to modern versions of that instrument. The very high prices fetched by many Italian violins of the 17th and 18th centuries results from

MUSICAL INSTRUMENTS / 597

Accordion, Italian, 20th Century

competition between collectors and *musicians,* who regard these specimens as the finest violins ever made. Many violinists will spend a fortune on an early instrument, believing it will further their career. On the other hand, wind instruments of that era, though interesting as antiques, are considered inferior to their modern counterparts from a musical standpoint.

For more in-depth information and listings, you may refer to *The Official Price Guide to Music Machines and Instruments,* published by the House of Collectibles.

	Current Price Range		Prior Year Average
☐ **Accordian,** German	225.00	300.00	238.00
☐ **Clarinet,** Wm. Nuernberger, German, silver-plate	60.00	80.00	65.00
☐ **Clavichord,** Heidelberg, rosewood case, four tapered legs, c. 1857	1300.00	1600.00	1350.00
☐ **Cornet,** Klemm and Bro., Philadelphia, brass body with nickel mounts, mid 19th c.	420.00	520.00	450.00
☐ **Drums,** Chinese, bodies of painted wood, set of four	130.00	170.00	140.00
☐ **Dulcimer,** Italian, fruitwood body, 19 strings, c. 18th c.	620.00	820.00	700.00
☐ **Fife,** rosewood and brass, 16" L., c. 1850-1870	100.00	125.00	102.00
☐ **Flute,** Henry Hill, carved ivory, six-keyed	500.00	575.00	512.00
☐ **Guitar,** Naples, rosewood fingerboard, c. 1891	650.00	775.00	682.00
☐ **Harmonica,** brass plates, c. 1875	90.00	130.00	100.00
☐ **Harp,** Swiss, enamel and gold, 19th c.	2600.00	3400.00	2900.00
☐ **Helicon,** Henry Pourcelle, Paris, brass body with three piston valves, 19th c.	1000.00	1300.00	1050.00

598 / NAPKIN RINGS AND HOLDERS

	Current Price Range		Prior Year Average
☐ **Oboe,** Klenig, ivory, three-keyed, 18th c.	7000.00	8500.00	7200.00
☐ **Rollmonica,** plus three rolls	75.00	95.00	80.00
☐ **Saxophone,** tenor, Buescher and Co., Elkhart, Indiana, brass body and brass mounts, c. 1935	950.00	1200.00	1025.00
☐ **Ukelele,** Arthur Godfrey, plastic, c. 1953	25.00	32.00	26.00
☐ **Viola,** German, one-piece back, 18th c.	425.00	525.00	450.00
☐ **Violin,** Hungarian, one-piece back, red brown color	275.00	355.00	290.00

ORGANS

☐ **Gem roller organ,** three rolls	475.00	550.00	480.00
☐ **Esteyreed,** full pedal keyboard	3300.00	3900.00	3500.00
☐ **Loring and Blake**	1200.00	1500.00	1250.00
☐ **Mason and Hamlin,** Church	4200.00	5200.00	4500.00
☐ **Pump,** Estey, c. 1880's	1500.00	1800.00	1550.00

PIANOS

☐ **Baby grand,** Smith, New York	12500.00	15500.00	13500.00
☐ **Grand,** Broadwood, 7½" L	3400.00	4200.00	3600.00
☐ **Chickering Ampico-A,** 5'4" L	6000.00	8000.00	6500.00
☐ **Grand concert,** Baldwin, 9' L	11500.00	13500.00	1200.00
☐ **Grand,** Emerson, rosewood	4500.00	5500.00	4500.00
☐ **Grand,** Steinway, Duo-Art player, walnut, c. 1929	15500.00	18500.00	16500.00
☐ **Grand,** Steinway, carved	5000.00	6000.00	5250.00
☐ **Grand,** Steinway, c. 1940's	5500.00	6750.00	5600.00
☐ **Grand,** square, Hallett and Cumston, c. 1860's	3200.00	4000.00	3350.00
☐ **Player,** Aeolian-Duo-Art, upright, c. 1905	2400.00	3000.00	2500.00
☐ **Player,** coin-operated	3500.00	4300.00	3700.00
☐ **Player,** Lindeman	1800.00	2500.00	2050.00
☐ **Player,** Steinway	2700.00	3300.00	2900.00
☐ **Square,** mahogany case with carved fleur-de-lys, c. 1830	650.00	900.00	720.00
☐ **Upright,** H. C. Bayes	1400.00	1900.00	1550.00

NAPKIN RINGS AND HOLDERS

The Victorian table was something to behold. There wasn't just a separate dish, and fork, or spoon for every kind of food that could possibly be served — there were many frilly little extras as well. Among these was the venerable napkin ring, which really had no excuse for its existence except that it added another touch of fussiness to the table. When you sat down to dinner in 1870 to 1900 (or thereabout), the napkin beside your plate was not folded but deftly stuffed into a silver plated, ornamental ring. These rings were sold by the millions, and came in every conceivable design. It takes no great insight to see that people must have been collecting them, even when they were new — otherwise the manufacturers would hardly have bothered putting out so many different types. If you look through a Sears Roebuck catalogue of the '90's, you'll find page after page devoted to napkin rings. And just about any variety store of that era displayed hundreds of them. They were the perfect gift: cheap, eye-catching, and always useful if the recipient wanted to be in style. Some specimens are found in wood but these are far in the minority.

NAPKIN RINGS AND HOLDERS / 599

Late Victorian Napkin Rings, devotion to elegant table settings, typical examples of rectangular and circular models. . . . . $35.00-$45.00

	Current Price Range		Prior Year Average
☐ **Angel** with butterfly	118.00	135.00	125.00
☐ **Bulldog** guarding ring	80.00	92.00	86.00
☐ **Cherub** with bird, flowers on side, square ring, silver-plate	95.00	110.00	102.00
☐ **Cherubs,** two playing, Meriden	40.00	50.00	44.00
☐ **Chick** looking over ring	95.00	110.00	102.00
☐ **Crossed rifles,** each side engraved, silver-plate . .	170.00	195.00	182.00
☐ **Cupid** with flute	140.00	160.00	150.00
☐ **Dog** chasing car	145.00	160.00	152.00
☐ **Dog** on each side of ring, Toronto Silver-Plate Co.	130.00	155.00	142.00
☐ **Eagle,** resilvered, 4" H.	140.00	180.00	160.00
☐ **Fans** on either side, ring above ballfooted base .	135.00	160.00	147.00
☐ **Floral engraving,** solid silver, ornate	60.00	75.00	67.00
☐ **Foxes and bird** in nest	110.00	130.00	120.00
☐ **Girl** with pigtail pushing ring, William Rogers . . .	240.00	300.00	260.00
☐ **Horseshoe** and ring	68.00	82.00	74.00
☐ **Kangaroo** on leaf	60.00	75.00	67.00
☐ **Kate Greenaway,** boy smiling, hands behind sailor hat	165.00	190.00	175.00
☐ **Kate Greenaway,** girl with dog, engraved flowers	70.00	85.00	75.00
☐ **Kate Greenaway,** girl holding gun	165.00	185.00	175.00
☐ **Kitten** batting air beside ring	80.00	90.00	84.00
☐ **Kitten** pulling cart	137.00	150.00	143.00
☐ **Laughing child** in nightgown	120.00	135.00	126.00
☐ **Leaf base** with acorn	62.00	75.00	68.00
☐ **Owls,** mother and owlettes on fancy footed base	235.00	280.00	250.00
☐ **Peacock** seated on ring	190.00	215.00	200.00
☐ **Rabbit,** ornate design, silver-plate	85.00	110.00	95.00
☐ **Rabbit,** sitting at side of ring	50.00	65.00	55.00
☐ **Ring and toothpick**	70.00	85.00	77.00
☐ **Rose and leaf,** on both sides, leaf engraving, silver-plate	100.00	140.00	120.00
☐ **Rustic boys,** each side of square ring, silver-plate	180.00	215.00	190.00

600 / NAUTICAL GEAR

	Current Price Range		Prior Year Average
☐ **Squirrel,** fancy design on ring, original condition	160.00	190.00	175.00
☐ **Sunflower,** leaves on sides, Meriden	45.00	60.00	52.00
☐ **Swan** on oval base	140.00	170.00	155.00
☐ **Turtles** with ring on back	115.00	135.00	125.00
☐ **Violin**	70.00	85.00	77.00
☐ **Waterlily,** Rogers	40.00	50.00	44.00
☐ **Wine barrel** on leaves and twigs	40.00	50.00	44.00
☐ **Wishbone,** "Best Wishes," four ball feet, Wilcox	35.00	42.00	38.50
☐ **Woman** on side of floral engraving	150.00	185.00	165.00

NAUTICAL GEAR

The age of sailing is long since gone, but the romantic era of ships and the sea lives on in nautical memorabilia. For anyone with even a slight fascination for the world of maritime adventure, these collectibles have an almost magical appeal. Hand-wrought in most cases, weathered from ages of salt spray, they're bold and proud reminders of a colorful age. When ships were scuttled, some of the components would invariably be salvaged. They might then be used on another ship or end up in the attic of a sea captain along with miscellaneous souvenirs of his travels. Most of what you'll find on the market dates to the 19th century, the final century for sailing ships, but occasionally some earlier items do turn up. They hardly ever bear markings, unless they happen to be of very late origin, and therefore can be dated only on the basis of style, material and workmanship. As a beginner you might want to confine your purchases to the specialist dealers, who are very knowledgeable and will tell you all the pertinent facts about each item. New England has traditionally been the primary source for nautical antiques, but there are now a number of specialist dealers in other parts of the country as well. Watch the auction sales, too, and even the flea markets.

☐ **19th century anchor,** sailing ship, 500 lbs.	475.00	675.00	550.00
☐ **Bell,** brass	45.00	75.00	55.00
☐ **Binnacles** (container holding a ship's compass), usually brass	425.00	625.00	500.00
☐ **Chest,** sea, canvas on lid, ship painting	600.00	775.00	660.00
☐ **Clock,** brass, Seth Thomas, 7" Dia.	180.00	240.00	200.00
☐ **Compasses,** in case, on gimbals	225.00	425.00	300.00
☐ **Figurehead,** carved, painted wood, 32" H., 19th c.	2200.00	3200.00	2500.00
☐ **Globe,** covered with linen, 28" Dia., c. 1875	425.00	625.00	500.00
☐ **Gold scales** with small weights	130.00	260.00	180.00
☐ **Guinea scales,** English scale used to weigh gold coins	145.00	195.00	170.00
☐ **Helmet,** brass and copper, deep sea, 17" Dia.	850.00	1100.00	900.00
☐ **Hydrometers,** in case with weights and thermometer	85.00	125.00	100.00
☐ **Ivory or boxwood rules,** used for measuring and drafting	55.00	110.00	75.00
☐ **Lamp,** copper with brass and copper, deep sea, 17" H.	850.00	1050.00	900.00
☐ **Lantern,** brass top, copper	75.00	110.00	88.00

NAVAJO BLANKETS AND SERAPES / 601

	Current Price Range		Prior Year Average
☐ **Octants,** Hadley quadrant, ebony, in case, used for ship's navigation	500.00	700.00	550.00
☐ **Pocket scales**	110.00	160.00	125.00
☐ **Porthole,** brass, 8" Dia.	45.00	65.00	50.00
☐ **Sextants,** brass, in case, late 19th to 20th c.	350.00	470.00	390.00
☐ **Ship's telegraph**	375.00	575.00	450.00
☐ **Slide rules**	65.00	85.00	70.00
☐ **Sovereign scales,** English scale used to weigh coins	70.00	95.00	82.00
☐ **Telescope,** brass, English, with case, 19¼" L., 19th c.	425.00	625.00	500.00
☐ **Telescopes,** long glass	200.00	325.00	235.00
☐ **Telescopes on stand,** astronomical or marine	850.00	3100.00	1800.00

OCEANLINER MEMORABILIA

☐ **Ashtray,** ceramic	10.00	13.00	10.50
☐ **Candy container,** tin, United States	10.00	13.00	10.50
☐ **Deck plan,** France	5.00	8.00	5.50
☐ **Deck plan,** Europa	5.00	8.00	5.50
☐ **Menu,** Queen Elizabeth, farewell dinner, c. 1941	5.00	8.00	5.50
☐ **Menu,** Swedish-American Lines, c. 1941	4.00	5.50	4.20
☐ **Menu,** Red Star Line, handprinted, c. 1900	8.00	11.00	8.50
☐ **Officer's hat**	20.00	27.00	21.50

(Note: Relics from the TITANIC are worth at least five times as much as a comparable item from another ship, but beware of reproductions as these have become abundant in recent years.)

NAVAJO BLANKETS AND SERAPES

Blanket weaving, one of the chief arts of the American Indian, was brought to fullest perfection among the Navajos of the southwest. Though much of the native production was for community use, some of the finest blankets were brought to trading posts and swapped for necessities. Proprietors of the trading posts always preferred to get such items from the Indians, rather than from a wholesaler in the East: the quality was better and payment could be made in merchandise. You will need some expertise to recognize the more valuable specimens. Many late creations as well as those of inferior quality and outright reproductions are on the market. The finest Navajo blankets were made in the mid to late 19th century.

☐ **Chief's blanket,** woven with nine-spot pattern of deep red, black, brown, orange and white rectangles enclosing geometric motifs with background stripe in black and white	1100.00	1600.00	1250.00
☐ **Germantown wearing blanket,** woven with a Chief's third phase nine-spot pattern of red, white and blue diamonds each having a cross in the center and black and white stripe background	1700.00	2100.00	1800.00
☐ **Serape,** Bosque Redondo (?), orange, light and dark blue, green and yellow on gray bands, zig-zag figures in other colors, 45" x 65", c. 1890	3000.00	3600.00	3100.00

602 / NEEDLEWORK

	Current Price Range		Prior Year Average
☐ **Serape,** late terraced style, indigo blue, white, red, 52″ x 68″, c. 1890	4100.00	4500.00	4100.00
☐ **Serape,** white and indigo blue on two-ply red ground, 54″ x 72″, c. 1880	8500.00	10500.00	9000.00
☐ **Wearing blanket** woven in handspun and Germantown yarn with a chief's fourth phase nine-spot pattern of red and blue, black diamonds enclose green and yellow geometric motifs	1450.00	1650.00	1460.00

NEEDLEWORK

This area of interest includes interesting, old, artistic, or simply curious specimens of embroidery and other needlework. The most familiar needlework collectibles are undoubtedly samplers, of which a few are listed here: the fabric pictures that once hung in nearly every home. Making pictures in needlework was considered an essential phase of becoming skilled in the sewing art — it was an exercise, like penmanship exercises, and most young girls in the 1650 to 1850 period turned out their share of samplers. Sampler making was likewise a profession, as they were sold in early shops and especially by the itinerant tradesmen who roamed America's streets in colonial times. The craft was not a native innovation, as samplers were being made in England before any such work was done in America. The value of a sampler depends on its age, size, subject, artistry, and state of preservation. Simple traditional patterns are not nearly as valuable as complex, original scenes. Fine embroidery is also avidly sought. If the specimen is especially rare or interesting, even a rather small scrap will have some value, as it may be the only existing fragment of that particular design. Embroidery makers often did not follow patterns in books but created their own, letting their imaginations run free. By making comparisons and studying the history of embroidery, fairly accurate estimates of dates can be arrived at.

EMBROIDERY

☐ **Apron,** Hungarian, brilliant color, c. 1930's	30.00	40.00	32.00
☐ **Chenille still-life,** French, urn and flowers, 10″ x 14″, dated 1824	235.00	335.00	275.00
☐ **Crazy quilt,** silk and velvet, slight damage, c. 1900	52.00	72.00	60.00
☐ **Crewel fragment,** four complete flowers, vines, c. 1810	60.00	75.00	62.00
☐ **Mandarin Square,** flying crane, 19th c.	210.00	290.00	240.00
☐ **Mandarin Square,** golden pheasant, metallic thread	75.00	105.00	85.00
☐ **Masonic emblems,** cotton floss on tan gabardine, 16″ sq., 19th c.	340.00	430.00	375.00
☐ **Pillowcase,** sunbonnet babies, red cotton on white linen, c. 1890	18.00	25.00	19.50
☐ **Pillowtop,** embroidery and beading bouquet of flowers, c. 1910	14.00	20.00	14.50
☐ **Robe,** Japanese, silk, very fine condition, c. 1890	260.00	335.00	282.00
☐ **Shawl,** paisley on olive green ground, good condition, large	210.00	260.00	225.00
☐ **Shawl,** Kashmir, black medallion, 84″ sq., c. 1900	250.00	325.00	260.00

	Current Price Range		Prior Year Average
☐ **Shawl,** peach silk, bright silk embroidered flowers, c. 1920's	150.00	200.00	165.00
☐ **Table cover,** Chinese, metallic thread, 45" sq., late 19th c.	34.00	42.00	36.00
☐ **Table cover,** machine-made paisley, 62" x 69"	45.00	55.00	47.00
☐ **Wall hanging,** velvet, silk floss flowers, 9" x 12", c. 1885	32.00	42.00	35.00

LACE

☐ **Collar,** Gros Point de Venise, mid-1600's	260.00	360.00	300.00
☐ **Doily,** tatted, intricate design, oval, 10" L.	9.00	13.00	10.00
☐ **Gloves,** cotton crochet, c. 1890's	14.00	20.00	14.50
☐ **Handkerchief,** linen with Point de Gaze lace, c. 1829	85.00	125.00	100.00
☐ **Mantilla,** cream-colored, Blonde de Caen lace, c. 1820	110.00	150.00	120.00
☐ **Rectangle,** Point Plat de Venise a Reseau, c. 1720	210.00	285.00	238.00

SAMPLERS

☐ **Alphabet and flowers,** faded, c. 1855	85.00	120.00	95.00
☐ **Alphabet and geometric designs,** English, long horizontal shape, c. 1680	1500.00	1900.00	1600.00
☐ **Alphabet and numbers only,** faded, c. 1842	85.00	115.00	95.00
☐ **Alphabet,** wool on linen, small, c. 1800's	55.00	75.00	60.00
☐ **Cain and Abel motif,** good color, c. 1801	725.00	925.00	820.00
☐ **Outdoor scene** with house, birds, cow, c. 1830's	620.00	820.00	700.00
☐ **Three alphabets,** dog, cat, house, good color, 18" x 22", c. 1841	300.00	360.00	310.00

NEEDLEWORKING TOOLS

Not only is fine old needlework collected, but the implements used to create it. These are usually found individually, though sometimes an old set or a partial set will turn up. The large-scale sets, intended mainly for gift-giving, began to come on the market around 1850: brides received them by the score as needleworking skills were deemed mandatory for a happy marriage. By 1890, they were being manufactured in great quantities, and hence, quality declined, but some very novel ones were made. Thimbles are a specialty in themselves for some hobbyists.

☐ **Basket,** wicker, 12" H.	22.00	27.00	22.50
☐ **Darner,** glass, red	30.00	38.00	31.00
☐ **Darner,** glove, sterling silver	40.00	52.00	44.00
☐ **Darner,** sock, brown	30.00	37.00	31.50
☐ **Needle case,** brass	15.00	20.00	14.50
☐ **Needle case,** carved ivory	34.00	42.00	36.00
☐ **Needle case,** sterling silver	26.00	32.00	27.00
☐ **Needle case,** tortoise shell	80.00	100.00	85.00
☐ **Pincushion,** ivory, pedestal base	45.00	58.00	48.00
☐ **Pincushion,** sterling silver	110.00	150.00	120.00
☐ **Pincushion,** patchwork, 8"	15.00	20.00	16.50
☐ **Scissors,** embroidery, stork, silver plate, 3" L.	30.00	37.00	31.50

604 / NURSERY COLLECTIBLES

	Current Price Range		Prior Year Average
☐ **Sewing bird,** brass	45.00	58.00	49.00
☐ **Sewing bird,** brass, clamp-on, large with cushion	150.00	200.00	165.00
☐ **Sewing bird,** iron, 6″ L.	35.00	42.00	35.00
☐ **Sewing bird,** sterling silver, 6″ L.	45.00	55.00	46.50
☐ **Sewing machine,** Singer, heavy duty	230.00	310.00	260.00
☐ **Sewing machine,** White, Cleveland, Ohio, early 1900's	140.00	180.00	150.00
☐ **Spinning wheel,** Norwegian, paint decorated, small	190.00	240.00	205.00
☐ **Spool cabinet,** Eureka, walnut, 22 drawers, 16 with glass	1100.00	1600.00	1250.00
☐ **Spool cabinet,** Brooks, four-drawer	285.00	360.00	312.00
☐ **Tape measure,** clock	70.00	90.00	75.00
☐ **Tape measure,** duck and hen	40.00	50.00	40.00
☐ **Tape measure,** figural turtle, sterling, brass enamel	55.00	70.00	57.00
☐ **Tape measure,** owl	24.00	32.00	26.00
☐ **Tape measure,** papoose, original box	14.00	18.00	14.50
☐ **Tape measure,** rabbit	35.00	42.00	36.00
☐ **Tape measure,** vault	25.00	32.00	26.00
☐ **Tatting shuttle,** tortoise shell	14.00	20.00	15.00
☐ **Thimble,** brass	17.00	24.00	18.50
☐ **Thimble,** celluloid	8.00	11.00	8.50
☐ **Thimble,** engraved bird, large size, 14k gold	75.00	100.00	82.00
☐ **Thimble,** gold with leather case	85.00	115.00	95.00
☐ **Thimble,** sterling silver	42.00	58.00	47.50
☐ **Thimble,** tortoise shell and sterling silver	105.00	130.00	107.00
☐ **Thimble holder,** wooden acorn with hinged leaf top	50.00	70.00	55.00
☐ **Thimble holder,** celluloid, with thread holder	16.00	20.00	16.50

NURSERY COLLECTIBLES

In our great-grandparents' time, there was not nearly as big a variety of items available for use in the nursery as there is today. But still, the baby had to be fed and amused, and manufacturers put forward a selection of items to serve that purpose. On the whole, they seem very crude and primitive by 1980's standards, but that aids in giving them collector appeal. For one thing, they were highly breakable, and breakable objects and babies do not mix well. Nursing bottles of the late 19th and 20th century were mostly glass; the average mother ran through dozens of them on the same infant, continually replacing ones that baby tossed on the floor or sidewalk. Earlier nursing bottles are of silver or pewter, and instead of rubber nipples have straw-like devices at the top. Ornate silver nursing bottles were restricted to children of socially prominent families. The colorful ABC plates, from which the slightly older baby ate, carried a variety of motifs. These had enormous popularity and are riding high again as collectors' items.

NURSERY COLLECTIBLES / 605

ABC PLATES

	Current Price Range		Prior Year Average
☐ Biblical scene, Samuel and Eli, 8″ Dia.	32.00	42.00	35.00
☐ Black children, 7″ Dia.	45.00	58.00	48.00
☐ Boys, reading a letter, 5″ Dia.	35.00	45.00	37.00
☐ Capitol, Washington, D.C., 7¼″ Dia.	40.00	52.00	44.00
☐ Cat and kittens, 7¼″ Dia.	36.00	48.00	39.00
☐ Clockface center, 8″ Dia.	55.00	75.00	60.00
☐ Dancing Master, 7¼″ Dia.	30.00	39.00	32.50
☐ Dog in center, 6½″ Dia.	35.00	46.00	39.00
☐ Eagle in center, 3″ Dia.	24.00	32.00	26.00
☐ Elephant in center, 6″ Dia.	30.00	42.00	30.00
☐ Farm scene, haywagon and oxen, 4″ Dia.	40.00	48.00	41.00
☐ Fisherman in pond, 8⅜″ Dia.	40.00	48.00	41.00
☐ Football scene, 7¼″ Dia.	45.00	60.00	47.50
☐ Hi Diddle Diddle, tin, 8″ Dia.	36.00	44.00	38.00
☐ Horse race scene, 7″ Dia.	42.00	52.00	44.50
☐ Hunting scene, 8½″ Dia.	40.00	49.00	41.50
☐ Ice cream, 7½″ Dia.	35.00	45.00	37.50
☐ Kitten and puppy in pitcher, 7″ Dia.	26.00	35.00	28.00
☐ Little bear, 7¼″ Dia.	38.00	49.00	41.00
☐ Little Bo Peep, glass, 7″ Dia.	32.00	42.00	35.00
☐ Little Miss Muffet, 6¼″ Dia.	35.00	45.00	38.00
☐ Man and dog sliding, 7″ Dia.	36.00	47.00	39.50
☐ Mary Had a Little Lamb, tin, 7″ Dia.	38.00	49.00	40.50
☐ Mother, daughter and verse, 7″ Dia.	36.00	47.00	39.50
☐ Pigs-in-Pen, pewter, 6¼″ Dia.	55.00	75.00	60.00
☐ Potter's art, 6¼″ Dia.	23.00	31.00	25.00
☐ Punch and Judy, 7″ Dia.	55.00	75.00	60.00
☐ Robinson Crusoe, 7″ Dia.	45.00	60.00	47.50
☐ Rosaline, 8½″ Dia.	100.00	130.00	105.00
☐ Sign language	250.00	325.00	262.00
☐ Soccer scene, 7¼″ Dia.	50.00	65.00	52.00
☐ Star in center, glass, 6″ Dia.	30.00	37.00	30.50
☐ Sunbonnet babies	150.00	200.00	165.00
☐ Titmouse, 7″ Dia.	32.00	40.00	34.00
☐ Tom the Piper's Son, alphabet border, 6¾″ Dia.	30.00	37.00	31.00
☐ Who Killed Cock Robin, tin, 7″ Dia.	40.00	49.00	41.00
☐ Youth and Maiden, Gothic attire, 5¾″ Dia.	34.00	41.00	35.50

BOTTLES

☐ Baby bottle, cylindrical, 20th c.	8.00	11.00	8.50
☐ Baby bottle, Egyptian	1100.00	1600.00	1250.00
☐ Baby bottle, silver	850.00	1050.00	900.00
☐ Baby bottle, turtle and tube, 19th c.	25.00	32.00	26.00

MISCELLANEOUS

☐ Bassinet, wicker, decorated	160.00	200.00	170.00
☐ Bed, baby, wicker, feather mattress	170.00	220.00	185.00
☐ "Buddy Pots" with long spout	230.00	310.00	260.00
☐ Cradles, pine, spindles, 36″ L.	120.00	150.00	125.00
☐ Cup, Peter Pan, engraved	75.00	95.00	80.00
☐ Highchair, oak, decorated	80.00	100.00	85.00
☐ Lantern, child's brass, battery-operated, wire handle, 10″ H.	35.00	45.00	36.00
☐ Rocker, child's, painted black with flower motif.	120.00	160.00	130.00

OPERA MEMORABILIA

It has often been said that fans of any kind of entertainment — sports, theatrical, or you-name-it — are no match for opera fans in enthusiasm and hero-worship. Very likely that's true, because opera devotees have been gathering and carefully preserving memorabilia for generations. The abundant supply of material on today's market, of such greats as Caruso and Geraldine Ferrar, is ample testimony to the collecting activities of early fans. In addition to autographed photos, letters and other signed items, opera memorabilia collectors also seek out old opera programs, posters, ticket stubs, passes, membership cards, and anything pertaining to the history of opera in printed or written form. Usually, items relating to the more famous opera houses such as LaScala or the Metropolitan automatically command a premium. Opening night programs of new operas, are the specialty of some collectors. Others want costumes used by noted opera stars, or stage props. It's all available on the market, and if you enjoy opera you will certainly find opera memorabilia an intriguing hobby.

	Current Price Range		Prior Year Average
☐ **Enrico Caruso,** caricature by Caruso, ink on drawing paper, figure of man in topcoat carrying a cane, signed	200.00	275.00	212.00
☐ **Enrico Caruso,** check for $800 endorsed by Caruso, bank stamp slightly obliterating signature, good specimen	110.00	160.00	125.00
☐ **Enrico Caruso,** 8" x 10" b/w photo in costume from "The Girl of the Golden West," wearing six-gallon hat and leather vest, signed	120.00	165.00	132.00
☐ **Enrico Caruso,** 5" x 7" b/w photo from a magazine signed and a larger portrait, unsigned, framed along with a phonograph record in a simple gold-plated metal frame against a background of dark blue silk	425.00	525.00	450.00
☐ **Enrico Caruso,** pair of typed letters signed by Caruso, one on hotel stationery written while on tour in Mexico, dealing with opera roles, etc.	100.00	130.00	105.00
☐ **Enrico Caruso,** poster of the Metropolitan Opera House advertising Caruso in "I Pagliacii"	250.00	325.00	262.00
☐ **Ezio Pinza,** holograph letter signed, sent from Milan, dealing with preparations for an operatic role	30.00	36.00	31.00
☐ **Ezio Pinza, small b/w photo signed and inscribed with a brief sentiment, c. 1932**	24.00	32.00	26.00
☐ **Metropolitan Opera House,** seat from the "old" Metropolitan Opera House, velvet-covered, worn, good condition overall	380.00	460.00	400.00
☐ **Metropolitan Opera House,** 6" x 6" fragment of curtain from the "old" Metropolitan Opera House, New York (closed 1964), framed with identifying card in a frame of polished oak, overall size, 12" x 17"	100.00	130.00	105.00
☐ **Metropolitan Opera House,** brick from the facade of the "old" Metropolitan Opera House, mounted on a teakwood stand	110.00	160.00	125.00

ORIENTALIA / 607

	Current Price Range		Prior Year Average
☐ **Metropolitan Opera House bills,** most bills prior to 1915 (that is, posters carrying announcements of operas to be performed, with listing of cast, conductor, etc., but not *illustrated*)*	40.00	65.00	47.50
☐ **Metropolitan Opera House bills,** most bills, c. 1915-1930	25.00	40.00	27.50
☐ **La Scala Opera House bill,** Milan, Italy, most bills c. 1900-1920	55.00	85.00	70.00
☐ **Beverly Sills,** large poster of the New York City opera, picturing her in roles from the *"Three Queens,"* signed by her in Magic Marker, c. 1975	15.00	20.00	14.50
☐ **Beverly Sills,** 11" x 14" b/w photo of her as Mary Stuart, pasted on heavy cardboard, signed and inscribed	85.00	110.00	88.00

(*The values of bills vary depending on the operas and stars named; Caruso bills invariably go higher than others.)

ORIENTALIA

Cloisonne Shallow Bowl, background of white with cloud cloison pattern, the multicolored decoration features a flower and vine design, 8"x2½"
.... **$450.00-$550.00**

ORIENTALIA

Orientalia has gone through a number of eras of widespread popularity in the west. It first became a fad in the 1700's to the point where even Chippendale and the other major furniture makers included Oriental styles in their lines — and the manufacturers of just about everything else did likewise. It was revived again in the Victorian age, then briefly in the 1920's, and today it is perhaps at the greatest peak of popularity in history. Orientalia has become within the past decade, not only one of the mostly hotly contested-for collectors' items but a favorite of the investors. Prices on most classes of Orientalia have soared, not just on such traditionally collected things as rugs and ceramics but furniture and even archaeological items from ancient China. Without question, most Orientalia is extremely attractive to the eye and carries more pure workmanship than a comparable article of western manufacture. The term "Orientalia" encompasses, in the main, objects of Chinese and Japanese origin; but it also technically extends to all collectibles originating in the Far East, including Thailand, Ceylon, Vietnam, Korea, and elsewhere. These areas all possess very ancient cultures and have produced vast arrays of craft items through the years. Orientalia poses some inevitable problems for the buyer, as there is often a difficulty in dating and even (in some cases) determining the place of origin; but the real thorn in the collector's side is the profusion of facsimiles and outright fakes. Much of what is sold today as antique jade is neither antique or jade, but modern soapstone carved to resemble antique jade. If you wish to buy Orientalia either for pleasure or as an investment, by all means patronize the specialist antique dealers rather than Chinatown shops or other doubtful sources.

MAJOR DYNASTIES AND PERIODS

CHINA

Shang Dynasty	1523 B.C.-1027 B.C.
Chou Dynasty	1027 B.C.- 221 B.C.
Spring & Autumn Period	770 B.C.- 475 B.C.
Warring States Period	481 B.C.-2211 B.C.
Ch'in Dynasty	221 B.C.- 206 B.C.
Han Dynasty	206 B.C.- 220 A.D.
Three Kingdoms	220 A.D.- 280 A.D.
Six Dynasties Period	280 A.D.- 589 A.D.
Northern Wei	385 A.D.- 535 A.D.
Northern Chi	550 A.D.- 577 A.D.
Northern Chou	557 A.D.- 581 A.D.
Sui Dynasty	589 A.D.- 618 A.D.
T'ang	618 A.D.- 906 A.D.
Five Dynasties	907 A.D.- 959 A.D.
Sung Dynasty	906 A.D.-1280 A.D.
Yuan Dynasty	1280 A.D.-1368 A.D.
Ming Dynasty	1368 A.D.-1643 A.D.
Ch'ing Dynasty	1644 A.D.-1912 A.D.

JAPAN

Jomon Period	1000 B.C.- 200 B.C.
Yayoi Period	200 B.C.- 500 A.D.
Tumulus or Great Tomb Period	300 A.D.- 700 A.D.
Asuka Period	552 A.D.- 645 A.D.
Early Nara Period	645 A.D.- 710 A.D.
Nara Period	710 A.D.- 794 A.D.
Early Heian Period	794 A.D.- 897 A.D.
Heian or Fujiwara Period	897 A.D.-1185 A.D.
Kamakura Period	1185 A.D.-1392 A.D.
Ashikaga or Muromachi Period	1392 A.D.-1573 A.D.
Momoyama Period	1573 A.D.-1615 A.D.
Tokugawa Period	1615 A.D.-1868 A.D.

ORIENTALIA / 609

	Current Price Range		Prior Year Average

CHINESE FURNITURE

☐ **Altar table,** hardwood, rectangular top, carved and pierced end supports, 29" x 50"	1500.00	2000.00	1550.00
☐ **Altar table,** hardwood, rectangular top, roll-over ends with straight carved legs, 36" x 5'6"	1800.00	2300.00	1950.00
☐ **Armoire,** red lacquered, rectangular cabinet with two red and gold doors on hardwood frame stand, 6' x 39½"	2600.00	3100.00	2750.00
☐ **Bed,** elaborate vermillion lacquered frame and canopy with figural panels, 7'4" x 7'4"	3600.00	4600.00	4000.00
☐ **Cabinet,** rosewood, front enclosed with cupboard doors, carved fruitwood, exotic birds and flowering bushes, 4'5" x 40"	560.00	660.00	600.00
☐ **Chair,** side, carved rosewood, solid back panel with bird and flowering branches, 19th c.	325.00	400.00	338.00
☐ **Club chairs,** upholstered in black velvet, set of four	360.00	435.00	382.00
☐ **Dressing table,** rectangular top, three drawers, above two pedestals with three drawers each, drawer fronts lacquered in red and gold, 30" x 4'6"	600.00	725.00	635.00
☐ **Floor lamp,** hardwood, elaborately carved with pierced bracket supports and dragon-carved feet, 6'5"	235.00	305.00	260.00
☐ **Panel,** lacquered red with gold, carved flowers, figures and precious objects, 4'6" x 45"	550.00	625.00	562.00
☐ **Table,** console, rectangular hardwood top inset with blue and white porcelain plaque, straight legs with carved feet, 33½" x 4'2½"	3000.00	3800.00	3100.00
☐ **Table,** low circular, decorated in red and black lacquer with figures and scrollwork, 16" x 31" ...	560.00	650.00	595.00
☐ **Table,** writing, black and gold lacquered, rectangular top with drawers and pair of cupboards on straight legs, 32" x 51"	3000.00	3800.00	3200.00

CHINESE JADE

☐ **Beaker,** white jade bronze-form, slender ku with raised median knop, wood stand 5½" H.	1200.00	1500.00	1250.00
☐ **Bowl,** gray and brown jade dragon, two handles, wood stand, 5¾" Dia.	340.00	400.00	350.00
☐ **Brush washer,** dark green jade, cluster of clouds, wood stand, 4¾" L.	650.00	775.00	682.00
☐ **Cats,** white and gray, reclining in playful manner	750.00	850.00	775.00
☐ **Jade elephant,** gray and brown, supporting on its back a small bronze form	200.00	250.00	215.00
☐ **Jade lotus,** grayish-white, undercut branches of blossoms and leafage, 4" L.	400.00	470.00	415.00
☐ **Jadeite dragon buckle,** pair of Ch'ih lung amid lotus scrolls in grayish-white, 4¾" L.	3300.00	3900.00	3500.00
☐ **Jadeite pendant,** small mottled apple green, carved and pierced with stems of leafage and tendrils, gold link, 1½" H.	2300.00	2900.00	2500.00
☐ **Tripod censer,** white jade, Ch'ien Lung period, petal-molded rim and three stump feet, wood stand, 5¼" Dia.	3100.00	3700.00	3300.00

CHINESE PAINTING

	Current Price Range		Prior Year Average
☐ **Birds and flowering branches,** hanging scroll, ink on silk, signed, 36¼" x 14", late 15th-16th c.	4300.00	5100.00	4600.00
☐ **Cat,** rock and flowers, hanging scroll, ink tones of red, green, lilac, pink and white on silk, signed, 48¼" x 13", 19th c.	1200.00	1500.00	1250.00
☐ **Ducks,** lotus and millet, hanging scroll, ink, tones of red and green on silk, signed, 105½" x 59½".	3100.00	3850.00	3375.00
☐ **Mountain landscape with travelers,** hanging scroll, ink, tones of red, green and blue on silk, K'ang Hsi period, signed, 77" x 40¼"	1300.00	1700.00	1400.00
☐ **Nomadic hunting scene,** hanging scroll, ink, tones of red, yellow, green, brown, black and white on silk, framed, 63" x 31¾", 18th c.	1000.00	1300.00	1025.00
☐ **Portrait of Lan Ts'Ai-Ho,** hanging scroll, ink, tones of red, green and white on silk, K'ang Hsi period, 44½" x 19⅝"	525.00	625.00	550.00
☐ **Portrait of Lu Hsing,** hanging scroll, ink, silk, character inscription, 19 seals, 89½" x 41⅝"	1200.00	1600.00	1300.00
☐ **Portrait of Shou Lao,** hanging scroll, ink, silk, character inscription, 19 seals, 89½" x 41⅝"	1200.00	1600.00	1300.00
☐ **Rams, Three San Yang,** hanging scroll, ink, tones of red and white on silk, 18¼" x 11⅜", late 17th-18th c.	460.00	560.00	500.00
☐ **River landscape,** with scholar and attendant, hanging scroll, tones of green, red and white on silk, 47½" x 20⅛"	3000.00	3800.00	3300.00
☐ **Scholar holding a rock,** hanging scroll, ink, tones of blue and red, signed, 51¾" x 20¾", dated 1645	1700.00	2200.00	1850.00
☐ **Spring plowing,** handscroll, ink, tones of red, green and blue on silk, signed with seals, 7¼" x 68¾", 18th c.	650.00	725.00	662.00

CHINESE SNUFF BOTTLES

☐ **Blue-flecked animal mask,** loop handles on edges with stopper	245.00	305.00	265.00
☐ **Blue and white,** with matching saucer, landscape scene, stopper and fitted box	500.00	575.00	512.00
☐ **Double overlay glass,** milk white body, overlaid in yellow relief with a tasselled pi disc on either side with stopper	1475.00	1850.00	1575.00
☐ **Gilt-bronze,** ear of maize with husk curled revealing the kernels with stopper	380.00	460.00	410.00
☐ **Gold fleck,** flattened form, black metal with gold markings and stopper	65.00	85.00	70.00
☐ **Green glass,** flattened form, foot and handles with dotted ju-i outline, a yin-yang medallion on both sides with stopper	850.00	1050.00	900.00
☐ **Interior-painted glass,** scene of a figure on horse firing an arrow at a bird and leading Chu Ko-liang and attendant through a snowy landscape, signed and dated with stopper, c. 1900	1500.00	2000.00	1650.00
☐ **Jade,** dot and grain pattern with stopper	390.00	490.00	395.00
☐ **Jasper,** simulated, flattened form on oval foot in tones of brown, yellow and red with stopper	190.00	240.00	205.00

	Current Price Range		Prior Year Average
☐ **Macaroni agate,** pale brown translucent stone with stopper	750.00	875.00	785.00
☐ **Overlay glass,** opaque lemon yellow metal, red relief with bat above peaches with stopper	500.00	575.00	512.00
☐ **Porcelain,** molded pear shape, scaly dragon with stopper	425.00	525.00	450.00
☐ **Red overlay,** flattened form with fruiting peach trees growing from rocks with stopper	335.00	410.00	362.00
☐ **Rock crystal,** children playing beside rocks and bamboo, dated second summer, with stopper, c. 1968	700.00	775.00	712.00
☐ **White jade,** standing on oval foot with saucer, stopper and fitted box	525.00	625.00	550.00
☐ **Yi-Hsing,** oval foot enameled with house and landscape in blue and green tones with stopper	1500.00	2000.00	1650.00
☐ **Yi-Hsing,** side decorated with prunus blossom, reverse with bamboo, flat circular form with stopper	1200.00	1500.00	1250.00

JAPANESE NETSUKE

☐ **Figure of Sennin,** bisque, porcelain figure standing and a gourd on his shoulder, unsigned	220.00	300.00	238.00
☐ **Flower,** ebony, form of an open flower, silver studs in the center, unsigned, 19th c.	285.00	350.00	308.00
☐ **Horn ashtray,** bowl formed by dragon with metal inlaid eyes, unsigned	500.00	575.00	512.00
☐ **Karako,** wood figure, youth beating on drum, unsigned, 19th c.	375.00	430.00	365.00
☐ **Mask,** man smiling wearing a soft cap, signed, 19th c.	150.00	180.00	155.00
☐ **Mask,** wood carving, open mouth and protruding inlaid eyes, one larger mask and one smaller, unsigned	340.00	400.00	350.00
☐ **Monkey,** feet crossed forming himotoshi, arms across eyes, "see no evil," signed, 19th c.	420.00	520.00	450.00
☐ **Mother and child,** slender woman bare-footed wearing a kimono holding baby boy in her arms, unsigned, 19th c.	410.00	490.00	430.00
☐ **Mother and children,** wood group, woman with child strapped to her back and holding a smaller child in her arms, signed	225.00	300.00	238.00
☐ **Rat group,** adult and two smaller rats munching on berries, unsigned, 19th c.	700.00	825.00	720.00
☐ **Snake,** ebony, coiled about itself, textured skin, inlaid horn eyes, unsigned, 11th c.	610.00	680.00	625.00
☐ **Turtle,** wooden group, adult turtle on lotus leaf with two smaller turtles on its back, signed, 19th c.	2400.00	2900.00	2550.00
☐ **Tiger,** wood, seated with its head turned backwards, tail across the back, signed, 19th c.	680.00	800.00	720.00
☐ **Wood group playing,** hermits both wearing garments seated on oval base on either side of go aboard, signed, 19th c.	475.00	550.00	485.00

IVORY CARVINGS

The art of ivory carving is believed to predate jade carving in China. Throughout the centuries, Chinese artisans fashioned ivory carvings and sculptures for local sale, then, in more recent times, in a much greater abundance for export. Most Chinese carved ivory is elephant tusk, obtained from Indian via Ceylon or other trading routes, or fossil ivory dug from the Chinese soil. Carvings made from fossil ivory are usually dark in color and heavier in weight. Some Chinese ivory carvings are made from walrus tusk or other non-elephant ivory, but these are far in the minority. These are difficult works to appraise if one is not keenly attuned to the subject: artistic style, execution, and the amount of fine detailing are vital considerations. Age is of less importance; nearly all specimens found on the market date from the 19th and 20th centuries despite their appearance of vast antiquity. Their antique appearance does not result from any intentional effort at deception; the Chinese carvers simply went on copying the traditional styles and topics generation after generation, and were skilled at doing so. Originality of subject, therefore, will sometimes add extra value — and if the subject is both original and novel, the piece is likely to be quite desirable. Some works show a marvelous complexity, and were intended to be admired (as they continue to be admired by collectors) as examples of the carver's steady hand and precision.

	Current Price Range		Prior Year Average
☐ **Ivory jar and lid,** high relief carvings of maidens attacking dragons, the lid surmounted by a large dragon head, 9½"	2300.00	2900.00	2500.00
☐ **Ivory figure** of a young woman, wearing long robe, holding fan and basket of fruit, 8¾", believed to date from c. 1900	650.00	900.00	720.00
☐ **Ivory statuette** of a man and a fox, man holding a length of knotted rope and a rifle, almost certainly made for European or U.S. export market, 6"	475.00	650.00	482.00
☐ **Ivory carving** of an elderly woman, eyes inlaid with horn, hold left arm upward with wrist bent, small bucket at her feet, 6½"	1300.00	1800.00	1400.00
☐ **Ivory carving** of a male dancer, in motion on one leg, 6", apparently 20th century	625.00	825.00	700.00
☐ **Ivory carving** of a fisherman, wearing robe with incised decoration, holding fishing rod in one hand and fish in the other, frog on his knee, well detailed, 4⅝"	800.00	1050.00	880.00
☐ **Ivory carving** of an umbrella manufacturer at work, seated, putting finishing touches to umbrella made of lashed reeds, very highly detailed, c. 1880-1895	900.00	1150.00	980.00

	Current Price Range		Prior Year Average

- **Ivory tusk,** whole elephant tusk with multitudes of small carvings along the entire length and circumference, representing gods, village scenes, pagodas, etc. 33″ 1300.00 1700.00 1400.00

(Note: The values of these carved tusks, which are not by any means rare, depend to some extent on their size. There are small ones only two feet long which sell usually in the $500 to $800 range, and large ones of four feet which can go for $4,000 to $7,000. Specimens of five feet and even larger are recorded, but seldom ever appear for sale. **Fakes are plentiful,** *in which the material is not ivory but a kind of plastic. Items of this nature should not be bought in giftshops or shops advertising "Oriental Imports," but from antique dealers who specialize in Orientalia.)*

IVORY NETSUKE

- **Buddha,** solid, seated with pendulous earlobes and loose robes, nose worn away, unsigned, 18th c. 235.00 285.00 250.00
- **Cat,** wearing a bib, looking into discarded paper lantern while mouse escapes, signed, 19th-20th c. 500.00 575.00 512.00
- **Erotic group,** amorous man and woman, insigned 500.00 580.00 530.00
- **Figure of a Sennin,** puzzled expression with hand on his head, unsigned, 18th century 400.00 455.00 405.00
- **Hotei,** seated with one knee raised, wearing loose robe, holding tama in palm, signed, 18th c. 775.00 890.00 815.00
- **Hunter,** wearing short belted tunic and straw hood, carries sword and smiling monkey, 18th c. 780.00 885.00 825.00
- **Kinko,** seated on carp, reading from a scroll, wearing robe and soft cap, signed, 19th c. 475.0 550.00 482.00
- **Marine cluster,** two fish, a squid and an octopus, eyes are inlaid horn, signed, 19th c. 625.00 725.00 650.00
- **Mask cluster,** depicting no drama characters, signed, 19th c. 575.00 650.00 582.00
- **Okame mask,** chubby face with black hair and two black dots on her forehead, signed, 19th c. ... 325.00 400.00 338.00
- **Puppy,** playing with rump in air, inlaid eyes, carved ear, signed 575.00 650.00 582.00
- **Sage,** seated, wearing a skull cap and leaning against a table, unsigned, 18th c. 425.00 500.00 438.00
- **Sake cup,** three characters seated back to back, signed, 19th c. 700.00 775.00 720.00
- **Tennin,** angel in flight beating on drum, signed .. 625.00 725.00 650.00
- **Wolf,** forepaw resting on skull, signed, 19th c. ... 235.00 295.00 255.00

OWLS

Snowy Owl, by William J. Stephenson . . . . $75.00-$85.00

    The owl was first used in artistic symbolism as a device on the coins of ancient Athens, which normally carried an owl on one side and the head of Athena (patron goddess of the state) on the other. This set of devices remained unchanged on the Athenian coins for hundreds of years. The owl was later a model for statuary of many kinds, emblems, shields, and (beginning in the 19th century) all sorts of commercially made novelties. The Age of Owls hasn't died yet: a visit to any giftshop will reveal many newly-made owls in ceramic, brass, wax, and other materials.

	Current Price Range		Prior Year Average
☐ **Bookends,** rookwood, tan glaze, pair	110.00	150.00	120.00
☐ **Book rack,** expanding, cast brass, two owls	34.00	42.00	36.00
☐ **Doorstop,** carved wood with glass eyes, c. 1920's	20.00	27.00	21.50
☐ **Fairy lamp,** bisque, owl face, glass eyes, 4½ " H.	170.00	220.00	165.00
☐ **Inkwell,** alabaster, owl on pile of books, 19th c. . .	110.00	160.00	125.00
☐ **Jar,** Atterbury, opal glass, inserted red eyes, 7" H.	120.00	155.00	125.00
☐ **Painting,** primitive, two owls, late 19th c.	105.00	130.00	107.00
☐ **Stickpin,** gold, two diamond chip eyes, 14K gold .	125.00	160.00	140.00

PAPERBACK BOOKS

The Case of the Wayland Wolf, by Erle Stanley Gardner, February 1962, Pocket Book, 4501 . . . **$2.50-5.50**

Although hobbyists have valued hardbound books for centuries, the collecting of paperbacks is a modern area. Paperbacks captured the reading audience during the Depression when price often determined the saleability of items in the market. Even after the economy recovered, the inexpensive, easy-to-carry books continued to sell widely. Naturally, most readers traded or gave their paperbacks away — with their low cost hardly anyone though of saving them. But, some readers collected all the paperbacks by their favorite authors, or even all the books of their favorite genre. For instance, science fiction buffs saved every science fiction book they bought, because they wanted to read them again. Such readers became the first collectors of paperback books.

As with hardbound books, first editions are the most valuable, but the author, the title, and the condition are important, also. Look for books in the best of condition — paperbacks are often printed on inexpensive paper which deteriorates more easily than quality paper, and once deterioration begins the process cannot be reversed.

For more in-depth information and an extensive listing, you may refer to *The Official Price Guide to Paperbacks and Magazines* by the House of Collectibles.

ADVENTURE

	Current Price Range		Prior Year Average

ACE
Ace Books, Inc./A.A. Wynn, Inc.

☐ D57 *Treachery In Trieste,* Charles L. Leonard; *Counterspy Express,* A.S. Fleischman, original, 1954 .... 6.50 21.00 12.00
☐ D222 *First On The Rope,* R. Frison-Roche 2.50 5.50 4.00
☐ D318 *Captain Crossbones,* Donald Barr Chidsey 2.50 5.50 4.00

ARMED SERVICES EDITIONS
Editions For The Armed Services, Inc.

☐ A-14 *The Ship,* C.S. Forester 2.00 6.50 4.00
☐ B-49 *My Friend Flicka,* M. O'Hara 3.00 6.00 4.00
☐ D-98 *The Trees,* Conrad Richter 2.00 5.50 4.00

BANTAM BOOKS
Bantam Books, Inc.

☐ 5 *Scaramouche,* Rafael Sabatini 3.00 8.00 5.00
☐ 33 *The Prisoner Of Zenda,* Anthony Hope ... 3.00 8.00 5.00
☐ 58 *Captain Courageous,* Rudyard Kipling .. 3.00 8.00 5.00

DELL
Dell Publishing Company, Inc.

☐ 144 *The White Brigand,* Edison Marshall, 1947 5.00 12.00 8.00
☐ 195 *Beam Ends,* Errol Flynn 3.00 8.00 5.00
☐ 320 *The Cave Girl,* Edgar Rice Burroughs 10.00 28.00 17.00

GOLD MEDAL
Fawcett Publications, Inc.

☐ 241 *Savage Interlude,* Dan Cushman 5.00 12.00 8.00
☐ S441 *Sow The Wild Wind,* John Vail 3.00 8.00 5.00
☐ S549 *Queen Of Sheba,* Gardner F. Fox 5.00 14.00 8.00

HARLEQUIN
Harlequin Books, Ltd.

☐ 66 *Royce Of The Royal Mounted,* Ames Moore 5.00 16.00 10.00
☐ 228 *Drums Of Dambala,* H. Bedford Jones ... 5.50 16.00 10.00
☐ 276 *Conflict,* E.V. Timms 5.00 10.00 7.00

POCKET BOOK
Pocket Books, Inc.

☐ 47 *Bring 'Em Back Alive,* Edward Anthony and Frank Buck 5.00 16.00 10.00
☐ 810 *The Freeholder,* Joe David Brown 2.00 6.00 3.00
☐ 1024 *The Barbarians,* F. VanWyck Mason 2.50 6.50 4.00

HUMOR

ACE
Ace Books, Inc./A.A. Wynn, Inc.

☐ D25 *The Code Of The Wooster,* P.G. Wodehouse 10.00 18.00 14.00
☐ S116 *Words Fail Me!,* Brant House 3.00 8.50 5.00
☐ D175 *Best TV Humor Of The Year,* Irving Settel . 3.00 8.00 5.00

PAPERBACK BOOKS / 617

		Current Price Range		Prior Year Average

ARMED SERVICES EDITIONS
Editions for the Armed Services, Inc.

	A11 *My World And Welcome To It,* James Thurber	3.00	8.50	5.00
	N2 *The Dream Department,* S.J. Perelman	3.00	6.00	4.00
	657 *Barefoot Boy With Cheek,* Max Shulman	2.50	5.50	4.00

AVON
Avon Book Company/New Avon Library/Avon Publishing Co., Inc./Avon Publications, Inc./Avon Book Division - Hearst Corporation

	202 *From Gags To Riches,* Joey Adams	6.00	16.00	10.00
	441 *A Mouse Is Born,* Antia Loos	5.00	14.00	10.00
	617 *Battle Of The Sexes,* Charles Preston	5.00	14.00	10.00

BALLANTINE BOOKS
Ballantine Books, Inc.

	8 *The World Of Li'l Abner,* Al Capp	5.00	16.00	10.00
	229 *Sergeant Bilko,* Nat Hiken	3.00	8.00	5.00
	337K *Live Among The Savages,* Shirley Jackson	1.00	2.50	2.00

DELL
Dell Publishing Company, Inc.

| | 39 *Murder Challenges Valcour,* Rufus King | 5.00 | 14.00 | 8.00 |
| | 754 *Laughing On The Inside,* Bill Yates | 3.00 | 8.00 | 5.00 |

POCKET BOOK
Pocket Books, Inc.

	4 *Topper,* Thorne Smith	25.00	78.00	50.00
	199 *Arsenic And Old Lace,* Joseph Kesserling	5.50	15.50	10.00
	280 *Life With Father,* Clarence Day	5.00	16.00	10.00

MYSTERY

ACE
Ace Books, Inc./A.A. Wynn, Inc.

	D7 *So Dead My Love,* Harry Whittington/*I, The Executioner,* Stephen Ransome	4.25	15.25	8.50
	S97 *Death Has Two Faces,* Norman Herries	3.00	8.00	5.00
	D273 *The Midnight Eye,* Mike Roscoe/*Shakedown Hotel,* Ernest Jason Fredicks	2.50	5.50	4.00

ARMED SERVICES EDITIONS
Editions for the Armed Services, Inc.

	M29 *The Moonstone,* Wilkie Collins	3.00	6.00	4.00
	P17 *Blood Upon The Snow,* Hilda Lawrence	2.50	5.50	3.50
	711 *Wings Of Fear,* Mignon G. Eberhart	3.00	8.00	5.00

AVON
Avon Book Company, New Avon Library/Avon Publishing Co., Inc./Avon Publications, Inc./Avon Book Division - Hearst Corporation

	61 *Murder In Three Acts,* Agatha Christie	6.00	16.00	10.00
	465 *The Tragedy of Z,* Ellery Queen	5.00	14.00	8.00
	792 *Murder In Lima,* Robert A. Leuey	2.50	6.00	4.50

BANTAM BOOKS
Bantam Books, Inc.

		Current Price Range		Prior Year Average
☐ 132	Date With Death, Eaton K. Goldthwaite ..	3.00	8.00	5.00
☐ 968	Dig Me A Grave, John Spain	3.00	8.00	5.00
☐ A1797	The Silent Speaker, Rex Stout	1.25	3.50	2.00

DELL
Dell Publishing Company, Inc.

☐ 59	Turn On The Heat, A.A. Fair	6.00	16.00	10.00
☐ 172	Sad Cypress, Agatha Christie	6.00	16.00	10.00
☐ 348	A Halo For Nobody, Henry Kane	3.00	8.00	5.00

GOLD MEDAL
Fawcett Publications, Inc.

☐ 152	The Killer, Wade Miller	3.00	12.00	7.00
☐ 235	The Avenger, Matthew Blood	5.00	12.50	8.00
☐ 648	Terror Over London, Gardner F. Fox	3.00	8.00	5.00

POCKET BOOK
Pocket Books, Inc.

☐ 71	The French Powder Mystery, Ellery Queen	5.00	16.00	10.00
☐ 268	The Maltese Falcon, Dashiell Hammett ..	8.00	18.00	12.00
☐ 507	She Died A Lady, Carter Dickson	5.00	14.50	9.00

SIGNET
New American Library of World Literature, Inc.

☐ 791	My Gun Is Quick, Mickey Spillane	5.00	14.00	9.00
☐ 932	The Long Wait, Mckey Spillane	4.00	11.50	7.00
☐ 1149	The Naked Angel, Jack Webb	3.00	8.00	5.00

NONFICTION

ACE
Ace Books, Inc./A.A. Wynn, Inc.

☐ D228	We Die Alone, David Howarth	2.50	5.50	4.00
☐ D269	Death In The South Atlantic, Michael Powell	3.00	8.00	5.00
☐ D334	Queen Of The Flat-tops, Stanley Johnston	2.50	5.50	4.00

ARMED SERVICES EDITIONS
Editions for the Armed Services, Inc.

☐ F170	Here Is Your War, Ernie Pyle	2.50	6.00	4.00
☐ R6	Psychology You Can Use, W.H. Roberts ..	3.00	8.00	5.00
☐ 1103	The Well-tempered Listener, Deems Taylor	2.50	5.50	4.00

AVON
Avon Book Company/New Avon Library/Avon Publishing Co., Inc. /Avon Publications, Inc./Avon Book Division - Hearst Corporation

☐ 330	Desperate Men, James D. Horan	6.00	16.00	10.00
☐ 700	Mirror Of Your Mind, Joseph Whitney	3.00	8.00	5.00
☐ T118	The Loves Of Liberace, Leo Guild	3.00	8.00	5.00

BALLANTINE BOOKS
Ballantine Books, Inc.

		Current Price Range		Prior Year Average
☐	101 *The Dam Busters*, Paul Brickhill	3.00	8.00	5.00
☐	221 *The Password Is Courage*, John Castle	1.50	3.50	2.50
☐	311K *Sex, Vice And Business*, Monroe Fry	1.50	3.50	2.50

BANTAM BOOKS
Bantam Books, Inc.

☐	845 *How To Survive An Atomic Bomb*, Richard Gerstell	6.00	14.00	8.00
☐	F1203 *The Kings Of The Road*, Ken W. Purdy	2.00	6.00	3.50
☐	1539 *A Night To Remember*, Walter Lord	1.00	2.50	2.00

CARDINAL EDITIONS
Pocket Books, Inc.

☐	C135 *The Exploration Of Space*, Arthur C. Clarke	1.00	2.50	2.00
☐	C146 *Call Me Lucky*, Bing Crosby	2.00	6.00	4.00
☐	C238 *Profiles In Courage*, John F. Kennedy	1.50	3.50	2.50

POPULAR AND CLASSICAL FICTION

ARMED SERVICES EDITIONS
Editions for the Armed Services, Inc.

☐	A26 *Lord Jim*, Joseph Conrad	3.00	8.00	5.00
☐	D117 *A Tree Grows In Brooklyn*, B. Smith	2.00	6.00	4.00
☐	E137 *Jamaica Inn*, Daphne DuMaurier	2.00	6.00	4.00

BANTAM BOOKS
Bantam Books, Inc.

☐	131 *The Pearl*, John Steinbeck	3.00	8.00	5.00
☐	712 *The African Queen*, C.S. Forester	3.00	8.00	5.00
☐	A867 *Tender Is The Night*, F. Scott Fitzgerald, 1951	2.00	6.00	4.00

POCKET BOOK
Pocket Books, Inc.

☐	1 *Lost Horizon*, James Hilton, 1939	28.00	98.00	60.00
☐	55 *Out Town*, Thornton Wilder	6.00	16.00	10.00
☐	215 *Magnificent Obsession*, Lloyd C. Douglas	5.00	14.00	8.00

SIGNET
New American Library of World Literature, Inc.

☐	664 *Portrait Of The Artist As A Young Man*, James Joyce	3.00	8.00	5.00
☐	1001 *The Catcher In The Rye*, J.D. Salinger	2.00	6.00	4.00
☐	1236 *The Rose Tattoo*, Tennessee Williams	1.25	3.25	2.00

ROMANCE

ACE
Ace Books, Inc./A.A. Wynn, Inc.

☐	D539 *Psychiatric Nurse*, Mary Mann Fletcher	2.00	3.50	2.50
☐	D558 *Campus Nurse*, Suzanne Roberts	2.00	3.50	2.50
☐	D565 *The Heart Of Dr, Hilary*, Ray Dorien	2.00	3.50	2.50

620 / PAPERBACK BOOKS

		Current Price Range		Prior Year Average

BANTAM BOOKS
Bantam Books, Inc.

	122	*A Certain French Doctor*, Elizabeth Seifert	2.00	6.00	4.00
☐	455	*Love Is A Surprise!*, Faith Baldwin	2.00	6.00	4.00
☐	1787	*What, Then, Is Love*, Emilie Loring	1.00.00	2.50	2.00

DELL
Dell Publishing Company, Inc.

☐	73	*Week-end Marriage*, Faith Baldwin	5.00	14.00	8.00
☐	189	*Kind Are Her Answers*, Mary Renault	3.00	8.00	5.00
☐	249	*Stars Still Shine*, Lida Larrimore	3.50	8.50	5.50

HARLEQUIN
Harlequin Books, Ltd.

☐	30	*Portrait Of Love*, Margaret Nichols	6.50	16.50	11.00
☐	308	*Doctor Paul*, Bette Allan	3.00	8.00	5.00
☐	348	*The Doctor On Elm Street*, Kay Hamilton	3.50	8.50	5.50

PYRAMID BOOKS
Almat Publishing Corp./Pyramid Books

☐	483	*My Heart Has Wings*, Elizabeth Hoy	3.00	8.00	5.00
☐	494	*Love Is My Reason*, Mary Burchell	3.00	8.00	5.00
☐	501	*Do Something Dangerous*, Elizabeth Hoy	3.00	8.00	5.00

SCIENCE FICTION

ACE
Ace Books, Inc./A.A. Wynn, Inc.

☐	D155	*Journey To The Center Of The Earth*, Jules Verne	2.00	6.00	4.00
☐	D461	*The Time Traders*, Andre Norton	2.00	6.00	4.00
☐	D548	*End Of The World*, Dean Owen	3.00	8.00	5.00

BANTAM BOOKS
Bantam Books, Inc.

☐	886	*The Martian Chronicles*, Ray Bradbury	5.00	14.00	8.00
☐	A1443	*Forbidden Planet*, W.J. Stuart	2.00	6.00	4.00
☐	A1646	*Pebble In The Sky*, Isaac Asimov	2.00	6.00	4.00

POCKET BOOK
Pocket Books, Inc.

☐	123	*Dr. Jekyll And Mr. Hyde*, Robert Louis Stevenson	10.00	32.00	20.00
☐	989	*Sands Of Mars*, Arthur C. Clarke	5.00	12.00	8.00
☐	1222	*The Winds Of Time*, Chad Oliver	3.00	8.00	5.00

PYRAMID
Almat Publishing Corp./Pyramid Books

☐	G214	*Tomorrow And Tomorrow*, Hunt Collins	3.00	8.00	5.00
☐	G397	*Off The Beaten Orbit*, Judith Merril	3.00	8.00	5.00
☐	G458	*Man Of Many Minds*, E. Everett Evans	3.00	8.00	5.00

SIGNET
New American Library of World Literature, Inc.

☐	882	*The Day After Tomorrow*, Robert A. Heinlein	2.00	6.00	4.00
☐	1007	*Destination: Universe!*, A.E. Van Vogt	3.00	8.00	4.00
☐	S1240	*The Caves Of Steel*, Isaac Asimov	3.00	8.00	4.00

WESTERN

ARMED SERVICES EDITIONS
Editions For The Armed Services, Inc.

		Current Price Range		Prior Year Average
☐	G195 *Raiders Of The Rimrock*, Luke Short	2.50	6.50	4.00
☐	R24 *The Long Chance*, Max Brand	2.00	6.00	4.00
☐	1107 *The Border Legion*, Zane Grey	2.50	6.50	4.50

BANTAM BOOKS
Bantam Books, Inc.

☐	720 *Action At Three Peaks*, Frank O'Rourke ..	2.50	6.50	4.50
☐	1067 *Nevada*, Zane Grey	2.50	6.50	4.50
☐	1893 *Rio Bravo*, Leigh Brackett	1.00	2.75	2.00

GOLD MEDAL
Fawcett Publications, Inc.

☐	411 *Black Horse Canyon*, Les Savage, Jr.	5.00	12.00	8.00
☐	457 *Many Rivers To Cross*, Steve Frazee	3.00	8.00	5.00
☐	760 *The Bounty Killer*, Marvin Albert	3.00	8.00	5.00

POCKET BOOK
Pocket Books, Inc.

☐	161 *The Spirit Of The Border*, Zane Grey	5.00	14.00	9.00
☐	487 *The Yukon Trail*, William MacLeon Raine .	3.00	8.00	5.00
☐	600 *The Big Sky*, A.B. Guthrie, Jr.	3.00	8.00	5.00

POPULAR BOOKS
Popular Library, Inc.

☐	102 *Duel In The Sun*, Niven Busch	5.00	14.00	9.00
☐	250 *Mavericks*, Walt Coburn	5.00	14.00	9.00
☐	367 *Shotgun Guard*, D.B. Newton	3.00	8.00	5.00

PAPER MONEY

Everybody talks about the declining value of the dollar, and the fact that today's currency is just "pieces of paper" unbacked by gold or silver. True enough, but those pieces of paper CAN and often DO rise in value as collectors' items paper money collecting has become as very popular hobby. But it's far from new. In fact it goes all the way back to 1865. After the Civil War, some people who got "stuck" with Confederate notes decided to keep them as a curiosity — and thus a new hobby was born, Today, all types of OBSOLETE U.S. notes are collectors' items, such as the large-size notes issued up to 1928. All U.S. currency up to that time was about 1½ times LARGER than our present notes. (The government reduced the size of our notes to save on production costs.) Even the current type of SMALL SIZE notes are collectible, too, as the following listings show. We have herewith listed various determinations of the small-size Federal Reserve Notes, which have consistently been among the most popular with collectors. Collecting Federal Reserve Notes offers the possibility for a really huge collection, since there are so many combinations of signatures and issuing cities (cities with Federal Reserve Banks, whose names appear right on the notes). Many of the later specimens are still in circulation and you come across them every day. However, you shouldn't bother putting circulated specimens of these notes

Ten Dollars Federal Reserve Note, face design, Hamilton facing left, series 1928 .... **$35.00-$48.00**

into your collection. When circulated they have no value over the face value. Instead, get your notes from a dealer, who will be able to sell you crisp uncircualted specimens. These fresh crisp notes will increase in value through the years, whereas circulated specimens are not likely to ever acquire any higher value. For more in-depth information and listings, you may refer to *The Official Blackbook Price Guide of United States Paper Money,* Published by the House of Collectibles.

SERIES OF 1963A GRANAHAN-FOWLER — GREEN SEAL

DISTRICT	UNC.	DISTRICT	UNC.
☐ 1A Boston	3.00	☐ 7G Chicago	3.00
☐ 2B New York	3.00	☐ 8H St. Louis	3.00
☐ 3C Philadelphia	3.00	☐ 9I Minneapolis	3.00
☐ 4D Cleveland	3.00	☐ 10J Kansas City	3.00
☐ 5E Richmond	3.00	☐ 11K Dallas	3.00
☐ 6F Atlanta	3.00	☐ 12L San Francisco	3.00

*The Dallas note of this series as shown, with the letter "K" in the black seal and the numbers "11" in the four corners does not have any more significance or value than any other notes with their respective district letter and corresponding number.

A false rumor was circulated several years ago the "K" was for Kennedy, the "11" was for November, the month in which he was assassinated, and that the note was issued by the Dallas bank to commemorate the occasion. The entire story is aporcryphal.

This note is in no way associated with the late President Kennedy. The notes were authorized by the act of June 4, 1963. This was five months before Kennedy was assassinated. The Federal Reserve district for Dallas is K-11.

SERIES OF 1963 GRANAHAN-DILLON — GREEN SEAL

DISTRICT	UNC.	DISTRICT	UNC.
☐ 1A Boston	3.00	☐ 7G Chicago	3.00
☐ 2B New York	3.00	☐ 8H St. Louis	3.00
☐ 3C Philadelphia	3.00	☐ 9I Minneapolis	3.00
☐ 4D Cleveland	3.00	☐ 10J Kansas City	3.00
☐ 5E Richmond	3.00	☐ 11K Dallas	3.00
☐ 6F Atlanta	3.00	☐ 12L San Francisco	3.00

PAPER MONEY / 623

John W. Barr served as Secretary of the Treasury from December 20th, 1968 to January 20th, 1969, filling the unexpired term of Henry H. Fowler. His signature appears on the $1.00 Federal Reserve notes of the series of 1963-B only.

During the one month term of Joseph W. Barr about 471 million notes were printed with his signature. These notes were for the following Federal Reserve Banks.

NOTES ISSUED

REGULAR NUMBERS		UNC.	STAR NUMBERS	UNC.
☐ 2B New York	123,040,000	3.00	3,680,000	4.25
☐ 5E Richmond	93,600,000	3.00	3,040,000	8.00
☐ 7G Chicago	91,040,000	3.00	2,400,000	4.25
☐ 10J Kansas City	44,800,000	4.00	None Printed	
☐ 12L San Francisco	106,400,000	3.50	3,040,000	4.25
	458,880,000		12,160,000	

ONE DOLLAR NOTES (1969) FEDERAL RESERVE NOTES

SERIES OF 1969—ELSTON-KENNEDY, GREEN SEAL

Boston	2.50	Cleveland	2.50	Chicago	2.50	Kansas City	2.50
New York	2.50	Richmond	2.50	St. Louis	2.50	Dallas	2.50
Philadelphia	2.50	Atlanta	2.50	Minneapolis	2.50	San Francisco	2.50

SERIES OF 1969A—KABIS-KENNEDY, GREEN SEAL

Boston	2.50	Cleveland	2.50	Chicago	2.50	Kansas City	2.50
New York	2.50	Richmond	2.50	St. Louis	2.50	Dallas	2.50
Philadelphia	2.50	Atlanta	2.50	Minneapolis	2.50	San Francisco	2.50

SERIES OF 1969B—KABIS-CONNALLY, GREEN SEAL

Boston	2.50	Cleveland	2.50	Chicago	2.50	Kansas City	2.50
New York	2.50	Richmond	2.50	St. Louis	2.50	Dallas	2.50
Philadelphia	2.50	Atlanta	2.50	Minneapolis	2.50	San Francisco	2.50

SERIES OF 1969C—BANUELOS-CONNALLY, GREEN SEAL

Boston	2.00	Cleveland	2.00	Chicago	2.00	Kansas City	2.00
New York	2.00	Richmond	2.00	St. Louis	2.00	Dallas	2.00
Philadelphia	2.00	Atlanta	2.00	Minneapolis	2.00	San Francisco	2.00

SERIES OF 1969D—BANUELOS-CONNALLY, GREEN SEAL

Boston	2.00	Cleveland	2.00	Chicago	2.00	Kansas City	2.00
New York	2.00	Richmond	2.00	St. Louis	2.00	Dallas	2.00
Philadelphia	2.00	Atlanta	2.00	Minneapolis	2.00	San Francisco	2.00

SERIES OF 1974—NEFF-SIMON, GREEN SEAL

Boston	1.75	Cleveland	1.75	Chicago	1.75	Kansas City	1.75
New York	1.75	Richmond	1.75	St. Louis	1.75	Dallas	1.75
Philadelphia	1.75	Atlanta	1.75	Minneapolis	1.75	San Francisco	1.75

SERIES OF 1977—MORTON-BLUMENTHAL, GREEN SEAL

Boston	2.00	Cleveland	2.00	Chicago	2.00	Kansas City	2.00
New York	2.00	Richmond	2.00	St. Louis	2.00	Dallas	2.00
Philadelphia	2.00	Atlanta	2.00	Minneapolis	2.00	San Francisco	2.00

SERIES OF 1977A-MORTON-MILLER, GREEN SEAL
This series is now in production. All notes are current.

TWO DOLLAR (1976) FEDERAL RESERVE NOTES

SERIES OF 1976 NEFF-SIMON — GREEN SEAL

DISTRICT	UNC.	DISTRICT	UNC.
1A Boston	4.75	7G Chicago	4.75
2B New York	4.75	8H St. Louis	4.75
3C Philadelphia	4.75	9I Minneapolis	4.75
4D Cleveland	4.75	10J Kansas City	4.75
5E Richmond	4.75	11K Dallas	4.75
6F Atlanta	4.75	12L San Francisco	4.75

FIVE DOLLAR NOTES (1928) FEDERAL RESERVE NOTES

SERIES OF 1928 — SIGNATURES OF TATE AND MELLON, GREEN SEAL

BANK	GOOD	V.FINE	UNC.	BANK	GOOD	V.FINE	UNC.
Boston	7.00	10.00	27.00	Chicago	7.00	10.00	21.00
New York	7.00	10.00	21.00	St. Louis	7.00	10.00	27.00
Philadelphia	7.00	10.00	23.00	Minneapolis	7.00	10.00	29.00
Cleveland	7.00	10.00	24.00	Kansas City	7.00	10.00	27.00
Richmond	7.00	10.00	29.00	Dallas	7.00	10.00	27.00
Atlanta	7.00	10.00	27.00	San Francisco	7.00	10.00	23.00

SERIES OF 1928A — SIGNATURES OF WOODS-MELLON, GREEN SEAL

BANK	GOOD	V.FINE	UNC.	BANK	GOOD	V.FINE	UNC.
Boston	7.00	10.00	40.00	Chicago	7.00	10.00	32.00
New York	7.00	10.00	33.00	St. Louis	7.00	10.00	43.00
Philadelphia	7.00	10.00	35.00	Minneapolis	7.00	10.00	45.00
Cleveland	7.00	10.00	35.00	Kansas City	7.00	10.00	45.00
Richmond	7.00	10.00	45.00	Dallas	7.00	10.00	45.00
Atlanta	7.00	10.00	40.00	San Francisco	7.00	10.00	40.00

SERIES OF 1928B—SIGNATURES OF WOODS-MELLON, GREEN SEAL
BLACK FEDERAL RESERVE SEAL NOW HAS A LETTER FOR DISTRICT IN PLACE OF THE NUMERAL

BANK	GOOD	V.FINE	UNC.	BANK	GOOD	V.FINE	UNC.
Boston	7.00	10.00	38.00	Chicago	7.00	10.00	38.00
New York	7.00	10.00	40.00	St. Louis	7.00	10.00	38.00
Philadelphia	7.00	10.00	38.00	Minneapolis	7.00	10.00	45.00
Cleveland	7.00	10.00	38.00	Kansas City	7.00	10.00	45.00
Richmond	7.00	10.00	42.00	Dallas	7.00	10.00	42.00
Atlanta	7.00	10.00	42.00	San Francisco	7.00	10.00	37.00

SERIES OF 1928C — SIGNATURES OF WOODS-MILLS, GREEN SEAL

BANK	GOOD	V.FINE	UNC.	BANK	GOOD	V.FINE	UNC.
Cleveland	37.00	75.00	260.00	San Francisco	42.00	85.00	300.00
Atlanta	37.00	75.00	260.00				

This series not issued by other banks.

SERIES OF 1928D — SIGNATURES OF WOODS-WOODIN, GREEN SEAL

BANK	GOOD	V.FINE	UNC.
Atlanta	75.00	185.00	600.00

This series not issued by other banks.

FIVE DOLLAR NOTES (1934) FEDERAL RESERVE NOTES

SERIES OF 1934 — JULIAN-MORGENTHAU, GREEN SEAL

"Redeemable in Gold" removed from obligation over Federal Reserve Seal
Note: *The Green Treasury Seal on this note is known in a light and dark color. The light seal is worth about 10% to 20% more in most cases.*

BANK	V.FINE	UNC.	BANK	V.FINE	UNC.
☐ Boston	10.00	32.00	☐ Kansas City	10.00	32.00
☐ New York	10.00	32.00	☐ Dallas	10.00	32.00
☐ Philadelphia	10.00	32.00	☐ San Francisco	10.00	32.00
☐ Cleveland	10.00	32.00	☐ San Francisco*	30.00	160.00
☐ Richmond	10.00	32.00			
☐ Atlanta	10.00	32.00			
☐ Chicago	10.00	32.00			
☐ St. Louis	10.00	32.00			
☐ Minneapolis	10.00	32.00			

*This note with BROWN Treasury Seal and surcharged HAWAII. For use in Pacific area of Operations during World War II.

SERIES OF 1934A — JULIAN-MORGENTHAU, GREEN SEAL

BANK	V.FINE	UNC.	BANK	V.FINE	UNC.
☐ Boston	8.00	29.00	☐ San Francisco	10.00	30.00
☐ New York	8.00	27.00	☐ San Francisco*	22.00	140.00
☐ Philadelphia	8.00	25.00			
☐ Cleveland	8.00	27.50			
☐ Richmond	10.00	30.00			
☐ Atlanta	10.00	27.00			
☐ Chicago	10.00	25.00			
☐ St. Louis	10.00	29.00			

*This note with BROWN Treasury Seal and surcharged HAWAII. For use in Pacific area of operations during World War II.

SERIES OF 1934B — SIGNATURES OF JULIAN-VINSON, GREEN SEAL

BANK & CITY	V.FINE	UNC.	BANK & CITY	V.FINE	UNC.
☐ Boston	14.00	35.00	☐ Chicago	11.00	35.00
☐ New York	11.00	35.00	☐ St. Louis	18.00	35.00
☐ Philadelphia	11.00	35.00	☐ Minneapolis	18.00	35.00
☐ Cleveland	11.00	35.00	☐ Kansas City	18.00	45.00
☐ Richmond	14.00	35.00	☐ Dallas	\.\.\.	Not Issued
☐ Atlanta	14.00	35.00	☐ San Francisco	14.00	38.00

SERIES OF 1934C — SIGNATURES OF JULIAN-SNYDER, GREEN SEAL

BANK & CITY	V.FINE	UNC.	BANK & CITY	V.FINE	UNC.
☐ Boston	9.00	27.00	☐ Chicago	9.00	27.00
☐ New York	9.00	27.00	☐ St. Louis	9.00	27.00
☐ Philadelphia	9.00	27.00	☐ Minneapolis	9.00	30.00
☐ Cleveland	9.00	27.00	☐ Kansas City	9.00	27.00
☐ Richmond	9.00	27.00	☐ Dallas	9.00	30.00
☐ Atlanta	9.00	27.00	☐ San Francisco	9.00	27.00

SERIES OF 1934D — SIGNATURES OF CLARK-SNYDER, GREEN SEAL

BANK & CITY	V.FINE	UNC.	BANK & CITY	V.FINE	UNC.
☐ Boston	7.50	19.00	☐ Chicago	7.50	17.50
☐ New York	7.50	16.00	☐ St. Louis	10.00	20.00
☐ Philadelphia	7.50	18.50	☐ Minneapolis	10.00	22.00
☐ Cleveland	7.50	20.00	☐ Kansas City	10.00	22.00
☐ Richmond	7.50	20.00	☐ Dallas	12.00	25.00
☐ Atlanta	9.00	20.00	☐ San Francisco	8.00	20.00

FIVE DOLLAR NOTES (1950) FEDERAL RESERVE NOTES
BLACK FEDERAL RESERVE SEAL AND GREEN TREASURY SEALS
ARE NOW SMALLER

SERIES OF 1950 — SIGNATURES OF CLARK-SNYDER, GREEN SEAL

BANK & CITY	V.FINE	UNC.	BANK & CITY	V.FINE	UNC.
☐ Boston	7.50	15.00	☐ Chicago	7.50	15.00
☐ New York	7.50	13.00	☐ St. Louis	7.50	16.00
☐ Philadelphia	7.50	14.50	☐ Minneapolis	7.50	18.50
☐ Cleveland	7.50	14.50	☐ Kansas City	7.50	16.00
☐ Richmond	7.50	14.00	☐ Dallas	7.50	16.00
☐ Atlanta	7.50	14.50	☐ San Francisco	7.50	15.00

SERIES OF 1950A — PRIEST-HUMPHREY, GREEN SEAL

Boston	14.00	Cleveland	14.00	Chicago	14.00	Kansas City	14.00
New York	14.00	Richmond	14.00	St. Louis	15.00	Dallas	14.00
Philadelphia	14.00	Atlanta	14.00	Minneapolis	15.00	San Francisco	14.00

SERIES OF 1950B — PRIEST-ANDERSON, GREEN SEAL

Boston	13.00	Cleveland	12.50	Chicago	11.50	Kansas City	14.00
New York	12.50	Richmond	12.50	St. Louis	15.00	Dallas	13.00
Philadelphia	12.50	Atlanta	12.50	Minneapolis	17.50	San Francisco	14.00

SERIES OF 1950C — SMITH-DILLON, GREEN SEAL

Boston	12.50	Cleveland	12.50	Chicago	14.00	Kansas City	14.00
New York	11.00	Richmond	12.50	St. Louis	12.50	Dallas	17.50
Philadelphia	12.50	Atlanta	12.50	Minneapolis	14.00	San Francisco	15.00

SERIES OF 1950D — GRANAHAN-DILLON, GREEN SEAL

Boston	12.00	Cleveland	12.00	Chicago	11.00	Kansas City	12.50
New York	12.00	Richmond	11.00	St. Louis	11.50	Dallas	12.50
Philadelphia	12.00	Atlanta	12.00	Minneapolis	12.50	San Francisco	12.00

SERIES OF 1950E — GRANAHAN-FOWLER, GREEN SEAL

New York ... 13.00   Chicago .... 15.00   San Francisco 14.00
This Note was issued by only three banks.

FIVE DOLLAR NOTES (1963) FEDERAL RESERVE NOTES
"IN GOD WE TRUST" IS ADDED ON THE BACK

SERIES OF 1963 — GRANAHAN-DILLON, GREEN SEAL

Boston	14.00	Cleveland	13.00	Chicago	13.00	Kansas City	16.00
New York	13.00	Richmond	NONE	St. Louis	13.00	Dallas	15.00
Philadelphia	12.00	Atlanta	13.00	Minneapolis	NONE	San Francisco	14.00

SERIES OF 1963A — GRANAHAN-FOWLER, GREEN SEAL

Boston	11.00	Cleveland	11.00	Chicago	11.00	Kansas City	12.00
New York	13.00	Richmond	NONE	St. Louis	11.00	Dallas	11.50
Philadelphia	11.00	Atlanta	11.00	Minneapolis	11.00	San Francisco	11.50

FIVE DOLLAR NOTES (1969-1977) FEDERAL RESERVE NOTES
WORDING IN GREEN TREASURY SEAL CHANGED FROM LATIN TO ENGLISH

SERIES OF 1969 — ELSTON-KENNEDY, GREEN SEAL

Boston 9.50	Cleveland 9.50	Chicago 10.00	Kansas City . 11.00
New York 9.50	Richmond ... 9.50	St. Louis 9.50	Dallas 10.50
Philadelphia . 9.50	Atlanta 9.50	Minneapolis . 10.00	San Francisco 10.00

SERIES OF 1969A — KABIS-CONNALLY, GREEN SEAL

Boston 8.50	Cleveland 8.50	Chicago 8.50	Kansas City .. 8.50
New York 8.50	Richmond ... 8.50	St. Louis 8.50	Dallas 8.50
Philadelphia . 8.50	Atlanta 8.50	Minneapolis . 8.50	San Francisco . 8.50

SERIES OF 1969B — BANUELOS-CONNALLY, GREEN SEAL

Boston 8.50	Cleveland 8.50	Chicago 8.50	Kansas City .. 8.50
New York 8.50	Richmond ... 8.50	St. Louis 8.50	Dallas 8.50
Philadelphia . 8.50	Atlanta 8.50	Minneapolis . 8.50	San Francisco . 8.50

SERIES OF 1969C — BANUELOS-SHULTZ, GREEN SEAL

Boston 8.00	Cleveland 8.00	Chicago 8.00	Kansas City .. 8.00
New York 8.00	Richmond ... 8.00	St. Louis 8.00	Dallas 8.00
Philadelphia . 8.00	Atlanta 8.00	Minneapolis . 8.00	San Francisco . 8.00

SERIES OF 1974 — NEFF-SIMON, GREEN SEAL

Boston 7.50	Cleveland 7.50	Chicago 7.50	Kansas City .. 7.50
New York 7.50	Richmond ... 7.50	St. Louis 7.50	Dallas 7.50
Philadelphia . 7.50	Atlanta 7.50	Minneapolis . 7.50	San Francisco . 7.50

SERIES OF 1977 — MORTON-BLUMENTHAL, GREEN SEAL

Boston 7.50	Cleveland 7.50	Chicago 7.50	Kansas City .. 7.50
New York 7.50	Richmond ... 7.50	St. Louis 7.50	Dallas 7.50
Philadelphia . 7.50	Atlanta 7.50	Minneapolis . 7.50	San Francisco . 7.50

SERIES OF 1977A — MORTON-MILLER, GREEN SEAL
Slight premium over face for uncirculated.

SERIES OF 1981 — BUCHANAN-REGAN, GREEN SEAL
This series is now in production.

TWENTY DOLLAR NOTES (1928) FEDERAL RESERVE NOTES

SERIES OF 1928 — SIGNATURES OF TATE-MELLON, GREEN SEAL

BANK	V.FINE	UNC.	BANK	V.FINE	UNC.
☐ Boston	28.00	70.00	☐ Chicago	28.00	55.00
☐ New York	28.00	60.00	☐ St. Louis	35.00	75.00
☐ Philadelphia	28.00	65.00	☐ Minneapolis	40.00	85.00
☐ Cleveland	28.00	65.00	☐ Kansas City	35.00	85.00
☐ Richmond	37.00	75.00	☐ Dallas	35.00	85.00
☐ Atlanta	35.00	70.00	☐ San Francisco	30.00	75.00

628 / PAPER MONEY

SERIES OF 1928A — SIGNATURES OF WOODS-MELLON, GREEN SEAL

CITY	V.FINE	UNC.	CITY	V.FINE	UNC.
☐ Boston	40.00	65.00	☐ Chicago	45.00	75.00
☐ New York	45.00	75.00	☐ St. Louis	50.00	70.00
☐ Philadelphia	45.00	65.00	☐ Minneapolis	NOT ISSUED	
☐ Cleveland	45.00	70.00	☐ Kansas City	55.00	100.00
☐ Richmond	50.00	75.00	☐ Dallas	40.00	80.00
☐ Atlanta	50.00	70.00	☐ San Francisco	NOT ISSUED	

SERIES OF 1928B — SIGNATURES OF WOODS-MELLON, GREEN SEAL
FACE AND BACK DESIGN SIMILAR TO PREVIOUS NOTE. NUMERAL IN FEDERAL RESERVE SEAL IS NOW CHANGED TO A LETTER.

BANK	V.FINE	UNC.	BANK	V.FINE	UNC.
☐ Boston	35.00	55.00	☐ Chicago	35.00	55.00
☐ New York	35.00	55.00	☐ St. Louis	35.00	65.00
☐ Philadelphia	35.00	55.00	☐ Minneapolis	35.00	60.00
☐ Cleveland	35.00	55.00	☐ Kansas City	35.00	60.00
☐ Richmond	35.00	55.00	☐ Dallas	35.00	70.00
☐ Atlanta	35.00	60.00	☐ San Francisco	35.00	60.00

SERIES OF 1928C — SIGNATURES OF WOODS-MILLS, GREEN SEAL
ONLY TWO BANKS ISSUED THIS NOTE.

BANK	V.FINE	UNC.	BANK	V.FINE	UNC.
☐ Chicago	45.00	110.00	☐ San Francisco	45.00	120.00

TWENTY DOLLAR NOTES (1934) FEDERAL RESERVE NOTES

FACE AND BACK DESIGN SIMILAR TO PREVIOUS NOTE. "REDEEMABLE IN GOLD" REMOVED FROM OBLIGATION OVER FEDERAL RESERVE SEAL. SIGNATURES OF JULIAN-MORGENTHAU, GREEN SEAL.

BANK	GOOD	V.FINE	UNC.	BANK	GOOD	V.FINE	UNC.
☐ Boston	——	32.00	55.00	☐ St. Louis	——	35.00	50.00
☐ New York	——	32.00	50.00	☐ Minneapolis	——	35.00	60.00
☐ Philadelphia	——	32.00	50.00	☐ Kansas City	——	35.00	50.00
☐ Cleveland	——	32.00	50.00	☐ Dallas	——	35.00	50.00
☐ Richmond	——	32.00	50.00	☐ San Francisco	——	35.00	50.00
☐ Atlanta	——	32.00	50.00	☐ *San Francisco			
☐ Chicago	——	32.00	50.00	(HAWAII)	50.00	165.00	875.00

*The San Francisco Federal Reserve Note with brown seal and brown serial numbers, and overprinted "HAWAII" on face and back, was a special issue for the Armed Forces in the Pacific area during World War II.

SERIES OF 1934A — SIGNATURES OF JULIAN-MORGENTHAU

BANK	V.FINE	UNC.	BANK	V.FINE	UNC.
☐ Boston	30.00	60.00	☐ St. Louis	30.00	65.00
☐ New York	30.00	60.00	☐ Minneapolis	30.00	75.00
☐ Philadelphia	30.00	60.00	☐ Kansas City	30.00	65.00
☐ Cleveland	30.00	60.00	☐ Dallas	30.00	60.00
☐ Richmond	30.00	60.00	☐ San Francisco	30.00	60.00
☐ Atlanta	30.00	60.00	☐ *San Francisco		
☐ Chicago	30.00	60.00	(HAWAII)	110.00	450.00

SERIES OF 1934B — SIGNATURES OF JULIAN-VINSON, GREEN SEAL

BANK	V.FINE	UNC.	BANK	V.FINE	UNC.
☐ Boston	30.00	60.00	☐ Chicago	30.00	45.00
☐ New York	30.00	50.00	☐ St. Louis	30.00	50.00
☐ Philadelphia	30.00	50.00	☐ Minneapolis	30.00	65.00
☐ Cleveland	30.00	55.00	☐ Kansas City	30.00	50.00
☐ Richmond	30.00	50.00	☐ Dallas	32.50	65.00
☐ Atlanta	30.00	45.00	☐ San Francisco	30.00	50.00

SERIES OF 1934C — SIGNATURES OF JULIAN-SNYDER, GREEN SEAL

BANK	V.FINE	UNC.	BANK	V.FINE	UNC.
☐ Boston	30.00	55.00	☐ Chicago	30.00	50.00
☐ New York	30.00	50.00	☐ St. Louis	30.00	50.00
☐ Philadelphia	30.00	50.00	☐ Minneapolis	30.00	60.00
☐ Cleveland	30.00	50.00	☐ Kansas City	30.00	55.00
☐ Richmond	30.00	50.00	☐ Dallas	30.00	55.00
☐ Atlanta	30.00	50.00	☐ San Francisco	30.00	50.00

SERIES OF 1934D — SIGNATURES OF CLARK-SNYDER, GREEN SEAL

BANK	V.FINE	UNC.	BANK	V.FINE	UNC.
☐ Boston	30.00	50.00	☐ Chicago	30.00	50.00
☐ New York	30.00	50.00	☐ St. Louis	30.00	50.00
☐ Philadelphia	30.00	50.00	☐ Minneapolis	30.00	55.00
☐ Cleveland	30.00	50.00	☐ Kansas City	30.00	55.00
☐ Richmond	30.00	50.00	☐ Dallas	30.00	52.50
☐ Atlanta	30.00	50.00	☐ San Francisco	30.00	52.50

TWENTY DOLLAR NOTES (1950) FEDERAL RESERVE NOTES

SERIES OF 1950 — SIGNATURES OF CLARK-SNYDER, GREEN SEAL

Black Federal Reserve Seal and Green Treasury Seal are slightly smaller.

BANK	UNC.	BANK	UNC.
☐ Boston	42.00	☐ Chicago	42.00
☐ New York	42.00	☐ St. Louis	42.00
☐ Philadelphia	42.00	☐ Minneapolis	48.00
☐ Cleveland	42.00	☐ Kansas City	45.00
☐ Richmond	42.00	☐ Dallas	45.00
☐ Atlanta	42.00	☐ San Francisco	42.00

SERIES OF 1950A — SIGNATURES OF PRIEST-HUMPHREY, GREEN SEAL
Issued for all Federal Reserve Banks. 32.50

SERIES OF 1950B — SIGNATURES OF PRIEST-ANDERSON, GREEN SEAL
Issued for all Federal Reserve Banks. 32.50

SERIES OF 1950C — SIGNATURES OF SMITH-DILLON, GREEN SEAL
Issued for all Federal Reserve Banks. 32.00

SERIES OF 1950D — SIGNATURES OF GRANAHAN-DILLON, GREEN SEAL
Issued for all Federal Reserve Banks. 32.00

SERIES OF 1950E — SIGNATURES OF GRANAHAN-FOWLER, GREEN SEAL
Issued only for New York, Chicago and San Francisco. 35.00

TWENTY DOLLAR NOTES (1963-1977) FEDERAL RESERVE NOTES

SERIES OF 1963 — SIGNATURES OF GRANAHAN-DILLON, GREEN SEAL
Issued for all Federal Reserve Banks except Philadelphia and Minneapolis. 30.00

SERIES OF 1963A—SIGNATURES OF GRANAHAN-FOWLER, GREEN SEAL
Issued for all Federal Reserve Bank. 29.00

SERIES OF 1969 — SIGNATURES OF ELSTON-KENNEDY, GREEN SEAL
Issued for all Federal Reserve Banks 26.00

SERIES OF 1969A — SIGNATURES OF KABIS-CONNALLY, GREEN SEAL
Issued for all Federal Reserve Banks 24.00

SERIES OF 1969B — SIGNATURES OF BANUELOS-CONNALLY, GREEN SEAL
Issued for all Federal Reserve Banks 24.00

SERIES OF 1969C — SIGNATURES OF BANUELOS-SHULTZ, GREEN SEAL
Issued for all Federal Reserve Banks 24.00

SERIES OF 1974 — SIGNATURES OF NEFF-SIMON, GREEN SEAL
Issued for all Federal Reserve Banks 22.00

SERIES OF 1977 — SIGNATURES OF MORTON-BLUMENTHAL, GREEN SEAL
Issued for all Federal Reserve Banks 22.00

SERIES OF 1977A — SIGNATURES OF MORTON-MILLER, GREEN SEAL
Issued for all Federal Reserve Banks . . . . Slight premium over face

SERIES OF 1981 — SIGNATURES OF BUCHANAN-REGAN, GREEN SEAL, current.

PAPERWEIGHTS

Decorative glass paperweights did not begin to be produced until the 19th century. In fact, paperweights as a whole — even including those of other materials — do not have an early origin. Apparently, the clerk of early times used whatever was at hand to secure the papers on his desk against breezes (which, considering the poor ventilation of early offices, was probably not a serious problem). Heavy coins are said to have sometimes served the purpose, such as the two-pence British copper of 1797. In any case, glass paperweights found a ready market. Some bought them for use, some out of pure admiration. Those of the leading manufactures such as Clichy and Baccarat were retailed in luxury shops of Europe and, to some extent, America. They were also extensively sold to tourists visiting France. The best and most valuable specimens are from the mid 1800's. The "millefiori" weights contain arrays of small ornamental glass beads or stems, of various colors, arranged to form striking patterns. There are also topical paperweights, such as those sold at World Fairs and Expositions, character weights, and various types of novelty weights. The advice is sometimes given, that the weight of a paperweight is an indication of quality. This is erroneous.

PENNY ARCADE COLLECTIBLES / 631

	Current Price Range		Prior Year Average
☐ **Baccarat,** millefiori canes on ground	140.00	190.00	150.00
☐ **Baccarat,** mushroom double overlay	280.00	330.00	300.00
☐ **Baccarat,** pansy	460.00	550.00	500.00
☐ **Banford,** pendant, animal figures	65.00	85.00	75.00
☐ **Clichy,** millefiori canes on turquoise ground	575.00	675.00	625.00
☐ **Clichy,** star garlands on rose cane	1500.00	2000.00	1750.00
☐ **D'Albret,** cameo of Jenny Lind	90.00	120.00	105.00
☐ **Fruit weight,** white ground	420.00	500.00	460.00
☐ **Journal American,** brass newsstand	20.00	28.00	24.00
☐ **Lundberg Studios,** butterfly	65.00	85.00	75.00
☐ **Lundberg Studios,** sunflower	65.00	85.00	75.00
☐ **Molded coal dust,** depicts coal breaker in Pennsylvania, c. 1910	12.00	18.00	15.00
☐ **Perthshire,** millefiori, factory signature in cane . .	37.00	45.00	41.00
☐ **Perthshire,** millefiori, with six clusters of canes .	120.00	150.00	135.00
☐ **Pressed glass star,** "lens" center frames photograph, 6" Dia., c. 1915	25.00	34.00	28.00
☐ **Rectangular glass lens,** factory photograph, c. 1910	22.00	32.00	27.00
☐ **Rectangular glass lens,** Madonna and Child, c. 1920	7.00	12.00	9.00
☐ **Snowball weight,** Lone Ranger and calf, c. 1955 .	22.00	30.00	26.00
☐ **Stankard,** wild rose, single flower	280.00	350.00	320.00
☐ **Stankard,** yellow meadowreath, single flower . . .	290.00	360.00	325.00
☐ **St. Louis,** flower with five petals, orange ground .	240.00	290.00	265.00
☐ **St. Louis,** red cherries on white basket	390.00	450.00	420.00
☐ **St. Louis,** white dahlia, mauve ground	250.00	310.00	280.00
☐ **Whittemore,** iris, Tennessee state flower	390.00	450.00	420.00
☐ **Whittemore,** wild prairie rose, North Dakota state flower	450.00	535.00	480.00

PENNY ARCADE COLLECTIBLES

The Penny Arcade was a special attraction at amusement parks across the country beginning in the late 1800's. It consisted of rows and rows of machines into which you fed pennies (later, nickels and dimes). Some were games, including forerunners of modern pinball machines; others contained little novelties that could be (if you were lucky) plucked out by the machine's mechanical scoop; and still others tested your strength, or told your fortune, or gave your weight on the moon. All of the old Penny Arcade machines are collectible today, as are tokens made for use in them (which are scarce, since most took ordinary coins), and all kinds of Penny Arcade advertising matter. Sometimes dealers in musical collectibles have these items, as strange as they may sound, as they buy up miscellaneous equipment from old amusement parks in order to get musical articles.

632 / PENS AND PENCILS

	Current Price Range		Prior Year Average
☐ **Baseball game,** electric, "Deposit 2¢," cast-lead pitcher throws ball, player pushes button to activate batsman, "fielders" include Cochrane, Gehrig, Simmons and other stars of 1930	4600.00	5300.00	4900.00
☐ **Flip-picture machine,** deposit 5¢, turn crank, look in viewer, pictures flip to give the appearance of a movie, World War I era, but these were still in use as late as the 1960's	975.00	1175.00	1050.00
☐ **"Fortune Teller,"** machine sometimes called "Gypsy Fortune Teller," nearly life-size half-length figure of a woman, dark gown, deposit 2¢, woman moves hand, takes card with printed fortune, passes it to person	2600.00	3300.00	2800.00
☐ **"Test Your Strength" machine,** deposit 1¢, squeeze handles	650.00	850.00	750.00
☐ **Ticket,** "Admit One to George C. Tillyou's Steeplechase," Coney Island, Brooklyn, New York, c. 1940	2.75	3.50	2.25
☐ **Wooden duck** from shooting gallery, target painted on side, 8"long, c. 1940	12.00	18.00	15.00

PENS AND PENCILS

Top to Bottom: **Fine Point Pencil, Safety Self Filling Fountain Pen,** Montgomery Ward . . . . **$7.00-$10.00**

    Writing instruments have extremely early origins and have gone through numerous changes in style and design over the centuries. Quill pens were not the first writing tools. They were not used until around the 6th century A.D., having been preceded by metal styluses. Once adopted, however, they became almost universal in use, and remained the standard writing instrument until the early 1800's. Normally, a goose quill was used. For an ordinary pen, the quill was simply shaped and pared at the tip, and used without any embellishment. But, obviously, the elite were not about to write with plain quills — *their* quill pens were encrusted with silver along the shank or other ornamentation, and sometimes personalized. The quill feather was frequently dyed a bright color. Writing cases were made containing one or more pens and an ink jar from as long ago as the 17th century in Europe and the 18th in America. These are extremely desirable as collectors' items but hard to get. The best ones have morocco-covered lids and sides, often gilt tooled. Fountain pens are much more numerous on the antique market than quills, and since they carry manufacturers' names and (often) model numbers, are particularly intriguing to collect. Some can be quite valuable as the following listings show. Excellent bargains can be found on collectible fountain pens by shopping the antique shops, as not one dealer in a dozen knows the values — they will price either too high or too low, out of guesswork.

ABBREVIATIONS FOR DESCRIPTION, METHOD OF FILLING, AND CONDITION

BC	- barrel and cap	M	-	mint condition (like new)
BF	- button actuated filler	MBL	-	marble-like plastic
CBHR	- chased black hard rubber	O	-	overlay
E	- excellent condition	P	-	poor condition
ED	- eyedropper filled	PF		- plunger filled
F	- fair condition	R		- ribbon
G	- good condition			(ladies' model, ring on top)
GF	- gold-filled	S		- sterling silver
GL	- gold-like (or plated)	SBHR		- smooth black hard rubber
GS14	- 14kt solid gold	SL		- silver-like (or plated)
GS18	- 18kt solid gold	T		- trim,
HR	- hard rubber			(clip, decorative bands, etc.)
LF	- lever actuated filler	W		- working condition

Example - 1899 Parker No. 20 pen, SBHR-ED-EW would be a Model 20 fountain pen manufactured by the Parker Pen Company; shown in their 1899 catalog; with a barrel and cap made from smooth black hard rubber; filled by removing the front of the pen and dropping ink into the barrel with an eyedropper; and in excellent working condition.

	Current Price Range		Prior Year Average
☐ 1899 Parker No. 10 pen, SBHR-ED-EW	23.00	30.00	26.00
☐ 1903 Moore Non-Leakable pen, CBHR-ED-EW	32.00	43.00	36.00
☐ 1904 Diamond Point pen, CBHR-"coin-filler"-EW	23.00	30.00	26.00
☐ 1905 Laughlin pen, SO-ED-EW	36.00	48.00	42.00
☐ 1905 F. R. Mooney pen, GFO-EW	27.00	35.00	31.00
☐ 1913 Waterman No. 12½ "PSF" Pen, SBHR-SLT-LF-FW	17.00	25.00	21.00
☐ 1913 Waterman No. 52V pen, CBHR-SLT-LF-MW	17.00	25.00	21.00
☐ 1913 Waterman No. 52V-½ R-pen, CBHR-SLT-LF-MW	17.00	25.00	21.00
☐ 1913 Waterman No. 54 pen, CBHR-SLT-LF-EW	26.0	38.00	32.00
☐ 1914 Waterman No. 52 pen, CBHR-SLT-LF-GW	10.00	15.00	12.00
☐ 1915 Parker No. 48-R pen, GFBC-BF-E	45.00	65.00	55.00
☐ 1915 Waterman No. 52V pen; CBHR (unusual pocket clip starts with globe on cap top)-SLT-LF-MW	24.00	38.00	31.00
☐ 1915 Waterman No. 452-½ V R-pen, SO-FW	22.00	34.00	28.00
☐ 1916 Parker Black Giant pen, MW	550.0	750.00	650.00
☐ 1917 Waterman No. 52 pen, CBHR (wide clip)-SLT-LF-EW	17.00	24.00	20.00
☐ 1917 Waterman No. 54 pen, CBHR-SLT-LF-MW	17.00	24.00	20.00
☐ 1918 Wahl pen, SO-ED-GW	23.00	30.00	26.00
☐ 1918 Waterman No. 55 pen, CBHR-SLT-LR-MW	60.00	80.00	70.00
☐ 1918 Waterman No. 454 pen and pencil, S (floral engraving) LF-EW	160.00	210.00	180.00

634 / PENS AND PENCILS

	Current Price Range		Prior Year Average
☐ 1919 **Sheaffer R-pen,** GFBC-LF-E (scratched section)	9.00	12.00	10.50
☐ 1920 **Dunn pen,** black with red barrel end-GLT	4.50	7.00	5.75
☐ 1920 **Eversharp pencil,** SL-EW	4.5	7.00	5.75
☐ 1920 **Sheaffer R-pencil,** GF-EW	7.00	10.00	8.00
☐ 1920 **Waterman No. 20,** MW	320.00	400.00	360.00
☐ 1920 **Waterman No. 52V pen,** CBHR (original price sticker) SLT-LF-MW	18.00	25.00	21.50
☐ 1920 **Waterman No. 52V pen,** CBHR-SLT-LF-MW	16.00	22.00	19.00
☐ 1920 **Waterman No. 52V pen,** CBHR-SLT-LF-EW	14.00	19.00	16.00
☐ 1920 **Waterman No. 52½V R-pen,** SBHR-GLT-LF-GW	9.00	12.00	10.00
☐ 1921 **Sheaffer R-pencil,** S-GW	7.00	10.00	8.50
☐ 1922 **Parker Duofold Jr., pen,** red HR-initial model-BF-E	45.00	65.00	55.00
☐ 1922 **Wahl pen,** GFBC-LF-EW	9.00	12.00	10.50
☐ 1922 **Waterman No. 52 pen,** CBHR-SLT-LF-EW	14.00	20.00	17.00
☐ 1923 **Conklin pen,** SBHR-"crescent filler"-GLT-F with E nib	7.00	10.00	8.00
☐ 1923 **Moore No. L-92 pen,** SBHR-GLT-MW	27.00	35.00	30.00
☐ 1923 **Parker Duofold Jr., pen,** red-HR-BF-E	32.00	40.00	36.00
☐ 1923 **Parker Duofold "Big Red" pen,** red-HR-BF-MW	85.00	115.00	100.00
☐ 1923 **Sheaffer "White Dot" pen,** green jade-GLT-LF-GW	45.00	65.00	55.00
☐ 1923 **Wahl Eversharp pen and pencil,** GF-LF-M	15.00	23.00	19.00
☐ 1923 **Wahl Eversharp R-pen and pencil,** GF-LF-M (in box)	12.00	19.00	14.50
☐ 1923 **Wahl Eversharp R-pencil,** GF-EW	4.00	7.00	5.50
☐ 1923 **Wahl pen,** GF-LF-EW	32.00	44.00	38.00
☐ 1923 **Waterman No. 7 pen,** red ripple HR-GLT-wide clip-LF-EW	60.00	80.00	70.00
☐ 1923 **Waterman No. 55 pen,** red ripple HR-GLT-wide clip-LF-GW	45.00	60.00	52.00
☐ 1924 **Parker Duofold Jr., pen,** red, HR-GLT-BF-EW	27.00	38.00	32.00
☐ 1924 **Parker Duofold Special pen,** red HR-GLT-BF-MW	36.00	45.00	40.00
☐ 1924 **Parker Duofold "Big Red" pen,** red HR-GLT-BF-GW	44.00	58.00	49.00
☐ 1924 **Sheaffer "White Dot" R-pen,** green jade, GLT-LF-GW	13.00	19.00	16.00
☐ 1924 **Sheaffer "White Dot" R-pen,** green jade, GLT-LF-MWE	22.00	30.00	26.00
☐ 1924 **Wahl pen,** GF-LF-GW	7.00	10.00	8.00
☐ 1924 **Wahl Eversharp R-pencil,** Ew	5.00	8.00	6.00
☐ 1924 **Wahl Eversharp pencil,** S (floral engraving)-MW	22.00	30.00	26.00
☐ 1924 **Waterman No. 52 pen,** red ripple HR-GLT-wide clip-EW	17.00	25.00	21.00
☐ 1925 **Conklin Endura R-pen,** green, MBL-GLT-LF-MW	22.00	30.00	26.00
☐ 1925 **Conklin Endura R-pen,** brown, MBL-GLT-LF-EW	20.00	27.00	23.00
☐ 1925 **Parker Duofold Jr., pen,** red HR-BF-EW	27.00	36.00	31.00
☐ 1925 **Sheaffer "White Dot" pen,** green jade, GLT-LF-EW	34.00	48.00	41.00

PENS AND PENCILS / 635

	Current Price Range		Prior Year Average
☐ Sheaffer "White Dot" pen, black, GLT-LF-EW ...	40.00	55.00	47.00
☐ 1025 Sheaffer "White Dot" R-pen, black, GLT-LF-MW	16.00	22.00	19.00
☐ 1925 Sheaffer pen, green jade, GLT-LF-EW with lifetime nib	9.00	12.00	10.00
☐ 1925 Wahl pen, GF-LF-EW	10.00	15.00	12.00
☐ 1926 Marxton pen, green, MBL-GLT-GW	7.0	10.00	8.00
☐ 1926 Parker pencil, green jade, GLT-GW	9.00	12.00	10.00
☐ 1926 Sheaffer "White Dot" large pen, pearl and black, GLT-LF-EW	60.00	80.00	70.00
☐ 1926 Sheaffer pen, green jade, LF-EW	14.00	20.00	17.00
☐ 1926 Wahl R-pen, S with GF-LF-MW	27.00	36.00	31.00
☐ 1926 Wahl pen, GF-LF-roller clip	20.00	27.00	23.00
☐ 1926 Waterman No. 5 pen, red ripple, HR-GLT-LF-EW	14.00	21.00	17.00
☐ 1927 Chilton pen, SBHR-GLT-PF-E	10.00	15.00	12.00
☐ 1927 Grieshaber pen, pearl and black, EW	40.00	55.00	47.00
☐ 1927 Parker Duofold Sr., pen, green jade, BF-EW .	45.00	65.00	55.00
☐ 1927 Parker Duofold Jr., pen, green jade, BF-EW .	22.00	30.00	26.00
☐ 1927 Wahl Eversharp "Big Boy" pencil, wood grain, GLT-EW	7.00	10.00	8.00
☐ 1927 Waterman No. 5 pen, black, SLT-LF-EW	14.00	19.00	16.00
☐ 1928 Wahl Eversharp "Gold Seal" pen and pencil, pearl and black, GLT-MW	45.00	60.00	52.00
☐ 1929 Parker Lady Duofold pen, pearl and black, MBL-GLT-BF-EW	20.00	28.00	24.00
☐ 1929 Parker Lady Duofold pen, red, BF-EW	27.0	38.00	32.00
☐ 1929 Parker Lady Duofold pen, green jade, BF-pocket clip-EW	22.00	30.00	26.00
☐ 1929 Waterman Lady Patricia pen, S-LF-GW	36.00	47.00	42.00
☐ 1929 Waterman Lady Patricia pen, onyx and terra cotta, GLT-LF-EW	14.00	19.00	16.50
☐ 1930 Parker Lady Duofold Streamlined pen, green, MBL-GLT-BF-MW	18.00	25.00	21.50
☐ 1930 Sheaffer "White Dot" R-pen, pearl and black, MBL-GLT-LF-GW	18.00	25.00	21.50
☐ 1930 Sheaffer "White Dot" Streamlined pen, black, GLT-LF-EW	45.00	60.00	52.00
☐ 1930 Sheaffer R-pen, pearl and black, LF-EW	22.00	30.00	26.00
☐ 1930 Wahl Eversharp R-pen, pearl and black, MBL-GLT-EW	9.00	12.00	10.50
☐ 1930 Wahl Eversharp "Gold Seal" pencil, pearl and black, GLT-EW	12.00	19.00	15.50
☐ 1930 Waterman No. 5 pen, black, GLT-GW	9.00	12.00	10.50
☐ 1931 Eversharp Doric pen, black, EW	10.00	15.00	12.50
☐ 1931 Parker Duofold Streamlined pen, burgundy, MBL-GLT-BF-EW	22.00	30.00	26.00
☐ 1931 Parker Lucky Curve Duofold "Big Red" pen, red, BF-EW	130.00	170.00	150.00
☐ 1931 Parker Duofold pen, green jade, BF-MW ...	22.00	30.00	26.00
☐ 1931 Parker Duofold pencil, green jade, MW	10.00	15.00	12.50
☐ 1931 Sheaffer "White Dot" combination pen and pencil, black, GLT-LF	36.00	47.00	42.00
☐ 1931 Sheaffer "White Dot" pen, green, MBL-GLT-LF-GW	14.00	19.00	16.50

636 / PENS AND PENCILS

	Current Price Range		Prior Year Average
☐ 1932 **Parker Duofold Streamlined pen,** black, GLT-BF-EW	32.00	43.00	38.00
☐ 1932 **Parker Parkette pen,** black, GLT-LF-FW	2.50	4.00	3.25
☐ 1932 **Sheaffer pen,** green jade, GLT-LF-EW	9.00	12.00	10.50
☐ 1932 **Waterman No. 92V pen,** burgundy pearl, MBL-GLT-LF-EW	7.00	10.00	8.50
☐ 1933 **Chilton pen,** black, GLT-EW	22.0	30.00	26.00
☐ 1933 **Parker Vacumatic pen,** burgundy, GLT-BF-G	4.00	7.00	5.50
☐ 1933 **Parker Parkette pen,** red and silver, MBL-GLT-LF-EW	3.50	5.00	4.25
☐ 1933 **Waterman No. 5 pen and pencil,** black, GLT-LF-EW	22.00	30.00	26.00
☐ 1934 **Parker Vacumatic pen,** burgundy and black, GLT-BF-EW	22.00	30.00	26.00
☐ 1935 **Eversharp Midget pen,** green, MBL-GLT-E	3.50	5.00	4.25
☐ 1935 **Parker Duofold pen,** green and black, GLT-BF-EW	9.00	12.00	10.50
Sheaffer desk pen with "Pen used by President Roosevelt to sign Guffey-Snyder Coal Bill Aug. 30, 1935" engraved on it	22.00	30.00	26.00
☐ 1935 **Waterman No. 94 pen,** green and brown, MBL-GLT-LF-EW	14.00	19.00	16.50
☐ 1936 **Cameleon two-nib pen,** salmon, GLT-EW	22.00	30.00	26.00
☐ 1936 **Packard combination pen and pencil,** red, MBL-LF-GLT-MW, boxed	4.00	7.00	5.50
☐ 1936 **Parker Duofold pen,** green and black, SLT-BF-EW	5.00	8.00	6.50
☐ 1936 **Parker Challenger pen,** green, MBL-LF-EW	6.50	9.00	7.75
☐ 1936 **Ronson Penciliter,** rodium plate and green, MBL-EW	22.00	30.00	26.00
☐ 1936 **Sheaffer "White Dot" pen and pencil,** red and black, GLT-LF-GW	33.00	45.00	39.00
☐ 1936 **Sheaffer "White Dot" pen,** black, GLT-LF-EW	40.00	60.00	50.00
☐ 1936 **Wahl Oxford pen,** green jade, GLT-EW	7.00	10.00	8.50
☐ 1936 **Waterman No. 3V pen,** red and gray, MBL-SLT-LF-EW	4.50	7.00	5.75
☐ 1936 **Waterman No. 92 pen and pencil,** red and green, MBL-GLT-LF-GW	10.00	15.00	12.50
☐ 1937 **Parker Vacumatic pen,** blue and black, GLT-BF-MW	20.00	25.00	22.50
☐ 1937 **Sheaffer pen,** green and black, GLT-LF-EW	9.00	12.00	10.50
☐ 1937 **Sheaffer "White Dot" pen,** black, GLT-LF-GW	7.00	10.00	8.50
☐ 1935 **Sheaffer "White Dot" pen,** silver and black, SLT-LF-EW	45.00	60.00	52.00
☐ 1938 **Parker Duofold pen,** gold and black, GLT-BF-EW	5.00	8.00	6.50
☐ 1938 **Sheaffer pen,** grey and black, SLT-LF-GW	4.59	6.75	5.10
☐ 1938 **Waterman No. 32 pen,** black, SLT-LF-GW	2.75	4.00	3.15
☐ 1939 **Parker "Blue Diamond" Major Vacumatic,** silver and black, BF-MW	14.00	19.00	16.50
☐ 1939 **Parker Challenger pen,** pearl, MBL-LF-MW	6.00	9.00	7.50
☐ 1939 **Sheaffer "White Dot" pen,** gold and black, BLT-PF-EW	10.00	15.00	12.50
☐ 1939 **Waterman No. 32X pen,** SLT-LF	5.00	7.50	6.25

	Current Price Range		Prior Year Average
☐ 1940 Parker Challenger pen, green, MBL-LF-GW .	3.50	5.00	4.25
☐ 1940 Sheaffer "White Dot" Crest pen and pencil, black, LF-EW	22.00	29.00	25.00
☐ 1940 Waterman pen, black, SLT-LF-EW	1.75	3.00	2.35
☐ 1940 Waterman pen, black, GLT-LF-EW	4.00	6.75	5.45
☐ 1942 Parker Vacumatic pen, black, GLT-BF-EW (unique blind cap)	18.00	27.00	22.50
☐ 1942 Parker "Blue Diamond" "51" pen, black, GF, cap, BF-EW	14.00	19.00	16.50
☐ 1942 Parker "Blue Diamond" "51" pen, blue, S, cap, BF-EW	10.00	15.00	12.50
☐ 1942 Sheaffer Crest Triumph pen, black GF, cap, PF-GW	10.00	15.00	12.50
☐ 1942 Sheaffer "White Dot" Triumph lady's pen, gray and black, SLT-PF-EW	18.00	27.00	22.50
☐ 1942 Sheaffer "White Dot" Triumph pen, green and black, GLT-PF-EW	14.00	19.00	16.50
☐ 1942 Sheaffer "White Dot" Triumph pen, silver and black, SLT-PF-GW	10.00	15.00	12.50
☐ 1942 Sheaffer "White Dot" pen, green and black, GLT-PF-GW	4.00	7.00	5.50
☐ 1943 Eversharp "64" pen and pencil, black, GS, 14 caps, LF-MW, boxed	50.00	70.00	60.00
☐ 1943 Eversharp "64" pen and pencil, black, GS, 14 caps, LF-MW	30.00	40.00	35.00
☐ 1943 Parker "Blue Diamond" "51" pen, gray, S, cap BF-MW	22.00	30.00	26.00
☐ 1943 Sheaffer "White Dot" Triumph pen, black, GS, 14 band on cap, PF-GW	10.00	15.00	12.50
☐ 1944 Parker "Blue Diamond" Vacumatic pen, blue and black, GLT-BF-MW	18.00	27.00	22.50
☐ 1944 Parker "Blue Diamond" Vacumatic pen, gold and black, GLT-BF-MW	8.00	12.00	10.00
☐ 1944 Parker "Blue Diamond" "51" pen, black-stainless cap, BF-EW	10.00	15.00	12.50
☐ 1944 Sheaffer "White Dot" Triumph Tuckaway pen, black, GLT-PF-GW	10.00	15.00	12.50
☐ 1945 Eversharp Skyline pen, green, GF, cap LF-EW	8.00	12.00	10.00
☐ 1945 Eversharp Skyline pen, gray, GF, cap, LF-EW	7.00	10.00	8.50
☐ 1945 Eversharp Skyline pen, black, GLT-LF-EW ..	4.00	7.00	5.50
☐ 1945 Eversharp Skyline pen, burgundy, LF-FW ..	4.00	7.00	5.50
☐ 1945 Eversharp Skyline pen, black-green and black cap, LF-EW	4.00	7.00	5.50
☐ 1945 Parker "Blue Diamond" Vacumatic pen, silver and black, SLT-E	10.00	15.00	12.50
☐ 1945 Parker "Blue Diamond" "51" pen, green, stainless cap, BF-EW	10.00	15.00	12.50
☐ 1945 Parker Vacumatic pen, green and black, BF-MW	7.00	10.00	8.50
☐ 1945 Sheaffer "White Dot" Crest Triumph pen, black, GF cap, LF-MW	18.00	27.00	22.50
☐ 1945 Sheaffer Tuckaway pen and pencil, green and black, LF-MW	18.00	27.00	22.50

638 / PENS AND PENCILS

	Current Price Range		Prior Year Average
☐ 1946 Parker Vacumatic pen and pencil, green and black, BF-MW, boxed	12.00	19.00	15.50
☐ 1946 Sheaffer "White Dot" Crest Triumph pen, blue, GF cap, MW	22.00	32.00	27.00
☐ 1946 Sheaffer "White Dot" pen, black, GLT-LF-GW	9.00	12.00	10.50
☐ 1946 Sheaffer "White Dot" Sentinel Triumph Deluxe pen, pencil and stratowriter, blue-chrome and GF caps, PF-EW	27.00	37.00	32.00
☐ 1946 Sheaffer "White Dot" Tuckaway, blue-chrome and GF cap, PF-MW	14.00	19.00	16.50
☐ 1946 Sheaffer "White Dot" Triumph pen, blue, GLT-PF-MW, price sticker	16.00	23.00	19.50
☐ 1946 Sheaffer "White Dot" Triumph pen, brown, GLT-PF-MW, price sticker	14.00	19.00	16.50
☐ 1946 Sheaffer "White Dot" pen, black, GLT-GW .	9.00	12.00	10.50
☐ 1946 Waterman pen, gray, MBL-SLT-LT-GW	4.50	7.00	5.75
☐ 1947 Sheaffer "White Dot" Tuckaway, black, GF cap, PF-EW	16.00	22.00	19.00
☐ 1947 Sheaffer "White Dot" Triumph pen, brown, SL and GF cap, PF-MW	20.00	28.00	24.00
☐ 1947 Waterman pen, black, SL and GL cap, LF-EW	5.00	8.00	6.50
☐ 1948 Parker "51" Special pen, gray-chrome cap, EW	4.50	7.00	5.75
☐ 1948 Sheaffer "White Dot" Triumph pen, SL and GF cap, PF-FW	7.00	10.00	8.50
☐ 1949 Parker "21" pen and pencil, blue, stainless caps, EW	9.00	12.00	10.50
☐ 1949 Parker "21" pen, blue, stainless cap, MW ..	4.00	6.75	5.40
☐ 1949 Waterman pen, brown, SL and GL cap, LF-EW	4.00	6.50	5.40
☐ 1950 Parker "21" pen, blue, stainless cap, EW ...	5.00	8.00	6.50
☐ 1950 Sheaffer "White Dot" Triumph pen, black, SL and GF cap, EW	7.00	10.00	8.50
☐ 1950 Shaeffer "White Dot" Triumph pen, maroon, SL and GF cap, EW	7.00	10.00	8.50
☐ 1950 Sheaffer pen, blue, GLT-LF-EW	3.50	5.75	4.60
☐ 1950 Sheaffer "White Dot" pen, black, GLT-PF-EW	5.00	7.50	6.25
☐ 1951 Sheaffer "White Dot" TM pen, black, SL and GFT cap, PF-EW	7.00	10.00	8.50
☐ 1951 Sheaffer "White Dot" TM pen, maroon, SL and GFT cap, PF-EW	7.00	10.00	8.50
☐ 1951 Sheaffer TM pen, maroon, GLT-EW	3.50	5.00	4.25
☐ 1953 Sheaffer Snorkel pen, black, GLT-MW, boxed	8.00	12.00	10.00
☐ 1953 Sheaffer "White Dot" Snorkel pen, black, GS 14 cap band, PF-GW	14.00	20.00	17.00
☐ 1954 Sheaffer "White Dot" Snorkel pen, maroon, GLT-PF-G	3.50	5.00	4.25
☐ 1954 Sheaffer Snorkel pen, maroon, GLT-PF-GW	2.75	4.00	3.45
☐ 1954 Sheaffer Snorkel pen, maroon, GLT-PF-EW .	3.50	5.00	4.25
☐ 1954 Sheaffer "White Dot" Snorkel pen, maroon, SL and GFT cap, PF-EW	9.00	12.00	10.50

PHARMACY ITEMS

Pharmacies have flourished in all parts of the world, since very early times, and sometimes have sold quite bizarre wares. Old Chinese pharmacies dispensed fossil bones, as they were believed by the Chinese to have curative powers when powdered and taken as medicine. In medieval England, the pharmacist (known, as he still is in England, as a chemist) was counted upon to carry the ingredients for witches' brews and every kind of Old Wives remedy; such shops must have truly been a house of horrors. Pharmacies were established in the American colonies from as early as the 17th century. Relics of this era are not likely to be found on the antiques market, but you will have no trouble locating pharmacy items from the 18th and 19th centuries, when the trade greatly expanded. Probably the most common pharmacy relic is the mortal and pestle, an iron bowl and club-like iron rod in which medicinal ingredients were pulverized. These are not, on the whole, very costly: good early ones can be bought for less than $50. Pharmacy jars and vials are the favorite specialties of some hobbyists. They often carry labels, which aid in dating them. The really serious student of pharmacy history also collects books on the subject as well as account ledgers kept by early pharmacies and anything else relating to the profession. Much more is available than you might imagine, and the best advice for a beginner is: concentrate on the EARLIEST items you can get.

	Current Price Range		Prior Year Average
☐ **American pharmacist's sign,** rectangular wood, a white ground with black hand-lettering, listing products and services, a few prices, c. 1840	525.00	600.00	562.00
☐ **Cork press,** cast iron, 19th c.	42.00	55.00	48.00
☐ **Mortar and pestle,** English, the mortar carved from a solid block of wood, 7½" H., 15th c.	200.00	300.00	250.00
☐ **Pharmacist's ledger book,** Roxbury, Mass., kept from September 1831 to March 1832, 162pp., marbled boards with morocco spine	32.00	40.00	36.00
☐ **Pill boxes,** turned wood, with lid, 1½" Dia.,	1.50	3.50	2.50
☐ **Pillmaking machine,** mahogany/brass, c. 1870's	150.00	200.00	175.00
☐ **Roman pharmacy jar,** cloudy whitish glass with bubbles and sand particles, 4" H., 2nd-3rd c. A.D.	75.00	100.00	87.00
☐ **Roman pharmacy vial,** brown glass, narrow, well formed, 3½" L., 2nd-3rd c. A.D.	32.00	45.00	38.00
☐ **Scrapbook** containing pharmacists' advertisements clipped from newspapers of 1780-1830, mostly New England, about 800 items, the album bound in pink cowhide	350.00	450.00	400.00
☐ **Wedgwood mortar and pestle,** 12" L., 19th c.	120.00	170.00	145.00

PHONOGRAPHS AND ROLLER ORGANS

In the early days of the phonograph, its chief competition was the roller organ. Phonographs had a major advantage in that they could reproduce speech and various sound effects, while the roller organ played music only. But early phonographs were not the devices of today. They were crude and

Columbia Type AJ Disc Phonograph .... **$450.00-$650.00**

primitive, and many people really preferred the big sound of the roller organ. The roller organ played itself — so long as you pedaled it (later ones worked by electricity, or were converted from pedal-power to electric.) Each roll contained selections of popular tunes of the day. When roller organ enthusiasm was at its height, just about any tune, new or old, domestic or foreign, could be found "on a roll." For a long time, these two devices, the phonograph and roller organ, vied for the top of the market. The phonograph eventually won out, after improvements had been made on it, but it was not until 1910 that the battle was finally decided. Unfortunately, the decline of roller organ popularity caused many owners to allow their machines to fall into neglect. They were taken up to the attic or down to the cellar and stored without proper covering, allowed to collect 30 or 40 years worth of dust. Diligent efforts by today's collectors and dealers have succeeded in bringing many of the surviving roller organs back to their original condition. When you buy these or ANY mechanical antique, thoroughly investigate the condition, because a very large portion of the value rests with it.

For more in-depth information and listings, you may refer to *The Official Price Guide To Music Marchines and Instruments* by Susan Gould and published by the House of Collectibles

PHONOGRAPHS AND ROLLER ORGANS

	Current Price Range		Prior Year Average
☐ **Celestina roller organ,** plays paper rolls, hand crank, several times on paper roll, with three rolls, c. 1880	360.00	440.00	400.00
☐ **Same as above, slightly different case and decals (see color section)**	360.00	440.00	400.00
☐ **Columbia "Eagle" Graphophone,** Model B, plays two-minute records, nickel horn, key-wind, c. 1898-1900	230.00	290.00	260.00
☐ **Columbia Graphophone,** Model Q, plays two-minute records, wax cylinders, metal horn, c. 1897	210.00	260.00	235.00
☐ **Columbia Graphophone,** 2nd Series, plays two-minute records, metal horn, key-wind, c. 1898	180.00	240.00	210.00
☐ **Columbia Graphophone,** Type AA, permanent reproducer, plays two-minute cylinders, smallest Columbia phono with enclosed works, c. 1908	320.00	400.00	360.00
☐ **Cylinder record cabinets,** many styles and sizes were made to house the cylinder records within their boxes, may have wooden or cardboard pegs	250.00	450.00	350.00
☐ **Concert roller organ,** plays wooden cobs with iron pins, hand crank (no spring), with 12 cobs, c. 1889	325.00	475.00	400.00
☐ **Edison Amberola 30,** oak case, inside horn, plays four-minute blue amberol records, diamond stylus, c. 1910-1916	200.00	300.00	250.00
☐ **Edison Amberola V.,** single spring motor with automatic stop, plays four-minute blue amberol records, mahogany case, telescopic tube connected to reproducer, c. 1912-1913	420.00	535.00	475.00
☐ **Edison diamond disc,** floor and table models, plays thick Edison 80 rpm disc records, internal horn, c. 1915	140.00	190.00	165.00
☐ **Edison Fireside Edition,** Model "A," plays two-minute cylinders, wooden cygnet horn, sapphire, c. 1910-1914	350.00	450.00	400.00
☐ **Edison Fireside phonograph,** plays two and four-minute records, wood base, morning glory horn and crane, painted horn, c. 1906-1910	310.00	390.00	350.00
☐ **Edison Gem phonograph,** plays two-minute wax cylinders, cast iron case on wooden base, c. 1906	260.00	340.00	300.00
☐ **Edison home phonograph,** plays two and four-minute records, metal cygnet horn, c. 1898-1910	290.00	380.00	335.00
☐ **Edison home suitcase-type,** latches and large scroll decal on cover, plays two-minute cylinder records, with painted morning glory horn and crane, c. 1888-1891	370.00	460.00	415.00
☐ **Edison Maroon Gem,** plays two and four-minute records, 24″ morning glory horn (very rare), c. 1916-1918	650.00	800.00	725.00
☐ **Edison and other manufacturers,** record cylinders, rarities and famous names (Caruso, Sousa, etc.)	4.00	9.00	6.50
☐ **Edison standard phonograph,** wooden base, 10″ tin horn, 18″ brass bell, plays two-minute records, c. 1898-1908	1250.00	1750.00	1500.00

642 / PHOTOGRAPHICA

	Current Price Range		Prior Year Average
☐ **Edison standard suitcase-type,** square top style with suitcase latches, no decal on case, plays two-minute cylinders, early model, c. 1897-1901 .	450.00	600.00	525.00
☐ **Edison Triumph,** Model D, oak case, plays two and four-minute cylinder records. Model C reproducer plays two-minute records. Model H reproducer plays four-minute cylinder records. c. 1908	400.00	550.00	475.00
☐ **Gem roller organ,** same type but with cheaper case	300.00	425.00	362.00
☐ **Helikon,** German reed organette, hand crank, plays cardboard 6¾" diameter, many types and slight variations in styles made with six discs, c. 1900	200.00	275.00	237.00
☐ **Pathe,** cylinder phonograph made in France, plays 3" diameter cylinder records, some models come with adaptors for smaller cylinders, aluminum horn	250.00	325.00	287.00
☐ **Portable phonographs,** several types made to look like a box or folding camera, they play 78 rpm records, all parts (i.e., reproducer, crank, tone arm, "horn," and turntable) fit inside the case for travel, quite small, c. 1920-1930's	200.00	285.00	242.00
☐ **Rol Monica,** harmonica installed in "genuine bakelite" case, plays small paper rolls which come in striped boxes, by blowing in or out on mouthpiece while turning crank one produces music, the Playasax works on the same principle and there are others, c. 1925-1928	85.00	120.00	102.00
☐ **Victor III,** double spring, plays 78 rpm records on 10" turntable. c. 1902	400.00	500.00	450.00
☐ **Victor Type E Disc phonograph,** mounted horn, black enameled with brass bell, 8" turntable, plays 78 rpm records, c. 1902	420.00	535.00	475.00
☐ **Victor table phonograph,** plays 78 rpm records, oak wood cabinet, c. 1908-1916	80.00	150.00	115.00
☐ **Zonophone Standard,** 7" turntable, plays 78 rpm records, front mounted bell horn, single spring motor, oak case, c. 1901	650.00	850.00	750.00
☐ **Zonophone,** Universal Talking Machine Manufacturing Co., 10" turntable, plays 78 rpm records, read mounted, large brass bell horn, oak case, slotted crank, c. 1900-1910	800.00	1000.00	900.00

PHOTOGRAPHICA

Early pioneer photographs have long been collected by historical societies and, to some extent, by private individuals. Interest in them was, traditionally, as documentary evidence of the things they picture, and only incidentally as relics of an important artform. Beginning in the 1960's this point of view changed, and the age of inspired photographica collecting was ushered in. Since then the hobby has greatly expanded and become the subject of numerous books, clubs, periodicals, and related activities.

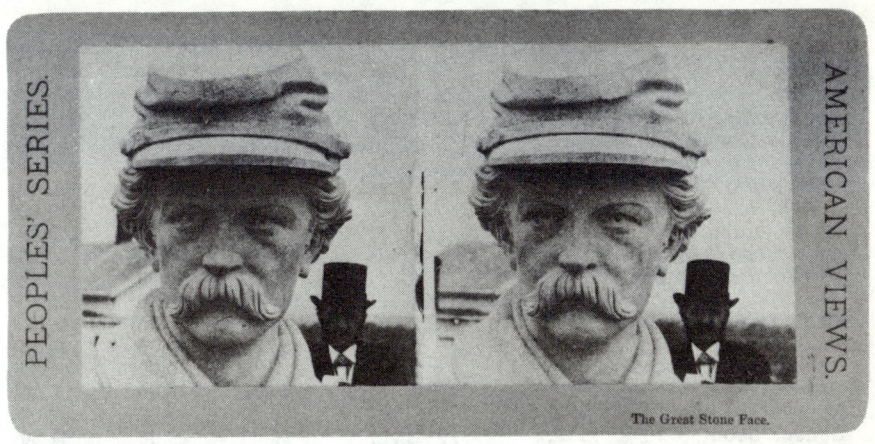

Photographica, stereograph, c. 1880 .... **$3.00-$15.00**

Today's collectors do not restrict themselves to photographs, but extend their vistas into the equipment used to create them: the cameras of yesteryear, and other paraphernalia of early photography studios. The more specialized collectors refuse to stop even there, but build supplemental collections of old camera ads, handbooks, vintage photography journals, and just about anything pertaining to photography which is early and appealing.

The uninformed buyer is in for a bad time of it in this field, as age, looks, and often, even the manufacturer's reputation count for little in the value of a camera. Study this subject thoroughly before making any sizeable investments.

BOX CAMERAS

	Current Price Range		Prior Year Average
☐ **Adlake,** 4″ x 5″, c. 1897	85.00	115.00	100.00
☐ **Adlake Repeater,** 4″ x 5″	70.00	85.00	77.00
☐ **Agfa Memo**	60.00	70.00	65.00
☐ **Blair Weno Hawkeye,** No. 6	65.00	85.00	75.00
☐ **Blair Weno Hawkeye,** No. 7	40.00	55.00	47.00
☐ **Blair Baby Hawkeye**	160.00	200.00	180.00
☐ **Brownie** No. 0	18.00	25.00	21.50
☐ **Brownie** No. 1, c. 1900	55.00	75.00	65.00
☐ **Brownie** No. 2	5.00	10.00	7.50
☐ **Bullit,** No. 4, 4″ x 5″ plate	75.00	100.00	87.00
☐ **Bullseye,** No. 4	70.00	90.00	80.00
☐ **Conley,** 4″ x 5″	45.00	75.00	57.00
☐ **Cyclone,** magazine type	70.00	90.00	80.00
☐ **Diamond** postcard gun camera	450.00	600.00	525.00
☐ **Ertee** photo button camera, c. 1920	800.00	1000.00	900.00
☐ **Eureke** (Kodak) No. 2	50.00	70.00	60.00
☐ **Falcon** No. 2, c. 1893	55.00	75.00	65.00
☐ **Flexo** (Eastman Kodak)	55.00	75.00	65.00
☐ **Harvard,** pinhole all metal	200.00	275.00	237.00

644 / PHOTOGRAPHICA

	Current Price Range		Prior Year Average
☐ Hawkeye, 4″ x 5″, c.1905	150.00	190.00	170.00
☐ Hicro color box box camera (Kodak)	75.00	100.00	87.00
☐ Kamaret (Blair Camera Company)	390.00	470.00	430.00
☐ Kewpie, Conley 2, 3, 3A	30.00	40.00	35.00
☐ Keystone Ferrotype camera	140.00	190.00	165.00
☐ Kodak, first made, c. 1888	2800.00	3700.00	3250.00
☐ Kodak, No. 4, 1890	330.00	410.00	370.00
☐ Kodak, ordinary, models B, C	600.00	700.00	650.00
☐ Kodak, speed No. 1A	130.00	170.00	150.00
☐ Mandel Ette camera, c. 1921	60.00	80.00	70.00
☐ New York, Ferrotype Co., camera, c. 1906	160.00	210.00	185.00
☐ Panorama Kodak, No. 1 Model D, c. 1900	120.0	170.00	145.00
☐ Premo, film pack	55.00	75.00	65.00
☐ Puck Special, 4″ x 5″	80.00	110.00	95.00
☐ Ray Box, c. 1895	55.00	75.00	65.00
☐ Rochester Optical Co., 4″ x 5″	38.00	48.00	42.00
☐ Seneca Scout, c. 1916	20.00	29.00	24.50
☐ Turret panoramic camera, c. 1904	300.00	385.00	342.00
☐ Univex "A", c. 1937	14.00	20.00	17.00
☐ Vive Tourist Mag, plate box, c. 1895	70.00	95.00	82.00
☐ Wonder Automatic Cannon, c. 1908	450.00	575.00	515.00

CARTES DE VISITE

☐ Architectural scene	3.00	5.00	4.00
☐ Civil War historical figure	15.00	65.00	40.00
☐ Lincoln	45.00	70.00	57.00
☐ Theatrical personality	15.00	40.00	27.00
☐ Tom Thumb family	16.00	25.00	20.50
☐ Unidentified personal portrait	1.25	5.00	3.15

DAGUERREOTYPE CASE

☐ Abstract rose	65.00	85.00	75.00
☐ Angel with trumpet	50.00	75.00	62.00
☐ Civil War theme	50.00	80.00	65.00
☐ Daniel in the Lion's Den	200.00	300.00	850.00
☐ Gypsy Fortune Teller	100.00	140.00	120.00
☐ Holy family	200.00	275.00	237.00
☐ Horse race	250.00	320.00	285.00
☐ Indian Chief	45.00	65.00	55.00
☐ Landing of Columbus	600.00	800.00	700.00
☐ Lion with nude lady	70.00	90.00	80.00
☐ Mary and her little lamb	70.00	100.00	85.00
☐ Scroll, Constitution and the Law	65.00	90.00	77.00
☐ Washington crossing Delaware	600.00	775.00	688.00

HIDDEN CAMERAS

☐ Ansco Vanity - made up box, c. 1927	1000.00	1500.00	1250.00
☐ Ensign pocketbook, c. 1926	2800.00	3500.00	3150.00
☐ Gray's patent vest camera	1800.00	2300.00	2050.00
☐ Krause photo revolver, c. 1920	1700.00	2200.00	1950.00
☐ Petal octagon shape	110.00	150.00	130.00
☐ Photoret, round, c. 1897	475.00	650.00	555.00
☐ Pocket Presto camera, c. 1896	800.00	1000.00	900.00
☐ Pocket Ticka camera	140.00	180.00	160.00
☐ Tom Thumb with original box	1600.00	2000.00	1800.00

MISCELLANEOUS

	Current Price Range		Prior Year Average
☐ **Album,** bird and floral, blue plush	55.00	75.00	65.00
☐ **Album,** black leather embossed, gold clasp	35.00	48.00	42.00
☐ **Album,** brown leather, brass fasteners, gold leaf	260.00	330.00	285.00
☐ **Album,** music box, brass trim	95.00	120.00	110.00
☐ **Album,** red plush, musical	130.00	170.00	150.00
☐ **Ambrotype,** Civil War soldier holding revolver	90.00	120.00	105.00
☐ **Ambrotype,** entertainment personality	150.00	400.00	275.00
☐ **Ambrotype,** girl with doll	40.00	70.00	55.00
☐ **Ambrotype,** historical figure	170.00	425.00	297.00
☐ **Ambrotype,** military leader	170.00	425.00	297.00
☐ **Ambrotype,** Niagara Falls, full plate	250.00	450.00	350.00
☐ **Ambrotype,** outdoor scene	190.00	280.00	235.00
☐ **Ambrotype,** school class picture	190.00	280.00	235.00
☐ **Ambrotype,** young man picking apples	100.00	140.00	120.00
☐ **Photographs,** storefronts, late 19th c.	12.00	40.00	26.00
☐ **Tintypes,** anonymous portraits, small	4.00	12.00	8.00

MOTION PICTURE CAMERAS

☐ **Bell & Howell Filmo** Model 70DA, 25mm	120.00	170.00	145.00
☐ **Bell & Howell Filmo** Model 75, c. 1928	70.00	100.00	85.00
☐ **Camex Reflex Zoom,** 8mm	120.00	170.00	145.00
☐ **Cine-Kodak,** Model K, 25mm	45.00	65.00	55.00
☐ **Simplex,** pocket movie camera, 25mm	18.00	25.00	21.50

PROJECTORS

☐ **B & L 300**	300.00	375.00	337.00
☐ **Kodak,** Model A, 16mm	110.00	140.00	125.00
☐ **Simplex,** multi-exposure, c. 1914	2000.00	2500.00	2250.00
☐ **Tourist,** multiple, 750 shot, c. 1914	3000.00	4000.00	3500.00

35mm CAMERAS

☐ **Agfa & Ansco Memo,** vertical camera	50.00	75.00	62.00
☐ **Argus A**	23.00	35.00	28.00
☐ **Argus K**	130.00	170.00	150.00
☐ **Compass, Lern, Le Coultre & Cie,** c. 1938	1100.00	1600.00	1350.00
☐ **Kodak, Ektra,** interchangeable lenses	300.00	375.00	337.00
☐ **Kodak 35,** c. 1938	23.00	30.00	26.50
☐ **Kodak Vollenda, Radionar,** c. 1932	60.00	80.00	70.00
☐ **Leica A, Elmax,** c. 1925	4800.00	6000.00	5400.00
☐ **Leica A,** c. 1926	500.00	700.00	600.00
☐ **Leica C,** c. 1929	4500.00	5750.00	5125.00
☐ **Leica D** (Body only), c. 1932	225.00	300.00	262.00
☐ **Leica III,** c. 1933	140.00	190.00	165.00
☐ **Leica IIIA,** c. 1935	110.00	150.00	130.00
☐ **Leica IIIB,** c, 1937	130.00	180.00	155.00
☐ **Leica IIIC,** c. 1940	115.00	185.00	150.00
☐ **Simplex,** multi-exposure	2000.00	2500.00	2250.00
☐ **Tourist,** multiple 750 shot, c. 1914	3000.00	3675.00	3400.00
☐ **Universal Mercury I,** c. 1939	40.00	55.00	47.00
☐ **Universal Mercury II,** c. 1938	40.00	55.00	47.00
☐ **Zeiss, Contaflex,** c. 1936	650.00	800.00	725.00
☐ **Zeiss, Contax I** with Tessar, c. 1932	220.00	310.00	265.00
☐ **Zeiss, Contax II,** c. 1936	110.00	140.00	125.00
☐ **Zeiss, Contax III** with built-in meter	135.0	190.00	160.00

PLATES

Life's Best Wishes Series, "1982 Happiness" Boehm Studio Artists, Hamilton Collection / Edward Marshall Boehm Studios . . . . **$70.00-$80.00**

    The world of collector plates ranges in theme from the beautifully serious to the rollicking humorous, from the highly esthetic to the sweet and sentimental. Subjects include children, holidays, wild life, literary and bibical topics, or even cartoon characters. Most people select their plates according to the subjects which interests them: visual impact attracts most collectors. For the most part, these are limited editions produced specifically for collectors.

    Many new plates are issued every year with most of the older plates still available through dealers and gift shops. You should buy plates which are in top condition only — poor condition will decrease their value greatly.

    For more in-depth information and a complete listing of all collector plates produced from 1895 to the present, you may refer to *The Official Price Guide to Collector Plates* by the House of Collectibles.

BAYEUTHER (GERMANY)

CHRISTMAS SERIES

		Current Price Range		Prior Year Average
☐	1969 **Christkindlemarkt,** artist: Hans Mueller, porcelain, blue underglaze, 8″, production: one year, issued price $12.00	23.00	28.00	25.00
☐	1975 **Snowman,** artist: Hans Mueller, porcelain, blue underglaze, 8″, production: unannounced, issued price $21.50	23.00	28.00	25.00
☐	1980 **Miltenberg,** artist: Hans Mueller, porcelain, blue underglaze, 8″, production quantity 10,000, issued price $37.50	35.00	40.00	37.00

DANISH CHURCH SERIES

☐	1970 **Marmor Kirken,** artist: unannounced, porcelain, blue underglaze, 8″, production: one year, issued price $13.00	9.00	13.00	11.00
☐	1974 **Broager Kirken,** artist: unannounced, porcelain, blue underglaze, 8″, production: one year, issued price $15.00	17.50	22.50	20.00
☐	1978 **Haderslav Cathedral,** artist: unannounced, porcelain, blue underglaze, 8″, production: one year, issued price $19.95	15.00	20.00	17.00

FATHER'S DAY SERIES

☐	1970 **Castle Pfalz,** artist: Hans Mueller, porcelain, blue underglaze, 8″, production: one year, issued price $12.50	17.50	22.50	20.00
☐	1977 **Castle Eltz,** artist: Hans Mueller, porcelain, blue underglaze, 8″, production: one year, issued price $24.50	23.00	28.00	25.00
☐	1981 **Castle Gutenfels,** artist: Hans Mueller, porcelain, blue underglaze, 8″, production quantity 2,500, issued price $39.50 ..	37.00	42.00	39.00

MOTHER'S DAY SERIES

☐	1971 **Mother And Children,** artist: Ludwig Richter, porcelain, blue underglaze, 8″, production quantity 5,000, issued price $12.75	17.50	22.50	20.00
☐	1976 **Rocking The Cradle,** artist: Ludwig Richter, porcelain, blue underglaze, 8″, production quantity 5,000, issued price $23.50	23.00	28.00	25.00
☐	1982 **Suppertime,** artist: Ludwig Richter, porcelain, blue underglaze, 8″, production quantity 5,000, issued price $39.50	37.00	42.00	39.00

THANKSGIVING SERIES

☐	1974 **Old Mill,** porcelain, blue underglaze, 8″, production quantity 2,500, issued price $19.00	17.50	22.50	20.00
☐	1977 **Horses,** artist: Hans Mueller, porcelain, blue underglaze, 8″, production quantity 2,500, issued price $24.50	23.00	28.00	25.00
☐	1981 **Gathering Wheat,** artist: Hans Mueller, porcelain, blue underglaze, 8″, production quantity 2,500, issued price $39.50	35.00	40.00	37.00

648 / PLATES

BING & GRONDAHL (DENMARK)
CHRISTMAS SERIES

		Current Price Range		Prior Year Average
☐	**1897 Sparrow,** artist: Frans August Hallin, porcelain, bas-relief, blue underglaze, 7", production: one year, issued price 75¢ ...	1000.00	1500.00	1250.00
☐	**1901 Three Wise Men,** artist: S. Sabra, porcelain, bas-relief, blue underglaze, 7", production: one year, issued price $1.00 .	375.00	450.00	415.00
☐	**1907 Little Match Girl,** artist: E. Plockross, porcelain, bas-relief, blue underglaze, 7", production: one year, issued price $1.00 .	115.00	150.00	132.00
☐	**1916 Sparrows,** artist: J. Bloch Jorgensen, porcelain, bas-relief, blue underglaze, 7", production: one year, issued price $1.50 .	90.00	110.00	100.00
☐	**1925 Child's Christmas,** artist: Achton Friis, porcelain, bas-relief, blue underglaze, 7", production: one year, issued price $2.50 .	80.00	90.00	85.00
☐	**1929 Fox Outside,** artist: Achton Friis, porcelain, bas-relief, blue underglaze, 7", production: one year, issued price $2.50	85.00	95.00	90.00
☐	**1942 Danish Farm,** artist: Ove Larsen, porcelain, bas-relief, blue underglaze, 7", production: one year issued price $4.00	150.00	190.00	170.00
☐	**1948 Watchman,** artist: Margrethe Hyldahl, porcelain, bas-relief, blue underglaze, 7", production: one year, issued price $5.50 .	85.00	97.00	91.00
☐	**1960 Village Church,** artist: Kjeld Bonfils, porcelain, bas-relief, blue underglaze, 7", production: one year, issued price $10.00	185.00	235.00	210.00
☐	**1969 Arrival Of Guests,** artist: Henry Thelander, porcelain, bas-relief, blue underglaze, 7", production: one year, issued price $14.00	32.00	38.00	33.00
☐	**1976 Christmas Welcome,** artist: Henry Thelander, porcelain, bas-relief, blue underglaze, 7", production: one year, issued price $27.50	25.00	30.00	27.50

MOTHER'S DAY SERIES

☐	**1971 Cat And Kitten,** artist: Henry Thelander, porcelain, bas-relief, blue underglaze, 6", production: one year, issued price $11.00	15.00	20.00	17.50
☐	**1975 Doe And Fawn,** artist: Henry Thelander, porcelain, bas-relief, blue underglaze, 6", production: one year, issued price $19.50	23.00	28.00	25.00
☐	**1979 Fox And Cubs,** artist: Henry Thelander, porcelain, bas-relief, blue underglaze, 6", production: one year, issued price $28.00	25.00	30.00	27.00

EDWARD MARSHALL BOEHM STUDIOS (GREAT BRITAIN)
BOEHM OWL COLLECTION *(The Hamilton Collection)*

☐	**1980 Snowy Owl,** artist: Boehm Studio Artists, English bone china 4-color illustration, 24 KT gold rim, 10½", production quantity 15,000, issued price $45.00	42.00	48.00	45.00

		Current Price Range		Prior Year Average
☐	1981 **Great Horned Owl,** artist: Boehm Studio Artists, English bone china 4-color illustration, 24 KT gold rim, 10½", production quantity 15,000, issued price $45.00	42.00	48.00	45.00
☐	1981 **Barred Owl,** artist: Boehm Studio Artists, English bone china 4-color illustration, 24 KT gold rim, 10½", production quantity 15,000, issued price $45.00	42.00	48.00	45.00

EUROPEAN BIRD PLATES SERIES

☐	1973 **Chaffinch,** production quantity 4,319, issued price $50.00	52.00	58.00	55.00
☐	1973 **King Fisher,** production quantity 4,319, issued price $50.00	52.00	58.00	55.00
☐	1973 **Linnet,** production quantity 4,319, issued price $50.00	52.00	58.00	55.00

WATERBIRD PLATE COLLECTION *(The Hamilton Collection)*

☐	1981 **Wood Ducks,** artist: Boehm Studio Artists, bone china, 24 KT gold band, 10½", production quantity 15,000, issued price $62.50	60.00	67.00	63.50
☐	1982 **Common Mallards,** artist: Boehm Studio Artists, bone china, 24 KT gold band, 10½", production quantity 15,000, issued price $62.50	60.00	67.00	63.50
☐	1982 **American Pintails,** artist: Boehm Studio Artists, bone china, 24 KT gold band, 10½", production quantity 15,000, issued price $62.50	60.00	67.00	63.50

FENTON ART GLASS (UNITED STATES)

AMERICAN CRAFTSMAN SERIES

☐	1971 **Printer,** carnival glass, production: one year, issued price $10.00	37.00	39.00	42.00
☐	1976 **Gunsmith,** carnival glass, production: one year, issued price $15.00	12.00	16.00	14.00
☐	1981 **Housewright,** carnival glass, production: one year, issued price $17.50	15.00	20.00	17.50

CHRISTMAS IN AMERICA SERIES

☐	1970 **Little Brown Church In Vale,** blue satin glass, production: one year, issued price $12.50	15.00	20.00	17.50
☐	1973 **Saint Mary's/Mountains,** blue satin glass, production: one year, issued price $12.50	32.00	38.00	35.00
☐	1977 **San Carlos Bormeo de Car.,** blue satin glass, production: one year, issued price $15.00	14.00	18.00	16.00
☐	1980 **Christ Church, Alexandria, VA,** carnival glass, production: one year, issued price $16.50	15.00	20.00	17.50

MOTHER'S DAY SERIES

	Current Price Range	Prior Year Average
☐ 1971 **Madonna With Sleeping Child,** blue satin glass, production: one year, issued price $12.50	25.00 30.00	27.50
☐ 1973 **Small Cowper Madonna,** blue glass, production: one year, issued price $12.50 ...	35.00 40.00	37.50
☐ 1975 **Taddei Madonna,** carnival glass, production: one year, issued price $13.50	22.00 26.00	24.00

FRANKLIN MINT (UNITED STATES)
AMERICAN REVOLUTION SERIES

☐ 1976- 77 **The Battle Of Concord Bridge,** artist: Paul Rickert, pewter, high-relief sculpture, 9½", production quantity 3,596, issued price $75.00	70.00 80.00	75.00
☐ 1976- 77 **Washington Crosses The Delaware,** artist: Alexander Farnham, pewter, high-relief sculpture, 9½", production quantity 3,596, issued price $75.00	70.00 80.00	75.00
☐ 1976- 77 **Victory At Yorktown,** artist: John Chumley, pewter, high-relief sculpture, 9½", production quantity 3,596, issued price $75.00	70.00 80.00	75.00

BIRDS AND FLOWERS OF THE ORIENT SERIES

☐ 1979- 80 **Lotus And Water Fowl,** artist: Naoka Nobata, porcelain, hand-decorated, 24 KT gold rim, 10¼", production quantity 32,373, issued price $55.00	52.00 60.00	56.00
☐ 1979- 80 **Mandarin Duck And Iris,** artist: Naoka Nobata, porcelain, hand-decorated, 24 KT gold rim, 10¼", production quantity 32,373, issued price $55.00	52.00 60.00	56.00
☐ 1979- 80 **Chinese Blue Pie And Cherry,** artist: Naoka Nobata, porcelain, hand-decorated, 24 KT gold rim, 10¼", production quantity 32,373, issued price $55.00	52.00 60.00	56.00

CURRIER AND IVES SERIES

☐ 1977- 79 **Winter Pastime,** artist: Currier and Ives, pewter, high-relief, sculptured, 6½", production quantity 1,836, issued price $39.50	40.00 45.00	42.50
☐ 1977- 79 **American Homestead — Winter,** artist: Currier and Ives, pewter, high-relief, sculptured, 6½", production quantity 1,836, issued price $39.50	40.00 45.00	42.50
☐ 1977- 79 **Haying Time — The Last Load,** artist: Currier and Ives, pewter, high-relief, sculptured, 6½", production quantity 1,836, issued price $39.50	40.00 45.00	42.50

FAIRY TALES MINIATURES SERIES

	Current Price Range		Prior Year Average
☐ 1979-84 **The Little Mermaid,** artist: Carol Lawson, fine bone china, 24 KT gold intricate border, 3″, production quantity 15,207, issued price $14.50	14.00	20.00	17.00
☐ 1979-84 **The Frog Prince,** artist: Carol Lawson, fine bone china, 24 KT gold intricate border, 3″, production quantity 15,207, issued price $14.50	14.00	20.00	17.00
☐ 1979-84 **The Nightingale,** artist: Carol Lawson, fine bone china, 24 KT gold intricate border, 3″, production quantity 15,207, issued price $14.50	14.00	20.00	17.00

GRIMM'S FAIRY TALES SERIES

	Current Price Range		Prior Year Average
☐ 1979 **Bremen Town Musicians,** artist: Carol Lawson, Bavarian porcelain, painted 24 KT gold border, 8½″, production quantity 27,006, issued price $42.00	40.00	45.00	42.50
☐ 1979 **Rapunzel,** artist: Carol Lawson, Bavarian porcelain, painted, 24 KT gold border, 8½″, production quantity 27,006, issued price $42.00	40.00	45.00	42.50
☐ 1979 **Rumplestiltskin,** artist: Carol Lawson, Bavarian porcelain, painted, 24 KT gold border, 8½″, production quantity 27,006, issued price $42.00	40.00	45.00	42.50

POOR RICHARD'S SERIES

	Current Price Range		Prior Year Average
☐ 1979-81 **Love Thy Neighbour, Yet Don't Pull Down Your Hedge,** pewter, sculptured, 2″, production quantity 13,133, issued price $12.50	13.00	18.00	15.50
☐ 1979-81 **There's A Time To Wink As Well As Time To See,** pewter, sculptured, 2″, production quantity 13,133, issued price $12.50	13.00	18.00	15.50
☐ 1979-81 **An Empty Bag Cannot Stand Upright,** pewter, sculptured, 2″, production quantity 13,133, issued price $12.50	13.00	18.00	15.50

SONGBIRDS OF THE WORLD SERIES

	Current Price Range		Prior Year Average
☐ 1977-81 **Baltimore Oriole,** artist: Arthur Singer, English bone china, painted, 24 KT gold border, 10½″, production quantity 20,225, issued price $55.00	52.00	58.00	55.00
☐ 1977-81 **Cardinal,** artist: Arthur Singer, English bone china, painted, 24 KT gold border, 10½″, production quantity 20,225, issued price $55.00	52.00	58.00	55.00

GORHAM COLLECTION (UNITED STATES)

CHRISTMAS SERIES

		Current Price Range		Prior Year Average
☐	1975 **Good Deeds,** artist: Norman Rockwell, china, 24 KT gold rim, 8½", production: one year, issued price $17.50	62.00	68.00	65.00
☐	1977 **Yuletide Reckoning,** artist: Norman Rockwell, china, 24 KT gold rim, 8½", production quantity 18,500, issued price $19.50 .	32.00	38.00	35.00
☐	1980 **Letter To Santa,** artist: Norman Rockwell, china, 24 KT gold rim, 8½", production: one year, issued price $27.50	25.00	30.00	27.50

FOUR SEASONS SERIES

☐	1975 **Me And My Pal,** artist: Norman Rockwell, china, 24 KT gold rim, 10½", production: one year, issued price $70.00	170.00	220.00	195.00
☐	1978 **The Tender Years,** artist: Norman Rockwell, china, 24 KT gold rim, 10½", production: one year, issued price $100.00	100.00	125.00	112.00
☐	1981 **Old Timers,** artist: Norman Rockwell, china, 24 KT gold rim, 10½", production: one year, issued price $100.00	90.00	110.00	100.00

MOPPETS CHRISTMAS SERIES

☐	1973 **Christmas March,** production quantity 20,000, issued price $10.00	32.00	38.00	35.00
☐	1976 **Christmas Tree,** production quantity 20,000, issued price $13.00	12.00	16.00	14.00
☐	1979 **Moppets,** production quantity 18,500, issued price $12.00	10.00	14.00	12.00

KAISER (GERMANY)

ANNIVERSARY SERIES

☐	1975 **Tender Moment,** artist: Kurt Bauer, porcelain, cobalt blue underglaze, 7½", production quantity 7,000, issued price $25.00	23.00	28.00	25.50
☐	1978 **Viking Toast,** artist: Toni Schoener, porcelain, cobalt blue underglaze, 7½", production: one year, issued price $30.00 ...	27.00	32.00	29.50
☐	1981 **Rendezvous,** artist: Hannelore Blum, porcelain, cobalt blue underglaze, 7½", production: one year, issued price $40.00 ...	37.00	42.00	39.50

CHRISTMAS SERIES

☐	1973 **Holy Night,** artist: Toni Schoener, porcelain, cobalt blue underglaze, 7½", production quantity 8,000, issued price $18.00	35.00	40.00	37.50
☐	1976 **Christ The Saviour Is Born,** artist: Carlo Maratti, porcelain, cobalt blue undeglaze, 7½", production: one year, issued price $25.00	17.50	22.50	20.00
☐	1980 **Joys Of Winter,** artist: Hannelore Blum, porcelain, cobalt blue underglaze, 7½", production: one year, issued price $40.00	37.00	42.00	39.50

MOTHER'S DAY SERIES

		Current Price Range		Prior Year Average
☐	1972 **Flowers For Mother,** artist: Toni Schoener, porcelain, cobalt blue underglaze, 7½", production quantity 8,000, issued price $16.50	20.00	25.00	22.50
☐	1976 **Swan And Cygnets,** artist: Toni Schoener, porcelain, cobalt blue underglaze, 7½", production quantity 7,000, issued price $25.00	20.00	25.00	22.50
☐	1980 **Raccoon Family,** artist: Joann Northcott, porcelain, cobalt blue underglaze, 7½", production: one year, issued price $40.00	37.00	42.00	39.50

REED & BARTON (UNITED STATES)

CHRISTMAS SERIES

☐	1970 **A Partridge In A Pear Tree,** artist: Robert Johnson, damascene silver, 11", production quantity 2,500, issued price $55.00	185.00	235.00	210.00
☐	1973 **Adoration Of The Kings,** artist: Rogier van der Weyden, damascene silver, 11", production quantity 7,500, issued price $60.00	56.00	63.00	59.50
☐	1976 **Morning Train,** artist: Maxwell Mays, damascene silver, 11", production quantity 7,500, issued price $65.00	62.00	70.00	66.00

FOUNDING FATHERS SERIES

☐	1975 **Thomas Jefferson,** production quantity 2,500, issued price $65.00	62.00	70.00	66.00
☐	1976 **Patrick Henry,** production quantity 2,500, issued price $65.00	62.00	70.00	66.00
☐	1976 **John Adams,** production quantity 2,500, issued price $65.00	62.00	70.00	66.00

ROYAL COPENHAGEN (DENMARK)

CHRISTMAS SERIES

☐	1913 **Spire Of Frederik Church,** artist: Arthur Boesen, porcelain, bas-relief, blue underglaze, 7", production: one year, issued price $1.50	130.00	170.00	150.00
☐	1921 **Market-place,** artist: Oluf Jensen, porcelain, bas-relief, blue underglaze, 7", production: one year, issued price $2.00	80.00	90.00	85.00
☐	1927 **The Ship's Boy At The Tiller Christmas Night,** artist: Benjamin Olsen, porcelain, bas-relief, blue underglaze, 7", production: one year, issued price $2.00	175.00	225.00	200.00
☐	1931 **Mother And Child,** artist: Gotfred Rode, porcelain, bas-relief, blue underglaze, 7", production: one year, issued price $2.50	100.00	120.00	110.00
☐	1937 **Christmas Scene In Copenhagen,** artist: Nils Thorsson, porcelain, bas-relief, blue underglaze, 7", production: one year, issued price $2.50	120.00	155.00	138.00

654 / PLATES

	Current Price Range	Prior Year Average

- ☐ **1947 The Good Shepher,** artist: Kai Lange, porcelain, bas-relief, blue underglaze, 7", production: one year, issued price $4.50 . — 200.00 — 250.00 — 225.00
- ☐ **1952 Christmas In The Forest,** artist: Kai Lange, porcelain, bas-relief, blue underglaze, 7", production: one year, issued price $5.00 .... — 120.00 — 155.00 — 138.00
- ☐ **1964 Fetching The Christmas Tree,** artist: Kai Lange, porcelain, bas-relief, blue underglaze, 7", production: one year, issued price $11.00 .... — 85.00 — 95.00 — 90.00
- ☐ **1970 Christmas Rose And Cat,** artist: Kai Lange, procelain, bas-relief, blue underglaze, 7", production: one year, issued price $14.00 .... — 27.00 — 32.00 — 29.50
- ☐ **1977 Immervad Bridge,** artist: Kai Lange, porcelain, bas-relief, blue underglaze, 7", production: one year, issued price $32.00 — 30.00 — 35.00 — 32.50

MOTHER'S DAY SERIES

- ☐ **1972 Oriental Mother,** artist: Kamma Svensson, porcelain, blue underglaze, production: one year, issued price $14.00 .... — 10.00 — 14.00 — 12.00
- ☐ **1975 Bird In Nest,** artist: Arne Ungermann, porcelain, blue underglaze, production: one year, issued price $20.00 .... — 17.50 — 22.50 — 20.00
- ☐ **1977 Twins,** artist: Arne Ungermann, porcelain, blue underglaze, production: one year, issued price $24.00 .... — 22.00 — 27.00 — 24.50

ROYAL CORNWALL (UNITED STATES)

THE CREATION SERIES *(First Release)*

- ☐ **1977 In The Beginning,** artist: Yiannis Koutsis, porcelain, 24 KT gold band, 9¼", production quantity 10,000 issued price $37.50 . — 110.00 — 140.00 — 125.00
- ☐ **1978 Noah And The Ark,** artist: Yiannis Koutsis, porcelain, 24 KT gold band, 9¼", production quantity 10,000, issued price $45.00 .... — 105.00 — 130.00 — 117.00
- ☐ **1980 Jacob's Wedding,** artist: Yiannis Koutsis, porcelain, 24 KT gold band, 9¼", production quantity 10,000, issued price $45.00 . — 70.00 — 80.00 — 75.00

THE CREATION SERIES *(Charter Release For Calhoun's Collector's Society)*

- ☐ **1977 The Tower Of Babel,** artist: Yiannis Koutsis, porcelain, 24 KT gold band, 9¼", production quantity 19,500, issued price $29.50 .... — 75.00 — 85.00 — 80.00
- ☐ **1978 Jacob's Ladder,** artist: Yiannis Koutsis, porcelain, 24 KT gold band, 9¼", production quantity 19,500, issued price $29.50 . — 75.00 — 85.00 — 80.00
- ☐ **1978 Joseph Interprets Pharoah's Dream,** artist: Yiannis Koutsis, porcelain, 24 KT gold band, 9¼", production quantity 19,500, issued price $29.50 .... — 75.00 — 85.00 — 80.00

THE PROMISED LAND SERIES

		Current Price Range		Prior Year Average
☐	1979 **Let My People Go,** artist: Yannis Koutsis, porcelain, 24 KT gold band, 9¼", production quantity 24,500, issued price $45.00.	42.00	48.00	45.00
☐	1980 **Miriam's Song Of Thanksgiving,** artist: Yiannis Koutsis, porcelain, 24 KT gold band, 9¼", production quantity 24,500, issued price $45.00	42.00	48.00	45.00
☐	1980 **The Ten Commandments,** artist: Yiannis Koutsis, porcelain, 24 KT gold band, 9¼", production quantity 24,500, issued price $45.00	42.00	48.00	45.00

THE REMARKABLE WORLD OF CHARLES DICKENS SERIES
(Wedgwood)

☐	1980 **Scrooge And Marley's Ghost,** artist: Konrad Hack, queensware, 9", production quantity 19,500, issued price $60.00.	56.00	63.00	59.50
☐	1981 **Mr. Pickwick And Friends,** artist: Konrad Hack, queensware, 9", production quantity 19,500, issued price $60.00	56.00	63.00	59.50
☐	1982 **Pip And Miss Havisham,** artist: Konrad Hack, queenware, 9", production quantity 19,500, issued price $60.00	56.00	63.00	59.50

WINDOWS ON THE WORLD SERIES

☐	1981 **Rainy Day In London,** artist: Higgins Bond, porcelain, 24 KT gold band, 9½", production quantity 19,500 issued price $45.00	42.00	48.00	45.00
☐	1981 **Harvesting In The Ukraine,** artist: Higgins Bond, porcelain, 24 KT gold band, 9½", production quantity 19,500, issued price $45.00	42.00	48.00	45.00
☐	1982 **Palace Of The Winds, Jaipur,** artist: Higgins Bond, porcelain, 24 KT gold band, 9½", production quantity 19,500, issued price $45.00	42.00	48.00	45.00

ROYAL DELFT (NETHERLANDS)

CHRISTMAS *(Large)*

☐	1916 **Star-Floral Design,** 10", production: one year, issued price $4.25	630.00	900.00	760.00
☐	1920 **Church Tower,** 10", production: one year, issued price $12.50	335.00	435.00	385.00
☐	1926 **Windmill Landscape,** 10", production: one year, issued price $12.50	415.00	515.00	465.00
☐	1930 **Church Entrance, Delft,** 10", production: one year, issued price $10.00	310.00	390.00	350.00
☐	1959 **Landscape,** 10", production quantity 250, issued price $26.25	310.00	390.00	350.00
☐	1965 **Corn-Mill In Rhoon,** 10", production quantity 300, issued price $35.00	325.00	405.00	465.00
☐	1978 **Winter Skating Scene,** 10", production quantity 1,000, issued price $277.00	235.00	320.00	278.00

CHRISTMAS SERIES

	Current Price Range	Prior Year Average
☐ 1956 **Christmas Bells,** 9″, production: one year, issued price $11.75	300.00 375.00	338.00
☐ 1929 **Church Spire,** 7″, production one year, issued price $3.00	290.00 360.00	325.00
☐ 1970 **Mill Near Haarlem,** 7″, production quantity 1,500, issued price $26.25	120.00 155.00	138.00

PLAYING CARDS

Playing cards have a distinct claim as historically important collectors' items. When the art of printing from engraved steel plates was developed early in the 15th century, sets of cards were among the first "publications." They could be printed easier than books, and apparently the public demand for them was assured. A debate is still raging among historians over whether Johann Gutenberg printed a set of cards before he printed any books. At any rate, card playing boasts a very antique heritage, and a colorful one. It long predates printing, as cards were drawn and painted by hand on scraps of parchment in the earlier Middle Ages. Cards were considered equally as popular as chess at the European courts, and in later times became even more popular, as a card set was bought (or self-made) more cheaply than chess pieces.

The earliest cards likely to be found by collectors date from the 1700's, and are of European origin. You may, at first, have some difficulty in estimating the ages of cards, because the designs tend to be retained for generations or even centuries with only minor changes. This is true even today: most decks are designed after the fashion of Restoration England (1660-1685), with the King of Spades bearing a strong resemblance to Charles II.

When a deck is incomplete, by even a single card, its value is seriously reduced. Conversely, a complete deck in the original packet, as marketed, carries a substantial premium. Packets do not exist for all decks, as some were retailed in paper wrappers that were torn off and discarded.

☐ **Battle Axe pinocle deck,** E. E. Fairchild, c. 1945	10.00	15.00	12.50
☐ **Believe It Or Not deck,** Stancraft, cartoons on all cards, c. 1963	30.00	38.00	34.00
☐ **Bicentennial deck,** United States Playing Card Company, set of six decks with Colonial Flags on back, 1976	22.00	27.50	24.75
☐ **Capitol #188 United States Playing Card Company,** 4-leaf clover backs, green printing, c. 1895	26.00	33.00	29.50
☐ **Chicago World Fair deck,** c. 1934	14.00	20.00	17.00
☐ **Civil War pack,** The Union Playing Cards, American Card Co., N.Y., two-color, eagles, stars, flags, shields, suits	500.00	700.00	600.00
☐ **Congress,** Magna Carta backs, c. 1950	4.00	6.00	5.00
☐ **Dougherty,** round corners, full deck (52), c. 1870, worn, one card damaged	40.00	50.00	45.00
☐ **Dougherty Piquet deck,** Civil War era, square corners	27.00	34.00	30.50

	Current Price Range		Prior Year Average
☐ **Eisenhower Presidential Portraits double deck,** one deck with Washington backs, one with Lincoln, both from paintings done by Dwight D. Eisenhower, Nu-Vue cards, c. 1960	40.00	50.00	45.00
☐ **Flatiron Pinocle deck** by New York Card Company, backs have color view of Flatiron Building, c. 1905	40.00	50.00	45.00

NOTE: *The Flatiron Building was a famous early skyscraper in New York, still standing, but no longer tall, compared to modern structures.*

☐ **Fleet Wing Gasoline,** advertising, c. 1910	12.00	18.00	15.00
☐ **French-suited pack,** L. I. Cohen, large size, gold trim	200.00	300.00	250.00
☐ **Flinch cards,** c. 1910	22.00	29.00	25.50
☐ **Gypsy Witch,** fortune telling deck	9.00	12.00	10.50
☐ **Hard-a-Port-Cut Plug,** tobacco giveaways, 52 plus joker, complete set, late c. 1880's	200.00	300.00	250.00
☐ **Hart's Squared Linen Eagle Pharo,** Sam Hart, N.Y., c. 1906	100.00	150.00	125.00
☐ **Initial #54 United States Playing Card Company,** backs carry initial M or W, c. 1907	15.00	20.00	17.50
☐ **Moorish deck,** Congress, dancing girl on backs, Moorish joker, gold edges, c. 1903	27.00	35.00	31.00
☐ **Movie Souvenir deck,** M. J. Moriarty, silent film era, has Charlie Chaplin joker, c. 1916	75.00	100.00	87.00
☐ **National Ramblers deck,** 52 cards plus joker, gold edges, marked "Aluminum Surface, Waterproof," c. 1895	24.00	30.00	27.00
☐ **Nestor deck,** Popular Playing Cards, N.Y., c. 1910	28.00	37.00	32.50
☐ **Panama souvenir cards,** 53 plus information cards, USPC, real photos, c. 1908	40.00	65.00	52.00
☐ **Richardson Round deck,** 4-colored suits, worn, soiled, c. 1880	50.00	70.00	60.00
☐ **Rustlers deck,** Willis Russell, dated 1906	40.00	55.00	47.00
☐ **Smart Set #400,** "The Flying Girl," Russell, green printing, c. 1912	25.00	32.00	28.50
☐ **St. Louis World's Fair,** Official Souvenir Cards, Samuel Cupples, c. 1904	80.00	110.00	95.00
☐ **Texas Whitehouse** (parody on Lyndon B. Johnson), c. 1966	12.00	16.00	14.00
☐ **Trumps Long Cut,** tobacco insert deck, complete set of 52, late 1800's	700.00	900.00	800.00

NOTE: *"Tobacco insert decks" were not sold in the usual way but distributed one-card-at-a-time in cigarette packets, like baseball cards. Hardly anyone succeeded in building a complete set, as numerous duplicates were acquired along the way. Hence, complete tobacco insert decks are the rarest in the hobby from their era. Also, because of the virtual unobtainability of complete decks, partially complete decks DO have value, which is usually not the case with decks that were sold in the ordinary manner. If the above deck (for example) had two cards missing, it would still be worth around $500.*

658 / POLICE MEMORABILIA

	Current Price Range		Prior Year Average
☐ **Turkish Playing Card Monopoly deck,** E. E. Fairchild, piquet deck, c. 1935	20.00	28.00	24.00
☐ **Uncle Sam's cabinet,** c. 1901	25.00	34.00	28.50
☐ **Vanity Fair transformation deck,** United States Playing Card Company, America's first true transformation deck, c. 1895	400.00	525.00	462.00
☐ **Victory Pinocle deck,** Arrco, 1945	45.00	60.00	52.00
☐ **Victory Playing Cards,** Arrco, Chicago, Uncle Sam (King), Statue of Liberty (Queen), Soldier and Sailor (Jacks), Hitler and Mussolini (Jokers), c. 1945	140.00	170.00	155.00

POLICE MEMORABILIA

Rubber Coat, Chicago Regulation Police, black **$50.00-$60.00**

Like almost everything else, police equipment has become more streamlined and efficient, thereby giving its ancestors a certain charm and collecting appeal. The changing nature of criminal activity is well-mirrored by these collectibles, as well as the evolution of police techniques. In the 19th century, most suspects were not likely to carry firearms and resistance to arrest was largely a matter of struggling about or fighting, so the officer of that time carried a variety of gear to subdue objecting suspects. Nippers, also referred to as "come-alongs," were the predecessor of handcuffs: a length of strong oxhide attached to handles, which was wound around the suspect's wrists and held tight. The only drawback was they had no locking mechanism, and required the constant attendance of an officer to hold them in place. Handcuffs, of designs much more primitive than today, were in use by most U.S. police departments by the third quarter of the 19th century. These old cuffs could easily be "slipped" by skilled criminals. The metal helmets worn by many police departments in the 19th century, and into the early 20th, were definitely not for looks; police were frequent targets of rocks, etc., hurled from buildings.

The available variety of items might astound you. If you include foreign material in your collection, it becomes virtually endless. Extremely antique items (prior to about 1820) are regarded as questionable by most collectors, as police patrols of very early times used equipment almost identical — or exactly identical — to that of the military, and no thorough distinction can be drawn.

	Current Price Range		Prior Year Average
☐ **Badge,** first worn by New York City Police, brass, c. 1845-57	110.00	150.00	130.00
☐ **Baton,** exquisitely grained rosewood, solid ivory sections hand-carved, solid gold shield inscribed "Presented to Sgt. William McCarthy - June 8, 1901," original silk cord and tassel	220.00	275.00	247.00
☐ **Belt and frog**	36.00	45.00	40.50
☐ **Day stick**	10.00	15.00	12.50
☐ **Handcuffs,** English Darby's, c. 1860's	28.00	39.00	33.00
☐ **Helmet,** removable spike, c. 1895	190.00	220.00	205.00
☐ **New style handcuffs**	22.00	29.00	25.50
☐ **Night stick**	17.00	23.00	20.00
☐ **Nippers**	10.00	15.00	12.50
☐ **Rosewood baton for parade**	22.00	28.00	25.00
☐ **Shield,** municipal police bade, c. 1875-89	28.00	36.00	32.00
☐ **Summer hat**	50.00	65.00	57.00
☐ **Winter hat**	50.00	65.00	57.00

POLITICAL SOUVENIRS

It may be ironic that collector interest in political memorabilia surged in this country at a time when criticism of the political system was strongest — in the mid sixties to early seventies. Some collectors freely admit that they take the hobby seriously, even though they don't take politics too seriously. Others are devoted historians. Regardless of your point of view, the competition for this material is avid, prices go on advancing, and each new campaign produces fresh supplies of it. Because the hobby has been around a while, most political articles (and nearly ALL the older ones) have been catalogued and evaluated in the market. Old does not necessarily mean best in this hobby, because rarity and the popularity of a candidate enter the picture, too. The name of Lincoln stands tall here, just as it does with autographs. But age does count for *something,* insofar as an item of 1910 or 1920, no matter the party or candidate, is certain to have more collector value than a similar one from 1970 or 1980. In fact, the likelihood of modern political memorabilia

660 / POLITICAL SOUVENIRS

achieving big values in the future is slim; it will rise in price, but probably slowly, since such an indiscriminately large total is now manufactured. Also, the hobby is being invaded with profiteers, who make buttons and such things of modern candidates simply for the purpose of selling them to collectors. This happened blatantly in 1972 when Sen. Eagleton was removed from the Republican Presidential ticket, and soon thereafter the hobbyist papers were deluged with ads for McGovern/Eagleton buttons that obviously were spurious.

	Current Price Range		Prior Year Average
CAMPAIGN BUTTONS			
☐ Barker-Donnley jugate	70.00	85.00	77.00
☐ Bryan-Sewall jugate	28.00	35.00	31.00
☐ Bryan-Watson jugate	75.00	95.00	85.00
☐ Coolidge-Dawes jugate	23.00	30.00	26.50
☐ Cleveland	12.00	18.00	15.00
☐ Davis-Bryan jugate	250.00	340.00	295.00
☐ Debs-Stedman jugate	150.00	200.00	175.00
☐ Dewey-Warren jugate	23.00	30.00	26.50
☐ FDR-Garner jugate	30.00	38.00	34.00
☐ FDR-Curley, 1932, "Work & Wages"	75.00	95.00	85.00
☐ FDR-Truman jugate	45.00	60.00	52.00
☐ Foster-Gitlow jugate	150.00	190.00	170.00
☐ Grant-Colfax jugate	50.00	65.00	57.00
☐ Hancock	80.00	100.00	90.00
☐ Harrison	85.00	110.00	98.00
☐ Hoover-Curtis jugate	42.00	55.00	48.00
☐ Hughes-Fairbanks jugate	50.00	70.00	60.00
☐ Hughes-Fairbanks, ornate brass jugate	200.00	300.00	250.00
☐ Landon-Knox jugate	36.00	45.00	40.00
☐ Kennedy-Johnson jugate, 7/8" Dia.	22.00	30.00	26.00
☐ Lincoln photo button, cardboard/brass, 3/4" x 1", c. 1894	170.00	240.00	205.00
☐ McClellan	60.00	80.00	70.00
☐ McKinley	22.00	29.00	25.50
☐ Seymour-Blair jugate	65.00	90.00	78.00
☐ Smith-Robinson jugate	45.00	60.00	52.00
☐ Taft-Sherman jugate	12.00	18.00	15.00
☐ T. Roosevelt-Fairbanks jugate	18.0	25.00	21.00
☐ T. Roosevelt-Johnson jugate	560.00	680.00	620.00
☐ Truman-Barkley jugate	55.00	75.00	65.00
☐ Wilkie-McNary jugate	45.00	60.00	52.00
☐ Wilson-Marshall jugate	18.00	25.00	21.50
CAMPAIGN RIBBONS			
☐ Abraham Lincoln, 1860	300.00	375.00	338.00
☐ Andrew Jackson, 1828	430.00	500.00	465.00
☐ Clay and Frelinghuysen, 1844	300.00	370.00	335.00
☐ James Buchanan, 1856	70.00	90.00	80.00
☐ Jefferson Davis, 1861	500.00	600.00	550.00
☐ Seymour and Blair, 1868	375.00	450.00	415.00

CAMPAIGN TOKENS

	Current Price Range	Prior Year Average
☐ Abraham Lincoln, 1860	30.00 40.00	35.00
☐ Andrew Jackson, 1828	38.00 50.00	44.00
☐ Benjamin Harrison, 1888	12.00 18.00	15.00
☐ Franklin, 1852	23.00 30.00	26.50
☐ George McClellan, 1864	23.00 30.00	26.50
☐ Grover Cleveland, 1888-1892	12.00 18.00	15.00
☐ Henry Clay, 1844	18.00 25.00	21.50
☐ Horace Greeley, 1872	22.00 29.00	25.50
☐ Horatio Seymour, 1868	22.00 29.00	25.50
☐ James Garfield, 1880	14.00 20.00	17.00
☐ John Bell, 1860	30.00 38.00	34.00
☐ John Breckinridge, 1860	100.00 130.00	115.00
☐ John C. Fremont, 1864	50.00 70.00	60.00
☐ Lewis Case, 1848	100.00 130.00	115.00
☐ Martin Van Buren, 1836	22.00 29.00	25.50
☐ Millard Fillmore, 1856	22.0 29.00	25.50
☐ R. B. Hayes, 1876	60.00 80.00	70.00
☐ S. J. Tilden, 1876	60.00 80.00	70.00
☐ Stephen Douglas, 1860	40.00 55.00	48.00
☐ U. S. Grant, 1868	23.00 30.00	26.50
☐ William Henry Harrison, 1840	12.00 18.00	15.00
☐ Winfield Scott, 1852	23.00 30.00	26.50
☐ Winfield S. Hancock, 1880	12.00 18.00	15.00
☐ Zachary Taylor, 1848	27.00 35.00	31.00

MISCELLANEOUS

	Current Price Range	Prior Year Average
☐ Bobby Kennedy caricature mug	7.00 10.00	8.50
☐ Bryan "Death to Trusts," mechanical skeleton pin	220.00 275.00	248.00
☐ Bryan silver bug, mechanical pin	110.00 150.00	130.00
☐ Bryan, Wm. Jennings, tin tray, worn, 13" x 16"	36.00 45.00	41.00
☐ Grant-Wilson lantern, engraved paper, c. 1872	250.00 310.00	280.00
☐ Harrison and Reform sulfide brooch	190.00 230.00	210.00
☐ Hayes, ferrotype badge, c. 1876	260.00 340.00	300.00
☐ McKinley-Roosevelt lantern, dinner pail shape, c. 1900	240.00 290.00	265.00
☐ Roosevelt-Cox watch fob, c. 1919	50.00 65.00	58.00
☐ Taft-Sherman Inaugural plate, tin, 9½" Dia., c. 1908	40.00 55.00	48.00
☐ Taft-Sherman postcard, colored, embossed	12.00 18.00	15.00

PORCELAIN AND POTTERY

Lenox Dinnerware, Ming, covered muffin dish . . . . **$90.00-$110.00**

    Pottery-making was among the first trades of civilization and has flourished in all parts of the world. The variety of pottery, in its forms, uses, styles, and the philosophies of its manufacturers, is without end. It is perhaps the most varied and most numerous of all collectibles, and therefore this brief introductory article cannot hope to provide comprehensive information. The one vital fact which must be pointed out is the difference between porcelain and other pottery: porcelain is a very hard ware, to which a surface gloss is applied in firing. Other pottery (which, as a generic species, is much older than porcelain) is fired without a glaze. However, a glaze can be added to ANY pottery by painting it on after the object has dried and hardened. Thus, porcelain is always glossy (though not always to the same degree); other pottery may or may not be glossy, and when glossy, it is usually pretty obvious that the gloss was applied after manufacturing.

    Porcelain tends to be more highly rated than the other potteries. This is not (as one might mistakenly presume) because the technique is any more laudable, but simply because most of the great potters have chosen to work in porcelain. Virtually all important Chinese pottery is porcelain. The vast majority of collectible European pottery of the 18th and 19th centuries is likewise porcelain. However, most colonial American pottery is NOT porcelain, yet can can be very valuable.

    For more in-depth information and listings, you may refer to *The Official Price Guide to American Pottery and Porcelain* published by the House of Collectibles.

PORCELAIN AND POTTERY / 663

ART POTTERY
AMPHORA

	Current Price Range		Prior Year Average
☐ **Vase,** black birds in flight against pale green ground, factory mark, 6½″ H., c. 1900	290.00	430.00	360.00
☐ **Vase,** butterflies on the base below four stylized cranes, factory mark, 11½″ H., after 1918	290.00	430.00	360.00
☐ **Vase,** colorful rooster incorporating stylized eggs and flowers against a textured deep ochre ground, 13½″ H., c. 1915	250.00	400.00	325.00
☐ **Vase,** deep blue body, green and gilt leafage tendrils terminating in scrolling handles, 8½″ H., c. 1915	250.00	400.00	325.00
☐ **Vase,** gilt spider webs above butterflies against an iridescent blue and green ground, factory mark, 8½″ H., c. 1905	350.00	600.00	475.00
☐ **Vase,** pink and green floral bosses, 6¾″ H., c. 1900	185.00	300.00	245.00
☐ **Vase,** roughly textured body with iridescent copper glaze and applied with variegated circular bosses, factory mark, 6½″ H., c. 1903	290.00	430.00	360.00

ROOKWOOD

☐ **Basket,** high glaze with spiders and webs, much gold, by Albert R. Valentien, 14″ H., c. 1882	685.00	750.00	715.00
☐ **Bookends,** standing rooks, molded, with blue matt finish, c. 1925	170.00	190.00	180.00
☐ **Bookends,** standing elephants, molded, with cream matt finish, c. 1934	130.00	160.00	145.00
☐ **Clock,** seated panther next to clock, electric, high glaze green, c. 1957	190.00	240.00	215.00
☐ **Ewer,** orange high glaze ground with fruiting leafy branches, factory mark and artist signed, 8″ H., c. 1897	180.00	220.00	200.00
☐ **Ewer,** standard brown glaze, yellow floral decoration, 5″ H.	1025.00	1200.00	1100.00
☐ **Paperweight,** standing thoroughbred horse, natural colors, c. 1922	120.00	160.00	140.00
☐ **Plaque,** vellum glaze, scenic, E. T. Hurley, original frame 5″ x 8″, c. 1916	900.00	995.00	948.00
☐ **Plate,** nature flowering dogwood on high glaze salmon-colored background, no artist signature, 8″ Dia., c. 1887	180.00	220.00	200.00
☐ **Vase,** cream matt finish, all over molded Mexican scene, 8″ H.	90.00	110.00	100.00
☐ **Vase,** gray body with calla lillies and leafage, factory mark and artist signed, 12″ H., c. 1904	195.00	230.00	212.00
☐ **Vase,** iris glaze (high glaze with pastel colors), flowering crocus, artist J. D. Wareham, 10″ H., c. 1901	555.00	620.00	588.00
☐ **Vase,** monumental, trumpet neck with printed roses and leafage in orange and green, factory mark and artist signed, 19½″ H., c. 1889	1500.00	1800.00	1650.00
☐ **Vase,** standard brown glaze with two handle, portrait of a cavalier by Sturgis Laurence, 8″ H., c. 1897	1150.00	1400.00	1275.00
☐ **Vase,** vellum glaze, all over scenic by Ed Dier, 6″ H., c. 1912	440.00	480.00	460.00

664 / PORCELAIN AND POTTERY

	Current Price Range		Prior Year Average
☐ **Vase,** vellum glaze, matt finish, floral rim pattern by E. T. Hurley, 6″ H., c. 1910	160.00	190.00	175.00
☐ **Vase,** yellow poppy and green leafage, factory mark and artist signed, 8½″, c. 1902	210.00	250.00	230.00

ROSEVILLE

☐ **Bushberry,** handled basket, brown, 12″ H.	80.00	110.00	95.00
☐ **Donatello,** jardiniere and pedestal	430.00	530.00	480.00
☐ **Falline,** vase, 9″ H.	100.00	130.00	115.00
☐ **Ferella,** console bowl with attached flower frog	120.00	150.00	135.00
☐ **Jonquil,** handled basket, brown, 10″ H.	38.00	48.00	42.00
☐ **Ming tree,** hanging basket, green	85.00	95.00	90.00
☐ **Mock orange,** experimental vase, high glaze, black shading to rose and back to black, experimental marks on base (Wee flake), 6″ H.	105.00	125.00	115.00
☐ **Pine cone,** vase, brown, 15″ H.	100.00	120.00	110.00
☐ **Rozanne azurine mug,** high glaze blues and whites, blackberry decoration, artist signed Myers	560.00	660.00	610.00
☐ **Rozanne della robbia,** three-color vase with carved cherries, 8″ H.	950.00	1100.00	1025.00
☐ **Roxanne Egypt,** covered inkwell	200.00	245.00	222.00
☐ **Rozanne Olympic,** vase with black transfer decor or Greek muses on high glaze red ground, broken and repaired top, 14″ H.	740.00	840.00	790.00
☐ **Rozanne royal light tankard pitcher,** gray shading cream, blackberry decor, artist signed	260.00	320.00	280.00
☐ **Rozanne,** standard brown glaze, two-handled vase, jonquils, excellent art work, unglazed, artist signed, 8″ H.	185.00	215.00	200.00

WELLER

☐ **Art Nouveau matte finish vase** with full length figure of blonde woman, 8″ H.	75.00	85.00	80.00
☐ **Eocean mug,** high glaze with mushrooms	155.00	175.00	165.00
☐ **Eocean,** high glaze vase, bird in cherry tree, artist: E. Roberts, 12″ H.	790.00	860.00	825.00
☐ **Eocean,** high glaze vase, cabbage roses, no artist, 14″ H.	195.00	220.00	108.00
☐ **Eocean,** high glaze vase, pansey decor, gray background, no artist, 9″ H.	110.00	130.00	120.00
☐ **Figural,** Aunt Jemima teapot	105.0	135.00	118.00
☐ **Figural,** crouched frog, life-size with natural colors	80.00	100.00	90.00
☐ **Figural,** life-size rabbit with natural colors	415.00	475.00	445.00
☐ **Figural,** pop-eyed dog, large	395.00	450.00	420.00
☐ **Figural,** pop-eyed dog, small	130.00	160.00	145.00
☐ **Figural,** seated wood elf with natural colors	395.00	450.00	420.00
☐ **Glendale** (molden line), vase, molded design of birds, nests and eggs in pastel background, 8″ H.	80.00	100.00	90.00
☐ **Japanese birdimal,** high glaze vase with geisha girl by tree, green background, signed Rhead, 10″ H.	850.00	925.00	888.00
☐ **Japanese birdimal,** high glaze vase, scenic squeeze bag, trees and full moon, all in various shades of blue, 10″ H.	295.00	340.00	317.00

PORCELAIN AND POTTERY / 665

	Current Price Range	Prior Year Average
☐ **Louwelsa**, blue vase, leaf decoration, 8″ H.	380.00 420.00	400.00
☐ **Louselsa**, brown glaze mug with berry decor, artist signed	100.00 120.00	110.00
☐ **Louselsa**, brown glaze vase of St. Bernard dog, artist: Blake, 12″ H.	900.00 975.00	938.00
☐ **Louwelsa**, brown glaze vase with floral decor, no artist signature, 10″ H.	120.00 145.00	132.00
☐ **Rosemont** (molden line), high glaze vase with black background, brightly colored birds molded all over, 10″ H.	140.00 180.00	160.00
☐ **Sabrinian**, vase with sea horse handles, pale lavender colors, 8″ H.	85.00 105.00	95.00
☐ **Warwick** (molded line), handled basket, 8″ H.	35.00 50.00	42.00
☐ **Warwick**, vase, 10″ H.	25.00 35.00	30.00
☐ **Wild rose**, handled basket, 8″ H.	18.00 22.00	20.00

MISCELLANEOUS

☐ **Boch Keramis**, vase, stylized birds, blossoms and leafage in blue, pink and green against a cream ground, factory mark, 8″ H., c. 1925	210.00 260.00	235.00
☐ **Cowan**, Queen of Hearts whiskey jug	160.00 180.00	170.00
☐ **Fulper**, vase, mirror black, 10″ H.	165.00 195.00	180.00
☐ **Grueby**, vase with molded design, all green color, 8″ H.	590.00 640.00	615.00
☐ **Hampshire**, oil lamp, green	290.00 340.00	315.00
☐ **Longwy**, lamp base, crackle glaze with nude female figure and two peacocks in tones of blues and grays against turquoise ground, 13¼″, c. 1925	320.00 520.00	420.00
☐ **Longwy**, vase, paneled shouldered vessel, molded and decorated with a narrow band of stylized flowers, factory mark, 10½″, c. 1925	180.00 240.00	210.00
☐ **Newcomb**, vase, sculted floral border by Henrietta Bailey, 5″ H.	400.00 480.00	440.00
☐ **Newcomb**, matte finish vase, scenic, full moon with Spanish moss in trees, 8″ H.	500.00 580.00	540.00
☐ **Newcomb**, high glaze scenic mug with three black cats	1280.0 1400.00	1340.00
☐ **Zsolnay**, bowl, shallow with irregular rim and deep oxblood interior with fish swimming against a deep blue lustered ground, factory mark, 5¼″ H., c. 1900	410.00 490.00	450.00
☐ **Zsolnay**, vase, lustered green leafage and grasses against a textured blue ground, factory mark, 17⅛″ H., c. 1900	510.00 590.00	550.00

BELLEEK

This is a form of porcelain which originated in Ireland in the 1850's. Irish Belleek is characterized by a nascent, pearlized glazing, and almost eggshell-thin walls. The first American Belleek pieces are imitative of the Irish, but soon the porcelain manufacturers began making their own distinctive designs. Some of the finest of American Belleek was made by the Ceramic Art Company (CAC) which later became Lenox. Look also in the Lenox section for an extensive listing of some of Lenox's many wares.

666 / PORCELAIN AND POTTERY

	Current Price Range		Prior Year Average
☐ **Animal,** white bird, second black mark	110.00	145.00	127.00
☐ **Basket,** three-stand, first mark, 11″ H.	600.00	720.00	660.00
☐ **Basket,** purse, second black mark, 6″ H.	245.00	285.00	265.00
☐ **Bowls,** oval, green trim, second black mark	175.00	200.00	188.00
☐ **Bowls,** shamrock, second black mar, 4½″ Dia. . .	60.00	85.00	72.00
☐ **Bowls,** shell, first black mark	135.00	165.00	150.00
☐ **Bowl,** Willets, brown, yellow roses, 8¼″ Dia.	65.00	85.00	75.00
☐ **Box,** heart-shaped, swirls and floral design, 6½″ H.	160.00	190.00	175.00
☐ **Card tray,** floral and butterfly decor, 4″ sq.	200.00	230.00	215.00
☐ **Centerpiece,** first black mark, 7″ x 10″	600.00	720.00	660.00
☐ **Coffee set,** coffeepot, creamer, covered sugar bowl with two cups and saucers, gold bands, Lenox	340.00	390.00	365.00
☐ **Cracker jar,** diamond pattern, second black mark	260.00	285.00	272.00
☐ **Creamer,** Echinus pattern, first black mark, 3¼″ H.	150.00	175.00	162.00
☐ **Creamer,** figural swan, black mark, 3¼″ H.	90.00	110.00	100.00
☐ **Creamer,** harp, shamrock pattern, second black mark, 3½″ H.	80.00	100.00	90.00
☐ **Creamer,** shamrock pattern, second black mark .	65.00	85.00	75.00
☐ **Creamer,** shell, second black mark	80.00	100.00	90.00
☐ **Creamer,** toy, second black mark	80.00	100.00	90.00
☐ **Cups and saucers,** artichoke, Farmer's, first black mark	165.00	195.00	180.00
☐ **Cups and saucers,** dragon, first black mark	100.00	125.00	112.00
☐ **Cups and saucers,** Erne, second black mark	100.00	125.00	112.00
☐ **Cups and saucers,** harp, shamrock, third black mark	90.00	110.00	100.00
☐ **Cups and saucers,** hexagon, third black mark . . .	50.00	70.00	60.00
☐ **Cups and saucers,** Tridacna, first black mark . . .	50.00	70.00	60.00
☐ **Cups and saucers,** Willets, demitasse, white body, gold handle	100.00	125.00	112.00
☐ **Figurine,** affection, first black mark, 14½″ H.	1150.00	1300.00	1225.00
☐ **Figurine,** leprechaun, green mark, 4½″ H.	50.00	70.00	60.00
☐ **Figurine,** sea horse and shell, first black mark, 4″ H.	230.0	275.00	252.00
☐ **Figurine,** swan, first black mark	100.00	125.00	112.00
☐ **Figurine,** woman and man, black mark, pair, 7½″ H.	175.00	200.00	188.00
☐ **Egg holder,** Ott and Brewer, gold bamboo, dolphin handle	105.00	130.00	118.00
☐ **Goblet,** pink trim, first black mark	70.00	90.00	80.00
☐ **Honey pot,** shamrook, second black mark	170.00	195.00	182.00
☐ **Kettle,** shamrock, second black mark	140.00	165.00	152.00
☐ **Marmalade jar,** shamrock, basket weave pattern, third black mark, 4½″ H.	55.00	75.00	65.00
☐ **Match holder,** Little Red Riding Hood, 3½″ H. . . .	100.00	125.00	112.00
☐ **Muffineer,** Lenox, 7″ H.	55.00	75.00	65.00
☐ **Mug,** Ceramic Art Co.*, Indian wearing headdress, title "Many Horns," signed, 5½″ H., c. 1901	190.00	220.00	205.00
☐ **Mug,** nut pattern, second black mark, 2½″ H. . . .	100.00	125.00	112.00
☐ **Mug,** portrait of Cavalier, signed, 5½″ H.	85.00	105.00	95.00
☐ **Mug,** yellow corn and husk, palette mark, 5″ H. . .	80.00	100.00	90.00
☐ **Pitcher,** Bacchus and grape, green mark, 6″ H. . .	52.00	72.00	62.00

	Current Price Range		Prior Year Average
☐ **Pitcher,** cider, beaded handle with florals, Ceramic Art Co.*	145.00	165.00	155.00
☐ **Pitcher,** ivy, rope handle, first black mark, 5" H.	105.00	130.00	118.00
☐ **Pitcher,** lemonade, grapes and leaves, Ceramic Art Co.*	90.00	110.00	100.00
☐ **Pitcher,** Neptune, third black mark	90.00	110.00	100.00
☐ **Plates,** grass, first black mark	38.0	58.00	48.00
☐ **Plates,** shamrock, basketweave, 6¼" Dia.	45.00	65.00	55.00
☐ **Plates,** Willets, wild flowers with gold trim, 7½" Dia.	48.00	58.00	52.00
☐ **Salt,** pink trim, first black mark	50.00	70.00	60.00
☐ **Salt,** shamrock, second black mark	25.00	32.00	28.00
☐ **Salt,** shell and coral, second black mark	48.00	58.00	52.00
☐ **Sugar and creamer,** Echinus, second black mark	100.00	125.00	112.00
☐ **Sugar and creamer,** mask, third black mark	90.00	110.00	100.00
☐ **Sugar and creamer,** Neptune, second black mark	100.00	125.00	112.00
☐ **Sugar and creamer,** shamrock, second black mark	100.00	125.00	112.00
☐ **Sugar and creamer,** third black mark	90.00	110.00	100.00
☐ **Sugar and creamer,** tangerine trim, black mark	70.00	90.00	80.00
☐ **Teapots,** cone, second black mark	175.00	195.00	185.00
☐ **Teapots,** Neptune, second black mark	175.00	195.00	185.00
☐ **Teapots,** shamrock, third black mark	115.00	135.00	125.00
☐ **Tea sets,** Limpet, black mark	925.00	1100.00	1010.00
☐ **Tea sets,** Neptune, second black mark	355.00	400.00	388.00
☐ **Tea sets,** shamrock, second black mark	310.00	360.00	335.00
☐ **Tea sets,** Tridacna, second black mark, seven pieces	340.00	385.00	368.00
☐ **Trays,** bread, Limpet, third black mark	80.00	96.00	88.00
☐ **Trays,** bread, Neptune, third black mark	90.00	110.00	100.00
☐ **Trinket box,** acorn pattern, third black mark	150.00	170.00	160.00
☐ **Tub,** butter, shamrock, second black mark	35.00	42.00	39.00
☐ **Vases,** Aberdeen, flowers, third black mark	125.00	145.00	135.00
☐ **Vases,** green shamrocks, third green mark, 5½" H.	35.00	42.00	39.00
☐ **Vases,** mermaid with child	390.00	460.00	425.00
☐ **Vases,** shell, second black mark	175.00	200.00	188.00
☐ **Vases,** Willets, and painted poppies, 11" H.	110.00	130.00	120.00
☐ **Vases,** Willets, lemon tree, 11½" H.	130.00	150.00	140.00
☐ **Vases,** Willets, purple peacocks, 12" H.	150.00	170.00	160.00

NOTE: *Ceramic Art Co. became Lenox.

BENNINGTON

Bennington Wares were made in Bennington, Vermont, and much of it was made in imitation of English Rockingham wares. The mottled glazes are typical. Many people lump all American mottled-brown and yellow-glazed wares under the name Bennington, but not by any stretch of imagination could all of these wares have been produced there without at least a million employees! The major names involved are Norton, Fenton, and United States Pottery.

668 / PORCELAIN AND POTTERY

	Current Price Range		Prior Year Average
☐ Cupidor, flint enamel glaze, c. 1849	140.00	160.00	150.00
☐ Cuspidor, Rockingham, small	50.00	60.00	55.00
☐ Candlestick, flint enamel glaze, 7″ H.	310.00	370.00	340.00
☐ Picture frame, scalloped edges, Rockingham glaze	315.00	375.00	345.00
☐ Pie plate, Rockingham glaze	80.00	95.00	88.00
☐ Vase, parian, grapes and tendrils, c. 1858	65.00	72.00	68.00

BOEHM

Edward Marshall Boehm made superior porcelain sculptures by hand. Most of his work was inspired by nature in the form of birds and flowers. Mr. Boehm died in 1969, but his work has been carried on at the Boehm Studios in Trenton, New Jersey.

☐ American redstarts	1650.00	1850.00	1750.00
☐ Catbird	1300.00	1450.00	1375.00
☐ Koala bear cub	490.00	580.00	535.00
☐ Mourning doves	925.00	1000.00	962.00
☐ Roadrunner	2950.00	3300.00	3150.00
☐ Sugarbirds	7225.00	8225.00	7725.00
☐ Swan centerpiece (Malvern)	2025.00	2400.00	2200.00
☐ Towhee	1475.00	1650.00	1550.00
☐ Tree creepers (Malvern)	3275.00	3800.00	3525.00
☐ Yellow daisies	650.00	730.00	690.00
☐ Young American eagle	1040.00	1200.00	1120.00

CHINESE EXPORT

This is one of the most difficult and rewarding fields within porcelain collecting. Wares such as teapots, plates and cups were made in China and exported to the West as long ago as the 16th century. Surprisingly, pieces from that time, in perfect or near perfect condition, are occasionally available to collectors. Very high prices and relative rarity have encouraged many collectors to search for fine examples of 19th century wares, which were considered unworthy just 40 or 50 years ago. Some of the most commonly found and most beautiful wares are Rose Medallion. The price of any piece is closely tied to its age, artistic appeal, beauty of shape, rarity, condition and the presence of armorial monograms.

☐ Bowl, Fitzhugh pattern, green, 9½″ Dia., c. 1920	740.00	820.00	780.00
☐ Bowl, Hawthorne, 14½″ Dia.	300.00	360.00	330.00
☐ Bowl, "Mandarin Palette" with blossoms and butterflies, 11¼″ Dia., c. 1780	775.00	850.00	815.00
☐ Cup and saucer, coffee, Famille Rose, c. 1750	740.00	830.00	775.00
☐ Cup and saucer, Fitzhugh pattern, blue	58.00	68.00	62.00
☐ Garniture set, three covered baluster vases and pair beakers, dragons, 19th c.	1200.00	1400.00	1300.00
☐ Jug, blue willow pattern, 9⅛″ H., 19th c.	420.00	490.00	455.00
☐ Plate, cloak and spade center, 10″ Dia.	85.00	95.00	90.00
☐ Plate, Judgement in Paris in iron red, 9¼″ Dia., c. 1750	650.00	750.00	700.00
☐ Punch bowl, "Grisaille" decor, hunt scene with naked lady, 14″ Dia., c. 1780	1650.00	1850.00	1750.00
☐ Rice bowl, "Famille Rose," covered, c. 1869	45.00	52.00	48.00

	Current Price Range		Prior Year Average
☐ **Tea cup,** armorial decor, applied handle, 2" H., 19th c.	75.00	85.00	80.00
☐ **Tureen and cover,** pagodas in river, rectangular shape, diaper border, 14 1/8" H., c. 1770	1025.00	1200.00	1105.00
☐ **Vase,** elephant head handles, dolphin, bronze, 4 1/4" H.	240.00	290.00	265.00
☐ **Vase,** Geisha woman in garden, teakwood base, 11" H.	300.00	360.00	330.00
☐ **Warming dish,** bird and butterfly, orange, 9 1/2" Dia.	340.00	400.00	370.00

ROSE MEDALLION CHINESE EXPORT

☐ **Canton 20-piece tea set,** c. 1890	850.00	960.00	895.00
☐ **Covered bowl,** rectangular, 9 1/2" L., c. 1840's	650.00	770.00	710.00
☐ **Covered box,** square, c. 1840	875.00	1000.00	935.00
☐ **Cream and sugar,** c. 1880's	110.00	140.00	125.00
☐ **Garden seat,** pierced sides, 22" H.	3500.00	4100.00	3800.00
☐ **Jardiniere,** 12" H., 13" Dia.	500.00	600.00	550.00
☐ **Pitcher,** milk, tapered handle, 6 1/2" Dia.	350.00	400.00	375.00
☐ **Urns,** pair, 13 1/2", c. 1840	1100.00	1300.00	1200.00
☐ **Vases,** pair, 8" H., c. 1850's	200.00	245.00	222.00
☐ **Vegetable dish,** large, covered, c. 1880's	350.00	400.00	375.00

NOTE: Most late 19th c. Rose Medallion plates range from $20 to $50 each.

FIESTA WARE

Fiesta Ware, first produced by the Homer Laughlin China Co. in 1936, was designed by Fred Rhead, an English potter. The most outstanding feature of this pottery is its very festive colors.

☐ **Ashtray,** experimental, basketweave, flowers in relief	35.00	42.00	38.00
☐ **Ashtray,** yellow, c. 1936	14.00	16.50	14.75
☐ **Candleholders,** blue, pair, c. 1936	60.00	70.00	65.00
☐ **Candleholders,** yellow, pair	30.00	35.00	32.00
☐ **Carafe,** three-pint, old ivory, c. 1941	28.00	32.00	30.00
☐ **Chop plates,** yellow, 6" Dia.	5.00	8.00	6.50
☐ **Coffeepot,** red, c. 1936	50.00	60.00	55.00
☐ **Compartment plates,** turquoise, 10 1/2" Dia., c. 1941	8.50	12.50	10.50
☐ **Cup and saucer,** red	12.00	15.00	13.50
☐ **Cup and saucer,** yellow	9.00	14.00	11.50
☐ **Dessert bowl,** chartreuse, 6" Dia., c. 1941	6.50	9.50	8.00
☐ **Dessert plate,** yellow, 6" Dia.	5.00	8.00	6.50
☐ **Dinner plate,** rose, 10" Dia., c. 1936	3.50	9.50	6.50
☐ **Egg cups,** red, c. 1941	16.00	20.00	18.00
☐ **Fruit bowl,** rose, 5 1/2" Dia., c. 1939	4.25	6.50	5.35
☐ **Juice tumblers,** ivory, turquoise, yellow	8.00	9.50	9.25
☐ **Ice pitcher,** two-quart, red	25.00	30.00	27.50
☐ **Mug,** turquoise	20.00	24.00	22.00
☐ **Mug,** yellow	20.00	24.00	22.00
☐ **Platter,** turquoise, 12" Dia., c. 1939	8.25	10.50	9.35
☐ **Relish tray,** green base, red center, multi-color inserts	35.00	40.00	38.00

670 / PORCELAIN AND POTTERY

	Current Price Range		Prior Year Average
☐ **Relish tray,** old ivory, c. 1939	32.00	42.00	37.00
☐ **Salad bowl,** yellow, 7⅝″ Dia., c. 1939	10.00	15.00	12.50
☐ **Salt and pepper,** blue, c. 1937	5.25	6.25	5.75
☐ **Sauceboat,** green, c. 1939	10.00	12.50	11.25
☐ **Sugar and creamer,** red, c. 1941	12.00	14.50	13.25
☐ **Teapot,** large, red, c. 1936	25.00	30.00	27.50
☐ **Utility tray,** yellow, c. 1941	6.25	8.50	7.35
☐ **Vase,** old ivory, 10″ H., c. 1936	20.00	25.00	22.50
☐ **Water pitcher,** disc, green	18.00	21.00	19.50
☐ **Water tumblers,** green and turquoise	3.00	4.25	3.50
☐ **Water tumblers,** red	4.50	5.50	5.00

HAVILAND

Production of Haviland was begun in the mid 19th century in Limoges, France by Americans. The background history is confusing because of the various partnerships of brothers involved. It continues in production today.

	Current Price Range		Prior Year Average
☐ **Bone dish,** white	15.00	18.50	16.75
☐ **Bowl,** Coromandel pattern, Limoges, 9¼″ x 10¾″	48.00	58.00	52.00
☐ **Bowl,** vegetable, covered, St. Lazatte	40.00	46.00	43.00
☐ **Butter dish,** Miramar pattern, Limoges, with cover	60.00	70.00	65.00
☐ **Butter pats,** Princess	9.00	12.50	10.75
☐ **Cake plate,** green leaf, gold trim, Charles Field Haviland, 12″ Dia.	34.00	44.00	39.00
☐ **Chocolate pot,** blue-green flowers, leaves, gold trim	70.00	80.00	75.00
☐ **Coffeepot,** moss rose, 8″ H.	50.00	60.00	55.00
☐ **Cup and saucer,** bouillon, Miami	9.00	12.00	10.50
☐ **Cup and saucer,** Marquis pattern	24.00	28.00	26.00
☐ **Cup and saucer,** Princess	22.00	26.00	24.00
☐ **Cup and saucer,** Ranson, gold trim, bouillon	32.00	38.00	35.00
☐ **Decanter,** floral decor with stopper, Haviland-Limoges, 9″ H.	52.00	62.00	57.00
☐ **Gravy boat,** Greek pattern, American	35.00	40.00	37.50
☐ **Gravy boat,** silver anniversary	45.00	52.00	48.00
☐ **Hatpin holder,** blue flowers, signed	35.00	40.00	37.50
☐ **Ice cream set,** platter with six plates, blue and white	135.00	165.00	150.00
☐ **Plate,** apple blossom pattern, 9″ Dia.	14.00	18.00	16.00
☐ **Plate,** bread and butter, Frontenac	9.00	12.50	10.75
☐ **Plate,** morning glory pattern, 8½″ Dia.	28.00	32.00	30.00
☐ **Plate,** Princess pattern, 9½″ Dia.	28.00	32.00	30.00
☐ **Plate,** luncheon, Frontenac, 8½″ Dia.	14.00	18.00	16.00
☐ **Plate,** luncheon, Princess	12.00	14.00	13.00
☐ **Plate,** luncheon, yellow and pink carnations, Charles Field Haviland	8.50	12.50	10.50
☐ **Platter,** Greek pattern, Theodore Haviland, 13″ Dia.	32.00	38.00	35.00
☐ **Platter,** Ranson pattern, 11½″	42.00	48.00	45.00
☐ **Relish dish,** violets, Theodore Haviland	28.00	32.00	30.00
☐ **Salad plate,** Ranson pattern with gold, Haviland	8.50	12.50	10.50
☐ **Soup plate,** Cambridge pattern, Theodore Haviland	12.00	14.00	13.00

	Current Price Range		Prior Year Average
☐ **Soup tureen,** pink florals with gold trim	130.00	160.00	145.00
☐ **Sugar bowls,** Ranson, covered, white	42.00	48.00	45.00
☐ **Sugar and creamer,** Limoges, covered, autumn leaves	60.00	70.00	65.00
☐ **Teapot,** cupid, gold trim, Charles Field Haviland, 5″ H.	70.00	85.00	78.00
☐ **Tea set,** moss rose pattern, set	160.00	180.00	170.00
☐ **Tray,** dessert, Limoges, 11″ x 8″	36.00	46.00	41.00
☐ **Vase,** peacock, brown and black, signed, 10″ x 11½″ H.	360.00	430.00	385.00
☐ **Vegetable dish,** Limoges, pink roses	35.00	40.00	37.50
☐ **Vegetable dish,** Princess pattern, handled	46.00	56.00	51.00
☐ **Vegetable dish,** Ranson pattern, covered	46.00	56.00	51.00
☐ **Vegetable dish,** St. Lazarre pattern, covered	38.00	48.00	42.00

LENOX

Lenox got its start on May 18, 1889, when it was incorporated in New Jersey as the Ceramic Art Company. The new company was set up to manufacture American porcelain which would rival Irish Belleek in form, delicacy and color. Jonathon Coxon, Sr. was the president of the new company, and Walter Scott Lenox was the secretary-treasurer. Lenox eventually bought out his partner's interest and renamed the company after himself. Coxon, meanwhile, went to Ohio and founded the Coxon Belleek Company. Over 4000 different shapes have been made. In addition to the factory-decorated items, blanks were sold to be decorated at home by amateurs.

As of today, no fakes or forgeries of Lenox are known. At least 15 marks have been noted, the most desirable being the CAC wreath mark. Artists' signatures to look for are those of Hans and J. Nosek, and George and William Morney. For more information and listings, you may refer to *The Official Price Guide to American Pottery and Porcelain,* published by The House of Collectibles.

DINNERWARE

☐ **Bread and butter plate,** Ming pattern	11.00	13.00	12.00
☐ **Bread and butter plate,** J-34 pattern	8.00	9.50	8.75
☐ **Cup and saucer,** bouillon, K344B pattern	18.00	38.00	28.00
☐ **Cup and saucer,** bouillon, Ming	20.00	28.00	24.00
☐ **Cup and saucer,** demitasse, Hawthorn pattern, white	15.00	20.00	17.50
☐ **Cup and saucer,** demitasse, Hawthorn pattern, eggshell thin, C.A.C. brown palette mark	45.00	58.00	52.00
☐ **Cup and saucer,** demitasse, Mandarin pattern	20.00	30.00	25.00
☐ **Cup and saucer,** demitasse, Monticello pattern	15.00	21.00	18.00
☐ **Cup and saucer,** full size, Alaris pattern	22.00	32.00	27.00
☐ **Cup and saucer,** full size, Apple Blossom, coral & white	22.00	32.00	27.00
☐ **Cup and saucer,** full size, blue dot enamel work	30.00	36.00	33.00
☐ **Cup and saucer,** full size, Trellis	17.00	22.00	19.50
☐ **Cup and saucer,** full size, Virginia	35.0	42.00	38.00
☐ **Cup and saucer,** full size, Washington/Wakefield	28.00	38.00	33.00
☐ **Dinner plate,** Belvedere	20.00	26.00	23.00
☐ **Dinner plate,** Beltane, yellow and white	20.00	26.00	23.00
☐ **Dinner plate,** Mandarin	22.50	28.00	24.50

672 / PORCELAIN AND POTTERY

	Current Price Range		Prior Year Average
☐ Dinner plate, Washington/Wakefield	14.00	20.00	17.00
☐ Dinner plate, Pagoda, blue and white	12.00	18.00	15.00
☐ Luncheon plate, Pinehurst blue	12.00	18.00	15.00
☐ Salad plate, Monterey	9.00	16.00	12.50
☐ Salad plate, S-62	10.00	16.00	13.00
☐ Salad plate, Trio	8.0	12.50	10.00
☐ Sugar and creamer, Ming	75.00	90.00	82.00
☐ Sugar and creamer, Priscilla	65.00	85.00	75.00
☐ Teapot, cattail	30.00	40.00	35.00
☐ Vegetable bowl, S-34 pattern	30.00	40.00	35.00

FIGURINES

☐ Crinoline, perfect	350.00	450.00	400.00
☐ Floradora, perfect	425.00	525.00	475.00
☐ Mistress Mary, minor damage to lace ruffles and tips of fingers	300.00	400.00	350.00
☐ Mistress Mary, perfect	350.00	450.00	400.00
☐ Natchez Belle, minor damage to lace	335.00	435.00	385.00
☐ Southern Belle, perfect	400.00	500.00	450.00
☐ Twin boy, perfect	150.0	220.00	180.00
☐ Twin girl, perfect	120.00	160.00	140.00
☐ Twins, pair, undecorated and unmarked	100.00	150.00	125.00

GIFTWARE AND NOVELTY ITEMS

☐ Angel candle holder, white	50.00	60.00	55.00
☐ Ashtray, large, pheasant design	30.00	40.00	35.00
☐ Ashtray, small teardrop shape, green with gold	9.00	15.00	12.00
☐ Bird, large, brown, holes for flower arranging	45.00	52.00	48.00
☐ Bird, large, flower holder, pink	30.00	40.00	35.00
☐ Bird, small, blue	25.00	32.00	28.00
☐ Bird, small, white	20.00	26.00	23.00
☐ Candlestick, gold trim, pair, 9" H.	35.00	42.00	38.00
☐ Candlestick, Grecian style, blue and white, pair, 4" H.	28.0	32.00	30.00
☐ Candy dish, coral and white, 6" Dia.	19.00	26.00	22.50
☐ Candy dish, covered, white with gold trim	25.00	32.00	28.00
☐ Candy dish, dark green, melon-ribbed, covered	38.00	42.00	40.00
☐ Candy dish, white and gold trim, 8" L.	15.00	20.00	17.50
☐ Cigarette lighter, gold trim	20.00	25.00	22.50
☐ Cigarette urn, gray with platinum trim	10.00	15.00	12.50
☐ Compote, Ming pattern	50.00	58.00	54.00
☐ Dog, running schnauzer, white	40.00	50.00	45.00
☐ Dog, standing bulldog, white bisque	125.00	150.00	138.00
☐ Elephant, large, white	150.00	175.00	162.00
☐ Horn of Plenty, small, white and coral	25.00	45.00	35.00
☐ Llama, white	90.00	115.00	102.00
☐ Pitcher, hammered finish, mask spout, light green	90.0	115.00	102.00
☐ Shell bonbon, pink with white, 6" H.	20.00	28.00	24.00
☐ Swan, medium, coral	25.00	32.00	28.00
☐ Swan, medium, Lenox Rose design	42.00	48.00	45.00
☐ Swan, pink, 2" H.	20.00	28.00	24.00
☐ Swan, white with gold, CAC mark (Belleek), 2" H.	30.00	36.00	33.00
☐ Toby mug, William Penn, white	125.00	150.00	138.00
☐ Vase, bud, one handle, gold wheat design	24.00	28.00	26.00

PORCELAIN AND POTTERY / 673

	Current Price Range		Prior Year Average
☐ **Vase,** square base, fluting, white and green	40.00	48.00	44.00
☐ **Vase,** square, raised flower design	30.00	36.00	33.00
☐ **Vase,** swan handles, white with gold trim	32.00	38.00	35.00
☐ **Vase,** tall cylinder, sea horse decoration (Belleek)	25.00	32.00	28.00
☐ **Wall pocket,** white bisque	50.00	56.00	53.00

HAND-PAINTED ITEMS (FACTORY ARTISTS)

☐ **Fern pot,** with separate strainer, small hand-pained flowers with gold trim, pink palette mark, CAC (Belleek, 9" Dia.	160.00	175.00	168.00
☐ **Mug,** monk scene, CAC wreath mark (Belleek), 5" H.	130.00	160.00	144.00
☐ **Plate,** fish, signed Morley, 9" Dia.	80.00	90.00	85.00
☐ **Plate,** grapes, signed Nosek, 9" Dia.	40.00	45.00	42.00
☐ **Stein,** sterling lid and thumb rest, golfer, monochromatic greens, CAC (Belleek)	200.00	245.00	222.00
☐ **Tobacco jar,** Canadian geese in flight, blue skies, clouds, green grass and swamp plants, signed Morley, Lenox wreath, pink	350.00	400.00	375.00
☐ **Vase,** covered, ceramic parts made in four section separated by bronze connectors, bronze pineapple finial, garlands of flowers on white ground, c. 1898	280.00	340.00	310.00
☐ **Vase,** flowering poppies, air-brushed brown background, signed Morley, CAC wreath mark (Belleek), 10" H.	350.00	400.00	375.00
☐ **Vase,** plume handles, roses in shades of pink and gold, signed Marsh, CAC (Belleek), 14" H.	325.00	375.00	350.00
☐ **Vase,** portrait of springer spaniel, signed Bakery, Lenox wreath mark, 8" H.	225.00	265.00	245.00
☐ **Whiskey jug,** fruit design, CAC (Belleek) mark ...	175.00	200.00	188.00

HAND-PAINTED ITEMS (NON-FACTORY ARTISTS)

☐ **Cornucopia,** roses	75.00	95.00	85.00
☐ **Covered box,** poppy design	75.00	95.00	85.00
☐ **Pin tray,** blue background, butterflies, 7" L.	25.00	30.00	27.50
☐ **Salt dip,** small roses	10.00	12.00	11.00
☐ **Tea set,** orange flowers with gold, three pieces ..	100.00	125.00	112.00
☐ **Vase,** green background, roses on both sides, gold handles, CAC palette mark (Belleek), 14" H.	150.00	180.00	165.00
☐ **Vase,** iridescent peacocks, inferior art work, 10" H.	60.00	70.00	65.00
☐ **Vase,** slightly rounded, no handles, orchid decoration, 10" H.	75.00	85.00	80.00

(Note: There is a considerable price spread on non-factory items since they could have been painted by — an amateur or a professional artist. Home-decorated items can usually be identified quickly from the inferior art work — lack of depth, crudely done designs, and over-zealous use of gold.)

LENOX LINERS IN SILVER HOLDERS

☐ **Bouillons,** CAC liners, hand-painted gold and green ribbons, Gorham holders, set of six (Belleek)	360.00	430.00	395.00
☐ **Bouillons,** CAC liners, hand-painted flowers with raised gold paste, set of eight (Belleek)	500.00	600.00	550.00

674 / PORCELAIN AND POTTERY

	Current Price Range		Prior Year Average
☐ **Bouillons,** plain gold trim, Gorham holders, set of 12	240.00	280.00	260.00
☐ **Butter tub,** plain gold trim, openwork holder	35.00	40.00	37.00
☐ **Demitasse cups and saucers,** raised gold paste flowers, Tiffany Chrysanthemum holders and saucers, set of six	500.00	600.00	550.00
☐ **Demitasse cups and saucers,** plain gold trim on liners, International holders and saucers, set of eight	160.00	180.00	170.00
☐ **Ramekins,** CAC, hand-painted liners, raised gold work, Gorham holders, set of six, (Belleek)	600.00	720.00	660.00
☐ **Ramekins,** plain gold trim, openwork Reed and Barton holders, set of 12	360.00	430.00	395.00
☐ **Salt dip,** plain gold trim liner, openwork holder	18.00	20.00	19.00
☐ **Sauce bowl,** CAC mark, hand-painted flowers, two-handled silver holder, footed, (Belleek)	75.00	85.00	80.00
☐ **Sherbert,** plain gold trim, scalloped rim, Shreve and Company holder, Art Nouveau	50.00	60.00	55.00
☐ **Sherbert,** plain gold trim, openwork Gorham holder	30.00	35.00	32.50

SILVER OVERLAY

☐ **Biscuit jar,** white	100.00	125.00	112.00
☐ **Bowl,** cherry blossom design, 9″ Dia.	125.00	155.00	140.00
☐ **Bowl,** skimpy silver, 10″ Dia.	60.00	70.00	65.00
☐ **Candlesticks,** white, pair, 6″ H.	75.00	85.00	80.00
☐ **Candy dish,** shell shape, CAC mark (Belleek)	60.00	70.00	65.00
☐ **Coaster,** oxblood, Lenox wreath mark, has been made over into necklace on silver chain	60.00	70.00	65.00
☐ **Compote,** small, white, average silver	35.00	40.00	37.00
☐ **Honey pot,** bees covered with silver	60.00	70.00	65.00
☐ **Hot water pot,** white with ornate silver, bottom covered with silver so mark can't be seen but shape verifiable as Lenox	65.00	75.00	70.00
☐ **Luncheon plate,** simple bands of silver, 9″ Dia.	15.00	18.00	16.50
☐ **Mustard pot,** cobalt, CAC mark (Belleek)	95.00	115.00	105.00
☐ **Tea tile,** turquoise	75.00	85.00	80.00
☐ **Tea set,** five-piece (coffeepot, teapot, sugar, creamer, tray), white with cherry blossom design	425.00	525.00	475.00
☐ **Tea set,** small, cobalt, CAC mark on one piece only, other pieces unmarked (Belleek)	110.00	150.00	130.00
☐ **Vase,** cobalt with heavy silver, CAC mark (Belleek), 8″ H.	85.00	95.00	90.00
☐ **Vase,** shading from orange-brown to dark olive green, ornate silver work, CAC mark (Belleek), 6″ H.	125.00	145.00	135.00

MAJOLICA

Majolica is a pottery characterized by a high glaze and bright colors. It was first made several centuries ago in Italy and those early wares are called "maiolica," but most of what is collectible today are Victorian wares from England and America. The most important American manufacturer was Griffen, Smith and Hill of Phoenixville, Pennsylvania. Their wares are called "Etruscan."

PORCELAIN AND POTTERY / 675

	Current Price Range		Prior Year Average
☐ Chesapeake butter dish, bunch of grapes	20.00	24.00	22.00
☐ Candlestick, figural pair, boy and girl with flowers	75.00	85.00	80.00
☐ Etruscan cup and saucer, "Bamboo," rose pink inside	95.00	115.00	105.00
☐ Etruscan cup and saucer, "Shell-and-Seaweed"	110.00	140.00	125.00
☐ Etruscan plate, "Cauliflower" design, 7" Dia.	22.00	26.00	24.00
☐ Etruscan oyster plate, six compartments, 10" Dia.	70.00	85.00	78.00
☐ Etruscan 65-piece set, "Shell-and-Seaweed," includes mustache cups, syrups, covered butter dish	2800.00	3200.00	3000.00
☐ Etruscan vase, hand with corncob	70.00	85.00	78.00
☐ Minton oyster plate, seven compartments, 9" Dia.	70.00	85.00	78.00
☐ Morley and Co., pitcher, owl-shaped, 7½" H.	75.00	90.00	82.00
☐ Wedgwood butter plate, butterfly design	40.00	45.00	42.50
☐ Wedgwood platform charger, scythe and sunburst, cobalt, 13" Dia.	250.00	300.00	275.00
☐ Wedgwood strawberry serving set, with sugar and creamer	80.00	90.00	85.00

NIPPON

Nippon porcelain was made by the Noritake Company, Ltd., in Nagoya, Japan until 1921. Hand-painted pieces of good quality are rising in price.

☐ Ashtray, warrior on horseback	30.00	36.00	33.00
☐ Basket, florals and pink ribbons with gold, 4" L.	35.00	45.00	40.00
☐ Berry set, house scene, five pieces	50.00	60.00	55.00
☐ Bottle, perfume, pink roses	60.00	70.00	65.00
☐ Bowl, blue with ruffled top, two swans	100.00	120.00	110.00
☐ Bowl, scalloped rim, florals in coral pink, 11" Dia.	90.00	110.00	100.00
☐ Bowl, violets, 9½" Dia.	25.00	30.00	27.50
☐ Box, biscuit, mosque scene, covered bisque finish	140.00	165.00	153.00
☐ Box, floral, covered with gold trim, 3" H.	15.00	18.00	16.50
☐ Candlesticks, yellow flowers with green leaves, black base, blue maple leaf mark, pair, 8½" H.	120.00	145.00	132.00
☐ Chocolate set, pink cherry blossom, green wreath mark, 29 pieces	450.00	530.00	490.00
☐ Cigarette box, enameled horse head, bisque finish	65.00	75.00	70.00
☐ Creamer and sugar, farm and water scene, green "M" in wreath mark	55.00	62.00	58.00
☐ Cup and saucer, white, floral, green mark	10.00	12.50	11.25
☐ Dish, lake scene with swans and lily pad, oval, 7¼" Dia.	70.00	80.00	75.00
☐ Dish, mayonnaise, yellow and gold flowers, three pieces	30.00	36.00	33.00
☐ Ewer, pink roses with gold beading, blue maple leaf mark	45.00	50.00	47.00
☐ Ginger jar, rose decor with gold trim	25.00	28.00	26.50
☐ Hair receiver, floral on blue background	38.00	45.00	41.00
☐ Hatpin holder, desert scene, bisque finish	30.00	36.00	33.00

676 / PORCELAIN AND POTTERY

	Current Price Range		Prior Year Average
☐ **Humidor**, green, white and gold floral decor, enameled maple leaf mark	185.00	220.00	200.00
☐ **Lemonade set,** floral decor, pitcher and mugs ...	150.00	180.00	165.00
☐ **Match holder,** farm house scene, green "M" mark	55.00	65.00	60.00
☐ **Mayonnaise bowl,** blue and gold trim, two pieces	24.00	28.00	26.00
☐ **Mayonnaise set,** rising sun mark, three pieces ..	24.00	28.00	26.00
☐ **Mustache cup and saucer,** scenic, green wreath mark	150.00	180.00	165.00
☐ **Napkin ring,** floral decor, gold trim	45.00	55.00	50.00
☐ **Nut bowl,** basketweave with black walnuts, 7½" D.	110.00	145.00	128.00
☐ **Peanut set,** peanuts and vines, bowl with five bowls, 8¼" L.	185.00	230.00	208.00
☐ **Pitcher,** bulbous, grape pattern, 6" H.	65.00	75.00	70.00
☐ **Pitcher,** bulbous, sparrow flying through blossoms, 9½" H.	175.00	200.00	182.00
☐ **Pitcher,** tankard, pink, white and deep rose chrysanthemums, green border, 11" H.	260.00	300.00	280.00
☐ **Planter,** Indian in canoe, green "M" in wreath mark	75.00	85.00	80.00
☐ **Planter,** ship decor, jeweled, green wreath mark, 7¼" sq.	150.00	180.00	175.00
☐ **Plaque,** Indian portrait, green "M" in wreath mark, 7¾" sq.	135.00	155.00	145.00
☐ **Plaque,** lion and lioness, in relief, 10¾" sq.	425.00	495.00	460.00
☐ **Plaque,** scenic, blue maple leaf, 9" sq.	65.00	75.00	70.00
☐ **Plate,** orange poppies on brown background, blue maple leaf mark, 11" Dia.	175.00	200.00	182.00
☐ **Plate,** red roses with green border, 10" Dia.	38.00	45.00	41.00
☐ **Rose bowl,** pink and white, gold decorations, 5½" x 3"	48.00	56.00	52.00
☐ **Salt and pepper,** floral and gold	16.00	20.00	18.00
☐ **Sugar shaker,** gold beading with poppies	45.00	50.00	47.00
☐ **Sugar and creamer,** pink roses, gold trim, cover .	30.00	36.00	33.00
☐ **Sugar and creamer,** pink blossoms, gold trim, green "M" mark	35.50	41.00	38.50
☐ **Tea set,** sailboat scene, three pieces	110.00	150.00	130.00
☐ **Teapot,** child's face in relief, covered, 3¼" H. ...	4500.00	5300.00	4900.00
☐ **Tray,** desert scene, 10½" x 7"	45.00	50.00	47.00
☐ **Tray,** flowers and parrot on limb, green wreath mark	80.00	92.00	86.00
☐ **Urn,** desert scene, 10½" x 7"	45.0	50.00	47.50
☐ **Vase,** camel scene, six-sided, 9¼" H.	100.00	120.00	110.00
☐ **Vase,** deep blue, hand-painted, green mark, 10" H.	100.00	120.00	110.00
☐ **Vase,** Egyptian animals and people, 9"	90.00	110.00	100.00
☐ **Vase,** lake scene, green wreath mark, 6" H.	45.00	50.00	47.00
☐ **Vase,** red and white roses, gold beading, maple leaf mark, 7" x 9"	150.00	180.00	165.00

PORCELAIN AND POTTERY / 677

NORITAKE

Noritake china is still being produced in Japan today. Large quantities have been exported to this country. A favorite pattern with collectors is Azalea.

	Current Price Range		Prior Year Average
☐ **Ashtray,** pine cones, Noritake-Nippon mark	42.00	50.00	46.00
☐ **Basket,** Azalea pattern	80.00	96.00	88.00
☐ **Bonbon,** Azalea pattern	30.00	36.00	33.00
☐ **Bowl,** cereal	16.00	20.00	18.00
☐ **Butter tub,** with liner, Azalea pattern	30.00	36.00	33.00
☐ **Cake set,** ivory with black and gold trim, blue urn with flowers	70.00	80.00	75.00
☐ **Chocolate set,** hand-painted, green mark, 11 pieces	50.00	60.00	55.00
☐ **Condiment set,** Azalea pattern, five pieces	35.00	42.00	38.00
☐ **Creamer,** Sahara	20.00	24.00	22.00
☐ **Cup and saucer,** Azalea pattern	15.00	18.00	16.50
☐ **Dinner set,** Hanover, 64 pieces	350.00	410.00	380.00
☐ **Eggcup,** Azalea pattern	20.00	24.00	22.00
☐ **Gravy boat,** Azalea pattern, with attached stand .	32.00	38.00	35.00
☐ **Inkwell,** figural clown	36.00	42.00	39.00
☐ **Hatpin holder,** forget-me-nots	10.00	12.50	11.25
☐ **Lemon plate,** Azalea pattern	16.00	20.00	18.00
☐ **Mayonnaise set,** bowl, underplate, ladle, rose decor, three pieces	24.00	28.00	26.00
☐ **Mustard jar,** with spoon, Azalea pattern	45.00	52.00	48.00
☐ **Pitcher,** jar, Azalea pattern	90.00	110.00	100.00
☐ **Plate,** Azalea pattern, 7½" Dia.	6.00	8.00	7.00
☐ **Plate,** dinner, Azalea pattern	14.00	16.00	15.00
☐ **Plate,** square, Azalea pattern	3200.00	3800.00	3500.00
☐ **Plate,** soup, Azalea pattern, green mark, 7½" Dia.	12.00	14.00	13.00
☐ **Plate,** tree at lake, 6" Dia.	25.00	28.00	26.50
☐ **Platter,** Azalea pattern, 12" oval	25.00	28.00	26.50
☐ **Platter,** Azalea pattern, 14" oval	35.00	42.00	37.00
☐ **Relish dish,** Azalea pattern, four-section, handled, 9" L.	50.00	60.00	55.00
☐ **Sauce dish,** Azalea pattern, 6" Dia.	8.00	10.00	9.00
☐ **Soup bowl,** Azalea pattern	12.00	14.00	13.00
☐ **Spooner,** Azalea pattern	48.00	56.00	51.00
☐ **Syrup and underplate,** white roses, gold trim	38.00	44.00	41.00
☐ **Tea set,** Azalea pattern, 15 pieces	100.00	120.00	110.00
☐ **Teapot,** tree in meadow pattern	4850.00	5600.00	5200.00
☐ **Toothpick holder,** Azalea pattern	75.00	85.00	80.00
☐ **Tray,** tree at lake pattern	25.00	28.00	26.50
☐ **Tureen,** gold handles, floral holder	35.00	42.00	38.00
☐ **Urn,** rose decor with gold, two handles	85.00	95.00	90.00
☐ **Vase,** fan-shaped, tree in the meadow pattern . . .	5000.00	6000.00	5500.00
☐ **Vase,** gold handles, pink roses, 3" H.	15.00	18.00	16.50
☐ **Vase,** lavender, four handles, green wreath mark, 8½" H.	30.00	35.00	32.00
☐ **Vase,** sunset lake scene, gold rim, red wreath, 8" H.	30.00	35.00	32.00

678 / PORCELAIN AND POTTERY

MUSTACHE CUPS WITH SAUCERS

The late Victorian era (1880-1900) introduced mustache cups. During this period they grew increasingly popular. Different from standard drinking mugs, they were constructed with a separate piece inserted along one rim of the cup to keep the gentleman's mustache out of his drink. "Left-handed" cups made for left-handed men are the scarcest and most valuable. Reproductions are frequently sold, so the buyer should purchase from a reputable dealer. Prices are for good condition with matching saucer.

Note: Sterling or "coin" are double these prices. Double price for left-handed cups.

	Current Price Range		Prior Year Average
☐ **Austrian-designed,** multicolored floral decoration	56.00	65.00	60.00
☐ **Bavarian,** medallion of pink roses, gold scroll work, marked Royal Bavarian China — Germany, PMB	45.00	50.00	48.00
☐ **Bird** with floral gold trim	30.00	36.00	33.00
☐ **Civil war drum decor,** left-handed, c. 1860	165.00	195.00	180.00
☐ **Cup and attached saucer,** Worcester	85.00	95.00	90.00
☐ **Daniel Webster's birthplace**	70.00	80.00	75.00
☐ **Floral design,** blue forget-me-nots and roses	50.00	60.00	55.00
☐ **Floral design,** gold beaded edge and foot	42.50	50.00	43.50
☐ **Floral design,** lavender and pink assorted flowers	40.00	48.00	44.00
☐ **Floral design,** lavender flowers (Carlsbad)	40.00	48.00	44.00
☐ **Floral design,** red roses with gold trim on cup	42.50	50.00	43.50
☐ **Hand-painted floral,** French	50.00	60.00	55.00
☐ **Inscribed,** "John Summer, 1883"	60.00	72.00	66.00
☐ **Inscribed,** "Think of Me," white, pink and gold	50.00	60.00	55.00
☐ **Raised floral design,** Germany	25.00	32.00	28.00
☐ **Silver-plated,** cup and saucer set	30.00	36.00	33.00
☐ **Swirled cup and saucer,** "Papa" lettered on side	50.00	60.00	55.00
☐ **Pink lusterware cup and saucer,** inscribed panel	65.00	75.00	70.00
☐ **Victorian porcelain,** pink luster	30.00	36.00	33.00

ROYAL BAYREUTH

Royal Bayreuth was made in Tettau, Germany, beginning in 1794. The popularity of this porcelain remains high and prices rise constantly.

☐ **Ashtray,** clown, blue mark	135.00	165.00	150.00
☐ **Ashtray,** elk, blue mark	80.00	96.00	88.00
☐ **Bell,** hand-painted farm scene	45.00	52.00	48.00
☐ **Berry bowl,** roses, gold trim, blue mark, 4¼" Dia.	60.00	70.00	65.00
☐ **Bonbon,** pink and white roses, footed blue mark	5500.00	6500.00	6000.00
☐ **Bowl,** Brittany girl, blue mark, 6¼" Dia.	45.00	55.00	50.00
☐ **Bowl,** Dutch girl, house, blue sky and white clouds, 9½" Dia.	180.00	225.00	200.00
☐ **Bowl,** poppy, blue mark, 8" x 4½"	65.00	75.00	70.00
☐ **Bowl,** tomato, 9½" Dia.	125.00	150.00	138.00
☐ **Box,** black and tan, covered, pin roses, 4" x 5"	80.00	96.00	88.00
☐ **Box,** card, men at table, green, blue mark	75.00	85.00	80.00
☐ **Box,** "Little Bo Peep," green, blue mark	125.00	150.00	138.00
☐ **Candlestick,** goosegirl and geese, blue mark, 4½" H.	55.00	65.00	60.00

PORCELAIN AND POTTERY / 679

	Current Price Range		Prior Year Average
☐ Celery, lobster, 13″ x 5″	75.00	85.00	80.00
☐ Cracker set, bowl and pitcher, lobster	210.00	250.00	230.00
☐ Creamer, apple	80.00	96.00	88.00
☐ Creamer, bear	110.00	132.00	121.00
☐ Creamer, butterfly, blue mark	165.00	195.00	180.00
☐ Creamer, clown, red mark	130.00	165.00	148.00
☐ Creamer, devil and cards	90.00	115.00	102.00
☐ Creamer, eagle, blue mark	95.00	120.00	108.00
☐ Creamer, pig	115.00	140.00	128.00
☐ Creamer, strawberry	85.00	100.00	92.00
☐ Creamer, water buffalo	105.00	120.00	114.00
☐ Cup and saucer, demitasse, devil and dice	70.00	82.00	76.00
☐ Cup and saucer, demitasse, Murex	75.00	85.00	80.00
☐ Dish, candy, clown, blue mark	160.00	180.00	170.00
☐ Dish, lettuce, blue mark, 7″ x 5½″	32.00	39.00	35.00
☐ Hair receiver, barnyard scene, blue mark	85.00	98.00	91.00
☐ Hatpin holder, owl, black mark	230.00	270.00	250.00
☐ Hatpin holder, red poppy, blue mark	160.00	190.00	185.00
☐ Match holder, penquin, hanging type	90.00	110.00	100.00
☐ Mustard jar, rose, covered with original spoon	150.00	180.00	165.00
☐ Nappy, swans on lake, handled, oval	40.00	48.00	44.00
☐ Pitchers, Brittany girl decor, 5¼″ H.	75.00	85.00	80.00
☐ Pitchers, clown, red	190.00	230.00	210.00
☐ Pitchers, hunting scene, 7½″ H.	90.00	130.00	110.00
☐ Pitchers, milk, monkey, blue mark	130.00	160.00	145.00
☐ Pitchers, milk, poppy, blue mark	140.00	170.00	155.00
☐ Pitchers, milk, tavern scene	130.00	160.00	145.00
☐ Pitchers, water, Murex	140.00	170.00	155.00
☐ Plates, devil and cards, 7″ Dia.	110.00	135.00	122.00
☐ Plates, leaf with handle, 5½″ Dia.	70.00	80.00	75.00
☐ Plates, little girl with dog	95.00	115.00	105.00
☐ Salt and pepper, grape, blue mark	110.00	125.00	118.00
☐ Shakers, conch, pair	90.00	110.00	100.00
☐ Shakers, grapes	70.00	80.00	75.00
☐ Shakers, lobster	115.00	130.00	122.00
☐ Sugar and creamer, hunter and dogs	100.00	120.00	110.00
☐ Sugar and creamer, lobster	115.0	130.00	122.00
☐ Tea set, apple	220.00	265.00	240.00
☐ Tea set, tomato, blue mark, three pieces	175.00	195.00	185.00
☐ Toothpick holder, deer head	75.00	85.00	80.00
☐ Tray, pink roses, green, 10″ x 7″	85.00	96.00	90.00
☐ Vase, cows grazing, green	75.00	85.00	80.00
☐ Vase, Dutch scene, 5½″ H.	75.00	85.00	80.00
☐ Vase, girls and ship scene, 3½″ H.	55.00	62.00	58.00
☐ Vase, "Little Bo Peep," handles, 2½″ H.	95.00	115.00	105.00
☐ Vase, man with dogs, 7″ H.	165.00	195.00	180.00
☐ Vase, polar bear in snow, blue mark, 5″ H.	70.00	80.00	75.00
☐ Vase, rose tapestry, two gold handles, 3″ H.	110.00	135.00	122.00

ROYAL COPENHAGEN

Royal Copenhagen has been produced in Denmark since 1771 and is still being made. The factory was under royal operation for a time. Items were imported into the United States from the late 1800's to the early 1900's.

680 / PORCELAIN AND POTTERY

	Current Price Range		Prior Year Average
☐ **Ashtray,** Langelinie	70.00	80.00	75.00
☐ **Bonbon**	35.00	42.00	38.00
☐ **Bottle,** Fredericksborg castle on front, crown on back, 10″ H.	80.00	96.00	88.00
☐ **Bowl,** green and gray with gold, square, 6″ x 3″	400.00	480.00	440.00
☐ **Coffee pot,** gold edge and handles with underglazed decor	170.00	210.00	190.00
☐ **Dish,** shape of leaf, blue flowers and handle, 9″ Dia.	20.00	24.00	22.00
☐ **Figurines,** baby duckling, 4½″ H.	35.00	42.00	38.00
☐ **Figurines,** cat sitting, gray and white, 5½″ H.	55.00	65.00	60.00
☐ **Figurines,** dog, dachshund lying down, 3¼″ H.	65.00	75.00	70.00
☐ **Figurines,** pup sitting, tan and brown, 3½″ H.	55.00	65.00	60.00
☐ **Figurines,** Siamese cat lying with head and forepaw raised, 4″ H.	70.00	80.00	75.00
☐ **Figurines,** stag, brown eyes	100.00	120.00	110.00
☐ **Figurines,** young boy holding pig, 6½″ H.	90.00	110.00	100.00
☐ **Inkwell,** with tray, 6″ x 8½″ L.	100.00	120.00	110.00
☐ **Plate,** commemorative, soldiers, ships and flag	105.00	125.00	117.00
☐ **Plate,** fruit center, pink border, 8″ Dia.	30.00	36.00	33.00
☐ **Plate,** portrait of Josephine, 10¾″ Dia., c. 1923	85.00	100.00	92.00
☐ **Plate,** portraits of Napoleon, Josephine, Pauline Bonaparte and husband, set of four, 10¾″ Dia.	265.00	320.00	290.00
☐ **Plate,** soup, blue and white with open chain edge, green mark, 7¾″ Dia.	35.00	42.00	38.00
☐ **Platters,** gray and white, gold, 8″ x 12″	80.00	96.00	88.00
☐ **Platters,** blue and white, 9″ x 12″	80.00	96.00	88.00
☐ **Platters,** blue and white, 12″ x 15″	110.00	135.00	122.00
☐ **Sugar and creamer,** doll's pink roses, crown mark	40.00	48.00	44.00
☐ **Soup tureen,** with cover and underplate, blue, 18″ L., 1897 mark	190.00	230.00	210.00
☐ **Tray,** blue and white floral, 6″ x 11″	35.00	42.00	38.00
☐ **Tray,** crackleware, gold edge, green, 8¼″ Dia.	45.00	55.00	50.00
☐ **Vases,** blue gray, white flowers, 5″ H.	35.00	42.00	38.00
☐ **Vases,** fuchsia flowers, leaves, 9½″ H.	100.00	120.00	110.00
☐ **Vases,** green crackle with gold decorations, pair, 12″ H.	250.00	300.00	275.00
☐ **Vases,** rhododendron, 10″ H.	100.00	120.00	110.00
☐ **Vases,** ship decor, 8″ H.	85.00	95.00	90.00

SHAVING MUGS

As an essential toiletry utensil, the shaving mug held soap and a softbristled brush used to make lather. Often, occupational mugs were stored at the local barber shop and had the owner's name and occupation painted or enameled on the outside.

☐ **Accordion**	145.00	170.00	158.00
☐ **Anchor,** with owner's name inscribed	90.00	110.00	100.00
☐ **Anvil, tongs and hammer**	125.00	140.00	132.00
☐ **Arc light**	130.00	145.00	135.00
☐ **Architect's insignia**	110.00	125.00	117.00
☐ **Athlete,** high jumper	150.00	165.00	158.00
☐ **Athlete,** track star	150.00	180.00	165.00
☐ **Automobile,** early	155.00	185.00	170.00
☐ **Baker**	145.00	170.00	158.00

PORCELAIN AND POTTERY / 681

	Current Price Range		Prior Year Average
☐ Baggage master with truck and car	145.00	170.00	158.00
☐ Bakery wagon, driver and horse	150.00	160.00	155.00
☐ Barber	130.00	160.00	145.00
☐ Bartender	135.00	160.00	148.00
☐ Baseball player	175.00	210.00	190.00
☐ Baseball with bats	140.00	155.00	148.00
☐ Beer bottle and glasses around barrel of beer	120.00	145.00	132.00
☐ Beer mug	110.00	135.00	122.00
☐ Beer wagon with horse and driver	165.00	195.00	180.00
☐ Bicycle	145.00	170.00	152.00
☐ Bill poster	165.00	200.00	182.00
☐ Billiard players	160.00	195.00	178.00
☐ Blacksmith shoeing horse	130.00	160.00	145.00
☐ Boilermaker at work	130.00	160.00	145.00
☐ Bookkeeper	115.00	130.00	122.00
☐ Bookmaker at work (bookbinding)	145.00	165.00	155.00
☐ Bowler, men in bowling alley	160.00	195.00	178.00
☐ Brakeman operating brake	140.00	160.00	150.00
☐ Brewmaster	185.00	220.00	192.00
☐ Bricklayer	125.00	145.00	135.00
☐ Bridge, steel	140.00	160.00	150.00
☐ Buggy, horse and driver	100.00	120.00	110.00
☐ Butcher killing steer	100.00	120.00	110.00
☐ Cabinetmaker	160.00	190.00	175.00
☐ Caboose	95.00	110.00	102.00
☐ Camera	175.00	200.00	182.00
☐ Carpenter at table	165.00	195.00	180.00
☐ Carpenter at work	100.00	120.00	110.00
☐ Cigar store	110.00	130.00	120.00
☐ Clothing store and cigar store	110.00	130.00	120.00
☐ Coal miner at work	130.00	160.00	145.00
☐ Cooper at work making barrels	155.00	175.00	165.00
☐ Cowboys lassoing steer with name, Limoges	190.00	220.00	205.00
☐ Dentist pulling teeth	185.00	210.00	197.00
☐ Dentist with false teeth	170.00	190.00	180.00
☐ Doctor tending patient (rare)	255.00	300.00	282.00
☐ Drug store	125.00	155.00	140.00
☐ Druggist at work	120.00	145.00	132.00
☐ Drum	100.00	120.00	110.00
☐ Engine in station	120.00	140.00	130.00
☐ Fire steam engine	195.00	210.00	202.00
☐ Flour and general store	110.00	130.00	120.00
☐ Furniture store	120.00	140.00	130.00
☐ Grocery store and clerk	120.00	140.00	130.00
☐ Guns, crossed rifles and targets	120.00	140.00	130.00
☐ Hardware store	120.00	140.00	130.00
☐ Hatter at work	140.00	160.00	150.00
☐ Hotel register	110.00	135.00	122.00
☐ Horse-drawn hearse	260.00	360.00	310.00
☐ Hunter, shooting at birds, pointer dog	125.00	145.00	135.00
☐ Ice wagon, horse and driver	135.00	155.00	145.00
☐ Jewelry store	120.00	145.00	132.00
☐ Jockey	145.00	165.00	155.00
☐ Judge	200.00	245.00	222.00
☐ Livery stable	150.00	180.00	165.00
☐ Livery stableman	135.00	155.00	145.00

682 / PORCELAIN AND POTTERY

	Current Price Range		Prior Year Average
☐ Locomotive	135.00	155.00	145.00
☐ Mail wagon	110.00	130.00	120.00
☐ Marble cutter at work	125.00	145.00	135.00
☐ Milk wagon, horse and driver	125.00	145.00	135.00
☐ Minister in pulpit	210.00	255.00	238.00
☐ Motorman and conductor	130.00	160.00	145.00
☐ Musicians	100.00	120.00	110.00
☐ Painter at work	135.00	155.00	145.00
☐ Photographer	175.00	195.00	185.00
☐ Piano player	110.00	130.00	120.00
☐ Plasterer	105.00	125.00	115.00
☐ Plumber	120.00	145.00	132.00
☐ Policeman	160.00	185.00	172.00
☐ Printer setting type	100.00	120.00	110.00
☐ Prizefighting (rare)	400.00	480.00	440.00
☐ Restaurant and bar	110.00	130.00	120.00
☐ Roller skater	100.00	120.00	110.00
☐ Sheep shearer	100.00	120.00	110.00
☐ Shoe dealer	100.00	120.00	110.00
☐ State senator	145.00	165.00	155.00
☐ Steamship	135.00	155.00	145.00
☐ Surveyor	140.00	165.00	152.00
☐ Tailor, with scissors and yardstick	130.00	155.00	142.00
☐ Teacher, class of 1898	105.00	135.00	120.00
☐ Telegrapher	110.00	140.00	125.00
☐ Telephone	120.00	150.00	135.00
☐ Tobacco store	120.00	150.00	135.00
☐ Tugboat	185.00	210.00	198.00
☐ Umbrella	100.00	120.00	110.00
☐ Undertaker (very rare)	450.00	550.00	500.00

STAFFORDSHIRE

Staffordshire is a general name for pottery made in the Staffordshire county of England — an area suited for a very large pottery and china industry because of the composition of the clay found there, and because of the vast amount of coal mined there, which was used to heat the firing furnaces. Generally speaking, Staffordshire wares are highly decorative, gaily colored, and were quite inexpensive when first made. Figurines and animal figures are among the most collectible items today.

☐ Bottle, scene, decorated, c. 18th c.	420.00	485.00	448.00
☐ Bottle, scent, c. 18th c.	400.00	475.00	438.00
☐ Bowl, flowers and castles, 12″ H.	90.00	110.00	100.00
☐ Box, trinket, spaniel	70.00	80.00	75.00
☐ Cat, salt-glazed, 7½″ H.	600.00	720.00	660.00
☐ Cats, black and white, pair, 7½″ H.	170.00	205.00	188.00
☐ Cottage, with people	35.00	42.00	38.00
☐ Dog, greyhound, pair, 10″ H.	220.00	260.00	240.00
☐ Dog, poodle, pair, 6″ H.	120.00	140.00	130.00
☐ Figurine, girl praying	100.00	120.00	110.00
☐ Figurine, G. Gordon, 17½″ H.	140.00	160.00	150.00
☐ Figurine, Mrs. Punch sitting on goat	100.00	120.00	110.00
☐ Figurine, Queen Victoria, c. 1850	100.00	120.00	110.00
☐ Figurine, Robin Hood, 12″ H.	100.00	120.00	110.00

PORCELAIN AND POTTERY / 683

	Current Price Range		Prior Year Average
☐ **Figurine,** Wallace	120.00	145.00	132.00
☐ **Figurines,** Victoria and Albert, pair, 7½″ H.	670.00	800.00	730.00
☐ **Group,** lion and leopard	200.00	240.00	220.00
☐ **Group,** lovers, 12″ H.	110.00	135.00	122.00
☐ **Hen,** carmel nest, 7″ H.	170.00	200.00	185.00
☐ **Inkwell,** girl with dog	220.00	260.00	240.00
☐ **Jug,** decorated with bands of checks, c. 1760	330.00	390.00	360.00
☐ **Jug,** milk, blue and white	80.00	90.00	85.00
☐ **Lions,** standing with one foot on ball, pair	220.00	260.00	240.00
☐ **Pitcher,** cherubs, 6¼″ H.	60.00	70.00	65.00
☐ **Plate,** Boston Statehouse, blue, 9¼″ H.	350.00	450.00	400.00
☐ **Snuffbox,** 3¼″ W., c. 1765	190.00	220.00	205.00
☐ **Snuffbox,** voyeurs, 3¼″ W., c. 1765	850.00	975.00	915.00

STEINS

Stein containers for drinking beer or ale are popular collectibles. Among the most desirable are those made by the German firm Mettlach. The numbers in the Mettlach listings refer to style numbers, and are often found on the bottom of steins. The address of the Mettlach Collectors' Society is P. O. Box 900A34, Manchester, N.H. 03105.

	Current Price Range		Prior Year Average
☐ **Art Nouveau,** copper and brass, 14″ H.	100.00	120.00	110.00
☐ **Bacchus,** silver, Sheffield, 11½″ H.	550.00	660.00	500.00
☐ **Character,** monkey, drunken, Musterschutz, 1-litre	375.00	450.00	415.00
☐ **Crying radish,** Musterschutz, ³⁄₁₀-litre	425.00	525.00	475.00
☐ **David and Goliath,** handle with four finger holes, ½-litre	550.00	660.00	605.00
☐ **Firefighting scene** with pewter top, ½-litre	300.00	360.00	330.00
☐ **Glass,** farm scene with pewter lid, ½-litre	45.00	55.00	50.00
☐ **Happy turnip,** Musterschutz, 3-litre	450.00	550.00	500.00
☐ **Ivory,** battle scene, carved, 13¾″ H.	2200.00	2800.00	2500.00
☐ **Lithophanes,** clown, ½-litre	375.00	450.00	415.00
☐ **Lithophanes,** German scene, 6½″ H.	100.00	120.00	110.00
☐ **Mettlach,** No. 1527, ½-litre	500.00	660.00	580.00
☐ **Mettlach,** No. 1675, Heidelberg, ½-litre	475.00	550.00	515.00
☐ **Mettlach,** No. 2002, Munich, ½-litre	375.0	450.00	415.00
☐ **Mettlach,** No. 2038, Black Forest, 4-litre	3800.00	4200.00	4000.00
☐ **Mettlach,** No. 2136, Brewmaster, ½-litre	325.00	395.00	365.00
☐ **Mettlach,** No. 2181, Pug, ½-litre	325.00	395.00	365.00
☐ **Mettlach,** No. 2388, pretzel, ½-litre	460.00	540.00	500.00
☐ **Mettlach,** No. 2958, bowling, 16″ H.	700.00	860.00	780.00
☐ **Monk,** Gesetzlicht, ½-litre	190.00	210.00	200.00
☐ **Pewter,** Kayserzinn, 10″ H.	180.00	200.00	190.00
☐ **Puss in Boots,** 6½″ H.	50.00	60.00	55.00
☐ **Regimental,** 18th infantry, 1-litre	325.00	395.00	360.00
☐ **Regimental,** Franco-Prussian War, 1-litre	325.00	395.00	360.00
☐ **Schlitz Beer,** ceramic, 7½″ H.	30.00	36.00	33.00
☐ **Singing Pig,** Musterschutz, ¼-litre	325.00	395.00	360.00
☐ **Stoneware,** warriors battling, pewter lid, 1-litre	100.00	120.00	110.00
☐ **Tower,** pewter lid, Geschuta, ½-litre	290.00	330.00	310.00

684 / PORCELAIN AND POTTERY

TOBY JUGS AND MUGS

These are rightly called "jugs," and date back to the 1760's in England, where the Ralph Woods, Staffordshire potters of great repute, made the first ones. The name "Toby" has alternately been ascribed to the subject of a popular 18th century English song, "The Brown Jug," and to Uncle Toby in Stern's novel *Tristram Shandy*. At any rate, though Staffordshire jugs (which got the name "mugs" from some collectors because they were used for drinking, not pouring) were the first, there have been thousands of imitations made right up to the present time. They are all in the shape of human figures, all somewhat caricaturized and exaggerated, many of which are seen to be tippling from a tiny jug themselves.

	Current Price Range		Prior Year Average
☐ Al Smith, porcelain, 6⅜" H., c. 1928	45.00	55.00	50.00
☐ Allerton, cobalt blue with copper trim, 4" H.	22.50	26.50	22.50
☐ Delft, man with beard, marked on lid, 9" H.	465.00	565.00	515.00
☐ Delft, man taking snuff with bug on nose, 11" H.	575.00	685.00	625.00
☐ Herbert Hoover, porcelain, 6½" H., c. 1928	45.00	55.00	50.00
☐ MacArthur, Douglas, 3¾" H.	35.00	42.00	38.00
☐ Royal Doulton, 'Ard of 'earing	340.00	400.00	370.00
☐ Royal Doulton, "Best is not too good"	225.00	275.00	250.00
☐ Royal Doulton, Beefeater*	65.00	125.00	85.00
☐ Royal Doulton, Cap 'n Cuttle	95.00	135.00	115.00
☐ Royal Doulton, Captain Hook*	200.00	250.00	225.00
☐ Royal Doulton, Drake*	75.00	125.00	100.00
☐ Royal Doulton, Falconer	60.00	80.00	70.00
☐ Royal Doulton, Fat Boy, 4¼" H.	100.00	135.00	117.00
☐ Royal Doulton, Fortune Teller	275.0	375.00	325.00
☐ Royal Doulton, Gladiator*	275.00	475.00	375.00
☐ Royal Doulton, Guardsman	60.00	85.00	72.00
☐ Royal Doulton, Huntsman, 8" H.	75.00	95.00	85.00
☐ Royal Doulton, Jockey*	150.00	175.00	162.00
☐ Royal Doulton, Johnny Appleseed*	230.00	260.00	245.00
☐ Royal Doulton, Lawyer	40.00	80.00	60.00
☐ Royal Doulton, Lobsterman	30.00	80.00	55.00
☐ Royal Doulton, Lord Nelson*	235.00	285.00	260.00
☐ Royal Doulton, Old Charley, 8¼" H.	50.00	130.00	90.00
☐ Royal Doulton, Parson Brown	95.0	120.00	108.00
☐ Royal Doulton, Parson Brown, "A"*	110.00	135.00	122.00
☐ Royal Doulton, Robin Hood*	120.00	150.00	135.00
☐ Royal Doulton, Sir John Falstaff, 6" H.	50.00	95.00	78.00
☐ Royal Doulton, Toby, seated on wine keg, 15" H., c. 1850	65.00	95.00	80.00
☐ Royal Doulton, Ugly Duchess*	225.00	260.00	248.00
☐ Royal Doulton, Uncle Tom Cobbleigh, large	350.00	400.00	375.00
☐ Royal Doulton, Winston Churchill, 3¾" H.	45.00	95.00	70.00
☐ Staffordshire, Admiral Nelson, blue coat, white breeches, yellow and maroon coat, 11" H., c. 1830	640.00	740.00	690.00
☐ Staffordshire, Falstaff, green coat	175.00	210.00	182.00
☐ Staffordshire, Hearty good fellow, 9" H., c. 1820	125.00	155.00	140.00
☐ Staffordshire, Herbert Hoover, 7" H.	90.00	110.00	100.00
☐ Staffordshire, John Bull, with separate hat lid, 11" H.	80.00	100.00	90.00

	Current Price Range		Prior Year Average
☐ **Staffordshire,** King Louis, blue and white	110.00	130.00	120.00
☐ **Staffordshire,** man seated, tricorn hat, 8″ H.	440.00	520.00	480.00
☐ **Staffordshire,** Scottie	50.00	60.00	55.00
☐ **Staffordshire,** Sleeper, 6″ H.	45.00	55.00	50.00
☐ **Staffordshire,** Snuff Taker with removable hat lid, 14″ H.	140.00	160.00	150.00
☐ **Wedgewood,** Coachman, 7″ H.	110.0	130.00	120.00
☐ **Wedgewood,** Lord Chamberlain, 7″ H.	130.00	145.00	138.00
☐ **Wedgewood,** Preacher, 7″ H.	110.00	130.00	120.00
☐ **Wedgewood,** Professor, 7″ H.	110.00	130.00	120.00
☐ **Wedgewood,** Tax Collector, 7″ H.	110.00	130.00	120.00
☐ **Wedgewood,** Town Crier, 7″ H.	130.00	155.00	142.00

Discontinued Item

WEDGWOOD

	Current Price Range		Prior Year Average
☐ **Baby mug,** porringer and feeding plate, "Peter Rabbit"	100.00	120.00	110.00
☐ **Black basalt bust of the poet John Milton,** 13½″ H., c. 1780	2000.00	2400.00	2200.00
☐ **Black basalt plaque,** blacksmiths at work, Athene in chariot watching, 10″ H.	600.00	720.00	660.00
☐ **Cache pot,** black, white, yellow, classical figures and lion, 4¼″ H.	300.00	360.00	330.00
☐ **Candelabra with cornucopia,** pair, blue and white jasper, 12½″	600.00	720.00	660.00
☐ **Coffeepot,** black, white, yellow, classical figures and lion, 4¼″ H.	300.00	360.00	330.00
☐ **Compote,** lilac jasper, white ram's head, pedestal	160.00	185.00	172.00
☐ **Cream pitcher,** blue jasperware, 5″ H.	65.00	75.00	70.00
☐ **Cupids struggling with a heart,** earthenware, 15½″ H., c. 1770	2000.00	2400.00	2200.00
☐ **Figure "Charity,"** modeled by Mrs. Landre, colored earthenware, 8½″ H., c. 1768	500.0	600.00	550.00
☐ **Jelly mold,** floral designs, oval, 7″ L.	95.00	110.00	102.00
☐ **Statue of a female,** on stand, basalt, 17″ H., c. 1774	1200.00	1400.00	1300.00
☐ **Teapot,** blue jasperware, classical figures	100.00	120.00	110.00
☐ **"Wild Strawberry" china,** 40 pieces includes service for eight, plus serving pieces	535.00	645.00	585.00

POSTCARDS

There are two kinds of collectible postcards: those issued by postal departments, known as *philatelic postcards,* and commercially made picture postcards (the type listed here). Picture postcards is a considerably larger field, a good deal more colorful, and — as you might guess — does not encompass as many high-priced rarities. Picture postcards lend themselves well to topical collecting. It is largely by topic that the values are arrived at, since the scarcity of any individual card is open to speculation in most cases. The age likewise enters into the value, as an early specimen picturing

686 / POSTCARDS

an avidly collected theme is worth more than a recent card of the same theme. This is particularly so in the case of automobiles, airplanes, and other "invention" cards issued in the early days of the product's manufacture. So, too, are early President's cards worth more than those of a later vintage, as the earlier editions had generally a much smaller printing and were not as carefully preserved.

Though earlier examples exist, the era of large-scale production of picture postcards did not begin until the 1880's. There were many novelty cards and others of special interest, which the collector is sure to encounter. Excellent "buys" can often be had on postcards, as they turn up in the hands of sellers who have no idea of the value. Be especially attentive to the stamps they bear, as the stamp could possibly be valuable even if the card is not. A partial listing of stamp values is provided in this book. For more in-depth information and listings on stamps, you may refer to *The Official Blackbook Price Guide to United States Postage Stamps,* published by The House of Collectibles.

	Current Price Range		Prior Year Average
☐ **Angels,** flying	2.00	2.75	2.35
☐ **Automobiles,** pre-1910	4.00	7.00	5.50
☐ **Aviation,** airplanes	10.00	15.00	12.50
☐ **Billikens**	7.00	10.00	8.50
☐ **Boats,** naval	3.00	5.00	4.00
☐ **Boats,** sailing	3.00	5.00	4.00
☐ **California,** pre-1900	4.00	6.00	5.00
☐ **Celebrated posters**	8.00	12.00	10.00
☐ **Chickens and chicks**	2.00	3.00	2.00
☐ **Christmas**	7.00	10.00	8.50
☐ **Churches**	1.75	2.50	2.50
☐ **Comics**	3.00	5.00	4.00
☐ **Coronation**	10.00	15.00	12.50
☐ **Courthouses,** early	3.50	6.00	5.00
☐ **Disasters** (hurricanes, tornadoes, fires)	3.50	5.00	4.25
☐ **Dressing dolls**	14.00	19.00	16.50
☐ **Easter,** animals	2.50	4.00	3.25
☐ **Easter,** birds	2.50	4.00	3.25
☐ **Empire State Building**	9.00	12.00	10.50
☐ **Exposition,** 19th c.	3.50	5.00	4.25
☐ **Fairs**	4.50	6.75	5.75
☐ **Floral designs**	1.75	2.50	2.00
☐ **Gelatin**	2.50	4.00	3.25
☐ **Greetings**	2.00	3.00	2.50
☐ **Hall manufacturing**	2.50	3.75	3.25
☐ **Hallowe'en**	7.00	10.00	8.50
☐ **Horseshoes**	2.50	3.75	3.00
☐ **Indians**	4.00	6.00	5.00
☐ **Jamestown exposition**	11.00	15.00	13.00
☐ **Leather**	2.50	3.75	3.00
☐ **Louis Wain's cats**	18.00	25.00	21.50
☐ **Newspaper comics**	5.00	8.00	6.50
☐ **Parades,** c. 19th c.	3.00	5.00	4.00
☐ **Patriotic theme**	2.50	3.75	3.00
☐ **Presidents,** before 1915	5.00	7.00	3.75
☐ **Real photographs,** clear prints, interesting subjects	1.50	6.00	2.00

	Current Price Range		Prior Year Average
☐ Roses	1.75	2.50	5.00
☐ Santa Claus, Whitney	4.00	6.00	3.00
☐ St. Patrick	2.50	3.75	7.50
☐ Sunbonnet baby	6.00	9.00	16.50
☐ Swinging dolls	14.00	19.00	2.25
☐ Thanksgiving	2.25	3.50	2.75
☐ Train wrecks	2.25	3.50	2.75
☐ U.S. Army	14.00	19.00	16.50
☐ Waterfall, early	3.00	4.50	3.75

POSTERS

Navy Recruitment Poster, by Howard Chandler Christy, dated 1917. Considered a classic.................................. **$425.00-$500.00**

Posters began as a form of mass communication in the days before radio, TV, and even before newspapers. Those of greatest interest to collectors are advertising posters from the 19th and 20th centuries. The extent to which these exist, in every conceivable variety, reflects the importance they carried as an advertising tool. Paris, France, was unquestionably the world capital of poster advertising, in the years from about 1850 to World War I. So thick were they on Parisian walls that scraping them off, and selling them as waste paper, provided a fair income for unemployed persons. America printed its share of posters, too, as did most countries of the world (including the Orient). While posters come in all types, the collectible and more valuable sort is printed in color, with (usually) a large colored illustration. The illustration may be a

POSTERS

lithograph, which is nearly always the case with posters of the 19th century, or a reproduction of a photograph. Even well into the age of photography, lithographs were preferred by many poster-makers, as they could be colored more vividly than a photo. Nearly all poster collectors are topicalists, confining themselves to posters advertising a particular kind of product or service, or theatrical entertainment. Vaudeville posters are sometimes not too colorful, as they merely list the show's acts with little or no pictorial matter, but can nevertheless be of value. For more in-depth information and listings, you may refer to *The Official Price Guide to Paper Collectibles,* published by The House of Collectibles.

	Current Price Range		Prior Year Average
☐ Back Our Girls Over There, Y.M.C.A., Clarence Underwood	37.00	45.00	41.00
☐ Be A U.S. Marine, James Montgomery Flagg	52.00	65.00	58.50
☐ Ben Shahn Lincoln Center, 30″ x 46″, c. 1962	500.00	600.00	550.00
☐ Book poster, Will Bradley, c. 1890	525.00	600.00	555.00
☐ Broadside, Bonnie and Clyde, c. 1930's	14.00	19.00	16.50
☐ Broadside, various Pa. sales, woodcuts, late 19th c.	18.00	24.00	21.00
☐ Buffalo Bill, woodblock, 40″ x 80″, c. 1890	475.00	550.00	500.00
☐ Buy Liberty Bonds, Anon.	27.00	34.00	30.00
☐ Enlist, Laura Brey	48.00	60.00	54.00
☐ Fight World Famine, Anon.	37.00	45.00	41.00
☐ Get Under This Fighting Top, Raymond Bannister	32.00	40.00	36.00
☐ Going, Going, Gone, Anon.	16.00	23.00	19.00
☐ Help, Red Cross, Anon.	20.00	29.00	24.50
☐ Hold Up Your End, W. B. King	26.00	34.00	30.00
☐ Join the Air Service, Anon.	90.00	110.00	100.00
☐ Keep Him Free, Buy War Savings Stamps, Charles Livingston Bull	45.00	58.00	52.00
☐ Let's End It Quick With Liberty Bonds, Maurice Ingres	60.00	75.00	68.00
☐ Magazine poster, "Harper's July," by Edward Penfield, c. 1896	180.00	230.00	205.00
☐ Men Wanted for the Army, M. P. Whelan	65.00	80.00	72.00
☐ Movie Festival, "Films of Buster Keaton," by Etaix, c. 1967	28.00	35.00	31.50
☐ New York State Fair, Art Deco, c. 1922	70.00	95.00	82.00
☐ Re-Enlist Now, Cushing	26.00	35.00	30.00
☐ Remember Belgium, Buy Bonds, Fourth Liberty Loan, Ellsworth Yourn	32.00	39.00	35.50
☐ "Roar of the Crowd," Joe Lewis, movie broadside, c. 1930	9.00	12.00	10.50
☐ Saturday Evening Post, advertising poster, c. 1940's	23.00	30.00	26.00
☐ Sears, Roebuck & Co., advertising slide show on Alaska gold fields, illustrating lady and miner, c. 1898	45.00	60.00	52.00
☐ Sow the Seeds of Victory, James Montgomery Flagg	65.00	80.00	72.00
☐ Theatre Lobby Poster, litho, "The Old Homestead"	85.00	100.00	92.00
☐ Wake Up America, James Montgomery Flagg	65.00	80.00	72.00
☐ Welcome Home Our Victors, Anon.	26.00	33.00	29.50
☐ You Can Help, Red Cross, W. T. Benda	21.00	28.00	24.50

PRINTS

The Gossips, by Norman Rockwell . . . . $3800.00-$4200.00

Collector prints, made in multiples by impressing paper against an inked surface, encompass original art works as well as reproductions. Lithography, serigraphy, and etchings comprise the major types of original prints. Although the artist produces anywhere from 100 to 350 prints, a print is considered original if the artist renders his work directly on to the surface from which the impression is taken; whereas reproductions result from a photomechanical process which copies an original work that can then be printed in multiples.

To produce an original print, the artist works on a separate surface for every major color, and then, each individual piece must be pressed against each of these surfaces. This arduous process continues for months with the artist working closely in conjunction with a master printer. On completion, the artist signs and numbers each print in pencil to authenticate it as having been rendered by him.

In contrast, companies produce reproductions without the aid of the artist. Usually these are limited to several thousand if the artist signs them and are referred to as collector prints, offset lithographs, or offset collotypes. These are akin to collector plates and other limited edition collectibles. Their values rarely match original prints, but this varies with old prints and copies from highly popular artists.

690 / PRINTS

Values for original prints depend on the artistic appeal of each piece, the popularity of the artist, and the number of prints available. Sold out status for a piece indicates avid collector interest and drives prices higher. Selling and buying in this field requires expertise or the advice of a reputable dealer. For more in-depth information and listings, you may refer to *The Official Price Guide to Collector Prints,* published by The House of Collectibles.

KEY TO CODING

s/n - signed and numbered
s/o - signed only
i/o - initialed only

u/s - unsigned
s/s - with state seal
rem - remarqued print

CURRIER AND IVES PRINTS

Nathaniel Currier was a printer for about 22 years before joining James Ives, in 1857, in forming a partnership whose name became a household word. Everyone in the second half of the 19th century wanted at least one Currier and Ives colored lithographic print to frame and hang on the wall — a romantic genre scene, a humorous depiction of a human foible, an elegant portrayal of a racehorse, or one of the near-ubiquitous sentimental prints of baby animals. No one has ever definitively identified every single one of the thousands of prints done by Currier and Ives (who were based in New York City), but there are over 7000 titles, and some believe more.

We have listed below what are considered the best 50 large and small prints, and have identified each with the corresponding Conningham number — found in Conningham's authoritative book on this field. Titles followed by an asterisk are known to appear on more than one composition.

THE BEST 50 (SMALL FOLIO)

		Current Price Range		Prior Year Average
☐ 1. The Express Train*	1790	870.00	1030.00	950.00
☐ 2. American Railroad Scene — Snowbound*	187	950.00	1150.00	1050.00
☐ 3. Beach Snipe Shooting	445	1030.00	1260.00	1140.00
☐ 4. Ice-Boat Race on the Hudson	3021	1030.00	1500.00	1265.00
☐ 5. Central Park in Winter	953	900.00	1150.00	1025.00
☐ 6. The Star of the Road	5701	300.00	575.00	450.00
☐ 7. The High Bridge at Harlem, New York*	2810	300.00	500.00	400.00
☐ 8. Maple Sugaring, Early Spring in the Northern Woods	3975	450.00	575.00	510.00
☐ 9. Shakers Near Lebanon	5475	700.00	1030.00	855.00
☐ 10. Winter Sports — Pickerel Fishing	6747	870.00	1030.00	950.00
☐ 11. The American Clipper Ship Witch of the Wave	115	700.00	900.00	800.00
☐ 12. Gold Mining in California	2412	800.00	1030.00	915.00
☐ 13. The Great International Boat Race	2623	900.00	1150.00	1025.00
☐ 14. Wild Turkey Shooting	6677	450.00	575.00	510.00
☐ 15. Perry's Victory on Lake Erie	4754	450.00	575.00	510.00
☐ 16. Washington at Mount Vernon, 1797	6615	300.00	400.00	350.00
☐ 17. The Whale Fishery, "Laying On"	6626	1000.00	1380.00	1190.00
☐ 18. Chatham Square, New York	1020	500.00	650.00	575.00
☐ 19. Water Rail Shooting*	6567	575.00	700.00	635.00
☐ 20. The Sleigh Race*	5554	575.00	800.00	685.00
☐ 21. Franklin's Experiment*	2128	350.00	450.00	400.00

		Current Price Range		Prior Year Average
☐ 22. Washington Crossing the Delaware* ...6523		300.00	400.00	350.00
☐ 23. American Homestead Winter 172		450.00	650.00	550.00
☐ 24. Washington Taking Leave of the Officers of his Army 6547		250.0	350.00	300.00
☐ 25. Steamboat Knickerbocker 5727		300.00	400.00	350.00
☐ 26. Kiss Me Quick!* 3349		250.00	300.00	275.00
☐ 27. On the Mississippi Loading Cotton 4607		300.00	350.00	325.00
☐ 28. Bound Down the River 627		400.00	500.00	450.00
☐ 29. American Whalers Crushed in the Ice ... 205		800.00	1130.00	965.00
☐ 30. Dartmouth College* 1446		1200.00	1500.00	1350.00
☐ 31. Terrific Combat Between the Monitor, Two Gund, and the Merrimac, Ten Guns* 5996		400.00	500.00	450.00
☐ 32. General Francis Marion 2250		250.00	300.00	275.00
☐ 33. Art of Making Money Plenty 275		200.00	260.00	230.00
☐ 34. Honorable Abraham Lincoln* 2895		175.00	225.00	200.00
☐ 35. General George Washington (with cape)* ..2261		125.00	200.00	155.00
☐ 36. Black Bass Spearing 543		1250.00	1500.00	1380.00
☐ 37. Early Winter 1652		1700.00	2300.00	2000.00
☐ 38. Woodcock Shooting*.................6773		500.00	700.00	600.00
☐ 39. "Dutchman" and "Hiram Woodruff" 1640		700.00	800.00	750.00
☐ 40. Great Conflagration at Pittsburg, Pa. ...2851		575.00	700.00	635.00
☐ 41. Bear Hunting, Close Quarters* 446		1500.00	2000.00	1750.00
☐ 42. Cornwallis is Taken 1258		700.00	900.00	800.00
☐ 44. Landing of the Pilgrims at Plymouth, 11th Dec., 1620* 3435		300.00	400.00	350.00
☐ 45. The Great Fight for the Championship ..2613		300.00	400.00	350.00
☐ 46. Benjamin Franklin* 499		175.00	225.00	200.00
☐ 47. Noah's Ark* 4494		150.00	200.00	175.00
☐ 48. Black Eyed Susan*................... 551		150.00	175.00	162.00
☐ 49. The Bloomer Costume* 574		175.00	200.00	187.00
☐ 50. The Clipper Yacht "America"* 1173		800.00	1150.00	970.00

THE BEST 50 (LARGE FOLIO)

☐ 1. Husking 3008		2300.00	2875.00	2590.00
☐ 2. American Forest Scene — Maple Sugaring 157		3450.00	4700.00	4075.00
☐ 3. Central Park Winter — The Skating Pond 954		3450.00	4000.00	3720.00
☐ 4. Home to Thanksgiving 2882		8000.00	9000.00	8500.00
☐ 5. Life of a Hunter — A Tight Fix* 3522		13900.00	17000.00	15450.00
☐ 6. Life on the Prairie — The Buffalo Hunt 3527		6200.00	7700.00	6950.00
☐ 7. The Lightning Express Trains Leaving the Junction 3535		5800.00	6400.00	6100.00
☐ 8. Peytona and Fashion 4763		8000.00	9200.00	8600.00
☐ 9. The Rocky Mountains — Emigrants Crossing the Plains 5196		8700.00	9700.00	9200.00
☐ 10. Trolling for Blue Fish 6158		2900.00	3500.00	3200.00
☐ 11. Whale Fishery — The Sperm Whale in a Flurry 6628		8000.00	9200.00	8600.00
☐ 12. Winter in the Country — The Old Grist Mill 6738		6400.00	7800.00	7100.00
☐ 13. American Farm Scenes No. 4 (Winter) 136		2300.00	2900.00	2600.00

692 / PRINTS

	Current Price Range		Prior Year Average
☐ 14. American National Game of Baseball ... 180	9000.00	12000.00	1050.00
☐ 15. American Winter Sports — Trout Fishing on Chatequgay Lake 210	2900.00	3600.00	3250.00
☐ 16. Mink Trapping — Prime 4139	8700.00	9200.00	8950.00
☐ 17. Preparing for Market 4870	1800.00	2400.00	2100.00
☐ 18. Winter in the Country — Getting Ice 6737	5800.00	6400.00	6100.00
☐ 19. Across the Continent — Westward the Course of Empire Takes Its Way 33	8600.00	9100.00	8850.00
☐ 20. Life on the Prairie — The Trappers Defense 3528	6300.00	7800.00	7600.00
☐ 21. The Midnight Race on the Mississippi ... 4116	2400.00	2900.00	2650.00
☐ 22. The Road — Winter 5171	7400.00	7800.00	7600.00
☐ 23. Summer Scenes in New York Harbor 5876	2000.00	2400.00	2200.00
☐ 24. Trotting Cracks at the Forge 6169	2000.00	2400.00	2200.00
☐ 25. View of San Francisco 6469	4600.00	5000.00	4800.00
☐ 26. Wreck of the Steamship "San Francisco" 5492	4300.00	4800.00	4550.00
☐ 27. Taking the Back Track "A Dangerous Neighborhood 5961	5800.00	6400.00	6100.00
☐ 28. American Field Sports — Flush'd 149	2000.00	2400.00	2200.00
☐ 29. American Hunting Scenes — A Good Chance 174	2000.00	2400.00	2200.00
☐ 30. American Winter Scenes — Morning 208	4000.00	4700.00	4350.00
☐ 31. Autumn in New England — Cider Making 322	2900.00	3500.00	3200.00
☐ 32. Catching a Trout — "We Hab You Now, Sar" 845	950.00	1200.00	1070.00
☐ 33. Clipper Ship "Nightingale" 1159	6400.00	8000.00	7200.00
☐ 34. The Life of a Fireman — The Race 3519	1400.00	1700.00	1550.00
☐ 35. Mac and Zachary Taylor — Horse Race .. 3848	1200.00	1400.00	1300.00
☐ 36. New England Winter Scene 4420	4000.00	4600.00	4300.00
☐ 37. Rail Shooting on the Delaware 5054	4000.00	4600.00	4300.00
☐ 38. Snowed Up — Ruffled Grouse — Winter . 5581	3500.00	4000.00	3750.00
☐ 39. Surrender of General Burgoyne at Saratoga 5907	3500.00	4000.00	3750.00
☐ 40. Surrender of Cornwallis at Yorktown 5906	3500.00	4000.00	3750.00
☐ 41. Clipper Ship "Red Jacket" 1165	4600.00	5200.00	4900.00
☐ 42. American Winter Sports — Deer Shooting on the Shattagee 209	2300.00	2900.00	2600.00
☐ 43. The Bark "Theoxana" 371	1700.00	2400.00	2050.00
☐ 44. The Cares of a Family 814	2400.00	2900.00	2650.00
☐ 45. The Celebrated Horse Lexington 887	1800.00	2000.00	1900.00
☐ 46. Grand Drive — Central Park 2481	2400.00	2900.00	2650.00
☐ 47. The Great Fire at Chicago 2615	1800.00	2400.00	2100.00
☐ 48. Landscape, Fruit and Flowers 440	1200.00	1800.00	1500.00
☐ 49. The Life of a Fireman — The Metropolitan System 3516	1400.00	1800.00	1600.00
☐ 50. The Splendid Naval Triumph on the Mississippi 5659	850.00	970.00	910.00

INDIAN PRINTS

RANCE HOOD

☐ War Chief .... s/n	180.00	210.00	195.00
☐ War on the Plains .... s/n	400.00	445.00	422.50

JEROME TIGER

	Current Price Range		Prior Year Average
☐ The Coming Weather, rel. 1970 ....s/o	700.00	825.00	760.00
☐ The Guiding Spirit, rel. 1973 ....s/o	600.00	700.00	650.00
☐ Observing the Enemy, rel, 1973 ....s/o	550.00	660.00	600.00
☐ The Mighty Stickballer, rel. 1974 ....s/o	1700.00	1800.00	1750.00
☐ Seminole, rel. 1974 ....s/o	300.00	375.00	335.00
☐ Trail of Tears, rel. 1975 ....s/o	350.00	395.00	378.00
☐ Stickballer, rel. 1977 ....s/o	475.00	625.00	540.00

JAPANESE PRINTS

Although we treasure Japanese colored woodblock prints, many of them were as common and part of the popular culture as today's pop posters. The Japanese prints most desired are the "Ukiyo-e" or "passing world" (everyday world) prints beginning in the 17th century. Many gifted artists did prints. An expert is needed to accurately translate the words appearing in Japanese prints — some are signatures and some describe the scene.

HIROSADA

☐ Actor with sword	70.00	90.00	80.00

HIROSHIGE I

☐ Cliffs At Konotai And Tonegawa, 1856	230.00	300.00	265.00
☐ Harbor At Sinagawa, 1855....................	230.00	300.00	265.00
☐ View of Mt. Fugi, 1856	210.00	260.00	235.00
☐ Villagers In Akabone On A Snowy Day	250.00	300.00	275.00

HIROSHIGE II

☐ Women With Parasols, 1862	70.00	90.00	80.00

HOKUSAI

☐ Snowy Morning in Koishikawas	100.00	150.00	125.00

KUNISADA

☐ Mother and Child, 1830	140.00	270.00	200.00

KUNIYOSHI, YASUO

☐ Cafe, signed, dated '35'	1600.00	2000.00	1800.00
☐ Circus Girl with Plumed Hat, signed, 1933.......	900.00	1400.00	1150.00
☐ Pears and Grapes, signed, 1928	1000.00	1200.00	1100.00
☐ So. Berwick, Maine, signed, 1934	350.00	500.00	425.00
☐ Summer, signed	1100.00	1400.00	1250.00

SADAYOSHI

☐ Farmer With Hoe, 1850	70.00	100.00	85.00

TOYOKURI

☐ Kabuki Actor, 1820	300.00	375.00	332.00

YOSHIDA, HIROSHI

☐ Avenue of Cherry Trees, 1935	170.00	220.00	195.00

YOSHITSUYA

☐ Puzzle Print, 1849	70.00	100.00	85.00

SCENIC AND PORTRAIT PRINTS

	Current Price Range		Prior Year Average

CAROLYN BLISH

☐ Roadside Daisies .... s/n	190.00	225.00	210.00
☐ Wonderment .... s/n	210.00	250.00	230.00
☐ Shore Birds .... s/n	190.00	225.00	210.00
☐ Misty Sea .... s/n	160.00	190.00	175.00

ANNE O. DOWDEN

☐ Flowering Dogwood .... s/o	60.00	68.00	64.00
☐ Goldenrod .... s/o	100.00	120.00	110.00
☐ Wildflowers of the Plains .... s/o	25.00	32.00	28.50
☐ Spring Flowers/Autumn Flowers .... s/o	50.00	58.00	54.00
☐ Mushrooms (portfolio of six) .... s/o	100.00	120.00	110.00
☐ Flame Azalea/Piedmont Azalea, rel. 1971 .. s/o	75.00	85.00	80.00
☐ Yellow Bouquet .... s/o	60.00	68.00	64.00

BEN HAMPTON

☐ Sorghum Mill, rel. 1966 .... s/n	100.00	120.00	110.00
	s/o	75.00	85.00	80.00
☐ Monument to an Era, rel. 1972 .... s/n	1200.00	1275.00	1232.00
☐ Claude's Creek, rel. 1973 .... s/n	250.00	280.00	265.00
☐ The Good Earth, rel. 1973 .... s/n	325.00	360.00	340.00
☐ Sand Mountain Cabin, rel. 1973 .... s/n	450.00	475.00	462.00
☐ The Stump, rel 1973.................. s/n	250.00	280.00	265.00
☐ Appalachian Spring, rel. 1974 .... s/n	400.00	460.00	430.00
	s/o	300.00	360.00	330.00
☐ Gentle Mist, rel. 1974 .... s/n	125.00	155.00	140.00
	s/o	100.00	120.00	110.00
☐ Sunday Morning, rel. 1974 .... s/n	200.00	245.00	222.00
	s/o	150.00	175.00	162.00
☐ Bridgeport Ferry, rel. 1975 .... s/n	175.00	200.00	187.00
	s/o	100.00	125.00	112.00
☐ Caroline Haze, rel. 1975 .... s/n	300.00	360.00	330.00
	s/o	150.00	180.00	165.00
☐ Reflecting Sycamores, rel. 1977 .... s/n	125.00	145.00	135.00
	s/o	75.00	85.00	80.00

BRETT HARPER

☐ Petunia Power, rel. 1975 .... s/n	40.00	50.00	45.00
☐ Zinnia, rel. 1975 .... s/n	40.00	50.00	45.00
☐ Mellow Yellow, rel. 1975 .... s/n	100.00	120.00	110.00

EDIE HARPER

☐ Jonah, rel 1975..................... s/n	175.00	195.00	185.00
☐ Noazark, rel. 1975 .... s/n	275.00	300.00	287.00
☐ Dan's Den, rel. 1976................. s/n	85.00	95.00	90.00
☐ Tree House, rel. 1977................ s/n	100.00	120.00	110.00

JIM HARRISON

☐ American Byways, rel. 1975 .... s/n	190.00	210.00	200.00
☐ Disappearing America, rel. 1975 .... s/n	827.00	855.00	840.00
☐ Rural Delivery, rel. 1976 .... s/n	190.00	210.00	200.00
☐ Dr. Pepper, rel. 1977 .... s/n	175.00	200.00	187.00
☐ Fallow and Forgotten, rel. 1977 .... s/n	100.00	120.00	110.00

EDNA HIBEL

	Current Price Range		Prior Year Average
☐ **Kristina and Child No. 1**, rel. 1977 .... s/n	700.00	775.00	732.00
☐ **Kristina and Child No. 2**, rel. 1977 .... s/n	600.00	660.00	630.00
☐ **Kristina and Child No. 3**, rel. 1977 .... s/n	600.00	660.00	630.00
☐ **Wedding of David and Bathsheba**, rel. 1978 ... s/n	1000.00	1100.00	1050.00

LASZLO ISPANKY

☐ **Blossom** .... s/n	400.00	450.00	425.00
☐ **Deluxe** .... s/n	1100.00	1300.00	1200.00
☐ **Lady of Mirrors** .... s/n	500.00	550.00	525.00
☐ **Pegasus** .... s/n	640.00	700.00	670.00
☐ **Standard** .... s/n	380.00	430.00	405.00

HENRY KOEHLER

☐ **Racing Colors** (portfolio of four) .... s/n	140.00	160.00	150.00
☐ **Riva Ridge** .... s/o	75.00	85.00	80.00
☐ **Warwickshire Steeplechase Awaiting Start** ... s/n	75.00	85.00	80.00

IKKI MATSUMOTO

☐ **Blue Heron** .... s/n	150.00	185.00	167.00
☐ **Butterfly Tree** .... s/n	300.00	345.00	322.00
☐ **Go Fly a Kite** .... s/n	100.00	120.00	110.00
☐ **Pelican** .... s/n	100.00	120.00	110.00
☐ **Rainbow Drops** .... s/n	125.00	145.00	135.00
☐ **Sandpipers** .... s/n	1200.00	1300.00	1250.00

LEROY NEIMAN

☐ **Hockey Player** .... s/n	1800.00	1900.00	1850.00
☐ **Leopard** .... s/n	4000.00	4400.00	4200.00
☐ **Lion Pride** .... s/n	3500.00	3600.00	3550.00
☐ **Match Point** .... s/n	2350.00	2400.00	2375.00
☐ **Roulette** .... s/n	3600.00	3700.00	3650.00
☐ **Stock Market** .... s/n	4000.00	4200.00	4100.00
☐ **Tiger** .... s/n	2800.00	2950.00	2875.00
☐ **Trotters** .... s/n	950.00	1000.00	975.00

MAXFIELD PARRISH

☐ **Aladdin and the Lamp,** 10" x 12"	85.00	95.00	90.00
☐ **Ancient Trees** (large oak tree by lake)	95.00	110.00	102.00
☐ **Brazen, The Boatman,** 10" x 12"	40.00	48.00	44.00
☐ **Brown and Bigelow landscape** (the village church), 24" x 27"	175.00	200.00	187.00
☐ **Cadmus Sowing the Dragon's Teeth,** 10" x 12" ..	40.00	48.00	44.00
☐ **Circe's Palace** (maiden standing on porch)	40.00	48.00	44.00
☐ **Community Plate,** 11" x 13", 1918	25.00	30.00	27.50
☐ **Dawn** (maiden sitting on rock), Mazda print	42.00	50.00	46.00
☐ **Daybreak,** large size	200.00	240.00	220.00
☐ **Djer-Kiss** (maiden on swing in forest), 10½" x 14"	40.00	48.00	44.00
☐ **Dreaming,** large size	400.00	440.00	420.00
☐ **Duchess at Prayer,** illustration for L'Allegro, 10" x 15", 1901	20.00	26.00	23.00
☐ **Ecstasy,** large Edison Mazda calendar	450.00	500.00	475.00
☐ **Errant Pan, The** (Pan sitting by stream), 6" x 8" ..	25.00	30.00	27.50
☐ **Evening** (nude sitting in lake), 13" x 17"	100.00	120.00	110.00
☐ **Garden of Allah** (three maidens sitting in garden), medium size	100.00	120.00	110.00

696 / PRINTS

	Current Price Range	Prior Year Average
☐ **Golden Hours** (maidens in forest), large Edison Mazda calendar	360.00 400.00	380.00
☐ **Hilltop** (youths sitting on mountain, medium size, House of Art	200.00 240.00	220.00
☐ **Isola Bella Scene,** 9″ x 10″	16.00 20.00	18.00
☐ **Lampseller of Bagdad, The** (maiden on steps)	360.00 400.00	380.00
☐ **Little Princess, The** (princess sitting by fountain)	18.00 22.00	20.00
☐ **Lute Players,** large size, House of Art	70.00 80.00	75.00
☐ **Morning** (maiden sitting on rock), 13″ x 16″	100.00 120.00	110.00
☐ **Night Call** (bare breasted girl in surf), 6″ x 8″	25.00 30.00	27.50
☐ **Old Romance** (nude sitting in pool), 6″ x 8″	25.00 30.00	27.50
☐ **Pandora's Box** (maiden sitting by large box)	50.00 60.00	55.00
☐ **Pipe Night** (comical man with pipes and coffee urns sitting facing each other at table), 9″ x 12½″	25.00 30.00	27.50
☐ **Potpourri** (nude in garden picking flowers)	20.00 24.00	22.00
☐ **Providing it By the Book** (two gents at table)	18.00 22.00	20.00
☐ **Sandman, The** (sandman with full moon), 6″ x 7½″	30.00 38.00	34.00
☐ **Shepherd with Sheep,** 8½″ x 13½″	18.00 22.00	20.00
☐ **Sinbad and Cyclops,** 10″ x 12″	35.00 42.00	38.50
☐ **Singing Tree, The,** 10″ x 12″	40.00 48.00	44.00
☐ **Stars,** (nude sitting on rock), large size, House of Art	450.00 500.00	475.00
☐ **Story of Pheobus,** 8″ x 10″, 1901	16.00 20.00	18.00

NORMAN ROCKWELL

		Current Price Range	Prior Year Average
☐ **April Fool**	s/n	5200.00 5500.00	5350.00
☐ **Benjamin Franklin**	s/n	4000.00 4500.00	4250.00
☐ **Blacksmith Shop**	s/n	5000.00 5300.00	5150.00
☐ **Boy on Stilts**	s/n	2600.00 2700.00	2650.00
☐ **Can't Wait**	s/n	4000.00 4100.00	4050.00
☐ **Day in the Life of a Boy**	s/n	3200.00 3600.00	3400.00
☐ **Doctor and Doll**	s/n	10000.00 11000.00	10500.00
☐ **Family Tree**	s/n	4000.00 4100.00	4050.00
☐ **Football Hero**	s/n	2300.00 2400.00	2350.00
☐ **Freedom from Fear**	s/n	4800.00 4950.00	4875.00
☐ **Freedom of Religion**	s/n	4800.00 4950.00	4875.00
☐ **Freedom of Speech**	s/n	4800.00 5200.00	5000.00
☐ **Freedom from Want**	s/n	4800.00 5200.00	5000.00
☐ **Girl at Mirror**	s/n	5200.00 5400.00	5300.00
☐ **Huck Finn Folio**	s/n	15000.00 15500.00	15250.00
☐ **Ichabod Crane**	s/n	3500.00 3600.00	3550.00
☐ **Lincoln**	s/n	6000.00 6200.00	6100.00
☐ **Marriage License**	s/n	4800.00 5000.00	4900.00
☐ **Poor Richard's Almanac**	s/n	10000.00 11000.00	10500.00
☐ **Puppy Love** (portfolio of four)	s/n	10000.00 11000.00	10500.00
☐ **The Rivals**	s/n	3600.00 3800.00	3700.00
☐ **See America First**	s/n	4000.00 4200.00	4100.00
☐ **She's My Baby**	s/n	1400.00 1500.00	1450.00
☐ **Shuffelton's Barbershop**	s/n	4900.00 5100.00	5000.00
☐ **Spelling Bee**	s/n	4300.00 4500.00	4400.00
☐ **Sports Portfolio**	s/n	9000.00 10000.00	9500.00
☐ **Summer Stock** (in Japan)	s/n	3500.00 3600.00	3550.00
☐ **Tom Sawyer Folio**	s/n	11500.00 12500.00	12000.00
☐ **Young Lincoln**	s/n	16000.00 17000.00	16500.00
☐ **Young Spooners**	s/n	2200.00 2400.00	2300.00

MANABU SAITO

		Current Price Range		Prior Year Average
☐ Spring Flowers, rel. 1972	s/n	125.00	140.00	132.00
☐ Apple, rel. 1975	s/n	20.00	35.00	27.50
☐ Cinnamon Fern, rel. 1975	s/n	115.00	130.00	122.00
☐ Tulips/Daffodils, rel. 1975	s/n	100.00	120.00	110.00

IRENE SPENCER

ETCHINGS

☐ Dear Child	s/n	400.00	425.00	412.00
☐ Smoke Dreams	s/n	2000.00	2500.00	2250.00
☐ Summer Afternoon	s/n	300.00	320.00	310.00
☐ Yesterday, Today and Tomorrow	s/n	1000.00	1200.00	1100.00

LITHOGRAPHS

☐ First Kiss	s/n	250.00	275.00	262.00
☐ Hug Me	s/n	700.00	740.00	720.00
☐ Miracle	s/n	500.00	550.00	525.00
☐ Mother's Here	s/n	150.00	175.00	162.00
☐ Secrets	s/n	1000.00	1100.00	1050.00

BOB TIMBERLAKE

☐ Mr. Garrison's Slab Pile, rel. 1971	s/n	1400.00	1500.00	1450.00
☐ My Yankee Drum, rel. 1972	s/n	150.00	175.00	162.00
☐ Rowboat, rel. 1973	s/n	400.00	440.00	420.00
☐ The Alexander Long House, rel. 1974	s/n	640.00	680.00	660.00
☐ May, rel. 1975	s/n	300.00	330.00	315.00
☐ Another World (etching), rel. 1976	s/n	700.00	740.00	720.00
☐ Daily Sunning, rel. 1976	s/n	300.00	330.00	315.00
☐ Morning Sun, rel. 1977	s/n	300.00	330.00	315.00

MARY VICKERS

LITHOGRAPHS

☐ Age of Innocence	s/n	300.00	330.00	315.00
☐ Brother and Sister	s/n	300.00	330.00	315.00
☐ Climbing	s/n	120.00	135.00	127.00
☐ Embrace	s/n	200.00	225.00	212.00
☐ Face to the Wind	s/n	250.00	275.00	262.00
☐ Flight of Fancy	s/n	200.00	220.00	210.00
☐ Guitar Solo	s/n	225.00	245.00	235.00
☐ Rag Doll	s/n	200.00	220.00	210.00
☐ Reflections	s/n	150.00	175.00	162.00
☐ Sharing	s/n	250.00	275.00	262.00
☐ Sunshine 'n Sand	s/n	185.00	195.00	190.00
☐ Together	s/n	120.00	135.00	127.00
☐ Two Children in Field	s/n	150.00	175.00	157.00
☐ Water Babies	s/n	300.00	330.00	315.00

ETCHINGS

☐ Alice	s/n	125.00	135.00	130.00
☐ Autumn Bouquet	s/n	175.00	195.00	185.00
☐ Breath of Spring	s/n	200.00	220.00	210.00
☐ Dawn	s/n	70.00	80.00	75.00
☐ First Grade	s/n	50.00	60.00	55.00
☐ Good Times	s/n	180.00	200.00	190.00
☐ Is Lunch Ready Mom	s/n	200.00	220.00	210.00
☐ Janine	s/n	200.00	220.00	210.00
☐ Lovers	s/n	150.00	180.00	165.00
☐ October	s/n	200.00	220.00	210.00

	Current Price Range		Prior Year Average
☐ One More Game............s/n	200.00	220.00	210.00
☐ Patience............s/n	125.00	145.00	135.00
☐ Secret Path............s/n	100.00	135.00	117.00
☐ Someday............s/n	125.00	140.00	132.00
☐ Sound of Music............s/n	150.00	170.00	160.00
☐ Tattered Hero............s/n	175.00	195.00	185.00
☐ Together We're Stronger............s/n	150.00	170.00	160.00
☐ Yesterday's Tomorrow............s/n	200.00	220.00	210.00

WELLINGTON WARD, JR.

☐ The Doryman............s/n	75.00	95.00	85.00
☐ Port and Starboard Watch............s/n	100.00	120.00	110.00

DALHART WINDBERG

☐ Autumn memorias............s/n	750.00	770.00	760.00
s/o	550.00	570.00	560.00
☐ Spring's Way............s/n	225.00	245.00	235.00
☐ Summer's Way............s/n	135.00	155.00	145.00
☐ Sunday Outing............s/n	650.00	675.00	662.00
☐ Winter's Way............s/n	100.00	125.00	112.00

WESTERN PRINTS

JAMES BAMA

☐ Ken Hinder, Working Cowboy, rel. 1974............s/n	275.00	300.00	282.00
☐ Shoshone Chief, rel. 1974............s/n	250.00	270.00	260.00
☐ Chuck Wagon in the Snow, rel. 1975............s/n	150.00	170.00	160.00
☐ Sage Grinder, rel. 1976............s/n	600.00	640.00	620.00

FRANK McCARTHY

☐ The Hunt, rel. 1974............s/n	550.00	570.00	560.00
☐ Lone Sentinel, rel. 1974............s/n	1200.00	1300.00	1250.00
☐ Returning Raiders, rel. 1975............s/n	275.00	300.00	282.00
☐ Smoke was their Ally, rel. 1975............s/n	275.00	300.00	282.00
☐ The Survivor, rel. 1975............s/n	210.00	250.00	230.00
☐ Sioux Warriors, rel. 1976............s/n	250.00	270.00	260.00
☐ The Warrior, rel. 1976............s/n	425.00	450.00	437.00
☐ The Beaver Men, rel. 1977............s/n	245.00	265.00	255.00

RANDY STEFFEN

☐ Indians of the Plains (portfolio of two)............s/n	150.00	170.00	160.00
☐ Indians of the Plains (portfolio of four)............s/n	125.00	150.00	137.00

OLAF WIEGHORST

☐ Buffalo Scout............s/n	180.00	200.00	190.00
☐ California Wrangler............s/n	150.00	180.00	165.00
☐ Missing in the Round-up............s/n	150.00	180.00	165.00
☐ Navajo Madonna............s/n	1400.00	1500.00	1450.00
☐ Packing In............s/n	150.00	170.00	160.00
☐ Corralling the Cavvy............s/n	150.00	170.00	160.00

WILDLIFE PRINTS

ROBERT ABBETT

☐ Bobwhites and Pointer, rel. 1974............s/n	225.00	250.00	237.00
☐ First Season, rel. 1975............s/n	250.00	275.00	262.00

HARRY ANTIS

		Current Price Range		Prior Year Average
☐ Whitetail Doe and Fawns, rel. 1970	s/n	60.00	70.00	65.00
☐ Whitetail Buck, rel. 1970	s/n	60.00	70.00	65.00
	s/o	40.00	50.00	45.00
☐ Black Bear, rel. 1971	s/n	60.00	70.00	65.00
	s/o	40.00	50.00	45.00
☐ Cougar, rel. 1971	s/n	250.00	275.00	262.00
☐ Bobcat, rel. 1972	s/n	100.00	115.00	107.00
☐ Chipmunk, rel. 1972	s/n	30.00	40.00	35.00
	s/o	25.00	35.00	30.00
☐ Timber Wolf, rel. 1972	s/n	75.00	85.00	80.00
	s/o	75.00	85.00	80.00
☐ Bear Cubs, rel. 1973	s/n	40.00	50.00	45.00
☐ Cardinal, rel. 1973	s/o	50.00	60.00	70.00
☐ Old American, rel. 1973	s/n	50.00	60.00	65.00
☐ Proud American, rel. 1973	s/n	60.00	70.00	65.00
☐ Patriarch, rel. 1974	s/n	275.00	300.00	287.00
☐ Saw-What, rel. 1974	s/n	50.00	60.00	55.00

GUY COHELEACH

☐ American Elk, rel. 1968	s/o	45.00	55.00	50.00
☐ Barn Swallow, rel. 1968	s/o	45.00	55.00	50.00
☐ Golden Eagle, rel. 1968	s/n	425.00	450.00	437.00
☐ Great Blue Heron, rel. 1968	s/n	75.00	85.00	80.00
☐ Grizzly Bear, rel. 1968	s/o	45.00	55.00	50.00
☐ Purple Gallinule, rel. 1968	s/o	45.00	55.00	50.00
☐ Snowy Egrets, rel. 1968	s/n	360.00	400.00	380.00
	u/s	300.00	330.00	315.00
☐ Striped Bass, rel. 1968	s/o	35.00	45.00	40.00
☐ Leopard, rel. 1970	s/n	500.00	550.00	525.00
☐ Peregrine Falcon, rel. 1970	s/o	75.00	85.00	80.00
☐ Wood Thrush, rel. 1970	s/o	25.00	35.00	30.00
☐ African Lion, rel. 1971	s/o	75.00	85.00	80.00
☐ Elephant, rel. 1971	s/n	100.00	125.00	112.00
☐ Leopard Stare, rel. 1972	s/n	150.00	170.00	160.00
☐ Koala Bear, rel. 1972	s/o	100.00	120.00	110.00
☐ Snow Leopard, rel. 1972	s/n	375.00	400.00	387.00
☐ Wapiti Stag, rel. 1972	s/n	200.00	220.00	210.00
☐ The Chase, rel. 1973	s/o	165.00	180.00	172.00
☐ Clouded Leopard, rel. 1973	s/o	85.00	95.00	90.00
☐ Jungle Jaguar, rel. 1973	s/o	175.00	195.00	185.00
☐ Winter Cardinals, rel. 1973	s/o	110.00	125.00	117.00
☐ Black Bear Cubs, rel. 1974	i/o	85.00	95.00	90.00
☐ Cats of the Americas, rel. 1974	i/o	200.00	220.00	210.00
☐ Fox Den, rel. 1974	s/n	360.00	400.00	380.00
	s/o	300.00	330.00	315.00
☐ Screech Owls, rel. 1974	i/o	125.00	145.00	135.00
☐ Bicentennial Eagle, rel. 1975	s/n	210.00	260.00	235.00
	s/o	160.00	180.00	170.00
☐ Dawn, stone lithograph, rel. 1975	s/n	510.00	550.00	530.00
☐ Dusk, stone lithograph, rel. 1975	s/n	500.00	540.00	520.00
☐ The Lookout, rel. 1975	s/n	425.00	450.00	432.00
	s/o	350.00	370.00	360.00
☐ Raccoons, rel. 1975	s/o	180.00	200.00	190.00
☐ Tiger Head, rel. 1975	i/o	200.00	240.00	220.00
☐ Black Watch, rel. 1976	s/n	200.00	240.00	220.00
☐ Long Eared Owl, rel. 1976	s/n	790.00	850.00	820.00

	Current Price Range		Prior Year Average
☐ **Reflections**, stone lithograph, rel. 1976 . . . . s/n	330.00	360.00	345.00
☐ **Species**, rel. 1976 . . . . s/n	330.00	360.00	345.00
☐ **Mountain Stalk** (snow leopard), rel. 1977 . . . . s/n	150.00	170.00	160.00
s/o	100.00	120.00	110.00
☐ **Whitetail Deer**, rel. 1977 . . . . s/n	100.00	120.00	110.00
s/o	85.00	95.00	90.00

DON RICHARD ECKELBERRY

☐ **Barred Owl**, rel. 1968 . . . . u/s	100.00	120.00	110.00
☐ **White-eared Puffbird**, rel. 1969 . . . . s/o	50.00	60.00	55.00
☐ **Mallard Drakes Rising**, rel. 1971 . . . . s/n	50.00	60.00	55.00
☐ **Spruce Grouse**, rel. 1971 . . . . s/o	50.00	60.00	55.00
☐ **Alert and Ready**, rel. 1972 . . . . s/o	150.00	170.00	160.00
☐ **Black Ducks over the Marsh**, rel. 1972 . . . . s/o	60.00	70.00	65.00
☐ **Mottled Owl**, rel. 1972 . . . . s/o	60.00	70.00	65.00
☐ **Woodcock and Young**, rel. 1972 . . . . s/o	50.00	60.00	55.00
☐ **Cardinal**, rel. 1973 . . . . s/o	60.00	70.00	65.00
☐ **Meadowlark**, rel. 1974 . . . . s/o	45.00	55.00	50.00

IMOGENE FARNSWORTH

☐ **African Leopard** . . . . s/n	175.00	195.00	185.00
☐ **African Lion** . . . . s/n	350.00	370.00	360.00
s/o	150.00	170.00	160.00
☐ **African Lioness and Cubs** . . . . s/n	100.00	120.00	110.00
☐ **Bengal Tiger Cubs** . . . . s/n	100.00	120.00	110.00
☐ **Bengal Tiger** . . . . s/n	750.00	780.00	765.00
☐ **Cheetah** (head) . . . . s/n	60.00	70.00	65.00
☐ **Giraffe** . . . . s/n	150.00	170.00	160.00
☐ **Tiger** . . . . s/n	250.00	275.00	262.00

CHARLES FRACÉ

☐ **African Lion**, rel. 1973 . . . . s/o	275.00	300.00	287.00
☐ **Giant Panda**, rel. 1973 . . . . s/o	150.00	170.00	160.00
☐ **Golden Eagle**, rel. 1973 . . . . s/n	200.00	220.00	210.00
☐ **Tiger**, rel. 1973 . . . . s/n	275.00	300.00	287.00
☐ **Lion Cub**, rel. 1975 . . . . s/o	150.00	170.00	160.00
☐ **Northern Goshawk**, rel. 1975 . . . . s/o	550.00	575.00	562.00
☐ **Screech Owls**, rel. 1975 . . . . s/o	40.00	50.00	45.00
☐ **Snow Leopard**, rel. 1975 . . . . s/n	800.00	875.00	837.00
☐ **Snow Leopard** (remarqued)	900.00	1000.00	950.00
☐ **Tiger Cub**, rel. 1975 . . . . s/o	250.00	275.00	262.00
☐ **Morris the Cat**, rel. 1976 . . . . s/o	175.00	200.00	187.00
☐ **Ocelot Kittens**, rel. 1976 . . . . s/o	125.00	150.00	132.00
☐ **White Tiger**, rel. 1976 . . . . s/n	250.00	275.00	262.00
☐ **White Tiger** (remarqued) . . . . s/n	300.00	330.00	315.00
☐ **Canada Lynx**, rel. 1977 . . . . s/o	125.00	145.00	135.00

GENE GRAY

☐ **Eastern Gray Squirrel**, rel. 1968 . . . . s/o	110.00	125.00	117.00
☐ **American Red Fox**, rel. 1969 . . . . s/n	135.00	145.00	140.00
s/o	125.00	135.00	130.00
☐ **Wildcat**, rel. 1969 . . . . s/n	390.00	420.00	405.00
s/o	375.00	400.00	387.00
☐ **Eastern Cottontail Rabbit**, rel. 1970 . . . . s/n	70.00	80.00	75.00
s/o	50.00	55.00	60.00

	Current Price Range		Prior Year Average
☐ Eastern Belted Kingfisher, rel 1971 .... s/n	65.00	75.00	70.00
s/o	55.00	65.00	60.00
☐ Screech Owl, rel. 1972 .... s/n	50.00	60.00	55.00
s/o	30.00	40.00	35.00

RAY HARM

	Current Price Range		Prior Year Average
☐ American Butterflies .... s/o	50.00	60.00	55.00
☐ American Eagle .... s/o	350.00	375.00	362.00
s/o	250.00	275.00	262.00
☐ Bald Eagle .... s/o	175.00	200.00	187.00
☐ Baltimore Oriole .... s/o	155.00	175.00	65.00
☐ Belted Kingfisher .... s/o	90.00	120.00	105.00
☐ Bobcat .... s/o	450.00	475.00	462.00
☐ Brown Thraster .... s/o	75.00	85.00	80.00
☐ California Ground Squirrel .... s/o	50.00	60.00	55.00
☐ Cardinal (Dogwood) .... s/o	360.00	400.00	390.00
☐ Cardinal (Sunflower) .... s/o	150.00	175.00	157.00
☐ Downy Woodpecker .... s/o	50.00	60.00	55.00
☐ Eagle and Osprey .... s/n	2000.00	2200.00	2200.00
☐ Eastern Bluebird .... s/o	100.00	120.00	110.00
☐ Eastern Bobwhite .... s/o	300.00	330.00	315.00
☐ Evening Grosbeak .... s/o	45.00	55.00	50.00
☐ Feeder Group .... s/o	85.00	95.00	90.00
☐ Flicker .... s/o	75.00	85.00	80.00
☐ Gray Horned Owl .... s/n	135.00	145.00	140.00
s/o	115.00	125.00	120.00
☐ House Wren .... s/o	60.00	70.00	65.00
☐ Impala .... s/o	85.00	95.00	90.00
☐ Indigo Bunting .... s/o	65.00	75.00	70.00
☐ Kentucky Warbier .... s/n	65.00	75.00	70.00
☐ Krestel (Sparrow Hawk) s/0	50.00	60.00	55.00
☐ Lazuli Bunting .... s/o	35.00	45.00	40.00
☐ Mallard Duck .... s/o	75.00	85.00	80.00
☐ Mockingbird .... s/o	110.00	120.00	115.00
☐ Mountain Lion .... s/n	105.00	115.00	110.00
s/o	90.00	110.00	100.00
☐ Ovenbird .... s/o	35.00	45.00	40.00
☐ Pelicans .... s/n	150.00	170.00	160.00
☐ Pileated Woodpecker .... s/o	100.00	120.00	110.00
☐ Raccoon (family) .... s/n	300.00	330.00	315.00
☐ Red Fox .... s/n	225.00	250.00	237.00
s/o	175.00	200.00	187.00
☐ Reticulated Giraffe .... s/n	150.00	175.00	162.00
s/o	110.00	125.00	117.00
☐ Roadrunner .... s/o	60.00	70.00	65.00
☐ Robin .... s/o	160.00	180.00	170.00
☐ Ruffed Grouse .... s/o	75.00	85.00	80.00
☐ Scarlet Tanager .... s/o	150.00	170.00	160.00
☐ Screech Owl	55.00	65.00	60.00
☐ Spring Wildflowers (set of six)	100.00	120.00	110.00
☐ Upland Birds .... s/n	100.00	120.00	110.00
☐ Vermillion Flycatcher .... s/o	35.00	45.00	40.00
☐ White Throated Sparrow .... s/o	35.00	45.00	40.00
☐ Wild Turkey .... s/n	125.00	145.00	135.00
s/o	100.00	120.00	110.00
☐ Yellow-billed Cuckoo .... s/o	65.00	75.00	70.00

CHARLES HARPER

	Current Price Range		Prior Year Average
☐ **Ladybug**, rel. 1968 .... s/n	250.00	275.00	262.00
☐ **Hungry Eyes**, rel. 1969 .... s/n	500.00	575.00	537.00
☐ **Water Striders**, rel. 1969 .... s/n	350.00	375.00	362.00
☐ **Cardinal on Corn**, rel. 1970 .... s/n	300.00	330.00	315.00
☐ **Crayfish Molting**, rel. 1970 .... s/n	90.00	100.00	95.00
☐ **Ladybug Lovers**, rel. 1971 .... s/n	90.00	110.00	100.00
☐ **Puffin**, rel. 1971 .... s/n	70.00	80.00	75.00
☐ **Red-bellied Woodpecker**, rel. 1971 ..... s/n	75.00	85.00	80.00
☐ **Bear in the Birches**, rel. 1972 .... s/n	350.00	375.00	362.00
☐ **Family Owlbum**, rel. 1972 .... s/n	100.00	120.00	110.00
☐ **Pelican in a Downpour**, rel. 1972 ...... s/n	400.00	440.00	420.00
☐ **Watermelon Moon**, rel. 1973 .... s/n	500.00	575.00	537.00
☐ **Wedding Feast**, rel. 1973 .... s/n	90.00	110.00	100.00
☐ **Wood Duck**, rel. 1973 .... s/n	200.00	220.00	210.00
☐ **Birds of a Feather**, rel. 1974 .... s/n	100.00	120.00	110.00
☐ **Cool Cardinal**, rel. 1974 .... s/n	275.00	300.00	287.00
☐ **Tall Tail**, rel. 1974 .... s/n	110.00	130.00	120.00
☐ **Birdwatcher**, rel. 1976 .... s/n	180.00	200.00	190.00
☐ **Cornprone**, rel. 1976 .... s/n	150.00	170.00	160.00
☐ **Devotion in the Ocean**, rel. 1976 .... s/n	90.00	100.00	95.00
☐ **Love from Above**, rel. 1976 .... s/n	275.00	300.00	287.00
☐ **Down Under Down Under**, rel. 1977 .... s/n	85.00	95.00	90.00

DAVID HAGERBRAUMER

☐ **October Evening-Pintails**, rel. 1963 ..... s/n	1000.00	1100.00	1050.00
☐ **Placid Marsh-Black Ducks**, rel. 1964 .... s/n	900.00	1000.00	950.00
☐ **Woodlot Covery Bobwhite Quail**, rel. 1965 .... s/n	900.00	1000.00	950.00
☐ **Green Wing Flurry-Green Wing Teal**, rel. 1969 . s/n	450.00	480.00	465.00
☐ **Hill Country Gobblers-Turkey**, rel. 1972 ...... s/n	400.00	440.00	420.00
☐ **Timber Pothole-Mallards and Widgeon**, rel. 1973 .... s/n	400.00	440.00	420.00
☐ **Over the Ridge-Pheasants**, rel. 1973 ..... s/n	400.00	440.00	420.00
☐ **The Old Duck Camp Mallard**, rel. 1974 .. s/n	150.00	170.00	160.00
☐ **Afternoon Squall-Canada Geese**, rel. 1975 .. s/n	175.00	200.00	182.00

J. FENWICK LANSDOWNE

☐ **Wood Duck**, rel. 1973 .... s/n	200.00	220.00	210.00

RALPH McDONALD

☐ **Whitetail and Descending Canvasbacks** ..... s/n	150.00	170.00	160.00
☐ **The Raccoons** .... s/n	160.00	180.00	170.00
	s/o	115.00	130.00	122.00
☐ **Bobwhite Quail** .... s/n	115.00	130.00	122.00
☐ **Cardinal** .... s/o	65.00	75.00	70.00
☐ **Largemouth Bass** .... s/n	65.00	75.00	70.00
☐ **Mockingbird** .... s/n	185.00	205.00	195.00

BICENTENNIAL SERIES OF FIVE PRINTS

☐ **The American Whitetail Deer** .... s/s	90.00	110.00	100.00
☐ **American Bald Eagle** .... s/n	350.00	390.00	370.00
☐ **American Wild Turkey** .... s/n	125.00	145.00	135.00
☐ **The Frontiersman** .... s/n	80.00	90.00	85.00
☐ **The Indian** .... s/n	90.00	110.00	100.00

CLAY McGAUGHY

		Current Price Range		Prior Year Average
☐ Bachelor, rel. 1970	s/n	300.00	330.00	315.00
	s/o	150.00	175.00	162.00
☐ Birds of a Feather, rel. 1970	s/n	200.00	225.00	212.00
	s/o	150.00	175.00	162.00
☐ Follow the Leader, rel. 1970	s/n	175.00	195.00	185.00
☐ Intruder, rel. 1970	s/n	175.00	195.00	185.00
☐ Checkin' In, rel. 1971	s/n	175.00	195.00	185.00
☐ Loafers, rel. 1972	s/n	175.00	195.00	185.00

PETER PARNALL

☐ Pygmy Owl, rel. 1972	s/n	130.00	150.00	140.00
☐ Richardson's Owl, rel. 1972	s/n	155.00	175.00	165.00
☐ Bee, rel. 1974	s/n	265.00	285.00	275.00
☐ Buffalo Sun, rel. 1974	s/n	250.00	275.00	262.00
☐ Coyote Pups, rel. 1975	s/n	150.00	175.00	162.00
☐ Frog, rel. 1975	s/n	140.00	160.00	150.00
☐ Goldfinch, rel. 1975	s/n	135.00	150.00	142.00
☐ Sea Otters, rel. 1976	s/n	250.00	280.00	265.00
☐ Sperm Whale, rel. 1976	s/n	275.00	300.00	282.00

ROGER TORY PETERSON

☐ Baltimore Oriole, rel. 1973	s/n	300.00	330.00	315.00
☐ Flicker, rel. 1973	s/n	300.00	330.00	315.00
☐ Great Horned Owl, rel. 1974	s/n	800.00	900.00	850.00
☐ Bobwhite, rel. 1975	s/n	425.00	460.00	442.00
☐ Golden Eagle, rel. 1976	s/n	250.00	275.00	262.00
☐ Snowy Owl, rel. 1976	s/n	650.00	725.00	688.00
☐ Bluebird, rel. 1977	s/n	225.00	250.00	237.00

MAYNARD REECE

☐ Pheasant Country, rel. 1963	s/n	200.00	220.00	210.00
☐ Bobwhites, stone lithograph, rel. 1964		650.00	725.00	688.00
☐ Buffleheads (color edition), rel. 1973	s/n	250.00	425.00	345.00
☐ Late Afternoon — Mallards, rel. 1973	s/n	300.00	330.00	315.00
☐ Courtship Flight — Pintails, rel. 1974	s/n	175.00	200.00	187.00
☐ Mallards — Dropping In, rel. 1974	s/n	150.00	170.00	160.00
☐ Solitude — Whitetail Deer, rel. 1974	s/n	150.00	170.00	160.00
☐ Winging South — Canada Geese, rel. 1974	s/n	275.00	300.00	287.00
☐ Wooded Seclusion — Turkey, rel. 1974	s/n	125.00	150.00	137.00
☐ Autumn Trio — Ring-Necked Pheasants, rel. 1976	s/n	250.00	275.00	262.00
☐ Dark Sky — Mallards, rel. 1976	s/n	550.00	625.00	587.00

JOHN A. RUTHVEN

AQUATINT SERIES

☐ Carolina Paraquet	s/n	1300.00	1500.00	1400.00
☐ Ivory Billed Woodpecker	s/n	750.00	850.00	800.00
☐ Passenger Pigeon	s/n	1200.00	1300.00	1250.00

NORTH AMERICAN SERIES

☐ Fox Family	s/n	900.00	1000.00	950.00
☐ New York State Bluebird	s/n	250.00	275.00	262.00
☐ Redheaded Woodpecker	s/n	350.00	450.00	400.00
☐ Ruddy Ducks	s/n	350.00	450.00	400.00

AMERICANA SERIES

☐ Great Horned Owl	s/n	300.00	330.00	315.00
☐ Herring Gulls	s/n	250.00	275.00	262.00
☐ Roadrunner	s/n	250.00	275.00	262.00

704 / PRINTING COLLECTIBLES

	Current Price Range		Prior Year Average
GEORGETOWN SERIES			
☐ Cinnamon Teal .... s/n	100.00	120.00	110.00
☐ Fox Masque .... s/n	75.00	85.00	80.00
REGAL SERIES			
☐ Bengal Tiger .... s/n	1500.00	1600.00	1550.00
☐ Red Fox .... s/n	1300.00	1400.00	1350.00
MASTERPIECE SERIES			
☐ Gray Fox .... s/n	1200.00	1300.00	1350.00
INITIAL SERIES			
☐ Pheasant .... s/n	500.00	600.00	550.00
☐ Quail .... s/n	800.00	900.00	850.00
☐ Ruffed Grouse .... s/n	300.00	350.00	325.00
☐ Wild Turkey .... s/n	400.00	460.00	430.00
☐ Wood Ducks .... s/n	300.00	350.00	325.00

PRINTING COLLECTIBLES

Amateur printers are the primary collectors of relics from the printing industry; some interest comes also from book collectors, especially those who make a specialty of limited editions, finely printed books, and "incunabula" (books printed in the 15th century). It isn't a large hobby, but that's all to the good since this material is scarce. With stronger competition, its prices would be far beyond the budgets of most collectors. The beginner is apt to be most captivated by the miniature or tabletop presses of the 19th and early 20th centuries. These are quaint and to some extent interesting, but really are not as historical or as worthwhile to collect as items from a commercial printing shop. Try to get the oldest pieces available. Printing relics as early as the 1700's turn up in America. If you browse in Europe, even older material will occasionally be found — but you may need some expertise to recognize it.

☐ **Brass ink can,** screw top, c. 1910	36.00	48.00	42.00
☐ **Brass rule,** pica and inches	14.00	19.00	16.50
☐ **Gutenberg press,** miniature, wood, 7" x 10" x 13" ..	1000.00	1400.00	1200.00
☐ **Ives Printing press,** c. 1897	200.00	275.00	237.00
☐ **Type drawers,** regularly and irregularly spaced compartments, 16½" x 11"	12.00	18.00	15.00
☐ **Wooden type,** various sizes, letters less than punctuation marks	2.00	15.00	8.50

PUPPETS

Though the making of puppets is an ancient art, it is rare for early specimens to come upon the market. In fact, few truly early puppets are preserved, even in museums, probably because the materials from which they were constructed did not lend themselves to preservation. Nothing remains of Greek or Roman puppets. Many Egyptian dolls in clay or wood do exist, but these do not qualify as puppets in the modern understanding of the word. The oldest European puppets likely to be found on the antique market date from the 18th century. Most are of Italian manufacture, though it is often not possible to accurately judge the country of origin of a puppet. (The French antique shops are, incidentally, much better hunting grounds for antique puppets than those of America, but prices are high.) Many puppets which appear very old are, in fact, no earlier than the middle 1800's, due to primitive or "folk" craftsmanship, old designing methods, and (often) lots of abuse. The style of *costume* is not a good indicator of a puppet's age, many being purposely clothed in outdated fashions to suit special requirements. Puppets for a Shakespearean play are attired in Elizabethan dress, but no one except a beginner would suspect they were made in 1600.

But the puppet collector does not look only for age. A very old puppet may be valuable on grounds of age, but one of much more recent date can be even more valuable. Materials, craftsmanship, originality, background and other factors all enter the picture, and all must be interpreted according to the specimen at hand. Of *all* considerations, theatrical fame counts the most. The sale of a celebrated puppet, such as the original Charlie McCarthy or Howdy Doody, would excite great interest, even though these are 20th century creations of no special brilliance in design or workmanship.

Also of interest for reasons other than antiquity or beauty are the products of well-known puppeteers. There are many collectors who would pay dearly for an original by Bil Baird or other modern puppet makers (the Baird puppets are not made personally by Baird but by a team of workers, including five woodcarvers, in a factory-like operation; nevertheless their appeal to collectors is equal to, say, a painting from the studio of da Vinci.)

Any puppet that has appeared in a television program is desirable for that reason alone, even if it's poorly designed and constructed.

The physical size of puppets is rarely an influence on their value. Large puppets are more expensive to construct. Anyone who orders a life-size puppet from a puppet maker will pay $4,000 to $8,000 for it, possibly more; but its value to collectors may be less, as not many collectors have the space to store or display large specimens.

Nor does style have more than a minimal effect on value. The four most common types of puppets are: marionettes (operated by strings); hand puppets; rod puppets; and ventriloquist dummies, the last being of fairly recent development. All other factors being equal, a good marionette would probably outsell a good specimen of the other varieties, but factors are never equal and the puppet market is, to say the least, unpredictable. Strict guidelines can never be set on prices because every puppet is different from another, excepting those mass-produced for the toy market. There are few private collectors, especially in America (Europe is the headquarters of puppet making, puppet collecting, and everything else to do with puppets). When a collection is sold, most of the buyers are dealers in antique dolls.

At the present time, Oriental puppets are just coming into popularity with American collectors. Their beauty and craftsmanship merit higher prices than are now being obtained. Within a very few years, they are likely to outsell most or all western puppets. Fine puppets are still being made in the Orient — not those sold in "Chinatown" shops but the puppets used in Japanese theatrical productions.

When buying old puppets, take care to see that all component parts are original or (at least) old. With some specimens this is not the case, and of course the value of such puppets is not comparable to those which have not been rebuilt or improved. The costume, if any, should also be old. Some signs of wear are inevitable. Much better to have marks of age than for the

706 / PUPPETS

face, hands, etc., to be repainted. Repainting greatly reduces the value and may even render the specimen valueless to collectors.

Puppet heads. Heads without bodies are frequently offered for sale. These are collectible, but the price should not be nearly so high as for a complete specimen. Anyone purchasing a puppet head should not attempt to reconstruct the body, unless intending it for theatrical use.

It is vital to stress that the prices given below are for specific specimens sold on the market or offered for sale, except where the word "estimate" is given. A similar specimen might sell considerably higher or lower, depending on circumstances. Estimates are given for puppets for which there are no sales records, but whose values can be judged in light of collector interest, rarity, etc.

For more in-depth information and listings, you may refer to *The Official Price Guide To Dolls* published by the House Of Collectibles.

MARIONETTES

	Current Price Range		Prior Year Average
☐ **"Black Sambo,"** composition head and hands, checkered shirt, brown striped pants, brown jacket, in original box with 78 r.p.m. phonograph record, America, 11½" H., c. 1947	65.00	85.00	75.00
☐ **"Buffalo Bill,"** composition head, dressed in western outfit, belt with two guns, one hand missing, signs of wear, 46" H.	1400.00	1800.00	1600.00
☐ **Figure in the likeness of a skeleton,** painted wood, two strings missing, some paint worn off face, Mexican (?), 16½" H., first half of the 20th c.	400.00	500.00	450.00
☐ **Figure of a dragon,** entirely of wood, green, purple and other colors, prominent eyes, Chinese, 56" H., 20th c.	900.00	1200.00	1050.00
☐ **Figure of Satan,** papier-mache head, garishly painted, the body made of red plush, wooden shoes, carved wooden pitchfork, some damage, 29" H., 20th c.	750.00	950.00	850.00
☐ **Figure of a woman,** possibly a princess, silk attire in multicolors, composition head, Japanese modern	75.00	95.00	85.00
☐ **Fish, carved and painted wood,** moveable lower jaw, fins and tail, approx. 2' H.	475.00	550.00	512.00
☐ **Howdy Doody,** replica of the TV puppet, reduced size sold in toy stores in the early 1950's, 12" H.	65.00	90.00	82.00
☐ **Howdy Doody,** the orginal puppet used when the TV program first appeared on the air in 1948	15000.00	25000.00	20000.00
☐ **Man with round face,** bulging eyes, in tuxedo, American, carved and painted wooden face, 37" H., 20th c.	900.00	1200.00	1050.00

HAND PUPPETS

These are puppets in which the hand is inserted into the puppet through a sleeve, rather than being operated by strings, rods or other means.

	Current Price Range		Prior Year Average
☐ **Figure of an old woman,** wearing long dress and apron, carved wood head, painted (the painting may not be original), French or Swiss, late 18th or early 19th c.	550.00	675.00	610.00
☐ **Oliver J. Dragon,** of the "Kukla, Fran and Ollie" television program, the original puppet made and used by Burr Tillstrom, c. 1940's .....(estimated)	6000.00	8000.00	7000.00
☐ **Policeman,** old style uniform and hat, the head carved of balsa wood, traces of paint and gilding, very worn, American, first quarter of the 20th c. .	150.00	200.00	175.00
☐ **Punch,** long crooked nose, red cheeks, brightly colored costume, porcelain head and hands, chipped, probably English, mid-Victorian	1100.00	1400.00	1250.00

ROD PUPPETS (Operated by sticks)

☐ **Man on a horse,** stuffed bodies, papier-mache heads, also some components in other materials, one of the rods, missing, soiled, but generally in good condition	350.00	500.00	425.00
☐ **Monkey with smiling face,** long arms, rods attached to arms, 21″ H.	300.00	400.00	350.00

VENTRILOQUIST "DUMMIES"

☐ Average price of a newly or recently made ventriloquist dummy, large enough for theatrical use (height at least 36″ with a head three-quarters life-size or larger) is higher for those with special features, such as moveable eyelids, eyeballs that can be moved from side to side, etc.	500.00	800.00	650.00
☐ **Jerry Mahoney,** composition head and hands, a small but exact replica, American, 21″ H., c. 1950 (was not sold with phonograph record)	90.00	120.00	105.00
☐ **Jerry Mahoney,** composition head and hands, wearing suit and white shirt, American, 32″ H., c. 1950	160.00	200.00	180.00
☐ **As above,** in original suitcase-like carrying case with phonograph record	300.00	400.00	350.00
☐ **Original Charlie McCarthy dummy** of radio fame, head of carved wood (for a long while Edgar Bergen worked with just a single model of Charlie, then made another in case something happened to the first)	25000.00	40000.00	32500.00
☐ **Original Jerry Mahoney** used by Paul Winchell, head of carved wood. Jerry was by far the best designed of all the "famous dummies," with many special features ....(estimated)	7000.00	10000.00	8500.00

QUILTS

Quilts have been absorbed into the category of Folk Art, though their creators seldom intended them as works of art. Early America, and especially early rural America, thrived on its self-sufficiency: its ability to cultivate foodstuffs and manufacture the necessities of everyday life. Quilts are one example (of many) of our ancestors using their creative skills and their sense of thrift: oddments of fabric were cut and sewn into various patterns, to make clothing, bed coverings, etc. Not only was some money saved, but the owner was sure to possess a very unique "original," which made the shopkeeper's merchandise seem pale by comparison. The more free-spirited quilters gave no attention whatever to matching colors, and, in fact, seemed intent on clashing them as much as possible. The results more than compensate in splash and zest, what they may lack in harmony. Collecting specimens of old quilts was once a very restricted hobby, which seemed destined never to get beyond rural New England, Pennsylvania and some other areas. It has blossomed to full flower today, aided by museum interest and antique shows. On the whole, *Amish* quilts are the leaders in hobbyist appeal and in value, though they are not invariably the most valuable. The self-contained Amish community (of western Pennsylvania) was intent on "doing for itself," unconcerned about what was fashionable in the world's eyes; its quilts are ample testimony to its artistic spirit.

Learn discrimination, if you get into quilt collecting. Not all specimens are good, or old, or worth taking into your collection. Museum visits will help here, as most museums (and historical societies) own specimens of better-class quilts. Study these, and look for similar examples on the market. Dealers who (in the hopes of selling inferior ones) claim that museum-grade quilts are unobtainable are not to be listened to.

	Current Price Range		Prior Year Average
☐ **Amish single Irish chain doll's quilt,** all wool with maroon, navy blue and gray patches and zigzag quilting	360.00	450.00	405.00
☐ **Appliqued calico quilt** with pink, red, yellow and green flowers	370.00	460.00	410.00
☐ **Double wedding ring,** scalloped edges, unused, 78" x 67"	100.00	140.00	115.00
☐ **Lavender and white appliqued quilt,** center panel with sunburst and S scroll, white cotton ground with leaf and flower quilting	90.00	120.00	105.00
☐ **Nine patch pattern,** machine-quilted, c. 1890	125.00	175.00	140.00
☐ **Patchwork quilt,** hand embroidered silk on velvet	140.00	190.00	165.00
☐ **Pieced Amish cotton and wool basket quilt** with maroon, rust, green, blue, purple wool and cotton patches forming baskets	410.00	500.00	445.00
☐ **Pieced Amish cotton basket quilt** with blue and black patches dated 1918	490.00	625.00	540.00
☐ **Pieced Amish sateen, cotton and wool crib quilt,** in the "Trip Around the World" pattern with maroon, gray, black, blue, magenta and rust patches with a navy blue border	370.00	460.00	415.00
☐ **Pieced Amish variable star cotton and sateen quilt** with black and shocking pink patches	260.00	330.00	290.00

QUILTS / 709

	Current Price Range		Prior Year Average
☐ **Pieced calico and chintz "Friendship" quilt** with red, green, brown, blue, and orange print and solid calico with chintz patches in the "Square" pattern	650.00	850.00	750.00
☐ **Pieced calico "Bow Tie" quilt** with blue, red, brown, maroon and black calico patches with cubes of white cotton	280.00	345.00	310.00
☐ **Pieced calico crib quilt** with pink, yellow, black and green calico patches with square quilting	260.00	320.00	290.00
☐ **Pieced calico "Philadelphia Pavement" quilt** with yellow, orange, pink, red and green calico patches	210.00	260.00	235.00
☐ **Pieced calico "Pinwheel Quilt"** with red, brown, yellow and black calico patches	210.00	275.00	242.00
☐ **Pieced calico quilt in the "Star of the East" pattern** with brown, pink and blue calico patches on white cotton ground	225.00	300.00	255.00
☐ **Pieced calico quilt, "Variable Star" pattern** with various colored patches on white ground	110.00	160.00	135.00
☐ **Pieced calico Star of Bethlehem quilt** with red, blue, orange, green, and pink calico patches on white cotton ground	280.00	360.00	320.00
☐ **Pieced calico zigzag quilt** with red, brown, green, blue, purple, pink and gray calico patches and red and white gingham check border	290.00	375.00	332.00
☐ **Pieced cotton and calico "Sawtooth Diamond" quilt,** pink calico patches on deep blue ground	290.00	375.00	332.00
☐ **Pieced cotton and sateen Amish quilt** in the "Old Maid's Puzzle" in various shades of red, rust and black patches	260.00	330.00	290.00
☐ **Pieced cotton quilt,** "Flower Basket" pattern, with brown and beige patches on white ground, diagonal and zigzag quilting	475.00	550.00	505.00
☐ **Pieced cotton quilt,** handmade pyramid design on white background	110.00	140.00	125.00
☐ **Pieced cotton quilt with Texas Star,** stars in green, gold and orange	110.00	140.00	125.00
☐ **Pieced Mennonite calico "Ocean Waves" quilt** with pink, blue, red, gray and green calico and cotton patches with wide pink border	275.00	350.00	305.00
☐ **Pieced trapunto,** pair, green and white, late 19th c.	675.00	850.00	735.00
☐ **Tulip applique,** red, green, gray and white, c. 1880	150.00	190.00	168.00
☐ **Tumbling blocks,** silk and velvet	220.00	270.00	245.00
☐ **Victorian crazy quilt** with variously shaped velvet and silk colored patches embroidered with leaves, pansies and petunias	1900.00	2300.00	2180.00
☐ **Wool quilt** with log cabin design, c. 19th c.	190.00	230.00	210.00

RADIO PREMIUMS

Not even chain letters brought so much extra work for the Post Office as radio premiums. During the 1930's and '40's, uncountable millions of children sent uncountable millions of boxtops and postcards to their local radio stations, for tin rings or plastic buttons picturing their heros. Adults, too, got into the swing of it, sending off for premiums aimed at them: such as recipe booklets and beauty tips. There was hardly a show in radio history — up to the advent of TV — that did not offer premiums, and the longer-running shows went through dozens of them. What was the purpose of the premium? When a proof-of-purchase was required, it was essentially to get listeners to try the sponsor's product. When the premium was totally free (for a postcard request, as was often the case), it was merely a testing to gauge the size of the audience. Naturally, premiums were very cheaply made, but their artistic quality has no bearing for hobbyists: they're authentic souvenirs of the days when that big wooden machine in the living room ... with all the static in it ... ruled the world.

	Current Price Range		Prior Year Average
☐ Booklet, "Breakfast Ideas from General Mills," four-color cover, wrappers, some recipes but mainly promotional material on various cereal products, c. 1940	1.00	1.50	1.25
☐ Booklet, "Cooking Hints from Betty Crocker," wrapper, unpaged, c. 1938	1.00	1.50	1.25
☐ Card with photo of Roy Rogers and His Singing Group, "The Sons of the Pioneers," facsimile signature, small, c. 1945	2.25	3.50	2.85
☐ "Little Orphan Annie" decoder ring, one of the classic radio premiums (millions must have been distributed but, as with other premiums, few survive), c. 1936	60.00	90.00	85.00
☐ Membership card in the Gene Autry fan club, small photo of Gene Autry with facsimile signature, place for recipient to write in name and address, late 1940's	3.50	5.00	4.20
☐ The Lone Ranger finger ring, all zinc, adjustable, portrait of the Lone Ranger (this price is for a sound specimen, many are broken), c. 1947	5.50	8.00	6.75

RADIOS

Your father, grandfather, or possibly even YOU cursed them back in the '30's and '40's. Radios of that era crackled with static and went dead just as Joe DiMaggio was driving a long one to the bleachers, or Fred Allen was in the midst of a seam-splitting punchline. When you needed to replace a tube, it was invariably the one that the hardware store didn't keep in stock. But lots of time has passed, radio has been toppled as kingpin of the media by TV, and those big clunky receivers look almost charming today. They've attracted plenty of collector attention and in most cases are bringing prices considerably higher than they sold for originally. While ALL old radios are collectible, going right up to about 1950, hobbyists are primarily interested in the early pioneer models from the twenties and specimens of unusual or creative styling. Basically, the pre-1925 sets are extremely short on looks, as a radio was considered a *machine* in those days and not a supplement to the dining room decor. Things changed sharply in the later twenties, as makers vied with each other to bring out the most eye-appealing models. Wooden cabinets were standard until the '40's, when plastic started coming in. Plug the radio in and try to play it before you buy. If it doesn't play, don't assume that one fresh tube or a simple turn of a screwdriver will put things right. Chances are you will be facing a rather expensive restorations job, which might be successful only if the whole mechanism is replaced with solid state transistors. In that case, what you're really buying is a shell, so proceed cautiously.

	Current Price Range		Prior Year Average
☐ **A. C. Dayton Co.,** crystal set, c. 1923	100.00	140.00	118.00
☐ **A. C. Dayton Co.,** Super Six, c. 1924	125.00	170.00	148.00
☐ **Adams-Morgan,** Paragon Regen, c. 1921	190.00	240.00	215.00
☐ **Adams-Morgan,** R10 Short Wave, c. 1921	245.00	300.00	268.00
☐ **Atwater Kent,** #10, c. 1923	255.00	310.00	282.00
☐ **Beaver Baby Grand,** c. 1924	110.00	145.00	125.00
☐ **Crosley,** Vlm, c. 1922	275.00	340.00	305.00
☐ **Crosley,** X, c. 1922	190.00	235.00	212.00
☐ **Crosley,** Pup, c. 1925	280.00	340.00	310.00
☐ **Crosley,** 5-38, c. 1926	185.00	230.00	205.00
☐ **DeForest,** D6, c. 1923	290.00	340.00	315.00
☐ **DeForest,** D10, c. 1923	380.00	435.00	405.00
☐ **DeForest,** Everyman, crystal, c. 1923	210.00	250.00	230.00
☐ **Federal,** 58DX, c. 1922	395.00	440.00	418.00
☐ **Federal,** 57DX, c. 1922	370.00	420.00	395.00
☐ **Federal,** 61DX, c. 1923	390.00	435.00	413.00
☐ **Freshman,** Masterpiece, c. 1924	230.00	280.00	255.00
☐ **Grebe,** CR6, c. 1919	460.00	530.00	495.00
☐ **Grebe,** CR5, c. 1921	260.00	310.00	285.00
☐ **Grebe,** Synchrophase, c. 1925	380.00	425.00	400.00
☐ **Magnavox,** TRF-5, c. 1925	235.00	270.00	250.00
☐ **Philco,** 551, c. 1928	125.00	155.00	145.00
☐ **Philco,** 525, c. 1929	85.00	110.00	98.00
☐ **Philco,** Super-heterodyne Cathedral, c. 1931	120.00	150.00	130.00
☐ **RCA,** Radiola X, c. 1925	390.00	450.00	420.00
☐ **RCA,** Radiola 26, c. 1925	470.00	560.00	515.00
☐ **RCA,** Radiola c. 1923	155.00	190.00	170.00
☐ **RCA,** Radiola special, c. 1923	160.00	190.00	175.00
☐ **RCA,** Aeriola Jr. (crystal), c. 1922	125.00	160.00	140.00
☐ **Zenith,** 835, c. 1932	135.00	175.00	150.00

RAILROADIANA

Nostalgia isn't confined only to the objects of our own childhoods but of America's childhood, too — and remnants of the Iron Horse rank high in that regard. The Industrial Age began with the laying of the first rail lines. The railroads opened the West, gave employment to thousands, and helped shape America into the military and industrial giant it later became. Railroadiana as a collector's hobby has been with us for more than a generation. Thanks to the early interest taken by collectors (and institutional collectors) in the subject, a great deal of material has been preserved that might otherwise be lost. Anything pertaining to railroads, even if the date is fairly modern, has appeal and a claim on the hobbyist's attention; however, the most desirable and valuable relics tend to be the earliest. Because so much *is* available, some devotees prefer to specialize, collecting nothing but (for example) railroad lanterns, or locks. Since some of this material can be costly, specialization has much to be said for it. Most collectors are in agreement on the following point, that any object actually made as a train component, or for use on board, has the first rank as a collectible. The secondary category (but still collectible) includes items that would be found in a railway station, such as timetables and brochures. Railroad *signs,* because of their pictorial character and strong historical flavor, are particularly alluring. Going further along the line, there are such collectibles as model trains and train-related toys.

	Current Price Range		Prior Year Average
☐ **Ashtray,** floor model, brass	115.00	122.00	130.00
☐ **Badge,** police	90.00	105.00	120.00
☐ **Bell,** brass, 12" H.	750.00	960.00	1100.00
☐ **Cuspidor,** Maine Central	45.00	52.00	60.00
☐ **Dish,** Pacific Railroad, silver	40.00	45.00	50.00
☐ **Glass,** bar, Erie Railroad	20.00	22.00	26.00
☐ **Key,** switch, brass	15.00	18.00	20.00
☐ **Key,** switch, New York Central	15.00	18.00	20.00
☐ **Lantern,** caboose, Wabash	85.00	100.00	118.00
☐ **Lantern,** switch, Missouri Central	110.00	130.00	160.00
☐ **Passes,** New York Central	25.00	30.00	35.00
☐ **Pin,** conductor's, enamel inlay	25.00	30.00	35.00
☐ **Plates,** set of thirteen	45.00	52.00	60.00
☐ **Postcards,** railroad scenes	2.50	3.50	4.50
☐ **Punch,** conductor's	20.00	23.00	27.00
☐ **Ring,** conductor's, enamel, 10K	50.00	58.00	65.00
☐ **Scrapbook,** magazine pictures, patches, postcards	70.00	80.00	90.00
☐ **Sign,** Atlantic Coast Line, round, 34" Dia.	35.00	40.00	45.00
☐ **Sign,** crossing, pre-1900	45.00	55.00	65.00
☐ **Ticket holder,** wood	58.00	68.00	78.00
☐ **Track maul,** five to ten pounds	13.50	15.50	18.50
☐ **Tumbler,** New York Central	6.00	7.50	9.00
☐ **Tumbler,** Pennsylvania Railroad	4.50	5.50	6.50

RAZORS

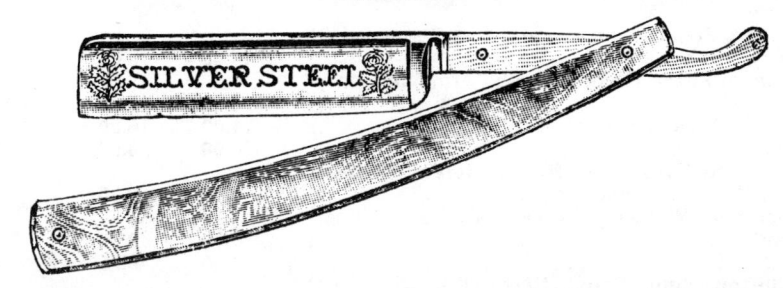

Razor, ⅝" wide blade, handle is celloloid reproductions of smoked pearl
.... **$10.00-15.00**

The old-fashioned straight razor is a deadly-looking instrument. Yet it was not too many years ago when nearly every man (except those who could afford the luxury of barbers) faced the straight razor each morning, groggy with sleep, and hoped he might survive to shave again next day. Thanks to its size, a shave went faster with straight razors — but that hardly compensated for the element of risk. Today, as collectors' items, straight razors and the folding variety have gained considerable appeal. The mere fact that they can be owned today, without the necessity of using them, is a great point in their favor. The earlier ones go back to the 19th century and are found with a wide variety of blade and handle types, and are imprinted with numerous manufacturers' names both United States and foreign. The common handles are wood painted black, hard rubber, or imitation bone. Better-class specimens have ivory, bone, or sterling silver handles, sometimes ornately decorated. These obviously were intended as gift items for the wealthy men of that time, who probably found a dozen or more of them beneath the tree each Christmas (but never used any, as they were shaved by valets). Old razors turn up frequently at knife shows, but the dealers exhibiting them at such events always ask the full market price. Bargains can often be found in antique shops, secondhand stores, or via rummaging about.

	Current Price Range		Prior Year Average
☐ **Antonio Tadros,** straight edge	7.00	10.00	8.50
☐ **Barber,** straight edge in original box	45.00	58.00	51.50
☐ **Cattaraugus Cutlery Co.** with "The Sovereign's Own" imprint	20.00	25.00	22.50
☐ **Chip-A-Way Cutlery Co., England** with "Chip-A-Way" imprint	9.00	12.00	10.50
☐ **Colquhoun and Cadman, Sheffield** with "Little Favorite" imprint	5.00	8.00	6.50
☐ **Electric Cutlery, New York** with "Arlington" imprint	5.00	8.00	6.50
☐ **Elsener, Switzerland** with "Ideal" imprint	6.00	9.00	7.50
☐ **G.R.S. Solinger, Germany** with "Extra Superb" imprint	6.00	9.00	7.50
☐ **Hamburg,** hollow ground with 'W. B. Speed" imprint	7.00	10.00	8.50

714 / REDWARE

	Current Price Range		Prior Year Average
☐ **Hibbard Spencer Bartlett and Co., Germany** with "May Flower" imprint	14.00	19.00	16.50
☐ **Imperial Razor, Germany** with "Army and Navy" imprint	15.00	20.00	17.50
☐ **Joseph Roger Cutler,** straight edge	11.00	15.00	13.00
☐ **Kinfolks, Inc.,** with "Real Red Point" imprint	5.00	8.00	6.50
☐ **Petty and Sons, John Manufacturers, Sheffield** with "Magnetic" imprint	6.00	9.00	7.50
☐ **Rector and Wilhelmy Co.** with "XX Clean Clipper" imprint	6.00	9.00	7.50
☐ **Reuter Bros**	4.50	6.75	5.60
☐ **Robeson Shur Edge, New York** with "The Nugget" imprint	5.00	8.00	6.50
☐ **Simmons Hardware Co.** with "Hornet" imprint	5.00	8.00	6.50
☐ **Simmons Hardware Co.** with "Royal Keen Kutter" imprint	14.00	19.00	16.50
☐ **Sterling Razor Works** with "Rattler" imprint	4.50	6.75	5.60
☐ **Victory Hone Co., Iowa** with "Victory Hollow #1" imprint	4.75	7.00	5.85
☐ **Winchester,** straight edge	60.00	80.00	70.00
☐ **Witte Hardware Co., Mo.** with "Witte's Rattler"	4.50	6.50	5.55

REDWARE

Redware is clay pottery, in the form of cooking utensils, storage containers and various household articles. It has been manufactured for thousands of years, and in the case of ancient specimens is usually called terracotta. Very early or amateurishly made redware was shaped entirely by hand like a freehand sculpture, and shows it. After the development of the potter's wheel it took on more regular shapes, but seldom reached the refined state of the more sophisticated potteries. Redware was extensively made in the early U.S., both as a commercial venture and to supply the immediate wants of local communities. The areas of heaviest manufacture were western Pennsylvania, Ohio, Kentucky, and Virginia. Redware falls clearly into the realm of "folk art," especially when it carries painted decoration (applied after firing). Our ancestors, though they did not wield the brush of a DaVinci, got an "A for effort" in decorating the things they made. Floral decoration is the most common to redware; also frequent are scenes of farm animals and birds. Other specimens carry strictly geometrical patterns and, in that case, are suggestive of Indian pottery. The SIZE, APPROXIMATE AGE, TYPE OF ARTICLE, and STATE OF PRESERVATION enter into determining the value, as well as, of course, artistic interest. Repairs can be made quite expertly, so do not assume a piece is "untouched" until closely scrutinized.

For further informaiton, consult *The Official Price Guide to Pottery and Porcelain,* published by The House of Collectibles.

ROGERS GROUP / 715

	Current Price Range	Prior Year Average
☐ **Bean pot,** brown, covered, two handles	32.00 40.00	36.00
☐ **Bed pan,** brown design, manganese splotching .	90.00 115.00	103.00
☐ **Candle sconce,** yellow and green, clear glaze ...	310.00 380.00	345.00
☐ **Crock,** ovoid, insect, 7½″ H.	425.00 500.00	468.00
☐ **Flask,** dark brown, 6″ H.	80.00 105.00	93.00
☐ **Jar,** green with brown splotches, two handles, 10½″ H.	110.00 140.00	125.00
☐ **Jug,** brown glaze, ovoid, two handles	90.00 115.00	102.00
☐ **Loaf pan,** brown splotches, glaze	160.00 200.00	180.00
☐ **Pitcher,** milk, spotted glaze, 15½″ Dia.	75.00 100.00	87.00
☐ **Spittoon,** speckled glaze	100.00 135.00	118.00

ROGERS GROUP

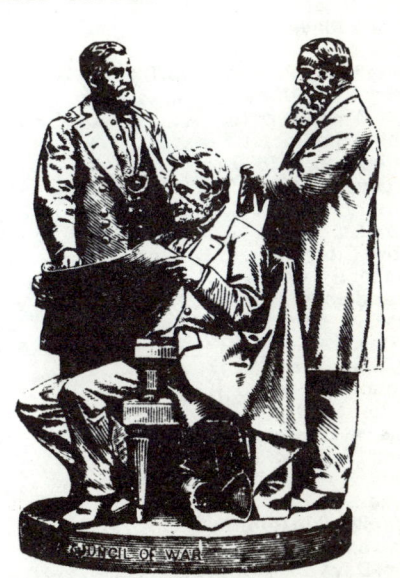

Left to Right: **Roger Group,** one more shot **$620.00-$775.00;** Council of War .... **$1200.00-$1500.00**

John Rogers, who flourished in the mid to late 19th century, could make a mighty boast: his sculptures adorned the homes of more Americans than those of any other artist. There was, however, a catch. While most sculptors created limited editions in bronze, or one-of-a-kind works in marble, John Rogers turned out prolific quantities of plaster models of his sculptures. They got into more homes because there were more of them, and they were both inexpensive and (for a while) fashionable. Rogers operated what amounted to a sculpture factory. His works were usually large in size, showing human subjects at various occupations or activities, or historical

ROGERS GROUP

characters. The Civil War, which he lived through, provided a good deal of subject matter. In terms of modeling, the Rogers Groups — as they're called — are quite skillful, and their large size gives them an imposing presence. Unfortunately, foolish approaches were often taken with their coloring, either by the studio or by early owners, who painted them (to give one example) solid black to suggest basalt sculpture. When found in the original greyish white they are more appealing AND OUGHT TO BE LEFT THAT WAY. Look carefully for small components that might be missing. These are delicate subjects and may have suffered accidents over the years. Their very heavy weight, coupled with their fragility, makes them a nightmare to ship.

	Current Price Range		Prior Year Average
☐ Balcony	750.00	900.00	825.00
☐ Bubbles	550.00	700.00	625.00
☐ Charity Patient	590.00	740.00	665.00
☐ Checkers Players	1250.00	1700.00	1500.00
☐ Chess	675.00	825.00	750.00
☐ Coming to the Parson, c. 1870	420.00	550.00	485.00
☐ Country Post Office	660.00	790.00	785.00
☐ Fairy's Whisper, c. 1881	1100.00	1700.00	1400.00
☐ Fetching the Doctor	710.00	880.00	790.00
☐ Fighting Bob, c. 1889	925.00	1175.00	1055.00
☐ First Love	450.00	525.00	483.00
☐ First Ride	670.00	830.00	750.00
☐ Football, c. 1891	1300.00	1850.00	1525.00
☐ Fugitive Story	820.00	975.00	895.00
☐ Going for the Cows	525.00	630.00	575.00
☐ Hide and Seek	710.00	840.00	775.00
☐ Home Guard	740.00	845.00	792.00
☐ Mail Day	650.00	770.00	710.00
☐ Miles Standish	375.00	485.00	430.00
☐ Neighboring Pews, c. 1884	680.00	790.00	735.00
☐ One More Shot	710.00	850.00	780.00
☐ Peddler at the Fair	740.00	860.00	810.00
☐ Playing Doctor, c. 1872	620.00	740.00	680.00
☐ Politics	600.00	715.00	657.00
☐ Referee	640.00	760.00	700.00
☐ Rip Van Winkle Returned	600.00	710.00	655.00
☐ Romeo and Juliet	520.00	610.00	565.00
☐ School Days	725.00	850.00	787.00
☐ Slave Auction	1600.00	2200.00	1800.00
☐ Slave Market	1800.00	2500.00	2150.00
☐ Taking the Oath, c. 1866	400.00	510.00	455.00
☐ Tap on the Window	530.00	640.00	585.00
☐ Traveling Magician, c. 1877	560.00	675.00	618.00
☐ Village Schoolmaster	775.00	900.00	835.00
☐ Washington	1000.00	1400.00	1200.00
☐ Watch on the Santa Maria	575.00	680.00	625.00
☐ Wounded Scout, c. 1864	1100.00	1475.00	1280.00
☐ Wrestler	1175.00	1500.00	1225.00

ROYAL DOULTON

Noelle, HN2179, c. 1957-67
.... **$350.00-$400.00**

Royal Doulton pottery has been manufactured since the 19th century. While the factory has produced many types of articles, for use and decoration, its figures are the most widely collected. The Royal Doulton figures are identified by an "HN" prefix, and then by numbers in a chronological sequence. The HN prefix is derived from the initials of Harry Nixon, who was at one time the company's art director. Figures from #1 to #359 are listed below. These are the earliest Royal Doulton figures and, on the whole, the most desirable for collectors. For more in-depth information and listings, you may refer to *The Official Price Guide to Royal Doulton* published by The House of Collectibles.

"HN" NUMERICAL LISTINGS OF FANCY AND CHARACTER FIGURES

	Current Price Range		Prior Year Average
☐ HN 1, Darling (1st version), 1913-28	1000.00	1150.00	1050.00
☐ HN 2, Elizabeth Fry, 1913-38	4000.00	4500.00	4200.00
☐ HN 3, Milking Time, 1913-38	3000.00	3500.00	3200.00
☐ HN 4, Picardy Peasant (female), 1913-38	1500.00	2000.00	1750.00
☐ HN 5, Picardy Peasant (female), 1913-38	1500.00	2000.00	1750.00
☐ HN 6, Dunce, 1913-38	2750.00	3000.00	2850.00
☐ HN 7, Pedlar Wolf, 1913-38	2000.00	2500.00	2200.00
☐ HN 8, The Crinoline, 1913-38	1250.00	1400.00	1350.00
☐ HN 9, The Crinoline, 1913-38	1250.00	1400.00	1350.00
☐ HN 9A, The Crinoline, 1913-38	1250.00	1400.00	1350.00
☐ HN 10, Madonna of the Square, 1913-38	1450.00	1600.00	1550.00
☐ HN 10A, Madonna of the Square, 1913-38	1000.00	1100.00	1050.00
☐ HN 11, Madonna of the Square, 1913-38	1650.00	1800.00	1750.00

718 / ROYAL DOULTON

	Current Price Range		Prior Year Average
☐ HN 12, Baby, 1913-38	2050.00	2200.00	2125.00
☐ HN 13, Picardy Peasant (male), 1913-38	1950.00	2000.00	1975.00
☐ HN 14, Madonna of the Square, 1913-38	1750.00	1850.00	1800.00
☐ HN 15, The Sleepy Scholar, 1913-38	1200.00	1300.00	1250.00
☐ HN 16, The Sleepy Scholar, 1913-38	1200.00	1300.00	1250.00
☐ HN 17, Picardy Peasant (male), 1913-38	1850.00	2000.00	1925.00
☐ HN 17A, Picardy Peasant (female), 1913-38	1850.00	2000.00	1925.00
☐ HN 18, Pussy, 1913-38	2500.00	2750.00	2600.00
☐ HN 19, Picardy Peasant (male), 1913-38	1000.00	1100.00	1050.00
☐ HN 20, The Coquette, 1913-38	2500.00	3000.00	2750.00
☐ HN 21, The Crinoline, 1913-38	1250.00	1400.00	1325.00
☐ HN 21A, The Crinoline, 1913-38	1250.00	1400.00	1325.00
☐ HN 22, The Lavender Woman, 1913-38	1750.00	2000.00	1850.00
☐ HN 23, The Lavender Woman, 1913-38	1750.00	2000.00	1850.00
☐ HN 23A, The Lavender Woman, 1913-38	1750.00	2000.00	1850.00
☐ HN 24, Sleep, 1913-38	2200.00	2400.00	2300.00
☐ HN 24A, Sleep, 1913-38	2200.00	2400.00	2300.00
☐ HN 25, Sleep, 1913-38	2500.00	2800.00	2650.00
☐ HN 25A, Sleep, 1913-38	2500.00	2800.00	2650.00
☐ HN 26, The Diligent Scholar, 1913-38	1050.00	1200.00	1125.00
☐ HN 27, Madonna of the Square, 1913-38	1650.00	1800.00	1750.00
☐ HN 28, Motherhood, 1913-38	1750.00	2000.00	1850.00
☐ HN 29, The Sleepy Scholar, 1913-38	1000.00	1250.00	1125.00
☐ HN 30, Motherhood, 1913-38	2250.00	2500.00	2350.00
☐ HN 31, The Return of Persephone, 1913-38	4000.00	5000.00	4500.00
☐ HN 32, Child and Crab, 1913-38	1250.00	1300.00	1275.00
☐ HN 33, An Arab, 1913-38	1500.00	1750.00	1625.00
☐ HN 34, Moorish Minstrel, 1913-38	2000.00	2200.00	2100.00
☐ HN 35, Charley's Aunt, 1914-38	700.00	800.00	750.00
☐ HN 36, The Sentimental Pierrot, 1914-38	1750.00	1900.00	1825.00
☐ HN 37, The Coquette, 1914-38	2500.00	3000.00	2750.00
☐ HN 38, The Carpet Vendor (1st version), 1914-38	2750.00	3000.00	2850.00
☐ HN 38A, The Carpet Vendor (1st version), 1914-38	2750.00	3000.00	2850.00
☐ HN 39, The Welsh Girl, 1914-38	2500.00	2750.00	2625.00
☐ HN 40, A Lady of the Elizabethan Period (1st version), 1914-38	1750.00	2000.00	1850.00
☐ HN 40A, A Lady of the Elizabethan Period (1st version), 1914-38	1750.00	2000.00	1850.00
☐ HN 41, A Lady of the Georgian Period, 1914-38	2000.00	2300.00	2150.00
☐ HN 42, Robert Burns, 1914-38	3000.00	3500.00	3200.00
☐ HN 43, A Lady of the Time of Henry VI, 1914-38	3000.00	3250.00	3100.00
☐ HN 44, A Lilac Shawl, 1915-38	1250.00	1500.00	1375.00
☐ HN 44A, A Lilac Shawl, 1915-38	1250.00	1500.00	1375.00
☐ HN 45, A Jester (1st version), 1915-38	1250.00	1500.00	1375.00
☐ HN 45A, A Jester (2nd version), 1915-38	1250.00	1500.00	1375.00
☐ HN 45B, A Jester (2nd version), 1915-38	1250.00	1500.00	1375.00
☐ HN 46, The Gainsborough Hat, 1915-38	1100.00	1200.00	1150.00
☐ HN 46A, The Gainsborough Hat, 1915-38	1100.00	1200.00	1150.00
☐ HN 47, The Gainsborough Hat, 1915-38	1100.00	1200.00	1150.00
☐ HN 48, Lady of the Fan, 1916-38	1650.00	1800.00	1725.00
☐ HN 48A, Lady with Rose, 1916-38	1650.00	1800.00	1725.00
☐ HN 49, Under the Gooseberry Bush, 1916-38	1650.00	1850.00	1750.00
☐ HN 50, A Spook, 1916-38	1100.00	1200.00	1150.00
☐ HN 51, A Spook, 1916-38	1250.00	1400.00	1325.00
☐ HN 51A, A Spook, 1916-38	1250.00	1400.00	1325.00
☐ HN 51B, A Spook, 1916-38	1250.00	1400.00	1325.00

ROYAL DOULTON / 719

	Current Price Range	Prior Year Average
☐ HN 52, Lady of the Fan, 1916-38	1650.00 1800.00	1725.00
☐ HN 52A, Lady with Rose, 1916-38	1650.00 1800.00	1725.00
☐ HN 53, Lady of the Fan, 1916-38	1650.00 1800.00	1725.00
☐ HN 53A, Lady of the Fan, 1916-38	1650.00 1800.00	1725.00
☐ HN 54, Lady Ermine, 1916-38	1250.00 1500.00	1375.00
☐ HN 55, A Jester (2nd version), 1916-38	1300.00 1500.00	1400.00
☐ HN 56, The Land of Nod, 1916-38	1750.00 2000.00	1825.00
☐ HN 56A, The Land of Nod, 1916-38	2000.00 2300.00	2100.00
☐ HN 56B, The Land of Nod, 1916-38	1750.00 2000.00	1825.00
☐ HN 57, The Curtsey, 1916-38	1500.00 1750.00	1625.00
☐ HN 57A, The Flounced Skirt, 1916-38	1650.00 1800.00	1725.00
☐ HN 57B, The Curtsey, 1916-38	1500.00 1750.00	1625.00
☐ HN 58, A Spook, 1918-38	1250.00 1400.00	1300.00
☐ HN 59, Upon her Cheeks She Wept, 1916-38	1500.00 1600.00	1550.00
☐ HN 60, Shy Anne, 1916-38	1500.00 1700.00	1600.00
☐ HN 61, Katharine, 1916-38	1500.00 1700.00	1600.00
☐ HN 62, A Child's Grace, 1916-38	1500.00 1700.00	1600.00
☐ HN 62A, A Child's Grace, 1916-38	1500.00 1700.00	1600.00
☐ HN 63, The Little Land, 1916-38	1950.00 2100.00	2000.00
☐ HN 64, Shy Anne, 1916-38	1500.00 1600.00	1550.00
☐ HN 65, Shy Anne, 1916-38	1550.00 1700.00	1625.00
☐ HN 66, The Flounced Skirt, 1916-38	1650.00 1800.00	1725.00
☐ HN 66A, The Curtsey, 1916-38	1550.00 1700.00	1625.00
☐ HN 67, The Little Land, 1916-38	1750.00 1900.00	1850.00
☐ HN 68, Lady with a Rose, 1916-38	1650.00 1800.00	1725.00
☐ HN 69, Pretty Lady, 1916-38	1250.00 1500.00	1375.00
☐ HN 70, Pretty Lady, 1916-38	1250.00 1500.00	1375.00
☐ HN 71, A Jester (1st version), 1917-38	1250.00 1500.00	1375.00
☐ HN 71A, A Jester (1st version), 1917-38	1250.00 1500.00	1375.00
☐ HN 72, An Orange Vendor, 1917-38	950.00 1100.00	1025.00
☐ HN 73, A Lady of the Elizabethan Period (1st version), 1917-38	1800.00 2000.00	1900.00
☐ HN 74, Katharine, 1917-38	1650.00 1800.00	1725.00
☐ HN 75, Blue Beard (1st version), 1917-38	4000.00 4500.00	4200.00
☐ HN 76, Carpet Vendor (2nd version), 1917-38	3000.00 3500.00	1750.00
☐ HN 77, The Flounced Skirt, 1917-38	1650.00 1800.00	1750.00
☐ HN 78, The Flounced Skirt, 1917-38	1650.00 1800.00	1750.00
☐ HN 79, Shylock, 1917-38	2500.00 2750.00	2600.00
☐ HN 80, Fisherwomen, 1917-38	3000.00 3500.00	3200.00
☐ HN 81, A Shepherd (1st version), 1917-38	2250.00 2500.00	2350.00
☐ HN 82, The Afternoon Call, 1918-38	2250.00 2500.00	2350.00
☐ HN 83, The Lady Anne, 1918-38	2750.00 3000.00	2850.00
☐ HN 84, A Mandarin (1st version), 1918-38	2250.00 2500.00	2350.00
☐ HN 85, Jack Point, 1918-38	2000.00 2200.00	2100.00
☐ HN 86, Out for a Walk, 1918-38	2250.00 2500.00	2375.00
☐ HN 87, The Lady Anne, 1918-38	2750.00 3000.00	2850.00
☐ HN 88, Spooks, 1918-38	1650.00 1800.00	1750.00
☐ HN 89, Spooks, 1918-38	1650.00 1800.00	1750.00
☐ HN 90, Doris Keene as Cavallini (1st version), 1918-38	2000.00 2500.00	2250.00
☐ HN 91, Jack Point, 1918-38	2000.00 2250.00	2100.00
☐ HN 92, The Welsh Girl, 1918-38	2500.00 2750.00	2600.00
☐ HN 93, The Lady Anne, 1918-38	2750.00 3000.00	2825.00
☐ HN 94, The Young Knight, 1918-38	2750.00 3000.00	2850.00
☐ HN 95, Europa and the Bull, 1918-38	3000.00 3500.00	3200.00

720 / ROYAL DOULTON

	Current Price Range		Prior Year Average
☐ HN 96, Doris Keene as Cavallini (2nd version), 1918-38	2250.00	2500.00	2375.00
☐ HN 97, The Mermaid, 1918-38	650.00	700.00	675.00
☐ HN 98, Guy Fawkes, 1918-38	1100.00	1200.00	1150.00
☐ HN 99, Jack Point, 1918-38	2000.00	2250.00	2125.00
HN 100 — HN 299 ANIMAL AND BIRD MODELS			
☐ HN 300, The Mermaid, 1918-38	1000.00	1100.00	1050.00
☐ HN 301, Moorish Piper Minstrel, 1918-38	2750.00	3000.00	2825.00
☐ HN 302, Pretty Lady, 1918-38	1500.00	1650.00	1570.00
☐ HN 303, Motherhood, 1918-38	2250.00	2500.00	2300.00
☐ HN 304, Lady with Rose, 1918-38	1650.00	1800.00	1725.00
☐ HN 305, A Scribe, 1918-36	1100.00	1200.00	1150.00
☐ HN 306, Milking Time, 1913-38	3250.00	3500.00	3350.00
☐ HN 307, The Sentimental Pierrot, 1918-38	1750.00	1900.00	1825.00
☐ HN 308, A Jester (2nd version), 1918-38	1250.00	1500.00	1350.00
☐ HN 309, A Lady of the Elizabethan Period (2nd version), 1918-38	1750.00	2000.00	1875.00
☐ HN 310, Dunce, 1918-38	2750.00	3000.00	2850.00
☐ HN 311, Dancing Figure, 1918-38	3250.00	3500.00	3350.00
☐ HN 312, Spring (1st version), The Seasons, 1918-38	1650.00	1800.00	1725.00
☐ HN 313, Summer (1st version), The Seasons, 1918-38	1650.00	1800.00	1725.00
☐ HN 314, Autumn (1st version), The Seasons, 1918-38	1650.00	1800.00	1725.00
☐ HN 315, Winter (1st version), The Seasons, 1918-38	1650.00	1800.00	1725.00
☐ HN 316, A Mandarin (1st version), 1918-38	2250.00	2500.00	1725.00
☐ HN 317, Shylock, 1918-38	2500.00	2800.00	2650.00
☐ HN 318, A Mandarin (1st version), 1918-38	2250.00	2500.00	2350.00
☐ HN 319, A Gnome, 1918-38	1000.00	1200.00	1050.00
☐ HN 320, A Jester (1st version), 1918-38	1250.00	1500.00	1350.00
☐ HN 321, Digger (New Zealand), 1918-38	1250.00	1500.00	1350.00
☐ HN 322, Digger (Australian), 1918-38	1250.00	1500.00	1350.00
☐ HN 323, Blighty, 1918-38	1250.00	1500.00	1350.00
☐ HN 324, A Scribe, 1918-38	1100.00	1200.00	1150.00
☐ HN 325, Pussy, 1918-38	2450.00	2600.00	2500.00
☐ HN 326, Madonna of the Square, 1918-38	1650.00	1800.00	1725.00
☐ HN 327, The Curtsey, 1918-38	1550.00	1700.00	1625.00
☐ HN 328, Moorish Piper Minstrel, 1918-38	2750.00	3000.00	2825.00
☐ HN 329, The Gainsborough Hat, 1918-38	1100.00	1200.00	1150.00
☐ HN 330, Pretty Lady, 1918-38	1450.00	1600.00	1525.00
☐ HN 331, A Lady of the Georgian Period, 1918-38	2000.00	2300.00	2100.00
☐ HN 332, Lady Ermine, 1918-38	1650.00	1800.00	1725.00
☐ HN 333, The Flounced Skirt, 1918-38	1550.00	1700.00	1620.00
☐ HN 334, The Curtsey, 1918-38	1500.00	1700.00	1620.00
☐ HN 335, Lady of the Fan, 1919-38	1650.00	1800.00	1750.00
☐ HN 336, Lady with Rose, 1919-38	1700.00	1800.00	1750.00
☐ HN 337, The Parson's Daughter, 1919-38	800.00	900.00	840.00
☐ HN 338, The Parson's Daughter, 1919-38	800.00	900.00	840.00
☐ HN 339, In Grandma's Days (A Lilac Shawl), 1919-38	1250.00	1500.00	1350.00
☐ HN 340, In Grandma's Days (A Lilac Shawl), 1919-38	1250.00	1500.00	1350.00
☐ HN 341, Katharine, 1919-38	1250.00	1500.00	1350.00
☐ HN 342, The Lavender Woman, 1919-38	1650.00	1800.00	1725.00

ROYALTY COLLECTIBLES / 721

	Current Price Range		Prior Year Average
☐ HN 343, An Arab, 1919-38	1750.00	2000.00	1825.00
☐ HN 344, Henry Irving as Cardinal Wolsey, 1919-38	1500.00	1750.00	1625.00
☐ HN 345, Doris Keene as Cavallini (2nd version), 1919-38	2750.00	3000.00	2875.00
☐ HN 346, Tony Weller (1st version), 1919-38	2750.00	3000.00	2875.00
☐ HN 347, Guy Fawkes, 1919-38	1750.00	2000.00	1875.00
☐ HN 348, The Carpet Vendor (1st version), 1919-38	1250.00	1400.00	1325.00
☐ HN 349, Fisherwomen, 1919-38	2750.00	3000.00	2825.00
☐ HN 350, The Carpet Vendor (1st version), 1919-38	3000.00	3500.00	3200.00
☐ HN 351, Picardy Peasant (female), 1919-38	3000.00	3250.00	3100.00
☐ HN 352, The Gainsborough Hat, 1919-38	1750.00	2000.00	1875.00
☐ HN 353, Digger (Australian), 1919-38	1250.00	1500.00	1350.00
☐ HN 354, A Geisha (1st version), 1919-38	2250.00	2500.00	2325.00
☐ HN 355, Dolly, 1919-38	1500.00	1700.00	1600.00
☐ HN 356, Sir Thomas Lovell, 1919-38	1500.00	1700.00	1600.00
☐ HN 357, Dunce, 1919-38	2750.00	3000.00	2825.00
☐ HN 358, An Old King, 1919-38	800.00	900.00	850.00
☐ HN 359, Fisherwomen, 1919-38	3250.00	3500.00	3350.00

ROYALTY COLLECTIBLES

The Royal Wedding of 1981, of Britain's Prince Charles, focused renewed attention on royalty collectibles. This is an ancient hobby, or (if not a hobby in the strict sense of the word) an ancient pursuit, as commoners from as long ago as medieval times sought relics of their sovereign. This is evident in early bookbindings, executed on order of the owners, who frequently chose to have the king's arms impressed on the covers rather than their own heraldic bearings. Much of what was produced in 1981 as "Royal Wedding souvenirs" was gimmicky and overly commercialistic. But for the more serious collector, who looks at the historical side of this interesting hobby, a great deal of intriguing, significant, worthy items from various reigns are available. Even if your interest stretches back into the dim past, there are suitable collectibles on the market. Autographs and printed proclamations exist for most kings and queens of the past 500 years or so. And when something of that nature cannot be obtained, a good addition to one's collection is a coin picturing the monarch. Small silver coins of (for example) Henry VIII, the most famous of the English kings, can be had for less than $100 when the condition is "average."

☐ Alexandra and Edward VII pressed glass creamer, Wedding Anniversary, c. 1888	60.00	80.00	70.00
☐ Elizabeth I document on vellum, unsigned but bearing a good impression of her Great Seal, attached to the document with silken twine, fleece-lined case, 7" x 4½"	1500.00	2000.00	1750.00
☐ Elizabeth II, Christmas card with her photo, signed by Prince Philip and Elizabeth II	350.00	500.00	425.00
☐ Elizabeth II, 8" x 10" b/w photo, signed and inscribed	600.00	900.00	750.00

722 / RUGS

	Current Price Range		Prior Year Average
☐ **Elizabeth II and Prince Philip,** creamware mug, Silver Wedding Anniversary, Wedgwood, 4″ H. ..	70.00	90.00	80.00
☐ **Henry VIII,** documents bearing Great Seal, but no signature	1000.00	1750.00	1315.00
☐ **Henry VIII,** document, vellum, stained, seal missing, genuine signature, dated 1532	1500.00	2500.00	2000.00
☐ **Kaiser Francis Joseph I,** enameled tin cup, 1898 Jubilee	160.00	200.00	180.00
☐ **Louis XIV of France,** a signature (removed from document or letter)	250.00	320.00	285.00
☐ **Queen Victoria stoneware flask,** c. 1837	200.00	250.00	225.00
☐ **Queen Victoria stoneware jug,** Golden Jubilee, c. 1887	80.00	110.00	95.00
☐ **Richard II,** document on vellum, no signature, 14″ c 8″	500.00	800.00	650.00

RUGS

HOOKED

Though the hooked rug is not an exclusively American artform, it is generally agreed that hooked rugs reached a higher level of quality in this country than anywhere else. The rising prices of imported rugs, and their general scarcity because of shipping difficulties and wars, turned more attention to the domestic products. Hooked rugs began to be made in the United States shortly after the War of 1812. The economic depression of the 1830's, known as the Hard Times Era, gave them a strong impetus, as it was an age of do-it-yourself, or do-without-it. A large proportion of hooked rugs of that era were homemade, for family use, and not for sale. However, manufacturers were not slow to see the commercial possibilities of hooked rugs. Before very long, small factories were springing up in the East to manufacture them; and many enterprising seamstresses (they were called "hookers," a perfectly innocent term at that time), made them on commission for retailers. This was one of the first big "piece work" projects for Americans — the seamstress turned in so many rugs, and got so much for each, as per prior agreement. Nobody got rich making them, but it put a few dollars in many pockets at a time when money was tight. The value of hooked rugs hinges on their size, age, pictorial matter, and, in general, the virtuosity of execution, as some makers were far more skilled than others. Original designs, rather than those copied from pattern books, are the highest prized. Minor fading is to be expected on the older specimens and perhaps light repair work may be needed. For display they should be framed under glass, in a frame large enough so that the edges need not be folded or crushed.

☐ **American,** depicting a lion lying between leaf and scrolling design in tones of blue, yellow, gray and red, 30″ x 56½″, 19th c.	550.00	725.00	613.00
☐ **American,** dog on grass in shades of red, brown, green and tan, 38″ x 59″ 19th c.	275.00	335.00	298.00

	Current Price Range		Prior Year Average
☐ **American Eagle and shield** in shades of gray and brown with a floral and leaf border, 30″ x 52″, 19th c.	650.00	775.00	710.00
☐ **American,** flag motif	575.00	675.00	710.00
☐ **American,** floral in tones of beige and black with garlands of green, red and yellow flowers, large	1800.00	2200.00	2000.00
☐ **American,** floral, with center of flowers and leaves, S-scroll devices in center on yellow ground, 19th c.	450.00	560.00	505.00
☐ **American,** geometric in strips of brown, yellow, gray and blue, 53″ x 10′3″	290.00	350.00	320.00
☐ **American,** geometric, red, black, yellow, green, 2′ x 3′, 1890's	55.00	70.00	63.00
☐ **American,** pictorial with animals on tan ground with tones of brown, red, beige, navy blue and black, 21″ x 33″	190.00	240.00	215.00
☐ **American,** pictorial with ducks, geese, stag and deer in landscape setting with beige, orange, green, blue, brown fabric, 21¼″ x 42″	270.00	330.00	300.00
☐ **American,** pictorial with horse surrounded by vines in tan, mauve, green and black fabric, 19″ x 39¾″	240.00	290.00	265.00
☐ **American,** pictorial with vessel flying the American flag in red, white and blue fabric, 29¼″ x 45″	260.00	320.00	290.00
☐ **American,** runner, flowers and leaves in center surrounded by squares, 25″ x 20″	285.00	345.00	315.00

Sometimes you will find so-called "rag" rugs offered by the same dealers who sell hooked rugs. These, while not strictly as collectible as hooked rugs, can be of some value depending on size and coloring, ranging from about $50 to several hundred for long runners. Then there are the "penny" and "tongue" rugs, the latter deriving its name from the shapes of its individual scrap components. These rugs are finished off with embroidery and can be quite handsome. The minimum price is usually in the $80-90 territory, with a stiff premium for specimens with creative embroidery or depicting topical themes.

ORIENTAL

The Oriental rug has long ranked as one of the classic collectors' items, not to mention classic status symbol, object d'art, and investment piece. Rugs were imported into Europe from the Orient as early as the 14th century by Genoese traders. Later, the Dutch East India Company made a specialty of them, in the 17th and 18th centuries, bringing thousands of fine examples from the East to the West. The term "Oriental rug" is loosely applied, as has been the case for centuries. It should technically designate Chinese and Japanese specimens, but is used to encompass those of Persia, Turkey, India, and in fact any territory that was east of Europe. For a long while the Persians were the acknowledged leaders in rugmaking, and their rugs now command great prices as antiques provided the style and period are "right." Values soared almost across-the-board on Oriental rugs in the mid to late 1970's, with many of them rising tenfold in value in a space of less than five years. Investor activity was partly to credit, and also the increased expertise in America, which has weeded out bad examples and made selection somewhat easier. Still, this is a field in which the unwary is soon parted from his money, if he buys from doubtful sources. The Oriental rugs sold by most importing companies are modern. Those in antiques shops are usually old, but not nearly old enough or fine enough to deserve high prices — and often are damaged from careless use by former owners. The safest source of supply are the specialist dealers in Oriental rugs, who cater to individuals and museums, and to investors as well. They advertise to buy and sell better-quality specimens and are quite accurate in their appraisals of age, condition, and market value.

	Current Price Range		Prior Year Average
☐ **Afghan Hatchli rug,** Holbein border and double "E" border, 6'8" x 4'2"	650.00	950.00	800.00
☐ **Belouchistan rug,** brown ground with geometric designs in brown, navy and red, 9'3" x 5'2"	900.00	1100.00	1000.00
☐ **Chinese rug,** rust ground with good luck symbol and lotus, 12" x 9"	1400.00	2000.00	1700.00
☐ **Daghestan rug,** ivory with flowerheads and geometric designs, red border, 4'6" x 3'2"	2750.00	3750.00	3250.00
☐ **Greek Island silk and metallic thread embroidery,** beige field embroidered with flowers and blossoming vines, 6' x 3'3"	550.00	800.00	680.00
☐ **Hereke rug,** ivory with floral medallion and stars, 16' x 12'8"	12000.00	15000.00	13500.00
☐ **Kirman rug,** red ground, sunburst medallion with floral spandrels, 11'7" x 9'	2500.00	3200.00	2850.00
☐ **Makal carpet,** flower latticework, rust ground with blue border, 24' x 14'	2700.00	3500.00	3100.00
☐ **Salor Bagface,** red with Salor guls within geometric border, 4' x 1'3"	1500.00	2200.00	1850.00
☐ **Sarouk carpet,** red ground, floral sprigs, blue border, 11'6" x 9'	1500.00	2200.00	1850.00
☐ **Silk embroidered Tucoman Bagface,** '8" x 1'9"	225.00	300.00	257.00
☐ **Spanish rug,** yellow with flower medallions, 12'8" x 9'8"	1100.00	1500.00	1300.00
☐ **Turkish embroidery,** gold metallic thread, arch design, red felt ground, 6'2" x 3'2"	1000.00	1400.00	1200.00
☐ **Turkish felt embroidery,** 4'10" x 4'10"	275.00	350.00	317.00
☐ **Veramin rug,** blue field with latticework, 10' x 7'	3500.00	4200.00	3850.00
☐ **Yomud rug,** burgundy with five rows of guls within a sunburst border, 13' x 8'5"	2250.00	3000.00	2600.00

NAVAJO

☐ **Black and white alternating strips,** 74" x 52", c. 1900	4500.00	5800.00	5100.00
☐ **Crystal rug,** gray center panel, black border, black and white figures, 38" x 60", c. 1890's	4200.00	5300.00	4800.00
☐ **Crystal rug (New Mexico),** black and white figures on red ground, 43" x 62", c. 1890's	5400.00	6500.00	5850.00
☐ **Four ply yarn** in green, white, brown and purple on red, 36" x 52" c. 1900	1700.00	2200.00	1950.00
☐ **Germantown yarn** in green, yellow, purple and white on red, 33" x 49", c. 1910	1400.00	1900.00	1650.00

	Current Price Range		Prior Year Average
☐ **Native yarn** analine dyed in red, black, white, orange, yellow, green, with addition of Germantown yarn, 34″ x 51″, c. 1900	2200.00	3100.00	2650.00
☐ **Terraced style**, black, white, indigo blue, red, 68″ x 56″, c. 1875	3900.00	4700.00	4100.00
☐ **White**, black, blue, red, 72″ x 60″, c. 1910	5750.00	7000.00	6390.00

SCIENCE FICTION AND SPACE

The Best From Fantasy And Science Fiction, Little, Brown and Company, (edited by Anthony Boucher and J. Francis McComas) .... **$14.00-$20.00**

Man's fascination with the unknown has made itself felt in various ways: by exploration, by invention, and often just by fantasizing about what COULD be or MIGHT be. Science and fantasy literature is now riding an unprecedented crest of popularity, but as a species it isn't new — as collectors have known for a long while. Books that might be classified as science fiction were penned as early as the 1700's, and works that unquestionably WERE science fiction date back to the 1800's — such as H. G. Wells' *War of the Worlds* and Jules Verne's *20,000 Leagues Under the Sea*. *Frankenstein*, which has to rate as science fiction, was first published in 1818. science fiction magazines and comics, listed here, had 20th century origins. Their first big push came with development of the airplane, which led to speculation about other forms of air travel. Originally, all of the publications listed below were very inexpensive. They were sold on newsstands and had paper covers. Though huge numbers were printed of the majority, the survival rate was rather low. You'll find them intriguing just to read, in addition to collecting them, as they show the vast changes in science fiction writing over the years. In the 1920's and '30's, almost all science fiction was of the "man from Mars" or "journey into the earth" variety, with occasional stories about timemachines. Anything more bizarre was considered (apparently) too esoteric for the readers of that day.

For a much more thorough listing of science fiction collectibles and advice on buying and selling, consult "The Official Price Guide to Comic and Science Fiction Books," published by The House of Collectibles.

PULP MAGAZINES

	Current Price Range		Prior Year Average
AVENGER (1939-1942)			
☐ Vol. 1, #1	28.00	41.00	33.00
☐ Vol. 1, #2	24.00	33.00	28.00
☐ Vol. 2, #1-6	15.00	22.00	18.00
☐ Vol. 3, #1-6	11.50	16.50	13.50
☐ Vol. 4, #1-6	9.20	13.40	11.10
CAPTAIN FUTURE (1940-1944)			
☐ Vol. 1, #1	19.50	27.50	22.00
☐ Vol. 1, #2, #3	16.00	22.00	18.00
☐ Vol. 3, #1-4, #3	12.60	17.60	15.60
DOC SAVAGE (1933-1949)			
☐ Vol. 1, #1	250.00	350.00	310.00
☐ Vol. 1, #2-2, #4	58.00	88.00	73.00
☐ Vol. 2, #5-4, #4	35.00	65.00	50.00
☐ Vol. 4, #6-8, #4	18.00	33.00	26.00
☐ Vol. 10, #5	12.00	22.00	17.00
☐ Vol. 31, #1	9.50	16.50	13.00
FLASH GORDON STRANGE ADVENTURES MAGAZINE (1936)			
☐ Vol. 1, #1	240.00	350.00	295.00
THE SHADOW (1931-1949)			
☐ Vol. 1, #1	350.00	580.00	420.00
☐ Vol. 1, #2	275.00	440.00	357.00
☐ Vol. 3, #3-4, #2	55.00	93.00	78.00
☐ Vol. 12, #3-16, #2	29.00	44.00	37.00
☐ Vol. 20, #1-23, #6	22.00	35.00	28.50
☐ Vol. 28, #1-31, #6	16.50	29.00	22.00
☐ Vol. 40, #1-43, #6	13.50	22.00	17.00
☐ Vol. 46, #5-48, #4	11.00	16.50	13.80
☐ Vol. 52, #5-54, #4	6.00	10.00	8.00
THE SPIDER (1933-1943)			
☐ Vol. 1, #1	66.00	100.00	83.00
☐ Vol. 1, #3	83.00	110.00	96.00
☐ Vol. 4, #1-7, #3	42.00	72.00	57.00
☐ Vol. 11, #1-13, #4	33.00	55.00	44.00
☐ Vol. 17, #1-19, #4	27.50	45.00	35.50
☐ Vol. 23, #1-25, #4	19.00	33.00	26.00
☐ Vol. 26, #1-28, #4	16.50	27.50	21.00
☐ Vol. 29, #1-30, #2	13.50	22.00	16.50
WU FANG (1935-1936)			
☐ Vol. 1, #1	132.00	178.00	156.00
☐ Vol. 1, #2	100.00	135.00	117.00

COMIC SPACE BOOKS

	Current Price Range		Prior Year Average
☐ Air Wonder Stories, Vol. 1, #1 (1929)	33.00	55.00	44.00
☐ Amazing Detective Tales, Vol. 1, #6 (1930)	45.00	68.00	57.00
☐ Amazing Stories, Vol. 1, #1 (1926)	165.00	275.00	220.00
☐ Amazing Stories Annual, Vol. 1, #1 (1927)	275.00	385.00	320.00
☐ Amazing Stories Quarterly, Vol. 1, #1 (1928)	33.00	55.00	42.00
☐ A. Merritt Fantasy Magazine, Vol. 1, #1 (1949)	6.75	10.00	8.25
☐ Astonishing Stories, Vol. 1, #1 (1940)	11.00	16.50	13.50

SCIENCE FICTION AND SPACE / 727

	Current Price Range		Prior Year Average
☐ Astonishing Stories, Vol. 1, #1 (1930)	550.00	880.00	700.00
☐ Authentic Science Fiction, #1 (1951)	16.50	27.50	21.50
☐ Avon Fantasy Reader #1 (1947)	6.75	10.00	8.25
☐ Avon Science Fiction Reader #1-3 (1951)	5.50	9.00	7.20
☐ Avon Science Fiction and Fantasy Reader, #1-2, (1953)	6.75	10.00	8.25
☐ Beyond Fantasy Fiction, Vol. 1, #1 (1953)	6.75	10.00	8.25
☐ Bizarre Mystery Magazine, Vol. 1, #1 (1965)	8.00	11.00	9.50
☐ Comet Stories, Vol. 1, #1 (1940)	9.00	13.50	11.50
☐ Cosmic Stories, Vol. 1, #1 (1941)	8.00	11.00	9.50
☐ Cosmos Science Fiction and Fantasy Magazine, Vol. 1, #1 (1953)	6.75	10.00	8.25
☐ Cosmos, Vol. 1, #1 (1976)	1.65	3.00	2.25
☐ Coven 13, Vol. 1, #1 (1969)	2.75	4.50	3.25
☐ Dime Mystery Magazine, Vol. 1, #1 (1932)	15.50	22.00	18.50
☐ Dream World, Vol. 1, #1 (1957)	4.50	6.75	5.20
☐ Dynamic Science Fiction, Vol. 1, #1 (1952)	3.50	5.50	4.50
☐ Dynamic Science Stories, Vol. 1, #1 (1939)	7.50	11.50	9.00
☐ Erie Mysteries, Vol. 1, #1 (1938)	27.50	38.00	32.00
☐ Famous Fantastic Mysteries, Vol. 1, #1 (1939) ...	16.50	24.00	19.50
☐ Famous Science Fiction, Vol. 1, #1 (1966)	4.40	6.50	5.50
☐ Fantastic, Vol. 1, #1 (1952)	5.50	8.80	6.85
☐ Fantastic Adventures, Vol. 1, #1 (1939)	11.00	16.50	13.50
☐ Fantastic Novels Magazine, Vol. 1, #1 (1940 and 1948)	13.00	20.00	16.50
☐ Fantastic Science Fiction, Vol. 1, #1 (1952)	2.75	4.50	3.35
☐ Fantastic Story Quarterly, Vol. 1, #1 (1950)	2.75	4.50	3.35
☐ Fantastic Universe, Vol. 1, #1 (1953)	4.50	7.80	6.30
☐ Fantasy Book, Vol. 1, #1 (1947)	2.75	4.00	2.85
☐ Fantasy Fiction, Vol. 1, #1 (1950)	4.50	7.80	6.30
☐ Fantasy Magazine, Vol. 1, #1 (1953)	2.75	4.50	3.35
☐ Fear, Vol. 1, #1 (1960)	2.75	4.50	2.85
☐ Forgotten Fantasy, Vol. 1, #1 (1970)	2.75	4.50	2.85
☐ Future Fiction, Vol. 1, #1 (1939)	13.50	20.00	16.50
☐ Galaxy Science Fiction, Vol. 1, #1 (1950)	4.50	7.80	6.30
☐ Galileo, Vol. 1, #1 (1976)	2.00	3.00	2.50
☐ Gamma, Vol. 1, #1 (1963)	2.25	3.50	2.85
☐ Ghost Stories, Vol. 1, #1 (1926)	22.00	33.00	27.00
☐ Golden Fleece, Vol. 1, #1 (1938)	22.00	33.00	27.00
☐ Horror Stories, Vol. 1, #1 (1935)	110.00	165.00	132.00
☐ Imagination Stories of Science and Fantasy, , Vol. 1, #1 (1950)	4.50	7.80	6.30
☐ Imaginative Tales, #1 (1954)	3.50	5.50	4.50
☐ Infinity Science Fiction, Vol. 1, #1 (1955)	3.50	5.50	4.50
☐ International Science Fiction, Vol. 1, #1 (1967) ...	1.65	2.75	2.35
☐ Isaac Asimov's Science Fiction, Vol. 1, #1 (1977) .	2.75	4.00	3.35
☐ Magazine of Fantasy and Science Fiction, Vol. 1, #1 (1949)	6.75	10.00	8.25
☐ Magazine of Horror and Strange Stories, Vol. 1, #1 (1963)	4.00	6.25	5.25
☐ Magic Carpet Magazine, Vol. 3, #1 (1933)	122.00	165.00	140.00
☐ Marvel Science Stories, Vol. 1, #1 (1938)	27.00	42.00	35.00
☐ Mind, Inc., Vol. 1, #1 (1929)	175.00	220.00	198.00
☐ Miracle Science and Fantasy Stories, Vol. 1, #1 (1931)	72.00	100.00	86.00

728 / SCIENCE FICTION AND SPACE

	Current Price Range		Prior Year Average
☐ The Mysterious Traveler Magazine, Vol. 1, #1 (1951)	3.50	5.80	4.30
☐ New World Science Fiction, Vol. 1, #1 - Vol. 1, #5 (American Reprints - 1960)	1.40	2.15	1.70
☐ Odyssey Science Fiction, Vol. 1, # (1976)	1.25	1.75	1.50
☐ Orbit Science Fiction, Vol. 1, #1 (1953)	1.55	2.25	1.75
☐ Oriental Stories, Vol. 1, #1 (1930)	110.00	155.00	135.00
☐ Other Worlds Science Stories, Vol. 1, #1 (1949)	4.50	7.75	6.00
☐ Out of This World Adventures, Vol. 1, #1 (1950)	6.50	10.00	8.25
☐ Planet Stories, Vol. 1, #1 (1939)	19.00	28.50	23.80
☐ Rocket Stories, Vol. 1, #1 (1953)	4.50	6.50	5.50
☐ Satellite Science Fiction, Vol. 1, #1 (1956)	4.50	7.75	6.00
☐ Saturn Magazine of Fantasy and Science Fiction, Vol. 1, #1 (1957)	2.25	3.50	2.85
☐ Science Fiction, Vol. 1, #1 (1939)	8.00	11.00	9.50
☐ Science Fiction Adventures, Vol. 1, #1 (1956)	2.50	4.50	3.55
☐ Science Fiction Digest, Vol. 1, #1 (1954)	2.75	4.50	3.55
☐ Science Fiction Plus, Vol. 1, #1 (1953)	4.50	6.50	5.50
☐ Science Fiction Quarterly, #1 (1940)	9.00	13.50	11.50
☐ Science Fiction Stories (1953)	3.00	4.15	3.55
☐ Science Stories, #1 (1953)	2.25	3.50	2.85
☐ Science Wonder Stories, Vol. 1, #1 (1929)	45.00	65.00	55.00
☐ Science Wonder Quarterly, Vol. 1, #1 (1929)	22.00	35.00	28.00
☐ Science Detective Monthly, Vol. 1, #1 (1930)	35.00	50.00	40.00
☐ Shock, Vol. 1, #1 (1948)	5.50	8.75	7.20
☐ Shock, Vol. 1, #1 (1960)	2.00	3.50	2.75
☐ Sinister Stories, Vol. 1, #1 (1940)	11.00	16.50	13.25
☐ Space Science Fiction, Vol. 1, #1 (1952)	2.25	4.00	2.85
☐ Space Science Fiction Magazine, Vol. 1, #1 (1957)	2.25	3.55	2.70
☐ Space Stories, Vol. 1, #1 (1952)	2.00	3.55	2.70
☐ Space Travel, Vol 5, #4 - Vol. 5, #6 (1958)	1.10	2.00	1.55
☐ Spaceway Science Fiction, Vol. 1, #1 (1953)	2.75	4.50	3.45
☐ Speed Mystery Stories, Vol. 1, #1 (1943)	4.50	7.25	5.80
☐ Spicy Mystery Stories, Vol. 1, #1 (1934)	60.00	90.00	75.00
☐ Star Science Fiction, Vol. 1, #1 (1958)	1.45	2.10	1.75
☐ Startling Mystery Magazine, Vol. 1, #1 (1940)	35.00	49.50	42.00
☐ Startling Stories, Vol. 1, #1 (1939)	11.00	16.50	13.25
☐ Stirring Science Stories, Vol. 1, #1 (1941)	6.50	10.00	8.25
☐ Strange Stories, Vol. 1, #1 (1939)	30.00	38.50	34.25
☐ Strange Tales, Vol. 1, #1 (1931)	165.00	245.00	200.00
☐ Super-Science Fiction, Vol. 1, #1 (1956)	2.25	3.50	2.85
☐ Super-Science Stories, Vol. 1, #1 (1940)	8.00	11.00	9.50
☐ Suspence, Vol. 1, #1 (1951)	2.25	3.50	2.85
☐ Tales of Magic and Mystery, Vol. 1, #1 (1927)	110.00	155.00	130.00
☐ Tales of the Frightened, Vol. 1, #1 (1957)	4.50	7.80	5.00
☐ Ten-Story Fantasy, Vol. 1, #1 (1951)	2.75	7.80	5.00
☐ Terror Tales, Vol. 1, #1 (1934)	100.00	135.00	117.00
☐ The Thrill Book, Vol. 1, #1 (1919)	1100.00	1650.00	1300.00
☐ Thrilling Mystery, Vol. 1, #1 (1935)	29.50	38.50	33.00
☐ Thrilling Wonder Stories, Vol 8, #1 (1936)	8.00	11.00	9.50
☐ Tops in Science Fiction, Vol. 1, #1 (1953)	1.95	3.10	2.50
☐ Two Complete Science Adventure Books, Vol. 1, #1 (1950)	2.75	4.50	3.35
☐ Uncanny Stories, Vol. 1, #1 (1941)	22.00	33.00	28.00
☐ Uncanny Tales, Vol. 2, #4 (1938)	33.00	50.00	41.00
☐ Unearth, Vol. 1, #1 (1976)	1.55	2.45	1.95

	Current Price Range		Prior Year Average
☐ Universe Science Fiction, #1 (1953)	1.55	2.45	1.95
☐ Unknown, Vol. 1, #1 (1939)	22.00	33.00	28.00
☐ Vanguard Science Fiction, Vol. 1, #1 (1958)	2.25	3.55	2.75
☐ Venture Science Fiction, Vol. 1, #1 (1957)	2.25	3.55	2.75
☐ Vertex, Vol. 1, #1 - Vol 3, #2 (1973)	1.55	2.45	1.95
☐ Vision of Tomorrow, Vol. 1, #1 (1969)	1.10	1.90	1.50
☐ Vortex Science Fiction, Vol. 1, #1 (1953)	1.50	2.25	1.80
☐ Weird Terror Tales, Vol. 1, #1 (1970)	3.85	6.05	4.95
☐ Weird Tales, Vol. 1, #1 (1923)	880.00	1320.00	1080.00
☐ Wonder Stories, Vol. 2, #1 (1930)	13.50	20.00	16.50
☐ Wonder Stories Annual, Vol. 1, #1 (1950)	2.25	3.50	2.85
☐ Worlds Beyond, Vol. 1, #1 (1950)	1.45	2.25	2.05
☐ Worlds of Fantasy, Vol. 1, #1 (1968)	1.45	2.25	2.05
☐ Worlds of If, Vol. 1, #1 (1952)	4.50	6.50	5.50
☐ Worlds of Tomorrow, Vol. 1, #1 (1963)	1.10	1.65	1.35

SCOUTING COLLECTIBLES

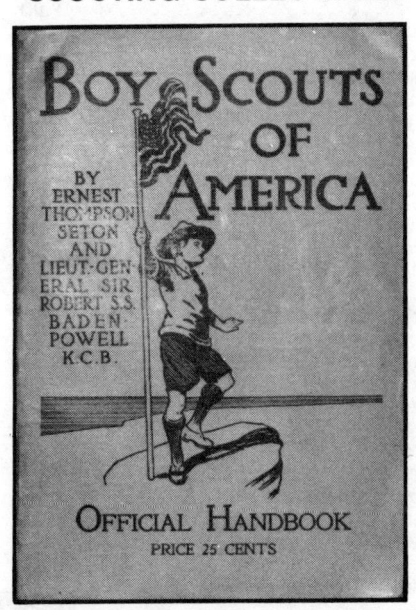

Official Boy Scout Handbook, by Seaton and Baden-Powell, first edition, c. 1910 .... **$225.00-$300.00**

They should give a badge for collecting scouting materials! Everything from cloth badges to metal neckerchief rings, from tools to backpacks, from uniforms to manuals are collected, and while Boy Scout collectors are a bit more numerous, Girl Scout collectors are remembering where those cookies came from. For more in-depth information and listings, you may refer to *The Official Price Guide to Scouting Collectible,* published by the House of Collectibles.

730 / SCOUTING COLLECTIBLES

	Current Price Range		Prior Year Average

MEDALLIONS

☐ **Excelsior Shoe Coin,** good luck symbols on back, dated July 1910	8.00	12.00	10.00
☐ **Rotary Club International,** good luck coin, 1½", 1920	10.00	18.00	14.00
☐ **Twenty-fifth Anniversary National Convention,** Alpha Phi Omega, silver, emblem, 1950	6.00	9.00	7.00
☐ **Youth Of The Scout World,** scouts signalling, eagle on back, bronze, 1952	4.00	6.00	5.00
☐ **Scout Tower At Valley Forge,** official, bronze, Washington praying on front, wording on back, 1957	12.00	15.00	13.00
☐ **Wonderful World Of Scouting,** sold at New York World's Fair, bronze, Boy Scout emblem on front, 1964	2.00	3.00	2.50
☐ **Pocket Piece,** official bronze, scout law and emblem on front, scout oath on back, 1968	2.00	4.00	3.00
☐ **Boy Power - Man Power,** official, silver or bronze, boy poser insignia on front, Scout oath on back, 1971	2.00	4.00	3.00
☐ **Pocket Piece,** official, bronze Cub Scouts, square, wolf on front, promise on back, 1972	2.00	4.00	3.00
☐ **Honoring Boy Scouts,** bronze, scout with staff on front, wording on back	3.00	5.00	4.00

MEDALS

☐ **General Douglas MacArthur Medal,** World War II for Victory Gardens	25.00	35.00	30.00
☐ **Grub Scout Button,** World War I	30.00	40.00	35.00
☐ **Hornaday Badge,** awarded to a Scout or Explorer for outstanding service or environmental quality within a council	35.00	50.00	40.00
☐ **Hornaday Conservation Silver Medal,** award for outstanding work in conservation	200.00	250.00	220.00
☐ **Medal Of Merit,** awarded for outstanding act of service not necessarily risking own life	200.00	300.00	240.00
☐ **Silver Antelope Award,** given to adult volunteers for distinguished service to youth in the region	150.00	200.00	170.00
☐ **Silver Beaver Award,** given to adult volunteers for outstanding service to youth on a council basis	50.00	75.00	56.00
☐ **Silver Faun,** the highest award made to lady scouters	250.00	300.00	275.00
☐ **Second Class,** heavy gold gilt medal, clasp pin back, c. 1916	18.00	22.00	20.00
☐ **Tenderfoot,** heavy gold gilt medal, highly polished clasp pin back, c. 1916	16.00	20.00	18.00

MERIT BADGES

☐ **Aerodynamics,** 6,693, 1942-1952.			
☐ **Type C,** 3,878 issued	5.00	6.00	5.50
☐ **Type D,** 2,795 issued	5.00	6.00	5.50
☐ **Airplane Design,** 5,938, 1942-1952.			
☐ **Type C,** 3,251 issued	5.00	6.00	5.50
☐ **Type D,** 1,687 issued	6.00	8.00	7.00

SCOUTING COLLECTIBLES / 731

	Current Price Range		Prior Year Average
☐ **American Business,** 22,015, 1967.			
☐ **Type E,** 6,832 issued	1.00	2.00	1.50
☐ **Type F,** 15,183 issued	.80	1.00	.90
☐ **Archery,** 377,138.			
☐ **Type A,** 3,056 issued	17.00	22.00	19.00
☐ **Type B,** 796 issued	14.00	18.00	16.00
☐ **Type C,** 3,466 issued	5.00	6.00	5.50
☐ **Type D,** 25,595 issued	2.00	3.00	2.50
☐ **Type E,** 122,931 issued	.80	1.00	.90
☐ **Type F,** 221,294 issued	.80	1.00	.90
☐ **Athletics,** 877,331.			
☐ **Type A,** 141,181 issued	5.00	7.00	6.00
☐ **Type B,** 47,466 issued	3.00	4.00	3.50
☐ **Type C,** 190,244 issued	1.00	2.00	1.50
☐ **Type D,** 169,022 issued	1.00	2.00	1.50
☐ **Type E,** 173,409 issued	.80	1.00	.90
☐ **Blacksmithing,** 27,147.			
☐ **Type A,** 13,148 issued	13.00	16.00	14.00
☐ **Type B,** 2,811 issued	7.00	9.00	8.00
☐ **Type C,** 7,893 issued	4.00	5.00	4.50
☐ **Type D,** 3,295 issued	5.00	6.00	5.50
☐ **Botany,** 71,783.			
☐ **Type A,** 12,196 issued	13.00	16.00	14.50
☐ **Type B,** 2,609 issued	7.00	9.00	8.00
☐ **Type C,** 7,632 issued	4.00	5.00	4.50
☐ **Type D,** 10,319 issued	3.00	4.00	3.50
☐ **Type E,** 17,658 issued	.80	1.00	.90
☐ **Type F,** 21,369 issued	.80	1.00	.90
☐ **Camping,** 2,373,138.			
☐ **Type A,** 117,797 issued	5.00	7.00	6.00
☐ **Type B,** 32,985 issued	4.00	5.00	4.50
☐ **Type C,** 149,658 issued	1.00	2.00	1.50
☐ **Type D,** 405,260 issued	.80	1.00	.90
☐ **Type E,** 920,817 issued	.80	1.00	.90
☐ **Type F,** 746,621 issued	.80	1.00	.90
☐ **Carpentry,** 548,539.			
☐ **Type A,** 207,097 issued	5.00	6.00	5.50
☐ **Type B,** 52,423 issued	3.00	4.00	3.50
☐ **Type C,** 199,254 issued	1.00	2.00	1.50
☐ **Type D,** 89,765 issued	1.00	2.00	1.50
☐ **Dog Care,** 298,839.			
☐ **Type D,** 89,005 issued	1.00	2.00	1.50
☐ **Type E,** 102,686 issued	1.00	2.00	1.50
☐ **Type F,** 107,148 issued	.80	1.00	.90
☐ **Electricity,** 504,829.			
☐ **Type A,** 81,489 issued	6.00	8.00	7.00
☐ **Type B,** 15,380 issued	5.00	6.00	5.50
☐ **Type C,** 61,766 issued	2.00	3.00	2.50
☐ **Type D,** 86,374 issued	1.00	2.00	1.50
☐ **Type E,** 152,477 issued	.80	1.00	.90
☐ **Type F,** 107,343 issued	.80	1.00	.90
☐ **Farm Layout,** 89,017, discontinued 1959.			
☐ **Type A,** 12,393 issued	13.00	16.00	14.50
☐ **Type B,** 9,232 issued	5.00	6.00	5.50
☐ **Type C,** 32,334 issued	2.00	3.00	2.50
☐ **Type D,** 35,058 issued	1.00	2.00	1.50

732 / SCOUTING COLLECTIBLES

	Current Price Range		Prior Year Average
Farm Records, 52,786, replaced by Farm and Ranch Management 1980.			
Type A, 6,445 issued	15.00	19.00	17.00
Type B, 3,019 issued	7.00	9.00	8.00
Type C, 9,185 issued	3.00	4.00	3.50
Type D, 12,125 issued	2.00	3.00	2.50
Type E, 11,095 issued	1.00	2.00	1.50
Type F, 10,917 issued	.80	1.00	.90
Fruit Culture, 11,865, discontinued about 1954.			
Type A, 3,267 issued	17.00	22.00	19.00
Type B, 1,499 issued	10.00	13.00	11.50
Type C, 4,180 issued	5.00	6.00	5.00
Type D, 2,919 issued	5.00	6.00	5.00
General Service, 32,876.			
Type F, 32,876 issued	.80	1.00	.90
Handicraft, 600,451.			
Type A, 249,506 issued	5.00	6.00	5.50
Type B, 88,837 issued	3.00	4.00	3.50
Type C, 262,108 issued	.80	1.00	.90
Home Repairs, 2,089,278, 1945.			
Type C, 118,897 issued	1.00	2.00	1.50
Type D, 749,846 issued	.80	1.00	.90
Type E, 700,707 issued	.80	1.00	.90
Type F, 519,828 issued	.80	1.00	.90
Insect Life, 96,463.			
Type A, 5,707 issued	16.00	20.00	18.00
Type B, 573 issued	14.00	18.00	16.00
Type C, 3,749 issued	5.00	6.00	5.50
Type D, 15,822 issued	2.00	3.00	2.50
Type E, 38,533 issued	1.00	2.00	1.50
Type F, 32,078 issued	.80	1.00	.90
Invention, 151 one of the original Merit Badges, it was discontinued in about 1917.			
Type A, 151 approximately issued	40.00	50.00	44.00
Leathercraft, 249,361, discontinued 1952.			
Type A, 121,612 issued	5.00	7.00	6.50
Type B, 23,919 issued	5.00	6.00	5.50
Type C, 69,142 issued	1.00	2.00	1.50
Type D, 34,688 issued	1.00	2.00	1.50
Lifesaving, 1,929,638.			
Type A, 143,360 issued	5.00	7.00	6.00
Type B, 43,372 issued	4.00	5.00	4.50
Type C, 189,730 issued	1.00	2.00	1.50
Type D, 355,295 issued	.80	1.00	.90
Type E, 705,809 issued	.80	1.00	.90
Type F, 492,072 issued	.80	1.00	.90
Mechanical Drawing, 174,673, 1933-1964.			
Type A, 2,491 issued	18.00	23.00	20.00
Type B, 7,827 issued	5.00	7.00	6.00
Type C, 46,835 issued	2.00	3.00	2.50
Type D, 68,554 issued	1.00	2.00	1.50
Mining, 8,036, discontinued in 1937.			
Type A, 6,677 issued	16.00	20.00	18.00
Type B, 1,359 issued	10.00	13.00	11.50

SCOUTING COLLECTIBLES / 733

	Current Price Range		Prior Year Average

- **Oceanography,** 51,457.
  - Type E, 14,039 issued .... .80 / 1.00 / .90
  - Type F, 37,418 issued .... .80 / 1.00 / .90
- **Pathfinding,** 598,085, discontinued in 1952.
  - Type A, 189,166 issued .... 5.00 / 7.00 / 6.00
  - Type B, 63,852 issued .... 3.00 / 4.00 / 3.50
  - Type C, 226,931 issued .... 1.00 / 2.00 / 1.50
  - Type D, 118,236 issued .... 1.00 / 2.00 / 1.50
- **Personal Health,** 1,014,833, discontinued in 1952.
  - Type A, 332,664 issued .... 5.00 / 6.00 / 5.50
  - Type B, 81,928 issued .... 3.00 / 4.00 / 3.50
  - Type C, 419,452 issued .... 1.00 / 2.00 / 1.50
  - Type D, 180,789 issued .... .80 / 1.00 / .90
- **Pets,** 392,614, started August, 1958.
  - Type D, 3,924 issued .... 4.00 / 5.00 / 4.50
  - Type E, 142,420 issued .... 1.00 / 2.00 / 1.50
  - Type F, 246,270 issued .... .80 / 1.00 / .90
- **Railroading,** 83,563.
  - Type D, 18,871 issued .... 3.00 / 4.00 / 3.50
  - Type E, 37,695 issued .... 1.00 / 2.00 / 1.50
  - Type F, 26,997 issued .... .80 / 1.00 / .90
- **Reptile Study,** 280,842.
  - Type A, 43,497 issued .... 9.00 / 11.00 / 10.00
  - Type B, 8,827 issued .... 5.00 / 7.00 / 6.00
  - Type C, 38,760 issued .... 2.00 / 3.00 / 2.50
  - Type D, 32,318 issued .... 2.00 / 3.00 / 2.50
  - Type E, 64,891 issued .... .80 / 1.00 / .90
  - Type F, 92,549 issued .... .80 / 1.00 / .90
- **Skating,** 26,729, new in 1973.
  - Type F, 26,729 issued .... .80 / 1.00 / .90
- **Small Boat Saling,** 83,400.
  - Type E, 12,745 issued .... 1.00 / 2.00 / 1.50
  - Type F, 70,655 issued .... .80 / 1.00 / .90
- **Traffic Study,** 22,662, new in 1975.
  - Type F, 22,662 issued .... .80 / 1.00 / .90
- **Water Skiing,** 81,312, 1969.
  - Type E, 12,551 issued .... .80 / 1.00 / .90
  - Type F, 68,761 issued .... .80 / 1.00 / .90

MISCELLANEOUS

- **Ash Tray,** Kit Carson House, Philmont, 1950 .... 6.00 / 8.00 / 7.00
- **Bank,** Conn., has another scout behind kettle, 1915 .... 200.00 / 300.00 / 250.00
- **Bank,** tin lithographed scout, 1912 .... 20.00 / 25.00 / 22.00
- **Binoculars,** tan leather, 1920's .... 70.00 / 85.00 / 77.00
- **Blotter,** BSA/Coca-cola, "Be Prepared, Be Refreshed" .... 5.00 / 7.00 / 6.00
- **Belt,** belt and buckle, gun medal, 1930's .... 6.00 / 9.00 / 7.50
- **Bookends,** metal, first class Emblem 6" x 6" .... 20.00 / 30.00 / 24.00
- **Bookmark,** green and gold, first class emblem, BSA National Council .... 4.00 / 5.00 / 4.25
- **Books,** Holy Bible, early BSA seal on cover ..... 40.00 / 50.00 / 45.00
- **Cachet Cover,** Boy Scout stamp club, 1932 ..... 8.00 / 10.00 / 9.00
- **Calendar holder,** cast metal, BSA perpetual, first class emblem .... 17.00 / 20.00 / 18.50

734 / SCOUTING COLLECTIBLES

	Current Price Range		Prior Year Average
☐ **Camera,** Official 7-Piece flash camera kit	10.00	15.00	12.00
☐ **Canteen,** Wearever seamless, felt cover, 1930's .	15.00	20.00	17.00
☐ **Cards,** 65 BSA job description cards, 1949-1962 .	4.00	6.00	5.00
☐ **Collar Monogram,** BSA, brass collar monograms, 1920's	30.00	50.00	40.00
☐ **Comb,** Official BSA comb and clippers in a case .	2.00	6.00	4.00
☐ **Compass,** Sylva pathfinder, BSA	1.00	3.00	2.00
☐ **Cut Outs,** Camping with the Scouts, gummed paper in book form, 1930's	20.00	25.00	22.00
☐ **Drum,** "Boy Scout Drum" tin, 6" round 3½" high, 1908	30.00	50.00	40.00
☐ **Figurine,** Head Scout, signaller, arms move, 2" ..	15.00	22.00	18.00
☐ **Figurine,** Kenner doll, Craig Cub Scout	12.00	18.00	15.00
☐ **Figurine,** Scout with pack and rifle, cardboard, 6" high	4.00	5.00	4.50
☐ **Figurine,** Lead Scout kneeling, frying eggs	10.00	12.00	11.00
☐ **Figurine,** Scout plastic figure, tree and flagpole, 3"	7.00	10.00	8.50
☐ **First Aid Kit,** Bauer and Black, gray, oval belt loop kit, rare, 1932	15.00	25.00	20.00
☐ **First Aid Kit,** Johnson and Johnson, swing clasp, 1942	12.00	20.00	16.00
☐ **Gadget Box,** imitation wood, cub, scout, and explorer emblems	3.00	5.00	4.00
☐ **Game,** game of Scouting by Milton Bradley, 1920's	60.00	100.00	80.00
☐ **Game,** target ball game, uses three marbles, like tiddlywinks, Boy Scout target shooting scene ...	40.00	60.00	50.00
☐ **Handkerchief,** set of 3, Scouts, contained in a Scout box	30.00	40.00	35.00
☐ **Light Bulb,** Boy Scout cheer light, Aerolux Light Corp.	5.00	7.00	6.00
☐ **Miror,** pocket signal disk, semaphore and morse, 1914	8.00	12.00	10.00
☐ **Paperweight,** Cub-Scout-Explorer, glass, 3" dome	15.00	25.00	20.00
☐ **Paperweight,** "Safety Good Turn 1958," tenderfoot emblem, Lucite	8.00	10.00	9.00
☐ **Pedometer,** Scouts hike-meter, also a compass .	7.00	12.00	9.00
☐ **Pin,** "I'm A Camper," pictures tent Scout and fire, 1" button	1.00	4.00	2.00
☐ **Pin,** "I Recruited One BSA"	1.00	1.50	1.25
☐ **Plaque,** imitation wood, first class emblem on shield 3½" x 5"	4.50	7.00	5.50
☐ **Postcards,** 12 Scout law postcards, 1917	50.00	75.00	60.00
☐ **Poster,** Bauer and Black Scout first aid chart, 20" x 32", 1920's	5.00	8.00	6.00
☐ **Poster,** "Is God Calling Me," Catholic Comittee on Scouting, 14" x 10", 1946	3.50	5.00	4.00
☐ **Poster,** scouts of Today Men of Leadership Tomorrow, 13½" x 19½" c. 1925	12.00	16.00	14.00
☐ **Poster,** religious awards, heavy cardboard, easel back, set of 8, 14" x 20"	12.00	15.00	13.50
☐ **Poster,** "We'll Help You to Win the War Dad," World War I, Scout and soldier, framed under glass, 12" x 18"	60.00	75.00	66.00

	Current Price Range		Prior Year Average
☐ **Record,** Brunswick label, 2 marches played by Boy Scout Band, 10″, 78 rpm	8.00	12.00	10.00
☐ **Record,** BSA, "Message from John Glenn," cardboard phonograph type	1.00	2.00	1.50
☐ **Record,** "The Explorers March," 45 rpm, 1950's ..	4.00	6.00	5.00
☐ **Ring,** first class, Scout, silver, square, 1970's ...	7.00	12.00	9.00
☐ **Ring,** recessed first class emblem, sterling c. 1920's	15.00	18.00	16.50
☐ **School Supplies,** tin pencil box, Mfg. by Wallace Pencil Co., Boy Scout scene in color	20.00	30.00	24.00
☐ **Serving Tray,** BSA, metal, Portrait of Boy Scout with Scout law on scroll, 6 camping scenes	10.00	15.00	12.00
☐ **Sheet Music,** Boy Scouts March, Hopkins, 1937 .	6.00	10.00	8.00
☐ **Sheet Music,** "Boy Scouts on Parade," Martin, 1930	6.00	10.00	8.00
☐ **Sheet Music,** "Hoe Your Little Bit in Your Own Back Yard," 1917	10.00	16.00	13.00
☐ **Sheet Music,** "Off to Camp March," Anthony, 1921	15.00	18.00	16.50
☐ **Sheet Music,** "The Boy Scout Dream," Jones, 1915	14.00	17.00	15.00
☐ **Signals,** BSA Signaller, 1937	12.00	15.00	13.00
☐ **Telescope,** Early British, brass and nickel "The B-P Telescout"	40.00	60.00	50.00
☐ **Tie Bars,** Cub Scout, wood	2.00	4.00	3.00
☐ **Tie Rack,** pressed wood, first class emblem and camp scenes, c. 1937	8.00	12.00	10.00
☐ **Tray,** tin, World War II, hinged lid showing Boy Scouts and British military leaders, 4″ x 5″ x 5″ .	20.00	30.00	24.00
☐ **Viewing Material,** glass langern slides, Scout Oath, Scout Law, set of 14, color	100.00	150.00	125.00
☐ **Watch,** Official BSA, Timex, first class emblem on face, expansion band	13.00	18.00	15.00
☐ **Watch Fob,** BSA Layman, white enamel, gold filled, 1915	40.00	50.00	44.00
☐ **Watch Fob,** Scout signalling (sideways) scene ..	15.00	25.00	20.00
☐ **Whistle,** "The Boy Scout," English with small compass, chrome over brass	12.00	17.00	14.00

BOY SCOUT HANDBOOKS

ORIGINAL 1910 EDITION VARIATIONS

☐ **Variation I,** brown and gold hardcover Seton and Baden Powell as authors, contains blank pages .	225.00	300.00	255.00
☐ **Variation V,** green and white soft cover, shows Seton as only author, "Price 25¢ net" on cover ..	200.00	300.00	240.00
☐ **Variation VII,** green hardcover with embossed "Campfire Edition"	180.00	250.00	215.00

HANDBOOK — FIRST EDITION

☐ **Black on brown cover,** some blank pages, title page marked "Proof Copy," proof, June 1911, 320 pages	160.00	200.00	180.00
☐ **Glossy Reprint,** same as above but soft cover, made in larger quantities	5.00	10.00	7.00
☐ **Reprint,** same as above, but hardcover, published for sale in commercial book stores	9.00	12.00	10.50

SECOND EDITION

	Current Price Range		Prior Year Average
☐ **Black on brown cover,** third printing, May 1912, 404 pages	125.00	160.00	145.00
☐ **Black on dark red cover,** fourth printing, July 1912, 404 pages	100.00	190.00	145.00
☐ **Black on dark red cover,** sixth printing, May 1913, 416 pages	100.00	150.00	125.00
☐ **Black on orange cover,** seventh printing, October 1913, 416 pages	90.00	150.00	120.00

THIRD EDITION

☐ **Silver cover,** twelfth printing, January 1915, 472 pages	125.00	200.00	160.00
☐ **Silver cover,** "13th edition 1916" on title page, reprint, thirteenth printing, April 1916, 464 pages	150.00	225.00	182.00
☐ **Red cover,** "sixteenth edition" on cover, sixteenth printing, May 1917, 498 pages	60.00	115.00	82.00
☐ **Light green cover,** "18th edition" on cover, eighteenth printing, May 1918, 498 pages	60.00	100.00	80.00
☐ **Every Boys Library Edition,** twentieth printing, May 1919, 496 pages	45.00	90.00	60.00
☐ **Light green cover,** twenty-third printing, January 1921, 488 pages	30.00	55.00	42.00

SCRIMSHAW

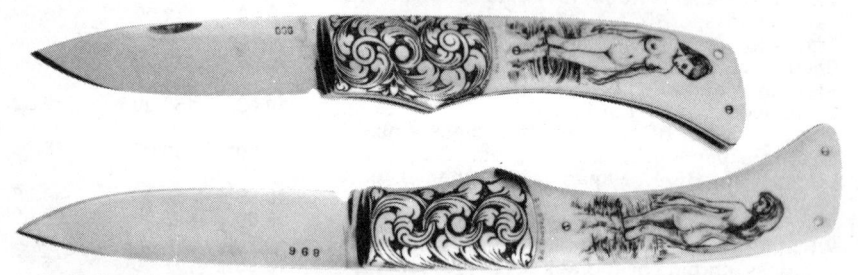

Bob Ogg Maker. The engraver is Mel Wood of Elgin, AZ. Scrimshander is Glen Stearns of Toledo, Ohio, the knife is by Bob Ogg and is valued at about .... **$400.00-$500.00**

Sailors had little free time on merchant and naval vessels in the 19th century, but what time they had was creatively employed: in fancy knot-tying, banjo-strumming, teaching parrots to say vulgar words, and manufacturing scrimshaw. Scrimshaw is artwork done on bone. Most commonly, whalebone was used, as many of the ships were whalers and had plenty of whalebone handy. Walrus tusk was also used, and sometimes other bones, depending on availability. When scrimshaw is found on an ox or cattle bone (which occasionally happens), quite likely the bone was fished up by the sailor-artisan from the kitchen's stewpot, or brought on board from a portside slophouse. When whale *teeth* or walrus tusk is used, the material is technically ivory, but is considered a low-grade ivory compared to elephant tusk. The age, size, artistic quality, subject matter, and state of preservation all go into determining the value of scrimshaw. There are two basic sorts: carved and painted. Carved scrimshaw, which seldom has any painted decoration, is mostly in the nature of little trinkets — boxes, pins, forks. Painted scrimshaw is done directly on the tooth or bone. It was accomplished by scratching the design into the surface with needles, then working India ink into the scratches. When a faded specimen is found, as is often the case, the scratches were either not deep enough; or bad ink was used; or the specimen was excessively handled and became "rubbed." On the other hand, beware of *very* bright designs, as these sometimes are modern. It is illegal to make scrimshaw any longer, because the whale is an endangered species, but this does not deter counterfeiters.

	Current Price Range		Prior Year Average
☐ **Box,** whalebone and wood, 10″ L.	505.00	730.00	655.00
☐ **Bust of man,** 4″ H.	138.00	190.00	166.00
☐ **Cane,** dove on knob, brass tip, 38″ H.	355.00	460.00	405.00
☐ **Carpenter's molding plane,** 9½″ L.	500.00	610.00	555.00
☐ **Carpenter's square,** teakwood handle	145.00	190.00	168.00
☐ **Corset stays,** whalebone, home scenes, 14″ L.	175.00	225.00	200.00
☐ **Hammer,** dolphin on handle, 7″ L.	247.00	330.00	282.00
☐ **Horn,** 10″ L., c. 19th c.	190.00	235.00	210.00
☐ **Napkin holder,** with cats	45.00	65.00	55.00
☐ **Pie crimper,** fancy with rosewood handle	165.00	210.00	188.00
☐ **Walrus' tusk,** cribbage board	880.00	1100.00	1000.00
☐ **Walrus' tusk,** dagger, 10″ L.	110.00	165.00	137.50
☐ **Walrus' tusk,** Indians, 6″ L.	660.00	880.00	720.00
☐ **Walrus' tusk,** mother and child on swing, 11″ L.	450.00	610.00	520.00
☐ **Whale's tooth,** crucifix, 6″ L.	275.00	355.00	315.00
☐ **Whale's tooth,** eagle and flag, 5″ L.	550.00	780.00	670.00
☐ **Whale's tooth,** children playing	575.00	800.00	685.00
☐ **Whale's tooth,** whaling scene, 5″ L.	650.00	880.00	770.00

SHAKER CRAFTS AND FURNITURE

Shakers settled in the United States after emigrating from England in the early 19th century. The name was applied by their critics. Shakers used considerable body motion in their religious services, and were said to "shake" (just as Quakers "quaked"). Like most other small religious communities in 19th century America, it strove for self-sufficiency and was willing to endure a modest existence, so long as it could satisfy its own needs. Thus, the Shakers grew their own produce, raised farm animals, knitted clothing, and made household goods. Nearly all of what they made was for their own use. As their only desire was for utilitarian use, their products were not lavishly decorated. Nevertheless, they have a certain charm and gracefulness, simply because of the no-nonsense styling, the fresh clean lines, and the total lack of commercialism. It is one of the few classes of furniture in the history of mankind that does not carry some touches to catch a prospective buyer's eye. A few decades ago, specimens of Shaker work could be turned up "at the source," by the site of old Shaker communities in western New York State and Pennsylvania. It has since been pretty thoroughly cleaned out and sent to market, and you will probably have to pay the full retail prices, or near them, for any that you want to buy. But do check the rural auctions and out-of-the-way antique shops, as luck still occasionally smiles on the determined collector.

	Current Price Range		Prior Year Average
☐ **Almanac,** 1885	55.00	75.00	65.00
☐ **Basket,** double handle, 7"	110.00	140.00	125.00
☐ **Basket,** cover, red-painted handle	210.00	265.00	232.00
☐ **Basket,** draining	75.00	95.00	85.00
☐ **Bonnet,** woven with straw	130.00	170.00	150.00
☐ **Box,** 8½" oval	100.00	135.00	117.50
☐ **Box,** 10½" oval	120.00	155.00	137.50
☐ **Box,** pincushion	180.00	240.00	210.00
☐ **Box,** sewing	210.00	265.00	232.00
☐ **Bucket,** wood with handle and lid, 12" H.	110.00	145.00	127.50
☐ **Bucker,** 1 gallon, dove-tailed, fair condition	10.00	15.00	12.50
☐ **Chair,** ladderback, woven tape seat	600.00	900.00	750.00
☐ **Clothes hanger**	60.00	80.00	70.00
☐ **Clothes hanger,** six-peg	45.00	65.00	55.00
☐ **Comb,** wood	22.00	30.00	26.00
☐ **Dust pan**	50.00	70.00	60.00
☐ **Foot stool,** decorated	210.00	265.00	232.00
☐ **Hay winder with rope**	40.00	60.00	50.00
☐ **Jelly cupboard,** red stained wood, c. 1890	450.00	600.00	525.00
☐ **Pegboard,** wood	180.00	240.00	210.00
☐ **Plantation desk**	700.00	1100.00	900.00
☐ **Rack,** spice dryer	170.00	210.00	190.00
☐ **Rocker,** ladderback, mushroom arms, splint seat	600.00	900.00	750.00
☐ **Sap bucket,** Enfield, New Hampshire	40.00	55.00	47.50
☐ **Soap shaver**	90.00	115.00	102.50
☐ **Spinning wheel**	280.00	370.00	325.00

SHIP MODELS

There are various types of ship models, some of which are hard to distinguish from others unless you have a little collecting (or at least looking) experience. They can be described roughly as follows. The *wright's model*, which is a very desirable kind, was constructed by a shipwright (ship builder) as a working model for an actual ship he was building, much like an architect's model of a skyscraper. A wright's model may not be correct down to the smallest detail, since changes in thought might have occurred along the way (perhaps leading to the construction of a second or third model). In fact, the ship may never have been built at all; the model was possibly submitted as a proposal but rejected. In any case these are well-admired models and when they can be identified nearly always go for high prices. A *sailor's model* is one made while the sailor served on that actual ship, for the purpose of selling when the ship called at port or for presentation to a relative. Sailors' models are usually rather crude because of the working conditions and shortage of proper tools, but are highly regarded. A *collector's model* is one made long after the ship itself was constructed, and often after it ceased to exist, by using photographs or drawings in books. Some collectors' models are fanciful, of ships that never existed at all, but the majority portray actual ships. The value of this type depends on the age, size, intricacy of detailing, and how well it is preserved. Models of steamships, no matter how big or nicely done, are not as strong on the market as sailing vessels — they just aren't as decorative looking. Then finally you have *kit models,* built from components and directions furnished in a commercially sold kit. These, understandably, are the least valuable of the lot.

	Current Price Range		Prior Year Average
☐ **American cargo ship "Explorer,"** masts and sails, mounted on a metal base, well-preserved except for portions of the rigging, 27" L., c. 1880	650.00	900.00	775.00
☐ **American gunner "Victory,"** meticulous workmanship, some detail work damaged, overall well-preserved, mounted on a new stand made of polished walnut, 41" L., c. 1900	1300.00	1800.00	1550.00
☐ **American battleship "Kentucky,"** the hull carved from a solid block of wood, painted, traces of original paint, one mast restored, the sails not original, mounted on a wooden platform painted deep blue, 19" L., c. 1870	1000.00	1400.00	1200.00
☐ **American battleship "Maine,"** the guns made of real brass, figures of seamen in carved wood, tins and crates on board, the work of a master modeler, 24" L., c. 1890	2200.00	3000.00	2600.00
☐ **American cargo ship "Explorer,"** masts and sails, mounted on a metal base, well-preserved except for portions of the rigging, 27" L., c. 1880	800.00	1100.00	950.00
☐ **American gunner "Victory,"** meticulous workmanship, some detail work damaged, overall well-preserved, mounted on a new stand made of polished walnut, 41" L., c. 1900	1600.00	2100.00	1850.00
☐ **English battleship "Great Harry,"** brass guns, made largely of oak, some components of other wood, gilded work with most of the original gilding intact, rare model, probably English or Scottish, of a ship dating to the 16th c., 57" L., c. 1810	6000.00	9000.00	7500.00
☐ **English liner "Titanic,"** wood and metal painted in various shades of gray, mounted on wooden stand, American or English, 32" L., recent	800.00	1000.00	900.00
☐ **English liner "Queen Mary,"** wood and metal, scale built by a modeler down to the smallest detail, rubber life preservers, scale-built lifeboats, etc., mounted on a copper and wood stand with engraved nameplate, 55" L., c. 1940	3750.00	5000.00	4350.00
☐ **English schooner "Admiral V,"** 26" L., c. 1900	400.00	550.00	475.00
☐ **German-built model of an unnamed sailing ship,** 15th c. design, well detailed, weathered wood, wormholes, some parts restored, unmounted, c. 1750-1800	2000.00	3000.00	2500.00
☐ **Model of an early Viking sailing ship,** 10th or 11th c. A.D., wood and canvas, probably German (not entirely accurate in design), 31" L., c. 1860	1750.00	2250.00	2000.00

SIGNS

Advertising Sign, c. 1920. Novel and scarce, this is a perfect example of the old-fashioned sign that got its point across — even if it wasn't too pretty . . .
. . . . **$65.00-$85.00**

Though signs have been with us for centuries, in one form or other, collecting them and taking a genuine historical interest in them is rather new. Hobbyists seek out a wide variety of signs, both commercial and non-commercial; into their sphere fall traffic and road signs, railway and bus depot signs, and the signs used atop (or alongside) shops, offices, and other places of business. Then, further, they collect the so-called "store signs" displayed *inside* shops, placed there by the suppliers of various brand-name products. It is obviously an immense field, in which the collector can hardly hope to compete by taking a "general " approach. Fortunately this hobby has now arrived at the stage where firm values are attached to most older signs, and there is no more need for blind buying. Nevertheless, some sales are still made "on emotion," to buyers who simply fancy a particular sign and willingly pay much more than its actual value.

Historically speaking, the most valuable signs would be those of English inns and taverns from the Elizabethan era up to the late 1600's. Unfortunately these are next to impossible to find. Only a very few are preserved, and are nearly all in English museum collections. Those still seen on the streets of London are, invariably, modern reproductions (but, despite that fact, some are periodically taken by thieves who believe them to be antiques). The most valuable American signs available to the collector are *topical shop signs* of the 19th century, such as a huge cigar denoting a tobacconist's shop, a pig that hung over a butcher's shop, etc. These signs are mostly made of wood that was cut to shape with a fretsaw, and painted.

	Current Price Range		Prior Year Average
☐ **Cardboard ice delivery sign,** window card	2.00	3.00	2.50
☐ **Cardboard Moxie sign,** "Feed the Nerves, Very Healthful," c. 1905	60.00	80.00	70.00
☐ **Enamelled Mobil Gas sign,** shield-shaped, 11" x 12"	45.00	65.00	55.00
☐ **Glass sign,** reverse painting, billiard parlour, New York City, framed, 5' x 9'	1175.00	1450.00	1280.00
☐ **Heavy paper Star Soap sign,** "Our Boy," large size	250.00	325.00	288.00
☐ **Paper and cardboard Horsford sign,** two children depicted, 9" x 12"	25.00	35.00	30.00
☐ **Porcelain Railway Express sign,** 11" L.	32.00	40.00	36.00
☐ **Porcelain sign,** Detroit Storage Batteries, 13¾" x 18¼"	30.00	37.00	33.50
☐ **Porcelain tobacco sign,** convex, polychrome, Dutch, 17" x 33"	225.00	300.00	257.00
☐ **Standing sign,** "Bus Stop," iron on shaft, set into weighted iron base, American, c. 1950	90.00	115.00	102.50
☐ **Tin Columbian Beer sign,** embossed polychrome, c. 1906	175.00	235.00	200.00
☐ **Tin Little Nipper sign,** with frame, 22" x 16"	260.00	340.00	300.00
☐ **Tin Moxie sign,** "The Drink That Made the Name Famous," with picture of horsemobile, embossed, c. 1933	110.00	145.00	127.50
☐ **Tin "Tivoli" Beer sing,** Alexandria, Virginia, 16" x 12", c. 1910	175.00	210.00	192.00
☐ **Tin Tractor Motor Oil sign,** lithographed, polychrome, raised letters, 12" x 16", c. 1940's	9.00	12.00	10.50
☐ **Wooden sign,** American, a high laced boot, painted brown and black, used either for a cobbler's shop or a shoe store, 78" x 51", c. 1890 ...	1700.00	2200.00	1950.00
☐ **Wooden sign,** American, a molar tooth, white, yellow, and dark gray, used over a dentist's office, approx. 43" x 41", c. 1870	2800.00	3600.00	3200.00
☐ **Wooden sign,** American, a pair of spectacles, painted light gray, orignal hangings attached, the wood mildewed, 6' W., c. 1880	1400.00	1900.00	1650.00
☐ **Wooden sign,** American or English, a pig painted in various shades of pink and red, advertising a butcher's shop, fixtures missing, slightly damaged, 54" W., c. 1870	1100.00	1400.00	1250.00
☐ **Wooden sign,** American, cigar-shaped, gaudily painted, some incised surface work, made of one plank of wood, 8½" L., c. 1880	1700.00	2200.00	1950.00

SILHOUETTES

Silhouettes originated in the age before photography, as an inexpensive way of making portraits. For the more affluent, there was the oil painter, and for many years the middle classes were content to think of portraiture as a rich man's division. Finally in the 1700's silhouette portraiture made some inroads and became, gradually, quite popular. Ironically the rich, amused with the craft as a novelty, patronized the silhouette makers just as much as the common folk. Silhouette portraits naturally showed the subject in profile at all times, since it is impossible, in the silhouette medium, to indicate facial features when the subject faces the artist. The majority are heads or busts, but others are half-lengths and even full-lengths, running to extremely elaborate detailing in some cases. This all depended upon the taste of the customer, the sum of money he was willing to spend (simple head silhouettes were very cheap), and the artist's dexterity. There were two basic ways of making a silhouette portrait, both used frequently. The first way was to cut out the subject's likeness on black paper, and paste this over white or buff paper (or the other way around; it made no difference so long as a sharp contrast was achieved). In the second technique, the cutting itself was discarded and the paper *from which it was cut* — bearing the outline of the cutting — was pasted atop contrasting paper. Unless one makes a close examination, it is usually difficult to notice which technique has been used. A third method, to blacken in the portrait with ink and do no cutting at all, was seldom employed except by amateurs. Silhouettes of famous persons are often found. In the vast majority of instances they were NOT made for the persons depicted, but as exhibit pieces by the artisans, to show what they could do.

	Current Price Range		Prior Year Average
☐ **Aaron Burr,** bust portrait, black watercolor, signed Jos. Wood, 3" x 2¾", 1812	330.00	400.00	365.00
☐ **Alexander Hamilton,** bust portrait wearing frilled stock, signed J. W. Jarvis, 4½" x 3½", 1804	475.00	550.00	505.00
☐ **Charles Carroll of Carrollton,** holding trowel and cane, 13" x 10¾", 1828	260.00	330.00	285.00
☐ **Double portrait of gentlemen and lady,** full length figures, signed Augn. Edouart Fecil, 9" x 7⅛", 1844	220.00	270.00	245.00
☐ **Gentleman wearing top hat,** landscape setting, signed Augn. Edouart Fecit, 8⅞" x 6⅝", 1829	250.00	320.00	285.00
☐ **Hon. Henry Clay,** bust portrait, inscribed J. W. Jarvis, 8" x 6¼", 1810	110.00	140.00	125.00
☐ **Miss Elizabeth Frobiser,** clad in bonnet, dress and white pantalettes, signed Frith, 1821	280.00	350.00	315.00
☐ **Portrait group,** two adults, six children, 19th c.	210.00	260.00	235.00
☐ **Portrait group,** Edouart, two adults, two children	575.00	680.00	625.00
☐ **Portrait group,** watercolor, two gentlemen and a lady, landscape setting, signed Cath, Ludlow, 8¾" x 9⅞", 1777	850.00	1000.00	925.00
☐ **Rev. Henry Jackson,** top hat and carrying walking stick, signed W. H. Brown, 9⅜" x 6¾", 1840	260.00	310.00	285.00
☐ **The Vegetable Huckster,** watercolor, signed G. Atkinson, 8¾" x 11", 1838	230.00	280.00	255.00
☐ **Watercolor portrait of Gen. Andrew Jackson,** head in black, signed S. L. Waldo, 5¼" x 3¾", 1820	640.00	770.00	705.00

SPORTS COLLECTIBLES

Poster For Ali Frazier, heavyweight title bout, closed-circuit TV shows . . . .
. . . . **$20.00-$25.00**

    This is a field of collecting to which nearly all of us can relate, as few people were not (in their younger days at least) collectors of some kind of sports mementos. The hobby has grown immensely through the years and has taken on a variety of twists. Yesteryear's collector of sport relics was almost always a "fan" first and a collector second, who concentrated on his favorite star or club. Today, there are many collectors to whom the hobby is much more vital than following the sports themselves. Also, the method of obtaining sports collectibles has undergone noticeable change. Twenty or thirty years ago, most enthusiasts took the strictly amateur approach of waiting at stadium gates to meet the players, or sending letters to them. When a collector paid for an item it was grudgingly, and the sum was always small (we can recall when nobody cared to give more than 50¢ for any baseball player's autograph, even an All-Star). Today, the hobby is served by a network of professional dealers, who operate just the same way as coin, stamp or other hobby dealers, keeping a stock of various merchandise for sale. The better quality sports collectibles now command high prices, and justifiably so, as they have a definite scarcity factor. Autographs of some old-time Hall of Fame baseball players are selling higher than autographs of some United States presidents. When buying autographs, be on guard for reproductions (printed signatures) and counterfeits (hand-drawn facsimiles). These unfortunately are plentiful but your chance of encountering them is reduced if you buy from the specialist dealers. As a general rule, skepticism is a worthwhile quality for the collector of sports items.

744 / SPORTS COLLECTIBLES

For more in-depth information and listings, you may refer to *The Official Price Guide to Baseball Cards,* published by the House of Collectibles.

BASEBALL GUIDES

Baseball guidebooks have extremely early origins — they were being issued even before the establishment of the first professional league in 1872. The early guides are all rare, because of limited printing and a high destruction ratio. Fans who saved a guide all year (and they were in the minority) usually discarded it when the following year's guide appeared.

	Current Price Range		Prior Year Average
☐ BEADLE 1860	110.00	150.00	130.00
☐ 1861	110.00	150.00	130.00
☐ 1862	105.00	140.00	122.00
☐ 1863	100.00	132.50	16.25
☐ 1864	98.00	128.00	113.00
☐ 1865	98.00	128.00	113.00
☐ 1866	105.00	130.00	112.00
☐ DeWITT 1868	110.00	140.00	125.00
☐ 1869	105.00	130.00	117.00
☐ 1870	100.00	120.00	110.00
☐ 1871	98.00	118.00	108.00
☐ 1872	95.00	115.00	105.00
☐ 1873	92.00	110.00	101.00
☐ 1874	85.00	100.00	92.00
☐ 1875	88.00	98.00	92.00
☐ REACH 1883	95.00	120.00	107.00
☐ 1884	93.00	117.00	105.00
☐ 1885	92.00	115.00	103.00
☐ 1886	91.00	113.00	102.00
☐ 1887	87.00	107.00	97.00
☐ 1888	86.00	105.00	95.00
☐ 1889	85.00	104.00	94.00
☐ 1890	83.00	101.00	91.00
☐ 1891	83.00	101.00	91.00
☐ 1892	82.00	100.00	90.00
☐ 1893	80.00	97.00	88.00
☐ 1894	79.00	96.00	87.00
☐ 1895	79.00	96.00	87.00
☐ 1896	78.00	95.00	86.00
☐ 1897	78.00	95.00	86.00
☐ 1898	77.00	93.00	85.00
☐ 1899	75.00	91.00	82.00
☐ 1900	67.00	82.00	74.00
☐ 1901	65.00	80.00	82.00
☐ 1902	65.00	80.00	82.00
☐ 1903	64.00	79.00	71.00
☐ 1904	63.00	77.00	70.00
☐ SPALDING 1877	115.00	160.00	138.00
☐ 1878	115.00	160.00	138.00
☐ 1879	112.00	155.00	134.00
☐ 1880	110.00	144.00	127.00
☐ 1881	107.00	140.00	123.00
☐ 1882	104.00	135.00	119.00
☐ 1883	102.00	133.00	117.00

SPORTS COLLECTIBLES / 745

	Current Price Range		Prior Year Average
☐ 1884	101.00	132.00	116.00
☐ 1885	100.00	130.00	115.00
☐ 1886	107.00	126.00	116.00
☐ 1887	92.00	117.00	104.00
☐ 1888	91.00	115.00	103.00
☐ 1889	90.00	114.00	102.00
☐ 1890	87.00	111.00	99.00
☐ 1891	86.00	110.00	98.00
☐ 1892	86.00	110.00	98.00
☐ 1893	86.00	110.00	98.00
☐ 1894	85.00	109.00	97.00
☐ 1895	83.00	105.00	94.00
☐ 1896	83.00	105.00	94.00
☐ 1897	83.00	105.00	94.00
☐ 1898	81.00	101.00	91.00
☐ 1899	79.00	97.00	86.00
☐ 1900	75.00	92.00	83.00
☐ 1901	74.00	91.00	82.00

BASEBALL YEARBOOKS

These differ from Guides (above) in that Yearbooks are published by the individual teams, and deal with the players on that team only. Yearbooks are of more recent origin than guides.

☐ BOSTON RED SOX 1953	17.00	25.00	21.00
☐ 1954	17.00	25.00	21.00
☐ 1955	16.00	23.50	19.50
☐ CALIFORNIA ANGELS 1967	13.00	19.00	16.00
☐ 1968	6.00	9.50	7.75
☐ CHICAGO WHITE SOX 1948	22.00	32.00	27.00
☐ 1949	22.00	32.00	27.00
☐ 1950	18.00	26.00	22.00
☐ CLEVELAND INDIANS 1955	17.00	25.00	21.00
☐ 1956	16.00	23.50	19.50
☐ 1957	14.00	20.00	17.00
☐ 1958	14.00	20.00	17.00
☐ 1961 (special oversize edition)	23.00	34.00	28.00
☐ KANSAS CITY ROYALS 1971	5.00	7.00	6.00
☐ MILWAUKEE BREWERS 1970	11.00	16.00	13.50
☐ MINNESOTA TWINS 1962	13.00	18.00	16.00
☐ 1963	13.00	18.00	16.00
☐ 1964	13.00	18.00	16.00
☐ NEW YORK METS 1962	135.00	200.00	168.00
☐ 1963	34.00	52.00	43.00
☐ 1964	28.00	45.00	36.00
☐ 1965	14.00	20.00	17.00
☐ NEW YORK YANKEES 1951	34.00	56.00	45.00
☐ 1952	34.00	56.00	45.00
☐ 1953	33.00	54.00	43.00
☐ 1954	33.00	54.00	43.00
☐ 1955	30.00	50.00	40.00
☐ 1956	24.00	40.00	32.00
☐ 1957	24.00	40.00	32.00
☐ PHILADELPHIA PHILLIES 1949	28.00	45.00	35.00
☐ 1950	27.50	43.00	35.00

746 / SPORTS COLLECTIBLES

	Current Price Range		Prior Year Average
☐ 1951	27.00	43.00	35.00
☐ 1952	23.00	37.00	30.00
☐ 1953	20.00	33.00	26.00
☐ PITTSBURGH PIRATES 1951	25.00	39.00	32.00
☐ 1952	23.00	36.00	28.00
☐ 1953	23.00	36.00	28.00
☐ 1954	22.00	34.00	28.00
☐ 1955	20.00	33.00	26.00
☐ 1956	17.00	25.00	21.00
☐ SAN FRANCISCO GIANTS 1958	23.00	36.00	28.00
☐ 1959	17.00	25.00	21.00
☐ 1960	17.00	25.00	21.00
☐ ST. LOUIS CARDINALS 1950	12.00	17.00	14.50
☐ 1951	20.00	28.00	24.00
☐ 1952	20.00	28.00	24.00
☐ 1953	20.00	28.00	24.00
☐ 1954	20.00	28.00	24.00
☐ 1955	19.00	27.00	23.00
☐ WASHINGTON SENATORS 1950	21.00	30.00	25.00
☐ 1951	21.00	30.00	25.00
☐ 1952	21.00	30.00	25.00

WORLD SERIES PROGRAMS

Special program-scorecards are printed for the World Series games, usually in a more "deluxe" style than programs for regular season games. These are among the most popular baseball collectibles. They are automatically scarcer when the Series runs only four or five games instead of the full seven (the World Series ends when one of the clubs wins four games), but this does not always have a bearing on value. Collectors are interested in other factors too, such as the teams and players involved and whether the Series produced any historic games.

☐ 1926	140.00	225.00	172.00
☐ 1927	170.00	250.00	210.00
☐ 1928	125.00	195.00	160.00
☐ 1929	115.00	180.00	147.00
☐ 1930	115.00	180.00	147.00
☐ 1931	115.00	180.00	147.00
☐ 1932	125.00	195.00	160.00
☐ 1933	105.00	160.00	130.00
☐ 1934	105.00	160.00	130.00
☐ 1935	100.00	145.00	122.00
☐ 1936	105.00	160.00	130.00
☐ 1937	105.00	160.00	130.00
☐ 1938	105.00	160.00	130.00
☐ 1939	100.00	150.00	125.00
☐ 1940	90.00	130.00	110.00
☐ 1941	100.00	145.00	122.00
☐ 1942	90.00	130.00	110.00

One of the most valuable sports collectibles is the program for the first World Series, played in 1903. This has a price range of $1,750 to $2,500.

SPORTS COLLECTIBLES / 747

BASEBALL — MISCELLANEOUS

	Current Price Range		Prior Year Average
☐ **Baseball uniform,** modern, known to have been worn (at least once) by a star major league player	500.00	680.00	590.00
☐ **Baseball uniform,** any age, known to have been worn by a Hall of Fame player	1350.00	1700.00	1520.00
☐ **Baseball uniform,** known to have been worn by Babe Ruth	6700.00	8900.00	7400.00
☐ **Baseman's mitt,** c. 1910	105.00	130.00	117.00
☐ **Catcher's chest protector,** c. 1905	265.00	305.00	285.00
☐ **Catcher's mask,** similar to one advertised in 1902 catalog	75.00	95.00	85.00
☐ **Fielder's glove,** c. 1890	125.00	175.00	150.00
☐ **Fielder's glove,** Early Wynn model, c. 1950's	23.00	28.00	25.00
☐ **Fielder's glove,** Larry Doby model, c. 1950's	23.00	28.00	25.00
☐ **First baseman's glove,** c. 1930	90.00	115.00	102.00
☐ **First baseman's glove,** Gil Hodges model, c. 1950's	34.00	45.00	39.00

FOOTBALL

☐ **Football dating before 1900,** depending on condition. (It should be noted that prices on such items as footballs, basketballs and other inflated sports balls vary according to whether or not they can be inflated to a point where they resemble the original shape.)	60.00	115.00	85.00
☐ **Football** known to have been thrown for a touchdown pass by Norm Van Brocklin, Los Angeles Rams, c. 1952	280.00	390.00	335.00
☐ **Football** used in the first year of the American Football League (shaped slightly different from National League ball)	115.00	160.00	138.00

GOLF

☐ **Driver,** wooden shaft, c. 1910	125.00	160.00	142.00
☐ **George Low Wizard 600 Putter,** flanged	470.00	610.00	490.00
☐ **Golf bag,** leather, c. 1930	195.00	245.00	120.00
☐ **Golf glove,** c. 1910	30.00	38.00	34.00
☐ **MacGregor R. Armour Set,** wood and irons, c. 1950	895.00	1250.00	1070.00
☐ **Marathon Wards set,** wood and irons, c. 1922	200.00	275.00	238.00
☐ **Power build driver,** c. 1950	105.00	135.00	120.00
☐ **Putter,** wooden shaft, c. 1930	54.00	68.00	61.00
☐ **Putter,** two-way blade with wooden shaft, c. 1920	64.00	78.00	71.00
☐ **Reuter Bull's Eye putter**	75.00	125.00	100.00
☐ **Score card,** Master's Tournament	40.00	78.00	59.00
☐ **Golfer's Manual** by H. B. Farnie, c. 1857	585.00	695.00	625.00
☐ **Tommy Armour wedge,** c. 1959	145.00	190.00	168.00
☐ **Wedge,** Walter Hagen, c. 1930	100.00	125.00	112.00
☐ **Wilson,** Sam Snead set, woods and irons, c. 1940	415.00	500.00	458.00
☐ **Wilson,** R-20 wedge, c. 1930	145.00	190.00	168.00

STAMPS

Stamp collecting — "philately" — has been the hobby of kings, presidents, and millions of very ordinary folk. Though so many new collecting hobbies have come on the scene, stamps have not only retained their popularity but have gained many new followers in recent years. At present, stamp collecting is ranked #2 behind coins as the top American hobby. You can start out by buying a beginner's kit in a department store, then write away to dealers and receive stamps on approval. If there are stamp shops in your vicinity, by all means visit them and look through the stamps they have available. Chances are as you progress in the hobby you'll want to specialize, as there are just too many stamps for any hobbyist to collect them all! With stamps there's always the possibility of finding a rarity, since a very minute difference from one stamp to another, can mean a tremendous difference in value. Below you'll find the current retail prices for all United States stamps issued up to 1907. These are considered the "classics" of the hobby because of their fine designing and historical appeal. Most collectors include at least some of them in their albums. For listing of later issues, as well as all special U.S. stamps such as Airmail, Tax, Registry, etc., you are invited to consult the standard handbook used by dealers and collectors: *The Official Blackbook Price Guide of United States Postage Stamps,* published by the House of Collectibles. *Condition* of course is a major factor in appraising any stamp. Some stamps can be found in MINT condition, just as they were originally sold by the Post Office and very nicely centered, but 19th century U.S. stamps are very difficult to get that way. When a stamp is described as FINE, the perforations do not touch the design, but the centering is not perfect. On a used stamp, the cancel may be heavy or smudgy. A stamp described as AVERAGE has the perforations cutting into the design, and if the stamp is USED its cancel is very heavy. It may also have other faults.

Scott No.		Fine Unused Each	Ave. Unused Each	Fine Used Each	Ave. Used Each
GENERAL ISSUES					
1847					
☐ 1	5¢ Red Brown	—	3250.00	1325.00	800.00
☐ 2	10¢ Black	—	15000.00	3000.00	1650.00
1875 REPRODUCTIONS OF 1847 ISSUE					
☐ 3	5¢ Red Brown	2000.00	1500.00	—	—
☐ 4	10¢ Black	3000.00	2000.00	—	—
1851-56 IMPERFORATE					
☐ 5A	1¢ Blue (Ib)	—	—	2800.00	1800.00
☐ 6	1¢ Blue (Ia)	—	—	3800.00	2400.00
☐ 7	1¢ Blue (II)	785.00	450.00	180.00	115.00
☐ 8	1¢ Blue (III)	—	—	1650.00	1000.00
☐ 8A	1¢ Blue (IIa)	—	1000.00	950.00	575.00
☐ 9	1¢ Blue (IV)	420.00	240.00	117.50	75.00
☐ 10	3¢ Orange Brown (I)	—	900.00	100.00	57.50
☐ 11	3¢ Dull Red (I)	215.00	125.00	11.00	6.50
☐ 12	5¢ Red Brown (I)	—	—	1300.00	775.00
☐ 13	10¢ Green (I)	—	—	1100.00	650.00
☐ 14	10¢ Green (II)	—	865.00	400.00	240.00

Scott No.		Fine Unused Each	Ave. Unused Each	Fine Used Each	Ave. Used Each
☐ 15	10¢ Green (III)	—	825.00	385.00	230.00
☐ 16	10¢ Green (IV)	—	—	1685.00	1000.00
☐ 17	12¢ Black	—	1075.00	360.00	225.00

1857-61 SAME DESIGNS AS PRECEDING ISSUE (EXCEPT PERFORATED 15)

Scott No.		Fine Unused Each	Ave. Unused Each	Fine Used Each	Ave. Used Each
☐ 18	1¢ Blue (I)	1025.00	545.00	600.00	340.00
☐ 19	1¢ Blue (Ia)	—	—	2500.00	1300.00
☐ 20	1¢ Blue (II)	775.00	425.00	230.00	130.00
☐ 21	1¢ Blue (III)	—	1800.00	1400.00	750.00
☐ 22	1¢ Blue (IIIa)	825.00	450.00	320.00	185.00
☐ 23	1¢ Blue (IV)	—	1350.00	420.00	225.00
☐ 24	1¢ Blue (V)	195.00	110.00	45.00	25.00
☐ 25	3¢ Rose (I)	—	485.00	40.00	22.50
☐ 26	3¢ Dull Red (II)	110.00	57.50	6.50	4.75
☐ 26a	3¢ Dull Red (IIa)	175.00	110.00	25.00	15.00
☐ 27	5¢ Brick Red (I)	—	3750.00	1085.00	560.00
☐ 28	5¢ Red Brown (I)	—	1275.00	450.00	230.00
☐ 28A	5¢ Indian Red (I)	—	—	1425.00	775.00
☐ 29	5¢ Brown (I)	1075.00	550.00	300.00	165.00
☐ 30	5¢ Orange Brown (II)	1000.00	525.00	1250.00	675.00
☐ 30A	5¢ Brown (II)	680.00	335.00	300.00	165.00
☐ 31	10¢ Green (I)	—	3250.00	700.00	365.00
☐ 32	10¢ Green (II)	1500.00	800.00	245.00	127.50
☐ 33	10¢ Green (III)	1450.00	775.00	240.00	125.00
☐ 34	10¢ Green (IV)	—	—	1365.00	710.00
☐ 35	10¢ Green (V)	350.00	180.00	135.00	70.00
☐ 36	12¢ Black (I)	540.00	275.00	150.00	80.00
☐ 36b	12¢ Black (II)	500.00	290.00	185.00	87.50
☐ 37	24¢ Gray Lilac	1100.00	575.00	420.00	220.00
☐ 38	30¢ Orange	1050.00	600.00	475.00	250.00
☐ 39	90¢ Blue	2125.00	1175.00	—	—

1875 REPRINTS OF 1857-61 ISSUE

Scott No.		Fine Unused Each	Ave. Unused Each	Fine Used Each	Ave. Used Each
☐ 40	1¢ Bright Blue	725.00	560.00	—	—
☐ 41	3¢ Scarlet	3450.00	2450.00	—	—
☐ 42	5¢ Orange Brown	1000.00	775.00	—	—
☐ 43	10¢ Blue Green	2600.00	1900.00	—	—
☐ 44	12¢ Greenish Black	2750.00	2000.00	—	—
☐ 45	24¢ Blackish Violet	3100.00	2200.00	—	—
☐ 46	30¢ Yellow Orange	3250.00	2350.00	—	—
☐ 47	90¢ Deep Blue	4675.00	3480.00	—	—

1861 FIRST DESIGNS (PERFORATED 12)

Scott No.		Fine Unused Each	Ave. Unused Each	Fine Used Each	Ave. Used Each
☐ 56	3¢ Brown Red	1185.00	685.00	—	—
☐ 62B	10¢ Dark Green	—	—	940.00	550.00

1861-62 SECOND DESIGNS

Scott No.		Fine Unused Each	Ave. Unused Each	Fine Used Each	Ave. Used Each
☐ 63	1¢ Blue	182.50	105.00	29.00	16.00
☐ 63b	1¢ Dark Blue	210.00	128.00	32.00	18.00
☐ 64	3¢ Pink	—	2175.00	510.00	280.00
☐ 64b	3¢ Rose Pink	365.00	220.00	58.00	35.00
☐ 65	3¢ Rose	75.00	45.00	2.30	1.35
☐ 66	3¢ Lake	—	1325.00	—	—
☐ 67	5¢ Buff	—	2175.00	525.00	330.00
☐ 68	10¢ Yellow Green	310.00	180.00	37.00	22.00
☐ 69	12¢ Black	580.00	350.00	80.00	48.00

750 / STAMPS

Scott No.		Fine Unused Each	Ave. Unused Each	Fine Used Each	Ave. Used Each
☐ 70	24¢ Red Lilac	720.00	415.00	105.00	60.00
☐ 70b	24¢ Steel Blue	—	—	235.00	140.00
☐ 70c	24¢ Violet	—	1500.00	775.00	455.00
☐ 71	30¢ Orange	640.00	365.00	110.00	65.00
☐ 72	90¢ Blue	1375.00	850.00	385.00	220.00

1861-66 NEW VALUES OR NEW COLORS

☐ 73	2¢ Black	230.00	128.00	48.00	29.00
☐ 74	3¢ Scarlet	6250.00	3850.00	1800.00	1400.00
☐ 75	5¢ Red Brown	1300.00	800.00	280.00	165.00
☐ 76	5¢ Brown	325.00	190.00	72.00	42.00
☐ 77	15¢ Black	900.00	510.00	112.00	65.00
☐ 78	24¢ Lilac	325.00	185.00	68.00	38.00

1867 GRILL WITH POINTS UP
A. GRILL COVERING ENTIRE STAMP

☐ 79	3¢ Rose	2400.00	1750.00	900.00	500.00

C. GRILL ABOUT 13 x 16 MM.

☐ 83	3¢ Rose	1600.00	1050.00	450.00	245.00

GRILL WITH POINTS DOWN
D. GRILL ABOUT 12 x 14 MM.

☐ 84	2¢ Black	2200.00	1775.00	1100.00	600.00
☐ 85	3¢ Rose	1300.00	825.00	500.00	280.00

Z. GRILL ABOUT 11 x 14 MM.

☐ 85B	2¢ Black	1300.00	720.00	390.00	210.00
☐ 85C	3¢ Rose	2500.00	1950.00	850.00	485.00
☐ 85E	12¢ Black	1600.00	1075.00	610.00	340.00

E. GRILL ABOUT 11 x 13 MM.

☐ 86	1¢ Blue	800.00	440.00	240.00	135.00
☐ 87	2¢ Black	385.00	205.00	95.00	52.00
☐ 88	3¢ Rose	320.00	178.00	11.50	6.00
☐ 89	10¢ Green	1225.00	680.00	170.00	95.00
☐ 90	12¢ Black	1400.00	775.00	180.00	100.00
☐ 91	15¢ Black	2775.00	1500.00	465.00	245.00

F. GRILL ABOUT 9 x 13 MM.

☐ 92	1¢ Blue	415.00	235.00	135.00	68.00
☐ 93	2¢ Black	215.00	117.50	38.00	20.00
☐ 94	3¢ Red	160.00	100.00	8.00	4.25
☐ 95	5¢ Brown	1475.00	850.00	320.00	165.00
☐ 96	10¢ Yellow Green	600.00	340.00	100.00	55.00
☐ 97	12¢ Black	635.00	370.00	100.00	55.00
☐ 98	15¢ Black	700.00	400.00	110.00	60.00
☐ 99	24¢ Gray Lilac	1600.00	835.00	635.00	340.00
☐ 100	30¢ Orange	1700.00	940.00	365.00	200.00
☐ 101	90¢ Blue	3500.00	2000.00	1000.00	545.00

1875 REISSUE OF 1861-66 ISSUES

☐ 102	1¢ Blue	—	450.00	—	525.00
☐ 103	2¢ Black	—	2200.00	—	2600.00
☐ 104	3¢ Brown Red	—	2375.00	—	2650.00
☐ 105	5¢ Light Brown	—	1350.00	—	1375.00
☐ 106	10¢ Green	—	1950.00	—	2050.00

Scott No.		Fine Unused Each	Ave. Unused Each	Fine Used Each	Ave. Used Each
☐ 107	12¢ Black	—	2700.00	—	2875.00
☐ 108	15¢ Black	—	2775.00	—	3000.00
☐ 109	24¢ Deep Violet	—	2800.00	—	3100.00
☐ 110	30¢ Brownish Orange	—	3500.00	—	4000.00
☐ 111	90¢ Blue	—	4250.00	—	5500.00

1869 PICTORIAL ISSUES
GRILL MEASURING 9½ x 9½ MM.

☐ 112	1¢ Buff	350.00	205.00	92.50	55.00
☐ 113	2¢ Brown	220.00	128.00	42.00	25.00
☐ 114	3¢ Ultramarine	180.00	105.00	8.30	5.20
☐ 115	6¢ Ultramarine	900.00	510.00	132.00	77.00
☐ 116	10¢ Yellow	1000.00	575.00	138.00	82.00
☐ 117	12¢ Green	820.00	480.00	135.00	77.00
☐ 118	15¢ Brown & Blue (I)	1750.00	1050.00	430.00	250.00
☐ 119	15¢ Brown & Blue (II)	975.00	560.00	160.00	95.00
☐ 120	24¢ Green & Violet	2375.00	1350.00	720.00	415.00
☐ 121	30¢ Blue & Carmine	2400.00	1350.00	450.00	280.00
☐ 122	90¢ Carmine & Black	7200.00	4250.00	1820.00	1050.00

1875
REISSUE OF 1860 ISSUE, HARD WHITE PAPER WITHOUT GRILL

☐ 123	1¢ Buff	520.00	310.00	360.00	205.00
☐ 124	2¢ Brown	715.00	420.00	400.00	235.00
☐ 125	3¢ Blue	2750.00	2200.00	1425.00	1065.00
☐ 126	6¢ Blue	—	725.00	—	550.00
☐ 127	10¢ Yellow	—	1200.00	—	825.00
☐ 128	12¢ Green	—	1250.00	—	830.00
☐ 129	15¢ Brown & Blue (III)	—	1275.00	—	550.00
☐ 130	24¢ Green & Violet	—	1200.00	—	520.00
☐ 131	30¢ Blue & Carmine	—	1650.00	—	950.00
☐ 132	90¢ Carmine & Black	—	3800.00	—	4750.00

1880
SAME AS ABOVE. SOFT POROUS PAPER

☐ 133	1¢ Buff	350.00	210.00	360.00	210.00

1870-71
PRINTED BY NATIONAL BANK NOTE CO. GRILLED

☐ 134	1¢ Ultramarine	700.00	395.00	80.00	50.00
☐ 135	2¢ Red Brown	435.00	255.00	50.00	28.00
☐ 136	3¢ Green	270.00	160.00	11.00	6.50
☐ 137	6¢ Carmine	1380.00	800.00	320.00	180.00
☐ 138	7¢ Vermilion	1320.00	775.00	270.00	165.00
☐ 139	10¢ Brown	1750.00	1050.00	550.00	330.00
☐ 140	12¢ Light Violet	—	—	2685.00	1550.00
☐ 141	15¢ Orange	1920.00	1250.00	875.00	520.00
☐ 142	24¢ Purple	—	—	—	9000.00
☐ 143	30¢ Black	—	2575.00	1325.00	825.00
☐ 144	90¢ Carmine	—	3450.00	775.00	440.00

1870-71 SAME AS ABOVE, WITHOUT GRILL

☐ 145	1¢ Ultramarine	220.00	127.50	10.50	6.00
☐ 146	2¢ Red Brown	105.00	58.00	6.50	4.25
☐ 147	3¢ Green	120.00	70.00	.65	.45

752 / STAMPS

Scott No.		Fine Unused Each	Ave. Unused Each	Fine Used Each	Ave. Used Each
☐ 148	6¢ Carmine.............	290.00	170.00	13.00	7.40
☐ 149	7¢ Vermilion...........	400.00	230.00	80.00	45.00
☐ 150	10¢ Brown	325.00	185.00	15.50	9.75
☐ 151	12¢ Dull Violet	720.00	420.00	62.50	36.00
☐ 152	15¢ Bright Orange.......	670.00	395.00	65.00	37.50
☐ 153	24¢ Purple	750.00	435.00	80.00	48.00
☐ 154	30¢ Black	1235.00	735.00	165.00	87.50
☐ 155	90¢ Carmine............	1400.00	850.00	295.00	167.50

1873
SAME DESIGNS AS 1870-71 ISSUE, WITH SECRET MARKS. PRINTED BY THE CONTINENTAL BANK NOTE CO. THIN HARD GRAYISH WHITE PAPER.

☐ 156	1¢ Ultramarine..........	85.00	50.00	3.50	1.95
☐ 157	2¢ Brown	200.00	120.00	10.00	6.00
☐ 158	3¢ Green...............	68.00	40.00	.30	.18
☐ 159	6¢ Dull Pink	275.00	155.00	11.50	6.75
☐ 160	7¢ Orange Vermilion	580.00	340.00	75.00	45.00
☐ 161	10¢ Brown	320.00	185.00	15.00	8.00
☐ 162	12¢ Black Violet	800.00	465.00	80.00	50.00
☐ 163	15¢ Yellow Orange	700.00	400.00	85.00	50.00
☐ 165	30¢ Gray Black	685.00	410.00	65.00	38.00
☐ 166	90¢ Rose Carmine.......	1420.00	820.00	300.00	175.00

1875

☐ 178	2¢ Vermilion............	280.00	165.00	6.50	4.50
☐ 179	5¢ Blue	270.00	160.00	12.00	7.00

1879
SAME TYPES AS 1870-75 ISSUES. PRINTED BY THE AMERICAN BANK NOTE CO. SOFT POROUS YELLOWISH WHITE PAPER.

☐ 182	1¢ Dark Ultramarine	180.00	100.00	2.90	1.75
☐ 183	2¢ Vermilion............	100.00	58.00	2.75	1.60
☐ 184	3¢ Green...............	90.00	55.00	.20	.12
☐ 185	5¢ Blue	270.00	155.00	10.50	6.00
☐ 186	6¢ Pink	730.00	420.00	15.00	8.25
☐ 187	10¢ Brown (no secret mark) ...	725.00	410.00	18.00	9.50
☐ 188	10¢ Brown (secret mark)......	490.00	280.00	16.50	10.00
☐ 188b	10¢ Black Brown	950.00	640.00	62.00	35.00
☐ 189	15¢ Red Orange	225.00	128.00	20.00	13.00
☐ 190	30¢ Full Black	550.00	320.00	30.00	16.50
☐ 191	90¢ Carmine............	1400.00	850.00	285.00	165.00

1882

☐ 205	5¢ Yellow Brown	175.00	100.00	7.50	4.50

1881-82 (N-H ADD 95%)
DESIGNS OF 1873 ISSUE, RE-ENGRAVED

☐ 206	1¢ Gray Blue	48.00	28.00	1.00	.65
☐ 207	3¢ Blue Green	70.00	42.00	.40	.22
☐ 208	6¢ Rose	400.00	230.00	75.00	44.00
☐ 208a	6¢ Brown Red	270.00	158.00	110.00	65.00
☐ 209	10¢ Brown	115.00	70.00	4.50	2.85
☐ 209b	10¢ Black Brown	175.00	100.00	13.50	7.65

STAMPS / 753

1,3948a

2,4,948b

5,9,18-24,40

10,11,25,26,41

12,27-30A,42

13-16,31-35,43

17,36,44

37,45

38,46

39,47

56,63,85A,86,
92,102

64-66,74,79,
88,94,104

57-67-75,76,
80,95,195

58-62B,68,
85D,89,96,106

59,69,85E,90,
97,107

60,70,78,99,
109

61,71,81,100,
110

62,72,101,11

73,84,85B,87,
93,103

77,85F,91,98,
108

754 / STAMPS

112, 123, 133

113, 124

114, 125

115, 126

116, 127

117, 128

118, 119, 129

120, 130

121, 131

122, 132

134, 156, 167, 182

135, 157, 168, 203

136, 158, 169, 214

137, 148, 159, 195, 208

138, 149, 160, 171, 196

139, 150, 161, 197, 209

140-151, 162, 173, 198

141, 152, 163, 189, 199

142, 153, 164, 175, 200

143, 154, 165, 201, 217

STAMPS / 755

144,155,166, 202,218

179,181,185, 204

205,205C,216

210,211B,213

211,211D,215

212

219

219D,220

221

222

223

224

225

226

227

228

229

230

231

756 / STAMPS

STAMPS / 757

256, 271, 282

257, 272

258, 273, 282C, 283

259, 273, 284

260, 275

261-261A, 276, 276A

262, 277

263, 278

285

286

287

288

289

290

291

292

293

294

295

296

758 / STAMPS

Scott No.		Fine Unused Each	Ave. Unused Each	Fine Used Each	Ave. Used Each
1883					
☐ 210	2¢ Red Brown	32.00	19.50	.20	.12
☐ 211	4¢ Blue Green	200.00	105.00	12.00	6.50
1887					
☐ 212	1¢ Ultramarine	77.00	45.00	1.25	.60
☐ 213	2¢ Green	23.00	13.00	.15	.08
☐ 214	3¢ Vermilion	105.00	60.00	47.00	28.00
1888					
☐ 215	4¢ Carmine	155.00	92.00	16.50	9.75
☐ 216	5¢ Indigo	150.00	87.50	7.00	4.25
☐ 217	30¢ Orange Brown	575.00	325.00	115.00	70.00
☐ 218	90¢ Purple	1150.00	650.00	320.00	180.00

1890-93 SMALL DESIGN (N-H ADD 95%)

		Fine Unused Block	Ave. Unused Block	Fine Unused Each	Ave. Unused Each	Fine Used Each	Ave. Used Each
☐ 219	1¢ Dull Blue	125.00	70.00	28.00	17.50	.20	.12
☐ 219D	2¢ Lake	625.00	370.00	145.00	92.00	.80	.45
☐ 220	2¢ Carmine	80.00	48.00	20.00	11.00	.12	.07
☐ 220a	"Cap on Left 2"	330.00	185.00	70.00	42.00	1.95	1.25
☐ 220c	"Cap on Both 2's"	1175.00	700.00	275.00	155.00	8.00	5.00
☐ 221	3¢ Purple	460.00	270.00	110.00	65.00	6.25	4.00
☐ 222	4¢ Dark Brown	450.00	265.00	105.00	62.00	2.90	1.85
☐ 223	5¢ Chocolate	450.00	265.00	105.00	65.00	2.85	1.80
☐ 224	6¢ Brown Red	460.00	270.00	105.00	65.00	20.00	11.90
☐ 225	8¢ Lilac	445.00	240.00	95.00	58.00	14.00	8.50
☐ 226	10¢ Green	830.00	500.00	185.00	110.00	4.00	2.45
☐ 227	15¢ Indigo	1300.00	750.00	300.00	160.00	28.00	16.25
☐ 228	30¢ Black	1600.00	925.00	385.00	230.00	33.00	20.00
☐ 229	90¢ Orange	2700.00	1550.00	630.00	355.00	185.00	110.00

1893
COLUMBIAN ISSUE (N-H ADD 95%)

☐ 230	1¢ Blue	220.00	130.00	55.00	32.00	.60	.35
☐ 231	2¢ Violet	200.00	110.00	50.00	28.00	.12	.08
☐ 231c	2¢ "Broken Hat"	330.00	195.00	78.00	50.00	.75	.40
☐ 232	3¢ Green	450.00	265.00	105.00	65.00	30.00	16.75
☐ 233	4¢ Ultramarine	665.00	380.00	155.00	87.00	12.00	7.00
☐ 234	5¢ Choclate	700.00	440.00	175.00	110.00	14.00	8.00
☐ 235	6¢ Purple	750.00	440.00	180.00	115.00	35.00	22.50
☐ 236	8¢ Magenta	525.00	300.00	150.00	85.00	17.00	11.00
☐ 237	10¢ Black Brown	1000.00	570.00	240.00	140.00	12.50	7.50
☐ 238	15¢ Dark Green	1750.00	1075.00	440.00	260.00	115.00	68.00
☐ 239	30¢ Orange Brown	2325.00	1350.00	535.00	325.00	180.00	110.00
☐ 240	50¢ Slate Blue	2950.00	1675.00	665.00	390.00	315.00	185.00
☐ 241	$1 Salmon	—	—	2100.00	1175.00	1100.00	675.00
☐ 242	$2 Brown Red	—	—	2650.00	1480.00	1050.00	615.00
☐ 243	$3 Yellow Green	—	—	4000.00	2275.00	1520.00	875.00
☐ 244	$4 Crimson Lake	—	—	5500.00	3350.00	2275.00	1275.00
☐ 245	$5 Black	—	—	6250.00	3675.00	2500.00	1450.00

1894
UNWATERMARKED (N-H ADD 95%)

Scott No.		Fine Unused Block	Ave. Unused Block	Fine Unused Each	Ave. Unused Each	Fine Used Each	Ave. Used Each
☐ 246	1¢ Ultramarine..	130.00	68.00	32.00	18.00	6.00	3.00
☐ 247	1¢ Blue	270.00	130.00	65.00	35.00	3.00	1.60
☐ 248	2¢ Pink, Type I ..	95.00	48.00	22.50	12.00	4.00	2.00
☐ 249	2¢ Carmine Lake Type I.......	635.00	330.00	160.00	78.00	2.00	1.00
☐ 250	2¢ Carmine, Type I.......	132.00	65.00	30.00	16.00	.40	.20
☐ 251	2¢ Carmine, Type II	1220.00	600.00	285.00	150.00	4.25	2.00
☐ 252	2¢ Carmine, Type III	535.00	265.00	125.00	65.00	5.75	3.00
☐ 253	3¢ Purple	525.00	260.00	125.00	65.00	11.00	5.50
☐ 254	4¢ Dark Brown ..	535.00	260.00	130.00	67.00	4.25	2.50
☐ 255	5¢ Chocolate ...	450.00	235.00	110.00	52.50	7.00	3.65
☐ 256	6¢ Dull Brown...	750.00	375.00	175.00	85.00	22.00	12.00
☐ 257	8¢ Violet Brown .	550.00	275.00	130.00	68.00	17.50	8.00
☐ 258	10¢ Dark Green ..	1275.00	610.00	310.00	150.00	11.00	5.65
☐ 259	15¢ Dark Blue....	1725.00	850.00	430.00	215.00	77.00	37.50
☐ 260	50¢ Orange......	2175.00	1100.00	500.00	250.00	150.00	72.00
☐ 261	$1 Black (I)	5450.00	2675.00	1275.00	650.00	425.00	215.00
☐ 261A	$1 Black (II).....	—	—	2200.00	1075.00	700.00	370.00
☐ 262	$2 Blue	—	—	2600.00	1300.00	850.00	420.00
☐ 263	$5 Dark Green ..	—	—	5000.00	2450.00	1875.00	925.00

1895
DOUBLE LINE WATERMARK "USPS" (N-H ADD 95%)

☐ 264	1¢ Blue	36.00	21.00	8.40	4.95	.12	.08
☐ 265	2¢ Carmine, Type I.......	180.00	100.00	42.00	25.00	1.00	.60
☐ 266	2¢ Carmine, Type II	210.00	120.00	50.00	30.00	4.00	2.35
☐ 267	2¢ Carmine, Type III	25.00	15.00	6.00	4.00	.10	.06
☐ 268	3¢ Purple	180.00	110.00	44.00	26.00	1.45	.95
☐ 269	4¢ Dark Brown ..	187.00	105.00	42.00	25.00	2.15	1.20
☐ 270	5¢ Chocolate ...	200.00	120.00	44.00	26.00	2.45	1.45
☐ 271	6¢ Dull Brown...	410.00	230.00	95.00	52.00	5.25	3.10
☐ 272	8¢ Violet Brown	160.00	87.00	35.00	22.00	1.70	1.00
☐ 273	10¢ Dark Green ..	375.00	220.00	87.50	55.00	2.10	1.20
☐ 274	15¢ Dark Blue....	1065.00	590.00	245.00	140.00	10.50	6.30
☐ 275	50¢ Dull Orange..	1570.00	885.00	360.00	210.00	34.00	20.00
☐ 276	$1 Black (I)	3575.00	2100.00	800.00	465.00	100.00	60.00
☐ 276A	$1 Black (II).....	—	—	1650.00	900.00	210.00	125.00
☐ 277	$2 Blue	—	—	1160.00	710.00	440.00	260.00
☐ 278	$5 Dark Green ..	—	—	2750.00	1500.00	540.00	325.00

1898 (N-H ADD 95%)

☐ 279	1¢ Deep Green ..	60.00	36.00	13.65	8.20	.12	.07
☐ 279B	2¢ Red.........	58.00	34.00	13.50	8.00	.10	.06
☐ 279C	2¢ Rose Carmine	800.00	425.00	175.00	125.00	40.00	20.00
☐ 279D	2¢ Orange Red ..	60.00	35.00	14.00	8.00	.28	.17
☐ 280	4¢ Rose Brown..	140.00	80.00	32.00	20.00	1.75	.80
☐ 281	5¢ Dark Blue....	180.00	105.00	39.50	24.00	1.30	.80

Scott No.		Fine Unused Block	Ave. Unused Block	Fine Unused Each	Ave. Unused Each	Fine Used Each	Ave. Used Each
☐ 282	6¢ Lake	210.00	115.00	45.00	28.00	3.75	2.20
☐ 282a	6¢ Purplish Lake	300.00	175.00	65.00	38.00	6.50	4.00
☐ 282C	10¢ Brown (I)	1000.00	525.00	235.00	138.00	4.50	3.00
☐ 283	10¢ Orange Brown (II)	925.00	500.00	210.00	115.00	4.00	2.25
☐ 284	15¢ Olive Green ..	1200.00	675.00	270.00	155.00	9.00	5.20

1898 TRANS-MISSISSIPPI EXPOSITION ISSUE (N-H ADD 90%)

☐ 285	1¢ Yellow Green .	225.00	135.00	53.00	32.00	10.50	6.25
☐ 286	2¢ Copper Red ..	220.00	125.00	50.00	30.00	3.75	2.00
☐ 287	4¢ Orange	1075.00	625.00	250.00	140.00	40.00	20.50
☐ 288	5¢ Dull Blue	950.00	565.00	220.00	127.00	36.00	20.00
☐ 289	8¢ Violet Brown .	1650.00	950.00	375.00	225.00	70.00	40.00
☐ 290	10¢ Gray Violet ..	1600.00	925.00	385.00	220.00	39.00	24.00
☐ 291	50¢ Sage Green ..	—	—	1175.00	675.00	335.00	180.00
☐ 292	$1 Black	—	—	2500.00	1450.00	1000.00	600.00
☐ 293	$2 Orange Brown	—	—	3775.00	2250.00	1450.00	800.00

1901 PAN-AMERICAN ISSUE (N-H ADD 75%)

☐ 294	1¢ Green & Black	235.00	130.00	58.00	33.00	9.00	5.25
☐ 295	2¢ Carmine & Black	230.00	130.00	55.00	32.00	3.00	1.75
☐ 296	4¢ Chocolate & Brown	850.00	500.00	210.00	120.00	42.00	24.00
☐ 297	5¢ Ultramarine & Black	865.00	510.00	215.00	125.00	42.00	24.00
☐ 298	8¢ Brown-Violet-Black	1000.00	620.00	235.00	145.00	95.00	57.00
☐ 299	10¢ Yellow-Brown-Black	1700.00	950.00	365.00	210.00	60.00	35.00

1902-03 PERF. 12 (N-H ADD 80%)

☐ 300	1¢ Blue Green ..	65.00	32.00	15.00	7.50	.12	.06
☐ 301	2¢ Carmine	68.00	35.00	16.00	8.25	.12	.06
☐ 302	3¢ Violet	400.00	200.00	90.00	44.00	5.25	2.80
☐ 303	4¢ Brown	400.00	200.00	90.00	44.00	2.00	1.00
☐ 304	5¢ Blue	425.00	210.00	100.00	50.00	1.95	.95
☐ 305	6¢ Claret	470.00	235.00	110.00	55.00	5.00	2.75
☐ 306	8¢ Violet Black..	270.00	130.00	65.00	32.00	4.25	2.20
☐ 307	10¢ Red Brown ..	600.00	265.00	140.00	65.00	2.10	1.20
☐ 308	13¢ Purple Black .	340.00	160.00	80.00	40.00	16.00	8.00
☐ 309	15¢ Olive Green ..	1520.00	775.00	375.00	185.00	10.00	5.00
☐ 310	50¢ Orange	3900.00	1850.00	900.00	440.00	62.00	32.00
☐ 311	$1 Black	5800.00	2750.00	1400.00	675.00	95.00	45.00
☐ 312	$2 Dark Blue	—	—	1750.00	850.00	335.00	170.00
☐ 313	$5 Dark Green ..	—	—	3380.00	1625.00	1175.00	625.00

1906-08 IMPERFORATED (N-H ADD 70%)

☐ 314	1¢ Blue Green ..	210.00	135.00	50.00	32.50	28.00	18.50
☐ 315	5¢ Blue	4000.00	2650.00	975.00	650.00	430.00	290.00

1903 PERF. 12 (N-H ADD 50%)

☐ 319	2¢ Carmine	65.00	30.00	10.25	6.50	.10	.06
☐ 319a	2¢ Lake	50.00	28.00	12.00	6.75	.20	.12

1906 IMPERFORATED (N-H ADD 70%)

Scott No.		Fine Unused Block	Ave. Unused Block	Fine Unused Each	Ave. Unused Each	Fine Used Each	Ave. Used Each
☐ 320	2¢ Carmine.....	210.00	142.00	55.00	35.00	25.00	16.50
☐ 320a	2¢ Lake........	425.00	285.00	110.00	70.00	40.00	28.00

1904
LOUISIANA PURCHASE ISSUE (N-H ADD 75%)

☐ 323	1¢ Green.......	275.00	155.00	65.00	37.50	8.50	5.00
☐ 324	2¢ Carmine.....	200.00	115.00	48.00	27.50	3.00	1.80
☐ 325	3¢ Violet.......	700.00	425.00	165.00	95.00	60.00	36.00
☐ 326	5¢ Dark Blue....	1050.00	600.00	245.00	150.00	42.00	25.00
☐ 327	10¢ Red Brown...	2000.00	1100.00	475.00	270.00	75.00	42.00

1907 JAMESTOWN EXPOSITION ISSUE (N-H ADD 75%)

☐ 328	1¢ Green.......	225.00	90.00	55.00	22.00	14.00	5.00

STEVENGRAPHS AND SILK PICTURES

The "Stevengraph" is a typical memorial to Victorian tastes, an era when ornament was king and the public's aesthetic senses were assaulted daily by manufacturers. Bibliophiles (book collectors) are familiar with the ornate bookbindings from earlier times. A good binding was counted on to sell a book in those days. And if the reader bought a book for its binding, would he (and more especially she) not want a pretty bookmark for keeping his place in it, rather than using a matchstick or hairclip? Thomas Stevens, an enterprising Englishman, figured the public could scarcely resist such a product, and he was proven correct. He brought out silk bookmarks, embellished with various colorful pictures. Around holiday time they outsold just about everything else in the giftshops. After manufacturing them for 20 years, beginning in 1854, Stevens added something new to his line — the Stevengraph, a large rectangular version of the Stevens bookmark, intended to be framed and hung as a picture. These, too, did exceptionally well, and became almost as commonplace on English walls as were the lithographs of Currier and Ives on those of America. As you will note, the values differ, sometimes sharply, depending on subject matter. Be careful of the condition and avoid specimens that are faded or stained. Bookmarks are often unevenly "mellowed" (faded), if they remained untouched in a book for ages with part of the bookmark inside and part outside. The mellowing of bookmarks can also be related to the acid content in paper, as those used to keep one's place in cheap publications with a high acid-content paper are usually badly browned.

BOOKMARKS

	Current Price Range		Prior Year Average
☐ Home Sweet Home	135.00	170.00	142.00
☐ Little Bo-Peep	50.00	65.00	58.00
☐ Merry Christmas	60.00	75.00	68.00
☐ Moses in the Bullrushes	110.00	150.00	130.00
☐ Remember Me	45.00	60.00	42.00
☐ To A Dear Friend	50.00	70.00	60.00
☐ Unchanging Love	25.00	32.00	28.50

STEVENGRAPHS

	Current Price Range		Prior Year Average
☐ Are You Ready	135.00	170.00	142.00
☐ Buffalo Bill	550.00	625.00	587.00
☐ Called To The Rescue	230.00	280.00	255.00
☐ Card, Birthday Greeting	45.00	60.00	52.00
☐ Crystal Place	280.00	340.00	310.00
☐ Death of Nelson	210.00	260.00	235.00
☐ Finish	170.00	210.00	190.00
☐ First Touch	360.00	420.00	390.00
☐ For Life or Death	260.00	310.00	285.00
☐ Fourth Bridge	350.00	415.00	382.00
☐ Full Cry	270.00	320.00	295.00
☐ Good Old Days	300.00	375.00	338.00
☐ Home Sweet Home	110.00	140.00	125.00
☐ Lady Godiva Procession	180.00	235.00	205.00
☐ Last Lap	260.00	320.00	290.00
☐ Louisiana Purchase	140.00	190.00	165.00
☐ Madonna and Child	500.00	600.00	550.00
☐ Meet, The	230.00	290.00	260.00
☐ Mrs. Cleveland	290.00	350.00	320.00
☐ Present Time	360.00	430.00	395.00
☐ Procession	170.00	210.00	190.00
☐ To The Rescue	140.00	190.00	165.00
☐ Water Jump	160.00	200.00	180.00

STOCK CERTIFICATES

Old paper instruments which have lost their face value, by one reason or another, often acquire a fresh value as collectors' items. There was once a saying, "Worthless as a used stamp," which the hobby of philately has disproved. Confederate currency, which many people just threw away after the Civil War, now has collectible value. And defunct stock certificates have certainly come into that group. The broken investor who cried, in '29, that his stocks were worthless could hardly have envisioned collectors eagerly buying them up. The hobby of collecting stock certificates, originally a minor branch of "paperana," has grown to sizable scope. Thousands upon thousands of different examples exist and, of course, new ones are coming along all the time, which will eventually go into the collectible catagory. Without any doubt, the most picturesque and artistically appealing certificates date from the 1850 to 1900 period. It was considered very important, at that time, for certificates to be complex in design, to discourage counterfeiters. The engraved detailing is sometimes as fine as found on banknotes of the same era, and is more impressive insofar as stock certificates are much larger.

764 / STOCK CERTIFICATES

Stock And Bonds, Confederate, 1864, Philadelphia, 1868 **$15.00-$40.00**

Specimens with pictures at the head, known as vignettes, are the most desirable to collectors, and their value depends largely upon the type of picture (which relates, in most instances, to the nature of the stock). A railroad company stock certificate, with a good vignette of a locomotive from 1870 or 1880, is highly prized. Shipping company stocks with views of sailing vessels are likewise sought. There are many ways to approach this intriguing hobby. If one's funds are tight, many certificates of the 20th century can be had for less than $1 apiece.

	Current Price Range		Prior Year Average
☐ **Acme Uranium Mines, Inc.,** Delaware, allegorical vignette of female and two males, used, 1950's ..	2.00	3.00	2.50
☐ **Boston Chamber of Commerce Realty Trust,** Massachusetts, vignette of old office building showing people and automobiles, used, 1923-1924	4.00	6.00	5.00
☐ **Buffalo Iron Company,** Tennessee, proxy used with battleship revenue stamp affixed, c. 1900's .	3.00	5.00	4.00
☐ **Citizens National Bank in Gastonia,** Gastonia, North Carolina, unissued, eagle with outspread wings	2.00	3.00	2.50
☐ **Eames Petroleum Iron Company,** New York, allegorical vignette representing New York, used, 1882	7.00	10.00	8.50

	Current Price Range		Prior Year Average
☐ **Fidelity Fund, Inc.,** Massachusetts, vignette features the statute of the mariner located at Gloucester, Massachusetts, used, early 1960's	2.50	4.00	3.25
☐ **International Resistance Company,** Delaware, vignette showing rocket, radar antenna, etc., representative of company's business, used, early 1960's	3.00	5.00	4.00
☐ **Louisville Railway Company,** two vignettes, streetcar and female holding lightning bolts, right edge trimmed close, used, early 1890's	10.00	15.00	12.50
☐ **National Tool Company,** Ohio, eagle with outstretched wings, used, 1940's	2.00	3.00	2.50
☐ **New England Gas and Electric Association,** topless female flanked by power lines on the left and gas storage tanks on the right, used, 1940's	3.00	5.00	4.00
☐ **New York, Ontario and Western Railway Company,** New York, vignette of steam engine pulling freight cars, used, 1920's	10.00	15.00	12.50

STONEWARE

Stoneware is a type of ceramic ware that was developed in the 18th century and used extensively for the next hundred years or so, in manufacturing all kinds of household items, giftware, and miscellaneous articles. At that time, pottery makers were in heated competition in a virtual war to capture the market. Each tried to bring out something new that would catch on. The real goal was to make porcelain in the Oriental manner, but technology (in Europe) had not quite reached that point. So a variety of almost-porcelains came and went, and other wares, all of which excited a great deal of attention as they were brought out. "Bone" china contained finely ground fish bones, and "Stone" ware actually had, as one of its ingredients, pulverized stone. The object was to make the ware more durable, as an objection to pottery was its breakability. While stoneware did have a tougher surface and resisted chipping better than other potteries, it broke just the same when dropped. In fact, the destruction rate was higher with stoneware, as its heavy weight caused it to fall with a greater impact. Nevertheless, stoneware succeeded in finding a market, and some very good work was done in it. After having its run in England, stoneware started becoming popular in America after the Revolution. The ware is non-porous and has a grey finish supplied by salt glazing (flinging salt into the kiln while the piece was being fired). Many specimens are painted but overall painting is rare; more often, a simple design is used over the natural finish.

☐ **Batter Pitcher,** blue floral design on gray ground, 10"H.	230.00	290.00	260.00
☐ **Bottle,** gray, inscribed E. C. Boyton, 10"H.	36.00	45.00	40.50
☐ **Bowl,** blue and grayware, 8" Dia.	42.00	52.00	47.00
☐ **Butter crock,** cobalt blue on white ground, 7½" Dia.	115.00	145.00	130.00
☐ **Canning jar,** cobalt blue, 8" H.	32.00	40.00	36.00
☐ **Crock,** blue floral design with handles, 10½" H.	85.00	110.00	102.50

766 / TELEGRAPH COLLECTIBLES

	Current Price Range		Prior Year Average
☐ **Crock,** blue snowflake design on gray ground, inscribed F. H. Cowden, Harrisburg	70.00	90.00	80.00
☐ **Crock,** blue sunflower on gray ground, inscribed O. L. & A. K. Ballard, Burlington, Vermont, 3-gal., 10½" H.	90.00	115.00	102.50
☐ **Ewer,** gray, cobalt with handles, 8" H.	60.00	80.00	70.00
☐ **Flask,** cobalt blue leaf sprays on upper body, 8½" H.	230.00	280.00	255.00
☐ **Jar,** blue grape cluster on gray ground, inscribed A. K. Ballard, Burlington, Vermont, 2-gal., 11" H.	90.00	115.00	102.50
☐ **Jar,** deep blue with flowers on gray ground, J. Heister, Buffalo, New York, 3-gal., 13½" H.	60.00	80.00	70.00
☐ **Jar,** gray and blue, Rice's Landing, Pennsylvania, 3-gal., 13" H.	85.00	110.00	95.00
☐ **Jug,** cobalt blue bird on gray, Whites, Utica, 1-gal., 10½" H.	85.00	110.00	95.00
☐ **Jug,** cobalt blue floral with handles, 10" H., 1800's	45.00	60.00	52.00
☐ **Jug,** cobalt blue leaves on gray, ovoid, I. Seymour, Troy, New York, 2-gal., 13¼" H.	45.00	60.00	52.00
☐ **Jug,** cobalt blue leaf decor on gray, ovoid, 1-gal, 9½" H.	42.00	57.00	48.00
☐ **Jug,** cobalt blue plant design on gray, ovoid, Gilson & Co., Reading, Pennsylvania, 13" H.	80.00	110.00	95.00
☐ **Jug,** impressed tulip, applied handles, ovoid, c. 1800	220.00	280.00	250.00
☐ **Pitcher,** butterfly, 10" H.	50.00	60.00	55.00
☐ **Pitcher,** cobalt blue flower on tan ground, applied handle, 8½" H.	210.00	265.00	235.00
☐ **Pitcher and jug,** cobalt blue flowers on gray ground, White's, Binghamton, 19th c.	300.00	360.00	330.00
☐ **Salt box,** blue and gray, embossed slat on front, 6" Dia.	52.00	65.00	57.00
☐ **Spittoon,** blue and gray	37.00	45.00	41.00
☐ **Water cooler,** urn form, flared top, impressed birds, cobalt blue on gray, Summerset Potters Works, 3-gal., 16" H.	1500.00	2000.00	1700.00

TELEGRAPH COLLECTIBLES

The telegraph, which pointed the way for radio and today's mass media, left behind many souvenirs. Collectors are mainly interested in items dating before 1900, with keys heading the list. Look for items bearing the maker's name and a patent date. These are always desirable, however the patent date is not necessarily the date of manufacture (the item could have been in production for many years after being patented). Avoid pieces with heavy corrosion.

Telegraph Set, sounds and key mounted on wood base, brass and aluminium .... **$85.00-$100.00**

	Current Price Range		Prior Year Average
☐ **Key,** Western Union Telegraph Co., Spies Electric Works Polechanger 1-B, black, bakelite base with nickel-plated fittings, 6⅛" x 3½" x 1⅝"	65.00	82.00	71.00
☐ **Sounder,** Bunnell & Co., wood base, japanned brass coil covers, 5½" x 3" x 4½"	38.00	52.00	45.00
☐ **Sounder,** Bunnell (? unmarked), one piece bronze casting on wood base, 5½" x 3" x 3½", probably 1870's	77.00	94.00	85.00

TELEPHONES

Telephones have had a varied history, not only in terms of technology but in physical styling. While the phone collector might be interested in the technical side of things, it's basically the telephone as an *object,* in its changing shapes and designs through the years, that arouses his attention. As with many revolutionary inventions (radio and the phonograph could be cited), all effort at first was in making it work, and design was completely ignored. The earliest pioneer phones were contained in wooden boxes, which either sat on a desk or, more usually, were mounted on a wall. In terms of physical appearance the box phone was far short of handsome, and in well-to-do homes care was taken to place the phone out of view because of its ugliness. Nevertheless, these venerable relics seem quite appealing today, so antique looking and so vastly different than their present counterparts. The so-called candlestick or "bell" type of phone, in which the earpiece resembles a bell and rests on a hook, became standard in the 1920's and remained in use during the thirties. It is often referred to as the "Elliot Ness" model, thanks to a TV program set in the 1920's. Almost any old phone can be set with modern equipment and actually placed in use, if you so desire (repairs will, however, be your responsibility and not the phone company's — as is always the case when you use your own equipment). Most collectors,

768 / TELEPHONES

Crank Phone, wall, oak, 20″ x 9″ . . . . **$180.00-$225.00**

however, are well content to keep their vintage phones just as they find them, to be displayed as in a museum. You will not have any trouble locating antique phones, and sometimes they can be had well below the real market values (shown here) if discovered in out-of-the-way locations. This is one hobby in which you need not be concerned over fakes. Usually the only matter to be settled, with any individual specimen, is whether or not any repainting has been done.

	Current Price Range		Prior Year Average
☐ **Bell,** brass receiver	154.00	210.00	184.00
☐ **Candlestick,** brass dial	93.00	127.00	110.00
☐ **Candlestick,** brass, Stromberg	160.00	220.00	180.00
☐ **Desk,** dial, c. 1920's	60.00	77.00	68.50
☐ **Lineman's monitor**	30.00	45.00	37.50
☐ **Portable,** forest service, model C, no cranks, pair	35.00	50.00	42.00
☐ **Wall,** Kellogg	210.00	275.00	242.50
☐ **Wall,** Stromberg Carlson	200.00	250.00	225.00
☐ **Wall,** walnut case, c. 1900's	210.00	280.00	245.00
☐ **Wall,** Western Electric	132.00	183.00	157.00
☐ **Wall,** oak, 20″ H.	120.00	170.00	145.00
☐ **Wall,** oak, carved, 23″ H.	187.00	245.00	214.00

THEATRICAL MEMORABILIA

Theatrical Program, for the musical production *My Fair Lady* when it was performed at the Theatre Royal on Drury Lane in London . . . . **$4.00-$5.00**

Vaudeville may be dead in the United States but collectors of its memorabilia, as well as that of the legitimate stage, motion pictures and other branches of show business, are going stronger than ever. All types of items qualify, from personal mementos of the stars themselves to playbills posted outside the theatres to actual remnants of old theatres themselves — such as swatches of curtains. The common "scrapbook" type of collection, that many of us kept in childhood, is seldom of much value as it usually contains little but clippings from magazines and newspapers. Such a collection would need to be highly specialized, and very meticulously assembled, to have a substantial value. Collectors are chiefly interested in the unusual, offbeat, and unique items, which are not available to the mass public. Some make a specialty of contracts, seeking out original agents' or booker' contracts with stars of the past. Though much of this material has gone into museums and other institutional collections, it is by no means impossible to find on the market. For signed items, autograph dealers are the best source of supply. For theatrical posters and related material, dealers in prints are your headquarters. And of course for books and other printed material, you will want to investigate the catalogues published by dealers in old and rare books and in Paper Americana. Auction sales are well worth attending. If you can find an old theater in the process of shutting down, you may be able to buy some of its momentos before demolition begins.

770 / THEATRICAL MEMORABILIA

	Current Price Range		Prior Year Average
☐ **David Belasco,** signed holograph letter	38.50	45.00	41.00
☐ **Card signed by Agnes Moorehead,** c. 1940's	9.00	12.00	10.50
☐ **Collection of curtain fragments** (ranging in size from 3" x 3" to about 8" x 8") from various U.S. Vaudeville playhouses, 17 in all, each matted in heavy colored cardboard with identifying card, the whole contained in a specially constructed wooden box covered in pink velvet and fitted with brass hinges and catches, soiled	500.00	680.00	590.00
☐ **Collection of 167 posters and lobby cards** from U.S. Vaudeville and legitimate playhouses, mostly 1910-30, mostly New York, good condition, a few duplicates	2200.00	2750.00	2450.00
☐ **Collection of 14 typed letters** signed and three holograph letters signed from Alfred Lunt, all to the same correspondent, c. 1953-1961	188.00	250.00	218.00
☐ **Lynn Fontanne,** costumed as Queen Elizabeth, matted and framed 8" x 10" b/w photo, signed and inscribed	92.00	122.00	106.00
☐ **Alfred Hitchcock,** 8" x 10" b/w photo, signed	30.00	40.00	35.00
☐ **DeWolf Hopper** (famous for his readings of "Casey at the Bat"), 8" x 10" sepia photo, signed and inscribed, c. 1900	80.00	100.00	90.00
☐ **Large poster advertisement of the B. F. Keith Circuit theatres,** listing twelve acts, along with addresses of the Keith theatres in various parts of the country, worn along folds, lightly damp-stained, framed in an oak frame, glazed	100.00	135.00	117.50
☐ **Pair of green silk gloves worn by Celeste Holm**	90.00	110.00	100.00
☐ **Poster advertising Lew Dockstadter Minstrels,** lightly damp-stained, rare, 17" x 26", c. 1922	135.00	190.00	160.00
☐ **Poster from the Palace Theater, New York,** advertising Judy Garland, covered in protective cellophane, one corner creased	330.00	400.00	365.00
☐ **Poster of the Riverside Theater, New York,** advertising Burns and Allen comedy, c. 1938	60.00	80.00	70.00
☐ **Set of seven scrapbooks,** 8½" x 11", containing 1,600 items pertaining to the English music halls of 1900-1920, with signed and (in some cases) inscribed photographs of actors, actresses, singers, and other entertainers, along with playbills, clippings, tickets, and miscellaneous memorabilia	1350.00	1750.00	1550.00
☐ **Silk scarf worn by Katherine Hepburn,** in an early role, c. 1938	155.00	190.00	178.00
☐ **Walking stick used by Nigel Bruce,** along with a pocket photo of him in a typical role and two letters from the owner of this memorabilia to a collector	120.00	155.00	137.00

TOBACCO COLLECTIBLES

Tobacco Jar, Lenox wreath mark, Canada geese in flight, signed by W.H. Morley .... **$460.00-$560.00**

When Columbus' men found the Indians smoking tobacco, they wondered what purpose could possibly be served by such a pasttime. But in less than a century, tobacco smoking had acquired a vast popularity in Europe and was to increase in later times, becoming one of the largest industries of the world. With it came various fashions, appliances, gadgets, gimmicks, and a stream of literature that has not stopped at the present day. For collectors, the history and "cult" of tobacco has, for generations, held a special lure. George Arents, a pioneer in the field who was active in the early 20th century, built the largest collection ever assembled on the subject. It was donated to the New York Public Library and now occupies a large room of its own. Many of the rarest broadsides, circulars and documents on tobacco are preserved because of Arents' efforts. The present day collector may choose to bypass documents and literature, and concentrate on the more colorful (though obviously less historical) cigar bands and box labels. The better examples of these made their appearance late in the 19th century and continued to be produced well up into the 20th, at least until the Depression. Cigar band collecting was a hobby of many youngsters of the past, who eagerly waited for dad to smoke a certain cigar so they could obtain the colorful band. Swapping and trading was done, just as with view cards. Regardless of how your cigar bands are obtained, they are best stored flat, opened out, in an album. They can be mounted in place with philatelic hinges, which are sold by stamp dealers.

CIGAR BANDS

	Current Price Range		Prior Year Average
☐ **Abraham Lincoln,** the 16th President, portrait	12.00	16.00	14.00
☐ **D.W.G. Corp.,** custom-made, Detroit, Michigan, silhouette of woman holding flower	1.00	1.75	1.50
☐ **El Generalisimo Arzenoy Rodriguez,** man in military hat, embossed seals at sides	1.25	2.00	1.58
☐ **El Kairo,** man wearing Egyptian headdress	1.50	2.50	2.00
☐ **El Rajah,** no other wording, man in Indian (Asian) headgear	1.25	2.00	1.58
☐ **Glorias de Guillermo 11,** very wide band in oval shape, embossed, portrait	12.00	16.00	14.00
☐ **Grover Cleveland,** band	9.00	12.00	10.50
☐ **Her Majesty Alexandra Victoria,** Elias Rojas, made in Tenerife, large half-length portrait with motto "God Save the Queen"	12.00	15.00	13.50
☐ **Jockey Club La Corona,** "rolled in U.S.A.," horse's head	1.00	1.50	1.25
☐ **John Tyler,** band	10.00	13.00	11.50
☐ **Judge Schemanske,** Detroit, Michigan, embossed	2.00	3.00	1.50
☐ **King Edward VII,** Hoja La Rica, wide label with portrait	9.00	12.00	10.50
☐ **King Solomon,** wide label, attractive portrait with scroll, swords and shield	4.00	7.00	5.50
☐ **Mi Carmen,** maker C. Fernandez	1.00	1.50	1.25
☐ **Millard Fillmore,** band	8.00	11.00	9.50
☐ **Regalia Coronation,** portrait of Edward VII, 1902	12.00	16.00	14.00
☐ **R. B. Hayes,** band	9.00	12.00	10.50
☐ **Robert Walker,** portrait of man in 18th century garb	2.00	3.50	2.75

PIPES

Pipes have a long history, going back (in Europe) to the 16th century and further in America. Originally the pipe was merely a vehicle by which tobacco could be smoked and little thought was given to its artistry or craftsmanship. The enthusiasm for pipe smoking in Europe in the 1600's and 1700's, and in America in the colonial era, knew no bounds. Coffeehouses and taverns kept pipes on hand for patrons who did not bring their own. These long-stemmed "tavern pipes" were made of clay and started out being nearly two feet in length. As each user lit up, he broke off about an inch of the stem, for sanitary considerations. Therefore the pipe got smaller and smaller, and eventually reached the point where it could no longer be smoked. Lavishly decorated pipes with intricate hand carving came into vogue in the 18th century and were made in various parts of the world. For a long while an ivory bowl was considered the mark of a better-class pipe, and the price depended upon whether it was plain or carved. Bowls carved into the likeness of animals, gargoyles, kings, fictional characters, and many other types will be found, displaying a greater or lesser degree of carving skill (which you will have no trouble detecting, with just a minimum of experience). The uniqueness of the subject counts toward the value, but the complexity and virtuosity of carving is of more importance. Some of this work is signed but much of it isn't. Decorative pipes still in their original cases always carry a premium, which can go as high as 50% depending on the type of case and its state of preservation. Hand-carved specimens dating after about 1880 were, in most cases, made for the export market by German firms.

	Current Price Range		Prior Year Average
☐ **Briar,** bull's head, glass eyes	27.00	36.00	31.50
☐ **Delft,** blue and white	18.00	25.00	21.50
☐ **Elk's head,** 6" L.	55.00	70.00	62.50
☐ **Lady,** Victorian, 6" L.	47.00	55.00	51.00
☐ **Lion,** devouring prey, 12" L.	70.00	90.00	80.00
☐ **Meerschaum,** deer, 14" L.	260.00	320.00	290.00
☐ **Meerschaum,** deer pursued by dog, 9" L.	120.00	165.00	142.00
☐ **Meerschaum,** floral design, silk-lined leather case	90.00	120.00	105.00
☐ **Meerschaum,** Fu Manchu	210.00	260.00	230.00
☐ **Meerschaum,** German, marked Arthur Schneider, Leipzig, 18" L., late 19th c.	4000.00	6000.00	5000.00
☐ **Meerschaum,** horse's head, 9½" L.	70.00	90.00	80.00
☐ **Meerschaum,** monk's head, 6" L.	45.00	60.00	52.00
☐ **Meerschaum,** running deer, leather case, amber stem	90.00	120.00	105.00
☐ **Meerschaum,** suede bowl, leather case	70.00	90.00	80.00
☐ **Meerschaum,** wold, amber stem	100.00	130.00	115.00
☐ **Opium,** cloisonne, 15" L.	265.00	315.00	290.00
☐ **Panther's head,** 10" L.	45.00	60.00	52.00
☐ **Porcelain,** German, painted decor	45.00	60.00	52.00
☐ **Porcelain,** landscape decor, handpainted	110.00	140.00	125.00
☐ **Pugs,** two on stem	30.00	40.00	35.00
☐ **Water,** cloisonne, 10" L.	145.00	180.00	162.00
☐ **Water,** snakeskin bowl	135.00	170.00	152.00

TOBACCO JARS AND HUMIDORS

Made of wood, china, pottery, iron and other metals, the tobacco jar was generally a combination of a humidor and pipe holder. Frequently, it was not only functional but also quite ornately decorated. Sculptured heads, figures or animals were quite common. Price ranges listed are for original jars in good condition.

☐ **Arab,** wearing headdress, 7" H.	60.00	75.00	67.50
☐ **Boy,** bisque, 6¾" H.	60.00	75.00	67.50
☐ **Buffalo,** pottery, Dedare ware	190.00	240.00	215.00
☐ **Bulldog,** Bristolware tan colored ceramic	55.00	70.00	62.00
☐ **Devil's head,** red, bee on side of head	50.00	65.00	57.00
☐ **Elephant,** Majolica	90.00	115.00	102.50
☐ **Egyptian Queen,** exotic face, very colorful, 4" H.	80.00	100.00	90.00
☐ **Frog with pipe**	85.00	110.00	97.00
☐ **Girl's face,** with light hair, hat functions as cover	85.00	110.00	97.00
☐ **Human skull**	95.00	120.00	107.00
☐ **Indian chief,** Majolica, feathered headdress, 10" H.	95.00	120.00	107.00
☐ **Jester with dog,** Staffordshire, 9½" H.	250.00	300.00	275.00
☐ **Lion's head,** Austrian hallmarks	50.00	70.00	60.00
☐ **Man,** with derby hat, pipe in mouth, Austrian	50.00	70.00	60.00
☐ **Man,** with skull cap, English pottery	95.00	120.00	97.00
☐ **Monk,** fat with laughing face, bisque chinaware	65.00	85.00	75.00
☐ **Monkeys,** face on lid and around base	140.00	175.00	157.00
☐ **Old Salt Sea Captain,** with cap and pipe	90.00	115.00	102.50
☐ **Ram's head,** Majolica	90.00	115.00	102.50
☐ **Royal Bayreuth,** tapestry ware, cows in field	275.00	340.00	302.00
☐ **Sea captian,** pipe in mouth, Majolica	100.00	135.00	117.50

TOOLS

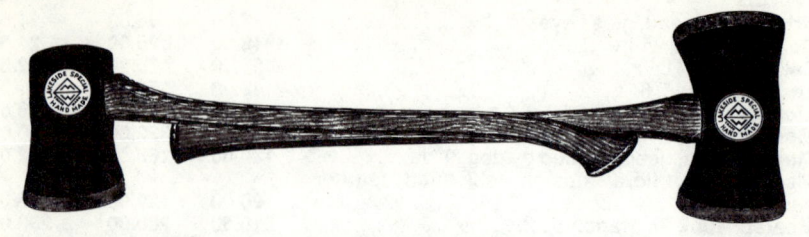

Left to Right: **Single And Double Bit Axes,** by Lakeside, rustless black finish, hickory handles, sold with and without handles . . . . **$20.00-$60.00**

If antiques are collected, why not collect the tools used to create them? Just as furniture and craftwork of yesteryear is uniquely different from today's, so too, were the craftsman's and artisan's tools. In addition, the tool collector can extend his interests to farming implements and anything that could, even in the broadest terms, be classified as a tool. Tools have, of course, existed in one form or another since prehistoric times, so the serious individual could well assemble a panoramic collection touching on many different cultures, uses, and time periods. Neolithic tools were stones sharpened or shaped in various ways. Though these surely qualify as "museum pieces," they can be had from dealers inexpensively ($40 to $100, depending on size). Roman-era tools are on the market, too, and aren't nearly as costly as you might fear. The really tough ones to find are European medieval, but they can be discovered on occasion. American wrought iron tools from as early as the first half of the 18th century turn up on the antique market. Tools of this early a vintage are exclusively blacksmith products, individually made and in most cases retailed by the maker in his local community (or used by himself). Makers' markings are infrequent and since these items were not made under patent or submitted for patent, there is no notice to that regard either. Generally the age can be closely estimated by style. With later specimens there is more regularity and usually more markings to help in identification. Tools dating after about 1840 are almost all factory-made, but are still interesting and collectible.

	Current Price Range		Prior Year Average
AUGERS			
☐ **Hand-forged stem is Y-shaped at hickory handle,** 24" x 1¼", c. 1850's	22.00	32.00	27.00
☐ **Hand-forged crude hickory handles,** unreadable mark, 15" x 1¼", c. 1850's	20.00	29.00	23.50
☐ **Stamped #5,** no manufacturer's mark, well-shaped hickory handle, 15" x 1½", c. 1880	14.00	20.00	17.00
BRACES			
☐ **Metal and wood,** set screw holds bits (hand-turned handles), c. 1840-1860	35.00	50.00	42.00
☐ **Metal and wood,** set screw holds bits, c. 1880-1900	20.00	29.00	23.50
☐ **Walnut with brass trim,** English mark, bit spring broken, c. 1810-1830	90.00	120.00	105.00

	Current Price Range		Prior Year Average

CHISELS

- ☐ **Common,** hand-forged, from file, 6½″ W. blade, iron ferrule, c. 1840-1860 .... | 8.00 | 12.00 | 10.00
- ☐ **Corner,** hand-forged, each side 11″ W., blade 7¼″ L., iron collar on handle, c. 1810-1883 ...... | 20.00 | 28.00 | 24.00
- ☐ **Marked "Charles Buck—Cast Steel,"** brass ferrule, blade ⅞″ W., maple with leather, handle striking surface, c. 1900-1920 .... | 7.00 | 10.00 | 8.50

CLAMPS

- ☐ **All wood,** two "bolts," 5″ jaw, marked "William J. Hood, maker, Valley Falls, R.I.," c. 1860-1880 .... | 14.00 | 19.00 | 16.50

DRAW KNIFE

- ☐ **Cooper's tangs bent through handles,** brass ferrule, c. 1830-1850 .... | 12.00 | 17.00 | 14.50
- ☐ **Leather working "Snell & Atherton,"** #5, all metal scraper, c. 1870........................... | 14.00 | 19.00 | 16.50
- ☐ **Open scorp,** brass ferrule, 19th c............. | 14.00 | 19.00 | 16.50
- ☐ **Wagon maker's,** "Ohio Tool Co." #9, 9″ blade, eggshaped handles, maple, c. 1870 .... | 15.00 | 20.00 | 17.50

HAMMERS

- ☐ **Caulking,** slotted head, iron wings, c. 1880's .... | 12.00 | 15.00 | 13.50
- ☐ **Cobbler's,** marked "Steel drop forged champion," handle replaced, c. 1920's .... | 5.00 | 8.00 | 6.50
- ☐ **Cobbler's or upholstery,** "Made in Germany," hand-forged tool, steel, unusually angled head, c. 1920's.. | 7.00 | 10.00 | 8.50

HAT BRIMMER

- ☐ **Tool used to cut felt for hats,** had adjustable blade holder that slides away from curved base so that brim can be cut to 2″-5″ W. as desired, maple with brass-locking nuts, c. 19th c. .... | 27.00 | 36.00 | 30.00

HATCHETS

- ☐ **LL beam,** 9″ straight handle, blade 2½″ W., c. 1920 .... | 12.00 | 17.00 | 14.50
- ☐ **Plumb,** boy scout holster, 10½″ curved handle, blade 3″ W., c. 1920 .... | 7.00 | 10.00 | 8.50

HOOK

- ☐ **Hay,** hand-wrought, hickory handle, c. 19th c. ... | 5.00 | 7.50 | 6.75

KNIVES

- ☐ **For trimming hooves,** c. 1890-1910 .... | 2.50 | 4.00 | 3.25
- ☐ **Hay,** brass ferrules on both handles, c. 1860-1880 | 17.00 | 24.00 | 20.00

LEVELS

	Current Price Range		Prior Year Average
☐ **All metal,** cast iron decorative body, 18″ x 2½″ x 1″, c. 1910	20.00	25.00	22.50
☐ **#2 stamped on butt,** horizontal and vertical bubbles, working, mahogany, 28″ x 3¼″ x 1¼″, c. 1880	55.00	75.00	65.00
☐ **"Stratton Brothers, Greenfield, Mass.,"** with eagle logo on brass plate, brass corners	30.00	40.00	35.00

PLANES

☐ **All wood except blade,** carpenter's plane, Boech, 12″ L., c. 19th c.	18.00	25.00	21.50
☐ **All wood except blade,** "Horn" plane, European, Boech, c. 19th c.	17.00	24.00	20.00
☐ **All wood except blade,** Ohio Tool Co., joining plane, Boech, 26″ L. c. 19th c.	18.00	25.00	21.00
☐ **All wood except blade,** toothing plane, Boech, c. 19th c.	17.00	24.00	20.00
☐ **Metal and wood,** Stanley Rule and Level Co., #33, 28″ L., c. 1900-1910	22.00	29.00	25.00
☐ **Molding plane,** "E. T. Burrones & Co., Portland, Me." printed on side of plane, "Use this tool for fitting Burrowes Patent Sliding Screens"	27.00	36.00	30.00
☐ **Molding plane,** fancy with brass plow planes, etc.	52.00	70.00	61.00
☐ **Molding plane,** standard, generally priced, up to 1½″ W.	11.00	16.00	13.50

RULERS, FOLDING

☐ **Chapin Stephens Co.,** brass trim all around, stamped "JRP," c. 19th c.	22.00	29.00	25.00
☐ **Ivory,** 24″ L., c. 19th c.	55.00	70.00	62.50
☐ **Lufkin #651,** brass trim, marked "Boxwood — Made in England"	14.00	19.00	16.50
☐ **Lufkin,** pat'd. 12/3/18, brass trim, marked "Boxwood," stamped "Maguire," c. 1918	13.00	18.00	15.00
☐ **Stanley,** #66½, brass at hinges and end, "Warrented Boxwood," 36″ L., c. 19th c.	22.00	29.00	23.00
☐ **Stanley,** #68, brass trim on hinges and ends, "Boxwood," c. 1900	14.00	19.00	16.50

SAWS

☐ **Backsaw,** Wright & Co. on blade, extra heavy back, beech handle, 11″ L., c. 1890	14.00	19.00	16.50
☐ **Keyhole,** W. B. Sears & Co. on blade, "C.B." stamped on maple handle, brass bolts, 7″ L., c. 1890	9.00	12.00	10.50

SCALES

☐ **Lumber,** J. Chatillon & Son, New York, in yellow paint, "200," black, c. 19th c.	60.00	90.00	75.00
☐ **Steelyard,** reversible, two hooks on "Heavy" measure, hand-forged, c. 1810-1830	50.00	70.00	60.00

SCRAPER

	Current Price Range		Prior Year Average

☐ **Unusual paint or wood scraper,** chestnut, turned handle, "W. S. Thompson," 19th century stamped in 3-sided U-shaped blade, handmade, 3½ " L., c. 19th c. **25.00 35.00 30.00**

SCREWDRIVERS

☐ **Clockmaster's,** brass ferrule, breech handle, marked "Sargent, Cast Steel," c. 1890 .... **8.00 12.00 10.00**
☐ **Primitive Yankee model** **20.00 30.00 25.00**
☐ **Winchester,** wood handle **9.00 13.00 10.50**

SCRIBE — MARKING GAUGES

☐ **Beech** with brass facing and trim **9.00 12.00 10.50**
☐ **Handmade,** all beech, hand-stamped inches and numbers, 8" L. **7.00 10.00 8.50**
☐ **Handmade,** beech and mahogany, no inches ... **7.00 10.00 8.50**
☐ **Rosewood** with brass facings and trim **22.00 29.00 25.00**

SHOVELS

☐ **Carved from one piece,** maple or chestnut, grain shovel, c. 1840-1880 .... **18.00 25.00 21.50**
☐ **Snow shovel,** handmade, wood with tin trim, c. 20th c. **12.00 17.00 14.50**

T-SQUARES

☐ **Rosewood handle,** brass plate and three-pointed diamond inlay, stamped "OWO," blade, 7½" x 1¾", c. 1890-1910 .... **14.00 19.00 16.50**
☐ **Rosewood handle,** brass plate and four-leaf clover inlay, "JM" carved in handle, blade 12" x 2⅛", c. 1870-1890 .... **17.00 23.00 20.00**
☐ **Rosewood handle,** "Miller's Falls, Made in U.S.A.," #1438, brass plate, 8" x 1½", c. 1920 ... **9.00 12.00 10.50**

WRENCHES

☐ **Monkey,** A-1, pat'd., 1900 and 1908, miniature, 2" opening, c. 1910 .... **5.00 7.50 6.75**
☐ **Wagon wrench,** hand-forged, curved body, c. 1840-1850 .... **12.00 17.00 14.50**

TOYS

Toys of the past probably mirror our culture, and tell us more about ourselves and how we got that way, than any other collectibles. Although the "nostalgia" craze of the sixties threw considerable extra attention toward toy collecting, it was far from a new hobby at that time. Large collections have been formed throughout the 20th century and the subject has been well covered in collectors' literature, going back generations. The hobby has, though, taken some new directions, and is ever-growing. It could never have been doubted that the beautiful hand-carved toys of 19th century America were well worth preserving,

Buck Rogers Space Gun, toy water pistol .... **$10.00-$15.00**

admiring, and collecting. Recently, other classes of toys, some of them quite modern, have been added to the collectible roster and in some instances are fetching substantial prices. Thus, a vital rule to keep in mind when browsing for collectible toys is: a *very* old toy can be valuable for its age alone, but a recently made one *could* be valuable as well, especially if it has some celebrity interest or other special appeal. Toys picturing or otherwise relating to comic characters, motion pictures, radio, TV or other celebrities nearly always command a premium. As far as 19th century carved wood and cast metal toys are concerned, these should not be expected to retain the full original paint. The general level of condition on toys of 100 years old (or older) is not too high, and the collector who refuses anything beneath pristine mint condition will not do much collecting. The basic criterian is that toys should be complete with no components missing, and not restored in any way. A *repainted* toy has practically no value, regardless of how valuable it would be otherwise. Learn to live with scratches, nicks and chipped paint (or no paint) and you ought to get far in this hobby.

For more information and listings, you may refer to the *Official Price Guide To Toys* published by the House of Collectibles.

ANIMAL-DRAWN VEHICLES

	Current Price Range		Prior Year Average
☐ **Animal Cage Circus Wagon,** Barclay, c. 1930's, lead and tin, slush lead, length 9$\frac{7}{8}$"	25.00	35.00	22.00
☐ **Artillery,** Wilkins, c. 1895, two-horse, rider on caisson, seat top lifts off, cannon, length 10" ...	250.00	350.00	260.00
☐ **Bakery Wagon,** Arcade, length 13"	300.00	400.00	330.00
☐ **Bakery Wagon,** Kenton, 1941, marked "Bakery" .	200.00	250.00	220.00
☐ **Band Wagon,** Kenton, musicians, driver, rider on horse	150.00	200.00	175.00

TOYS / 779

	Current Price Range		Prior Year Average
☐ **Beer Delivery Wagon,** Kenton, c. 1930's, cast iron, two-horse, driver, 10 wooden kegs, length 14½".	170.00	225.00	195.00
☐ **Black Man In Cart Whipping Mule,** Stevens, c. 1890, painted cast iron, mechanical, length 9"..	300.00	400.00	340.00
☐ **Boar Cart,** Kenton, c. 1910, cast iron, Egyptian driver, length 8"	400.00	500.00	450.00
☐ **Carriage,** Wilkins, driver in derby, one-horse, passenger	600.00	775.00	680.00
☐ **Cinderella Coach,** Bliss, c. 1890, paper lithograph on wood, two-horses, four coachmen, lift off roof, blocks inside tell Cinderella story, length 26"...	2000.00	3500.00	2500.00
☐ **Circus Cage,** Barnum and Bailey, c. 1930, elephant drawn, painted, stained and lithographed wood, length 35"	180.00	280.00	220.00
☐ **Circus Cage Wagon,** Kenton, two horses, two riders, driver, animal in cage	150.00	200.00	175.00
☐ **Circus Wagon,** iron and tin, two horses, lion cage, length 9"	150.00	200.00	175.00
☐ **Circus Wagon,** cast iron and wood, containing carved wood bear, length 13"	150.00	200.00	175.00
☐ **City Truck,** Wilkins, cast iron, two-horse with driver	400.00	600.00	500.00
☐ **Coach And Four,** Barclay, c. 1930's, slush lead, length 10¼"	12.00	18.00	14.00
☐ **Coal Car,** Arcade, with horse	50.00	70.00	58.00
☐ **Coal Cart,** Kenton, donkey pulling, black driver..	200.00	300.00	250.00
☐ **Covered Wagon,** tin, driver and horse, Indian head lithographed on side	18.00	22.00	20.00
☐ **Delivery Wagon,** Kenton, No. 5, driver and two horses	100.00	150.00	120.00
☐ **Delivery Wagon,** Wilkins, driver, prancing horse team, length 21"	150.00	200.00	175.00
☐ **Dispatch Wagon,** Chein, one-horse, 11½"	50.00	70.00	60.00
☐ **Dog Cart,** Kenton, greyhound pulling dog riding, length 7"	150.00	200.00	175.00
☐ **Dry Goods,** c. 1860, cloth and wood two horse drawn wagon pull-toy, length 26"	125.00	175.00	150.00
☐ **Dump Cart,** Carpenter, two horse	200.00	300.00	240.00
☐ **Dump Cart,** Dent, black man, mule	80.00	120.00	100.00
☐ **Dump Cart,** Fallows, c. 1890, one horse, tin, length 16"	300.00	400.00	350.00
☐ **Dump Cart,** George Brown, c. 1885, painted tin, length 8¼"	80.00	120.00	100.00
☐ **Dump Cart,** George Brown, c. 1880, tin, back gate lifts out for dumping, length 13"	80.00	120.00	100.00
☐ **Delivery Cart,** Kenton, donkey, cast iron	100.00	150.00	120.00
☐ **Dump Cart,** Hard and Soft Coal, tin, length 19"..	400.00	600.00	500.00
☐ **Dump Cart,** horse pulling cart pull toy, length 7¾"	50.00	70.00	60.00
☐ **Dump Truck,** cast iron and tin, one horse	50.00	70.00	60.00
☐ **Dump Wagon,** Kenton, two horses, lever releases bottom of wagon	80.00	120.00	100.00
☐ **Dump Wagon,** Kenton, c. early 1900's, length 10¼"	60.00	80.00	70.00
☐ **Eagle Chariot,** George Brown, c. 1870, painted tin, length 11"	300.00	400.00	340.00

780 / TOYS

	Current Price Range		Prior Year Average
☐ **Essex Trap,** Hubley, c. 1890, cast iron, driver and horse, length 13″	200.00	300.00	240.00
☐ **Expandable Wagon,** Hubley, with wood bed, cast iron, two horse, driver, length 26″	200.00	300.00	240.00
☐ **Express Wagon,** Kenton, length 11″	40.00	50.00	44.00
☐ **Express Wagon,** Kenton, horse, driver cast iron .	120.00	180.00	150.00
☐ **Farm Wagon,** Arcade, two horse, driver	200.00	300.00	240.00
☐ **Farm Wagon,** Kenton, driver, one horse, early, length 15″	150.00	200.00	175.00
☐ **Fire Wagon,** Kenton, two horse, driver, equipment, bell, wagon nickel-plated, length 23″	200.00	300.00	240.00
☐ **Gentleman's Cart,** Wilkins, c. 1900, gentleman driver, white horse, length 10″	120.00	180.00	150.00
☐ **Gig,** George Brown, tin, one horse, length 10″ ...	150.00	200.00	170.00
☐ **Gig,** Hubley, lady driver, horse-drawn, length 15″	450.00	650.00	525.00
☐ **Gig,** Ives, c. 1890's, driver with top hat, length 5½″	40.00	50.00	45.00
☐ **Gig,** Pratt and Letchworth, cast iron and pressed steel, seven colors, one horse, one rider, length 10½″	200.00	300.00	240.00
☐ **Gig,** Wilkins, fancy, and driver, length 10″	60.00	80.00	70.00
☐ **Gig,** cast iron, one horse, figure	70.00	90.00	80.00
☐ **Gloomy Gus,** Harris, standing in tin cart pulled by iron horse, length 7½″	70.00	90.00	80.00
☐ **Goat Cart,** Harris, shell-type, cast iron, length 5″	50.00	60.00	54.00
☐ **Goat Cart,** Kenton, figure with large ears, length 7″	100.00	150.00	120.00
☐ **Goat Cart,** iron goat and wheels, tin cart, length 7½″	50.00	60.00	54.00
☐ **Gong Bell Pull Toy,** two cast iron horses	50.00	70.00	60.00
☐ **Gravel Wagon,** Kenton, with two horses, length 13″	80.00	120.00	100.00
☐ **Hansom Cab,** Dent, No. 57, two-wheeled, one horse	100.00	150.00	120.00
☐ **Hansom Cab,** Dent, c. 1905, cast iron, lady passenger, driver, length 14″	300.00	400.00	340.00
☐ **Hansom Cab,** Hubley, driver cast in window, horse	70.00	90.00	80.00
☐ **Hansom Cab,** Kenton, figures, horse, length 15½″	175.00	225.00	200.00
☐ **Hook And Ladder,** Kenton, two horse, driver, length 20″	150.00	200.00	175.00
☐ **Hook And Ladder,** Kenton, nickel-plated, two horse, driver, length 20″	120.00	180.00	150.00
☐ **Ice Wagon,** Hubley, two horse, cast iron, length 15″	550.00	750.00	650.00
☐ **Ice Wagon,** Hubley, c. 1906, two horse, cast iron, black horses pulling green wagon, with driver, length 15½″	550.00	750.00	650.00
☐ **Ladder Wagon,** cast iron, with two horses, three sections of ladder, bell, length 25½″	175.00	225.00	200.00
☐ **Landau Carriage,** Hubley, c. 1905, painted cast iron, length 16½″	550.00	750.00	650.00
☐ **Landau,** Kenton, c. 1910, cast iron, white horse pulling green carriage with driver, length 15″	400.00	500.00	450.00

	Current Price Range		Prior Year Average
☐ **Landau,** four horse, with driver, length 24″	200.00	300.00	225.00
☐ **Log Wagon,** Hubley, c. 1905, two oxen, driver, length 15″	175.00	225.00	200.00
☐ **Log Wagon,** Kenton, one horse with driver, length 14½″	80.00	120.00	100.00
☐ **Log Wagon,** Kenton, c. early 1900's, black man, two oxen, cast iron, length 15″	300.00	400.00	340.00
☐ **Log Wagon,** cast iron with driver and two oxen, length 15¼″	250.00	350.00	300.00
☐ **Mail Cart,** tin, horse-drawn	50.00	70.00	60.00
☐ **McCormick Deering Farm Wagon,** Arcade, two horse	60.00	80.00	70.00
☐ **McCormick Deering Manure Spreader,** Arcade, with team of horses	80.00	120.00	100.00
☐ **McCormick Deering Farm Wagon,** two horse, cast iron, length 12½″	35.00	45.00	40.00
☐ **Mess Cart,** WWI-type, tin, two horse-drawn, painted	40.00	50.00	45.00
☐ **Milk Cart,** Althoff Bergman, c. 1880, "Pure Milk", length 14″	650.00	850.00	750.00
☐ **Milk Wagon,** Kenton, with horse and driver	120.00	180.00	150.00
☐ **Milk Wagon,** goat-drawn, possibly George Brown, painted tin, length 6″	80.00	120.00	100.00
☐ **Milk Wagon,** driver and one horse, length 12¾″	50.00	70.00	60.00
☐ **Mower,** two horses and driver, cast iron, length 10″	100.00	150.00	120.00
☐ **One Horse Truck Wagon,** Dent, stake sides, with driver, length 16″	80.00	120.00	100.00
☐ **One Horse Wagon,** Kenton, No. 3, with driver, length 15″	80.00	120.00	100.00
☐ **Overland Circus,** Kenton, c. 1940's-1950's, two horse, cast iron with driver, cage containing bear, length 13¾″	50.00	60.00	55.00
☐ **Overland Circus,** Kenton, c. 1940's, cast iron, two horse with driver, cage containing cast iron bear, length 14″	250.00	350.00	300.00
☐ **Overland Circus,** Kenton, cast iron, two horse with driver, cage containing cloth bear, length 14″	350.00	450.00	400.00
☐ **Pull Toy,** horse-drawn carriage, tin, length 12″	80.00	120.00	100.00
☐ **Pull Toy,** horse pulling water wagon, tin, iron wheels, length 7¼″	60.00	80.00	70.00
☐ **Pumper,** Carpenter, No. 33, two horse, length 18″	200.00	300.00	340.00
☐ **Pumper,** Dent, c. 1915, painted cast iron, moving horses, length 14½″	150.00	200.00	175.00
☐ **Pumper,** Kenton, three horses, length 18″	250.00	350.00	300.00
☐ **Pumper,** cast iron, three horses with figure, length 13″	50.00	60.00	54.00
☐ **Pumper,** driver part of casting, two horse, early, length 15½″	100.00	150.00	120.00
☐ **Pure Milk Wagon,** Fallows, c. 1895, painted and stenciled tin, length 12½″	500.00	700.00	600.00
☐ **Rabbit,** Kenton, pulling cart with two wheels and seat, cast iron, length 5″	65.00	75.00	70.00

Description	Current Price Range		Prior Year Average
☐ **Road Cart,** Dent, one horse, driver in top hat, two seats, length 16″	300.00	400.00	350.00
☐ **Royal Circus Lion Cage,** Hubley, length 9″	150.00	200.00	175.00
☐ **Royal Circus Polar Bear Cage,** Hubley, c. 1920's, length 11¾″	150.00	200.00	175.00
☐ **Royal Circus Tiger Wagon,** Hubley, c. 1920's, length 11½″	175.00	225.00	200.00
☐ **Royal Circus Tiger Wagon Cage,** Hubley, c. 1920, driver, two tigers, length 16″	450.00	550.00	500.00
☐ **Royal Circus Wagon,** two horses with driver and animal in cage	250.00	350.00	300.00
☐ **Sleigh,** Hubley, c. 1900, one horse, painted cast iron, nickel plated, length 15″	200.00	300.00	240.00
☐ **Sleigh,** Hubley, c. 1910, two horse, painted and nickel plated cast iron, length 15″	250.00	350.00	300.00
☐ **Spring Wagon,** Hubley, horse, driver, cast iron	175.00	225.00	200.00
☐ **Sulky,** horse and driver pull toy, comic style, length 10″	20.00	30.00	24.00
☐ **Surrey,** Hubley, c. 1894, clockwork, cast iron, brass works, five colors, length 9″	350.00	450.00	400.00
☐ **Surrey,** Kenton, two horse, cast iron with driver and passenger, length 12½″	30.00	40.00	34.00
☐ **Surry,** Kenton, with fringe top, driver and passenger, two horse, length 13″	60.00	80.00	70.00
☐ **Surrey,** Kenton, c. 1940, one horse, length 16″	125.00	175.00	150.00

AUTOMOBILES AND MOTORCYCLES

Description	Current Price Range		Prior Year Average
☐ **Auto,** c. 1920's, length 4″	40.00	50.00	44.00
☐ **Auto,** c. 1930's, two door, very low cab, long body	65.00	95.00	80.00
☐ **Auto,** c. 1930's, cab open on front seat, length 6¾″	75.00	100.00	90.00
☐ **Auto Express 546,** with drivers and barrels, length 6″	120.00	160.00	135.00
☐ **Auto With Trailer,** c. 1938, both auto and trailer very streamlined, length 2½″	45.00	60.00	52.00
☐ **Auto With Trailer,** c. 1930's, two door, total length 23″	60.00	70.00	64.00
☐ **Buick Sedan,** Arcade, c. 1920, rubber tires, length 8½″	700.00	1000.00	850.00
☐ **Buick Sedan,** 103, Tootsietoy, c. 1930	8.00	10.00	9.00
☐ **Buick Sedan,** 4657, Tootsietoy, c. 1930, tinplate garage	40.00	50.00	45.00
☐ **Buick,** Arcade, c. 1928, two-door, spare tire on rear, length 8″	500.00	700.00	600.00
☐ **Cadillac Brougham,** 6103, Tootsietoy, c. 1926	25.00	35.00	30.00
☐ **Cadillac Station Wagon,** Wyandotte, c. 1941, length 21″	20.00	30.00	25.00
☐ **Champion Motorcycle,** c. 1930, cast iron, rubber tires on wood hubs, length 7¼″	60.00	80.00	70.00
☐ **Checker Cab,** c. 1920's, with driver, thin white rubber tires, with rear tire	450.00	600.00	525.00
☐ **Chevrolet Coupe,** Arcade, c. 1928, white rubber tires, spare tire on rear, length 8″	180.00	240.00	210.00
☐ **Chevrolet Coup,** 6202, Tootsietoy, c. 1926	20.00	30.00	25.00
☐ **Chevrolet Coupe,** 6204, Tootsietoy, c. 1926	20.00	30.00	25.00

	Current Price Range		Prior Year Average
☐ **Chevrolet Coupe,** Arcade, c. 1928, spare tire on back, length 8″	175.00	250.00	200.00
☐ **Chevrolet Sedan,** Arcade, c. 1928	180.00	260.00	220.00
☐ **Chrysler Airflow,** Barclay, c. 1936, length 4″	6.00	8.00	7.00
☐ **Chrysler Airflow,** Hubley, take-apart body, length 4½″	80.00	100.00	90.00
☐ **Chrysler Airflow Auto,** Sun Rubber, white rubber tires	25.00	35.00	30.00
☐ **Ford Sedan and House Trailer,** Kingsbury, c. 1937, pressed steel, length 23″	90.00	120.00	100.00
☐ **Ford Thunderbird,** Tootsietoy, black rubber tires	12.00	16.00	13.50
☐ **Ford Touring Model T,** Arcade, with driver	60.00	80.00	70.00
☐ **Ford V-8 Convertible Sedan,** 0115, Tootsietoy, c. 1934	15.00	22.00	18.00
☐ **Ford V-8 Coupe,** 0112, Tootsietoy, c. 1934	22.00	30.00	24.00
☐ **Ford V-8 Sedan,** 0111, Tootsietoy, 1935, in catalog 1936-1939	7.50	11.25	15.00
☐ **Friction Auto,** Clark, manufactured from 1899-1909	160.00	240.00	320.00
☐ **Funnies Set,** 5102, Tootsietoy, "Uncle Walt" roadster, in catalog 1932-1933, standard version	75.00	112.50	150.00
☐ **Harley-Davidson With Side Car,** Hubley, c. 1930's, three-wheeler	70.00	80.00	75.00
☐ **Gang Buster Car No. 7200,** Marx, c. 1930's, length 14″	70.00	90.00	80.00
☐ **Golden Arrow Racer,** Barclay, slush lead, length 4½″	4.00	5.00	4.50
☐ **Graham Convertible Coupe,** 0514, Tootsietoy, c. 1932, five-wheeler	25.00	35.00	30.00
☐ **Graham Coupe,** 0612, Tootsietoy, c. 1932, six wheel	30.00	40.00	35.00
☐ **Graham Roadster,** 0511, Tootsietoy, c. 1932, five-wheel	40.00	50.00	45.00
☐ **Graham Town Car,** 0616, Tootsietoy, c. 1932, six-wheel	40.00	50.00	45.00
☐ **Jaguar Auto,** Tootsietoy, black rubber tires	2.00	3.00	2.25
☐ **Jaguar XK140,** Tootsietoy, black plastic tires	25.00	35.00	30.00
☐ **Limousine,** 4528, Tootsietoy, c. 1910	15.00	20.00	18.00
☐ **LaSalle Convertible Sedan,** 0715, Tootsietoy, c. 1935	60.00	80.00	70.00
☐ **LaSalle Sedan,** 230, Tootsietoy, c. 1939	7.00	9.00	8.00
☐ **LaSalle Sedan,** 0713, Tootsietoy, c. 1935	60.00	80.00	70.00
☐ **Lark Auto,** Tootsietoy, black plastic tires	1.00	2.00	1.50
☐ **Midget Race Car,** Ohlsson and Rice, c. 1940's, aluminum body, rubber tires	40.00	50.00	45.00
☐ **Model A Ford,** Arcade, c. 1928-1931, with driver, length 6½″	150.00	200.00	175.00
☐ **Model A Ford,** Hubley, c. 1950, die-cast assembled kit	20.00	30.00	25.00
☐ **Model A Coupe,** Arcade, spare tire on back, length 4¼″	50.00	70.00	60.00
☐ **Oldsmobile Brougham,** 6303, Tootsietoy, c. 1926	20.00	30.00	25.00
☐ **Oldsmobile Roadster,** 6301, Tootsietoy, c. 1926	20.00	30.00	25.00
☐ **Open Touring Car,** 232, Tootsietoy, c. 1939	7.00	9.00	8.00
☐ **Packard Car,** American National, c. 1920's, coupe	150.00	200.00	175.00

	Current Price Range		Prior Year Average
☐ **Packard,** Pedal Car, early, wire wheels	100.00	150.00	120.00
☐ **Police Car No. 317,** Barclay, c. 1930's, slush mold, length 3¾"	25.00	35.00	30.00
☐ **Radio Police,** c. 1940, slush mold police car coupe, white rubber tires	8.00	10.00	9.00
☐ **Rio Coupe,** Arcade, rumble seat	180.00	240.00	200.00
☐ **Roadster,** 704, Manoil, futuristic, Pat. No. 95791	9.00	12.00	10.00
☐ **Roadster,** c. 1930's, no cab, length 3½"	20.00	30.00	25.00
☐ **Roadster,** c. 1930's, convertible, spare tire on side of car, length 4½"	20.00	30.00	25.00
☐ **Roadster,** c. 1910's, box-shaped body, driver, length 6"	75.00	100.00	88.00
☐ **Roadster,** cast iron, early, driver, length 7"	90.00	120.00	100.00
☐ **Runabout Auto,** Kenton, cast iron, resembles a 1910 Franklin, driver, length 7"	400.00	500.00	440.00
☐ **Sedan,** A. C. Williams, c. 1931, cast iron, interchangeable body, length 6¾"	100.00	150.00	125.00
☐ **Sedan,** Arcade, c. 1937, cast iron, length 8"	90.00	120.00	100.00
☐ **Sedan,** Barclay, c. 1935, two door, rubber wheels, slush lead, XX, length 3⅛"	12.00	16.00	13.50
☐ **Sedan,** Barclay, c. 1936, four door, Chrysler, length 5"	8.00	10.00	9.00

BATTERY OPERATED

	Current Price Range		Prior Year Average
☐ **Amtrak Locomotive,** S-T Company, c. 1960's, length 16"	18.00	28.00	20.00
☐ **Animated Santa On Rotating Globe,** HTC Company, c. 1950's, four actions, height 11½"	40.00	50.00	42.00
☐ **Army Radio Jeep,** c. late 1950's, radio lights, driver signals with arm, goes forward and reverse, tin litho	28.00	34.00	30.00
☐ **Automoball,** T-N Company, c. early 1960's, tin car with tin driver, mystery action, blows ball on top of radiator smokestack	45.00	55.00	48.00
☐ **Ball Blowing Clown,** T-N Company, c. 1950's, three actions with ball, height 11"	80.00	100.00	85.00
☐ **Balloon Blowing Bear,** Alps Company, c. 1950's, plush bear on tin seat, eyes light, arms rise, feet kick, no air for balloons, height 11⅛"	40.00	50.00	45.00
☐ **Balloon Blowing Monkey,** Alps Company, c. 1950's, five actions with balloon, height 11½"	55.00	70.00	60.00
☐ **Buick,** San, based on a 1950's model, length 6"	55.00	65.00	58.00
☐ **Bulldozer,** M-T Company, c. 1950's, six actions, length 11"	40.00	50.00	45.00
☐ **Bulldozer,** T-N Company, c. 1950's, five actions, length 7½"	45.00	60.00	55.00
☐ **Burger Chef,** plush, cloth-dressed dog, tin, lighted stove, dog shakes salt, moves pan over stove, sniffs, ears and eyes go up and down	80.00	95.00	85.00
☐ **Cable Train,** T-N Company, c. 1940's, four piece set, length 12"	55.00	70.00	60.00
☐ **Calypso Joe,** Linemar, c. 1950's, four actions, height 11"	75.00	100.00	85.00
☐ **Candy Vending Machine Bank,** Wonderful Toy Company, c. 1950's, five actions, height 9"	150.00	200.00	175.00

Item	Current Price Range		Prior Year Average
☐ **Capitol Airlines Viscount 321,** Linemar, c. 1950's, four actions, wingspan 14″, length 11″	60.00	80.00	70.00
☐ **Champion Weight Lifter,** Y-M Company, c. 1960's, five actions, height 10″	45.00	60.00	52.00
☐ **Charlie Weaver Bartender,** Rosko, c. 1961, cloth dressed, vinyl face and hands, body sways, shakes cocktail, pours, smacks lips, face reddens, smoke emits from ears	35.00	45.00	38.00
☐ **Chief Robotman,** K.O. Company, c. 1950's, four actions, height 12″	150.00	200.00	175.00
☐ **Circus Fire Engine,** M-T Company, c. 1960's, four actions, length 11″	60.00	80.00	70.00
☐ **Circus Lion,** Rock Valley Toy Company, c. 1950's, four actions, includes whip and flannel carpet with levers, height 11″	150.00	200.00	165.00
☐ **Clancy Roller Skating Monkey,** Ideal, c. mid 1960's, colorful plastic, rollerskates forward, height 20″	35.00	45.00	38.00
☐ **Climbing Fireman,** c. late 1950's, realistic looking, fireman climbs up and down tin ladder	125.00	175.00	150.00
☐ **Dapper Jigger Dancer,** Haji Company, c. 1950's, height 12″	75.00	100.00	85.00
☐ **Dennis The Menace Playing Xylophone,** plays "London Bridge"	100.00	145.00	125.00
☐ **Dino Robot,** S-H Company, c. 1960's, five actions, height 11″	115.00	150.00	130.00
☐ **Dino The Dinosaur And Fred Flintstone,** Marx, c. 1961, eight actions, length 22″	150.00	200.00	175.00
☐ **Dippie The Whale,** c. 1950's, tin, whale swims and spouts water, length 12″	35.00	45.00	40.00
☐ **Dog With Caterpillar,** plush dog on tin lithograph base, spring-like caterpillar moves back and forth,			
☐ **Double Barrel Gun,** T-N Company, machine gun, tin, tripod base, sound, light flashes, barrels move in and out alternately, height 17″	20.00	26.00	22.00
☐ **Dozo Clown,** cloth-dressed clown, lithograph base, sweeps with broom, face lights, smoke emits from rear end, face reddens	80.00	100.00	90.00
☐ **Drumming Mickey Mouse,** Linemar, c. 1950's, three actions, height 10″	375.00	475.00	400.00
☐ **Drumming Polar Bear.** Alps Company, c. 1960's, three actions, height 12″	30.00	40.00	34.00
☐ **Dump Truck,** T-N Company, c. 1960's, No. 7343, seven actions, length 10¼″	45.00	60.00	48.00
☐ **El Toro,** Cragstan, plush and tin lithograph, tin matador swings back and forth in front of bucking bull, bull snorts	80.00	100.00	90.00
☐ **Feeding Bird Watcher,** Linemar, c. 1950's, five actions, height 9″	60.00	78.00	68.00
☐ **Fire Boat,** M-T Company, c. 1950's, five actions, length 15″	45.00	55.00	50.00
☐ **Fire Boat,** Y Company, c. 1950's, ladder extends 16″, six actions, length 12″	45.00	60.00	48.00
☐ **Fishing Bears Bank,** Wonderful Toy Company, c. 1950's, six actions, height 9½″	150.00	200.00	175.00
☐ **Fishing Kitty,** Linemar, c. 1950's, seven actions, includes tray and plastic fish, height 9″	70.00	90.00	80.00

786 / TOYS

	Current Price Range		Prior Year Average
☐ **Hootin' Hollow Haunted House,** Marx, c. 1960's, eight actions, height 11"	200.00	275.00	250.00
☐ **Hooty The Happy Owl,** Alps Company, c. 1960's, six actions, height 9"	70.00	90.00	80.00
☐ **HyQue Monkey,** Rosko, c. early 1960's, cloth-dressed, fur, vinyl face and hands, stands on heavy gauge tin pedestal, squeeze his hand and hands go up to mouth, eyes, and ears, face lights and reddens as he blushes, eyes blink, shuts off	175.00	225.00	200.00
☐ **Indian Joe,** Alps Company, c. 1960's, four actions, height 12"	45.00	60.00	48.00
☐ **Jaguar car,** T-T Company, c. 1960's, minor toy, length 10½"	22.00	30.00	26.00
☐ **James Bond-007 Car-M101,** Daiwa Company, c. 1960's, seven actions, includes ejectable driver, length 11"	90.00	120.00	110.00
☐ **Jeep,** Cragstan, No. 10560, length 5½"	15.00	20.00	18.00
☐ **Jocko Drinking Monkey,** Linemar, c. 1950's, cloth-dressed, tin lithographed monkey, pours liquid into cup, opens mouth, drinks, eyes light	25.00	35.00	28.00
☐ **Jolly Bambino Eating Monkey,** Alps, small monkey in high chair holds can of candy, drops one candy in hand and pops it into mouth	125.00	175.00	140.00
☐ **Jolly Penguin,** Japan, c. early 1940's, key-wind, plush, tin, plastic, waddles, wings flap, height 5½"	20.00	30.00	25.00
☐ **Josie The Walking Cow,** T-N Company, c. 1950's, seven actions, two cycles, length 14", height 8½"	100.00	140.00	115.00
☐ **Jumbo The Bubble Blowing Elephant,** Y Company, c. 1950's, three actions, includes plastic bowl for bubble solution, height 7¼"	45.00	60.00	48.00
☐ **Jungle Jumbo,** B.C. Company, c. 1950's, five actions, height 9"	90.00	120.00	100.00
☐ **Key-Wind Santa,** cloth-dressed Santa rings bell, waves, height 6½"	20.00	30.00	25.00
☐ **Kissing Couple,** auto with "Just Married" printed on side, couple turn heads, kiss, groom's face blushes red	18.00	22.00	20.00
☐ **Mechanical Juggling Clowns,** TPS Company, cloth-dressed, tin, balances plate on his nose, arms spin, looks as if he is going to fall over	45.00	55.00	50.00
☐ **Mickey Magician,** Linemar, Japan, c. early 1960's, tin lithograph, rubber hands and ears, Mickey stands behind table, raises and lowers hat, squeaks, waves wand	250.00	350.00	280.00
☐ **Mickey Mouse Drummer,** Linemar, c. late 1950's, Mickey walks, eyes light up, beats drum	175.00	275.00	225.00
☐ **Mickey Mouse And Donald Duck Fire Engine,** M-T Company, c. 1960's, three actions, length 16"	80.00	100.00	90.00
☐ **Mickey Mouse Trolley,** T-M Company, tin and plastic, trolley pictures of Minnie Mouse, Pinocchio, Bambi, Dumbo, cats, bear	65.00	75.00	70.00

TOYS / 787

	Current Price Range		Prior Year Average
☐ **Mighty Mike,** plush covered tin bear on tin lithograph base, lifts barbells, barbells light	50.00	60.00	55.00
☐ **Military Police Car,** Linemar, c. 1950's, six actions, length 8½"	70.00	90.00	80.00
☐ **Milk Drinking Dog,** Japan, c. late 1950's, plush dog sits on tin chair, eyes light, pours, drinks ...	35.00	45.00	40.00
☐ **Minnie Mouse In Rocking Chair,** Linemar, key-wind tin, Minnie knits as she rocks back and forth in tin lithographed chair	150.00	200.00	175.00
☐ **Mischievous Monkey,** M-T Company, c. 1950's, six actions, includes tree and monkey, height 18" ...	70.00	90.00	80.00
☐ **Miss Friday The Typist,** girl with tin body and rubber head, long hair, types at tin desk, turns head to look at typewriter	125.00	160.00	140.00
☐ **Mix-ette Mixer,** KDP Company, c. 1940's, includes mixer stand and bowl, when assembled height 9"	22.00	30.00	26.00
☐ **New Space Capslule,** tin lithograph, plastic, blinking light, bump n' go action, tin astronaut pops out, length 9"	60.00	70.00	65.00
☐ **Ninja,** tin, cloth-dressed spy figure clad in black cape, pull string and he climbs string, arms move	65.00	75.00	60.00
☐ **Nutty Mad Indian,** Marx, c. 1960's, four actions, height 12"	45.00	60.00	48.00
☐ **Nutty Nibs,** Linemar, c. 1950's, minor action, includes lithograph bowl of nuts and steet ball, height 11½"	150.00	200.00	165.00
☐ **Pan Am 727,** tin friction jet, wingspan 9½"	10.00	15.00	12.00
☐ **Panda In Rocker,** plush panda in tin rocker on tin lithographed base, raises pipe to mouth, pipe lights up, smoke emits from mouth	55.00	65.00	60.00
☐ **Pago Pago,** TPS Company, tin lithographed native holds spear and shield, key-wind, head rocks back and forth as he turns around	70.00	80.00	72.00
☐ **Picnic Bear,** c. 1950's, plush covered tin bear seated on tin lithographed stump, pours from bottle, raises cup, drinks, eyes light up	25.00	35.00	30.00
☐ **Picnic Rabbit,** Alps Company, c. 1950's, rabbit pours carrot juice into eggshell, drinks, eyes light up, height 9"	65.00	75.00	70.00
☐ **Picnic Poodle,** STS Company, c. 1950's, four actions, two cycles, length 7", height 7"	30.00	40.00	35.00
☐ **Pinnochio-Playing London Bridge,** Rosko, c. 1950's, three actions, includes xylophone, height 10"	80.00	100.00	90.00
☐ **Popcorn Vendor,** S And E Company, c. 1960's, No.s-4035, six actions, includes lithograph umbrella, length 7"	90.00	120.00	100.00
☐ **Pop Drinking Panda,** M-T Company, c. 1950's, five actions, base 4" x 4", height 10"	60.00	80.00	70.00
☐ **Red Gulch Bar,** K Company, c. 1950's, five actions, height 9½"	100.00	150.00	125.00
☐ **Rex The Reckoning Dog,** key-wind, plastic dog on tin lithographed base, head nods, numbers appear on base	25.00	35.00	30.00

788 / TOYS

	Current Price Range		Prior Year Average
☐ **Roaring Gorilla,** c. late 1950's, tin lithographed gorilla on tin base, hit the chestand his eyes light up, arms rise, he roars	70.00	80.00	75.00
☐ **Rocket Launcher T-12,** Daiya Company, c.1960's, six actions, length 10", width 5½"	150.00	200.00	165.00
☐ **Rocking Chair Panda,** T-M Company, c. 1950's, five actions, height 10"	60.00	80.00	70.00
☐ **Sammy Wong-The Tea Totaler,** T-N Company, c. 1950's, four actions, height 10"	90.00	120.00	100.00
☐ **Santa Claus Bank,** c. 1961, cloth-dressed tin, vinyl face, Santa sits atop tin house, bell in one hand, packages in other, operates on coin or switch	125.00	175.00	150.00
☐ **Santa Drummer,** cloth-dressed, remote control Santa, celluloid face, beats drum as he walks, light bulb in hat	70.00	80.00	72.00
☐ **School Bus,** Cragstan, c. 1950's, a minor toy, length 20½"	30.00	40.00	34.00
☐ **Scissors Dog,** Linemar, tin, lithographed dog, electric scissors mouth	35.00	45.00	38.00
☐ **Shoe-Shaking Dog,** M-T Company, c. 1950's, five actions, height 6", length 8"	30.00	40.00	34.00
☐ **Shooting Gorilla,** M-T Company, c. 1950's, four actions, includes gun and darts, height 12"	80.00	100.00	90.00
☐ **Shrunken Head,** looks like cow hide covered with real human hair	35.00	45.00	40.00
☐ **Shuco Mouse,** U.S. Zone Germany, key-wind tin mouse, mouse scurries forward	20.00	30.00	24.00
☐ **Shuco V.W.,** key-wind beetle, length 4"	22.00	30.00	24.00
☐ **Shutterbug Photographer,** T-N Company, c. 1950's, five actions, height 9"	120.00	175.00	145.00
☐ **Skipping Monkey,** plastic, tin, monkey skips wire rope	25.00	35.00	30.00
☐ **Sky Patrol,** tin boy in tin lithograph space vehicle	150.00	200.00	170.00
☐ **Singing Bird In Cage,** yellow tin canary in round tin cage, tail moves, warbling sound	90.00	120.00	115.00
☐ **Sleeping Bear,** Linemar, c. 1950's, six actions, length 9"	65.00	80.00	70.00
☐ **Smoking Popeye,** Linemar, c. 1950's, five actions, height 9"	275.00	375.00	200.00
☐ **Smoking Pop Locomotive-The General,** San Company, c. 1950's, four actions, length 10¼"	45.00	60.00	52.00
☐ **Talking Parrot,** Marx, felt-covered parrot on tin lithographed pedestal, wings flap, eyes light, head turns, talks via tape recorder in base	175.00	250.00	215.00
☐ **Tank M-56,** M-T Company, c. 1940's, wheel drive, seven actions, length 7½"	45.00	60.00	52.00
☐ **Tank M-35,** HTC Company, c. 1950's, three actions, length 8"	40.00	50.00	44.00
☐ **Tarzan,** San Company, c. 1960's, tin, vinyl head, remote control, dressed in loincloth, Tarzan walks, raises arms, roars, height 13"	100.00	150.00	120.00
☐ **Teddy The Artist,** Y Company, c. 1950's, three actions, includes patterns, height 9"	90.00	120.00	100.00

CLOCKWORK AND WINDUPS

	Current Price Range	Prior Year Average
☐ **Acrobat,** celluloid type body, long running clockwork motor, turns and performs, height 6″	4.00 6.00	4.25
☐ **Acrobatic Marvel,** c. 1930's, monkey on pole performs tricks	30.00 40.00	32.00
☐ **Boy On Ice Cream Bicycle,** lithographed metal, runs in circle as boy's feet peddle, height 4″	4.00 6.00	4.50
☐ **Bumper Car,** Marx, c. 1930's	20.00 30.00	23.00
☐ **Capitol Hill Racer,** Unique Art, c. 1930's	40.00 50.00	42.00
☐ **Cat And Ball,** Marx, c. 1950's, lithographed tin and plastic, cat lying down holds ball between front paws	18.00 22.00	20.00
☐ **Charlie McCarthy,** c. 1930, top hat has his name, dressed in tuxedo and monocle	70.00 80.00	74.00
☐ **Chirping Bird,** sings flap, bird chirps, length 7″	2.00 3.00	2.25
☐ **Circus Cage,** c. 1928, decorative circus wagon	150.00 200.00	175.00
☐ **Clever Bear,** Japan, c. 1948, dressed tin, furry bear walks	25.00 35.00	32.00
☐ **Clown In Cart,** Marx, c. 1930, drawn by small horse	30.00 40.00	34.00
☐ **Clown "Roli Zoli,"** clown on scooter, lithographed metal, long run clockwork motor, moves in circles, zigzags, bumps into obstacles and reverses, stops and starts, height 5½″	4.00 6.00	3.00
☐ **Donald Duck And Goofy Duet,** Marx, c. 1946, lithographed tin clockwork, Donald plays drum, Goofy dances, height 10″	150.00 250.00	160.00
☐ **Double Jiggers,** c. 1920's, lithographed tin, two black figures made of tin dance in front of a lithographed scene	400.00 500.00	450.00
☐ **Drummer On Horseback,** c. 1920's, wears striped outfit, two drums carried on both sides of the horse's neck	40.00 50.00	42.00
☐ **Ernest Plank Boat,** German, c. 1895	100.00 150.00	115.00
☐ **Feeding Bird,** lithographed metal, bird pecks around, his tail bobs up and down, height 4½″	1.00 3.00	1.50
☐ **Ferdinand The Bull,** Marx, c. 1938	30.00 40.00	34.00
☐ **Ferris Wheel,** c. 1900's	200.00 250.00	215.00
☐ **Fireman,** Marx, c. 1930, climbs ladder on a stand	30.00 40.00	35.00
☐ **Fire Truck,** Germany, c. 1930, lithographed tin, tin characters, firefighting equipment, bell rings	125.00 145.00	135.00
☐ **Flash Gordon Rocket Fighter,** c. 1930's, length 12″	70.00 80.00	72.00
☐ **Flippo The Dog,** Marx, USA, c. 1940's, lithographed tin, sitting dog somersaults	30.00 40.00	32.00
☐ **French Wind-Up Pig Herder,** c. 1914, tin	150.00 200.00	165.00
☐ **George The Drummer Boy,** c. 1940's, soldier in British uniform, name of toy on the drum	10.00 20.00	14.00
☐ **Hopping Frog,** China, lithographed metal, plastic lifelike frog colors, height 3½″	1.00 3.00	1.50
☐ **Horse And Cart,** c. 1930's, tin	25.00 35.00	28.00
☐ **Interstate Bus,** Strauss, c. 1920's, open stairs lead to luggage area on top of the bus	70.00 80.00	74.00
☐ **Ice Cream Cart,** Cortland, c. 1940's, ice cream man rides at back of cart	15.00 25.00	18.00
☐ **Model T Ford,** Bing, c. 1920's, four door	70.00 80.00	72.00
☐ **Model T Ford,** Bing, c. 1920's, two door	70.00 80.00	75.00
☐ **Monkey And Candy Cart,** c. 1950's, monkey rides at back of cart and pedals	2.50 6.50	4.50

790 / TOYS

	Current Price Range		Prior Year Average

- ☐ **Monkey On Horse,** China, lithographed metal, wind-up, horse prances, bell rings, furry mane and tail, height 6″ **5.00 7.00 4.75**
- ☐ **Motorcycle With Sidecar,** wind-up, heavy lithographed metal, rubber side wheels, length 7″ **7.00 10.00 8.00**
- ☐ **Police Squad Motorcycle,** Marx, c. 1950, lithographed tin, sidecar and loud siren **60.00 70.00 62.00**
- ☐ **Popeye In The Cart,** Marx, c. 1937, USA, lighographed tin, Popeye rides in a cart pulled by a very small pony **150.00 180.00 160.00**
- ☐ **Popeye On Bicycle,** Linemar, c. 1950, Japan, lithographed tin, Popeye rides bike around in circles, bell rings **150.00 185.00 160.00**
- ☐ **Porter,** Germany, c. 1930's, lithographed tin, figure hand-painted, porter pushes baggage, hops on it for a ride, then jumps off **70.00 80.00 72.00**
- ☐ **Prancing Horse,** Germany, c. 1930's, lithographed tin, white horse with saddle and bridle **50.00 60.00 55.00**
- ☐ **Racer,** Structo, c. 1920's, very plain with wheels set at very end of car **30.00 40.00 34.00**
- ☐ **Racer,** England, streamlined with large fin at the back **18.00 22.00 20.00**
- ☐ **Racer,** c. 1914, old-fashioned square shape, length 11″ **100.00 150.00 115.00**
- ☐ **Railroad Handcar,** c. 1920's, two men, one at each end of the handlebar which pumps up and down . **30.00 40.00 32.00**
- ☐ **Red Cap Porter,** Marx, c. 1930's **45.00 55.00 48.00**
- ☐ **Red Ranger Ridem Cowboy,** Wyandotte, c. 1930's **30.00 40.00 42.00**
- ☐ **Toonerville Trolley,** Fisher, Germany, c. 1922, lithographed tin, based on Fontaine Fox cartoon, conductor stands at back, erratic movement **550.00 750.00 600.00**
- ☐ **Toy Boat,** J. Chein Co., c. 1940's, USA, all lithographed metal, spring wound motor, length 8½″ **7.00 10.00 6.00**
- ☐ **Toyland Milk Wagon,** Marx, c. 1930's, USA, lithographed tin, dairy delivery wagon, fine details **90.00 110.00 100.00**
- ☐ **Wind-Up Truck,** Structo, c. 1920's, very simple design, length 12″ **100.00 140.00 115.00**
- ☐ **Two-Speed Motorcycle,** Germany, (US Zone), c. 1950, lithographed tin, two-speed motor and control switch **55.00 75.00 60.00**
- ☐ **Waddling Duck,** lithographed metal, paddle-action in circular pattern, height 4″ .... **1.00 3.00 .75**
- ☐ **Walking Porter,** Marx, c. 1935, USA, lithographed tin, wood wheels, head moves as porter walks .. **145.00 185.00 155.00**
- ☐ **Whiz Skyfighter,** Girard Toy, c. 1920's, double-wing airplane **25.00 35.00 28.00**
- ☐ **Whoopie Cowboy,** Marx, c. 1938, USA, lithographed tin, one of the early crazy cars, tractor with farmer at wheel **150.00 200.00 185.00**
- ☐ **Wild West Bucking Bronco,** Lehmann, c. 1910, front legs attached to platform, the rear legs kick up **80.00 110.00 90.00**
- ☐ **World War I Soldier,** Marx, stretched out on his stomach aiming his rifle, wheel underneath propels him forward **18.00 22.00 20.00**

SOLDIERS

	Current Price Range		Prior Year Average
☐ **Anti-Aircraft With Range Finder 82,** Manoil	8.00	12.00	10.00
☐ **At Attention 45/10,** Manoil	12.00	18.00	15.00
☐ **Aviator 34,** Manoil	10.00	15.00	12.00
☐ **Aviator 941,** Barclay	4.00	6.00	5.00
☐ **Aviator Holding Bomb 85,** Manoil	15.00	20.00	17.00
☐ **Bomb Thrower 31,** Manoil, three grenades in pouch	8.00	12.00	10.00
☐ **Bugler 909,** Barclay	3.00	5.00	4.00
☐ **Bugler,** Jones, early	5.00	7.00	6.00
☐ **Bugler 10,** Manoil, hollow base version	12.00	18.00	14.00
☐ **Bugler 10,** Manoil	8.00	12.00	10.00
☐ **Cook's Helper With Ladle 60,** Manoil, normal helmet	8.00	12.00	10.00
☐ **Drummer 11,** Manoil, hollow base version	12.00	18.00	15.00
☐ **Drummer 11,** Manoil, stocky version	7.00	11.00	9.00
☐ **Drummer 11,** Manoil, vertical drum	10.00	15.00	12.00
☐ **Falling With Rifle 780,** Barclay, cast helmet	8.00	12.00	10.00
☐ **Field Doctor 42,** Manoil, crawling	12.00	18.00	15.00
☐ **Fifer 739,** Barclay, tin helmet	10.00	15.00	12.00
☐ **Grenade Thrower 738,** Barclay, rifle off ground, tin helmet	12.00	18.00	15.00
☐ **Kneeling,** Jones, firing rifle, no stand	40.00	50.00	44.00
☐ **Kneeling 703,** Barclay, firing, long stride, tin helmet	8.00	12.00	10.00
☐ **Kneeling 703,** Barclay, firing, short stride	12.00	18.00	15.00
☐ **Kneeling With AA Gun,** Jones	7.00	11.00	8.00
☐ **Kneeling With Binoculars,** Auburn Rubber	4.00	6.00	5.00
☐ **Machine Gunner 12,** Manoil, prone, spaces under body	8.00	12.00	10.00
☐ **Officer 778,** Barclay, with gas mask, cast helmet .	12.00	18.00	14.00
☐ **Officer 708,** Barclay, with sword, short stride	15.00	20.00	17.50
☐ **Officer 708,** Barclay, with sword, tin helmet, long stride	7.00	11.00	9.00
☐ **Soldier 45/14,** Manoil, with shell for bazooka	25.00	35.00	30.00
☐ **Sitting Soldier 33,** Manoil	12.00	18.00	15.00
☐ **Sitting,** Barclay, with rifle, tin helmet	8.00	12.00	10.00
☐ **Sound Detector,** Auburn Rubber	15.00	20.00	17.00
☐ **Sniper 26,** Manoil	8.00	12.00	10.00
☐ **Sniper,** Manoil, thin	4.00	6.00	5.00
☐ **Standing 747,** Barclay, firing rifle, cast helmet ...	8.00	12.00	9.00
☐ **Standing 747,** Barclay, firing rifle, long stride	7.00	11.00	9.00
☐ **Standing 747,** Barclay, firing rifle, short stride ...	12.00	18.00	15.00
☐ **Stretcher Bearer,** Auburn Rubber	3.00	5.00	4.00
☐ **Stretcher Bearer 539,** Manoil	4.00	6.00	5.00
☐ **U.S. Infantry 4,** grey iron, port arms, early	8.00	12.00	10.00
☐ **U.S. Infantry 3/1,** grey iron, port arms	6.00	8.00	7.00
☐ **U.S. Infantry 3,** grey iron, shoulder arms, early ...	4.00	6.00	5.00
☐ **U.S. Machine Gunner 13/1,** grey iron	6.00	8.00	7.00
☐ **U.S. Marine 9,** grey iron	6.00	8.00	7.00
☐ **U.S. Naval Officer 14AW,** grey iron, early, in white	6.00	8.00	7.00
☐ **U.S. Sailor 14,** grey iron, early, in blue	5.00	7.00	6.00
☐ **U.S. Sailor 14,** grey iron, in blue	5.00	7.00	6.00
☐ **U.S. Sailor Signalman 14/1W,** grey iron	7.00	11.00	9.00
☐ **U.S. Sailor 14W,** grey iron, in white	4.00	6.00	5.00
☐ **Tank Defender,** Auburn Rubber	5.00	7.00	6.00
☐ **Tank Soldier,** Auburn Rubber, running with box ..	4.00	6.00	5.00

SPACE TOYS

Item	Current Price Range		Prior Year Average
☐ **Apollo 15 EVA And Toy Lunar Module,** DSK Company, Astronaut James Irwin, pilot of the lunar module, salutes Astronaut David Scott who records this EVA (extravehicular activity) of the 1971 mission to the moon	45.00	55.00	48.00
☐ **Busy Robot,** S-H Company, Japan, c. 1965-70, battery-operated, construction worker robot, yellow hard hat, body and wheelbarrow, height 11″	350.00	450.00	375.00
☐ **Capsule 6,** M-T Company, Japan, c. 1960-65, battery-operated, authentic details, inauthentic shape, length 11½″	75.00	100.00	85.00
☐ **Fire Bird,** Japan, c. 1960-65, battery-operated, controlled by the sound of a big plastic whistle, length 13½″	100.00	150.00	120.00
☐ **Flash Gordon Set Of Plastic Figures,** Premier Products Company, Brooklyn, NY, c. 1952, comes with plastic space rocket	10.00	15.00	11.00
☐ **Lunar Robot,** Y Company, Japan, c. 1965-70, wind-up, a small mechanical robot, height 7″	150.00	250.00	175.00
☐ **Martian Super Sensitive,** Japan, c. 1955-60, battery-operated, a jeep with a strange radar apparatus, length 9½″	275.00	375.00	280.00
☐ **Mechanized Robot,** Japanese adaptation of robots designed after the robot Robby from the film ForbiddenPlanet, but apparently not authorized, height 13½″	300.00	400.00	325.00
☐ **Remote Control Robot,** Masudaya Toys, made over a ten year period, earlier models have a tin decorated battery box, later models have a plain battery box and control cylinder	75.00	85.00	78.00
☐ **Robot,** Yone, Japan, c. 1970-75, wind-up, height 3″	75.00	85.00	75.00
☐ **Robot,** Japan, c. 1955-60, wind-up, mechanical robot that sparks, height 5″	125.00	175.00	150.00
☐ **Space Explorer,** Ichiko, Japan, c. 1965-70, battery-operated, length 8″	150.00	180.00	160.00
☐ **Space Explorer,** M-T Company, Japan, c. 1960-65, battery-operated, saucer-shaped with fins, height 12″	125.00	160.00	115.00
☐ **Super Cycle,** B Company, Japan, c. 1955-60, friciton, futuristic motorcycle driven by an all green man in a helmet, length 12″	45.00	55.00	48.00
☐ **Super Space Giant,** S-H Company, Japan, c. 1965-70, battery-operated, stop n' go, swing open door, blinking and shooting gun, realistic shooting noise, rotating body, height 16½″	600.00	700.00	625.00
☐ **Thunder Robot,** Asakusa, Japan, c. 1960-65, battery-operated, strange monster appearance, height 11″	500.00	600.00	525.00
☐ **Universe Car,** China, c. 1970-75, battery-operated, tin, spaceship, small dome in the center, two fins at the back, length 10″	55.00	65.00	58.00
☐ **Universe Rocket,** T-N Company, Japan, c. 1960-65, battery-operated, red and black trim on a white body, rocket stands on its end, two large wings on the sides, height 21½″	75.00	125.00	80.00

TRAINS AND ENGINES
LIONEL O GAUGE SETS

	Current Price Range		Prior Year Average
☐ **#1665 0-4-0 Switcher,** with slope back tender	180.00	280.00	220.00
☐ **#226E Locomotive,** with #2226W Tender; #3859 Dump; #3820 Floodlight; #2817 Caboose; #3814 Merchandise	900.00	1000.00	940.00
☐ **#1054 Freight Train,** with #1681 Engine and Tender; #1680 Tank; #1682 Caboose; #1677 Gondola, lithographed	250.00	350.00	300.00
☐ **#1862 General,** with Tender; #1875 Coach, with whistle; #1876 Mail; #1877 Horse	500.00	600.00	540.00
☐ **#1862 General Sears Special,** with #1862 Tender; #1887 Horse, yellow fence with horses and cattle; #1866 Mail, yellow, brown; #1885 Coach, blue, white, brown	900.00	1200.00	1000.00

LIONEL PASSENGER SETS

☐ **#2360 Solid Stripe,** GG-1, twin motor maroon with #2544 Molly Pitcher; #2543 William Penn; #2541 Alexander Hamilton	1000.00	1300.00	1150.00
☐ **#2421 Maplewood,** with #2422 Chatham; #2423 Hillside, silver, black stripe, people in windows ..	150.00	250.00	190.00
☐ **#2530 Railway Express Baggage,** with #2531 Tail Car; #2534 Silver Bluff Coaches	225.00	275.00	240.00
☐ **#8466 A Unit,** with #8467 A Dummy; #8475 B Unit, Amtrak set, with five Williams Amtrak Aluminum coaches, Vista domes, two coaches, one baggage, one observation	350.00	450.00	400.00
☐ **#8568 Lionel Preamble Express Twin A's,** with four car Williams set, Bicentennial special, Minuteman, Liberty Bell, Paul Revere, and George Washington	250.00	350.00	300.00

LIONEL ROLLING STOCK

☐ **#610 Coach,** dark green	45.00	55.00	50.00
☐ **#653 Hopper,** pea green, nickel trim	35.00	45.00	40.00
☐ **#804 Tank Car,** gray, rubber stamped	25.00	35.00	30.00
☐ **#807 Caboose,** red, peacock	20.00	30.00	24.00
☐ **#810 Crane,** black, burnt orange, maroon, peacock boom	75.00	85.00	80.00
☐ **#812 Gondola,** light green, nickel trim	30.00	40.00	34.00
☐ **#812 Gondola,** dark green, brass trim	20.00	30.00	24.00
☐ **#812 Gondola,** mohave, brass trim	40.00	50.00	45.00
☐ **#813 Cattle Car,** orange, brass trim	80.00	90.00	82.00
☐ **#815 Sunoco Tank Car,** nickel trim	125.00	175.00	150.00
☐ **#815 Tank Car,** green	90.00	100.00	94.00
☐ **#816 Hopper,** red, nickel trim	125.00	175.00	150.00
☐ **#6176 Hopper,** light yellow, black lettering	20.00	30.00	24.00
☐ **#6257 Caboose,** red, Lionel lettering	6.00	8.00	7.00
☐ **#6282 Wheel Car**	18.00	22.00	20.00
☐ **#6357 Caboose,** brown	16.00	20.00	18.00
☐ **#6405 Lionel Horse Car,** no stakes	12.00	18.00	15.00
☐ **#6415 Tank Car**	18.00	24.00	21.00
☐ **#6425 Gulf Tank Car,** three dome	10.00	16.00	13.00
☐ **#6446 N And W Hopper,** Norfolk and Western, light gray	28.00	38.00	33.00
☐ **#6446-25 N And W Hopper,** black	20.00	30.00	23.00
☐ **#6446-25 N And W Hopper,** gray	30.00	40.00	33.00

794 / TOYS

	Current Price Range		Prior Year Average
☐ #6448, Target Car, red, white	35.00	45.00	38.00
☐ #6457 Caboose, brown, Lionel Lines	10.00	16.00	12.00
☐ #6457 Caboose, light and smokestack	8.00	12.00	10.00
☐ #6462 Gondola, maroon	6.00	10.00	8.00
☐ #6464 Great Northern Box Car	20.00	30.00	24.00
☐ #6464-75 Rock Island Box Car	60.00	70.00	64.00
☐ #6464-150 Eagle Merchandise Car	44.00	54.00	48.00
☐ #6464-225 Southern Pacific Box Car, black, red, yellow	95.00	115.00	105.00
☐ #6464-400 B And O Box Car	45.00	55.00	48.00
☐ #6464-450 Great Northern, green, yellow, orange	80.00	90.00	84.00
☐ #6476 Hopper, red, white lettering	8.00	12.00	10.00
☐ #6572 Railway Express, green, gold	70.00	80.00	73.00
☐ #6736 Detroit And Mackinac Hopper	30.00	40.00	33.00

AMERICAN FLYER S GAUGE ROLLING STOCK

☐ #20 Western Type Franklin Coach	32.00	42.00	36.00
☐ #40 Western Type Baggage Express Car	40.00	50.00	44.00
☐ #628 Lumber Car, W.L., metal base	12.00	18.00	15.00
☐ #630 Caboose, dark red	10.00	16.00	13.00
☐ #631 T And P Gondola, green	6.00	10.00	8.00
☐ #632 Hopper, dark gray	4.00	8.00	6.00
☐ #633 Box Car, B and O	25.00	35.00	28.00
☐ #634 Searchlight Car	15.00	23.00	18.00
☐ #636 Depressed Center Cable Car, 12 wheel	20.00	30.00	24.00
☐ #638 Caboose, A.F.L., red	4.00	8.00	6.00
☐ #640 Hopper, gray, four hoppers	6.00	10.00	8.00
☐ #640 Wabash Hopper, black	20.00	30.00	24.00
☐ #644 A.F. Industrial Brown Hoist, 12 wheel	100.00	175.00	140.00
☐ #648 Track Cleaning Car	12.00	18.00	15.00
☐ #660 Baggage, chrome	40.00	50.00	44.00
☐ #718 Railway Express Car, red	35.00	45.00	40.00
☐ #801 B And O Hopper, black	18.00	24.00	22.00
☐ #906 Crane	30.00	40.00	34.00
☐ #914 Log Unloading Car	35.00	45.00	38.00
☐ #921 Hopper, brown, white	20.00	30.00	24.00
☐ #925 Gulf Tank Car	12.00	18.00	15.00
☐ #935 Bay Window Caboose	70.00	80.00	75.00
☐ #970 Seaboard Box Car	35.00	45.00	40.00
☐ #24039 Rio Grande Cookie Box Car	55.00	65.00	60.00
☐ #24328 Shell Tank Car	25.00	35.00	30.00
☐ #24533 Service Car	30.00	40.00	34.00
☐ #24549 Generator Car, with searchlight, yellow, brown	25.00	35.00	30.00

TRUCK AND SERVICE VEHICLES

☐ American Railway Express Truck, Sturditoy, c. 1920's	75.00	100.00	88.00
☐ Anti-aircraft Truck, Barclay, c. 1940, no driver, man firing AA gun, double barrel, length 2¾"	6.00	8.00	7.00
☐ Bank Of America Armored Truck, Smitty, No. 602-B, length 14½"	35.00	45.00	40.00
☐ Bekins Van, Smitty No. 406, six-wheel tractor and four-wheel trailer, length 29"	165.00	220.00	195.00
☐ Bell Telephone Truck, Hubley, c. 1938, towing device at rear of truck, length 13"	80.00	120.00	100.00

TRADE CARDS AND CATALOGS / 795

	Current Price Range	Prior Year Average
☐ **Coca Cola Truck,** Metalcraft, c. late 1920's-30's, pressed steel, rubber tires, 10 bottles in rack, "Every Bottle Sterilized", length 11"	225.00 300.00	260.00
☐ **Double-Decker Bus,** Arcade, c. 1928, length 8"	125.00 175.00	140.00
☐ **Double-Decker,** Arcade, c. 1930's, length 8"	100.00 175.00	130.00
☐ **Electrically Lighted Truck And Trailer Set,** Marx, No. T-5715, c. 1930's, length 15"	30.00 40.00	35.00
☐ **Emergency Truck,** Kenton, c. 1930's, black rubber tires, takes batteries for headlights and spotlight	60.00 80.00	70.00
☐ **Firetruck,** Buddy L, c. 1930, length 29"	70.00 80.00	72.00
☐ **Firetruck,** Hubley, with searchlight, white rubber tires with wooden rims	9.00 12.00	10.00
☐ **Greyhound 1939 World's Fair Bus,** Arcade, rubber wheels, length 6½"	80.00 100.00	90.00
☐ **Greyhound Deluxe Bus,** Tootsietoy 1045, c. 1935	15.00 20.00	17.00
☐ **Moving Van,** Structo, c. 1929, open cab, length 16"	95.00 125.00	115.00
☐ **Moving Van,** c. 1930, length 25"	80.00 120.00	100.00
☐ **Nucar Transport,** Hubley, c. 1938, length 16½"	175.00 275.00	225.00
☐ **Oil Tank Truck,** Tootsietoy 235, c. 1940	7.00 9.00	8.00
☐ **Oliver Tractor,** Arcade, black rubber wheels	22.00 30.00	26.00
☐ **Overland Circus Cage Truck,** Kenton, with driver, length 7½"	165.00 220.00	185.00
☐ **Pumper,** Sturditoy, c. 1920's, length 26"	50.00 100.00	75.00
☐ **Pumper,** Tommy Toy, c. late 1930's, large, red hubs	15.00 20.00	17.00
☐ **Railway Express Truck,** c. early 1930's, cast iron, length 5"	60.00 80.00	70.00
☐ **Truck,** c. 1930's, towing device at back, length 5"	20.00 30.00	24.00
☐ **Truck,** Wyandotte, c. 1930's, with stake sides, length 12"	35.00 45.00	40.00
☐ **U.S. Mail,** Steelcraft, c. 1928, length 27¼"	280.00 380.00	320.00
☐ **Water Tower Truck,** Keystone, c. 1920's, with pump, length 36"	70.00 80.00	74.00
☐ **Water Truck,** Sturditoy, c. 1920's, length 24"	80.00 120.00	100.00

TRADE CARDS AND CATALOGS

Barnum said that it pays to advertise, but long before the venerable showman gave this advice it was being taken: advertising, in one form or another, goes back a very long time. Elsewhere in this book are listed other advertising collectibles, such as posters. Trade cards and catalogues are a special group of advertising relics insofar as they were intended, in most cases, to go through the mails. Trade catalogues have a longer history than cards. In Europe they date back extremely far; in America, to the 18th century. The earliest examples were intended really as handlists, explaining the manufacturer's product or products and stating its cost. Trade catalogues became more numerous, more pictorial, and decidedly more puffed-up in terms of advertising claims in the 19th century. All are collectible but they fall into many categories and the level of interest, as well as the values, varies considerably. Among the most valuable (which can run into the hundreds of dollars) are the earliest catalogues of famous manufacturers, such as the big firearms companies of the 1800's. Trade cards are of a number of kinds. They nearly always carried a picture along with the advertising message, and of course the company name in distinctive letters. But insofar as the style of the card was concerned, there were such novelties as metamorphics (cards that showed two different pictures, depending on how they were turned), mechanicals (with moving parts), and see-throughs in which the paper is thin in strategic places and showed a design when held up to a light. There is really much more available in this field than we could hope to enumerate. A bit of digging among the stocks of "paper Americana" dealers will reveal much more.

	Current Price Range		Prior Year Average
☐ Ayer's Sarsaparilla	18.00	23.00	20.50
☐ "Give the Babies Nestle's Food"	3.00	5.00	4.50
☐ Herrick's Pills & Plasters	11.00	16.00	13.50
☐ Hutzler Bros., Importers, Baltimore, comic face of old woman with wording, "Sweet 16 and 60"	6.00	9.00	7.50
☐ Morgan's Sapolio, watermelon opening to reveal face of black youth	6.00	9.00	7.50
☐ Rising Sun stove polish	6.50	9.25	7.80
☐ Rough on Rats, "15¢ Per Box. It Clears Out Rats, Mice, Bed Bugs, Flies, Roaches"	7.00	10.00	8.50
☐ Soapine, Kendall Manufacturing Co., Providence, R.I., illustration of whale	2.00	3.00	2.50
☐ Sterling Stoves, card reads "Light Bread, the New Sterling Did It," with illustration of woman standing atop stove	2.50	4.00	3.20

TRAMP ART

A relatively unnoticed group of collectibles until the 1960's, tramp art has now gone into prestigeous museum collections and is reaching high price levels on the market. Gradually, "tramp art" is becoming a more and more loosely applied designation, now encompassing just about any object of the late 19th/early 20th centuries that have a rustic, amateurish, yet ingenious appearance. Obviously collectors, or at any rate, many of them, are not as concerned about the actual origins as they used to be. True examples of tramp art were manufactured by bonafide tramps, with which every era in history was well supplied. Establishment of coast-to-coast rail lines made tramping a thriving career in the later 1800's. The more enterprising members of the group made handicrafts to sell or exchange for food or (more likely) drink, using whatever scraps could be found along the road. Some had skill in carving wood, but usually when a tramp artist made something of wood he "built it up" from many small pieces, such as dowels or matchsticks, rather than starting with a large block and cutting it down. How they obtained the glue is an unanswered question. But if they made a small investment on glue, they stopped there, as tramp artists very seldom painted or otherwise finished their creations. The most common articles are boxes of all sorts (some of them quite large) combs, mirrors, birdcages, and clothing hooks. By around 1920, the manufacture of tramp art was dying out.

	Current Price Range		Prior Year Average
☐ **American eagle statuette,** wingspan not stated, carved from wood, the feathers indicated by incised lines, possibly western Pennsylvania origin, very good specimen, 14" H., c. 1870	600.00	800.00	700.00
☐ **American eagle statuette,** carved from wood, the wings carved separately and attached, no traces of paint, rough, 9½" H., wingspan 16", c. 1870 ..	325.00	400.00	357.00
☐ **Birdcage,** constructed of matchsticks, twigs and other materials, domed top with ring for hanging, well preserved, 14" H., late 19th c.	325.00	390.00	355.00
☐ **Birdcage,** twelve perches, constructed of thin galvanized and other wire, matchsticks, etc., 27" H., c. 1870	425.00	500.00	457.00
☐ **Jewel chest,** made of planks of several different kinds (and thicknesses) of wood, joined with glue and nails, the lid opening on English-style hinges, covered over in seashells, the interior lined with green felt, somewhat damaged, 14" x 12" x 5", c. 1910	175.00	225.00	200.00
☐ **Jewel chest,** made of pine slats, incised carving of birds on lid, columns at the sides constructed from matchsticks, 10" x 8" x 4½", c. 1880	180.00	230.00	205.00
☐ **Jewel chest,** the interior compartmented, made of sheet tin partially painted, traces of tar or similar substance at the joints, 11½" x 8" x 6¼", c. 1880	110.00	140.00	125.00
☐ **Jewel (or other) box** made from a cardboard cigar box, the lid and exterior sides covered with matchsticks to form decorative patterns, c. 1910	80.00	100.00	90.00
☐ **Mirror in frame,** frame made of tree branches, wooden plank at the back, burn holes at the back, overall size 8" x 6", c. 1880	90.00	120.00	105.00
☐ **Pencil box,** made of orange-crate wood, glued, the top section sliding, painted in shades of red and green with foliage decorations in other colors, some incised linework done with jacknife or similar tool, good condition, c. 1900	40.00	50.00	45.00
☐ **Pocket mirror,** oval, probably a fragment of wall mirror set into a discarded photo mount (one of the favorite "throw-aways" used by tramp artists were broken mirrors, which could be cut down), 4", c. 1870 or earlier	90.00	120.00	105.00
☐ **Small box,** made of several hundred wooden dowels glued together, geometrical pattern at the top also formed by dowels, 6" x 4", c. 1880 ..	260.00	330.00	295.00
☐ **Small box,** lid missing, carved entirely from a solid block of wood, decorative work at the sides, traces of gilding, some damage, 5" x 4", c. 1870 .	110.00	140.00	125.00
☐ **Small box,** sliding lid (broken), the box made of thin wood, the lid of wood set with a mirror, 5" x 4½", c. 1890	105.00	130.00	118.00

TRIVETS

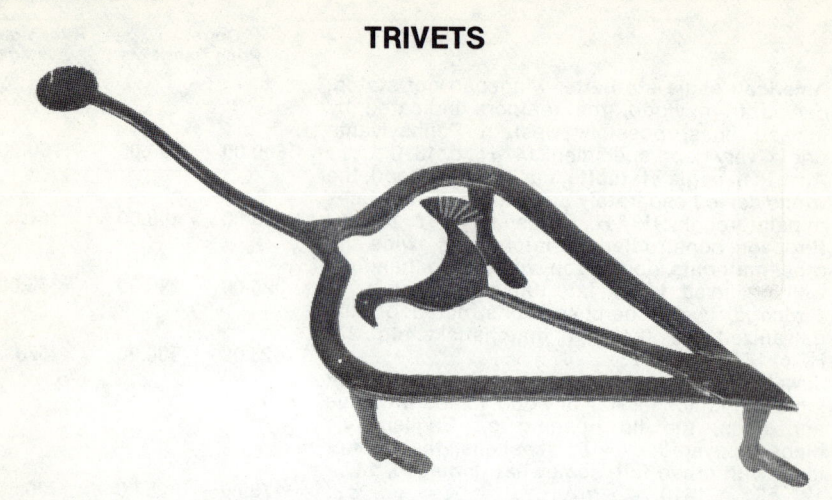

Trivet, cast iron, heart shape with rooster in center, three feet **$50.00-75.00**

Trivets are wrought-iron stands, with little feet on them, used to rest something hot upon so it would not mar the surface beneath. They were used in the kitchen for cooking vessels brought to the table, which might scorch the tablecloth or the table veneer, and on the ironing board to rest the sadiron on. A plain coaster-type device would of course have served the purpose, but the 19th century — the grand era of trivets — liked ornamental things. So you will find trivets with designs of ships, bunnies, flowers, and even famous celebrities of the time such as Jenny Lind. Any celebrity or character types are worth a large premium. Do not repaint a trivet, and if there is some patina (corrosion) it is better left alone than removed.

	Current Price Range		Prior Year Average
☐ **Geometric design,** c. 1890	6.00	9.00	7.50
☐ **"Jenny Lind,"** fine large trivet with full figure portrait, c. 1850	37.00	45.00	41.00
☐ **"Odd Fellows,"** horseshoe shape, clasped hands with eagle above, early	32.00	40.00	36.00
☐ **Small trivet,** horseshoe shape, c. 1890	14.00	19.00	16.50
☐ **Trailing vine or lattice work,** wedge-shaped, c. 1894	6.00	9.00	7.50

TRUNKS

Trunk, solid brass lock, steel brass plated trimmings, sole leather strap around trunk, three-ply veneer lumber . . . . **$175.00-$225.00**

Trunks are nothing more than overgrown traveling boxes. Most are rather more heavy-duty than boxes, and have protection in the form of iron bands or metal plates.

	Current Price Range		Prior Year Average
☐ **Camelback trunk,** original	75.00	100.00	88.00
☐ **Canvas-covered trunk,** relined, lock works, c. 1900	150.00	220.00	185.00
☐ **Dolls's trunk,** canvas-covered"	20.00	45.00	32.50
☐ **Jenny Lind trunk,** wood with iron bands, arched lid	100.00	200.00	150.00
☐ **Leather-covered trunk,** small, c. 1820's	150.00	200.00	175.00
☐ **Leather-covered trunk,** pine, bras studs, original hardware	90.00	115.00	102.00
☐ **Oak trunk,** dovetailed and pegged	335.00	365.00	350.00

TYPEWRITERS

Typewriter, by Reliance, pica or elite, 25 lbs. . . . . **$80.00-$120.00**

    Various attempts to make "mechanical writing machines" occurred in the 19th century, but practical typewriters were not on general sale until the late 1870's. Even then, they were so troublesome that writing could be done faster and easier by hand. Advances in design followed in the eighties, and it was not long before portables and even a folding portable (made by Corona) hit the market. Typewriter collecting has never enjoyed widespread popularity, because of the storage difficulties and the fact that most antique specimens are, when found, in a rather bad state of condition. For those interested in this hobby, the minuses could well add up to a plus, as they've helped to keep the prices of old typewriters within a very reasonable range — hardly ever as high as $200. It would take an extremely early model in almost mint condition to command that kind of sum. In fact, typewriters are among the comparatively few products of which antique specimens can be bought cheaper than the modern version. And you can, unquestionably, get some attractive "buys" by looking through the antique shops. Few antique dealers have any established customers for typewriters, and therefore place a modest pricetag on the odd specimen or two they chance to acquire. This is a "strictly for pleasure" hobby — don't buy with the intent of making an investment, as you might have difficulty finding anyone to buy such a collection.

UMBRELLAS / 801

		Current Price Range		Prior Year Average
☐	**Blickensderfer,** wooden case, c. 1880	90.00	120.00	105.00
☐	**Corona,** portable, folding, c. 1920	45.00	60.00	53.00
☐	**Corona,** office model, c. 1910	80.00	100.00	90.00
☐	**Merritt,** wooden case, c. 1890	125.00	175.00	150.00
☐	**Olivetti,** office model, c. 1910	85.00	105.00	95.00
☐	**Underwood,** office, c. 1920	75.00	95.00	85.00

UMBRELLAS

Left to Right: **Umbrellas: Men's,** taffeta silk, 28" **$250.00-$350.00; Four Women's,** all of taffeta silk-ebony, mother of pearl and silver figure on handles **$400.00-$500.00 each; Men's Umbrella,** taffeta silk, sterling silver nose .... **$550.00-$700.00**

It cannot be denied that for every object with a long history of use, there are some people interested in collecting specimens of it. Umbrellas of one form or another go back hundreds of years, and the variety in styles and designs is astronomical. Those made for well-dressed citizens of the past were sometimes much more colorful than their clothing. Basically they followed the taste in fashions, in terms of color and pattern, but could carry considerable detailing or "extras" such as fringes, ruffles, or even fur trim. Umbrellas made prior to about 1850 have a delicate appearance and seem very unsuited for battling foul weather. One can only conclude that fashion ruled the day, and that owners would rather get a bit wet if they stayed in style. Of course, many umbrellas of that era were intended for the sun or for light showers only. Check the condition before buying. If the fabric is damaged or any of the spokes are missing, the specimen should sell at a reduced price. If the handle has a carved knob, the value will depend in part on the quality and preservation of the carving and the material from which it's made. Unless very exceptional, umbrellas of the 20th century are not of interest to collectors.

802 / VACUUM CLEANERS

	Current Price Range		Prior Year Average
☐ **American,** painted floral pattern on cover, oak handle 35½" L., 39" Dia. when open, c. 1850	280.00	340.00	310.00
☐ **American,** pine handle 33½" L., 39" Dia. when open, c. 1820	85.00	105.00	95.00
☐ **American,** walnut handle 34" L., 41" Dia. when open, late 18th c.	390.00	460.00	425.00
☐ **American,** men's, sold by Sears, Roebuck & Co., c. 1900	18.00	25.00	21.50
☐ **English,** ebony handle fitted with silver plate and ivory knob, 35" L., 43" Dia. when open, mid 18th c.	575.00	700.00	632.00
☐ **English or Irish Victorian,** cover knitted in shades of pink, light blue and green floral pattern	130.00	180.00	155.00
☐ **French,** high domed model, cherrywood handle 39" L., 35½" Dia. when open, c. 1800	260.00	330.00	295.00

VACUUM CLEANERS

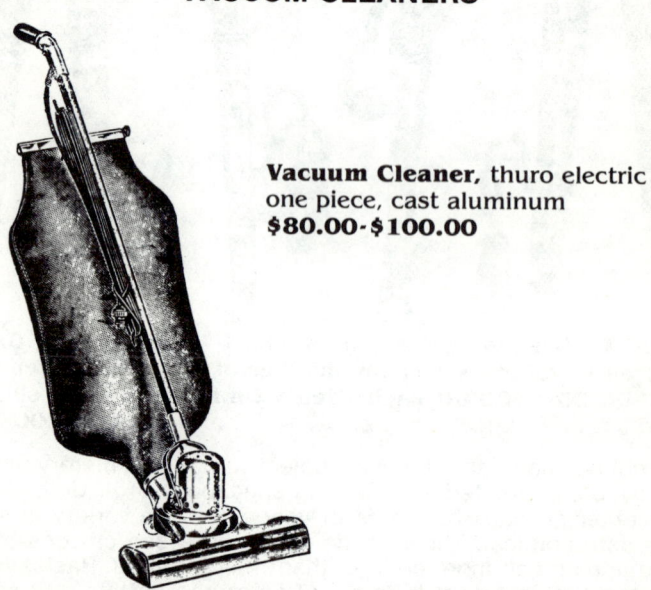

Vacuum Cleaner, thuro electric one piece, cast aluminum
$80.00-$100.00

The last thing anyone thought of as a potential collectors' item, when they began coming on the market, was vacuum cleaners. As this was a strictly utilitarian product, makers gave no attention to styling for design. But even if they may not be good-looking, early vacuum cleaners are intriguing from a mechanical point of view and are certainly a slice of "Americana." When the mechanism is housed in wood, this is unquestionably an early model. If the cord is frayed or appears in any way questionable, it should not be plugged in, as it might cause a fire. Old vacuum cleaners can be restored to original working condition, but most collectors prefer to keep them just "as found" — which is considerably cheaper and simpler. There are no specialist dealers on these — just rummage about the antiques shops, shows, and country auctions.

	Current Price Range		Prior Year Average
☐ **Bissell,** hand sweeper	28.00	36.00	32.00
☐ **Bissell,** Grand Rapids, hand sweeper	45.00	55.00	50.00
☐ **General Electric,** 110 volt	55.00	68.00	61.50
☐ **Thuro Electric,** 110 volt, c. 1910	80.00	100.00	90.00
☐ **Wardway Electric,** 110 volt, c. 1922	42.00	52.00	47.00
☐ **Wardway,** hand sweeper	17.00	23.00	20.00

WEATHER VANES

Eagle Weather vane, clawed feet resting on ball, old green patina, 5' wing span .... **$850.00-$1250.00**

WEATHER VANES

Weather vanes dotted the skyline in the 18th and 19th centuries — not only on homes but on schools, churches, and public buildings of all sorts. The purpose they served was chiefly ornamental. Weather vanes began as an aid to travelers, to show the wind velocity and direction; or to farmers, or anyone for whom such information might be useful. But as they became more and more numerous, the original purpose was forgotten, and attractive ornamentation was, eventually, the only consideration. Vane-making developed into a major American industry, centered largely in New England. There were basically two types, the better kind made of cast copper, cast in a foundry just like statuary. These are often referred to as "full models," because of their three-dimensional nature. The cheaper sort was flat, usually cut from a piece of sheet tin used as is or nailed over a wooden cutout. While all are collectible, if old and authentic, the full models are definitely the more valuable in most instances. Some are really handsome and original, showing a great deal of creative effort and careful modeling that even decades of exposure to harsh weather has not impaired. When corrosion is found on weathervanes, it should not be removed. Sad to say, many fine old vanes have been destroyed in recent years, as the result of being stolen from historic buildings and melted down for scrap copper, in some cases reducing a rare $50,000 weather vane antique to $10 or $15 worth of metal.

	Current Price Range		Prior Year Average
☐ **American eagle** with spread wings mounted on wooden block	600.00	800.00	700.00
☐ **Automobile,** open roadster, intricate detail, heavy copper, gilded gold leaf, full bodies, 26" L.	400.00	550.00	475.00
☐ **Automobile,** open top, complete with goggled old green patina navigator and driver, heavy copper, full bodied, 24" L.	900.00	1200.00	1050.00
☐ **Banneret and scroll,** ornately gilded copper, 3' L.	90.00	125.00	110.00
☐ **Beaver,** Quebec, made of tin, c. 1860	1000.00	1500.00	1250.00
☐ **Cannon,** mounted on spoked gun carriage, reinforced barrel and stand, copper	175.00	225.00	200.00
☐ **Chicken,** old decorations made of tin with iron rods	700.00	1000.00	850.00
☐ **Cow,** mounted on 20½" arrow, 9½" L.	150.00	200.00	175.00
☐ **Crowing cock,** made of copper, 28½" L.	1000.00	1400.00	1200.00
☐ **Deer,** running buck with curved antlers, full bodies, copper, old green patina with traces of old gilt, 50" L.	275.00	400.00	335.00
☐ **Dragon,** winged beast with snake-like tail, crouching on stand above scrolled direction indicators, 54" L.	200.00	300.00	250.00
☐ **Eagle,** hollow copper, spreadwing, 24" W., c. 19th c.	1100.00	1700.00	1400.00
☐ **Eagle,** clawed feet resting on ball, old green patina, 5' wing span	185.00	230.00	205.00
☐ **Eagle,** perched on sphere, cast iron with directional lettering	1000.00	1500.00	1250.00
☐ **Fish,** contemporary folk art, painted galvanized tin, 18" L.	50.00	70.00	60.00
☐ **Fish,** copper, 26" L.	900.00	1200.00	1050.00
☐ **Fiske running horse,** black hawk #201, 33" L.	3750.00	5000.00	4200.00

WOODENWARE / 805

	Current Price Range		Prior Year Average
☐ **Flag,** unfurled 48-star banner with pointed standard	120.00	160.00	140.00
☐ **Fox,** running, scrolled pointers, copper, full-bodied, 30″ L.	170.00	250.00	210.00
☐ **Goose,** cast iron, 23″ wing span	600.00	900.00	750.00
☐ **Greyhound,** long-legged animal standing on reinforced pedestal, ¾ full-bodied, green patina, 30″ L.	175.00	230.00	197.00
☐ **Heraldic arrow with lions,** wrought iron with scrolling base	275.00	375.00	325.00
☐ **Horse and arrow,** gold globe	300.00	450.00	375.00
☐ **Horse and rider,** hollow copper, directional roof finial	2200.00	3000.00	2600.00
☐ **Locomotive with tender,** large model of late 19th c. railroad machine, full-bodied copper, 5′ L.	300.00	400.00	350.00
☐ **Lion,** large head with carved mane, copper, ¾ full-bodied, 4′ L.	200.00	275.00	237.00
☐ **Race horse with jockey,** Kentucky thoroughbred, full-bodied copper, 32″ L.	300.00	400.00	350.00
☐ **Sailing vessel,** painted green	275.00	350.00	315.00
☐ **Standing Indian,** original zinc finish, single direction indicator	400.00	575.00	480.00

WOODENWARE

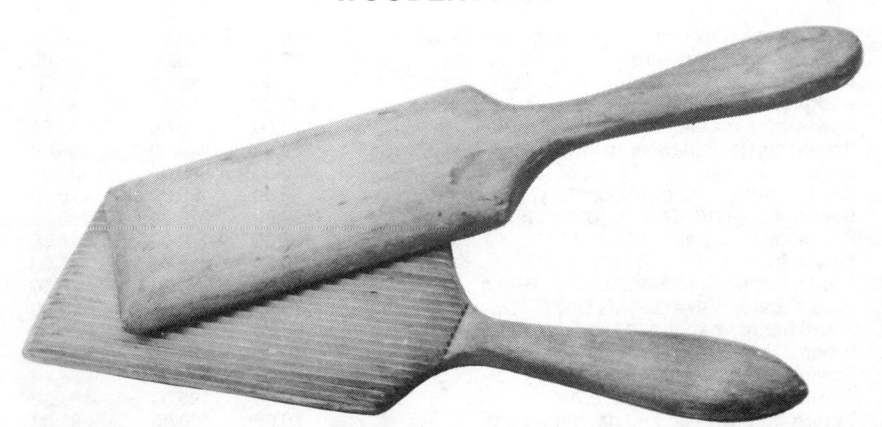

Butter Hands, wood, 1890-1920 .... $30.00-$40.00

806 / WOODENWARE

Early America relied heavily on rustic kitchen equipment, manufactured in the local community by whatever artisans luck had supplied. As sales appeal was hardly important, the most convenient materials were always used, including the cheapest and most abundant of all: wood. Woodenware is frequently called "treen," which undoubtedly derives from "tree." By taking solid blocks of wood and carving, whittling, and sanding, nearly any kind of kitchen utensil could be made. It was slow work and grueling, but the finished product, if not exactly pleasing to the eye, at least had durability. Woodenware far outlasted all forms of pottery, and many users firmly believed that foodstuffs stored in wood containers acquired better flavor. Woodenware was manufactured in virtually all parts of the early United States, from New England to the West Coast. It continued to be made somewhat longer in the west, into the late 1800's in isolated regions, because of the shortage of factory-made goods. However the majority of woodenware found on the antique market falls into the 1830-1870 era and some few pieces will be earlier, though precise dating is never easy. Symmetry of form should not be expected. This is "folk art" in one of its purest and rawest states. A premium is attached whenever the artisan felt moved to include some decoration, such as incised lines or raised bosses (made by gouging out the surrounding wood). Woodenware nearly always shows evidence of considerable use and acquires its own special kinds of patina, depending on the use to which the specific item was placed.

	Current Price Range		Prior Year Average
☐ **Apple butter scoop**	80.00	110.00	95.00
☐ **Apple tray,** old red stain	23.00	30.00	26.50
☐ **Barber pole,** hanging, original decorations, 22" L.	230.00	290.00	260.00
☐ **Baskets,** peck measure	27.00	35.00	31.00
☐ **Bellows,** pine	50.00	70.00	60.00
☐ **Bootjack**	27.00	35.00	31.00
☐ **Bowls,** burl, maple, 6" x 2½"	220.00	290.00	255.00
☐ **Bowls,** burl (refinished), 15" Dia.	360.00	440.00	400.00
☐ **Bowls,** burl, walnut, 17" Dia., c. 18th c.	410.00	480.00	445.00
☐ **Bowls,** maple, turn-of-the-century, 14" Dia.	60.00	80.00	70.00
☐ **Bowls,** maple, 16" Dia., c. 18th or 19th c.	250.00	310.00	280.00
☐ **Bowls,** original paint, 14" x 23"	120.00	170.00	145.00
☐ **Bowls,** turned, 22" L., 8" Dia.	160.00	210.00	185.00
☐ **Bowls,** turned maple, 12" Dia., c. 1920's	18.00	23.00	20.50
☐ **Bread board,** "Give Us This Day"	75.00	100.00	88.00
☐ **Bread board,** maple, 11" Dia.	50.00	70.00	60.00
☐ **Brooms,** fireplace	15.00	20.00	17.50
☐ **Brooms,** long handle, kitchen	27.00	40.00	33.50
☐ **Butterchurn,** painted blue, c. 1890's	140.00	190.00	165.00
☐ **Butterchurn with lid and dasher,** refinished	70.00	100.00	85.00
☐ **Butter prints,** cow, factory made	60.00	80.00	70.00
☐ **Butter prints,** flowers and leaves, factory made	35.00	50.00	42.50
☐ **Butter prints,** handcarved cow	160.00	210.00	185.00
☐ **Butter prints,** large round with leaf design, factory made	40.00	55.00	47.50
☐ **Butter prints,** paddle type	37.00	45.00	41.00
☐ **Butter prints,** paddle with handle and bowl	12.00	17.00	14.50
☐ **Butter prints,** round, pineapple, factory made	65.00	85.00	75.00
☐ **Butter prints,** sheaf of wheat	70.00	90.00	80.00
☐ **Cabbage cutter**	130.00	180.00	155.00
☐ **Cabbage cutting board**	45.00	60.00	52.50

WOODENWARE / 807

	Current Price Range		Prior Year Average
☐ Candle box, open or sliding lid type	110.00	170.00	135.00
☐ Carrying yoke, oxen	40.00	60.00	50.00
☐ Cheese drainer	90.00	115.00	102.50
☐ Cheese ladle	40.00	55.00	47.50
☐ Chopping bowl, owl, burled wood	120.00	260.00	190.00
☐ Church rail	80.00	120.00	105.00
☐ Clothes drying rack, pat'd turn of century	60.00	110.00	85.00
☐ Clothes mangler	70.00	100.00	85.00
☐ Clothes winder	16.00	22.00	19.00
☐ Collection box	75.00	100.00	85.00
☐ Cookie spoon	22.00	30.00	26.00
☐ Cranberry rake	100.00	140.00	120.00
☐ Curd knife, 20″ L.	70.00	100.00	85.00
☐ Darning egg, with handle	16.00	23.00	19.50
☐ Dippers	70.00	100.00	85.00
☐ Dough box, with cover	130.00	180.00	155.00
☐ Drinking cup	40.00	65.00	52.50
☐ Eating spoons, origianl old finish	10.00	18.00	14.00
☐ Flour sifter	17.00	26.00	21.50
☐ Foot warmer, for charcoal, with pierced tin	80.00	110.00	95.00
☐ Grater box, handmade, pierced tin grater	25.00	40.00	32.50
☐ Hasty pudding stick	14.00	20.00	17.00
☐ Herb box, with cover	33.00	48.00	40.50
☐ Hobby horse, in swing standard, 41″ x 33″, c. 1945 .	65.00	90.00	77.50
☐ Knife boxes, pine	42.00	55.00	48.50
☐ Knife boxes, walnut	75.00	90.00	82.50
☐ Knife tray, plain, painted, heart cutout	75.00	110.00	92.50
☐ Lemon squeezer	26.00	34.00	30.00
☐ Letter writing box, lap desk	50.00	100.00	75.00
☐ Maple syrup stirrer	8.00	11.00	9.50
☐ Meat pounder	11.00	15.00	13.00
☐ Mixing bowl, medium size, burled wood	140.00	230.00	165.00
☐ Mortar and pestles, lignum vitae	130.00	170.00	150.00
☐ Mortar and pestles, maple...................	70.00	100.00	85.00
☐ Noggins	130.00	180.00	155.00
☐ Nutcracker, carved, 11½″ L., c. 1900	40.00	55.00	47.50
☐ Ox yokes, with bows	110.00	150.00	130.00
☐ Ox yokes, without bows....................	80.00	110.00	95.00
☐ Pantry box, with cover, round, depending on size	50.00	90.00	70.00
☐ Pie crimper, ebony and ivory, 5½″ L., c. 1860's ..	60.00	95.00	77.50
☐ Pill box, mass-produced for pharmacists	1.00	3.00	2.00
☐ Pitchfork, four-tine	40.00	55.00	47.50
☐ Pitchfork, made from trained tree root	19.00	33.00	26.00
☐ Plates, good finish, old, approx. 8″ Dia.	17.00	30.00	23.50
☐ Platter, beaded, turning edge	32.00	50.00	41.00
☐ Potato masher	14.00	20.00	17.00
☐ Propeller, airplane	120.00	160.00	140.00
☐ Rolling pin, lignum vitae	50.00	70.00	60.00
☐ Rolling pin, mahogany inlay	55.00	75.00	65.00
☐ Rolling pin, maple with handles	45.00	60.00	52.50
☐ Rum keg, rundlet	55.00	85.00	70.00
☐ Salt box, covered pine, original condition, 5½″ x 6¼″ x 6″	65.00	90.00	72.50
☐ Salt box, hanging pine, Pennsylvania Dutch type (refinished)	80.00	110.00	95.00
☐ Sap bucket	40.00	55.00	47.50

	Current Price Range		Prior Year Average
☐ **Sewing box,** Singer sewing machine parts, unfolds	35.00	50.00	42.50
☐ **Soap dish** with drainer inset	55.00	70.00	62.50
☐ **Soap scoop**	60.00	80.00	70.00
☐ **Spatula**	11.00	16.00	13.50
☐ **Spice box,** oval, probably Shaker, 10"	40.00	55.00	47.50
☐ **Spice box,** round, not Shaker, 10"	22.00	24.00	23.00
☐ **Spoon holder**	27.00	35.00	31.00
☐ **Sugar box,** turned on lathe, footed	50.00	65.00	57.50
☐ **Sugar bin**	150.00	190.00	170.00
☐ **Sugar tub**	70.00	90.00	85.00
☐ **Swiggers**	35.00	45.00	40.00
☐ **Tankards,** with cover	42.00	60.00	51.00
☐ **Tankards,** with toddy hole	55.00	70.00	62.50
☐ **Utensil rack,** pine with wrought iron hooks	70.00	90.00	80.00
☐ **Wagon seat,** crude, seats two, plank	100.00	200.00	150.00
☐ **Wagon wheel,** different sizes	150.00	190.00	170.00
☐ **Wall bucket**	30.00	40.00	35.00
☐ **Washboards,** slat	32.00	45.00	38.50
☐ **Washboards,** spool	55.00	75.00	65.00
☐ **Washtub**	70.00	90.00	80.00
☐ **Water pump**	36.00	45.00	40.50
☐ **Whetstone,** foot-operated, bench style	140.00	180.00	160.00

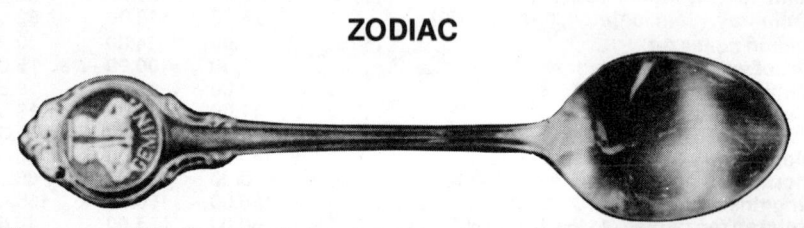

ZODIAC

Zodiac, one of twelve, Gemini, per set . . . . $480.00-$600.00

Growing interest in astrology and the occult has been reflected in the collectibles' market, where such articles are now in greater demand than ever. The hobbyist is likely to think first in terms of books or other printed matter but there is actually a much wider variety of material available. Anything bearing an astrological symbol or relating in some way to the science of astrology qualifies. A beginning collector would be well advised to look for the older and more unusual items. This is one field in which oddity definitely carries a plus.

☐ **Ashtray,** brass, Art Deco, all 12 animals, 4½" Dia.	9.00	12.00	10.50
☐ **Charm,** gold, pair of Pisces fish, ⅞" L., c. 1930's-40's	70.00	90.00	80.00
☐ **Ring,** gold band with zodiacal symbols, West Africa, c. 19th C.	400.00	500.00	450.00
☐ **Rug,** hooked, round, 48" Dia., c. 1930's	200.00	300.00	250.00
☐ **Sundial,** engraved bronze, symbols and animals, Portuguese, c. 18th c.	700.00	900.00	800.00
☐ **Woodblock print** of zodiacal animals from book, small, c. 1780's	14.00	19.00	16.50

COLLECTIBLE REFERENCE INDEX

HOW TO USE THIS INDEX: Locate the particular *item* or *subject category* in question in the alphabetical listing below.

— A —

ABC Plates, 605
Advertising Collectibles, 62-67, 117, 123, 124, 126, 127, 710, 796
Agata Glass, 381
Airplanes, 543
Airplanes (Motif), 195, 542, 543
Airplanes, Toy, 248, 785, 787
Alarm Clocks, 64, 229, 234, 236, 282
Albums, Photograph, 292
Alligators (Motif), 155, 560
Almanacs, 67-70, 738
Amberina Glass, 382-383
Ambrotypes, 645
American Eagles (Motif), 70-71, 314, 668, 723, 797, 804, *See also: Eagles*
American Indian Artifacts, 71-75
Amish Quilts, 708, 709
Amphora Art Pottery, 663
Ancient Coins, 250
Andirons, 84, 338-339
Angels, Cherubs, Cupids (Motifs), 122, 191, 194, 209, 211, 212, 407, 433, 510, 511, 557, 599, 672, 683, 685, 686
Animation Film Art, 75-83
Ansonia Clocks, 229-230
Antiques, Investing In, 30-34
Antiques, Selling Your, 34-40
Antiques, What's New In?, 53, 54
Antiques, World of, 1
Apothecary Items, 362
Aprons, 241, 602
Art Deco, 83-85, 209, 219, 258, 317, 397, 398, 417, 418, 420, 498, 511, 513, 514, 536, 538, 688, 808
Art Glass, 316, 380-408
Art Nouveau, 85-87, 258, 259, 364, 397, 399, 417, 418, 419, 433, 498, 509, 556, 664, 683
Art Pottery, 663-665
Ashtrays, 84, 243, 281, 556, 559, 601, 669, 672, 675, 676, 678, 680, 712, 733, 808, *See also: Glassware*
Auction, Selling By, 40-42
Augers, 774
Aurene Glass, 380
Autographs, 87-99, 117, 589, 591, 593, 606, 607, 721, 722, 770

Autos And Automobilia, 99-119
Automobiles (Motif), 99-116, 680, 686, 804
Automobiles and Motorcycles, Toy, 782-784
Automobilia, 117-119
Avon Bottles, 186-190

— B —

Baby Bottles, 605
Baccarat Glass, 383-384
Badges, 225, 659, 661, 712
Banks: Mechanical, 120-122; Still, 122-127, 219, 244, 277, 279, 280, 281, 283, 284, 733
Bar Pin, 84
Barbed Wire, 127-129
Barber Bottles, 385, 401
Baseball Cards, 129-153
Baseball Collectibles, 744-747
Baskets, 154-157, 340, 357, 373, 374, 375, 603, 738; Ceramic, 663, 666, 675, 676, 806; Glass, *See: Glassware;* Silver, 86
Bathing Beauties, 244, 246, 247, 248
Batons, Police, 659
Battery Operated Toys, 784-788
Bayonets, 225, 576
Bayreuther Porcelain, 647; *See also: Royal Bayreuth,* 678-679
Beaded Bag, 242
Beam, Jim, Bottles, 190-197
Bears (Motif), 121, 194, 222, 314, 679
Beds, 359, 368, 372, 605, 609
Bed Pans, 561, 715
Bed Warmers, 558, 559, 561, 574
Beds, 359, 368, 372
Bee Hive Clocks, 236
Beer Cans, 157-166
Belleek Porcelain, Irish and American, 295, 665-667, 673
Bellows, 339, 806
Bells, 86, 166-169, 282, 286, 337, 556, 600, 678, 712; *See also: Glassware*
Benches, Stools, 84, 359-360, 367, 369, 372
Bennington Pottery, 667-668
Bentwood, 360

Bibles, 178, 733
Bicycles, 169-170
Big Little Books, 179-180
Bing and Grondahl Plates, 648
Birds (Motif), 84, 119, 187, 191, 206, 211, 212, 220, 222, 288, 314, 342, 508, 509, 510, 513, 556, 599, 604, 650, 651, 665, 666, 668, 672, 678; See also: American Eagles; Chickens; Decoys; Ducks; Eagles; Parrots; Peacocks; Swans
Bitters Bottles, 198-200, 416
Blacks, 121, 206, 219, 310, 314, 779
Black Clocks, 238
Blanket Chests, 362, 372
Blotters, 244
Bobeche, 404
Boehm Birds, 648-649
Boehm Porcelain, 648-649, 668
Bohemian Glass, 384
Books, 172-185, 224, 225-226, 284, 542, 589, 639; Almanacs, 67-70, 738; American Indian, 73-75; Automobile, 117-119; Bibles, 178, 733; Children's, 179-182; Cookbooks, 182-184; Detective Fiction, 185; Disney, 179, 180, 181; Paperbacks, 615-621
Bookcases, 368-369, 556
Bookends, 86, 219, 220, 278, 283, 286, 614, 663, 733; See also: Glassware
Bookplates, 170-172
Bookmarks, 244, 763
Bootjacks, 559, 806
Bottle Openers, 246, 557
Bottles, 186-207, 385, 542, 680; See also: Avon, Barber, Beam, Bitters, Coca-Cola, Cordial, Historical Flasks, Ink, Jars, Milk, Perfume, Poison, Whiskey
Bowls, See Glassware, Porcelain and Pottery
Bowls, Wooden, 526, 529, 806
Box Cameras, 643-644
Boxes, 207-210, 281, 316, 556, 559, 666, 675, 678, 682, 737, 738, 797, 807, See also: Glassware
Bracelets, 417, 507-508
Braces, 774
Brass, 84, 167, 208, 211, 218, 314, 337, 338, 339, 359, 364, 498, 518-519, 555-558, 600, 601, 604, 659, 712, 808
Breweriana, 63, 64, 66, 67
Bristol Glass, 385-386

Bronze, 84, 86, 87, 167, 168, 314, 357, 498
Bronze Figurals, 84, 86
Brooches, 84, 86, 508-510
Brooks, Ezra, Bottles, 205-206
Brooms, 806
Buffalo (Motif), 288, 560, 679, 773
Buicks, 100-101
Buildings (Motif), 121, 122, 123, 125
Building A Collection, 3
Building A Reference Library, 57
Burmese Glass, 386-387
Butterflies (Motif); See: Insects
Butter Molds or Prints, 526, 806
Buttons, 211-212, 226
Buttons, Pinback and Political, 277, 279, 281, 282, 283, 286, 542, 660
Buying At Auction Sales, 11
Buying From Dealers, 7
Buying From Other Sources, 14

— C —

Cabinet Clocks, 229, 232, 235
Cabinets, Music, 365, 370
Cadillacs, 101-102
Calendars, 63, 117, 244
Calendar Clocks, 229, 230-231, 233-234, 236, 238, 239
Cambridge Glass, 387-390
Camels (Motif), 123, 222
Cameo Glass, 85, 86, 87, 399
Cameos, 509, 510
Cameras, 278, 643-645, 734
Campaign Memorabilia, 357, 660-661
Candleholders, Candlesticks, 84, 518, 526, 556, 561-562, 668, 669, 672, 674, 675, 678; See also: Glassware
Candle Snuffers, 558, 560
Candlestands, 360-361, 372
Candy Containers and Dishes, 574, 601, 672, 674, 679, See also: Glassware
Canes and Walking Sticks, 213, 737, 770
Canning Tools, 506
Cards, See: Baseball Cards; Football Cards, Greeting Cards; Playing Cards; Postcards
Care and Storage, 42-52
Caricatures and Cartoons, 213-214, 606
Carnival Glass, 167, 408-414
Carousel Animals, 214-215
Cars, See: Automobiles
Cartes de Visite, 644

Cartoons Cels, 76-80
Cartoon Strips, 215-217
Carvings, Wood, 71, 291, 292-294, 342
Cash Registers, 217-218
Cast Iron Toys, 779-784
Cats (Motif), 123, 124, 191, 218-219, 220, 314-315, 432, 433, 498, 508, 560, 599, 609, 613, 680, 682, 737
Celebrity Dolls, 300, 301, 306, 307-308, 311
Celluloid Items, 211, 258, 319, 604
Ceramic Art Company, *See: Lenox*
Chairs, 360, 361, 369, 371-372, 373, 374, 375, 376, 609
Chalkware, 219-220
Character Dolls, 277, 278, 280, 282, 297, 298, 300
Cherubs, *See: Angels*
Chess Sets, 220-221
Chests, 362, 369, 372, 600
Chevrolets, 102-105
Chickens and Roosters (Motifs), 315, 433, 557, 599, 683, 686, 804
Children's Books, 179-182
Children's Furniture, 359, 360, 361, 365, 368, 371, 373, 374, 375, 605
Children's Tableware and Flatware, 421, 435, 685
China Bottles, 190-197
China Cabinets, 369
Chinese Collectibles, 608, 609, 610
  See also: Cloisonne
Chinese Export Porcelain, 668-669
Chinese Furniture, 609
Chinese Jade, 609
Chinese Painting, 610
Chinese Snuff Bottles, 610
Chippendale Furniture, 360, 361, 362, 363, 364-365, 366, 367
Chisels, 775
Christmas Greeting Cards, 481-482, 721
Christmas Plates, 647, 648, 649, 652, 653, 655-656
Christmas Tree Holder, 560
Christmas Tree Ornaments and Lights, 221-223, 282, 284
Chrysler, 106
Churns, 526, 806
Cigar Bands, 772
Cigarette Cases and Boxes, 84, 209, 245, 574, 675, *See also: Glassware*
Cigarette Lighter, 245, 672
Circus Memorabilia, 223-225
Civil War Memorabilia, 91, 225-227, 579-582, 645, 656, 716

Clamps, 775
Clocks, 63-64, 84, 86, 117, 227-240, 245, 397, 600, 663
Cloisonne Enamel, 212, 498, 773
Clothing, 240-242, 226, 289, 290, 770; Sports Uniforms, 747
Clowns (Motif), 121, 127, 167, 222, 677, 678, 679
Coca-Cola Collectibles, 63, 64, 65, 66, 243-249, 795
Coffee Mills, 521
Coffee Pots, 518, 520, 524, 556, 558, 562, 669, 670, 680, 685
Coins, 250-257
Collectible Plates, 646-656
Collector Publications, 54-57
Colt Firearms, 324
Comb Case, 574
Combs, 258-259, 738
Comic Art, 259-263
Comic Books, 248, 264-275
Comic Character Spinoffs, 276-286
Comic Space Books, 265-275, 726-728
Comic Strips, 215-217
Compacts, 84
Condition: A Major Influence On Value, 18-20
Connecticut Shelf Clocks, 233, 236-237, 239
Cookbooks, 182-184, 710
Cooking Utensils, 518-529, 558-561
Copper, 519-520, 558-559
Coralene Glass, 390
Cork Press, 639
Corkscrews, 287-288, 518, 520
Corner Cupboards, 362
Cosmetic Labels, 526
Cottage Clocks, 234, 236
Country Music Collectibles, 587-589
Coverlets, 288-289
Cowboy Gear, 289-290
Cows (Motif), 804
Cradles, 360
Crazy Quilts, 602, 709
Crèches, 290, 291
Crocheting, 288, 603
Crystal Regulators, 229, 240
Cuff Links, 245
Cupboards, 364, 372, 527
Cupids, *See: Angels*
Currier and Ives, 226, 650
Cuspidors, 561, 562, 668, 712, 715, 766
Custard Glass, 414-416
Cut Glass, 416-420, 498

— D —

Daguerreotype Cases, 645
Dance Memorabilia, 291-292
Darners, 403, 603
Daum Nancy, 380-381
Decanters, 190-196, 543, 670 *See also: Glassware*
Decoys, 292-294
Deer (Motif), 207, 220, 384, 385, 499, 556, 804
Delft, 655-656, 684
Depression Glass, 421-431
Desks, 84, 363, 369
Detective Fiction, 185
Devils (Motif), 498, 557, 679, 773
Disney Character Collectibles, 76-83, 277, 278, 279, 280, 282, 284, 285, 286, 298, 305, 482
Dodges, 106-107
Dogs (Motif), 121, 122, 126, 127, 156, 213, 219, 220, 295, 314, 315, 338, 432, 556, 557, 560, 561, 599, 664, 672, 679, 680, 682, 722, 773, 805
Dollhouse Furniture, 313
Dollhouses, 312
Dolls, 277, 280, 281, 282, 286, 296-312, 342
Dolphins (Motif), 87, 168, 383, 407, 737
Donkeys, *See: Mules and Donkeys*
Doorbells, 167, 556
Doorknobs, 384
Doorknockers, 556, 560
Doorstops, 282, 313-315, 560, 614
Dragons (Motif), 212, 556, 557, 609, 666, 804
Dressers, 370
Drysinks, 363, 370, 372
Ducks (Motif), 123, 207, 220, 292-294, 432, 604, 632, 680
Durand Glass, 390-391
Dynasty Chart, 608

— E —

Eagles (Motif), 86, 121, 124, 201, 202, 220, 288, 339, 433, 498, 560, 561, 574, 599, 679, 764, 765, 803, 804, *See also American Eagles*
Earrings, 510
Eggs (Motif), 315-316, 433
Egyptians (Motif), 123, 192, 397, 511, 676, 773
Electric Irons, 503
Elephants (Motif), 121, 122, 123, 206, 222, 314, 557, 560, 609, 669, 672, 773
Embroidery, 708, 724
Enamels, 84, 212, 498
Erotic Netsuke, 613
Export China, *See: Chinese Export Porcelain*
Eyeglasses, 317, 587
Eyeglass Cases, 317
Ezra Brooks Bottles, 205-206

— F —

Faberge, 316
Fairies, Gnomes, Leprechauns, Brownies, Elves (Motifs), 220, 651, 664, 666
Fairy Lamps, 219, 386, 614
Fakes, 20-28
Fan Magazines, 586-587
Fans, 117, 317-319
Farm Machinery, 319-320
Fenton Art Glass, 649-650
Fiesta Ware, 669-670
Figureheads, 600
Figurines, Ceramic, 277, 278, 279, 280, 281, 282, 283, 284, 286, 666, 672, 680, 682-683
Firearms, American, 227, 289, 290, 320-335, 577-579
Fire Engines, 336-337
Fire Engines, Toy, 780, 781, 785, 786, 789
Firefighting Equipment, 336-338
Fire Marks, 337
Fireplace Equipment, 338-340
Fish (Motif), 155, 222, 804, 809
Fishing Tackle, 340-341
Flashlight, 246
Flasks, 86, 200-202, 715, 722
Flight Collectibles, 542-543, 808
Flower Prints, 692, 694, 697, 698
Folk Art, 341-342, 558, 804
Football Cards, 343-356
Football Collectibles, 747
Footwarmers, 562, 574
Fords, 107-113
Foreign Coins, 250
Forks, 86, 565-566, 568-570
Foxes (Motif), 206, 314, 599, 805
Fraktur, 342
Frames, 284, 668
Franklins, 650-651
Frogs (Motif), 121, 122, 314, 357, 664, 773
Fruit Crate Labels, 535
Fruit Jars, 504, 505
Fulper Art Pottery, 665
Furniture, 86, 357-376

INDEX / 813

— G —

Gallé, Emile, Glass, 391-392
Games, 244, 277, 279, 284, 342, 376-379, 632, 734
Garnier Bottles, 206-207
Gasoline Pump Globes, 117-118
Gasoline Signs, 64, 65, 741
Gilbert, Wm. L., Clocks, 230-232
Giraffes (Motif), 206
Girandole Clocks, 222, 223
Glassware, 380-479; *See also: Bells, Bottles, Marbles, Plates*
Glasses, *See Eyeglasses*
Globe, 246, 600
Globes (Motif), 65, 66, 121, 124, 190, 498
Godey's Lady's Book, 547
Golf Collectibles, 747
Greenaway, Kate, 181, 481, 599
Greeting Cards, 480-482
Greeting Postcards, 686
Gregory, Mary, Glass, 316, 401
Greuby Art Pottery, 665
Guns, *See: Firearms*

— H —

Hairpins, 258
Hair Receiver, 675, 679
Hall Racks, 85, 370
Hammers, 737, 775
Handbags and Wallets, 242, 245, 248
Handcuffs, 659
Handel Lamps, 538
Hand-painted China, 673
Hand Puppets, 707
Hat Rack, 560
Hatchets, 775
Hatpin Holders, 670, 675, 677, 679
Hatpins, 557
Hats, 241, 242, 659
Haviland, 670-671
Hearts (Motif), 188, 223, 433, 434, 510, 512, 557
Heisey Glass, 392-396
Helmets, 337, 583, 587, 600, 659
Hepplewhite Furniture, 360, 361, 362, 363, 364, 366, 367, 368
Hidden Cameras, 644
Highboys and Lowboys, 364
Highchairs, 360, 361, 371, 373, 605
Historical Flasks, 200-202
Hitchcock Furniture, 372
Hobby Horse, 807
Hood Ornaments, 118

Hooked Rugs, 722-723
Hooks, 340, 775
Horns, Auto, 118
Horse-Drawn Carriages, 483-484
Horses (Motif), 125, 126, 315, 498, 499, 681, 682, 804, 805
How To Use This Book, 60
Hubcaps, 118
Humidors, Tobacco Jars, 411, 557, 676, 771, 773
Hummels, 291, 485-497

— I —

Ice Boxes, 370
Ice Cream Molds, 562
Indian Arrowheads, 72-73
Indian Baskets, 155-157
Indian Blankets and Serapes, 601-602
Indian Head Pennies, 251-253
Indian Prints, 692-693
Indian Rugs, 724-725
Indians (Motif), 125, 190, 220, 315, 557, 676, 686, 773, 805
Ingraham Clocks, 232-233
Ink Bottles, 498-499
Inkwells and Inkbottles, 380, 384, 390, 399, 401, 419, 497-499, 557, 562, 614, 664, 677, 680, 683
Insects (Motif), 87, 380, 392, 508, 510, 556, 559, 679
Insulators, 449-502
Irons, 502-503, 560
Ironware, 71, 314, 339, 340, 498, 520-523, 559-561
Ithaca Clocks, 234
Ivory, 212, 213, 220, 221, 258, 318, 319, 511, 600, 603, 612-613

— J —

Jacquard Weavings, 288-289
Jade, 84, 609
Japanese Collectibles, 608, 611
Japanese Netsuke, 611
Japanese Prints, 693
Jardiniere, 422, 557, 669
Jars, 380, 384, 386, 404, 411, 413, 419, 504-506, 614, 639, 766, 771
Jazz, 589-591
Jerome, Chauncey, Clocks, 234-235
Jewelry, 84, 85, 87, 278, 282, 357, 506-513
Jewelry Boxes, 209, 417, 797
Jukeboxes, 513-517

814 / INDEX

— K —

Kabar Knives, 532
Kachina Dolls, 206
Kewpies, 281
Key Chains, 246
Keys, *See: Locks & Keys*
Kitchen Clocks, 231, 233, 237, 240
Kitchen Collectibles, 517-529
Kitchen Cupboards, 364
Kitchen Utensils, 517-529, 806-808
Knife Rests, 397, 419
Knives, 86, 226, 529-535, 576-577; Paper Knives, 86; Silver Knives, 566-567; Tools, 775

— L —

Labels, 535-536
Lace, 603
Lalique, 396-398
Lamps and Lighting Devices, 86, 87, 118, 219, 222, 337, 374, 375, 376, 484, 524, 537-541, 557, 562, 574, 600, 605, 609, 614, 665, 712, *See also: Glassware*
Lanterns, 540, 661
Latticinio Glass, 400
Laundry Stoves, 503
Legras Glass, 398
Leica Cameras, 645
Lenox Porcelain, 666, 667, 671-674
Levels, 776
Libbey Glass, 398-399, 417, 418, 419, 420
Liberty Head Dimes, 253-254
Liberty Head Half Dollars, 256-257
Liberty Head Quarters, 254-256
License Plates, 118-119
Lightbulbs, 538, 714
Lighting Devices, *See: Lamps*
Lightning Rod Ornaments, 541
Limited Edition Plates, 647-656
Lincoln, Abraham, Collectibles, 98, 227, 660, 661, 772
Lincolns, 113-114
Lindbergh Memorabilia, 542-543
Liners, Lenox, 673-674
Lions (Motif), 125, 223, 315, 556, 683, 722, 773, 805
Lithophane Steins, 683
Lockets, 510-511
Locks and Keys, 543-545, 712
Loetz Glass, 399-400
Lone Ranger, 710
Lorgnettes, 317
Love Seats, Sofas, Settees, 364, 366, 373, 375, 376
Lunch Boxes, 209
Lutz Glass, 400
Luxardo Bottles, 207

— M —

Magazines, 545-550
Magician's Memorabilia and Collectibles, 550
Majolica, 168, 674-675, 773
Mandarin Squares, 603
Maps, 551-552
Marbles, 378-379
Marinot Art Glass, 380, 381
Marionettes, 278, 706
Mary Gregory Glass, 316, 401
Market Trends, What Makes, 28-30
Masonic Emblems, 200, 602
Matchbox Labels, 536
Matchsafes and Holders, 519, 522, 524, 527, 557, 560, 666, 676, 679
Mechanical Banks, 120-122
Mechanical Toys, 784-790
Medals, 543, 552-553, 730
Meerschaum Pipes, 773
Menus, 554-555, 591, 601
Mercedes-Benz, 114
Merit Badges, 730-733
Metals, 555-574
Mettlach Steins, 683
Mickey Mouse Collectibles, 82, 216, 262, 271, 278, 785, 786
Militaria, 322, 324, 328, 331, 553, 575-585
Milk Glass, 195, 222, 246, 316, 431-434, 498, 540, 541
Millefiori Glass, 402
Mineral Water Bottles, 202-204
Miniatures, 313, 342, 540-541
Mirrors, 87, 219, 246, 364, 370, 797
Mission Oak Furniture, 371
Model Soldiers, 585-586
Molds, 557, 558, 562, 685
Monkeys (Motif), 121, 127, 213, 315, 433, 560, 679, 773
Mortar and Pestles, 519, 522, 527, 639
Mother's Day Plates, 647, 648, 650, 653, 654, 807
Mourning Pictures, 342
Motion Picture Cameras, 645
Movie Memorabilia, 586-587, 657
Mugs, 558, 562, 661, 664, 666, 669, 673, 721, *See also: Glassware*
Mules and Donkeys (Motifs), 122, 123, 127
Music, 587-594
Music Boxes, 277, 281, 283, 284, 285, 594-596
Music Memorabilia, 589, 591, 593
Musical Instruments, 337-338, 342, 596-598
Mustache Cups, 676, 678
Mystery Books, 617-618

INDEX / 815

— N —
Napkin Rings And Holders, 598-600, 676
National Geographic, 548
Nativity Scenes, 290-291
Nature Prints, 698-704
Nautical Gear, 600-601
Navajo Blankets and Serapes, 601-602
Navajo Rugs, 724-725
Nazi Militaria, 577
Necklaces, 511
Needle Cases, 603
Needlework, 602-603
Needleworking Tools, 603-604
Neiman, LeRoy, 695
Netsuke, 613
New Haven Clock Co. Clocks, 235-238
Nippon Porcelain, 675-676
Noritake Porcelain, 677
Nudes, 84, 86, 397, 398
Nursery Collectibles, 604-606
Nutcrackers, 522, 557, 560, 807

— O —
Oak Clocks, 231, 232, 235
Oak Furniture, 84, 368-371
Occupational Mugs, 680-682
Ocean Liner Memorabilia, 601
OG Clocks, 233, 236, 239
Ogee Clocks, 236, 239
Oldsmobiles, 114-115
Opera Memorabilia, 606-607
Organs, 598, 641
Oriental Rugs, 723-724
Orientalia, 607-613
Owls (Motif), 121, 126, 212, 432, 433, 557, 599, 604, 614, 679

— P —
Packards, 115-116
Painted Furniture, 371-372
Paintings, 219, 342, 610, 614
Pairpoint Lamps, 539
Paperclips, 557, 560
Paper Collectibles, 63-65, 67-70, 73-75, 76-83, 87-99, 117-119, 129-153, 170-172, 172-185, 214, 216-217, 219, 224, 226, 244, 245, 260-263, 265-275, 278, 291, 292, 311-312, 338, 343-356, 480-482, 506, 535-536, 545-550, 551-552, 554, 587, 589, 591, 606, 607, 615-621, 621-630, 632, 656-658, 661, 685-687, 687-688, 689-704, 710, 712, 721, 722, 733, 734, 735-736, 741, 742, 744, 748-762, 763-765, 795-796

Paper Dolls, 311-312
Paper Money, American, 621-630
Paperweights, 246, 248, 295, 557, 560, 630-631, 663, 734; *See also: Glassware*
Paper-Mâché, 71, 317
Parasols, 242
Parrish, Maxfield, 695-696
Parrots (Motif), 121, 222, 315, 557, 560
Pattern Glass, 434-480
Patriotic Symbols, 71, 205, 288, 686, 723, 804; *See also: American Eagles*
Peach Blow Glass, 402, 403
Peacocks (Motif), 86, 223, 399, 404, 599, 667
Pen Collector's Abbreviations, 633
Pencil Boxes and Holders, 210, 247, 543, 735, 797
Pencil Sharpeners, 247
Pendants, 511-512
Pennsylvania-German Collectibles, 208
Penny Arcade Collectibles, 631-632
Penny Rugs, 723
Pens and Pencils, 632-638
Pepsi Collectibles, 64, 65, 66
Perfume, Cologne, Scent Bottles and Atomizers, 187-190, 675, 682; *See also: Glassware*
Pewter, 87, 284, 285, 286, 498, 561-563
Pharmacy Items, 639
Phonographs And Roller Organs, 639-642
Photographica, 95-98, 291, 550, 642-645
Pianos, 598
Picture Frames, *See: Frames*
Pie Crimper, 522, 737, 807
Pigs (Motif), 122, 126, 679, 741
Pillmaking Machine, 639
Pincushions, 603, 738
Pipes, 772-773
Pistols, 577, 578, 579
Pitchers, 87, 520, 557, 559, 666, 667, 669, 672, 676, 677, 679, 683, 685, 715, 765, 766; *See also: Glassware*
Planes, Carpenters', 737, 776
Plant Stands, 87, 370, 374, 375
Plates, Collectible, 397, 646-656
Playboy, 548-549
Player Pianos, 598
Playing Cards, 247, 282, 656-658
Poison Bottles, 204-205

816 / INDEX

Police Memorabilia and Collectibles, 658-659, 712
Political Souvenirs, 659-661
Popeye, 315, 790
Porcelain, 662-685
Poor Richard's Almanac, 70
Porringers, 563
Postcards, 219, 247, 543, 593, 661, 685-687, 712, 734
Posters, 224, 227, 247, 291, 292, 550, 589, 606, 607, 687-688, 734, 770
Pottery, 662-685
Pressed and Pattern Glass, 434-479, 498, 540-541, 631, 721
Prices In This Book, About The, 59-60
Printing Collectibles, 704
Prints, 226, 689-704
Projectors, 645
Pulp Magazines, 726
Punch Magazine, 549
Puppets and Marionettes, 278, 281, 704-707

— Q —
Quezal, 380, 381, 538
Quilts, 708-710

— R —
Rabbits (Motif), 122, 126, 220, 315, 432, 599, 604, 664
Radiator Caps, 119
Radio Premiums, 710
Radios, 247, 710-711
Rag Rugs, 723
Railroadiana, 63, 712, 765
Razors, 713-714
Recordings, 558-589, 590-591, 592, 735
Redware, 714-715
Reels, 341
Remington Firearms, 227, 329, 330-332, 579, 580
Rifles, 227, 326-328, 329-330, 332-333, 334, 580, 582
Rings, 85, 512, 710, 712, 735, 808
Rock 'n' Roll, 591-593
Rocking Chairs, 360, 361, 365, 370, 373, 374, 375, 605
Rockwell, Norman, 652, 696
Rod Puppets, 707
Rogers Groups, 715-716
Roller Organs, 598, 639-642
Rolling Pins, 433, 808
Rookwood Pottery, 614, 663-664

Roosters, *See: Chickens*
Rose Medallion Chinese Export Porcelain, 669
Rosemaling, 372
Roseville Pottery, 664
Royal Bayreuth, 167, 210, 316, 678-679, 773
Royal Copenhagen, 653-654, 679-680
Royal Doulton, 295, 684, 717-721
Royalty Collectibles, 721-722
Rubena Verde Glass, 403-404
Rugs, 722-725, 808
Rulers, 776
Rushlight Holder, 561

— S —
Saddles, 290
Sadirons, 503, 560
Salt and Pepper Shakers, 283, 284, 285, 667, 670, 676, 679; *See also: Glassware*
Salt Box, 210
Samplers, 603
Sandwich Glass, 400, 401
Santa Claus (Motif), 66, 127, 220, 222, 223, 432, 687
Satin Glass, 404-405, 541
Saturday Evening Post, 549
Saws, 320, 776
Scales, 522, 600, 601, 776
Schoenhut Toys, 312
Science Fiction And Space, 725-729
Scissors, 603
Scooter, 170
Scouting Collectibles, 729-736
Scrimshaw, 736-737
Secretaries, 366
Sewing Birds, 604
Sewing Machines, 604
Shaker Crafts and Furniture, 210, 361, 365, 528, 737-738
Shaving Mugs, 680-682
Shawls, 242, 602-603
Sheep, Lambs, Rams (Motif), 220, 315, 508
Sheet Music, 224, 279, 281, 284, 589, 593-594, 735
Sheraton Furniture, 360, 361, 362, 363, 364, 366, 367
Ship Models, 738-739
Ships (Motif), 556, 739
Shoes (Motif), 125

INDEX / 817

Shovels, 777
Sideboards, 366, 370
Signatures, *See: Autographs*
Signs, 64, 65, 71, 247, 639, 712, 740-741
Silhouettes, 741-742
Silk Pictures, 762, 763
Silver and Silverplate, 258, 259, 510, 563-573, 599, 604, 674
Sleds, 484
Smith & Wesson Firearms, 334
Smoking Collectibles, *See: Ashtrays, Matchbooks, Tobacco Collectibles*
Snakes (Motif), 156, 157, 338, 508, 510
Snuff Containers, Boxes and Bottles, 210, 574, 610-611, 683
Sofas and Settees, 366, 373, 375, 376
Space Collectibles, 726-729
Space Toys, 792
Spinning Wheels, 604, 738
Spittoons, *See: Cuspidors*
Spool Cabinets, 604
Spoons, 564-565, 570-573
Sports Collectibles, 743-747
Sports Equipment, 747
Sports (Motif), 681
Squirrels (Motif), 220, 315, 600
Staffordshire Pottery, 682-683, 684-685
Stamps, 748-762
Stationery, 224, 550
Steeple Clocks, 234
Steins, 401, 673, 683
Steuben Glass, 408
Stevengraphs And Silk Pictures, 762-763
Stickpins, 420, 614
Still Banks, 122-127, 219
Stock Certificates, 119, 763-765
Stoneware, 219, 722, 765-766
Stoves, Laundry, 503
Sunbonnet Babies, 602, 687
Sundials, 808
Swans (Motif), 223, 389, 407, 432, 434, 600, 666, 672, 673, 679
Swords, 227, 584-585

— T —

Tables, 87, 360, 367-368, 370-371, 372, 373, 374, 375, 376, 587, 609
Taffeta Glass, 408-414
Tape Measures, 604
Tea Caddies, 528, 557, 574; Miniature, 313

Teapots, 520, 557, 559, 561, 563, 667, 670, 671, 672, 676, 677, 685
Telegraph Collectibles, 766-767
Telephones, 767-768
Telescopes, 557, 601
Theatre Seats, 606
Theatrical Memorabilia, 769-770
Thermometers, 65, 66
Thimbles, 247, 284, 604
Thomas, Seth, Clocks, 238-239, 600
Tiebacks, 404, 557
Tiffany, 405-406, 513, 539
Tin, 523-525, 574; *See also: Toleware*
Tin Toys, 278, 284, 782, 784, 785, 786, 787, 788, 789
Tobacco Collectibles, 63, 64, 65, 66, 67, 84, 411, 657, 673, 771-773; *See also: Ashtrays, Cuspidors*
Toby Mugs and Jugs, 672, 684-685
Tokens, Campaign, 661
Toleware, 574
Tools, 774-777
Toothbrush Holders, 285
Toothpick Holders, 677, 679; *See also: Glassware*
Tortoise Shell, 259, 318, 319, 511, 603, 604
Toy Soldiers, 791
Toys, 219, 224-225, 247-248, 277-286, 342, 596, 777-794
Tractors, 320
Trade Cards and Catalogs, 795-796
Trains, Model and Toy, 793-794
Tramp Art, 210, 796-797
Trays, Metal, Glass, Ceramic, 66, 67, 87, 248, 558, 563, 661, 671, 676, 677, 679, 680, 735, 806; *See also: Glassware*
Trivets, 519, 523, 561, 798
Trumpet, Fireman's, 337-338
Trunks, 372, 799
Turtles (Motif), 155, 169, 383, 508, 556, 561, 600, 604
Typewriters, 800-801

— U —

Umbrella Stand, 375
Umbrellas, 801-802
Umbrellas and Parasols, 248
Uncle Sam (Motif), 432, 658
U.S. Presidents, 98

818 / INDEX

— V —

Vacuum Cleaners, 802-803
Valentines, 482
Vases, 85, 87, 119, 188, 558, 559, 563, 663, 664, 665, 667, 668, 669, 670, 671, 672, 673, 674, 675, 676, 677, 679, 680; *See also: Glassware*
Vending Machines, Toy, 784, 787
Venetian Glass, 168, 407
Ventriloquist's Dummies, 707
Verre de Soie Glass, 408, 420
Victorian Furniture, 361-362, 363, 365, 366, 367, 368, 373-374

— W —

Waffle Irons, 519, 523, 561
Wagon Jacks, 808
Wagons, 484
Walking Sticks, *See: Canes*
Wallets, *See: Handbags and Wallets*
Walnut Clocks, 230, 232, 235, 238
Wardrobes, 371
Washboards, 519, 529, 808
Washington, George, 98
Watches, 84, 282, 286, 513
Waterbury Clocks, 239-240
Weathervanes, 803-805
Weavings, 288, 289
Webb Glass, 380, 381

Wedgwood, 169, 212, 285, 316, 509, 639, 655, 675, 685, 722
Weller Art Pottery, 664-665
Western Prints, 698
Whetstone, 808
Whirligig, 342
Whiskey Bottles, 205-207, 417
Whiskey Labels, 536
Wicker, 372-376, 603, 605
Wildlife Prints, 698-699
Willets Belleek, 666, 667
Winchester Firearms, 290, 334-335
Windup Toys, 789-790
Wolf (Motif), 315, 613
Woodenware, 526-529, 805-808
World of Antiques, 1-3
World War I and II Memorabilia, *See: Militaria*
World's Fair Memorabilia and Collectibles, 195, 399, 434, 656, 657, 795
Wrenches, 777

— XYZ —

Yokes, 807
Zeppelins (Motif), 222
Zodiac (Motif), 809
Zsolnay Ceramics, 665

Central Florida's Biggest tourist attraction for
COLLECTORS
DECORATORS,
and **NOSTALGIA FANS**

SHIRLEY'S ANTIQUES

It's like walking through a museum and being able to BUY the items that you RARELY FIND on the open market — brought together in one great treasure-trove. An antique shop, where the collector's dreams comes true! You can shop in full confidence, and be assured that you are always paying a fair price! Over 6,500 square feet for your antique shopping pleasure. Specializing in: Oak Furniture, Old Cars, Advertising and Country Store Items, Stained Glass, Brass Beds, Unusual Bathroom Plumbing and Hardware — anything unique or unusual. Items for every taste — and every budget.

Of course, Shirley's is always interested in PURCHASING fine collectors' items. Whether BUYING or SELLING, Shirley's invites you to CALL or VISIT at:

SHIRLEY'S ANTIQUES
750 HWY. 50
WINTER GARDEN, FL 32787
(305) 656-6406

An experienced staff will courteously assist you in every way. Shirley's is located just 10 minutes west of Orlando, FL, entertainment capital of Florida, and 25 minutes north of DISNEY WORLD.

Members report
SAVINGS of $1,000.00 and more
as a result of American Collector Club membership

American Collector Club
Membership Number: 0111OMSM0110
Expiration Date: 10/87

MARY M MCSMITH
0110 EAST ANYWHERE
TIMBUCKTOO US 01110

is an Associate in good standing and entitled to all Associate benefits and opportunities through the expiration date shown above.

James K. Barker
Associate Director

This card can save you money too!

Watch for this emblem

10 in shops offering automatic discounts to members.

Members receive American Collector each month

Featuring collectables of the last 100 years, special American Collector editions spotlight

* Roseville   * Americana   * Paper
* Modern Dolls   * Porcelain   * Glass
* Clocks & Watches   * Political   * Pottery
* Antique Dolls   * Patriotic   * Toys
* Limited Editions   * Advertising   * Jewelry

There are regular columns for collectors of:
* Books   * Bottles   * Photographica   * Dolls
* Records   * Nippon   * Barberiana   * Jars
* Stoneware   * Glass   * Stocks & Bonds   * Paper

Questions are answered in "Readers Ask." "What Is It?" challenges. It's helpful, fun and informative!

American Collector is just one of many ACC member Benefits!

Your member-only newsletter

brings you news reference info, book discounts up to 70%, other special money-savers, FREE member bonuses several times a year.

* Book Discounts
* Barter through ACE
* Discounts on Collectables
* FREE bonus gifts
* Publication Discounts
* A sample of Member Benefits

Members often save more than annual dues in the first month of membership.

For buyers of this Official Guide, 5-month trial membership, $9.95; 12 months, $20.

Send your application to:

American Collector Club
P.O. Drawer C (HC), Kermit, TX 79745

How did your plates do?

Reco's "Little Boy Blue" by John McClelland

UP 214% in 1 Year

Some limited edition plates gained more in the same year, some less, and some not at all... But Plate Collector readers were able to follow the price changes, step by step, in Plate Price Trends, a copyrighted feature appearing in each issue of the magazine.

Because The Plate Collector is your best source guide... has more on limited editions than all other publications combined ... and gives you insight into every facet of your collecting... you too will rate it

**Your No. 1. Investment
In Limited Editions.**

In 1972, Plate Collector was the first to feature limited editions only. It's expanded, adding figurines, bells and prints, earning reader raves like you see below.

To bring you the latest, most valuable information, our editors crisscross the continent. Sometimes stories lead them to the smaller Hawaiian Islands, or to the porcelain manufacturers of Europe.

Their personal contact with artisans, hobby leaders, collectors, artists and dealers lets you share an intimate view of limited editions.

Each fat, colorful issue brings you new insight, helps you enjoy collecting more.

You'll find Plate Collector a complete source guide. Consider new issue information and new issue announcements, often in full color. Use the ratings of new releases and wide array of dealer ads to help you pick and choose the best.

Read regular columns, including one on Hummels, and check current market values in Plate Price Trends to add to your storehouse of knowledge.

You'll profit from tips on insurance, decorating, taxes... just a sample of recurring feature subjects.

Read Plate Collector magazine to become a true limited edition art insider. Order now. See new and old plates in sparkling color. Enjoy 2 issues every month, delivered to your home at savings up to 37% from newsstand price.

**12 issues (6 months) $17.50
24 issues (year) $28
The PLATE COLLECTOR**
P.O. Box 1041-HC   Kermit, TX 79745

To use VISA and MasterCard, include all raised information on your card.

Here is Plate Collector, as viewed by our readers in unsolicited quotes...

"Objective and Impartial," has "great research," yet is warm and personal... "I am delighted in 'our' magazine." A New York couple says flatly, "It is the best collector magazine on the market."

"Quality printing is valuable to me because there are no stores near me where I can view and decide," says an Arizona reader. It is "a major guide to the plates I buy," says a Massachusetts reader, while "It is the best investment in a magazine I ever made," comes from Illinois.

"I enjoy your articles on artists," "The full-color pictures are great," "Your staff was most helpful," "I depend on Plate Collector," and "I look forward to receiving it twice a month," are other reader reactions.

A California reader said simply, "I am glad there is a Plate Collector."

There is only one...
THE OFFICIAL® PRICE GUIDE

THE <u>MULTI-PURPOSE</u> REFERENCE GUIDE!!

THE OFFICIAL PRICE GUIDES SERIES has gained the reputation as the <u>standard barometer of values</u> on collectors' items. When you need to check the market price of a collectible, turn first to the OFFICIAL PRICE GUIDES . . . for impartial, unbiased, current information that is presented in an easy-to-follow format.

• **CURRENT VALUES FOR BUYING AND SELLING.** ACTUAL SALES that have occurred in all parts of the country are CAREFULLY EVALUATED and COMPUTERIZED to arrive at the most ACCURATE PRICES AVAILABLE.

• **CONCISE REFERENCES.** Each OFFICIAL PRICE GUIDE is designed primarily as a *guide to current market values.* They also include a useful summary of the information most readers are seeking: a history of the item; how it's manufactured; how to begin and maintain a collection; how and where to sell; addresses of periodicals and clubs.

• **INDEXED FORMAT.** The novice as well as the seasoned collector will appreciate the unique alphabetically *indexed format* that provides *fast retrieval* of information and prices.

• **FULLY ILLUSTRATED.** All the OFFICIAL PRICE GUIDES are richly illustrated. Many feature COLOR SECTIONS as well as black-and-white photos.

Over 20 years of experience has made
THE HOUSE OF COLLECTIBLES
the most respected price guide authority!

PRICE GUIDE SERIES

American Silver & Silver Plate
Today's silver market offers excellent opportunities *to gain big profits* — if you are well informed. *Over 15,000 current market values* are listed for 19th and 20th century American made Sterling, Coin and Silverplated flatware and holloware. Special souvenir spoon section. *ILLUSTRATED.*
$9.95-2nd Edition, 576 pgs., 5⅜" x 8", paperback, Order #: 184-5

Antique Clocks
A pictorial price reference for all types of American made clocks. Detailed listings insure positive identification. Includes company histories. *ILLUSTRATED.*
$9.95-1st Edition, 576 pgs., 5⅜" x 8", paperback, Order #: 364-3

Antique & Modern Firearms
This unique book is an encyclopedia of gun lore featuring over *21,000 listings with histories* of American and foreign manufacturers *plus a special section on collector cartridges values.* *ILLUSTRATED.*
$9.95-3rd Edition, 544 pgs., 5⅜" x 8", paperback, Order #: 363-5

Antiques & Other Collectibles
Introduces TODAY'S world of antiques with *over 100,000 current market values* for the most complete listing of antiques and collectibles IN PRINT! In this *new — 832 PAGE edition, many new categories have been added to keep fully up-to-date with the latest collecting trends.* *ILLUSTRATED.*
$9.95-4th Edition, 832 pgs., 5⅜" x 8", paperback, Order #: 374-0

Antique Jewelry
Over *8,200 current collector values* for the most extensive listing of antique jewelry ever published, Georgian, Victorian, Art Nouveau, Art Deco. *Plus a special full color gem identification guide. ILLUSTRATED.*
$9.95-2nd Edition, 672 pgs., 5⅜" x 8", paperback, Order #: 354-6

Bottles Old & New
Over *22,000 current buying and selling prices* of both common and rare collectible bottles . . . ale, soda, bitters, flasks, medicine, perfume, poison, milk and more. *Plus expanded sections on Avon and Jim Beam. ILLUSTRATED.*
$9.95-6th Edition, 672 pgs., 5⅜" x 8", paperback, Order #: 350-3

Collector Cars
Over *36,000 actual current prices* for 4000 models of antique and classic automobiles — U.S. and foreign. Complete with engine specifications. *Special sections on auto memorabilia values and restoration techniques. ILLUSTRATED.*
$9.95-4th Edition, 544 pgs., 5⅜" x 8", paperback, Order #: 357-0

Collector Handguns
Over *15,000 current values* for antique and modern handguns. Plus the most up-to-date listing of current production handguns. *ILLUSTRATED.*
$9.95-1st Edition, 544 pgs., 5⅜" x 8", paperback, Order #: 367-8

Collector Knives
Over *13,000 buying and selling prices* on U.S. and foreign pocket and sheath knives. *Special sections on bicentennial, commemorative, limited edition, and handmade knives.* By J. Parker & B. Voyles. *ILLUSTRATED.*
$9.95-5th Edition, 704 pgs., 5⅜" x 8", paperback, Order #: 324-4

Collector Plates
Destined to become the "PLATE COLLECTORS' BIBLE." This unique price guide offers the most comprehensive listing of collector plate values — *in Print!* Special information includes: *company histories; artist backgrounds; and helpful tips on buying, selling and storing a collection.* *ILLUSTRATED.*
$9.95-1st Edition, 672 pgs., 5⅜" x 8", paperback, Order #: 349-X

For your convenience use the handy order form.

PRICE GUIDE SERIES

Collector Prints
Over **14,750 detailed listings** representing over 400 of the most famous collector print artists from Audubon and Currier & Ives, to modern day artists. *Special feature includes gallery/artist reference chart.* ILLUSTRATED.
$9.95-4th Edition, 544 pgs., 5⅜" x 8", paperback, Order #: 189-6

Comic & Science Fiction Books
Over **31,000 listings with current values** for comic and science fiction publications *from 1903-to-date. Special sections on Tarzan, Big Little Books, Science Fiction publications and paperbacks.* ILLUSTRATED.
$9.95-6th Edition, 544 pgs., 5⅜" x 8", paperback, Order #: 353-8

Glassware
Over **25,000 listings** for all types of American made glassware, pressed and pattern, depression, cut, carnival and more. *ILLUSTRATED.*
$9.95-1st Edition, 544 pgs., 5⅜" x 8", paperback, Order #: 125-X

Hummel Figurines & Plates
The most complete guide ever published on every type of Hummel — including the most recent trademarks and size variations, with **4,500 up-to-date prices.** *Plus tips on buying, selling and investing.* ILLUSTRATED.
$9.95-3rd Edition, 448 pgs., 5⅜" x 8", paperback, Order #: 352-X

Kitchen Collectibles
This beautiful pictorial guide has over **1,100 illustrations** - truly a MASTERPIECE of reference. This first really complete *History of America in the Kitchen* describes hundreds of implements and lists their current market values. *ILLUSTRATED.*
$9.95-1st Edition, 544 pgs., 5⅜" x 8", paperback, Order #: 371-6

Military Collectibles
This detailed historical reference price guide covers the largest accumulation of military objects — 15th century-to-date — listing over **12,000 accurate prices.** *Special expanded Samuri sword and headdress sections.* ILLUSTRATED.
$9.95-2nd Edition, 576 pgs., 5⅜" x 8", paperback, Order #: 191-8

Music Machines
Virtually every music related collectible is included in this guide — over **11,000 current prices.** *78 recordings, mechanical musical machines, and instruments.* ILLUSTRATED.
$9.95-2nd Edition, 544 pgs., 5⅜" x 8", paperback, Order #: 187-X

Old Books & Autographs
Descriptions of the finest literary collectibles available, with over **11,000 prices for all types of books:** Americana, bibles, medicine, cookbooks and more. *Plus an updated autograph section.* ILLUSTRATED.
$9.95-4th Edition, 512 pgs., 5⅜" x 8", paperback, Order #: 351-1

Oriential Collectibles
Over **15,000 detailed listings and values** for all types of Chinese & Japanese collectibles, pottery, rugs, statues, porcelain, cloisonne, metalware. *ILLUSTRATED.*
$9.95-1st Edition, 544 pgs., 5⅜" x 8", paperback, Order #: 375-9

Paper Collectibles
Old Checks, Invoices, Books, Magazines, Newspapers, Ticket Stubs and even Matchbooks — any paper items that reflects America's past — are gaining collector value. This book contains **over 25,000 current values** and descriptions for all types of paper collectibles. *ILLUSTRATED.*
$9.95-2nd Edition, 608 pgs., 5⅜" x 8", paperback, Order #: 186-1

Pottery & Porcelain
Over **10,000 current prices and listings** of fine pottery and porcelain, plus an extensive Lenox china section. *Special sections on identifying china trademarks and company histories.* ILLUSTRATED.
$9.95-2nd Edition, 576 pgs., 5⅜" x 8", paperback, Order #: 188-8

For your convenience use the handy order form.

PRICE GUIDE SERIES

Records
Over **31,000 current prices** of collectible singles, EPs, albums, plus 20,000 memorable song titles recorded by over 1100 artists. *Rare biographies and photos are provided for many well known artists.* ILLUSTRATED.
$9.95-4th Edition, 544 pgs., 5⅜" x 8", paperback, Order #: 356-2

Royal Doulton
This authoritative guide to Royal Doulton porcelains contains over **3,500 detailed listings** on figurines, plates and Toby jugs. Includes tips on buying, selling and displaying. *Plus an exclusive numerical reference index.* ILLUSTRATED.
$9.95-2nd Edition, 544 pgs., 5⅜" x 8", paperback, Order #: 355-4

Wicker
You could be sitting on a *fortune!* Decorators and collectors are driving wicker values to unbelievable highs! This pictorial price guide *positively identifies all types* of Victorian, Turn of the century and Art Deco wicker furniture. *A special illustrated section on wicker repair is included.* ILLUSTRATED.
$9.95-1st Edition, 416 pgs., 5⅜" x 8", paperback, Order #: 348-1

Encyclopedia Of Antiques
The House of Collectibles, the world's largest publisher of collector price guides opens its vast archives of knowledge to the public in an easy to use volume that ranks as an **absolute must** for the library of every collector and investor. A total of more than **10,000 definitions, explanations, consise factual summeries of names, dates, histories, confusing terminology** . . . for every popular field of collecting. *An exclusive appendix* includes many trademark and pattern charts as well as a catagorized list of museums and reference publications.
$9.95-1st Edition, 672 pgs., 5⅜" x 8", paperback, Order # 365-1

Buying & Selling Guide To Antiques
Covers every phase of collecting from beginning a collection to its ultimate sale . . . examines in detail the collecting potential of over **200 different catagories** of items in all price ranges — from razors to Rembrant paintings. Learn how the collectibles market operates, which factors determine the value of a collectors item. *Special features include a dealer directory, a condition grading report, list of museums and reference publications, plus a discussion of buying and selling techniques.* ILLUSTRATED.
$9.95-1st Edition, 608 pgs., 5⅜" x 8", paperback, Order #: 369-4

MINI PRICE GUIDE SERIES

Antiques & Flea Markets
Discover the fun and profit of collecting antiques with this handy pocket reference to **over 15,000 types of collectibles.** Avoid counterfeits and learn the secrets to successful buying and selling. ILLUSTRATED.
$2.50-1st Edition, 240 pgs., 4" x 5½", paperback, Order #: 308-2

Antique Jewelry
A handy-pocket sized up-date to the larger *Official Price Guide to Antique Jewelry*, lists **thousands of values** for bracelets, brooches, chains, earrings, necklaces and more. *Special sections on gold, silver and diamond identification.*
$2.95-1st Edition, 240 pgs., 4" x 5½", paperback, Order #: 373-2

Baseball Cards
This guide lists **over 70,000 current market values** for baseball cards – Bowman, Burger King, Donruss, Fleer, O-Pee-Chee and Topps. ILLUSTRATED.
$2.95-3rd Edition, 288 pgs., 4" x 5½", paperback, Order #: 376-7

For your convenience use the handy order form.

MINI PRICE GUIDE SERIES

Beer Cans
The first pocket-sized guide to list *thousands of values* for cone and flat top beer cans produced since the mid 1930's. Each listing is graphically detailed for positive identification.
$2.95-1st Edition, 240 pgs., 4" x 5½", paperback, Order #: 377-5

Comic Books
Young and Old are collecting old comic books for fun *and Profit!* This handy ''pocket-sized'' price guide lists current market values and detailed descriptions for the most sought-after ''collectible'' comic books. *Buying, selling and storing tips are provided for the beginning collector. ILLUSTRATED.*
$2.50-1st Edition, 240 pgs., 4" x 5½", paperback, Order #: 345-7

Dolls
Doll collecting is one of America's favorite hobbies and this guide lists *over 3,000 actual market values* for all the manufacturers! Kewpies, Howdy Doody, Shirley Temple, GI Joe plus comprehensive listings of Barbies. *ILLUSTRATED.*
$2.95-1st Edition, 240 pgs., 4" x 5½", paperback, Order #: 316-3

O.J. Simpson Football Cards
The world famous O.J. Simpson highlights this comprehensive guide to football card values. *Over 21,000 current collector prices* are listed for: Topps, Bowman, Fleer, Philadelphia and O-Pee-Chee. *Includes a full color O.J. SIMPSON limited edition collector card. ILLUSTRATED.*
$2.50-2nd Edition, 256 pgs., 4" x 5½", paperback, Order #: 323-6

Hummels
How much are your Hummels worth? You can become an expert on these lovely figurines with this guide, *FULLY ILLUSTRATED*, with a handy numerical index that puts descriptions and *3,000 market prices* at your fingertips. Learn why the slightest variation could mean hundreds in value.
$2.95-1st Edition, 240 pgs., 4" x 5½", paperback, Order #:318-X

Paperbacks & Magazines
Old discarded paperbacks and magazines could be worth 50-100 times their original cover price. Learn how to identify them. *Thousands* of descriptions and prices show which issues are rare. *ILLUSTRATED.*
$2.50-1st Edition, 240 pgs., 4" x 5½", paperback, Order #: 315-5

Pocket Knives
This mid-season up-date to the larger *Official Price Guide to Collector Knives* lists *over 4,000 collector values* for Case, Kabar, Cattaraugus, Remington, Winchester and more. *Special sections on buying and selling plus a list of limited edition pocket knives.*
$2.95-1st Edition, 240 pgs., 4" x 5½", paperback, Order #: 372-4

Scouting Collectibles
Discover the colorful history behind scouting, relive childhood memories and profit from those old family heirlooms. *Thousands of prices* are listed for all types of Boy and Girl Scout memorabilia. *ILLUSTRATED.*
$2.50-1st Edition, 240 pgs., 4" x 5½", paperback, Order #: 314-7

Star Trek/Star Wars Collectibles
The most startling phenomena in decades! Star Trek and Star Wars fans have created a space age world of collectibles. *Thousands of current values* for book, posters, photos, costumes, models, jewelry and more . . . *plus tips on buying, selling and trading.ILLUSTRATED.*
$2.95-1st Edition, 240 pgs., 4" x 5½", paperback, Order #: 319-8

Toys
Kids from eight to eighty enjoy collecting toys and this comprehensive guide has them all! Trains, trucks, comic and movie character, space toys, boats and **MORE.** *Over 8,000 current market values* of toys, old and new, plus investment tips and histories. *ILLUSTRATED.*
$2.95-1st Edition, 240 pgs., 4" x 5½", paperback, Order #: 317-1

For your convenience use the handy order form.

— NUMISMATIC SERIES —

THE BLACKBOOKS are more than just informative books, they are the most highly regarded authority on the nation's most popular hobbies.

1983 Blackbook Price Guide of United States Coins
A coin collector's guide to current market values for all U.S. coins from 1616 to date—over **16,000 prices**. THE OFFICIAL BLACKBOOK OF COINS has gained the reputation as the most reliable, up-to-date guide to U.S. Coin values. This new special 1983 edition features, an exclusive gold and silver identification guide. Learn how to test, weigh and calculate the value of any item made of gold or silver. Proven professional techniques revealed for the first time. Take advantage of the current "BUYERS' MARKET" in gold and silver. ILLUSTRATED.
$2.95-21st Edition, 288 pgs., 4" x 5½", paperback, Order #: 342-2

1983 Blackbook Price Guide of United States Paper Money
Over **8,200 buying and selling prices** covering U.S. currency from 1861 to date. Every note issued by the U.S. government is listed and priced, including many Confederate States notes. Error Notes are described and priced, and there are detailed articles on many phases of the hobby for beginners and advanced collectors alike. ILLUSTRATED.
$2.95-15th Edition, 240 pgs., 4" x 5½", paperback, Order #: 343-0

1983 Blackbook Price Guide of United States Postage Stamps
Featuring all U.S. stamps from 1847 to date pictured in full color. Over **18,750 current selling prices**. You will find new listings for the most current commemorative and regular issue stamps, a feature not offered in any other price guide, at any price! There were numerous important developments in the fast moving stamp market during the past year and they are all included in this **NEW REVISED EDITION**. ILLUSTRATED.
$2.95-5th Edition, 240 pgs., 4" x 5½", paperback, Order #: 344-9

— INVESTORS SERIES —

The Official Investor's Guide Series shows you, *step by step*, how to select the right items for your investment program, how to avoid the many pitfalls that can foil new investors, with full instructions on when to sell and **How And Where To Sell** in order to realize the **Highest Possible Profit**.

Investors Guide to Gold, Silver, Diamonds
All you need to know about making money trading in the precious metals and diamond markets. This practical, easy-to-read investment guide is for everyone in all income brackets. ILLUSTRATED.
$6.95-1st Edition, 208 pgs., 5⅜" x 8", paperback, Order #: 171-3

Investors Guide to Gold Coins
The first complete book on investing in gold coins. Exclusive price performance charts trace all U.S. gold coin values from *1955 to date*. ILLUSTRATED.
$6.95-1st Edition, 288 pgs., 5⅜" x 8", paperback, Order #: 300-7

Investors Guide to Silver Coins
The most extensive listing of all U.S. silver coins. Detailed price performance charts trace actual sales figures from *1955 to date*. ILLUSTRATED.
$6.95-1st Edition, 288 pgs., 5⅜" x 8", paperback, Order #: 301-5

Investors Guide to Silver Dollars
Regardless of your income, you can *become a successful silver dollar investor*. Actual sales figures for every U.S. silver dollar *1955 to date*. ILLUSTRATED.
$6.95-1st Edition, 192 pgs., 5⅜" x 8", paperback, Order #: 302-3

For your convenience use the handy order form.

FOR IMMEDIATE DELIVERY

VISA & MASTERCARD CUSTOMERS
ORDER TOLL FREE!
1-800-327-1384

This number is for orders only, it is not tied into the customer service or business office. Customers not using charge cards must use mail for ordering since payment is required with the order — sorry no C.O.D.'s. Florida residents call (305) 857-9095 — ask for order department.

OR SEND ORDERS TO

THE HOUSE OF COLLECTIBLES, ORLANDO CENTRAL PARK
1900 PREMIER ROW, ORLANDO, FL 32809   PHONE (305) 857-9095

☐ Please send me the following price guides—(don't forget to add postage & handling):
☐ I would like the most current edition of the books checked below.

☐ 184-5 @ 9.95	☐ 125-X @ 9.95	☐ 365-1 @ 9.95	☐ 372-4 @ 2.95
☐ 364-3 @ 9.95	☐ 352-X @ 9.95	☐ 369-4 @ 9.95	☐ 314-7 @ 2.50
☐ 363-5 @ 9.95	☐ 371-6 @ 9.95	☐ 308-2 @ 2.50	☐ 379-1 @ 2.95
☐ 374-0 @ 9.95	☐ 191-8 @ 9.95	☐ 373-2 @ 2.95	☐ 319-8 @ 2.95
☐ 354-6 @ 9.95	☐ 187-X @ 9.95	☐ 376-7 @ 2.95	☐ 317-1 @ 2.95
☐ 350-3 @ 9.95	☐ 351-1 @ 9.95	☐ 377-5 @ 2.95	☐ 342-2 @ 2.95
☐ 357-0 @ 9.95	☐ 375-9 @ 9.95	☐ 345-7 @ 2.50	☐ 343-0 @ 2.95
☐ 367-8 @ 9.95	☐ 186-1 @ 9.95	☐ 316-3 @ 2.95	☐ 344-9 @ 2.95
☐ 324-4 @ 9.95	☐ 188-8 @ 9.95	☐ 323-6 @ 2.50	☐ 171-3 @ 6.95
☐ 349-X @ 9.95	☐ 356-2 @ 9.95	☐ 318-X @ 2.95	☐ 300-7 @ 6.95
☐ 189-6 @ 9.95	☐ 355-4 @ 9.95	☐ 378-3 @ 2.95	☐ 301-5 @ 6.95
☐ 353-8 @ 9.95	☐ 348-1 @ 9.95	☐ 315-5 @ 2.50	☐ 302-3 @ 6.95

Add $1.50 postage and handling for the first book and 50¢ for each additional book. Add $2.50 to each order for insurance and special handling. Florida residents add 5% sales tax.

☐ Check or money order enclosed $_____ (include postage and handling)
☐ Please charge $_____ to my: ☐ MASTERCARD ☐ VISA

Charge Card Customers Not Using Our Toll Free Number Please Fill Out The Information Below.

Account No. (All Digits) _____ Expiration Date _____
Signature _____

NAME (please print) _____ PHONE _____
ADDRESS _____ APT. # _____
CITY _____ STATE _____ ZIP _____